THE VICTORIA HISTORY OF THE COUNTIES
OF ENGLAND

A HISTORY OF GLOUCESTERSHIRE
VOLUME XII

INSCRIBED TO THE MEMORY OF HER LATE MAJESTY

QUEEN VICTORIA

WHO GRACIOUSLY GAVE THE TITLE TO AND

ACCEPTED THE DEDICATION OF THIS HISTORY

THE VICTORIA HISTORY OF THE COUNTIES OF ENGLAND

JOHN BECKETT DIRECTOR AND GENERAL EDITOR
ALAN THACKER EXECUTIVE EDITOR
ELIZABETH WILLIAMSON ARCHITECTURAL EDITOR

THE UNIVERSITY OF LONDON
INSTITUTE OF HISTORICAL RESEARCH

The Leadon valley at Pauntley

A HISTORY OF
THE COUNTY OF
GLOUCESTER

VOLUME XII

NEWENT AND MAY HILL

A. R. J. JUŘICA

PUBLISHED FOR THE
INSTITUTE OF HISTORICAL RESEARCH
BY BOYDELL & BREWER · 2010

© University of London 2010

All rights reserved. Except as permitted under current legislation
no part of this work may be photocopied, stored in a retrieval system,
published, performed in public, adapted, broadcast,
transmitted, recorded or reproduced in any form or by any means,
without the prior permission of the copyright owner

First published 2010

A Victoria County History publication
in association with The Boydell Press
an imprint of Boydell & Brewer Ltd
PO Box 9 Woodbridge Suffolk IP12 3DF UK
and of Boydell & Brewer Inc.
668 Mt Hope Avenue Rochester NY 14620 USA
website: www.boydellandbrewer.com
and with the
University of London Institute of Historical Research

ISBN 978–1–90435–636–3
ISSN 1477–0709

A catalogue record for this book is available
from the British Library

Typeset by Tina Ranft, Woodbridge
Printed in Great Britain by
CPI Antony Rowe, Chippenham and Eastbourne

CONTENTS OF VOLUME TWELVE

	Page
Dedication	ii
Contents	vii
List of Illustrations	viii
List of Maps	x
VCH Advisory Board	xi
Editorial Note	xii
Classes of Documents in the National Archives	xiii
Gloucestershire Archives (formerly Gloucestershire Record Office) Accumulations	xiv
Note on Abbreviations	xvi

TOPOGRAPHY

Architectural descriptions prepared by Elizabeth Williamson and for Newent town also by Duncan James

NEWENT AND MAY HILL

A. R. J. JUŘICA — 1

PARISH HISTORIES

Newent — 7
N. M. HERBERT

Bromesberrow — 95
S. A. DRAPER

Dymock — 122
A. R. J. JUŘICA

Huntley — 174
A. R. J. JUŘICA

Kempley — 196
A. R. J. JUŘICA

Longhope — 223
A. R. J. JUŘICA

Oxenhall — 254
N. M. HERBERT

Pauntley — 281
A. R. J. JUŘICA

Preston — 301
A. R. J. JUŘICA

Taynton — 317
A. R. J. JUŘICA

Index — 347

LIST OF ILLUSTRATIONS

THANKS are offered to English Heritage for allowing the reproduction of material from the National Monuments Record (NMR) at Swindon and for arranging new photography for the volume; unless stated otherwise the photographs dated 2008 were taken by Michael Hesketh-Roberts of English Heritage. For permission to reproduce material in its possession thanks are offered to Gloucestershire Archives (GA). Copying of that material was by Shaun Carroll.

Frontispiece The Leadon valley at Pauntley 2008.

Figure		Page
1	May Hill 2008. Photograph by S.A. Draper.	1
2	Aerial view of Newent town 1972. Aerofilms photograph A237512: ©English Heritage. NMR. Aerofilms collection.	15
3	Broad Street, Newent, *c.*1910. Photograph by R.H. Bisco (GA, GPS 225/41).	16
4	Roof of the former boothall, Newent, 2008.	22
5	Newent market house *c.*1840. Water colour by a member of the Foley family (copy in GA, GPS 225/50).	22
6	Black Dog inn, Newent, 2008.	24
7	Tan House, Newent, *c.*1966. Photograph by Amanda Simpson (née Tomlinson). Reproduced by permission of Dr Simpson.	25
8	High Street, Newent, *c.*1910. Photograph by R.H. Bisco (GA, GPS 225/45).	25
9	Land Settlement Association houses at the Scarr, Newent, 2008. Photograph by S. Draper.	29
10	Briery Hill, Newent, 2008.	35
11	The Court House, Newent. Photograph from 1910 sale particulars (GA, SL 13).	41
12	Clifford Manor, Newent. Photograph from 1932 sale particulars (GA, D 2299/5994).	43
13	Great Boulsdon, Newent, 2008.	44
14	Carswalls Manor, Newent, 2008.	45
15	Conigree Court, Newent, 2008.	47
16	The Moat, Newent. Photograph from 1910 sale particulars (GA, SL 13).	52
17	Stardens, Newent. Photograph from 1910 sale particulars (GA, SL 80).	53
18	Traditional cider making at Newent in the mid 20th century. Photograph, probably by W.R. Bawden, for Eagle Photos published in *Gloucestershire Countryside*, January–March 1951.	59
19	Packing market-garden produce at the Scarr, Newent. Photograph, probably by W.R. Bawden, for Eagle Photos published in *Gloucestershire Countryside*, January–March 1951.	60
20	Three Choirs Vineyard 2008. Photograph by S. Draper.	61
21	Friendly society procession in Broad Street, Newent, *c.*1910. Photograph by R.H. Bisco (GA, GPS 225/40).	79
22	Ancient cross shaft at Newent church 2008.	91
23	Newent church, interior, 2008.	93
24	St Peter's church, Clifford's Mesne, 2008.	94
25	Bromesberrow 2008.	96
26	Bromesberrow Place *c.*1800. Plate published in T.D. Fosbrooke, *Abstracts of Records and Manuscripts Respecting the County of Gloucester, Formed into a History* (1807).	97
27	Russell's End, Bromesberrow, 1995. NMR photograph BB95/12273: ©Crown copyright.NMR.	101
28	Bromesberrow Place 1991. NMR photograph BB91/11019: ©Crown copyright.NMR.	105
29	Roof of Toney's Farm, Bromesberrow, 2008.	107
30	Bromesberrow church tower 2008.	121
31	The Old Cottage, Dymock, 1948. Photograph by S. Pitcher. NMR photograph AA49/1842: reproduced by permission of English Heritage.NMR.	128
32	Greenway House, Dymock, 2008.	135
33	Hillash, Dymock, 1975. Photograph for Dymock Women's Institute (GA, D 3295/I/6).	136
34	The Old Grange, Dymock. Photograph from 1920 sale particulars (GA, D 3028/5).	140
35	Boyce Court, Dymock, 1975. Photograph for Dymock Women's Institute (GA, D 3295/I/6).	142

List of Illustrations

36	Outbuildings at Callow Farm, Dymock, 2008.	143
37	Pound Farm, Dymock, 1975. Photograph for Dymock Women's Institute (GA, D 3295/I/6).	146
38	Ann Cam's school, Dymock. Drawing from the office of Waller, Son, & Wood, Gloucester, 1884 (GA, D 2593/2/454).	164
39	Dymock church 1948. Photograph by S. Pitcher. NMR photograph AA49/1837: reproduced by permission of English Heritage.NMR.	169
40	Dymock church, south doorway, 1948. Photograph by S. Pitcher. NMR photograph AA49/1838: reproduced by permission of English Heritage.NMR.	169
41	Dymock church, interior, 1948. Photograph by S. Pitcher. NMR photograph AA49/1839: reproduced by permission of English Heritage.NMR.	173
42	Huntley church and school 1968. Photograph by G. Barnes. NMR photograph AA01441: reproduced by permission of English Heritage.NMR.	178
43	Huntley Manor. Lithograph by Martin & Hood, London, in 1884 sale particulars (GA, SL 10).	182
44	Huntley Court. Photograph from 1924 sale particulars (GA, D 2299/3139).	183
45	Making tent pegs at Forest Products Ltd, Huntley, 1939. Photograph by C.E. Hart (GA, D 3921/II/19).	187
46	Huntley church, interior, 1968. Photograph by G. Barnes. NMR photograph AA79/2269: reproduced by permission of English Heritage.NMR.	196
47	Medieval barn at Friar's Court, Kempley, 2008.	201
48	Ceiling at Stone House, Kempley, 2008.	205
49	St Mary's church, Kempley, south doorway 1975. NMR photograph BB75/5864: ©Crown copyright. NMR.	217
50	St Mary's church, Kempley, interior 1970. Photograph by G. Barnes. NMR photograph BB84/1384: reproduced by permission of English Heritage.NMR.	218
51	Church of St Edward King and Confessor, Kempley, 1970. Photograph by G. Barnes. NMR photograph AA79/224: reproduced by permission of English Heritage.NMR.	221
52	Pound House, Longhope, 2008.	227
53	Marle Cottage, Longhope, 2008. Photograph by S. Draper.	230
54	Upper Boxbush House, Longhope, 2008.	230
55	Hart's Barn, Longhope, 1996. NMR photograph AA96/956: ©Crown copyright.NMR.	231
56	The premises at Longhope of James Constance & Sons Ltd in the early 20th century. Undated photograph (GA, D 3824).	239
57	Products of the turnery of James Constance & Sons Ltd, Longhope. Photograph 1927 (GA, D 3824).	240
58	Lock Cottage, Oxenhall, 2008. Photograph by S. Draper.	258
59	Oxenhall church *c.*1840. Water colour by a member of the Foley family (copy in GA, GPS 241/3).	259
60	Quince Cottage near Shaw common, Oxenhall, 2008.	261
61	Kew's Farm, Kilcot, 2008.	263
62	Holder's Farm, Oxenhall, 2008.	264
63	Building thought to have been the charcoal store of the Ellbridge ironworks, Oxenhall, 2008.	275
64	Font at Oxenhall church 2008.	281
65	Little Place, Pool Hill, 2008.	286
66	Pauntley Court 1996. NMR photograph BB96/3786: ©Crown copyright.NMR.	288
67	Payford mill, Pauntley, 2005. Photograph by Elizabeth Williamson.	293
68	Pauntley church, south doorway, 1996. NMR photograph BB96/3808: ©Crown copyright.NMR.	299
69	Preston Court 1945. Photograph by S. Pitcher. NMR photograph A45/5533: reproduced by permission of English Heritage.NMR.	307
70	Preston church, detail of north doorway, 1945. Photograph by S. Pitcher. NMR photograph A45/5529: reproduced by permission of English Heritage.NMR.	315
71	Preston church 1975. Photograph by B.R. Edwards published on Images of England website.	316
72	Byfords, Taynton, 2008.	323
73	Outbuildings at Taynton House. Photograph *c.*1952 (GA, D 2299/10703).	324
74	Hall and stair at Hownhall, Taynton, 2008.	325
75	Former workhouse at Taynton 2008. Photograph by S. Draper.	337
76	Former school in Taynton 2008. Photograph by S. Draper.	340
77	Taynton church, seating plan created in 1825 (from faculty papers: Gloucester Diocesan Records, F 1/4).	345
78	All Saints' church, May Hill, 2008.	346

LIST OF MAPS

The maps were drawn by Cath D'Alton. The original drafts, prepared by S.A. Draper, N.M. Herbert, and A.R.J. Jurica, were based on first edition 6" and 1/2,500 OS maps with the exception of number 14. That was prepared from a plan of Preston parish made in 1843 by Robert Jones of Ledbury: Gloucester Diocesan Records, G 3/43.

Map *Page*

1. Gloucestershire parishes in the Newent and May hill area 1850 — xxii
2. Newent parish 1882 — 7
3. Newent town 1840 — 14
4. Newent, Compton tithing 1882 — 27
5. Newent, Malswick tithing 1882 — 31
6. Newent, Boulsdon and Cugley tithings 1882 — 33
7. Bromesberrow 1882 — 95
8. Dymock 1880 — 123
9. Huntley 1840 — 175
10. Kempley 1880 — 197
11. Longhope 1870 — 223
12. Oxenhall, Kilcot, and part of Gorsley 1882 — 255
13. Pauntley (main part) 1880 — 282
14. Preston 1834 — 302
15. Taynton 1880 — 318

VICTORIA HISTORY OF GLOUCESTERSHIRE ADVISORY BOARD 2008–9

Chairman
MR D. SETCHELL, former Chairman of Council, University of Gloucestershire

Members
PROFESSOR J. BECKETT, Director VCH
MS HEATHER FORBES, County and Diocesan Archivist
MR N.W. KINGSLEY, Chairman of the VCH Advisory Board
MR J. LOOSLEY
SIR NICHOLAS MANDER BT
MAVIS, LADY DUNROSSIL, Gloucestershire County Council
DR SHELLEY SAGUARO, Head of the Department of Humanities and Associate Dean for Research, University of Gloucestershire
F.M. SKINNER, Gloucestershire County Council

EDITORIAL NOTE

VOLUME TWELVE of the *Victoria History of Gloucestershire* has been produced under the partnership of the University of Gloucestershire (formerly the Cheltenham and Gloucester College of Higher Education) and Gloucestershire County Council with the University of London's Institute of Historical Research. The partnership, first formed in 1996, has been renewed for a further five-year term from April 2006 and the University of London wishes to thank the University of Gloucestershire and the County Council for their generous support.

Dr Nicholas Herbert, County Editor since 1970, retired in 2003 to be replaced by Dr Carrie Smith until 2006. In 2007 Dr John Juřica, Assistant Editor since 1973, was appointed County Editor and Dr Simon Draper was appointed in turn Research Assistant and Assistant Editor.

The authors and editors of the volume have drawn widely on information and advice from many people and bodies, too numerous to be mentioned here but named in the footnotes to the articles with which they helped. All are warmly thanked. Particular thanks are owed to the late David Bick of Newent, the late Brian Frith of Gloucester, Ms E.M. Goulding of Newent, Mrs Rosalind Lowe of Goodrich (Herefs.), Mr John Rhodes of Gloucester, Mr Donald Sherratt of Taynton, Mr Brian Smith of Vowchurch (Herefs.), Mrs Jennifer Thick of Dymock, the late Kenneth Tomlinson of Newent, Mrs Jill Voyce of Huntley, and Mr Eric Warde of Newent.

For allowing access to records in their possession thanks are owed to His Grace the Duke of Beaufort for items in the Badminton Muniments, for which Mrs Margaret Richards was archivist, to the late Andrew Foley of Stoke Edith (Herefs.) for items in the Hereford Record Office, to the trustees of the Madresfield estate, to Dymock parish council, to the county archivists of Hampshire, Herefordshire, and Worcestershire, to the deans and chapters of Gloucester, Hereford, and Westminster, and to the archivists of Birmingham City Archives, the House of Lords Record Office, and the Shakespeare Centre Library and Archive (formerly Shakespeare Birthplace Trust) at Stratford-upon-Avon (Warws.). The staff of Gloucestershire Archives under the county and diocesan archivist, Mr N.W. Kingsley and from 2005 Heather Forbes, continued their indispensable aid. The office was renamed Gloucestershire Archives in 2005 following the transfer to it from Gloucester Library of the Gloucestershire Collection. The library of the Bristol and Gloucestershire Archaeological Society housed at the Francis Close Hall campus of the University of Gloucestershire remained an invaluable resource.

The structure, aims and progress of the Victoria History as a whole are described on the VCH website (www.victoriacountyhistory.ac.uk).

LIST OF CLASSES OF DOCUMENTS IN THE NATIONAL ARCHIVES (FORMERLY THE PUBLIC RECORD OFFICE)

CHANCERY
Proceedings
- C 1   Early
- C 2   Series I
- C 3   Series II
- C 44   Common Law Pleadings, Tower Series
- C 54   Close Rolls
- C 66   Patent Rolls
- C 78   Decree Rolls
- C 93   Commissioners for Charitable Uses: Inquisitions and Decrees

Masters' Exhibits
- C 108   Farrar
- C 115   Duchess of Norfolk Deeds (including Llanthony cartularies and registers)

Inquisitions post mortem
- C 138   Series I, Hen. V
- C 139   Hen. VI
- C 140   Edw. IV and V
- C 141   Ric. III
- C 142   Series II
- C 143   Inquisitions ad quod damnum

COURT OF COMMON PLEAS
Feet of Fines
- CP 25/1   Series I
- CP 25/2   Series II
- CP 40   De Banco Rolls

CROWN ESTATE COMMISSIONERS
- CRES 36   Office of Woods, Forest, and Land Revenues, General Department, Registered Files
- CRES 38   Title Deeds, etc.

DUCHY OF LANCASTER
- DL 7   Inquisitions post mortem
- DL 13   Drafts and Particulars for Patents

EXCHEQUER, TREASURY OF THE RECEIPT
- E 32   Forest Proceedings

EXCHEQUER, KING'S REMEMBRANCER
- E 101   Accounts, Various
- E 134   Depositions taken by Commission
- E 142   Extents, Inquisitions and Valors of Forfeited Lands
- E 159   Memoranda Rolls
- E 164   Miscellaneous Books, Series I
- E 178   Special Commissions of Inquiry
- E 179   Subsidy Rolls, etc.

EXCHEQUER, AUGMENTATION OFFICE
- E 301   Certificates of Colleges and Chantries
- E 309   Enrolment of Leases
- E 310   Particulars of Leases
- E 315   Miscellaneous Books
- E 321   Legal Proceedings

EXCHEQUER, FIRST FRUITS AND TENTHS OFFICE
- E 331   Bishops' Certificates of Institutions to Benefices

MINISTRY OF EDUCATION
- ED 7   Public Elementary Schools, Preliminary Statements

FORESTRY COMMISSION
- F 9   Director of Forestry for England, Correspondence and Papers, Dymock Forest

REGISTRY OF FRIENDLY SOCIETIES
Indexes to Rules and Amendments
- FS 2   Series I
- FS 4   Series II

HOME OFFICE
- HO 107   Census Returns 1841 and 1851
- HO 129   Ecclesiastical Returns

BOARD OF INLAND REVENUE
- IR 18   Tithe Files
- IR 29   Tithe Apportionments
- IR 30   Tithe Maps

JUSTICES ITINERANT
- JUST 1   Eyre Rolls, Assize Rolls, etc.

MINISTRY OF AGRICULTURE, FISHERIES, AND FOOD
- MAF 68   Agricultural Returns: Parish Summaries

PROBATE
- PROB 11   Registered copies of wills proved in Prerogative Court of Canterbury

BRITISH TRANSPORT HISTORICAL RECORDS
RAIL 836   Herefordshire and Gloucestershire Canal Navigation Company

COURT OF REQUESTS
REQ 2   Proceedings

GENERAL REGISTER OFFICE
RG 9	Census Returns	1861
RG 10		1871
RG 11		1881
RG 12		1891
RG 13		1901

SPECIAL COLLECTIONS
SC 2	Court Rolls
SC 6	Ministers' and Receivers' Accounts
SC 12	Rentals and Surveys: Portfolios

COURT OF STAR CHAMBER
STAC 2   Proceedings, Hen. VIII

COURT OF WARDS AND LIVERIES
WARD 7   Inquisitions post mortem

LIST OF ACCUMULATIONS IN GLOUCESTERSHIRE ARCHIVES (FORMERLY GLOUCESTERSHIRE RECORD OFFICE)

DEPOSITED COLLECTIONS

D 22	Daglingworth manor and miscellaneous deeds
D 23	Probyn family of Newland
D 36	Colchester-Wemyss family of Westbury-on-Severn
D 48	Huntley family of Boxwell
D 127	Scott & Fowler of Gloucester and Berkeley (solicitors)
D 177	Haines & Sumner of Gloucester (solicitors), including Pringle of Longhope records
D 182	Mullings, Ellett, & Co. of Cirencester (solicitors)
D 185	Society of Genealogists
D 204	Haines & Sumner (solicitors), records of turnpike trusts
D 245	Hughes & Tanner of Cheltenham (solicitors)
D 326	Guise family of Elmore
D 332	Vizard & Son of Monmouth (solicitors)
D 365	Weldon, Thomson, & Co. of Tewkesbury (solicitors)
D 412	Newent: manors of Kilcot and Boulsdon
D 413	Slade & Co. of Newent (solicitors)
D 421	Bathurst family of Lydney
D 537	Cadle family of Westbury-on-Severn
D 543	Yearsley & Wadeson of Mitcheldean (solicitors)
D 602	Newent and Upleadon deeds
D 892	miscellaneous deeds and papers
D 897	Perrys of Brighton (solicitors)
D 917	Newent deeds
D 936	dean and chapter of Gloucester
D 936A	dean and chapter of Gloucester
D 963	Bromesberrow: Hall Place (Brookend) estate
D 1142	Lord & Parker of Worcester (solicitors)
D 1272	Treasures of Gloucester (solicitors)
D 1297	Scott & Fowler of Gloucester and Berkeley (solicitors)
D 1349	miscellaneous deeds
D 1381	Waller & Son of Gloucester (architects)
D 1388	Mullings, Ellett, & Co. of Cirencester (solicitors)
D 1466	Newent charities
D 1589	Price family of Tibberton
D 1604	Curtler & Hallmark of Worcester (solicitors)
D 1618	Ricardo family of Minchinhampton and Bromesberrow
D 1677	Hall and Gage families of Highmeadow
D 1803	Octavius Price of Newent (solicitor)
D 1810	C.T. Price of London (solicitors)
D 1842	Fisher family of Stroud
D 1882	Radcliffes & Co. of London (solicitors)
D 1927	miscellaneous deeds
D 1938	Guiting Power, Newent, and Painswick deeds
D 1998	Newent deeds
D 2052	notes on nonconformity compiled by G. Dutton
D 2079	Brookes & Badham of Tewkesbury (solicitors)
D 2099	Stallard & Co. of Worcester (solicitors)
D 2176	Price family of Tibberton
D 2184	Foley family abstract of title

D 2245	Hooke family of Newent	D 16	sequestration papers
D 2263	Clark & Lees of Newent (tanners)	F 1	faculties
D 2299	Bruton, Knowles, & Co. (estate agents)	F 4	parsonage house papers
D 2428	land valuation records compiled under the Finance Act of 1910	G 2	leases
		G 3	estate books and papers
D 2528	Foley family of Newent and Oxenhall	T 1	tithe awards
D 2592	Tennant family of Upton upon Severn	V 1	bishop's transcripts
D 2593	ASTAM Design Partnership (architects: Fulljames & Waller papers)	V 5	glebe terriers
		V 6	parish papers
D 2689	Gloucester Methodist circuit	V 15	archdeacon's papers
D 2700	Badminton estate	vols.	volumes of the diocesan registry
D 2710	Slade & Co. of Newent (solicitors)	wills	probate copies of wills proved in consistory court
D 2957	deeds transferred from the Gloucestershire Collection		

QUARTER SESSIONS RECORDS

Clerk of the Peace

D 3028	papers of Canon D. Gethyn-Jones	Q/CB	bonds
D 3168	Gloucestershire rural community council	Q/CI	lists and indexes
D 3269	Gloucester municipal charity trustees	Registration	
D 3270	Governors of Gloucester United schools	Q/REl	elections, land tax
D 3295	Gloucestershire Federation of Women's Institutes	Q/RI	inclosure awards
		Q/RNc	papists' estates
D 3398	Hannam Clark & Son of Gloucester (solicitors)	Q/RSf	friendly societies
		Q/RUm	public works
D 3403	Madge, Lloyd, & Gibson of Gloucester and Newent (solicitors)	Q/RZ	miscellaneous
		The Court in Session	
D 3469	charities review papers compiled by L.S. Duirs	Q/SIb	indictment books
		Q/SO	order books
D 3921	documents and papers deposited by Dr C.E. Hart	Q/SR	order rolls
		Q/SRh	highway diversions
D 4317	Blythe, Dutton, & Holloway of London (solicitors)		

OTHER RECORDS

D 4587	Davis, Foster, & Finley of Malvern (solicitors)	A	prints
		C	county council
D 4647	Bridges, Sawtell, & Adams of London (solicitors)	DA	district councils and superseded authorities
D 4858	Young & Gilling of Cheltenham (estate agents)	DC	post 1974 district councils
		EL	catalogues of records in other archive repositories
D 4869	Probyn family of Huntley and Newland		
D 5570	miscellaneous deeds	G	boards of guardians
D 6026	Gloucester and Hereford Congregational Union	GBR	Gloucester borough
		GPS	photographs
D 6854	Lloyds Bank plc	HB	highway boards
D 6913	Frere, Cholmeley, & Co. of London (solicitors)	P	parishes
		S	schools
D 7723	Clifford Manor estate		
D 7457	notes on Bromesberrow compiled by R.L. Steynor	PAMPHLETS	
		ED	education
D 9125	documents transferred from the Gloucestershire Collection	GE	genealogy
		NC	nonconformity
		PA	parish histories

GLOUCESTER DIOCESAN RECORDS (GDR)

B 4	court papers	SL	sale particulars
D 5	advowson papers		

NOTE ON ABBREVIATIONS

Abbrev. Rot. Orig.	*Rotulorum Originalium in Curia Scaccarii abbreviatio*, ed. H. Playford and J. Caley (2 vols., Rec. Com. 1805–10)
Acreage Returns, 1905	Board of Agriculture Returns of 1905, from a MS copy in possession of the editor, VCH Glos.
Alumni Cantab.	J.A. Venn (ed.), *Alumni Cantabrigienses 1752–1900* (6 vols. Cambridge, 1940–54)
Alumni Oxon.	J. Foster (ed.), *Alumni Oxonienses 1500–1714* (4 vols. Oxford, 1891–2); *1715–1886* (4 vols. Oxford, 1887–8)
Atkyns, *Glos.*	R. Atkyns, *The Ancient and Present State of Glostershire* (London, 1712)
Bibliotheca Glos.	*Bibliotheca Gloucestrensis: Collections of Scarce and Curious Tracts Illustrative of and Published during the Civil War* (Gloucester, priv. printed, 1825)
Bigland, *Glos.*	*Historical, Monumental, and Genealogical Collections Relative to the County of Gloucester, Printed from the Original Papers of Ralph Bigland* (3 vols. 1791–1889, issued in parts; vol. III is unpaginated)
BGAS	Bristol and Gloucestershire Archaeological Society
BL	British Library
Book of Fees	*Book of Fees* (3 vols., HMSO 1920–31)
Bp. Benson's Surv. of Dioc. of Glouc. 1735–50	*Bishop Benson's Survey of the Diocese of Gloucester, 1735–1750*, ed. J. Fendley (Gloucestershire Record Series 13, BGAS 2000)
Bryant, *Map of Glos.* (1824)	A. Bryant, *Map of the County of Gloucester in the years 1823 & 1824* (1824)
Cal. Chart.	*Calendar of the Charter Rolls preserved in the Public Record Office* (HMSO 1903–27)
Cal. Close	*Calendar of the Close Rolls preserved in the Public Record Office* (HMSO 1892–1963)
Cal. Cttee for Compounding	*Calendar of the Proceedings of the Committee for Compounding with Delinquents, etc.* (HMSO 1889–92)
Cal. Doc. France	*Calendar of Documents preserved in France illustrative of the history of Great Britain and Ireland*, ed. J.H. Round (HMSO 1899)
Cal. Fine	*Calendar of the Fine Rolls preserved in the Public Record Office* (HMSO 1911–62)
Cal. Inq. Misc.	*Calendar of Inquisitions (Chancery) preserved in the Public Record Office* (HMSO 1916–68)
Cal. Inq. p.m.	*Calendar of Inquisitions post mortem preserved in the Public Record Office* (HMSO 1904–95)
Cal. Inq. p.m. Hen. VII	*Calendar of Inquisitions post mortem, Henry VII* (HMSO 1898–1955)
Cal. Pat.	*Calendar of the Patent Rolls preserved in the Public Record Office* (HMSO 1891–1986)
Cal. Regs. Priory of Llanthony	*Calendar of the Registers of the Priory of Llanthony by Gloucester 1457–1466, 1501–1525*, ed. J. Rhodes (Gloucestershire Record Series 15, BGAS 2002)
Cal. SP Dom.	*Calendar of State Papers, Domestic Series* (HMSO 1856–1972)
Cal. Treasury Books	*Calendar of Treasury Books* (HMSO 1904–69)
Calamy Revised	A.G. Matthews, *Calamy Revised: being a Revision of Edmund Calamy's Account of the Ministers and Others Ejected and Silenced, 1660–2* (1934)
Cat. Ancient Deeds	*Descriptive Catalogue of Ancient Deeds in the Public Record Office* (HMSO 1890–1915)
Citizen	*Citizen* (newspaper, established at Gloucester 1876)
Close	*Close Rolls of the reign of Henry III preserved in the Public Record Office* (HMSO 1902–75)
Complete Baronetage	*Complete Baronetage*, ed. G.E.Cockayne (6 vols. 1900–9)
Complete Peerage	G.E.Cockayne and others (eds.), *The Complete Peerage…*(2nd edn, 13 vols. 1910–50)
Compton Census	*Compton Census of 1676: a critical edition*, ed. A. Whiteman (British Academy Records of Social and Economic History, new series X, Oxford, 1986)
1801 Crop Returns Eng.	*1801 Crop Returns for England*, I, ed. M. Turner (List and Index Society 189, 1978)
Cur. Reg.	*Curia Regis Rolls* (HMSO 1923–72)
DoE List	Department of the Environment List of Buildings of Special Architectural or Historic Interest
Dugdale, *Mon.*	W. Dugdale, *Monasticon Anglicanum*, ed. J. Caley, H. Ellis, and B. Bandinel (1849)
Eccl. Misc.	*Ecclesiastical Miscellany* (Records Section 11, BGAS 1976), including A.C. Percival and W.J. Sheils (eds.), 'A Survey of the Diocese of Gloucester, 1603'

Educ. Enq. Abstract	*Education Enquiry Abstract* (Parliamentary Papers 1835 (62), xli)
Educ. of Poor Digest	*Digest of Returns to the Select Committee on Education of the Poor* (Parliamentary Papers 1819 (224), ix (1))
EHR	*English Historical Review*
Eng. Episc. Acta VII	*English Episcopal Acta VII: Hereford 1079–1234*, ed. J. Barrow (British Academy 1993)
Feudal Aids	*Inquisitions and Assessments relating to Feudal Aids preserved in the Public Record Office* (6 vols., HMSO 1899–1920)
Flaxley Cart.	*Cartulary and Historical Notes of the Cistercian Abbey of Flaxley*, ed. A.W. Crawley-Boevey (Exeter, priv. printed, 1887)
Fosbrooke, *Glos.*	T.D. Fosbrooke, *Abstracts of Records and Manuscripts Respecting the County of Gloucester, formed into a history* (2 vols. Gloucester, 1807)
Fosbrooke, *Glouc.*	T.D. Fosbrooke, *An Original History of the City of Gloucester, almost wholly compiled from new materials…including also the original papers of Ralph Bigland* (London, 1819)
GA	Gloucestershire Archives (formerly Gloucestershire Record Office: see above, Gloucestershire Archives Accumulations)
GBR	Gloucester Borough Records (in Gloucestershire Archives)
GDR	Gloucester Diocesan Records (in Gloucestershire Archives)
Glos. Ch. Bells	M. Bliss and F. Sharpe, *Church Bells of Gloucestershire* (Gloucester, 1986)
Glos. Ch. Notes	S.R. Glynne, *Gloucestershire Church Notes*, ed. W.P.W. Phillimore and J. Melland Hall (1902)
Glos. Ch. Plate	*Gloucestershire Church Plate*, ed. J.T. Evans (BGAS 1906)
Glos. Colln.	The Gloucestershire Collection (in Gloucestershire Archives, transferred from Gloucester Library), comprising printed works, manuscripts, prints and drawings, etc.
Glos. Feet of Fines 1199–1299	*Abstracts of Feet of Fines relating to Gloucestershire 1199–1299*, ed. C.R. Elrington (Gloucestershire Record Series 16, BGAS 2003)
Glos. Feet of Fines 1300–59	*Abstracts of Feet of Fines relating to Gloucestershire 1300–1359*, ed. C.R. Elrington (Gloucestershire Record Series 20, BGAS 2006)
Glos. N&Q	*Gloucestershire Notes and Queries* (10 vols. 1881–1914)
Glos. Subsidy Roll, 1327	*Gloucestershire Subsidy Roll I Edw. III, 1327* (priv. printed by Sir Thomas Phillipps [? 1856])
Glouc. Apprentices Reg. 1595–1700	*Calendar of the Registers of Apprentices of the City of Gloucester 1595–1700*, ed. J. Barlow (Gloucestershire Record Series 14, BGAS 2001)
Glouc. Cath. Libr.	Gloucester Cathedral Library
Glouc. Freemen Reg. 1641–1838	*Calendar of the Registers of the Freemen of the City of Gloucester 1641–1838*, ed. J. Juřica (Gloucestershire Record Series 4, BGAS 1991)
Glouc. J.	*Gloucester Journal* (established 1722)
Greenwood, *Map of Glos.* (1824)	C. and J. Greenwood, *Map of the County of Gloucester in the Year 1823* (1824)
GRO	Gloucestershire Record Office (renamed in 2006 Gloucestershire Archives)
HCA	Hereford Cathedral Archives
Herefs. RO	Herefordshire Record Office, Hereford
Hist. & Cart. Mon. Glouc.	*Historia et Cartularium Monasterii Sancti Petri Gloucestriae*, ed. W.H. Hart (RS no 33, 3 vols. 1863–87)
Hist. Parl. Commons	*The History of Parliament: The House of Commons* (The History of Parliament Trust)
HMSO	Her (His) Majesty's Stationery Office
Hockaday Abs.	The 'Hockaday Abstracts' (in Gloucestershire Archives), being abstracts of ecclesiastical records relating to Gloucestershire, compiled by F.S. Hockaday mainly from diocesan records
Hodgson, *Queen Anne's Bounty*	C. Hodgson, *An Account of the Augmentation of Small Livings, by 'The Governors of the Bounty of Queen Anne, for the Augmentation of the Maintenance of the Poor Clergy'* (1st edn 1826; 2nd edn 1845 with supplement of 1864)
Inq. p.m. Glos.	*Abstracts of Inquisitions post mortem for Gloucestershire, 1236–1413, 1625–42* (6 vols. issued jointly by the British Record Society, Index Library vols. xxx, xl, xlviii, and ix, xxi, xlvii, and the BGAS, 1893–1914)
L&P Hen. VIII	*Letters and Papers, Foreign and Domestic, of the Reign of Henry VIII* (HMSO 1864–1932)
LJ	*Journals of the House of Lords*
MCA	Madresfield Court Archives

Military Surv. of Glos. 1522	*Military Survey of Gloucestershire, 1522*, ed. R.W. Hoyle (Gloucestershire Record Series 6, BGAS 1993)
Nat. Soc. files	Schools files of the National Society, Church of England Record Centre, South Bermondsey, London
Nat. Soc. *Inquiry, 1846–7*	*Result of the Returns to the General Inquiry made by the National Society* (1849)
Nonarum Inquisitiones	*Nonarum Inquisitiones in Curia Scaccarii*, ed. G. Vandersee (Rec. Com. 1807)
Notes on Dioc. of Glouc. by Chancellor Parsons	*Notes on the Diocese of Gloucester by Chancellor Richard Parsons, c.1700*, ed. J. Fendley (Gloucestershire Record Series 19, BGAS 2005)
NRA	National Register of Archives
OED	*Oxford English Dictionary*
Oxford DNB	*Oxford Dictionary of National Biography* (2004)
Pat.	*Patent Rolls of the reign of Henry III preserved in the Public Record Office* (HMSO 1901–13)
Pipe R	*Pipe Roll*
Plac. de Quo Warr.	*Placita de Quo Warranto…in Curia Receptae Scaccarii Westm. Asservata*, ed. W. Illingworth and J. Caley (Rec. Com. 1818)
Pleas of the Crown for Glos. ed. Maitland	*Pleas of the Crown for the County of Gloucester, 1221*, ed. F.W. Maitland (1884)
PN Glos.	*The Place-Names of Gloucestershire* (English Place-Name Society vols. 38–41, 1964–5)
Poor Law Abstract, 1804	*Abstract of Returns Relative to the Expense and Maintenance of the Poor* (printed by order of the House of Commons, 1804)
Poor Law Abstract, 1818	*Abstract of Returns to Orders of the House of Commons Relative to Assessments for Relief of the Poor* (Parliamentary Papers 1820 (294), xii)
Poor Law Com. 2nd Rep.	*Second Report of the Poor Law Commission* (Parliamentary Papers 1836 (595), xxxix (1))
Poor Law Returns (1830–1)	*Account of the Money Expended for the Maintenance and Relief of the Poor for the five years ending 25th March 1825, 1826, 1827, 1828, and 1829* (Parliamentary Papers 1830–1 (83), xi)
Poor Law Returns (1835)	*Account of the Money Expended 1830, 1831, 1832, 1833, and 1834* (Parliamentary Papers 1835 (444), xlvii)
PRO	Public Record Office (renamed The National Archives)
Proc. CNFC	*Proceedings of the Cotteswold Naturalists' Field Club*
Public. Elem. Schs. 1906	*List of Public Elementary Schools in England and Wales on 1 Jan. 1906* (Parliamentary Papers 1906 [Cd 3182], lxxxvi)
Rec. Com.	Record Commission
Reg. Bothe	*Registrum Caroli Bothe, Episcopi Herefordensis, 1516–35*, ed. A.T. Bannister (Canterbury and York Society 1921)
Reg. Cantilupe	*Registrum Thome de Cantilupo, Episcopi Herefordensis, 1275–82*, ed. W.W. Capes (Canterbury and York Society 1907)
Reg. Gilbert	*Registrum Johannis Gilbert, Episcopi Herefordensis, 1375–89*, ed. J.H. Parry (Canterbury and York Society 1915)
Reg. Lacy	*Registrum Edmundi Lacy, Episcopi Herefordensis, 1417–20*, ed. A.T. Bannister (Canterbury and York Society 1918)
Reg. Mascall	*Registrum Roberti Mascall, Episcopi Herefordensis, 1404–16*, ed. J.H. Parry (Canterbury and York Society 1917)
Reg. Mayew	*Registrum Ricardi Mayew, Episcopi Herefordensis, 1504–16*, ed. A.T. Bannister (Canterbury and York Society 1921)
Reg. Myllyng	*Registrum Thome Myllyng, Episcopi Herefordensis, 1474–92*, ed. A.T. Bannister (Canterbury and York Society 1920)
Reg. of Dymock	*The Registers of the Church of St. Mary, Dymock, 1538–1790*, ed. I. Gray and J.E. Gethyn-Jones (Records Section 4, BGAS 1960)
Reg. Orleton	*Registrum Ade de Orleton, Episcopi Herefordensis, 1317–27*, ed. A.T. Bannister (Canterbury and York Society 1908)
Reg. Spofford	*Registrum Thome Spofford, Episcopi Herefordensis, 1422–48*, ed. A.T. Bannister (Canterbury and York Society 1919)
Reg. Stanbury	*Registrum Johannis Stanbury, Episcopi Herefordensis, 1453–74*, ed. A.T. Bannister (Canterbury and York Society 1919)
Reg. Swinfield	*Registrum Ricardi de Swinfield, Episcopi Herefordensis, 1283–1317*, ed. W.W. Capes (Canterbury and York Society 1909)

Reg. T. de Charlton	*Registrum Thome de Charlton, Episcopi Herefordensis, 1327–44*, ed. W.W. Capes (Canterbury and York Society 1913)
Reg. Trefnant	*Registrum Johannis Trefnant, Episcopi Herefordensis, 1389–1404*, ed. W.W. Capes (Canterbury and York Society 1916)
Reg. Trillek	*Registrum Johannis de Trillek, Episcopi Herefordensis, 1344–61*, ed. J.H. Parry (Canterbury and York Society 1912)
12th Rep. Com. Char.	*12th Report of the Commissioners Appointed to Enquire Concerning Charities* (Parliamentary Papers 1825 (348), x)
16th Rep. Com. Char.	*16th Report of the Commissioners Appointed to Enquire Concerning Charities* (Parliamentary Papers 1826–7 (22), ix (1))
18th Rep. Com. Char.	*18th Report of the Commissioners Appointed to Enquire Concerning Charities* (Parliamentary Papers 1828 (62), xx (1))
1st Rep. Com. Employment in Agric.	*1st Report of the Royal Commission on the Employment of Children, Young People and Women in Agriculture* (Parliamentary Papers 1867–8 [C 4068-I], xvii)
Richardson, *Wells and Springs of Glos.*	L. Richardson, *Wells and Springs of Gloucestershire* (HMSO 1930)
Rot. Chart.	*Rotuli Chartarum in Turri Londinensi asservati, 1199–1216*, ed. T.D. Hardy (Rec. Com. 1837)
Rot. Litt. Claus.	*Rotuli Litterarum Clausarum in Turri Londinensi asservati, 1204–27*, ed. T.D. Hardy (2 vols., Rec. Com. 1833–44)
Rot. Parl.	*Rotuli Parliamentorum* (6 vols. [1783])
RS	Rolls Series
Rudder, *Glos.*	S. Rudder, *A New History of Gloucestershire* (Cirencester, 1779)
Rudge, *Agric. of Glos.*	T. Rudge, *General View of the Agriculture of the County of Gloucester* (London, 1807)
Rudge, *Hist. of Glos.*	T. Rudge, *The History of the County of Gloucester* (2 vols. Gloucester, 1803)
Smith, *Men and Armour*	*The Names and Surnames of all the Able and Sufficient Men in Body fit for His Majesty's Service in the Wars, within the County of Gloucester, 1608, Compiled by John Smith* (London, 1902)
SMR Glos.	Gloucestershire Sites and Monuments Record (Gloucestershire county council archaeology service)
Tax. Eccl.	*Taxatio Ecclesiastica Angliae et Walliae auctoritate P. Nicholai IV circa A.D. 1291*, ed. S. Ayscough and J. Caley (Rec. Com. 1802)
Taylor, *Domesday Glos.*	C.S. Taylor, *Analysis of the Domesday Survey of Gloucestershire* (BGAS 1887–9, issued in parts)
Taylor, *Map of Glos.* (1777)	I. Taylor, *Map of the County of Gloucester* (1777), republished in *A Gloucestershire and Bristol Atlas* (BGAS, 1961)
Turner, *Agric. of Glos.*	G. Turner, *General View of the Agriculture of the County of Gloucester* (London, 1794)
TNA	The National Archives (formerly Public Record Office: see above, Classes of Documents in The National Archives)
Trans. BGAS	*Transactions of the Bristol and Gloucestershire Archaeological Society*
Univ. Brit. Dir.	*Universal British Directory of Trade, Commerce, and Manufacture*, ed. P Barfoot and J. Wilkes (5 vols. 1791–8)
Valor Eccl.	*Valor Ecclesiasticus temp. Hen. VIII auctoritate regia Institutus*, ed. J. Caley and J. Hunter, (6 vols., Rec. Com. 1810–34)
VCH	*Victoria County History*
Verey and Brooks, *Glos.* II	D. Verey and A. Brooks, *Gloucestershire*: vol. II, *The Vale and the Forest of Dean* (The Buildings of England 2002)
Visit. Glos. 1623	*Visitation of the County of Gloucester, 1623*, ed. J. Maclean and W.C. Heane (Harleian Society 21, 1885)
Visit. Glos. 1682–3	*Visitation of the County of Gloucester, 1682, 1683*, ed. T. FitzRoy Fenwick and W.C. Metcalfe (Exeter, priv. printed, 1884)
Walker Revised	A.G. Matthews, *Walker Revised: being a Revision of John Walker's Sufferings of the Clergy during the Grand Rebellion, 1642–60* (1948)
Westminster Abbey Mun.	Westminster Abbey Muniments
Williams, *Parl. Hist. of Glos.*	W.R. Williams, *The Parliamentary History of the County of Gloucester* (Hereford, priv. printed, 1898)
Worcs. RO	Worcestershire Record Office, Worcester

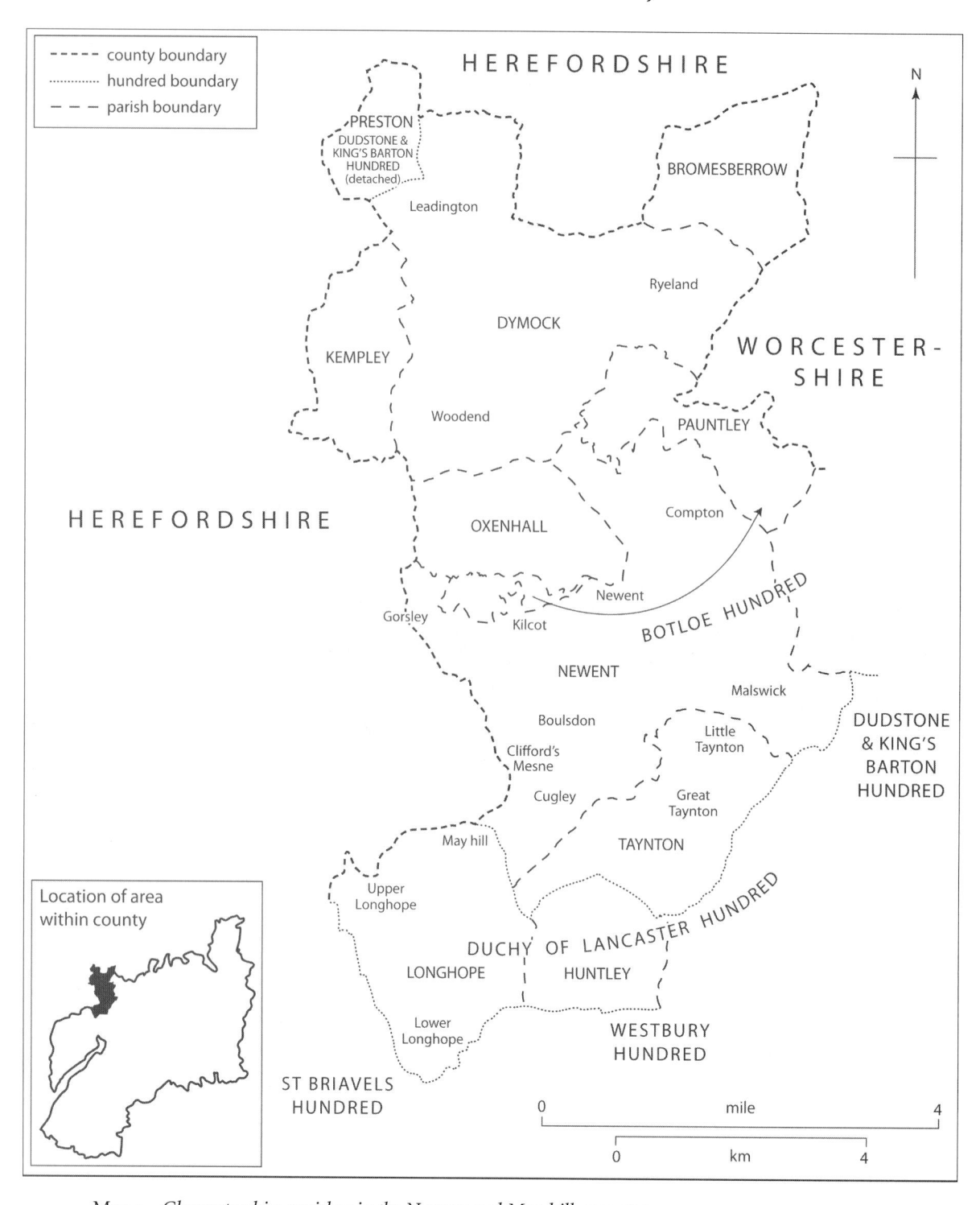

Map 1. *Gloucestershire parishes in the Newent and May hill area 1850*

NEWENT AND MAY HILL

1. May hill: view from the south-west at the Wilderness, Mitcheldean

THIS volume of the county history covers an area in the north-west corner of Gloucestershire adjoining the ancient counties of Hereford and Worcester. The area, a belt of land extending northwards to the county boundary with the town of Newent at its centre, contained ten ancient parishes, namely Bromesberrow, Dymock, Huntley, Kempley, Longhope, Newent, Oxenhall, Pauntley, Preston, and Taynton. The whole of each parish is treated here. The area's identity has been shaped by its proximity to the Forest of Dean and in its physical characteristics has affinities with south Herefordshire.

TOPOGRAPHY

In a rolling landscape streams form tributaries of the river Leadon that on its winding course towards the river Severn passes through a ravine marking the county's ancient boundary with Worcestershire.[1] Away from the Leadon the hills are steeper and the northern end of the area rises on foothills of the Malverns. To the south the landscape is dominated by May hill, an eminence formerly known as Yartleton hill[2] that is partly in Herefordshire and is crowned by trees at 296 m.[3] The valley of the Longhope brook to its south-west drains southwards towards the Severn.

The area has substantial tracts of woodland including ancient woods and plantations created between the 18th and 20th centuries. The older woods are vestiges of expanses of wooded and waste land, which on the hilly northern end in Bromesberrow was within the medieval Malvern Chase. The whole of the southern half of the area up to Newent was for a time until the early 14th century within the jurisdiction of the Forest of Dean.[4] Over much of the area a pattern of small

---

1 Above, frontispiece.
2 *PN Glos.* III, 192; Bodleian, Top. Glouc. c. 3, f. 194; *Notes on Dioc. of Glouc. by Chancellor Parsons*, 188; Rudder, *Glos.* 504.
3 Above, frontispiece.
4 *VCH Glos.* V, 285, 296–7.

hedged fields and scattered farmsteads emerged from the clearance of the ancient woodland, a process well advanced by the late Anglo-Saxon period. Open fields never occupied more than a small area on some of the less hilly land and most were inclosed early in a piecemeal process and converted to pasture and orchard. Much more extensive were common woods and pastures, some of which occupied the steeper slopes of May hill until their inclosure in the later 19th century.

COMMUNICATIONS

The area is covered by a network of narrow lanes. Among those crossing the Leadon is a possible salt way running southwards from Worcestershire. The main roads are routes from Gloucester that fan out west of the Severn towards South Wales and Herefordshire and are based in part on Roman roads. In the coaching era roads forked in the south, in Huntley, for Monmouth and for Hereford, the latter route crossing the south side of May hill towards Ross-on-Wye (Herefs.). Another route to Hereford passed north of the hill by way of Newent. In the north a road from Gloucester passing through Bromesberrow on an Anglo-Saxon route was one of several roads converging on Ledbury (Herefs.). Despite the turnpiking of some of the principal roads the countryside between Newent town and the county boundary remained relatively inaccessible in the later 18th century.[1] In the early 19th century the major routes were altered in places to mitigate the steepness of their gradients and other improvements in the turnpike era included the building of a new way into Herefordshire beyond Dymock in the 1830s. The M50 motorway, opened in 1960 across the northern end of the area, has a junction with the Gloucester–Ledbury road within Bromesberrow.

The Hereford and Gloucester canal leading from the Severn at Gloucester opened across the area in 1798 on its completion as far as Ledbury. Passing near Newent town, it ran through a tunnel between Oxenhall and Dymock and in the north it closely followed the course of the Leadon. It closed in 1881 to be replaced by a railway opened between Gloucester and Ledbury in 1885. Another branch railway running through the area, the Gloucester and Hereford line up the Longhope valley, had been finished in 1855. Both railways closed in 1964 and part of the track of the Ledbury line was adapted as a road bypassing Newent town.

SETTLEMENT, SOCIETY, AND BUILDINGS

The greatest concentration of known sites from the Romano-British period within the area is in Dymock. In the late Anglo-Saxon period there were extensive adjacent royal estates at Dymock and Newent, the latter an outpost of that at Westbury-on-Severn. In addition in 1066 King Harold was lord of Bromesberrow and Oxenhall and thegns were in possession of Longhope (then called Hope) and possibly of other estates such as Carswalls, Huntley, Kempley, and Oxenhall. While Dymock, the largest estate, had a church, Newent's church was probably older, established by the 8th or 9th century, and the churches at Pauntley and Taynton originated as chapels of it. In 1086 all the estates were in Botloe hundred[2] apart from Longhope in the south, which was in Westbury hundred,[3] and Preston in the north-west, which was a detached part of Longbridge hundred,[4] itself perhaps created out of Botloe.[5] The estates were all to form separate parishes apart from two estates at Taynton, which made a single parish, from Carswalls and *Hege* (identified as Hayes), which were taken into Newent parish, and from Ketford and Kilcot, which belonged to Pauntley parish, Kilcot as a detached part.[6]

At the time of Domesday Book, when most arable land was in tenant holdings rather than in demesne, probably only Dymock and Newent had villages as their primary settlements. Most settlement was in solitary farmsteads and many of the tenants, usually villans, were the precursors of later yeomen who occupied scattered freehold and copyhold farms throughout the area. The building of farmsteads on cleared land continued after the Norman Conquest, when new settlement also included a substantial earthwork in Taynton, but with the consolidation of farms from the later Middle Ages numerous farmhouses and farmsteads were abandoned. Despite moves in the 13th century to foster trade on the royal manor of Dymock the only market centre to emerge was at Newent. In the 18th and 19th centuries squatter settlement on common and waste land created a number of hamlets, as on May hill and at Gorsley on the Herefordshire border,[7] and road improvements facilitated the growth of villages in Huntley, Kempley, and Longhope. Increased residential development in the later 20th century centred on Newent town, which expanded into the surrounding fields, and led to hamlets such as Bromesberrow Heath, Clifford's Mesne, and May Hill despite their irregular road patterns becoming regarded as villages.

At the Norman Conquest Dymock and Newent, the largest parishes, remained largely royal territory and Preston, the smallest, belonged to Gloucester abbey. Newent passed to Cormeilles abbey (Eure), which established a priory there, and in the 12th century the larger estate at Dymock was broken up, part of it passing to the local Cistercian house at Flaxley. While

---

1 Rudder, *Glos.* 408, 508, 561–2.
2 *Domesday Book*, I, 164, 166, 167–8, 170.
3 Ibid. 167.
4 Ibid. 165v.
5 F.R. Thorn, 'Hundreds and Wapentakes', *The Gloucestershire Domesday* (1989), 44.
6 The histories of Rudford, Tibberton, and Upleadon, which also belonged to Botloe hundred (*Domesday Book*, I, 165v., 167, 170v.), will be given in another volume of this county history.
7 Turner, *Agric. of Glos.* 50.

several other religious houses and hospitals acquired bits of land in the area, in Kempley including St Katherine's hospital at Ledbury, most of the land remained in lay hands. Prominent baronial families with manors in the area and almost invariably non-resident included the Lacys and the lords of Monmouth and Kilpeck (Herefs.) and later the Greys of Wilton, in Bridstow (Herefs.), and the Talbots. Among smaller lay lords the most prominent and the wealthiest at the end of the medieval period were the Whittingtons of Pauntley. Yeoman families with farms that perhaps originated in the holdings of Domesday tenants became significant landowners in the manors, occupying the medieval farmsteads scattered throughout the area.

From the 16th century, save for Preston which passed to the bishops of Gloucester, the parishes contained few big estates, most of their land belonging to gentry and yeomen. The property of Cormeilles abbey, which Fotheringhay college (Northants.) had owned from the early 15th century until its surrender to the Crown, came to the Winters of Lydney. Destruction during the Civil War included the sacking of Taynton church[1] and there were minor military engagements after the siege of Gloucester was lifted in 1643 and the area west of the Severn was filled with opposing garrisons.[2] Landowners and farmers incurred financial damage by giving free quarter to both sides in the conflict.[3] After hostilities ceased leading royalists, notably Sir John Somerset at Pauntley, suffered financial penalties but there was no great transfer of land, apart from sales of property in Dymock and Newent by Sir John Winter, the chief supporter of the Crown in the Forest of Dean area.

From the mid 17th century the Foleys, a dynasty of ironmasters, were among the leading landowners, particularly in Newent and Oxenhall. Among the resident gentry the Wynniatts and Cams of Dymock were families that had prospered locally as yeomen. The Pyndars, who came to Kempley from Derbyshire in the later 17th century, changed their name to Lygon and moved to Madresfield (Worcs.) on inheriting an estate there in the mid 18th. Substantial yeoman families remained the backbone of local society, notably the Hookes in Pauntley, the Hills in and around Dymock and Newent, and from the 17th century the Holders in Taynton. With the non-residence of its more substantial landowners, of whom the Roman Catholic Somersets abandoned the enlargement of their house at Pauntley Court in the later 17th century, and the absence of large estates the area has few grand houses. Bromesberrow Place, the principal exception, standing in the north-east on the former county boundary, was enlarged in the later 18th century for the Yate family. In the 19th and early 20th century most of the area's major landowners were resident, among them the Onslows, the Foleys' successors, in Newent, the Thackwells and Drummonds (later Deane-Drummonds) in Dymock, and the Ricardos in Bromesberrow. The Probyns of Newland built a modest country house in Longhope but they later occupied Huntley Manor and sold most of their land in the later 19th century to the Ackers family, which thereby became the dominant influence in the south of the area. Farming families continued to own a large part of the land in the early 21st century.

Within the landscape the houses of the yeomanry are an ubiquitous feature. Many are situated on a hillside or an outcrop, having complex sections with wings at different levels (Winter's Farm; Russell's End) and ancillary buildings on separate terraces (Byfords; Kew's Farm). Some on flatter land stand within or next to moats (Bellamy's Farm; the Moat; Taynton Court). Many houses date from the 16th and 17th centuries but among survivals of late medieval architecture Toney's Farm, one of several early stone-built houses at the foot of the Malvern hills, and Crooke's Farm have elaborate roofs. The remains of several jettied houses form part of the building stock of Newent town.

In the modern period some manor houses and farmhouses evolved into small country houses. One of the earliest is Preston Court, a large timber-framed house of the late 16th or early 17th century. Local stone, used for plinths, gable walls, and chimneys, was occasionally employed for entire houses such as an early 17th-century manor house (Stone House) in Kempley. While new building in the later 17th and early 18th century included fashionable houses such as Kempley Court, Hart's Barn, Boyce Court, Hownhall Farm, Briery Hill, and, in Newent town, the Tan House, the adoption of brick for outer walls rather than just for the infill of timber frames was gradual. The technique of building entirely in brick reputedly became standard practice for smart houses in Newent town at the very end of the 17th century[4] but it was used earlier, as at Huntley Court, and it was extended in the 1690s to a collection of outbuildings at Taynton House. Light timber framing continued to be used in the construction of humbler houses in the 18th century. Cider houses from the period survive in many of the farmyards and several retain mill machinery.

In the 19th century roadside villas were built in the countryside and the remodelling and enlargement of main houses such as Taynton House and Boyce Court continued. One entirely new country house, Clifford Manor, was built on the lower slopes of May hill. Farm buildings were also improved, in the early years in Oxenhall and Newent and latterly in Dymock and

---

1 *LJ* 9, 665.
2 *Bibliotheca Glos.* pp. lxxxi, 68, 72–5; *Cal. SP Dom.* 1644–5, 269. See F.A. Hyett, 'The Civil War in the Forest of Dean, 1643–5', *Trans. BGAS* 18 (1893–4), 94–106.
3 TNA, E 134/1657/Mich. 47.
4 GA, D 412/Z 3, Nourse MS, p. 15.

Kempley, where the Madresfield estate provided new houses, outbuildings, and cottages. In Huntley, where a model farmstead at Woodend was among buildings erected for the Probyns in the 1850s, the rector Daniel Capper rebuilt the church and parsonage (later Huntley Manor) in the early 1860s. In the 20th century, particularly after the sale of their land, many farmhouses were modernized and their outbuildings converted as dwellings.

In church architecture Dymock, dating from the late 11th century, is by far the largest in a local group of early Norman churches with decoration ascribed to a 'Dymock school' of sculptors.[1] Kempley's 12th-century church is virtually complete, retaining its nave roof and much of its wall decoration. Medieval additions to the area's churches were modest, except perhaps at Newent, and 19th-century restorations were usually pedestrian. Notable individual buildings are a mid 17th-century church aligned north–south at Taynton, a late 17th-century nave at Newent constructed primarily as a self-contained auditorium, an ornate Victorian church by S.S. Teulon at Huntley, and an 'Arts and Crafts' church of 1903 by A. Randall Wells at Kempley. The last is a reminder of the High Churchmanship of the Lygons (Earls Beauchamp), the imposition of which provided a challenge to the religious traditions and practice in Dymock and Kempley in the later 19th century. In the course of the 19th century nonconformists built a few, small chapels and from the 1860s Anglicans provided places of worship for growing settlements at Bromesberrow Heath, Clifford's Mesne, and Gorsley.

ECONOMY

In an area often devoted primarily to dairying and cattle and sheep rearing, the lighter and friable sandy soils of the north were used primarily for growing rye in the Middle Ages. The countryside extending deep into Herefordshire became known as 'the ryelands' and, more particularly, a division of Dymock took its name from the cultivation of rye.[2] The Ryeland breed of sheep, reared for meat and wool, was named from the area.[3] Agricultural improvements were often delayed in the 18th century and despite a decline in the cultivation of rye well over half of the crop returned in Gloucestershire in 1801 was grown in Bromesberrow, Dymock, and Newent.[4] There were numerous apple and pear orchards in the mid 16th century and the countryside was likened in the later 18th century to a garden overspread in spring with flowers and to a forest of fruit trees.[5] The ryelands were particularly suitable for cider apples[6] and the area around Dymock became noted for the quality of its drink made from the Red Streak variety,[7] said to have been introduced to England from France by John Scudamore, Viscount Scudamore, of Holme Lacy (Herefs.) in the late 1630s.[8] Taynton, which was associated with a variety of squash pear by the 1670s,[9] was esteemed for its cider and perry in the later 18th century[10] and Huntley, Kempley, and Newent had businesses producing cider and perry until well into the 20th century. In the later 20th century viniculture was established in several places. The area's role in soft fruit and market-garden cultivation developed in the 20th century, notably through a scheme applied to a Newent estate in the 1930s. A long celebrated feature of the area's natural flora are the daffodils that flower in its lanes and fields in the spring.

With its weekly market, a right granted to Cormeilles abbey in 1253, the town of Newent became the area's principal trading centre. The market dealt in corn and Welsh cattle at the start and a market house built in 1668 was used for sales of butter. Annual fairs came to deal mainly in livestock and cheese. From the Middle Ages the town's inhabitants were predominantly tradesmen and craftsmen supplying goods to the surrounding villages. Cloth making continued in the town into the early modern period and leather tanning was an important industry there in the 17th century. With the discovery of coal deposits close by and the building of the canal from Gloucester the town's economic prospects looked promising in the later 18th century. A small spa was also developed but the various initiatives failed to prosper. While the poor state of many local roads had offered some protection to its trade, road improvements from the early 19th century increasingly drew Newent into the economic orbit of the county town, and regional centre, of Gloucester. Newent's market business ceased in the mid 20th century but its onion fair was revived later as a pleasure fair.

Industrial activity was based on the area's mineral resources and woodland. French immigrants operated a glassworks near the foot of May hill for a few decades from the late 16th century. In the 17th century blast

---

1 E. Gethyn-Jones, *The Dymock School of Sculpture* (Chichester, 1979), reviewed by S.E. Rigold in *Medieval Archaeology* 25 (1981), 242–3.

2 Rudge, *Agric. of Glos.* 20, 138; Turner, *Agric. of Glos.* 48.

3 W. Marshall, *The Rural Economy of Gloucestershire* (1796), II, 199.

4 W.E. Minchinton, 'Agriculture in Gloucestershire during the Napoleonic Wars', *Trans. BGAS* 68 (1949), 170.

5 Rudder, *Glos.* 409; Marshall, *Rural Econ. of Glos.* II, 253.

6 J. Beale, 'Aphorisms Concerning Cider', in J. Evelyn, *Sylva, or a Discourse of Forest-Trees, and the Propagation of Timber in His Majesties Dominions* (1664 edn), 21–6; D. Colwall, 'An Account of Perry and Cider out of Gloucestershire', in ibid. (1679 edn), 401–2.

7 Bodleian, Top. Glouc. c. 3, f. 196v.

8 GA, D 412/Z 3, Nourse MS, p. 8; for Scudamore, *Complete Peerage*, XI, 572–3.

9 Colwall, 'Account of Perry and Cider', 401.

10 Rudder, *Glos.* 725; Turner, *Agric. of Glos.* 53; Marshall, *Rural Econ. of Glos.* II, 222, 229.

furnaces in Longhope and elsewhere smelted locally-mined ore and cinders, the latter being the iron-rich slag produced and deposited, often in large tips, during earlier iron-ore working. All the ironworks within the area were short-lived apart from the Ellbridge furnace, north of Newent town, which was taken over by the Foley family, the main players in the industry. It remained in production until the mid 18th century and the building thought to have been its charcoal store is one of the most significant reminders of the area's past industry.[1] Mining within the Newent coalfield was only sporadic despite the coalfield's development being one of the principal objects for the construction of the Hereford and Gloucester canal. Quarrying of stone took place throughout the area, notably on the sides of May hill where substantial quarries were worked periodically in the 18th and 19th centuries. In the same period brickworks in Kempley, Newent, and Taynton supplied the needs of local builders and gardeners.

Coppicing for charcoal production, an early feature of the woodland economy, intensified in the 17th and 18th centuries to satisfy the requirements of ironworks within and beyond the area. The Foleys bought a number of woods to secure charcoal supplies and the Probyns were among landowners establishing new plantations. During the same period oak bark was regularly harvested for tanning purposes. Other woodland crafts used the small wood to make products such as handles, hoops, and laths and the most successful business in that field, the turnery established in Longhope by the Constance family in the later 18th century, survived until the early 1980s. During the 20th century deciduous woodland gave way to conifer plantations, one of the agents in the change in timber production being the Forestry Commission, which took over the commercial management of a number of woods, including those in the west known collectively as Dymock Woods. In the south C.P. Ackers (d. 1960) increased the woodland on his Huntley estate and businesses he fostered to make woodland products and provide advice on woodland management continued in the early 21st century.

Tradesmen moving goods along the roads into Herefordshire and South Wales included in the early 17th century a carrier operating in London from the south of the area at Longhope. Residents on the duchy of Lancaster manor there could obtain exemption from fair and market tolls in England.[2] Local carriers and hauliers continued to serve the agricultural economy in the era of motorised transport, one of the more successful businesses being founded at Longhope by Henry Read in the 1920s. From the mid 20th century the area became increasingly a dormitory for Gloucester and other large towns. Several small business parks were established to provide manufacturing and service jobs within the area and in the early 21st century Newent town retained a role as a centre for shopping, professional services, and schools.

ADMINISTRATION

Hundredal rights in Botloe remained with the Crown[3] but about half of the parishes and tithings obtained total or partial exemption from the jurisdiction of the hundred court. In Newent, where Cormeilles abbey enjoyed extensive franchises including view of frankpledge by the 13th century and granted liberties piecemeal to the inhabitants of the town, the supremacy of the abbey's manor court was confirmed in 1297. A separate town court was held until at least the late 15th century and there were also lesser courts for other manors. The roof of Newent's former boothall, probably its early court and market house, is an elaborate and rare example from a late medieval town building. In Dymock the lords of the manor held a view of frankpledge for the whole parish apart from the estate of Flaxley abbey. The two lords of Taynton probably held their own views by the later 13th century; in 1287 Cecily de Mucegros claimed that right in Great Taynton and Bevis de Knovill asserted his entitlement to a number of franchises in Little Taynton.[4] Tithingmen for Bromesberrow, Kempley, Oxenhall, and Pauntley were answerable in the hundred view of frankpledge according to records of the years 1641–5;[5] the sheriff or his deputy held that view in the later 18th century.[6]

The ties of Huntley and Longhope with their respective hundreds were loosened in the later Middle Ages, probably in the 15th century. The manor courts in both places, which had become estates of the duchy of Lancaster and were eventually to form part of a new hundred made up of duchy estates,[7] exercised leet jurisdiction in the early modern period. Preston, where Gloucester abbey had leet jurisdiction in the early 16th century, belonged between 1483 and 1662, through the addition of Longbridge hundred to Dudstone and King's Barton hundred,[8] to a separate county, the inshire, administered by Gloucester corporation.[9]

Botloe's historic meeting place was a green at its centre high above the Leadon on the boundary between

---

1 Below, Fig. 63.
2 See TNA, DL 13/53/61.
3 *Feudal Aids*, II, 263; Herefs. RO, E 12/G/9.
4 *Plac. de Quo Warr.* 243–4, 246.
5 Herefs. RO, E 12/G/9.
6 Glos. Colln. JF 6.70(6, 10).
7 *Military Surv. of Glos. 1522*, 199, 206; Smith, *Men and Armour*, 68, 71. See *VCH Glos.* X, 1.
8 *Domesday Book*, I, 165v.; Taylor, *Domesday Glos.* 31.
9 *VCH Glos.* IV, 54, 113; see TNA, PROB 11/287, f. 145v.

Newent and Pauntley,[1] but the mound represented in the second element of its name is possibly the earthwork at Castle Tump, 1.6 km to the north-west at the limits of Dymock, Newent, Oxenhall, and Pauntley.[2] It has been postulated that the road running west of the mound represents a Roman route from Gloucester.[3] In the mid 17th century the hundred court met further south at Ell bridge,[4] where the same road crossed a tributary of the Leadon near Newent town.

In 1835 Newent became the centre of a poor-law union made up of 18 parishes, including Aston Ingham and Linton in Herefordshire and Redmarley D'Abitot and Staunton in Worcestershire.[5] The town continued to have a role in the government of a wide area until 1974, from 1895 as the centre of a rural district that comprised the union's Gloucestershire parishes. Its two Worcestershire parishes technically formed a separate rural district[6] until they were added to Gloucestershire in 1931.[7] Huntley and Longhope, the two southernmost parishes in this volume, became part of the Westbury-on-Severn poor-law union in 1835[8] and thus belonged from 1895 to East Dean and United Parishes Rural District,[9] reorganised in 1935 as East Dean Rural District.[10] From 1974 all of the area in the volume was within Forest of Dean District.

---

1 *PN Glos.* III, 174; see GDR, T 1/140 (no 232).
2 *PN Glos.* IV, 139; OS Map 6", Glos. XVII.NW (1884 edn).
3 T. Catchpole, T. Copeland, and A. Maxwell, 'Introduction' to 'Roman Dymock: archaeological investigations 1995–2002', *Trans. BGAS* 125 (2007), 132–3.
4 Herefs. RO, E 12/G/9.
5 *Poor Law Com. 2nd Rep.* p. 523.
6 GA, DA 30/100/5, pp. 1, 37, 57, 76.
7 Ibid. 100/13, p. 371.
8 *Poor Law Com. 2nd Rep.* p. 524.
9 See GA, DA 24/100/1, pp. 1–2, 193.
10 *Census*, 1931 (pt. ii).

NEWENT

THE town of Newent stands 12 km (7½ miles) north-west of Gloucester close to the county boundary with Herefordshire in a large parish that extends to within 7.5 km (4¾ miles) of the city. The settlement, which was of evident importance in Anglo-Saxon times, was formed into a town by the Norman abbey of Cormeilles which in the 13th century maintained a priory and established a market there. It enjoyed modest success as a trading centre, particularly in the 17th century and the early 18th when tanneries, cloth making, and the nearby Ellbridge iron furnace all contributed to its livelihood. In the late 18th century hopes of greater prosperity were kindled by the building of the Hereford and Gloucester canal, the associated development of a coalfield, road improvements, and the promotion of a spa, but Newent remained small, providing marketing and local government services to surrounding villages. In the late 20th century it was much enlarged by new housing and became principally a dormitory town for Gloucester.

From the early Middle Ages Newent parish comprised several manors and numerous freehold and tenant farms. In later centuries the number of farmsteads was reduced as farms were enlarged, and cottages accumulated on commons and waste land. The largest of the new settlements were the dispersed hamlets of Gorsley and Kilcot, formed on part of Gorsley common adjoining the Herefordshire boundary, and Clifford's Mesne, on the northern slopes of May hill. Smaller hamlets were based on roadside greens at the parish boundaries. A later community, of a more planned nature, was established in the 1930s as a project of the Land Settlement Association.

BOUNDARIES AND DIVISIONS

The ancient parish, one of the largest in the county, comprised 8,091 a. (3,276 ha) and bordered 11 other Gloucestershire and Herefordshire parishes (including both parts of Pauntley and a detached part of Much Marcle).[1] Its boundaries, which in many places crossed

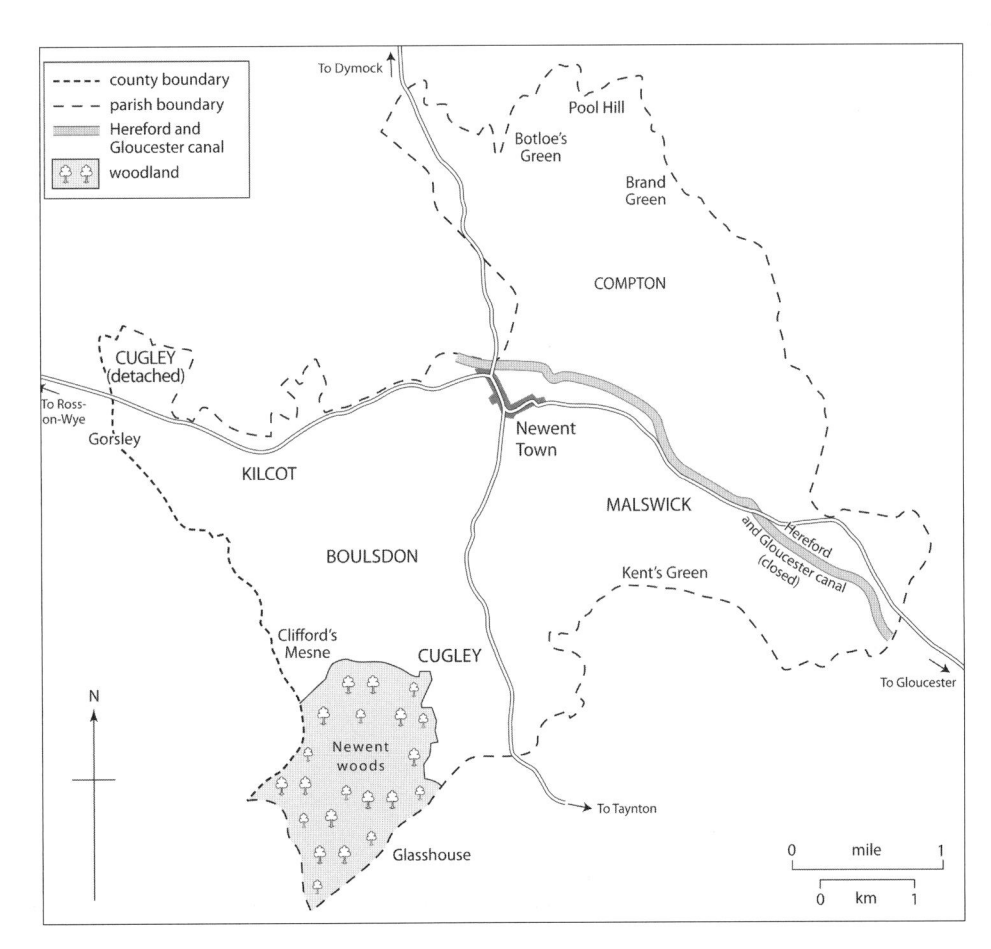

Map 2. Newent parish 1882

---

1 *OS Area Book* (1883). This account was written between 2004 and 2007 and revised in 2009.

common land and woodland, were not in the main marked by distinctive features. In places they followed a lane or a water course, including on part of the east a small stream known by 1618 as Knowles's brook,[1] but frequently they respected those features for only a short distance, as in the north where the Ell brook and a tributary and roads from Newent to Ross-on-Wye (Herefs.) and to Dymock were all touched. Even the county boundary, where it crossed Gorsley common, had few defining features; in 1719 the lord of Kilcot manor planted a series of oak trees to mark off his part of the common from Aston Ingham (Herefs.) to the south-west, as well as from a part to the north belonging to Newent manor.[2] On Pool hill common in the north-east the parishioners of Pauntley marked out the boundary in 1616 but were accused in the Newent manor court of taking in 6 a. of Newent.[3] Most of the settlements that formed on commons and greens straddled parish boundaries. In 1820 Newent and Aston Ingham agreed a minute diversion of the boundary to make it follow the party wall in a pair of cottages, so avoiding potential disputes over poor-relief allocation.[4]

Within its boundaries the parish comprised six ancient tithings known in the early 16th century as 'aliwaters',[5] a term of obscure origin that later appears in the form 'holywater'.[6] Newent tithing, which was also termed the borough or liberty of Newent,[7] occupied the north central part of the parish and included the market town with a wide area of demesne land of Newent manor and a few small tenant farms. Its boundaries can be roughly identified to include Ell brook on the north-east and north, Boulsdon Lane on the south, and a small tributary stream (once known as Ploddy or Bloody brook)[8] on the south-east.

The tithings of Compton, Malswick, and Cugley adjoined Newent tithing on the north-east, the south-east, and the south respectively and contained early farmsteads, mostly owing allegiance to Newent manor, and later hamlets on the parish boundaries. Compton tithing included Carswalls, recorded as a separate manor from the time of Domesday Book, and on the tithing's boundary with Pauntley were the hamlets called Brand Green, Compton Green, Pool Hill, and Botloe's Green.[9] Malswick tithing, straddling Ell brook and the main Gloucester–Newent road, included a distinct area of ancient estates called Okle and part of the hamlet of Kent's Green on the boundary with Taynton. The main part of Cugley tithing, centred on the road from Newent town to Taynton, included a manor called Southorle, based on the house called the Moat and recorded as a separate vill of Newent in 1300, and, adjoining it, an ancient estate called Stalling (later Stallions), recorded from 1181.[10] At its south end Cugley included the large tract of woodland called Yartleton woods on May hill, and adjoining the woods, just within the boundary with Taynton, there was once a small hamlet called Glasshouse Green. A detached part of Cugley tithing in the north-western arm of the parish formed part of Gorsley common[11] and from the early modern period was settled by cottages.

Boulsdon tithing occupied the south-western part of the parish, bounded from Cugley tithing by the Boulsdon brook; it probably took the second element of its name from the low ridge rising west of that brook. Originating as a separate manor in the late 11th century, it comprised ancient farmsteads near and on the road from Newent to Clifford's Mesne, a hamlet formed in the early modern period on the lower slopes of May hill at the south end of the tithing. The sixth tithing of the parish, Kilcot, occupied most of the north-western arm of the parish. Apart from the Conigree, site of one of its ancient manors, and a few other farmsteads at its east end, it comprised scattered cottages built as encroachments on Gorsley common. The nomenclature of Kilcot is confusing. As a manorial name it included at least a substantial part of the detached portion of Pauntley manor on the tithing's north side, while later as a settlement name it tended to be limited to the houses within the east part of the tithing, particularly those on the Newent–Ross road. Gorsley was also sometimes used as a manorial name, applied to some small farmsteads in and adjoining the detached part of Pauntley,[12] while as a settlement name it was applied loosely to all the houses on the common, both within Newent and over the county boundary in Linton.

Major adjustments were made to Newent's boundaries in the late 20th century. In 1965 part of Aston Ingham, including the Oaks farmhouse and other houses adjoining Clifford's Mesne, was added to Newent.[13] In 1992 the parish was reduced in area by the transfer of houses near Glasshouse hamlet on May hill and at Kent's Green to Taynton, to the south, and by the redrawing of its boundary on the north-east and east to transfer land and houses at Pool Hill, Compton Green, and Brand Green to Pauntley, at Hook's Lane, Grinnell's hill, and Madam's wood to Upleadon, and at

---

1 Herefs. RO, E 12/G/7, ct. 23 Apr. 1618; TNA, HO 107/350.
2 GA, D 412/Z 3, Nourse MS, p. 13.
3 Herefs. RO, E 12/G/7, ct. 23 Oct. 1616.
4 GA, P 225/VE 2/2.
5 TNA, REQ 2/2/153.
6 Smith, *Men and Armour*, 62; Rudder, *Glos.* 563.
7 Herefs. RO, E 12/G/3, ct. (6 Mar.) 7 Edw. III; G/7, ct. 13 Apr. 1615; GA, D 2957/212/130; D 332/T 8, deed 2 Oct. 1705; *Census*, 1831.
8 Herefs. RO, E 12/G/3, ct. (10 Oct.) 2 Hen. VI; G/5, survey 1624, pp. 5, 33; and for the identification of the fields adjoining the brook: GDR, T1/126 (for the map, missing from this copy of the Newent tithe award, see GA, D 2710).
9 BL, Add. MS 18461, f. 1v.; below, settlement (outlying settlements: Compton).
10 C.E. Hart, 'Metes and Bounds of the Forest of Dean', *Trans BGAS* 66 (1945), 187; BL, Add. MS 18461, f. 1v.; below, manors.
11 Below (landscape).
12 Below, manors (Kilcot); Oxenhall, manor (estates in detached part of Pauntley).
13 *Census*, 1971; OS Map 1:25,000, SO 62/72 (1977 edn).

Layne's Farm, Red hill, and Leachford (formerly Lydenford) to Rudford and Highleadon.[1] In 2000 Kilcot and the part of Gorsley within Newent were formed into a separate civil parish called Gorsley and Kilcot.[2] The settlement of Gorsley thus remained for civil purposes divided between parishes and counties, though the parts within Newent and Linton, together with a wider area in the west of Newent including Kilcot and Clifford's Mesne, had formed a separate ecclesiastical district since 1872.[3]

LANDSCAPE

The land is formed mainly by the Triassic New Red sandstone in the north-east and the Old Red sandstone of the Devonian period in the south-west. On the slopes of May hill older, Silurian sandstones outcrop, forced to the surface by the fold known as the Malvern fault.[4] The New Red sandstone is revealed in some deep-sided lanes, including one south of the house called the Conigree (Conigree Court) where a cutting was made in 1807,[5] Hill Top Lane by the Ell brook north-east of Newent town, and others near Botloe's Green and Compton Green. At the break between the Devonian and Triassic rocks, running through Boulsdon and Kilcot tithings, coal strata occur near the surface[6] and were worked sporadically, the main period of activity being the late 18th century and early 19th.[7] On May hill, the dominant feature of the landscape, land within Newent climbs to above the 260-m contour. Most of the rest of the parish is gently rolling countryside at around 30–50 m but the hilly nature becomes more pronounced again at its north end, around Botloe's Green and Pool Hill, where the land rises to between 70 and 80 m.

Much of the land drains to the Ell brook, which in its long progress through the parish flows northwards through Kilcot tithing, turns eastwards along part of the north boundary, and then arcs south-eastwards through Malswick tithing to join the river Leadon on the boundary between Upleadon and Highleadon. The brook's main tributary is the Boulsdon brook,[8] which rises on May hill and flows northwards through Boulsdon tithing to Newent town. Near the town it was usually called in the Middle Ages Coleford brook, after the ford where it crossed Boulsdon Lane,[9] but within the town it has been called since at least 1329 Peacock's brook,[10] probably after a local family.[11] Among smaller tributaries are those mentioned above, the brook forming part of the parish's north boundary before joining Ell brook on the boundary between Oxenhall and the detached part of Pauntley, Ploddy brook rising in Cugley near the house called the Moat, and Knowles's brook forming part of the east boundary in Malswick. In the more low-lying parts of the parish several houses attached to manor estates were protected by moats. In the 17th century three large ponds were built on Gorsley common to store spring water for the Ellbridge iron furnace several miles away in Oxenhall parish.[12] The Great Pool and the Middle Pool, built before 1670,[13] straddled the boundary with Linton; covering together 25 a., they fed a watercourse which ran north-eastwards to join the tributary of Ell brook at the north boundary of the parish.[14] Smallbrook Pool was built in 1694 where a brook of that name crossed the boundary with Aston Ingham before continuing over the common to join Ell brook at Gorsley ford.[15] The ponds and associated watercourses were maintained until the ironworks went out of use in the mid 18th century.[16] The ponds were drained[17] and the sites became pasture closes, but the rubble and earth dams that had contained them survived largely intact but much overgrown in 2007.

The main tract of woodland in what was generally a well wooded parish clothed the northern slopes of May hill and was known in the Middle Ages as Yartledon woods (from the old name of the hill). The name later took the form Yartleton, and from the early 19th century the woods were usually known as Newent woods. Mentioned in 1181,[18] Yartleton woods remained one of the chief assets of Newent manor for many centuries. For a period up to the early 14th century, however, management of the woods, with others further north belonging to Boulsdon and Kilcot manors, was curtailed by the inclusion of part of Newent in the bounds of the Forest of Dean. Yartleton woods were long managed as oak coppice, but in the early 20th century after being acquired by the Huntley

---

1 The Forest of Dean (Parishes) Order 1991 (unpublished Statutory Instrument 1992 no 2283; information (Sept. 2003) from Mr G. Ellison (environment directorate, Glos. co. council); OS Map 1:25,000, OL 14 (2005 edn). See *Rudford & Highleadon Chronicle*, II (copy in Glos. Colln. R 255.4), 17, 19.

2 The Forest of Dean (Parishes) Order 1999 (unpublished Statutory Instrument 1999 no 3279).

3 Below, religious hist. (religious life in 19th and 20th cents.).

4 Geol. Surv. Map (solid and drift edn 1988), sheet 216; W. Dreghorn, *Geology Explained in the Severn Vale and Cotswolds* (Newton Abbot, 1967), 179–81.

5 GA, P 225A/SU 2/1.

6 D. Bick, *The Mines of Newent and Ross* (Newent, 1987), 7.

7 Below, econ. hist. (coal mining).

8 GA, D 892/T 57, deed 12 Mar. 1760; D 5570/2.

9 Herefs. RO, E 12/G/1, ct. (15 Jan.) 19 Edw. II; G/3, ct. (10 Sept.) 7 Edw. III; for the ford (which has been culverted), GA, Q/SRh 1819B.

10 Herefs. RO, E 12/G/3, ct. (26 June) 3 Edw. III; G/7, ct. 28 Apr. 1620; GA, D 1810/10, deed 22 Nov. 1803.

11 BL, Add. MS 15668, f. 43; 18461, f. 105.

12 *Chapters in Newent's History* (Newent Local Hist. Soc. 2003), 157–8.

13 Herefs. RO, E 12/G/12, notes 30 Aug. 1670.

14 Ibid. G/13, lease (of the parts in Linton parish) 15 May 1749; GA, D 2528, p. 7; photocopy 5.

15 GA, D 412/Z 3, Nourse MS, p. 13; Herefs. RO, G/13, lease 25 May 1749.

16 Herefs. RO, E 12/G/25, accts.; G/29, vouchers 1746.

17 OS Maps 6", Glos. XVI.SE (1889 edn); XVII.SW (1884 edn).

18 BL, Add. MS 18461, f. 1v.; 15668, ff. 4, 23v.

Manor estate much was replaced with conifers.[1] The woods were said to cover 595 a. in 1660 and were surveyed as 674 a. in 1775. The parts on the higher slopes, south-west of the lane leading from Clifford's Mesne to Glasshouse, were known in the 18th century as Cockeridge hill and College wood, the latter presumably in reference to Fotheringhay college, owner of Newent manor in the late Middle Ages. On the lower slopes the main part was known as Fair Oak wood, a part adjoining Clifford's Mesne as Mesne (Mine) wood, and a smaller part adjoining the farm called Black House as Jordan's grove.[2] That Jordan's grove was tithable, unlike the rest of Yartleton woods which as demesne of the former lords, Cormeilles abbey, were tithe-free,[3] indicates that it was included in the abbey's grant of land in that area to Robert Jordan in the early 13th century.[4] The grove belonged to the owners of the adjoining farmland in the mid 17th century[5] and was sold to Thomas Foley, the lord of the manor, in 1665.[6] Robert Jordan's grant included an assart, which, with other evidence of assarting in Cugley tithing in the 12th and 13th centuries,[7] suggests considerable early medieval clearance of woodlands on the slopes below Yartleton woods. About 1315 two tenants of Newent manor, who had houses at or near the sites of Little Cugley and Ploddy House Farms, held parts of an alder grove (*alnetum*) called Black moor (*Blakemore*),[8] which was probably absorbed later into their farmland.

Woods near the west boundary of the parish, north of May hill, originally belonged to Boulsdon manor. They included Acorn (or Hacking) wood, the north part of which was sometimes called Lady grove,[9] and Spring wood; in 1838 the former covered *c*.80 a. and the latter 23 a. Further north Kilcot wood, originally part of the Kilcot manor based on the house called the Conigree, covered 72 a. in 1838. On the east boundary of the parish, adjoining the larger Collin Park wood in Pauntley, Madam's wood (also sometimes called Collin's Hill wood) covered 41 a. in 1838.[10] In 1516 the manor of Okle Clifford, in Malswick, included three small groves and a wood called Gravenhill;[11] the wood was in the area of Grinnell's hill on the Upleadon boundary and was partly converted to farmland before 1819.[12] Small groves and coppices remained on many other farms in the early modern period.[13]

The main tract of common land, Gorsley common, occupied much of the north-western arm of the parish and extended into the adjoining Herefordshire parishes. Within Newent the northern part of the common, bounded by the Oxenhall woodlands on the north, the boundary with Linton on the west, and ancient inclosures forming Gorsley Court and Brassfields farms on the east, belonged to Newent manor as a detached part of Cugley tithing,[14] while the southern part, between Aston Ingham on the south-west and Kilcot wood on the east, belonged to Kilcot manor. The northern part may represent the wood on Newent manor that was mentioned as *Tedeswode* in 1181 and 1286,[15] for that name, which survives at Tedgewood Farm in Upton Bishop (Herefs.), appears to have been used in the early Middle Ages for the whole of the large tract of woodland that straddles the county boundary.[16] Possibly all of Gorsley common was part of that woodland in the early Middle Ages, being cleared later by uncontrolled commoning of animals and taking of timber. In 1624 the part belonging to Newent manor was estimated at *c*.240 a. and described as covered with gorse and heath. It had already been subjected to some encroachment by cottagers,[17] and by 1775, when an accurate survey extended it at 246 a., 91 a. had been encroached.[18] The part belonging to Kilcot manor probably covered 200 a. or more. It was subject to similar encroachment in the late 18th century, and in 1806 over 40 a. was said to have been inclosed and many cottages built within the previous 20 years.[19] By 1838, except for a patch of land known as Kilcot green on the Newent–Ross road and a few strips of roadside waste, that process had engulfed all of Gorsley common within Newent parish.[20]

On the lower slopes of May hill the common called Clifford's Mesne by 1677 belonged to Boulsdon manor.[21] Encroachment there had begun by the late 18th century[22] and what remained of the common was mostly inclosed by the owner of the manorial rights in the late 19th century.[23] The smaller commons in the parish were also subject to gradual encroachment by cottage building. In 1775, of those belonging to Newent manor in Compton tithing, 5 a. at Botloe's green, 10 a. on the part of Pool hill common within Newent, and 8 a. at Brand green remained uninclosed;[24] all of Picklenash

---

1 Below, econ. hist. (woodland management).
2 Herefs. RO, E 12/G/15, mortgage 28 May 1660; GA, D 2528, plan A; GDR, T 1/126.
3 GDR, V 5/212T 3; T 1/126.
4 BL, Add. MS 15668, f. 36v.
5 Herefs. RO, E 12/G/15, mortgage 28 May 1660; G/17.
6 Below, settlement (outlying settlements: Cugley).
7 BL, Add. MS 18461, f. 1v.; 15668, f. 39v.
8 Ibid. Add. MS 18461, f. 110 and v.; and for those holdings (of Wal. de Farley and Wm. Emelot), below, settlement (outlying settlements: Cugley).
9 Herefs. RO, E 12/G/15, mortgage 28 May 1660; GA, D 2528, plan D; D 2245/T 8.
10 GDR, T 1/126.
11 *Cal. Regs. Priory of Llanthony*, p. 140.
12 GA, D 3269, deeds of Okle Clifford 1819–1914.
13 e.g. Herefs. RO, E 12/G/5, survey 1624, pp. 45, 97; GA, D 332/T 4, deed 2 Oct. 1606; D 2245/T 3, deed 21 Apr. 1637.
14 GA, D 245/I/13, ct. 27 Oct. 1777; TNA, HO 107/1960.
15 BL, Add. MS 18461, f 1v.; Herefs. RO, E 12/G/3, ct. (19 Apr.) 14 Edw. I.
16 Below, Dymock, introd. (landscape).
17 Herefs. RO, E 12/G/5, survey 1624, p, 15.
18 GA, D 2528, pp. 6–7.
19 Ibid. D 412/E 1; D 245/I/22.
20 GDR, T 1/126.
21 GA, D 332/T 5.
22 Ibid. D 412/E 1.
23 Ibid. E 2, letter 11 Dec. 1916; D 7723/1.
24 Ibid. D 2528, plan D.

green on the Ross road north of the town had been encroached by then.[1] By the time of the Commons Registration Act of 1965 the former commons of the parish, which included also Okle green in Malswick tithing and part of Highleadon common at Red hill on the east boundary,[2] were represented only by small patches of roadside waste.[3]

COMMUNICATIONS

Roads

The principal route through the parish came from Gloucester through Malswick to Newent town, from where it branched westwards to Ross and northwards to Dymock. It gave Newent a modest importance in the pattern of travel in the Middle Ages. Henry III passed through the town on his way from Gloucester to Hereford in 1226,[4] and cattle drovers from Wales came regularly through towards Gloucester in the 13th century.[5]

The road through Malswick, entering the town at its eastern end, was described as the 'great street' in 1228.[6] It appears to have been always the preferred route from Gloucester to Newent,[7] but there may have been an alternative in a road branching from it in Rudford parish, passing through Tibberton and Kent's Green, and entering Newent by Bury Bar Lane, which leads into the town's central market area.[8] The course of the latter route from near Caerwents Farm, west of Kent's Green, survives only as an ill-defined footpath but near the town, where it climbs a low ridge to the place called Bury Bar, it forms a deep hollow way. At Bury Bar it was referred to in 1657 as the lane leading from the town to Nelfields[9] (a farmhouse reached by a footpath from the lower end of the hollow way), suggesting that it was not then a recognized route to Gloucester. It may, however, have been one of two routes to Newent referred to by the Gloucester and Hereford turnpike trustees in 1727 when they decided to concentrate their efforts on only one.[10]

The Ross-on-Wye road, running westwards from the town through Kilcot tithing, formerly traversed Gorsley common by a winding lane that crosses the Ell brook at Gorsley ford. The Dymock road crosses the Ell brook north of the town at Ell bridge, for the repair of which the prior of Newent had a grant of oak timber in 1266.[11] Newent and Oxenhall parishes later took joint responsibility for repairing the bridge[12] and co-operated in rebuilding it in 1710.[13] North of the bridge, where within Oxenhall it climbs a hill known as Lambsbarn pitch, the road was recorded in 1693 as the highway to Dymock.[14] It seems likely, however, that in ancient times the route to Dymock ran along the Newent–Oxenhall parish boundary further east, following part of a lane called by 1344 Sandy way[15] before branching north-westwards to join the present route near a place called Three Ashes. A croft in Newent parish described in 1363 as adjoining highways from Newent to Dymock and to Botloe's green,[16] probably lay within the angle made by the lane to Three Ashes and the northern continuation of Sandy way. The lane linking Sandy way and Three Ashes was among a number of roads in Newent that were declared redundant and closed as highways in 1819.[17] The continuation of Sandy way, running by way of Botloe's green and Pool hill to cross the Leadon at Ketford, was described as the road from Newent to Ledbury (Herefs.) in 1776,[18] but possibly the road through Dymock was the more usual route between the two towns even before it was turnpiked in 1768.

The network of minor roads and narrow lanes in the parish was particularly complex south and south-west of Newent town. The principal road in that area left the town by Culver (formerly Coleford) Street and ran southwards through Cugley tithing to Taynton and Huntley. It was crossed by various routes giving access to the main Newent–Gloucester road in the east. One route, presumably used as a way to Gloucester by inhabitants of Gorsley and Kilcot and by travellers on the Ross road not needing to go through the town, followed Conigree Lane, running south-west of the house of that name, and Boulsdon Lane and crossed the Taynton road at the south end of Culver Street. East of Culver Street, where it was described in 1333 as the road from Boulsdon to Gloucester,[19] it continued south of Southend Farm to join the road mentioned above, running from Newent town by way of Caerwents Farm, Kent's Green, and Tibberton; most of its course east of the crossroads on Culver Street was discontinued as a highway in 1819.[20]

---

1 Ibid. p. 7; photocopy 5.
2 Ibid. D 245/I/13, ct. 27 Oct. 1777; I/20, letter 12 Nov. 1822; I/21; D 2528, plan C.
3 Ibid. DA 30/132/11.
4 *Rot. Litt. Claus.* II, 132–3.
5 BL, Add. MS 18461, f. 60.
6 *Close* 1227–31, 99.
7 e.g. BL, Add. MS 18461, f. 98; Herefs. RO, E 12/G/5, survey 1624, p. 25.
8 D. Bick, *Old Newent and District* (Newent, 1992), 13.
9 GA, D 421/T 34; and for the land called Deda furlong, which it adjoined, GDR, T 1/126.
10 GA, D 204/2/2, mins. 19 Oct. 1726, 27 Aug. 1727.
11 *Close* 1264–8, 211.
12 GDR wills 1559/360.
13 Glos. Colln. RQ 212.4.
14 GA, D 127/588.
15 Herefs. RO, E 12/G/2, ct. (6 Oct.) 18 Edw. III.
16 Ibid. ct. (11 Mar.) 37 Edw. III.
17 GA, Q/SRh 1819B.
18 Ibid. D 2957/212/92; D 2528, plan D; below, Pauntley, introd. (roads).
19 Herefs. RO, E 12/G/3, ct. (29 May) 7 Edw. III; and see Rudder, *Glos.* 562, where it is described as the cross way from Gloucester to Boulsdon.
20 GA, Q/SRh 1819B.

Further south on the Taynton road another junction was marked by a small green called by the 1520s Bromwich (or Bromage) green[1] and in 1624 Bromwich Oak green. The Taynton road was once joined there by a lane running from Great Boulsdon Farm and crossing the Boulsdon brook to the north-west[2] and by another climbing over Stallions hill to the south-west; the latter was used by Newent priory as a route to its Yartleton woods in 1285 when the owner of the Stallions estate attempted to stop its wagons passing through his court.[3] South of the green a lane from Clifford's Mesne to Kent's Green forms a crossroads that was called Anthony's Cross by the 1520s.[4] Near the parish boundary Judge's Lane, leading down from Glasshouse hamlet, joins the Taynton road, which crosses the brook on the boundary by a bridge built at the joint expense of Newent and Taynton in 1813.[5]

A lesser route leaves Newent town on the south-west by Watery Lane and traverses Boulsdon tithing to Clifford's Mesne. It was crossed in Watery Lane (by the site of the 19th-century cemetery) by a route from Oxenhall, which in turn crossed the Ross road at Stoney bridge on the parish boundary and beyond Watery Lane continued to join Boulsdon Lane at the ford by Lower Boulsdon Farm; parts of that route were closed in 1819 and survive only as footpaths, but the section north-west of Watery Lane remained open and with a branch running north-eastwards to Picklenash green is called Bradford's Lane.[6]

Compton tithing in the north-east part of the parish was criss-crossed by a similar network of lanes with crossroads and greens forming minor focuses, as at Compton green, Botloe's green, Limetree on Sandy way, and the place called by 1768 Three Cocks[7] on the road from Newent to Upleadon and Tewkesbury. The last road leaves the Dymock road north of Ell bridge to reach the parish boundary at Eden's Hill. In Malswick tithing a road from Gloucester to Upleadon by way of Highleadon green crosses Ell brook at the parish boundary by Lydenford bridge, for which the lords of Newent and Upleadon shared responsibility in 1387.[8]

The Gloucester–Newent road was made a turnpike in 1726 under an Act which covered routes leading from Gloucester towards Hereford and South Wales.[9] In 1768 the road running northwards from Newent to Dymock and thence to Ledbury was included in the same trust.[10] In the late 18th century, however, the roads around Newent remained in a very poor state of repair, their condition among the worst encountered by Samuel Rudder, the Gloucestershire historian, in his travels in the county in the 1770s.[11] Under an Act of 1802 powers were given to build a new line for the Newent–Ross road to join an existing turnpike from Mitcheldean to Hereford at Crow Hill, in Upton Bishop.[12] It was completed in 1810[13] and included a new straight course across Gorsley common, branching from the existing road at a place in Kilcot that became known as Cross Hands.[14] Also turnpiked under the same Act was a road leading south from the Ross road at Kilcot to join the main Gloucester–Ross road at Lea Line. At the same period there were also improvements to the Gloucester turnpike to Newent,[15] enabling the route through Newent town to be promoted as an alternative coaching route between Gloucester and Hereford;[16] by 1822 a coach service ran through the town on six days a week.[17] In 1812 a separate district of the Gloucester and Hereford trust was created to cover the Gloucester road from the south boundary of the parish and its continuation from the town through Dymock towards Ledbury,[18] and an Act of 1824 consolidated that district with the Ross road trust to create a new Newent trust.[19] In the early 1830s tolls were collected at gates near Layne's Farm, where the Gloucester road entered the parish, at the junction with Cleeve Lane at the entrance to the town, on the Dymock road at Ell bridge, and on the Ross road just west of the junction with Conigree Lane.[20] The Newent trust's roads ceased to be turnpikes in 1874.[21] During the 20th century the network of roads in the parish remained little changed, but the Gloucester and Ross roads became increasingly busy as a result of new building around the town and the opening in 1960 of the M50 motorway with a junction on the Ross road 5 km west of the town, in Linton parish. The increase of traffic led to the opening in 1968 of a short bypass, skirting the town from the Gloucester road on the east to the junction of the Ross and Dymock roads on the north.[22]

---

1 Herefs. RO, E 12/G/4, ct. *c*.1523 (approx. dated by presentment of Roger Porter's death).
2 Ibid. G/5, survey 1624, p. 6; GA, D 332/T 5, deed 6 Mar. 1625; D 1810/1, deed 23 May 1789. The green, hardly discernible in 2007, was at OS Nat. Grid SO 712242: see GA, Q/SRh 1819B, where it is named 'Broomageham green'.
3 BL, Add. MS 15668, f. 71 and v.; Herefs. RO, E 12/G/3, ct. (3 July) 13 Edw. I.
4 Herefs. RO, E 12/G/4, ct. *c*.1523; G/5, survey 1624, p. 6.
5 GA, P 225/VE 2/1.
6 Ibid. Q/SRh 1819B.
7 Ibid. D 412/T 2, abs. of title to estates of Isabella Beale; GDR, T 1/126.
8 *Public Works in Medieval Law* I, ed. C.T. Flower (Selden Soc. 32), 151.

9 Glouc. and Heref. Roads Act, 12 Geo. I, c. 13.
10 Ibid. 9 Geo. III, c. 50.
11 Rudder, *Glos.* 561.
12 Newent Roads Act, 42 Geo. III, c. 45 (Local and Personal).
13 *Glouc. J.* 10 Sept. 1810.
14 GA, SL 12; GDR, T 1/126 (nos 817A, 2021).
15 Fosbrooke, *Glouc.* 213; GA, D 204/2/5, mins. 9 Dec. 1819, 25 Apr., 11 May, 7 Oct. 1820.
16 *Glouc. J.* 27 Mar. 1815; 1 May 1820.
17 *Pigot's Dir. Glos.* (1822–3), 62.
18 GA, D 204/2/5, mins. 20 June 1812.
19 Newent Roads Act, 5 Geo. IV, c. 11 (Local and Personal).
20 OS Map 1", sheet 43 (1831 edn); GA, P 225/IN 3/3.
21 Annual Turnpike Acts Continuance Act, 1874, 37 & 38 Vic. c. 95.
22 *Citizen*, 29 Nov. 1960; 17 Feb. 1968.

Canal and Railway

The Hereford and Gloucester canal traversed the east side of Newent parish running close to the Ell brook for several miles. The first Act for the project, passed in 1791, envisaged a route along the valley of the river Leadon with a branch to Newent, but the plan was revised to take the main line through Newent, where the development of the coalfield was the chief incentive. Under powers granted by a new Act of 1793 work began from the Gloucester end, and by 1795 the canal had progressed to Newent and by 1798 as far as Ledbury.[1] Although new pits were opened, the results of the coalfield development were disappointing[2] and the completion of the canal, to Hereford, was not achieved until 1845.[3] A wharf to serve Newent town was established on the canal near Ell bridge.[4]

In 1870 the Great Western Railway took over full management of the canal with the option to convert it to a railway. Work on the railway began in 1881 and was completed in 1885. For much of its course through Newent it made use of the canal bed. A station for Newent was built near Ell bridge and in 1938 a halt was opened in Malswick. The railway was closed for passenger traffic in 1959 and for freight in 1964.[5] Later in the 1960s part of its course north-east of Newent town was used as the route of the new bypass road.

POPULATION

The 34 tenants mentioned at Newent in 1086 are probably not a good indication of the number of households at that time as most of their holdings were large.[6] By the early 14th century, when 137 houses were recorded in the town and there were probably another 150–200 in the outlying areas,[7] the population is likely to have been well over 1,000; 105 wealthier inhabitants were assessed for the subsidy in 1327.[8] Loss of some smaller farms in the late Middle Ages presumably led to a decline in population. In 1551 there were said to be $c.712$ communicants,[9] and in 1563 190 households.[10] During the early modern period, with the general prosperity of agriculture, a diversity of occupations in Newent town, and the building of new cottages on the parish's commons, there was a gradual growth in population. In 1650 the parish was said to contain 300 families,[11] about 1710 $c.$1,100 inhabitants in 270 houses,[12] and about 1775 $c.$1,560 inhabitants.[13] In 1801 2,354 people in 459 houses were enumerated, and a steady rise continued in the early 19th century, reaching 2,859 by 1831 (1,346 in the town and adjoining parts of Newent tithing and 1,513 in the five other tithings) and 3,306 by 1851. There was then a gradual fall to 2,485 by 1901 and to 2,299 by 1931. By 1951 the addition of housing estates to the town and the influx of over 50 families as part of the Land Settlement Association scheme had caused a rise to 2,912. With further new building the population reached 3,807 by 1971 and 5,373 by 1991. In 2001 the population of Newent civil parish was 5,073 and that of the new civil parish of Gorsley and Kilcot 277.[14]

SETTLEMENT

In the late Anglo-Saxon period Newent, as a substantial constituent of the royal estate at Westbury-on-Severn,[15] was an important local centre. The early ecclesiastical status of the large parish, of which Pauntley remained a chapelry in the Middle Ages,[16] is indicated by the discovery there of a cross shaft of the late 8th or early 9th century.[17] Following the Norman Conquest the manor of Newent became the property of Cormeilles abbey, which supported a reeve with his own tenants in 1086 and set up a priory in the principal settlement.[18]

THE DEVELOPMENT OF NEWENT TOWN

Streets and Street Names

The town of Newent developed from the 13th century on an irregular plan, probably inherited in its essentials from the Anglo-Saxon and early Norman village. Its

---

1 D.E. Bick, *The Hereford & Gloucester Canal* (Newent, 1979), 7–4.
2 Below, econ. hist. (coal mining); Oxenhall, econ. hist. (coal mining).
3 Bick, *Heref. & Glouc. Canal*, 21–9.
4 GA, P 225/IN 3/3.
5 Bick, *Heref. & Glouc. Canal*, 37–8, 58–62.
6 *Domesday Book* (Rec. Com.), I, 166, 167v.
7 Below, settlement (development of Newent town: the Middle Ages; outlying settlements).
8 *Glos. Subsidy Roll, 1327*, 35.
9 J. Gairdner, 'Bishop Hooper's Visitation of Gloucester', *EHR* 19 (1904), 119.
10 Bodleian, Rawl. C. 790, f. 28.
11 C.R. Elrington, 'The Survey of Church Livings in Gloucestershire, 1650', *Trans. BGAS* 83 (1964), 98.
12 Atkyns, *Glos.* 569.
13 Rudder, *Glos.* 565.
14 *Census*, 1801–2001.
15 *Domesday Book* (Rec. Com.), I, 163; *VCH Glos.* X, 85.
16 Below, Pauntley, religious hist.
17 Below, religious hist. (ch. bldgs.: the parish ch.).
18 *Domesday Book*, I, 166; below, econ. hist. (agric.).

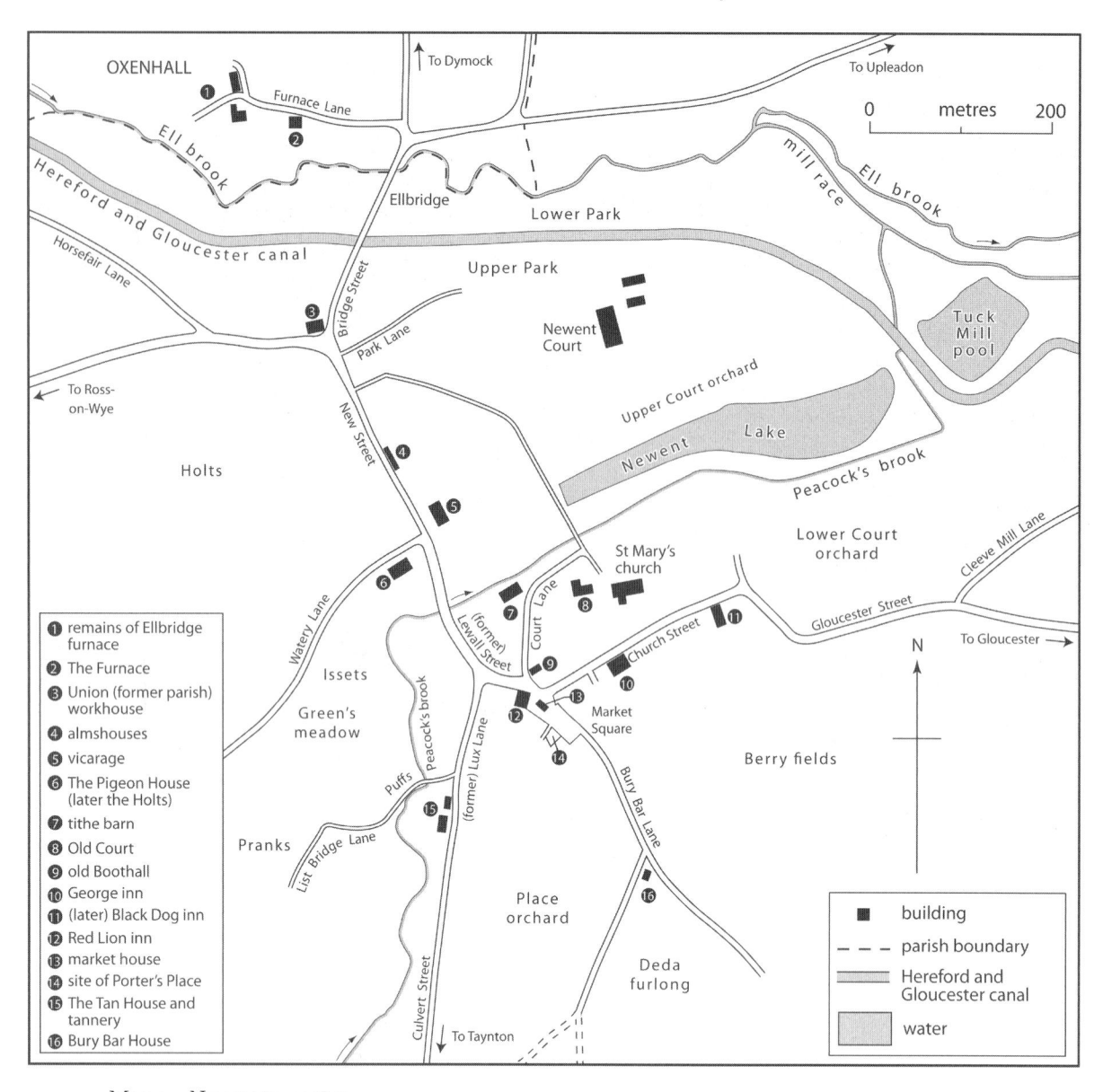

Map 3. *Newent town 1840*

Key:
1. remains of Ellbridge furnace
2. The Furnace
3. Union (former parish) workhouse
4. almshouses
5. vicarage
6. The Pigeon House (later the Holts)
7. tithe barn
8. Old Court
9. old Boothall
10. George inn
11. (later) Black Dog inn
12. Red Lion inn
13. market house
14. site of Porter's Place
15. The Tan House and tannery
16. Bury Bar House

main trading street follows a convoluted course with several changes of alignment.[1] The road from Gloucester enters the town from the east and after performing two almost right-angled bends reaches the town centre from a north-easterly direction, while the road from Ross-on-Wye enters at the north, where it joins the route from Dymock and Ledbury. A third street, of less importance but probably equally well built-up in the Middle Ages, enters the town from the south on the road from Huntley and Taynton.

The names of the town's streets have undergone several changes but their earlier forms can be recovered from records including a list published in the 1770s.[2] The Gloucester road in the east of the town was recorded as Church (or Churchend) Street from 1368[3] and its outer part, beyond the first of the two sharp bends, was distinguished in the 17th and 18th centuries as Old Church Street[4] or Bartholomew's Street. The short stretch of Church Street[5] between the two bends became known as Upper Church Street by the late 19th century,[6] while the name Gloucester Street had become established as the name of the outer part, between there and the junction with Cleeve Mill Lane.

Where it curves towards the north-west through

---

1 Map 3 and below, Fig. 2.
2 See Rudder, *Glos.* 561–2. For street names as used 1882: OS Maps 1:2,500, Glos. XVII.10, 14 (1884 edn).
3 Herefs. RO, E 12/G/1, cts. (7 July) 39 Edw. III, (12 Oct.) 40 Edw. III.
4 Ibid. G/5, survey 1624, p. 9; GA, D 2957/212/5, 12; D 421/M 81 (s.vv. 'Porter's rents', 'chantry rents').
5 GA, D 3403, deed 8 Sept. 1747.
6 Ibid. D 2957/212/18; DA 30/132/8.

2. *Newent in 1972, looking north-east over the town centre and former market place*

the centre of the town, the main thoroughfare was known by 1539 as Le Wall[1] (later Lewall Street), a name apparently derived from the wall of the priory precinct bordering it to the north-east. Beyond the crossing of Peacock's brook, known as Peacock's bridge in 1369, the thoroughfare continued to the junction with the Ross and Dymock roads as New Street,[2] a name recorded from 1300.[3] The part of the Dymock road continuing down to the bridge over Ell brook was known as Ellbridge Street in 1365.[4] By the 18th century the use of parts of the streets for livestock sales had given the alternative names of Beast Fair to New Street[5] and of Horse Fair to the beginning of the Ross road,[6] though the latter was also called Crown Hill from an inn at its junction with New Street.[7] By 1841 Lewall Street had become known as Broad Street[8] and by 1882 the name Lewall Street had been transferred to the section of New Street between Peacock's brook and the junction with Watery Lane. Also by 1882 the northern part of New Street had been renamed High Street. Ellbridge Street was usually known simply as Bridge Street by the early 19th century and was often called Station Street after the opening of the railway in 1885.[9] The entrance to the Ross road was from the late 19th century known as Ross Street.

The inner part of the long street entering the town from the south was known by 1300 as Lux Lane,[10] while its outer part was called by 1410 Coleford (or Culford) Street, taking its name from the brook flowing close to its western side and the ford near by on Boulsdon Lane.[11] From the early 18th century Coleford Street was

---

1 Herefs. RO, E 12/G/5, rental 31 Hen. VIII; GA, D 421/E 13, ff. 14–15.
2 Herefs. RO, E 12/G/1, cts. (30 Nov.) 43 Edw. III, (20 Feb.) 11 Hen. IV.
3 Hart, 'Metes and Bounds of the Forest of Dean', 187.
4 Herefs. RO, E 12/G/1, ct. (7 July) 39 Edw. III.
5 GA, D 2957/212/136; D 185/IV/38.
6 For this usage, see also TNA, HO 107/1960, where the union workhouse is listed as in Horsefair.
7 GA, Q/SRh 1819B.

8 TNA, HO 107/350. Below, Fig. 3.
9 e.g. T. Ward, *Around Newent* (Old Photographs Series, 1994), 21–2.
10 Hart, 'Metes and Bounds of the Forest of Dean', 187; Herefs. RO, E 12/G/1, ct. (20 Oct.) 7 Edw. III.
11 Herefs. RO, E 12/G/1, ct. (18 Apr.) 11 Hen. IV; and for the brook, ibid. ct. (15 Jan.) 19 Edw. II. Rudder (*Glos.* 562) made the unlikely assumption that it was named from a route to Coleford, in the Forest of Dean.

3. Broad Street looking north c.1910

more usually known as Culvert or Culver Street.[1] By the end of the century those names had come to be applied to the whole length of the southern street (Culver Street becoming established as the form in the 20th century); the name Lux Lane, for the northern part, was not generally used after c.1775.

Among minor lanes, for the most part little built on, Cleeve Mill Lane, recorded from 1366,[2] ran from the Gloucester road at the east entrance of the town down to a mill on Ell brook, and the short Currier's Lane, so called by 1624,[3] ran northwards from the double bend in Church Street into the manorial grounds north of the town. Symoundes Lane, which in 1410 adjoined part of the orchard of the former priory,[4] was possibly an alternative name for Currier's Lane. In the town centre a short lane, later known as Court Lane, led north into the priory precinct through a gateway that survived until the early 19th century.[5]

At the north end of the town a lane known as Park Lane by the 1770s led eastward from the junction of the Dymock and Ross roads into the manorial lands called the Parks and in the early 19th century became the drive to a new mansion called Newent Court.[6] Bury Bar Lane, so called by 1370,[7] enters the town from the south-east to join the main thoroughfare at the junction of Church Street and Lewall Street, traversing the north-east side of an open area known later as Market Square or in the early 19th century (from an adjoining inn) Red Lion Square.[8] Bury Bar Lane, which may have been the end of another route from Gloucester,[9] was evidently named from a gate standing at the top of a low ridge[10] that runs south of the town, roughly parallel with Church Street. Possibly that ridge was itself the 'Bury' which gave its name to gate and lane and to the adjoining Bury (or Berry) fields.[11] A long lane leading south-westwards from New Street and known as Watery Lane by the early 19th century[12] was apparently that called Isetts Lane in 1410 from a family of customary tenants whose house stood near its junction with New Street.[13] A small alley called List Bridge Lane in the 1770s led westwards from Lux Lane across a footbridge over Peacock's brook, which in 1423 was referred to at that point as the List brook.[14] 'Souhares' Lane mentioned in 1333 in the area at the south end of

1 e.g. GA, D 332/T 8, abs. of title to Porter's Place; D 2957/212/37, 52, 57, 157.
2 Herefs. RO, E 12/G/1, ct. (9 Apr.) 40 Edw. III.
3 Ibid. G/5, survey 1624, p. 77.
4 Ibid. G/1, ct. (18 Apr.) 11 Hen. IV; and see GA, P 225A/MI 9, for the location of 'Lower Court Orchard'.
5 Below, manors (Newent manor: Newent priory).
6 GA, P 225A/MI 9.
7 Herefs. RO, E 12/G/1, ct. (14 Oct.) 44 Edw. III; GA, D 421/M 80/3, ct. 2 Aug. 20 Ric. II.
8 GA, D 1810/1, deed 2 Feb. 1831.
9 Above (communications: roads).
10 GA, D 421/T 34, deed 7 May 1657; D 1810/5.
11 Ibid. D 1810/4.
12 Ibid. Q/SRh 1819B.
13 Herefs. RO, E 12/G/1, ct. (20 Feb.) 11 Hen IV; G/5, survey 1624, p. 67; and for the bounding fields mentioned in the second source, GDR, T 1/126.
14 Herefs. RO, E 12/G/2, ct. (4 Apr.) 1 Hen. VI; G/5, rental 31 Hen. VIII (s.v. 'Culford Lane').

Coleford Street[1] may have been that called later Southends Lane running south-eastwards from Coleford Street, but it may equally have been the part of the old Boulsdon–Gloucester road which Southends Lane joins near a house called Southerns or Southends.

The Middle Ages

Newent parish church, recorded from 1181, stands on the north-west side of Church Street, very probably on a pre-Conquest site.[2] West of the church the domestic and farm buildings of Newent priory, from which Cormeilles abbey administered estates it acquired locally following the Conquest, occupied a large precinct in the 13th and 14th centuries, bounded to the south and west by a long wall following the curving course of the town's main thoroughfare.[3]

The market town that formed around those features after the grant of market rights in 1253 shows few signs of planning. It was evidently built up piecemeal during the later 13th century and the early 14th and therefore probably inherited its irregular street plan from an existing, but much more dispersed, settlement. A rental of 1278 listed 99 renters within Newent tithing and a more detailed rental of much the same period, undated and possibly incomplete, listed 76 tenements. Of the latter 6 were burgages owing cash rents alone, 30 were cottages owing rents and work in the lord's meadows with pitchfork or rake, and 8 were customary tenements owing a full quota of labour services.[4] The burgages presumably represent the beginnings of the enlargement and infilling of the existing settlement, while the others are probably its older constituents. Of the cottages 16 can be roughly identified (from their haymaking service as recorded in a rental of c.1315) as being in Church Street (most of them probably in the later Gloucester Street), another 5 near Ell bridge, and others in Lux Lane or in the part of Lewall Street between that lane and Peacock's brook.[5] Of the customary holdings those held by tenants surnamed Prank, Isett, and Puff (Pouf) were, from the later evidence of field names, located in the area between Peacock's brook and Watery Lane.[6] A burgage held by John Anketil was part of a row of tenements on the south-east side of the inner part of Church Street,[7] where long plots running back from the street to the top of the ridge behind are the only ones in Newent resembling the burgage plots of planned towns elsewhere. Other burgages may have been in New Street, whose name, recorded from 1300,[8] suggests that it was built up after the founding of the market; there, however, the plots are shorter and the houses, which in the early 16th century mostly only merited the description 'cottages',[9] were probably quite humble dwellings. Later terminology is of little help when trying to distinguish old and new additions to the town: the rental of c.1315 called all its dwellings messuages, and in the late medieval and early modern period the term burgage, when used, was applied indiscriminately to any dwelling wherever situated and of whatever origin.

Enlargement and infilling in the town continued during the late 13th century. Four new burgages on adjoining sites, probably in Lewall Street, were granted in the manor court in 1286,[10] and during the next decade the market place, a term then applied to a wider area than the narrow space later called Market Square, was being built up. Various transactions in the 1290s evidently relate to the block of property bounded by Market Square on the north-east and Lewall Street on the north and that bounded by Market Square on the south-west and Church Street on the north-west. In the former area, in 1290 John Deerhurst was granted a plot with permission to build on it[11] and in 1298 Geoffrey Fillol and his wife had a grant of a burgage opposite the priory gateway (the entrance to Court Lane) and bounded by Deerhurst's house and the market place. By c.1315 Fillol's plot had apparently been sub-divided, for three of his sons had houses in that part of the market place. One son also held an unbuilt plot of land adjoining his house and to that of a neighbour, Richard Plumtree, whose house to the west also was described as opposite the priory gateway[12] and adjoining the market place.[13] Further to the east, the market place evidently included what became the inner end of Church Street. Encroachment on the market from that direction was under way in 1297 when Henry Isett had a grant of two selds adjoining the south-western side of a structure called the market gate, with the right to build a solar there.[14]

The market gate, providing the entrance to the market area from the Gloucester road, may have stood several plots along Church Street where the longer property boundaries on its south-east side give way to shorter ones and where a narrow yard still makes a break in the street frontage. Four other selds mentioned c.1315 adjoined the priory wall on the north-west side of Church Street,[15] evidently occupying part of the site of the range of houses that extends from the churchyard to the entrance of Court Lane; if nearer the Court Lane

---

1 Ibid. G/3, ct. (27 Mar.) 7 Edw. III.
2 Below, religious hist.
3 Below, manors (Newent manor: Newent priory).
4 BL, Add. MS 15668, ff. 7, 41v.–43.
5 Ibid. 18461, ff. 98–105v.
6 GDR, T 1/126 (nos 1040, 1046A, 1047).
7 BL, Add. MS 18461, ff. 65, 99v.
8 Above (streets).
9 Herefs. RO, E 12/G/5, rental 31 Hen. VIII.

10 Ibid. G/3, ct. (12 Jan.) 14 Edw. I; the rents and two of the tenant names appear to identify them with four listed in BL, Add. MS 18461, f. 101.
11 Herefs. RO, G/2, ct. (4 Feb.) 18 Edw. 1.
12 Ibid. ct. (1 June) 25 Edw. I; BL, Add. MS 18461, ff. 74v., 100v.
13 Herefs. RO, E 12/G/3, ct. (6 Oct.) 13 Edw. II.
14 Ibid. G/2, ct. (22 Nov.) 26 Edw. I; BL, Add. MS 18461, f. 100.
15 BL, Add. MS 18461, f. 99v.

end of that range, they too would be within the market gate. The gate was among measures taken by Cormeilles abbey to control access to the market. All occupants of houses adjoining the market place were forbidden to have back entrances to their plots and were enjoined to keep up their parts of the walls and fences. Dwellers there also paid a premium for their advantageous position for trade. About 1315 their annual rents were mostly over 4s. compared to the usual 2s. or 1s. elsewhere in the town; Henry Isett paid 9s. 4d. and another householder 8s. 6d.[1]

The rental drawn up c.1315 listed 137 dwellings and 9 selds or shops in the town. Although few landmarks and no street names are included, it can be deduced that c.30 of the houses stood in the eastern part of the town on Church Street, c.20 in the central area including the market place and part of Lewall Street, c.40 in the southern part including Lux Lane and Coleford Street, and another 40 or so in the northern part on New Street and Ellbridge Street. The rental described the entrance of the Gloucester road on the east and that of the road from Yartleton (i.e. the south end of Coleford Street) as the two 'heads' of the town. The use of that description for the end of Coleford Street rather than the junction of the Ross and Dymock roads at the north end of the town seems to reflect the large number of houses then on the southern street; as a built-up part of the settlement it was perhaps earlier than New Street.[2] Also c.1315 there were six customary tenants with houses and small farms within Newent tithing, at least four of them probably in the area between Watery Lane and Peacock's brook.[3] The houses at the south end of the town in the late 13th century and the early 14th included some on the Boulsdon–Gloucester road. Near its junction with the end of Southends Lane a group of dwellings formed a small hamlet called Shaw:[4] four men surnamed of Shaw (*de la Sawe*) paid rent in Newent tithing in 1278[5] and a family surnamed 'atte Cross' had houses in that area in 1333, some within and some outside the liberty (Newent tithing), the south boundary of which appears to have followed the Boulsdon–Gloucester road.[6] John de la Pludie, a rent payer in the tithing in 1278,[7] probably had a dwelling near by on the north-east side of the road, where a group of closes was later called Ploddy fields. Further to the south-east, beyond Ploddy brook, a field called Batteridge was presumably the site of a customary tenement known by that name in 1404.[8]

In the town centre infilling with new houses continued into the mid 14th century. A plot for building on was granted in 1333[9] and three more in 1338; two of the latter adjoined the wall of the priory precinct, into which their owners were forbidden to make entrances.[10] Five new selds were mentioned in 1344, perhaps additions to the row at the entrance to Church Street where there were at least eight selds in 1367. The building of hearths in the new ones presumably marked a stage in their conversion into dwellings.[11] The central area of the town generally seems to have taken on its present form by the close of the 14th century. Two houses in Bury Bar Street adjoining the manor pound in 1396[12] probably formed part of the range on the north-east side of Market Square; the pound may then, as in the early 19th century, have been near the south-east end of the square.[13] The town's high cross, mentioned in 1405[14] seems to have occupied the site at the north-west end of Market Square where a new market house was built in 1668.[15] The erection in the 15th century of a boothall, used presumably as a court and market house, at the entrance to Court Lane also emphasises that the area was the focal point of the town.[16] Another prominent building in the central area was Porter's Place, the home of the lawyer Roger Porter (d. 1523) on the south-west side of Market Square.[17]

In the Middle Ages some or all of the entrances to the town were marked by gates. The Bury Bar at the top of Bury Bar Lane is mentioned above. Cleeve Bar, recorded in 1405,[18] was probably at the east end of the town at the junction of the later Gloucester Street and Cleeve Mill Lane, a place that was referred to as 'Townsend' in 1539.[19] Redes Bar, mentioned in 1367,[20]

---

1 BL, Add. MS 18461, ff. 99v.–100v.; for the ban on entrances, see also Herefs. RO, E 12/G/3, cts. (6 Oct.) 13 Edw. II, (2 Aug.) 14 Edw. II.
2 BL, Add. MS 18461, ff. 98–105v. The topography and dating of this rental are deduced partly from comparison with property transactions in the court rolls of the period (in Herefs. RO, E 12/G/1–3). Although a perambulation (in the order Church Street, the market area, Lux Lane, Coleford Street, New Street, and Ellbridge Street), it jumps from one side of a street to another and is further complicated by the insertion in the succession of houses of land elsewhere in the manor held by the householders.
3 BL, Add. MS. 18461, f. 115 and v. Apart from those mentioned above, held by the Prank, Puff, and Isett families, the house and land of Wm. Carles was probably represented later by Green meadow, adjoining the east side of Watery Lane: Herefs. RO, E 12/G/5, rental 31 Hen. VIII (s.v. 'Culford Street'); GDR, T 1/126 (no 1046).
4 For fields called Shaw, Ploddy, and Batteridge, Herefs. RO, E 12/G/5, survey 1624, pp. 5, 73; GDR, T 1/126 (nos 1439, 1446).
5 BL, Add. MS. 15668, f. 7.

6 Herefs. RO, E 12/G/3, cts. (6, 27 Mar., 29 May, 14 July) 7 Edw. III.
7 BL, Add. MS 15668, f. 7.
8 Herefs. RO, E 12/G/2, ct. 10 Oct. 6 Hen. VI. For the southern part of the town, see Map 6.
9 Ibid. G/1, ct. (24 Nov.) 7 Edw. III.
10 Ibid. ct. (14 Oct.) 12 Edw. III.
11 Ibid. G/2, ct. (6 Oct.) 18 Edw. III; G/1, cts. (12 Oct.) 40 Edw. III, (27 Apr.) 41 Edw. III.
12 GA, D 421/M 80/3.
13 Ibid. D 1810/1, deed 2 Feb. 1831.
14 Herefs. RO, E 12/G/2, ct. (29 Apr.) 6 Hen. IV.
15 GA, D 332/T 5, deed 6 Mar. 1625; D 365/T 3.
16 Below (bldgs. of Newent town); see also below, manors (Newent manor: Newent priory).
17 Below, manors (Boulsdon manor).
18 Herefs. RO, E 12/G/2, ct. 29 Apr. 6 Hen. IV.
19 Ibid. G/5, rental 31 Hen. VIII (s.v. 'Cleves Myll Lane'); survey 1624, p. 72.
20 Ibid. G/1, ct. (14 Oct.) 41 Edw. III; GA, D 421/M 80/3.

may have been at the junction of the Ross and Dymock roads or at the south end of Coleford Street.

By the end of the Middle Ages the town had assumed the form it was to retain with little enlargement for four centuries. A rental of 1539 enumerated 124 houses in the town. Of those 38 were in Church Street, where 22, mainly on its north side, were described as cottages, evidently the smaller houses sited at the bends in the street and in the later Gloucester Street, and 14 as messuages, mostly those on the longer plots on the south-east side of the street's inner part. Four shops remained near the entrance to the street in the range of buildings south-west of the churchyard and a cottage there had formerly been three shops. The 25 dwellings listed under the heading Lewall Street evidently included those on the south-west side of Market Square as Porter's Place was among them. Those on the north and north-east side of the street, backing on the former priory precinct, were classed mainly as cottages and those on the south and south-west side mainly as messuages. New Street, the description probably including also Ellbridge Street, had 40 houses, the majority classed as cottages. Lux Lane had 10 houses and Coleford Street 11:[1] the settlement on the long south street had evidently been much reduced in the late Middle Ages. Presumably by 1539 there was a considerable gap between the houses in Lux Lane and those in Coleford Street, which in the early 19th century comprised mainly a group of cottages at the far south end, between the junctions with Southends Lane and the Boulsdon–Gloucester road.[2]

The Early Modern Period and Nineteenth Century

The main change within the town in the early modern period was the refronting of many of its timber-framed houses with brick. The prosperous years of the late 17th century and early 18th prompted also some more extensive and prestigious rebuildings: the most notable were at the Tan House in Lux Lane, at the house of the Skinner family at the far end of the inner part of Church Street,[3] and at the two largest houses in the town, almost the only ones standing detached in their own grounds, namely the manor house (the Court House) on the Newent priory site, remodelled soon after 1713,[4] and the vicarage on the east side of New Street, rebuilt in 1729.[5]

On the outskirts of the town most of the dwellings recorded in the 13th and 14th centuries had been demolished by the 17th. Of the customary tenements in the fields between Watery Lane and Peacock's brook, that called Puffs was ruinous in 1624 and the site an empty 'toft' in 1659, and that called Isetts was described in 1624 as a 'meese place', also presumably demolished.[6] Further south, however, a small farmhouse survived, reached by a lane that left Coleford Street opposite Southends Lane and crossed the brook by a footbridge.[7] Known at different times as Curtis Place (or the Hill), Reeces, and Tallys, the house and small farm belonged to John Curtis in 1539 and was sold in 1595 to William Rice (or Reece). He enlarged the farm and sold it in 1597 to Walter Nourse, whose heirs and successors, lords of Boulsdon manor, retained it to the mid 19th century.[8] East of Coleford Street the hamlet of Shaw had vanished or been much reduced by the 16th century,[9] its site being absorbed eventually into the farm called Southerns based on the house at the junction of Southends Lane and the old Boulsdon–Gloucester road.[10] The closes called Ploddy fields, lying north-east of those lanes, formed a small customary farm with a barn in 1624[11] and a house called Skeeles had been provided for the farm by 1709.[12] In the early 17th century the only building on a wide tract of manorial demesne land south of the town, then leased among several tenants, apparently was a barn. Shortly before 1657, however, a new house, Nelfields Farm, was built on a low hillock[13] as the centre of a compact farm formed by the lords of the manor.[14] It was apparently of timber-frame which was replaced in stages in brick and stone. On the same side of the town but much closer to it, a small house built before 1692 at the top of the ridge at Bury Bar was rebuilt on a larger scale shortly before 1791, when it was bought by the Newent attorney Benjamin Aycrigg (d. 1822),[15] it was remodelled again in the late 19th century.

On the Ross road north-west of the town a farmhouse called Mantleys in the early 17th century[16] seems to derive its name from *Mammeclive*, used for that area in the Middle Ages. A family styled 'de Mammeclive' had a freehold estate in the 13th and 14th centuries, but as they held it originally from the

---

1 Herefs. RO, E 12/G/5, rental 31 Hen. VIII.
2 OS Map 1", sheet 43 (1831 edn); GDR, T 1/126; see also, Rudder, *Glos.* 562.
3 Below (bldgs. of Newent town).
4 Below, manors (Newent manor: Newent priory).
5 Below, religious hist. (endowment and patronage).
6 Herefs. RO, E 12/G/ 5, survey 1624, pp. 67, 77; G/16, deed 24 Nov. 1659.
7 GDR, T 1/126 (no 1057) and GA, SL 12, where ownership by Isabella Beale and the name 'Reece's estate' identify it.
8 Herefs. RO, E 12/G/5, rental 31 Hen. VIII (s.v. ' Culford Lane'); GA, D 332/T 3–5; D 1810/1–2.

9 Herefs. RO, E 12/G/5, rental 31 Hen. VIII (s.v. 'Culford Lane'); GA, D 421/E 13, f. 15v.
10 Below, manors (other manors and estates: Southends); GA, D 1810/1, deed 23 May 1789.
11 Herefs. RO, E 12/G/5, survey 1624, p. 73.
12 GA, D 2957/212/130; D 1810/4, deed 20 Sept. 1727; GDR, T 1/126 (where the names of the fields have changed).
13 GA, D 421/E 13, f. 16; Herefs. RO, E 12/G/5, survey 1624, pp. 2–5; G/15, deed 24 Feb. 1657.
14 GA, D 2528, plan B.
15 Ibid. D 1810/5–6; and for Aycrigg, *Univ. Brit. Dir.* IV, 62.
16 Herefs. RO, E 12/G/7, ct. 13 Apr. 1615.

lords of Pauntley manor[1] it is possible that their dwelling was further west, within the detached part of Pauntley. Mantleys with its farm was sold before 1615 to the Hooke family of Crooke's Farm in Pauntley,[2] and a family called Matthews owned it for several generations from the 1770s when the house was remodelled with a new brick front.[3] Near by, a cluster of cottages formed at the green called Picklenash in the angle of the Ross road and Bradford's Lane. A cottage was built there soon after 1598 on a plot leased from the lord of Newent manor, Sir Edward Winter,[4] and another had joined it by 1624.[5] In the early 18th century the lords of the manor granted a number of leases of cottages at Picklenash[6] and in 1775 there were six small dwellings around the green.[7]

By 1831 the number of inhabited dwellings within Newent tithing had risen to 271.[8] With no expansion of the town beyond its ancient limits, population growth was accommodated by subdivision of existing dwellings or housing plots.[9] That was a feature particularly in the upper part of Culver Street (the part formerly called Lux Lane) and also in Gloucester Street where the party walls of the small dwellings came to bear little relation to the old boundaries of the plots behind them.[10] On the part of Church Street within the double bend and on the north side of Gloucester Street uniform rows of brick and tiled cottages were put up in the late 18th century or the early 19th.[11] Almost the only addition to the town's area was a row of cottages built on the east side of Bury Bar Lane in the mid 19th century.[12] More significant was the building of Newent Court in the old manorial grounds on the north side of the town c.1810. With its extensive landscaped grounds, drives, and lodges it took on the character of the town's 'big house' in the later 19th century when it was owned by Andrew Knowles.[13] Within the town a dwelling called by 1661 the Pigeon House, sited within the angle of the main street and Watery Lane,[14] was rebuilt in the mid 19th century as a substantial villa facing south-east on a large garden.[15] It was probably built for the Newent solicitor Thomas Cadle, who owned it in 1828.[16] Cadle sold the house in 1849 to his partner Edmund Edmonds, who renamed it the Holts, the ancient name of a group of closes on the opposite side of Watery Lane, and fitted and furnished it on a lavish scale. Edmonds or his mortgagee offered the land opposite for sale for building c.1880,[17] and in the 1890s a few brick houses were built there, including a short terrace on what became Holts Road.[18]

The Twentieth Century

During the first quarter of the 20th century new building was limited to a few dwellings on the town's outskirts, including several on the south-east side of the Ross road between the junction with Horsefair Lane and Picklenash[19] and a substantial residence called Mantley Chase west of Bradford's Lane, the latter built in 1909 for the Conder family of the Conigree.[20] In 1931 and 1932 Newent Rural District Council built a row of 12 houses north-east of the town in Compton tithing where Hill Top Lane joins the Upleadon road.[21] Its next schemes were west of the town, where during 1935 and 1936 it built eight pairs of houses on the north-west side of Watery Lane.[22] Another 24 houses on a plot north of the parish cemetery were completed in 1939[23] when wartime restrictions confined council building to a few cottages for agricultural workers.[24]

The RDC resumed building in 1947[25] and during the next 18 years it added c.160 houses in the area west of Watery Lane, mainly pairs and short terraces but from the early 1960s also bungalows for older tenants. Among the ground covered was the site a prisoner-of war-camp established in 1944.[26] There was also private building on individual plots adjoining the council's estate, and in the mid 1960s there were two larger private developments, one of 50 houses and the other of 22 bungalows, off Watery Lane. By the late 1960s housing filled much of the land between Watery Lane and Bradford's Lane, leaving the cemetery, recreation ground, and council allotments as the remaining open spaces in that area. In the same period private development proceeded between Watery Lane and Culver Street: the main estates there were 58 dwellings built during 1959 and 1960 on Johnstone Road and 50 houses and bungalows built in the mid 1960s further

---

1 BL, Add. MS 18461, ff. 116v., 122.
2 *Inq. p.m. Glos.* 1625–42, III, 84–5; GA, D 421/M 81 (s.v. 'Porter's rents').
3 GA, D 245/I/13; P 225/CW 3/1; GDR, T 1/126; 'Newent, Past and Present' (Newent W.I. 1975: copy in GA, D 3295/II/5).
4 Herefs. RO, E 12/G/14, lease 1 Apr. 1598; GA, D 421/E 13, f. 20.
5 Herefs. RO, E 12/G/5, survey 1624, p. 9.
6 GA, EL 148 (leases 6, 11 July 1720, 30 June 1731, 10 July 1740, 14 June 1749).
7 Ibid. D 2528, p. 7; photocopy 5.   8 *Census*, 1831.
9 e.g. GA, D 2957/212/12, 57; D 1810/10, deed 22 Nov. 1803; 11, deed 6 June 1829.
10 OS Map 1:2,500, Glos. XVII.14 (1884 edn).
11 Ward, *Around Newent*, 78–80.
12 Some of them were apparently put up shortly before 1838 and others added later: OS Map 1", sheet 43 (1831 edn); GDR, T 1/126.

13 Below, manors (Newent manor: Newent Court).
14 GA, D 185/IV/36.
15 Ward, *Around Newent*, 40.
16 GA, P 225/CW 3/1–2; TNA, HO 107/350.
17 GA, D 2299/27, 3311; K.M. Tomlinson, 'A Country Tomb tells a Victorian True Story', *Trans. BGAS* 113 (1995), 168–9, 178.
18 GA, DA 30/100/5, pp. 62, 74; OS Map 1:2,500, Glos. XVII.14 (1902 edn).
19 GA, DA 30/100/8, pp. 330–1, 407; 100/10, pp. 22, 75.
20 Ibid. 100/9, pp. 222, 478; D 2428/1/24.
21 Ibid. DA 30/100/13, pp. 354, 409, 431, 435.
22 Ibid. 100/14, pp. 98, 132, 158, 196.
23 Ibid. pp. 265, 272, 378, 407.
24 Ibid. 100/15, pp. 193, 196, 282, 338.
25 Ibid. 100/16, pp. 6, 21; 100/17, pp. 47, 137. The next three paras. are based primarily on the RDC minutes in ibid. 100/17–42.
26 Ibid. 100/15, pp. 229, 249, 292.

south. Individual houses and bungalows were built along Culver Street in a process that by the mid 1970s linked the older groups of houses at its northern and southern ends.[1]

From the mid 1960s housing plans were directed to the Bury Bar area south of Church Street and Gloucester Street.[2] Between 1970 and 1972 the RDC completed 67 houses in short terraces on the north side of a new road (Foley Road) running roughly parallel with Church Street and Gloucester Street and 24 bungalows adjoining it. In the early 1970s a private developer began building on a continuation of Foley Road to the south-west; that development eventually comprised c.100 small dwellings in short closes laid at angles to the road. Amid concern that Newent was becoming a dormitory of Gloucester, private development on the south-east side of Foley Road was limited to no more than 130 houses[3] built in the late 1980s[4] on a series of roads running down to Onslow Road. Onslow Road, which curved back northwards past the east end of Foley Road to the Gloucester road, provided access to all the new estates on the south-east side of Newent. Land east of its junction with the Gloucester road was developed as an industrial estate in the mid 1990s.[5]

On the north side of the town, where Wildsmith & Son, a local firm of builders, bought Newent Court and its grounds in the late 1950s, an estate of c.80 houses was built south of the grounds' ornamental lake in the early 1970s; the entry was from the Gloucester road at what had been the eastern drive to the mansion. In 1979 another estate was begun based on the site of the mansion and the drive leading to it from north end of High Street.[6]

Within the old town the only area to have been much altered by the beginning of the 21st century was Upper Church Street and Gloucester Street. The row of cottages on the south-west side of Upper Church Street was demolished under a slum clearance order obtained in 1963 and its site was used partly for road widening and extending the car park of the Black Dog inn.[7] On the same street during 1967 and 1968 the RDC built 21 flats and bungalows and a warden's house in a scheme (St Bartholomew's) for elderly people designed by its consultant architect Jean Elrington.[8]

Following a slum clearance scheme of the early 1970s[9] the north-east side of Upper Church Street and the north side of Gloucester Street were developed as low-rise blocks of flats, including one completed in 1979 for the British Legion Housing Association.[10] Changes incidental to the building of the bypass in the late 1960s included the demolition of the houses on the east side of Bridge Street.[11] In the central area the principal changes were the demolition of the Holts, replaced in the early 1970s by the county council with a group of public buildings (library, health centre, and police station),[12] and the opening in 2000 of a supermarket behind the houses on the south-west side of Market Square.[13]

THE BUILDINGS OF NEWENT TOWN

Boothall and Market House

The most significant medieval building in Newent town is the former boothall, which presumably, as with structures so designated elsewhere, served as both court and market house.[14] Surviving as the northern end of no 1 Broad Street (a grocery shop since the mid 19th century),[15] details indicate a construction date in the mid to late 15th century.[16] The building, which comprised a hall open to the roof ridge above an undercroft, had a high standard of finish inside and out. The side walls are close studded, implying that they were exposed to the approaches from the former priory and the town, and the end walls have curved tension braces and near square panels; the western end was attached to the gateway at the entrance to Court Lane. The roof[17] has four bays and the arch-braced collar truss spanning the centre of the building has V-shaped struts above the collar, forming a diamond that has been cusped to create a quatrefoil design. The two intermediate trusses also have arch bracing and quatrefoils but a less massive cross section. Two tiers of heavy purlins are threaded through the principal rafters and three tiers of slightly curved windbraces (48 in total) have cusping at the top, so that each pair forms a semicircular cutout. The upper end was probably towards the east, as the bay lengths are marginally longer than those towards the west. A repaired or replacement window in the hall's north wall, perhaps a copy, has two lancet-headed openings, and there may

---

1 OS Map 1: 25,000, SO 62/72 (1977 edn).
2 See *Glos. Life and Countryside*, Apr.–May 1967, 21; *Citizen*, 13 Oct. 1967.
3 See *Glos. and Avon Life*, Jan. 1983, 26; *Citizen*, 31 May 1984.
4 Information from Mrs D.M.A. Rosser, town clerk of Newent.
5 'Archaeological Review 1993', *Trans. BGAS* 112 (1994), 209; 'Archaeological Review 1996', ibid. 115 (1997), 290.
6 Information from Mrs Rosser.
7 GA, DA 30/132/8; 100/35, pp. 36, 117.
8 Ibid. 100/35, pp. 43, 94, 162, 277; 100/36, pp. 34, 197.
9 Ibid. 100/40, pp. 56, 214; 100/41, p. 169; Ward, *Around Newent*, 80.
10 Plaque on bldg.
11 Ward, *Around Newent*, 22.
12 'Newent, Past and Present' (Newent W.I. 1975: copy in GA, D 3295/II/5).
13 Information from Mrs Rosser.
14 See *VCH Glos.* IV, 248; IX, 111.
15 GA, D 2957/212/28–9; D 917, deed 2 June 1874.
16 The descriptions of the boothall and market house are based on a report by Mr Duncan James, which notes that the boothall shares details with Upper Limebrook Farm (1447–8) at Wigmore (Herefs.), and with Abbot's Lodge (1480) and the Master's House (1487) at Ledbury (Herefs.).
17 Below, Fig. 4.

4. *The roof of the former boothall*

5. *The market house in the mid 19th century*

have been three other similar windows to light the room. No evidence for original windows is visible in the undercroft, although a doorhead survives in its north side. The timber, of better quality than that used in many Newent buildings, may have been supplied from holdings of the owner of the manor, Fotheringhay college, which possibly employed a team of peripatetic craftsmen rather than local builders.

In the later 16th century or the early 17th a floor was inserted in the hall, but it was later removed from the western two bays. In 1624, when referred to as the old boothall, the building had presumably ceased to be used for its original purpose; it was then held on lease by James Morse,[1] members of whose family owned it in the early 18th century.[2]

The town's market house, built in 1668 at the north-west end of Market Square,[3] is modest compared with market halls near by in Herefordshire at Ledbury, Ross-on-Wye, and Leominster. The decoration is principally on the gable facing Church Street, a feature which could be an addition. Its original length, 9 m (30 ft), repeats that of the boothall and close studding on the walls is a clear reference to the earlier building. The chamber, standing on eight posts, has three bays. The central one is the largest and the south-eastern, judging by the position of the entrance and the way in which the main trusses face towards it, was apparently the upper end. The two internal trusses each have two pairs of raking struts rising to the (hidden) principal rafters, a design possibly related to the later lining of the roof. The construction, originally with large braces from the soffit of the tiebeams to the wall posts, suggests that the chamber may have been built for trading activity rather than meetings. The posts (some of which are replacements) supporting the chamber lack decoration, similarly the jowels to the corner posts, the close studding, and the straight braces: they could be the re-used remnants of an earlier structure. In 1864, when the building was restored, the windows were replaced in late medieval style and an apsidal-ended south-east room was added. The chamber was probably ceiled then.

Domestic Buildings

In Newent's old centre many houses, of a fairly uniform size and type, were built between about 1400 and 1660 with timber frames, of which only a few are not hidden behind later fabric. Many, especially in the parts of Church, High, and Culver Streets most distant from Market Square, remained in domestic use in 2007. Those described here can only give an indication of character and uses. In this section modern street names are used.

The buildings of the 15th century and early to mid 16th tended to be fairly plain. Seven jettied cross wings can be traced, some still associated with their 15th-century open halls or with 16th-century floored hall ranges. In Culver Street no 3 is probably the cross wing of a cruck-framed range at nos 5–7, and no 14 Broad Street almost certainly belonged to a two-bayed hall to its south (no 1 Culver Street). The plausible but unauthenticated date 1465 has been painted on no 14, which has a deep jetty under its first floor, and a shallow one under its second, both now underbuilt. On the top floor the gable also projects slightly, with a moulded and crenellated tiebeam and curved tension braces down to the second-floor bressumer, both typical 15th-century features. Evidence of a large mullioned window on the ground floor suggests that floor was not occupied by a shop, but a passage (once much wider) through the cross wing to rear premises might indicate the building had a commercial use.

Other cross wings or hall-and-cross wing houses are incorporated in later buildings. Behind the 19th-century front at no 28 Church Street stands a cross wing where one roof truss with cusped braces and the date 1481 survives together with a cusped single-light window.[4] The house to its east (nos 30–32) had a two-bayed hall with open hearth and probably single-bayed ends in line; the eastern end was remodelled as a cross wing in the 16th century, a chimneystack inserted in the hall in the 17th, and the house partly refaced in brick c.1700. A 16th-century cross wing also survives at nos 25–7 on the south-east side of Church Street attached to what may have been a hall range, divided much later into cottages. Similar cross wings occur on the east side of Lewall Street at the long, partly refaced property which in 2007 included the 'Good News Centre' and at nos 1–2 High Street, built in the 16th century with a deep jetty to the wing.

A greater number of the timber-framed houses in the central area appear to date from the late 16th century and the 17th. They are more richly decorated, particularly Harwood House and no 4 Church Street, which have diagonal and square-patterned framing. Several have more than two jettied storeys, and most appear to have been built or rebuilt to occupy the full width of the original plots, as can be seen from the large square plot occupied by the Red Lion inn on the corner of Market Square and Broad Street, the wide frontage of Harwood House south of it, and the five-bayed refronted house at nos 17–19 Church Street: that suggests that the pressure to increase density, even close to the market, was not great at that period. Three-storeyed houses were fitted into prominent positions at the western entrance to Church Street, presumably replacing the buildings that were part of the early encroachments on the market area. They no doubt had shops on the ground floor with great chambers over, but evidence for the former has been destroyed. No 2 and nos 1–3, jettied on two sides, were clearly designed for their corner positions, though the latter was encased in brick in the early 19th century, as was the two-storeyed and jettied Red Lion which is built round a courtyard. No 2 Church Street seems to have been added to its jettied easterly neighbour, no 4, which is one of the most decorated houses of the period, having carved angle posts and a great chamber with an elaborate ceiling including a plaster panel of a griffin. Some houses of the late 16th century and the 17th,

---

1 Herefs. RO, E 12/G/5, survey 1624, pp. 1, 8.
2 GDR wills 1673/1; 1726/266.
3 Fig. 5. For its history, below, econ. hist. (markets and fairs).
4 Information (2004) from David Bick of Newent.

6. The Black Dog inn, Church Street

particularly those away from the market area in Culver Street (e.g. nos 1, 32, 50–52, and Queen Anne's Cottage), were built on a more rural pattern, detached and single-storeyed with garrets, many of which have been raised. Several such houses with narrow fronts were only cottages, and nos 62–70 Culver Street is a cottage row. Many houses in Culver Street have cellars which were apparently excavated later.[1]

Several houses were replaced or refronted in brick in the late 17th century and the early 18th. Alterations, most commonly the insertion of shop fronts, were made during the 19th and 20th centuries but little wholesale replacement has been carried out since 1800. Entire houses of brick were reputedly introduced in 1698, with the exception of one built in 1660 for the mercer Thomas Master.[2] Good quality stone was scarce and used sparingly, many details which elsewhere would have been of stone being expressed in brick or timber. Early examples of brick casing appear at no 5 Broad Street and at the house now the Black Dog inn. The former incorporates an earlier L-plan house with basement and three storeys and two rooms on each floor. A well staircase with 'barley sugar' balusters in the angle of the L and panelling in a rear room go with the new work; there are vestiges of brick pilasters on the façade. The Black Dog, facing north-east at the far end of Church Street, was a large farmhouse when it was built in the earlier 17th century, having a two-storeyed hall range, a long south-eastern cross wing, and a north-west wing. About 1700 it was converted into a gentleman's residence for Stephen Skinner,[3] whose father, a Newent clothier, had acquired the nearby manorial demesne land called Bury fields.[4] The house was given a brick front with fashionable stone quoins, modillion cornice, casement windows, and timber doorcase.[5] The parlour, at the west end, was also refitted in the early 18th century, though some of the detail inside and out may be the work of the Gloucester architect H.A. Dancey in 1910.[6] Skinner, whose family remained in possession until the mid 18th century,[7] apparently intended to transform part of his adjoining land into pleasure grounds in 1705 when he leased it, reserving the right to build a summer house.[8] The house became the Black Dog inn in the mid 19th century,[9] while the land was farmed from Town Farm, a new farmhouse built at the west end of Gloucester Street.[10] The detached Tan House, on the west side of the part of Culver Street formerly called Lux Lane, may be slightly earlier than Skinner's house and contemporary with the upper part of the adjoining brick barn which is dated 1695. It was built by the

---

1 Information (2004) from David Bick.
2 GA, D 412/Z 3, Nourse MS, pp. 7, 15; and for Master, ibid. D 2957/212/145.
3 Ibid. D 412/Z 3, 'MS no II'; D 2957/212/124.
4 GDR wills 1674/112; Bigland, *Glos.* II, 245; GA, D 1810/4.
5 Fig. 6.

6 Verey and Brooks, *Glos.* II, 605; for Dancey, see also *VCH Glos.* IV, 235.
7 GA, D 1810/4.
8 Ibid. D 2957/212/127.
9 Ibid. D 412/Z 3, Newent notes, 1900.
10 Ibid. D 2299/3311.

7. The Tan House, Culver Street, c.1966

Bower family, owners of the tannery there,¹ as a symmetrical composition in brick with hipped roofs, wooden mullion-and-transom windows on the first floor, and sashes on the ground floor. The house is set behind a narrow forecourt and approached through gateposts with ornamental finials.²

The style of the major houses of the period was repeated in rebuilding and refacing work elsewhere in the town, at for example nos 16 and 29 Broad Street, and at the five-bayed no 27 Broad Street. The grandest brick town house, no 8 Broad Street (in 2007 Lloyds Bank), was designed with a hipped roof as if it were a detached house. It has a first-floor Venetian window, a central pediment with a Diocletian window, and a Doric doorcase, unusually for Newent made of stone; surviving details suggest the interior was comparable in quality. At the north end of the town a large brick house, of five bays with a central pediment with a circular window, was built in the early or mid 18th century on a prominent site at Crown Hill, on the corner of the Ross road and Bridge Street facing down High Street.³ It was used from c.1768 as the parish workhouse and later as the Newent union workhouse; in the mid 1860s a new range was added to it and in the 1920s, when it became a school, the 18th-century house was replaced.⁴ Many buildings in High Street were remodelled or rebuilt in the early 18th century. A long row on the west side includes Shirley House, which appears to conceal a substantial timber-framed structure, and the brick-built Malt House, which has a long, partly non-domestic range alongside it and maltings at the rear, said to be of c.1800.⁵

Modernization continued into the late 18th century and the early 19th.⁶ Doorcases and windows were changed, and a few timber-framed buildings were given completely new brick façades, for example no 12 Broad Street at the corner with Culver Street, nos 39–41 Church Street, and the almshouses on the east side of High Street which were refaced with a uniform frontage in 1810.⁷ An extensive but plain rebuilding was carried

8. High Street looking north c.1910, showing the almshouses on the right and the union workhouse in the distance

---

1 Ibid. D 412/Z 3, Nourse MS, p. 6; 'Newent, Past and Present'.
2 Fig. 7.
3 Ward, *Around Newent*, 23, 30.
4 Below, local govt. (parochial govt.; local govt. after 1834); social hist. (education: secondary schools).
5 *Chapters in Newent's History*, 24.
6 See Fig. 8.
7 Below, social hist. (charities: almshouses); GA, GPS 225/29.

out c.1800 at the George inn, Church Street, where an assembly room was provided. In the mid and late 19th century a few houses were rebuilt or refaced (for example no 5 Church Street and no 1 Broad Street), mostly replacing older houses and with only two or three bays. The few distinctive changes to the appearance of the town's streets in the Victorian era included the Congregational church, built on the south-west side of Broad Street in 1845 with a Gothic façade of Cotswold stone,[1] and the police station and magistrates' court in Court Lane, designed by James Medland in variegated red and blue brick in 1878.[2] Late 20th-century additions, including the library and health centre in Lewall Street, a terrace of new houses on the site of the almshouses in High Street, and the new flats with which Gloucester Street and Upper Church Street were redeveloped, generally adopted plain and unobtrusive designs in accord with the traditional, small-scale townscape.

OUTLYING SETTLEMENTS AND BUILDINGS

Outside the town the parish was populated in the early Middle Ages in a pattern of small scattered farmsteads. A rental of Newent manor c.1315 listed 81 houses in Compton, Malswick, and Cugley, the tithings where most of its tenant lands lay.[3] With an unknown quantity of tenant houses on the smaller manors in those tithings and on the Boulsdon and Kilcot manors, the total in the five rural tithings is likely to have been at least double that number. Depopulation and amalgamation of holdings in the later Middle Ages[4] are reflected in the total of only 48 dwellings listed on Newent manor in Compton, Malswick, and Cugley in 1539[5] and the 40 listed c.1607.[6] The abandonment of houses and the creation of larger farms continued in the early modern period, the formation of Green farm providing one example of a process evident generally in the parish.[7] The principal farmhouses, those attached to the manors or large freeholds, are described with their estate history.[8] Among the lesser farmhouses are some timber-framed structures, mostly of the 17th century, but the majority were rebuilt or extended in brick in the late 18th century or the early 19th.

From the mid 18th century the building of cottages on the commons and waste land increased the population in outlying areas of the parish, and in 1831 328 houses were enumerated in the five rural tithings.[9] Gorsley common and Clifford's Mesne were most affected by that process, and among the smaller commons Brand green acquired a compact hamlet. Some of the cottages were described as being very poor in quality and accommodation in the late 19th century,[10] remarks which may have referred particularly to those of the earliest date. The later cottages, dating from the early 19th century, were usually of two storeys with four or five rooms.[11] For many, particularly in the western parts of the parish, the yellow Gorsley stone was the chosen material, while others were of brick or, in a few cases, of thin timber framing with brick infilling. Abandonment or demolition much reduced the numbers of cottages during the 20th century. By 1921, for example, of 18 built before 1775 on the north part of Gorsley common within the parish only 7 remained though supplemented by a few of more recent date.[12] Demolitions continued under the statutory powers of Newent Rural District Council after the 1930s[13] and surviving cottages were provided with new bathroom and kitchen extensions in the 1950s and 1960s.[14] In the later 20th century many cottages underwent a more wholesale remodelling and enlargement and new houses and bungalows were built among them.

Compton

In the large north-eastern tithing of Compton there were 27 tenants of Newent manor in 1278,[15] and 23 tenancies there had houses attached c.1315, most of them held by customary tenure and with small farms varying in size from 8 to 36 a.[16] Settlement in the tithing was probably always of a dispersed nature, but in the 14th century it was regarded as forming two groups of dwellings called Great and Little Compton; the latter included houses by Sandy way leading from near Newent town northwards to Botloe's green in the west part, while the former was perhaps based on Compton green in the north-east part.[17] About 1607 there were still 16 houses on Newent manor in Compton,[18] but the process had begun by which many were demolished on being absorbed into the large farms, of 100–300 a., that covered most of the tithing by the 19th century.[19]

---

1 Below, religious hist. (religious life in 19th and 20th cents.: Congregationalists).
2 J. Douglas, *Historical Notes of Newent with Oxenhall and Pauntley* (1912), 12; Verey and Brooks, *Glos.* II, 604.
3 BL, Add. MS 18461, ff. 106–14.
4 Below, econ. hist. (agric.).
5 Herefs. RO, E 12/G/5, rental 31 Hen. VIII.
6 GA, D 421/E 13.
7 Below (Cugley).
8 Below, manors.
9 *Census*, 1831.
10 Douglas, *Notes of Newent*, 9; GA, D 1882/5/3.

11 e.g. GA, SL 79; DA 30/100/25, p.11; 100/28, p. 49; 100/32, p. 6.
12 Ibid. D 2528, pp. 6–7; photocopy 5; OS Maps 1:2,500, Glos. XVI.12, 16, XVII.9, 13 (1923 edn).
13 e.g. GA, DA 30/100/14, pp. 221, 238, 272–3, 354; 100/25, p. 52.
14 e.g. ibid. 100/24, p. 255; 100/25, pp. 8, 41; 100/27, pp. 49, 51, 132; 100/28, p. 49; 100/31, p. 180; 100/32, p. 6.
15 BL, Add. MS 15668, f. 7v.
16 Ibid. 18461, ff. 108, 111v.–113v.
17 Herefs. RO, E 12/G/1, ct. (14 Oct.) 12 Edw. III; G/2, cts. (6 Oct.) 18 Edw. III, (11Mar.) 37 Edw. III.
18 GA, D 421/E 13, ff. 17 and v., 18v.
19 GDR, T 1/126; TNA, HO 107/1960. Below, Map 4.

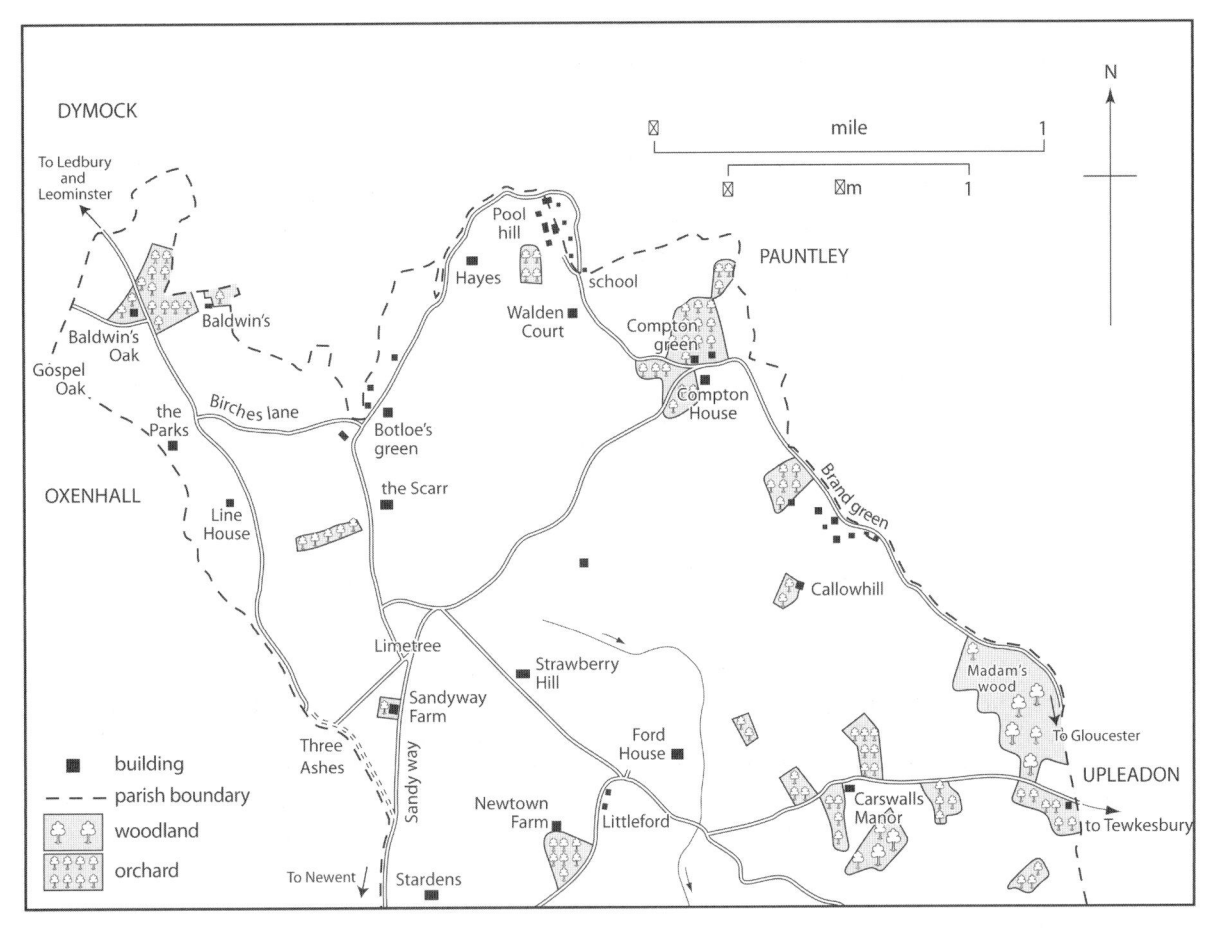

Map 4. *Newent, Compton tithing 1882*

Farmsteads north-east of Newent town By the early modern period the two principal farms in the north-east of Compton were Hayes and Walden Court. Both probably represented early freehold estates, and the latter was enlarged by absorbing three customary farms, Hillhouse, Nashes, and Greaves, which were granted in reversion to its owner in 1563.[1] The first two were possibly those held from the manor by Roger 'de la Hulle' and Simon 'Atennasse' c.1315.[2] The sites of the three dwellings were probably between Walden Court and Compton green. Three other customary farmhouses of Newent manor were recorded in the same area in 1624. Of these Wallys stood at the south side of Compton green on or near the site of Compton House[3] and presumably represented the dwelling of tenants with that surname in the 13th century and early 14th.[4] Its farm was among the few tenant holdings retained by the manor after the mid 17th century. Compton House, the centre of one of the main farms on the estate in 1775,[5] was rebuilt c.1820 as a large, stuccoed villa. It was sold some time before 1838 to the Pauntley Court estate and became the centre of a large farm in Newent and Pauntley parishes. A long, low house on the north side of the green, apparently a rebuilding of the 18th century, also belonged to Compton House farm in 1838.[6] It was probably the house on Newent manor called Walters in the early 17th century,[7] passing to a branch of the Pauncefoot family by the early 18th century and to the owner of Pauntley Court in 1819.[8]

Further south at Callowhill, near Brand Green, a house and one of the larger farms (72 a.) of the early Middle Ages was recorded as a freehold on the manor from the 13th century. Robert of Callowhill was succeeded there c.1240 by Robert Dobyns, whose family retained the farm for several generations.[9] The farmhouse, which by 1435 and until the mid 17th century belonged to the Hooke family of Crooke's Farm, Pauntley,[10] was rebuilt or extensively remodelled in the 17th century as a three-bayed range of timber frame with brick infilling. Lean-to extensions of a

---

1 Below, manors (other manors and estates: Walden Ct.); Herefs. RO, E 12/G/15, deed 14 Feb. 1563.
2 BL, Add. MS 18461, ff. 112v.–113.
3 Herefs. RO, E 12/G/5, survey 1624, pp. 83, 91, 99.
4 BL, Add. MS 15668, f. 41; 18461, f. 112v.
5 GA, D 2957/212/68; D 2528, plan D.
6 GDR, T 1/126, 140; TNA, HO 107/1960.
7 Herefs. RO, E 12/G/5, survey 1624, p. 83; GA, D 421/M 81 (s.v. Compton copyholders).   8 GA, D 4647/8/3.
9 BL, Add. MS 15668, ff. 7v., 41, 52, 54v.; 18461, f. 108.
10 Below, Oxenhall, manor (estates in detached part of Pauntley); GA, D 421/M 81 (s.v. Compton freeholders).

similar build mask both sides of the north-west bay and a small timber-framed barn adjoins the house.

Carswalls Manor, on the Upleadon road in the south-east of Compton, was the site of a manorial estate recorded from 1086. The large farm based there in the early modern period[1] had presumably absorbed some medieval tenant holdings of its manor. Moor House, recorded on the farm in 1778[2] was probably at the south edge of its land at the place later called Little Carswalls; there were a pair of cottages and farm buildings there in 1838,[3] the cottages being replaced by a bungalow c.1959.[4] A house site called Rosehill mentioned on Carswalls Manor farm in 1778 was near Little Carswalls, on the opposite side of the lane.[5] A dwelling called Bullock's in 1624[6] stood at the source of a spring by the Upleadon road 600 m to the east of Carswalls Manor. It was probably the home of William Bullock (Bolloc), a customary tenant on Newent manor c.1315. The house later took the name Kerry's from its early 17th-century tenant.[7] It still belonged with its small farm to the Newent manor estate in 1775[8] but had been sold and demolished by 1838.[9]

Farmsteads north of Newent town The Scarr (formerly Atherland's Place), south of Botloe's green, was the principal farmhouse on the lanes in the west part of Compton tithing in the early modern period. Probably of early medieval origin,[10] its farm too was enlarged at the expense of some of the smaller tenancies of Newent manor. Customary tenants in Compton in the early 14th century included members of the Coppe family and Walter Ysett;[11] in 1401 the lord of the manor granted the site of two houses called Coppehayes to new tenants with a provision for building a new house there,[12] and in the mid 17th century tenements called Coppes Place and Ysetts were held with Scarr farm by the Dobyns family.[13] Other house sites mentioned on the farm in 1685 included Broad Woodward's,[14] which probably represented lands called Great Woodward's held freely by Robert of Compton in 1278.[15]

Farmhouses further south, near the Upleadon road, included Stardens which is at or near a site occupied in the late 13th century; it was later part of the manor estate, whose owner enlarged and remodelled it as his own residence in the 1860s.[16] Newtown Farm, in the same area, was recorded from 1676[17] and was rebuilt in brick in the late 18th century when it belonged to the owners of Carswalls; they sold it to the tenants, the Cummins family, in 1811.[18] Further east there was probably a number of dwellings around a ford through a stream crossing the Upleadon road in the 13th and 14th centuries, when several Compton tenants were surnamed 'de la Forde'.[19] Ford House Farm, standing some way north of the ford, was presumably the house of that name belonging to the Cooke family of Highnam in the early 17th century[20] and it was rebuilt as a large, rectangular brick house shortly before 1789, when as the centre of a farm of 220 a. it was sold to John Wood of Preston Court.[21] A small group of houses at a place called Littleford on the Upleadon road west of the ford includes two 17th-century timber-framed cottages. Small farmhouses established in the same part of Compton by the early modern period included Strawberry Hill, on the lane of that name leading from the Upleadon road to the junction called Limetree, and Farthings on Sandy way close to Limetree. Farthings, apparently built shortly before 1733, was renamed Sandyway Farm before 1819.[22]

The area around Limetree was possibly the part of Newent manor that was distinguished as *Lindam* in 1181[23] and the area of Compton tithing where a number of tenants surnamed 'de la Linde' lived in the 13th and 14th centuries.[24] There was, however, also a farm called by 1778 Line (or Linde) House[25] at the western edge of the tithing, beyond the Dymock road. Baldwin's Oak, a small farmhouse on the Dymock road in the north-west of Compton, was recorded from 1675,[26] and the same family gave its name to Baldwin's, a farmhouse on the east side of the road,[27] which in the later 20th century became the centre of the Three Choirs Vineyard. Shortly before 1882 a new house called the Parks was built west of the road between Line House and Baldwin's Oak. Part of the Newent manor estate, but named from a medieval park of the lords of Oxenhall which overlapped the parish boundary there,[28] the substantial residence, of polychrome brickwork, was leased separately from its

---

1 Below, manors.
2 GA, D 1938, deed 21 May 1778.
3 GDR, T 1/126; and for the probable location, ibid. (nos 420, 438).
4 GA, DA 30/100/27, p. 145.
5 GDR, T 1/126 (nos 476–7).
6 Herefs. RO, E 12/G/5, survey 1624, pp. 95, 97.
7 BL, Add. MS 18461, f. 113v.
8 GA, D 2528, plan C.
9 GDR, T 1/126 (nos 449–52, 460–3).
10 Below, manors (other manors and estates).
11 BL, Add. MS 18461, ff. 111v.–112.
12 Herefs. RO, E 12/G/3, ct. (10 Jan.) 2 Hen. IV.
13 Ibid. G/6, rental c.1655; GA, D 421/M 81 (s.v. Compton freeholders).
14 GA, D 4647/6/1.
15 BL, Add. MS 15668, f. 7v.; 18461, f. 103v.
16 Below, manors (other manors and estates).
17 GDR wills 1680/184.
18 Below, manors (Carswalls); GA, D 1938.
19 BL, Add. MS 15668, 7v.; 18461, f. 108.
20 GA, D 421/E 13, f. 17; Herefs. RO, E 12/G/6, rental c.1655.
21 *Glouc. J.* 3 Mar. 1788; GA, D 2299/138.
22 GA, D 4647/8/3.
23 BL, Add. MS 18461, f. 1v.
24 Ibid. Add. MS 15668, f. 7v.; 18461, f. 112 and v.; Herefs. RO, E 12/G/1, ct. (15 Jan.) 19 Edw. II; G/2, ct. (17 Mar.) 18 Edw. III.
25 GA, D 1938.
26 GDR wills 1685/218.
27 Ibid. T 1/126; GA, D 2710.
28 Below, Oxenhall, introd. (landscape); OS Map 6", Glos. XVII.NW (1884 edn).

9. Land Settlement Association houses of the 1930s at the Scarr

farmland in the early 20th century.[1] Tenants surnamed 'de Castello' who held land in Compton under Newent manor in the 13th century were named from the earthwork by the roadside just within Dymock parish[2] and probably lived within Dymock.

Land Settlement Association Much of the western side of Compton was transformed by the purchase in 1937 of Scarr farm by the Land Settlement Association. During the following two or three years 57 small houses were built for the Association's tenants. Some stood along concrete-surfaced roads laid east and west of Scarr farmhouse and its buildings, which became a packing and processing depot. Others were further north, on Birches Lane, and further south, on the lanes around Limetree. The chalet bungalows, designed in brick with tiled gambrel roofs and weather-boarded gables, each contained two bedrooms, living room, kitchen, and downstairs bathroom. They were improved in the 1950s and 1960s with rear extensions, and most holdings were given new glasshouses,[3] which with the glasshouses of other farms covered a significant acreage of the western part of Compton by 1976.[4] Some of the houses were further enlarged after the Association was wound up in the early 1980s, but most retained their distinctive appearance in 2008[5] and a few still had the timber piggeries and poultry houses provided at the start of the scheme.

Hamlets on the parish boundary In the late 18th century and the early 19th the building of cottages on waste land on the boundary between Compton and Pauntley parish created the hamlets of Botloe's Green, Brand Green, and Pool Hill. At Botloe's Green, a high point on the boundary, an old road from Newent town to Ledbury (by way of the Leadon crossing at Ketford) is joined by Birches Lane, leading from the Newent–Dymock road to the west. There were two houses adjoining the green in 1565,[6] and in 1749 the lord of Newent manor leased a cottage on a patch of roadside waste on Birches Lane just to the west of the green. The earliest to be built on an encroachment taken from the green itself was apparently one built shortly before 1776, presumably by the carpenter who then took a lease of it.[7] Further building followed, producing a scatter of *c.*10 cottages on the green by 1838, and some others were built on the waste on the south side of Birches Lane.[8] By 2007 most of the cottages had been demolished or rebuilt.

At Pool Hill, at the extreme northern point of Newent parish, most of the settlement that formed on the hillside common was within Pauntley. Only one cottage had been built by 1775 on the higher part of the common within Newent,[9] presumably the same leased by the lord of the manor to a blacksmith in 1759.[10] Another was leased in 1819,[11] and by 1838 there were six or seven in the Newent part of the hamlet.[12] They include two which, though built after 1775, have thin timber framing, a feature also of a cottage at Botloe's Green and others at Brand Green.

Brand Green surmounts a ridge on the lane that

---

1 GA, D 1882/5/3; SL 79.
2 BL, Add. MS 15668, ff. 7v., 14v.; Herefs. RO, E 12/G/2, ct. (4 Aug.) 18 Edw. I.
3 *Kelly's Dir. Glos.* (1939), 271; *Glos. Countryside*, June 1958, 47–8; *The Countryman* (1961), 583–91. See below, econ. hist. (agric.).
4 OS Map 1:25,000, SO 72 (1977 edn).
5 Fig. 9.

6 GA, D 2957/212/2.
7 Ibid. EL 148 (lease 29 Apr. 1749); D 2957/212/92; D 2528, plan D.
8 GDR, T 1/126.
9 GA, D 2528, plan D.
10 Ibid. EL 148 (lease 14 Nov. 1759).
11 Ibid. D 2957/212/99.
12 GDR, T 1/126.

marked the north-eastern boundary of Newent. A cottage built on an encroachment there before 1624[1] was possibly the early timber-framed dwelling that survived near the north end of the former green in 2007. It may have remained an isolated dwelling until the mid 18th century when the lords of Newent granted further leases of cottages.[2] By 1775 there were three on the green and another on a smaller patch of roadside waste further north.[3] Further building formed Brand Green into the largest of the hamlets in Compton; by 1838 there were over 20 cottages on the former green, where a pattern of narrow lanes had formed, and on the patch of waste further north.[4] In 1947 the RDC built two pairs of houses of 'Swedish timber' type on the lane north of the hamlet.[5] Some bungalows were built among the older cottages in the early 1960s[6] and other houses were added later in the century.

Malswick

In Malswick, the south-eastern tithing of the parish, the farmsteads were based on the Newent–Gloucester road. On the north-east side of the road they mostly belonged in the Middle Ages to three estates called Okle Clifford, Okle Grandison, and Okle Pitcher, while in the remainder of the tithing they were customary or freehold tenancies of Newent manor. Those on Newent manor included 22 dwellings c.1315.[7] Roughly half that number of farmsteads survived in the early 19th century and few can be identified with medieval predecessors. Coxmore, Malswick, and Yate's Farms, on the south-west side of the road in fields bounded by Ploddy brook on the north-west and Grange Lane on the south-east, illustrate the fairly close spacing of the medieval farmsteads. Coxmore (where only derelict farm buildings remained in 2007) was presumably at the site of the dwelling of John of Coxmore, a customary tenant c.1315[8] and remained a copyhold of the manor in the early 17th century.[9] Yate's, where the small timber-framed farmhouse dates from the 17th century, remained a tenancy on the manor estate in 1742.[10] Another early 14th-century tenant, John Horsman,[11] presumably had a house in fields called Horsman's by Ploddy brook to the south-west of Coxmore Farm. A toft (empty site) of that name was mentioned in 1482.[12]

The small copyhold farm that included the fields in 1624 had a farmhouse[13] but it had been demolished by 1838 when the fields were part of Malswick farm.[14]

Grange Lane On Grange Lane remains of a large moat survive from what may have been an outlying farmyard for Newent priory's demesne farm.[15] Further to the south-east on the same side of the main road another such feature gave its name to Moat Farm, though that farmhouse stands a short way west of the moat's remains.[16] Presumably the site of a dwelling of some importance in the Middle Ages, it may have belonged to a Malswick family of freeholders surnamed 'de Chemino', who in the 13th and 14th centuries held c.90 a. (a large farm for the parish at that period).[17] The present farmhouse comprises a 17th-century timber-framed range, enlarged c.1800 by the addition of a parallel brick range on the south.

Other dwellings that were apparently in the same part of Malswick in the 13th and 14th centuries were those of freehold tenants surnamed 'of Cowmeadow' and 'of Slowe';[18] the former took their name from a large common meadow on the boundary with Tibberton, while the name of the latter accords with the low-lying (and then doubtless poorly-drained) nature of the area.[19] A tenancy called Slow's Place was mentioned in 1464[20] and a house, or possibly two houses, called Slow's was a copyhold on Newent manor in 1640.[21] Layne's Farm, standing by the Gloucester road where it enters the parish, was a copyhold on the manor held by the Layne family in the late 17th century and remained a leasehold in 1775.[22] By the early 1820s it belonged, together with Yate's Farm, to the Foleys' land agent William Deykes (d. 1827), whose nephew, William Deykes, succeeded to the two farms.[23] Layne's Farm comprises timber-framed and brick ranges of similar type and date to those at Moat Farm.

Rymes Place On the north-east side of the Gloucester road a house at or near the site of Rymes Place Farm was the centre of the largest copyhold estate (92 a.) on the manor in 1624. It had presumably absorbed other holdings, for it was then said to include three messuages. The other two houses may have stood on

---

1 Herefs. RO, E 12/G/5, survey 1624, p. 9.
2 GA, D 2957/212/84; EL 148 (leases 8 Dec. 1752, 23 Sept. 1757).
3 Ibid. D 2528, plan D.
4 GDR, T 1/126.
5 GA, DA 30/100/16, pp. 34, 84, 154; 100/17, pp. 17, 23.
6 Ibid. 100/30, p. 275; 100/32, p. 141; 100/33, p. 48.
7 BL, Add. MS 18461, ff. 106–107v., 113v.–114v.
8 Ibid. f. 114v.
9 Herefs. RO, E 12/G/4, ct. 8 Aug. 23 Eliz.; G/5, survey 1624, pp. 37, 39.
10 GA, EL 148 (lease 1742); D 2528, plan C.
11 BL, Add. MS 18461, f. 114v.
12 Herefs. RO, E 12/G/2, acct. roll 22 Edw. IV (s.v. allowed and defective rents).
13 Ibid. G/5, survey 1624, pp. 33, 35.
14 GDR, T 1/126.
15 Below, manors (other manors and estates).
16 GDR, T 1/126; GA, D 2710; OS Map 6", Glos. XXIV.NE (1888 edn). See below, Map 5.
17 BL, Add. MS 15668, ff. 7v., 40; 18461, f. 106; Herefs. RO, E 12/G/1, ct. (30 Nov.) 43 Edw. III.
18 BL, Add. MS 15668, ff. 7v., 39v.; 18461, f. 106; Herefs. RO, E 12, G/1, ct. (31 Apr.) 45 Edw. III.
19 PN Glos. IV, 172.
20 Herefs. RO, E 12/G/1, ct. 1 Oct. 4 Edw. IV.
21 GA, D 421/M 81 (s.v. Malswick copyholders).
22 Ibid. EL 148 (lease 1728); D 2528, plan C.
23 Ibid. Q/REl 1, Botloe hundred 1826–30; TNA, PROB 11/1730, ff. 257–260v.; GDR, T 1/126.

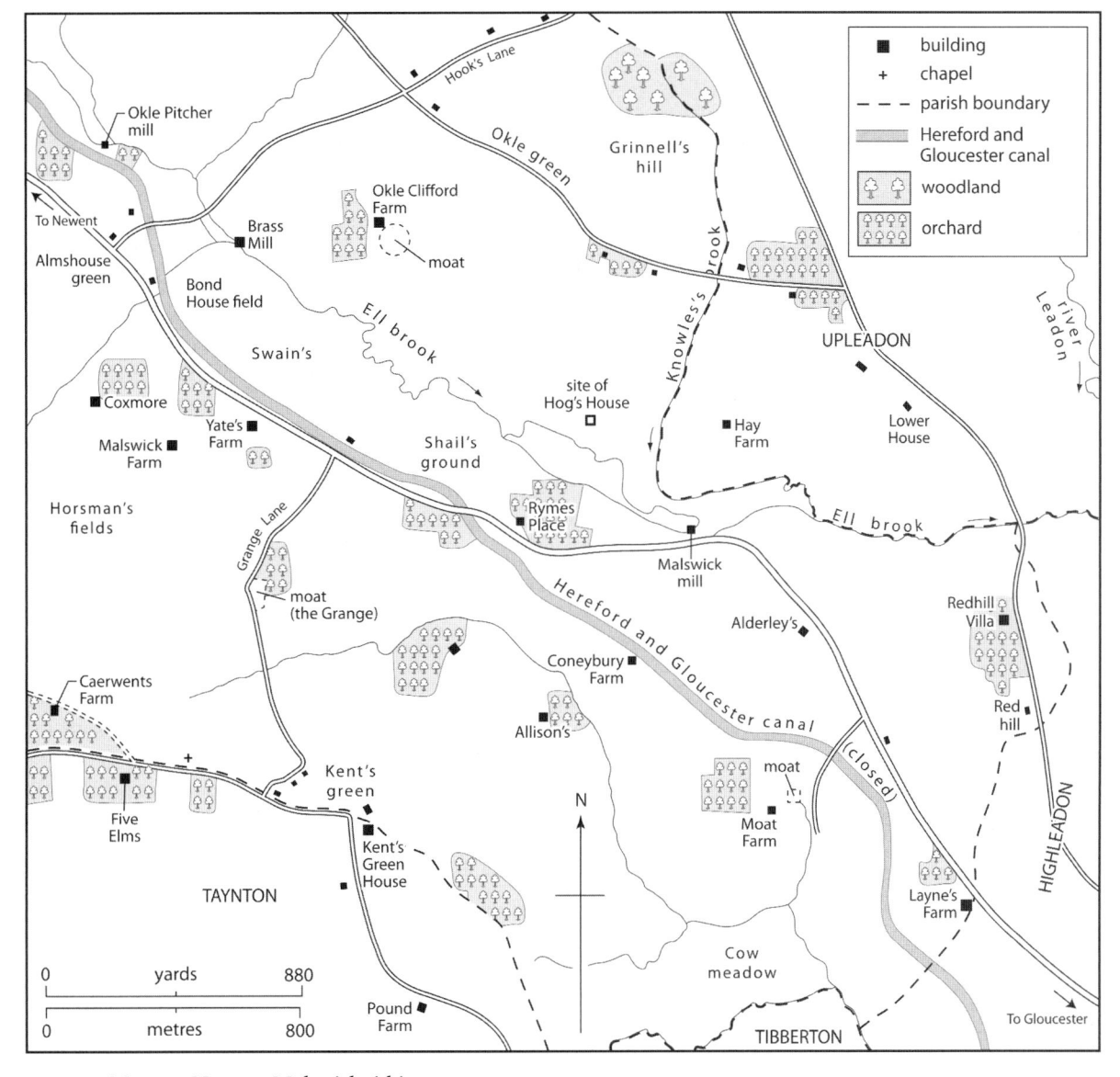

Map 5. *Newent, Malswick tithing 1882*

the opposite side of the road, in the angle with Grange Lane, where much of the farm's land lay.[1] Rymes Place was the centre of a larger farm in the mid 19th century when its farmhouse, a plain late 18th-century brick range, was enlarged by the addition of a block of red and yellow brickwork with a deep hipped roof and tripartite windows; at the same time it was provided with a set of new farm buildings.[2]

A copyhold farmhouse called Hog's House or Hogsend,[3] probably named from the family of Robert Hog, a mid 13th-century customary tenant,[4] stood north of Rymes Place in the angle made by the Ell brook and its tributary, Knowles's brook. The farm was among those sold by the lord of the manor in the 1650s.[5] By 1713 it belonged to the Beale family of the Court House and later was tenanted for many years with their Hay farm, in Upleadon parish.[6] The house, described as a cottage in 1838, was demolished later in the 19th century.[7] A former customary tenement in Malswick granted as freehold to Reynold Mile in 1307[8] was possibly that later called Mile House, at Red hill beside the road from Highleadon green to Upleadon. In 1634 John Maddocks of Hartpury leased Mile House to a tenant who was to build a new house beside an existing cottage there.[9] Two houses standing close together at Red hill in 1838 were replaced a few years

---

1 Herefs. RO, E 12/G/5, survey 1624, pp. 19, 21, 23.
2 GDR, T 1/126; GA, D 1388/SL 4, no 18.
3 Herefs. RO, E 12/G/4, ct. 25 Apr. 24 Eliz.; G/5, survey 1624, pp. 29, 31.
4 BL, Add. MS 15668, f. 40; 18461, f. 113v.
5 GDR wills 1681/82.
6 GA, D 4587/2; Q/REl 1, Botloe hundred 1776.
7 GDR, T 1/126; OS Map 6", Glos. XVII. SE (1889 edn).
8 BL, Add. MS 18461, ff. 74 and v., 106v.
9 Herefs. RO, E 12/G/15.

later by a substantial residence called Redhill Villa (later Redhill Farm).[1]

Okle Okle Clifford manor, the largest of the three estates in the area called Okle, was based on a moated site between Ell brook and Okle green.[2] In the late 16th century the estate included seven tenant farmhouses, as well as a mill on the brook. At least two of those houses, Bond House and Swain's,[3] stood between the brook and the Gloucester road, at the south-eastern edge of the large farm that was based on the manorial site in the early modern period.[4] In 1819 a cottage and small farm remained at Swain's and another cottage and small farm, called Shail's, fronted the main road further to the south-east. Their farmland was then leased with Okle Clifford farm[5] and both cottages were later removed. The sites of Okle Grandison manor and the six tenant houses recorded on its estate in 1659[6] have not been identified. The area to the north-east of Okle Clifford farm, beyond Okle green and adjoining Hook's Lane which runs from the north-west end of the green to join the former parish boundary with Upleadon, seems the most likely location. The third estate, Okle Pitcher, appears to have been based on a house at Okle Pitcher mill, on the Ell brook upstream of Okle Clifford farm.

Almshouse green and Kent's green   Scattered building of cottages on roadside waste included a few around Almshouse green, at the junction of the Newent–Gloucester road and a lane leading north-eastwards over Ell brook towards Hook's Lane. The junction may be that called Deadman's Cross where a cottage and blacksmith's shop stood in 1728.[7] Its later name, recorded from 1841, may derive from the use of one of the cottages to house parish paupers. The construction of the canal, passing near by between the main road and the brook, appears to have encouraged the building of additional dwellings around the junction in the late 18th century and the early 19th.[8] At the same period a few cottages were built along Okle green, along the north-west side of Hook's Lane, and on roadside waste at Red hill where one squatter long defied the lord of Newent manor's attempts to establish rights over his cottage.[9]

Kent's green, on the south boundary of the tithing, attracted another small group of dwellings, some within Taynton parish.[10] A house called Kent's had been built by 1624 to farm demesne land of Newent manor adjoining Grange Lane.[11] In 1775 there were only two dwellings on or adjoining the Newent part of the green,[12] but five or six more cottages had been added within the parish by 1838.[13]

Cugley

In the main part of Cugley tithing,[14] based on the road running south from Newent town to Taynton, tenant farmhouses of Newent manor provided the core of the settlement. In 1278 39 Cugley tenants paid rent to the manor,[15] and c.1315 37 houses were listed on the manor in the tithing. Only 15 of the latter, mainly customary tenancies, had a significant holding of land; most comprised only a freehold messuage and curtilage.[16] It is possible that the landless tenants lived mostly on the northern edge of the tithing, perhaps engaged in occupations connected with the town and its trade. At that period there were houses along the south-west side of the old Boulsdon-Gloucester road, where it marked the boundary with Newent borough,[17] and others may have formed an extension into Cugley of the settlement on Coleford Street. All the minor freeholds and their houses appear to have been abandoned in the later Middle Ages: in 1539 fewer than 12 houses were enumerated on the manor in Cugley tithing[18] and c.1607 only 10.[19]

Farmsteads south of Newent town   In the north of Cugley were two ancient freehold estates, Stallings, at Stallions hill between the Taynton road and the Boulsdon brook, and Southorles manor, based on a moated house (the Moat) on the opposite side of the road.[20] During the 17th century, under the Woodward family, the farm based on the Moat absorbed a number of house sites: at the close of the century it contained five such sites. One called Paradise, standing near Anthony's Cross in the angle of the Taynton road and a lane leading to Clifford's Mesne, had perhaps belonged to the Stallings estate. Another, in Hill fields south-east of Anthony's Cross, was a former copyhold of Newent manor.[21]

The surviving farmsteads in the central part of the tithing all derive from early medieval tenant holdings of Newent manor, though it is not clear which occupy medieval sites. The tenants listed in 1278 and c.1315 included three men with the surname 'de la Pludie'; their dwellings were presumably on or near the site of

---

1   GDR, T 1/126; GA, D 2957/212/133.
2   Below, manors (Okle).
3   TNA, SC 12/32/15, f. 1 and v.
4   GDR, T 1/126 (nos 517–18).
5   GA, D 3269, deeds of Okle Clifford 1819–1914.
6   Herefs. RO, E 12/G/9, rental 1659.
7   GA, EL 148 (lease 13 Apr. 1728).
8   TNA, HO 107/350; HO 107/1960.
9   GA, D 245/I/21.
10 See below, Taynton, settlement.
11 Herefs. RO, E 12/G/5, p. 41.
12 GA, D 2528, plan C.
13 GDR, T 1/126.
14 For the other part of the tithing, below (Kilcot and Gorsley).
15 BL, Add. MS 15668, f. 7v.
16 Ibid. 18461, ff. 108v.–111v.
17 Above (development of Newent town: the Middle Ages).
18 Herefs. RO, E 12/G/5, rental 31 Hen. VIII.
19 GA, D 421/E 13, ff. 17v., 18v.–19.
20 Below, manors (other manors and estates).
21 TNA, C 142/398, no 109; GDR wills 1710/26; Herefs. RO, E 12/G/5, survey 1624, p. 61; and for Paradise and Hill fields (later called Hither and Far Copyhold), GDR, T 1/126 (nos 1510–11, 1567).

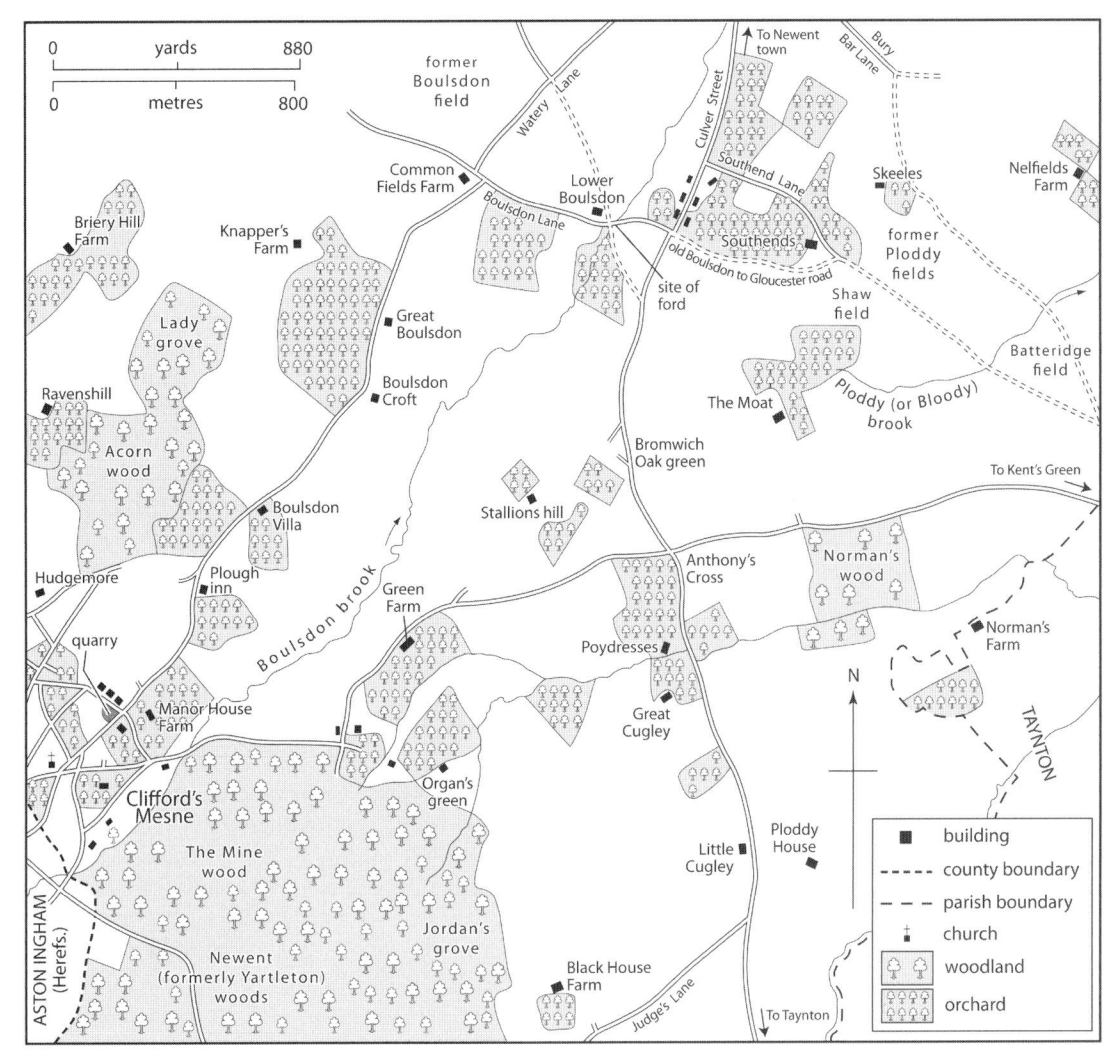

Map 6. *Newent, Boulsdon and Cugley tithings 1882*

Ploddy House Farm on the east side of the Taynton road. Two other tenants at those dates were surnamed Emlett;[1] a house of that name was in the lord's hands in 1482,[2] and in 1624 its site was part of a 77-a. copyhold based on Ploddy House.[3]

Other medieval holdings evidently passed into a farm based on Great Cugley on the opposite side of the road. They included probably a house held by Adam Ely *c.*1315 and mentioned as Ely's Place in 1409, and another held by John Dyne *c.*1315 and recorded as Dyne's Place in 1416.[4] In 1624 a number of small copyholds, held by members of the Woodward family, included a close called Ellys Hay and land called Vines and Deanes. The only house apparently then remaining on those holdings was one called Rabbit's; that was later the name of a field just to the west of Great Cugley Farm, which may be a new farmhouse built later in the 17th century.[5] Little Cugley Farm, standing by the Taynton road further south with land around the junction of Judge's Lane, seems to represent the customary holdings of 13th- and 14th-century tenants surnamed 'of Farley'.[6] In the early 17th century a house and large copyhold farm in that area, belonging to the Astman family, was called Farley and Woolrick,[7] and by the close of that century John Astman held it as a freehold.[8] The origins of the farm based on Poydresses, a partly 17th-century timber-framed house north of Great Cugley, have not been discovered.

Farmsteads below Newent woods An ancient freehold on the hillside north-west of Judge's Lane close to Yartleton woods formed the basis of the farm called

---

1 BL, Add. MS 15668, f. 7v.; 18461, ff. 110–11.
2 Herefs. RO, E 12/G/2, acct. roll 22 Edw. IV (s.v. allowed and defective rents).
3 Ibid. G/5, survey 1624, pp. 47–9.
4 BL, Add. MS 18461, f. 111; Herefs. RO, E 12/G/1, cts. 6 Nov. 11 Hen. IV, (4 Dec.) 4 Hen. V.

5 Herefs. RO, E 12/G/5, survey 1624, pp. 51–7; GDR, T 1/126 (no 1689).
6 BL, Add. MS 15668, ff. 7v., 39; 18461, f. 110.
7 Herefs. RO, E 12/G/5, survey 1624, pp. 43–7; GA, D 421/E 13, f. 18v.; M 81 (s.v. Cugley copyholders).
8 GA, D 365/T 2.

Black House. Land there granted by Cormeilles abbey to Robert Jordan (also called Jordan of Cugley) in the early 13th century[1] belonged to William de Gardino c.1315.[2] By 1523 it was part of the estate of Roger Porter, under whose descendants[3] it was leased as two farms, both with houses, known from their respective tenants as Skinner's Jordans and Astman's Jordans. After the dispersal of the Porters' estate in the early 17th century the farms passed through various owners before being sold in 1665 and 1668 to Thomas Foley, lord of Newent manor, who bought a third house and land in the same area in 1668.[4] The Foleys later leased the whole as a single farm based on Black House, which presumably occupies the site of one of the earlier houses.[5]

Further north Green Farm, facing a green on the road leading from Anthony's Cross to Clifford's Mesne, became the centre of a farm that incorporated at least six earlier holdings and house sites. A family surnamed Boverel had a freehold, a house and 18 a., in Cugley in the 14th century.[6] Called Boverallys, it was among Roger Porter's lands in 1523[7] and belonged to Henry Hartland in 1664. Thomas Hartland enlarged the farm in the early 1730s by purchasing houses and farms called Botgrove (later Arthur's) and Birches, together with three other holdings on which houses were recorded in 1607. By 1817 the whole formed a unit of 131 a. based on Green Farm, which is probably on the site of the medieval Boverallys. Arthur's, standing at the north end of the green, was then the only other house remaining;[8] it was presumably the cottage on the farm that burnt down before 1940.[9] The farmhouse was rebuilt in the early 19th century as a symmetrical building of coursed stone rubble with brick dressings and has contemporary stables and coach house.

Glasshouse green   An early group of cottages formed at the south end of the tithing at a place called Yartleton waste or Glasshouse green; the site adjoins Yartleton woods within the angle formed by the junction of Judge's Lane and a lane coming through the woods from Clifford's Mesne. The cottages were established around a glassworks which also gave the name to the adjoining part of Taynton parish.[10] At least two cottages stood there by 1607,[11] and by 1624 there were nine held from Newent manor on or around the green. Some were apparently built for those working the glasshouse, but in 1624 four occupants were paupers excused payment of rent by the lord of the manor.[12] In 1659 five cottages remained[13] and in 1775 four stood on the green, which was then divided into small closes and orchards, and within Newent there were two others near by.[14] All those on the former green had been removed by 1838[15] and by the early 21st century all the old close boundaries had been taken out, leaving a single field. In 1882 P.R. Cocks (later Lord Somers) built a residence called Clifford Manor at the top of Judge's Lane facing the former green.[16] In 2007 it was the only house in the area within the former Newent boundary apart from Home Farm, a farmhouse of c.1800 to its north-east.

A small group of cottages, probably of later origin than those at Glasshouse green, was established on Organ's green which adjoins the northern edge of Yartleton woods. One was leased from the manor in 1732[17] and three stood there in 1838.[18]

Boulsdon

In Boulsdon, which formed a separate manor from the 11th century,[19] the few farmsteads of the early modern period were presumably, as in the other tithings, survivors of a denser pattern of dwellings. They stand on the road from Newent town to Clifford's Mesne, on Boulsdon Lane which joins that road near the north end of the tithing, and on the higher, well-wooded land of the tithing's western edge.

Great Boulsdon   Great Boulsdon Farm on the Clifford's Mesne road is on or near the site of the medieval manor house.[20] Further south on the road were farms based on Little Boulsdon, renamed Boulsdon Croft before 1882, Clifford's Mesne Farm, which for a time in the late 19th century housed an inn called the Plough, and Manor House Farm,[21] which was probably given that name only in the late 19th century when acquired by Lord Somers, owner of the residual manorial rights of Boulsdon.[22]

Common Fields Farm, north of Great Boulsdon at the junction with Boulsdon Lane, was built or rebuilt c.1800 as a tall, symmetrical brick farmhouse with new farm buildings, probably for the Hooke family of Crooke's Farm, Pauntley, which accumulated a large holding in open fields lying north of the house.[23] A house built shortly before 1719 on an inclosure made

---

1   BL, Add. MS 15668, ff. 36v., 39.
2   Ibid. 18461, f. 109.
3   Herefs. RO, E 12/G/4, ct. c.1523; for the Porters' estate, below, manors (Boulsdon manor).
4   Herefs. RO, E 12/G/17; TNA, C 142/398, no 109.
5   GA, D 2528, plan A.
6   BL, Add. MS 18461, f. 108v.; Herefs. RO, E 12/G/1, ct. (31 Apr.) 45 Edw. III.
7   Herefs. RO, E 12/G/4, ct. c.1523.
8   GA, D 365/T 1; D 537/T 16; GDR, T 1/126.
9   GA, D 2299/6085.
10 See below, Taynton, settlement.
11 GA, D 421/E 13, f. 20.
12 Herefs. RO, E 12/G/5, survey 1624, pp. 11–12.
13 Ibid. G/16.
14 GA, D 2528, plan A.
15 GDR, T 1/126.
16 Below, manors (Boulsdon manor: Clifford Manor).
17 GA, D 2957/212/83.
18 GDR, T 1/126.
19 Below, manors.
20 Ibid. Above, Map 6.
21 OS Map 6", Glos. XXIV.NW (1887 edn).
22 GA, D 7723/1.
23 Ibid. D 2245 (acc. 7541), envelope nos 12–13, 15, 17. See GDR, T 1/126.

10. *Briery Hill: the north-west front*

from an open field called Mill field, lying south of Boulsdon Lane, was probably at Common Fields Cottage near the west end of the lane;[1] the present house there is later in date. Lower Boulsdon Farm, standing on the north side of the ford by which Boulsdon Lane crossed the Boulsdon (or Coleford) brook, has not been found mentioned before 1779, when it was called Beach House.[2] A house that stood east of Great Boulsdon on a lane, since discontinued, that crossed Boulsdon brook to join the Newent–Taynton road was called Tanner's in 1607 when it belonged to the Porters' manor estate. Its name may have derived from an occupation, for its tenant, Thomas Curtis,[3] was perhaps the tanner of the same name then at Boulsdon.[4] Known later as 'Tanner's or Curtis's', the house remained standing, as a part of the Boulsdon manor estate, until at least 1789.[5]

Briery Hill Briery Hill Farm in the north-west part of Boulsdon tithing, near Kilcot wood, is apparently the survivor of a small group of medieval farmhouses. Part of a small farm owned in 1640 by John Pitt, a weaver,[6] its later owners included, from 1721, George Cowcher (d. 1745), a Gloucester attorney,[7] who was probably responsible for rebuilding the house as a fashionable residence with a formal garden. The house and its farm, which was enlarged in 1790, were sold in 1811 to Elizabeth Hooke, widow of an owner of Crooke's Farm,[8] and remained part of her family's estate until the mid 20th century.[9] The early 18th-century house is of two storeys on an L plan and built of red brick. It has main façades with tall segment-headed casement windows, a staircase, a partly hipped roof, and cellars with brick vaulting. A two-storeyed addition was built in the angle of the L soon after the house was finished. In the early 19th century the north-west front was given sash windows and a columned porch[10] and the main parlour and bedroom new chimneypieces: many details are like those at Crooke's Farm.[11] Single-storeyed buildings on the west side were later attached to form a service wing. The north-western garden slopes to a large rectangular pond, possibly converted from remains of brick pits created during building, and other elements, such as ramped walls and a brick alcove, survive from what was apparently an elaborate formal garden; in 1824 an area to the south-west of the house included a serpentine walk.[12] On the south side of the south-eastern garden or yard an early 18th-century detached kitchen or brewhouse, later used as a coach house, is built of stone but brick-faced towards the house. To the east an 18th-century barn, in which crucks were used as principal rafters, a cart shed, and stables are grouped round the former farmyard. Other outbuildings were built north-east of the house and farmyard between 1824 and 1882.[13]

Lands to the north and north-east of Briery Hill

---

1 GA, D 2245/T 4.
2 Ibid. D 1803/4; and for the identification, GDR, T 1/126.
3 GA, D 365/ T 1.
4 Smith, *Men and Armour*, 64.
5 GA, D 332/T 5, deed 6 Mar. 1625; T 8; D 1810/1.
6 Ibid. D 421/M 81 (s.v. Porter's rents).
7 Ibid. D 2245 (acc. 7541), envelope 10A; Fosbrooke, *Glouc.* 167.
8 GA, D 2245 (acc. 7541), envelope 10A.
9 Ibid. file no 7; DA 30/100/34, p. 57.
10 Fig. 10.
11 See below, Oxenhall, settlement (bldgs.).
12 GA, photocopy 232.
13 Account based partly on a report by N.J. Moore (1994, in possession of the owners).

added to its farm in 1790 were called Croker's, White's, and Romer's.[1] Croker's, comprising a house and 12 a., was recorded from 1607, and White's, a house site and 24 a., from 1673;[2] both were possibly medieval customary tenancies of Boulsdon manor. One house remained on the land in 1790, standing just south of Wyatt's Farm at the boundary with Kilcot tithing. Romer's, apparently a former tenancy of Kilcot manor, was evidently represented in 1838 by fields called Greasy Romans and Stony Romans adjoining Wyatt's Farm on the north-west.[3] Land called Ravenshill belonged to the Boulsdon manor estate in the early 17th century[4] and perhaps already included the small farmhouse of that name standing on a hilltop site to the south of Briery Hill. The house and farm belonged in 1778 to the owners of the Carswalls estate in Compton.[5] A small house called Hudgemore, further south, also stands on land belonging to Boulsdon manor in the early 17th century.[6]

Apart from Clifford's Mesne hamlet (described below), few dwellings were added in Boulsdon tithing in the modern period. Two brick villas were built in the late 19th century on the stretch of road between Little Boulsdon and Clifford's Mesne Farm. Boulsdon Villa, the southern one, and its park-like grounds became a falconry centre in 1967.[7]

Clifford's Mesne The hamlet of Clifford's Mesne grew up from the late 18th century in the south part of Boulsdon tithing on the flanks of May hill below Yartleton woods. The second element of its name, the regional name for a tract of common or waste land, referred originally to a hillside common covering the north-western slope of a coomb formed by the headwaters of the Boulsdon brook. Late additions to the hamlet have given the road from Newent town, leading across the common some way above the brook, the character of a village street, but the earliest cottages were dispersed above and below that road. The earliest known lease of a cottage was made by the lord of Boulsdon, owner of the manorial rights in the common, in 1761,[8] and most of six cottages with inclosures paying rent to that manor in 1791 were probably at Clifford's Mesne.[9] As with similar hamlets in the parish, the pace of settlement quickened at the start of the next century, and by 1838 there were c.35 small dwellings within a pattern of minor lanes and small closes. One group of cottages, rather more regularly placed than the rest, stood alongside a track leading down the hillside near the common's northern edge and was perhaps built in connexion with the working of a quarry at the junction of that track and the road from Newent. A more irregular group stood along the bottom of the common, close to the brook, and others were scattered along the higher slopes near the boundary with Aston Ingham.[10]

In the late 19th century Clifford's Mesne hamlet was given a more definite identity by the provision of a building for a school and chapel at a junction of lanes with the road from Newent and, in 1882, a church further to the north-east on the road.[11] Although more cottages had been added and most of the waste land inclosed by then, the hamlet retained its dispersed character.[12] The building of new houses, mainly bungalows, among the old cottages was under way in the 1950s and early 1960s,[13] and the RDC built a group of six houses called Southall Terrace near the church in 1954 and 1955.[14] New building on a larger scale continued in the last quarter of the 20th century, mainly on the principal road of the hamlet, and by 2007, apart from its irregular street plan, Clifford's Mesne had the appearance of a modern residential development.

Kilcot and Gorsley

This section describes settlement within Kilcot tithing and the adjoining detached part of Cugley tithing, an area where boundaries and settlement names are difficult to define.[15] As much of the western part of the area was anciently part of Gorsley common, early settlement was presumably in the east end of Kilcot. One of the few known medieval sites is that of the Conigree (Conigree Court), which occupies a low hill in sight of Newent town and was the centre of one of several manors called Kilcot in the 13th century.[16] In 1307 its manor had 13 tenants,[17] whose dwellings were presumably in the same area of the tithing. The location of some is indicated by chief rents that were owed to the lord in the early 19th century from, among other lands, Bradford's farm on the eastern edge of the tithing at a bend in Bradford's Lane, Wyatt's farm to the south-west of the Conigree, the fields (part of Briery Hill farm) called Romans adjoining Wyatt's, and fields north of the Ross road at the boundary with the detached lands of Pauntley.[18] The part of the Ross road to the north-west of the Conigree was referred to as Kilcot Street in 1624,[19] suggesting that other medieval farmhouses had stood along that section of it.

---

1 GA, D 2245 (acc. 7541), envelope 10A (deed 2 Aug. 1790).
2 Ibid. D 332/T 4.
3 GDR, T 1/126.
4 GA, D 332/T 4, deed 2 Oct. 1606; D 421/M 81 (s.v. Porter's rents).
5 Ibid. D 1938.
6 Ibid. D 892/T 57, deed 26 Aug. 1607.
7 *Glos. Life*, Jan. 1974, 19.
8 GA, D 412/T 1. 9 Ibid. M 1/1.
10 GDR, T 1/126.
11 Below, religious hist. (religious life in 19th and 20th cents.).
12 OS Map 6", Glos. XXIV.NW (1887 edn); GA, D 7723/1.
13 GA, DA 30/100/22, p.122; 100/29, p. 63; 100/32, p. 166; 100/34, p. 122.
14 Ibid. 100/22, p. 90; 100/23, pp. 99, 170; 100/42, p. 25.
15 Above, introd. (boundaries and divisions); for map see below, Map 12.
16 Below, manors.
17 *Inq. p.m. Glos.* 1301–58, 97–8.
18 GA, D 412/M 1/2; GDR, T 1/126.
19 GA, D 2245/T 2; and for the identification of Barn Close, mentioned as adjoining the street: GDR, T 1/126 (nos 895, 907–8).

Kilcot In the early modern period the Conigree remained the centre of a modest-sized demesne farm and the only other dwellings attached to it were a few cottages on the Ross road to the north-east. One called the Squirrel,[1] standing near Stoney bridge where a small stream marked the boundary between Kilcot and Newent tithings, was mentioned from 1686[2] and may have once been a roadside alehouse. Bradford's, a small 17th-century timber-framed farmhouse, took its name from a family that owned it in the mid 18th century.[3] Wyatt's was recorded from 1615, when it was called Roodes Place or Rudgeaton; it was acquired with its farm by the clothier Stephen Skinner in 1625[4] and remained part of his family's Newent estates until the mid 18th century.[5]

Another focus of early settlement in Kilcot seems to have been near the centre of the tithing, where the Ross road meets a number of minor lanes. Judging from the various closes in the area called Kilcot field and Kilcot orchard,[6] it was there that the place name originated. By the early 19th century a loose cluster of cottages had formed there,[7] having as its eastern limit the Kilcot inn, standing at the junction with Kew's Lane (leading to a farmstead of that name in the detached part of Pauntley), and as its lower, western limit the junction called Kilcot Cross or Cross Hands, where after 1810 the old and new lines of the Ross turnpike road diverged. By 1838 there were over 20 cottages in the area, almost all owner-occupied and with just a garden or small closes belonging to them.[8] Of the older cottages that survive most appear to date from the late 18th century or the early 19th and are of brick or the local Gorsley stone. One, Lodge Farm, incorporates timber framing. The Kilcot inn (formerly the Welsh Harp) was established by the early 18th century,[9] but was rebuilt *c.*1800 as a double-pile building of brick, the symmetrical front having ground-floor bays; a lower outbuilding of the local stone adjoins it on the west.

In the north-west part of Kilcot tithing lands called Broadgrove and Bleisfield, lying between Hillhouse grove (part of Pauntley) and the old course of the Ross road, were once occupied by a number of dwellings, possibly of medieval origin. The lands were apparently among those, including also a large part of the detached lands of Pauntley, granted to Cormeilles abbey, lord of Newent, in the mid 13th century.[10] In 1624 Newent manor had eight tenant houses (two of them described as decayed) on Broadgrove and Bleisfield[11] and there were ten there in 1640,[12] all of them evidently with only very small holdings of land. By 1775 the houses had been removed and the sites included in a single 94-a. farm based on the farmhouse called Brassfields Farm.[13] The tall late 18th-century brick house with its large contemporary barn and other buildings constitutes the only substantial farmstead in the west part of Kilcot and was given more prominence by the building of the new Ross road just to the north of it in the early 19th century.

Gorsley common The tract of waste that once covered *c.*400 a. within Newent as well as extending into Linton and Aston Ingham was the site of the most extensive cottage building in Newent parish during the early modern period. Some were in the detached part of Cugley tithing belonging to Newent manor in the north of the common, and others were further south within the west end of Kilcot tithing, on part of the common belonging to the manor based on the Conigree. In the former part settlement began early: four cottages were built there before 1624,[14] and five were included in the sale of Newent manor to Thomas Foley in 1659.[15] Between 1711 and 1769 sixteen leases of cottages were granted by the Foleys,[16] and in 1775 eighteen cottages were widely dispersed over their part of the common.[17] The total had risen to over 30 by 1838, by which time inclosure of most of the common within Newent had produced a complex pattern of small lanes and a patchwork of paddocks and orchards.[18]

On Kilcot manor's part of the common building was under way by 1771, and between 1783 and 1786 the new owner of the manor, J.N. Morse, granted leases of eight cottages, probably to regularize the status of dwellings in existence for some years.[19] Morse also began a programme of token hedge-breaking on the inclosures of other squatters to prevent them gaining ownership by uninterrupted possession and persuade them to accept him as owner.[20] At least seven more cottagers agreed to take leases between 1808 and 1815.[21] By 1838 there were *c.*25 cottages on Kilcot manor's part of the common, dispersed among closes and orchards on both sides of Ell brook and to the east of the road leading from Kilcot Cross to Aston Ingham.[22]

Most of the cottages on the common seem to have been built of the local stone, though some were of

---

1 GA, SL 12; GDR, T 1/126.
2 GA, D 412/T 1.
3 Ibid. D 2592, deeds of Kew's estate 1668–1796.
4 Ibid. D 2957/212/101–2.
5 Ibid. D 1810/4.
6 GDR, T 1/126 (nos 860–1, 877–8, 897).
7 Bryant, *Map of Glos.* (1824); OS Map 1", sheet 43 (1831 edn).
8 GDR, T 1/126.
9 Below, social hist. (inns and public houses).
10 Below, manors (Kilcot).
11 Herefs. RO, E 12/G/5, survey 1624, pp. 13–14.
12 GA, D 421/M 81 (s.v. Broadgrove tenants).
13 Ibid. D 2528, p. 7; photocopy 5.
14 Herefs. RO, E 12/G/4, survey 1624, pp. 14–15.
15 Ibid. G/16.
16 GA, EL 148 (leases 14 Sept. 1711, 3 Apr. 1717, 27 Sept. 1727, 27 Mar. 1732, 29 Apr., 14 June, 20 Sept. 1749, 5 Nov. 1750, 20 Sept. 1754, 10 July 1769); D 2957/212/79, 88.
17 Ibid. D 2528, pp. 6–7; photocopy 5.
18 GDR, T 1/126; GA, D 2710.
19 GA, D 412/T 1.
20 Ibid. E 1.
21 Ibid. M 1/1.
22 GDR, T 1/126.

brick.¹ One of those established on Newent manor before 1775² stands by the stream that marked the old boundary between Newent and the detached land of Pauntley and in part has thin timber framing. Another of the early dwellings in the same area, Brockmore Farm (formerly Brockmore Head) near the north boundary, has its lower courses of stone and the rest of brick; the cottage that existed there by 1775 was apparently enlarged in the early 19th century when the original encroachment was expanded to create a small farm on the Foleys' estate.³

The settlement on Gorsley common retained its widely dispersed character. The new line of the Ross turnpike formed in 1810⁴ attracted few dwellings, and a building for a school and chapel, built beside it to the west of Brassfields Farm in 1872, and a church, built adjacent twenty years later,⁵ have remained an isolated group. In the 20th century many of the old cottages in the Gorsley area were abandoned or demolished, but some new bungalows were built in the 1950s and 1960s.⁶ The surviving older dwellings were almost all remodelled and extended later in the century, often retaining very little of their original character.

MANORS AND ESTATES

At the time of the Norman Conquest the royal manor of Newent covered the bulk of Newent parish as later constituted, but a manor called Carswalls which was later part of the parish was in separate ownership and another, called Kilcot, included part of the later parish at Gorsley. By 1086, when Newent manor had passed to the abbey of Cormeilles in Normandy, Boulsdon had been alienated to form a distinct manor. By the 13th century two more manors had been formed at Kilcot, and other small ones had been established at Okle and Stalling (later Stallions) under the overlordship of the abbey, to which they owed riding and other services. Other substantial freeholds had emerged by the close of the Middle Ages, and in the early modern period the pattern of landholding became even more complex, with the creation, and later dispersal, by the Porter family of a large estate based on Boulsdon, and by sales made from Newent manor by the royalist Winter family following sequestration of its estate under the Commonwealth.

From 1659 Newent manor belonged to the Foley family, notable ironmasters, who were probably first attracted to it by the opportunity of exploiting the manorial woodland to fuel their Ellbridge furnace, adjoining the parish in Oxenhall, though they added some farmland to the estate in the late 17th century. Later, as non-resident owners with large estates elsewhere, the Foleys were less interested in enlarging their Newent estate, but their 19th-century successors, the Onslows, added farms and established a residence on it, at Stardens. A local tradesman, John Nourse Morse, became an important landowner by purchases in the 1780s but his estate remained intact only for his lifetime, as was the case with a large estate created by Andrew Knowles in the late 19th century. Other attempts to build up estates, including one based on a new house called Clifford Manor on the slopes of May hill, were also short-lived. In much of the parish, however, the general pattern from the 17th century was one of modest-sized freehold farms and that pattern was reinforced in the early years of the 20th by the sale and break-up of the Newent manor and Newent Court estates.

NEWENT MANOR

In 1066 Newent manor, comprising six hides, was held by Edward the Confessor and, as part of an estate based on Westbury-on-Severn, contributed to the one night's royal farm. Soon after the Conquest it passed to the abbey of Cormeilles (Eure). According to the abbey's cartulary, that was by the grant of its founder William FitzOsbern (d. 1071), earl of Hereford, to whom King William had given the manor, but the Domesday survey credits the earl's son Roger of Breteuil as the grantor.⁷ A large part of FitzOsbern's lands passed later to Robert (d. 1168), earl of Leicester, by his marriage to Amice de Gael, and their son Robert ès Blanchemains, earl of Leicester,⁸ included Newent in a confirmation to Cormeilles of Norman and English possessions in 1181. That grant, which was confirmed by Henry II, extended Newent at five hides, including lands in Compton, Malswick, Boulsdon, Cugley, Okle, Stalling, and 'Lindam' and the woods called Yartleton and 'Tedeswode'.⁹ By the early 13th century Cormeilles had established a priory at Newent and had given the prior,¹⁰ who was also styled bailiff of Newent, the duty of

---

1 GA, SL 79.
2 Ibid. D 2528, photocopy 5.
3 GDR, T 1/126; GA, D 1882/5/3; SL 79.
4 Above, introd. (communications: roads).
5 Below, religious hist. (religious life in 19th and 20th cents.).
6 GA, DA 30/100/24, p. 83; 100/25, p.227; 100/26, pp. 61, 128; 100/27, p. 37; 100/30, pp. 94, 255.
7 *Domesday Book* (Rec. Com.), I, 163, 166. The cartulary, in a confused entry, calls the founder 'William FitzOsbert' and implies that Robert, earl of Leicester, who confirmed the manor to the abbey in 1181, was FitzOsbern's son; further confusion was evident in 1262 when a Newent jury stated that Newent was given to Cormeilles by ' William son of Osbert, earl of Leicester': BL, Add. MS 18461, ff. 1, 51v.
8 *Complete Peerage*, VII, 527–33.
9 BL, Add. MS 18461, ff. 1v.–4v.
10 The prior of Newent was mentioned in 1221: *Pleas of the Crown for Glos.* ed. Maitland, p. 85.

administering the manor and supervising the abbey's other English possessions.[1]

In 1294 at the outbreak of war with France Edward I took Newent manor in hand but gave temporary custody to Cormeilles abbey and the prior of Newent for the payment of a farm.[2] Manor and priory were again seized by the Crown at the time of brief fighting in 1324 and returned to the prior for an annual farm of £130.[3] They were once more forfeit from 1337, the beginning of the long French war, during which custody was usually left with the prior in return for the same annual farm.[4] Before 1342, however, a grant of custody was made to Henry of Lancaster, earl of Derby, but, after it was confirmed that royal policy for the lands of alien monasteries was that the dispossessed house should have the first option of taking them at farm, priory and manor were re-delivered to the prior.[5] In 1382 the king gave Cormeilles licence to grant Newent manor to John Devereux and others of his family for their lives, paying the Crown a farm of £126 13s. 4d. while the war continued.[6] Devereux was released from payment of the farm in 1385[7] and remained in possession in 1390 when the former prior, John Smith (*Faber*), whose establishment was presumably dissolved at the time of the grant to Devereux, was receiving a pension from the profits of the manor.[8] Henry IV at his accession in 1399 granted Newent at farm to John Cheyne of Beckford (Glos., later Worcs.), who became a member of his council and a trusted diplomat.[9] Cheyne played a part in the suppression of Owen Glendower's revolt, employing in the campaign a number of his Newent tenants, who were reimbursed by a levy on the manor in 1405.[10] In 1411, following the permanent dispossession of the lands of the alien monasteries, Newent was included in the endowment of Fotheringhay college (Northants.), a new foundation of Edward, duke of York; the college was to take possession on Cheyne's death, which occurred in 1413 or 1414. In 1419 the college, for which buildings at Fotheringhay were not completed for many years,[11] considered moving its establishment to Newent.[12]

Fotheringhay college, which leased Newent manor before 1540 to (Sir) Nicholas Arnold of Highnam,[13] surrendered the freehold to the Crown in 1547.[14] The Crown granted it the same year to Sir Richard Lee[15] and he sold it in 1555 to Edward Wilmot, a merchant of Witney (Oxon.).[16] Edward conveyed it in 1556 to his son, also Edward, reserving his right to the site of the manor from after his death (which occurred in 1558) to his wife Christian, with reversion to a younger son Alexander.[17] The younger Edward Wilmot sold the freehold of the manor in 1567 to William Winter of Lydney,[18] who in 1569 was attempting to oust the tenant, Sir Nicholas Arnold, for non-payment of rent and for waste in the manor woods.[19] Winter was knighted in 1573 and died in 1589, and the manor passed to his son (Sir) Edward (d. 1619) and then to Sir Edward's son (Sir) John. As a result of Sir John Winter's activities on the royalist side in the Civil War, Newent with his other possessions was in sequestration until 1647, was confiscated in 1649, and was bought back by Winter in 1651 or 1652.[20] To meet his debts Winter and his son William mortgaged the estate heavily and sold off parts,[21] and in 1659 they and the mortgagees sold the manor to the wealthy ironmaster Thomas Foley of Great Witley (Worcs.),[22] who already owned the adjoining Oxenhall manor and Ellbridge iron furnace.[23]

During the 1660s Thomas Foley and his second son Paul added to the farmland of the manor by the purchase of several small estates.[24] Thomas died in 1677, having settled Newent and Oxenhall on Paul,[25] with whose estate at Stoke Edith (Herefs.) the manors subsequently descended. Paul Foley, who became M.P. for Hereford and, in 1695, Speaker of the House of Commons, died in 1699.[26] He was succeeded by his son Thomas (d. 1737), and Thomas by his son Thomas (d. 1749), who in 1738 conveyed his Gloucestershire estates, reserving the woodland and ironworks, to his son, also Thomas. The last Thomas was created Lord Foley in 1776 after inheriting Great Witley and the estates of the older branch of the family.[27] His Newent estate then comprised 2,072 a. and included the manor house called the Court House, farms based on Nelfields, Stardens, Compton House, Black House, and Brassfields at Gorsley, numerous smaller holdings and cottages, and

---

1 BL, Add. MS 18461, ff. 32–3; *VCH Glos.* II, 105–6.
2 BL, Add. MS 18461, ff. 92–3; Herefs. RO, E 12/G/2, ct. (7 May) 26 Edw. I, where a writ addressed by the king to 'his bailiffs of Newent' is enrolled; ct. (19 July) 26 Edw. I, where the prior is described as the king's minister.
3 BL, Add. MS 15668, ff. 81v.–84; TNA, SC 6/1125/15.
4 *Cal. Close* 1337–9, 195; 1341–3, 221; BL, Add. MS 15668, ff. 90 and v., 94–98v.
5 *Cal. Close* 1341–3, 588.
6 *Cal. Pat.* 1381–5, 123.
7 Ibid. 1385–9, 13.
8 Herefs. RO, E 12/G/5, acct. roll 14 Ric. II.
9 *Cal. Pat.* 1399–1401, 205; for Cheyne, J.S. Roskell, 'Sir John Cheyne of Beckford', *Trans. BGAS* 75 (1956), 43–72.
10 Herefs. RO, E 12/G/2, cts. (12 Mar.), 29 Apr. 6 Hen. IV.
11 Roskell, 'Sir John Cheyne', 70–1; *VCH Northants.* II, 170–1.
12 Herefs. RO, E 12/G/2, ct. 12 Feb. 6 Hen. V.

13 TNA, E 315/82, f. 8v.
14 *Cal. Pat.* 1547–8, 4–5.
15 Ibid. 107–9.
16 Ibid. 1555–7, 94.
17 Ibid. 409–10; TNA, C 142/118, no 54.
18 Herefs. RO, E 12/G/16.
19 TNA, C 3/195/2.
20 Ibid. C 142/227, no 204; C 142/378, no 147; *VCH Glos.* V, 61.
21 GA, D 421/T 14, articles of agreement 24 Aug. 1652; D 1810/4, deed 1663; deeds 1656–7, in Herefs. RO, E 12/G/14–15, 18, 31.
22 Herefs. RO, E 12/G/16; for Thos., *Oxford DNB*.
23 Below, Oxenhall, manor.
24 Herefs. RO, E 12/G/17–18.
25 GA, D 2184.
26 *Oxford DNB*.
27 GA, D 2184; Herefs. RO, E 12/G/32, notice to tenants 23 Mar. 1737/8; *Burke's Peerage* (1963), 936–7.

945 a. of woodland, common, and waste land.[1] At his death in 1777 Lord Foley left his Gloucestershire estates to his third son Andrew Foley (d. 1818) of Newport House, Almeley (Herefs.), who was succeeded in turn by his children Thomas (d. 1822), William Andrew (d. 1828), and Elizabeth (d. 1861).[2]

Elizabeth Foley was succeeded by her nephew Richard Foley Onslow, the son of her sister Harriet and Richard Onslow, formerly vicar of Newent. R.F. Onslow, who made Stardens his residence, died in 1879, and Newent and Oxenhall passed to his son Andrew George Onslow (d. 1894), and to Andrew's son Andrew Richard Onslow, who lived at the house called the Furnace in Oxenhall.[3] The estate underwent several changes in composition, including the addition of Newtown farm before 1878, the sale of Nelfields in 1890,[4] and the addition of Great Cugley farm in 1893.[5] It was put up for sale in two portions, in 1910 and 1913, as a result of which it was divided into separate freehold farms; Newent woods, comprising 688 a.,[6] were acquired by the Huntley Manor estate of the Ackers family.[7]

Newent Priory and the Court House

Newent priory occupied a walled precinct on the north side of the town, bounded by the vicarage garden on the north-west, by part of New Street and by Lewall Street (as those names were originally used) on the south-west and south, part of Church Street on the south-east, and the churchyard on the north-east. To the north, between the precinct and Ell brook, lay a park and other demesnes with a coney warren, fishponds, dovecot, and, by the late 13th century, a fulling mill.[8] The gate of the precinct opened on to the town's market place at what was later the south end of Court Lane and had a porter's lodging adjoining in 1368.[9] The gateway survived until the early 19th century, and in 1673 a chamber over its arch belonged to the adjoining house, formerly the boothall.[10] The domestic buildings were apparently close to the west end of the parish church on or near the site of the later manor house. It was presumably there that the farmer of the manor, John Devereux, built himself a new 'great chamber' in 1390.[11] The buildings near the east end of the precinct also included a barn and a carthouse in 1338;[12] the former was perhaps beside Court Lane where a barn, used to store the rectory tithes, was replaced in 1889 by the town's police station and magistrates' court.[13] The north-west part of the precinct, beyond the course of Peacock's brook, was occupied by other farm buildings, including in the early 15th century two barns, an oxhouse, a hayhouse, and a mares' stable.[14] The priory establishment was probably very small, perhaps comprising only the prior and one or two other monks, but 11 household and farm servants were employed in 1347.[15]

The manor house, occupying the north-east end of the priory precinct was called the Court House until the early 19th century, when to distinguish it from a new mansion built near by (Newent Court) it became known as Old Court. Few, if any, of the post-medieval lords used it, the Winters living at Lydney, the Foleys at Stoke Edith or Almeley, and the Onslows locally at Stardens or the Furnace. For much of the 18th century the Court House was leased to the Beale family:[16] it was successively the home of the clothier Miles Beale[17] (d. 1713), his son Miles (d. 1748), who rebuilt the house,[18] and the younger Miles's son John (d. 1775), who served as High Sheriff of the county in 1752.[19] A later tenant was Samuel Richardson,[20] who was High Sheriff in 1787.[21] By 1805 the Richardson family had sublet the house to James de Visme, who occupied it for a few years[22] before moving into his new house, Newent Court. Richard Onslow, vicar of Newent 1803–49, occupied Old Court for most of his incumbency.[23] It was alienated from the manor in 1870 when R.F. Onslow sold it to Charles James Cooke, a Newent solicitor, whose mortgagee took possession of the house before 1879 and sold it to Andrew Knowles of Newent Court. At the sale of the Newent Court estate it was bought in 1910 by Clara, Amy, and Gertrude Hutchinson;[24] Amy was living there in 1935.[25] In the late 20th century it became a hotel, which closed in 1999 when the house (once again known as the Court House) was bought by Mr and Mrs R. Morris.[26]

The main eastern and southern ranges of the Court House,[27] as rebuilt in the early 18th century, form a **T** and are of brick, of two storeys with dormered attics and brick-vaulted cellars. The eastern range presents a

---

1 GA, D 2528.
2 Ibid. D 2957/212/22.
3 Ibid. D 1882/5/1–2; *Burke's Peerage* (1963), 1863.
4 GA, D 1882/5/1; SL 13.
5 Ibid. D 2299/6.
6 Ibid. SL 79–80.
7 J. Douglas, *Historical Notes of Newent with Oxenhall and Pauntley* (1912), 15.
8 Herefs. RO, E 12/G/5, acct. roll 22 Edw. IV; G/5, survey 1624, p. 1; below, econ. hist. (mills).
9 BL, Add. MS 18461, f. 100v.; Herefs. RO, E 12/G/1, cts. (8 May) 42 Edw. III, (14 Oct.) 44 Edw. III.
10 GDR wills 1673/1; 1726/266. For the boothall, above, settlement (bldgs. of Newent town).
11 Herefs. RO, E 12/G/5, acct. roll 14 Ric. II.
12 Ibid. G/1, ct. (14 Oct.) 12 Edw. III.
13 GA, D 412/Z 3, Newent notes, 1900.
14 Herefs. RO, E 12/G/1, ct. 18 Apr. 11 Hen. IV; G/2, ct. 12 Feb. 6 Hen. V; G/3, ct. (1 Aug.) 9 Hen. IV.
15 Ibid. G/1, acct. roll 21 Edw. III.
16 For whom, Bigland, *Glos.* II, 241.
17 GA, D 412/Z 3, 'MS no II'; D 892/T 57, deed 1703.
18 Ibid. D 412/Z 3, Nourse MS, p. 15; EL 148 (lease 10 Nov. 1733).
19 Ibid. D 2957/212/89.
20 Ibid. 212/94; *Glouc. J.* 3 Aug. 1789.
21 *Glos. N&Q* III, 414.
22 GA, D 2957/212/95–6.
23 Hockaday Abs. ccxciii, 1816 sqq.
24 *Kelly's Dir. Glos.* (1870), 604–5; deeds in possession of Mr R. Morris of the Court House.
25 *Kelly's Dir. Glos.* (1935), 266.
26 Information from Mrs Morris.
27 Fig. 11.

11. *The Court House (formerly Old Court) from the south in 1910*

symmetrical five-bayed façade to the church, formerly reached by a gate, now blocked, in the churchyard wall. The rebuilding incorporated on the north-west a slightly lower wing from an earlier house, which may have influenced the irregular plan. The southern bay of the older wing was remodelled at the rebuilding, but the remainder, apparently of the 16th century, was timber-framed, of two storeys and attics, and with four star-plan brick chimneys on an internal stack.[1] That older part of the wing was replaced in 1871.[2] Also in the 19th century single-storeyed service additions were built to the west. The main rooms in the eastern range comprise a three-bayed panelled room, a smaller southern room extended *c.*1800 by a Gothic bay, and on the first floor two rooms, separated by closets, which were also redecorated *c.*1800. The southern range contains the main staircase.

Newent Court

The former demesnes to the north of the priory precinct, including lands called Upper and Lower Park, Upper and Lower Court Orchard, and meadows beside Ell brook, were leased under the manor from the late 15th century. In 1624 they were divided among several tenants, the Parks being held by copy.[3] They remained part of the manor, subject to mortgages by the Winter family, in 1657[4] but were apparently alienated soon afterwards and passed to Sir Edmund Bray[5] (d. 1684). They then descended with the Walden Court and (later) Okle Clifford estates to James de Visme,[6] who *c.*1810 built a mansion called Newent Court (or New Court) and landscaped the grounds to provide a setting for the house and walks for visitors to the nearby Newent spa. He incorporated as features the stretch of the new Hereford and Gloucester canal that traversed his land and the old mill pond on the far side of the canal, and he made a large new lake covering *c.*4 a. in Court Orchard south of the house.[7] He died in 1826 and was succeeded by his son Revd James Edward de Visme (*fl.* 1838).[8] Later, house and grounds passed to George Reed, a West India merchant, and before 1856 they were acquired by John B.H. Burland (*fl.* 1870).[9] In the mid 1870s Newent Court was bought by Andrew Knowles, who built up a large estate in Newent and Taynton, his purchases including the Moat farm in 1877 and Nelfields farm in 1890. At his death in 1909 the estate comprised *c.*2,000 a.[10] It was split up by sales in 1910 and 1911.[11]

Newent Court with its grounds was bought in 1911 by Everard Charles de Peyer[12] (d. 1925).[13] The house was badly damaged by a fire in 1942 but later that year it was bought for the use of Ribston Hall High school, Gloucester; the cost, because of wartime restrictions on expenditure, was borne by the headmistress Gertrude Whitaker who was reimbursed by the governors after the war. Until the early 1950s pupils stayed there for a few weeks at a time to gain practical experience in

---

1 Photog. seen (2005) in possession of K.M. Tomlinson of Newent.
2 Datestone on bldg.
3 Herefs. RO, E 12/G/2, acct. rolls 22 Edw. IV, 22 Hen. VII; G/5, survey 1624, pp.1, 67; GA, D 421/E 13, ff. 15v.–16.
4 Herefs. RO, E 12/G/14, 18.
5 GA, D 127/572; D 4647/7/1, deed 1734.
6 Below (other manors: Walden Ct.; Okle: Okle Clifford).
7 GA, D 412/Z 3, Newent notes, 1900; P 225A/MI 1/8–9; *Glouc. J.* 27 Mar. 1815; *Pigot's Dir. Glos.* (1822–3), 61.
8 Below (Okle: Okle Clifford); GDR, T 1/126.
9 GA, D 412/Z 3, Newent notes, 1900; *Kelly's Dir. Glos.* (1856), 333; (1870), 604.
10 GA, SL 13.
11 Ibid. PA 225/2.
12 Ibid. D 2299/4664.
13 Ibid. P 225/VE 2/4.

horticulture and animal husbandry.[1] Later the house was unoccupied for some years before being demolished c.1970[2] to make way for new housing. James de Visme's house was a substantial Regency mansion with a Doric portico on the west entrance front and a semicircular bay on the east front. It was altered in the late 19th century when a small tower was added on the entrance front. Ornamental lodges with mock timber framing stood at the drive entrances on High Street to the west and Gloucester Street to the south-east;[3] the latter survived at the entrance to a new housing estate in 2005. The lake and adjoining part of the grounds were restored and landscaped as a public amenity by Newent town council in the late 1990s.[4]

BOULSDON MANOR

A hide of land that formed part of Newent manor in 1066 and which Durand, sheriff of Gloucestershire, held from Cormeilles abbey in 1086[5] was evidently the later manor of Boulsdon. In the 14th century Boulsdon, with an estate in Frampton on Severn, was held from Durand's descendants, the de Bohuns, earls of Hereford;[6] it also owed a chief rent of 5s. to the lord of Newent[7] and in 1597 Boulsdon manor was said to be held directly from Newent manor.[8] One of the manorial assets of Boulsdon was the tract of common land on the slopes of May hill called Clifford's Mesne, suggesting that the Cliffords, lords of Frampton, may have held the manor in the 12th century, though the common may have been named from a later member of that family, owner of part of the manor at the start of the 17th century.

Thomas of Boulsdon owned woodland in Boulsdon, presumably as part of the manor, in 1258,[9] and a man of that name paid the chief rent for the manor in 1278.[10] It passed by the early 14th century to William of Boulsdon,[11] who was a principal taxpayer in Newent parish in 1327[12] and evidently owned Boulsdon together with the estate in Frampton.[13] In 1346 Margery of Foxcote was licensed to hear mass in a private oratory at her manor house at Boulsdon.[14] In 1373 Richard le Ward held ½ knight's fee in Boulsdon and Frampton.[15]

Thomas Boulsdon held the manor of Boulsdon and lands in Frampton at his death in 1473, when he was succeeded by his daughter Elizabeth.[16] It seems that the two estates were later subject to a partition, perhaps among daughters of Elizabeth and her husband John Alley. Roger Porter was dealing with a third of Boulsdon manor in 1517[17] and his descendants retained a manor at Boulsdon. In the early 17th century, however, there was another manor there, belonging with part of Frampton to James Clifford (d. 1613)[18] of Fretherne, whose executors and trustees were engaged in litigation over it in the 1620s;[19] it has not been traced later.

Roger Porter, a lawyer from an established Newent family,[20] died in 1523[21] when his Boulsdon manor passed to his son Arthur. Arthur was under-steward of Llanthony priory, Gloucester, and at the Dissolution purchased several of the priory's estates and took up residence at the Newark, Hempsted.[22] He was succeeded at his death in 1558 by his son Sir Thomas Porter[23] (d. 1597) and Sir Thomas by his son (Sir) Arthur Porter.[24] Sir Arthur owned an extensive, though scattered, estate in Newent, and, as much of the land lay outside Boulsdon tithing, the original estate had evidently been augmented, probably by Roger Porter. Roger incurred an unusually high tax assessment (£50 on lands and £26 13s. 4d. on goods) at Newent in 1522,[25] and in 1539 his son Arthur owned 18 houses and numerous parcels of land in Newent town.[26] Sir Arthur Porter's estate comprised that town property and many small farms in Boulsdon, Cugley, Malswick, Compton, and the rural part of Newent tithing. He dispersed it by sales, including a group of small farms in Cugley and Boulsdon to Thomas Hill of Oxenhall and John Pitt of Cugley in 1607,[27] the manor of Southorles to Thomas Woodward before 1610, and the house in Newent town called Porter's Place to John Latton before 1615;[28] most of the houses in the town went to individual owners. Parts of the estate were further subdivided by the new owners, and by 1640 the chief rents, totalling £4 17s., that Sir Arthur had owed to Newent manor for his various properties had become the responsibility of 32 separate owners.[29]

The manorial rights of Boulsdon passed from Sir

---

1 GA, D 3398/2/2/53; *Chapters in Newent's History* (Newent Local Hist. Soc. 2003), 261.
2 D. Bick, *Old Newent & District* (Newent, 1992), 8.
3 For illustrations of the ho., GA, SL 13; D 2299/4664; Glos. Colln. prints 199.1.
4 Information board at W. end of lake.
5 *Domesday Book* (Rec. Com.), I, 166.
6 *Cal. Inq. p.m.* XIII, p. 141; *Cal Close 1381–5*, 513.
7 BL, Add. MS 18461, f. 109v.; Herefs. RO, E 12/G/7, ct. papers 1615.
8 TNA, C 142/253, no 97.
9 Ibid. E 32/28, rot. 2d.
10 BL, Add. MS 15668, f. 8.
11 Ibid. 18461, f. 109v.
12 *Glos. Subsidy Roll, 1327*, 35.
13 *VCH Glos.* X, 147.
14 *Reg. Trillek*, 59.
15 *Cal. Inq. p.m.* XIII, p. 141.
16 TNA, C 140/48, no 16.
17 *VCH Glos.* X, 147 and n.
18 TNA, C 142/339, no 181.
19 Ibid. C 3/398/187.
20 *Cal. Regs. Priory of Llanthony*, p. xv; Herefs. RO, E 12/G/2, acct. roll 22 Hen. VIII (s.vv. farm of demesne land, farm of rectories).
21 Hockaday Abs. ccxcii.
22 *Cal. Regs. Priory of Llanthony*, p. xxxii; *VCH Glos.* IV, 395, 424.
23 TNA, C 142/122, no 74.
24 Ibid. C 142/253, no 97.
25 *Military Surv. of Glos. 1522*, 52.
26 Herefs. RO, E 12/G/5, rental 31 Hen. VIII.
27 GA, D 365/T 1.
28 Herefs. RO, E 12/G/7, ct. papers 1615.
29 GA, D 421/E 13, f. 13; M 81.

12. Clifford Manor from the north-east in 1932

Arthur Porter, apparently through one or more intermediate sales, to John Latton and his brother Edward Latton, who released his right to John in 1615.[1] The manor passed to John's son, also called John, who sold it with Porter's Place and other lands to Thomas Estcourt of Taynton in 1626. In 1629 Thomas and Richard Estcourt sold the manor, on which Clifford's Mesne was then mentioned, to Walter Nourse. Walter (d. 1652) was succeeded by his son, also Walter, who died in 1663 and was succeeded by his wife Mary. Mary surrendered it in 1677 to her son, another Walter Nourse, who retained it until his death in 1743.[2] It passed to Walter's son John (d. 1754), rector of Damerham (Wilts., later Hants), who left it to his sister Elizabeth (d. 1757). She left it to a kinsman, William Nourse of Weston under Penyard (Herefs.). William died in 1788, and his son John[3] sold off his estate in parcels, Boulsdon manor with some land in the tithing and Porter's Place, together with Southends farm, being acquired in 1789 by John Nourse Morse. Morse, a Newent mercer who had acted as the Nourse family's steward or agent for some years,[4] died in 1830, leaving Boulsdon manor and Southends to his son John and after John's death, which occurred in 1842, to trustees for sale.[5] The manorial rights of Boulsdon, which in 1788 comprised only chief rents of £1 3s. owed by freeholders in the tithing, the right of soil in the waste of Clifford's Mesne and Kent's green, and the right to hold courts,[6] have not been traced for some years after 1842. Later in the century, however, they were believed to belong to P.R. Cocks of Clifford Manor, who had the quarry rights on Clifford's Mesne.[7]

Clifford Manor

Philip Reginald Cocks, who succeeded to the title of Lord Somers in 1883,[8] became owner of a group of smallholdings and cottages on Clifford's Mesne, partly by carrying out inclosures of common land.[9] In the late 1870s and early 1880s he also formed an estate at Glasshouse elsewhere on the slopes of May hill by a series of small purchases of land (some of it in Taynton parish),[10] and in 1882 he built himself a house at Glasshouse which he named Clifford Manor.[11] Described as 'lord of the manor of Clifford's Mesne',[12] he died in 1899. By the following year his house and estate had been acquired by Theodore Grimké-Drayton, who added Green farm, north of Newent woods, to give himself a total estate of 295 a. In 1912 Grimké-Drayton put his estate up for sale[13] and the manorial rights of Boulsdon were bought with Clifford Manor by Francis Frederick Grafton.[14] The rights, which a few years later — the chief rents deemed uncollectable — were thought to comprise only a quarry on Clifford's Mesne,[15] apparently passed to later owners of Clifford Manor, John Richard Glasson (*fl.* 1931) and Lt.-Cmdr. F.C.R.R. Younghusband (*fl.* 1939).[16]

---

1 Ibid. D 332/T 6.
2 Ibid. T 5; Bigland, *Glos.* II, 245–6.
3 GA, D 332/T 4; TNA, PROB 11/807, ff. 14–15v.
4 GA, D 1810/1; D 245/I/19, letters 29 Oct., 17 Dec. 1803; D 2245/T 8, deed 1792.
5 Ibid. D 1810/2; D 1927/8, deed 2 Feb. 1844.
6 Ibid. D 412/E 2.
7 Ibid. Z 2.
8 *Burke's Peerage* (1900), 1391.
9 GA, D 7723/1; D 412/E 2, letter 11 Dec. 1916.
10 Ibid. D 413/T 2–5, 7–12.
11 Ibid. D 412/Z 2.
12 *Kelly's Dir. Glos.* (1897), 202.
13 GA, D 2299/951.
14 Ibid. D 4858/2/4/1932/2.
15 Ibid. D 412/E 2, letter 11 Dec. 1916.
16 *Kelly's Dir. Glos.* (1931), 214; (1939), 220.

Clifford Manor was designed in grand baronial style, but on a small scale, by Medland & Son,[1] its most eye-catching feature an embattled tower with a taller circular stair turret.[2] The rock-faced Gorsley stone contrasts with clay tiles and brick chimneys. The house was converted as several dwellings c.1963.[3]

Great Boulsdon Farm

According to a tradition recorded by the lord of the manor Walter Nourse c.1725 the early medieval lords of Boulsdon had a castle standing on a mound,[4] which was later identified as being close to the Newent–Clifford's Mesne road, near Great Boulsdon Farm.[5] The farm was possibly the estate described as the site of the manor of Boulsdon that was owned in 1640 by Edward Gwillim and perhaps had been included in a conveyance made to Edward or a predecessor of the same name by Sir Arthur Porter in 1610.[6] If Great Boulsdon was Gwillim's estate, it returned to the ownership of the lords of the manor before 1703 when Walter Nourse remodelled its farmhouse, then known as Panhills (or Pennells).[7] John Nourse sold Great Boulsdon c.1789 to Edward Hartland,[8] who sold the 139-a. farm back to the lord of the manor J.N. Morse in 1819.[9] At his death Morse left it to be put up for sale, but William Morse, apparently his grandson, bought it from his devisees in 1831. William died in 1837, and in 1842 Great Boulsdon was sold for the benefit of his creditors to Edmund Rudge, a Tewkesbury tanner.[10] Rudge (d. 1843) was succeeded by his nephew Edmund Rudge, who held it, subject to complex transactions resulting from mortgages and his divorce from his wife Frances, until his death in 1886. His trustee sold the farm in 1891 to Octavius Price, a Newent solicitor.[11]

Great Boulsdon was a timber-framed L-plan house of the 17th century, with two storeys, attics, and a cellar under one wing. Each wing contained two rooms a floor, with hall and kitchen in the main range. At the early 18th-century remodelling the west wing was extended in brick to five bays and the west face cased in brick. In the early 19th century the east face was also brick clad, and later in the century the west face was refenestrated and large dormers inserted.[12] Alterations in the late 20th century included an extension to give access to an upper flat, and a lean-to on the entrance front.

13. *Great Boulsdon: the west front*

Porter's Place

The house called Porter's Place that descended with Boulsdon manor for many years was the home of Roger Porter (d. 1523).[13] It stood on the south-west side of the market square in Newent town with c.40 a. of closes and orchards belonging to it, extending southwards towards Southends Lane.[14] It was the home of the Nourse family in the 17th century and the early 18th,[15] but it was demolished before 1789 and the site was sold by J.N. Morse's devisees in 1831.[16] A new house of modest proportions (Albion House) was built on part of the site c.1870.[17]

CARSWALLS MANOR

In 1066 Wulfhelm held 1 hide at Carswalls, in Compton tithing on the east side of the parish, and in 1086 Roger de Lacy held the same with Odo as his tenant.[18] In 1236 an estate there, described as ⅕ knight's fee, was held by Gerard de Hussemane from Walter de Lacy,[19] while another estate, comprising ½ hide and rents, belonged to Parnel, widow of Randal de Solers.[20] Ingram de Solers quitclaimed ½ yardland at Carswalls to William

---

1 Verey and Brooks, *Glos.* II, 312.
2 Above, Fig. 12.
3 GA, DA 30/100/32, p. 75.
4 Ibid. D 412/Z 1.
5 Ibid. Z 2.
6 Ibid. D 421/M 81; TNA, CP 25/2/297/7 Jas I Hil. no 29.
7 GA, D 421/Z 1; see ibid. D 1810/2, deed 24 Dec. 1842.
8 Ibid. D 245/I/19, letter 17 Dec. 1803; D. Bick, *The Mines of Newent and Ross* (Newent, 1987), 15.
9 GA, D 412/M 1/1, f. 90v.; *Glouc. J.* 17 Aug. 1818.
10 GA, D 1810/2.
11 Ibid. D 1927/7.
12 Fig. 13.
13 Inscr., describing him as 'of the Place', on stone slab of his brass in Newent ch.
14 GA, D 332/T 5, deed 6 Mar. 1625; T 8.
15 TNA, PROB 11/228, f. 66v.; Bigland, *Glos.* II, 245.
16 GA, D 1810/1.
17 Ibid. D 2299/27.
18 *Domesday Book* (Rec. Com,), I, 167v.
19 *Book of Fees*, I, 439, 443.
20 *Glos. Feet of Fines 1199–1299*, p. 53.

14. Carswalls Manor

de Hussemane in 1255[1] but had an acknowledgement of his right to a house and ploughland from Roger de Solers in 1268.[2] Also known as Ingram of Carswalls, he retained his estate in 1278 when it owed a chief rent of 5s. to Newent manor.[3] John of Carswalls held ¼ knight's fee at Carswalls in 1303[4] and was probably the man called John Ingram who owed the chief rent for Carswalls c.1315;[5] the ¼ fee had passed by 1346 to Richard Carswalls.[6]

No later record of Carswalls has been found until c.1523 when John Heylond was succeeded there by his daughters Isabel, wife of John Haverd, and Joan, wife of John Westerdale.[7] In 1560 John Gooding and his wife Elizabeth conveyed Carswalls manor to Elizabeth's son Philip Haverd[8] and in 1575 Philip, with his wife Anne, conveyed it to Richard Green[9] (d. by 1596).[10] Green's son, also Richard, married Dorothy Pauncefoot, and it was presumably through her that her brother Grimbald Pauncefoot (d. 1668)[11] held Carswalls in 1640.[12] It passed to Grimbald's son Poole Pauncefoot (d. 1687), to his son William (d. 1691),[13] and to William's son, another William Pauncefoot (d. 1711).[14] After a division between coheirs half of the Carswalls estate was settled in 1728 on the marriage of Sarah Pauncefoot and William Bromley[15] (d. 1769). In 1778, when the estate comprised Carswalls Manor, Newtown, and Line House farms in Compton and Ravenshill farm in Boulsdon, William's son Robert Bromley of Abberley (Worcs.) sold half of it to Sir George Smith Bt, of East Stoke (Notts.), the owner of the other half. Sir George, who was the county sheriff for 1775–6, changed his name in 1778 to Bromley and in 1803 to Pauncefote. At his death in 1808 his estate, comprising over 700 a., passed to his son Sir Robert Howe Bromley, who in 1811 sold Newtown and Line House farms to James Cummins (d. 1834).[16] Carswalls Manor farm, comprising 300 a., belonged by 1838 to Paul Hawkins Fisher[17] (d. 1873) of Stroud, who was succeeded by his son Charles Hawkins Fisher (d. 1901).[18] The Fisher family sold the farm in 1902 to the tenant T.B. Holloway, who offered it for sale in 1914, when it included farm buildings at Little Carswalls.[19] In 2005 Carswalls Manor farm, comprising c.81 ha (c.200 a.), was owned and farmed by members of the Carter family.

The large farmstead, occupying a prominent site beside the road to Upleadon, retains the remnants of a moat and a derelict brick dovecot of c.1700. The house and the farm buildings were rebuilt in brick in the late 18th century or the early 19th. The L plan of the house, of two storeys and attics over a cellar, may repeat that of its predecessor, and the double-pile south wing, which contains a dog-leg stair and a single chimneystack with

1 Ibid. p. 109.
2 Ibid. p. 146.
3 BL, Add. MS 15668, f. 7v.
4 *Feudal Aids*, II, 250.
5 BL, Add. MS 18461, f. 108.
6 *Feudal Aids*, II, 285.
7 Herefs. RO, E 12/G/4, ct. c.1523 (approx. dated by presentment of Roger Porter's death).
8 GA, D 1349/23.
9 TNA, CP 25/2/142/1822, no 26.
10 GA, D 48/T 51.
11 *Visit. Glos. 1682–3*, 76; for the Pauncefoots, ibid. 131; Bigland, *Glos.* II, 315–16.
12 GA, D 421/M 81.
13 GDR wills 1687/176.
14 Ibid. 1715/82; Atkyns, *Glos.* 568.
15 GA, D 602, deed 1779.
16 GA, D 1938; *Glouc. J.* 9 Sept. 1811; *Complete Baronetage*, V, 108 and n; *Burke's Peerage* (1900), I, 202; Rudder, *Glos.* 54.
17 GDR, T 1/126.
18 GA, D 1842/E 2; *Kelly's Dir. Glos.* (1879), 709; (1902), 250.
19 GA, SL 113, 311.

diagonal fireplaces, may incorporate fabric of c.1700. The windows are segment-headed.[1] West of the house stands a ruinous single-storeyed outbuilding on an L plan; the farmyard to the east contains a large barn to which an engine house was added c.1900.

KILCOT

Three medieval manors are recorded at Kilcot, a name that was formerly applied to a large area in the north-west part of Newent parish and the adjoining detached portion of Pauntley parish (transferred to Oxenhall in 1883). A manor called Kilcot was held in 1086 by Ansfrid of Cormeilles, lord of Pauntley, and in the mid 13th century part of that manor, including lands at Gorsley and in the detached bit of Pauntley, was granted by Ansfrid's successors to Cormeilles abbey, lord of Newent manor, reserving a chief rent of 8s. The lands in that grant were sometimes accorded the status of a separate manor, and evidently formed the ⅓ knight's fee at 'Gorsley' that the prior of Newent was said in 1398 to have formerly held.[2] Two other manors recorded at Kilcot from the 13th century were connected tenurially with Taynton and seem to have emerged independently of Newent manor, for there is no record of a chief rent paid from them to the lords of Newent. One belonged to Robert de Mucegros at his death in 1254, when it was described as a ploughland held of Arnald du Boys as of Taynton for ⅙ knight's fee.[3] It descended with Robert's manor of Great Taynton to the Ferrers family, whose estate in both places was held in chief as ½ fee during the 14th and early 15th centuries.[4] In 1351 it was styled the manor of Taynton and Kilcot.[5] The Kilcot land of that estate has not been traced after the Middle Ages. The other manor, based later on the house called the Conigree, was held by Bevis de Knovill in the late 13th century and descended with the manor of Little Taynton.[6] Presumably it was created by subinfeudation from the Mucegros manor, for Kilcot wood was held by John de Mucegros in 1258 but by Bevis de Knovill in 1270[7] and Bevis's successors were later said to hold their manor from the Ferrers family.[8]

Gorsley and Brassfields

By 1390 part of the estate that derived from the grant to Cormeilles abbey in the mid 13th century had become known as the 'court of Gorsley' and was charged, as it also was in 1482, with payment of the 8s. rent owed to the lords of Pauntley.[9] It adjoined the west side of the detached portion of Pauntley parish and in 1624, though not apparently later, was itself regarded as within Pauntley.[10] The name Gorsley Court became attached to a small house in that area in the late 19th century, but as that house was built on an encroachment made on Gorsley common after 1775 it is unlikely to have formed part of the medieval estate.[11] In 1482 the court of Gorsley was in the hands of the lords of Newent, following the death or forfeiture of the tenant Walter Hill.[12] In 1539 it was held from Newent manor by copy, together with two fields to the south-east called Broadfield and Blethefield (later Broadgrove and Bleisfield) which may also have been included in the mid 13th-century grant. By the early 17th century those lands had been divided into small leaseholds, the tenant of the court of Gorsley, Thomas Hill, having five under-tenants in 1624 and Broadgrove and Bleisfield being divided among nine tenants.[13] Later, under the Foleys, the tenancies were consolidated, Broadgrove and Bleisfield becoming a single farm called Brassfields.[14] Also attached to Newent manor, but probably deriving from another source, was the adjoining part of Gorsley common forming a detached part of Cugley tithing; it was progressively inclosed by cottagers.[15] At the start of the 20th century the Onslows' estate in the Gorsley area comprised Brassfields farm, smaller farms based on Brockmore Head, Bull Hill, and the house called Gorsley Court, and numerous cottages and smallholdings.[16] At the sale of the estate in 1913 all those appear to have passed to separate owners, presumably in most cases the sitting tenants.

Kilcot Manor and the Conigree

In 1270 Kilcot wood, and evidently a manor, belonged to Bevis de Knovill,[17] who in 1285 had a grant of free warren in his demesne lands in Kilcot and Little Taynton.[18] After his death in 1307 his Kilcot manor descended with Little Taynton manor, following a divided ownership in the late Middle Ages before passing to the Cassey family of Wightfield, in Deerhurst. It remained in the same ownership as Little Taynton until the mid 17th century[19] save that in 1580 Henry Cassey settled Kilcot wood on the marriage of his son Thomas, who succeeded him in the whole estate in 1595.[20]

In 1653 John Atkinson of Stowell conveyed Kilcot

---

1 Above, Fig. 14.
2 Below, Oxenhall, manor (estates in detached part of Pauntley).
3 *Cal. Inq. p.m.* I, p. 82.
4 *Feudal Aids*, II, 250, 284, 298; below, Taynton, manors.
5 *Inq. p.m. Glos.* 1301–58, 341–2.
6 Below (Kilcot manor).
7 TNA, E 32/28, rot. 2d.; E 32/29, rot. 8.
8 *Inq. p.m. Glos.* 1301–58, 97–8; TNA, C 142/84, no 39.
9 Herefs. RO, E 12/G/5, acct. roll 13 Ric. II; G/2, acct. roll 22 Edw. IV.
10 Ibid. G/5, survey 1624, p. 7.
11 OS Map 6", Glos. XVII.SW (1884 edn); GA, photocopy 5.

12 Herefs. RO, E 12/G/2, acct. roll 22 Edw. IV.
13 Ibid. G/5, rental 31 Hen. VIII (s.v. Kilcot); survey 1624, pp. 7–8, 13–14; GA, D 421/E 13, ff. 19v.–20.
14 Above, settlement (outlying settlements: Kilcot and Gorsley).
15 GA, D 2528, pp. 6–7; photocopy 5.
16 Ibid. D 1882/5/3.
17 TNA, E 32/29, rot. 8.
18 *Cal. Chart.* 1257–1300, 289.
19 Below, Taynton, manors; *Cal. Close* 1360–4, 532; J.N. Langston, 'Old Catholic Families of Gloucestershire: the Casseys of Wightfield in Deerhurst', *Trans. BGAS* 74 (1955), 131, 141–2.
20 TNA, C 142/246, no 106.

15. *Conigree Court: the west front*

manor to John Bourne,[1] who in 1686 was living at the house called the Conigree (later Conigree Court), apparently the ancient site of the manor.[2] Bourne (d. *c.*1709)[3] was succeeded by his daughter Dorothy, the wife of Walter Nourse (d. 1743). Kilcot passed with Walter's Boulsdon manor in turn to his son Revd John Nourse (d. 1754) and daughter Elizabeth (d. 1757) and then, under the provisions of John's will, it went to their cousin Mary, wife of John Lewis of Llantilio Crossenny (Mon.). She by will dated 1760 left it to her youngest son John Lewis, who sold Kilcot in 1782 to John Nourse Morse; under him it returned to the same ownership as Boulsdon manor.[4] Morse was diligent in attempting to preserve his rights over part of Gorsley common that belonged to his Kilcot manor,[5] but he alienated Kilcot wood in 1792.[6] At his death in 1830 he left the estate, comprising a farm based on the Conigree and numerous cottages on Gorsley common, to his daughter Isabella Beale and after her death in 1856 his trustees sold the manorial rights and some cottages and land to a Newent solicitor Edmund Edmonds and the Conigree to Charles Clarke of Ashleworth.[7] Edmonds retained the lordship in 1882.[8] The Conigree was offered for sale by the heirs or executors of John Cannock in 1896[9] and was bought then or shortly afterwards by Edward Conder, who also acquired the manorial rights of Kilcot.[10] Conder (d. 1910) was succeeded by his son Edward. He died in 1934 and his widow Bertha[11] and executors offered the Conigree with 94 a. for sale in 1952.[12] By 1960 it was owned and farmed by J.M. Smith,[13] who was succeeded there by his son Mr M.J. Smith.[14]

Conigree Court, which occupies a low hill near the east side of Kilcot tithing just south of the Newent–Ross road, was presumably medieval in origin and named from a rabbit warren maintained by the early lords of Kilcot. In the earlier 17th century the house was leased to various wealthy tenants, one of whom is said to have carried out much building work.[15] John Bourne was apparently one of the few owners to live at the Conigree, and after his death it was usually leased as a farmhouse[16] until Edward Conder remodelled it as his

1 Ibid. CP 25/2/553/1653 Trin. no 31.
2 GA, D 332/T 4.
3 GDR wills 1709/120.
4 TNA, PROB 11/807, ff. 14–15v.; GA, D 412/T 2, deed 9 July 1782; see above (Boulsdon manor).
5 GA, D 412/E 1; M 1/1.
6 Ibid. D 2245/T 8.
7 Ibid. D 412/T 2; and for the estate in 1838, GDR, T 1/126.
8 GA, D 1882/5/2.
9 Glos. Colln. RX 212.
10 GA, D 412/E 1, receipt 1906; *Kelly's Dir. Glos.* (1897), 249.
11 GA, D 412/M 2; *Burke's Landed Gentry* (1937), 249.
12 GA, D 2299/10782; DA 30/100/18, p. 87.
13 Ibid. DA 30/100/29, p. 50; *Glos. Life and Countryside*, Apr.–May 1967, 23.
14 Information from Mrs Smith of the Conigree.
15 GA, D 412/Z 3, Nourse MS, p. 13.
16 Ibid. D 412/M 1/1–2.

own residence in 1897.[1] The earliest part of the house is the projecting north-western wing, probably built in the early to mid 17th century as a self-contained timber-framed house of two or three bays facing south-west. The entrance was north of the stone stack on the southern side. The western end is raised on a high stone plinth and possibly had an agricultural use, perhaps as a cider house and cellar. The eastern end may have functioned as a kitchen open to a roof which retains some smoke-blackened timbers. In the late 17th century or the early 18th the eastern end of the house was extended or rebuilt in brick, and a range at right angles, extending north, was built or rebuilt. Conder's alterations in the 1890s doubled the house in size by adding a second, west pile of rooms to the east range and a northern wing of reception rooms. The front, with new work built in red brick and decorative half timbering, became an asymmetrical **E**.[2] The east front was partly tile-hung, and a small extension was made to its south end. The floor was removed from the northern bay of the old house to create a double-height library as part of that suite. The southern wing was devoted to service rooms, and was made into a separate house in the 20th century.

OKLE

The area called Okle in Malswick tithing, on the east side of the parish, was divided among freehold estates in the Middle Ages. In the mid 13th century three men surnamed 'of Okle' (*de Acle*) held estates from Newent manor by performing riding service and suit at the county and hundred courts for the lords.[3] One of them, Reynold of Okle, was apparently the man of that name who was sheriff of Gloucestershire in several years at that period.[4] Members of the three families still held the estates c.1315.[5] Joan 'ate' Okle had licence for a private oratory in her house at Newent in 1347[6] and John of Okle of Newent served as a verderer of the Forest of Dean before 1358.[7]

Okle Clifford

One of the Okle estates was later known as the manor of Okle Clifford, having presumably passed at some time to a branch of the Clifford family. Its descent has not been traced until the late 15th century when it was probably the estate at Okle for which Henry Pauncefoot was liable for suit to Newent manor in 1473.[8] Later (before 1501) Llanthony priory purchased Okle Clifford manor from Robert Hyett of Newland and N. Pauncefoot of Twyning. The manor was also claimed by John Roberts of Newland and his wife Maud, daughter of William Dulle, in her right, but in 1507 they released their claim to Llanthony for a payment of £60.[9] The priory retained Okle Clifford until the Dissolution, by which time the site of the manor and demesne lands were held on a long lease by John Morgan.[10] The Crown leased the site and demesne in 1578 to Freeman Young[11] and sold the freehold of the manor before c.1600, when William Garnett sold it to Jeffrey Suckley (d. 1610 or 1611). Suckley's son Edward,[12] with his wife Anne, conveyed the manor in 1616 to Revd Timothy Gate,[13] and in 1627 Gate and others conveyed it to John Keys, whose widow Barbara and son William were in possession and living at Okle Clifford in 1646.[14]

Okle Clifford manor was later acquired by William Rogers (d. 1662). His second son Richard Rogers owned it at his death in 1677 and devised it to his elder brother William on condition of the payment of legacies to their three sisters.[15] William died in 1690, leaving it to his brother John (d. 1721),[16] who was succeeded by his son, also John Rogers[17] (d. 1735). The younger John was succeeded by his brother Edward (d. 1763), who devised Okle Clifford to his wife Elizabeth, and it was later divided between their daughters Laetitia, who married Charles Jones, and Elizabeth, who married Edward Bearcroft, a prominent barrister. The half share of Elizabeth (d. 1774) and Edward (d. 1796) passed in turn to their son Philip Rogers Bearcroft (d. c.1806) and their daughter Elizabeth, who inherited the other half of the manor on the death of her aunt Laetitia Jones in 1806 or 1807. Elizabeth married James de Visme[18] (d. 1826) of Newent Court, whose son Revd James Edward de Visme sold Okle Clifford, comprising a large moated manor house and 309 a. between the Newent–Gloucester road and Okle green, to the Gloucester municipal charity trustees in 1858. The trustees, who added the estate to the endowments of St Kyneburgh's hospital in the city,[19] maintained it as a single tenant farm, rebuilding the house in 1860.[20] Okle Clifford farm remained part of the estates of the Gloucester

---

1 Inscr. over porch.
2 Above, Fig. 15.
3 BL, Add. MS 15668, f. 41v.
4 Ibid. 18461, ff. 52–4; Rudder, *Glos.* 51–2.
5 BL, Add. MS 18461, f. 107 and v.
6 *Reg. Trillek*, 102.
7 *Cal. Close* 1354–60, 483.
8 Herefs. RO, E 12/G/3, ct. (28 Oct.) 13 Edw. IV.
9 *Cal. Regs. Priory of Llanthony*, pp. 86–8.
10 *Valor Eccl.* II, 425; TNA, E 164/39, f. 378.
11 *Cal. Pat.* 1575–8, pp. 524–5.
12 TNA, REQ 2/410/134; below (Okle Pitchard).
13 TNA, CP 25/2/298/14 Jas. I Mich. no 38.
14 GA, D 22/T 10.
15 *Visit. Glos.* 1682–3, 145, 147; GDR wills 1678/119.
16 TNA, PROB 11/407, ff. 56v.–58v.; GA, P225/IN 1/2, burials.
17 TNA, PROB 11/579, ff. 42–3.
18 GA, D 4647/7/1; Bigland, *Glos.* II, 241–2; and for the Bearcrofts, *Hist. Parl. Commons* 1754–90, II, 70.
19 GA, D 3269, Okle Clifford deeds 1819–1914.
20 Ibid. Okle Clifford papers 1928–31; D 3270/19679, pp. 133, 169, 190.

municipal charities in 2005.[1] The farmhouse of 1860, standing outside and just to the north of the remnants of the moat, was designed in classical style and built of orange-red brick with stone dressings. It is of two storeys with a very deep plan under a single pitched roof and has projecting bay windows, a porch on the main west front, and cellars. A north-east wing contains a cheese room accessible both from inside the house and by an outside stair. In the farmyard west of the house contemporary barns have big ventilated bays, and there is also a cock barn, cow stalls, and a stable, the last perhaps a survival from the 18th century.

Okle Grandison

A manor called Okle Grandison, evidently another of the three estates recorded from the mid 13th century, was in the possession of the lords of Oxenhall by 1437, and its name suggests that it had belonged to members of the Grandison family who held Oxenhall manor in the mid 14th century.[2] The 'lady of Grandison' mentioned in a Newent manor account roll in 1390[3] may have been Alice de Brian, then owner of Oxenhall. Okle Grandison continued to descend with Oxenhall,[4] whose lord leased the manorial rights and demesne lands to Philip Bradford in 1444.[5] Francis Finch and another man (probably Finch's creditor) sold the manor of Okle Grandison to Thomas Foley in 1660,[6] two years after Foley bought Oxenhall from Finch. It seems that his purchase comprised only the manorial rights, for the Foleys later had no land in the Okle area and after the mid 18th century ceased to distinguish Okle Grandison as a separate unit in the records of their Newent and Oxenhall estate. A part of the manor's tenant land, called Rough Birches, lay on the north-east side of Okle green, and presumably its other land and the manor house mentioned in 1536 and 1659 were in the same area.[7]

Okle Pitchard

The third of the estates held by men surnamed 'of Okle' in the 13th century was possibly that later called Okle Pitchard (or Pitcher). The origin of the subjoined name, perhaps a family name, has not been discovered. Arnold Colwall held Okle Pitchard as a freehold under Newent manor c.1607,[8] and he conveyed it in 1610 to Jeffrey Suckley,[9] owner of Okle Clifford. At Suckley's death in that or the following year his heir was his son Edward,[10] but in 1612 some of the lands of the estate and a mill, the later Okle Pitcher mill, belonged to Edward's younger brother, Peter Suckley, who left them to Edward at his death in 1618.[11] The estate passed to Roland Suckley, who conveyed it in 1624 to John Bradford[12] (*fl.* 1640).[13] About 1775 Okle Pitchard was said to belong to George Smith.[14] In 1838 the estate, or its residue, was represented by a house, Okle Pitcher mill, and a few adjoining fields, all owned by the miller James Humpidge. The mill was on Ell brook north of the lane leading from the Gloucester–Newent road towards Upleadon.[15]

OTHER MANORS AND ESTATES

The Grange at Malswick

A large moat known as the Grange, in Malswick tithing beside the lane running from the Gloucester–Newent road southwards towards Kent's Green,[16] may have originated as the site of an outlying set of farm buildings for Newent priory. Described as a messuage called the Grange, it was leased under Newent manor in 1539,[17] and in 1563 the lord of the manor, Edward Wilmot, sold it in reversion, from the end of Sir Nicholas Arnold's lease of the manor, to William Dobyns, owner of Walden Court.[18] It remained in the possession of the owners of Walden Court in the mid 17th century,[19] but was sold later to Charles Jones of Malswick (d. 1716) who was succeeded by his son Charles (d. 1740). The Joneses, both styled gentleman of Malswick,[20] presumably occupied a substantial dwelling-house at the Grange, but in the mid 19th century, when it formed part of Rymes Place farm, there was only a small cottage and a barn on the site.[21] Both buildings had been removed by 2005.

Hayes Farm

Hayes farm, in Compton tithing west of Pool Hill hamlet, may take its name from a small manor called '*Hege*' which in 1086 was held, together with Pauntley manor, by Ansfrid of Cormeilles.[22] There is, however, no definite record of the farm before the mid 16th century and no evidence of any claim by its owners to

---

1 Information from the tenant, Mr Garlick.
2 TNA, C 139/87, no 46; for the Oxenhall descent, below. For the Grandisons, also see below, Dymock, manors (Dymock manor).
3 Herefs. RO, E 12/G/5.
4 e.g. *Cal. Pat.* 1461–7, 486; *L&P Hen. VIII*, VIII, p. 147; Herefs. RO, E 12/G/9.
5 Westminster Abbey Mun. 3535.
6 Herefs. RO, E 12/G/12.
7 Ibid. G/9, rental 1659; TNA, SC 6/Hen. VIII/6044; GDR, T 1/126 (no 539).
8 GA, D 421/E 13, f. 17.
9 TNA, CP 25/2/297/7 Jas. I Hil. no 21.
10 Herefs. RO, E 12/G/7.
11 GDR wills 1618/149; GA, D 185/IV/32; and for the lands mentioned in these sources, GDR, T 1/126 (nos 426, 428, 434).
12 TNA, CP 25/2/299/21 Jas I Hil. no 10.
13 GA, D 421/M 81; Herefs. RO, E 12/G/6, rental (n.d., *c.*1645).
14 Rudder, *Glos.* 563.
15 GDR, T 1/126; GA, D 2710.
16 GDR, T 1/126; GA, D 2710; D 2299/979.
17 Herefs. RO, E 12/G/5, rental 31 Hen. VIII.
18 Ibid. G/15; TNA, C 3/49/112.
19 GA, D 421/E 13, f. 17; M 81.
20 GDR wills 1717/274; 1742/170; Bigland, *Glos.* II, 249.
21 GDR, T 1/126; GA, P 225A/MI 1/10.
22 *Domesday Book* (Rec. Com), I, 170.

manorial status. There were possibly dwellings on or near the site of the farmhouse c.1315, when the free tenants of Newent manor in Compton included Peter de Heye, holding a messuage and ½ yardland, and Thomas de Heye, holding recently enfranchised customary land.[1] In 1542 Hayes farm belonged to the Newent chantry of SS James and Anne, whose chaplain leased it to William Wall.[2] After the dissolution of the chantries the Crown sold it in 1550 to two speculators,[3] who sold it later to the tenant; Wall, then described as of Pauntley, retained it in 1565.[4] Another William Wall paid a free rent to Newent manor for Hayes in 1640,[5] and another William Wall was said to have a handsome house and a good estate there c.1710.[6] He died in 1717 and Hayes farm then descended with his estate at Lintridge, in Dymock, until the early 19th century.[7] In 1816 John and Mary Terrett sold Hayes to John Matthews, a Newent mercer, who sold it in 1841 to Henry Thompson, another mercer of the town. In 1849 Thompson sold the farm to another John Matthews,[8] who was declared bankrupt before 1855 when the farm was bought by the Newent solicitor Edmund Edmonds. Edmonds sold it to Mary Harrison of Birkenhead, who died in 1866 leaving the farm to her daughter Susan, the wife of James Henry Frowde.[9] Frowde, who had performed for many years as a clown with Hengler's Circus before retiring in 1861,[10] also became owner of the adjoining Walden Court farm. In the 1890s his son James Charles William Frowde was farming at Hayes, then a farm of 147 a., and in 1901, after his parents' deaths, he joined other members of the family in selling Hayes and Walden Court to John Leather Stelfox. Stelfox's executors sold Hayes farm in 1925 to the tenant Wilfred Barton, whose widow Edith sold it in 1957 to Walter Maddox.[11] He transferred it soon afterwards to his son Mr Gerald Maddox, who farmed there until 2003 when he sold the house and 28.5 ha (70 a.) to Mr Nigel Freeman and the remainder of the land to another purchaser.[12] The farmhouse is in part of the 17th century and timber-framed but has large additions of the 19th century.[13]

The Scarr

A farm in the north part of Compton tithing, originally called Atherlard's Place but from the 18th century usually known as the Scarr, presumably took its name from the Atherlard family which was recorded at Newent c.1315.[14] It was evidently the 'Atherleys' held c.1607 by Guy Dobyns[15] and later by Samuel Dobyns, probably the same who died in 1679.[16] It apparently passed to Guy Dobyns (d. 1682), whose son Samuel[17] settled Atherlard's Place on his marriage to his wife Hester in 1685, subject to his mother Bridget's life interest in a half share.[18] Bridget died in 1689, Samuel in 1709, and Hester in 1727.[19] The estate passed to Samuel's son also Samuel (d. by 1743) and to his widow Elizabeth, from 1754 the wife of Edward Sergeaunt of Mitcheldean. In 1800 Edward died and Elizabeth sold the farm, then 228 a., to Joseph Hankins of Upleadon.[20] From Hankins, later also owner of Walden Court, it passed to his son Thomas (d. 1864).[21] William John Phelps of Dursley owned the Scarr in 1879[22] and N. Phelps in 1900. By the latter date the farm had been enlarged to 356 a. and had a modern farmhouse with extensive new farm buildings, as well as outlying buildings and farm cottages at Newbarn and Strawberry Hill.[23] In 1912 the farm was owned by A.W. Clifford of Dursley.[24] In 1937 Scarr farm was bought by the Land Settlement Association and divided into numerous smallholdings.[25] The original farmhouse, part of which remains as a farm cottage, stood close to the lane leading from Newent to Botloe's Green.[26] It was replaced shortly before 1882 by a large, symmetrical, three-bayed house of red brick to the south-east.[27]

Southends (or Southerns)

In 1539 a farm based on the house called Southends (or Southerns) in Southends Lane was occupied, apparently as a freehold under Newent manor, by Robert ap Powell in right of his wife.[28] It was later held by Christopher Bradley, and c.1607 belonged to John

---

1 BL, Add. MS 18461, ff. 108, 113v.
2 GA, D 2957/212/1.
3 *Cal. Pat.* 1549–51, 280.
4 GA, D 2957/212/2.
5 Ibid. D 421/M 81.
6 Atkyns, *Glos.* 568.
7 GA, D 1604/T 1; covenant for production of deeds 11 Oct. 1816 (citing schedule of deeds), in possession of Mr G.V. Maddox of Putley (Herefs.); below, Dymock, manors (other estates).
8 Deeds in possession of Mr Maddox.
9 E. Warde, *They Didn't Walk Far: a History of Pool Hill* (priv. printed, 2000), 33–4.
10 *Chapters in Newent's History*, 74–7; press cuttings in possession of Mr Maddox.
11 *Kelly's Dir. Glos.* (1894), 244–5; (1897), 249; deeds and sale partics. in possession of Mr Maddox.
12 Information from Mr Maddox.
13 DoE List, Newent (1985), 3/69; the ho. was not seen for the purposes of this account.
14 BL, Add. MS 18461, f. 113.
15 GA, D 421/E 13, f. 19v.
16 Ibid. M 81; Bigland, *Glos.* II, 242.
17 Bigland, *Glos.* II, 242; GDR wills 1682/163.
18 GA, D 4647/6/1.
19 Ibid. P 225/IN 1/2.
20 Ibid. D 4647/6/1.
21 Ibid. 7/2–3; below (Walden Ct.).
22 *Kelly's Dir. Glos.* (1879), 709.
23 GA, D 2299/108.
24 Douglas, *Notes of Newent*, 14.
25 Below, econ. hist. (agric.).
26 GDR, T 1/126; GA, D 2710.
27 OS Map 6", Glos. XVII.NW (1884 edn).
28 Herefs. RO, E 12/G/5, rental 1539.

Mayle (fl. 1624).[1] By 1640 it belonged to Walter Nourse[2] (d. 1652), lord of Boulsdon manor and owner of the nearby Porter's Place estate, and it passed to his younger son Timothy.[3] Timothy Nourse was ordained and became a preacher and theologian at Oxford, but in 1672 he converted to Roman Catholicism and retired to Southends, where he remodelled the house. He died in 1699,[4] leaving Southends to his wife Lucy but with the option of taking other lands in its place. It presumably passed then, or on Lucy's death in 1732, to Timothy's heir, his nephew Walter Nourse[5] (d. 1743). In 1789 John Nourse, Walter's eventual successor to Boulsdon manor, sold Southends, a farm of 110 a., to J.N. Morse.[6] Morse (d. 1830) left it to his son John (d. 1842) and in 1844 his trustees sold the house and part of the farm to Thomas Cadle of Ross-on-Wye (Herefs.) and the rest of the farm to Thomas's brother John,[7] who added it to his adjoining Moat farm. Thomas Cadle (d. 1859) left his Southends estate to support his wife Harriet and his daughters during her lifetime and then to his son Joseph Draper Cadle, who emigrated to Australia before 1863.[8] By 1877 Southends belonged to Henry Thomson,[9] who used most of the land as orcharding for his cider-making business until that failed in 1911. Southends was later bought by John Wilkins of Billinghurst (Sussex), who in 1918 sold Southends house and the land, then let separately with a modern farmhouse called Southcote, to his respective tenants.[10]

Southends is a two-storeyed house on an irregular three-pile plan. It may originally have been a late 16th- or early 17th-century timber-framed house that faced east with hall and perhaps two cross wings, of which the southern one has survived almost intact. By Timothy Nourse's late 17th-century alterations the sizeable house was encased in brick, and it was altered further in the 18th century when a tall single-storeyed kitchen was added (or perhaps rebuilt) at the west end of the southern wing. Other 18th-century alterations included the insertion of a tall window to light the (probably original) dog-leg stair in the southern wing. At that time or in the next century the north side of the northern wing became the entrance front, and in the mid 19th century the wing was reroofed and a symmetrical façade applied to its front. Service additions were made to the western side and a two-storeyed bay-window created on the south front facing the garden, which incorporates a slightly sunken area due south of the house. The surviving farm buildings include two 17th-century barns, both altered during the 18th and 19th centuries.

Southorles Manor and the Moat

An estate known as the manor of Southorles or Lower Southerns was based on the house called the Moat in the north part of Cugley tithing. Early owners were perhaps Roger of Southorle, a free tenant of Newent manor in Cugley in 1290,[11] John of Southorle, who was appointed a collector of rents on Newent manor in 1342,[12] and William Southorle (apparently also known as William Southern), who was involved in disputes with the farmer of the manor, John Cheyne, and his tenants in 1407.[13] Ownership has not been clearly traced until the early 17th century when Sir Arthur Porter sold Southorles manor and the Moat to Thomas Woodward before 1610. Thomas, who by the time of his death in 1623 had added various other houses and lands in Cugley to his estate, settled the Moat and the manor on his second son Thomas with remainder to his third son Christopher.[14] Christopher was living at Worcester at his death in 1656 or 1657 and may by then have made the Moat estate over to his son Christopher.[15] The younger Christopher (d. 1699) added to it the adjoining Stallions farm as well as some lands in the area that had passed from his grandfather to other family members. He left his whole estate, a total of 379 a., to his son Thomas (fl. 1717).[16] Thomas's heir was apparently his nephew Christopher Woodward, who was described as of the Moat at his death, aged 21, in 1731,[17] and the following year the estate was settled on the marriage of Christopher's sister Elizabeth to Edward Chinn of Newnham.[18] In 1768 Elizabeth, by then widowed, settled the estate on the marriage of her son Edward Chinn (d. 1791). Edward was succeeded by his son, also Edward, who sold the estate to Henry Fowke of Tewkesbury in 1802.[19] Fowke sold it in 1810 to Revd William Beale (d. 1827).[20] Beale devised it to his youngest son Theophilus, who sold the 113-a. estate in 1830 to his father-in-law Joseph Cadle of Westbury-on-Severn. Cadle (d. 1833) was succeeded by

---

1 Ibid. G/5, survey 1624, p. 73; GA, D 421/E 13, f. 15.
2 GA, D 421/ M 81.
3 Bigland, *Glos.* II, 245; above (Boulsdon manor).
4 *Oxford DNB*; GA, D 412/Z 3, Nourse MS, p. 4.
5 GDR wills 1700/57.
6 GA, D 332/T 5; D 1810/1; above (Boulsdon manor).
7 GA, D 1927/8.
8 Ibid. 5, mortgage 1863.
9 Sale partics. 1877, in possession of Mr M.H. Keene of the Moat.
10 GA, D 2299/1552.
11 Herefs. RO, E 12/G/2, ct. roll 17–18 Edw. I (list of suitors on dorse).

12 *Cal. Pat.* 1340–3, 387.
13 *Cal. Close* 1405–9, 349; 1399–1402, 492.
14 Herefs. RO, E 12/G/7, ct. papers 13 Apr. 1615; TNA, C 142/398, no 109; GDR wills 1622/186; for the Woodwards, *Visit. Glos. 1682–3*, 208 (where the elder Thomas's death date is incorrect).
15 TNA, PROB 11/264, ff. 384–6.
16 GDR wills 1710/26.
17 Bigland, *Glos.* II, 246; see also GA, P 241/IN 1/1, baptisms 1704/5, 1706, 1710 (for Chris. Woodward, d. 1710, younger brother of Thos., and his family).
18 GA, D 892/T 57.
19 Ibid. D 1927/4.
20 Ibid. 6.

16. *The Moat in 1910*

his son John (d. 1859), whose trustee sold it in 1861 to Charles Richardson of Almondsbury. In 1877 Richardson sold the Moat with 170 a. to Andrew Knowles.[1] At the dispersal of Knowles's Newent Court estate[2] the Moat was sold with 342 a. in 1911 to Charles Priday, a Gloucester corn miller who died in 1926. Priday's family retained the Moat until 1957 when they sold it to Harold Keene,[3] whose son, Mr M.H. Keene, owned and farmed it together with the neighbouring farms of Stallions and Caerwents in 2005.[4]

The Moat house stands on an almost rectangular island in the centre of a rectangular moat, very wide from east to west, perhaps having been widened in relatively recent times. The building contains fabric of earlier than *c*.1800, when the present double-pile gentrified farmhouse was built in red brick with 5 bays, 2½ storeys, and a hipped slated roof. The entrance to the island is across a bridge from the farmyard to the north, and the main front faces south over a garden which fills the rest of the island.[5] The plan of the main block is regular with central hall and staircase flanked by drawing and dining rooms, pantries and large servants' hall, which suggests an extensive farm establishment. A one- and two-storeyed north-eastern wing contained a kitchen and cellar. The farmyard has contemporary barns and shelter sheds, a red brick barn of high quality being decorated with Gothic panels.

Stallions (Stalling)

Land called Stalling, on what was later known as Stallions hill west of the Moat estate, formed a freehold under Newent manor in the 13th century. It was apparently held by Robert of Stalling in the 1240s,[6] and the same or another Robert held it in 1285, when he unsuccessfully disputed Newent priory's right to use a way over his land towards Yartleton woods.[7] Robert of Stalling died before 1293, holding a house and 43½ a. by the same riding service as was owed by the three Okle estates.[8] His son and heir John of Stalling came of age in 1304,[9] but Reynold Ayleway held the estate *c*.1315.[10] Its later medieval descent is not known, but at some date it was acquired in fee by the lords of Newent manor: in the early 17th century lands called Stalling comprised a leasehold under the manor.[11] The lessee in 1640 was Christopher Woodward,[12] of the Moat, whose son Christopher bought the freehold from the Winter family in the late 1650s.[13] In the 18th century Stallions (as the estate was by then usually known) comprised a

---

1 GA, D 1927/8.
2 Ibid. SL 13.
3 Schedule of deeds, in possession of Mr M.H. Keene of the Moat; GA, D 2299/5477; *The Times*, 16 Nov. 1926; 3 Feb. 1927.
4 Information from Mrs Keene.
5 Fig. 16.
6 BL, Add. MS 15668, ff. 54v., 65.

7 Ibid. f. 71 and v.; Herefs. RO, E 12/G/3, ct. roll 13–14 Edw. I.
8 *Cal Inq. p.m.* III, p. 256; BL, Add. MS 15668, f. 41v.
9 *Cal. Inq. p.m.* IV, pp. 223–4.
10 BL, Add. MS 18461, f. 107v.
11 GA, D 421/E 13, f. 16; Herefs. RO, E 12/G/5, survey 1624, pp. 5–6.
12 GA, D 421/M 81.
13 GDR wills 1710/26; above (Southorles manor).

17. *Stardens: the south front in 1910*

barn and *c.*100 a.,[1] and a small farmhouse was built there before 1806. The farm descended with the Moat until 1806 when Henry Fowke sold it to John Hartland. Hartland sold it in 1811 to Thomas Hartland, later of Nelfields Farm, who died in 1844; his trustees sold it the following year to Thomas Cadle (d. 1859), owner of Southends farm. The mortgagee, Lindsey Winterbotham of Stroud,[2] later acquired possession and sold Stallions in 1864 to Henry Thomson. Thomson sold it in 1884 to Andrew Knowles of Newent Court,[3] and ownership then passed once more with the Moat.[4] The farmhouse was rebuilt in 1979.[5]

Stardens

A substantial freehold estate in Compton tithing accumulated by Nicholas of Stardens (*fl.* 1292, *c.*1315),[6] was possibly the origin of Stardens farm lying north of the town near the Upleadon road. Half of a house called Stardens and other lands called Stardens were among possessions of Newent's two chantries, St Mary and SS James and Anne, at their dissolution in 1548.[7] In the early 17th century the farm belonged to William Pauncefoot, who sold it to Peter Leigh, steward of Newent manor.[8] Leigh's son William settled it, comprising a house and 127 a., on the marriage of his son, also William, in 1653. The younger William died before 1658 when his widow Marianne and her husband Robert Barber sold Stardens to George Dalton. Dalton sold it in 1664 to Thomas Foley[9] and it then descended as a tenant farm on Newent manor.[10] R.F. Onslow remodelled and enlarged Stardens as his own residence in 1864,[11] and in 1911 at the sale of the Onslow estate the house was bought with *c.*48 a. by Col. William Frederick Noel (d. 1923).[12] The house later passed through various hands before being converted to three dwellings in 1952;[13] one part housed a country club for some years from 1963.[14] Stardens appears to have been rebuilt in the late 18th century, and in 1840 was a three-bayed, 2½-storeyed brick range with a hipped roof.[15] Onslow's rebuilding, to a design by John Middleton of Cheltenham,[16] turned that house into a Gothic mansion, giving it large tripartite windows and irregular wings built of local stone with limestone dressings.[17] The more elaborate eastern wing contained the principal rooms, which faced west, the drawing room being lit by a projecting traceried bay; the

1 GA, D 892/T 57, lease 1764; D 1927/4, mortgage 1785.
2 Ibid. D 1927/5.
3 Ibid. D 2957/212/135.
4 Above (Southorles manor).
5 Information from Mrs Keene of the Moat.
6 BL, Add. MS 18461, f. 103 and v.; see ibid. f. 108; Herefs. RO, E 12/G/1, rental 1292.
7 Hockaday Abs. ccxcii, 1549; *Cal. Pat.* 1548–9, 187.
8 Herefs. RO, E 12/G/7, letter 1616; G/5, survey 1624, p. 1.
9 Ibid. G/18.
10 GA, D 2528, plan B.
11 *Kelly's Dir. Glos.* (1870), 604.
12 GA, D 2299/3023.
13 Bick, *Old Newent*, 81; Verey and Brooks, *Glos.* II, 607.
14 *Glos. Countryside*, Apr.–May 1963, 39.
15 GA, P 225A/MI 1/13.
16 Verey and Brooks, *Glos.* II, 607.
17 Fig. 17.

entrance front was on the eastern side. The interior was quite plainly finished, but in 1910 had a staircase lit by a window with armorial glass and wood panelled ceilings in the main rooms.[1]

Walden Court

Walden (or Walden's) Court farm, based on a house in Compton tithing south of Pool Hill and including land in Pauntley parish, has not been found recorded before the mid 16th century. The origin of the name, presumably derived from early owners, is not known. It was apparently the estate, described as the site of the manor of Compton and said (probably incorrectly) to have been once held from Gloucester abbey, that Guy Dobyns owned at his death in 1544; Guy was probably the man of that name who in 1522 had a high assessment (£20) on his goods at Compton.[2] In 1544 Guy's son and heir John Dobyns was under sentence of outlawry for the murder in 1538 of the constable of Newent.[3] William Dobyns owned Walden in 1563 when the lord of Newent manor sold him the reversion of three nearby copyholds in Compton tithing[4] that were subsequently absorbed into the farm.[5] In 1604 Walden was settled on Randall and Philip Dobyns and the heirs of Philip,[6] and Randall Dobyns owned it in 1640.[7] Later the estate was acquired by Sir Edmund Bray of Great Barrington, who died in 1684, leaving it to his grandson Reginald Bray (d. 1712). It passed to Reginald's brother Edmund (d. 1725), who left Walden Court to his son and namesake. The younger Edmund (d. 1728) was succeeded by his elder brother Reginald Morgan Bray. In 1734 he sold the estate to John Rogers of Okle Clifford,[8] with which it then descended until 1813 when James and Elizabeth de Visme sold it, comprising the house and 233 a., to Joseph Hankins.[9] Joseph (d. 1824) left it with the Scarr, his adjoining farm, to trustees, who were to use it to support his wife Mary and sons during her life and then to sell it. His youngest son Thomas, one of the beneficiaries of the trust, bought the farms from the trustees in 1835.[10] He died in 1864,[11] and Walden Court passed later to James Henry Frowde, who was living there in 1879 and 1885.[12] His family sold the farm in 1901 with Hayes farm to J.L. Stelfox. Stelfox's executors sold it in 1925[13] to Henry Hinds, whose family owned and farmed Walden Court farm, comprising 48.5 ha (120 a.), in 2005.[14]

Walden Court was built in the late 16th or early 17th century as a two-storeyed timber-framed house with a large hall with a rear stack and probably two cross wings. The exterior displays close-studding and large mullioned and transomed windows, somewhat enhanced in the 19th century. The service end was replaced in the 19th century and the rear of the other wing, which contains the parlour, has also been replaced. In the 19th century the hall was partitioned into hall and sitting room. Cusped lights in the windows may relate to the use of the hall for religious services in the time of J.H. Frowde,[15] and many small piecemeal additions were made at that period and later. A large brick barn with two threshing floors dates from the late 17th century or the early 18th, and in the 19th century other farm buildings were provided, one dated 1872.

Newent Rectory

The rectory of Newent, comprising all the grain and hay tithes, descended with the Newent manor estate until the early 18th century. In 1291, including the profits of the annexed chapel of Pauntley, it was valued at £26 13s. 4d.[16] From 1382, when the manor passed from Cormeilles abbey, it was let at farm for £80 a year,[17] and in 1506 the farmer was the prominent Newent landowner Roger Porter.[18] In 1535 the rectory tithes were on lease from Fotheringhay college for £14 a year[19] (presumably not intended as a reflection of their value) and in 1555 Sir Richard Lee included them at the same rent in a renewal of the lease of the manor to Sir Nicholas Arnold.[20] Paul Foley, at his death in 1699 gave the rectory tithes, said a few years later to be worth £140 a year,[21] to trustees who were to hold them for 31 years to augment three Herefordshire churches (St Peter's in Hereford, Dormington, and Mordiford) and at the end of the term to assign them to the vicarage of Newent or another church or charity at their discretion.[22] The trustees chose to convey the tithes to Newent vicarage c.1728.[23]

---

1 GA, SL 80.
2 *Military Surv. of Glos. 1522*, 51.
3 TNA, C 142/73, no 78; *L&P Hen. VIII*, XIII (2), pp. 194, 203.
4 TNA, C 3/49/112; Herefs. RO, E 12/G/15, deed 14 Feb. 1563.
5 GA, D 4647/7/1, deed 9 Feb. 1734.
6 J. Maclean, 'Pedes Finium or Excerpts from the Feet of Fines, in the County of Gloucester', *Trans. BGAS* 17 (1892–3), 212.
7 GA, D 421/M 81.
8 Ibid. D 4647/7/1, deed 9 Feb.1734; TNA, PROB 11/379, ff. 6–7v.; A.L.Browne, 'The Brays of Great Barrington', *Trans. BGAS* 57 (1935), 158–75.
9 Above (Okle: Okle Clifford); GA, D 4647/7/1.
10 GA, D 4647/7/2.
11 Ibid. 7/3.
12 *Kelly's Dir. Glos.* (1879), 709–10; (1885), 534.
13 Above (Hayes farm).
14 Information fom Mrs M. Hinds of Walden Ct.
15 Plaque in hall; *Kelly's Dir. Glos.* (1885), 532. See below, Pauntley, religious hist. (religious life).
16 *Tax. Eccl.* 161.
17 Herefs. RO, E 12/G/5, acct. roll 14 Ric. II.
18 Ibid. G/2, acct. roll 22 Hen. VII.
19 *Valor Eccl.* IV, 287.
20 TNA, C 3/195/2.
21 Atkyns, *Glos.* 567.
22 TNA, PROB 11/453, ff. 167v.–168.
23 GDR, V 5/212T 4.

ECONOMIC HISTORY

The small town of Newent was created in a predominantly agricultural area and hosted a succession of crafts and industries drawing on the natural resources of the countryside. Although the development of a coalfield near by foundered in the 19th century and Newent was drawn ever more into the economic orbit of Gloucester, the town continued to supply goods and services to its residents and to those of surrounding communities.

AGRICULTURE

To the Mid Seventeenth Century

In 1086 there were two slaves on the demesne land of Cormeilles abbey's Newent manor and it was worked by three ploughteams. The tenants were 9 villans and 9 bordars with 12 ploughteams, and a reeve held another part of the estate comprising 1½ villan holdings and 5 bordars. In addition all the tenants of the manor worked jointly another 5 ploughteams. Durand of Gloucester's estate, the later Boulsdon manor, had 2 slaves and 1 team in demesne and a tenantry of 5 bordars with 2 teams.[1] On Carswalls manor there was 1 team in demesne and the tenants were 3 villans and 1 bordar with two teams.[2] The large number of ploughteams listed (26) shows that the parish was extensively cultivated but appears disproportionate to the number of individual tenant holdings (33½ in all). Presumably the holdings were large and employed considerable numbers of dependent labourers: in the early 14th century the yardland on Newent manor, possibly the equivalent of the 11th-century villan holding, comprised 72 a.[3] The existence in 1086 of a manorial reeve with his own group of tenants, and presumably greater administrative responsibility than was usual, probably arose from the ownership of the manor by a religious house in Normandy. Cormeilles later established a cell at Newent with a prior who acted ex officio as bailiff of its manor. The need for regular communication between Newent and the mother house probably led to the creation of four sub-manors (Stalling and three at Okle) which were held from the abbey by riding service.[4]

Newent manor demesne   In 1291 the abbey's demesne, cultivated by Newent priory, was extended at six ploughlands.[5] Much of its arable formed a tract south-east of Newent town, including fields called Upper and Lower Berry field (80 a. in 1624), Crockwardines, and Nelfield. North of the town and priory precinct were pasture closes, orchards, and a small park, and beyond was meadowland bordering Ell brook. The demesne also included a meadow called Lydenford, presumably by Ell brook upstream of the crossing of that name on the boundary with Upleadon and Highleadon, and parcels in a large common meadow called Cowmeadow adjoining Tibberton and Taynton. There was also demesne adjoining Kent's green[6] and it was probably to aid the cultivation of the abbey's lands in the south-east of the parish that a farmstead known as the Grange was established on the lane to the green.[7]

During the 13th century the demesne was intensively cultivated for the priory and opportunities to enlarge its holdings in the parish were taken. Most of the acquisitions were by purchase or lease rather than by gift in free alms.[8] The meadowland evidently proved insufficient for the numbers of livestock on the demesne farm. Between 1278 and 1296 the priory took leases of parcels in Cowmeadow and elsewhere, usually for terms of six years, from 19 or more of its tenants and freeholders.[9] Ploughing and harvest work on the demesne was done mainly by the labour services of the customary tenants,[10] but the priory servants included a cowherd in 1298[11] and a shepherd in 1310.[12] In the early 15th century, under John Cheyne and later Fotheringhay college, parcels of demesne land and some of the farm buildings at the priory precinct were leased out.[13] Probably from that time the lords gave up all demesne farming, as they certainly had by 1482.[14] In 1539 the demesne land was held by 11 separate tenants,[15] and by 1624 it was divided among 18 tenants.[16]

Holdings and services   In the 13th and 14th centuries the parish supported a multitude of small agricultural holdings. About 1315 on the Newent manor estate, including only those for whom a dwelling is mentioned,

---

1   *Domesday Book* (Rec. Com.), I, 166.
2   Ibid. 167v.
3   BL, Add. MS 18461, ff. 103v., 115 (John Prank's holding).
4   Above, manors; for similar arrangements on Caen abbey's manor of Minchinhampton, see *VCH Glos.* IX, 193.
5   *Tax. Eccl.* 171.
6   Herefs. RO, E 12/G/2, acct. roll 22 Edw. IV; G/5, survey 1624, pp. 1–7; and for location of the lands, GDR, T 1/126; GA, D 2710.
7   Above, manors (other manors and estates: the Grange at Malswick).
8   BL, Add. MSS 15668, 18461, passim.
9   Ibid. MS 15668, ff. 1v., 4–5, 13.
10   Ibid. ff. 5–6v.; 18461, ff. 110–115v.
11   Herefs. RO, E 12/G/2, ct. (17 Dec.) 26 Edw. I.
12   GA, D 421/M 80A, ct. (28 Apr.) 3 Edw. II.
13   Herefs. RO, E 12/G/1, cts. (20 Feb., 3 June) 11 Hen. IV; G/2, ct. (12 Feb.) 6 Hen. V; G/3, cts. (28 Mar., 1 Aug.) 9 Hen. IV.
14   Ibid. G/2, acct. roll 22 Edw. IV.
15   Ibid. G/5, rental 31 Hen. VIII.
16   Ibid. survey 1624, pp. 1–7.

there were 87 tenants, 36 of them holding freely and 51 by customary tenure; many other holdings comprising just land were listed, often it seems occupied by inhabitants of the town. The customary tenants with dwellings mostly held half or quarter yardlands (36 or 18 a.) and included 18 living in Compton tithing, 14 in Cugley, 13 in Malswick, and 6 in the parts of Newent tithing adjoining the town.[1] In 1307 Bevis de Knovill's Kilcot manor had eight free tenants and five neifs (four of them holding 30 a. each and one with 6 a.).[2] For the other six manors recorded in the parish no comparative evidence has been found for the period, but in the late 16th century and the mid 17th (by which time numbers of holdings had probably been reduced) Okle Clifford and Okle Grandison respectively had eight and six resident tenants.[3] From what is known about the chief manor and Kilcot, and can be surmised about the others (which included the substantial Boulsdon manor), it might be assumed that in the years before the Black Death 150 or more small farmers inhabited and cultivated the rural parts of Newent parish.

On Newent manor many of the services owed by the customary tenants had been commuted permanently for fixed cash rents by the beginning of the 14th century. Among the few still liable to the full quota of works were four quarter-yardlanders in Compton, who might be required to work every fourth week for five days (their duties including ploughing and harrowing 13 a.) and perform 16 bedrips; their whole obligation, if commuted at the will of the abbot, was worth 10s. a year.[4] Most of the other holdings then owed ploughing service on a few acres, together with some haymaking and carrying duties at the hay harvest. Other obligations owed by certain tenants included guarding the lord's swine at pasture, carrying salt to the manor, providing labour for the repair of the mill dyke at Malswick, contributing to a payment for millstones, and brewing ale when the abbot of Cormeilles visited the manor.[5] Many of the inhabitants of Newent town, though otherwise free of labour services, were liable to provide a worker, armed with a pitchfork or rake, for the hay harvest in Lydenford or other demesne meadows.[6] Resistance to the labour services is recorded in the mid 1280s when six men were presented in the manor court for sending insufficient men to work in the hay harvest, another for sending his wife, and another for withdrawing his service altogether.[7] In 1365 20 tenants were absent from the haymaking and in 1368 a large number failed to appear at the corn harvest.[8] Some ploughing, harrowing, harvest, and carrying works were still being used in 1390,[9] but the remaining obligations presumably lapsed or were commuted with the leasing out of the demesne in the 15th century. By 1482 the value of commuted works was subsumed in the sum for tenant rents in the bailiff's annual account.[10] On the Kilcot manor of Bevis de Knovill in 1307 only one of the five customars still owed labour service, the others paying cash rents.[11]

From the mid 14th century the decay and abandonment as separate units of many tenant holdings on Newent manor and a general shortage of tenants becomes clear. In 1354 two half-yardland customary tenements in Cugley were leased to a single tenant for a term of six years;[12] in 1369 two decayed houses were ordered to be taken into the lord's hands;[13] and in 1397 a tenant died in possession of a holding which included the land once attached to five houses but possessed no cattle or sheep to provide a heriot.[14] In 1401 another of the Cugley customary tenements was waste, and a lease was granted of the sites of two former houses in Compton.[15] In 1482 many holdings were on lease at a reduced rent, seven of them including the sites of demolished houses (tofts).[16] By 1539 the number of free and customary tenancies on Newent manor which had houses had been reduced to 46,[17] and c.1607 the equivalent number, increased by a few new cottage tenements, was 58.[18] In 1624 customary tenements (copyholds) with houses attached numbered only 6 in Cugley tithing, 5 in Malswick, and 4 in Compton, but, as a result of the amalgamation of holdings, they included good-sized farms: in Malswick one farm, apparently that later called Rymes Place, had 92 a., Hogsend farm had 51 a., and Horsman's farm had 48 a.; in Cugley a farm based on a house at or near the site of Little Cugley had 86 a. and Ploddy House farm had 77 a.; and in Compton two farms based on houses near Compton green had 56 a. and 43 a. respectively. Various other copyholds, mostly small, comprised lands only, though some, including two of the old customary tenements in Newent tithing, had ruined houses or tofts. Some parts of the former demesne were also tenanted as copyhold in the early 17th century,

---

1 BL, Add. MS 18461, ff. 106–116v. Omitted from this analysis are eight tenants listed in 'Kilcot', most of whose land was probably in the detached part of Pauntley, and the holders of some of the smaller manors of the parish, who are listed as paying chief rents.
2 *Inq. p.m. Glos.* 1301–58, 97–8.
3 Below, this section.
4 BL, Add. MS 18461, f. 111v.–112.
5 Ibid. ff. 106–116v.; Add. MS 15668, ff. 5v.–6v.
6 Ibid. 15668, f. 5v.; 18461, ff. 98–105v.
7 Herefs. RO, E 12/G/3, cts. (3 July) 13 Edw. I, (15 June, 27 July) 14 Edw. I.
8 Ibid. G/1, cts. (7 July) 39 Edw. III, (5 Oct.) 42 Edw. III.
9 Ibid. G/5, acct. roll 14 Ric. II.
10 Ibid. G/2, acct. roll 22 Edw. IV.
11 *Inq. p.m. Glos.* 1301–58, 97–8.
12 Herefs. RO, E 12/G/1, ct. (14 Oct.) 28 Edw. III; BL, Add. MS 18461, f. 110.
13 Herefs. RO, E 12/G/1, ct. (16 July) 43 Edw. III.
14 GA, D 421/M 80A, ct. 12 Feb. 20 Ric. II.
15 Herefs. RO, E 12/G/3, ct. (10 Jan.) 2 Hen. IV.
16 Ibid. G/2, acct. roll 22 Edw. IV.
17 Ibid. G/5, rental 31 Hen. VIII.
18 GA, D 421/E 13, ff. 15v.–20.

including the land adjoining Kent's Green.¹ Most of the copyholds were later enfranchised, apparently by the Winter family in the 1650s. By the late 18th century only three or four of those recorded in 1624 still belonged to the manor.²

Among the other manors of the parish, Okle Clifford in the late 16th century had eight tenants with houses and land (six free and two customary) as well as a larger number of tenancies comprising land only.³ Okle Grandison in 1659 had six tenants (freehold, leasehold, or copyhold) with houses and land.⁴

Fields and closes   Most of the cultivated land of the parish was in closes from antiquity, but there were a few small open fields, the principal ones lying west of Newent town, bordered on the south-east by Watery Lane. In the northern part of that area was Worsden field, where the strips were apparently held originally by townspeople or inhabitants of the outlying parts of Newent tithing; in the south-western part, separated from Worsden field by Bradford's Lane, Boulsdon field was probably reserved to inhabitants of Boulsdon tithing.⁵ In the Middle Ages Newent tithing also included an open field called Cleeve field, on the east side of the town in the angle of the Gloucester road and the lane to Cleeve Mill,⁶ and Boulsdon tithing contained at least one other, Mill field, straddling the Boulsdon brook to the east of Great Boulsdon farm.⁷ A field called Withycroft near Stardens farm was recorded in the late 12th century⁸ and still had uninclosed strips in the mid 17th.⁹ In Compton tithing in the early 17th century some tenants held strips in fields called Newlands and Stonylands near Compton green,¹⁰ and in Kilcot strips remained in a field called Mouse field, lying in the area between the Ross road and Wyatt's farm.¹¹

In the early 14th century the demesne arable of Newent manor was cropped on a conventional three-course rotation. On parts the courses were wheat, oats, and a fallow,¹² but large quantities of rye were grown on other parts in 1347, and in Newent generally rye was for long the main cereal crop.¹³ The diverse nature of the soil, some parts clay and some parts sand, led to many closes being distinguished by names such as Wheat field or Rye field.¹⁴ Fruit growing, mainly for the production of cider and perry, was widespread by the late 16th century when leases of former demesne land usually included a provision for planting apple and pear stocks.¹⁵

Commons   The strips and common rights in Cowmeadow, on the south boundary, were held by occupiers from all parts of the parish in the late 13th century and later.¹⁶ Common pasture rights in the woodlands on the slopes of May hill were apparently restricted to freeholders of Newent manor in the early 17th century; in 1632 the commoners secured an agreement with the lord of the manor, Sir John Winter, to protect their claims, which, however, lapsed later that century.¹⁷ Gorsley common straddling the north-western boundary of the parish was described in 1624 as fit for pasturing horses and young cattle and sometimes sheep. The tenants of Newent manor, the Kilcot manor based on the Conigree, and Oxenhall, Linton, and Aston Ingham manors all intercommoned there, but the boundaries of the parts belonging to the respective manors were defined and the commoners kept their cattle as much as possible within their own areas.¹⁸ Among the smaller commons of the parish, Okle green was being overburdened with stock in 1424,¹⁹ and on Brand green, Pool hill, and Botloe's green, on the boundary with Pauntley, the animals of Newent and Pauntley tenants grazed together without stint in 1619.²⁰

From c.1650 to c.1850

The pattern of landholding in Newent became more complex by the dismemberment of Boulsdon manor and other parts of the Porter family's estate in the early 17th century and the sale of much demesne and tenant land on Newent manor during the Commonwealth period.²¹ Holdings ranged later from temporary groupings of closes rented by Newent butchers²² to substantial ring-fenced farms based on ancient manorial sites such as Okle Clifford and Carswalls. The engrossment of farms continued, with the Foleys leading the way after their purchase of the manor by

---

1 Herefs. RO, E 12/G/5, survey 1624.
2 GA, D 2528, plans C, D.
3 TNA, SC 12/32/15.
4 Herefs. RO, E 12/G/9, rental 1659.
5 *Cal. Pat.* 1548–9, 189; 1550–3, 5; GA, D 332/T 3, deed 10 Aug. 1597; T 4, deed 19 Aug. 1595; Herefs. RO, E 12/G/5, survey 1624, pp. 69, 71.
6 BL, Add. MS 18461, f. 68; Herefs. RO, E 12/G/2, acct. roll 22 Edw. IV (s.v. farm of demesne); G/3, ct. (10 Oct.) 2 Hen. VI.
7 GA, D 2245/T 4, deed 10 Apr. 1730.
8 *Glos. Feet of Fines 1199–1299*, p. 2; BL, Add. MS 18461, ff. 63, 66; TNA, SC 12/32/15, f. 1; GDR, T 1/126 (no 392).
9 Herefs. RO, E 12/G/18, deed 25 July 1653.
10 Ibid. G/5, rental 1624, pp. 85, 87; GDR, T 1/126 (nos 292–3).
11 GA, D 2957/212/101; D 2245/T 2.
12 BL, Add. MS 16461, ff. 110, 111v.
13 Herefs. RO, E 12/G/1, acct. roll 21 Edw. III.
14 Rudge, *Agric. of Glos.* 138; Herefs. RO, E 12/G/5, survey 1624, pp. 21, 29, 43, 47, 87.
15 Herefs. RO, E 12/G/14, bundle marked 'leases, Newent demesnes'; GA, D 2957/212/115.
16 BL, Add. MS 15668, ff. 1v., 4–5; Herefs. RO, E 12/G/5, survey 1624, pp. 25, 27, 46, 49, 55, 83, 93, 101; GA, D 2710.
17 Below (woodland management: charcoal production).
18 Herefs. RO, E 12/G/5, survey 1624, p. 15.
19 Ibid. G/3, ct. (10 Oct.) 2 Hen. VI.
20 GA, D 1803/1.
21 Above, manors (Newent manor; Boulsdon manor).
22 GA, D 2957/212/44, 127; D 1810/4, deed 20 Sept. 1727; D 2245/T 4, deed 19 Jan. 1745; GDR wills 1726/267.

buying a number of free holdings in the south of Cugley tithing in the 1660s to form Black House farm (87 a. in 1775).[1] The Hartland family formed Green farm near by (131 a. in 1817) by a similar process in the early 18th century, and in Boulsdon tithing Briery Hill farm's 89 a. was made up of four former tenancies in 1802.[2] Those acreages were typical of the main farms of Newent parish at the turn of the 18th century; Carswalls farm, with 286 a. in 1808, was an unusual size.[3]

Land use and agricultural improvement During the early modern period farming shared the strong pastoral basis of much of the surrounding region: dairying for cheese making, the raising of cattle and the Ryeland breed of sheep, and the cultivation of cider orchards were the most significant enterprises.[4] As elsewhere in west Gloucestershire and Herefordshire, the repeal of the cider tax in 1766 was marked by lavish celebrations, including a public dinner in the market place, a sheep-roast, bonfires, and a ball.[5] Almost every farm in the parish made cider and some came to specialize in its production. In 1818 Great Boulsdon farm had c.50 a. of its 139 a. given over to orcharding,[6] and in 1826 on Caerwents farm 44 a. out of 70 a. was planted with apple and pear trees, said to be capable of producing over 200 hogsheads of cider and perry in a good year.[7] J.N. Morse, a leading landowner in Newent from the 1780s,[8] dealt in cider as well as in apple and pear stocks, raised in nurseries on his estate.[9] Some houses in Newent town had cider-making equipment,[10] and some of its tradesmen, including the mercer and chandler William Nelme (d. 1702), dealt in cider as a sideline.[11] Cattle raising had long been an important feature of local farming, reflected in the strength of the butchering trade in the town,[12] and 15 of Newent's farmers were styled graziers in a trade directory of the early 1790s.[13]

Improvements in arable farming were hampered by a general reluctance to try new techniques. By the late 18th century, however, manuring and liming of some areas of sandy soil had made them more suitable for growing wheat, and turnips and clover were being introduced to the rotation. A spirit of improvement was also evident in livestock farming, with Ryeland ewes being cross-bred with Dorset and Shropshire rams.[14] In 1801, when c.2,400 a. of land in Newent was returned as under crops, wheat accounted for 1,238 a. and rye for only 60 a.; barley (572 a.), peas, beans, and oats accounted for most of the remainder and there was 147 a. of turnips.[15] Inclosure of the remaining open-field land proceeded slowly during the period. Two closes called New Tynings taken out of Worsden field were mentioned in 1705[16] and a 13-a. inclosure from Mill field in 1719.[17] Much of Boulsdon field remained in strips to the mid or later 19th century.[18] The principal tract of common, at Gorsley, was described in the early 1790s by a writer on agriculture as suitable for raising corn and for orcharding but 'in its present state nearly useless'.[19] In 1806 some freeholders tried to promote an inclosure of the part of the common lying within Newent, including in their plans the more recent encroachments made by cottagers. The lords of the two manors with rights there, Andrew Foley and J.N. Morse, and their agents were reluctant, however, having regard both for the welfare of the cottagers and the difficulties involved in ejecting them.[20] Later some Newent landowners, influenced by the contemporary movement to provide allotments as a support for the poor, divided and rented out parts of their estates as small gardens. By 1836 there were some on John Hartland's estate south of the town, adjoining the continuation of Bury Bar Lane, and others on land west of Watery Lane belonging to Benjamin Hooke's Common Fields farm and to another owner. Those allotments were presumably occupied mainly by inhabitants of Newent town.[21]

The Late Nineteenth Century and the Twentieth

In 1851 Newent parish had 48 farms (using 20 a. as a minimum size for that description). The typical size remained around 80 to 130 a., worked by the family and two or three labourers. The main exceptions were based in Compton tithing, where the Pauntley Court estate's Compton House farm had 500 a., about half of it in Pauntley parish, and employed 20 labourers, Carswalls farm had 320 a. and 18 labourers, Scarr farm had 290 a. and 11 labourers, and Hayes farm had 280 a. and 16 labourers. Okle Clifford farm, with 300 a. and 10 labourers, was the only other farm of similar size.[22] Also

---

1 Herefs. RO, E 12/G/17; GA, D 2528, plan A.
2 GA, D 2245 (acc. 7541), envelope 10A; D 2245/T 5–6; D 332/T 4.
3 Ibid. D 1938.
4 Turner, *Agric. of Glos.* 46, 52–3; Rudge, *Agric. of Glos.* 309–10; Rudder, *Glos.* 561.
5 *Glouc. J.* 14 July 1766.
6 Ibid. 17 Aug. 1818.
7 Ibid. 24 Apr. 1826.
8 Above, manors (Bouldson manor; Kilcot: Kilcot manor and the Conigree).
9 *Chapters in Newent's History* (Newent Local Hist. Soc. 2003), 68; GA, D 245/I/22, letter 21 Mar. 1809.
10 e.g. GDR wills 1708/201; GA, D 1998, deed 23 Jan. 1796.
11 TNA, PROB 11/ 470, f. 92.
12 Below (distributive and service trades).
13 *Univ. Brit. Dir.* IV (1798), 62.
14 Turner, *Agric. of Glos.* 47–8; Rudge, *Agric. of Glos.* 138; Rudder, *Glos.* 597.
15 *1801 Crop Returns Eng.* I, 175.
16 GA, D 332/T 8.
17 Ibid. D 2245/T 4, deed 10 Apr. 1730.
18 GDR, T 1/126; GA, D 2710.
19 Turner, *Agric. of Glos.* 50.
20 GA, D 245/I/21, letters 12 Nov., 28 Dec. 1806, 25 Jan., 21 Mar. 1809.
21 Ibid. Q/RUm 148; GDR, T 1/126 (nos 1033, 1036, 1138).
22 TNA, HO 107/1960; for Compton House farm, see GDR, T 1/126, 140.

by the mid 19th century there was a proliferation of holdings comprising only a cottage, orchard, and a few acres taken from the waste; most were on Gorsley common and others were on Clifford's Mesne. Some cottagers followed a trade or craft to supplement their income but, as encroachment diminished the area of waste available to pasture animals, others probably worked at least part-time for the larger farms. In 1896 a total of 95 agricultural holdings was returned[1] and in 1926 114 including 43 of under 20 a.[2]

Land use   Arable predominated in the mid 19th century. In 1866 (when the total acreages suggest that some farms failed to make a return) 3,263 a. was returned as under crops and 1,927 as permanent grassland. Wheat, roots, and grass seeds were then the main constituents of the rotation; the amount of rye grown was then only 33 a. and dwindled to a few acres by end of the century. The slump in cereal prices produced the usual reversal in the proportion of arable to pasture and meadow. In 1896 2,842 a. of land was returned under crops as against 4,060 a. permanent grass, and the number of livestock showed a considerable increase, with 1,154 cattle and 3,399 sheep and lambs compared to 835 and 2,618 in 1866.[3] Scarr farm was unusual as still being an arable enterprise, with all but 25 of its 347 a. under the plough, cropped mainly with barley and roots. When offered for sale in 1900 it was reported to be well farmed but nevertheless losing money: the previous owner had spent £30,000 in purchasing it and putting up new buildings but the farm was expected to realize no more than £10,000.[4] The 64-a. Ravenhill farm, which was over two thirds arable in 1869[5] and a noted supplier of seed-wheat at that period, was all farmed as pasture or orchard by 1916.[6] Some owners, including those of Ford House, Great Cugley, and Great Boulsdon, took their farms in hand in the 1880s and 1890s and managed them through bailiffs.[7]

Between the wars even more land was converted to pasture, and there was a further increase in livestock, with 1,608 cattle returned in 1926, including a large contingent of dairy cows.[8] Dairying benefited at that period from Newent's rail links to Gloucester, Ledbury, and Hereford, and *c.*1921 Cadbury Ltd, the chocolate makers, established a milk collection depot near Newent station.[9] In 1928 over half of the arable on Okle Clifford farm had recently been laid down to grass and landlord and tenant agreed to share the cost of

18. *Cider making on the premises of Andrew Ford in 1951*

providing a water supply for dairy farming.[10] In 1932 on the 103-a. Black House farm only 2 a. was ploughed,[11] and in the following year Callowhill farm's 143 a. included only *c.*22 a. under the plough.[12] In 1926 the crops returned for the parish included 99 a. of sugar beet, which remained an important cash crop for some farms to the end of the century.[13] An unusual feature of farming in the early 20th century was the survival of Cowmeadow as a common meadow comprising in 1903 40 plots divided among *c.*9 farmers. In 1908 the Gloucester estate agent and auctioneer Henry Bruton, having become one of the principal owners by his purchase of the adjoining Moat farm, began an annually renewable exchange of plots with the owner of Layne's farm to give each a compact holding.[14] Similar temporary arrangements, apparently involving all the owners of strips in the meadow, continued in 1921.[15]

Almost every farm had a cider mill and press in the late 19th century and early 20th. They were also to be found on many of the cottage holdings in the western arm of the parish,[16] where about half of the former Gorsley common was under orchard in the 1880s.[17] The Kilcot inn was among premises making cider in that area to the mid 20th century.[18] In 1896 366 a. of land in Newent parish was returned as orchard.[19] The firm of Henry Thompson & Co., based at Southends farm, won many prizes for its draught and bottled cider and perry; when it failed in 1911, a collapse attributed to financial mismanagement, the trade was said to be thriving in the area.[20]

---

1   TNA, MAF 68/1609/15.
2   Ibid. MAF 68/3295/15.
3   Ibid. MAF 68/25/4; MAF 68/26/12; MAF 68/1609/15.
4   GA, D 2299/108.
5   Ibid. 1557.
6   Ibid. 1361.
7   *Kelly's Dir. Glos.* (1894), 245.
8   TNA, MAF 68/3295/15.
9   GA, DA 30/100/12, pp. 283, 299.
10 Ibid. D 3269, Okle Clifford farm papers 1928–31.
11 Ibid. D 2299/4933.
12 Ibid. 5035.
13 TNA, MAF 68/3295/15.
14 GA, D 2299/447.
15 Ibid. 2441.
16 Ibid. SL 79.
17 OS Maps 6", Glos. XVI.SE (1889 edn); XVII.SW (1884 edn).
18 *Millennium Memories: the History of Gorsley and Kilcot*, ed. L. Hines (2001), 62–3, 75. See Fig. 18.
19 TNA, MAF 68/1609/15.
20 GA, D 2299/1552.

19. Packing market-garden produce at the Scarr in 1951

Market gardening and poultry farming In the 20th century there was a growth in market gardening, particularly the growing of soft fruit in upland parts of the parish. About 30 a. was returned as devoted to that sort of agriculture in 1896,[1] and there were several specialist market gardens in the parish in 1937[2] when the Land Settlement Association bought Scarr farm for one of its schemes for settling unemployed people on the land. The Association divided the 360-a. farm into 57 smallholdings of between 3 and 8 a., each with a small dwelling, piggery, glasshouse, and poultry house. The scheme was run on the co-operative system under a committee and estate manager; supplies and equipment were provided from a pool and packing and marketing of produce were done centrally.[3] During the Second World War the criteria for granting tenancies were changed to benefit any man of non-military age, and after the war new tenants were required to have experience in horticulture. In the 1950s and 1960s, while the manager ran part of the land as a nursery, the tenants, of whom there were 49 in 1961, produced vegetables, soft fruit, and chrysanthemums.[4] In 1969 the packing station employed 40 people and each tenant two or three part-time workers in the busy months. A programme of improvements then under way included the replacement of the glasshouses to provide each holding with 1 a. under glass.[5] In the later 20th century poultry farming, in which some farmers specialized by the early 1930s,[6] expanded with the establishment of large egg and rearing units. The principal firms were Stallard Bros., which in the early 1960s built a complex of sheds for battery chickens south-west of Compton Green,[7] and a business run by the Freeman family of Town Farm, which in 1983 employed c.60 people in rearing and processing oven-ready chickens.[8]

Farming in the later 20th century In the mid and later 20th century the proportion of arable in the parish showed a modest rise and livestock farming retained its strength, with 2,124 cattle, mainly in dairy herds, and 4,711 sheep and lambs returned in 1986. In 1956 1,815 a. was returned as growing general crops and 356 a. growing vegetables, glasshouse crops, and soft fruit, while 3,890 a. was returned as permanent grassland and 277 a. as orchard. In 1986 the equivalent figures were 755 ha (1,865 a.), 170.3 ha (421 a.) including 15.7 ha (39 a.) under glass, 1,146 ha (2,833 a.), and 48.3 ha (119 a.). The 1,777 pigs returned in 1956 (compared with 683 in 1926) were mainly accounted for by the piggeries on the Land Settlement Association estate. That estate also contributed to the large numbers of poultry then kept, but the later increase in the number of chickens returned, over 43,000 birds in 1986 compared with c. 25,000 in 1956, was mainly accounted for by the two large businesses mentioned above.[9] In the early 1980s, following the winding up of the Land Settlement Association, its holdings were sold, many to the tenants. Most were formed into larger units, which continued to grow soft

---

1 TNA, MAF 68/1609/15.
2 *Kelly's Dir. Glos.* (1931), 266.
3 Fig. 19.
4 *Kelly's Dir. Glos.* (1939), 271; *Glos. Countryside*, June 1958, 47–8; *The Countryman* (1961), 583–91.
5 GA, DA 30/100/37, p. 239; see also, ibid. pp. 69, 131, 238; 100/35, p. 101; 100/38, pp. 87, 271.
6 *Kelly's Dir Glos.* (1931), 266–7; (1935), 266–7; GA, D 2299/6045.
7 GA, DA 30/100/31, p. 158; 100/39, pp. 76, 224.
8 *Glos. and Avon Life*, Jan. 1983, 29.
9 TNA, MAF 68/4533/168; MAF 68/6005/14/168.

20. The Three Choirs Vineyard

fruit and market garden produce.¹ In 1986 a total of 42 full-time farming units was returned in Newent parish: 8 were described as dairy farms, 6 as mainly devoted to cattle and sheep raising, 5 to pigs or poultry, and the others to general cropping or fruit and vegetable growing; 92 other units worked on a part-time basis were mainly small market gardens or fruit farms. The latter gave the parish an unusually high proportion of people still employed full- or part-time in agriculture, a total of 389 in 1986.²

The main features in farming at the end of the 20th century and the beginning of the 21st included a reduction in dairying and other general trends in agriculture such as the amalgamation of farms into larger units and the sale of farmhouses, often with a field or two attached, to non-farming owners. In 2007 the larger farms were mainly engaged in cattle and sheep raising, but fruit growing and market gardening remained the principal enterprises in the north part of the parish, where much produce was then grown under 'Spanish polytunnels', many of the glasshouses having gone out of use. A successful new enterprise was a vineyard called the Three Choirs, which began in 1972 with the planting of a vines on a fruit farm at Welsh House Lane in Pauntley³ and was later based on the farmhouse formerly called Baldwin's, just within Newent's northern boundary.⁴ By 2007 its vines covered 75 a. in Newent and Pauntley and the buildings comprised a winery, which also processed grapes for other English vineyards, a 'real ale' brewery begun in 2002, a restaurant, and a small hotel.⁵

WOODLAND MANAGEMENT AND WOODLAND CRAFTS

Yartleton woods on the northern slopes of May hill were an important asset of Newent manor, but during the 13th century and the early 14th the benefit the lords could derive from them was restricted because the south-western part of Newent was within the Forest of Dean and subject to forest law. During the 13th century the Forest's north-eastern boundary followed the Gloucester–Newent road through Malswick tithing and passed along the main street of the town to Ell bridge. For most of the remainder of its course within the parish it ascended Ell brook to Gorsley ford, 700 m north of the boundary with Aston Ingham (Herefs.), but whereas according to a perambulation of 1282 it followed a road from Ell bridge to rejoin the brook at Oxenhall bridge, south of Oxenhall church, according to another of 1300 it followed the brook all the way from Ell bridge to Gorsley ford. The perambulations also appear to disagree whether its course south of the ford into Aston Ingham continued on the brook or by a nearby lane. The south-western

---

1 Information from Mr Eric Kneen of Newent; http://www.grantsforhorticulturists.org.uk/LSA-guide.rtf (accessed 14 Oct. 2007).
2 TNA, MAF 68/6005/14/168.
3 *Citizen*, 21 Oct. 1975; *Glos. Life*, Aug. 1989, 468.
4 Fig. 20.
5 Information from Mr T. Shaw of Three Choirs Vineyard.

part of Newent was finally confirmed as being outside the Forest in 1327.[1]

In the 13th century Newent priory was several times presented at Forest eyres for committing waste in its woods[2] and in 1308 and the early 1320s it sought the intervention of the Crown and the justices of the forests when its claim to take estovers without supervision by Dean's foresters was challenged.[3] The use of other woods on the west side of the parish, belonging to Boulsdon and Kilcot manors, was similarly restricted before 1327, though the owners were permitted to appoint their own woodwards subject to approval by the justices-in-eyre.[4] Lands called Great and Little Woodwards in Compton tithing, held by a free tenant of Newent manor c.1315, may have been charged with the service of acting as a manorial woodward[5] but possibly only within Compton, which lay outside the Forest's bounds.

Charcoal Production

In the early modern period much of Newent's woodland was managed as coppice to provide charcoal for the iron industry. That was no doubt the case with Yartleton woods by 1448 when Fotheringhay college leased them to a Mitcheldean man, reserving the standards and large timber trees.[6] Charcoal burning was a significant source of livelihood in Newent in 1608 when seven colliers were recorded in the parish. Five lived in Compton,[7] presumably operating in the small woods and groves of that tithing: fields called Coalpits and Coalpit Piece in the south part of Carswalls farm and others called Colliers Leaze and Pit field to the west of Madam's wood[8] probably got their names from charcoal burning.

Sir John Winter, lord of Newent manor, was supplying his Forest of Dean ironworks from Yartleton woods in 1632. By agreement with leading freeholders he was to enclose certain coppices for a period of six years before felling, and during the following six years the commoners were to exercise their rights, an arrangement presumably intended to rotate among various parts of the woods. To protect the woods against encroachment, it was agreed that cottages there without good title were to be demolished and no more built except those necessary to house workmen cutting and charcoaling the coppices.[9] In 1660, when Thomas Foley, the new owner of the manor, was using the woods to supply his Ellbridge furnace, 417 of their 595 acres were described as coppice. By arrangement with fellow landowners, Foley also managed other coppices in Newent, including 30 a. of Kilcot wood on Kilcot manor and 35 a. in Boulsdon belonging to the owner of Ravenshill farm.[10] Under the Foleys the commoners came under increasing pressure to abandon their rights at Yartleton. The Cugley freeholders led by one of the Woodward family resisted and Paul Foley is said to have secured their acquiescence by paying off Woodward and reducing the chief rents owed to the manor by the others.[11] During the late 17th century and the early 18th the Foleys cut and corded the Yartleton coppices on a 14-year cycle.[12] In the 1680s at least seven Newent parishioners worked as charcoal burners and others followed the trade of 'corder', cutting and stacking the coppice wood.[13] During the second half of the 19th century, under the Onslow family, annual sales of timber and coppice wood in Yartleton woods were held by the Gloucester auctioneers Bruton & Knowles.[14] About 1911, at the sale of the Onslows' estate, the woods were bought by C.P. Ackers,[15] heir to the Huntley Manor estate, and from that time they were managed with adjoining woodland in Huntley and Taynton, most of the oak coppice being replaced by conifers for commercial timber production.[16]

Other Woodland Crafts

The woods, by supplying oak bark, contributed to the tanning industry of the town and parish and, by supplying material for hoops and staves, to the manufacture of barrels for local cider production: seven or more coopers were working in Newent during the 1680s.[17] Other crafts connected with the woodlands were lath and broom making, carried on by a number of cottagers at Clifford's Mesne during the early 19th century. In 1851 four inhabitants of the hamlet were employed as wood cutters.[18] Brand Green had a lath maker in 1820. In the same period wood cutting and charcoal burning employed cottagers of the Gorsley and Kilcot area, possibly working in the adjoining Oxenhall woods,[19] and in 1851 two Gorsley men made hurdles for sheep pens.[20] Several timber merchants

---

1 C.E. Hart, 'Metes and Bounds of the Forest of Dean', *Trans. BGAS* 66 (1945), 172, 175–8; *VCH Glos.* V, 297.
2 TNA, E 32/29, rot. 8d.; BL, Add. MS 15668, f. 9v.
3 BL, Add. MS 15668, ff. 4, 22v.
4 TNA, E 32/28, rott. 2d., 8; E 32/29, rot. 8 and d.; E 32/30, rot. 6; *Cal. Pat.* 1307–13, 77, 380.
5 BL, Add. MS 18461, f. 103v.
6 Herefs. RO, E 12/G/1, ct. (7 May) 26 Hen. VI.
7 Smith, *Men and Armour*, 62–4.
8 GDR, T 1/126 (nos 264, 267, 474–5); GA, D 2710.
9 Herefs. RO, E 12/G/6.
10 Ibid. G/15, mortgage 1660; G/19, survey of woods c.1668.
11 GA, D 412/Z 3, Nourse MS, p. 8.

12 Herefs. RO, E 12/G/12, table of woods 1698–1711.
13 GA, P 225/IN 1/2.
14 Ibid. SL 79–80.
15 J. Douglas, *Historical Notes of Newent with Oxenhall and Pauntley* (1912), 15.
16 GA, D 2299/3851; below, Huntley, econ. hist. (woodland management).
17 GA, P 225/IN 1/2.
18 Ibid. IN 1/4, baptisms 1822; TNA, HO 107/1960.
19 GA, D 412/T 1, assignment of lease 4 July 1801; P 225/IN 1/4, baptisms 1815, 1818, 1820, 1823–4.
20 TNA, HO 107/1960 (where the north part of Gorsley within the parish is included under Cugley tithing).

operating in the parish in the late 18th century and the early 19th[1] presumably traded in timber from the local woodlands. A Monmouth timber merchant and ship builder, Hezekiah Swift, contracted to buy Kilcot wood and woodland in Boulsdon, though the sale was concluded in 1818 with the owner of the Pauntley Court estate.[2] There were timber yards on the canal, north of Newent town, by 1841,[3] and Herbert Lancaster established a saw mill and timber yard beside the railway in Horsefair Lane shortly before 1900.[4] Lancaster's firm, one of the main employers in the parish during the early 20th century, continued there until c.1970,[5] when a firm making fencing and ladders took over the site.[6]

COAL MINING, QUARRYING, AND BRICK MAKING

The coal measures underlying part of the parish were exploited from the beginning of the 17th century or earlier.[7] In 1607 two mines were being worked on lands belonging to John Beach[8] and John Pitt in Boulsdon tithing, where fields adjoining the lane to Clifford's Mesne later had names such as Coal grounds and Coal orchard. The mine on Pitt's land was leased to four miners, who paid him the fifth penny of their profits; two of them were natives of the Mendip region of the Somerset coalfield.[9] A coal miner recorded at Kilcot in 1608[10] possibly worked in the detached part of Pauntley parish near by. Working of the deposits in Boulsdon apparently continued sporadically. At his death in 1652 Walter Nourse, lord of Boulsdon manor, left timber for use in the coal mines and the proceeds from them to his widow.[11] New pits were sunk by William Nourse, who inherited the manor and Great Boulsdon farm in 1757, and they presumably produced the coal that was sent from Newent to Gloucester in the winter of 1763. Nourse is said to have concluded that the operation was not worth the labour and closed his pits.[12]

A new incentive for working the deposits in and around Newent came with the promotion of the Gloucester and Hereford canal in 1789. New pits were sunk in Newent the following year and the owners sent a wagon of coal to the mayor and corporation of Gloucester as a sample of what they hoped would be a regular trade to the city.[13] At Boulsdon the main proprietors were J.N. Morse, who bought the manor in 1789, and Edward Hartland, who bought Great Boulsdon farm then or soon afterwards. In 1794 Hartland offered a lease of his land, which was said to include seams 7–8 ft deep,[14] and later, together with Morse and some Gloucester men, he formed the Boulsdon Coal Co. to develop the field and purchase pumping machinery.[15] The works in the Newent area failed to fulfil the expectations: the seams proved thin and the coal failed to compete, even in its own immediate area, with supplies brought down the Severn from Staffordshire and, increasingly from c.1811, from the developing Forest of Dean coalfield. Paradoxically, the canal intended to open up the coalfield made supplies from elsewhere easy to transport to Newent.[16] Although efforts to win coal commercially continued in nearby parts of Pauntley and Oxenhall,[17] mining at Boulsdon was said to be extinct in 1856.[18] Two disused shafts survived on Great Boulsdon farm in 1882.[19]

Stone for local purposes was dug at small quarries in various parts of the parish, notably at Clifford's Mesne where quarries in the sandstone, one of the assets of Boulsdon manor, were used for repairing the farm buildings on the estate in 1784.[20] The main quarry there, situated beside the lane from Newent near the north entrance to the hamlet, was worked commercially for building stone in the 1870s[21] but was described in 1916 as almost exhausted.[22] A similar stone, known as Gorsley stone, was used in many buildings in the parish but was produced mainly from quarries beyond its boundary in Linton.[23]

Clay was being dug for brick making in the parish by 1660[24] and at a number of sites during the 18th and 19th centuries. There was a brick kiln on Stallions farm in 1764,[25] and another small works was in production on the south part of Gorsley common by 1790 and until the mid 19th century.[26] Another, at Clifford's Mesne, operated for a few years in the 1890s.[27] A works,

---

1 *Univ. Brit. Dir.* IV, 62; *Pigot's Dir. Glos.* (1822–3), 62.
2 GA, D 2245/T 8, abs. of title 1844; for Swift, *VCH Glos.* V, 156.
3 TNA, HO 107/350.
4 OS Map 1:2,500, Glos. XVII.10 (1903 edn).
5 *Chapters in Newent's History*, 165; GA, DA 30/100/15, p. 388; 100/31, p. 84.
6 *Glos. and Avon Life*, Jan. 1983, 29.
7 For a detailed account of coal mining in the parish and area, D. Bick, *The Mines of Newent and Ross* (Newent, 1987).
8 Beach, described as a bailiff in 1608, perhaps occupied lands under Sir Arthur Porter: Smith, *Men and Armour*, 64.
9 GDR vol. 100, depositions 20 Oct. 1607, 15 Mar., 7 June 1608; and for the field names, ibid. T 1/126 (nos 1538, 1966–7, 1977).
10 Smith, *Men and Armour*, 63.
11 TNA, PROB 11/228, f. 66v.
12 Bigland, *Glos.* II, 238; Glos. Colln. R 22.1, diary entry for 1 Feb. 1763.
13 *Glouc. J.* 12, 19 July 1790.
14 Ibid. 7 July 1794; above, manors (Boulsdon manor).
15 Bick, *Mines of Newent and Ross*, 14–19; Turner, *Agric. of Glos.* 55; GA, D 245/I/25, letters 30 Oct. 1810, 16 Mar., 30 Apr. 1811.
16 Bick, *Mines of Newent and Ross*, 11; D. Bick, *The Hereford & Gloucester Canal* (Newent, 1979), 16.
17 Below, Oxenhall, econ. hist. (coal mining).
18 *Kelly's Dir. Glos.* (1856), 332.
19 OS Map 6", Glos. XVII.SW (1884 edn).
20 GA, D 332/T 5.
21 *Kelly's Dir. Glos.* (1870), 604; (1879), 709; GA, D 7723/1.
22 GA, D 412/E 2, letter 11 Dec. 1916.
23 Verey and Brooks, *Glos.* II, 30.
24 GA, D 412/Z 3, Nourse MS, p. 7.
25 Ibid. D 892/T 57.
26 Ibid. D 412/E 1, notes by J.N. Morse; sale partics. 1857.
27 *Chapters in Newent's History*, 163.

producing bricks, tiles, and drain pipes, was established on the Gloucester road just to the east of Newent town before 1882 by the Onslows, lords of the manor, and continued in production until c.1900.[1]

MILLS

There were three mills on Newent manor in 1086, two held in demesne and one held by the tenants.[2] The Ell brook later drove four mills in its course through the parish. The highest, Cleeve Mill on Cleeve Lane to the east of Newent town,[3] was recorded as part of the manor from 1235.[4] It remained a corn mill on lease from the manor until 1913,[5] except that it was briefly alienated in the 1650s and passed to George Dalton, who sold it with Stardens farm back to the lord of the manor in 1664. Described then as two overshot mills[6] and in 1714 as three mills under one roof,[7] Cleeve Mill ceased to work by water power in 1959 when a flood damaged its race, but for some years afterwards it was powered by an oil engine and ground animal feed.[8] The mill and mill house, rebuilt in brick c.1800, remained in place with an iron water wheel in 2007.

Okle Pitcher mill, c.400 m above the point where Ell brook was crossed by a lane leading from the Gloucester–Newent road towards Upleadon,[9] was known as Little New Mill in 1612 when it was part of a small freehold estate (Okle Pitchard).[10] Later it may have been used to grind bark for a tannery, for it was named as 'the leather mill' on a map of 1824,[11] but it was worked as a corn mill in 1817 by James Humpidge,[12] its owner in 1838.[13] It went out of use in the 1930s when the machinery was removed and the building converted as a dwelling.[14]

Okle mill, later known as Brass Mill, stood just below the lane to Upleadon. It was recorded from 1436[15] and probably belonged, as in the early 17th century, to Okle Clifford manor. It was a corn mill in 1627 and was converted as a brass hammer mill possibly in 1639 when it was leased to John Broughton and Richard Ayleway.

In 1646 the owners of Okle Clifford, Barbara and William Keys, sold the mill to Stephen Skinner, a Newent clothier,[16] whose family remained the owners until 1727 or later. By 1690 it had been turned once more to a corn mill.[17] Thomas Green of Linton, a mealman, owned and worked it in 1827[18] and it had an adjoining malthouse in 1838.[19] In 1919, after a damaged sluice-gate caused the mill to flood, the owner intended to give up working it,[20] and in the 1930s the building was converted as part of the adjoining mill house.[21]

Malswick mill, further downstream at a point where the Ell brook borders the Gloucester road, was recorded as a corn mill on the Newent manor estate from 1235.[22] About 1315 it was kept in hand by the lords, whose customary tenants maintained its dyke and leat as part of their services, and it was presumably the mill to which most of the tenants, both free and customary, were then required to bring their corn.[23] Malswick mill was on lease by 1389[24] and was held by copy in the late 15th century and in the early 17th.[25] It was probably alienated from the manor by the Winters in the 1650s. Shortly before 1781 William Taylor sold it to Thomas Trounsell, a local farmer.[26] It continued in use until after the Second World War.[27]

In 1289 the prior of Newent leased a fulling (or tuck) mill on Newent manor to John the fuller.[28] The mill was powered from Peacock's brook and stood in the demesne lands north of the town, a short way above the confluence of the brook and the Ell brook (at a site adjoining the line of the later canal). In 1482, known as Pool Mill, it was in decay and was on lease to the bailiff of the manor together with two fishponds and other parts of the demesne.[29] It was in the same ruinous state in 1506[30] but it was possibly in use again in the early 17th century when two tuckers lived in the town.[31] In 1624 James Morse held it on lease with the fishponds.[32] It was sold together with the adjoining demesne lands soon after 1657 and passed with them through the Bray, Rogers, and de Visme families.[33] The building had

---

1 OS Map 6", Glos. XVII.SE (1889 edn); *Kelly's Dir.Glos.* (1889 and later edns).
2 *Domesday Book* (Rec. Com.), I, 166.
3 OS Map 1:25,000, SO 72 (1952 edn).
4 BL, Add. MS 15668, f. 54v.; 18461, f. 62.
5 Herefs. RO, E 12/G/2, acct. roll 22 Edw. IV; G/5, survey 1624, p.1; GA, SL 79.
6 Herefs. RO, E 12/G/18.
7 GA, D 2957/212/71.
8 G.M. Davies, 'Mills of the River Leadon and Tributaries', *Glos. Soc. Ind. Archaeol. Newsletter* 7 (Apr. 1966), p. 41.
9 For its site and those of the two mills further downstream below, OS Map 6", Glos. XVII.SE (1889 edn).
10 GDR wills 1618/149; GA, D185/IV/32. For the estate, above, manors (Okle: Okle Pitchard).
11 Bryant, *Map of Glos.* (1824).
12 *Glouc. J.* 28 Apr.1817; *Pigot's Dir. Glos.* (1822–3), 62.
13 GDR, T 1/126.
14 Davies, 'Mills of the River Leadon', p. 41.
15 Herefs. RO, E 12/G/1, ct. (30 Oct.) 15 Hen. VI; G/3, ct. 10 Oct.

21 Hen.VI.
16 GA, D 22/10.
17 Ibid. D 2957/212/119, 124; D 1810/4.
18 Ibid. D 922/T 2.
19 GDR, T 1/126; GA, D 2710.
20 GA, DA 30/100/12, p. 170.
21 Davies, 'Mills of the River Leadon', p. 42.
22 BL, Add. MS 15668, f. 54v.; 18461, f. 62v.
23 Ibid. 18461, ff.110 and v., 112v.
24 Herefs. RO, E 12/G/5, acct. roll 14 Ric. II.
25 Ibid. G/2, acct. roll 22 Edw. IV; G/5, rental 31 Hen. VIII; survey 1624, p. 25.
26 GA, D 4587/2.
27 Davies, 'Mills of the River Leadon', p. 42.
28 BL, Add. MS 15668, f. 4.
29 Herefs. RO, E 12/G/2, acct. roll 22 Edw. IV.
30 Ibid. acct. roll 22 Hen. VII.
31 Below (other industry and crafts).
32 Herefs. RO, E 12/G/5, survey 1624, p.1.
33 Above, manors (Newent manor: Newent Court).

probably been demolished by the 1770s[1] but the large mill pond called Tuck Mill pool, evidently one of the fishponds mentioned earlier, survived until the railway was built over the site in the 1880s.[2]

In 1612 Edward Gwillim, who was possibly then owner of Great Boulsdon farm, joined in a conveyance of a water mill and land in Boulsdon to George Shipside.[3] The mill may have been on the Boulsdon brook to the east of the farm, where fields were later called Mill fields.[4]

OTHER INDUSTRY AND CRAFTS

Henry II, when confirming the earl of Leicester's grant of 1181 to Cormeilles abbey, gave it the right to work a forge on Newent manor and burn charcoal in the woods to sustain it.[5] That and presumably other bloomery forges operating in the Middle Ages left deposits of cinders in various parts of the parish, apparently adding to others left by Roman iron working.[6] Cinders were being used to fill potholes in the town's streets in 1485[7] and large quantities were dug for the use of Ellbridge furnace established in the adjoining part of Oxenhall by the late 1630s.[8] Francis Finch, the furnace's owner, bought deposits found in a field called Cinder pits, probably in Compton tithing, in 1639 and others from the Moat estate, in Cugley, in the 1650s.[9] His successors to the furnace, the Foleys, reserved cinders in leases of their lands on Newent manor,[10] where sites yielding them included a field called Cinders adjoining Cleeve Mill[11] and Cinder field and Cinder meadow on Nelfields farm.[12] In 1727 they were being dug on the Skinner family's estate, adjoining the Gloucester road on the east side of the town.[13]

Among Newent men employed at Ellbridge furnace were two iron founders recorded in the 1680s and two 'furnace men' in the early years of the next century.[14] As mentioned above, other inhabitants found work cutting and charcoaling the coppices in local woodland, and many must have been employed from time to time in carrying and labouring tasks, including maintenance of the ponds and watercourses on Gorsley common associated with the furnace.[15] A small nail making industry recorded at Newent from the 1680s[16] was presumably established in connexion with the furnace but survived its closure c.1750. Three nailers worked in the parish in 1822[17] and the trade was represented there in the 1850s.[18]

A glassworks, operated by French Huguenot families, was established in the late 16th century at Yartleton on the lower slopes of May hill. It gave its name to a small hamlet and inn in Taynton parish but the main site was on land known as Yartleton waste (later Glasshouse green) in the adjoining part of Newent in the angle made by the junction of lanes from Cugley and Clifford's Mesne. Between 1598 and 1634 several glassmakers were recorded in Newent, including Abraham Liscourt,[19] who c.1607 was paying a rent of £10 for the Yartleton glasshouse to the lord of Newent manor,[20] and John Bulnoys (or Bolonies), who in 1624 occupied one of a small group of cottages that had been built on the green. Another of the cottages was then occupied by Francis Davis, a potter.[21] Glass making at Yartleton had probably ceased by 1640, when a widow Davis occupied the glasshouse and paid a rent of £1 for it,[22] but pottery making appears to have continued at the site until the mid 18th century: between 1676 and 1746 six potters, four of them members of the Davis family, were mentioned among inhabitants of Newent parish.[23] On Glasshouse green, from which all the dwellings were later removed, many fragments of glass and pottery have been unearthed.[24]

In the late 13th century and the early 14th, when a fulling mill operated next to Newent town[25] the town's tradesmen included weavers, fullers, and dyers.[26] In the early modern period cloth making was probably the town's principal industry. Several clothiers were based there at the end of the 16th century,[27] and townspeople listed for the muster of 1608 included two fullers (tuckers) and 14 weavers, the latter including three employed as journeymen by clothier or master weaver Roger Hill;[28] another six weavers were listed then in outlying parts of the parish.[29] The industry maintained

---

1 Rudder, *Glos.* 562.
2 GA, P 225A/MI 9; D 421/Z 3, Nourse MS, p. 10 (a note added to this transcript by E. Conder).
3 TNA, CP 25/2/298/10 Jas. I Mich. no 49.
4 GDR, T 1/126 (nos 1560, 1562).
5 BL, Add. MS. 18461, f. 4 and v.
6 Rudder, *Glos.* 562.
7 Herefs. RO, E 12/G/2, ct. 13 Oct. I Hen. VII.
8 Below, Oxenhall, econ. hist. (Ellbridge furnace).
9 Herefs. RO, G/15, deed 20 Apr. 1639; G/12, agreement 12 Dec. 1655.
10 e.g. GA, D 2957/212/68, 88.
11 Herefs. RO, E 12/G/18, deed 23 Apr.1664.
12 GA, D 2528, plan B. 13 Ibid. D 1810/4.
14 Ibid. P 225/IN 1/2, burials 1686, 1716, baptisms 1689, 1704.
15 Above, introd. (landscape).
16 GA, P 225/IN 1/2, burials 1682, baptisms 1685.
17 *Pigot's Dir. Glos.* (1822–3), 62.
18 TNA, HO 107/1960.
19 *Chapters in Newent's History*, 171–5.
20 GA, D 421/E 13, f. 16v.
21 Herefs. RO, E 12/G/5, survey 1624, p. 11; GDR wills 1634/70; for the group of bldgs., GA, D 2528, plan A.
22 GA, D 421/M 81 (s.v. 'Yarkelton' tenants).
23 Ibid. P 225/IN 1/2, baptisms 1676, 1683, 1706, 1711, 1714, 1721, 1729–30, burials 1711; D 2957/212/73.
24 *Chapters in Newent's History*, 176–83.
25 Above (mills).
26 Herefs. RO, E 12/G/1, ct. (5 Oct.) 17 Edw. II; rental 1291; G/2, cts. (22 Nov., 10 Feb.) 26 Edw. I; BL, Add. MS 18461, ff. 104v.–105.
27 GA, D 332/T 3, deed 12 Aug. 1595; GDR, V 1/164, baptisms 1600; Hockaday Abs. ccclxv, 1587.
28 Smith, *Men and Armour*, 60–2.
29 Ibid. 62–3.

its importance during the 17th century, when leading clothiers included Stephen Skinner (d. 1674), who purchased demesne land from the manor in 1657,[1] and Miles Beale (d. 1698). The latter's son, Miles Beale (d. 1713),[2] had racks for drying cloth in the grounds of the Court House.[3] In the 1680s there were c.5 clothiers in Newent[4] and c.20 or more men engaged in weaving and dyeing[5] but, as in other small Gloucestershire towns (outside the Stroud and Dursley areas), Newent's cloth-making industry was in decline by the early 18th century. Few cloth workers were recorded after the 1720s, and the clothier Ailway Parsons (d. 1764) appears to have been the last representative of the entrepreneurial class of the industry,[6] which had apparently died out entirely in Newent ten years later.[7]

Three stocking weavers were mentioned in Newent town in 1766[8] but that industry, evidently the frame-knitting mentioned c.1775,[9] seems to have been short-lived. Flax dressing employed some Newent men in the late 17th century and the early 18th,[10] and the town had two linen manufacturers in 1830.[11] In the late 16th century and the early 17th several men were presented in the manor court for soaking hemp in the pond and millstream at Cleeve Mill and in Peacock's brook in the town.[12] The fibres were perhaps supplied to rope makers in Gloucester or elsewhere. In the mid and later 19th century the wives of cottagers in the Kilcot area made gloves, probably as outworkers for Worcester firms.[13]

Tanning was an important trade in Newent, where the woodlands provided the required oak bark and the butchering trade a ready supply of hides. In 1611 and 1619 the manor court was at pains to enforce on the butchers from surrounding villages who sold meat in the Newent market a statutory obligation to bring their hides and tallow as well.[14] Seven tanners were listed in the parish in 1608, four under Boulsdon and one each under the town, Malswick, and Cugley,[15] and between 1631 and 1640 four Newent farmers apprenticed their sons to tanners in Gloucester.[16] A tannery was established in the town, backing onto Peacock's brook on the west side of Culver Street, shortly before 1652 and was bought by Edward Bower in 1671.[17] Eleven tanners recorded in Newent in the 1680s included four members of the Bower family, which, with the White family, dominated the trade in Newent during the 18th century.[18] The Culver Street tannery remained in use until 1914, worked in its final years by F.W.H. Lees & Co.[19] Some of the buildings survived in 2007 adjoining the substantial dwelling (the Tan House) built by the Bowers in the late 17th century.[20]

MARKETS AND FAIRS

In 1226 Henry III, while passing through Newent, granted Cormeilles abbey the right to hold an annual fair on the eve, feast day, and morrow of the Purification (2 February). The grant was provisional until the king's majority[21] and was perhaps not confirmed when he declared himself of full age the next year, for in 1253 he made another grant to the abbey of a four-day fair around the feast of St Peter ad Vincula (1 August), together with a weekly Tuesday market.[22] In 1313 Edward II made a new grant of a market on Friday and a four-day fair around the feast of SS Philip and James (1 May);[23] the new market day replaced the existing one but later that century the fair was still being held in August rather than at the new date.[24]

Markets

An inquisition appointed to find out if the market established in 1253 was harming markets near by at Gloucester and Newnham concluded in 1258 that it fitted well into the pattern of local trade, as Welsh cattle dealers could circulate between the markets at Ross-on-Wye on Thursdays, Gloucester on Saturdays and Wednesdays, Newnham on Sundays, and Newent. The Newent market was said to receive the corn formerly carried from the surrounding area to Gloucester.[25] The town proved capable of carving out for itself a sufficient trading area between those of Gloucester and Ledbury and was probably a major factor in the demise of an older market at Dymock. In 1291 the tolls taken by the lords of Newent manor from the market and fair produced on average £5 a year.[26] There was evidently a

---

1 GDR wills 1674/112; GA, D 1810/4, deed 30 Apr. 1663.
2 TNA, PROB 11/445, ff. 181v.–182; PROB 11/536, ff. 186–8; GA, P 225/IN 1/2, burials 1683, baptisms 1699, 1702.
3 GA, EL 148 (lease 10 Nov. 1733). See above, manors (Newent manor: Newent priory and the Court Ho.).
4 GA, P 225/IN 1/2, burials 1683, 1687–8, 1691; *Glouc. Apprentices Reg. 1595–1700*, p. 221.
5 GA, P 225/IN 1/2, passim.
6 Bigland, *Glos.* II, 245.
7 Rudder, *Glos.* 562.
8 GA, P 225/IN 1/2, baptisms 1766, burials 1766.
9 Rudder, *Glos.* 562.
10 GA, P 225/IN 1/2, baptisms 1687, 1690, 1711, 1718, marriages 1705.
11 *Pigot's Dir. Glos.* (1830), 382.
12 Herefs. RO, E 12/G/2, ct. papers 1583, 1618, 1620.
13 TNA, HO 107/1960; RG 11/2526.
14 Herefs. RO, E 12/G/7, ct. papers 1611, 1618–19.
15 Smith, *Men and Armour*, 61, 63–4.
16 *Glouc. Apprentices Reg. 1595–1700*, 75, 77, 83, 94.
17 GA, D 185/IV/35.
18 Ibid. P 225/IN 1/2, passim; and for the Bowers and Whites, also GDR wills 1680/169; 1698/212; 1727/387; *Univ. Brit. Dir.* IV, 62; Bigland, *Glos.* II, 250.
19 GA, D 2263/8–11; DA 30/100/11, p. 241.
20 Date and inits. on adjoining bldg.
21 *Rot. Litt. Claus.* II, 132.
22 *Cal. Chart.* 1226–57, 435.
23 Ibid. 1300–26, 206.
24 Herefs. RO, E 12/G/5, acct. roll 19 Ric. II; G/2, acct. roll 22 Edw. IV.
25 BL, Add. MS 18461, f. 60 and v.
26 *Tax. Eccl.* 171.

falling off in the volume of trade later in the Middle Ages: the tolls from the fair produced 20*s.* in the year 1394–5[1] and those of both market and fair only 10*s.* in 1481–2 and 29*s.* in 1505–6, over and above the cost of stationing men, presumably toll collectors, at the entrances to the town at fair time.[2]

About 1775 the Newent market was said to suffer from the poor state of the local roads.[3] Bad roads appear, however, to have been to some extent a protection to its trade, for, according to another writer, the improvements made by turnpike trusts in the early 19th century ruined it by laying it open to competition from Gloucester, where local farmers now found it practical to go on market days.[4] No doubt smaller producers and market customers were also finding the trip more practicable in 1822 when three carriers ran from Newent to Gloucester on its two market days; one of the carriers also ran to Ross-on-Wye on its market day.[5] The Newent market was described as very small in 1830,[6] and by 1870 it was being held only once a month, mainly for the sale of livestock.[7] The opening of the railway link with Gloucester in 1885 reduced the amount of stock brought to Newent for sale,[8] though the market still produced £20 a year in tolls in 1902[9] and its meetings were increased again, to once a fortnight, before 1910. It apparently continued on that basis until the Second World War.[10]

From the 13th century the market was held south of the Newent priory precinct in the central part of the town's main thoroughfare, where there was probably once a larger open area than the small market place that later survived in the entrance to Bury Bar Lane. Market trading apparently extended into the west part of Church Street where there was a row of selds *c.*1315. Part of the building called the boothall, standing by the priory gate on the north side of the market place, was presumably used for trade in the Middle Ages,[11] and before 1625 a separate market house was built. That was replaced in 1668 by a new building on a different site, at the north end of the market place.[12] The open, arcaded lower floor of the new market house was used mainly for the sale of butter in the late 18th century,[13] while the room above was used for town meetings. The building was in a dilapidated state by 1864 when the lord of the manor, R.F. Onslow, restored and enlarged it.[14] In the 1870s Onslow moved livestock sales from the market place to a cattle market, fitted with iron pens, on an adjoining site further along Bury Bar Lane.[15] At the sale of the manor estate in 1913 the auctioneer James Clark bought the rights to the market and tolls. The following year he sold the market house to two sons of Henry Bruton (d. 1894) of Gloucester, an auctioneer who had begun his business in Newent, and they donated it to the parish council in his memory.[16] In 1944 G.H. Smith sold the remaining rights and assets of the market to a committee formed to build a war memorial hall for the town; it conveyed the market place to Newent Rural District Council[17] and, some years later, built the hall on part of the old cattle market site.

Fairs

By the start of the 18th century a total of four fairs were held at Newent, on the Wednesday before Easter, the Wednesday before Whitsun, 1 August, and the Friday after 8 September; according to one account, the two spring fairs had been granted by Henry VIII and the two summer fairs granted (presumably confirmed in the case of the August fair) by James I.[18] Newent's four annual fairs apparently did a modest amount of trade in 1735 when Thomas Foley granted a 21-year lease of his tolls, together with a small farm at Malswick, at a total annual rent of £32 10*s.*[19] In the 1760s they dealt mainly in cattle, horses, and cheese, and the September fair was a sheep sale; the calendar change of 1752 had altered the day of the last to the Friday after 19 September and the August fair to 12 August.[20] The fairs were held in the streets of the north part of the town in the 18th century when New Street had the alternative name of the Beast Fair[21] and Crown Hill, the adjoining part of the Ross road, was sometimes known as the Horse Fair.[22] Later, however, horse sales were held a bit further out of town, in a field in the angle of the Ross road and the lane leading to Oxenhall (Horsefair Lane).[23] In the mid 19th century the fair on 12 August was apparently the principal one, doing a good trade in sheep and horses,[24] but the September fair was the only one that survived

---

1 Herefs. RO, E 12/G/5, acct. roll 19 Ric. II.
2 Ibid. G/2, acct. rolls 22 Edw. IV, 22 Hen. VII.
3 Rudder, *Glos.* 562.
4 Fosbrooke, *Glouc.* 213.
5 *Pigot's Dir. Glos.* (1822–3), 62.
6 Ibid. (1830), 382.
7 *Kelly's Dir. Glos.* (1870), 604.
8 J. Douglas, *Hist. Notes of Newent with Oxenhall and Pauntley* (1912), 9.
9 GA, D 1882/5/3.
10 *Kelly's Dir. Glos.* (1910), 258; (1939), 271; see below.
11 Above, settlement (development of Newent town).
12 GA, D 412/Z 3, Nourse MS, pp. 6–7, 10; GDR wills 1625/122.
13 GA, D 412/Z 3, Nourse MS, p. 10; D 602, where it was called the butter cross in 1777.

14 *Kelly's Dir. Glos.* (1870), 604; (1889), 848.
15 Douglas, *Notes of Newent*, 9; OS Map 1:2,500, Glos. XVII.14 (1902 edn).
16 GA, P 225A/PC 4/3.
17 Ibid. DA 30/100/15, pp. 313, 316, 322.
18 Atkyns, *Glos.* 568; Bodleian, Top. Glouc. c. 3, f. 139v.
19 GA, EL 148 (lease 26 May 1735).
20 *Glouc. J.* 2 Apr., 28 May, 30 July, 3 Sept. 1764 (the August fair was advertised for the 10th that year, the 12th falling on a Sunday).
21 GA, D 2957/212/136; D185/IV/38.
22 Rudder, *Glos.* 562; and for the Horse Fair, see also TNA, 107/1960 (entry for the union workhouse).
23 GDR, T 1/126 (no 1011).
24 GA, D 412/Z 3, Newent notes, 1900.

by the end of the century when onions, brought from the Vale of Evesham, were an important commodity sold at it.[1] The Onion Fair, as it became known, was revived in the late 20th century as a pleasure fair.[2]

DISTRIBUTIVE AND SERVICE TRADES

The economy of Newent town in the Middle Ages was typical of small inland market centres, with a predominance of tradesmen supplying foodstuffs and basic crafts to the surrounding area. Townspeople listed in rentals of 1278 and c.1315 included those surnamed cordwainer, glover, skinner, tailor, smith, hooper, tiler, carpenter, wheelwright, cook, baker, butcher, mustard seller, and mercer.[3] In 1297 a group of men attempting to secure from Cormeilles abbey greater powers for the town court included four bakers, two cordwainers, a cook, a brewer, and a tailor, and, representing Newent's cloth-making industry, a weaver and a dyer.[4] For commodities not available locally the town looked to Gloucester, to which in 1258 dealers were said to go for products such as salt, fish, and leather[5] and through which John Anketil, a Newent man trading in wine in 1287, presumably got his supplies.[6] The purchase of items for local distribution was probably the business of the group of Newent men who traded regularly in Gloucester's markets in the late 14th century.[7] Eels and herrings were sold in Newent in the 1360s,[8] and in 1500 at least five townspeople retailed fish.[9] The processing and sale of meat, probably connected with the Welsh cattle trade mentioned in 1258, was long a major occupation of the town. In 1323 17 Newent men were presented for infringing the assize of meat,[10] and as many as 10 butchers were regularly presented for the same in the early 15th century.[11] Fourteen men had infringed the assize of bread in 1333,[12] though later the bakers feature in the presentments in more modest numbers. Larger numbers were engaged in the brewing and selling of ale, often a trade for women: in 1367 22 people were described as ale sellers or alehouse keepers, in 1408 11 as brewers and 14 as alehouse keepers, and in 1527 17 as brewers.[13] The numbers involved in the presentments indicate that large volumes of staple foodstuffs were produced for surrounding villages and hamlets rather than for the town alone.

In the early modern period, while manufacturing activities gave Newent parish as a whole a varied economic character, for Newent town its role as a provider of foodstuffs and minor crafts and services to its area remained the defining characteristic. In the early 18th century one account said that its trade depended chiefly on its markets and fairs[14] and another described its 'manufacture' as that carried on by such as tanners, tailors, shoemakers, blacksmiths, innkeepers, and butchers.[15] About 1775 its business was defined as the supply of 'common necessaries' to surrounding villages.[16] Apart from the cloth workers, millers, and tanners mentioned above, the muster roll of 1608 listed 47 tradesmen and craftsmen in the town, including 8 shoemakers, 7 tailors, 6 butchers, and 5 smiths. Inhabitants of the outlying parts of the parish at that time included 3 smiths, 2 carpenters, and a cooper.[17] A similar trading character is revealed in the parish registers of the late 17th century and the early 18th, where almost all the male parishioners mentioned are identified by trade. In the 1680s some 190 men pursued 46 different occupations and, apart from those engaged in cloth working and tanning, the largest categories were shoemakers (29), butchers (24), carpenters (11), blacksmiths (9), and tailors (9).[18] The number of butchers reflects the town's role in supplying meat beyond its immediate area. About 1725 it was recorded that Newent butchers attended markets at Gloucester, Ledbury, Ross, and Mitcheldean and claimed to slaughter twice as many animals as did the butchers of Gloucester.[19] The building trades were represented chiefly by the carpenters and by a few thatchers in the late 17th century; men described as masons became more numerous in the first few decades of the next century but were probably mostly builders in brick rather than stone.[20] A handful of tradesmen of a more specialist character recorded at the period included two gunsmiths, a clockmaker, a locksmith, a pewterer, and a millwright.[21]

The town also offered scope for a wealthier class of

---

1 *Kelly's Dir. Glos.* (1889), 848.
2 *Glos. Life*, Jan. 1974, 21; *Chapters in Newent's History*, 51.
3 BL, Add. MS 15668, f. 7; 18461, ff. 98–105v.
4 Herefs. RO, E 12/G/2, cts. (1 June) 25 Edw. I, (22 Nov.) 26 Edw. I.
5 BL, Add. MS 18461, f, 60.
6 TNA, JUST 1/278, rot. 58d.; he was the highest rent-payer in the town in 1278: BL, Add. MS 15668, f. 7.
7 *VCH Glos.* IV, 47.
8 Herefs. RO, E 12/G/1 ct. (12 Oct.) 40 Edw. III; G/2, cts. (4 Mar.) 36 Edw. III, (11 Mar.) 37 Edw. III.
9 Ibid. G/4, ct. (31 Mar.) 12 Hen. VII.
10 Ibid. G/1, ct. (5 Oct.) 17 Edw. II.
11 e.g. ibid. G/1, cts. (6 Nov, 20 Feb., 18 Apr.) 11 Hen. IV, 2 Nov. 3 Hen. V; G/2, cts. 29 Apr., (6 Aug.) 6 Hen. IV; G/3, ct. 27 Apr. 9 Hen. IV.
12 Ibid. G/3, ct. (10 Sept.) 7 Edw. III.
13 Ibid. G/1, cts. (14 Oct.) 41 Edw. III, (Oct.) 19 Hen VIII; G/3, ct. 27 Apr. 9 Hen. IV.
14 Bodleian, Top. Glouc. c. 3, f. 140.
15 GA, D 412/Z 3, 'MS no II'.
16 Rudder, *Glos.* 562.
17 Smith, *Men and Armour*, 60–4.
18 GA, P 225/IN 1/2.
19 Ibid. D 412/Z 3, 'MS no II'.
20 Ibid. P 225/IN 1/2, passim.
21 Ibid. baptisms 1682, burials 1683, 1686; GDR wills 1686/209; *Glouc. Freemen Reg. 1641–1838*, p. 57; Bigland, *Glos.* II, 250.

retailer in the late 17th and 18th century. The mercers and chandlers William Nelme (d. 1702),[1] Acton Woodward (*fl.* 1686, 1714) and his son Acton (d. 1718),[2] and Edward Morse (d. 1759) and his son J.N. Morse were dealers in and mortgagees of property both in the town and the surrounding area.[3] Among the professions two or three surgeons and apothecaries were usually practising in the town in the 18th century, including several members of the Richardson family.[4] An attorney mentioned in 1713[5] is the sole representative of the legal profession recorded in the early 18th century, but *c.*1792 five attorneys were based in the town.[6] The number at the latter date presumably reflected the extra business promised by the schemes for the canal, coalfield, and Newent spa; when the attorney Matthew Paul died in 1801 two men competed to succeed to his practice.[7]

Although the prospects for development and expansion in the late Georgian period were largely unfulfilled and some parts of its marketing role were assumed by Gloucester, Newent town remained a busy centre during the 19th century. In 1851 151 of the heads of households enumerated in the town were engaged in trades and crafts, usually on a small scale. The largest employers were a builder with 10 men at work for him, a fell monger and woolstapler with 8, and a master carpenter with 6. Shoemakers (24), carpenters (12), and tailors (11) formed the largest groups, and there was a range of retailers such as grocers, drapers, and ironmongers but no shops dealing in luxury items. Only four townsmen were butchers, indicating that the trade was by then confined to supplying only the town and its immediate area. The canal provided little direct employment – in 1851 only a barge owner, a wharfinger, and a few watermen lived in the town or at Almshouse Green in Malswick[8] – but the main cargo it carried kept in business a number of coal merchants in the early 19th century. Two surgeons and two firms of solicitors were in business in the 1820s; the principal solicitors, occupying most of the official posts, were the partners Oliver Ainsworth and Thomas Cadle. Four solicitors working in Newent in 1851 included Edmund Edmonds,[9] an influential figure until 1872 when the circumstances of his wife's death ruined his reputation.[10] Newent's first bank appears to have been a branch of the Gloucestershire Banking Co. opened in 1866;[11] earlier, banking was no doubt one of the services provided by Gloucester. The larger of the outlying hamlets of the parish, Kilcot, Gorsley, Clifford's Mesne, and Brand Green, had men pursuing basic rural trades and crafts, such as blacksmiths, masons, carpenters, wheelwrights, and hauliers, until the mid 20th century, as well as one or two shopkeepers. Blacksmiths and carpenters were also to be found in some smaller hamlets, including Botloe's Green.[12]

Locally-based trades and crafts continued to provide the livelihood of the majority of the working population of Newent town up to the mid 20th century, when people began to commute to work in Gloucester and, in the 1970s, also to the Rank Xerox factory at Mitcheldean. Its character as a dormitory town for workers in Gloucester and also Cheltenham became more marked with the addition of large new housing estates in the late 20th century,[13] though some local employment was provided by the development of a business park on the Gloucester road, east of the town, from 1993;[14] manufacturers of double-glazing, security doors, and computer software were among firms that established themselves at the site. Another small development comprised a group of office buildings with geodesic domes on Cleeve Lane. The growth in the town's population preserved its main thoroughfare as a shopping street at the beginning of the 21st century, with over 40 small shops remaining in 2007, together with a supermarket opened in 2000[15] and a range of other businesses including four public houses, two banks, and two firms of solicitors.

---

1 TNA, PROB 11/470, ff. 92–3; Bigland, *Glos.* II, 247; GA, P 225/IN 1/2, burials 1685, 1702.

2 GA, D 365/T 1; D 892/T 57, deeds 1703, 1714; GDR wills 1703/17; 1718/21; Bigland, *Glos.* II, 245.

3 GA, D 892/T 57, deed 1715; GDR wills 1760/107; Bigland, *Glos.* II, 248.

4 GA, P 225/IN 1/2, burials 1728, 1745, baptisms 1747; ibid. IN 1/3, burials 1795; *Glouc. J.* 30 Mar. 1756; *Univ. Brit. Dir.* IV, 62; Bigland, *Glos.* II, 241, 248.

5 GA, P 225/IN 1/2, baptisms 1713.

6 *Univ. Brit. Dir.* IV, 62.

7 *Glouc. J.* 28 Sept. 1801.

8 TNA, HO 107/1960.

9 *Pigot's Dir. Glos.* (1822–3), 62; TNA, HO 107/350, 1960.

10 *Kelly's Dir. Glos.* (1856), 333; K.M. Tomlinson, 'A Country Tomb tells a Victorian True Story', *Trans BGAS* 113 (1995), 167–78.

11 *Kelly's Dir. Glos.* (1870), 605; *Chapters in Newent's History*, 78.

12 *Kelly's Dir. Glos.* (1856 and later edns), s.v. Newent and (from 1897) Gorsley with Clifford's Mesne; TNA, HO 107/1960; RG 11/2526.

13 *Glos. Life and Countryside*, Apr.–May 1967, 21, 23; *Glos. Life*, Jan. 1974, 21.

14 'Archaeological Review 1993', *Trans. BGAS* 112 (1994), 209; 'Archaeological Review 1996', ibid. 115 (1997), 290.

15 Information from Mrs D.M.A. Rosser, town clerk of Newent.

LOCAL GOVERNMENT

MANORIAL AND BOROUGH GOVERNMENT

Despite the creation of the town and the granting of liberties to its inhabitants by Cormeilles abbey, the Newent manor court retained a paramount position against the townspeople's wish for greater independence in the late 13th century. Although manor courts were also held for Boulsdon and Kilcot in the late 18th and early 19th century, the courts of the smaller manors of the parish, including that for Okle Clifford held by the prior of Llanthony once a year in 1516,[1] probably lapsed at an early date when those manors lost their few tenants. For Carswalls no court had probably been held for many years before 1806 when its owner Sir George Pauncefote was concerned to find the Foleys' steward unaware that he had any manorial rights.[2]

The Middle Ages

It was presumably from the time of the royal grant of a market at Newent in 1253 that Cormeilles abbey allowed its tenants in the principal settlement of the parish separate liberties from those of its tenants elsewhere in the manor. The granting of those liberties appears to have been in piecemeal awards to individuals rather than in a comprehensive charter enfranchising all the townspeople. That procedure resulted in part from the fact that the new market town had as its basis an established village, and probably also reflected the abbey's reluctance to allow the inhabitants too independent a status. In the abbey's records the town is consistently designated 'the market town of Newent'.[3] The term 'borough' is first found recorded in 1384,[4] after the abbey had relinquished all rights in the lordship, and the first reference found to the townspeople as 'burgesses' is in 1464.[5] Some holdings in the town were styled 'burgages' in the 13th century, but later, until the end of the 14th, that term was rarely, if ever, used.[6]

A rental of the town, compiled within 20 or 30 years after the market grant, lists *c*.70 holdings, of which 16 are described as burgages and most of the others as cottages. The former were presumably new or newly-enfranchised tenements, while the latter, some of which were held for lives or at will and 30 of which owed agricultural work in the hay harvest, were presumably tenements of earlier, purely manorial, origin. Most of the holdings, both burgages and non-burgages, owed annual rents of 1*s*. or 2*s*.,[7] and four burgages granted to new tenants in 1286 owed 2*s*.[8] In later grants of houses and building plots, however, the lords required a greater monetary return: among 137 houses listed in the town *c*.1315, 32, mainly situated on the market or in other central areas, owed rents of between 3*s*. and 14*s*.[9] Some houses in the town remained on tenures for lives until the 1290s or later when they were upgraded by charter to tenure by heredity.[10] By *c*.1315 almost all were heritable and held by a form of tenure that was described as 'according to the manner and custom of the town' but also as '*per bill(etum) abbatis mutabilem*', suggesting that the terms were changeable at the will of the abbot. The obligations owed to the lord under that tenure were service as catchpoll and ale-taster, custody of prisoners at the tenant's own cost, apprehending thieves and (in some cases) conveying them to the county gaol at Gloucester, suit of court and mill, and payment of fines under the assizes of bread and ale, toll on the brewing of ale, entry fines, heriots, and mortuaries (the last to the abbey in its role as rector of Newent). In addition 30 or so houses were still required to provide a man to work in the hay harvest with a pitchfork or rake.[11]

Courts In the 1290s the townspeople attempted to assert a degree of independence from the lord and emphasize their separate status within the manor. In 1297 20 townsmen refused their suit to the manor court, known usually as 'the great court', claiming that they should answer only to a separate court held for the market town and at the summons of the town bailiff rather than the hayward of the manor. The steward presiding decided that minor matters between inhabitants of the town might be dealt with in the town court but more serious matters should come before the great court. A jury of suitors, who were probably free tenants from the rural parts of the manor, also gave a judgement asserting the supremacy of the great court: all inhabitants of the town should answer there in all matters affecting the rights of the lord and reply there to anyone who

---

1 *Cal. Regs. Priory of Llanthony*, p. 140.
2 GA, D 245/I/23, letters 22, 24 Nov. 1806.
3 e.g. BL, Add. MS 18461, f. 98; Herefs. RO, E 12/G/1, ct. (14 Oct.) 12 Edw. III; G/2, cts. (1 June) 25 Edw. I, (19 July) 26 Edw. I.
4 Herefs. RO, E 12/G/1, ct. (28 Dec.) 8 Ric. II.
5 Ibid. G/1, ct. I Oct. 4 Edw. IV.
6 The term is not used in a rental of *c*.1315: BL, Add. MS 18461, ff. 98–105v.
7 Ibid. 15668, ff. 41v.–43.
8 Herefs. RO, E 12/G/3, ct. (12 Jan.) 14 Edw. I.
9 BL, Add. MS 18461, ff. 98–105v.
10 Ibid. f. 104; Herefs. RO, E 12/G/2, ct. (1 June) 25 Edw. I.
11 BL, Add. MS 18461, ff. 98–105v. (for recital of services, see tenement of Adam Barnot at f. 98).

brought suit against them. The dissidents admitted their guilt and were fined, but there was further unrest in the following year when some townsmen refused their obligation to guard prisoners.[1] Later in 1298 the abbot of Cormeilles granted charters of three tenements in the town and, mindful of recent events, in them reserved his right to call the two courts together in joint session and, if he thought it desirable, overrule in the great court any judgements made in the town court. He also reserved to himself the right to appoint the town officers, specified as a catchpoll, serjeants, and ale-tasters.[2] In 1307 the great court, as if to emphasize its primacy in manor and town, was styled 'the court of the out-dwellers and in-dwellers (*curiam forincecorum et intrinsecorum*)';[3] by 1322 it had reverted to its former style.[4]

In the 1360s the town court convened for two or three sessions a year under the style of *curia intrinseca*.[5] In the late 15th century, styled variously as the portmoot, 'the little court of the town', or 'the court of the bailiff of the borough and his burgesses', it held one or two sessions a year. Its business, which included hearing pleas of trespass and debt, enforcing the assizes of bread and ale and other regulations on tradesmen, and maintaining the town streets, duplicated in many ways that of the great court and view of frankpledge held for both town and manor, but it never seems to have challenged again the great court, which maintained its supremacy, in particular as the venue for the election of the officers of the town. The last record found of the town court was in 1482[6] and it had almost certainly expired by the mid 16th century. A single record survives of a court of pie-powder, convened on a market day (Friday) in 1376 over a matter of two oxen taken as distraint and released from the pound by the owner.[7]

In the late 13th century the great court[8] usually met in ordinary session once a month, but, as later, there were probably two or three other sessions when it exercised frankpledge jurisdiction. In the early 15th century there were usually two or three ordinary sessions a year and views of frankpledge in spring and autumn, and by the end of that century only two sessions a year for all of the court's business. That business included civil pleas, tenurial matters such as admissions and payment of entry fees by new heirs or assignees of town houses, grants of customary tenements in the manor, and enforcement of the obligations owed by all classes of tenant, road maintenance, the election of officers for both town and the rural tithings of the manor, and, at its frankpledge sessions, presentments by the officers of tradesmen's offences, bloodshed, and affray. In the early 15th century the court was also collecting annual payments of 4*d.* each from certain individuals for the right of trading toll-free in the town,[9] presumably regular market traders who were not eligible by right of holding houses in the town. In 1326 the great court defended its jurisdiction against the Botloe hundred court, where one tenant had impleaded two others,[10] and in 1415 it took action against a man who entered the manor to make an arrest without warrant.[11]

Apart from view of frankpledge and assize of bread and ale, the franchises that the abbot of Cormeilles exercised within the manor included infangthief.[12] That right (to execute justice on thieves taken with the stolen goods) was enforced through the great court in 1319.[13] According to local tradition the gallows stood at a place called Woeful hill, by the Ross road north of the Conigree,[14] which, apart from being on the main road out of the town, probably marked the boundary between the Newent manor liberty and Kilcot manor.[15] In 1287 Newent priory was apparently claiming the right to have its own prison on the manor,[16] though the duties of the town tenants listed *c.*1315 show that thieves (at least those not taken with the goods) were expected to be conveyed to the county gaol.

Officers The officers annually elected for Newent town in the great court in the 1320s were a catchpoll and two ale-tasters. The former is clearly the officer who is later styled bailiff of the town. His duties included presenting in the court affrays leading to bloodshed or the raising of the hue and cry and offenders against the assize of bread. In 1366 the court disciplined the bailiff for failing to weigh bread sold in the town and, at the same time, the ale-tasters for failing in their office. In 1344 the town bailiff and ale-tasters were elected at the October frankpledge court by the townspeople, showing a considerable advance in their freedoms since 1298 when the abbot reserved the appointments as his prerogative. By 1423 the court was also electing two carnells to enforce fair

---

1 Herefs. RO, E 12/G/2, ct. roll 25–6 Edw. I.
2 BL, Add. MS 18461, ff. 74v.–75v.
3 Herefs. RO, E 12/G/1, ct. (15 June) 35 Edw. I.
4 Ibid. G/3, ct. (26 Nov.) 13 Edw. II.
5 Ibid. G/1, ct. roll 37–8 Edw. III; G/2, ct. roll 35–7 Edw. III.
6 Ibid. G/2, ct. (23 Sept.) 13 Edw. IV; ibid. acct. roll 22 Edw. IV; G/3, ct. (26 Sept.) 14 Edw. IV.
7 Ibid. G/3, ct. (25 July) 50 Edw. III.
8 What follows, on the court and officers, is based generally on the court rolls in Herefs. RO, E 12/G/1–4 and GA, D 421/M 80/1–3.
9 Herefs. RO, E 12/G/1, cts. 6 Nov. 11 Hen. IV, 2 Nov. 3 Hen. V.
10 Ibid. ct. (15 Jan.) 19 Edw. II.
11 Ibid. ct. 2 Nov. 3 Hen. V.
12 *Plac. de Quo Warr.* 263. See BL, Add. MS 15668, ff. 1v., 69.
13 Herefs. RO, E 12/G/3, ct. (26 Nov.) 13 Edw. II.
14 GA, D 412/Z 1, notes on Boulsdon and Kilcot, *c.*1725; Rudder, *Glos.* 564.
15 Above, introd. (boundaries and divisions).
16 TNA, JUST 1/278, rot. 58d.

trading by butchers, an office that was termed 'victual-taster' in the early 15th century when it also had responsibility for fishmongers. No further record has been found of the office of serjeant mentioned in 1298.[1] That office was perhaps served by the townspeople by a rota of houses, as may have been the case with the town watchmen mentioned in 1307.[2] From 1410, however, two constables were elected in the court annually, and by 1527 they had been joined by two men styled serjeants-at-mace.

In the late 13th century the men of Compton, Cugley, Malswick, and Newent tithings made presentments concerning the rural parts of the manor, and by the 1320s they elected a tithingman in the great court for each of their respective tithings. The officer for Newent tithing was elected by, and had responsibility for, the small number of customary tenants who lived within the bounds of that tithing in or adjoining the town.[3] From the 1440s a fifth tithingman, for Boulsdon, also appeared in the court. He presumably represented only a few tenants within that tithing who owed suit to Newent manor, and his presentment usually stated that all was well (*omnia bene*).[4] A bailiff of the manor also occasionally appeared in the court to report on tenurial matters[5] and is presumably the same officer who accounted annually for the whole manor, both town and rural areas, in the late Middle Ages.[6]

From the Mid Sixteenth Century

In the late 16th century and the early 17th the Newent manor court continued to meet in two annual sessions in April and October as a joint view of frankpledge and court baron. Tenurial matters, such as grants of copyholds and enforcement of the payment of chief rents by freeholders, provided much of its business. Among its other concerns were nuisances, encroachments on the waste land of the manor, and householders taking in lodgers without giving security against their becoming chargeable to the parish. In 1579 the absence of a pillory and cucking-stool was presented, a lack which had not been remedied 30 years later. The officers for the town, elected at the October court, were the bailiff, two constables, who were now responsible for presenting affrays and bloodshed, two serjeants-at-mace, and two carnells. By 1617 there were also two men styled sealers, or searchers, of leather. The five tithingmen continued to be elected for each of the tithings where the manor had tenants. The office of town bailiff had acquired greater stature: his name headed the list of presentments at the court, and some who served were, as well as having property in the town, prominent local landowners, for example Thomas Hooke of Crooke's Farm, in Pauntley, in 1581 and Randall Dobyns of Walden Court in 1622.[7] In the 1630s the bailiff was ex officio a trustee of the town's almshouse charity.[8]

No further records of the court have been found until 1777 when one annual session was held in October, as continued to be the case until 1822 or later. The office of town bailiff had lapsed by the early 18th century, and the officers elected by the court in the late 18th century and the early 19th were two constables, who then had responsibility for the whole parish, one man as victual-taster and leather-sealer, the five tithingmen, and a hayward. The court dealt with the few small parcels that were still copyhold, but its main concern was unsanctioned encroachment on the greens and roadside waste.[9] The Foleys' agent, William Deykes, and their steward, Robert Hughes of Cheltenham, both regarded the court as vital in combating encroachments and in fixing its date went to considerable trouble to avoid local fair and market days which might cause poor attendance.[10]

Among the other manors of the parish, a manor court for Kilcot, which also claimed leet jurisdiction, was held at the Conigree in the early 18th century.[11] In the late 18th century and the early 19th when J.N. Morse was lord of Kilcot his court was much preoccupied with encroachments on the part of Gorsley common that belonged to the manor.[12] The Kilcot court convened at the Kilcot inn in the first decade of the 20th century, but whether it had had a continuous existence up to then or was a revival by the antiquarian-minded lord of the manor, Edward Conder, is not known.[13] For Boulsdon it was said in 1788 that a manor court had been continuously held and had appointed constables for the manor.[14] Then, and in 1806, encroachments on Clifford's Mesne and other waste of the manor provided the main business.[15]

PAROCHIAL GOVERNMENT

The early history of parish government is sparsely documented; many records were probably in a boxful of old papers burnt on the orders of the rector in 1877.[16] By the late 18th century, when overseers of

---

1 BL, Add. MS 18461, f. 75.
2 Herefs. RO, E 12/G/1, ct. (15 June) 35 Edw. I.
3 Ibid. G/3, ct. (6 Oct.) 13 Edw. II.
4 e.g. ibid. G/3, cts. 15 May, 10 Oct. 21 Hen. VI.
5 Ibid. G/1 ct. (26 Sept.) 8 Ric. II, (24 Jan.) 11 Hen. IV.
6 Ibid. G/2, acct. roll 22 Edw. IV; G/5, acct. roll 14 Ric. II.
7 Court papers and draft ct. rolls, in ibid. G/2, 4, 7–8.
8 GA, P 225/CH 1/1.
9 Ibid. D 245/I/13.
10 Ibid. I/19–20, 24.
11 Ibid. D 412/Z 1; ibid. Z 3, Nourse MS, p. 13.
12 Ibid. MI 1/1, f. 153 and passim; T 1.
13 Ibid. M 2.
14 Ibid. E 2, no 1.
15 Ibid. E 2, no 9.
16 Ibid. Z 3, Newent notes, 1900.

the poor and surveyors of the highways were being appointed for each of the parish's six tithings, poor relief was centralized and from 1815 road maintenance was also jointly administered. By the early 1830s the officers for the individual tithings were little more than rate collectors.

In 1768 the parish vestry drew up regulations for a workhouse[1] accommodated in a substantial house at Crown Hill at the north end of the town.[2] A management committee, comprising the vicar, the churchwardens, an overseer (presumably for the town), and six other inhabitants, was to supervise the workhouse and its master and two of its members to act as inspectors of the house. The vestry ruled in 1770 that no one was to receive weekly pay outside the house, though it continued to authorize one-off payments for nursing care, clothing, and other needs of individual paupers. The ban on out-relief was evidently lifted later under pressure of increasing numbers of poor. Under the system for financing the workhouse in place in 1784 the overseers of the five entirely rural tithings paid two thirds of the produce of their rates to the overseer of the town tithing for the workhouse, while retaining the other third for their casual poor. In 1792 paupers needed the sanction of the overseer of their home tithing before they were given relief by the town overseer.

The master of the workhouse, appointed at a salary of £10 a year in 1768, was required not only to direct the work of the paupers but also to teach their children to read and write and the girls also to sew and knit. In 1771 the vestry contracted with James Bamford of Gloucester to employ the poor for two years at spinning. Spinning and knitting seem to have remained the usual work performed in the house, though in 1819 some children were employed in heading pins.[3] In 1772 the vestry extended free instruction in reading, spinning, and knitting to children of poor families not in receipt of relief, and it bought 12 new spinning wheels for use in the house. Some able-bodied paupers were sent out of the house to do agricultural labour, which in 1772 included hop picking, and in 1819 some were employed on road repairs.[4] In 1816 the leading ratepayers agreed to institute the roundsman system of relief, taking turns to provide employment for six-day spells, but that was apparently a temporary expedient at a time of severe distress. Apprenticeships of pauper children to farmers and tradesmen were made regularly in the late 18th century, with as many as 22 placed out in 1788. In 1785 the vestry offered a monopoly of the supply of shoes for the paupers to any shoemaker who would employ two of them. Some apprenticeships were made with charity funds given for that purpose, and various pieces of parish land were also applied in support of the poor rates.

During the late 18th century ratepayers were often reluctant to attend vestry meetings and apply themselves to the task of parish government. In 1773 22 signed an undertaking to attend regularly on pain of a fine, and later there were several similar attempts to enforce attendance. At the close of the year ending Easter 1784, when the cost of relief at £671 had more than doubled since 1776,[5] the vestry appointed a new management committee to improve the situation: measures to be undertaken and enforced included the badging of the poor, the expulsion of vagrants from the town, a petition to the magistrates against granting licences for alehouses, and the reduction of the constables' expenses while on parish business. From 1798 an assistant overseer, first appointed at a salary of £25, administered all relief and managed the workhouse under the direction of two prominent ratepayers, one as visitor of the house and treasurer and the other as guardian of the poor. Under Joseph Hankins, owner and farmer of the Scarr, who served the former post from 1800 to 1816, that system seems to have been fairly successful in containing the cost of relief. In the year ending Easter 1803, when 108 paupers received permanent relief and 89 occasional relief, £1,247 was spent,[6] and in the year 1810–11 £1,159; expenditure rose to £1,369 in 1813–14, when 120 (including 68 inmates of the workhouse) received permanent relief and 24 occasional relief,[7] but it fell in the two next years to just over £1,000. During the next 20 years the cost was usually around £1,200, but a peak of £1,484 was reached in 1830–1.[8] In the severe winters of 1799–1800 and 1800–1 subscriptions were opened to run soup kitchens and subsidize the price of bread and other provisions to the poor. There were similar schemes in 1814 and 1830. In 1810, to circumvent profiteering by shopkeepers, Hankins bought a quantity of flour for resale to the poor at market price, the vestry agreeing to make up out of the rates any losses he incurred.

In the early years of the 19th century road repairs were managed by surveyors for the tithings, two acting for the town and Kilcot tithings and one each for Compton, Cugley, Malswick, and Boulsdon. In 1815 a general surveyor was appointed at a salary of £40; he was given overall control of repairs

---

1 The following account of poor relief is based on the vestry minutes for 1768–1818, in GA, P 225/VE 2/1.
2 Illustrated in T. Ward, *Around Newent* (Old Photographs Series, 1994), 23.
3 GA, P 225/VE 2/2.
4 Ibid.
5 *Poor Law Abstract, 1804*, 172–3.
6 Ibid.
7 Ibid. *1818*, 146–7.
8 *Poor Law Returns* (1830–1), 66; (1835), 65.

throughout the parish and received from the elected surveyors all the rates and money collected as composition for statutory road work.[1]

LOCAL GOVERNMENT AND PUBLIC SERVICES AFTER 1834

From 1835 Newent was the centre of a poor-law union comprising 18 parishes in Gloucestershire, Herefordshire, and Worcestershire.[2] Its workhouse became the union workhouse, though not bought from the parish until 1843,[3] and the union added a new range to the west side of the building in 1867–8.[4] The workhouse closed in 1918,[5] and in 1922 it was conveyed to the county education authority for use as a school.[6] In 1863 Newent became the centre of a highway board,[7] whose powers passed in 1899 to Newent Rural District Council.[8] Other roles that Newent played in the local administration of its north-western area of the county in the 19th and 20th centuries were as the centre of a petty sessional division[9] and, from 1846 to the late 1940s, of a county court district.[10]

The Newent rural district, formed in 1895, administered the union's fourteen Gloucestershire parishes and two Worcestershire parishes.[11] Its council met in the union workhouse but later had offices in Broad Street[12] and 1951 moved them to the former rectory house.[13] Its principal projects for Newent town were the provision of mains water in 1910, an improved sewerage scheme of 1965,[14] and substantial housing estates built between the mid 1950s and early 1970s.[15] It was dissolved in 1974 when Newent parish became part of the new Forest of Dean District.

The earliest schemes to provide public services for the town were initiated by the parish vestry, where disagreements between town and rural ratepayers sometimes hampered implementation. The Newent parish council formed in 1894 assumed the vestry's powers as the lighting and cemetery authority for the town.[16] Later it took responsibility for allotments, a recreation ground, and other public areas,[17] and, in 1914, became owner of Newent market house, where it held its meetings.[18] In 2007, under the style of Newent Town Council, it retained those responsibilities, apart from lighting, and also carried out street cleaning as agent for the district council. From 1983 a mayor of Newent, a purely honorary office, was elected annually.[19] In 2000 a separate parish council was established for the new civil parish of Gorsley and Kilcot.[20]

Water Supply

Newent town drew its water from numerous private wells, the right of access to which was often specified in title deeds and householders' wills.[21] In the early 1890s Gloucester corporation's plans to extract water locally were opposed by the parish vestry and the Newent union (in its role as a rural sanitary authority) from fear of damage to existing sources of supply.[22] When the works, comprising a pumping station beside the Ell brook in Oxenhall and a reservoir at Madam's wood at the east boundary of Newent, were opened in 1896[23] the newly-formed RDC became interested in tapping the supply but it was several years before a majority of Newent ratepayers agreed on a scheme. There was a complication in that some houses and farms on the Onslows' estate had been provided with a free piped supply under the agreement for building the works.[24] In 1907 the RDC reached agreement with the corporation for a supply to an area of 250 a. in and around the town. Laying the mains began in 1909 and was completed the following year. Initially most of the town was supplied from standpipes, only c.37 private houses paying to be connected.[25] Supplies to outlying parts of the parish, financed by the RDC but engineered by the city corporation, were provided after the Second World War, the mains to the Kilcot and Gorsley area being laid in 1954 and 1955.[26] The control of the supply passed from Gloucester corporation to the North-West

---

1 GA, P 225A/SU 2/1; VE 2/1, min. 8 Jan. 1815.
2 *Poor Law Com. 2nd Rep.* p. 523; above, Newent and May Hill (administration).
3 GA, P 225/VE 2/3, min. 22 Dec. 1842; G/NE 8A/4.
4 Ibid. G/NE 8A/11–12; Ward, *Around Newent*, 23.
5 GA, G/NE 8A/30.
6 Ibid. CE/M 2/16, pp. 116, 155. See below, social hist. (education: secondary schools).
7 GA, HB, catalogue.
8 Ibid. DA 30/100/6, p. 248.
9 *Glos. QS Archives*, 73; *Kelly's Dir. Glos.* (1856), 332; (1879), 710.
10 *Slater's Dir. Glos.* (1852–3), 146; GA, DA 30/100/17, p. 102.
11 GA, DA 30/100/5, pp. 1, 37, 57, 76; above, Newent and May Hill (administration).
12 *Kelly's Dir. Glos.* (1906), 254; (1939), 272.
13 GA, DA 30/100/18, p. 155; 100/19, pp. 8, 141, 187.
14 Below.

15 Above, settlement (development of Newent town: the 20th cent.).
16 GA, P 225A/PC 1/1, pp. 1, 24–6, 48.
17 Ibid. PC 1/1–6, passim.
18 Ibid. PC 1/2, pp. 250, 258.
19 Information from Mrs D.M.A. Rosser, town clerk.
20 *Millennium Memories: History of Gorsley and Kilcot*, ed. L. Hines (2001), 95.
21 e.g. GA, D 602, deed 1693; D 1998, deed 1695; GDR wills 1558/337; 1673/1; 1701/201; 1709/61.
22 GA, P 225/VE 2/4, min. 5 Apr. 1894.
23 *VCH Glos.* IV, 264; below, Oxenhall, introd. (landscape).
24 GA, P 225A/PC 1/2, p. 81; DA 30/100/8, pp. 189–90, 215, 312; 100/9, pp. 37, 130–1.
25 Ibid. DA 30/100/8, pp. 433–4; 100/9, pp. 20–1, 24, 107, 426, 446; 100/10, pp. 37–8.
26 Ibid. 100/23, pp. 61, 89, 250.

Gloucestershire Water Board in 1965 and to the Severn-Trent Water authority in 1974.[1]

Sewerage and Drainage

In 1866 the parish vestry drew up a scheme for a sewerage system for the town, with the intention of forming a 'special drainage district' under new legislation, but decided it was impractical to implement without a mains water supply to flush the sewers.[2] Proposals for a special drainage district were revived in 1870 but led to several months of argument over the limits of the area to be rated to the district; a threat from the Home Office to appoint an official to implement a scheme resolved the matter.[3] The laying of the sewers and the construction of basic outfall works by the Ell brook in Cleeve Lane were completed by 1875.[4] In 1895 the system was taken over by the RDC, which made improvements to it in 1913. The system long remained inadequate,[5] however, even after 1938 when a small works was constructed near the railway station just above Ell bridge to serve c.30 houses at the north end of the town.[6] Modern treatment works completed in 1965[7] on the opposite side of Cleeve Lane from the old works were enlarged in 1972. In 1974 the town's sewerage system passed to the Severn-Trent Water authority, which continued for some years to employ the Forest of Dean district council as its agent for maintaining the system.[8]

Surface drainage was another long-standing concern of the RDC in the 20th century. Peacock's brook tended to flood at the point where it passed through a culvert under Broad Street, and after the Second World War new building in the Culver Street and Watery Lane area threatened further problems in that part of the town. Measures to remedy the situation included improving the section of the brook south of the main street in 1955, the laying of a new drain in Watery Lane in the early 1960s, and the building of another from the main street to Newent Lake in the early 1970s.[9]

Gas Supply

The Newent Gas Light & Coke Co. formed in 1850 opened a small works on the east side of Watery Lane the following year.[10] The parish vestry appointed lighting inspectors, but a majority of ratepayers did not vote a rate to provide gas lamps in the town until 1852[11] and the limits of supply were left undetermined, as rural ratepayers objected to the inclusion of the whole parish.[12] In 1869 the company made a new contract with the inspectors to light 24 lamps in the town in the winter months.[13] In 1892, when it became a limited company, it constructed a second gasholder at its works, and a few years later it had 170 private customers in the town.[14] The vestry's lighting powers passed in 1895 to the parish council; the question of the area of supply was finally resolved at a parish meeting which decided on a radius of 50 chains around the market house.[15] The gas company was nationalized in 1949 as part of the South-West Gas Board. The Newent works closed c.1956 and from then the town was supplied by mains from Gloucester, though one of the gasholders remained in use until the advent of natural gas in the early 1970s.[16]

Electricity Supply

The Shropshire, Worcestershire, & Staffordshire Electric Power Co. acquired powers to serve Newent and adjoining parishes in 1930[17] and laid on supplies to the town the following year.[18] Electricity was brought to the outlying parts of the parish later in the century by the Midland Electricity Board: Brand Green and Pool Hill were connected in 1956[19] and Kilcot, Gorsley, and Clifford's Mesne in the early 1960s.[20]

Fire Service

The town had acquired a fire engine by 1820 when its maintenance was the churchwardens' responsibility.[21] In 1845 the vestry rented a building to house a new engine bought from the London firm of W.J. Tilley by subscription and set up a management committee.[22] In 1876 a new committee was formed of representatives of the ratepayers and insurance companies, but the service was still funded by subscription.[23] In 1885 the engine was operated and hauled to the site of fires by a voluntary brigade of nine men.[24] In 1893 the parish decided to make it the

---

1 *VCH Glos.* IV, 264.
2 GA, P 225/VE 2/3, mins. 3 Oct. 1866, 28 Jan. 1869.
3 Ibid. VE 2/4, mins. 1870–1.
4 Ibid. min. 19 Mar. 1875; *Chapters in Newent's History* (Newent Local Hist. Soc. 2003), 117.
5 GA, DA 30/100/10, pp. 79–80, 438, 241.
6 Ibid. 100/14, pp. 313, 344; 100/21, p. 139.
7 Ibid. 100/30, pp. 126–7; 100/33, pp. 218, 294.
8 *Chapters in Newent's History*, 118.
9 GA, DA 30/100/9, pp. 250, 259; 100/13, p. 218; 100/15, p. 138; 100/16, p. 80; 100/39, pp. 149, 152, 201.
10 *Chapters in Newent's History*, 119; OS Map 1/2,500, Glos. XVII.14 (1884 edn).
11 GA, P 225/VE 2/3, mins. 13, 17 June 1850, 23 Jan., 1 Sept. 30 Oct. 1851, 16 Sept. 1852.
12 Ibid. P 225A/PC 1/1, pp. 60–1.
13 Ibid. P 225/LW 1/1.
14 *Chapters in Newent's History*, 121.
15 GA, P 225A/PC 1/1, pp. 24–6, 60–1, 66–7, 81.
16 *Chapters in Newent's History*, 122.
17 GA, Q/RUm 666.
18 Ibid. P 225A/PC 1/4, pp. 80, 102.
19 Ibid. DA 30/100/25, p. 25.
20 Ibid. 100/31, p. 29; *Millennium Memories*, 22.
21 GA, P 225/CW 2/1.
22 Ibid. VE 2/3, mins. 22 Jan., 7 Feb., 23 Mar. 1845.
23 Ibid. VE 2/4, mins. 15, 29 Sept. 1876.
24 *Kelly's Dir. Glos.* (1885), 532.

responsibility of the lighting inspectors and finance it from their rates,[1] and the parish council ran the service from 1895[2] until 1940 when under wartime measures the RDC was charged with maintaining a brigade.[3] From 1948 the county fire service maintained a station, manned by a part-time crew, in the old cattle market,[4] and in 1962 a new fire and ambulance station was opened in Bridge Street.[5]

Other Services

A burial board for the parish formed in 1863 laid out a cemetery, including twin mortuary chapels and a sexton's lodge, on the west side of Watery Lane.[6] Management of the cemetery passed to the parish council in 1895.[7] Newent had no hospital, apart from a temporary building for infectious diseases provided by the RDC in Bury field south of the town and moved to Coldharbour Lane in Oxenhall in 1897.[8] A new health centre for the town was built in 1974 at the junction of Watery Lane and the main street.[9] From soon after the formation of the county police force in 1839 a small detachment, comprising in 1851 a sergeant and two constables, was based in the town. The police occupied various rented houses until 1878 when a police station and magistrates' court were built in Court Lane.[10] That remained in use until 1974 when the police moved to a new station beside the new health centre.[11] On an adjoining part of the site a new building for the Newent branch of the county library, formerly housed in part of the old rectory, opened in 1987.[12]

SOCIAL HISTORY

SOCIAL LIFE AND SOCIAL STRUCTURE

In the early Middle Ages Cormeilles abbey[13] dominated Newent as founder of its market town, chief lord of much of the parish, owner of a large demesne farm, and rector of the parish church. Its local administrators, the priors of Newent, were all or mostly Frenchmen from Normandy, including Simon of Moyaux (*fl.* 1241, 1253),[14] John of Moyaux (*fl.* 1260),[15] Simon of Goupillières (*fl.* 1277, 1298),[16] and William of Hacqueville (*fl.* 1303, 1311).[17] Possibly that contributed to tensions between the lords and their tenants in the late 13th century when the inhabitants of the town attempted to assert their separate status within the manor.[18] The priors remained in control of the manor as farmers after the outbreak of the wars with France, but in the early 15th century Newent passed to a new lord, Fotheringhay college, under whom more freedom and control was apparently given to manor and town officials.

Most of the post-medieval lords were not resident, though for the Winters of Lydney and their successors the Foleys of Stoke Edith, influential families in nearby parts of Gloucestershire and Herefordshire, Newent with its woodland and other assets formed an important part of their estates. In the Civil War the ownership of Sir John Winter, leader of the royalists in west Gloucestershire, put Newent in the royalist camp, and during 1643 and 1644 a force based in the town under Colonel Nicholas Min was among garrisons attempting to contain the parliamentarians at Gloucester.[19] Many Newent people had family and other connexions with the city and when Min's troops first arrived they met opposition, requiring conciliation by Winter's steward to defuse the situation.[20] Under the Foleys the day-to-day running of the manor estate was left to agents such as John Spicer, manager of the Ellbridge ironworks in the 1660s and 1670s,[21] and William Deykes, who served three successive owners for 50 years until his death in 1827.[22] The incumbents of Newent were often active figures in the community, among them John Foley (d. 1803) and Richard Onslow (d. 1849) who married into the Foley family.[23] The latter's son, Richard Foley

---

1 GA, P 225/VE 2/4, min. 13 Apr. 1893.
2 Ibid. P 225A/PC 1/1, p. 52.
3 Ibid. DA 30/100/15, p. 3.
4 Ibid. 100/17, p. 81; 100/21, p. 214.
5 'Newent, Past and Present' (Newent W.I., 1975: copy in GA, D 3295/II/5).
6 GA, P 225/VE 2/3, min. 26 Jan. 1863; P 225A/PC 3/7.
7 Ibid. P 225A/PC 1, p. 48.
8 Ibid. p. 99; DA 30/100/5, pp. 168–9, 226; 100/6, pp. 30, 50.
9 'Newent, Past and Present'.
10 J. Douglas, *Historical Notes of Newent with Oxenhall and Pauntley* (1912), 12; TNA, HO 107/1960.
11 'Newent, Past and Present'.
12 *Newent Official Guide* (*c.*1955: copy in GA, D 3168/4/8/15), 12; *Citizen*, 3, June 1987.
13 For the landowners mentioned in this section, above, manors.
14 BL, Add. MS 15668, ff. 55v., 61; 18461, ff. 121v., 130v.
15 Ibid. 15668, ff. 69, 70v.
16 Ibid. 18461, ff. 33, 63v., 65v.
17 Ibid. ff. 29v., 95v.
18 Above, local govt. (manorial and borough govt.).
19 *Bibliotheca Glos.* I, 68, 72–5, 86, 90–2.
20 GA, D 412/Z 3, Nourse MS, pp. 8–9.
21 Ibid. p. 3; TNA, E 134/20 Chas. II/East. 37.
22 TNA, PROB 11/1730, ff. 257–60v.; inscription on tomb in Newent churchyard.
23 Below, religious hist. (religious life in 17th and 18th cents.; religious life in 19th and 20th cents.).

Onslow, who succeeded to the manor estate in 1861, became Newent's first truly resident squire for many years. He enlarged one of its farmhouses, Stardens, as his own dwelling, was prominent as a local magistrate, and was master of a pack of harriers, which he kennelled in a building in Watery Lane.[1] Later in the 19th century Andrew Knowles, who became owner of Newent Court, the largest house in the parish, shared the role of squire with the Onslows. The sale and dispersal of both the Knowles and Onslow estates in the years 1910 to 1913 marked the end of the era of large landowners in Newent.

Throughout the centuries the lords of Newent manor were only the leading landowners among many; there were several families of minor gentry, with manorial estates, and a large body of freehold farmers. In 1522 of 151 people assessed in the parish for a military survey 40 had an assessment on land as well as goods. The wealthiest inhabitant was then Roger Porter,[2] who occupied a large house in the town's market place and probably had by then built up an estate with houses in the town and farms outside it that his family held for the next 100 years or so. As a lawyer and a man of influence beyond the parish, it was to Porter that the Newent parishioners turned for help c.1515 when contesting what they regarded as an unjust levy of tax.[3] The muster roll for 1608 reflects the diverse character of the large parish, with (of those whose status or occupation was given) 11 persons styled as gentlemen, 25 as yeomen, 18 as husbandmen, 60 as labourers, 20 as servants, and 90 as tradesmen of various kinds (64 in the town and adjoining parts of Newent tithing and the remainder in the rural tithings).[4] Among the gentry in the early modern period the families of Dobyns, Rogers, Woodward, Nourse, and Morse were prominent, and among the yeoman farmers, a class that was strengthened by the enfranchisement of copyholds and the general amalgamation of holdings, the Hartlands, Astmans, and Hankinses were represented for many generations.

Cottagers who established themselves around commons and greens on the fringes of the parish were a growing element. That was a process that the landowners generally sanctioned as long as their rights were acknowledged by the acceptance of leases at small reserved rents. The plots of land and orchard taken in around the cottages, together with the opportunities of working part-time in the local woodlands and doing harvest work and fruit picking on the farms, gave the settlers a life-style that was independent and often characterized as feckless.[5] Gorsley common, which attracted the largest body of settlers, was known sometimes as 'Heathen's Heath' before benefiting during the 19th century from the influence of a Baptist chapel and later an Anglican church.[6]

Newent town remained integrated institutionally with the large manor and parish and, having few wealthy inhabitants of its own, its administration tended to be dominated by the resident landowners and farmers of the rural tithings. At the rebuilding of the parish church in the 1670s the lead was taken by the landowners, whose status was underlined by their appropriating the most prestigious seating in the new church.[7] Poor relief, though centralized in a workhouse in the town from the 1760s, was also directed mainly by the landowners and leading farmers. In the 19th century and the early 20th the financing of public services for the town sometimes created tension between the townspeople and the rural ratepayers.[8] In the absence of many wealthy tradesmen or shopkeepers, professional men, doctors among them, often took the lead in the town's affairs.[9] The solicitor Edmund Edmonds gained a prominent position in the town's public life in the mid 19th century, with the result that his trial (and acquittal) in 1872 for the manslaughter of his wife attracted much sensational interest and revealed some of the jealousies and tensions of life in the small town.[10] Newent preserved its small-town character until the mid 20th century, when the addition of new housing estates began to have an impact. Gloucester city, which at less than eight miles away had long been a factor in the town's history as a provider of services, a competitor for agricultural market trade,[11] and a magnet for young men seeking apprenticeships,[12] loomed even larger as the employer of the bulk of the inhabitants. In the 1960s there was local concern that Newent was becoming merely a dormitory suburb[13] and the end of its administrative role as centre of a rural district in 1974 appeared as a further loss of identity. By the beginning of the 21st century the establishment of some light industry, the enlargement of its secondary school, and the provision of new community facilities had to some extent redressed the balance.

---

1 GA, D 412/Z 3, Newent notes, 1900; D. Bick, *Old Newent and District* (Newent, 1992), 2.
2 *Military Survey of Glos. 1522*, 51–3, 56–7.
3 TNA, REQ 2/2/153.
4 Smith, *Men and Armour*, 60–4.
5 Turner, *Agric. of Glos.* 50; *Glos. Chron.* 29 Aug. 1868 (letter); *1st Rep. Com. Employment in Agric.* app. II, pp. 126, 132.
6 *Millennium Memories: Hist. of Gorsley and Kilcot*, ed. L. Hines (2001), 20; *Chapters in Newent's History* (Newent Local Hist. Soc. 2003), 201.

7 Below, religious hist. (religious life in 17th and 18th cents.).
8 Above, local govt. (parochial govt.; local govt. and public services).
9 *Chapters in Newent's History*, 103–5; GA, D 2299/1059.
10 K.M. Tomlinson, 'A Country Tomb tells a Victorian True Story', *Trans. BGAS* 113 (1995), 167–78.
11 Above, econ. hist. (markets and fairs).
12 *Glouc. Apprentices Reg. 1595–1700*, passim.
13 *Glouc. J.* 14 Oct. 1967; *Glos. Life and Countryside*, Apr.–May 1967, 18–23.

Among Newent inhabitants who have achieved a more than local reputation was Timothy Nourse (d. 1699) of Southends Farm, theologian and writer.[1] His nephew and fellow-landowner Walter Nourse (d. 1743) compiled *c*.1725 a discursive but informative account of recent Newent events.[2] Revd John Lightfoot (1735–88), the son of a yeoman farmer of the parish, became a distinguished naturalist and the author of *Flora Scotica*. The composer Rutland Boughton (1878–1960), who enjoyed success with *The Immortal Hour* and other works in the 1920s, lived in his later years on a smallholding at Kilcot. Robert ('Joe') Meek (1929–67), who was born in Newent town, became known in the field of popular music for introducing experimental techniques to record production.[3]

Inns and Public Houses

In the late Middle Ages the town had numerous small alehouses, usually kept by women or as a sideline by minor tradesmen.[4] In 1596 eight men were indicted for keeping unlicensed alehouses,[5] and two years later a butcher and labourer were among those keeping ale- and cider-houses and allowing illegal games at them.[6] The King's Head adjoining the churchyard was at one time the principal inn of the town but by 1711 it had apparently closed.[7] In the late 18th century the George, on the opposite south side of Church Street, was regarded as the town's chief inn.[8] Following the improvement of the Ross road in the early 19th century, it became a posting-house and a stopping-place for Gloucester and Hereford coaches, as well as having an assembly room for balls and concerts, putting up commercial travellers, and providing the venue for the Newent court leet.[9] The only comparable establishment was the Red Lion, at the north-west corner of the market place. Recorded from 1776,[10] it was the only other public house accorded the status of an inn and posting-house in 1822.[11] In 1856 a main part of its trade was catering for commercial travellers and for farmers on market days,[12] and by 1870 it too had an assembly room for concerts and meetings.[13]

Among other public houses in the town, the Bull on the corner of Church Street and the market place had opened by 1702[14] and survived until *c*.1916.[15] Adjoining it on the south side, facing the market place, was the Royal Oak, open by 1719[16] and until the early 20th century.[17] North-east of the Bull, in Church Street, a public house called the Bell closed *c*.1779.[18] A house at the other end of Church Street became an inn, under the sign of the Black Dog, in the mid 19th century.[19] On the north-east side of Lewall Street (as that name was originally used) an inn called the Horseshoe opened in the late 17th century,[20] but before 1732 its sign moved to a house on the other side of the street that was replaced by the Congregational chapel in 1845.[21] At the corner of Lewall Street and Culver Street, an inn called the Black Swan changed its name to the Duke of Marlborough's Head in the early 18th century (presumably in the first decade); it closed before 1832, but by 1892 and until *c*.1917 part of the building on the same site was the Nag's Head inn.[22] On the west side of Culver Street an inn called the Pied Horse in 1726 later took the sign of the King's Head but closed before 1800.[23] In New Street the Crown, at the north end on the corner with the Ross road, was open by 1660[24] and until the mid 19th century.[25] In 1700 New Street also had an inn called the Lamb, whose site has not been identified.[26] The New inn on the west side of the street (at the house later called Noent House) had opened by 1891[27] but closed *c*.1915.[28] The King's Arms, on the north side of the Ross road, had opened by 1822,[29] and by 1861 and until the early 20th century there was a small public house called the Anchor on the west side of Bridge Street by the old canal.[30] Of the nine public houses that were open in the town in 1891,[31] the George, Red Lion, Black Dog, and King's Arms survived in 2007.

In the rural parts of the parish there were only a few public houses, though some of the hamlets no doubt had unnamed and unrecorded ale- or cider-

---

1 *Oxford DNB*.
2 GA, D 412/Z 3, Nourse MS.
3 *Oxford DNB*.
4 Above, econ. hist. (distributive and service trades).
5 BL, Harl. MS 4131, f. 484.
6 Ibid. f. 531.
7 GA, D 412/Z 3, Nourse MS, p. 11; D 917.
8 *Univ. Brit. Dir.* IV (1798), 61.
9 *Glouc. J.* 16 Nov. 1801; 8 Aug. 1825; *Pigot's Dir. Glos.* (1822–3), 62; *Slater's Dir. Glos.* (1852–3), 146.
10 *Glouc. J.* 29 Jan. 1776.
11 *Pigot's Dir. Glos.* (1822–3), 62.
12 *Kelly's Dir. Glos.* (1856), 332.
13 Ibid. (1870), 604.
14 TNA, PROB 11/470, f. 92.
15 T. Ward, *Around Newent* (Old Photographs Series, 1994), 70; GA, D 2299/1459.
16 GA, D 365/T 3; OS Map 1:2,500, Glos. XVII.14 (1884 edn).
17 *Licensed Houses in Glos. 1903*, 122.
18 GA, D 602.
19 Ibid. D 412/Z 3, Newent notes, 1900; *Kelly's Dir. Glos.* (1879), 711.
20 GA, D 412/Z 3, Nourse MS, p. 11; D 5570/2.
21 Ibid. D 412/Z 3, Newent notes, 1900; *Glouc. J.* 21 Mar. 1732.
22 GA, D 3403, deeds of former Black Swan inn 1723–1953; Ward, *Around Newent*, 45, 49.
23 GDR wills 1726/166; GA, D 5570/2.
24 GDR wills 1701/172.
25 GA, Q/SRh 1819B; *Glouc. J.* 8 Mar. 1725.
26 *Slater's Dir. Glos.* (1852–3), 146.
27 *Licensed Houses in Glos. 1891*, 140; Ward, *Around Newent*, 30.
28 GA, D 2299/1287.
29 *Pigot's Dir. Glos.* (1822–3), 62.
30 TNA, RG 9/1759; Ward, *Around Newent*, 22.
31 *Licensed Houses in Glos. 1891*, 140.

21. *Procession of members of the Ancient Order of Foresters in Broad Street c.1910*

houses. In Kilcot an inn called the Welsh Harp had opened on the Ross road 2 km west of the town by 1736.[1] It still bore that sign, possibly connected with Welsh cattle drovers using the route, in the early 19th century[2] but was more usually known as the Kilcot inn. A house standing by Gorsley ford, where the Ross road in its original course crossed the Ell brook, was known as Dun Cow and may have been an inn; it was burnt down before 1719.[3] On the Gloucester road south-east of the town, near the road junction at Almshouse Green, the Traveller's Rest public house had opened by 1841[4] and remained open in 2007. A public house called the Plough, to the north of Clifford's Mesne on the Newent road, was open for a short period in the late 19th century.[5] In 2007 Clifford's Mesne was served by the Yew Tree inn at the south side of hamlet, part of Aston Ingham (Herefs.) until the boundary change of 1965.

Clubs, Societies, and Public Meeting Places

Until the late 19th century the public houses provided the main meeting places in the town, among other things for its friendly societies: one met at the Bull in 1819 and another at the Red Lion in 1844.[6] From the 1860s until the early 20th century a branch of the Odd Fellows met at the Red Lion[7] and a branch of the Ancient Order of Foresters at the George.[8] Outside the town a friendly society met at the Kilcot inn from 1854 until 1878,[9] and at Clifford's Mesne in the early 1850s there were two societies, for men and women respectively.[10] The upper room in Newent's market house was used for a variety of official purposes both before and after 1914 when the building became the property of the town and parish.[11] The adjoining market place was the site of ox-roasts and public dinners to mark special events, such as the repeal of the cider tax in 1766[12] and the start of new reigns in 1820, 1830, and 1837; at the latter occasions there was particularly lavish ceremonial, perhaps promoted by the vicar Richard Onslow.[13] A bull-baiting ring adjoining the market house was in use until 1795 or later.[14] The Crown inn had a cockpit in 1725.[15]

Concerts of secular music at the chief inns appear to have been fairly frequent events in the late 18th

---

1 *Glouc. J.* 30 Nov. 1736.
2 GDR wills 1818/18; Bryant, *Map of Glos.* (1824).
3 GA, D 2957/212/131; GDR, T 1/126 (no 2107).
4 TNA, HO 107/350.
5 OS Map 6", Glos. XXIV.NW (1887 edn).
6 TNA, FS 2/3, Glos. nos 179, 291. See Fig. 21.
7 TNA, FS 2/3, Glos. no 739; FS 4/12, Glos. no 739.
8 Ibid. FS 2/3, Glos. no 877; Ward, *Around Newent*, 48.
9 TNA, FS 2/3, Glos. no 499; FS 4/12, Glos. no 291.
10 Ibid. FS 2/3, Glos. nos 457, 475.
11 Above, econ. hist. (markets and fairs); *Newent Official Guide* (*c.*1955: copy in GA, D 3168/4/8/15), 9–10.
12 *Glouc. J.* 14 June 1737; 14 July 1766.
13 GA, P 225/VE 2/2, mins. 6, 9 Feb. 1820, 4, 9 July 1830, June 1837.
14 Ibid. D 412/Z 3, Newent notes, 1900.
15 *Glouc. J.* 8 Mar. 1725.

century and early 19th. In 1818 a musical festival included concerts at the George and at the parish church.[1] Among the church congregation a concern for church music had long been evident. An organ was acquired as early as 1737,[2] and the interior layout of the late 17th-century nave lent itself to musical performances, including those held annually in the 1770s and 1780s in support of the town's charity school.[3] In 1813 doubts about the competency of the organist then employed provided an item for discussion in the parish vestry,[4] and in 1837 the choice of a new organist was decided by vote after members had heard the candidates perform. The post, which included instructing the choir boys in the singing gallery, carried a salary of £40 in 1850.[5] The choir had existed from at least the 1750s: when Richard Warjohn, a Newent tailor, died in 1834, his fellow-choristers provided a headstone, displaying the words and score of a hymn or psalm, to celebrate his 77 years as a member.[6] An annual music festival was held at Newent in the late 19th century, and the town's musical tradition was continued in the mid 20th by a choral society.[7]

From 1885 an institution known as the Newent (or Albion) club occupied Albion House adjoining the market place where there were reading rooms and a billiard room; the premises, and presumably with it the club, closed in 1935.[8] Before 1902 a Newent shopkeeper Cornelius Thurston opened a hall in Culver Street for lectures, concerts, and other functions. In 1922 the hall was being used as a cinema and on some evenings for amateur dramatics; the cinema, called the Plaza,[9] closed in the early 1970s, but within a few years another was started at the Community Centre on the Ross road.[10] After the First World War a Comrades' Club for veterans was opened in the town,[11] and in 1954 a new public meeting room opened alongside Bury Bar Street on part of the site of the old cattle market; the room was paid for by subscription as a memorial to the dead of the Second World War and was promoted chiefly by a local doctor, W.M.L. Johnstone.[12] The grammar school building on the Ross road became a youth centre after the school left it in 1965[13] and continued to be the venue for youth groups when, c.1980, it became the Community Centre.[14] In the outlying areas the schools and churches founded at Clifford's Mesne and Gorsley in the later 19th century provided the main focuses of community activities. The school building at Clifford's Mesne was used as a village hall after the school's closure in 1935, and that at Gorsley served as a church hall from 1954 until replaced in the early 1990s by a room added to the church building.[15] The Land Settlement Association estate founded at the Scarr farm in 1937 organized its own social activities in the mid 20th century, having a recreation hall and a branch of the Women's Institute.[16]

In 1898 Andrew Knowles of Newent Court gave land on the west side of Watery Lane to the parish council for use as a recreation ground, and in 1912 his trustees gave other land which enlarged the ground to 7 a.[17] Among other amenities later managed by the council were Newent Lake and the adjoining part of the grounds of Newent Court, landscaped and opened as a public park in 1998,[18] and an arboretum, planted beside Bradford's Lane to mark the millennium of 2000.[19]

A cricket team had been formed at Newent by 1872.[20] In the early 20th century the town had clubs for football, tennis, hockey, and bowling and a small golf course. Some of those clubs were defunct by the 1960s, when there was a lack of sporting facilities.[21] The situation had improved by the 1980s, partly through the development of the large new Newent school, which made its swimming baths, gymnasium, and sports hall available for public use out of school hours.[22] In the early 21st century the Newent cricket club had its pitch in Oxenhall parish and the town's football club a ground adjoining the Gloucester road in Malswick.

In the early 20th century the wild daffodils which flower in and around Newent attracted visitors to the area each spring. Special trains were laid on from Gloucester, and the flowers were gathered by local schoolchildren and sent by rail to London hospitals.[23] A later attraction was the National Birds of Prey Centre started in 1967 at a house and grounds

---

1 *Glouc. J.* 6 Feb. 1775; 29 Jan. 1776; 3 Aug. 1818; 8 Aug. 1825.
2 Ibid. 14 June 1737.
3 Ibid. 9 Aug. 1779; 13 Aug. 1781.
4 GA, P 225/VE 2/1, min. 14 Nov. 1813.
5 Ibid. VE 2/3, mins. 12 Jan. 1837, 10 May 1850.
6 Headstone in churchyard.
7 J. Douglas, *Historical Notes of Newent with Oxenhall and Pauntley* (1912), 9; *Glos. Countryside*, Jan.–Mar. 1951, 375.
8 GA, D 2299/299, 5463.
9 *Kelly's Dir. Glos.* (1902), 250; (1927), 275; *Chapters in Newent's History*, 32–3.
10 *Glos. Life*, Jan. 1974, 21; *Glos. and Avon Life*, Jan. 1983, 29.
11 *Kelly's Dir. Glos.* (1927), 275.
12 *Newent Official Guide* (c.1955), 10; *Glos. Life and Countryside*, Apr.–May 1967, 23.
13 'Newent, Past and Present' (Newent W.I. 1975: copy in GA, D 3295/II/5).
14 *Glos. and Avon Life*, Jan. 1983, 29.
15 GA, P 225/CH 3/6; below, religious hist. (religious life in 19th and 20th cents.: Gorsley and Clifford's Mesne churches).
16 *Glos. Countryside*, June 1958, 47.
17 GA, P 225A/PC 1/1, pp. 152–3, 157; PC 1/2, pp. 183–4, 214.
18 *Glos. and Avon Life*, Jan. 1983, 27; plaque at town end of lake.
19 Information board at arboretum.
20 GA, D 3028/5.
21 Ibid. D 2299/4664; 'Newent, Past and Present'; *Glos. Life and Countryside*, Apr.–May 1967, 23.
22 *Glos. and Avon Life*, Jan. 1983, 31.
23 Ward, *Around Newent*, 44; *Newent Official Guide* (c.1955), 7.

in Boulsdon, where courses in training the birds and demonstrations of flying them were held.[1] In Newent town the Shambles Museum, a re-creation of a street of Victorian shops, with a large collection of contemporary artefacts, was opened in Church Street in 1988.[2] Those remained Newent's main tourist attractions in 2007, together with the Three Choirs Vineyard, one of the largest English vineyards, on a hillside at the north boundary of the parish.[3]

Newent Spa

In the late 18th century Thomas Richardson, a Newent doctor, promoted the drinking of water from a spring[4] rising beside the Ell brook near Cleeve Mill.[5] In 1789 the spa was advertized by distributing samples of the water to local towns, and, aping established spas, by publishing a list of visitors, though only 12 people, and nobody of great note, were then listed.[6] By 1815 a small spa house had been built by the spring, and one of the attractions for those taking the waters was the walk to it from the town, passing through the grounds of Newent Court, ornamented by two large ponds and the Hereford and Gloucester canal.[7] Like most other such projects in the vicinity of Cheltenham, the spa's success was limited, although ambitious claims for it were still made by Newent innkeepers and others in the 1820s.[8] By 1852 the spa cottage was derelict.[9]

CHARITIES FOR THE POOR

Almshouses

The Newent almshouses, a row of small dwellings on the east side of New Street, originated in the gift by Giles Nanfan of Birtsmorton (Worcs.) c.1580 of a half burgage for an almshouse; the townspeople implemented his bequest before 1614, apparently paying for a new building on the site. The deed of Nanfan's gift had been lost by 1635 when his grandson John Nanfan confirmed it to a group of trustees, including the vicar, churchwardens, and town bailiff. In 1639 Randall Dobyns of Walden Court gave a half burgage adjoining the almshouses for the same purpose,[10] and later in the century William Rogers (d. 1690) of Okle Clifford gave two newly built almshouses at the north end of the site.

In 1750 the almshouses formed eight dwellings.[11] There was no regular endowment for the support of the occupants or for the upkeep of the buildings, which had become ruinous by 1810; the almshouses were then repaired by the parish at the cost of £336, raised by the sale of stock acquired with an accumulation of funds from other charities and by the sale of timber on charity land.[12] The repair evidently gave the almshouses the form they had in the mid 20th century, a range of building with a uniform brick frontage concealing older timber framing and divided into ten small apartments of two rooms each.[13] In the mid 1820s they were occupied by 20 people, chosen by the vicar and churchwardens, making no distinction between those receiving or not receiving parish relief.[14]

Hester Severne by will dated 1862 gave £100 to provide a fund for repairing the buildings,[15] but in 1895 they were described as in a disgraceful condition. Despite the trustees' wish to transfer management to the new parish council[16] the almshouses remained under the trusteeship of the rector (formerly the vicar), churchwardens, and overseers, the last acting for Newent poor-law union which gave assistance to some of the occupants.[17] In 1970 the trustees secured a Scheme empowering them to sell the almshouses once all the occupants had died and apply the proceeds, with the income of the Severne charity, to a general relief in need charity; that became in 1972 part of the Newent United charity.[18] In 1974 the almshouses were demolished and the site sold for a development of small houses.[19]

Other Charities

In the course of the 17th and early 18th century 20 different parishioners, including members of the Nourse, Rogers, and Pauncefoot landowning families and two of the vicars, Thomas Avenant and John Craister, gave bequests for the poor of Newent parish in the form of cash, small parcels of land, or rent charges. Among gifts which specified a use other than general relief were the educational bequests by Thomas Avenant and Eleanor Green, mentioned below, and three to finance apprenticeships: Walter Nourse (d. 1652) gave 40s. a year to apprentice two

---

1 *Glos. Life*, Jan. 1974, 19, 23; http://www.nbpc.co.uk (accessed 15 Nov. 2007).
2 *Glos. Echo*, 16 Feb. 1987; *Citizen*, 18 Mar. 1988.
3 Above, econ. hist. (agric.: late 19th cent. and 20th).
4 Douglas, *Notes of Newent*, 9.
5 OS Map 1", sheet 43 (1831 edn); GDR, T 1/126 (nos 386–7).
6 *Glouc. J.* 18 May, 27 July 1789.
7 Ibid. 27 Mar. 1815; *Pigot's Dir. Glos.* (1822–3), 61.
8 *Glouc. J.* 4 May 1818; 1 May 1820; 28 Apr. 1827.
9 *Slater's Dir. Glos.* (1852–3), 146.
10 GA, P 225/CH 1/1–2.
11 Ibid. D 1466; and for Rogers, TNA, PROB 11/407, ff. 56v.–58v.
12 GA, P 225/CH 3/1, accts. 1810.
13 Ibid. GPS 225/29; P 225/CH 3/10. Street front shown above, Fig. 8.
14 *18th Rep. Com. Char.* 284–5.
15 GA, P 225/CH 3/10.
16 Ibid. P 225A/PC 1/1, pp. 62, 205–6; P 225/VE 2/4, min. 17 Apr. 1900.
17 Ibid. P 225/CH 3/10.
18 Ibid. D 3469/5/110.
19 Ibid. P 225A/CH 2/21.

children to farming, William Rogers (d. 1690) gave £3 a year to apprentice one boy to a trade, and Timothy Nourse (d. 1699) gave £10 a year to apprentice five boys. Timothy Nourse also gave £2 10s. a year to buy cloth for old people, to which his widow Lucy (later Lucy Stokes) added a bequest to provide gowns for poor widows. By 1750 the principal sums of the charities given in the form of cash amounted to £283,[1] of which £37 was later laid out on land and the remainder lent to individuals on bonds. During the 18th century the charities were administered in an imprecise manner, and by 1793 £86 of the funds in hand in 1750 had been lost. Apprenticeships were made on a regular, if not annual, basis but what use was made of the funds from the other, less specific bequests is not clear. In 1793 the vicar John Foley drew up a full statement of the situation and attempted to improve the administration of the charities. His efforts led to fuller accounting and the recording of disbursements, including the distribution of garments under the clothing charities.[2] The commissioners reporting on charities, who collected their evidence for Newent in 1827,[3] found that the intentions of the donors were for the most part being fulfilled but objected to the application of some of the funds to those in receipt of parish relief.[4]

Two more parish charities were established in the 19th century: John Harvey Ollney by will proved 1836 left £200 to Newent to be invested in stock to support a Christmas distribution of coal and blankets and William White in 1859 gave £150 similarly to provide blankets.[5] In 1906 a separate foundation was formed in respect of the Avenant and Green charities. Under a Scheme of 1925 regulating the other charities, apprenticeships were to continue and income was also to be assigned to such things as healthcare, the provision of bedding and clothing, and subscriptions to provident clubs. Their total income was then £42 a year, some of it still derived from land and rent charges. In 1972 those charities were combined with the fund resulting from the planned sale of the Newent almshouses to form a general 'relief in need' charity under the title of the Newent United charity. In 1975 the three apprenticeship charities were removed from it and added to the Avenant and Green educational foundation, to be applied to apprenticeships or other help for young people with vocational training.[6] In 2007 the annual income of the Newent United charity was £1,752 and that of the apprenticeship and educational charity £131.[7]

EDUCATION

Charity and National Schools

In 1712 two charity schools at Newent taught a total of 50 children,[8] but when and by whom they were established and financed has not been discovered. Charles Jones mentioned as a schoolmaster at Newent in 1710 may have taught in one of them.[9] Anne Knowles, who at her death in 1726 was said to have taught in the town for 46 years,[10] had perhaps kept a small dame school. At his death in 1728 the vicar Thomas Avenant left £20 for instructing two children in the catechism,[11] and before 1750 Eleanor Green gave £40, the bulk of the proceeds to be used for teaching poor children.[12] In 1772 leading parishioners, wishing 'to prevent vice [rather] than punish it', set up a school financed out of the rates at the workhouse; children of poor parents not on parish relief could receive instruction there in reading, knitting, and spinning, and those who made good progress were to be rewarded with the gift of a warm garment.[13] In 1775, presumably as a development of that project though differently financed, there was a recently established charity school with over 50 children. The children were taught reading and the catechism, and the girls also sewing and knitting; the more promising pupils were taught writing. The school was supported by voluntary contributions, and an annual subscription of 10s. 6d. entitled a subscriber to recommend a pupil for entry. When necessary, the funds were supplemented by a collection at a charity sermon preached by the vicar or curate.[14]

The charity school was still well supported in 1781,[15] but had apparently lapsed by 1818 when a Sunday school was the only parish school recorded.[16] By 1833 a day school was run in association with the Sunday school, but weekday attendance was only 10 compared to 100 on Sundays. The school was supported by subscriptions and church collections, together with £2 10s. a year produced by the Avenant and Green bequests.[17] By

---

1 GA, D 1466; and for detail of the Nourse and Rogers charities, GDR wills 1700/57; TNA, PROB 11/228, ff. 66v.–7; PROB 11/407, ff. 56v.–58v.
2 GA, P 225/CH 3/1.
3 Ibid. CW 2/1.
4 *18th Rep. Com. Char.* 284–8.
5 GA, P 225/CH 3/2–4, 10.
6 Ibid. D 3469/5/110.
7 http://charity-commission.gov.uk/registeredcharities (accessed 20 Mar. 2009: nos 202871, 311610).
8 *Glos. N&Q* I, 294.
9 GA, P 225/IN 1/2, baptisms 1710.
10 Ibid. burials 1726.
11 GDR wills 1727/32.
12 GA, D 1466.
13 *Glouc. J.* 9 Nov. 1772; GA, P 225/VE 2/1, min. 30 Oct. 1772.
14 *Glouc. J.* 7 Aug. 1775.
15 Ibid. 13 Aug. 1781.
16 *Educ. of Poor Digest*, 304.
17 *Educ. Enquiry Abstract*, 322.

1847 the school had been much expanded and a master and two mistresses were teaching 112 children on both weekdays and Sundays; school pence were charged to supplement subscriptions. The two rooms used were regarded as inadequate, but the vicar Richard Onslow had by then obtained grants of £354 and £100 from the government and the National Society respectively,[1] enabling the parish to build a new school the following year with accommodation for 300 children. The site, north of the town at Picklenash, was given by the lady of the manor Elizabeth Foley and her heir R.F. Onslow.[2] An extra classroom was added in 1873, the cost met by subscription and part of the principal of Hester Severne's charity.[3] In the mid 1870s attendance at the Picklenash National school, organized as boys', girls', and infants' departments, was usually around 150.[4]

At Clifford's Mesne a building was put up in 1863 for use as both a National school and a chapel. In 1868 an untrained mistress taught c.30 infants there, the older children of the hamlet attending the Picklenash school. Kilcot also had a small school by 1868, attended by c.25 children. It probably ceased in 1872 when a National school (also doubling as a chapel) was built at Gorsley.[5] In its first year the Gorsley school, with mixed and infant departments, had an average attendance of 64.[6] In 1868 there was a night school at Newent, attended mainly by boys after their farm work; it was run by the curate Morris Burland and four other teachers and was said to be the best such school in the district.[7]

In the mid 1870s the committee managing the three National schools (Picklenash, Clifford's Mesne, and Gorsley) was forced by financial problems to consider the formation of a school board to meet the requirements for the parish under the 1870 Education Act. Many parishioners were opposed to a board and a voluntary rate was introduced in an attempt to make up the shortfall in funds. In 1877, however, the committee had to raise the weekly pence paid at Picklenash and Gorsley to 2*d*., and in 1879 it considered closing Gorsley and Clifford's Mesne after government grants to those schools had been reduced. In 1882 it handed over all three schools to a newly elected school board.[8]

Board and Council Schools

In 1885 Picklenash school had an average attendance of 220 in mixed and infant departments,[9] and in 1897 the Gorsley and Clifford's Mesne schools, both comprising single, all-age departments, had average attendances of 60 and 51 respectively.[10] The three became council schools under the Act of 1902,[11] and in 1910 Picklenash had an average attendance of 276 in separate boys', girls', and infants' departments, Gorsley had an average attendance of 51 in mixed and infant departments, and Clifford's Mesne, similarly organized, one of 45.[12] Attendance at Gorsley school had fallen to 30, including 13 from the adjoining part of Herefordshire, by 1926 when it was closed.[13] At Clifford's Mesne, where average attendance was 43 in 1922,[14] the older children were removed to Picklenash school in 1928 and only 13 attended by 1935 when the school was closed.[15]

At Picklenash school average attendance had fallen by 1922 to 208, rising again by 1932 to 269 and by 1938, as the only council school in the parish, to 323.[16] In 1947 it had 353 pupils on its roll and a staff of 12.[17] From 1949 it received the older pupils from schools serving 15 neighbouring parishes, swelling its numbers to c.500 aged between 5 and 15, some of them housed in temporary classrooms. In 1952 the children aged over 11 were transferred to the new Newent bi-lateral school, leaving just over 300 at Picklenash.[18] In the mid 1960s the school was divided into separate junior and infant schools, the latter, known as Glebe Infant school, housed in a new building near by. In 1984 a new building for the junior school was opened and the old school building of 1848 was sold and converted as dwellings.[19] In 2007 Picklenash Junior school had 246 children on its roll and Glebe Infant school had 132.[20]

Secondary Schools

By 1910 many of the older children of the parish were travelling by train to attend schools in Gloucester.[21] In 1922 the county council acquired the old Newent union workhouse on the Ross road for use as a secondary grammar school for the area, planned to accommodate 160 boys and girls in six classrooms. The older part of the premises was

---

1 Nat. Soc. *Inquiry*, 1846–7, Glos. 12–13.
2 GA, P 225/SC 1/6; *Kelly's Dir. Glos.* (1856), 332.
3 GA, P 225/CH 2/7. For Hester Severne's char., above (charities for the poor: almshouses).
4 GA, P 225/SC 1/1.
5 Below, religious hist. (religious life in 19th and 20th cents.: Gorsley and Clifford's Mesne churches); *1st Rep. Com. Employment in Agric.*, app. II, p. 132.
6 TNA, ED 7/35/230.
7 *1st Rep. Com. Employment in Agric.* app. II, pp. 132–3.
8 GA, P 225/SC 1/1.
9 *Kelly's Dir. Glos.* (1885), 533.
10 Ibid. (1897), 202.
11 *Public Elem. Schs.* 1906, 107.
12 *List 21*, 1911 (Board of Education), 165.
13 GA, C/CE/M 2/18, pp. 165–6, 188.
14 *List 21*, 1922 (Board of Education), 106.
15 GA, C/CE/M 2/22, pp. 387–8; M 2/23, pp. 13–14.
16 *List 21*, 1922 (Board of Education), 106; 1932, 116; 1938, 128.
17 GA, C/CE/M 2/30, f. 182.
18 *Newent Official Guide* (c.1955), 11–12.
19 *Chapters in Newent's History*, 135.
20 *Schools and Establishment Dir. 2007–8* (Glos. co. council), 22, 37.
21 GA, DA 30/100/10, p. 76.

demolished and replaced with a new classroom block, and a house near by was bought as a headmaster's residence.[1] The school opened in 1925.[2] In 1952 it was reorganized as a 'bi-lateral school', an early experiment in the comprehensive system: it combined the grammar school with a secondary modern stream formed of the children aged over 11 from Picklenash council school. It opened with a staff of 26 teachers and c.480 children, who were taught in the existing building and in others on the south side of the Ross road;[3] by the early 1960s there were c.650 pupils.[4] In 1965 the school moved into new buildings on a large site on the east side of Watery Lane. Extensions to the buildings were made in 1973, and by 1975 the school had c.1,200 pupils drawn from over 20 surrounding parishes.[5] In 2007 the school, then styled Newent Community school, had 1,334 pupils on its roll.[6]

Other Schools

The Wesleyan Methodists had a Sunday school at their chapel in Culver Street in 1833,[7] and in 1868 they also ran a day school, with c.20 pupils taught by an elderly schoolmistress.[8] In 1846 the Congregationalists opened a British day school with c.100 pupils at their new chapel in Broad Street.[9] It continued on a smaller scale in 1868 when, supported by voluntary contributions and pence, between 30 and 40 children were taught by an untrained mistress.[10] Those two nonconformist schools evidently closed before the establishment of the school board for the parish. Goff's school, attached to Gorsley Baptist chapel in Linton (Herefs.) from c.1819, probably attracted some pupils from the Newent part of Gorsley in the mid 19th century.[11]

In the early 19th century, in the absence of any large-scale provision for education by the parish, small private day schools proliferated in Newent. In 1833 seven were in existence, most of them recently founded, ranging from one with 7 pupils to one with 24. Three day and boarding schools were evidently seminaries or classical academies for children from a wealthier background.[12] An earlier example of that type of school was kept in the town from c.1786 by Revd William Beale and taken over 1811 by another clergyman,[13] who described it in 1815 as a seminary for educating boys for commercial pursuits or for the university.[14] In 1867 Revd Joseph White opened an establishment called Newent Grammar school at the Porch House on the south side of Church Street; it included a department which specialized in teaching divinity students preparing for ordination.[15] A later occupant of the Porch House, Dr K.M. Tomlinson, a Newent general practitioner, ran a small preparatory school there in the 1960s as a non-profit making venture with the costs shared among the parents.[16]

RELIGIOUS HISTORY

ORIGIN AND STATUS OF THE PARISH CHURCH

The early ecclesiastical status of the large parish is indicated by a cross shaft of the late 8th or early 9th century discovered, probably *in situ*, in Newent churchyard. A second carved stone, a small rectangular tablet possibly dating from the early 11th century, was also found on that site.[17] That the church originally served an even wider area is supported by the fact that the churches of three adjoining parishes were in the same ownership in the late 12th century. In 1181 Newent church with its tithes, together with the churches of Taynton and Dymock and the chapel of Pauntley, was confirmed to Cormeilles abbey by the earl of Leicester. In 1195 the bishop of Hereford licensed Cormeilles to appropriate the churches of Newent, Dymock, and Kingstone (Herefs.) and Pauntley chapel on the deaths of their then incumbents,[18] and in 1247 the bishop ordained a vicarage in Newent church. In the early 18th century the vicarage was endowed with the rectory tithes of the parish, but the incumbents continued to be called vicars until the 1870s when the style of rector was adopted. In 1872 a new ecclesiastical district of Gorsley with Clifford's

---

1 GA, C/CE/M 2/16, pp. 116, 155, 285–6; M 2/17, pp. 63, 85, 157–8. See Ward, *Around Newent*, 24.
2 *Kelly's Dir. Glos.* (1927), 276.
3 *Glos. Countryside*, July–Sept. 1955, 273–4.
4 *Newent Official Guide* (c.1962: copy in Glos. Colln. R 212.19), 7.
5 'Newent, Past and Present'.
6 *Schools and Establishment Dir. 2007–8*, 60.
7 *Educ. Enquiry Abstract*, 322.
8 *1st Rep. Com. Employment in Agric.* app. II, p. 132.
9 *Glouc. J.* 10 May 1845; 9 May 1846.
10 *1st Rep. Com. Employment in Agric.* app. II, p. 132.
11 *Millennium Memories*, 18.
12 *Educ. Enquiry Abstract*, 322; *Pigot's Dir. Glos.* (1830), 382.
13 *Glouc. J.* 22 Apr. 1811; 14, 21, 28 Nov. 1814.
14 Ibid. 9 Jan. 1815.
15 *Kelly's Dir. Glos.* (1885), 533; *Chapters in Newent's History*, 132; OS Map 1:2,500, Glos. XVII.14 (1884 edn).
16 *Chapters in Newent's History*, 133–4.
17 Below (ch. bldgs).
18 BL, Add. MS 18461, ff. 1v., 8v.

Mesne was created from the western part of the parish with an adjoining part of Linton (Herefs.).[1] In 1985 that living was added to that of Newent to form a united benefice.[2]

ENDOWMENT AND PATRONAGE

On its creation in 1247 the vicarage was endowed with the small tithes of the parish, offerings made at the altar, a meadow, and a wagon of hay each year from the meadow of Robert of Stalling. Cormeilles abbey retained the grain and hay tithes, offerings at the feasts of the Purification and St Blaise, and all tithes from its demesne lands; those profits passed to its successors as lords of Newent manor.[3] The meadow awarded to the vicarage was presumably the acre beside Ell brook which was the vicar's only glebe in 1684. The vicar then received the load of hay from the Moat estate, which had absorbed Robert of Stalling's land, and took tithe of fruit or, if turned into cider and perry (as much was), a twelfth of the liquor, and tithe of coppice wood. The largest tract of woodland, Yartleton woods, was exempt as former demesne of Cormeilles abbey,[4] but the remaining coppices produced c.£40 in composition in the 1830s.[5] In 1607 the vicar claimed tithe from coal pits being worked in Boulsdon.[6] The total value of the profits assigned in 1247 was said to be 14 marks[7] (£9 6s. 8d.) but in 1291 the vicarage was valued at only £4.[8] In 1535 it was worth £23[9] and in 1650 £50.[10]

In the late 1720s the vicarage was augmented by the gift of the rectory tithes under the will of the former lord of the manor Paul Foley,[11] and in 1762 it was said to be worth c.£250.[12] In 1804, however, it was valued at £1,069. In 1835 the vicar was receiving £1,240 in compositions,[13] and in 1838 he was awarded a corn rent charge of £1,542.[14] The value of the tithes rents, a share of which was assigned to the new benefice of Gorsley with Clifford's Mesne in 1872,[15] was later reduced and in 1906 the living was worth £600.[16] A tithe barn in the old priory precinct near the Court House passed to the vicarage when it was endowed with the rectory tithes; it remained part of the benefice until 1861 when the vicar exchanged it and the glebe meadow for land adjoining the vicarage house.[17]

The vicarage house, standing on the north-east side of New Street, was recorded from 1369.[18] It was rebuilt in 1729 by the vicar John Craister[19] as a substantial residence of brick with a five-bayed front of two storeys raised on cellars. In the mid 1860s it was much altered and enlarged by a new north range.[20] The house was sold in 1949 or 1950 to become the offices of Newent Rural District Council,[21] and a new residence for the incumbent was built in Culver Street.[22]

The advowson of the vicarage descended with the manor estate. In the 14th century, during the war with France, the Crown made the presentations,[23] and during the late 16th century and the 17th most presentations were made by assignees of the patrons: Anthony Bourchier presented in 1550, Alexander Dobyns in 1564, William Winter of Coleford, brother of the lord of the manor, in 1617, John Hanbury in 1627, and Thomas Foley, presumably the eldest son of the lord of the manor, in 1691.[24] In the 1870s the Onslow family conveyed the advowson to St Catherine's college, Cambridge,[25] which sold it in 1921 or 1922 to A.E. Lark.[26] Lark (*fl.* 1939)[27] devised it to C.J.K. Burrell, rector of Newent 1925–49. He devised it to Trinity college, Dublin, and the college conveyed it in 1962 to the bishop of Gloucester.[28]

RELIGIOUS LIFE IN THE MIDDLE AGES AND THE SIXTEENTH CENTURY

The priory established by Cormeilles abbey at Newent by the early 13th century and dissolved c.1382 was apparently a very small community, mainly occupied with the administration of Newent manor and the abbey's other possessions in England. There is no record of a church or chapel among its buildings and probably the prior and monks worshipped in the parish church close to their quarters.[29] It was probably the abbey or priory which

---

1 Below (religious life in 19th and 20th cents.).
2 *Dioc. of Glouc. Dir.* (1997–8), 62.
3 BL, Add. MS 18461, f. 13; above, manors (other manors and estates: Newent rectory).
4 GDR, V 5/212T 3.
5 Glos. Colln. RQ 212.3.
6 GDR vol. 10, depositions 20 Oct. 1607.
7 BL, Add. MS 18461, f. 13.
8 *Tax. Eccl.* 161.
9 *Valor Eccl.* II, 500.
10 C.R. Elrington, 'The Survey of Church Livings in Gloucestershire, 1650', *Trans. BGAS* 83 (1964), 98.
11 Above, manors (other manors and estates: Newent rectory).
12 Hockaday Abs. cxciii.
13 Glos. Colln. RQ 212.3.
14 GDR, T 1/126.
15 Below (religious life in 19th and 20th cents.).
16 *Kelly's Dir. Glos.* (1906), 253.

17 GA, D 412/Z 3, Newent notes, 1900; P 225/IN 3/1.
18 Herefs. RO, E 12/G/1, ct. (30 Nov.) 43 Edw. III; G/3, ct. (1 Aug.) 9 Hen. IV.
19 Hockaday Abs. ccxciii.
20 Verey and Brooks, *Glos.* II, 606–7.
21 GA, DA 30/100/18, pp. 63, 155; 100/19, pp. 8, 187.
22 Ibid. 100/18, p. 193; P 225/IN 3/6.
23 BL, Add. MS 15668, f. 85; *Cal. Pat.* 1343–5, 6; 1367–70, 434; 1391–6, 335–6.
24 Hockaday Abs. ccxciii; and for Wm. Winter (d. 1626), Herefs. RO, E 12/G/14, bundle marked 'living and rectory'; below, Dymock, manors (other estates: Dymock rectory).
25 *Kelly's Dir. Glos.* (1870), 604; (1879), 709.
26 *Dioc. of Glouc. Kalendar* (1921), 51; (1922), 51; GA, P 225/IN 4/5, entry for 13 Sept. 1922.
27 *Kelly's Dir. Glos.* (1939), 271.
28 Newent church guide (2000), p. 15.
29 Above, manors (Newent manor).

founded within the church a chantry of St Mary, recorded from the mid 13th century when a Newent tenant gave 2s. rent to support the chaplain and provide lights in the chapel;[1] the priory was later its patron.[2] The lady chapel, housing the chantry, was rebuilt wholly or partly in 1361,[3] probably by the efforts of lay parishioners rather than the priory, which then held the manor and its revenues as a farmer under the Crown. The nature of the chantry's endowments, which at its dissolution in 1548 comprised 13 houses dispersed throughout the town[4] and scattered lands in other parts of the parish,[5] suggests that most were acquired piecemeal from different parishioners; In 1510 a townsman devised the reversion of a house to it.[6]

In the late Middle Ages the donations of parishioners established and maintained a second chantry, dedicated to SS James and Anne and housed in a chapel standing in the churchyard.[7] It was stated, in the course of a 16th-century lawsuit, that it had been constituted by a deed of 1447 or 1448.[8] In 1484 it was said to have been founded for the benefit of the souls of John Marcle, Walter Marcle, and others,[9] and later John Hooke and another were credited as founders.[10] Evidently, as with St Mary's chantry, the endowments of the founders were supplemented by later gifts; at the time of its dissolution the chantry owned nine houses in the town and lands scattered through the parish, including small farms at Stardens and Hayes.[11] The chantry priest was presented by Llanthony priory, Gloucester, in 1484,[12] but in 1538 the right of patronage belonged to St Bartholomew's hospital in the same town.[13] At the dissolution of chantries its lands were valued at £10 6s. 8d. a year and those of St Mary's chantry at £9 7s. 3d.[14] Most of their lands were sold to various dealers between 1549 and 1554,[15] though the Crown retained some of them until 1570 or later.[16]

A chapel mentioned in 1181, and apparently attached to Boulsdon,[17] may have been that dedicated to St Helen which the vicar of Newent was licensed to use as an oratory in 1404.[18] By later accounts a chapel, dedicated to St Helen or St Hilary and demolished in Henry III's reign, stood in Kilcot and served both that tithing and Boulsdon.[19] Its site was perhaps on ground later called Chapel meadow by the parish boundary to the north-west of the Kilcot inn.[20] In the 1340s the lord of Boulsdon and a landowner at Okle were licensed to have private oratories in their houses.[21]

Medieval vicars of Newent included Hugh of Martley, named from a Worcestershire manor owned by Cormeilles abbey.[22] In 1311 he was licensed to travel to Rome on the business of his church.[23] Two or more men surnamed Hooke, presumably of the family that owned Crooke's farm in the part of Pauntley parish adjoining Newent, held the vicarage in the late Middle Ages. Robert Hooke was instituted in 1393[24] and John Hooke, his successor in 1434,[25] was possibly the same who occurs as vicar in 1459 and 1482.[26] William Porter, who held the vicarage by 1515 and to his death in 1524,[27] had numerous other ecclesiastical preferments, including the precentorship of Hereford cathedral. A native of Newent,[28] he was apparently the brother of the local landowner Roger Porter.[29]

Edward Horne was burned for heresy at Newent during the Marian persecution but how strong a body of Protestant feeling in the parish he represented is unknown. Although not recorded in Foxe's martyrology,[30] local traditions about his death survived for many years. By one account, a cave on May hill known as Crocket's Hole was used as a hiding place by Horne and a man called Crocket,[31] possibly a memory of John Crocket of Highnam who was condemned for heresy in 1556.[32]

Service of the cure in the mid and later 16th century was erratic and often inadequate. In 1544 two

---

1 BL, Add. MS 15668, f. 61v.
2 *Cal. Pat. 1343–5*, 235, 375.
3 *Cal. Inq. p.m.* XVI, p. 28.
4 Herefs. RO, E 12/G/5, rental 31 Hen. VIII.
5 Hockaday Abs. ccxcii, 1549.
6 Ibid. 1510.
7 Ibid. 1538, 1547.
8 TNA, C 3/57/48.
9 *Reg. Myllyng*, 194.
10 J. Maclean, 'Chantry Certificates, Gloucestershire', *Trans. BGAS* 8 (1883–4), 291.
11 Hockaday Abs. ccxcii, 1549, 1550, 1553.
12 *Reg. Myllyng*, 194.
13 Hockaday Abs. ccxcii, 1538.
14 Maclean, 'Chantry Certificates', 290–1.
15 *Cal. Pat.* 1548–9, 187, 429; 1549–51, 29, 101, 280; 1550–3, 5; 1553, 147; 1553–4, 96.
16 TNA, E 310/14/50, f. 39; E 309/Box 4/13 Eliz./33, no 6.
17 BL, Add. MS 18461, f. 1v.
18 *Reg. Mascall*, 190.
19 GA, D 412/Z 1, notes on Boulsdon and Kilcot, c.1725; Z 3, Nourse MS, p. 13.
20 Atkyns, *Glos.* 569; GDR, T 1/126 (no 855).
21 Above, manors (Boulsdon manor; Okle).
22 *VCH Glos.* II, 105.
23 *Reg. Swinfield*, 464.
24 *Cal Pat.* 1391–6, 335–6, 347.
25 Herefs. RO, E 12/G/2, cts. 29 Apr. 6 Hen IV, (28 July) 1 Hen. VI; *Reg. Spofford*, 360.
26 Hockaday Abs. ccxcii, 1459; Herefs. RO, E 12/G/2, acct. roll 22 Edw. IV (s.v. farm of demesne).
27 Hockaday Abs. ccxcii.
28 A.B. Emden, *A Biographical Register of the University of Oxford to 1500* III (1959), 1503.
29 Hockaday Abs. ccxcii, 1523; *Visit. Glos. 1623*, 127.
30 K.G. Powell, 'Beginnings of Protestantism in Gloucestershire' *Trans. BGAS* 90 (1971), 154.
31 GA, D 412/Z 3, Nourse MS, p. 16; ibid. 'MS no. II'; Rudder, *Glos.* 563–4. For Crocket's Hole, below, Longhope, introd. (landscape).
32 Powell, 'Beginnings of Protestantism', 154.

men claimed to hold the profits of the benefice under lease from the vicar, Richard Ward, or a previous incumbent and another man occupied the vicarage house, claiming it under a separate lease.[1] In 1548 Ward was non-resident and, though he or a lessee had provided a curate, there had been no sermons preached for a year and the giving of alms to the poor had been omitted.[2] In 1551 Ward's successor John Cutler was unable to repeat the Commandments; he could repeat the Articles but not prove them from scripture.[3] Later in the 1550s two other clerics in succession laid claim to the vicarage,[4] but Cutler remained vicar until 1564 when the former curate Henry Donne was instituted.[5] In 1570 Donne was cited for expressing contempt of the authority of the diocesan bishop and being absent without dispensation.[6] In 1576 he was described as a reasonably good divine,[7] but during his absence prayers had been read and communion administered by an unordained minister.[8] Donne remained vicar until his death in 1605 and was succeeded by Nathaniel Dodd, a professor of theology.[9]

RELIGIOUS LIFE IN THE SEVENTEENTH AND EIGHTEENTH CENTURIES

During the Civil War and Commonwealth period the vicar of Newent was John Wilse. Instituted in 1643, he was described as a preaching minister in 1650. He subscribed in 1662[10] but died soon afterwards, apparently in prison.[11]

On 18 January 1674 the nave roof of the parish church collapsed under the weight of snow lying on it, making necessary the rebuilding of the nave and adjoining south aisle. That work[12] was carried out between 1675 and 1679 and provided scope for much debate within the parish.[13] Among those most active in the project were the resident landowners Richard and William Rogers of Okle Clifford and Christopher Woodward of the Moat and the vicar Thomas Jackman, a conscientious incumbent who served the living from 1663 to his death in 1690.[14] Eventually it was decided to rebuild the church 18 ft shorter than the old one, a plan said to have been urged on Jackman by his wife who thought it would be easier for him to preach in. Work began but the plan with a central row of columns related to pilasters around the walls was abandoned as too restrictive of space and the parishioners decided on a single-span roof proposed by Newent carpenter Edward Taylor. He had recently worked under Wren at St Bride's church in Fleet Street (London) and his design for the roof is said to have adopted structural principles employed at the Sheldonian Theatre in Oxford.[15] The oak timber for the rafters was given by Charles II from his Forest of Dean,[16] and a number of Gloucestershire gentry subscribed to the cost, as did Paul Foley, the lord of the manor,[17] though apparently not closely involved with the rebuilding. Large pews in the new building were allocated to six of the main ratepayers, Foley, Christopher Woodward, William Rogers, Poole Pauncefoot of Carswalls, Sir Edmund Bray, owner of Walden Court and other lands, and Stephen Skinner, holder of former demesne land adjoining the town. Other leading ratepayers, Mary and Walter Nourse, owners of Boulsdon manor, and Walter's uncle Timothy Nourse of Southends, later claimed to have been unfairly treated and made attempts to alter the seating so as to exclude Skinner. The pews were aligned to face the north wall, against which was installed a pulpit given by Elizabeth Rogers of Okle Clifford,[18] and galleries ran around the other walls, including one that partially blocked the entrances to the chancel and lady chapel.[19]

The form of the new building[20] was regarded as innovative for the parish church of a small provincial town and became an object of considerable interest and local pride.[21] A thanksgiving for the escape without loss of life was instituted by Jackman on the anniversary of the fall of the old church, which had occurred on a Sunday night a few hours after the departure of a large congregation, and a parishioner, Eleanor Green, later left a bequest for a sermon on that day.[22]

John Craister, a Cambridge divine who was instituted vicar in 1728, was the first incumbent to benefit from the augmentation of the living. He rebuilt the vicarage house and housed there his

---

1 *L&P Hen. VIII, Addenda* I, p. 553.
2 Hockaday Abs. xxxi, 1548 visit. f. 33; ccxcii, 1548.
3 J. Gairdner, 'Bishop Hooper's Visitation of Gloucester', *EHR* 19 (1904), 119.
4 Hockaday Abs. ccxciii, 1554; TNA, C 3/34/19.
5 Bodleian, Rawl. C. 790, f. 28; Hockaday Abs. ccxciii, 1564.
6 GDR vol. 9, p. 11.
7 Hockaday Abs. xlvii, 1576 visit. f. 116.
8 GDR vol. 40, f. 229v.
9 Hockaday Abs. ccxciii.
10 Elrington, 'Surv. of Church Livings', 98.
11 *Notes on Dioc. of Glouc. by Chancellor Parsons*, 169, 173.
12 See below (ch. bldgs.).
13 The account given here is based on that by Walter Nourse (d. 1743), who witnessed the events as a young man: GA, D 412/Z 3, Nourse MS, pp. 1–4. Part of his account is quoted in H. Colvin, *A Biographical Dictionary of British Architects 1660–1840* (3rd edn, 1995), 959-60.
14 GA, D 412/Z 3, Nourse MS, p. 15; P 225/IN 1/2, burials 1690; *Notes on Dioc. of Glouc. by Chancellor Parsons*, 172.
15 Colvin, *Biog. Dict. Brit. Architects* (4th edn, 2008), 518, 584, 1019–20.
16 *Cal. Treasury Books 1672–5*, 625.
17 Bodleian, Top. Glouc. c. 3, f. 140 and v.
18 Probably the widow of Wm. Rogers (d. 1662): Bigland, *Glos.* II, 242; GDR wills 1678/119.
19 GA, D 412/Z 3, Newent notes, 1900.
20 See below (ch. bldgs.).
21 Bodleian, Top. Glouc. c. 3, f. 140; GA, D 412/Z 3, 'MS no II'.
22 GA, D 412/Z 3, Nourse MS, p. 15; D 1466.

library of over 1,000 volumes, which at his death in 1737 he left for the use of later vicars.[1] For at least part of the incumbency of the next vicar, James Griffith, curates served the parish and lived in the vicarage house. Griffith died in 1762 and for the next 100 years the living was held by relatives of the patrons. Robert Foley, instituted in 1762 on the presentation of his brother Thomas, later Lord Foley, was also rector of Kingham (Oxon.) and became dean of Worcester.[2] He gave Newent church two sets of plate, one for use in administering communion to parishioners in their homes.[3] John Foley (d. 1803), Robert's successor in 1783,[4] was a leading magistrate,[5] residing at Newent where he played an active role in the organization of poor relief and regularized the administration of the parish charities.[6]

For a parish containing a small town and several outlying hamlets and having a church with little seating for its numerous poor, there was surprisingly little challenge to the established church from nonconformity in the 17th and 18th centuries. No nonconformists were returned for Newent in 1676,[7] and in 1735 only six Presbyterians and a Quaker were recorded, and in 1750 only two Presbyterians and a Baptist.[8] The first registration of a nonconformist meeting place found was in 1779,[9] by an unidentified group, possibly Methodists.

RELIGIOUS LIFE IN THE NINETEENTH AND TWENTIETH CENTURIES

In 1803 Richard Francis Onslow was instituted vicar of Newent on the presentation of his father-in-law Andrew Foley. Onslow, who was vicar of Kidderminster and in 1815 became archdeacon of Worcester, lived in the Court House at Newent for most of his incumbency.[10] His longest serving curate, William Beale (d. 1827), who married into the Morse family, became vicar of Dymock.[11] Onslow died in 1849 and was succeeded as vicar by his son Arthur Andrew Onslow (d. 1864). In 1846 one of Richard Onslow's curates, John Skally,[12] issued a pastoral address which earned accusations of 'Puseyism' from a dissenting minister,[13] but High Church views and liturgy seem otherwise to have made little impact on church life at the period. Clergy and congregation showed no urgency in altering their late 17th-century church interior to conform to modern ideas of worship. The gallery across the east end of the nave, obscuring the view of chancel and altar, was not removed until 1865; it was not until 1884, under Peter Wood (rector 1878–97), that the nave was reseated with pews facing east; and the lady chapel remained in use as a vestry until refitted for worship in 1912.[14]

Nonconformity gained a permanent presence in the parish only at the start of the 19th century with the building of a Wesleyan Methodist chapel. The group faced some violent opposition, the motivation for which is not clear but seems unlikely to have stemmed from rival sectarian convictions.[15] The Wesleyans remained the only dissenting group firmly established in the town[16] until the 1840s when the Congregationalists built a chapel. Neither congregation was ever very numerous or financially well-based. Some of the outlying hamlets had missions from dissenting groups from the 1820s onwards, but the only group that became firmly rooted were the Baptists in Gorsley and Kilcot, whose base was outside the parish at a chapel in the Linton part of Gorsley.

The provision by the established church for the outlying hamlets began in 1863 with the building of a chapel at Clifford's Mesne. Another was built at Gorsley in 1872 when the two hamlets were formed into a separate ecclesiastical district.[17] A wooden chapel-of-ease to the parish church had opened at Kilcot by 1870[18] but is not recorded later, perhaps discontinued when the new arrangements of 1872 were put in place. In 1885 the owner of Walden Court, J.H. Frowde, was holding services for the inhabitants of Pool Hill in his main hall, licensed for that purpose.[19] In 1899 a mission room was opened at Almshouse Green, in Malswick, supported by Andrew Knowles of Newent Court,[20] but it was demolished c.1909 to make way for road improvements.[21]

During 1968 and 1969 when the parish church was closed during examination and partial removal of its spire, services were held in the town's

---

1 Hockaday Abs. ccxciii; TNA, PROB 11/684, ff. 34v.–36; Bp. Benson's Surv. of Dioc. of Glouc. 1735–50, 11.
2 Hockaday Abs. ccxciii; *Burke's Peerage* (1963), 936.
3 GA, P 225/CH 3/1.
4 Hockaday Abs. ccxciii.
5 E. Moir, *Local Government in Gloucestershire, 1775–1800* (BGAS Records Section 1969), 73–5, 77, 104, 124.
6 GA, P 225/VE 2/1; CH 3/1. See above, social hist (charities for the poor: other charities).
7 *Compton Census*, 544.
8 Bp. Benson's Surv. of Dioc. of Glouc. 1735–50, 11.
9 Hockaday Abs. ccxciii.
10 Ibid.; *Burke's Peerage* (1963), 936–7, 1863.
11 Morse fam. pedigree, compiled by P. Rowlandson: copy seen (2005) in possession of Dr K.M. Tomlinson of Newent.
12 *Burke's Peerage* (1963), 1863; Hockaday Abs. ccxciii.
13 Reuben Partridge, *High-Church Principles, Anti-Scriptural; being an answer to the Revd J.J. Skally's address to the parishioners of Newent* (Newent, 1846: copy in Glos. Colln. R 212.3).
14 GA, D 412/Z 3, Newent notes, 1900; Newent church guide (2000), pp. 15–16.
15 Below.
16 See GDR vol. 383, no cxxii.
17 Below (Gorsley and Clifford's Mesne churches).
18 *Kelly's Dir. Glos.* (1870), 604.
19 Ibid. (1885), 532; above, manors (other manors and estates: Walden Ct.). See below, Pauntley, religious hist. (religious life).
20 GA, P 225/VE 2/4.
21 Ibid. DA 30/100/9, p. 428.

Congregational and Methodist chapels, the former providing the venue for the institution of a new rector in 1969.[1] That spirit of cooperation encouraged the establishment of a local ecumenical partnership between the Anglicans and Methodists in 1970. From that date the two congregations held joint services in the parish church and shared pastoral work.[2] In 1998 those arrangements were extended to include the Baptists in the parish,[3] and in 2007 the united benefice was served by a team ministry comprising an Anglican priest-in-charge, a Methodist minister, and a part-time Baptist minister.[4]

Gorsley and Clifford's Mesne Churches

In 1872 a separate ecclesiastical district of Gorsley with Clifford's Mesne was created from part of the west side of Newent parish and an adjoining part of Linton. The living, styled a perpetual curacy and later a vicarage, was endowed with tithe rent charges to the value of £120 a year and £49 a year, given up respectively by the vicars of Newent and Linton, and with £38 a year granted by the Ecclesiastical Commissioners. The right of patronage was shared between the incumbents of the parent parishes, the vicar of Newent taking two turns and the vicar of Linton the third.[5] In 1879 the living was worth £207 a year. A vicarage house was built at Gorsley, on the north side of the Newent–Ross road opposite Brassfields Farm, in 1876.[6] In 1882 the church at Clifford's Mesne was declared the official parish church of the ecclesiastical district,[7] but the location of the vicarage house and the larger size of a new Gorsley church opened in 1893 resulted in Gorsley coming to be regarded as its centre. In 1985 the benefice was united with Newent and ceased to have a resident incumbent.[8]

At Clifford's Mesne a building to serve as both as chapel-of-ease to Newent and as a National school was built in 1863 at what became the centre of the growing hamlet. The site was bought for that purpose by Morris Burland,[9] curate of Newent parish and later the first incumbent of Gorsley with Clifford's Mesne.[10] In 1882 a new church, dedicated to St Peter, was built 150 m further to the north-east on the Boulsdon road. The cost, £1,021, was raised by voluntary subscriptions and grants.[11] The old building remained a school until 1935[12] and later was used as a village hall. In 2007 Clifford's Mesne church, as one of the three churches of the united benefice but with its own churchwardens and parochial church council, held services each Sunday.[13]

At Gorsley a building for use as a chapel and school was built in 1872 within the Newent part of the new ecclesiastical district and was enlarged by the addition of a chancel in 1877.[14] The site, beside the Newent–Ross road, was an isolated one but reasonably central to the scattered cottages and smallholdings it was intended to serve. A new church begun on an adjoining site to the east in 1892 was consecrated as Christ Church the following year. The site was given by the Onslow estate and the cost, £1,030, was met by grants and voluntary contributions including £404 from the vicar S.R. Cambie. The old building continued in use as a school until 1926 and became the church hall in 1954. In 1992 it was sold and became a house, and in 1997 a room for meetings was added to the west end of Christ Church.[15] In 2007 the church, managed under the united benefice by a local 'ministry team' of five lay members, was used for services every Sunday.[16]

Wesleyan Methodists

A group which registered a house in Culver Street for dissenting worship in 1792 was probably Wesleyan Methodist. In 1805 Wesleyans opened a small chapel owned by and adjoining the house of a builder, Thomas Warne, in Culver Street.[17] Hostility and intimidation from mobs of townspeople continued for several months in the summer of that year and led to the temporary closure of the chapel.[18] There was further trouble in 1820.[19] In its first years the meeting was led by local preachers, who in 1805 were under the general direction of J.M. Byron;[20] a minister based in Gloucester,[21] and later the chapel was attached to the Ledbury circuit.[22] The congregation, which presumably used some of the

---

1 *Dean Forest Mercury*, 7 Nov. 1969; GA, P 225/CW 3/18; *Newent United Reformed Church* (Souvenir Booklet, 1996), 35.

2 *Glos. Life*, Jan. 1974, 23.

3 *Millennium Memories: the History of Gorsley and Kilcot*, ed. L. Hines (2001), 26.

4 Information from the Revd S. Mason, priest-in-charge.

5 GA, P 225/IN 3/8.

6 *Kelly's Dir. Glos.* (1879), 709; OS Map 6", Glos. XVII.SW (1884 edn).

7 Glos. Colln. R 140A.3.

8 'Christ Church, Gorsley: a brief history' (church pamphlet, 2005).

9 Glos. Colln. R 140A.3; GA, P 225/SC 1/2.

10 GDR vol. 385, pp. 110, 153.

11 Glos. Colln. R 140A.3.

12 Above, social hist. (education: board and council schools).

13 Newsletter of the united benefice (2007); information from Revd S. Mason.

14 *Kelly's Dir. Glos.* (1879), 709.

15 *Millennium Memories*, 23–5.

16 'Christ Church, Gorsley: a brief history'; Newsletter of united benefice (2007).

17 Hockaday Abs. ccxciii, 1792, 1805; GA, D 917.

18 Glos. Colln. R 212.5.

19 *Glouc. J.* 3 Jan. 1820.

20 Glos. Colln. R 212.5.

21 G.R. Hine, *Methodist Church Gloucester Circuit Records* (1971), 5.

22 *Chapters in Newent's History* (Newent Local Hist. Soc. 2003), 199.

houses in the town that were registered during that period,[1] aided the establishment of meetings in several nearby parishes.[2] A chapel opened in 1815 at Pool Hill, within Pauntley parish, attracted some of its congregation from adjoining parts of Newent parish;[3] a house at Brand Green that was registered for worship by a minister of the Ledbury circuit in 1820 was perhaps connected with it.[4]

On the Sunday of the ecclesiastical census of 1851 the Culver Street chapel had a morning congregation of 46 (including 27 Sunday school children) and an evening congregation of 56.[5] It was replaced by a new chapel, begun in 1855 and opened the following year. The building of the chapel and the work of its ministry were aided by a gift of £1,000 from a Mr Wellin,[6] perhaps the Newent woolstapler and fellmonger William Wellin.[7] The new chapel continued in use for worship until c.1970 when it closed following the agreement between the Wesleyans and Anglicans to share worship in the parish church.[8]

Congregationalists

Congregationalists under the auspices of the Gloucester Southgate church held services and a Sunday school in the town from 1844.[9] In 1845 they built a chapel (opened the following year) on the south-west side of Broad Street (the former Lewall Street).[10] In 1851 there was a church membership of 18 but the adult congregations at three services held on the Sunday of the ecclesiastical census that year were estimated at 37, 56, and 73.[11] A manse for the minister was built in Culver Street in 1869.[12] The congregation established several cottage meetings in outlying hamlets in the mid 19th century: in the late 1840s they were held at Kent's Green and Brand Green[13] and in 1858 at Brand Green, Clifford's Mesne, and Stoney bridge, on the Ross road north of the Conigree. In 1900 the Broad Street chapel had a membership of 43.[14] Its strength remained at around that figure in the early 20th century, though in 1906 under a popular minister membership rose to 56 and the average congregation to 120, with over 40 pupils attending the Sunday school. The finances of the church were never secure, though the congregation added a vestry to the chapel and, in 1940, replaced the dilapidated manse with a new house in Bradford's Lane[15] From 1937 the church was served as a joint pastorate with the Ledbury Congregational church, but from 1960 it ceased to have a settled minister.[16] In 2007 (as the Newent United Reformed church) it had a membership of 25 and services were conducted by lay preachers or retired ministers living locally.[17]

Baptists

From the early 19th century Baptists obtained a strong following in Gorsley and Kilcot, and after 1821 many cottagers attended a chapel and schoolroom (Goff's school) opened at Blindman's Gate on the Ross road within the Linton part of Gorsley. In 1819 the minister of Ryeford chapel, in Weston-under Penyard (Herefs.), from which the Gorsley chapel and school were founded,[18] registered two houses in Newent for worship.[19] Those meetings apparently soon lapsed, as did another mission started in the town in 1831 by John Hall, a long-serving minister at Gorsley chapel.[20] By the 1930s a building in Kilcot, beside the Aston Ingham road just south of Kilcot Cross, was used as a Sunday school in connexion with Gorsley chapel, and in 1934 a small chapel was built alongside it. That chapel remained in use until the early 1990s,[21] when it was remodelled as a dwelling.[22]

Christian Brethren

From 1930 an independent evangelical group based at Cinderford, known as the Brethren or Christian Brethren, held meetings at Clifford's Mesne in a tent or in the open air. Later they met at Ravenshill Farm, to the north of Clifford's Mesne, and from 1932 in a small building of timber and corrugated iron in the hamlet. From the early 1940s the Christian Brethren held meetings in Newent town, and from 1948 they used a building known as the Gospel Hall on the Ledbury road. In 1950 the group, led by Alfred Cracknell and Arthur Goulding, began to raise money for building a chapel in the town. That was achieved in 1962 with the opening of a small chapel in Glebe Close,[23] among the new housing estates on the north-west side of Watery Lane. The Brethren

---

1 Hockaday Abs. ccxciii.
2 Ibid. ccl, 1816; cclxxx, 1814; ccxciii, 1816; cccx, 1814.
3 E. Warde, *They Didn't Walk Far: a History of Pool Hill* (priv. printed, 2000), 117, 120; below, Pauntley, religious hist. (religious life).
4 Hockaday Abs. ccxciii.
5 TNA, HO 129/335/1/4/7.
6 *Glouc. J.* 10 Nov. 1855; 21 June 1856.
7 TNA, HO 107/1960.
8 Above, this section.
9 GA, D 6026/9/1; Hockaday Abs. ccxciii; *Glouc. J.* 16 Nov. 1844.
10 *Glouc. J.* 10 May 1845; 9 May 1846.
11 *Newent United Reformed Church*, 4; TNA, HO 129/335/1/4/6.
12 *Newent United Reformed Church*, 7.
13 GA, D 6026/9/1.
14 Ibid. D 2052.
15 *Newent United Reformed Church*, 10–11, 16,19.
16 Ibid. 19, 30–1.
17 Information from Mrs D. Jones, former chapel sec.
18 *Millenium Memories*, 17–18, 20.
19 Hockaday Abs. ccxciii.
20 *Chapters in Newent's History*, 201.
21 *Millennium Memories*, 21.
22 *Citizen*, 4 Mar. 1993.
23 *Chapters in Newent's History*, 201–2.

continued to worship there in 2007, led by elders and deacons among whom the Cracknell and Goulding families remained prominent. The chapel then had a membership of 80 and was usually attended by congregations of c.130 drawn from Newent and surrounding parishes.[1] From 1974 the group also ran a Christian bookshop in the town. That moved in 1980 to a house opposite the junction of the main street and Watery Lane and remained open as the 'Good News Centre', combining the bookshop with a café, in 2007.[2]

Other Protestant Dissenting Groups

During 1835 and 1836 the missionary Thomas Kington registered houses in many hamlets near Newent, including Brand Green, Botloe's Green, and Kilcot. Presumably, like Kington's chapel at Broom's Green in Dymock, they remained in use for only a short time.[3] From 1935 Plymouth Brethren met in part of the old tannery buildings in Culver Street.[4] In the late 20th century they occupied successively a small chapel in Church Street and another in Glebe Close; the latter closed in 1999. From 1981 the Newent Community Centre (the former grammar school building at the entrance to the Ross road) was used for services by the Newent Christian Fellowship, a group allied to the pentecostalist sect the Assemblies of God.[5]

Roman Catholics

In 1939 the Salesian Fathers, who ran a school at Blaisdon Hall, opened a Roman Catholic mass centre at a house at the Scarr in the north of Newent parish. In 1943, a time when the congregation was enlarged by Italian and German prisoners-of-war housed in a camp outside the town, the services were transferred to Newent market house. In 1952 the congregation, under Fr. William Boyd, acquired a site on the Ross road and began raising money for a church. The church, dedicated to Our Lady of Lourdes, was begun in 1957 and opened at the end of 1959, much of the building work being done by volunteers.[6] In 2007 it was the centre of a parish covering a large area of north-west Gloucestershire and having another mass centre at Blaisdon.[7] The usual attendance at mass at the Newent church, often including people from the adjoining part of Herefordshire extending to Ledbury and Ross-on-Wye, was c.120.[8]

CHURCH BUILDINGS

The Parish Church

Newent parish church, which by the early 15th century bore the dedication to St Mary the Virgin,[9] is likely to have been an Anglo-Saxon foundation. In 1907 a cross shaft (kept in the porch in 2007) was found in a prominent position on the south side of the churchyard next to the road. Carved with figurative scenes which depict Adam and Eve after their expulsion from Eden, the angel restraining Abraham from the sacrifice of Isaac, and the victory of David over Goliath, it probably dates from the late 8th century or the early 9th, being related both in

22. *Ancient cross shaft at Newent church*

---

1 Information from Mr T. Cracknell, chapel sec.
2 *Chapters in Newent's History*, 202.
3 Hockaday Abs. ccxciii. For Kington, below, Dymock, religious hist. (religious life).
4 *Kelly's Dir. Glos.* (1939), 272; GA, DA 30/100/14, p. 144.
5 *Chapters in Newent's History*, 199–200.
6 Ibid. 197.
7 http://www.newentcatholic.org.uk (accessed 21 Sept. 2007).
8 Information from the parish priest, Fr. A. Murray.
9 Hockaday Abs. cxcii, 1416, 1489, 1502.

style and iconography to sculpture from high-status Mercian sites of that period.[1] A carved tablet possibly of the early 11th century and displaying on one face a crudely-exectued representation of the Crucifixion[2] was also unearthed in the early 20th century.[3]

Of the medieval church, represented by its chancel, south lady chapel, and south-west tower and spire, nothing earlier than the late 13th century survives, and no details of its nave and south aisle are recorded. After the collapse of the nave roof in 1674, reconstruction of the body of the church was completed in 1679 in the form of an undivided auditorium.[4] The character of the new work of that period is still evident, particularly inside, but the whole church displays the zeal of 19th-century restorers who altered both medieval and 17th-century work.[5]

The medieval fabric is of squared coursed sandstone. The earliest parts, dating apparently from a rebuilding in the late 13th century or early 14th, seem to be the chancel and the arcade with a simple round column dividing it on the south from the lady chapel. The chapel, possibly already in existence in the mid 13th century,[6] was (according to a statement of 1383) rebuilt by a group of parishioners in 1361,[7] but as a result of later restoration and renewal it is difficult to relate much of the fabric to that period. Both chancel and chapel have arch-braced collar rafter roofs, the chapel's with a moulded longitudinal rib, and the chapel has a priest's door and an aumbry with ball-flower decoration. The three-stage tower with diagonal buttresses was built in the mid 14th century and has rich mouldings, including ribbed arrises on the recessed octagonal spire. The tower's lowest stage is open as the south porch: it has a fan vault with bell hole, and its northern buttresses project into the body of the church, the north-eastern one incorporating a spiral staircase.

The principal medieval survival within the church is a late 14th-century tomb with effigies of a knight and lady which stood originally against the south wall of the lady chapel.[8] It had been badly damaged by the start of the 19th century when it was repaired,[9] and in 1912, after further restoration, it was moved to a site under the arcade between chapel and chancel.[10] The effigies were identified in the early 18th century as members of the Grandison family, though no inscription was then visible[11] and the heraldry now surviving is fragmentary. An image of the Virgin stood at the east end of the chapel in 1523 when Roger Porter asked to be buried before it;[12] his brass, originally set in the floor, has been re-set in the east wall.[13] Externally, a timber-framed porch was added to shelter the chapel's south door, probably early in the 17th century, and by the late 18th the chapel had acquired a tall eastern bellcot,[14] which was removed at a later restoration.

In the rebuilding of the 1670s James Hill of Cheltenham and Francis Jones of Hasfield were the chief masons and the local carpenter Edward Taylor was designer and overseer of the work on the roof.[15] Externally the nave is ashlar-faced with large segment-headed mullioned and transomed windows with arched lights and classical mouldings; the battlemented parapet has urns. The internal walls, originally plastered, are articulated by the unfluted Ionic pilasters of ashlar. Their tall bases were designed to accommodate box pews, parts of which were re-used in new pews at the late 19th-century restoration. The pilasters, applied to the walls to correspond to the central row of stone columns originally intended to support the roof, survived the change in plan to an undivided space with galleries along all but the north wall, where the pulpit was placed.[16] The ceiling is almost flat and was originally plastered. The wide span was made possible by the roof structure said to have been based on principles developed by Wren: it is of eight bays with single-span king-post trusses, four pairs of purlins, no ridge piece, scissor bracing between king posts, and windbraces between trusses in the lower part of the slope.[17] The medieval east wall was retained but modified, with the openings into the chancel and lady chapel given square heads and flanking pilasters. The stone font, a classically decorated bowl on a stem, is of the late 17th century, as is the stone reredos, which has been moved to the west end together with a reversed wrought-iron overthrow.

---

1 Fig. 22; R. Cramp, 'Schools of Mercian Sculpture', in *Mercian Studies*, ed. A. Dornier (Leicester, 1977), 193, 225, 228–9; information from Michael Hare, forthcoming in R. Bryant, *Corpus of Anglo-Saxon Stone Sculpture, X; the Western Midlands*.

2 D.P. Dobson, 'Anglo-Saxon Buildings and Sculpture in Gloucestershire.', *Trans. BGAS* 55 (1933), 265, 272–3; G. Zarnecki, 'The Newent Funerary Tablet', ibid. 72 (1953), 49–55.

3 GA, P 225/IN 4/5. The tablet is kept in Gloucester museum and the ch. contains a cast of it : information from Michael Hare of Gloucester.

4 Above (religious life in 17th and 18th cents.).

5 The description of the fabric takes account of Verey and Brooks, *Glos.* II, 601–4.

6 Above (religious life in Middle Ages and 16th cent.).

7 *Cal. Inq. p.m.* XVI, pp. 27–8.

8 Roper, *Glos. Effigies*, 431–4.

9 GA, D 412/Z 3, Newent notes, 1900.

10 Ibid. P 225/IN 4/5.

11 Bodleian, Top. Glouc. c. 3, f. 140v.

12 Hockaday Abs. ccxcii, 1523.

13 Davis, *Glos. Brasses*, 129–30.

14 Bigland, *Glos.* II, pl. facing p. 238; *Glos. Ch. Notes*, 78.

15 Inscr. inside E. gable of nave, quoted in ch. guide (2000), 13.

16 GA, D 412/Z 3, Newent notes, 1900.

17 Fig. 23.

23. *Newent church looking south-east, showing the 17th-century nave*

During the 18th century some high-quality wall monuments were placed in chancel and nave for leading families of the parish, including one designed by John Flaxman for Barbara Bourchier (d. 1784), daughter of James Richardson of Newent. In the churchyard many of the town's tradesmen of the period are commemorated by ornate and deeply-carved headstones in the local sandstone. By the 1770s the church had a ring of six bells,[1] including two cast by John Pennington in 1638 and 1644 and another by Abraham Rudhall of Gloucester in 1724; most were recast later,[2] and the ring was augmented to eight in 1983.[3] In 1737 an organ, built by local carpenter Thomas Warne, was installed in the church;[4] it was moved from the south gallery to the west gallery c.1839, re-sited on the south of the chancel in 1870,[5] and moved to the north of the chancel in 1912.[6]

In 1827 and 1828, at the cost of a group of leading townsmen, the west gallery was rebuilt on cast-iron columns by Richard Jones of Ledbury.[7] The gallery across the entrances to the chancel and lady chapel was removed in 1865.[8] The major 19th-century restoration was carried out under John Middleton of Cheltenham between 1879 and 1884, starting with the chancel (partly using plans by Gilbert Scott), and continuing with the reorganization of the nave to face east, the removal of the pulpit (reduced in height) to the north-east corner, the scraping of the walls, and the creation of the present panelled and boarded ceiling. The work on the chancel included the reconstruction of the large east window,[9] which had remained blocked since most of the tracery had collapsed in 1651.[10] Waller & Son continued the restoration between 1909 and 1912, their work including the addition of a north vestry to the chancel as a memorial to Andrew Knowles of Newent Court, the restoration of the lady chapel (until then used as the vestry), and, in the nave, alterations to the ceiling and removal of the south gallery.[11]

In 1968 the top section of the church spire, which was built of limestone rather than the local sandstone of the lower stages, was declared dangerous and was removed; the discrepancy in materials evidently resulted from the loss of part of

1 Rudder, *Glos.* 564.
2 *Glos. Ch. Bells*, 445–6.
3 Ch. guide (2000), 18.
4 *Glouc. J.* 7 June 1737.
5 GA, D 412/Z 3, Newent notes, 1900; P 225/CW 3/2.
6 Ibid. PA 225/2.

7 Ibid. P 225/CW 3/1.
8 Ibid. D 412/Z 3, Newent notes, 1900.
9 Ibid. P 225/CW 3/5; *Kelly's Dir. Glos.* (1885), 532.
10 GA, D 412/Z 3, Nourse MS, p. 11; 'Transactions at Newent', *Trans. BGAS* 10 (1885–6), 244.
11 GA, P 225/CW 3/5; IN 4/5; PA 225/2.

the spire in a gale in 1662[1] and rebuilding and repair carried out in 1771,[2] 1829,[3] and probably at other times. The church was closed for almost two years, and the missing section of the spire was replaced during 1971 and 1972.[4] In 1979 the north vestry was extended to form a church room and office. The space below the west gallery was converted to a children's room in 1985.[5]

Other Anglican Churches

The late 19th-century churches at Clifford's Mesne and Gorsley are both simple Gothic buildings, mainly of the local sandstone and with aisleless naves and chancels. St Peter, Clifford's Mesne, built in 1882 to designs of E. Swinfen Harris, is the more attractive building, influenced by the Arts and Crafts Movement and distinguished by a prominent roof with central bellcot and a well-preserved interior with scissor-braced roof and original furnishings.[6] Christ Church, Gorsley, built during 1892 and 1893 to a more stolid design by S. Rollinson & Son, has short transepts and an eastern apse and a timber-framed porch as elaborations of the basic plan; the bellcot is on the west gable. The furnishings, of several dates, have been imported.[7]

Nonconformist and Roman Catholic Buildings

Of Newent's nonconformist chapels the Congregational (later United Reformed) chapel opened in Broad Street in 1846 was designed by William Rees of Gloucester as a simple box but was given an old-fashioned Gothic façade of Painswick stone with an embattled gable. It also included a schoolroom for a British school.[8] A vestry was added to the building in 1926.[9] The Wesleyan chapel completed in Culver Street in 1856[10] was built in a Gothic manner with a steeply-gabled street front of polychromatic brickwork. In 2007 it was used as an auction room.

The Roman Catholic church on Ross Road opened in 1959 was enlarged and given a glass front in a programme of modernization completed in 2007.[11]

24. *Detail of ironwork at St Peter's church, Clifford's Mesne*

---

1 *Notes on Dioc. of Glouc. by Chancellor Parsons*, 169.
2 *Glouc. J.* 9 Sept. 1771.
3 GA, P 225/CW 2/1.
4 Ibid. CW 3/18; *Dean Forest Mercury*, 2 Feb. 1968; 7 Nov. 1969; *Citizen*, 17 Dec. 1969; 30 Apr. 1971.
5 Ch. guide (2000), 19.
6 Verey and Brooks, *Glos.* II, 312. See Fig. 24.
7 Verey and Brooks, *Glos.* II, 510.
8 Ibid. 604; *Glouc. J.* 10 May 1845; 9 May 1846.
9 *Newent United Reformed Church*, 10–11, 16,19.
10 *Glouc. J.* 10 Nov. 1855; 21 June 1856.
11 http://www.newentcatholic.org.uk (accessed 21 Sept. 2007).

BROMESBERROW

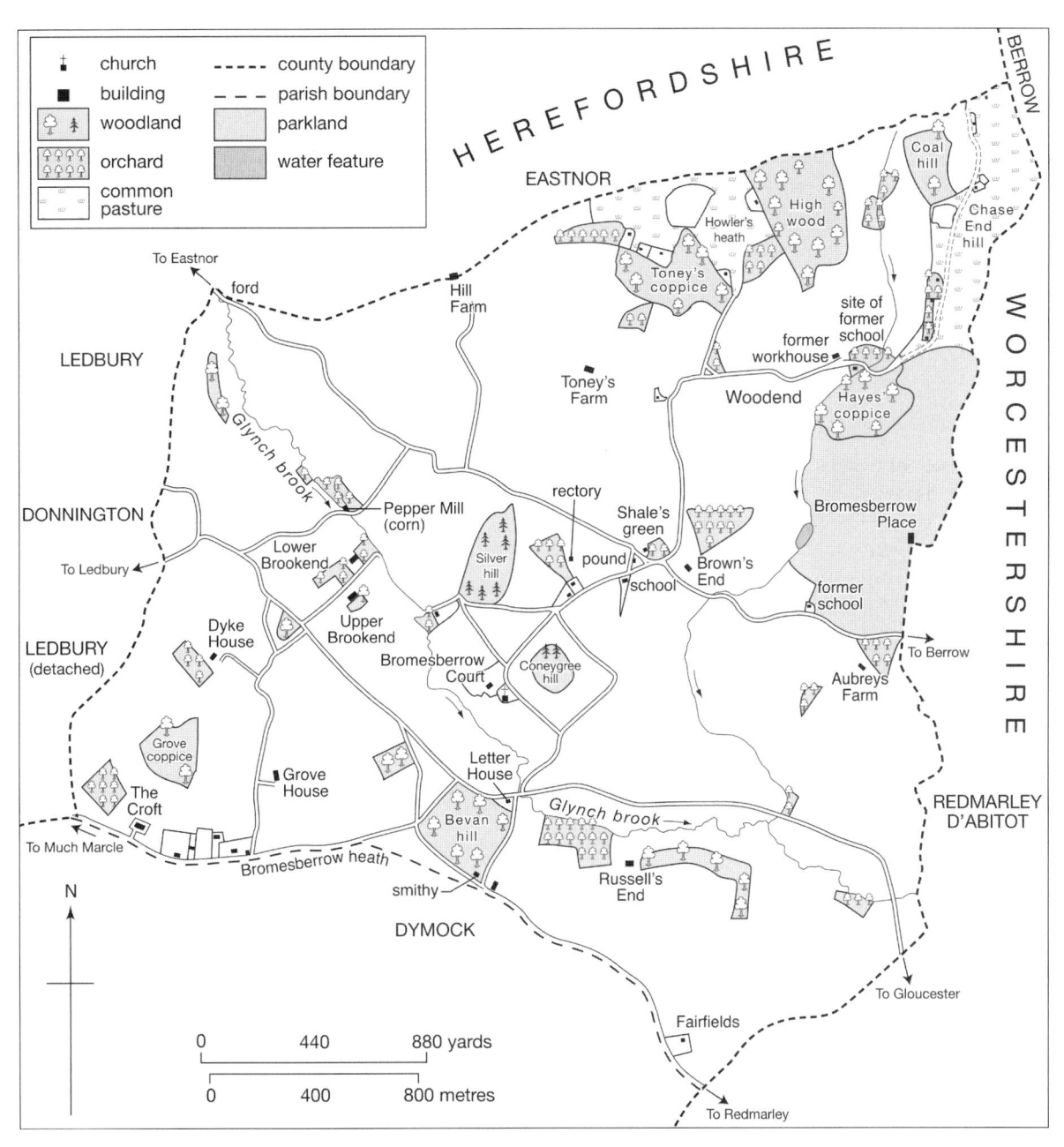

Map 7. *Bromesberrow 1882*

BROMESBERROW is a small rural parish 18 km NNW of Gloucester and 5 km south-east of Ledbury (Herefs.). Situated at the southern tip of the Malvern hills, the ancient parish was bordered by Herefordshire to the north and west and Worcestershire to the east. Before disafforestation in the 17th century part of the parish lay within Malvern Chase[1] and the lord of Bromesberrow was expected to attend the chase court at Hanley Castle (Worcs.).[2] The parish boundaries, which enclosed 1,809 a. (732 ha),[3]

---

1 Bigland, *Glos.* II, 257; B. Smith, *A History of Malvern* (2nd edn, 1978), 25–40.
2 GA, D 333/Z 3; J. Toomey (ed.), *Records of Hanley Castle, Worcestershire, c.1147–1547* (Worcs. Rec. Soc. N.S.. 18, 2001), 111, 114, 151.
3 OS Area Book (1883).

25. Bromesberrow: view from the south-west showing the church and Coneygree hill

remained the same until 1992, when Bromesberrow gained land from Redmarley D'Abitot (Glos., formerly Worcs.) to the east and its boundary on the south-west was moved to the line of the M50 motorway to take the village of Bromesberrow Heath from Dymock.[1]

LANDSCAPE

The landscape of Bromesberrow, included within the Malvern Hills Area of Outstanding Natural Beauty in 1959,[2] is well wooded and rises steeply from Toney's Farm (80 m) to Howler's heath (180 m). Chase End hill (191 m)[3] in the north-east of the parish, called *wærlafes dune* ('Wærlaf's hill') in the 10th century,[4] is the southernmost of the Malvern hills and is formed from a mixture of Precambrian igneous rocks and Cambrian shale. Howler's heath, recorded in the early 14th century,[5] lies on Silurian May Hill (Llandovery) sandstone,[6] which was quarried there for building stone.[7]

South of Toney's Farm the relief is gentler, typically between 50 and 75 m, and the Glynch brook crosses the parish from north-west to south-east. On the east side a small stream rising in Eastnor (Herefs.) runs north–south through Woodend to join the brook south of Aubreys Farm. In the centre of the parish, close to its church, two prominent rounded hills have given rise to place names in Old English *beorg*.[8] Coneygree hill, probably the mound from which Bromesberrow took its name,[9] was a rabbit warren (*le Conynger*) in 1393[10] and was landscaped in the 18th century in an aborted attempt to build a new manor house on its summit.[11] Bevan hill, rising south of the Glynch brook and east of Bromesberrow heath, was recorded in 1369.[12] Much of the land in the south of the parish is formed from Permian Bridgnorth and Triassic Bromsgrove sandstones, giving light and well-drained soils red in colour, although Dyke House (86 m) in the south-west stands on a patch of boulder clay.[13]

In 1086 Bromesberrow had woodland measuring 2 by 1 leagues.[14] Early woods mentioned in the parish

---

1 The Forest of Dean (Parishes) Order 1991 (unpublished Statutory Instrument 1992 no 2283); information (Sept. 2003) from Mr Gareth Ellison (environment directorate, Glos. co. council). This history, written in 2007 and incorporating research conducted by Dr Carrie Smith, is concerned with the parish as it existed up to 1992.
2 *The Times*, 27 Oct 1959.
3 OS Map 1:25,000, sheet 190 (2006 edn).
4 *PN Glos*. III, 186; Finberg, *Early Charters of W. Midlands*, 56. It was recorded as *Warlowesdowne* in 1467: GA, D 247/61.
5 E. Scroggs, 'The Shrewsbury (Talbot) Manuscripts', *Trans. BGAS* 60 (1938), 274; *PN Glos*. III, 167.
6 Geol. Surv. Map 1:50,000, solid and drift, sheet 216 (1988 edn).

7 Below, econ. hist. (industry and trade).
8 Bromesberrow and Silver hill: *PN Glos*. III, 166–7, 168; IV, 102; Harvard Law School, Cambridge (Mass.), MS Lat. 14, Box 85, no 51 (copy in GA, MF 1524).
9 Fig. 25. M. Gelling and A. Cole, *The Landscape of Place Names* (2000), 146, 148.
10 Harvard Law School, MS Lat. 14, Box 85, no 53; see SMR Glos. no 5359.
11 Below, manor (manor: Hook Ho.).
12 Harvard Law School, MS Lat. 14, Box 85, no 51.
13 Geol. Surv. Map 1:50,000, solid and drift, sheet 216 (1988 edn).
14 *Domesday Book* (Rec. Com.), I, 168.

26. *Bromesberrow Place from the west c.1800*

included High wood (*Overwode*), Hayes' coppice (*le hey*), and *Bernewode* near Toney's Farm.[1] The name Whiteleaved Oak, associated with the meeting-point of the three counties at the north-east corner of Bromesberrow, referred in 1584 to a great tree that was a landmark on the boundary of Malvern Chase.[2] The light sandy soils covering much of the parish are generally poor and historically were used for growing rye, although numerous orchards are recorded from the late 16th century and fertile river meadows line the Glynch brook and its tributary through Woodend. The extent and number of Bromesberrow's medieval open fields are not known and most arable farming in the parish appears to have taken place in small closes. Inclosure seems to have been a long and informal process that was largely complete by the early 19th century. Bromesberrow heath, the greater part of which belonged to Dymock, was inclosed under awards dated 1864 and 1866,[3] but Howler's heath, recorded as *Oulithe* ('owl's slope') in the 14th century,[4] and much of Chase End hill remained common land in 2007.[5]

Following the building of Bromesberrow Place on the eastern boundary in the later 18th century a park containing several plantations and a fishing lake was created around the house;[6] a boat house had been erected beside the lake by 1903.[7] In the late 20th century a new park, designed by Hal Moggridge, was laid out to the west of the existing one and shelter belts of trees were planted around the fringes of the parkland. A reservoir was created to the north of the fishing lake in the 1980s.[8] In 1905 Malvern Urban District Council began pumping water from a well west of Bevan hill[9] and under an agreement of 1908 with Newent Rural District Council it provided a free supply to some Bromesberrow residents.[10]

ROADS

Bromesberrow is crossed by a network of minor lanes and paths, several of which have formed deep hollow ways.[11] Many of Bromesberrow's farmsteads can only be reached along narrow dead-end lanes, but it is likely that the settlements around the church and at Brookend stand on a former route to Ledbury along the Glynch brook, perhaps the highway referred to in the 13th century.[12] Among the lanes converging on a small triangular green in the centre of the parish are routes westwards towards Eastnor by way of Clencher's mill ford, northwards over Chase End hill, and eastwards towards Berrow (Worcs.). A hollow lane running NE–SW past Pepper Mill crossed a small bridge over the Glynch brook in the early 18th century.[13] The crossing in

---

1 Scroggs, 'Shrewsbury (Talbot) Manuscripts', 273–5; Harvard Law School, MS Lat. 14, Box 85, no 52.
2 Smith, *Hist. of Malvern*, 29.
3 Below, econ. hist. (agric.); Dymock, econ. hist. (agric.).
4 Scroggs, 'Shrewsbury (Talbot) Manuscripts', 274; *PN Glos.* III, 167.
5 Reg. of Common Land (Glos. co. legal services dept.), no CL 290; ibid. (Worcs. co. legal services dept.), no CL 10.
6 GA, photocopy 924; Fosbrooke, *Glos.* II, facing p. 248, reproduced as Fig. 26.
7 OS Map 6", Glos. X.NE (1903 edn).
8 Information from Dr The Hon. G. Greenall of Bromesberrow Place.
9 Richardson, *Wells and Springs of Glos.* 63–5.
10 GA, DA 30/100/9, pp. 268–70.
11 See SMR Glos. nos 22123, 22127, 22129, 22134.
12 GA, D 963, undated deed no 3.
13 Ibid. D 1388, Pitt and Yate, Bromesberrow deeds 1620–1711.

2007 was marked by a narrow stone-built bridge, which was possibly the same bridge repaired in 1811.[1]

The ancient road from Gloucester to Ledbury entered the parish from the east along its southern boundary, following a route recorded in the 10th century.[2] At the eastern end of Bromesberrow heath, the road turned northwards around the western side of Bevan hill and down a steep slope known in 1811 as the 'old cut'[3] to continue westwards along the line of the present main road. The road was turnpiked from Ledbury to Bromesberrow in 1722[4] and the rest of the road through and alongside the parish was included in an Act of 1764 that created a turnpike route between Ledbury and the Gloucester–Worcester road.[5] In the early 19th century, before 1811, the Gloucester–Ledbury road adopted a new course, entering the parish by the Glynch brook and passing north of Bevan hill.[6] A branch road running westwards from Bevan hill towards Much Marcle (Herefs.) was turnpiked in 1833[7] and its line was straightened following the inclosure of Bromesberrow heath.[8] Both of Bromesberrow's turnpike roads were disturnpiked in 1871.[9] Construction of the M50 motorway, opened in 1960,[10] necessitated the demolition of one cottage on its route across the south of the parish, from the Glynch brook in the east to Bromesberrow Heath in the west,[11] and included the creation of a junction with the Gloucester–Ledbury road.[12]

POPULATION

Nineteen tenants were recorded in Bromesberrow in 1086[13] and eighteen persons were assessed for tax there in 1327.[14] A muster in 1542 named 29 Bromesberrow men[15] and in 1563 the parish was said to contain 30 households.[16] The number of communicants in the parish was given as *c.*80 in 1551[17] and 120 in 1603[18] and there were 50 families in 1650.[19] There were at least 132 inhabitants in 1676[20] and an estimate of 80 *c.*1710[21] is likely to have been too small, for the population in 1770 was put at 138.[22] The recorded population rose from 235 in 1801 to 337 in 1831 before falling back to 260 in 1851. During the later 19th century it recovered to a little below 300 but it dropped to 255 in 1901,[23] when a number of agricultural labourers left to seek work in the Welsh coalfields.[24] Despite a partial revival in its size, reaching 269 in 1911, the parish's population decreased steadily throughout the 20th century to 182 in 1991. Reflecting the boundary changes of 1992 it was 411 in 2001.[25]

SETTLEMENT

Bromesberrow is settled in scattered farmsteads and cottages. The settlement pattern was established by the 13th century, when several residents bore surnames indicating the locations of their dwellings, including a brook, a grove, a hill, a heath, and a ditch.[26] A few early inhabitants also lent their names to small hamlets, most with the suffix 'end'.[27] Between the 14th and 19th centuries several dwellings in the parish were abandoned, their former identity occasionally being preserved in field names.[28] Squatter settlement is recorded at Chase End from the later 18th century[29] and the number of inhabited houses in the parish grew from 40 in 1801 to 64 in 1871[30] as more cottages were erected on all three of Bromesberrow's commons.[31] Following a reduction in the number of houses to 52 in 1901, new building in the 20th century increased the total to 68 in 1951 and 74 in 1991.[32]

---

1 GA, P 63/SU 2/1.
2 *PN Glos.* III, 186; Finberg, *Early Charters of W. Midlands*, 61.
3 GA, D 1618, Ricardo fam. papers, memos to surveyors 1811.
4 Ledbury Roads Act, 7 Geo. I, c. 23.
5 Ibid. 4 Geo. III, c. 62.
6 Birmingham City Archives, Barnard Colln. 886/1; GA, D 1618, Ricardo fam. papers, memos to surveyors 1811. See Bryant, *Map of Glos.* (1824); OS Map 1", sheet 43 (1831 edn).
7 Ledbury Roads Act, 3 Wm. IV, c. 58 (Local and Personal).
8 GA, Q/RI 31.
9 Annual Turnpike Acts Continuance Act, 1871, 34 & 35 Vic. c. 115.
10 *Citizen*, 29 Nov. 1960.
11 GA, D 7547/7/2 (par. mag. Aug. 1958).
12 OS Map 1:2,500, SO 7433–7533 (1971 edn).
13 *Domesday Book* (Rec. Com.), I, 168.
14 *Glos. Subsidy Roll, 1327*, 36.
15 *L&P Hen. VIII*, XVII, 499.
16 Bodleian, Rawl. C. 790, f. 27.
17 J. Gairdner, 'Bishop Hooper's Visitation of Gloucester', *EHR* 19 (1904), 119.
18 *Eccl. Misc.* 100.
19 C.R. Elrington, 'The Survey of Church Livings in Gloucestershire, 1650', *Trans. BGAS* 83 (1964), 98.
20 *Compton Census*, 544.
21 Atkyns, *Glos.* 304.
22 Rudder, *Glos.* 314.
23 *Census*, 1801–1901.
24 GA, S 63/2, p. 42.
25 *Census*, 1911–2001.
26 GA, D 963, undated deeds nos 1, 3; *Pleas of the Crown for Glos.* ed. Maitland, pp. 88, 90; Scroggs, 'Shrewsbury (Talbot) Manuscripts', 274.
27 Below, this section.
28 cf. GA, D 9125/Austin cat. 7287; GDR, T 1/40.
29 Below, this section.
30 *Census*, 1801–71.
31 *1st Rep. Com. Employment in Agric.* app. II, p. 124; above, introd. (landscape); below (the northern hills).
32 *Census*, 1901–91.

BESIDE THE GLYNCH BROOK

The medieval church stands north of the Glynch brook next to Bromesberrow Court. The latter, a farmhouse, incorporates much of the late medieval manor house;[1] in 1382 expenses were paid for a hedge enclosing both it and the church.[2] Upstream is the hamlet known by the mid 13th century as Brookend.[3] Upper and Lower Brookend are two substantial 17th-century farmhouses, the former perhaps incorporating fragments of a late medieval hall.[4] Nearby Pepper Mill, a former water mill likely to be on the site of the manorial mill,[5] belonged with Lower Brookend to the Eastnor estate from 1735[6] and has an 18th-century house. Midway between Lower Brookend and Bromesberrow Court a small farmhouse known as Lodwicks (or Grants), acquired by Rice Yate from the lord of the manor in 1669,[7] was demolished in the mid 20th century.[8]

In the south-west of the parish Dyke House and Grove House are former farmsteads that presumably mark the sites inhabited by Robert Dyke and Robert Grove in the early 13th century.[9] The farmsteads, which in 1487 belonged respectively to Alice Dyke and Richard Grove,[10] both have houses constructed according to classical principles in the 17th or 18th centuries.[11] Further south towards Bromesberrow heath a cottage called Watts belonged to Dyke House in 1776[12] and a squatter cottage had been erected on the heath by 1812.[13] In 1838 c.10 dwellings were strung out along the northern side of the road to Much Marcle; the small farmstead at the west end[14] was known later as the Croft.[15] Further east Newent Rural District Council built six houses next to the Malvern waterworks below Bevan hill in the 1930s.[16]

In the south-east Russell's End, so named in 1320,[17] was possibly home to a man surnamed 'of Russeley' in 1268.[18] The 15th-century farmhouse standing there below Bevan hill near the Glynch brook was presumably William Brooke's dwelling called Russhleys in 1487.[19] In the late 20th century it became a private house and two or three new houses were built near by. To the south Fairfields, a two-storeyed 19th-century gentleman's residence on the Redmarley road, incorporates parts of an older timber-framed farmhouse. Further west on the road a 17th-century farmhouse near Bevan hill[20] probably occupies the site of Hill Place, recorded in 1487[21] and purchased by John Bromwich in 1580.[22] Letter House, located below Bevan hill on the main Gloucester–Ledbury road, was one of two post houses in the parish in 1822.[23] In 2007 there was a residential caravan park c.500 m east of Russell's End, close to the M50 motorway junction.

By the eastern parish boundary stand Bromesberrow Place and Aubreys Farm. The former was originally a farmhouse known as Hook House and was renamed in the later 18th century, when it was remodelled for the lords of the manor as a country house.[24] Aubreys Farm is on the site of a medieval farmstead occupied by members of the Aubrey family[25] established in Bromesberrow by 1327.[26] The brick farmhouse, part of the Bromesberrow Place estate in 1812,[27] was divided into two cottages in the early 20th century[28] and was used as offices in 2007. In 1638 an adjacent trapezoidal moat[29] surrounded a plot known as 'the vineyard'.[30]

To the west of Aubreys Farm a loose cluster of dwellings is focused on the small triangular green mentioned above.[31] The green is likely to have been near the home of Walter Green (*atte Grene*) in 1327[32] and it was known in the 19th century as Shale's green.[33] Brown's End, east of the green on the site of Robert Baker's dwelling in 1388,[34] has a 17th-century farmhouse with a contemporary detached bakehouse.[35] Hatch Farm, built north of the green c.1900,[36] stands adjacent to a pair of 19th-century

---

1 Below, manor (manor: Bromesberrow Ct.).
2 Harvard Law School, MS Lat. 14, Box 85, no 52.
3 TNA, JUST 1/275, rot. 4. See also GA, D 1448/T 3.
4 Below (bldgs.); manor (other estates: Upper Brookend).
5 SMR Glos. no 6547; GA, D 9125/Austin cat. 7287; below, econ. hist. (mills and fishponds).
6 W. Wynn-Lloyd, 'Bromesberrow', *Trans. BGAS* 45 (1923), 145.
7 GA, D 1618, deeds of Lodwicks and Jacketts 1668–86; photocopies 192, 194.
8 OS Map 6", Glos. X.NE (1924 edn).
9 GA, D 963, undated deed no 1.
10 Ibid. D 9125/Austin cat. 7287.
11 Below (bldgs.).
12 GA, Q/REl 1, Botloe hundred. See also GDR, T 1/40.
13 GA, photocopy 924. See also ibid. photocopy 192.
14 GDR, T 1/40.
15 OS Map 6", Glos. X.SW (1883 edn).
16 GA, DA 30/100/14, pp. 251, 384; above, introd. (landscape).
17 BL, Add. Ch. 72661.
18 TNA, JUST 1/275, rot. 4.

19 GA, D 9125/Austin cat. 7287; below (bldgs.).
20 Bavenhill Farmhouse: below (bldgs.).
21 GA, D 9125/Austin cat. 7287, s.v. Hyllehouse.
22 Ibid. D 1388, Pitt and Yate, Bromesberrow deeds 1580–1703.
23 Ibid. photocopy 192; below, econ. hist. (industry and trade).
24 Below, manor (manor: Hook Ho.).
25 GA, D 9125/Austin cat. 7287.
26 *Glos. Subsidy Roll, 1327*, 36.
27 GA, photocopy 924.
28 Wynn-Lloyd, 'Bromesberrow', 152.
29 SMR Glos. no 5365.
30 GA, D 326/R 2.
31 Above, introd. (roads).
32 *Glos. Subsidy Roll, 1327*, 36.
33 GDR, T 1/40.
34 GA, D 9125/Austin cat. 7286. See also Harvard Law School, MS Lat.14, Box 85, no 54.
35 Below, manor (other estates: Brown's End).
36 cf. OS Map 6", Glos. X.NE (1883, 1903 edns): it was known in the early 20th cent. as Brownsend Farm.

estate cottages[1] on the site of a medieval farmhouse called Hatches.[2] South-west of the green are the early 19th-century rectory house[3] and a cottage known as Holt's on the site of a dwelling owned by the church lands charity in 1620.[4] On the south side of the green, where a parish pound stood in the later 19th century,[5] Bromesberrow school dates from 1871.[6] Twentieth-century dwellings include four houses erected by the RDC opposite Brown's End in the 1940s[7] and, near by, a new rectory house of the 1950s in Albright Lane[8] and a pair of cottages on the east side of Coneygree hill.[9]

THE NORTHERN HILLS

Hill Farm in the north-west of the parish on the boundary with Eastnor may stand on the site of the dwelling of the Lythe (*atte Lythe*, 'slope')[10] family in the 14th century;[11] it belonged to Richard Beauchamp, Lord Beauchamp, in the late 15th century.[12] The house at Toney's Farm to the south-east dates from the 14th century[13] and the farm included four or five cottages on or around Howler's heath to the north in the 15th century;[14] two of those cottages appear to have preserved the surnames ('of Cock hill' and 'of Howler's heath') of men resident in the early 14th century.[15] During the early 19th century squatter cottages were erected on the waste.[16] At least three were taken into the Ricardos' Bromesberrow Place estate[17] and the ruins of one were visible close to the boundary of High wood in 2007.[18]

The hamlet of Woodend, recorded in the mid 14th century,[19] was located on rising ground to the north of Bromesberrow Place. Containing cottages called Jacketts and Soters in 1547[20] and Charmers in 1671,[21] the hamlet comprised two houses in the early 18th century[22] and was chosen in 1751 as the site of the parish poorhouse (later workhouse). Following its closure in 1835, that house was retained by the parish as two dwellings and was sold in 1964.[23] The only other cottage to survive at Woodend in 2007 was known in the mid 19th century as Keeper's House.[24] Two dwellings called Chylhead (Chelnage) and Longelees (Longneys) in 1424[25] appear to have stood south-east of Woodend and were presumably occupied by William 'of Chelenhed' and Richard 'of Langley' in 1327:[26] the former derived his surname from a location on the boundary with Redmarley D'Abitot documented in the 10th and 11th centuries.[27]

Chase End in the north-east corner of the parish was long known as Keys End, perhaps after the Keys family, members of which were resident in the mid 14th century.[28] It was the location of a cottage called Partridges in 1547[29] and Rice Yate bought a cottage near the common there in 1669.[30] A small 17th-century house stands at the northern end of the settlement close to the hamlet of Whiteleaved Oak in Berrow.[31] Squatter cottages were erected on the waste in the later 18th and early 19th century[32] and most had been taken into the Ricardos' estate by 1870;[33] one had outbuildings that in 1850 included a cider mill, pigsty, cow barn and stable.[34] In 1871 James Howell rebuilt one cottage in brick as two semi-detached dwellings.[35] During the 20th century the settlement at Chase End remained largely unchanged, although improvements were made to existing buildings.[36]

---

1 GA, D 7547/1/10. The cottages were on the Brown's End estate in the 1930s: ibid. D 2299/6537.
2 See Scroggs, 'Shrewsbury (Talbot) Manuscripts', 273–4; GA, D 9125/Austin cat. 7287; D 1262, Bromesberrow deeds 1366–1743, deed 4 Aug. 1527.
3 Below, religious hist. (patronage and endowment).
4 GA, D 963.
5 OS Map 6", Glos. X.NE (1883 edn).
6 Below, social hist. (education).
7 GA, DA 30/100/17, pp. 245, 354.
8 Below, religious hist. (patronage and endowment).
9 cf. OS Maps 6", Glos. X.SE (1924 edn); 1:2,500, SO 7433–7533 (1971 edn).
10 *PN Glos.* III, 167.
11 Scroggs, 'Shrewsbury (Talbot) Manuscripts', 275–6.
12 GA, D 9125/Austin cat. 7287. For the descent of Beauchamp's land, see below, manor (introductory para.).
13 Below, manor (other estates: Toney's Farm).
14 GA, D 247/61; D 9125/Austin cat. 7287; Harvard Law School, MS Lat. 14, Box 85, no 56.
15 Scroggs, 'Shrewsbury (Talbot) Manuscripts', 274, 276. Fields named 'Cockles' lay to the east of Toney's Farm: GDR, T 1/40.
16 GA, D 1618, Yate fam. deeds and papers 1807–20, letter 15 Nov. 1818.
17 Ibid. D 3527/13; D 6913, Ricardo fam. deeds 1823–90.

18 Personal observation. See GDR, T 1/40 (no 29); GA, DA 30/100/25, p. 52.
19 GA, D 1262 Bromesberrow deeds 1366–1743.
20 GDR wills 1547/195–6.
21 Herefs. RO, D 96/43; below, econ. hist. (mills and fishponds).
22 Atkyns, *Glos.* 304.
23 Below, local govt. (parochial govt.).
24 GDR, T 1/40; below, econ. hist. (woodland management).
25 GA, D 9125/Austin cat. 7287. See below, manor (manor: Hook Ho.).
26 *Glos. Subsidy Roll, 1327*, 36.
27 *PN Glos.* III, 186; Finberg, *Early Charters of W. Midlands*, 56, 225–7.
28 Scroggs, 'Shrewsbury (Talbot) Manuscripts', 275. See e.g. OS Map 1", sheet 43 (1831 edn).
29 GDR wills 1547/195–6.
30 GA, D 1618, deeds of Woodend 1623–86.
31 Yewtree Cottage: below (bldgs.).
32 GA, D 3527/12; D 6913, Ricardo fam. deeds 1823–90; photocopy 192.
33 Ibid. D 3527/12; D 6913, Ricardo fam. deeds 1823–90; *1st Rep. Com. Employment in Agric.* app. II, p. 124.
34 GA, D 6913, Ricardo fam. deeds 1823–90.
35 Ibid. D 7547/2/5; datestone inscribed 'J.H. 1871'.
36 DoE List, Bromsberrow (1987), 3/21; GA, D 7547/2/5.

27. Russell's End from the west

BUILDINGS

Medieval houses survive from four of the estates and farms that had been established by the late Middle Ages. Two are stone-built. That at Toney's Farm, sited on a hillside platform, dates from the 14th century and displays very high-quality timberwork.[1] The manor house, set within a complex of much more recent farm buildings west of the church at Bromesberrow Court, is similar in plan but probably later.[2] The other two medieval houses are timber-framed and probably of the 15th century; Upper Brookend stands on a level site close to the Glynch brook[3] and Russell's End is at the foot of a steep slope down to the brook. The latter preserves at its core a cruck-framed range[4] comprising a hall of two bays and a 1½-storeyed chamber end of one bay: the hall retains the north door to its cross passage. Altered floor levels suggest that the chamber end originally had two full storeys before the surrounding ground was made up. The upper part of the present cellar represents the lower part of the range's ground floor; with a higher floor level than at present the solar would have been open to the roof.

There was much building activity in the parish in the 16th and 17th centuries. Major improvements were made at Russell's End, leading the house to be described in 1592 as new.[5] The east, service end of the medieval range was rebuilt and it is likely that the insertion of an upper floor in the hall, the erection of a massive south chimneystack, and the construction of a larger cellar were also contemporary. The chamber end was extended southwards by the addition of a 2½-storeyed block with a large room on each floor and three-light mullioned windows (now blocked) on the east front. It was heated by a west chimneystack of brick on a stone base, whilst the frame, infilled with brick, has some close studding for display. The new block was adjacent to a buttery and it contained the parlour and upper chambers that in 1617 John Brooke, on assigning the house to his widowed daughter-in-law for her life, retained for his own use.[6] In the late 17th century the parlour was refitted with panelling and a new chimneypiece.

Improvements were made at the other three medieval houses in the parish, that at Upper Brookend being almost completely rebuilt on a larger scale in the 17th century.[7] Brown's End, which is mainly 17th-century in date, is very similar in character to Upper Brookend and both houses, in addition to the manor house and Russell's End, had five hearths each in 1672.[8] One hearth at Brown's End perhaps belonged to a surviving bakehouse.[9]

In the 17th and 18th centuries several new houses were also raised in Bromesberrow. The timber-framed house at Lower Brookend was built in the mid 17th century to a T plan and possesses high-quality brick nogging. The slightly raised chamber wing to the south is marked out as superior by close studding on the main, east elevation and two star

---

1 Below, manor (other estates: Toney's Farm); Fig. 29.
2 Below, manor (manor: Bromesberrow Ct.).
3 Ibid. (other estates: Upper Brookend).
4 Fig. 27.
5 TNA, PROB 11/79, ff. 111v.–112v.
6 GA, D 6854/1/5.
7 Below, manor (manor: Bromesberrow Ct.; other estates: Upper Brookend, Toney's Farm).
8 TNA, E 179/247/14, rot. 36 and d.
9 Not seen: DoE List, Bromsberrow, 5/18.

chimneys on the south. The main range appears to have been rebuilt on a larger scale with two storeys and attic rooms in the late 17th century and a rear outshut was added shortly afterwards. Near Bevan hill Bavenhill Farmhouse, a thatched timber-framed dwelling with an L plan, is of the late 17th century and at Chase End a small timber-framed cottage, initially of one bay, was erected at a similar date.[1] Grove House, a large brick house of the late 17th or early 18th century, was possibly the first building in the parish to be designed in the neo-classical style. The tall, main block has two storeys over a high basement, taking advantage of its position on a slope, a symmetrical south front, long segment-headed windows, hipped roofs, and prominent flanking chimneystacks.[2] A range of farm buildings to the south includes stables contemporary with the house.

The major building project of the later 18th century was Bromesberrow Place. A scheme of John Yate (d. 1758) for a small house on top of Coneygree hill proved impractical and instead the timber-framed farmhouse at Hook House, the Yates' existing residence, was extensively remodelled as a brick mansion, perhaps completed in 1772.[3] Dyke House was rebuilt c.1790 in red brick on an L plan and incorporates part of an earlier stone-built house retained as a kitchen with a cellar beneath. A plain single-pile front range of three bays and two storeys with sash windows has a cider cellar under the south end, and a north wing with casements incorporates a staircase and former dairy.

The 19th century was mainly a period of improvements to existing houses, Toney's Farm among them.[4] Grove House was enlarged and given new dormers and Dyke House gained a new kitchen. Alterations at Russell's End included new windows, tiled roofs, and new north and west entrances. Some walls were rebuilt in brick and the interior was reconfigured. At Bromesberrow Court a polite brick front facing the church was built in the early 19th century and an almost free-standing block towards the farmyard was added later in the century.[5] Farm buildings were rebuilt or added at Brown's End in 1839, possibly to designs by J.G. Price,[6] and an early 19th-century brick barn was constructed at Lower Brookend. The farmhouse near Bevan hill gained a lean-to cider house.[7] At Dyke House, where a barn is dated 1838, many new farm buildings were constructed in the 1880s. Bromesberrow Place was the property most thoroughly transformed. There Osman Ricardo through his architect created a stuccoed neo-Greek country house c.1823.[8] A contemporary or slightly later south-west lodge, a *cottage ornée*, was used for a time as a school.[9]

New buildings in the 19th century were few, the chief one being a rectory house built in brick in 1802 in the neo-classical style on a site above its predecessor.[10] Also important to the local community was a school of 1871, a small plain building in Malvern stone with polychrome window heads.[11] Other additions in the 18th and 19th centuries were restricted to a few cottages, notably those surviving on and close to Bromesberrow's three ancient commons. Although ten council houses were erected in the parish during the 1930s and 1940s,[12] the 20th century saw only limited new development. Despite the erection of new farm buildings at Bromesberrow Court and apple-packing sheds at Dyke House in the second half of the century, by 2007 many farmhouses had lost their agricultural purpose and were occupied as country homes. Several outbuildings had been converted for residential or commercial purposes, those at Russell's End being made dwellings in the 1990s.[13]

MANOR AND ESTATES

Following the Norman Conquest Bromesberrow became the possession of the de Tony family and from the later 14th century the manor belonged to the Bromwich family. Estates under the manor included a yardland held in 1287 by Flaxley abbey as farmer of Dymock manor.[14] Land on the boundary with Eastnor (Herefs.) acquired in 1483 by Richard Beauchamp, Lord Beauchamp, was granted by Henry VII to the Talbots of Grafton (Worcs.), later earls of Shrewsbury, and descended with Bronsil castle in Eastnor.[15]

With the amalgamation of many holdings a

---

1 DoE List, Bromsberrow, 5/14; 3/21.
2 Only one of the chimneystacks survives: see GA, D 7547/6/5.
3 Below, manor (manor: Hook Ho.).
4 Ibid. (other estates: Toney's Farm).
5 Ibid. (manor: Bromesberrow Ct.).
6 Ibid. (other estates: Brown's End).
7 DoE List, Bromsberrow, 5/14.
8 Below, manor (manor: Hook Ho.).
9 DoE List, Bromsberrow, 6/4; below, social hist. (education).
10 Below, religious hist. (patronage and endowment).
11 Below, social hist. (education).
12 Above (beside the Glynch brook).
13 Information from Valerie Lester of Russell's End.
14 *Cal. Inq. p.m.* II, 305.
15 E. Scroggs, 'The Shrewsbury (Talbot) Manuscripts', *Trans. BGAS* 60 (1938), 273–80; GA, D 9125/Austin cat. 7287; *Military Surv. of Glos. 1522*, 61. For the Talbots, see *Complete Peerage*, XI, 731.

pattern of substantial freehold farms emerged in Bromesberrow by the 17th century. Starting in 1663 the Yate family built up an estate that from 1708 included the manor, the principal seat of which was transferred from Bromesberrow Court to Hook House (later Bromesberrow Place). The estate continued to be enlarged until 1929, when two farms were sold off,[1] and it fragmented further following the death of Dinah Albright in 1990.[2] The Eastnor estate acquired Lower Brookend and Pepper Mill in 1735[3] and sold them in the 1960s.[4] Dyke House was part of the Haffield estate from 1871 to 1927.[5]

BROMESBERROW MANOR

An estate of five hides at Bromesberrow held in 1066 by Earl (i.e. King) Harold belonged in 1086 to Ralph de Tony (Tosny).[6] Ralph, who granted part of the demesne tithes to Conches abbey (Eure),[7] died c.1102 and his estates passed to his son Ralph (d. c.1126).[8] The manor was held for a knight's fee of Thomas de Beauchamp (d. 1401), earl of Warwick,[9] whose overlordship evidently descended from the marriage of Guy de Beauchamp (d. 1315), earl of Warwick, with Alice, daughter of Ralph de Tony and sister of Robert de Tony.[10] Later the manor was held from Hanley Castle (Worcs.).[11] Its lords, who had a jurisdiction in Bromesberrow as the chief lords of Malvern Chase,[12] included the successive husbands of Isabel le Despenser, namely Richard de Beauchamp (d. 1422), earl of Worcester, and from 1423 Earl Thomas's son and heir Richard de Beauchamp.[13]

In 1200 when held by Roger de Portes the manor was taken temporarily in hand by the Crown.[14] Later Matthew de Portes was lord of Bromesberrow[15] and the manor passed to Richard de Portes, the ward of Richard du Boys in the 1280s. Richard de Portes, who came of age by 1291,[16] was lord of Bromesberrow in 1316[17] and had a house there[18] after William de Whitefield was granted free warren in the demesne in 1320.[19] William died by 1349 and his widow Constance, who married Stephen de Casynton, retained a life interest in the manor in 1367, when it belonged to John Bromwich[20] (d. 1388).[21] John's widow Catherine married in turn Hugh Waterton (d. 1409)[22] and Roger Leech and on her death in 1420 the manor passed to John's nephew Thomas Bromwich.[23] Another John Bromwich presented to the rectory in 1447[24] and a second Thomas Bromwich held his first manor court in 1467. In 1473 William Botte, vicar of Norton (Herefs.), held the court, presumably as a guardian. In 1476 the manor belonged to John Bromwich (d. 1485) and his wife Maud. Their son and heir John, who held his first court in 1487,[25] died in 1512. His widow Ann or Agnes (née Payne)[26] married William Whittington, son of John Whittington of Pauntley, c.1514 and on her death c.1540 the manor reverted to her son John Bromwich of Tarrington (Herefs.).[27] John (d. 1567) was succeeded in turn by his son John[28] (d. 1592) and the latter's nephew Edward Bromwich of Frampton on Severn.[29] On Edward's death in 1624 the manor passed to his son Isaac, a minor.[30] Isaac, lord in 1641,[31] died by 1667, leaving the manor to his son Robert,[32] who settled it on his son Edmund in 1703. Edmund sold it in 1706 to John Hyett of Gloucester and he conveyed it in 1708 to Walter Yate of Hook House.[33]

From Walter Yate, who in 1736 acquired Aubreys farm through an exchange of lands with the trustees of a Sandhurst charity,[34] the manor passed at his death in 1744 to John Yate, son of Richard Yate of Arlingham. John died in 1749 and under Walter's will the estate reverted to John Yate, only son of Charles

---

1 Bromesberrow Court and Russell's End: GA, D 4914/1.
2 Below (other estates: Toney's Farm).
3 Above, settlement (beside the Glynch brook); see Fosbrooke, *Glos.* II, 250.
4 GA, D 7547/1/3; below, econ. hist. (mills and fishponds).
5 GA, D 7547/1/6; NRA Report, Bromesberrow (R.L. Steynor).
6 *Domesday Book* (Rec. Com.), I, 168. For Ralph, *Oxford DNB*, s.v. Tosny.
7 *Eng. Episc. Acta VII*, pp. 96–7; Dugdale, *Mon.* VI (2), 994–5.
8 *Complete Peerage*, XII (1), 762.
9 *Inq. p.m. Glos.* 1359–1413, 228.
10 *Complete Peerage*, XII (1), 371–2.
11 *Cal Inq. p.m.* XXI, 175–6. See GA, D 333/Z 3; TNA, C 142/29, no 57; C 142/146, no 132; *Inq. p.m. Glos.* 1625–42, II, 189–90; Bigland, *Glos.* I, 257.
12 GA, D 9125/Austin cat. 7286.
13 *Complete Peerage*, I, 26–8; see *VCH Worcs.* IV, 96.
14 *Pipe R* 1200 (PRS 12), 121; 1202 (PRS 15), 174; 1204 (PRS 18), 153.
15 GA, D 963, undated deed no 3.
16 *Cat. Ancient Deeds*, IV, 282.
17 *Feudal Aids*, II, 265.
18 *Cal. Pat.* 1321–4, 445.
19 *Cal. Chart.* 1300–1326, 428.
20 TNA, CP 25/1/78/74, no 462; J. Toomey (ed.), *Records of Hanley Castle, Worcestershire, c.1147–1547* (Worcs. Rec. Soc. N.S. 18, 2001), 111.
21 *Complete Peerage*, XII (I), 614.
22 *Inq. p.m. Glos.* 1359–1413, 228, 258–9.
23 *Cal Inq. p.m.* XXI, 175–6; *Cal. Close* 1419–22, 198.
24 Fosbrooke, *Glos.* II, 249; *Visit. Glos.* 1623, 29; Hockaday Abs. cxxxv.
25 Harvard Law School, Cambridge (Mass.), MS Lat. 14, Box 85, no 56 (copy in GA, MF 1524); *Cal. Inq. p.m. Hen. VII*, III, 64; GA, D 9125/Austin cat. 7287.
26 TNA, C 142/29, no 57; *Visit. Glos.* 1623, 29.
27 GDR vol. 32, pp. 36–41; Hockaday Abs. cxxxv; cccx, Pauntley, 1525.
28 TNA, C 142/146, no 132.
29 Ibid. PROB 11/79, ff. 111v.–112v.; GA, P 63/IN 1/1; *VCH Glos.* X, 146.
30 *Inq. p.m. Glos.* 1625–42, II, 189–90.
31 W. Wynn Lloyd, 'Bromesberrow', *Trans. BGAS* 45 (1923), 107.
32 GA, D 1142/3; D 1388, Pitt and Yate, Bromesberrow deeds 1623–99.
33 Ibid. D 1142/3; below (Hook Ho.).
34 GA, P 281/CH 2/5; *16th Rep. Com. Char.* 60–1.

Yate of Arlingham. On John's death in 1758 it passed to Robert Dobyns of Evesbatch (Herefs.), grandson of Walter's sister Catherine, on condition that he adopted the surname Yate.[1] Robert, known therefore as Robert Dobyns Yate,[2] was High Sheriff of Gloucestershire in 1765[3] and died the following year, leaving the manor to his son Robert Gorges Dobyns Yate.[4] Robert, under whom the family seat at Hook House was transformed into the mansion known as Bromesberrow Place,[5] died in 1785.[6] His son and heir Walter Honywood Yate came of age in 1799[7] and sold the manor in 1811 subject to his life interest to Joseph Pitt of Cirencester. In 1818 Pitt sold the estate to the political economist David Ricardo of Gatcombe Park, in Minchinhampton,[8] who later the same year purchased W.H. Yate's interest and, a year later, agreed to settle some of his debts.[9]

When David Ricardo died in 1823[10] his Bromesberrow estate passed to his eldest son Osman, who owned *c*.875 a. in the parish in 1838.[11] Osman (d. 1881) was succeeded by his nephew Frank Ricardo (d. 1897),[12] who had in 1876 inherited Russell's End farm from his father Mortimer.[13] Frank's son and heir Frank lived at Bure Homage in Christchurch (Hants) and broke up the estate in 1929, selling the bulk of it with Bromesberrow Place to George Stacey Albright and Bromesberrow Court and its farm to Beatrice Waudby-Griffin. Russell's End was sold to George Chance of Stourbridge (Worcs.).[14] On Albright's death in 1945[15] his estate, extending across *c*.1,500 a. in Bromesberrow, Redmarley D'Abitot, and Berrow (Worcs.),[16] passed to his niece Dinah Albright. Following her death in 1990[17] some farms were sold to their tenants,[18] but most of the estate was purchased with Bromesberrow Place by Dr The Hon. Gilbert Greenall.[19] Beatrice Waudby-Griffin married A.R. Rowden (d. 1947)[20] and following her death in 1976 Bromesberrow Court was sold to William Sargeant. He died in 1996 and his son Mr Peter Sargeant owned the house and farm in 2007.[21]

Bromesberrow Court

The medieval manor house, west of the church at Bromesberrow Court, was constructed largely from red sandstone rubble on an L-shaped plan with hall and service end in line and an east chamber wing projecting south. The hall range, into which a floor was inserted in the 17th century, retains a pair of principal rafters, one purlin, and part of a ridge-piece, all smoke-blackened. The east wing has massive beams with broach stops supporting the upper floor and a timber-framed north extension of two storeys that probably dates to the 18th century. In the early 19th century the building was raised and extended in brick. A neo-classical front of three bays and two storeys with sash windows was created to face the church and the hall range was extended northwards, later being converted into cottages with a late 19th-century two-storeyed block on its north side. In the 20th century the internal circulation was improved with the creation of new entrances and the insertion of a staircase at the south end of the house. The extensive farm buildings of 19th- and 20th-century date include a tallet house with unusual diagonal framing.

Hook House

Hook House, the residence of the lords of the manor from 1708, stood on Bromesberrow's eastern boundary and was rebuilt in the 18th century with the name Bromesberrow Place.[22] Members of the Hook family are documented from 1369, when Reynold Hook (*atte Hoke*) was bailiff.[23] In 1424 William Hook, rector of Redmarley D'Abitot (Worcs., later Glos.) and former rector of Bromesberrow, held a property called Hook's Place.[24] It passed to his nephew Thomas Hook by 1463[25] and was held by Thomas's son Guy in 1487.[26] Roger Bradford (d. 1552) left Hook House to his eldest son John (d. 1561)[27] and William Bradford enlarged the estate by the purchase in 1565 of property called Chelnage and Longneys from Francis

---

1 TNA, PROB 11/740, ff. 103–6; Bigland, *Glos.* I, 260; GA, D 1142/3.
2 GA, D 1618, Yate fam. deeds and papers 1754–1820.
3 Rudder, *Glos.* 54.
4 Bigland, *Glos.* I, 261; GA, D 1142/3.
5 For Bromesberrow Place, see below (Hook Ho.).
6 Bigland, *Glos.* I, 260.
7 GA, D 182/III/155.
8 Ibid. D 6913, Ricardo fam. deeds 1811–25. For Pitt, see *Hist. Parl. Commons* 1790–1820, IV, 806. For Ricardo, see *Oxford DNB*; *VCH Glos.* XI, 190.
9 GA D 6913, Ricardo fam. deeds 1811–25.
10 For the Ricardos, see *Burke's Landed Gentry* (1937), II, 1912.
11 GDR, T 1/40.
12 GA, D 7547/2/1.
13 Ibid. D 3527/19.
14 Ibid. D 4914/1; D 7547/1/4; 2/1; *Kelly's Dir. Glos.* (1927), 58; (1931), 55.

15 *The Times*, 29 Dec. 1945.
16 Ibid. 14 Mar. 1946.
17 Memorial window in Bromesberrow ch.
18 Below (other estates: Toney's farm).
19 Information from Dr Greenall.
20 *The Times*, 26 June 1933, 11 Feb. 1947.
21 GA, D 7547/1/4; information from Mr P. Sargeant of Lintridge, Dymock.
22 Atkyns, *Glos.* 304; Rudder, *Glos.* 314; OS Map 6", Glos. X.NE (1883 edn).
23 Harvard Law School, MS Lat. 14, Box 85, nos 51–4; GA, D 9125/Austin cat. 7286.
24 GA, D 9125/Austin cat. 7287; below, religious hist. (religious life: the middle ages).
25 Harvard Law School, MS Lat. 14, Box 85, no 55.
26 GA, D 9125/Austin cat. 7287.
27 GDR wills 1552/105; GA, P 63/IN 1/1.

28. *Bromesberrow Place: the south front in 1991*

Miles, a Leicester fishmonger.[1] William died in 1613[2] and Edmund Bradford sold the estate by deeds of 1648 and 1655 to Humphrey Morton of Eastnor. Humphrey sold it in 1663 to Rice Yate of, in turn, Llangandeirne (Carmarthenshire) and Gloucester.[3] Rice, who acquired more property in Bromesberrow[4] including woodland,[5] died in 1690 and was succeeded by his son Walter.[6]

Walter (d. 1744) continued to live at Hook House after purchasing the manor.[7] A small house begun according to his wishes[8] by John Yate (d. 1758) on the summit of Coneygree hill was in 1762 the subject of plans with a grandiose Palladian design by Ferdinando Stratford.[9] The site proved impractical and instead Hook House was greatly enlarged to make Bromesberrow Place. The new brick mansion, finished perhaps in 1772,[10] retained part of the timber-framed farmhouse in the south-east angle. The west-facing entrance front was of nine bays and two storeys with a central canted bay reminiscent of Stratford's design for the wings of the aborted house rising the full height. Whilst the back of the house looked more old-fashioned with three storeys, bands between them, and slightly-projecting end bays, the south front was similar with an off-centre two-storeyed canted bay and a west wing of one bay. A cupola lit a central staircase and, to the north, an adjacent H-plan stable block in the same idiom incorporated a service range; the staircase and stables are the most complete survivals from that house.[11]

Shortly after 1823 Osman Ricardo and his architect, probably George Basevi,[12] created a stuccoed neo-Greek house with a sequence of handsomely decorated rooms (drawing room, entrance hall, and dining room) along the west front. Doric porticoes were placed to the west and south and a camellia house with a cast- and wrought-iron structure was built on the south-east side.[13] Inside, a second staircase was inserted immediately to the south of the existing one. In the late 19th century a billiard room was added on the north-west side. Alterations in the 20th century included the insertion before 1961 of twin arches opening the staircase compartments.[14]

---

1 GA, D 1618, deeds of Chelnage and Longneys 1565–1671; above, settlement (the northern hills).
2 GA, P 63/IN 1/1.
3 Ibid. D 1618, deeds of Chelnage and Longneys 1565–1671.
4 Ibid. deeds of Lodwicks and Jacketts 1668–86.
5 Ibid. deeds of Woodend 1623–86.
6 Bigland, *Glos.* I, 267; GA, D 1388, Pitt and Yate, Bromesberrow deeds 1652–1744.
7 Above; Atkyns, *Glos.* 304.
8 TNA, PROB 11/740, ff. 103–106.
9 GA, D 7547/4/12; photocopy 181. For Stratford, see H. Colvin, *A Biographical Dictionary of British Architects 1660–1840* (1978), 788.
10 Rainwater heads are dated 1768 and 1772: N. Kingsley, *The Country Houses of Gloucestershire*, II (1992), 88–9.
11 See Fosbrooke, *Glos.* II, plates facing pp. 57, 248; Fig. 26.
12 Colvin, *Biog. Dict. Brit. Architects*, 93–5.
13 Fig. 28.
14 B. Little, 'Bromesberrow Place – a mansion of character and interest', *Glos. Countryside*, Oct.–Nov. 1961, 10–13.

OTHER ESTATES

Upper Brookend

An estate based on the house at Upper Brookend sometimes known as Hall Place belonged in 1424 to Joan Pendock and in 1475 to John Beale. John's son and heir John had the freehold in 1487 and John Beale of Bushley (Worcs.) owned it in 1506. In 1527 William Grove sold the estate, described as a manor, to Thomas Stone[1] (d. 1546),[2] from whom Upper Brookend descended in the direct line to Roger (d. 1591), Thomas (d. c.1658), William (d. 1683), and Thomas (d. 1693). Thomas was succeeded by his brother Guy (d. 1743), a London cutler, and the descent in the Stone family from father to son resumed, the estate (c.100 a. in the later 18th century) passing to Samuel (d. 1758), Revd Guy (d. 1779), Samuel (d. 1825), Guy (d. 1862), and Samuel (d. 1921). Samuel's sister Elizabeth Stone (d. 1944) left the estate to her niece Marion Edith Fry, wife of Sir Charles Fawcett.[3] In 1944 Lady Fawcett sold Upper Brookend to A.R. Rowden (d. 1947) and following the death of Rowden's widow Beatrice in 1976 it was sold to Alan McKechnie. He sold it in 1992 to Mr Anthony McClellan.[4]

Heavy timber framing in the hall range at Upper Brookend appears to date from the 15th century and may represent the hall with a chamber of three bays that William Stone was required to build anew for John Beale in 1475.[5] In the 17th century the house was almost entirely rebuilt to an H plan by the addition or redevelopment of a north chamber wing with diamond chimneystacks and close studding in the gable and the provision of a plainer south service range. In 1672 it was one of the five largest houses in the parish, taxed at five hearths.[6] Extensive outbuildings were erected around a farmyard to the west in the 18th or early 19th century;[7] some were demolished or converted to living accommodation in the 1980s, when the house also was much remodelled,[8] the upper parts of the timber framing and the interior being recreated. Further alterations and additions were made c.2000 to designs by Craig Hamilton: a new north-west wing of sandstone with entrance hall formed the south side of an entrance court enclosed on the north by a garage and a cloister garden was laid out to the west of the house.[9]

Brown's End

An estate at Brown's End included a house called Hatches which Christopher Hooke of Pauntley sold in 1559 to John Stone (d. 1578). The latter's son John owned the estate in 1614[10] and it passed at his death in 1632 to his son John (d. 1633), whose son John (d. 1695)[11] held it in 1672.[12] Another John Stone owned Brown's End in 1707 and left it at his death in 1742 to his sister Mary[13] (d. 1767), wife of Revd Giles Nanfan, rector of Birtsmorton (Worcs.).[14] Another Mary, the widow of John Nanfan of Brown's End (d. by 1749),[15] had the estate in 1775[16] and Margaret (née Walford), the widow of John Nanfan, son of Giles and Mary, owned it in 1787. Margaret was succeeded by 1794 by her daughter Margaret Nanfan, who married in turn Thomas Webb of Sherbourne and Revd. James Davenport of Stratford-upon-Avon (both Warws.) and by will proved 1830 left an estate of 170 a. to her son John Webb.[17] John (d. 1845) left the estate to his nephew Thomas Townsend Webb[18] (d. 1859), who was succeeded by his son Elias (d. 1930).[19] Brown's End passed to Elias's son John Elias Nanfan Webb, who sold part of the estate to G.S. Albright in 1938.[20]

The former farmhouse at Brown's End, which was sold in 1956 to R.F. Clarke,[21] is a timber-framed H-plan house of 17th-century date with a 2½-storeyed central range of four bays and east and west wings of two and three bays. In 1672 it was one of four houses in the parish with five hearths,[22] one of them perhaps in a surviving detached timber-framed bakehouse of 1½ storeys. The house was enlarged in brick in the late 18th century and a porch and rear extension were added in the early 20th. Farm buildings include a shelter shed and barn of the early 19th century. The latter incorporates re-used crucks and bears a stone giving the date 1839 and the name J.G. Price.[23]

---

1 GA, D 9125/Austin cat. 7287; D 963.
2 GDR wills 1546/187.
3 GA, D 963, map of Upper Brookend 5 Jan. 1788; TNA, PROB 11/726, ff. 274–276v. For the descent in the Stone family, see GA, D 963, list compiled by Guy Stone 1 Feb. 1828 with later additions; P 63/IN 1/1–2. For Lady Fawcett, see *The Times*, 10 Mar. 1952 (obituary of Sir Charles Fawcett).
4 GA, D 7547/1/2; PA 63/8; *The Times*, 11 Feb. 1947; information from Mrs J. McClellan.
5 GA, D 963, deed 17 May 1475.
6 TNA, E 179/247/14, rot. 36 and d.
7 Aerial photograph before 1977 in owner's possession.
8 *Malvern Gazette & Ledbury Reporter*, 8 June 1990.
9 Information from Mrs McClellan.
10 GA, D 1262, Bromesberrow deeds 1366–1743; P 63/IN 1/1. For Hatches, see above, settlement (beside the Glynch brook).
11 GDR wills 1632/47; 1633/73; GA, P 63/IN 1/1.
12 TNA, E 179/247/14, rot. 36 and d.
13 GA, D 1262, Bromesberrow deeds 1366–1743, deed 1707, will of John Stone 1741/2; P 63/IN 1/1.
14 Bigland, *Glos.* I, 261.
15 Shakespeare Birthplace Trust, Stratford-upon-Avon (Warws.), DR 574/413.
16 Rudder, *Glos.* 314.
17 GA, Q/REl 1, Botloe hundred; Shakespeare Birthplace Trust, ER 3/1680; ER 11/17/18; Fosbrooke, *Glos.* II, 249.
18 Shakespeare Birthplace Trust, ER 5/860–1; GA, D 5646/44.
19 GA, D 7547/2/3.; *The Times*, 2 July 1930.
20 GA, D 2299/6537, 7066.   21 Ibid. D 7547/2/3.
22 TNA, E 179/247/14, rot. 36 and d.
23 DoE List, Bromsberrow (1987), 5/17; Verey and Brooks, *Glos.* II, 208 give the barn's date as 1739.

29. Roof timbers of Toney's Farm

Toney's Farm

Toney's Farm, named after a family resident in Bromesberrow by the early 13th century,[1] was part of an estate that passed from Robert Toney (*fl.* 1424)[2] to his son John. John's son and heir Richard, a minor in 1472, was dead by 1473 and the estate passed to John's brother Robert[3] (*fl.* 1487).[4] In 1522 Henry Toney's landholding in Bromesberrow was second in value only to that of the lord of the manor.[5] Richard Smith and his wife Eleanor, formerly wife of Roland Wrenford, the son and heir of Thomas Wrenford of Castlemorton (Worcs.), owned Toney's farm in 1606 and Eleanor's children Richard Wrenford and Frances, wife of Thomas Tracy, sold it in 1620 to William Coxe[6] (d. 1666).[7] In 1667 William's son William conveyed the estate (*c.*150 a.) to John Wodley (d. 1670 or 1671), who left it to his son William. In 1677 John Coxe of Tarlton bought the farm for his brother Richard, then living in Ireland. Richard sold it the following year to Rice Yate,[8] the owner of Hook House, with which the farm descended, from 1708 as part of the manor estate,[9] until it was bought in 1992 by Mr Francis Windsor Clive.[10]

The house at Toney's Farm preserves at its core a 14th-century hall range built of Malvern stone with a roof of three heavy cruck trusses: that over the centre of the two-bayed hall has arched braces and cusped quatrefoil above the collar.[11] Perhaps in the early 16th century the hall was floored with massive beams with bar stops and a large chimneystack was inserted in the east bay, apparently the cross passage. In the 17th century the chamber end was reconstructed as a 2½-storeyed cross wing, perhaps retaining earlier fabric in its stone-walled ground floor.[12] The east service end was replaced or remodelled in the 19th century, when some refacing and refenestration of the hall range took place.

---

1 GA, D 963, undated deed no 1.
2 Ibid. D 9125/Austin cat. 7287.
3 Harvard Law School, MS Lat. 14, Box 85, no 56.
4 GA, D 9125/Austin cat. 7287.
5 *Military Surv. of Glos. 1522*, 60.
6 GA, D 1388, Pitt and Yate, Bromesberrow deeds 1620–1711.
7 Ibid. P 63/IN 1/1.
8 Ibid. D 1618, deeds of Toney's farm 1649–79.
9 Above (Bromesberrow manor); GA, photocopy 924; D 2428/1/17, f. 5; GDR, T 1/40.
10 Information from Mr F. Windsor Clive.
11 Fig. 29.
12 The chamber and service ends of the house were not inspected in 2007.

ECONOMIC HISTORY

Part of the 'the ryelands' area,[1] Bromesberrow remained an agricultural parish with a significant woodland economy.

AGRICULTURE

The Middle Ages

In 1086 Bromesberrow manor had 1 plough in demesne and 14 ploughs belonging to 11 villans and 8 bordars. A slave was also recorded.[2] Four ploughteams were recorded in Bromesberrow in 1220.[3] Evidence for open-field agriculture is limited, but in the later Middle Ages many tenants possessed parcels in a field called 'Haseldene' in the south-east corner of the parish.[4] Most arable farming seems to have taken place within closes, some of which bore names such as 'Rudyng'[5] and 'Heyrudyng'[6] signifying their origins in clearings from woodland or waste.[7]

In the late 14th century parcels of the demesne were let to tenants for annual cash rents. Much of that land lay in meadows beside the Glynch brook that were cropped for hay or used as pasture. Every third year certain meadows became common pasture, whilst arable fields on the demesne were commonable after each harvest. Each year the crop from a proportion of the tenanted demesne was reserved for the lord, a custom known as the third sheaf. Grain harvested from the demesne typically comprised barley, oats, and rye, the last commanding the highest price at threshing and at market in Newent.[8]

In 1487 there were 20 free and 13 customary tenants in the manor.[9] Many of the former held more than one messuage (one as many as four), implying the consolidation of earlier holdings into larger farms.[10] Throughout the late 14th and 15th century customary tenants owed cash rents to the lord rather than labour services[11] and payments in kind included hens[12] and a goose, which by 1487 was owed by two tenants jointly.[13] Holdings in the 15th century included yardlands and half-yardlands. In 1467 John Beale, a freeholder, owed 20s. a year for two yardlands[14] and in 1475 he instructed his tenants at Hall Place (Upper Brookend) to sow a close annually with flax, which they were to pull, dress, and steep for his profit.[15] The cultivation of vines in medieval Bromesberrow is suggested by the field name 'Vynnyng'.[16] In 1518 William Whittington was storing fruits and wool, brewing beer, and dressing pig carcasses in a small chapel close to the church.[17] Cows, sheep, and pigs were among animals kept on farms in the early 16th century[18] and tenants had rights to common pasture on Howler's heath and in High wood.[19]

The Early Modern Period

In the early 17th century 6 yeomen, 7 husbandmen, and 5 labourers were resident in Bromesberrow.[20] No detailed record of holdings exists for the period, but among the larger farms were Hill Place,[21] Aubreys,[22] and Toney's, the last of which comprised c.150 a. in 1667.[23] In 1787 Bromesberrow Court, which had absorbed the land worked from Hill Place,[24] was the largest farm and the farmers at Toney's and Aubreys were among five other tenants of the Yates' manor estate. Russell's End was a farm on the Grove House estate and Lower Brookend and Hill farm belonged to the Eastnor estate.[25]

Much of the parish continued to be given over to arable cultivation. In 1667 the manor was said to include 360 a. of arable, 40 a. of meadow, and 60 a.

---

1 See above, Newent and May Hill (economy).
2 *Domesday Book* (Rec. Com.), I, 168.
3 *Book of Fees*, I, 307.
4 GA, D 247/61; D 9125/Austin cat. 7287; Harvard Law School, Cambridge (Mass.), MS Lat. 14, Box 85, nos 51–6 (copy in GA, MF 1524). The name survives in Hazeldine wood in the adjoining parish of Redmarley D'Abitot: OS Map 1:25,000, sheet 190 (2006 edn).
5 Harvard Law School, MS Lat. 14, Box 85, no 55.
6 Ibid. no 56.
7 *PN Glos.* III, 167; IV, 167.
8 Harvard Law School, MS Lat. 14, Box 85, nos 51–4; GA, D 9125/Austin cat. 7286.
9 GA, D 9125/Austin cat. 7287.
10 See above, settlement.
11 Harvard Law School, MS Lat. 14, Box 85, nos 51–4; GA, D 9125/Austin cat. 7286–7.
12 Below (woodland management).
13 GA, D 9125/Austin cat. 7287. Two adjacent small fields, each called Goose Acre, are identified in the tithe award: GDR, T 1/40.
14 GA, D 247/61.
15 Ibid. D 963.
16 Harvard Law School, MS Lat. 14, Box 85, nos 51–4. Vineings is the name of a field recorded close to Russell's End in the 19th cent.: GDR, T 1/40.
17 Hockaday Abs. cxxxv.
18 GA, D 963, will of Joan Stone proved 25 Jan. 1530/1; GDR wills 1545/198; 1547/195–6.
19 E. Scroggs, 'The Shrewsbury (Talbot) Manuscripts', *Trans. BGAS* 60 (1938), 273–5; below (woodland management).
20 Smith, *Men and Armour*, 67–8.
21 GA, D 1388, Pitt and Yate, Bromesberrow deeds 1580–1703, deeds 1580, 1594; above, settlement (beside the Glynch brook).
22 GA, D 326/R 2.
23 Ibid. D 1618, deeds of Toney's Farm 1649–79.
24 Ibid. D 1388, Pitt and Yate, Bromesberrow deeds 1580–1703, deeds 1580, 1594.
25 Ibid. Q/REl 1, Botloe hundred; above, manor.

of pasture.[1] 'Haseldene' remained an open field into the 18th century.[2] Meadows continued to be valued for both hay and pasture[3] and many were subdivided into smaller closes by new quickset hedges.[4] On Howler's heath a sub-circular close known as Priest's Meadow had been created within the common by 1671.[5] In the west of the parish water meadows are recorded in the early 18th century beside the Glynch brook in an area known as 'the bans'[6] (later Banks or Bance).[7]

Mixed agriculture was practised by most farms. There was dairying and pig farming at Russell's End, its owner having 40 cheeses, 3 gallons of butter, and bacon flitches in 1659,[8] and in 1671 the rectory buildings included two barns and a sheepcot.[9] About 1703 it was noted that rye from the parish 'sometimes sold dearer than wheat' and was transported for up to 60 miles around.[10] In 1801, of the 477 a. of arable recorded in the parish, over half produced wheat and barley, whilst other notable crops were turnips (70 a.), rye (54 a.), and peas (29 a.).[11]

Orchards are recorded from the late 16th century.[12] The local practice of planting fruit trees on arable land is attested at Aubreys in 1662[13] and the rectory house as well as many of the farmsteads had a cider mill in the later 17th century.[14] Field and yard names indicate that hops were, or had been, grown in several places[15] and a moat at Aubreys Farm[16] enclosed a piece of land known in 1662 as 'the vineyard'.[17] The brewing of beer is suggested by the presence of a malt mill at Upper Brookend in 1592.[18]

The Nineteenth and Twentieth Centuries

In 1807 the manor estate included farms at Bromesberrow Court (360 a.), Bromesberrow Place (146 a.), Toney's (190 a.), and Aubreys (124 a.). Other holdings over 50 a. were Brown's End (166 a.), Upper Brookend (144 a.), Russell's End (136 a. including Lodwicks farm, part of the manor estate), Grove House (94 a.), Lower Brookend (81 a.), and Dyke House (60 a.).[19] Ten occupiers employed 67 agricultural labourers in 1831.[20] In 1851 both Bromesberrow Court and Brown's End farms were managed by bailiffs and Richard Brooke at Grove House provided work for 20 men, women, and boys.[21] Throughout the 19th and early 20th century the major farms remained much the same size[22] and the number of farmers recorded in Bromesberrow fluctuated between seven and nine.[23] In 1926 five of the 20 holdings returned for the parish exceeded 100 a.[24] In 1956 the equivalent number was seven (out of 18 holdings) and 47 workers had regular employment in agriculture.[25] In 1986 only 17 individuals worked on eight farms, two of which had over 100 ha (c.247 a.), one between 20 and 30 ha (c.49 and 74 a.), one between 10 and 20 ha (c.25 and 49 a.), and four less than 10 ha (c.25 a.).[26] In 2007, whilst Aubreys and Hill farms remained tenant holdings on the Bromesberrow Place and Eastnor estates respectively,[27] much of Bromesberrow's farmland was worked from farmsteads outside the parish.[28]

In 1838 the parish contained 1,000 a. of arable, 381 a. of meadow and pasture, and 100 a. of waste. There was no trace of open fields, the piecemeal inclosure of 'Haseldene' presumably having been completed much earlier.[29] Although rye was still grown, Bromesberrow's reputation for the crop had faded[30] and only 8 a. was returned in 1866.[31] Most farms were mixed in the early 19th century and one with meadows beside the Glynch brook kept oxen for ploughing and raised Herefordshire cattle and pigs in 1810.[32] The churchwardens' accounts for the period 1816–38 contain cures for cracked cows'

---

1 GA, D 1388, Pitt and Yate, Bromesberrow deeds 1623–99.
2 Ibid. D 6854/1/5.
3 Ibid. D 1388, Pitt and Yate, Bromesberrow deeds 1580–1703, deeds 1580, 1594.
4 Ibid. D 1262, Bromesberrow deeds 1366–1743, deed 1646; D 1388, Pitt and Yate, Bromesberrow deeds 1623–99, deed 1654.
5 Herefs. RO, D 96/43. See also GA, D 1388, Pitt and Yate, Bromesberrow deeds 1623–99, deed 11 Feb. 1698.
6 Ibid. D 963, memo 16 July 1705.
7 Ibid. map 1788; GDR, T 1/40.
8 TNA, PROB 11/299, ff. 12–13.
9 GDR, V 5/59T 1.
10 *Notes on Dioc. of Glouc. by Chancellor Richard Parsons*, 152.
11 *1801 Crop Returns Eng.* I, 169.
12 GA, D 1388, Pitt and Yate, Bromesberrow deeds 1580–1703, deeds 1580, 1594; Bromesberrow deeds 1652–1744, deed 1652/3; D 326/R 2.
13 Ibid. D 326/R 2; see ibid. D 1618, deeds of Dunnings Croft 1623–1726, deed 1725; Rudder, *Glos.* 408–9.
14 GDR, V 5/59T 1; TNA, PROB 11/299, ff. 12–13; PROB 11/427, ff. 174–5.
15 GA, D 1618, deeds of The Hopgate 1635–76; Shakespeare Birthplace Trust, DR 574/413; GA, D 1262, Bromesberrow deeds 1366–1743, will of John Stone 1741/2.
16 SMR Glos. no 5365.
17 GA, D 326/R 2.
18 TNA, PROB 11/81, f. 283 and v.
19 GA, D 1142/3.
20 *Census*, 1831.
21 TNA, HO 107/1960.
22 GA, photocopy 924; GDR, T 1/40; GA, D 2428/1/17, ff. 1–6.
23 *Kelly's Dir. Glos.* (1856–1906 edns).
24 TNA, MAF 68/3295/15; see *Kelly's Dir. Glos.* (1931), 55.
25 TNA, MAF 68/4533/162.
26 Ibid. MAF 68/6005/162.
27 Information from Dr The Hon. G. Greenall of Bromesberrow Place and Mr J. Hervey-Bathurst of Eastnor Castle.
28 Information from Mr P. Sargeant of Lintridge, Dymock; Mr V.P. Steynor of Dyke House; and Mr F. Windsor Clive of Toney's Farm.
29 GDR, T 1/40.
30 Fosbrooke, *Glos.* II, 252; Rudge, *Agric. of Glos.* 138.
31 TNA, MAF 68/26/16.
32 GA, D 2080/81.

udders and inflammation in sheep[1] and Brown's End farm, which gained a new barn with a paved stone threshing floor in 1839,[2] employed a dairymaid in 1851.[3]

The early 19th century saw a number of smallholdings established on Bromesberrow's commons.[4] In 1848 a property on Chase End hill included stables, pigsties, and a cow house in addition to two orchards and a cider mill.[5] Several other dwellings possessed cider mills[6] and Bromesberrow was known for its perry made from Oldfield pears.[7] Orchards of apples, pears, and cherries were common throughout the parish and hop gardens were mainly at Chase End.[8] In 1827 there was a hop kiln at a cottage known as The Box.[9]

In 1838 the main areas of common land were Chase End hill (38 a.), Howler's heath (30 a.), and Bromesberrow heath (10 a.).[10] The last was inclosed under an award dated 1864, in which less than an acre was given to Osman Ricardo for his manorial rights and the rest was sold to Richard Brooke of Grove House.[11] In 1866 the 856 a. of rotated crops returned for the parish included 250 a. of wheat, 219 a. of grass and clover, 166 a. of turnips and swedes, 121 a. of barley, and 51 a. of peas. Some 608 a. was under permanent grass and animals kept on Bromesberrow farms included 1,028 sheep, 165 cattle (including 40 milch cows), and 90 pigs.[12]

During the late 19th and early 20th century arable land was converted to meadow or pasture. In 1896 Bromesberrow returned 784 a. of permanent grass and 694 a. of rotated crops, the latter including 331 a. of cereals, 159 a. of grass and clover, and 152 a. of roots. In 1926 the area of permanent grass was 919 a. and the reported arable included 223 a. of cereals, 147 a. of grasses and clover, and 90 a. of roots. Dairying continued to be important, 74 milch cows being returned in 1926 when the numbers of beef cattle, sheep, and pigs were 318, 913, and 290 respectively. In 1896 there were 58 a. of orchards and in 1926 64 a. of orchards and soft fruit were returned.[13] There was a fruit farm at Hatch farm (Brownsend farm) in the early 1930s.[14] In the late 19th century children from the parish found casual employment picking wild daffodils in the spring and blackberries in the autumn for sale locally.[15]

By 1956, although the area of permanent grass returned for the parish had shrunk to 492 a., the number of cattle had grown to 484, including 161 milch cows. There were also 658 sheep, 327 pigs, and 3,736 poultry birds.[16] Plans for a new dairy on the Eastnor estate at Lower Brookend were approved in 1959.[17] Of the 1,037 a. of arable land returned in 1956, 431 a. were under grass and clover, 397 a. cereals, and 138 a. roots. The area of orchards and soft fruit returned was 90 a.[18] Dairying remained important and in 1986, when 171 milch cows were returned, at least 56 ha (138 a.) of horticultural crops were produced and one farm specialized in market gardening. Most of the 30 ha (74 a.) of apple and pear orchards returned in 1986[19] were at Dyke House, where a fruit farm established after the Second World War remained in business until the late 1990s.[20] In 2007 new farming ventures in Bromesberrow included alpaca rearing on Howler's heath and a small vineyard at Hatch farm.[21] A company specializing in sheep breeding was the tenant of Aubreys farm.[22]

WOODLAND MANAGEMENT

In the 14th century High wood, high up on the north side of Bromesberrow, was a common wood[23] and the lord of the manor received customary payments of hens ('woodhens') from tenants at Christmas for the right to collect wood.[24] In 1370 part of the lord's income derived from the sale of an old ash tree.[25] In the 15th century the lord's wood was on *Warlowesdowne* (Chase End hill) and was managed by a woodward (often the manorial bailiff), who regularly seized timber felled without permission. Those fined for trespass or theft[26] included in 1473 William Dene, rector of Redmarley D'Abitot (Worcs.), for taking pheasants and partridges.[27] In 1546, having inclosed part of High wood, John

---

1 GA, P 63/CW 2/2.
2 DoE List, Bromsberrow (1987), 5/17.
3 TNA, HO 107/1960.
4 Above, settlement (the northern hills).
5 GA, D 6913, Bromesberrow deeds 1823–90.
6 Ibid. D 3527/12; D 6913, Bromesberrow deeds 1823–90; P 63/CW 2/2; photocopy 924.
7 Kelly's Dir. Glos. (1870–1939 edns); W. Marshall, *The Rural Economy of Gloucestershire* (1776), II, 222; Rudge, *Agric. of Glos.* 235.
8 GA, D 3527/13; photocopy 924; GDR, T 1/40.
9 GA, D 3527/12.
10 GDR, T 1/40.
11 GA, Q/RI 31.
12 TNA, MAF 68/25/4; MAF 68/26/16.
13 Ibid. MAF 68/1609/6.; MAF 68/3295/15.
14 GA, D2299/7066; see also *Kelly's Dir. Glos.* (1931), 55.
15 GA, P 63/SC 1/1; S 63/2, pp. 26, 34–5; 3, pp. 44, 54.
16 TNA, MAF 68/4533/162.
17 GA, DA 30/100/28, p. 23.
18 TNA, MAF 68/4533/162.
19 Ibid. MAF 68/6005/162.
20 Information from Mr Steynor.
21 http://www.video-webs.co.uk/camelids/breeders.php (acccessed 14 May 2007); personal observation.
22 http://www.innovis.org.uk/centres (accessed 14 May 2007); information from Dr Greenall.
23 Scroggs, 'Shrewsbury (Talbot) Manuscripts', 275.
24 GA, D 9125/Austin cat. 7286; Harvard Law School, MS Lat. 14, Box 85, nos 51–4.
25 Harvard Law School, MS Lat. 14, Box 85, no 51.
26 GA, D 247/61; D 9125/Austin cat. 7287; Harvard Law School, MS Lat. 14, Box 85, nos 55–6; above, introd. (landscape).
27 Harvard Law School, MS Lat. 14, Box 85, no 56.

Bromwich was ordered before commissioners of the Court of the Marches to respect his tenants' right to gather wood for fuel and fencing there.[1]

In the 1660s part of Bromesberrow's woodland was managed as a source of charcoal for Thomas Foley's iron furnace in Oxenhall.[2] By 1776 an area of woodland in the north-east of the parish was known as Cole (later Coal) hill[3] and remains of charcoal-burning hearths have been noted in Toney's coppice and Hayes' coppice.[4] The former, belonging to Toney's farm, was cut after 12 years' growth in the late 17th century.[5] The latter was one of five coppices on the manor estate, which in 1667 included 50 a. of woodland.[6] In the mid 18th century colliers (i.e. charcoal burners) were active on the Upper Brookend estate[7] and later in the century, when most coppiced wood from Bromesberrow was used to make laths, hurdles, and hoops, some was sold as cordwood to iron furnaces at Powick (Worcs.), Lydney, and Flaxley.[8] In 1789 W.H. Yate derived £100 from the sale of coppiced wood, as well as £7 from timber and £1 6s. 8d. from bark.[9]

In the early 19th century the manor estate included 87 a. of oak coppices, of which the largest was High wood (29 a.).[10] In 1838, when those woods were in hand, most of the other major landholdings included at least one coppice. A keeper's cottage is recorded at Woodend[11] and gamekeepers were resident in Bromesberrow throughout much of the 19th century,[12] when, by the 1870s, local boys acted as beaters during the shooting season.[13] During the late 19th and early 20th century timber, mainly elm and oak, and coppiced wood from Bromesberrow were periodically sold at auction.[14] Sporting rights on the Bromesberrow Place, Lower Brookend, and Dyke House estates were enjoyed by their owners in 1910[15] and the Bromesberrow Place estate employed a gamekeeper in the early 21st century.[16] In 2007 there was a nursery of woodland trees at Russell's End.[17]

MILLS AND FISHPONDS

The Millward family, established in Bromesberrow by 1327,[18] held parcels of demesne land called 'mill field' and 'mill croft' in the late 14th century[19] and Lower Brookend in 1424.[20] In 1370 the lord of the manor profited from the sale of an old millstone[21] and in 1394 William Walker held a fulling mill that he had constructed with timber from the manorial demesne.[22]

The manorial water mill, apparently that recorded in 1472,[23] was held in 1487 by Robert Bradford.[24] Pepper Mill on the Glynch brook,[25] probably the mill which John Jones and his wife Anne owned in 1610,[26] belonged to the Stock family and operated as a corn mill in 1671.[27] Built partly of red sandstone, it became part of the Eastnor estate in 1735[28] and was remodelled. Successive millers lived there in the 19th century,[29] of whom James Jauncey employed two men in 1851.[30] The mill ceased to operate c.1900[31] and the Eastnor estate sold its buildings in 1963.[32]

In 1288 there was a fishpond close to the boundary between Bromesberrow and Eastnor (Herefs.)[33] and in the late 14th century John Clinton leased a pond from the lord of Bromesberrow and stocked it with 2,000 fish. Situated in 'the chase',[34] the lord's pond was called 'Chermersh' in 1472.[35] Its location is likely to have been that of 'Chevernissh pole', described as a boundary mark of Malvern Chase in the 14th century and known as 'Charmill pool' in 1584, by which time it had been drained and was used as meadow.[36] A cottage and lands called 'Charmers' are recorded in the 17th century at Woodend[37] and a field beside a tributary of the Glynch brook there bore the name 'pool meadow' in the 19th century.[38]

---

1 GA, D 963.
2 Below, Oxenhall, econ. hist. (Ellbridge furnace).
3 GA, Q/REL 1, Botloe hundred; Bryant, *Map of Glos.* (1824); OS Map 1", sheet 43 (1831 edn).
4 SMR Glos. nos 22122, 22128.
5 TNA, PROB 11/405, ff. 238v.–40.
6 GA, D 1388, Pitt and Yate, Bromesberrow deeds 1623–99, deeds 8 Oct., 5 Nov. 1667.
7 Birmingham City Archives, Barnard Colln. 20.
8 Turner, *Agric. of Glos.* 54.
9 Birmingham City Archives, Barnard Colln. 29.
10 GA, D 1142/3; photocopy 924.
11 GDR, T 1/40.
12 GA, P 63/IN 1/6; TNA, RG 9/1761.
13 GA, S 63/1, pp. 417, 492; 2, pp. 40, 54.
14 Ibid. D 2299/2/3/3–4; 2/4/83–4, 87; 2/7/89; 2/8/36; 2/11/84.
15 Ibid. D 2428/1/17.
16 Information from Dr Greenall.
17 http://www.wyevalenurseries.co.uk/html/wyevale_transplants.html (accessed 14 May 2007).
18 *Glos. Subsidy Roll, 1327*, p. 87.
19 Harvard Law School, MS Lat. 14, Box 85, nos 53–4.
20 GA, D 9125/Austin cat. 7287.
21 Harvard Law School, MS Lat. 14, Box 85, no 51.
22 Ibid. no 53.
23 Ibid. no 56.
24 GA, D 9125/Austin cat. 7287.
25 Incorrectly named 'paper mill' on Taylor, *Map of Glos.* (1777); cf. GA, P 63/IN 1/2 for the name Pepper Mill in 1782.
26 TNA, CP 25/2/297/8 Jas. I Mich. no 17.
27 Ibid. CP 25/2/657/23 Chas. II Mich. no 3.
28 W. Wynn-Lloyd, 'Bromesberrow', *Trans. BGAS* 45 (1923), 145.
29 GA, P 63/IN 1/2; *Harrison's Dir. Glos.* (1859), 419; *Kelly's Dir. Glos.* (1856–94 edns).
30 TNA, HO 107/1960.
31 OS Map 6", Glos. X.NE (1903 edn).
32 GA, D 2299/22493.
33 Scroggs, 'Shrewsbury (Talbot) Manuscripts', 273–4.
34 Harvard Law School, MS Lat. 14, Box 85, no 53.
35 Ibid. no 56.
36 B. Smith, *A History of Malvern* (2nd edn, 1978), 27, 30.
37 Herefs. RO, D 96/43.
38 GDR, T 1/40.

INDUSTRY AND TRADE

The field name 'lime pits', documented in the 14th and 15th centuries,[1] presumably records the digging of lime high up on the boundary with Eastnor close to Hill Farm.[2] In the 19th century sandstone from Howler's heath and Chase End hill was used on local roads[3] and at the church.[4] Some of the numerous masons living in Bromesberrow at that time were presumably involved in quarrying[5] but in 1883 only one of the quarry scoops visible in the north of the parish remained in use.[6] A small quarry at Russell's End in 1883 had been abandoned by 1903.[7]

The crafts or trades of butcher, baker, carpenter, gardener, and tailor are represented in surnames in medieval Bromesberrow[8] and a skinner was resident in 1436.[9] The place name 'Smytheshey', documented in 1424 and 1487, suggests the presence of a smith.[10] A butcher and a glover are recorded in 1596[11] and eight tradesmen were listed in 1608: three weavers, a tailor, a carpenter, a glover, a cooper, and a shoemaker.[12] A wool-winder and a broadweaver were also resident in the early 17th century[13] and members of two families worked as tailors and weavers at that time.[14] Two shoemakers are recorded in the 18th century.[15] A smithy standing on church land in 1683[16] continued to function in 1769.[17]

Eleven carpenters are recorded between 1763 and 1848 and a sawyer lived on Howler's heath in 1808.[18] Other parishioners engaged in woodland crafts in the early 19th century included a cooper, who also worked as a grafter,[19] and two hurdle-makers, one of whom was based in Toney's coppice.[20] Bricks were being made in 1802,[21] perhaps at the old brickyard recorded in 1812,[22] and a resident of Chase End in 1819 was a bricklayer.[23] A blacksmith's shop was established on the south side of Bevan hill by 1803.[24]

Several bakers and butchers are recorded in Bromesberrow in the 19th century[25] and two shopkeepers, a grocer, a tailor, and a shoemaker were in business there in 1863. The grocer also operated a carrying service to Gloucester three times a week from Letter House on the Ledbury road,[26] but in 1870 the only carrier serving the parish was based in Pendock (Worcs.).[27] In 1935 a daily bus service between Gloucester and Ledbury ran through Bromesberrow.[28]

In the 1930s a cycle repairer worked at Bromesberrow Heath. The smithy below Bevan hill[29] later became the site of an engineering firm[30] that in the early 21st century was in business in Preston.[31] In the late 20th century the former rectory house was a nursing home[32] and in 2000 the parish had 17 businesses engaged in agriculture, retail, services, and construction. Only two of them employed more than four people.[33] In 2007 Grove House was run as a guesthouse[34] and converted farm buildings at Dyke House and Toney's Farm were used for holiday accommodation.[35] A company manufacturing bird tables and nesting boxes was based in the former smithy at Bevan hill.[36] Bromesberrow's post office, established by 1924 and open in 2007, stood just outside the ancient parish in Redmarley D'Abitot.[37]

---

1   Scroggs, 'Shrewsbury (Talbot) Manuscripts', 275–6; Harvard Law School, MS Lat. 14, Box 85, no 56; GA, D 9125/Austin cat. 7287.
2   GDR, T 1/40.
3   GA, P 63/SU 2/1.
4   R.L. Steynor, 'Bromesberrow Church' (1984: typescript in GA, PA 63/5), 37.
5   GA, P 63/IN 1/6.
6   OS Map 6", Glos. X.NE (1883 edn). See also SMR Glos. nos 22133, 22137–8, 27152.
7   OS Map 6", Glos. X.SE (1883, 1903 edns).
8   GA, D 963, undated deeds nos 2–3; D 9125/Austin cat. 7286–7; BL, Add. Ch. 72661; Scroggs, 'Shrewsbury (Talbot) Manuscripts', 274–5.
9   *Reg. Spofford*, 217.
10 GA, D 9125/Austin cat. 7287.
11 BL, Harl. MS 4131, f. 512 and v.
12 Smith, *Men and Armour*, 67–8.
13 TNA, PROB 11/127, ff. 254v.–55; GDR wills 1620/100.
14 GA, D 1388, Pitt and Yate, Bromesberrow deeds 1621–81; D 1618, deeds of Woodend 1623–86; deeds of Lodwicks and Jacketts 1668–86.
15 Ibid. P 63/IN 1/2, 3.
16 GDR, V 5/59T 1.
17 GA, P 63/CW 2/6.
18 Ibid. P 63/IN 1/2, 3, 6.
19 Ibid. D 3527/12.
20 Ibid. P 63/IN 1/6.
21 Herefs. RO, BB 88/1.
22 GA, photocopy 924.
23 Ibid. P 63/IN1/2, 6.
24 Ibid. D 1142/2; Q/RI 31.
25 Ibid. P 63/IN 1/6; *Kelly's Dir. Glos.* (1870), 482.
26 *Kelly's Dir. Glos.* (1863), 212–13; above, introd. (roads).
27 *Kelly's Dir. Glos.* (1870), 482.
28 Ibid. (1935), 56.
29 Ibid. (1931–9 edns).
30 Bavenhill Mechanics Ltd: GA, D 7547/2/4.
31 See below, Preston, econ. hist.
32 GA, D 7547/7/2 (par. mag. July 1959). It was then known as The Laurels.
33 *Bromesberrow 1999–2000: Parish Appraisal* (copy in VCH Glos. office), 10.
34 http://www.the-grovehouse.com (accessed 30 April 2007).
35 Information from Mr Steynor and Mr Windsor Clive.
36 http://www.birdtable.co.uk (accessed 30 April 2007).
37 OS Map 6", Glos. X.NE (1924 edn).

LOCAL GOVERNMENT

MANORIAL GOVERNMENT

A manor court was held from at least 1325.[1] In the later 14th century it met once or twice a year,[2] but in 1389, despite the arrival of the lord's steward for that purpose, none was held.[3] In the 15th century the court punished trespassers and poachers on the demesne. A woodward, often the bailiff, made regular presentments for illicit felling of timber in the lord's wood and fines were levied on those who obstructed highways or failed to maintain watercourses. The bailiff regularly impounded stray cattle; on at least two occasions their owners retrieved them by force.[4] In 1476, following the leading tenants' agreement not to take up office or settle their differences in any higher jurisdiction without the lord's permission, the court fined Robert Cocks for his appointment as constable of Hanley (Worcs.) and a number of people for pursuing justice in the hundred court.[5]

The manor court lapsed after 1605.[6] In 1773 R.G.D. Yate attempted to revive it by convening on 11 May a court described as both a court leet with view of frankpledge and a court baron. Its main purpose was to prosecute the petty constables for their failure to maintain the village stocks and whipping post and to erect a pound.[7] Very few tenants attended and the court never met again.[8]

PAROCHIAL GOVERNMENT

Bromesberrow's two churchwardens are mentioned in 1385 as *custodes ecclesie*.[9] In the later 17th century, when one was chosen in rotation from the major householders, Rice Yate and Robert Bromwich appointed deputies to serve in their stead and by the mid 18th century the appointment of substitutes was common.[10] In some years in the 19th and early 20th century there was only one churchwarden.[11] In 1777 the vestry resolved to hold a parish meeting on the first Sunday of every month and in 1792 it agreed to pay the parish clerk an annual salary.[12] The parish meeting was given the powers of a parish council in 1970.[13]

The office of constable is recorded in Bromesberrow from the 1630s[14] and the holder in 1664 failed to return any presentments to the quarter sessions.[15] In 1802 the lack of a petty constable for Bromesberrow obliged the high constable of Botloe to issue a warrant against an unruly apprentice.[16]

In the 18th century poor relief was administered by one or two overseers of the poor, serving like the churchwardens in a rotation of the main householders.[17] The income for relief came in part from the rent of a parcel of land (4 a.) known in 1747 as 'the poors' land'.[18] That parcel formed part of the church lands charity, originally given for the repair of the church and used by the churchwardens by the 1630s also to fund apprenticeships of children to local farmers and occasional payments to the tramping poor.[19] In 1785 the overseers paid each household with an apprentice 10s. 6d.[20] One farmer bypassed his obligation to take on an apprentice in 1796 by paying a fine of 7 gns.[21] Expenditure by the overseers included repairs to stocks and a whipping post in the year 1796–7.[22]

In 1751 the vestry decided to build a poorhouse on church land by Woodend Street[23] and in 1781 it entered an agreement for placing the parish's paupers for a year in the Dymock workhouse. In 1784, during an outbreak of smallpox in the poorhouse, the parish paid the funeral expenses of those who died and later the cost of inoculating 12 inhabitants against the disease.[24] By 1826 the poorhouse was run as a workhouse under a governor[25] and in 1829 many of its inmates were set to work on local farms, the men earning 1s. 4d. daily

---

1 Bigland, *Glos.* I, 257; GA, D 1618, Ricardo fam. papers, letter from Mr Strachan Mar. 1818.
2 Harvard Law School, Cambridge (Mass.), MS Lat. 14, Box 85, nos 51–4 (copy in GA, MF 1524).
3 GA, D 9125/Austin cat. 7286.
4 Ibid. D 247/61; D 9125, Austin cat. 7287; Harvard Law School, MS Lat. 14, Box 85, nos 55–6; above, econ. hist. (woodland management).
5 GA, D 247/61; Harvard Law School, MS Lat. 14, Box 85, no 56.
6 GA, D 247/61; D 1618, Ricardo fam. papers, letter from Strachan 1818.
7 GA, D 7547/4/5; W. Wynn-Lloyd, 'Bromesberrow', *Trans. BGAS* 45 (1923), 108.
8 GA, D 1618, Ricardo fam. papers, letter from Strachan 1818.
9 Ibid. D 963.
10 Ibid. P 63/CW 2/1; IN 1/1.
11 Ibid. VE 2/2.
12 Ibid. VE 2/1.
13 Ibid. D 7547/7/2 (par. mag. July 1970).
14 Ibid. P 63/CW 2/1.
15 Ibid. Q/SIb 1, f. 103.
16 Herefs. RO, BB 88/1, p. 111.
17 GA, P 63/OV 2/1; VE 2/1.
18 Ibid. OV 2/1; GDR, T 1/40, where it is called the 'poors' ground'.
19 GA, P 63/CW 2/1. See also ibid. OV 4/2–3; VE 2/1.
20 Ibid. VE 2/1.
21 Ibid. OV 4/2.
22 Ibid. OV 2/1.
23 Ibid.; photocopy 192; GDR, V 5/59T 2.
24 GA, P 63/VE 2/1.
25 Ibid. OV 7/1.

and the women 8*d*.[1] In 1835, when Bromesberrow joined the Newent poor-law union,[2] the poorhouse closed and its 12 occupants were admitted to Newent workhouse.[3] The house at Woodend Street was let as two dwellings and was rebuilt in 1848 following a fire.[4] It was sold by the parish in 1964.[5]

Annual expenditure on poor relief, which had rarely exceeded £15 in the 1730s, rose to £79 in 1783,[6] following an increase in weekly pay to offset the high price of bread that year.[7] In 1795 the farmers were advised to allow the poor to glean their fields following the corn harvest.[8] In 1803, when the annual cost stood at £138, 6 people received permanent and 15 occasional help. Some 35 non-parishioners were also relieved that year, an unusually high number that is perhaps explained by the rapid growth of squatter settlement on the fringes of the parish.[9] By 1815 annual expenditure had grown to £226, with 23 people receiving permanent and 29 occasional help,[10] and in 1826 it reached a peak of £429, before dropping back in the following decade to a little over £300.[11]

The accounts of the parish's surveyor of the highways survive for the period 1768–1818.[12] Before 1800 his annual expenditure on road and bridge repairs rarely exceeded £10, but in 1805 it grew to £24 and in 1814 it stood at £70. The rise in expenditure, funded by increased highway rates, resulted from much building work: in the year 1815–16 alone 310 tons of stone was purchased from quarries on Chase End hill and Howler's heath.[13] In 1834 magistrates ordered the parish to devote a third of the highway rates towards the maintenance of turnpike roads in its area[14] and from 1854 Bromesberrow was expected to pay for all of its turnpike repairs. The vestry first elected a waywarden to the newly-formed Newent Highway Board in 1863[15] and the parish's inclusion within the Newent highway district was confirmed in 1867.[16]

SOCIAL HISTORY

SOCIAL STRUCTURE

In 1327 William de Whitefield, lord of the manor, was assessed for tax in Bromesberrow at 4*s*. 6*d*. Of the other residents, Walter Aubrey and Richard Grove were taxed at 5*s*. 6*d*. and 5*s*. respectively, whilst two were taxed at just over 3*s*., five at just over 2*s*., and eight at 1*s*. 8*d*. or less.[17] John Bromwich, lord of the manor by 1367, was MP for Gloucestershire in 1365 and was appointed justiciar of Ireland in 1379.[18] In 1388 and 1390 those harvesting the lord's grain in Bromesberrow were rewarded with bread and ale.[19]

By the late 15th century customary tenants on the manor owed cash rents rather than labour services. The majority of the population were freeholders, many owning substantial farms.[20] John Beale held a court for his tenants at Upper Brookend twice yearly in 1475 and the owner held it once every seventh year by 1506 and required his tenants to provide board and lodging for himself and his steward on such occasions. The description in 1527 of Upper Brookend (then called Hall Place) as a manor perhaps reflects the tradition of courts being held there.[21] The Bromesberrow manor house, known as Bromesberrow Court in 1487,[22] was occupied by William and Ann Whittington from *c*.1514 to *c*.1540; their household included servants, one of whom William later married.[23] In 1522 William with goods worth £20 was the wealthiest inhabitant of Bromesberrow. Of thirty other inhabitants, excluding the rector, four had goods valued between £6 and £10, three at £4, four at £2, and three at £1; for the rest no valuation was made.[24]

Among later lords of Bromesberrow, John Bromwich (d. 1592) resided at Bromesberrow Court.[25] Never marrying, he fathered several children, the eldest of whom, Robert Bromwich alias

---

1 GA, P 63/OV 7/3.
2 *Poor Law Com. 2nd Rep.* p. 523.
3 GA, G/NE 60/1, pp. 1–3.
4 Ibid. P 63/CW 2/3; CW 2/8; GDR, T 1/40; above, settlement (the northern hills).
5 R.L. Steynor, 'Bromesberrow Church' (1984: typescript in GA, PA 63/5), 19.
6 GA, P 63/OV 2/1.
7 Ibid. VE 2/1.
8 Birmingham City Archives, Barnard Colln. 884/4.
9 *Poor Law Abstract, 1804,* 172–3; above, settlement (the northern hills).
10 *Poor Law Abstract, 1818,* 146–7.
11 *Poor Law Returns* (1830–1), 66; (1835), 64.
12 GA, P 63/SU 2/1.
13 Ibid.; OV 1/1; SU 1/1–3. See above, econ. hist. (industry and trade).
14 GA, P 63/SU 3/1.
15 Ibid. VE 2/2.
16 *London Gazette,* 24 Mar. 1867, pp. 1707–8.
17 *Glos. Subsidy Roll, 1327,* 36.
18 *Cal. Close,* 1364–8, 168; *Cal. Pat.* 1377–81, 380, 402–3; above, manor (manor).
19 GA, D 9125/Austin cat. 7286; Harvard Law School, Cambridge (Mass.), MS Lat. 14, Box 85, no 54 (copy in GA, MF 1524).
20 GA, D 247/61; D 9125/Austin cat. 7287; Harvard Law School, MS Lat. 14, Box 85, nos 55–6.
21 GA, D 963; above, manor (other estates: Upper Brookend).
22 GA, D 9125/Austin cat. 7287.
23 GDR vol. 32, pp. 36–45.
24 *Military Surv. of Glos. 1522,* 60–1.
25 GDR vol. 32, pp. 36–45; see above, manor (manor).

Dyer,[1] inherited a farm in Bromesberrow that John purchased in 1580.[2] In 1608 James Bromwich, uncle of Edward Bromwich,[3] occupied the manor house with a household including at least one servant. The other men listed in Bromesberrow that year comprised 6 yeomen, 7 husbandmen, 5 labourers, and 8 craftsmen or tradesmen.[4] Between 1640 and 1700 eight Bromesberrow boys were apprenticed to Gloucester masters.[5] Of Bromesberrow's 29 householders in 1672, 10 were excused payment of hearth tax, 9 were assessed at one hearth each, 2 had two hearths, and 3 had three hearths. Robert Bromwich, lord of the manor, was among 4 residents to have five hearths each and John Stock had ten hearths.[6]

Robert Bromwich and Rice Yate were the only Bromesberrow residents summoned to attend the heralds' visitation of 1682 and 1683.[7] Yate (d. 1690), a former Royalist cavalry officer,[8] had purchased Hook House in 1663[9] and the Bromwich family's Frampton on Severn estate in 1670.[10] After acquiring the manor in 1708 Walter Yate (d. 1744) continued to use Hook House as his principal residence.[11] His heir John Yate (d. 1749) worked in London as a barrister.[12] The Stone family, owners of Upper Brookend, took up residence in Ireland in the mid 18th century and let their estate to tenants.[13] In the late 18th and early 19th century most farms, including Bromesberrow Court, were occupied by tenants,[14] some of whom are commemorated in elaborate chest tombs in the churchyard.[15]

R.G.D. Yate (d. 1785), lord of Bromesberrow from 1766, oversaw the completion of Bromesberrow Place c.1772, paid for improvements to the church's fabric, and installed his brother H.G.D. Yate (d. 1812) as rector.[16] The latter frequently embellished parish records with his poetry and quotations from classical sources.[17] Bromesberrow Place, which in the later 1780s was let to John Somers Cocks (later Earl Somers) during the minority of W.H. Yate,[18] was celebrated in the early 19th century for Yate's museum of curiosities incorporating many items originally collected by the antiquary Richard Greene (d. 1793).[19] In 1812 a Hygeian temple was among buildings in its grounds.[20]

In the late 18th and early 19th century a number of squatter cottages were built on Bromesberrow's commons,[21] one of which at Chase End was erected with the lord's permission by a Yate family servant.[22] In 1851 twelve households included servants and in 1861 those employing five or more were Bromesberrow Place (10), the rectory (7), Grove House (5), and Brown's End (5). Fairfields was occupied in 1851 by Thomas Hill, rector of Staunton, and in 1861 by Henry Moore, a banker in Ledbury (Herefs.).[23] Osman Ricardo (d. 1881), who inherited the manor in 1823, was resident and active as a landlord, buying up several cottages in the parish.[24] He and his wife Harriet established new schools.[25]

In 1929 Bromesberrow Place was sold to G.S. Albright (d. 1945), its tenant from 1904.[26] He was a member of a Birmingham Quaker family and a director of Albright & Wilson Ltd, manufacturers of phosphorus for the match industry.[27] Other prominent landowners in Bromesberrow in the early 20th century included several military officers,[28] in addition to J.E.N. Webb, owner of Brown's End, who worked as a railway engineer in India.[29] Albright's niece Dinah Albright developed one of the largest private orchid collections in the country at Bromesberrow Place[30] and in 1978 established the Albright Trust, a charity which in

---

1 GA, P 63/IN 1/1; D 7547/6/1.
2 Ibid. D 1388, Pitt and Yate, Bromesberrow deeds 1580–1703; TNA, PROB 11/79, ff. 111v.–112v.
3 *Visit. Glos. 1623*, 29.
4 Smith, *Men and Armour*, 67–8.
5 J. Barlow (ed.), *A Calendar of the Registers of the Apprentices of the City of Glouc. 1595–1700* (BGAS, Gloucestershire Record Series 14, 2001), 98, 106, 186, 197, 199, 211, 233, 260.
6 TNA, E 179/247/14, rot. 36 and d.
7 Bigland, *Glos.* I, 258.
8 Fosbrooke, *Glos.* II, 251. For his Civil War banners, see below, religious hist. (religious life).
9 Above, manor (manor: Hook Ho.).
10 *VCH Glos.* X, 146.
11 Atkyns, *Glos.* 304.
12 Bigland, *Glos.* I, 260.
13 Ibid. 257; GA, D 7547/1/2; Stone family monument in churchyard.
14 GA, Q/REl 1, Botloe hundred; P 63/OV 1/1.
15 In particular those of Josiah Tibbatts (d. 1801) and Thomas Jones (d. 1802): DoE List, Bromsberrow (1987), 5/6, 9.
16 Above, manor; below, religious hist. (religious life).
17 See GA, P 63/IN 1/2.
18 Birmingham City Archives, Barnard Colln. 913/7; *Complete Peerage*, XII(1), 32–3.
19 Fosbrooke, *Glos.* II, 252–3; *A Catalogue of the Curiosities in the Museum of W.H. Yate at Bromesberrow Place* (Gloucester, c.1801: copy in Glos. Colln. R 59.1). For Richard Greene, see *Oxford DNB*.
20 GA, photocopy 924.
21 Above, settlement (the northern hills).
22 GA, photocopy 924.
23 TNA, HO 107/1960; RG 9/1761.
24 Above, settlement (the northern hills).
25 Below (education).
26 GA, D 7547/2/1; *Kelly's Dir. Glos.* (1906), 51.
27 http://www.open.ac.uk/ou5/Arts/chemists/person.cfm?SearchID=5680 (accessed 30 May 2007: no 277367); *Oxford DNB*, s.v. Arthur Albright.
28 *Kelly's Dir. Glos.* (1906–39 edns.).
29 GA, D 7547/6/9; *Ledbury Reporter*, 5 Aug. 1960.
30 *Evesham Journal*, 6 Dec. 2002.

CHARITIES FOR THE POOR

In 1683 Robert Bromwich held £9 10s. for an annual distribution to the poor on the feast of St Thomas (21 December).[2] The charity's principal, later recorded as £10 donated by the Leadington family,[3] was enlarged by £30 left by Walter Yate by will proved 1745.[4] A gift of £30 by Catherine Yate (d. 1711), by will proved 1751, for a distribution on the anniversary of her burial[5] was included in the St Thomas's day charity by the 1780s.[6] Revd H.G.D. Yate, who paid for doles of bread during the harsh winter and spring of 1795,[7] left by will proved 1813 the income from £70 stock to be distributed to the second poor on St Thomas's day. The gift was subject to life interests[8] and had not become effective by 1829. By that date £10 from the St Thomas's day charities had been added to £100 (£90 after legacy duty)[9] which under the will, proved 1818, of H.G.D. Yate's sister Anne Foote was to be used by the rector to provide for blankets and clothing for sick and elderly churchgoers on that day.[10]

The St Thomas's day charities, which are recorded on a charity board erected in the church c.1845,[11] yielded an income of c.£7 in 1870[12] and continued to be distributed on the appointed day in the late 19th and early 20th century, mostly in the church after matins[13] but occasionally in the school.[14] Anne Foote's charity was given as clothing in 1932[15] and the four charities were managed together by 1963.[16] Revd F.F. Rigby, rector 1962–73,[17] distributed the charities in cash, 14 parishioners receiving 10s. each in one year,[17a] but by 2000 all the charities had ceased to exist.[19]

The educational charity of Thomas Eckley, given by will dated 1716, provided for binding poor children of the parish apprentices.[20]

EDUCATION

In 1678 the rector, Richard Eaton, was licensed as the headmaster of a school in Bromesberrow.[21] William Stone, rector of Eastnor (Herefs.), by will proved 1702 left £5 to instruct one Bromesberrow child in the English language and the catechism.[22] Thomas Eckley of Grove House by will dated 1716 left £50 towards keeping poor children in school and binding them apprentices, the principal being vested initially in Joseph Weale, heir to Grove House.[23] Both charities are recorded in 1791[24] but had lapsed by 1818. In that year a mixed day school supported by voluntary contributions taught c.30 children.[25] The same school had 29 pupils in 1826, when there was also a Sunday school,[26] and 19 in 1833.[27]

In 1826 a school educating girls at parental expense was established in the lodge at Bromesberrow Place. It taught c.30 girls in 1833[28] and, with the support of Harriet Ricardo, continued in 1868.[29] Sarah Hodges was schoolmistress there for 40 years.[30] A Sunday school begun in 1828 was privately funded and taught 20–30 boys in 1833.[31] In 1836 Osman Ricardo established a day school for boys and from 1838 it occupied a new stone building at Woodend next to the teacher's cottage. In 1852, when as Bromesberrow Church school it had an average attendance of 38, pupils paid pence and Ricardo met any shortfall in income.[32] It had closed by 1868, when boys from Bromesberrow attended schools in Pauntley and Berrow (Worcs.)[33]

An infant school is recorded in the late 1850s,[34] and in 1861 an assistant schoolmaster lived at Bromesberrow Heath,[35] where there was a school in

---

1 http://www.charity-commission.gov.uk/registeredcharities (accessed 30 May 2007: no 277367); information from Revd Dr P. Newing of The Rectory, Albright Lane.
2 GDR, V 5/59T 2.
3 Ibid. 5; *20th Rep. Com. Char.* 10.
4 TNA, PROB 11/740, ff. 256v.–258.
5 GDR wills 1751/139; GA, P 63/IN 1/1.
6 *20th Rep. Com. Char.* 10. See also GDR, V 5/59T 5; GA, D 7547/6/10.
7 GA, D 7547/6/10.
8 TNA, PROB 11/1542, ff. 84-86v.
9 *16th Rep. Com. Char.* 67; *20th Rep. Com. Char.* 10.
10 TNA, PROB 11/1611, ff. 132v.–140.
11 Located in 2007 in the first stage of the tower.
12 *Kelly's Dir. Glos.* (1870), 482.
13 GA, P 63/CH 1.
14 Ibid. S 63/1, p. 493; 2, p. 5.
15 Ibid. P 63/CH 1.
16 http://www.charity-commission.gov.uk/registeredcharities (accessed 30 May 2007: no 220633).
17 R.L. Steynor, 'Bromesberrow Church' (1984: typescript in GA, PA 63/5), 19, 21.
18 GA, D 3469/5/23.
19 http://www.charity-commission.gov.uk/registeredcharities (accessed 30 May 2007: no 220633).
20 GDR, V 7/59T 5; below (education).
21 Hockaday Abs. cxxxv.
22 GA, D 1262, Bromesberrow deeds 1366–1743.
23 GDR, V 5/59T 5; GA, D 2957/116/23.
24 Bigland, *Glos.* I, 258.
25 *Educ. of Poor Digest*, 193. See *20th Rep. Com. Char.* 11.
26 GDR vol. 383, p. 107.
27 *Educ. Enq. Abstract*, 309.
28 Ibid.
29 *1st Rep. Com. Employment in Agric.* app. II, p. 125.
30 TNA, HO 107/1960; RG 9/1761; gravestone in churchyard to N. of vestry.
31 *Educ. Enq. Abstract*, 309.
32 TNA, ED 7/34/53; GDR, T 1/40.
33 *1st Rep. Com. Employment in Agric.* app. II, p. 125.
34 *Kelly's Dir. Glos.* (1856), 235; *Harrison's Dir. Glos.* (1859), 419.
35 TNA, RG 9/1761.

1863.[1] In 1868 some younger children attended the nearby Haffield school, in Dymock.[2]

A new school erected on glebe land close to the rectory house opened in 1872 and as Bromesberrow National school taught 34 boys, girls, and infants in its first year.[3] The building, constructed in Malvern stone to designs by Middleton & Goodman,[4] comprised a teacher's house and a schoolroom used also for a Sunday school[5] and was largely paid for by subscription, of which £120 came from the sale of land to Richard Brooke at the inclosure of Bromesberrow heath.[6] The school was funded by pence and by subscriptions from Osman and Harriet Ricardo, Henry Moore, and Revd R.P. Hill, all of whom were regular visitors.[7] In 1904 the average attendance was 52.[8]

Throughout much of the late 19th and early 20th century attendance was often low and the turnover of staff high.[9] Following a series of inspections highlighting cramped accommodation,[10] a new classroom for infants was built in 1900.[11] The school changed its name to Bromesberrow C. of E. school in 1906. The average attendance dropped to 27 in 1918[12] but recovered to 45 in 1922 and 67 a decade later.[13] The older boys were transferred to a school in Ledbury (Herefs.) in 1942.[14] In 1967 and 1968 the school was remodelled and enlarged, partly at the expense of Dinah Albright,[15] and from 1969 it was known as Bromesberrow St Mary's C. of E. Primary school.[16] It retained voluntary aided status in 2005, when 55 children were on the roll.[17] A nursery was established in 2001[18] and a school hall was completed in 2004.[19]

SOCIAL LIFE

A church house, long demolished in 1725, stood in a corner of the churchyard.[20] The parish vestry usually convened in the church and in the 1860s Letter House hosted meetings to decide the inclosure of Bromesberrow heath.[21] Bromesberrow appears never to have had a licensed public house, but in the late 19th century the Bell inn at Bromesberrow Heath was the meeting place of a friendly society with a membership drawn from Bromesberrow and Dymock.[22]

Soon after G.S. Albright's arrival at Bromesberrow Place in 1904 a reading room and a parish library were established, the room being accommodated in the rectory coach house.[23] In 1909 a temperance society drew members from the parish[24] and c.30 individuals subscribed to coal and clothing clubs run by the rector.[25] There was a village cricket club in 1912.[26] In the conflict of the First World War 12 parishioners lost their lives and in 1921 a stone cross[27] was unveiled on the green in front of the school as their memorial.[28]

A village club, opened in 1922 and enlarged in 1928,[29] had G.S. Albright as its president.[30] In 1939 the building burned down and in 1950 a replacement village hall was erected east of Coneygree hill on land owned by Dinah Albright. A sports field was also created there.[31] The hall was rebuilt using entirely local voluntary labour in 1992[32] and, having been extended in 2002,[33] was used by local organisations, including a bowls club and a gardening and social club, in 2007.[34]

---

1 GA, Q/RI 31.
2 *1st Rep. Com. Employment in Agric.* app. II, p. 125; below, Dymock, social hist. (education: after 1826).
3 TNA, ED 7/34/53; GA, D 7547/4/2 (par. mag. Mar. 1911).
4 Verey and Brooks, *Glos.* II, 208.
5 TNA, ED 7/34/53.
6 GA, P 63/VE 2/2; F.F. Rigby, *To Our Lady of Bromesberrow* (Evesham, 1970: copy in Glos. Colln. R 59.8), 44–7; above, econ. hist. (agric.: the 19th and 20th cents.).
7 GA, P 63/SC 2/1; S 63/1, pp. 1, 4, 28.
8 *Public Elem. Schs. 1906*, 182.
9 GA, P 63/SC 1/1–2; S 63/1–4.
10 Ibid. S 63/1, pp. 411–12, 428, 444; *The Times*, 22 July 1896.
11 GA, S 63/2, pp. 38–9.
12 Ibid. P 63/SC 1/1.
13 *List 21*, 1922 (Board of Education), 102; 1932, 113.
14 GA, C/CE/M 2/27, f. 88.
15 F.F. Rigby, *Bromesberrow Saint Mary's School* (Evesham, 1972: copy in Glos. Colln. R 59.9), 21.
16 Ibid. 3.
17 *Schools and Establishments Dir. 2005–6*, 9.
18 http://www.charity-commission.gov.uk/registeredcharities (accessed 4 June 2007: no 1091157).
19 *Droitwich Advertiser*, 13 Feb. 2004; information from Revd Dr P. Newing.
20 Hockaday Abs. cxxxv.
21 GA, P 63/VE 2/1–2.
22 TNA, FS 3/85, no 1108; below, Dymock, social hist. (social life: meeting places, societies, clubs, and events).
23 GA, D 7547/5/13.
24 Ibid. S 63/2, p. 238.
25 Ibid. P 63/MI 2.
26 Ibid. D 963, par. mag. Oct. 1912.
27 http://www.smilodon.plus.com/WarMems/bromsberrow.html (accessed 4 June 2007).
28 GA, D 7547/3/14; Wynn-Lloyd, 'Bromesberrow', 116; Rigby, *To Our Lady*, 54–5.
29 GA, D 7547/3/2.
30 *Kelly's Dir. Glos.* (1939), 58.
31 GA, C/CE/M 2/32, pp. 51–2, 176; D 7547/3/2.
32 *Bromesberrow 1999–2000: Parish Appraisal* (copy in VCH Glos. office), 16.
33 *Redditch Advertiser*, 14 June 2002.
34 Ibid. 6 Dec. 2002; 5 Dec. 2003; *Bromsgrove Advertiser*, 4 Mar. 2005.

RELIGIOUS HISTORY

EARLY HISTORY AND STATUS OF THE PARISH CHURCH

In the late 11th century Ralph de Tony granted the greater part of his demesne tithes to the abbey founded at Conches (Eure) by his father Roger.[1] A parson is recorded in Bromesberrow in the early 13th century[2] and in the 1260s a rector disputed Conches abbey's title to some of the tithes.[3] The living has remained a rectory and from 1935 it included Bromesberrow Heath, Lintridge, and part of Ryton in Dymock, to the south.[4] In 1981 the benefice merged with four others to form the united benefice of Redmarley D'Abitot and Bromesberrow with Pauntley, Upleadon and Oxenhall.[5] From 2000 the united benefice also included Dymock with Donnington and Kempley and Preston.[6]

PATRONAGE AND ENDOWMENT

The advowson of the church descended with the manor until the early 19th century. In the 1280s Richard du Boys made three presentations during the minority of Richard de Portes.[7] The bishop presented to the living in 1488[8] and upheld the right of William Whittington and his wife to the patronage against the claim of John Bromwich in 1521.[9] The Crown was patron by lapse in 1596 and patrons for a turn were Richard Stone, rector of Redmarley D'Abitot, in 1601, Sir Richard Tracy in 1620, and Thomas Webb and John Abbot in 1709.[10] In 1809 W.H. Yate sold the advowson to William Lygon, Lord (later 1st Earl) Beauchamp. Of the earl's successors[11] the 6th earl sold it in 1867 to Mortimer Ricardo[12] (d. 1876), from whom it passed to his son Frank. On Frank's succession to the Bromesberrow estate in 1881 the advowson was reunited with the manor[13] and in 1933 it was transferred to the bishop.[14]

The rectory was valued at £10 in 1291.[15] Conches abbey's interest in Bromesberrow presumably passed to the priory of Great Malvern (Worcs.), which in 1271 the bishop confirmed was entitled to half the demesne tithes.[16] The rector later received all the tithes and paid the priory a pension of 4s. for a share of the corn tithes. The living was worth £7 15s. in 1535.[17] In 1671 the rector took all the tithes in kind[18] but by 1730 a standard modus had been established for payment of the small tithes.[19] The tithes were commuted for a corn rent charge of £362 in 1838.[20] In 1671 the glebe included strips in the open fields[21] and in 1725 Walter Yate gave the rector ¼ a. in exchange for a corner of the churchyard.[22] In 1838 the glebe comprised 55 a. in closes mostly near the rectory house[23] and in 1939 it covered c.45 a.[24] The living was worth £65 in 1650,[25] £100 in 1750,[26] and £356 in 1856.[27]

The rectory house contained five bays and had six outbuildings in 1671.[28] In 1802 a new brick house (The Old Rectory) was built on a more elevated site close by at the expense of Revd H.G.D. Yate and his nephew W.H. Yate to designs by James Millard of Gloucester.[29] Standing c.500 m north-east of the church, it has a neo-classical front of three bays and 2½ storeys and a plain two-storeyed rear.[30] Minor alterations were made chiefly to the service rooms in 1877 and 1878[31] and the house was sold in 1955. A new rectory house (The Rectory) built in 1958 in Albright Lane was sold in 1979 to Dinah Albright and was owned in 2007 by the Albright Trust.[32]

---

1 *Eng. Episc. Acta VII*, pp. 96–7; Dugdale, *Mon.* VI (2), 994–5.
2 GA, D 963, undated deed no 3.
3 King's College Cambridge Archive, 6/2/181/01/10/01.
4 GA, P 125/IN 4/1; see below. Dymock, religious hist. (early hist.).
5 GDR, D 5/4/2/8.
6 *Dioc. of Glouc. Dir.* (2001–2), 24–5.
7 *Reg. Cantilupe*, 251; *Reg. Swinfield*, 527; above, manor (Bromesberrow manor).
8 *Reg. Myllyng*, 196.
9 *Reg. Bothe*, 99–100, 334.
10 Hockaday Abs. cxxxv.
11 Worcs. RO, 705:99 (BA 3375), Dymock deeds 1633–1811. For William Lygon and his successors, below, Kempley, manor (manor).
12 GA, D 6854/1/7.
13 *Burke's Landed Gentry* (1937), II, 1912; *Kelly's Dir. Glos.* (1889), 683; (1927), 58.
14 *London Gazette*, 14 Feb 1933, p. 1014.
15 *Tax. Eccl.* 161.
16 *Reg. Swinfield*, 308.
17 *Valor Eccl.* II, 500; III, 240; Dugdale, *Mon.* III, 240.
18 GDR, V 5/59T 1.
19 Ibid. 3.
20 Ibid. T 1/40.
21 Ibid. V 5/59T 1.
22 Hockaday Abs. cxxxv.
23 GDR, T 1/40.
24 *Kelly's Dir. Glos.* (1939), 55.
25 C.R. Elrington, 'The Survey of Church Livings in Gloucestershire, 1650', *Trans. BGAS* 83 (1964), 98.
26 *Bp. Benson's Surv. of Glouc. 1735–50*, 4.
27 GDR vol. 384, f. 46.
28 Ibid. V 5/59T 1.
29 Birmingham City Archives, Barnard Colln. 931, 933; R. Gunnis, *Dict. of British Sculptors 1660–1851* (1968), 259.
30 DoE List, Bromsberrow (1987), 5/19.
31 GA, D 2593/2/333.
32 R.L. Steynor, 'Bromesberrow Church' (1984: typescript in GA, PA 63/5), 18, 24; GDR, A 8/3/2; information from Revd Dr P. Newing of The Rectory. For the trust, above, social hist. (social structure).

RELIGIOUS LIFE

The Middle Ages

The medieval parish church comprised chancel and nave with a low belfry over the west end.[1] The earliest surviving fabric dates from the early 13th century, when the west end of the nave was built in coursed red sandstone rubble with narrow lancet windows. A round 13th-century cross head removed from the east wall in 1858 and later incorporated in a churchyard monument may originally have been mounted on one of the roof gables.[2] The font is a featureless limestone tub, which if *in situ* may indicate that there was already a church at Bromesberrow in the late 12th century.[3] In the 14th century the chancel was rebuilt, a south-east window was inserted in the nave, a timber-framed south porch was added, and a tower with a timber-framed belfry was built within the west end of the nave.[4] The belfry may have been renewed in the early 16th century.[5]

The dedication of Bromesberrow church to St Mary the Virgin is attested in the early 13th century, when Hugh of Walford gave parishioners 4 a. of land in Bromesberrow to provide lamps in the church on specified festivals.[6] Other gifts by parishioners to support lights included a house and garden let for 12*d*. a year in the late 13th century.[7] The church or parish property was administered by the two churchwardens in 1385.[8]

Walter, chaplain of Bromesberrow, was indicted for larceny and other crimes in 1255.[9] Walter Marsh, rector from 1280,[10] was among men accused in 1284 of the death of Walter of Blakeney[11] and with his patron Richard du Boys, constable of Corfe castle (Dorset),[12] was appointed by the king in 1286 to lay out a new town in Studland (Dorset).[13] In 1297 George de Criketot, who was in minor orders, became rector and the living was given *in commendam* to his brother Roger.[14] George was given leave of absence for study in 1301,[15] as were a number of his immediate successors.[16] In 1392 Walter Skenfrith, chaplain of Bromesberrow, had escaped from the bishop's prison.[17] In 1411 William Hook exchanged the rectory for that of Redmarley D'Abitot.[18] William Skinner, rector on an exchange in 1419,[19] retained the living, despite accusations of sexual incontinence,[20] until his death in 1447.[21]

In 1518 William Whittington, the lord of the manor who often attended church with his hawk,[22] was found guilty of threatening the rector John Jennings as he was about to celebrate Mass and of using a chapel near the church for secular purposes.[23] The chapel may have been the building that served later as a charnel house.[24] In 1521, on the settlement of the dispute over the right of patronage, Guy Whittington became rector in preference to Robert Jennings.[25] Joan Stone, by will proved 1531, left a kerchief to the church.[26]

From the Reformation to the Restoration

In 1540 Guy Whittington stepped down as rector in favour of Robert Jennings in return for an annual pension of 4 marks during the latter's incumbency. Thomas Harwell, Robert's successor in 1546, held the living in plurality with Tarrington (Herefs.) and later Pendock (Worcs.).[27] Unable to recite the Ten Commandments in 1551,[28] he was deprived of Bromesberrow in 1554 but had been reinstated by 1563, when he was residing at Pendock.[29] In 1576 he was presented for not preaching quarterly sermons and for wearing a surplice in perambulations. John Bromwich was noted as being regularly absent from church and failing to maintain the churchyard,[30] despite having asserted his right to occupy the seat in church traditionally reserved for the lord of the manor.[31] James Price, rector from 1583, had no other

---

1 GA, photocopy 242; Verey and Brooks, *Glos.* II, 207–8; *Ledbury Reporter*, 22 Feb. 1957.
2 Verey and Brooks, *Glos.* II, 207–8; W. Wynn-Lloyd, 'Bromesberrow', *Trans. BGAS* 45 (1923), 123. The monument is located N. of the chancel.
3 A.C. Fryer, 'Gloucestershire Fonts: Norman', *Trans. BGAS* 37 (1914), 126.
4 Verey and Brooks, *Glos.* II, 208; *Ledbury Reporter*, 22 Feb. 1957.
5 The bressummer (not seen in 2007) is said to bear the date 1502: Wynn-Lloyd, 'Bromesberrow', 109.
6 GA, D 963, undated deed no 3.
7 Ibid. no 2.
8 Ibid. deed 19 June 1385; above, local govt. (parochial govt.).
9 *Close* 1254–6, 201.
10 *Reg. Swinfield*, 251.
11 *Cal. Pat.* 1281–92, 143.
12 Ibid. 1272–81, 385.
13 Ibid. 1281–92, 217.
14 *Reg. Swinfield*, 531.
15 Ibid. 545.
16 *Reg. Orleton*, 391; *Reg. Trillek*, 396, 397.
17 *Cal. Pat.* 1391–6, 203.
18 Ibid. 1408–13, 285; *Reg. Mascall*, 177.
19 *Reg. Lacy*, 119.
20 Hockaday Abs. cxxxv.
21 *Reg. Spofford*, 367.
22 GDR vol. 32, pp. 36–45.
23 Hockaday Abs. cxxxv; see above, econ. hist. (agric.: the middle ages).
24 Below (from the Reformation to the Restoration).
25 *Reg. Bothe*, 99–100, 334.
26 GA, D 963.
27 Hockaday Abs. cxxxv.
28 J. Gairdner, 'Bishop Hooper's Visitation of Gloucester', *EHR* 19 (1904), 119.
29 Hockaday Abs. cxxxv.
30 GDR vol. 40, f. 238.
31 Ibid. vol. 32, pp. 36–45.

benefice and was neither a graduate nor a preacher; he had held the living while Thomas Harwell had been deprived of it.[1] A chalice and paten dated 1588 are among the church goods.[2]

Henry Hooper, rector from 1591,[3] became embroiled in lawsuits and was accused of assaulting a parishioner.[4] He was deprived for simony in 1596.[5] For the duration of his incumbency the parish register contains very few entries. His successor Thomas Higgs, who was serving the parish in 1593,[6] was presented in 1600 for not preaching and reading the homilies and for engaging a layman to say services in his absence.[7] By the early 17th century several parishioners did not attend church or receive the Easter Communion.[8] John Stock, rector from 1601, resigned in 1620 to be replaced by Christopher Stock,[9] whose first wife Elizabeth (d. 1621) has a stone memorial in the chancel.[10] In the 1630s a prayer book and communion cushions were bought and repairs made to the church porch, the ring of bells, and a charnel house.[11] Income for the upkeep of the church came from the land given by Hugh of Walford and other church property, all of it vested in 1545 in five parishioners.[12] In 1620, following a period in which the income had been static, the scattered pieces of land and several cottages were entrusted to six feoffees.[13]

After the Restoration: the Yate family and the parish church

Christopher Stock remained rector until his death in 1674. Richard Eaton, his successor,[14] was found in 1707 to have failed to adhere to the Book of Common Prayer and to have worn a surplice.[15] After his death in 1709 he was followed in turn by his son Richard, rector until his death in 1745,[16] Robert Harden, also rector of Evesbatch (Herefs.) and vice-principal of Hertford College, Oxford,[17] and in 1771 William Hayward, also vicar of Dymock.[18]

At the church repairs were made to the porch in 1635 and 1636 and the steeple in 1669 and 1681. Three of the bells were recast into four by Alexander Rigby at Tewkesbury in 1682.[19] In 1725 Walter Yate provided a new altar piece[20] and about the same time he built a chapel on the north side of the chancel as his family's mortuary chapel.[21] In 1773 the church was repaired under the direction of R.G.D. Yate, who at his own expense built a west gallery and had the church's five bells recast as six by Thomas Rudhall of Gloucester in 1773.[22] A painting of the royal arms was placed in the church in 1779.[23]

In 1781 R.G.D. Yate gave the rectory to his brother Henry Gorges Dobyns Yate and over the next five years the latter carried out repairs in the church, whitewashed its walls, inserted a new round-headed ashlar arch and wrought-iron gates between the chancel and the Yate chapel, and donated a silver paten, velvet furnishings, and brass sconces.[24] The 14th-century window of the Yate chapel, perhaps moved from the chancel north wall, contains glass from the manor house at Quedgeley donated by H.G.D. Yate. That glass includes late medieval pieces bearing the arms of Prior Edmund Forest of Llanthony priory.[25] By the end of the century the chapel, for the maintenance of which Walter Yate had left two parcels of land,[26] also contained several notable monuments, as well as two Civil War cavalry standards, one Royalist and the other Parliamentarian, that had come into the possession of Rice Yate (d. 1690).[27] H.G.D. Yate, who also held the livings of Evesbatch and Fretherne,[28] introduced reforms to services at Bromesberrow, holding collections, reviving psalmody, and instructing the ringers to observe modern rather than traditional holidays.[29] He remained rector until his death in 1812.[30]

Four nonconformists were recorded in Bromesberrow in 1676[31] and one parishioner was regularly absent from church between 1677 and

---

1 Hockaday Abs. cxxxv; xlix, state of clergy 1584, f. 43, in which Price's Christian name is given as Humphrey.
2 GDR, V 5/367/1; *Glos. Ch. Plate*, 30.
3 Hockaday Abs. cxxxv.
4 BL, Harl. MS 4131, ff. 482v., 503 and v., 510 and v.
5 Wynn-Lloyd, 'Bromesberrow', 135.
6 GA, P 63/IN 1/1.
7 GDR vol. 87, f. 290.
8 GA, D 2052.
9 Hockaday Abs. cxxxv.
10 Wynn-Lloyd, 'Bromesberrow', 137; F. Rigby, *To Our Lady of Bromsberrow* (Evesham, 1970: copy in Glos. Colln. R 59.8), 7–8.
11 GA, P 63/CW 2/1.
12 Ibid. D 963.
13 Ibid.; TNA, C 93/8/7.
14 Hockaday Abs. cxxxv.
15 GDR, B 4/1/368.
16 Hockaday Abs. cxxxv.
17 GA, P 63/IN 1/2.

18 Hockaday Abs. clxxxvii; see below, Dymock, religious hist. (religious life).
19 GA, P 63/CW 2/1; *Glos. Ch. Bells*, 169–71.
20 Bigland, *Glos*. I, 258.
21 Hockaday Abs. cxxxv.
22 Bigland, *Glos*. I, 258; GA, P 63/CW 2/6; *Glos. Ch. Bells*, 169–71.
23 GA, P 63/VE 2/1.
24 Ibid. D 7547/6/10; P 63/CW 2/6; IN 1/2; VE 2/1; Verey and Brooks, *Glos*. II, 208.
25 Bigland, Glos. I, 260 n.; Verey and Brooks, *Glos*. II, 208. For the Quedgeley manor house, see VCH *Glos*. X, 218
26 TNA, PROB 11/740, ff. 256v.–258.
27 Bigland, *Glos*. I, 260–1; Wynn-Lloyd, 'Bromesberrow', 111–14; E. Fraser, 'Notes on two cavalry standards of Cromwell's time', *J. of Hist. Army Research* 2.8 (1923), 74–7.
28 Wynn-Lloyd, 'Bromesberrow', 138–9; VCH *Glos*. X, 166.
29 GA, P 63/VE 2/1.
30 His memorial tablet is fixed on the exterior of the Yate chapel.
31 *Compton Census*, 544.

1683.¹ The house of Joseph Stock was licensed for nonconformist meetings in 1702² and that of John Stock was similarly licensed in 1733.³ Two Presbyterians were recorded in 1735 and a Presbyterian family was resident in 1750.⁴ A protestant dissenter who had received relief from a London charity was buried in the churchyard in 1786.⁵

The Nineteenth Century and Later

Under George Turberville, who was dispensed in 1812 to hold the rectory with the vicarage of Hanley Castle (Worcs.), Bromesberrow church was served by a succession of curates residing in the rectory house. Charles Hill, his last curate, became rector in 1823 and remained resident after acquiring the rectory of Madresfield (Worcs.) in 1832.⁶ At his death in 1856 he was succeeded at Bromesberrow by his son Reginald Pyndar Hill, who retained the living until his death in 1887.⁷

In 1825 the church had *c.*200 seats, many of them free, and an average congregation at its two Sunday services of 130; the number of communicants was put at *c.*50–60. The church also ran a Sunday school.⁸ The previous year Osman Ricardo had repaired the west gallery, Charles Hill had installed a north gallery to accommodate his servants and the poor, and books of prayers and psalms had been issued to the singers.⁹ The church lands, comprising 5–6 a.,¹⁰ were mortgaged to Hill in 1827 to pay for repairs to the tower¹¹ and from 1845 they included an acre given by Osman Ricardo as compensation for three small pieces lost by the charity by the mid 18th century.¹² In 1851 attendance at the church's morning and evening services rarely exceeded 90.¹³ Later in the century a family at Chase End hill counted itself among members of the Latter Day Saints.¹⁴

Bromesberrow church was extensively restored and enlarged in 1857 and 1858 to designs by Frederick Preedy. The galleries were removed, the nave south wall was rebuilt using local stone, a north aisle with a three-bay arcade in the Decorated style was added, the windows were renewed, and the tower roof was replaced at a steeper pitch with Welsh slates. Amongst the new fittings were a stone pulpit and communion rails and a lectern carved in yew by David Smith of Ledbury. The sanctuary was tiled with Minton, Hollins, & Co. tiles and given a pillar piscina and

30. *Bromesberrow church tower from the north-east*

aumbry.¹⁵ In 1875 the tower was reconstructed with a timber spire in the French Gothic style¹⁶ and the Norman font set within an ornate stone casing (removed in 1938) and mounted on an octagonal plinth.¹⁷ In the later 1880s three windows were filled with glass memorials to Osman Ricardo (d. 1881), Charles Hill, and R.P. Hill, all designed by John

---

1 GA, D 2052.
2 Ibid. Q/SO 3.
3 Hockaday Abs. cxxxv. For John Stock and Lower Brookend, see Wynn-Lloyd, 'Bromsberrow', 145.
4 *Bp. Benson's Surv. of Glouc. 1735–50*, 4.
5 GA, P 63/IN 1/2.
6 Hockaday Abs. cxxxv.
7 *Alumni Cantab. 1752–1900*, III, 368, 373.
8 GDR vol. 383, no cvii.
9 GA, P 63/VE 2/1.
10 *20th Rep. Com. Char.* 10–11.
11 GA, P 63/CW 2/9.
12 Ibid. CW 2/3; GDR, V 5/59T 5.
13 TNA, HO 129/335/2/4/7.
14 GA, P 63/IN 1/9; see ibid. D 7547/2/5.
15 *Glos. Ch. Notes*, 123–4; Verey and Brooks, *Glos.* II, 207–8; GA, P 63/CW 3/1; GDR, V 5/367/1.
16 Fig. 30.
17 Wynn-Lloyd, 'Bromesberrow', 109; *Ledbury Reporter*, 22 Feb. 1957; Steynor, 'Bromesberrow Church', 8, 15.

Kempe, and a window in the tower was filled with new glass to mark the Golden Jubilee. Another window displays a memorial by Kempe to Frank Ricardo (d. 1897);[1] he had donated land for an extension to the churchyard consecrated in 1892.[2]

In 1910 a vestry room designed by Waller & Son was added to the north side of the tower.[3] Part of its cost was met by W.P. Robinson, who, following the death in 1908 of Revd H.D.Y. Scott, a descendant of the Yate family, had taken responsibility for maintaining the Yate chapel;[4] the chapel had served as a vestry since the 1850s.[5] Another benefactor was G.S. Albright, a member of the Society of Friends,[6] whose gifts included in 1908 a chamber organ (restored in 1975)[7] and in 1914 a clock installed in the tower.[8] Land given by Beatrice Waudby-Griffin was incorporated in the churchyard in 1933.[9] The church continued to be served by a resident rector until 1977, one of the longer incumbencies being that of W. Wynn-Lloyd (1904–21).[10] The church lands were sold off, part in 1942 and the cottage at Woodend in 1964.[11] Following Dinah Albright's death in 1990 a window in the church was glazed in her memory.[12] A Sunday school met twice monthly in the village school in 1999.[13] Although the priest-in-charge of Bromesberrow lived in Redmarley D'Abitot from 1979, the former rectory house in Albright Lane was occupied by a serving clergyman in 2007.[14]

DYMOCK

DYMOCK is a large rural parish straddling the river Leadon midway between the market towns of Newent and Ledbury (Herefs.) and 18 km northwest of Gloucester. Its village, standing in an area of Romano-British roadside settlement, was in the late Anglo-Saxon period the centre of a large royal estate, much of it in the hands of a tenantry that included numerous peasant farmers. The village remained primarily an agricultural settlement and in the medieval period the parish was largely populated in scattered farmsteads. One of several small hamlets formed later grew into the village of Bromesberrow Heath in the 19th and 20th centuries. Although the farmers were involved in parish life, after the 16th century Dymock was dominated by the owners of its several estates with the Lygons of Madresfield (Worcs.) being particularly prominent in the half century before the First World War. In the 20th century orcharding, long the main business of many farms, declined but agriculture continued at the heart of Dymock's economy. In the later 20th century the main settlements grew as they became residential areas for retired people and people working elsewhere.

BOUNDARIES AND DIVISIONS

The ancient parish covered 7,009 a. (2,836 ha).[15] Two thirds of it lay west of the Leadon, which after being augmented by the waters of the Preston and Kempley brooks turns eastwards from its southwards course and at Ketford follows the channel of a former mill leat flowing north of its original twisting course.[16] The parish extended northwards into the Leadington, to the west of the Leadon, and eastwards to Cut Mill and Lintridge, to the north of the river. Its boundaries, which on the east and on parts of the north and west were those of the county,[17] mostly followed natural and ancient features, including the Ludstock brook, a tributary of the Preston brook, west of the Leadington.[18] East of the Leadon the northern boundary closely followed a road that further east once formed the main route linking Ledbury with Gloucester.[19] The long southern

---

1 Verey and Brooks, *Glos.* II, 208; GDR, V 5/367/1; Steynor, 'Bromesberrow Church', 10.
2 GA, P 63/VE 2/2.
3 Ibid. D 2593/2/712.
4 Ibid. P 63/IN 3/3.
5 Ibid. VE 2/2.
6 Ibid. D 3028/1.
7 Steynor, 'Bromesberrow Church', 11, 21.
8 GA, D 3028/1; D 7547/5/7.
9 Ibid. P 63/IN 3/5; Steynor, 'Bromesberrow Church', 14.
10 Wynn-Lloyd, 'Bromesberrow', 140.
11 Steynor, 'Bromesberrow Church', 15, 19. For the cottage at Woodend, above, settlement (the northern hills); local govt. (parochial govt.).
12 It is located in the aisle.
13 *Bromesberrow 1999–2000: Parish Appraisal* (copy in VCH Glos. office), 18.
14 *Glouc. Dioc. Year Book* (1980), 79; above, social hist. (social structure).
15 *OS Area Book* (1884). This account was written between 2002 and 2006 and revised in 2009.
16 See Worcs. RO, 705:99 (BA 3375), Dymock deeds 1633–1811, copy ct. roll 24 Oct. 1633.
17 OS Maps 6", *Glos.* IX.SE (1883 edn); X.SE, SW, NW (1883 edns); XVI.NE (1889 edn); XVII.NE (1889 edn); NW (1884 edn).
18 See perambulation of Dymock manor in Worcs. RO, 705:99 (BA 5540), Dymock ct. book 1784–1822, cts. 9 and 10 June 1790.
19 Above, Bromesberrow, introd. (roads).

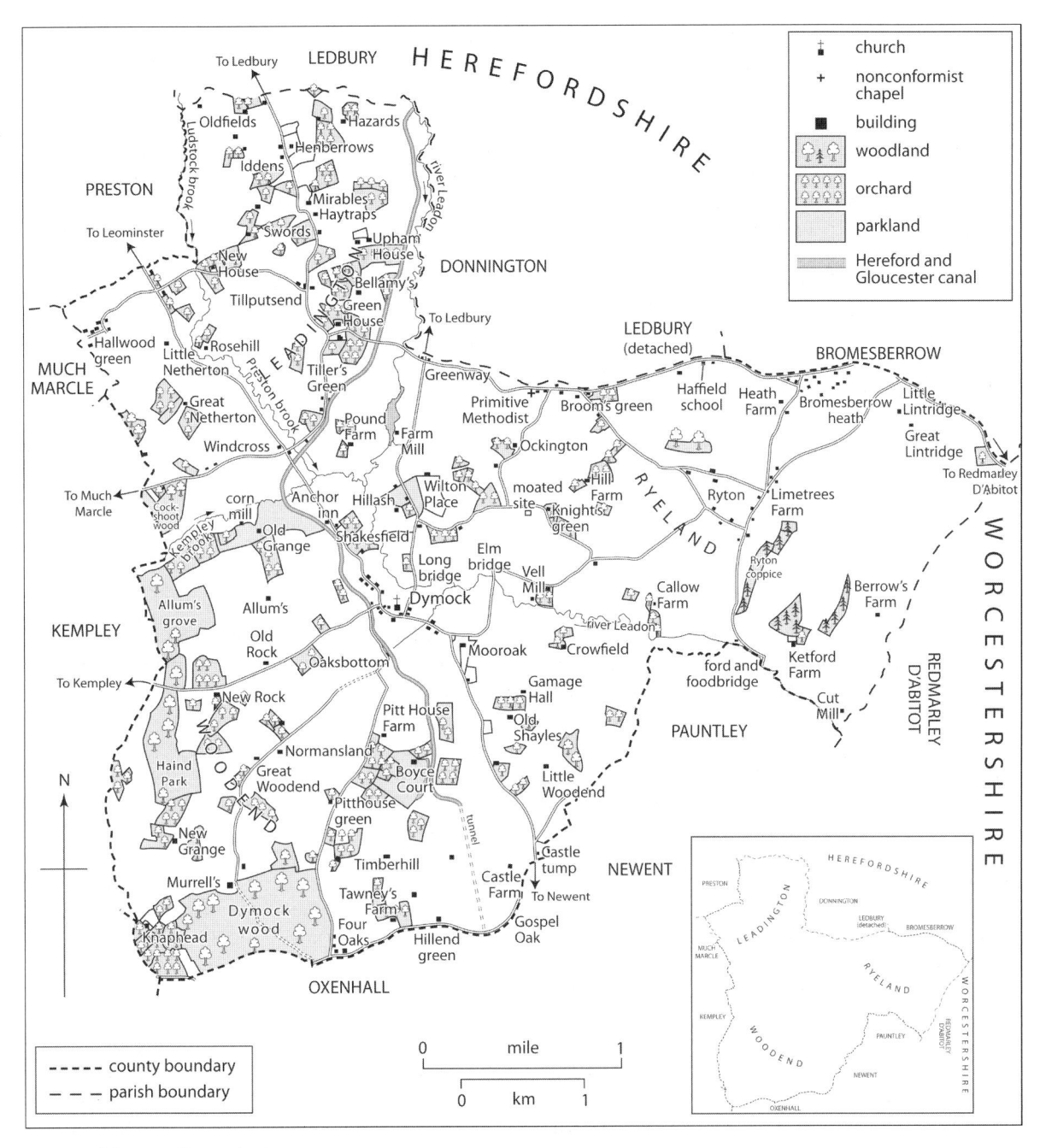

Map 8. *Dymock 1880*

boundary followed a road but in the east took a series of irregular turns (field boundaries) to include a substantial mound known as Castle Tump. Further west it passed a tree called Gospel Oak standing where Dymock met Newent and Oxenhall.[1] The tree, presumably a place where Bible readings were given on parish perambulations, died some time before its remains were blown down in 1893.[2] The slightly more irregular western boundary followed a short section of the Kempley brook and further north passed a tree called the Stonehouse Oak in 1796.[3] In 1935 the parish of Preston, 897 a. to the north-west, was added to Dymock[4] and in 1992 the village of Bromesberrow Heath in the north-east was transferred to Bromesberrow, the revised boundary following the M50 motorway, and Cut Mill in the east to Redmarley D'Abitot (Glos., formerly Worcs.).[5] The following account deals with the parish as it was constituted before 1935.

Dymock, on the eve of the Conquest a royal

---

1 OS Map 6", Glos. XVII.NW (1884 edn); GA, P 125/IN 1/18, p. 271.
2 GA, P 125/IN 1/18, p. 271.
3 Ibid. VE 2/2.
4 *Census*, 1931 (pt. ii).

5 Dymock par. council, par. meeting min. book, p. 202; The Forest of Dean (Parishes) Order 1991 (unpublished Statutory Instrument 1992 no 2283); information (Sept. 2003) from Mr Gareth Ellison (environment directorate, Glos. co. council).

manor, later contained five tithings with Flaxley in the south-west and Woodend (also known as Gamage Hall) in the south being based on manors created by grants in the 12th century. Leadington was in the north-west, and the land east of the Leadon was divided between Ockington and, to its east, Ryton (sometimes called Ryeland).[1] By later medieval times the parish also had three divisions or hamlets: Woodend, Leadington, and Ryeland.[2] The units of civil government in the parish,[3] they came to a single point in the parish churchyard.[4] Woodend, which was made up of Gamage Hall and Flaxley tithings, included all of the parish south of the Kempley brook and the river Leadon apart from a bit north of Dymock village street. Leadington, based on the tithing of the same name, extended from the street to take in the area north of the Kempley brook. Ryeland, comprising Ockington and Ryton tithings, covered the area east of the Leadon.[5]

LANDSCAPE

The Leadon flows through Dymock in a valley at c.30 m. Most of the parish is gently rolling countryside rising to over 60 m in places and reaching 90 m at Gospel Oak on the south boundary, but there is flatter land beside the Preston and Kempley brooks in the north-west and west and steep hills hem in the Leadon near Ketford in the east. The land is drained by small tributary streams, of which the Preston and Kempley brooks meet before flowing into the Leadon north-west of Dymock village near Windcross. The stream flowing north of the village was called Jordan's in the mid 16th century.[6] Land by the river and its principal tributaries is alluvial. Elsewhere it is mostly formed of sandstone[7] and the lighter soil on the higher land in the east, part of 'the ryelands',[8] is especially prone to erosion.

Early dispersed settlement and the abundance of ancient closes point to the emergence of much of the parish from ancient woodland. A wood measuring three leagues by one league was recorded in Dymock in the late 11th century[9] and the south-western part of the parish once belonged to a great wood called Teds (Tetills) wood that extended across the county boundary.[10] In the 1840s, when the parish had 457 a. of woodland or plantation, Dymock wood, on the south-western boundary, covered 171 a. and Haind (Hen) Park (75 a.), Allum's (70 a.), and Cockshoot (22 a.) woods formed a wide and almost continuous band of woodland on the west side.[11] Of those three woods, part of an estate of Flaxley abbey in the Middle Ages,[12] Haind Park was presumably the park or hay recorded in the 13th century.[13] The park of Chesterford recorded in 1394 was elsewhere in the parish.[14] Beginning in the later 19th century a new wood was planted in the east on the hillsides above Ketford,[15] but the total area of woods and plantations, 326 a. in 1905,[16] was reduced by the felling of Cockshoot wood in the early 1920s.[17]

Open fields and common meadows, existing in all parts of the parish save the south-west, were inclosed at an early date[18] and the former commons of the parish were represented at the time of the Commons Registration Act of 1965 primarily by two small pieces of Hallwood green in the north-west corner on the boundary with Much Marcle (Herefs.).[19] Orchards, already numerous in the mid 16th century,[20] were a major feature of the landscape in the later 18th century.[21] In the 18th and 19th centuries several landowners created small parks next to their houses, one of the first being at Boyce Court in the south of the parish.[22] The park at the Old Grange, in the west, was made a golf course in the 1990s.[23]

COMMUNICATIONS

Roads and Bridges

The highway from Newent that entered Dymock beside Castle Tump in the late 13th century[24] was part of a way from Gloucester into Herefordshire. After passing Portway Top,[25] presumably on the rise once

---

1 Below, manors; local govt.; see Bigland, *Glos.* I, 527; Dymock manor ct. books for 1704–84 and 1784–1822 in Worcs. RO, B705:99 (BA 3375) and 705:99 (BA 5540) respectively.
2 *Military Surv. of Glos. 1522*, 54–6.
3 Below, local govt.; in GA, P 125/VE 3/1 the divisions are called townships.
4 Rudder, *Glos.* 411.
5 Bigland, *Glos.* I, 527. The division boundaries used in this account are those indicated by 17th- and 18th-cent. rate and tax assessments: GA, P 125/OV 2/2; VE 2/1, ff. (at end) 117–19; Q/REl 1, Botloe hundred. See above, Map 8.
6 GDR wills 1565/106; MCA, J 6i, bdl. 100, no 1; GA, P 125A/SD 2/1–2 (no 1535).
7 Geol. Surv. Map 1:50,000, solid and drift, sheet 216 (1988 edn).
8 Rudge, *Agric. of Glos.* 20, 138; Turner, *Agric. of Glos.* 48.
9 *Domesday Book* (Rec. Com.), I, 164.
10 See *Inq. p.m. Glos.* 1359–1413, 132, 193; Teds wood became more particularly the name of woodland in Upton Bishop (Herefs.): MCA, F 5v, deed 1365; I 5i, bdl. 88A, nos 1, 4; I 5ii, bdl. 88, nos 17, 19.
11 GA, P 125A/MI 1/1–2; SD 2/1–2.
12 Below, manors (Old Grange manor)
13 *Flaxley Cart.* p. 128; see MCA, F 5iii, deed 1271.
14 *Inq. p.m. Glos.* 1359–1413, 188.
15 See below, econ. hist. (woodland management).
16 Acreage Returns, 1905.
17 GA, D 2299/3126.
18 Below, econ. hist. (agric.).
19 GA, DA 30/132/11.
20 Below, econ. hist. (agric.).
21 Rudder, *Glos.* 409
22 Taylor, *Map of Glos.* (1777); Bryant, *Map of Glos.* (1824).
23 Local information; see GA, SL 417.
24 BL, Add. MS 15668, f. 14v.
25 OS Map 6", Glos. XVII.NW (1884 edn). The place was called Porter Top in Dymock ct. book 1784–1822, cts. 8 and 17 Oct. 1784, 17 Oct. 1785.

known as port hill,[1] it turns west along the village street which also marks closely the line of a Roman route coming from the east, probably from Tewkesbury, and continuing towards Stretton Grandison (Herefs.).[2] Beyond the village, where Stoneberrow (Stanborough) bridge carried it over Jordan's brook in the late 16th century,[3] the medieval road continued to Windcross from where it ran north-westwards to Hallwood green, passing by Great and Little Netherton.[4]

A number of other roads or lanes linked the village with nearby towns in the early 18th century. Counters Lane, the way northwards to Ledbury,[5] dipped from the eastern end of the village street into the Leadon valley, where it followed a causeway known as Long bridge, and continued northwards up to the Lynch and on past Hillash to Greenway. Earlier occupants of Hillash had made bequests for the causeway's maintenance.[6] Ways to Ross-on-Wye (Herefs.) and Mitcheldean followed lanes leading westwards and southwards to Kempley and Four Oaks respectively.[7] The parish had other lanes and also an extensive network of footpaths that, together with the footbridges on them, the Dymock manor court sought to maintain in the 18th century; many of the paths linked outlying farmsteads to the village and several were called church ways.[8] The path known as Yokeford's Way in the 16th century branched off the Four Oaks lane near Oaksbottom towards Normansland and Dymock wood.[9] In the south-west, where a woodland path was known as 'Staurnchesway' in the mid 13th century,[10] a lane running south-westwards through Haind Park wood to Kempley green was closed in 1819.[11]

The road from Newent to Ledbury by way of Dymock village was turnpiked in 1768[12] and was the responsibility of the Newent turnpike trust from 1824.[13] Tollgates were placed at the east end of the village, including one across the entrance to the main street, and at crossroads at Greenway.[14] About 1835, on the construction of a new road beyond Windcross to Preston, the village street became part of a route linking Newent and Leominster (Herefs.)[15] and the road past Little Netherton was abandoned[16] The new road was a turnpike until 1871. The Newent–Ledbury road remained a turnpike until 1874.[17]

Long bridge, from which timbers were stolen in 1754,[18] was improved in 1789 and 1790, when brick culverts were constructed under the causeway.[19] The county repaired the main span, as well as a small bridge carrying the Newent road over a stream east of the village, in 1847.[20] Elm bridge downstream on the Ryton road, leading off the Newent road, provided an alternative crossing of the Leadon but in 1790 the road running north-westwards from the bridge towards the Lynch was closed.[21] The bridge was rebuilt in 1901[22] and the junction of the Newent and Ryton roads was widened by removing the parish pound in 1921.[23] Another way from Newent to Ledbury crossed the Leadon into Dymock downstream at Ketford and ran northwards through Ryton.[24]

The road crossing the Dymock–Ledbury road at Greenway is part of a route that led westwards across Bromesberrow heath from the Gloucester–Ledbury road. Its crossing of the Leadon, not far from Roman occupation in Donnington (Herefs.),[25] was known in the late 18th century as Chester's bridge[26] and is presumably the place called Chester ford in 1394.[27] West of the river the road forks, one branch leading northwards through the Leadington towards Ledbury and the other leading southwards and then westwards by way of Tiller's green, Windcross, and Kempley to a junction in Much Marcle with the road from Ledbury to Ross-on-Wye. The road to Much Marcle was a turnpike between 1833 and 1871[28] and tollgates were sited at the west end of Bromesberrow heath and at Windcross.[29]

1 BL, Add. MS 18461, ff. 82v.–83v.
2 SMR Glos. nos 7677, 9338; I.D. Margary, *Roman Roads in Britain*, II (1957), 60; see E. Gethyn-Jones, 'Roman Dymock. A Personal Record', *Trans. BGAS* 109 (1991), 91–8; T. Catchpole, T. Copeland, and A. Maxwell, 'Introduction' to 'Roman Dymock: archaeological investigations 1995–2002', *Trans. BGAS* 125 (2007), 132–4.
3 GDR wills 1565/106; 1747/66; TNA, E 310/14/54, f. 44.
4 Bryant, *Map of Glos.* (1824); OS Map 1", sheet 43 (1831 edn).
5 Dymock ct. book 1704–84, f. 9 and v.; see GA, P 125A/SD 2/1–2 (nos 1506–7).
6 GDR wills 1579/87; 1592/36; 1609/118.
7 GA, D 2545/1–2.
8 Dymock ct. book 1704–84, passim.
9 GA, D 214/T 17, deed 3 Nov. 1630.
10 *Close 1251–3*, 136.
11 GA, Q/SRh 1819D/2; see Bryant, *Map of Glos.* (1824).
12 Glouc. and Heref. Roads Act, 9 Geo. III, c. 50.
13 Newent Roads Act, 5 Geo. IV, c. 11 (Local and Personal).
14 OS Map 1", sheet 43 (1831 edn); GA, Q/RUm 129.
15 Ledbury Roads Act, 3 Wm. IV, c. 58 (Local and Personal); GA, Q/RUm 129.
16 See GA, P 125/VE 2/3, min. 29 Apr. 1840.
17 Annual Turnpike Acts. Continuance Acts, 1871, 34 & 35 Vic. c. 115; 1874, 37 & 38 Vic. c. 95.
18 GA, P 125/VE 2/1, f. (at end) 22.
19 Ibid. VE 2/2; Q/SRh 1790C/2.
20 Ibid. D 2593/2/71; Q/CI 2, pp. 16, 18.
21 Ibid. Q/SRh 1790C/2; P 125/VE 2/2.
22 Ibid. DA 30/100/7, pp. 95, 146.
23 Ibid. 100/12, pp. 318, 326; see OS Map 6", Glos. X.SW (1883 edn).
24 MCA, J 2viii, bdl. 111C, no 20. For the crossing at Ketford, see below, Pauntley, introd. (roads).
25 G.H. Jack, 'Some Notes on Roman Herefordshire', *Trans. Woolhope Naturalists' Field Club* (1908–11), 69; 'Roman Road between Monmouth and Gloucester', ibid. 108.
26 Dymock ct. book 1784–1822, cts. 9 and 10 June 1790.
27 *Inq. p.m. Glos.* 1359–1413, 188.
28 Ledbury Roads Act, 3 Wm. IV, c. 58 (Local and Personal); Annual Turnpike Acts Continuance Act, 1871, 34 & 35 Vic. c. 115.
29 GA, P 125A/SD 2/1.

The M50 motorway, opened in 1960,[1] crosses the parish from the north-east at a point near Bromesberrow Heath to the south at Four Oaks. Of the lanes it severed that at Four Oaks from the village was diverted to a junction with the lane in Dymock wood.

Canal and Railway

The Hereford and Gloucester canal opened across the centre of Dymock in 1798 following the construction of the Oxenhall tunnel.[2] It emerged from the tunnel in a deep cutting near Boyce Court and its northwards course passed immediately west of Dymock village before curving by the Old Grange and Tiller's green to adopt a route close to the river Leadon.[3] A tramroad following the line of the lane between the village and Four Oaks in 1807 was possibly laid to carry materials for the canal's construction. No later record of it has been found.[4] In 1881 the canal was closed between Gloucester and Ledbury to make way for a railway. The line, which opened in 1885, carried passenger traffic until 1959 and closed in 1964.[5] It took a more westerly route than the canal to enter Dymock at Four Oaks and north of the village it followed a direct route east of Tiller's green to follow the canal's course alongside the Leadon. There was a station next to the village[6] and, from 1937, a halt by the road west of Greenway.[7]

Among the remains of the canal, the section in the cutting north of the Oxenhall tunnel has been dammed to form a stretch of water, which in 2002 was overgrown and silted up towards the tunnel entrance.

POPULATION

Sixty-eight tenants, including a priest, lived on Dymock manor in 1066[8] and sixty-three parishioners were assessed for tax in 1327.[9] A muster roll of 1542 named 108 men of the parish,[10] which was said to have c.440 communicants in 1551,[11] 106 households in 1563,[12] 400 communicants in 1603,[13] and 140 families in 1650.[14] About 1710 the population was estimated at 1,000 living in 250 houses.[15] About 1775 it was estimated at 1,116[16] and in 1801 it was 1,223. Despite a small drop in the 1840s, the population grew to 1,870 in 1861, after which it fell to 1,149 in 1931. The addition of Preston in 1935 brought only a small increase and Dymock's population, having risen to 1,283 in 1991, was reduced by the loss of the Bromesberrow Heath area in 1992. In 2001 it was 1,141.[17]

SETTLEMENT

Archaeological investigations reveal that Romano-British settlement took place along the ancient road to Stretton Grandison on ground rising above the river Leadon to the north. Part of that settlement lies under the present village of Dymock[18] and in the 1770s ancient foundations and causeways were reported in fields 'above a quarter of a mile from the church'.[19] Although the village was the focus of substantial settlement in the late Anglo-Saxon period, the pattern of medieval settlement was largely one of scattered farmsteads. They dotted the surrounding countryside in the 14th century, some houses standing on earth platforms or in or next to moated enclosures. Many farmsteads were later abandoned[20] while the filling of encroachments on roadside wastes and common land with clusters of cottages from the 17th century led to the formation of several small hamlets.[21] Building in the 19th and 20th centuries latterly included new houses and bungalows beside several of the remaining farmsteads and many more dwellings in Dymock village and in the newer village of Bromesberrow Heath.

---

1 *Citizen*, 29 Nov. 1960.
2 D.E. Bick, *The Hereford & Gloucester Canal* (Newent, 1979), 14.
3 GA, P 125A/SD 2/1; OS Maps 6", X.NW and SW (1883 edn); XVII.NW (1884 edn).
4 GA, D 1272, Dymock deeds 1794–1885; see Bryant, *Map of Glos.* (1824); OS Map 1", sheet 43 (1831 edn).
5 Bick, *Heref. & Glouc. Canal*, 41, 59, 62; E.T. MacDermot, *Hist. GWR*, revised C.R. Clinker (1964), II, 185.
6 OS Maps 6", Glos. X.NW (1905 edn); X. SW (1903 edn); XVII.NW (1903 edn).
7 Bick, *Heref. & Glouc. Canal*, 62.
8 *Domesday Book* (Rec. Com.), I, 164.
9 *Glos. Subsidy Roll, 1327*, 5.
10 *L&P Hen. VIII*, XVII, 499.
11 J. Gairdner, 'Bishop Hooper's Visitation of Gloucester', *EHR* 19 (1904), 119.
12 Bodleian, Rawl. C. 790, f. 28.
13 *Eccl. Misc.* 102.
14 C.R. Elrington, 'The Survey of Church Livings in Gloucestershire, 1650', *Trans. BGAS* 83 (1964), 98.
15 Atkyns, *Glos.* 396.
16 Rudder, *Glos.* 411.
17 *Census*, 1801–2001.
18 In 'Roman Dymock. A Personal Record', *Trans. BGAS* 109 (1991), 91–8, E. Gethyn-Jones proposed that the village occupies the site of the town of Macatonium (Macatonion). For a discussion of more recent archaeological evidence, 'Roman Dymock: Archaeological Investigations 1995–2002', ibid. 125 (2007), 131–245.
19 Rudder, *Glos.* 409.
20 See GA, D 185/IV/16, copy ct. roll 16 May 1759; GDR, B 4/1/913.
21 See *1st Rep. Com. Employment in Agric.* app. II, p. 129.

DYMOCK VILLAGE

The village has one main street along the road from Newent to Leominster. The size of its church, at the eastern end, indicates the presence of a large congregation in the late Anglo-Saxon period and the early Middle Ages. Burgage holdings created probably after the justiciar Hubert de Burgh ordered the sheriff to hold a market and a fair on the royal manor in 1222[1] were not developed to form a market town but several properties in the village street, including copyhold cottages and a close west of the churchyard, continued to be described as burgages in the 17th and 18th centuries.[2]

The church, standing west of the Newent–Ledbury road, is set back from the street behind a green. The green, known in 1791 as Wintour's green,[3] was enlarged in the late 19th century following the demolition of the vicarage house on its west side.[4] A church house (later the parish workhouse) stood at the south-eastern corner of the churchyard[5] and until the 1920s there was an old building near by known, like one once occupied by a chantry priest, as the Priest's House.[6] Of the buildings on the east side of the green the Beauchamp Arms, facing the street next to the entrance to the Ledbury road, was formerly known as the Plough.[7] The White House, across the street from the green, is a former farmhouse on the rectory estate.[8] It stands in the place of a house that was the birthplace of John Kyrle (1637–1724), the 'Man of Ross',[9] and the home of the Winter family in the later 17th and early 18th century.[10] High House, west of the churchyard, is a tall, mid 18th-century house that was remodelled in 1878 as the vicarage house by the 6th Earl Beauchamp,[11] who shortly afterwards demolished the old vicarage, incorporating part of its site in the garden of High House and adding the rest to the green.[12] The parish pound against the churchyard wall was removed about the same time.[13] The churchyard, which included the sexton's dwelling in the mid 19th century,[14] was approached from the west by a walk replanted with lime trees in 1874[15] and was enlarged to the north in 1911.[16]

The village straggles along the street and its oldest houses are on the north side towards the west end. Two date possibly from the 15th century, another probably from the 16th century.[17] New building in the early 19th century, after the construction of the canal near by, included Great Wadley and the former George inn together on the site south of the street of a meeting place called Society Lodge.[18] To the east the former Ann Cam's school was built in the mid 1820s in place of an earlier school.[19] In the early 1840s the new Stoneberrow Place, in the centre of the village, was among a group of cottages close to the canal[20] and a tollhouse stood in the road at the east end of the street.[21]

In the early 1880s a railway station was built off the street next to the abandoned canal.[22] A police station (closed in 1971) was erected opposite it on the Kempley lane in 1898[23] but little other new building took place in the village before the mid 20th century.[24] Newent Rural District Council built a pair of houses in the street in 1948 and four pairs on the Kempley lane between 1949 and 1952.[25] In 1953 a new parsonage was erected north-west of High House.[26] The latter, which the RDC acquired, was converted as flats in 1957[27] and two new bungalows were built in its grounds in 1963.[28] The village's growth away from the main street continued after the railway's closure in 1964, the site of the station being filled with an old people's home and several houses[29] and a housing estate being built off the Kempley lane.[30] Among new developments by the street were a council estate of 21 dwellings on the south side completed in 1966[31] and a small estate of detached houses on the north side finished in 2001.[32]

---

1 Below, econ. hist. (markets and fairs); local govt.
2 Worcs. RO, 705:99 (BA 3375), Dymock deeds 1633–1811; GA, D 1604/T 1, deed 6 Mar. 1731/2; MCA, I 5iv, bdl. 89, no1.
3 Dymock ct. book 1784–1822.
4 GA, P 125A/SD 2/1–2 (no 1516); below, this section.
5 GA, P 125/VE 2/1, ff. (at end) 89–90; MCA, J 2ii, bdl. 103, no 1.
6 Hockaday Abs. clxxxvii; J.E. Gethyn-Jones, *Dymock Down the Ages* (1966), 50, 123.
7 GA, P 125A/SD 2/1–2 (no 1514).
8 See Rudder, *Glos*. 410.
9 Rudge, *Hist. of Glos*. II, 30; for Kyrle, *Oxford DNB*.
10 TNA, PROB 11/323, ff. 328–9; E 179/247/14, rot. 35d.; MCA, I 2vi, bdl. 67, no 3; Atkyns, *Glos*. 394.
11 GA, D 1381/54.
12 MCA, J 2ii, bdl. 104, no 17; GA, P 125/IN 1/18; IN 4/21; OS Map 6", Glos. X.SW (1883 edn).
13 GA, P 125A/SD 2/1–2, (no 1515); OS Map 6", Glos. X.SW (1883 edn).
14 GA, P 125/IN 1/15, burial 30 Nov. 1862.
15 Ibid. IN 4/19.
16 Ibid. IN 1/21, f. 140.
17 Below (bldgs.).
18 MCA, J 2vii, bdl. 111D, nos 25–8; bdl. 111E, no 43.
19 GA, P 125/SC 5.
20 Ibid. P 125A/MI 1/1–2 (nos 1550–1).
21 Ibid. (no 1514A).
22 Above, introd. (communications: canal and railway); OS Map 6", Glos. X.SW (1903 edn).
23 Inscr. on bldg.; GA, D 3295/I/ 6.
24 See *Heref. J.* 20 Sept. 1924.
25 GA, DA 30/100/17, pp. 210, 245; 100/18, pp. 3, 33, 133; 100/20, pp. 85, 164.
26 Verey and Brooks, *Glos*. II, 346.
27 GA, DA 30/100/25, pp. 149, 161, 166; 100/26, p. 62.
28 Ibid. 100/30, p. 115; 100/32, pp. 150, 228.
29 *Village Voices: Dymock Parish Appraisal 1990* (1991: copy in Glos. Colln. RR 116.9), 15; T. Ward, *Around Newent* (1994), 92.
30 OS Map 1:2,500, SO 7031–7131 (1973 edn).
31 Below (bldgs.).
32 Dymock par. council, par. meeting min. book, p. 256.

31. *The Old Cottage, Dymock, in 1948*

New building also took place on the fringes of the village next to long-established dwellings. It began in the mid 1930s when the RDC built five pairs of houses, two north of Long bridge on the Ledbury road, one to the east on the Newent road, and two further east at Batchfields on the Ryton road.[1] A schoolmaster's house was erected on the Ryton road in 1935[2] and another pair of council houses was placed there during the Second World War.[3] Later private building contributed to the spread of the village. Some of the new houses were to the north-west at Shakesfield where in the 17th century several cottages had stood in the area of Maypole Farm, a farmstead north of a way then known as Butcher's Lane.[4] Others were to the south, on the line of the former railway, towards Oaksbottom, where in 1811 a new cottage and limekiln had stood.[5]

OUTLYING SETTLEMENT

Woodend

Boyce Court, south of Dymock village, is of medieval origin and for a time from the later 17th century was the seat of the lords of Dymock manor.[6] Further south the homestead at Timberhill was the centre of the largest farm on the Boyce Court estate in the mid 19th century.[7] Of the smaller farmsteads in the area Farr's, part of Little Dymock manor, was presumably inhabited by the de la Lynde family in the mid 13th century for it was known also as Lynde House or Place in the mid 16th.[8] Moor's Farm in the late 17th century was part of a holding called Hulker's and Bulker's.[9] Tawney's, close to the south boundary, is named after a local family in the mid 16th century[10] and contains a small 17th-century house.

On the eastern outskirts of the village a small farmstead at Mooroak, east of the Newent road, was occupied by the Loveridge family in the early 17th century.[11] In the 20th century several new houses were built to the north, including the council houses at Batchfields mentioned above. In 1962 the county council erected a small farmhouse to the north-east on the lane to Crowfield,[12] where a homestead is recorded from the mid 17th century.[13] Further south Gamage Hall is a farmstead on the site of the medieval manor of Little Dymock.[14] Two farmsteads near by were among copyholds of that manor,[15] which included a farmstead called 'Crekwardens' in 1515,[16] and both have been associated by name with the Shayle family.[17] The house at Old Shayles, so called in 1577,[18] was replaced in 1909.[19] Little Woodend, previously known as the Woodend or Shayles,[20] was the home of Edward Shayle in the early 16th century[21] and part of the Ricardos' estate in the

---

1 GA, DA 30/100/14, pp. 52, 98, 204; 100/20, p. 192.
2 Nat. Soc. files.
3 GA, DA 30/100/15, pp. 196, 292; 100/20, p. 192.
4 MCA, I 6i, bdl. 93A, nos 15, 19, 26.
5 GA, D 1272, Dymock deeds 1794–1885.
6 Below, manors (other estates: Boyce Ct.).
7 GA, P 125A/SD 2/1–2.
8 TNA, C 142/100, no 44; C 142/185, no 86; JUST 1/274, rot. 10d.
9 GA, D 4317/6, rental 1692; 12, copy of 1703 terrier.
10 *Reg. of Dymock*, 1, 5.
11 GA, P 125/VE 3/1; Smith, *Men and Armour*, 59 calls it Moorhouse.
12 Datestone with inits. on ho.
13 *Reg. of Dymock*, 125.
14 Below, manors.
15 See GA, D 4317/6, rental 1692.
16 TNA, STAC 2/12/221.
17 For the Shayle fam. in the later 14th cent.: *Inq. p.m. Glos. 1359–1413*, 148.
18 *Reg. of Dymock*, 35.
19 Gethyn-Jones, *Dymock Down the Ages*, 125; see GA, SL 415.
20 GA, D 892/T 25/3; D 1618, Woodend deeds 1746–1819; GDR wills 1695/211.
21 *Military Surv. of Glos. 1522*, 54.

early 19th.[1] In the mid 18th century the land farmed from Old Shayles took in the site of a tenement called Chancellors.[2] Mere Hills Farm, to the east in Welsh House Lane, was established by the county council on land bought in 1919; its house is dated 1921.[3] In the later 19th century a farmhouse to the west on the Newent road at Beaconshill (formerly Bickenshill)[4] was rebuilt as a small private house.[5] A lodge to Boyce Court stands on the opposite side of the road.[6]

In the west of the parish the Old Grange, so called in 1555,[7] stands on the site of a grange of Flaxley abbey and until the early 20th century was the centre of a large estate.[8] The farmstead to the south at Allum's, recorded from 1539,[9] passed into the estate in the late 17th century.[10] Further south there are two old farmsteads and a few other, mostly later 20th-century, dwellings on the Kempley lane. Of the farmsteads the Old Rock, known as the Rock in 1509,[11] belonged to the Hill family until the early 20th century.[12] The New Rock, further west, was so called in 1657[13] and has a 17th-century house. Clutterbucks, a copyhold tenement on the Old Grange estate[14] that was destroyed by fire in the 18th century, probably stood to the south-west close to the parish boundary behind Haind Park wood.[15] There was a keeper's cottage up against the wood until after the First World War.[16]

Of the farmsteads established in the south-west of the parish that known in 1543 as the New Grange stands on Flaxley abbey's former (Old Grange) estate.[17] Blacklands and Normansland, on opposite sides of the way to Dymock wood, were copyholds of the estate.[18] Blacklands has an early house encased in brick[19] and a timber-framed outbuilding that until 1922 stood near the parish church.[20] Normansland, so called in 1612,[21] was known earlier as Yokeford.[22] It was inherited in 1808 by Joseph Thackwell,[23] who added the farmstead at Great Woodend, further along the lane, to his estate in 1832.[24] Among the few houses built on or near the way to the wood in the 20th century were a pair of farm cottages near Normansland[25] and a house of 1925 east of the New Grange.[26] Walnut Tree Farm, on the edge of the wood, was occupied in the early 18th century by Thomas Murrell[27] and was later known as Murrell's or Upper Murrell's. Murrell's Cottage, a small 17th-century house a little to the north, was one of two adjacent cottages in the mid 19th century.[28] The farmstead at Knaphead, on the side of the valley west of the wood, was inhabited in 1684.[29]

Pitt House Farm, by the lane to Four Oaks, may be the place inhabited by men surnamed of or at the pit in the 14th century.[30] Occupied by the Wills family in the mid 16th century, the house was known variously in the mid 18th century as the Pitt House and Edulus Place.[31] Several houses and cottages once stood further south on the lane at Pitt House green,[32] one on the west side being called the Heath House in 1680.[33] A house called Sherlocks that had been pulled down by the early 18th century was near by.[34] The house at Farmer's, east of the lane, was empty in 1956 and was later demolished.[35]

The position of the mound at Castle Tump right on the parish's south boundary points to its antiquity and makes it an unlikely candidate for the site of the medieval manor of Dymock. In the later 13th century, when it was known as the castle of Dymock, the site inhabited by men surnamed of the castle may have been off the mound.[36] At Castle Farm, to the south-west, the timber-framed house standing within a moat was rebuilt and parts of the surrounding ditch were filled in following a fire in

---

1 GA, photocopy 192; P 125A/SD 2/2 (no 1287).
2 Ibid. D 4317/6, ct. papers (Old Shayles and Chancellors).
3 Ibid. C/CC/M 5/31, pp. 125–6; see OS Map 6", Glos. XVII.NW (1924 edn).
4 GA, P 125A/SD 2/1–2 (no 1297).
5 *Kelly's Dir. Glos.* (1889), 763.
6 Below, manors (other estates: Boyce Ct.).
7 Worcs. RO, 705:99 (BA 5540), Kempley and Wilton ct. rolls 1526–68, rot. 37.
8 Below, manors (Old Grange manor).
9 TNA, E 101/59/10, rot. 1.
10 GA, D 214/T 17.
11 *L&P Hen. VIII*, I (1), p. 266.
12 Below, manors (other estates).
13 GA, P 125/VE 3/1.
14 Ibid. D 4317/6, rental 1692.
15 MCA, J 2iv, bdl. 105D, no 29; bdl. 105E, no 40; GA, P 125A/SD 2/1–2 (nos 1695, 1699).
16 GA, D 2299/3515; see ibid. P 125A/SD 2/1–2 (no 1600).
17 GDR wills 1544/79; GA, P 125A/VE 3/2; SL 417.
18 GA, D 4317/6, rental 1692.
19 Ibid. D 2299/10355.
20 Gethyn-Jones, *Dymock Down the Ages*, 50, 123.
21 *Reg. of Dymock*, 81.
22 See GA, D 214/T 17, deed 3 Nov. 1630; Dymock ct. book 1704–84, f. 89.
23 TNA, PROB 11/1481, ff. 367v.–368. For Thackwell (d. 1859), see *Burke's Landed Gentry* (1898), II, Ireland, 438; H.C. Wylly, *The Military Memoirs of Lieut.-General Sir Joseph Thackwell* (London, 1908).
24 GA, D 2299/530.
25 OS Map 6", Glos. XVII.NW (1903, 1924 edns).
26 GA, DA 30/100/13, pp. 59, 63, 75.
27 Ibid. D 2957/116/11, 17.
28 OS Map 6", Glos. XVII.NW (1884 edn); GA, P 125A/SD 2/1–2 (nos 1668, 1663, 1663A).
29 GA, P 125/VE 3/1.
30 *Glos. Subsidy Roll, 1327*, 5; *Inq. p.m. Glos. 1359–1413*, 148.
31 Below, manors (other estates: Pitt Ho. Farm).
32 GA, D 1272, Dymock deeds 1794–1885; TNA, CRES 38/681.
33 GA, D 2545/2–3.
34 Ibid. D 4317/6, rental 1692; D 1272, Dymock deeds 1736–1901.
35 Ibid. DA 30/100/25, p. 52.
36 BL, Add. MS 15668, f. 14v.; 18461, ff. 88v., 89v.

the 19th century.[1] In the mid 20th century a house was built on the drive to the house.[2] A small group of cottages beside the mound, the oldest of which dates from the 17th century, originated in settlement of waste land by the Newent road.[3]

Cottages were also erected to the west along the road marking the boundary with Oxenhall. A handful of early cottages stood on the western part of Hillend green,[4] where encroachment had begun by the mid 18th century.[5] Two pairs of identical cottages were built there in the early 20th century and the RDC erected two pairs of timber houses further east in 1947.[6] Among other new houses is a late 20th-century farmhouse set back from the road. Further west at Four Oaks, where two men were building on encroachments in 1753,[7] cottages followed the lane northwards into Dymock.[8] The hamlet, which includes 20th-century council houses within Oxenhall,[9] has remained small.

Ryeland

The farmhouse at the Lynch, on the Ledbury road north of Dymock village, was a public house in the mid 19th century.[10] A cottage to the east at Little Lynch, on the lane to Broom's green and Ryton, was later replaced by farm outbuildings.[11] Hillash, west of the Ledbury road, was owned and occupied by the Hill family in the mid 16th century.[12] Its 18th-century farmhouse became a private house in the 1850s.[13] Wilton Place, a large 18th-century house east of the road, replaced a farmhouse known as the Farm presumably on the spot where the Wilton family lived in the 16th century.[14] Farm Mill, on the river Leadon to the north-west, has a 17th-century house and remained a working mill until the 20th century.[15]

Ockington There was settlement to the east at Ockington in the early 13th century.[16] Its main farmhouse, owned by the Weale family for much of the 18th century,[17] was rebuilt as a private house in the 1980s.[18] The house next to it at Burtons,[19] occupied as two cottages in the mid 19th century,[20] was replaced by a new farmhouse in the early 20th century.[21] Hill Farm (formerly the Hill), on a hillside further east, was a copyhold of Dymock manor that belonged to the Hill family in the early 17th century.[22] Among the property that the Cams acquired from the Holmes family in the early 18th century,[23] it has late 17th-century outbuildings and an 18th-century house.[24]

To the south, beside the lane from the Lynch to Ryton, there is a moated site in a field known as Knight's Meadow.[25] Further along the lane there was encroachment on Knight's green in the mid 18th century[26] and one of two houses standing there in the mid 19th century[27] was a copyhold of Dymock manor.[28] Further east the house at a farmstead called Oysters (Heisters) was demolished before 1775 but its barn remained in use.[29]

Vell Mill in the fields beside the river Leadon to the south had medieval origins and a mill operated there until the early 18th century.[30] Its house, which belonged to Oxenhall vicarage from 1818,[31] was enlarged in the later 20th century. In the late 17th century Edward Puckmore, a wheelwright, built a house to the north-east, on the lane from Dymock village to Ryton; it was also known as Vell Mill, sometimes as Little Vell Mill.[32] In the late 19th century a pair of estate cottages was built to the west near Elm bridge.[33] Further east Callow Farm, an ancient farmstead on the far side of a hill next to the Leadon, has a house dating from the late 16th century and was part of the Madresfield estate for much of the 19th.[34] A homestead called Shayles abandoned after the late 1680s was a copyhold of Dymock manor and stood by the way from the Ketford river crossing to Ryton.[35]

---

1 Gethyn-Jones, *Dymock Down the Ages*, 125.
2 GA, D 2299/8511.
3 Ibid. D 4317/6, memo. of wastes 5 Nov. 1703; Dymock ct. book 1704–84, f. 44.
4 GA, P 125A/SD 2/1; OS Map 6", Glos. XVII.NW (1884 edn).
5 Dymock ct. book 1704–84, f. 76v.
6 GA, DA 30/100/17, pp. 17, 49, 58.
7 Dymock ct. book 1704–84, f. 66v.; MCA, F 5viii, deed 1503.
8 GA, P 125A/SD 2/1.
9 Below, Oxenhall, settlement.
10 GA, P 125A/SD 2/1–2 (no 631).
11 Ibid. (nos 626–7); D 2299/8701.
12 GDR wills 1579/87; 1611/76.
13 Below (bldgs.: outlying farms).
14 Below, manors (other estates).
15 Below, econ. hist. (mills).
16 *Pleas of the Crown for Glos. 1221*, ed. Maitland, p. 89; BL, Add. MS 18461, ff. 82v.–83v.
17 GA, P 125A/VE 3/2; Bigland, *Glos.* I, 527.
18 Information from Mrs J. Lewis, whose family bought the house in the later 1980s.
19 The name is recorded from 1565: GA, D 5980/1.
20 GA, P 125A/SD 2/1–2 (no 654).
21 Ibid. D 2299/8701.
22 Smith, *Men and Armour*, 60; TNA, C 115/43, no 2575.
23 GA, P 125/OV 2/2; P 125A/VE 3/2; TNA, PROB 11/797, ff. 131v.–134; MCA, I 3v, bdl. 74, no 9. For the Cams' acquisition, see below, manors (other estates): Great Netherton).
24 Below (bldgs.: outlying farms).
25 GA, P 125A/SD 2/1–2 (no 1183).
26 Dymock ct. book 1704–84, f. 53v.
27 GA, P 125A/SD 2/1–2 (nos 741, 744).
28 Ibid. D 1142/5.
29 MCA, I 4i, bdl. 77, nos 1, 7–11, 17–20; GA, P 125A/SD 2/1–2 (no 1179); D 2299/8701.
30 GA, P 125A/SD 2/1–2 (no 1169); see below, econ. hist. (mills).
31 GA, P 241/IN 3/4.
32 MCA, J 3iv, bdl. 132, nos 1–26; GA, P 125A/SD 2/1–2 (no 1167).
33 OS Map 6", Glos. X.SW (1883, 1903 edns).
34 Below, manors (other estates).
35 Dymock ct. book 1704–84, f. 42v.; GA, D 1142/2, abs. of ancient deeds.

Ryton   Ryton from where a local landholder in the mid 13th century took his name,[1] is made up of a hamlet strung out along a lane leading northwards towards Ledbury from Ketford bridge and more widely scattered cottages lower down to the west in the valley of a tributary of the Leadon followed by the M50 motorway. There are several early dwellings on a lane leading from the southern end of the hamlet towards Broom's green. At least one (no 333) dates from the late 16th or early 17th century. A smaller house (no 331), standing to the north beyond the motorway, is older.[2]

At the hamlet's south end, high up to the east of the lane from Ketford, a small timber-framed cottage and an adjacent stone building made three cottages known as the Gallows in 1901.[3] Adapted as a single dwelling in the early 20th century, they fell into ruin and were rebuilt as a house at the end of the century.[4] To the north used to be a copyhold farmhouse known in 1666 as the Line[5] and a tiny cottage called the Round House that was removed in the late 19th century from an island at a junction with a lane to Redmarley.[6] Limetrees Farm (formerly the Line Tree)[7] became part of the Madresfield estate in 1811[8] and was the largest farmstead on the lane in the mid 19th century.[9] Two pairs of council houses were built at the north end of the hamlet in the mid 1930s[10] and a few private bungalows have been built elsewhere on the lane. Half way along the lane's west side a cottage formerly attached to a smithy[11] was rebuilt in 2002.

Ketford   The hills of the east end of the parish overlooking the river crossing at Ketford are more sparsely populated than the rest of Dymock.[12] Walter of Ketford, a tenant of Dymock manor in the early 13th century,[13] had property in Little Ketford[14] and Robert Ketford had a house in the parish in 1373.[15] In the 18th century the two principal farms, centred on Great Ketford and Hill Place, were taken into the Yate family's estate and merged.[16] Great Ketford (later Ketford Farm),[17] which has survived, is set back from the Leadon below the crossing and has belonged to the Madresfield estate since 1810.[18] Upstream of the crossing a mill house was taken into the Madresfield estate in 1866[19] and was rebuilt before 1882.[20]

Of the few dwellings in the side valley to the northeast, only Berrow's Farm, which was taken into the Madresfield estate in 1869,[21] remained in the late 19th century and it was abandoned in the 20th century.[22] A cottage further north, in a place known both as Winter's Land and Little Ketford,[23] was demolished in the mid 19th century.[24] The farmstead at Cut Mill, at the bottom of the valley near the Leadon, was the site of a medieval mill.[25]

Lintridge   In the far north-east of the parish Lintridge Farm was formerly known as Little Lintridge.[26] Originally a copyhold of Dymock manor, it was the sole farmstead there from 1858 and belonged to the Madresfield estate from 1868.[27] Some way to the west is a pair of 20th-century farm cottages. A little to the south-east stands the surviving part of the house of Great Lintridge,[28] occupied after 1858 as cottages.[29]

Bromesberrow Heath   Much of the nearby village of Bromesberrow Heath stands on the former common of Bromesberrow heath. At least one homestead stood on or by the heath in the early 16th century[30] and piecemeal encroachment on it increased in the 18th century.[31] In the mid 19th century some 40 small cottages were scattered randomly on the common.[32] Most were south of the turnpike road running east–west across the heath but in the west, where the

---

1   *Cal. Inq. Misc.* I, 151.
2   DoE List, Dymock (1987), 5/100, 99; see below (bldgs.: outlying farms).
3   TNA, RG 13/2422; see GA, P 125A/SD 2/2 (no 998); MI 1/1, p. 40.
4   K. Clark, *The Muse Colony* (1992), 22, 114–15; Gethyn-Jones, *Dymock Down the Ages*, 116.
5   GA, P 125/VE 3/1; Dymock ct. book 1704–84, f. 17; see GA, P 125A/SD 2/1–2 (no 996).
6   MCA, J 2viii, bdl. 111C, nos 20, 24; OS Map 1:2,500, Glos. X.14 (1884, 1902 edns).
7   GA, P 125A/VE 3/2; Q/REl 1, Botloe hundred.
8   Worcs. RO, 705:99 (BA 3375), Dymock deeds 1802–13.
9   GA, P 125A/SD 2/1–2 (no 923); OS Map 1:2,500, Glos. X.14 (1884 edn).
10   GA, DA 30/100/14, pp. 52, 98, 204.
11   OS Map 6", Glos. X.SW (1883 edn).
12   For settlement at Ketford south of the Leadon, see below, Pauntley, settlement.
13   *Rot. Litt. Claus.* I, 504.
14   GA, D 214/T 16.
15   TNA, C 143/381, no 10.
16   Bigland, *Glos.* I, 527; GA, D 1142/4.
17   GA, P 125A/SD 2/1–2 (no 1031).
18   Worcs. RO, 705:99 (BA 3375), Dymock deeds 1633–1811; information from Madresfield estate office (2002).
19   Below, econ. hist. (mills).
20   MCA, H 5ii, bdl. 50, no 25; OS Map 6", Glos. X.SW (1883 edn); see GA, P 125A/SD 2/1–2 (no 1036).
21   GA, D 2079/III/20; MCA, I 2iii, nos 1, 6.
22   OS Map 6", Glos. X.SE (1883 edn); Archaeology Data Service (http://ads.ahds.ac.uk/catalogue: accessed 3 May 2005).
23   Worcs. RO, 705:99 (BA 3375), Dymock deeds 1633–1811.
24   GA, P 125A/SD 2/1–2 (no 976); OS Map 6", Glos. X.SE (1883 edn).
25   Below, econ. hist. (mills).
26   OS Map 6", Glos. X.SE (1883 edn).
27   Below, manors (other estates: Lintridge).
28   OS Map 6", Glos. X.SE (1883 edn).
29   TNA, RG 9/1761; RG 10/2609; see below, manors (other estates: Lintridge).
30   TNA, E 101/59/10, rot. 1.
31   Dymock ct. book 1704–84, ff. 17, 27v., 55, 76v., 84v.–85.
32   TNA, HO 107/350/6; HO 107/1960.

common extended northwards into Bromesberrow, building had spilled over the parish boundary.[1] Although the common was inclosed in the late 1850s, few new houses were built until the early decades of the 20th century[2] and there were 50 or so dwellings in 1965.[3] More houses and bungalows were built in the 1970s, most south of the road,[4] and new building continued in 2002. A small business park has been created to the south-west between the village and the farmstead of Heath Farm.

Several farmsteads stood by the road leading west from the heath. At Great Heath, part of William Gordon's Haffield estate in the 1820s,[5] a pair of cottages was built west of the farmstead in 1861 and the farmhouse was later demolished.[6] In 1862 the estate's owner, W.C. Henry, built a school church nearer the heath opposite the drive to Haffield, in Ledbury (Herefs.).[7] After the school's closure in 1951 it was used as a piggery before being restored as a house in the 1980s.[8]

Broom's Green Higher up to the west, Broom's Green is a hamlet strung out along both sides of the road over a former green. Most of its houses and cottages, which numbered just over a score in the mid 19th century,[9] date from the 18th or 19th century but at its east end Laurel Farm stands on the site west of the Ryton lane of a house known as Hunts in 1411[10] and White's Farm, further east, has a 17th- or 18th-century timber-framed barn.[11] Towards the west end a timber-framed house probably of the late 17th century is set back north of the road on the edge of the former green.[12]

Greenway Further west on the road Greenway is a cluster of dwellings around the crossroads on the Dymock–Ledbury road. On the west side the Old Nail Shop, built in the 16th or 17th century,[13] was occupied by a nailer in the early 19th.[14] On the east side Stone House (formerly Longtown Hall) has an early 19th-century front and was two dwellings in the mid 19th century.[15]

Leadington
Pound Farm, standing between the river Leadon and the Preston brook north of Dymock village, was the principal house on the estate of a branch of the Cam family in the late 16th century.[16] Further north Greenway House, standing north of the road that runs westwards from the river, was formerly known as the Green House and was part of a farmstead long owned by the Hankins family from 1411.[17] The house at Drew's Farm, immediately to the south across the road, was enlarged in the early 20th century.[18] Bellamy's Farm, slightly lower down to the north-east, was presumably the centre of George Bellamy's estate in the late 14th century.[19] Its house, which had a new wing in 1739 and was later rebuilt,[20] stands inside a moat with an earlier barn among farm buildings outside.[21] Leadington Farm (also called Leadington Place), owned by the Hodges family in the 18th century, was a farmstead a little to the north-west.[22]

Tiller's Green To the south the hamlet of Tiller's Green is scattered randomly over a green beside the Much Marcle road. There was a homestead there in the mid 17th century[23] and squatter cottages were among a dozen dwellings on the green in the mid 19th century.[24] A small house was built further south on the road soon afterwards.[25] Several cottages in the hamlet have been enlarged and a bungalow was among a few new dwellings built there in the later 20th century.

At Windcross, where the Much Marcle road crosses the road to Leominster, a 17th-century cottage with a thatch roof stands north-west of the crossroads.[26] A later timber-framed farmhouse to the south-east below the main road was enlarged in 1962.[27] Further west on the Much Marcle road Hill Grove was built in the place of a farmstead known

---

1 GA, P 125A/SD 2/1; Q/RI 31, 59.
2 OS Map 1:2,500, Glos. X.11 (1884–1923 edns).
3 GA, DA 30/100/34, p. 117.
4 *Bromesberrow 1999-2000: Bromesberrow Parish Appraisal* (copy in VCH Glos. office), 4.
5 GA, Q/REl 1, Botloe hundred; P 125A/MI 1/1, p. 19; SD 2/1–2 (no 836); for Gordon at Haffield, see C.J. Robinson, *A History of the Mansions and Manors of Herefordshire* (1873), 168; *Pigot's Nat. Commercial Dir.* (1835), 98.
6 Date on cottages; Verey and Brooks, *Glos.* II, 209; see OS Map 6", Glos. X.SW (1883 edn).
7 TNA, ED 7/34/117.
8 Local information.
9 GA, P 125A/SD 2/1; TNA, HO 107/1960.
10 Herefs. RO, AA 26/II/82; GA, P 125A/SD 2/1.
11 DoE List, Dymock, 5/66.
12 Ibid. 5/65.
13 Below (bldgs.).
14 GA, D 4243/1, deed 30 Jan. 1833.

15 Ibid. P 125A/SD 2/1–2 (no 672); TNA, HO 107/1960; DoE List, Dymock, 5/71.
16 Below, manors (other estates).
17 Herefs. RO, AA 26/II/82; see R. Lowe, 'Field Meeting to Dymock', *Herefordshire Archaeological News* 70 (Woolhope Club Archaeological Research Section 1999), 23–6.
18 GA, D 2299/1804.
19 *Inq. p.m. Glos.* 1359–1413, 188.
20 Dymock ct. book 1704–84, f. 45; GA, D 185/IV/16.
21 Lowe, 'Field Meeting to Dymock', 21–2; information from Mr Wilesmith of Bellamy's Farm.
22 GA, P 125A/VE 3/2; D 2099, Dymock deeds 1704–1851; GDR wills 1790/30.
23 GA, P 125/ VE 3/1.
24 Ibid. P 125A/SD 2/1; TNA, HO 107/1960; see Dymock ct. book 1704–84, f. 9 and v.
25 OS Map 6", Glos. X.SW (1883 edn).
26 DoE List, Dymock, 4/90.
27 GA, D 3295/I/6.

alternatively as Lady Grove and the Bush[1] for James John Wynniatt in the 1860s.[2] In the later 20th century six houses and bungalows were built next to it.

The Leadington The north end of the parish beyond Greenway House rises on the west side of the river Leadon, besides which Roman remains have been identified,[3] and contains many medieval homesteads. In 1539 Thomas Wynniatt lived at Upham and his younger namesake at Judgements immediately to the west.[4] Upham House, to the east, is a villa built in the 1830s by the owner of Upham farm[5] and let from the early 1860s as a private house.[6] Near by is a cluster of three early farmsteads east of the Ledbury lane. Haytraps, a copyhold of Dymock manor owned by the Gamond family in the mid 16th century,[7] was inhabited in 1287, Swords bears a name used locally as a surname at that time,[8] and Mirabels was presumably the centre of Richard Amyrable's estate in the late 14th century.[9] In the mid 19th century there were four small cottages to the south at Tillputsend, two on opposite sides of the Ledbury lane and an 18th-century pair on the lane to Hallwood green.[10] Two new cottages were built there later, the first by Thomas Gambier Parry after 1863,[11] and one was pulled down before 1963.[12] Two of the remaining dwellings were enlarged in the early 21st century.

Further north the farmhouse at Henberrows was rebuilt in the 19th century. Little Iddens, west of the Ledbury lane, is a small 17th-century farmhouse and the house at Glyniddens, to its north, was built in 1830.[13] Some of the scattered cottages or small farmhouses in the Oldfields area to the west and in the fields to the east[14] have been demolished and others have been modernized and enlarged.[15] A cottage on the east side at the site of a homestead called Hazards in the mid 17th century[16] had been abandoned by 1920.[17] A pair of cottages built on the lane by Gambier Parry[18] has been converted as a single dwelling.

Among the farmsteads that stood lower down towards the Ludstock and Preston brooks Lower House and several others that were all owned by the Hooper family in the late 17th and 18th century[19] have been abandoned almost without trace. To the south the homestead at New House, near the Preston brook on the lane to Hallwood green, was established following a small inclosure of open-field land not long before 1739.[20] Further south the farmstead at Rosehill, on the east bank of the Preston brook, was in the part of the Old Grange estate tenanted by the Wynniatt family in the late 16th century.[21]

Netherton There were at least two households at Netherton, in the open land west of the Preston brook, in the early 14th century.[22] The farmstead at Great Netherton, presumably the site of John Wills's house in the mid 16th century,[23] was the centre of an estate created by Robert Holmes in the mid 17th century.[24] Little Netherton, to the north-west, has also been known as Lower Netherton.[25] The farmstead there, perhaps that occupied by John Wynniatt in the early 16th century,[26] served an estate acquired by the Fawke family in the late 18th century.[27] In the 1860s a villa was built on the Leominster road to the north and in the following decade a farmhouse (Cropthorne Farm) was built near by, next to the lane from the Leadington to Hallwood green.[28] A pair of council houses was built near the farmhouse in 1934[29] and a bungalow was erected next to them in the 1950s.[30]

Hallwood Green Hallwood Green is a small hamlet that grew up in the north-west corner of Dymock next to Much Marcle on waste land known

---

1   Ibid. D 2099, Dymock deeds 1704–1851; OS Map 6", Glos. X.SW (1883 edn).
2   MCA, I 6i, bdl. 93, nos 31–2; see TNA, RG 2/1761; RG 10/2608.
3   G.H. Jack, 'Some Notes on Roman Herefordshire', *Trans. Woolhope Naturalists' Field Club* (1908–11), 69; 'Roman Road between Monmouth and Gloucester', ibid. 108.
4   TNA, E 101/59/10, rot. 1; GA, P 125A/SD 2/1–2 (nos 228, 140).
5   GA, D 5646/17.
6   TNA, RG 9/1761; RG 10/2608; GA, G/NE 160/3/1, f. 56.
7   GDR wills 1545/268; GA, D 1142/4.
8   TNA, JUST 1/278, rot. 58.
9   *Inq. p.m. Glos.* 1359–1413, 188.
10 GA, P 125A/SD 2/1–2 (nos 133–6).
11 E. Gambier Parry, 'Highnam Memoranda' (1902), f. 255: a copy of MS is in GA, D 2586; see OS Map 6", Glos. X.SW (1883 edn); GA, D 2299/1907.
12 See GA, DA 30/100/32, p. 74.
13 Below (bldgs.: outlying farms).
14 GA, P 125A/SD 2/1.

15 Theodora C. Reeves, 'History of Little Marcle and of Preston Parish' (1972: typescript in Glos. Colln. 36709), 2; information from Mabel McCulloch of Hallwood Green.
16 GA, P 125/VE 3/1; P 125A/SD 2/1–2 (no 172).
17 Ibid. D 2426/E 11/3.
18 E. Gambier Parry, 'Highnam Memoranda', ff. 254–5; GA, D 2426/E 11/3.
19 GA, D 2099, Dymock deed 1692; Dymock deeds 1730–40; Dymock deeds 1758–1859; P 125A/SD 2/1–2 (no 67).
20 Ibid. D 2099, Dymock deeds 1723–1820.
21 Ibid. D 214/T 17.
22 *Glos. Subsidy Roll, 1327*, 5.
23 GDR wills 1550/57; 1551/152; see MCA, I 3v, bdl. 74, no 2.
24 Below, manors (other estates).
25 GA, D 4317/6, rental 1692; 12, copy of 1703 terrier; P 125A/VE 3/2.
26 MCA, I 6i, bdl. 93A, no 2; *Military Surv. of Glos. 1522*, 55.
27 GA, Q/REl 1, Botloe hundred.
28 TNA, RG 10/2608; OS Map 6", Glos. IX.SE (1883 edn).
29 GA, DA 30/100/14, p. 52.
30 Ibid. 100/19, p. 218.

sometimes as Hollister's or Hollis's green.[1] There was settlement there in the 1670s, when the place was known as Hollowshuttes green,[2] and more building took place in the 18th century as squatters encroached on the green, six encroachments being reported in 1765.[3] The hamlet was bypassed by a new road into Herefordshire in the 1830s and it contained a score of dwellings[4] when, in 1848, parts of the green were inclosed.[5] It remained a backwater mostly of thatched cottages in the early 1940s.[6] In 1948 three pairs of council houses were built on the lane to the east[7] and in the later 20th century private bungalows and houses were erected by the green and some older houses were rebuilt.

BUILDINGS

Amongst the farmsteads and cottages which stand along Dymock village street and throughout the parish, building patterns and methods are consistent. Timber framing, often with brick infill in the 17th century, gave way to brick with stone slate or tile for roofing in the 18th. A long phase of rebuilding in the 17th century was followed by another phase between the mid 18th and mid 19th century, when distinctive two-storeyed, three-bayed farmhouses, usually with casement windows under segmental heads, were built and farmhouses were improved by adding extra storeys and service wings, remodelling façades, and building cider houses and other farm buildings. The ebb and flow of building activity is evident particularly among the main houses on Dymock's manors and larger farms.[8] Several dwellings have evolved into small country houses.

Dymock Village

The village street is lined with buildings from end to end but before the 19th century farmhouses and cottages were scattered along it. None of the farmhouses are now used for that purpose, although the White House, opposite the church, retains some farm buildings.

At the western end the Old Cottage and Wood's Cottage are late medieval cruck-framed houses, the former originally with two rooms.[9] The box-framed Laburnum Cottage is of similar size and was built probably in the 16th century.[10] No other early houses survive in the street but some of the fabric of the White House, which in the late 17th century with 9 hearths was the largest establishment in the village,[11] was incorporated in plain rebuilding of the house in the mid 18th century. In the early 19th century its front wall was raised to allow a storey of windows to light the attic, accommodating a cheese store, a new western wing containing a brewhouse and dairy was added, and a timber-framed outbuilding was rebuilt as stables and a cider house.[12] A barn burnt down in 1890.[13]

The work at the White House was part of a transformation of the village in the 18th century and the early 19th. Red brick was used both for new work and for remodelling existing property. Building work at the vicarage house (since demolished) included in 1806 a cider house with a granary over it.[14] Among the more ambitious designs was that by Richard Jones of Ledbury for Ann Cam's school, built in 1825. It combined Gothic and classical elements in a façade that screened the teachers' house and flanking schoolrooms.[15] High House, the largest and most prominently sited new house, was owned until 1771 by Revd James Brooke of Pirton (Worcs.).[16] Plain and urban in style with polychrome brickwork seen most clearly on its eastern end, it had five bays, three storeys, and a basement: in the early 19th century the windows on the façade were lengthened and reglazed. The house at Great Wadley was created in chequer brick soon after 1806 in a development that included rebuilding an adjacent structure as the George inn; the datestone on Great Wadley records its purchase in 1884 by the 6th Earl Beauchamp.[17] Several other buildings had rubbed brick dressings and classical doorcases.

New building in the mid 19th century is represented by Stoneberrow Place, a terrace of three composed c.1840 to look like a single house.[18] An early 18th-century cottage was refronted to make Stoneberrow House.[19] A more substantial change took place at High House, which in becoming the vicarage house in 1878[20] was doubled in size to the north, the original staircase being incorporated in the new work, and in 1884 Ann Cam's school was extensively remodelled to plans by Waller, Son, & Wood of Gloucester.[21] The only substantial brand-

---

1 GA, D 4317/6, ct. papers (The Moors); P 125/CH 1/3; P 125A/SD 2/1.
2 *Reg. of Dymock*, 151.
3 Dymock ct. book 1704–84, ff. 27v., 35, 38, 52v., 84v.–85.
4 TNA, HO 107/350/7; HO 107/1960.
5 GA, D 4317/12, 19th-cent. copy of 1703 terrier.
6 J. Douglas, *From Summer Lane* (Birmingham, 1979), 57–62, relates the reminiscences of a war-time evacuee at Hallwood Green.
7 GA, DA 30/100/17, pp. 57, 173.
8 See below, manors.
9 DoE List, Dymock, 4/120–1; GA, D 3828/2; Fig. 31.
10 DoE List, Dymock, 5/122.
11 Below, social hist. (social structure).
12 DoE List, Dymock, additional bldgs. 4–5/134–5.
13 Gethyn-Jones, *Dymock Down the Ages*, 118.
14 GDR, V 5/116T 4.
15 GA, P 125/SC 5; D 2593/2/454. See below, Fig. 38.
16 MCA, I 5iv, bdl. 89, no 2.
17 Ibid. J 2vii, bdl. 111D, nos 25–8; bdl. 111E, no 43.
18 GA, P 125A/MI 1/1–2 (no 1550).
19 Ibid. (no 1552).
20 Ibid. D 1381/54.
21 Ibid. D 2593/2/454; P 125/SC 18; SC 35.

32. *Greenway House: the south front*

new building late in the century was the police station of 1898 built on the Kempley lane to look like a suburban villa.[1] During the 20th century building activity was mainly restricted to small houses and bungalows in gaps in the street frontage. Among those designed by Jean Elrington for Newent Rural District Council in the 1960s was an estate of 18 houses and 3 bungalows.[2] The Rectory, built as the parsonage in 1953, is in a neo-Georgian style.[3]

Outlying Farms and Cottages

Although many of the farms scattered throughout the parish are on medieval sites, almost none has medieval fabric. At Little Netherton the core of the house, which contained a truncated cruck and perhaps dated from the 15th century or early 16th,[4] was rebuilt in the 1980s.[5] A two-bayed medieval hall was part of the house at Berrow's Farm that fell into ruin in the 20th century.[6] A small farmhouse at Ryton (no 331) has a cruck truss.

Some cottages or small farmhouses, such as the Old Nail Shop at Greenway and no 333 at Ryton, were built in the late 16th or 17th century with 1½ storeys.[7] One at Castle Tump had an original plan with two rooms and staircase against the central partition in 1989.[8] During the 17th century much rebuilding with square panelled timber framing was undertaken. At Little Netherton the house was extended by one bay and timber-framed outbuildings were built. Some of the farmhouses of that time, for example Little Iddens and Allum's, seem to have been plain rectangular houses of two or three units and two storeys. Among others with more elaborate plans, New Rock, Swords, and Upham were each built on an **L**. At Swords a large cruciform chimneystack is at the rear of the hall range, whereas at Upham the hall range is heated from one end and a dog-leg staircase rises in a tower in the angle with the cross wing, which retains wattle and daub infill. A **T** plan was used for the tall house at Great Woodend[9] and for the house at Lintridge Farm.[10] The farmhouse at Ockington, probably one of the largest mid 17th-century houses not associated with one of the manors or principal estates, was built as a substantial gentleman's residence of two storeys and **H** plan with asymmetrical cross wings and a massive chimneystack at the rear of the hall range. In the late 17th or early 18th century some of it was reclad in brick and a cider house with granary over was built.

Greenway House may have been built in the later 16th century with an **L** or **H** plan, of which a two-storeyed hall range and southern cross wing survive. The room above the hall was originally open to the roof which has some windbraces and was heated by one of the four diamond-set brick chimneys on the stack at the rear of the hall range. In the later 17th

---

1 Inscr. on bldg.; GA, D 3295/I/ 6.
2 GA, DA 30/100/32, p. 267; 100/33, p. 70; 100/34, pp. 79, 282.
3 Verey and Brooks, *Glos.* II, 346.
4 DoE List, Dymock, 4/93.
5 Information from Linda Horniblow of Little Netherton.
6 Archaeology Data Service.
7 DoE List, Dymock, 5/70, 100.
8 Images of England (http://imagesofengland.org.uk: accessed 23 Apr. 2008).
9 DoE List, Dymock, 4/94.
10 Below, manors (other estates: Lintridge).

33. Hillash: the east front in 1975

century or the early 18th the wing was widened, reroofed and faced in brick, the hall range was refaced and partly reroofed, and a detached two-storeyed cider house with brick cellar was built. In 1776 the building of a northern wing, perhaps in place of a service end, made the house a smart home for its owner Thomas Hankins.[1] Venetian and Diocletian windows in the wing's front elevation lit a reception room and bedrooms above,[2] and the rest of the wing was filled with a fashionable staircase. In the 19th century the house was enlarged by the addition of a dairy and a later stone extension at right angles to the southern wing. The western end of that wing appears to have been added as a kitchen slightly later and a bell turret was added to the gable, either when the house accommodated a school[3] or afterwards.

The high quality 18th-century building work at Greenway House included stone dressings, unusual for a farmhouse in an area where dressings were then usually of brick, as for example at the three-storeyed New House, which has segment-headed windows, paired on the ground floor, and band courses. The three-bayed houses at Hill Farm and Ketford Farm, the latter with its original rear outshut, seem to be the result of mid 18th-century rebuilding. At Hill Farm, where in 1648 the house had a chamber over a buttery and a closet called the study over a porch,[4] a detached timber-framed cider house and barn, the former of two storeys, were built not long before the house was rebuilt.[5] At Hillash, which was rebuilt as a superior farmhouse in the 18th century with four bays, 2½ storeys, and an elaborate well staircase, the façade was rendered and given a Doric portico in the early 19th century.[6] Low service ranges were added then[7] and new building after 1852, when it became the country house of Thomas Holbrook, included an entrance lodge.[8] The house at Pitt House Farm, made by knocking two dwellings into one by 1736, was known for a time as Edulus Place[9] and in 1795 its rooms included a hall and several parlours and its farm buildings a dairy house with an upper cheese room, cider houses, two barns, and cow sheds.[10]

Several houses were completely rebuilt in the first half of the 19th century. At Haytraps, which in 1622 had a hall range with parlour next to it and a cross wing with three rooms and attics,[11] the 18th-century pattern of a three-bayed front with segmental headed windows was developed. Mirabels followed the same model but has a second, later pile of rooms and large outbuildings. The new house at Crowfield Farm

---

1 Datestone above entrance to cellar. For Thomas Hankins, GA, Q/REl 1, Botloe hundred 1776. See J.W. Tonkin, 'Buildings, 1998', *Trans. Woolhope Naturalists' Field Club* 49.2 (1998), 313–15; Verey and Brooks, *Glos.* II, 347.
2 Above, Fig. 32.
3 Below, social hist. (education: after 1826).
4 TNA, C 115/43, no 2575.
5 DoE List, Dymock, 5/82.
6 Fig. 33.
7 The cellar has a datestone of 1833.
8 GA, D 2079/II 2/T 4; G/NE 160/3/1, f. 66; see TNA, RG 9/1761.
9 GA, D 1272, Dymock deeds 1736–1901.
10 *Glouc. J.* 20 Apr. 1795.
11 GA, D 1142/4.

incorporated early fabric.[1] Glyniddens, built in 1830 for Joseph Davies[2] in late Georgian style with sash windows, the larger Upham House, built slightly later for William Chichester[3] with a symmetrical three-bayed front and porch, and Heath Farm, which has a symmetrical five-bayed rendered front and Ionic porch, imitated fashionable villas.

Many small improvements to houses and farm buildings were carried out in the early 19th century. At Allum's, where rebuilding had begun in the 18th century, the house's easternmost room was replaced by a brick range set at right angles to form an L plan with a three-bayed entrance façade facing east, a central staircase, and a rear outshut. An additional wing with outside stairs to a probable cheese room had a cider house and cellar at one end where the ground drops to a farmyard cut out of the slope. A timber-framed barn stands at the upper level and there are animal sheds around the yard. At Little Netherton the house's T plan includes a two-bayed brick-faced block with hipped roof built in 1843 above a stone basement.[4] Later barns, one large and one small, are dated 1860 and 1861 respectively. Improvements were also carried out at New Rock, where a cider house was added to the rear of the cross wing. Among new buildings provided in the 1860s and 1870s for farms on the Madresfield estate[5] was an outbuilding at Limetrees Farm in 1877.[6]

Among the more radical changes in the 20th century, the upper storey and the interior of the house at Ockington were reconstructed and a number of its barns and other outbuildings were removed in the mid and late 1980s.[7] At Hillash the house was extended as a nursing home in the late 1980s and outbuildings were converted as residential accommodation.[8]

MANORS AND ESTATES

In the late Anglo-Saxon period Dymock was a major royal estate in which there was a possible intrusion shortly after the Norman Conquest. In the 12th century parts of the manor were granted to Flaxley abbey and William de Gamages to create two new manors, known later as Old Grange (or Dymock) and Little Dymock (or Gamage Hall). The manor of Dymock, occasionally called Great Dymock,[9] finally passed from royal hands in the later 13th century. The history of the manor of Rye, mistakenly regarded as part of Dymock,[10] has been given under Tirley, in an earlier volume.[11]

In the 14th century Dymock contained numerous farms including freehold and copyhold land held under the manors of Dymock and Little Dymock.[12] Many belonged in the 16th century to yeoman families that retained them for generations.[13] In the early 17th century the largest estate, based on the Old Grange, passed together with Little Dymock to the Wynniatt family. An estate amassed by a branch of the Cam family was broken up after 1790, part going to the Thackwells, and in the mid 19th century the Wynniatts (1,036 a.) and the Thackwells (657 a. and 417 a.) remained the principal landowners. At that time the rest of the parish was divided between well over forty estates or farms and the Lygons (the Earls Beauchamp) of Madresfield, who first purchased land in Dymock in the early 19th century, were one of four other families with 300 a. or more. The other estates were 13 holdings of between 100 and 200 a., 9 of between 50 and 100 a., 12 of between 20 and 50 a., and numerous smaller holdings.[14] The larger estates were broken up by sales in the early and mid 20th century.[15]

DYMOCK (GREAT DYMOCK) MANOR

Four years after the Norman Conquest the estate at Dymock that had belonged to Edward the Confessor, and was assessed at 20 hides, passed to William FitzOsbern, earl of Hereford. William, who possibly acquired the estate without royal consent for the Domesday jurors were ignorant of his title, died in 1071 and was succeeded at Dymock and in the earldom by his son Roger of Breteuil. Roger forfeited his estates by his rebellion against the king in 1075 and the manor remained in royal hands[16] probably until it was acquired by Miles of Gloucester. Miles, who was created earl of Hereford in 1141, died in 1143 and the manor and the earldom passed to his son Roger,[17] who gave part of Dymock to his foundation

---

1 Ibid. D 3295/I/6.
2 DoE List, Dymock, 4/78, mentions a datestone with Davis's inits. For Davis, GA, P 125A/MI 1/1, p. 12; SD 2/1–2 (no 58).
3 GA, D 5646/17.
4 Datestone with inits. 'JF' (for Joseph Fawke) and 'JHB'. For Fawke, GA, D 892/T 35/24; P 125A/SD 2/1–2 (no 467).
5 See below, manors (other estates: Callow Farm).
6 Datestone with init. 'B' for Earl Beauchamp.
7 Information from Mrs J. Lewis.
8 Information from Mr T. Huckerby, owner of the nursing home.

9 *Inq. p.m. Glos. 1625–42*, I, 155.
10 Rudder, *Glos.* 411.
11 *VCH Glos.* VIII, 98.
12 *Inq. p.m. Glos. 1301–58*, 253, 366–7; *1359–1413*, 148.
13 Below, social hist. (social structure).
14 GA, P 125A/SD 2/2.
15 See *Heref. J.* 20 Sept. 1924.
16 *Domesday Book* (Rec. Com.), I, 164. For the earls of Heref., *Complete Peerage*, VI, 447–57.
17 *Rot. Chart.* 53.

of Flaxley abbey.[1] The manor was among former royal demesne estates that Henry II confirmed to Earl Roger in 1154 or 1155[2] and granted to Roger's brother Walter of Hereford following the earl's rebellion and death in 1155.[3] On Walter's death c.1160 the manor reverted to the Crown[4] and in 1200 it was among the estates in which Henry de Bohun, heir to the earls of Hereford, quitclaimed all his rights on becoming earl.[5] Richard I had granted another part of Dymock to William de Gamages.[6]

The manor, which Walter de Clifford the younger held by grant from King John in 1216,[7] was taken in hand for the Crown in 1221 or 1222[8] and was granted in 1226 to the leading inhabitants (*probi homines*) at a fee farm.[9] They farmed the manor until 1244 or 1245, when it was granted to Morgan of Caerleon,[10] and Ela Longespée, countess of Warwick, held it under royal grant from 1249.[11] Ela, who in 1251 was awarded free warren on her demesnes,[12] married Philip Basset and with him granted the manor in 1257 to Flaxley abbey for her lifetime, the abbey paying an annuity of £50 to her and a stipend to her chaplain serving in the parish church.[13] Philip, who was justiciar from 1261 to 1263, died in 1271[14] and Ela had surrendered the manor to Edward I by 1287, when he granted her a £50 annuity in return[15] and gave the manor in exchange for two Sussex manors to William de Grandison, his wife Sibyl, and her heirs.[16] William was dead by 1335 and his son and heir Peter de Grandison[17] held Dymock manor at his death in 1358. Peter was succeeded by his brother John, bishop of Exeter,[18] and John (d. 1369) by his nephew Thomas de Grandison.[19]

At Thomas's death in 1375 the manor was divided between his aunts' descendants with a third going to William de Montagu, earl of Salisbury, another third to John Northwood, and the other third to Roger Beauchamp, Thomas Fauconberge, Alice wife of Thomas Wake, and Catherine widow of Robert Todenham.[20] Thomas Fauconberge's share, forfeited by his support of the king's enemies in France, was the subject of grants from 1377 until Thomas secured possession in 1406.[21] Roger Beauchamp's share passed at his death in 1380 to his son or grandson Roger Beauchamp.[22] Roger Northwood, who succeeded his father John (d. 1379),[23] and John Todenham, who succeeded his mother Catherine (d. 1383),[24] sold their shares to Richard Ruyhale and his wife Elizabeth by 1394.[25] William de Montagu sold his share by 1395 to his nephew Richard de Montagu[26] (d. 1429), who granted it in 1407 to Richard Ruyhale in return for an annuity.[27]

Richard Ruyhale died in 1408 holding two thirds of his estate, called the manor of Dymock, jointly with his wife Elizabeth and leaving an infant son Richard as his heir.[28] The younger Richard died a minor in 1415,[29] and in 1421 Elizabeth and her then husband Richard Oldcastle obtained a grant of the manor from Edmund Ruyhale, the younger Richard Ruyhale's uncle and heir.[30] Richard Oldcastle died childless in 1422[31] and on Elizabeth's death in 1428 the manor reverted to Edmund Ruyhale's trustees and passed to John Merbury,[32] a chief justice in south Wales,[33] who in 1432 acquired the interest in the manor that had descended from Alice Wake to Thomas Wake of Blisworth (Northants.).[34]

John Merbury died in 1438. His daughter and heir Elizabeth, wife of (Sir) Walter Devereux,[35] survived in 1453[36] and Walter died in 1459, having settled the manor on Anne, the wife of his son Walter, later Lord Ferrers. Following Anne's death in 1469 Walter held the manor by courtesy and after his death at the battle of Bosworth in 1485 his widow Jane (or Joan) took possession of it. She married in turn Thomas Vaughan (*fl.* 1492), Sir Edmund Blount (d. 1499), and Thomas Poyntz[37] of Alderley, who held the manor in

---

1 Below (Old Grange manor).
2 *Rot. Chart.* 53; D. Walker, '"Honours" of the Earls of Hereford', *Trans. BGAS* 79 (1960), 180.
3 *Pipe R* 1156–8 (Rec. Com.), 49.
4 Ibid. 1160 (PRS 2), 28.
5 *Rot. Chart.* 53, 61.
6 Below (Little Dymock manor).
7 *Rot. Litt. Claus.* I, 282.
8 Ibid. 334, 504; *Pipe R* 1220 (PRS N.S. 47), 74; 1221 (PRS N.S. 48), 233.
9 *Pat.* 1225–32, 61.
10 *Cal. Pat.* 1232–47, 2; *Abbrev. Rot. Orig.* I, 7–8.
11 *Close* 1247–51, 141; *Cal. Pat.* 1247–58, 42, 529.
12 *Cal. Chart.* 1226–57, 369.
13 *Glos. Feet of Fines* 1199–1299, p. 121.
14 *Handbook of Brit. Chronology* (1961), 71; *Complete Peerage*, XII (2), 365.
15 *Cal. Pat.* 1281–92, 269.
16 Ibid. 1334–8, 105.
17 *Cal. Inq. p.m.* VII, 460–1.
18 Ibid. X, 347–8.
19 Ibid. XII, 340–1.
20 Ibid. XIV, 136–40; see ibid. XVII, 194–5.
21 *Cal. Fine* 1377–83, 2; 1399–1405, 118; *Cal. Pat.* 1388–92, 303; 1391–6, 660; 1405–8, 139–40.
22 *Cal. Inq. p.m.* XV, 374–6.
23 Ibid. 49.
24 Ibid. XVI, 22.
25 *Cal. Pat.* 1391–6, 515–16; see TNA, CP 25/1/78/81, no 78.
26 *Cal. Fine* 1391–9, 145–6.
27 *Inq. p.m. Glos.* 1359–1413, 249; TNA, C 139/45, no 39.
28 *Inq. p.m. Glos.* 1359–1413, 249.
29 *Cal. Inq. p.m.* XX, 92.
30 *Cal. Pat.* 1416–22, 439–40; TNA, C 139/39, no 41.
31 *VCH Worcs.* III, 489; cf. TNA, C 139/148, no 12.
32 TNA, C 139/39, no 41; C 139/57, no 22; *Cal. Pat.* 1416–22, 439–40; 1429–36, 141.
33 *Complete Peerage*, V, 321–2.
34 *Cal. Close* 1429–35, 184.
35 TNA, C 139/87, no 43; for the Devereux fam., *Complete Peerage*, V, 321–9.
36 *Cal. Fine* 1452–61, 66.
37 *Cal. Inq. p.m. Hen. VII*, II, 342–3.

her right in 1522.[1] By 1537 the manor had passed to Anne and Walter Devereux's grandson Walter Devereux, Lord Ferrers.[2] Walter, who was created Viscount Hereford in 1550, died in 1558 and was succeeded by his grandson Walter Devereux, who was created Lord Bourchier in 1571 and earl of Essex in 1572. He left the manor at his death in 1576 to his widow Lettice.[3] She married in turn Robert Dudley (d. 1588), earl of Leicester, and Sir Christopher Blount (ex. 1601)[4] and retained the manor in 1604.[5]

In 1606 the manor was acquired by Giles Forster,[6] the owner of Boyce Court.[7] In 1611 Giles conveyed the manor to Sir George Huntley[8] (d. 1622). His son and heir William Huntley[9] was lord in 1631[10] but the manor court was held in the name of Giles Forster, his relative, in 1633[11] and of John Stratford in 1638.[12] In 1640 the owner was Sir John Winter of Lydney, also a relative of the Huntleys.[13] Sir John, a prominent royalist, suffered heavy financial penalties after the Civil War[14] and in 1656 he sold the manor to Evan Seys[15] of Boverton (Glam.). Evan, who was MP for Gloucester after the Restoration,[16] sold it in 1680 to Edward Pye of Much Dewchurch (Herefs.).[17] Edward, a merchant with business in Barbados, died in 1692 having settled the manor in trust for his grandnephew Edward Pye Chamberlayne. Edward, who lived for a time on Barbados,[18] took possession in 1704[19] and gave the estate to his son Edward Pye Chamberlayne in 1717.[20] The latter died in 1729 and his widow Elizabeth held the estate as guardian of their infant son Edward Pye Chamberlayne until 1740.[21] The son sold the manor and the rest of the estate in 1769 to Ann Cam of Battersea (Surrey),[22] heiress to other lands in Dymock.[23]

Ann Cam died in 1790[24] leaving the manor with part of her estate to John Moggridge of Bradford-on-Avon (Wilts.), a clothier.[25] John (d. 1803) was succeeded by his son John Hodder Moggridge[26] and he sold the manor in 1811 to Samuel Beale.[27] By 1812 Samuel had sold it to William Lygon, Lord Beauchamp of Powick (Worcs.),[28] who had already added several farms in Dymock to his estate at Madresfield in Worcestershire.[29] William, who was created Earl Beauchamp in 1815, died in 1816[30] and his successor at Madresfield owned c.550 a. in Dymock in the mid 19th century.[31] Most of that land was sold c.1919 but William Lygon, the 8th earl, retained the lordship of the manor in the mid 1960s[32] and the Madresfield estate included a farm at Ketford in 2002.

OLD GRANGE MANOR

Roger (d. 1155), earl of Hereford and lord of Dymock,[33] included the Dymock demesne and half of the Dymock wood in his endowment of Flaxley abbey. Henry II confirmed the gifts in 1158[34] and William de Gamages later granted the abbey other land in Dymock.[35] The abbey retained its estate based on a grange (later the Old Grange) on the west side of the parish until the Dissolution[36] when, in 1537, its possessions were acquired by Sir William Kingston.[37]

Sir William died in 1540 and his son and heir Sir Anthony Kingston[38] sold his Dymock property to Thomas Wenman in 1544.[39] Thomas was later knighted and his son Thomas[40] settled the estate, known as the manor of Dymock or Old Grange, on himself and his wife Jane (or Joan) in 1570. Thomas and Jane later acquired the manor of Little Dymock and after his death in 1582[41] she married in turn Thomas Fisher (d. by 1592) of Bampton (Oxon.)

---

1 *Military Surv. of Glos. 1522*, 17, 54.
2 TNA, C 142/59, no 72.
3 Ibid. WARD 7/18, nos 39–40.
4 *Complete Peerage*, V, 141.
5 GA, D 1142/4.
6 TNA, CP 25/2/297/4 Jas. I Mich. no 46.
7 Below (other estates: Boyce Ct.).
8 TNA, CP 25/2/297/8 Jas. I Hil. no 13.
9 *VCH Glos*. X, 172.
10 See *Inq. p.m. Glos. 1625–42*, I, 155.
11 Worcs. RO, 705:99 (BA 3375), Dymock deeds 1633–1811; *Visit. Glos. 1623*, 94.
12 TNA, C 115/43, no 2575.
13 GA, D 421/19/15; *Visit. Glos. 1623*, 94.
14 *Cal. Cttee for Compounding*, III, 2143.
15 P Gladwish, 'The Sale of Royalist Lands after the English Civil War: Two Case Studies from the West Midlands', *Midland History* XXIX (2004), 39; TNA, CP 25/2/554/1656 Trin. no 19.
16 *Hist. Parl. Commons 1660–90*, III, 424–6.
17 GA, D 3810.
18 TNA, PROB 11/416, ff. 337–9; Bigland, *Glos.* I, 529.
19 Worcs. RO, B705:99 (BA 3375), Dymock ct. book 1704–84, f. 3.
20 GA, D 3810.
21 Bigland, *Glos.* I, 529; Dymock ct. book 1704–84, ff. 50–2.
22 GA, D 3810.
23 Below (other estates: Wilton Place).
24 Monument in Dymock ch.
25 TNA, PROB 11/1189, ff. 204–207v.; Worcs. RO, 705:99 (BA 5540), Dymock ct. book 1784–1822.
26 Fosbrooke, *Glos.* II, 238.
27 GA, D 2592, deeds 1841–82, schedule of deeds 1842.
28 Dymock ct. book 1784–1822.
29 Below (other estates: Callow Farm).
30 For the Lygons, see *Burke's Peerage* (1963), 190; below, Kempley, manor.
31 GA, P 125A/MI 1/1, pp. 1–5; see *Kelly's Dir. Glos.* (1856 and later edns).
32 GA, SL 310; Gethyn-Jones, *Dymock Down the Ages*, 30, 59.
33 Above (Dymock manor).
34 *Flaxley Cart*. pp. 16, 18–19; see *Pipe R* 1160 (PRS 2), 28.
35 *Rot. Hund.* I, 183.
36 *Pipe R* 1221 (PRS N.S. 48), 233; *Valor Eccl.* II, 486.
37 *L&P Hen. VIII*, XII (1), p. 353.
38 W.C. Heane, 'Flaxley Grange', *Trans. BGAS* 6 (1881–2), 285; see *L&P Hen. VIII*, XVIII (1), p. 124; XIX (1), p. 379.
39 *L&P Hen. VIII*, XIX (1), p. 505.
40 TNA, C 3/195/9.
41 Ibid. C 142/202, no 179; below (Little Dymock manor).

34. *The Old Grange from the north-east in 1920, showing the medieval stonework on the east side*

and Richard Unett of Woolhope (Herefs.). She died in the early 17th century and her estate passed to her granddaughter Jane, the daughter of Richard Wenman (d. 1598) and wife of John Wynniatt.[1]

Jane Wynniatt died in 1633 and her husband in 1670. Their son Wenman Wynniatt (d. 1676)[2] was succeeded in the estate by his son Wenman, a minor.[3] He died in 1731 and after the death of his wife Penelope[4] in 1732 the Old Grange descended in the direct line to Reginald Wynniatt (d. 1762),[5] who inherited an estate on the Cotswolds at Stanton,[6] Revd Reginald Wynniatt (d. 1819), and Thomas Wynniatt (d. 1830).[7] Thomas left the Old Grange to his nephew Reginald Wynniatt, a minor.[8] At Reginald's death in 1881 it passed to his brother James John Wynniatt but his right of succession to the estate was quashed and Reginald's widow Caroline took possession.[9] She married Horace Drummond Deane and on her death in 1919[10] the estate passed to Reginald's only child Harriett, who had married Henry Mildmay Husey. Under Harriett (d. 1944)[11] much of the estate was sold[12] and the Old Grange and its grounds, which passed to her son Ernest Wynniatt Husey (d. 1958),[13] had a succession of owners after their sale in 1965.[14]

The Old Grange stands south of the Kempley brook on the site of Flaxley abbey's grange and within a park created probably in the 19th century.[15] The core of the house is a late medieval stone dwelling, the home in 1522 of the abbey's servant John Wynniatt,[16] of which a section of high-quality ashlar has been incorporated in a canted projection on the eastern side. In the 17th century when it was both owned and occupied by the Wynniatts[17] the house was rebuilt and enlarged in brick with mullioned and transomed windows, the hall being subdivided and the roof raised as shown by the timber-framed north-eastern gable and beams inside. Some fittings of that period survive but not necessarily *in situ*. A stable court was built close to the southern end of the house. Piecemeal changes to the house in the 18th and early 19th century are difficult to interpret but they included the addition of a porch on the north entrance front and a loggia on the south end, both in Greek revival style, and the washing of the house to make it all look stone-built.[18] In alterations of 1896 the northern end was rebuilt and extended

---

1 GA, photocopy 19; GA, D 214/T 17; for Ric. Wenman, TNA, C 142/254, no 84.
2 For the Wynniatt fam., pedigree in GA, photocopy 19.
3 See TNA, C 78/1453, no 5; Atkyns, *Glos.* 394.
4 MCA, F 3iii, deed 1271.
5 *Bp. Benson's Surv. of Dioc. of Glouc. 1735–50*, 6.
6 Rudder, *Glos.* 688.
7 Bigland, *Glos.* I, 527; GA, D 4262/T 17.
8 GA, D 4317/9, deed 25 Mar. 1868.
9 Ibid. deed 9 Aug. 1882; *Kelly's Dir. Glos.* (1894), 144; see Gethyn-Jones, *Dymock Down the Ages*, 73–4.
10 *Burke's Landed Gentry* (1937), I, 647.
11 Gethyn-Jones, *Dymock Down the Ages*, 73; *The Times*, 29 Mar. 1944.
12 See GA, SL 417.
13 B. Little, 'Dymock Grange', *Glos. Countryside*, Aug. 1957, 235; Gethyn-Jones, *Dymock Down the Ages*, 91.
14 GA, D 7322 (par. mag. Nov. 1965).
15 Cf. Bryant, Map of Glos. (1824); OS Map 1:2,500, Glos. X.13 (1884 edn).
16 *Military Surv. of Glos. 1522*, 54; *Valor Eccl.* II, 486.
17 Above; see below, social hist. (social structure).
18 The interior is described in Little, 'Dymock Grange', 233–5; DoE List, Dymock (1987), 4/88.

westwards to make a new entrance façade[1] and soon afterwards an east lodge was built on the Leominster road and an avenue planted along the drive between it and the house.[2] Farm buildings west of the house include a large 17th-century barn with a timber frame on a high stone plinth.

LITTLE DYMOCK MANOR

About 1197 Richard I granted part of Dymock manor to William de Gamages.[3] William's estate, which perhaps remained in his possession in the mid 1230s,[4] passed to Godfrey de Gamages (d. *c*.1253)[5] and was inherited by Godfrey's daughters Elizabeth and Euphemia, minors who married Henry of Pembridge and William of Pembridge repectively.[6] William and Euphemia held the estate or manor, assessed as ½ knight's fee, in 1285[7] and William held it by courtesy after her death. In 1317 it passed to their son William[8] and in 1342 he granted it to his son Henry and his wife Margaret.[9] The estate, based on Gamage Hall in the south-east of the parish, passed at Henry's death in 1362 to his son John, a minor,[10] and was later known as the manor of Little Dymock or Gamage Hall.[11] John (d. 1376)[12] was succeeded by his son John, who came of age in 1388.[13] The manor passed to the younger John's son Thomas and his son John[14] (d. 1505) was succeeded by his son Walter[15] and Walter (d. by 1515) by his daughter Elizabeth, who married (Sir) Roland Morton.[16] Roland survived Elizabeth and at his death in 1554 the manor passed to their son Richard Morton[17] (d. 1559), who was succeeded by his son Anthony.[18] After he sold the manor in 1571 to Thomas and Jane Wenman[19] it descended with the Old Grange,[20] John and Jane Wynniatt being lord and lady of the manor in 1631.[21] Revd Reginald Wynniatt reserved the manorial rights on selling Gamage Hall *c*.1770.[22] The house, which long had been occupied by tenants[23] and remained the manor court's meeting place,[24] is described below.[25]

OTHER ESTATES

Boyce Court

Boyce Court, formerly known as the Boyce, stands in the south of the parish near Dymock wood and in the 16th century was the principal house on an estate that previously had belonged to the du Boys (Boyce) family. In the late 12th or early 13th century Richard du Boys acquired from Flaxley abbey an assart of 4 a. between its wood and his land[26] and in the 13th century Walter du Boys held some of his land in Dymock of the fee of William Cauvey.[27] In 1299, Richard du Boys, a knight, granted two of his Dymock tenants their liberty[28] and in 1327 Edmund du Boys was assessed for tax in Dymock.[29] Walter Boyce, a freeholder in Little Dymock manor in 1385,[30] was possibly the Walter Boyce of Dymock who quitclaimed property in Bodenham (Herefs.) to Edmund Bridges and his wife Ellen in the early 15th century.[31] The Bridges family[32] also acquired land in Dymock, some through the marriage by 1457 to Maud, daughter and heiress of Thomas Henbarrow, of Thomas Bridges.[33] Their son William, who had a residence in Woodend division and was among Dymock's richest landowners,[34] died in 1523.[35] His son William lived at Boyce Court in 1530[36] and John, another son, owned the estate, sometimes called a manor, in 1558.[37] John was succeeded by his nephew Humphrey Forster in 1561.[38] In 1604 Humphrey and his wife Martha gave the estate to their son Giles in return for an annuity[39] and in 1611 Giles sold it, together with Dymock manor, to Sir George Huntley.[40] Later in 1611 Sir George sold Boyce Court

---

1 Fig. 34.
2 Kelly's Dir. Glos. (1897), 147; OS Maps 1:2,500, Glos. X.13 (1884, 1902, 1923 edns).
3 *Pipe R* 1197 (PRS N.S. 8), 121.
4 *Book of Fees*, I, 51, 439.
5 *Cal. Inq. p.m.* I, 66.
6 TNA, JUST 1/275, rot. 17d.; see *Abbrev. Rot. Orig.* I, 13.
7 *Glos. Feet of Fines 1199–1299*, p. 176; *Feudal Aids*, II, 243.
8 *Cal. Inq. p.m.* VI, 69; *Cal. Fine* 1307–19, 349.
9 *Cal. Pat.* 1340–3, 561.
10 *Cal. Inq. p.m.* XI, 317–18.
11 TNA, C 1/541/19.
12 *Cal. Inq. p.m.* XIV, 276.
13 *Cal. Close* 1385–9, 417.
14 TNA, C 1/541/19.
15 *Cal. Inq. p.m. Hen. VII*, III, 64.
16 TNA, C 1/336, no 47.
17 Ibid. C 142/102, no 75.
18 Ibid. C 142/122, no 67.
19 Ibid. CP 25/2/142/1805/13 Eliz. I Easter, no 14.
20 Above (Old Grange manor); see GA, D 185/IV/5, 10.
21 TNA, C 78/1453, no 5.
22 Rudder, *Glos.* 410.
23 *Military Surv. of Glos. 1522*, 54; GDR wills 1693/140.
24 Bigland, *Glos.* I, 527; below, local govt. (manorial govt.).
25 Below (other estates).
26 *Flaxley Cart.* pp. 158–9.
27 BL, Add. MS 18461, f. 82 and v.
28 *Cat. Ancient Deeds*, V, 300.
29 *Glos. Subsidy Roll, 1327*, 5.
30 *Cal. Inq. p.m.* XVI, 107–8.
31 *Cat. Ancient Deeds*, VI, 347.
32 For the Bridges fam., *Visit. Worcs. 1569* (Harl. Soc. 27), 25.
33 TNA, CP 25/1/293/73, no 423; C 1/118, no 44.
34 *Military Surv. of Glos. 1522*, 54.
35 T. Nash, *Hist. of Worcs.* II (1782), 107–8.
36 TNA, PROB 11/23, f. 166 and v.
37 Ibid. CP 25/2/71/589, no 44.
38 Ibid. C 142/129, no 99; PROB 11/44, ff. 286v.—287.
39 Ibid. CP 25/2/297/2 Jas. I Mich. no 30; *Reg. of Dymock*, 25.
40 TNA, CP 25/2/297/8 Jas. I Hil. no 13; above (Dymock manor).

35. Boyce Court: the south front in 1975

and its land to William Bourchier[1] (d. 1623), the lord of Barnsley manor who was succeeded by his son Walter (d. 1648).[2] Under Walter's will the manor of Boyce was sold in the early 1650s to Evan Seys,[3] later the owner of Dymock manor, with which Boyce Court passed,[4] becoming the residence of Edward Pye (d. 1692) and his successors[5] and descending after Ann Cam's death to John Hodder Moggridge.[6] John Drummond, who bought Boyce Court shortly before 1814,[7] died in 1835[8] and his son John[9] inherited an estate that covered 321 a. of Dymock[10] and passed after his death in 1875[11] to his daughter Georgiana Matilda (d. 1904) and her husband George Onslow Deane (d. 1929). Their son Horace Drummond Deane-Drummond (formerly Deane) died in 1930 and his son John Drummond Deane-Drummond[12] sold Boyce Court in 1935 to G.H. Goulding, a farmer.[13] The house belonged in 2004 to Goulding's daughter Sylvia.[14]

Although Evan Seys was assessed for tax on 13 hearths in 1672[15] the oldest surviving part of Boyce Court is a fragment of a two-storeyed brick house probably built in the early 18th century. That house, which incorporated fabric of the earlier house,[16] had an H plan with a south front of eight bays[17] and was probably double-pile.[18] In granting a lease in 1746 E.P. Chamberlayne reserved several rooms and outbuildings together with a new part of the house and a deep cellar.[19] In the early 19th century the eastern wing of the H was replaced by a larger neo-classical block and the principal 18th-century room was remodelled to match. The new block, rectangular and double-pile in plan with northerly projections, of which only the north-eastern is original, had a five-bayed stuccoed southern façade of 2½ storeys with a central porch and contained an entrance hall flanked by two large rooms. In the later 1930s it was altered slightly and all but three bays of the earlier house was demolished.[20]

The house stands close to the home farm in a park made picturesque probably when the house was enlarged in the early 19th century.[21] In the mid 18th century avenues led northward to the village and south-eastwards to the Newent road[22] and the grounds included a walled garden and a lower garden.[23] In the early 19th century wooded walks were laid out east of the house alongside the Hereford and Gloucester canal, cut through the park in the 1790s,[24] a stream was dammed to form an ornamental fishpond probably controlled to supply

1 TNA, CP 25/2/298/9 Jas. I Trin. no 6.
2 Ibid. C 142/399, no 138; VCH Glos. VII, 16.
3 TNA, PROB 11/205, ff. 111–114v.; GA, D 2592, deeds 1841–82, schedule of deeds 1842.
4 TNA, E 179/247/14, rot. 35d.; GA, D 3810; above (Dymock manor).
5 TNA, PROB 11/416, ff. 337–9; Bigland, Glos. I, 529.
6 Rudge, Hist. of Glos. II, 29.
7 GA, Q/REl 1, Botloe hundred.
8 Ibid. P 125/IN 1/15.
9 Burke's Landed Gentry (1898), I, 424.
10 GA, P 125A/MI 1/1, pp. 15–16; SD 2/2.
11 Ibid. P 125/IN 1/31.
12 Burke's Landed Gentry (1937), I, 647; see GA, D 2428/1/17, ff. 14–15.

13 Gethyn-Jones, Dymock Down the Ages, 123; Kelly's Dir. Glos. (1935), 157; (1939), 159.
14 Information from Sylvia Goulding of Boyce Court.
15 TNA, E 179/247/14, rot. 35d.
16 A ceiling dated variously 1603 or 1634 is recorded in Kelly's Dir. Glos. (1870), 540; (1931), 158.
17 Fosbrooke, Glos. II, pl. facing p. 238.
18 See Glos. Colln. 32481(11).
19 GA, D 892/T 25/20.
20 Gethyn-Jones, Dymock Down the Ages, 123; Kelly's Dir. Glos. (1935), 157; (1939), 159. See Fig. 35.
21 See Glos. Colln. 32481(11).
22 Taylor, Map of Glos (1777).
23 GA, D 892/T 25/20.
24 Above, introd. (communications: canal and railway).

36. Outbuildings at Callow Farm, showing ranges dated 1861 (right) and 1870

power to the farm buildings, and a drive was created running eastwards to a lodge on the Newent road.[1] Also in the 19th century a stable block was built and most of the farm buildings were replaced, all in brick. One timber-framed barn survives. The east lodge was rebuilt in 1865.[2]

Callow Farm

Callow farm, in the east of the parish, was perhaps represented by the land that William Callow, a chaplain, held from Dymock manor in 1394.[3] It was occupied by the Shayle family in the early 16th century[4] and Thomas Shayle (d. 1540) left it to his wife Elizabeth with reversion to his son Thomas.[5] John Shayle (d. 1685)[6] of Redmarley was succeeded by his nephew Thomas Shayle, a Gloucester mercer who sold the farm (159 a.) in 1687 to Rice Yate of Bromesberrow. Rice (d. 1690) and his son Walter (d. 1744) acquired other farms in the east of Dymock[7] and in 1810 W.H. Yate sold them all to William Lygon, Lord Beauchamp, owner of the Madresfield estate.[8] About 1919 the estate sold Callow farm (248 a.) to its tenant farmer, A.H. Chew.[9] He died in 1947[10] and the farm passed to his son R.S. Chew[11] (*fl.* 1964).[12] The brothers Malcolm and John Stallard bought it in 1978 and they farmed there in 2004.[13]

The two-storeyed farmhouse was built in the late 16th century on an H plan and has square-panel timber framing with intermediate close studding and, to the west, a high plinth and a cellar where the ground falls away to the north. The northern end of the east wing and the hall block, which has a stone northern stack with two diagonally-set brick shafts, seem to predate the western wing, which contained the parlour. That room has elaborately moulded beams and the wing a large stone stack with a pair of square-set chimneys. In the 19th century additional brick nogging was inserted in the frame and a single-storeyed addition was built across the northern side of the hall, part of which, together with the end of the west range, was refaced in brick. In the 20th century the southern end of the east wing, which has two large chimneystacks, was replaced; evidence of weathering suggests that it had fallen into disrepair. A staircase was inserted in the hall range and a conservatory added to the front. Later in the century a northern porch was added, the timber-framed north wall of the eastern wing was rebuilt as original, and the windows were returned to their earlier 20th-century pattern. Internal subdivision in the wings created bedrooms, bathrooms, and an entrance passage.

The development of the farmyard to the east follows that of the house. A 17th-century barn on a high stone plinth has a timber frame with a wattle infill that was renewed in the late 20th century. A brick cheese room next to the house was altered in the early 19th century and the adjoining animal shelters and sheds forming a long L were completed by the Madresfield estate in 1861. Stables adjoining the barn were built in 1870.[14]

---

1 Bryant, *Map of Glos.* (1824); see OS Map 1:2,500, Glos. XVII.1 (1903 edn).
2 Datestone on bldg.
3 *Inq. p.m. Glos.* 1359–1413, 188, 193.
4 Hockaday Abs. clxxxvii, 1509; *L&P Hen. VIII*, I (1), p. 217.
5 GDR, dispersed wills 8.
6 *Reg. of Dymock*, 158.
7 GA, D 1142/2. For the Yate fam., above, Bromesberrow, manor.
8 Worcs. RO, 705:99 (BA 3375), Dymock deeds 1633–1811; for the Lygons of Madresfield, below, Kempley, manor.
9 GA, SL 310; *Kelly's Dir. Glos.* (1906–39 edns).
10 Plaque in Dymock ch.
11 *Who's Who in Glos.* (1934), 44–5; GA, DA 30/100/23, p. 90.
12 GA, DA 30/100/32, p. 174.
13 Information from Malcolm Stallard of Callow Farm.
14 Datestones of 1861 and 1870 with letter 'B' for Earl Beauchamp. See Fig. 36.

Gamage Hall

About 1770 Gamage Hall was detached from Little Dymock manor and bought by Richard Hall.[1] At his death in 1780[2] the house passed with its land to his nephew Revd John Sergeaunt.[3] From John (d. 1780) it descended with Hart's Barn in Longhope to Richard Hall and in 1861 he sold the house with c.180 a. to Guy Hill,[4] owner and farmer of the Old Rock. Guy's son Henry[5] sold Gamage Hall farm to A.H. Chew in 1909[6] and the county council bought 260 a. with the house in 1919.[7] The council remained the owner in 2003.[8]

The house at Gamage Hall was rebuilt in the mid 17th century as a two-storeyed timber-framed farmhouse with four hearths in 1672.[9] The square-panelled frame is exposed inside and at the rear and original timbers have been incorporated in a south porch. In the 18th century the front, south wall of the eastern rooms, including the hall, was rebuilt in brick with segment-headed windows and in the early 19th century the rest of the south front was faced in brick and the house given sash windows front and back. A long partly timber-framed north-eastern wing, added in the late 17th or 18th century, has steps to a first-floor room, probably a cheese room.

Lintridge

In the mid 17th century Thomas Wall owned the estate or farm in the far north-east of the parish that became Great Lintridge. Thomas, the son of William Wall,[10] died in 1665. His son William, the county sheriff in 1682,[11] later lived in Ledbury and at his death in 1717 the estate passed to his grandson William Wall.[12] He sold it in 1727 to John Skipp of Ledbury and it was settled the following year on the marriage of John's daughter Jane and George Pritchard, heir to an estate at Hope End, in Colwall (Herefs.), and from 1749 owner of Dymock rectory. Great Lintridge descended with the rectory to Sir Henry Tempest Bt.,[13] on whose separation from his wife Susan in 1815 it was sold to John Terrett of Hanley Castle (Worcs.). At his death in 1820 the estate (434 a.) passed to his widow Mary, later wife of Joseph Harris of Claines (Worcs.), but in 1824 trustees for John's creditors sold it to Joseph Hill, the owner of Little Lintridge.[14]

Little Lintridge was an estate centred on a house formerly called Tops Tenement, a copyhold of Dymock manor that had belonged to the Weale family.[15] The Weales farmed at Lintridge in the mid 17th century[16] and John Weale sold the estate or farm to Decimus Weale and his wife Rachael (née Benson) in 1721. Their children, Decimus, Elizabeth wife of Robert Symonds, and Rachael wife of Matthew Kidder, sold it in 1746 to Thomas Hill. Thomas, later of Bromesberrow, settled Little Lintridge on his son Joseph in 1769[17] and from Joseph (d. 1800) it passed to his son Joseph. Joseph, the purchaser of Great Lintridge in 1824, was succeeded at his death in 1833 by his son Joseph[18] but in 1837 the representatives of Mary Harris (d. 1830) sold most of Great Lintridge (301 a.) to William Laslett of Worcester. William, who was elected MP for that city in 1852, released his estate to his sister Sophia Laslett in 1841 and she conveyed it back to him in 1851.[19] In 1858 he purchased Little Lintridge from Joseph Hill[20] and, having made its house the centre of his enlarged estate or farm,[21] sold it with 382 a. to Earl Beauchamp, owner of the Madresfield estate, in 1868.[22] The farm remained part of the Madresfield estate until c.1919[23] and was owned by Mr Peter Sargeant in 2004.[24]

The core of the Lintridge farmhouse (formerly Little Lintridge) has a **T** plan and timber framing with some close studding and decorative bracing. It was built with a hall range and a western wing with a cellar under the south end. A tall brick range added parallel to the north side of the hall range in the mid 18th century contains a staircase with two balusters per tread and carved tread ends. In the early 19th century a brick skin was applied to the earlier fabric, two full-height bows were added to the north front, and an extension with catslide roof was made to the east. Later in the century new outbuildings were provided around a courtyard west of the house.

---

1 Rudder, *Glos.* 410.
2 *Reg. of Dymock*, 278.
3 GA, D 1202.
4 Below, Longhope, manor (other estates); GA, DC/S 34/1–2; D 640/T 108.
5 Below (The Old Rock).
6 GA, SL 415; D 2428/1/17, f. 19.
7 *Mins. of Glos. County Council*, XXXI, 125–6.
8 Information from Mrs Jennifer Thick, sec. to Dymock par. council.
9 TNA, E 179/247/14, rot. 35d.
10 *Visit. Glos.1682–3*, 192–3.
11 Bigland, *Glos.* I, 528.
12 TNA, PROB 11/557, ff. 192–3; *Reg. of Dymock*, 252.
13 GA, D 1604/T 1; below (Dymock rectory).
14 MCA, H 5iv, bdl. 56A, nos 1, 5; H 6ii, bdl. 56A, nos 6–7.
15 GA, D 1604/T 1.
16 Ibid. D 1388, Pitt and Yate, Bromesberrow deeds 1623–99; GDR wills 1687/175; 1698/88.
17 GA, D 1604/T 1.
18 MCA, H 6ii, bdl. 56C, nos 36–52.
19 Ibid. bdl. 56A, nos 24–30; W.R. Williams, *The Parliamentary History of the County of Worcester* (Hereford, priv. printed 1897), 112.
20 MCA, H 6ii, bdl. 56C, no 51.
21 TNA, RG 9/1761; RG 10/2609.
22 MCA, H 6iv, bdl. 56I, nos 79–80.
23 GA, SL 310.
24 Information from Mr Sargeant.

Great Netherton

In the mid 17th century Robert Holmes, a London merchant, built up an estate at Great Netherton, in the north-west of the parish, purchasing land from among others John Wills,[1] whose family had lived at Netherton since at least the mid 16th century.[2] Robert, who settled there, came to own the largest estate in Leadington division and by 1670 it had passed to his eldest son John[3] (d. by 1685). John's son and heir John, of Ross-on-Wye[4] and later of Carwardine in Madley (Herefs.), died in 1700[5] and his son William sold his Dymock lands in 1712 to Joseph Cam, citizen and haberdasher of London.[6] Joseph died in 1729 leaving land in Dymock and Kempley in turn to his wife Mary (d. 1752) and daughter Mary. From Mary (d. 1774), wife of William Cam[7] (d. 1767),[8] Great Netherton passed to her daughter Ann Cam (d. 1790),[9] and at a division of land between Ann's heirs, confirmed in 1808, became the property of Hercules Hailes Dancocks.[10] At his death in 1818 he left Great Netherton (c.150 a.) to his widow Sarah and the reversion to his eldest son, also called Hercules Hailes Dancocks (fl. 1849).[11] Edmund Edmonds, the owner in 1859,[12] sold Great Netherton in 1873 to Reginald Wynniatt,[13] and John Wenman Wynniatt (d. 1934), the son of James John Wynniatt,[14] owned it in the early 20th century.[15] In the mid 20th century E. Wynniatt Husey sold the farm to the Hawkins family, the tenants since the late 19th century, and they retained it in 2004.[16]

The house at Great Netherton was built in the 17th century, probably with a timber frame and an **H** plan. The **H** was infilled on the east side in the 18th century, embracing the hall range stack and creating a new east front. The other outer walls have also been rebuilt in brick. The north wing was fitted as kitchen and dairy in the 19th century. Among the outbuildings to the west is a three-bayed barn with brick grilles built in 1809 for H.H. Dancocks,[17] whose son appears to have continued to improve the buildings.[18]

The Old Rock

The Old Rock, south-west of the village on the Kempley road, was occupied by Thomas Hill in 1539[19] and belonged to a farm owned by the Hill family of Hillash in the later 16th century.[20] It remained the property of the Hill family until the early 20th century, the ownership passing in the early 17th century to William Hill[21] (d. 1631)[22] and belonging in 1715 to Thomas Hill.[23] Thomas Hill (d. 1815 or 1816) left the Old Rock and its land (c.180 a.) to his nephew Thomas Hill (d. 1843), from whom they passed to his son Guy.[24] Guy, who purchased several other farms in Dymock and Pauntley,[25] died in 1888. Under his son Henry the farms were sold off, the Old Rock (157 a.) in 1911 to William Henry Stuart. Owned in 1944 by Robert Fielding Stuart,[26] the Old Rock changed owners in the later 1940s and S.J.S. Walker sold the farm (171 a.) to F.N. Cross in 1949.[27]

Pitt House Farm

In the mid 1660s Pitt House Farm, south of the village, was the centre of a customary estate owned by the Wills family,[28] which lived at the Pitt House by the mid 16th century.[29] The estate, over which the owners of the Old Grange had lordship, passed to the Hill family.[30] Richard Hill of Staunton (Worcs.) settled it on his marriage in 1736 and took up residence in the house, which was made up of two dwellings knocked into one sometimes called Edulus Place. Richard died in 1772 and his widow Mary in 1776 and their son Richard (d. 1794) left the house and most of the land to his nephew Noah Hill Neale. William Cummins, the owner from 1796,[31] sold the estate in 1803 to Samuel Neate (d. 1807) and Samuel Beale (d. 1840) of Upton upon Severn (Worcs.), the owner from 1811,[32] left it to his daughter Mary, the widow of William

---

1 MCA, I 3v, bdl. 74, no 2.
2 GDR wills 1550/57; 1621/36; *Reg. of Dymock*, 41, 62–3, 101.
3 GA, P 125/OV 2/2; TNA, PROB 11/332, ff. 170v.–171v.
4 MCA, I 3v, bdl. 74, no 1.
5 C.J. Robinson, *A History of the Mansions and Manors of Herefordshire* (1873), 21; TNA, PROB 11/458, ff. 135–6.
6 MCA, I 3v, bdl. 74, no 2.
7 Monument in Dymock ch.; TNA, PROB 11/632, ff. 237–243v.; PROB 11/797, ff. 131v.–134.
8 Below (Wilton Place).
9 TNA, PROB 11/999, ff. 201v.–202; PROB 11/1189, f. 204; monument in Dymock ch.
10 MCA, I 3v, bdl. 74, no 9.
11 GDR wills 1818/145; 1849/62. GA, P 125A/MI 1/1, pp. 12–13; SD 2/2.
12 GA, P 125/VE 2/3.
13 Ibid. D 1223/T 2.
14 Gethyn-Jones, *Dymock Down the Ages*, 73–4; GA, P 125/IN 1/41.
15 GA, D 2428/1/17, f. 8; SL 417.
16 Information from Mr Hawkins of Great Netherton.
17 Datestone.
18 Among the dated features is a stone tank of 1843.
19 TNA, E 101/59/10, rot. 1.
20 GDR wills 1579/87.
21 Ibid. 1611/76; GA, D 1734/1.
22 *Inq. p.m. Glos.* 1625–42, I, 154–5.
23 GA, D 1734/2.
24 Ibid. D 2545/4; see ibid. P 125A/MI 1/1, pp. 26–7.
25 Ibid. DC/S 34/1–3; DC/S 35; G/NE 160/3/1, ff. 30–2.
26 Ibid. D 2545/4; SL 415.
27 Ibid. D 2299/9539.
28 Ibid. P 125/OV 2/2.
29 TNA, E 101/59/10, rot. 1; *Reg. of Dymock*, 58; GDR wills 1593/26; Smith, *Men and Armour*, 59.
30 GA, D 4317/6, rental 1692; 12, copy of terrier 1703.
31 Ibid. D 1272, Dymock deeds 1736–1901; monument in Dymock ch.
32 GA, D 2592, deeds 1841–82, schedule of deeds 1842.

37. Pound Farm from the south-east in 1975

Symonds. On her death in 1859 it passed to her son James Frederick Symonds[1] (d. 1911) and in 1918 the house and 204 a. were sold to S.W. Bennion.[2] The farm was later owned by the Goulding family by whom it was sold in the early 21st century.[3]

Pound Farm

Pound Farm, north of the village, was a copyhold of Dymock manor[4] and part of an estate or farm owned in 1586 by William Cam.[5] William, who lived in the house, died in 1623 and the house and its land descended to John Cam (d. 1753). He was succeeded by his son John (d. 1769), a surgeon in Hereford, and his son and heir John, also a medical practitioner in Hereford,[6] died in 1809 leaving as heirs his daughters Ann (d. 1827), wife of Abraham Whittaker of Llanwarne (Herefs.), and Mary, wife of Nicholas Sykes of Kingston upon Hull (Yorks. E.R.). In 1844, just before Mary's death, the estate (125 a.) was sold to Edward Hankins of Ledbury and in 1852 he sold it to Thomas Dewell of Corsham (Wilts.). Thomas, a captain in the Royal Artillery, died in 1853 and his son Charles Goddard Dewell conveyed the farm in 1863 to William and Thomas Brindle. William Pope, the tenant farmer,[7] died in 1878 having acquired the freehold[8] and his family retained it in the early 20th century.[9] In 1954 the owner and farmer were J.F. Samuel[10] and in 2002 they were Mr L. Samuel.

The farmhouse,[11] standing on a high platform, is a fine and large building of two storeys with attics. It seems to have originated in the 16th century as a smaller house (see the western end of the northern wing) and to have been enlarged in the mid 17th century by the Cams into a **U** with wings projecting west and a porch on the east front in line with a rear stair tower. The low, southern end and the hall occupy four bays of close-studded framing on a rubble plinth. The high end is separately framed and distinguished by square panelling in the upper storey, close studding below, and well-dressed stone facing the plinth. Each wing is served by an internal chimney with diagonal brick stacks and the hall by a rear chimney with three. The interior is plain but has decorative mouldings in the hall and a dog-leg staircase. A considerable amount of work was done on the house and its outbuildings in the 18th and early 19th century, despite the owners living elsewhere. In the 18th century the house's south wall was rebuilt in brick, probably when an entrance was made there, its roof was replaced, a rear corridor was added (and later made two-storeyed), and a barn and cowhouse built. In the early 19th century single-storeyed extensions, one of them a cider house, were added to the house's wings and the barn and cowhouse were altered.

---

1 TNA, PROB 11/1935, f. 326 and v.; GA, D 1272, Dymock deeds 1736–1901.
2 TNA, CRES 38/681.
3 Information from Ms E.M. Goulding of Newent.
4 GA, D 185/IV/12.
5 TNA, PROB 11/70, f. 22 and v.
6 *Reg. of Dymock*, 95, 170, 267, 274; GA, P 125A/VE 3/2; Rudder, *Glos.* 410; Bigland, *Glos.* I, 527.
7 GA, D 2099, Dymock deeds 1800–45; D 9149, Dymock deeds; see ibid. G/NE 160/3/1, f. 62.
8 Ibid. reg. wills 1878, ff. 124v.–126.
9 Ibid. D 2428/1/17, f. 26.
10 Ibid. DA 30/100/23, p. 90.
11 Fig. 37.

Wilton Place

Wilton Place, known until the early 19th century as the Farm,[1] is named after a family descended presumably from John of Wilton, a mid 13th-century landowner in Dymock.[2] In 1522 Thomas Wilton was the wealthiest inhabitant of Ryeland division.[3] His estate[4] passed from his son John (d. 1560) to his son Thomas.[5] John Cam, who lived at the Farm in 1624,[6] died in 1662. The house and land passed to his son John[7] (d. 1680) and he was succeeded by his son John (d. 1707), from whom the estate passed in turn to his sons John (d. 1739)[8] and William, a London merchant.[9] William (d. 1767) was survived by his son John for only a few weeks[10] and by his daughter Ann,[11] who bought Dymock manor in 1769.[12] At her death in 1790 she left the Farm and four other farms in Dymock to John Thackwell.[13] John, who had estates and seats in Berrow and Birtsmorton (both Worcs.),[14] died in 1808 and his eldest son John inherited the Dymock farms apart from Normansland that went to a younger son Joseph.[15] John, who received the Hill estate at a division between Ann Cam's heirs in 1808,[16] died in 1829 and his widow and eldest son, John Cam Thackwell,[17] between them owned 657 a. in Dymock in the 1840s.[18] J.C. Thackwell died in 1892 and Wilton Place passed to John Thackwell (d. 1914). The estate remained intact until John's son and heir, John Henry Cam Thackwell,[19] sold off the house and farms in 1947.[20]

The red brick house,[21] reached along a short drive eastwards from the Ledbury road,[22] was built in the mid 18th century presumably for William Cam.[23] Of 2½ storeys throughout, it lacks stone dressings, ornament, or emphasis to any part of the façades and, standing at the top of a rise, looks particularly tall and austere from the north. To the south the plan formed a shallow U; to the north a western wing projects to make an L. In the later 19th century there were c.20 rooms with a large entrance and staircase hall in the centre of the south front flanked on the west by a dining room, kitchen, and lean-to bakery and yard and on the east by a drawing room and larder. On inheriting the estate in 1892 John Thackwell employed Waller & Son to enlarge and remodel the house. They placed the entrance on the west and altered the south garden front by adding a drawing room in a single-storeyed square bay between the wings and a conservatory in front of the south-east room. In the west wing they made a library and entrance hall and in the east a dining room linked to service rooms in a new single-storeyed extension to the north. The main staircase was replaced and the others reorganised.[24] After a brief period in the 1950s as a hotel[25] the house was converted as flats.[26] It was presumably during the conversion that the conservatory was removed. A few of the outbuildings, to the east and west, have been retained as separate dwellings. The remains of a walled garden lie to the east.

Dymock Rectory

The rectory estate originated in a grant of Dymock church with its tithes, including those of the manorial demesne, and a yardland to Cormeilles abbey (Eure) presumably in the late 11th century.[27] The abbey, which appropriated the church and its revenues under an episcopal licence of 1195,[28] agreed in 1207 that the Flaxley monks would pay 6s. 8d. a year for tithes from their demesne with nothing from assarts they cultivated in their woodland[29] and in 1289 it relinquished the right to corn tithes from William and Sibyl de Grandison's demesne in return for a grant of land.[30] Cormeilles administered its estate through its priory at Newent and the Crown, which at times during wars with France seized the priory, granted it at farm with other of the abbey's

---

1 The name Wilton Place is recorded from 1829: TNA, PROB 11/1764, f. 276v.
2 BL, Add. MS 18461, ff. 14 and v., 77v.–78v., 82–9.
3 *Military Surv. of Glos. 1522*, 55.
4 See TNA, C 1/916, no 42.
5 TNA, PROB 11/44, f. 193; *Reg. of Dymock*, 22. For the Wiltons, *Visit. Glos. 1623*, 270.
6 GA, P 125/VE 3/1.
7 *Reg. of Dymock*, 135; see ibid. 90.
8 Bigland, *Glos.* I, 530; see Atkyns, *Glos.* 394.
9 GDR wills 1739/181; GA, P 125/VE 2/1, f. (at end) 118.
10 Bigland, *Glos.* I, 530.
11 GA, D 4317/6, ct. presentments 1 June 1768.
12 Above (Dymock manor).
13 TNA, PROB 11/1189, ff. 204–207v.
14 *VCH Worcs.* III, 259; IV, 32.
15 *Burke's Landed Gentry* (1846), II, 1382; TNA, PROB 11/1481, ff. 365–368v.
16 MCA, I 3v, bdl. 74, no 9.
17 *Burke's Landed Gentry* (1846), II, 1382–3; TNA, PROB 11/1764, ff. 267v.–279.
18 GA, P 125A/MI 1/1, pp. 45–9; SD 2/2.
19 *Burke's Landed Gentry* (1937), II, 2222; see GA, D 2428/1/17, ff. 11, 14, 24, 31–2.
20 Gethyn-Jones, *Dymock Down the Ages*, 100, 121; GA, D 2299/8701.
21 The interior was not seen.
22 OS Map 1", sheet 43 (1831 edn).
23 See Taylor, *Map of Glos.* (1777).
24 GA, D 2957/2/580; see Gethyn-Jones, *Dymock Down the Ages*, pl. 24.
25 Advt. in J.E. Gethyn-Jones, *St Mary's Church, Dymock* (1952 ch. guide: copy in Glos. Colln. R 116.7).
26 Gethyn-Jones, *Dymock Down the Ages*, 121.
27 BL, Add. MS 18461, ff. 1–2v.
28 *Eng. Episc. Acta VII*, pp. 136–8.
29 BL, Add. MS 18461, f. 86 and v.
30 Ibid. ff. 89v.–90v.

possessions in the late 14th century.[1] In 1411 the rectory passed with the priory to Fotheringhay college (Northants.)[2]

After the college's surrender of its estates in 1547 the rectory passed with Newent manor down to Sir William Winter (d. 1589).[3] His son William possessed the rectory in 1603[4] and was succeeded at his death in 1626 by his son Giles[5] (d. 1630), whose son William[6] was temporarily ousted as owner during the Commonwealth.[7] From William (d. 1667)[8] the impropriation passed to his son William.[9] He lived at the White House in the village[10] and in 1710 his surviving heirs, his daughters Hester, wife of John Devall, and Margaret, conveyed the rectory to his brother Robert and brother-in-law Sir William Humphreys. Sir William (d. 1735), a London ironmonger who acquired a baronetcy in 1714, left his moiety to his grandson Robert Humphreys (d. 1737) and from him it passed to his sisters Mary, wife in turn of William Ball Waring and Thomas Gore, and Ellen, who married Charles Gore. Robert Winter (d. 1719) left the other moiety to his nephew Orlando Humphreys (d. 1737), heir to the baronetcy in 1735, and he left it to Ellen, his daughter. In 1749 the sisters and their husbands sold the rectory to George Pritchard of Hope End (Herefs).[11]

George (d. 1765)[12] was succeeded by his only child Jane. She died in 1767 and her husband Henry Lambert held the rectory estate until their only child Susan came of age.[13] Susan, who used the surname Pritchard,[14] married Sir Henry Tempest Bt.[15] and he sold off tithes piecemeal, in 1803 reserving those from 1,000 a. for payments including the vicar's stipend and Robert Winter's clothing charity.[16] The vicar, Evan Evans, bought the rectory later in 1803[17] and was succeeded both as rector and vicar in 1817 by his brother David (d. 1820).[18] The rectory, which David left to their sister Mary Collins,[19] was sold in 1825 to Abraham Thompson of Powick (Worcs.)[20] and in 1848 its tithes were commuted for a corn rent charge of £300.[21] Abraham died in 1853 and his executors sold the impropriation in 1857 to John Drummond of Boyce Court. He sold it to Earl Beauchamp in 1871.[22]

Medieval Monastic Estates

Aconbury priory (Herefs.), founded in the early 13th century by Margery de Lacy,[23] received an early grant of land in Dymock from Richard son of Robert le Rich of Gloucester. William de Gamages granted the priory a rent from a mill at Ketford and in the early 15th century the mill was farmed under the priory.[24] Wormsley priory (Herefs.) had a pasture in Dymock called Maidenpole in 1501[25] and retained it until the Dissolution. The Crown granted it to Daniel and Alexander Peart of Tewkesbury in 1553.[26]

ECONOMIC HISTORY

Despite attempts in the 13th century to bolster Dymock's trading role,[27] the parish's economy settled primarily on supplying the immediate needs of a large and scattered farming community. Large numbers of people were engaged in rural crafts and trades and farming was varied, with an emphasis in the early modern period on apple and pear cultivation. The Hereford and Gloucester canal and the railway that succeeded it[28] stimulated some commercial activity in the 19th and early 20th century.

AGRICULTURE

The Middle Ages

In 1066 the royal estate at Dymock had 2 ploughs in demesne while its tenants possessed a total of 45 ploughs, four of them belonging to 4 radknights and

---

1 VCH Glos. II, 105–6; see Cal. Fine 1391–9, 177; 1399–1405, 12.
2 Rot. Parl. III, 652–5.
3 Above, Newent, manors; Cal. Pat. 1547–8, 4–5, 108–9; 1555–7, 94; TNA, C 142/118, no 54; C 142/227, no 204; Herefs. RO, E 12/G/20.
4 Eccl. Misc. 102; Visit. Glos. 1682–3, 206.
5 Inq. p.m. Glos. 1625–42, I, 39.
6 Ibid. 135–6.
7 Bigland, Glos. I, 525: the rectory was sold in 1652 to Thomas Millard and Daniel Wycherley.
8 Bigland, Glos. I, 529.
9 TNA, PROB 11/323, ff. 328–9.
10 Notes on Dioc. of Glouc. by Chancellor Parsons, 156.
11 MCA, I 2vi, bdl. 67, nos 10–12, 15, 20–1; Complete Baronetage, V, 21–2 and n.; Bigland, Glos. I, 529.
12 TNA, PROB 11/913, ff. 355–7.
13 GA, P 125/CH 1/1. Henry retained the rectory in the late 1780s: ibid. Q/REl 1, Botloe hundred; Hockaday Abs. clxxxvii, 1787.
14 Bigland, Glos. I, 525.
15 Complete Baronetage, III, 293.
16 GA, P 125/CH 1/1.
17 MCA, I 2v, bdl. 67, no 26.
18 TNA, PROB 11/1592, f. 98 and v.; monument. in Dymock ch.
19 TNA, PROB 11/1637, f. 90 and v.
20 MCA, I 2v, bdl. 67, nos 34–5.
21 GA, P 125A/SD 2/2.
22 MCA, I 3ii, bdl. 67, nos 43, 45.
23 Dugdale, Mon. VI (1), 489.
24 TNA, E 315/55, pp. 41–2, 53–4; see below, econ. hist. (mills).
25 TNA, SC 6/Hen. VIII/7323, rot. 42d.
26 Cal. Pat. 1553, 146.
27 Below (markets and fairs).
28 Above, introd. (communications).

the rest to 11 freedmen, 42 villans, and 10 bordars.[1] Although only 12 ploughteams were recorded in Dymock in 1220,[2] more land was brought into cultivation in the 12th and 13th centuries as woodland in the south-west was cleared.[3] While much of the land won was put in closes and there is scant early documentary evidence of strip farming,[4] open arable fields as indicated by areas of former ridge and furrow existed in various parts of the parish, particularly in the east.[5] Open-field land in the south-east included one or more areas by Castle Tump known in the 13th century as Castle field and the bailey.[6] Later evidence suggests that Leadington tithing, in the north-west, had a separate system of agriculture.[7]

There had been some retreat from cultivation by 1340, when five yardlands in the parish lay uncultivated because of the poverty of the tenantry.[8] The sandy soils of the eastern part of the parish were suited particularly to the growing of rye,[9] amounts of which were among corn and pulses sold in 1347 probably by the receiver of the tithes.[10] That division of the parish became known as Ryeland, the name Ryton having been recorded in the 13th century,[11] and according to one tradition the Ryeland breed of sheep originated there.[12] The riverine land in the Leadon valley above and below Ketford, and also in the broad tributary valley west of Ryton, was possibly cultivated as water meadows later if not in the medieval period.[13] King's Meadow, between the Leadon's two channels at Ketford,[14] belonged to Dymock manor but was open as a common between haymaking and Candlemas in the mid 14th century.[15] At that time the manor's woodland was also common pasture.[16] The production of cider on many farms in the mid 16th century indicates that there were numerous orchards by the end of the medieval period.[17]

Many of Dymock's farms probably derived from the holdings of the manor's Domesday tenants. In the mid 13th century, when its demesne comprised 93 a. arable, 8 a. meadow, and 5 a. pasture, the manor received cash rents from 16 free tenants holding 12 yardlands and a number of assarts, 14 men holding other land, the tenants of 66 burgages, and customary tenants. The pattern of customary tenements was based on 11 yardland and 22 half-yardland holdings owing services mostly for sowing and harvesting corn, the tenants supplying seed for the winter ploughing and providing the labour of additional men during the harvest. Lesser customary tenants, of whom there were a score or more, also owed services and children and other adults owed small works in return for the Crown's protection.[18] Military and other free tenants witheld their service in the late 13th and early 14th century[19] and the demesne was let out before 1335, when the estate's value came almost entirely from tenants' rents (£28).[20] Robert Ketford held a ploughland and 40 a. meadow by military service in 1373[21] and rents from 25 tenants were assigned to the widow of Thomas de Grandison (d. 1375) as part of her dower.[22] In 1317 Little Dymock manor had 80 a. arable and 2 a. meadow in demesne but its main value was free tenants' rents (£8).[23] The dower awarded in 1385 to John of Pembridge's widow included rents from thirteen freehold and two customary tenants.[24] Customary tenants on both manors came to enjoy a favourable form of copyhold, their tenements being heritable by their legitimate children and subject, after the death of the owner, to the payment of a heriot and a relief of one year's rent.[25]

Flaxley abbey, according to one 13th-century rental, had 31 tenants in Dymock and they owed cash rents ranging from 2½d. to 17s. 8d. and totalling £4 9s. 9½d. Two tenants, both paying 8s., owed ploughing services, themselves supplying seed in the winter, and had to send men to the harvest on four days and a man to haymaking on one day. Nineteen other tenants also owed harvest services, most with three men.[26] Cormeilles abbey's tenants in the mid 14th century were mostly cottagers. Only a few held land, the largest holding being a half yardland, and in 1335 the cash rents for 31 holdings, of which two were in dual occupation, ranged from 4d. to 13s. 6d.[27] Under Fotheringhay college the rectory estate was

---

1 *Domesday Book* (Rec. Com.), I, 164.
2 *Book of Fees*, I, 307.
3 Below (woodland management).
4 See *Flaxley Cart*. p. 177.
5 Archaeology Data Service (http://ads.ahds.ac.uk/catalogue: accessed 3 May 2005).
6 BL, Add. MS 18461, ff. 86v.–87v., 89v.; 15668, f. 14v.
7 Below (the early modern period).
8 *Nonarum Inquisitiones*, 415.
9 Turner, *Agric. of Glos.* 48; Rudge, *Agric. of Glos.* 138.
10 Herefs. RO, E 12/G/1.
11 Above, introd. (boundaries and divisions); settlement (outlying settlement: Ryeland).
12 Rudder, *Glos.* 408; see W. Marshall, *The Rural Economy of Gloucestershire* (1796), II, 199.
13 Archaeology Data Service.
14 Worcs. RO, 705:99 (BA 3375), Dymock deeds 1633–1811, copy ct. roll 24 Oct. 1633; GA, P 125A/SD 2/1–2 (nos 1039–41).
15 *Inq. p.m. Glos.* 1301–58, 366.
16 Ibid. 253.
17 Below (the early modern period).
18 *Cal. Inq. Misc.* I, 151; *Glos. N&Q* IX, 21–3.
19 *Rot. Parl.* II, 83.
20 *Inq. p.m. Glos.* 1301–58, 253, 366–7; 1359–1413, 54.
21 TNA, C 143/381, no 10.
22 *Inq. p.m. Glos.* 1359–1413, 188–9.
23 Ibid. 1301–58, 168.   24 Ibid. 1359–1413, 148.
25 Bigland, *Glos.* I, 526–7 n.; TNA, C 78/1453, no 5.
26 *Flaxley Cart*. pp. 176–8; for another rental, see ibid. pp. 128–9.
27 BL, Add. MS 18461, ff. 79v.–81v.

held by a lessee in the late Middle Ages.¹ In 1522 Dymock's most prosperous farmer was John Wynniatt, the occupant of Flaxley abbey's grange (later Old Grange). Among other leading farmers Thomas Hill of Gamage Hall was the lessee of Little Dymock manor.²

The Early Modern Period

In 1608 some fifty farmers lived in Dymock with eleven of them, 6 yeomen and 5 husbandmen, working on Giles Forster's estate. The principal tenant farmer was John Wynniatt at the Old Grange.³ His farm included Rosehill and land in Kempley.⁴ Much land was copyhold, on Old Grange manor and some other estates for lives⁵ and on Dymock and Little Dymock manors by inheritance. The customs of those two manors, those of Dymock being rehearsed in an agreement of 1565 to which its lord and tenants were parties, permitted tenants to dispose freely of their land with the lord's consent and to grant leases for up to 21 years without it.⁶ As a result very little copyhold property on the two manors was enfranchised before the 19th century.⁷

By the mid 17th century the pattern of customary holdings within Dymock had been largely obscured. Holdings had been amalgamated and many houses had been abandoned. For the Wynniatt family's Old Grange estate, which in 1665 included five or six large farms on the west side of the parish as well as Gamage Hall,⁸ a rental of 1692 listed 41 holdings in Dymock held by 31 tenants, half of whom had free land as part or as the whole of their holding. Of the estate's 22 customary tenements 12 or 13 owed heriots and the rest were without houses.⁹ A number of other farms were absorbed into other estates, as in the east of the parish where substantial farms at Callow, Ketford, and Ryton were added to the lands of the Yate family of Bromesberrow in the later 17th and the early 18th century.¹⁰ In 1731, when five or six farms in the south belonged to the Chamberlayne family, the parish's largest farms were centred on the Old Grange and Boyce Court and there were substantial farms at Lintridge, Great Netherton, and Hill Farm.¹¹

Open fields and small common meadows were scattered throughout the parish apart from the southwest. Reduced in size by piecemeal inclosure,¹² the fields were mostly small. West of the village they included Monk Down (or Old field) south of the Kempley road and Stoneberrow and Mickle field further north.¹³ North of the village a field called Lower Lynch lay by the Ledbury road north of the Leadon.¹⁴ Leadington had more than seven open fields. North field and Heddens (later Iddens) field were in the north near the lane to Ledbury and Old (later Gloucestershire Old) field and Great and Little Sneads (later Sneadge) fields were lower down to the west towards the Ludstock and Preston brooks.¹⁵ Another field called Toplay (or Suffield) lay to the south, some way north-east of Tiller's green,¹⁶ and one called Haw field lay beyond the Preston brook near Hallwood green.¹⁷ Sneads field was also known as Eatons field¹⁸ and the open-field land in the north near the river Leadon became known as Far Eatons field.¹⁹ Leadington's common meadows probably included Sneads Moor and Redding Meadow on the east bank of the Preston brook.²⁰

An open field called Sidderdine²¹ lay midway between the village and Ryton. The open fields in the east of the parish also included Hemland to the east of Broom's green²² and East field and Warford to the east of Ryton and Horse Croft (or High field) to the north-east of it.²³ Bromesberrow heath and Broom's green on the northern boundary were common pastures in the 17th century.²⁴ South of the Leadon there was an open field called Crow field close to the river by the way to Ketford.²⁵ At the end of the 18th century King's Meadow, the riparian meadow at Ketford, was owned severally by three farms at Ryton and Bromesberrow Heath with the grazing on it between 20 July to 2 February reserved to Heath farm.²⁶

The parish contained numerous orchards with

---

1 TNA, E 315/52, no 140; C 1/983, no 28; Herefs. RO, E 12/G/5.
2 *Military Surv. of Glos. 1522*, 54–6; TNA, CP 40/978, Carte rot. 6 and d.
3 Smith, *Men and Armour*, 58–60.
4 GA, D 214/T 17.
5 Ibid.; ibid. D 2464/T 1, deed 15 Sept. 1649.
6 Bigland, *Glos*. I, 526–7 n.; TNA, C 78/1453, no 5.
7 GA, D 2545/2, deed 9 Apr. 1680; see below (the 19th and 20th cents.).
8 GA, P 125/OV 2/2.
9 Ibid. D 4317/6.
10 Bigland, *Glos*. I, 527; GA, D 1142/2, abstract of ancient deeds.
11 GA, P 125A/VE 3/2.
12 Ibid. D 892/T 25/2, 6, 15; D 2957/116/1; DC/S 34/3.
13 Ibid. D 214/T 17; Worcs. RO, B705:99 (BA 3375), Dymock ct. book 1704–84, f. 6v.
14 GA, D 892/T 25/14.
15 Ibid. D 1142/4, deeds 20 July 1604–6 Apr. 1629.
16 Ibid. D 185/IV 9; Q/RI 58.
17 Dymock ct. book 1704–84, f. 5 and v.
18 Worcs. RO, 705:99 (BA 5540), Dymock ct. book 1784–1822, ct. 18 May 1786.
19 GA, Q/RI 58.
20 Ibid. D 1142/4, deed 20 July 1604; D 892/T 25/4; for locations of the meadows, ibid. P 125A/SD 2/1–2.
21 Ibid. D 892/T 25/2; TNA, C 142/100, no 44.
22 GA, D 897, misc. deeds 1698–1825, deed 26 Sept. 1699; see ibid. Q/RI 58.
23 Ibid. D 1142/2, abs. of ancient deeds; Dymock ct. book 1704–84, ff. 3v.–4; see GA, Q/RI 58.
24 GA, D 2079/II 2/T 2, deed 29 June 1785; D 897, misc. deeds 1698–1825, deed 26 Sept. 1699; Dymock ct. book 1704–84, f. 3.
25 GA, DC/S 34/3, deed 9 Sept. 1709.
26 Ibid. D 2079/II 2/T 2, deed 25 Aug. 1801; MCA, H 5ii, bdl. 50, no 13.

many farms producing cider and presumably perry in the mid 16th century, some in large quantities.[1] Apple and pear trees were traditionally planted in widely-spaced rows in arable fields,[2] including open fields and newly inclosed land.[3] Some inclosed land was converted to pasture[4] but orcharding became the major enterprise of many farms[5] and the area became noted for the quality of its cider made from Red Streak apples. In the mid 17th century John Wynniatt of the Old Grange was a major producer of[6] and authority on such cider[7] and in 1767 the Old Grange farm comprised 88 a. arable, of which 75 a. contained orchards, 35 a. meadow, and 85 a. pasture.[8] Cider mills, operated on the larger farms by horse power, were usually housed in a separate outbuilding. In the later 18th century new orchards were planted in grassland as older trees became less productive. Favoured fruits at that time included the native Dymock Red and Royal Wilding apples and the local Oldfield pear.[9]

In the early 18th century wheat fields were abundant[10] but, with orcharding a priority, cereal cultivation was sometimes poor, land was not drained, and meadows were not watered. Many farmers devoted more land to pastoral than to arable farming,[11] Greenway House and Pitt House being among farmsteads with dairies and cheese stores as well as cider mills.[12] Sheepcots were scattered around the parish[13] and Ryeland sheep, kept traditionally for their wool,[14] remained the predominant breed, although improved by cross-breeding in the later 18th century.[15] Under Richard Hall (d. 1780) Gamage Hall farm was entitled to pasturage in a meadow in Minsterworth.[16] In Dymock hops were grown in a few, sometimes new, places[17] and hemp and flax were cultivated before 1624, when the vicar was entitled to the tithe of the crop.[18] Large quantities of flax were grown at Little Netherton and another place between 1788 and 1794.[19] Roots became part of the rotation and in 1801 turnips accounted for 147 and potatoes for 23 of the 1,715 a. returned in that year as under crops, mostly cereals and pulses. Wheat remained the main cereal[20] and rye, although it had a greater yield, was a comparatively trifling crop even on sandy soils.[21]

The Nineteenth and Twentieth Centuries

During the 19th century there were some 50–60 farms in Dymock and in 1896 the number of agricultural occupiers, including the smallholders, was 74.[22] In the early 19th century many farms had over 100 a., including Great Ketford and Callow farms which passed by sale in 1810 with other farms in the east of Dymock from the Yate family's estate to Lord Beauchamp's Madresfield estate.[23] In 1811, following its acquisition of a farm at Ryton,[24] the Madresfield estate owned 508 a. divided between five farms with Great Ketford and Callow farms having 151 a. and 144 a. respectively.[25] In the west there were equally large farms based on the Old Grange, Allums, New Grange, and Rosehill on the Old Grange estate.[26] About 1850 some twenty-five farms had at least 100 a., another ten 50 a., and twenty 20 a. The largest was Great Lintridge farm (300 a.) at the east end of the parish. Other large farms included the home farm (270 a.), Hill farm (210 a.), and Ockington (127 a.) on the Wilton Place estate in the north and east, Swords (193 a.), Mirabels (137 a.), and Upham (122 a.) in the Leadington, and Castle farm (200 a.), Gamage Hall (178 a.), Normansland (174 a.), and Old Rock (162 a.) in the south, where the greater part of the Boyce Court estate was farmed from Timberhill (200 a.). Other farms with between 100 a. and 140 a. were Pounds, Drews, Great Netherton, and Little Netherton farms in the north-west. Smaller farms were found throughout the parish.[27]

The creation of even larger farms was well advanced by the mid 1860s. Guy Hill, owner of the Old Rock,[28] acquired the farms at Crowfield, Gamage Hall, Bickenshill, and Old Shayles to create for

---

1 GA, D 1142/4, deed 2 June 1551; GDR wills 1547/191; 1550/57; 1553/39; 1560/117; 1563/110; 1577/166.
2 Rudder, *Glos.* 408–9.
3 Dymock ct. book 1704–84, ff. 26v.–27, 95 and v.; 1784–1822, ct. 18 May 1786; GA, D 892/T 25/18; D 1142/4; D 185/IV/18.
4 GA, D 185/IV/15.
5 Atkyns, *Glos.* 395.
6 Bodleian, Top. Glouc. c. 3, f. 196v.
7 J. Beale, 'Aphorisms Concerning Cider', in J. Evelyn, *Sylva, or a Discourse of Forest-Trees, and the Propagation of Timber in His Majesties Dominions* (London, 1664), 26.
8 *Glouc. J.* 16 Nov. 1767.
9 Marshall, *Rural Econ. of Glos.* II, 205–6, 212, 220–2, 237, 273; Turner, *Agric. of Glos.* 52–4; Rudge, *Agric. of Glos.* 220–38; *Glouc. J.* 20 Apr. 1795; 17 Aug. 1812; 15 Jan. 1816.
10 *Notes on Dioc. of Glouc. by Chancellor Parsons*, 155.
11 Rudder, *Glos.* 409.
12 R. Lowe, 'Field Meeting to Dymock', *Herefordshire Archaeological News* 70 (Woolhope Club Archaeological Research Section 1999), 25; *Glouc. J.* 20 Apr. 1795.
13 GA, D 1142/4, deed 6 Apr. 1629; D 1604/T 1, copy ct. roll 11 Apr. 1723.
14 Rudder, *Glos.* 408.
15 Turner, *Agric. of Glos.* 47; Rudge, *Hist. of Glos.* II, 27.
16 TNA, PROB 11/1063, f. 365 and v.
17 GDR wills 1662/89; MCA, I 4i, bdl. 77, no 7; GA, D 892/T 25/19–20.
18 GDR, V 5/116T 1.
19 GA, Q/CB 2; Q/SO 11, p. 501.
20 *1801 Crop Returns Eng.* I, 171.
21 Ibid. 186; Rudge, *Agric. of Glos.* 138.
22 GA, P 125A/MI 1/1; SD 2/2; TNA, HO 107/1960; MAF 68/1609/6.
23 Worcs. RO, 705:99 (BA 3375), Dymock deeds 1633–1811.
24 Ibid. Dymock deeds 1802–13.
25 MCA, A 3ii, 16.
26 GA, D 4317/6, rental 1820–5.
27 Ibid. P 125A/SD 2/1–2; TNA, HO 107/1960.
28 Above, manors (other estates).

himself a farm of 478 a. south and east of the village, and on the Old Grange estate the farm at Allums was enlarged to 357 a. by the addition of land formerly farmed from the manor house.[1] Shortly after inheriting the Madresfield estate in 1866 the 6th Earl Beauchamp[2] bought more farms in the east of Dymock[3] and in 1875 the estate's principal farms included Lintridge (383 a.), Great Ketford (248 a.), Callow (238 a.), and Limetrees in Ryton (182 a.).[4] By the early 20th century Guy Hill's former farm had been divided between several units[5] and soon after the First World War the Madresfield and Old Grange estates began selling off their farms.[6] To foster small-scale farming the county council bought 260 a., including the farmhouses at Gamage Hall and Crowfield, in 1919[7] and built a new farmstead at Mere Hills.[8] It later bought Maypole farm (44 a.).[9] Although the enfranchisement of copyhold land gathered pace at the end of the 18th century,[10] the process was piecemeal[11] and continued after the First World War.[12]

Among the 87 holdings returned in 1926 were 55 farms with over 20 a. Ten of them had at least 150 a. and one more than 300 a. The agricultural workforce included 125 labourers employed full time and 34 employed on a part-time or casual basis.[13] In 1956, although there was a similar number of farms and smallholdings, there were fewer smaller and more larger farms, four of them having over 300 a. In the later 20th century the incorporation of smaller farms into larger units continued and the number of farms and smallholdings was much reduced. In 1986, in a total of 58 holdings returned that year, there were 38 farms of over 10 ha (25 a.), among them seven with over 100 ha (250 a.) and two with over 200 ha (500 a.). The holdings provided employment for a total of 135 people, including 38 full-time farmers and a salaried manager, but 29 of the holdings were worked on a part-time basis. The number of hired labourers with full-time employment on the farms was 111 in 1956 and only 12 in 1986.[14] In 2004 the farms varied considerably in size and the county council retained ownership of several of them, including a group east of the Newent road.[15]

In 1842 the farmland comprised 3,584 a. of arable and 2,677 a. of meadow and pasture.[16] At that time arable farming usually followed a four course rotation with heavier soils being left fallow for a year and turnips being grown only on lighter soils.[17] The common of Bromesberrow heath was inclosed in the late 1850s at the instigation of William Laslett, the owner of the Lintridge estate,[18] the inclosure being confirmed in two awards dated 1864 and 1866 and dealing respectively with 9 a. in Bromesberrow and 28 a. in Dymock. On the Dymock side Earl Beauchamp as lord of Dymock manor and the churchwardens and overseers received small allotments, Laslett bought 20 a. next to Lintridge, and the rest of the land was divided between 19 other landholders, each one buying under an acre and some considerably less.[19] The remaining fragments of the open fields, at Stoneberrow, in the Leadington, and around Ryton, were inclosed together with King's Meadow under an award of 1862. That award dealt with 208 a., including old closes, and of its 28 beneficiaries E.J. Thackwell of Normansland received 50 a., another party 31 a., Earl Beauchamp 25 a., and the others all less than 10 a. each.[20]

In 1866 the 2,934 a. of arable returned for the parish included 1,198 a. under wheat, 745 a. under other cereals and pulses, and 987 a. under clover, grass leys, and roots.[21] Sheep farming and dairying remained important, the former particularly in the east of the parish, and several farms had resident cowmen and dairymaids.[22] Beef cattle and pigs were also raised and in 1866 totals of 2,399 sheep, 208 milch cows, 474 other cattle, and 320 pigs were returned.[23] In the late 19th century arable land was converted to meadow or pasture and in 1905 Dymock contained 1,920 a. of arable and 4,065 a. of permanent grassland.[24] In 1896, when more dairy and beef cattle and pigs were kept than thirty years earlier and horses were also raised, orchards covered at least 566 a.[25] John Pullen (d. 1908), a stonemason of the Leadington, was reputed for his skill in propagating fruit trees.[26] Some farmers grew hops, 50 a. on Old

---

1 GA, G/NE 160/3/1, passim; see ibid. DC/S 34/1–3; D 4317/7, undated terrier.
2 See below, Kempley, manor.
3 MCA, H 6iv, bdl. 56I, nos 79–80; I 2iii, bdl. 63, no 6.
4 Ibid. L 1i (5).
5 GA, SL 415.
6 Ibid. SL 310; SL 417.
7 Ibid. C/CC/M 5/31, pp. 125–6.
8 Above, settlement (outlying settlement: Woodend).
9 GA, D 2299/5385.
10 Dymock ct. book 1784–1822.
11 Worcs. RO, 705:99 (BA 3375), Dymock deeds 1802–13; 1633–1811; GA, D 2079/II 2/T 1, 2, 5; D 2099, Dymock deeds 1862–75; D 2545/4, deed 15 July 1825; MCA, J 2vi, bdl. 108A, no 22; J 6i, bdl. 99, no 33; bdl. 100, no 2.
12 GA, D 2299/1907.
13 TNA, MAF 68/3295/15.
14 Ibid. MAF 68/4533/164; MAF 68/6005/14/164.
15 Information from Mrs Eckley of Allums.
16 GA, P 125A/MI 1/1; SD 2/2.
17 TNA, IR 18/2714.
18 MCA, H 6iv, bdl. 56F, no 75; bdl. 56G, no 76.
19 GA, Q/RI 59, 31.
20 Ibid. Q/RI 58. The figure for Thackwell includes land allotted by the award to his late father, Sir Joseph: for the Thackwells, see *Burke's Landed Gentry* (1898), II, Ireland, 438.
21 TNA, MAF 68/26/16.
22 Ibid. HO 107/1960; RG 9/1761.
23 Ibid. MAF 68/25/4.
24 Acreage Returns, 1905.
25 TNA, MAF 68/1609/6.
26 Theodora C. Reeves, 'History of Little Marcle and of Preston Parish' (1972: typescript in Glos. Colln. 36709), 107–8.

Rock farm being newly planted with hops and 9 a. with fruit trees in the 1890s,[1] and in 1899 two new hop kilns were built at Gamage Hall.[2] Market gardening and soft fruit growing, mainly berries and currants, were established[3] and the wild daffodils that abounded in the woods, hedgerows, and fields of the parish were picked for a trade that continued well into the 20th century.[4] In 1901 two market gardeners and fruit growers lived at Ryton and fruit and flower dealers occasionally lodged at the Beauchamp Arms.[5]

In 1926 the area under cereals was returned as 643 a. and livestock farming was represented by 1,649 cattle, including 487 milch cows, 2,966 sheep, 432 pigs, and 7,997 poultry, including 6,920 chickens.[6] Hop cultivation had ceased by that time,[7] the remaining hop kilns being demolished,[8] but orcharding and fruit farming remained important, cider and perry being made on Hill farm in the early 1930s. A nurseryman was among the people listed in Dymock in 1931.[9] In the mid 20th century the area devoted to cereal production increased considerably and livestock numbers, including those of pigs and chickens as well as dairy and beef cattle, rose.[10] Farms were usually mixed and many had fruit trees and bushes.[11] In the south of the parish Castle farm (86 a.), a specialist fruit farm producing dessert and culinary apples, plums, and blackcurrants, included a new house for a foreman and a store that had been accommodation for pickers.[12] In 1956, when 1,234 a. of cereals was returned, orchards covered at least 361 a. and market gardens and fruit fields another 112 a.[13] Although many farms grew cereals, mostly wheat and barley, farming in the late 20th century was dominated by dairying. In 1986, when totals of 2,659 cattle, including 718 cows in milk or calf, and 6,300 sheep and lambs were returned, eleven of the holdings returned were dairy farms, seven were beef or sheep farms, three were fruit farms, and one was a cereal farm.[14] There were several dairy farms in 2004[15] and a cheese maker farming at Broom's Green, an enterprise started in 1973 and originally using milk from a herd of Old Gloucester cattle,[16] remained in business.

In the later 20th century orchards were grubbed up to make larger fields for cereal and dairy farming. Most of those cultivated in 1986, when 74 ha (183 a.) of orchards and 20 ha (49 a.) of fruit fields were returned, grew apples for eating or apples and pears for cider and perry making.[17] In 2004 the largest area of orchards was on Castle farm which extended into Oxenhall and produced and bottled apple juice. Soft fruit was grown under plastic at Lintridge and there were several market and nursery gardens. Intensive, large-scale poultry farming continued at a unit established near Mooroak in the 1960s.[18]

WOODLAND MANAGEMENT

In the mid 12th century the lord of Dymock gave half of the woodland there, together with half of his nets, to the monks of Flaxley abbey.[19] Parts of the wood were cleared by the abbey[20] and eight men, including two smiths, a forester, and a charcoal burner, had assarts on them in the early 13th century.[21] The woodland retained for the manor was wasted by its keeper during the wars immediately following Henry III's accession in 1216 but the undergrowth had regenerated by the mid 1240s.[22] At that time several freeholders held assarts from the manor[23] and in 1252 the Crown permitted Ela Longespée, the holder of the manor, to clear and inclose all the wood east of a path called 'Staurnchesway', an area of three yardlands.[24] The manor's woodland was common pasture in 1335.[25] Charcoal burning, an activity dependant on woodland material, may have been an occupation of those parishioners surnamed of or at the pit in the 14th century.[26]

Dymock wood, which had been inclosed by the early 16th century,[27] was long managed as coppice. In 1665 it supplied cordwood to the ironmaster Thomas Foley. Then it was owned by John Kyrle,[28] who

---

1 *Kelly's Dir. Glos.* (1902), 150.
2 GA, D 2299/690.
3 TNA, MAF 68/1609/6.
4 *The Times*, 7 Apr. 1928; 14 Mar. 1945. See Gethyn-Jones, *Dymock Down the Ages*, 147; K. Clark, *The Muse Colony: Rupert Brooke, Edward Thomas, Robert Frost and Friends: Dymock 1914* (1992), 9–10.
5 TNA, RG 13/2422.
6 Ibid. MAF 68/3295/15.
7 GA, P 125/MI 25, text of BBC radio broadcast 24 Dec. 1952.
8 Ibid. GPS 125/101.
9 *Kelly's Dir. Glos.* (1931), 158–9.
10 TNA, MAF 68/4533/164.
11 GA, D 2299/8701, 8870, 10355; P 125/MI 25, text of BBC radio broadcast 24 Dec. 1952.
12 Ibid. D 2299/8511.
13 TNA, MAF 68/4533/164.
14 Ibid. MAF 68/6005/14/164.

15 Information from Mrs Eckley and from Mr. G. Humphris of Gamage Hall.
16 *Citizen*, 17 Dec. 1973; *Sunday Telegraph*, 25 Jan. 1981; *Farmers Weekly*, 16 Dec. 1983.
17 TNA, MAF 68/6005/14/164.
18 GA, DA 30/100/34, p. 19; see OS Map 1:2,500, SO 7030–7130 (1970 edn).
19 *Flaxley Cart.* pp. 16, 18.
20 Ibid. pp. 158–9.
21 BL, Add. MS 18461, f. 86 and v.
22 *Cal. Inq. Misc.* I, 9.   23 Ibid. 151.
24 *Close* 1251–3, 136.
25 *Inq. p.m. Glos.* 1301–58, 253.
26 *Glos. Subsidy Roll, 1327*, 5; *Inq. p.m. Glos.* 1359–1413, 148.
27 GA, D 2597/116/14.
28 Herefs. RO, E 12/G/19; see J. Duncumb, *Hist and Antiquities of Herefs.* (continuation by W.H. Cooke), iii (1882), 136. For the Foleys, *Burke's Peerage* (1900), I, 605–6.

derived £100 a year from felling timber in it,[1] and among later owners were John Weale of Ockington from 1727 and George Terry of Hereford from 1763. In 1789, when Andrew Foley bought the wood,[2] most wood cut locally was used for laths, hurdles, and hoops and the rest was sent to ironworks at Powick (Worcs.), Lydney, and Flaxley.[3] As lord of Dymock manor Lord Beauchamp joined a landowners' association for the prosecution of poachers in 1814[4] and several parishioners worked as gamekeepers in the mid 19th century.[5] Later in the century the woods on the west side of the parish belonging to the Old Grange estate[6] were patrolled by a keeper living nearby in Kempley.[7] In the east of the parish conifer planting on the side of the Leadon valley between Ketford and Ryton, begun by the Madresfield estate by the early 1880s, led to the creation of a large wood around the remains of an older copse.[8] In 1901 the parish's woodlands gave employment to three woodmen and woodcutters, one of them at Ketford, a gamekeeper lived next to Haind Park wood, and a timber merchant at Broom's Green had employees.[9]

Dymock wood and adjoining woods in Oxenhall, in all 639 a., were acquired by the Crown in 1914[10] and were administered by the Forestry Commission from 1924 under the name of Dymock Woods.[11] Charcoal burning having ended in the 1920s, the woods supplied oak bark to the tanning industry until the mid 20th century.[12] Under the Commission conifer plantation was introduced and in the late 20th century provision for public access increased and some woodland was set aside for nature conservation in collaboration with Gloucestershire's wildlife trust. In the early 1960s the Commission employed nine foresters but by the end of the century it contracted out work in the woods.[13] In the early 21st century Dymock Woods covered an area of 506 ha (1,214 a.) on both sides of the county boundary, approximately half of it coniferous plantation and the remainder mostly oak and beech.[14] Ryton wood provided timber for use in Welsh mines during the First World War[15] and under the management of the Forestry Commission[16] included a private shoot in the early 21st century.

MILLS

There were seven mills in Dymock in 1340[17] and one on Dymock manor was described at that time as in ruins.[18] Dymock's mills driven by the river Leadon and its tributaries were usually never more than corn mills[19] but the name Walker's Close, recorded near a mill pond in the area of Maypole Farm, upstream of Dymock village, in 1513, suggests that a mill there may have been used for fulling.[20] Among the water mills whose precise sites have not been identified is one at Ketford from which William de Gamages granted Aconbury priory (Herefs.) 9s. rent in the late 12th or early 13th century.[21] In the mid 14th century the priory took a rent of 18s., sometimes reducing it when there was a lack of water in the summer.[22] The rent was later fixed at 13s. 4d.[23] and in 1406, the tenant having defaulted in its payment, the priory granted the mill for half that amount.[24] The location of Ryton mill, a water grist mill demolished before 1721 that was a copyhold of Dymock manor, is also not known.[25]

Farm Mill, one of two mills on the stretch of Leadon above Dymock village in the later 18th century,[26] was part of the Farm (later Wilton Place) estate in the later 17th century.[27] Sold to the tenant, James Hill, in 1805, it was taken back into the estate in 1894[28] and remained in use until just before the First World War.[29] The long box-framed thatched building on a rubble plinth dated from the late 17th century and incorporated at its east end a house of two bays, its frame infilled with brick. In the 19th century the house was extended east by a bay (since

1 Oxford DNB.
2 GA, D 2597/116/14–16, 22, 28.
3 Turner, *Agric. of Glos.* 54.
4 GA, D 9125/continuation cat. 795.
5 TNA, HO 107/350/6; GA, P 125/CH 4/4.
6 MCA, F 5iii, deed 1271; GA, P 125A/SD 2/1–2.
7 *Kelly's Dir. Glos.* (1889), 825; (1894), 216.
8 OS Map 6", Glos. X.SE. (1883–1924 edns); GA, D 2428/1/17, f. 11; see MCA, H 5ii, bdl. 50, no 22.
9 TNA, RG 13/2422.
10 Ibid. CRES 38/674.
11 Ibid. CRES 36/266.
12 Gethyn-Jones, *Dymock Down the Ages*, 146.
13 *The Oxenhall Anthology* (Oxenhall Parish History Group, 1999), 21–6.
14 Forestry Commission (http://www.forestry.gov.uk/website/ searchall: accessed 7 Dec. 2006).
15 L. Hart, *Once They Lived in Gloucestershire: A Dymock Poets Anthology* (1995), 24.
16 OS Map 1:25,000, SO 63/73 (1982 edn); J. Everard, W. Heselgrave, and D. Langford, *The Management of Broadleaf Woodland in the Forest of Dean* (Forestry Commission, 1994), 9 and app. D.
17 *Nonarum Inquisitiones*, 415.
18 *Inq. p.m. Glos.* 1301–58, 253, 366–7.
19 See G.M. Davies, 'Mills of the River Leadon and Tributaries', *Glos. Soc. Ind. Archaeol. Newsletter* 7 (Apr. 1966), 26–43.
20 MCA, I 6i, bdl. 93, nos 1–2; see GA, P 125A/SD 2/1–2 (no 1532).
21 TNA, E 315/55, pp. 53–6.
22 Ibid. SC 6/1107/2, m. 1; SC 6/1107/3, m. 1.
23 Ibid. SC 2/175/71, rot. 2.
24 Ibid. SC 6/1107/4, m. 2; SC 6/1107/5, m. 1.
25 GA, D 1142/2, abstract of ancient deeds; Dymock ct. book 1704–84, f. 21v.
26 See Taylor, *Map of Glos.* (1777).
27 TNA, CP 25/2/659/30 Chas. II Trin. no 19; CP 25/2/927/11 Anne Easter, no 7. For the estate, above, manors (other estates: Wilton Place).
28 GA, DC/S 114.
29 *Kelly's Dir. Glos.* (1906), 152; (1910), 155; R. and P. Palmer, *Secret River: an exploration of the Leadon Valley* (2004), 37.

raised). The west end of the mill was demolished apparently in the 1930s[1] and the rest of it was given domestic style windows in the 1970s. An oak-framed conservatory was built over part of the original footprint in 2003. A wooden fireplace dated 1634 has been imported.[2] An 18th-century brick building to the south was formerly stables.

Vell Mill, on the river downstream of the village, was known as the mill 'of the field' (*de la felde*) in the 13th century.[3] A copyhold of Little Dymock manor,[4] it had two ponds in the late 17th century[5] and had gone out of use by the time it was the residence of Thomas Hill (d. 1756).[6]

In the east of the parish Ketford mill, standing by the river below the lane leading up to Ryton, was a copyhold of Dymock manor. Probably worked by John Cooper, the only man in Dymock identified as a miller in the muster roll of 1608, it housed two pairs of millstones in the early 18th century.[7] In 1794 it was bought by John Hartland[8] and from the mid 1830s, under John Hartland Gladwin, it was usually let to a tenant. Despite being rebuilt at that time, it was demolished soon after being taken into the Madresfield estate in 1866.[9]

Cut Mill, downstream at the bottom of a tributary valley, belonged to an estate that passed from Robert Malet to John de Peneys and his first wife Rose. John (d. 1283) was succeeded by their daughter Agnes, wife of Ives of Clinton,[10] and her descendants, the Clintons of Eastnor (Herefs.), owned the mill in the mid 16th century.[11] The site was part of Woodchurch Clarke's estate sold in 1657 to Thomas Wall of Lintridge[12] and left by Thomas (d. 1665) to his daughter Catherine.[13] She married Rice Yate of Bromesberrow[14] and Cut Mill served as a farmstead on his successors' estate.[15]

In the west of the parish a mill on the Kempley brook at the Old Grange was powered from a leat starting in Kempley,[16] where in 1531 John Wynniatt, the occupant of Flaxley abbey's grange,[17] was reported for diverting the stream.[18] The mill, later let as part of a farm on the Old Grange estate,[19] stopped working in the later 19th century[20] and its building was used for farm purposes after the First World War.[21] The abbey may have had an earlier mill downstream at the confluence of the Preston brook where a field was called Monk Mill.[22] In the early 18th century there may have been a mill in the north-west below the Leadington, either on the Preston brook or a tributary.[23]

There have been several windmills in Dymock. Thomas Wynniatt and others quitclaimed one to John Wynniatt in 1649.[24] Another stood in the south of the parish by the Newent road in the later 18th century.[25]

INDUSTRY AND CRAFTS

At Bromesberrow Heath, where digging continued on the common in 1812,[26] sand and gravel workings were enlarged in the late 19th century[27] and extensive quarries were later formed. The deeper one, south of the M50 motorway,[28] has been closed and the largest one, north of the motorway, was used as a depot for crushing stone in 2003. Several quarries have been worked in the north of the Leadington.[29] One provided stone for Preston church in the mid 19th century[30] and another that had supplied stone for Eastnor Castle, Ledbury church, and Haffield school was reopened in the mid 1890s by E. Gambier Parry to provide stone for Preston church and a Ledbury institute.[31]

The area around Castle Tump in the south of the parish marks the northern limit of the Newent coalfield. Although a field there was known in 1801 as Coal Pit field[32] and some coal and iron-ore has been mined, the area was, prospecting apart, little touched

---

1 DoE List, Dymock (1987), 5/83.
2 Information from Mr Mason of Farm Mill. The fireplace bears the inits. 'TMB'.
3 BL, Add. MS 18461, f. 83v.
4 GA, D 185/IV/5.
5 Ibid. D 4317/6, ct. papers (Clutterbucks).
6 GDR wills 1792/19; *Reg. of Dymock*, 268.
7 Smith, *Men and Armour*, 60; Worcs. RO, B705:99 (BA 3375), Dymock ct. book 1704–84, f. 10.
8 MCA, H 5ii, bdl. 50, nos 5–7.
9 Ibid. nos 13–14, 22, 25; J 2vi, bdl. 108A, no 25; OS Map 6", Glos. X.SW (1883 edn).
10 *Cal. Inq. p.m.* II, 305.
11 BL, Add. Ch. 24762; TNA, C 142/59, no 72; C 3/48/52; CP 25/2/141/1770/1 Eliz. I Trin. no 3.
12 TNA, CP 25/2/555/1657 Mich. no 40.
13 Ibid. PROB 11/328, ff. 280–1; Bigland, *Glos.* I, 528.
14 GA, D 1142/2, abstract of ancient deeds.
15 Ibid. P 125A/VE 3/2; photocopy 917.
16 OS Maps 6", IX.SE, X.SW (1883 edn).
17 *Military Surv. of Glos. 1522*, 54; *Valor Eccl.* II, 486.
18 Worcs. RO, 705:99 (BA 5540), Kempley and Wilton ct. rolls 1526–68, rot. 4.
19 *Glouc. J.* 16 Nov. 1767; GA, P 125A/SD 2/1–2; G/NE 160/3/1, ff. 63–4.
20 OS Map 6", Glos. X.SW (1883, 1903 edns).
21 GA, SL 417.
22 Ibid. P 125A/SD 2/1–2 (no 319).
23 Ibid. D 2099, Dymock deeds 1730–40.
24 TNA, CP 25/2/553/1649/50 Hil. no 4.
25 Taylor, *Map of Glos.* (1777).
26 Dymock ct. book 1784–1822, cts. 24 Oct. 1803, 19 Oct. 1812.
27 OS Map 6", Glos. X.SE (1883 and 1903 edns).
28 Ibid. Map 1:1,250, SO 7232–7332 (1970 edn).
29 e.g. GA, P 125A/SD 2/1–2 (nos 170–1); OS Map 6", Glos. X.NW (1883 edn).
30 GA, P 256/CW 2/2.
31 E. Gambier Parry, 'Highnam Memoranda' (1902), ff. 254v.–255: a copy of MS is in GA, D 2586; *Ledbury Free Press*, 21 Jan. 1896 (Ledbury intelligence). GA, P 125A/SD 2/1–2 (nos 170–1); OS Map 6", Glos. X.NW (1883 edn)
32 GA, D 897, Dymock deeds 1743–1801; P 125A/SD 2/1–2 (no 1284).

by the coalfield's development in the late 18th and early 19th century.[1]

In the Roman period iron working and the manufacture of copper-alloy objects took place at several sites in Dymock.[2] Smiths were active in the parish in the 13th century and personal names during that period also included those derived from the trades of baker, shoemaker, tailor, and walker or fuller.[3] In 1537 one or more tanners were resident.[4] Excluding a miller, 34 tradesmen were listed in the parish in 1608, among them 7 masons, 5 shoemakers, 4 tailors, 3 butchers, and other usual village craftsmen as well as 2 sawyers. There were also 4 weavers of whom one had a servant[5] and another was later described as a broadweaver.[6] A few weavers lived in the parish in the early 18th century, including a broadweaver at Lintridge.[7] The potmaker recorded in 1608[8] may have worked a kiln operating in Haind Park wood in the 17th century.[9]

There was a distillery in the village in 1696[10] and another near Broom's green in 1785.[11] The Cripps family were distillers and maltsters in the mid 18th century.[12] Thomas Dance was described at his death in 1804 as an eminent maltster and his malthouse at Ryton[13] remained in business in the mid 19th century.[14] In the early 19th century James Thurston and Thomas Forty ran a malting business in the village at High House.[15]

The more usual rural crafts were well represented throughout Dymock in the 18th and 19th centuries and were invariably humble in character.[16] Bricks mostly for local use were made at many places,[17] as at Allums in the mid 18th century[18] and at Tiller's Green in the mid 19th,[19] and there was a new limekiln at Oaksbottom in 1811.[20] In the mid 19th century there was a timber yard in Dymock village and a builder's yard just outside it.[21] Several parishioners made laths, hurdles, and mopsticks and another was a basket maker. Members of the Sadler family at Broom's Green and Greenway were nailers and in the 1830s a pump maker was recorded.[22] In 1851 just over 100 tradesmen and craftsmen representing about 20 different trades were scattered around the parish.[23] Blacksmiths operated at several places, including the village and Bromesberrow Heath, in the 1870s.[24] In 1901 a house-building business in the village provided a little employment. Thatching, hoop making, and brush and broom making were among the traditional crafts to survive into the 20th century[25] and there were several bakeries, one of them at Hallwood Green, in the 1920s.[26] The only craftsmen listed in the parish in 1931 were a blacksmith, a builder, a carpenter, and a wheelwright. In 1939 there was a small sauce factory in the village.[27] In 1990 a saddler, a basket maker, and a jigsaw maker ran small businesses in the parish, several builders, plumbers, electricians, and fencing contractors were based there, and a bakery was in production.[28] A garden furniture maker, who moved to Gamage Hall from London in 2001,[29] ran one of the parish's many and varied small businesses in 2003.[30]

MARKETS AND FAIRS

In 1222 the justiciar Hubert de Burgh ordered the sheriff to hold a Thursday market and a fair on 14 September on the royal manor until the king came of age.[31] Henry III took control of his estates a year or so later, although he did not declare himself of age until 1227,[32] and the fortunes of the market and fair, if any, are unrecorded. Although market centres were established near by at Newent and Ledbury,[33] the

---

1 D. Bick, *The Mines of Newent and Ross* (Newent, 1987), 7, 53–6.
2 E. Gethyn-Jones, 'Roman Dymock – A Personal Record', *Trans. BGAS* 119 (1991), 94, 96; 'Archaeological Review 1993', ibid. 112 (1994), 199; 'Archaeological Review 1995', ibid. 114 (1996), 172; 'Roman Dymock: archaeological investigations 1995–2002', ibid. 125 (2007), 131–245.
3 *Flaxley Cart.* pp. 128–9, 176–7; BL, Add. MS 18461, ff. 79v.–81, 86 and v.
4 Worcs. RO, 705:99 (BA 5540), Kempley and Wilton ct. rolls 1526–68, rot. 13.
5 Smith, *Men and Armour*, 58–60.
6 GA, D 2464/T 1; GDR wills 1635/58.
7 GA, D 1604/T 1, deed 22 Oct. 1746; D 2957/116/6; Worcs. RO, 705:99 (BA 3375), Dymock deeds 1633–1811, deed 25 Oct. 1715.
8 Smith, *Men and Armour*, 59.
9 *Glos. Soc. Ind. Arch. Newsletter*, no 5 (July 1965), 16.
10 GA, D 185/IV/13.
11 Dymock ct. book 1784–1822, ct. 17 Oct. 1785.
12 Dymock ct. book 1704–84, f. 46 and v.; GDR wills 1773/179.
13 GA, P 125/IN 1/11.
14 Ibid. P 125A/SD 2/1–2 (no 1098); D 9149, Dymock deeds.
15 GDR wills 1826/79.
16 Dymock ct. books 1704–1822; TNA, HO 107/350/6–7; HO 107/1960; RG 9/1761.
17 See GA, P 125A/SD 2/1–2 (nos 1123, 1344, 1453, and 1624); Gambier Parry, 'Highnam Memoranda', f. 255.
18 GA, D 4317/6, ct. papers (The Moors).
19 A. Watkins, 'A "Cottage" Pottery near Kempley', *Trans. Woolhope Naturalists' Field Club* (1927–9), 146.
20 GA, D 1272, Dymock deeds 1794–1885.
21 Ibid. P 125A/SD 2/1–2 (nos 1497, 1538).
22 Ibid. P 125/CH 4/4.
23 TNA, HO 107/1960.
24 Ibid. RG 10/2608; RG 10/2609; *Kelly's Dir. Glos.* (1879), 639.
25 TNA, RG 13/2422.
26 Information from Mabel McCulloch of Hallwood Green.
27 *Kelly's Dir. Glos.* (1931), 158–9; (1939), 159.
28 *Village Voices: Dymock Parish Appraisal 1990* (1991: copy in Glos. Colln. RR 116.9), 5, 16–17.
29 *Forester*, 27 Sept. 2001.
30 'Dymock Parish Development Plan Spring 2003', 43.
31 *Rot. Litt. Claus.* I, 507.
32 M. Powicke, *The Thirteenth Century 1216–1307* (Oxford Hist. of England, 1962), 24–5, 38; see above, manors (Dymock manor).
33 H.P.R. Finberg, 'An Early Reference to the Welsh Cattle Trade', *Agricultural History Review* 2 (1954), 12–14. See above, Newent, econ. hist. (markets and fairs).

lord of the manor claimed the right to hold a market in 1287.[1] There is no evidence that Dymock had a regular market and fair after that.

DISTRIBUTIVE AND SERVICE TRADES

A family of mercers held land in Dymock in the 13th and 14th centuries[2] and a resident was presented in 1397 as a common usurer.[3] In 1576 a parishioner was presented for selling meat on Sundays and on religious festivals[4] and the muster roll of 1608 included a chapman and a horse rider.[5]

A haberdasher lived in Dymock in 1712.[6] In the later 18th century there was at least one shop in the parish[7] and in the mid 19th several shopkeepers, including two grocers, lived in the village and there were shopkeepers at Bromesberrow Heath, Broom's Green, and Ryton.[8] There was a co-operative store in 1876[9] and Tiller's Green, Hallwood Green, and the Leadington were among places with shops in 1901.[10] Post offices were opened in Dymock village by 1851[11] and at Greenway and Bromesberrow Heath later in the century.[12] Postal services employed a handful of men in 1901[13] and Dymock had its own sorting office until 1962.[14] There were shops at several places in 1939[15] but there was only one shop, in the village, in 1990.[16] Both the village and Bromesberrow Heath had post offices in 2002.

A cider merchant lived in Dymock in the mid 18th century[17] and a succession of excise officers was stationed there by 1770 and until at least 1785.[18] Although some farmers sold directly in Bristol, at the end of the century the cider and perry trade was largely controlled by a few merchants meeting at Ledbury.[19] A cider merchant living in Dymock in 1859[20] ran a business that continued in the trade until the early 20th century.[21] In 1775 the heir to the Ockington estate was an attorney in Dymock.[22] In 1841 a veterinary surgeon lived on Bromesberrow heath.[23]

The opening of the Hereford and Gloucester canal in 1798 fostered new commercial activity in Dymock. Goods were handled at a wharf next to the village and in the mid 19th century there was also a wharf at the Anchor inn on the Leominster road and another on the road west of Greenway.[24] In the 1810s stone was delivered by canal for road repairs[25] and in 1841 the Anchor's landlord was one of two coal dealers living by the canal.[26] A handful of families worked as boatmen[27] but in 1871, when the only boatmen recorded in Dymock were two women in the village, canal trade was of little significance.[28] The railway replacing the canal in the 1880s brought jobs. In 1901 the staff of the village station included two clerks and two porters as well as the station master, and a signalman and several platelayers also lived in the parish.[29] The station handled local produce, including cider and perry, and during the daffodil season special trains brought pickers and visitors to the area.[30]

On the roads three men offered carrying services from Dymock to Ledbury and Gloucester on market days and one of them a service to Ross-on-Wye in the mid 19th century. In 1856 there was also a bus service from the Plough inn to the Gloucester and Ledbury markets and a mail coach running daily between the two towns called at the inn.[31] Although a carrier operated between Bromesberrow Heath and Gloucester in 1885, fewer carrying businesses ran out of Dymock in the later 19th century. There was a weekly service to Ledbury in 1906.[32] In the early days of the railway horses and coaches were available for hire at the Beauchamp Arms (formerly the Plough).[33] In 1939 a bus proprietor was resident and the village had a petrol station.[34] There were two petrol stations there in 2002, one with a car workshop on the site of an old smithy at the corner of the Ledbury road.[35]

---

1 *Plac. de Quo Warr.* 259.
2 BL, Add. MS 18461, ff. 80–1.
3 A.T. Bannister, 'Visitation Returns of Diocese of Hereford in 1397', *EHR* 44 (1929), 453.
4 GDR vol. 40, f. 249v.
5 Smith, *Men and Armour*, 59.
6 Worcs. RO, BA 892/8, p. 218.
7 GA, P 63/IN 1/2, burial 12 Jan. 1799.
8 TNA, HO 107/1960.
9 GA P 125/IN 4/19.
10 TNA, RG 13/2422.
11 Ibid. HO 107/1960.
12 *Kelly's Dir. Glos.* (1885), 449; (1897), 147.
13 TNA, RG 13/2422.
14 Gethyn-Jones, *Dymock Down the Ages*, 145.
15 *Kelly's Dir. Glos.* (1939), 58, 159.
16 *Village Voices*, 16; see Gethyn-Jones, *Dymock Down the Ages*, 149.
17 *Glouc. J.* 27 Apr. 1772.
18 *Reg. of Dymock*, 220, 274, 281; GA, P 125/VE 2/1, f. (at end) 119; Q/REl 1, Botloe hundred, Ryeland division 1776, 1777.
19 Turner, *Agric. of Glos.* 53; see Marshall, *Rural Econ. of Glos.* II, 347–8.
20 GA, P 125/CH 4/4.
21 *Kelly's Dir. Glos.* (1885), 449; (1902), 151.
22 MCA, I 4i, bdl. 77, no 11.
23 TNA, HO 107/350/6.
24 GA, P 125A/SD 2/1–2 (nos 1554, 586, 302).
25 Ibid. P 125/SU 2/2.
26 TNA, HO 107/350/6–7.
27 GA, P 125/CH 4/4; TNA, HO 107/1960; RG 9/1761.
28 TNA, RG 10/2609–10.
29 Ibid. RG 13/2422.
30 Clark, *The Muse Colony*, 9–10; GA, D 7799/1.
31 *Kelly's Dir. Glos.* (1856), 281–2; *Hunt's Glouc., Heref. and Worc. Dir.* (1847), 215.
32 *Kelly's Dir. Glos.* (1885), 449; (1906), 152.
33 GA, D 5292, 29 Oct. 1898; MCA, E 1iii, 6.
34 *Kelly's Dir. Glos.* (1939), 159.
35 OS Map 6", Glos. X.SW (1883 edn).

Domestic service continued to provide a number of jobs in the larger houses and their grounds in the early 20th century.[1] A nursing home opened at Hillash in 1988[2] had a staff of over 30 in 1990[3] and continued there in 2004. The Old Grange was used for a time from the mid 1970s for a business selling stoves[4] and in the 1990s a golf centre was established there.[5]

LOCAL GOVERNMENT

Following Hubert de Burgh's instruction in 1222 to the sheriff to hold a market and fair in Dymock[6] some tenants on the royal manor evidently enjoyed liberties denied to others. In 1226 residents described as *probi hominess* were granted the manor at a fee farm of £33 6s. 8d.[7] and in an extent of the manor compiled some years later 66 holdings on it were styled 'burgages'.[8] Several individual burgages were recorded[9] and two tenants of Flaxley abbey held half burgages.[10] No comprehensive grant of liberties was apparently issued and in 1244 or 1245, when its tenants were in arrears with their payment, the manor was granted to Morgan of Caerleon at a fee farm of £26 13s. 4d.[11] Among the favoured tenants may have been the occupants of the port lands recorded much later in various parts of the parish.[12]

MANORIAL GOVERNMENT

Manor courts were held for both Dymock and Little Dymock in the 13th century.[13] The Dymock court exercised view of frankpledge in the parish[14] and only Flaxley tithing, the manor of Flaxley abbey, was not in that jurisdiction.[15] The abbey presumably had its own court but later owners of the Old Grange do not appear to have held a court there after acquiring Little Dymock manor in the late 16th century.[16] Newent priory convened a separate court for the rectory estate in the early 15th century.[17]

The main business of the Dymock and Little Dymock courts became the issuing of licences for the disposal of copyhold land.[18] The Dymock court, which Richard Howell and Richard Guy held as trustees in the years immediately after Edward Pye's death in 1692,[19] customarily met twice a year, after Michaelmas and Hocktide, in general session and every three weeks to deal with matters including pleas of debt and trespass.[20] The Hocktide or May court was held until at least 1623 but by the later 17th century there was one general session a year, in the autumn,[21] and the court convened occasionally to deal with tenurial business.[22] Attempts in 1783 and 1788 to revive the May court failed because too few people were present to empanel a jury. The autumn court was attended by the four tithingmen chosen by rota to represent Woodend (Gamage Hall), Ockington, Ryton (Ryeland), and Leadington. It dealt with encroachments on waste land and with obstructions on lanes and paths. It also heard reports of neglected lanes and bridges and their railings and from the later 18th century it occasionally ordered individuals and sometimes the surveyors of the highways to make repairs. In 1782 the lady of the manor was presented for replacing stiles on the way from the church towards Ledbury with gates. The court formally elected constables for the parish's three divisions and it fined a man for not serving as Woodend's constable in 1769. The constable chosen for Ryeland in 1780 appealed his election.[23] In the mid 18th century the lord of the manor allowed the stocks and pound to fall into disrepair and in 1762 it was reported that there were no stocks. The court chamber was also in disrepair in 1755. In 1796 stocks and a whipping post as well as the pound all needed repairing. The court's bailiff acted as cryer in the early 19th century.

In addition to tenurial matters the Little Dymock

---

1 TNA, HO 107/350/360/6–7; RG 10/2608; RGRG 13/2422.
2 Information from Mr. T. Huckerby.
3 *Village Voices*, 5.
4 *Glos. and Avon Life*, July 1985, 29; *Citizen*, 24 Sept.1986.
5 Local information.
6 *Rot. Litt. Claus.* I, 507; above, econ. hist. (markets and fairs).
7 *Pat.* 1225–32, 61; see *Cal. Pat.* 1232–47, 2.
8 *Cal. Inq. Misc.* I, 151.
9 BL, Add. MS 18461, ff. 89v.–90v.
10 *Flaxley Cart.* p. 177.
11 *Abbrev. Rot. Orig.* I, 7–8.
12 *Cal. Pat.* 1549–51, 101; TNA, E 310/14/54, f. 44; MCA, I 6i, bdl. 93A, nos. 7, 15; Worcs. RO, B705:99 (BA 3375), Dymock ct. book 1704–84, f. 9 and v.; GA, D 2079/II 2/T 2, deed 3 Feb. 1857.
13 *Inq. p.m. Glos.* 1301–58, 168, 253, 366–7; 1359–1413, 54–5; *Glos. Feet of Fines 1199–1299*, p. 176.
14 GA, D 2464/T 1; D 185/IV/7–9, 21.

15 Below, this section; for the tithings, above, introd. (boundaries and divisions).
16 GA, D 214/T 17, deed 3 Nov. 1630, refers to the ct. of Richard and Jane Unett in 1600.
17 Herefs. RO, E 12/G/3.
18 Bigland, *Glos.* I, 526–7 n.; TNA, C 78/1453, no 5; see GA, D 2464/T 1; D 789; D 185/IV/5.
19 GA, D 185/IV/11; D 897, misc. deeds 1698–1825; MCA, J 6i, bdl. 99, no 24; see TNA, PROB 11/416, f. 337 and v.
20 Bigland, *Glos.* I, 526 n.
21 GA, D 789; D 1142/4; D 185/IV/7–9.
22 The rest of this para. is based on ct. books for the period 1704–84 and 1784–1822 in Worcs. RO, B705:99 (BA 3375) and 705:99 (BA 5540) respectively.
23 GA, Q/SR 1780 A, no 7A; B, no 9B. For the divisions, above, introd. (boundaries and divisions); below (parochial govt.).

court in the late 17th and the 18th century was concerned with encroachments on waste land and on lanes and paths and with the cleansing of ditches.[1] The meetings of the Dymock and Little Dymock courts became less regular in the early 19th century as their role in the sale and mortgage of land decreased.[2] The Dymock court, which had continued its assemblies in the church house after it became the workhouse in the mid 18th century,[3] met in general session in 1853.[4] The Little Dymock court, which had met at the Harrow in the 1760s and 1770s, was held at Gamage Hall, its traditional meeting place, until at least 1877.[5]

PAROCHIAL GOVERNMENT

The system of government operated by the parish vestry was in place by the early 17th century. Each of the parish's divisions or hamlets, namely Woodend, Ryeland, and Leadington, had its own overseer of the poor, surveyor of the highways, and constable. Householders held the offices for a year in rotation and only occasionally served out of turn or appointed a deputy in their stead. A rota had long applied in the selection of Dymock's two churchwardens and three sidesmen.[6]

The rates granted by the vestry could vary from one division to another and in the 18th century one churchwarden accounted for the church rates from Ryeland and the other for those from Woodend and Leadington.[7] The vestry took initiatives to enforce law and order, in 1764 offering a reward for the arrest of a thief and in 1786 ordering the constables to help the churchwardens prosecute people playing unlawful games on Sundays. In 1777 it authorized the churchwardens to offer rewards for the destroying of mad dogs and in 1824 it determined that no one with a dog was to receive parish relief.[8]

The business of the elected council established for the parish in 1894 included the upkeep of Wintour's green and from 1907 to 1940 was conducted under the chairmanship of A.H. Chew. The council obtained electricity for street lighting in Dymock village by agreement with the Shropshire, Worcestershire, & Staffordshire Electric Power Co. in 1931.[9]

Poor Relief

In the mid 1660s the parish's three divisions between them regularly assisted 28 people with weekly payments, paid a few house rents, and gave other help to the poor according to need. The number of families receiving weekly assistance was similar in 1700[10] and in 1750. The burden of relief was considerable and in 1730 several landowners mounted a challenge to rating valuations.[11] The dispute went to arbitration and a new assessment was made the following year.[12] In the early 1760s about 100 families, a third of the population, were dependent in one way or another on the parish. A plan to build new poorhouses was abandoned in 1753 because of the cost and the church house was later used as a poorhouse. Sixteen people were ordered to leave the parish in 1755 and the vestry instructed the overseers to remove people without legal settlement in 1769, 1779, and 1782. In the mid 18th century medical services were obtained from doctors from Ledbury and elsewhere. Children were usually bound apprentice to local farmers, the choice of master being determined either by rota or by ballot. For a few years from 1757 some people were set to work spinning flax and hemp — men who couldn't spin were to be employed on highway maintenance — and in 1758 it was planned to lodge the poor for a year in the Ledbury workhouse. Single men and women without work were instructed in 1764 to find employment.[13]

In 1769 the parish opened a workhouse in the church house and appointed a salaried master to take charge of the poor. The workhouse quickly proved a major drain on the parish's finances and in 1770, in what was not the last move to check expenditure on relief, the vestry established a committee to control spending. In 1772 the dispensing of relief was contracted out for £158 but the following year it was again entrusted to a salaried official in charge of the workhouse. The workhouse had 40 residents in 1774. In 1775 the choice of a woman as workhouse manager was quashed and the overseers for Ryeland and Leadington contracted to administer relief for a year for £134, one of them serving as the workhouse master. The administration of relief remained contracted out to local men on an annual basis until 1796. In 1790 a subscription was paid to the Gloucester infirmary and 264 parishioners were inoculated against smallpox. With the failure of the wheat harvest in 1795 the vestry ordered bakers not to make fine white bread and corn was sold to the poor at a reduced price.[14]

From 1796 the vestry employed a resident master of the workhouse acting also as assistant overseer. John Hill, a parishioner, fulfilled those duties for over thirty years[15] and the parish continued to engage

---

1 GA, D 4317/6, ct. papers.
2 Ibid. D 1142/4; D 892; D 185/IV/7–10, 16, 21; D 897; D 4317/6; D 1618; Dymock ct. books 1704–1822.
3 GA, P 125/VE 2/1, ff. (at end) 89–90; VE 2/3, vestry min. 13 Apr. 1836; MCA, J 2ii, bdl. 103, no 1.
4 GA, P 125A, deeds 1782–1990.
5 Ibid. D 4317/6; see Bigland, *Glos.* I, 527.
6 GA, P 125/VE 3/1; for the constables, Dymock ct. books 1704–1822.
7 GA, P 125/VE 2/1; CW 2/8.
8 Ibid. VE 2/1–2.
9 Ibid. P 125A, par. council min. book 1894–1949.
10 Ibid. P 125/OV 2/2.
11 Ibid. VE 2/1.
12 Ibid. P 125A/VE 3/2.
13 Ibid. P 125/VE 2/1.
14 Ibid. VE 2/1–2.
15 Ibid. VE 2/2.

a workhouse master until it ceased to be directly responsible for its poor in 1835. In the early 1830s, when another man receiving a salary accounted for the poor rate of the three divisions, just over 30 people received out-relief.[1] The number of inmates in the workhouse was 37 in 1803 and declined from 35 in 1813 to 28 in 1815.[2] The taking of apprentices, which some farmers avoided by paying a fine,[3] was shared proportionately between wealthier and poorer farmers in the early 19th century; between 1810 and 1835 well over 50 children were articled to local farmers.[4]

The cost of relief rose from £173 in 1776 to £504 in 1803 when 4 persons other than those in the workhouse had regular help and 14 occasional help. By 1813 the cost had risen to £739 and 32 persons outside the workhouse received regular help and 102 occasional help. Fewer people were helped in 1815 when the cost was £545.[5] The cost was lower in the later 1820s and the early 1830s, save in 1832 when it was unusually high at £603.[6] Dymock became part of the Newent poor-law union in 1835[7] and the church house containing the parish workhouse was sold in 1838.[8]

Highway Repair

Each division looked after some of the lanes and bridges in its area and Leadington and Woodend thus had responsibility for the repair of the village street.[9] In 1790 and 1791 the vestry assigned half of the highway rates in Woodend and Ryeland to maintaining their respective sections of the improved turnpike road across the Leadon valley and in 1796 it additionally dedicated half of the rates in Leadington to the repair of the road through Windcross towards Much Marcle.[10] As Ryeland's surveyor of the highways John Thackwell increased expenditure considerably in the years 1816–18, when parts of the road at Bromesberrow Heath and Broom's Green were repaired. The surveyor in office from 1822 supervised much work in the division, including repairs to Ketford bridge[11] which was also maintained by Pauntley parish.[12] A subsidy to Kempley parish, a major item of expenditure for the Woodend ratepayers in 1819, was presumably for improvements to the chief road between the two parishes.[13]

Each division had its own surveyor until 1836 when, the vestry having failed to act, the Newent magistrates appointed a paid surveyor for the whole parish. The new surveyor, whose work was monitored by the vestry, was dismissed in 1843 and the vestry reverted to the appointment of a surveyor for each division. A new road to Hallwood Green remained unfinished in 1845 because the purchase money for part of the old road had not been received. In 1863 responsibility for the maintenance of the parish roads passed to the new Newent Highway Board on which Dymock was represented by two waywardens.[14]

SOCIAL HISTORY

SOCIAL STRUCTURE

In the mid 11th century Dymock's community included, in addition to a priest, 4 radknights, owing riding or escort services to the king as their lord, 11 freedmen, and 52 peasant farmers.[15] Although some inhabitants had burgage holdings in the mid 13th century, it remained essentially an agrarian society. Labour services were required on some estates but in the later Middle Ages both free and customary tenants owed only cash rents.[16] Of 63 parishioners assessed for tax in 1327 at least seven were rated at over 6s.: they included Alice Habgood (10s. 6d.) and William the smith (*faber*) (7s. 1d.). Thirteen people were assessed at between 2s. 0d. and 3s. 4d. and a bare majority for less than 2s. The presence of William of Pembridge (8s.),[17] lord of Little Dymock,[18] is significant as the owners of the other manors were non-resident throughout the Middle Ages.

In 1522, when perhaps a score of prosperous yeoman farmers lived in the parish, the wealthiest inhabitant by far, with goods valued at £40, was John Wynniatt, the agent of Flaxley abbey. Nine other men with goods valued at over £10 included the landowner William Bridges and members of the Bradford, Gamond, Hankins, Hill, Wills, and Wilton farming families. Members of the Cam and Weale families were among thirteen men with goods worth

---

1   GA, P 125/CW 2/1.
2   *Poor Law Abstract, 1804*, 172–3; *1818*, 146–7.
3   GA, P 125/CW 2/8.
4   Ibid. OV 4/1–2.
5   *Poor Law Abstract, 1804*, 172–3; *1818*, 146–7.
6   *Poor Law Returns* (1830–1), 66; (1835), 64.
7   *Poor Law Com. 2nd Rep.* p. 523.
8   MCA, J 2ii, bdl. 103, no 1.
9   Dymock ct. book 1784–1822.
10 GA, P 125/VE 2/2.
11 Ibid. SU 2/2.
12 Ibid. Q/SO 1, f. 106.
13 Ibid. P 125/VE 2/2.
14 Ibid. VE 2/3.
15 *Domesday Book* (Rec. Com.), I, 164.
16 Above, econ. hist.; below, local govt.
17 *Glos. Subsidy Roll, 1327*, 5.
18 Above, manors.

more than £5. Another 39 men had goods assessed at £2 or more and 25 at £1 or more.[1] The owners of the main estates usually remained non-resident until the late 16th or early 17th century. Among 166 Dymock men listed in 1608 were 30 yeomen, 20 husbandmen, 37 labourers, 36 tradesmen, and 28 servants. Six yeomen and five husbandmen were employed by the landowner Giles Forster. Most of the servants worked for one or other of the yeomen, eight of them for John Wynniatt[2] whose acquisition, by marriage, of the Old Grange estate established his family among the few resident landed gentry.[3] The yeomen took charge of parish government and during the Commonwealth period, when landowners Robert Holmes and Thomas Wall were among local magistrates conducting civil marriages, John Cam the younger acted as civil registrar.[4] Holmes was one of the Gloucestershire members nominated to the 'Barebones' Parliament' of 1653.[5] The parliamentary franchise enjoyed by some copyholders was confirmed following the county contest of 1776.[6]

In the late 17th century the local gentry, leading farmers, and landowners lived outside Dymock village with the exception of the Winters, who had their home at the White House.[7] In 1672, when 126 out of 172 householders in the parish had a single hearth, 18 had five hearths or more. The largest numbers belonged to Evan Seys at Boyce Court (13) and William Wall at Great Lintridge (10) followed by the heads of the Winter (9), Cam (8), and Wynniatt (7) families and John Holmes (7).[8] Seys was replaced as lord of Dymock manor by Edward Pye, a West Indies merchant, and he and his successors, the Chamberlaynes, made substantial alterations to Boyce Court.[9] In the early 18th century some 40 freeholders lived in Dymock.[10] Farming families, many long-established, continued along with the few gentry to dominate the parish and some joined a subscription started in 1785 for a local school.[11] Poor labourers made up a substantial part of the population. In 1672 some 68 householders were poor enough to be exempted from hearth tax[12] and in the 1760s about a third of the population, 100 families representing 359 individuals, were dependent in one way or another on the parish.[13]

The oldest surviving memorials of parishioners on the church walls[14] are small monuments to the landowners Thomas Wall (d. 1665) and John Wynniatt (d. 1670).[15] Robert Winter (d. 1719), part owner of the rectory[16] and the founder of a clothing charity,[17] was commemorated on a more prominent tablet and William Hankins (d. 1771) of Greenway House on a substantial monument made by W.H. Stephens of Worcester.[18] The memorial to Richard Hill (d. 1772) of Edulus Place (Pitt House Farm) displays heraldry reflecting his family's pretensions as country gentlemen.[19] His son Richard (d. 1794) had a small deer park next to the farmhouse[20] and played a prominent role in the opening of a village school in 1786.[21]

Several landowners and farmers rebuilt or substantially enlarged their houses during the century.[22] Particularly prosperous were the Cams. The rebuilding of their main house (later Wilton Place) was presumably commissioned by William (d. 1767), a London merchant[23] who is commemorated by the largest monument in the churchyard.[24] His daughter Ann, whose inheritance included land bought by Joseph Cam (d. 1729), a London haberdasher,[25] became lady of Dymock manor on buying Boyce Court in 1769[26] and, although she continued to live in London,[27] was possibly in Dymock at her death in 1790.[28] Part of her large fortune was used to provide a new village school[29] and a family memorial in the church was altered to give pride of place on it to her.[30]

Leading families in the 19th century included the

---

1 *Military Surv. of Glos. 1522*, 54–6; for John Wynniatt, see *Valor Eccl.* II, 486.
2 Smith, *Men and Armour*, 58–60.
3 Above, manors (Old Grange manor).
4 *Reg. of Dymock*, pp. xix–xx, 125–33.
5 Williams, *Parl. Hist. of Glos.* 54–5. Robert was also a local magistrate in the mid 1650s: *Reg. of Dymock*, 127, 129.
6 Worcs. RO, 705:99 (BA 5540), Dymock ct. book 1784–1822; Williams, *Parl. Hist. of Glos.* 67.
7 TNA, PROB 11/323, ff. 328–9; Atkyns, *Glos.* 394.
8 TNA, E 179/247/14, rott. 35d.–36; for Margaret Winter, ibid. PROB 11/323, ff. 328–9,
9 Above, manors (Dymock manor; other estates: Boyce Ct.).
10 Atkyns, *Glos.* 396.
11 GA, P 125/CH 4/1, 5, 7.
12 TNA, E 179/247/14, rott. 35d.–36.
13 GA, P 125/VE 2/1.
14 The monuments are recorded in Bigland, *Glos.* I, 528–9 in their early positions.
15 See above, manors (other estates: Lintridge; Old Grange manor).
16 See ibid. (other estates).
17 Below (charities for the poor).
18 Verey and Brooks, *Glos.* II, 346.
19 See F. Were, 'Notes on Heraldry seen at Spring Meeting', *Trans. BGAS* 31 (1908), 284.
20 GA, D 1272, Dymock deeds 1736–1901; *Glouc. J.* 20 Apr. 1795. For the Hills, above, manors (other estates: Pitt House farm).
21 Below (education: before 1826).
22 e.g. Hillash and Greenway House: see above, settlement (bldgs.: outlying farms).
23 Above, manors (other estates: Wilton Place).
24 Situated at E. end of the ch.
25 Above, manors (other estates: Great Netherton, Wilton Place); below, Kempley, manor (other estates: Saycell's farm).
26 Above, manors.
27 Rudder, *Glos.* 410.
28 GA, P 125/IN 1/11.
29 Below (education: after 1826).
30 Bigland, *Glos.* I, 529, records the monument before the alteration and gives the year of Joseph Cam's death as 1726. For a copy of Ann's portrait, Gethyn-Jones, *Dymock Down the Ages*, pl. 11.

Thackwells,[1] John Thackwell (d. 1829) being active in parish life.[2] The Drummonds, also newcomers, enlarged Boyce Court in the early 19th century,[3] and in the mid 19th century Boyce Court and Wilton Place along with the Old Grange, still an occasional residence of the Wynniatt family, were the main country houses in Dymock.[4] The grounds of Boyce Court and the Old Grange included ponds with boat houses at the end of the century.[5] In the mid 19th century, when there were some 50 or 60 farmers in Dymock, the population was made up largely of the families of farm labourers, unskilled workers, and tradesmen living often in outlying communities or scattered cottages. Among the farmers, several of them substantial landowners in their own right, about a score retained one or two domestic servants. Several people were in service in the village with the vicar's family and others with local tradesmen.[6]

From the mid 19th century the ranks of the landed and officer class were swelled by incomers, some with civil service backgrounds and some as tenants, taking up residence in the smarter houses and staffing them with domestic servants. Hillash, which was acquired by Thomas Holbrook, a naval captain, in 1852,[7] was the home of Stanley Napier Raikes in the late 1860s and both he and Edmund Story, then of Upham House and formerly of the Madras civil service, joined the Wynniatts and Drummonds and farming families such as the Hills and Thurstons in sponsoring events and treats for local residents and children.[8] Chief among Dymock's patrons in the later 19th and early 20th century were the 6th and 7th Earls Beauchamp, lords of Dymock manor who lived at Madresfield (Worcs.).[9] The church bells were rung to mark events in their lives[10] and their tenants, like those at Kempley, joined in celebrations marking the future 7th earl's birth in 1872 and his coming of age in 1893.[11] The 6th earl gave land for an enlargement of Wintour's green[12] and parishioners subscribed to a memorial to him placed in the window of the church's south chapel in 1893.[13] The 7th earl provided a building near the church for the use of a rifle club in 1906[14] and a piece of his land was allotments in 1910.[15] In the Bromesberrow Heath area the landowner William Charles Henry (d. 1892) of Haffield, in Ledbury (Herefs.), made provision for church services and schooling and founded clothing and coal clubs.[16]

In the early 20th century there were six country houses, including Greenway House, with resident servants. Among the population in 1901 were c.40 farmers, of whom 25 employed labourers and 12, notably Henry Hill at the Old Rock and Samuel Bennion at Rosehill, also had domestic servants living with them. The vicar's household included a governess and three women in service. A handful of businessmen and women, most of them resident in the village, provided jobs for non-family members.[17] The continuing involvement of landowners and farmers in local government was exemplified in the work of A.H. Chew (d. 1947),[18] a member of the parish council from its formation in 1894[19] and also of the rural district and county councils.[20]

In the mid 20th century gentry families disposed of their land and eventually left Dymock, the Deane-Drummonds in 1935 and the Thackwells in 1947.[21] The Wynniatts' connexion with Dymock ended with the death of Ernest Wynniatt Husey in 1958.[22] Although there continued to be many farmers, in the later 20th century the numbers of labourers and traditional craftsmen dwindled[23] and outsiders bought unwanted farm dwellings for their homes.[24] New housing became available, particularly in Dymock village and Bromesberrow Heath, and at the end of the century three quarters of the population lived in their own property.[25] Among the few people living in tied accommodation were the farming tenants of the county council but most farmers in the early 21st century owned their farms, with the Bennions owning most land.[26]

---

1 Above, manors (other estates: Wilton Place).
2 Below (education: before 1826); above, local govt. (parochial govt.: highway repair).
3 Above, manors (other estates: Boyce Ct.).
4 See TNA, HO 107/1960; RG 9/1761.
5 OS Maps 1:2,500, Glos. X.13 (1902 edn); XVII.1 (1903 edn).
6 *Census*, 1851: TNA, HO 107/1960.
7 GA, D 2079/II 2/T 4; see TNA, RG 9/1761.
8 GA, P 125/MI 17 (par. mags. Sept. and Oct. 1867); *Kelly's Dir. Glos.* (1870), 540; TNA, RG 10/2608.
9 GA, P 125/MI 17 (par. mag. Sept. 1867); IN 1/21, f. 52. For the earls' estate, above, manors (Dymock manor).
10 GA, P 125/IN 4/19, 20 Feb. 1872, 5 July 1876; IN 1/21, ff. 39, 50.
11 Ibid. IN 4/19, 6 Sept. 1872; MCA, P 1, no 4; see below, Kempley, social hist. (social structure).
12 GA, D 7322 (par. mag. Aug. 1882).
13 Ibid. P 125/IN 1/18, pp. 282, 284; VE 2/3.
14 Ibid. D 2428/1/1/17, f. 23; D 2299/5385; SL 310. The date is on the bldg.
15 GA, D 2428/1/1/17, f. 10.
16 Ibid. P 125/IN 1/18, p. 232; see below (education: after 1826); religious hist.
17 *Census*, 1901; TNA, RG 13/2422.
18 See Dymock par. council, par. meeting min. book, passim. For Chew, see above, manors (other estates: Callow farm).
19 GA, P 125A, par. council min. book 1894–1949.
20 *Who's Who in Glos.* (1934), 44–5.
21 Gethyn-Jones, *Dymock Down the Ages*, 100–1.
22 Ibid. 91.
23 See above, econ. hist.
24 See Theodora C. Reeves, 'History of Little Marcle and of Preston Parish' (1972: typescript in Glos. Colln. 36709), 2.
25 *Village Voices: Dymock Parish Appraisal 1990* (1991: copy in Glos. Colln. RR 116.9), 6.
26 Information from Mrs Jennifer Thick, sec. to Dymock par. council.

Boyce Court was reduced in size in 1935 to serve as a farmhouse[1] and of the other large houses Wilton Place was divided into flats by the mid 1960s[2] and Hillash was converted as a nursing home in the 1980s.[3] Greenway House, Upham House, and the Old Grange remained private dwellings.

CHARITIES FOR THE POOR

A custom for the rector, presumably in the person of the prior of Newent, to give the poor two bushels of mixed corn each week had been discontinued by the later 1370s.[4] By will proved 1530 Sir John Bridges, a London alderman, stipulated that future occupants of Boyce Court should give the poor the bread and ale intended for people attending his obit if none other than his kin was present.[5]

At his death in 1647 William Skinner of Ledbury, the chancellor of Hereford diocese,[6] apparently gave a rent charge of 4s. a year for Dymock's poor[7] but no record of the charity's distribution has been found.[8] William Wall by will proved 1717 left a rent charge of 20s. from a cottage in the village street for a bread charity[9] and William Weale, a London haberdasher, by nuncupative will proved 1719 left £100 for a corn charity.[10] A charity that Robert Winter by will proved 1719 endowed with a rent charge of £30 clothed 10 men and 10 women each Christmas.[11] Thomas Murrell by will proved 1738 left £10 for cash payments to 10 widows on the feast of St. Thomas (21 December).[12]

William Wall's charity was perhaps never distributed and the cottage providing its income had been pulled down by the 1750s.[13] William Weale's charity, which was distributed at Christmas using £5 given annually by his family from its land at Ockington, lapsed c.1772.[14] The recipients of Robert Winter's charity were required by its founder to attend church in their new clothes on Christmas day and from 1769 those clothes were distinguished by blue capes on the men's coats and blue cuffs on the women's gowns.[15] Thomas Murrell's charity, the principal of which had been doubled by 1807,[16] benefited between 14 and 20 widows in the following years[17] and it again paid 10 widows 1s. each after 1819, when the original endowment was entrusted to John Thackwell. Later known as Thomas Murzell's charity,[18] by the late 19th century it was distributed at or soon after Candlemas (2 February).[19] The distinctive trimmings worn by the recipients of Robert Winter's charity were scrapped as degrading badges in a revision of the charity's rules in 1829.[20] The requirement to wear the charity clothes in church on Christmas day was dropped in 1893.[21] In 1898 the use of less expensive cloth allowed the number of beneficiaries to be increased from 22 to 24.[22]

Thomas Murrell's charity continued to go to 10 widows and was paid by the Thackwell family until the mid 20th century,[23] after which the 10s. (50p) income was a rent charge on Ockington Farm.[24] Robert Winter's charity distributed clothes in the later 1930s[25] and vouchers by the later 1960s. In 1972 it was amalgamated with the Murrell charity to provide relief both generally and individually to the poor of Dymock[26] and in 2004 the combined charity had an income of £94.[27]

In 1866, following the inclosure of the common at Bromesberrow Heath, an acre there was set aside for the benefit of the labouring poor.[28]

EDUCATION

Before 1826

There was a school in Dymock in 1600[29] and schoolmasters were recorded there in 1608[30] and in 1612.[31] A schoolmaster licensed in 1708[32] was teaching in 1716.[33] William Hooper, by will proved 1747, left £3 a year from his Woodend estate for a dame school for 4 boys and 4 girls of poor parents not receiving relief from the parish. The school's

---

1   Gethyn-Jones, *Dymock Down the Ages*, 123.
2   Ibid. 121.
3   Above, settlement (bldgs.: outlying farms).
4   A.T. Bannister, 'Visitation Returns of Diocese of Hereford in 1397', *EHR* 44 (1929), 453.
5   TNA, PROB 11/23, ff. 166–168v.
6   *Alumni Oxon. 1500–1714*, IV, 1362.
7   Rudder, *Glos.* 411; receipt of the gift in 1650 is recorded on a board in the ch. porch: *20th Rep. Com. Char.* 11.
8   See GA, P 125/VE 2/1, f. (at end) 237; GDR, V 5/116T 3.
9   TNA, PROB 11/557, ff. 192–3.
10 Ibid. PROB 11/570, f. 51 and v.; *20th Rep. Com. Char.* 11.
11 MCA, I 2vi, bdl. 67, no 11; *20th Rep. Com. Char.* 11.
12 GDR wills 1738/113.
13 GA, P 125/VE 2/1, f. 13; Rudder, *Glos.* 411.
14 *20th Rep. Com. Char.* 11; GA, P 125/VE 2/1, f. (at end) 237.
15 GA, P 125/CH 3/1.
16 GDR, V 5/116T 4.
17 GA, P 125/CH 1/3.
18 Ibid. CW 2/8; *20th Rep. Com. Char.* 12.
19 GA, P 125/CH 1/4.
20 Ibid. CH 1/3.
21 Ibid. D 3469/5/49.
22 Ibid. P 125/IN 1/18, p. 451.
23 Ibid. P 125/CH 1/4.
24 Ibid. D 3469/5/49.
25 Ibid. P 125/CH 1/4.
26 Ibid. D 3469/5/49.
27 http://www.charity-commission.gov.uk/registeredcharities (accessed 22 June 2007: no 253500).
28 GA, Q/RI 59.
29 GDR vol. 87, f. 283.
30 Smith, *Men and Armour*, 58.
31 GA, D 2052.
32 Hockaday Abs. clxxxvii.
33 GA, Q/SO 4.

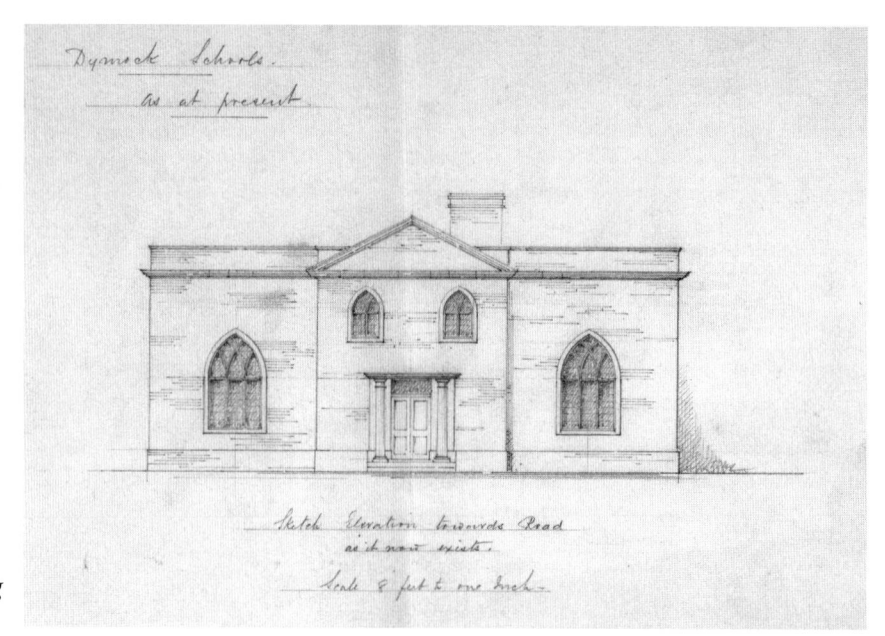

38. Ann Cam's school: the street front before rebuilding in 1884

curriculum was to include the Church catechism.[1] Payment of the rent charge ceased some years before 1775[2] and a schoolmaster living in Dymock in the late 1760s was not associated with the charity.[3]

In 1785 a group led by Richard Hill of Edulus Place and Revd H.G.D. Yate of Bromesberrow opened a subscription for a charity day and Sunday school at Dymock. The school, begun in the village the following year, was supported by voluntary contributions and the Hooper charity with the parish paying for children from its workhouse. Although income was supplemented in 1790 by a grant from Ann Cam's executor, the project was jeopardized by lack of funds and by 1803 the school buildings were leased and the tenant's wife taught a handful of children in them.[4] In 1818 there were also several dame schools in the parish and some parents sent their children to schools in Newent and Ledbury. The subscribers' school, which John Thackwell managed for several years,[5] was revived as a girls' school and at the end of 1824 it taught and clothed 12 pupils.[6]

After 1826

With the failure of the subscribers' scheme plans emerged to use the large fortune that Ann Cam had left for charitable purposes[7] for a new school in Dymock and in 1807 part of her estate was set aside for building and endowing one.[8] Known as Ann Cam's Charity School, it opened in 1826 on the site of the subscribers' school and was run as a Church school, although not to the National Society's plan. Under the charity two teachers, usually husband and wife, taught 50 boys and 50 girls aged from 7 to 11 from Dymock and its neighbourhood in separate departments[9] and the school's income included the Hooper charity and weekly pence for each child; the payment of pence was suspended between 1832 and 1848.[10] In 1833 two other day schools in Dymock taught 10 boys and 20 girls at their parent's expense[11] and in the mid 1840s some children attended schools in adjoining parishes. Ann Cam's school taught 64 boys and 52 girls on weekdays and Sundays in the mid 1840s[12] and had an average attendance of 55 in 1868.[13] There was at least one dame school in the village in the mid 19th century.[14]

Several schools were opened outside the village. Haffield School, first recorded in 1859,[15] was founded for the settlement on Bromesberrow heath by William Charles Henry and was established in 1863 as a National school in a new building west of the heath. With Henry and his wife managing it under the direction of the vicar of Dymock and supplying all its income other than pence, the

1 GDR wills 1747/66.
2 GA, P 125/VE 2/1, f. (at end) 237.
3 Ibid. DC/S 34/3; D 185/IV/10.
4 Ibid. P 125/CH 4/1, 5; for H.G.D. Yate, above, Bromesberrow (social hist.; religious hist.).
5 *Educ. of Poor Digest*, 298.
6 GA, P 125/SC 5.
7 See TNA, PROB 11/1189, f. 205v.
8 Fig. 38.
9 *20th Rep. Com. Char.* 12–13; GA, P 125/SC 5; Nat. Soc. files, Dymock.
10 GA, P 125/CH 4/2.
11 *Educ. Enq. Abstract*, 314.
12 Nat. Soc. *Inquiry, 1846–7*, Glos. 8–9.
13 *1st Rep. Com. Employment in Agric.* app. II, p. 130.
14 TNA, HO 107/1960, Dymock Leadington, no 124.
15 GA, P 125/CH 4/4.

school taught girls and infants[1] and had an average attendance of 50 in 1868.[2] In 1870 Miss Story of Upham House ran a small school in the Leadington.[3] Some of the new schools were small boarding establishments. Sarah Pitt's seminary, opened by 1856, accommodated 13 pupils, mostly boys, at Beaconshill in 1861.[4] It occupied Stoneberrow House in Dymock village in the 1870s and early 1880s and Revd Joseph White ran a middle-class school at Beaconshill in the early 1870s.[5] At Greenway House the East family taught boarders of both sexes in 1867 and the girls' school remained open in 1879.[6]

In 1871, when it became a public elementary school, Ann Cam's school affiliated to the National Society and its master since 1844 was dismissed. The school then had an average attendance of 98.[7] The managers' attempt to establish a night school ended in 1872[8] and a school they opened at Upham for the Leadington in 1875 closed for want of accommodation in 1876.[9] A National school was recorded at Greenway in the 1870s.[10] Ann Cam's school contained more classrooms from 1884[11] but the infants continued to be taught as part of the girls' department.[12] The school's average attendance fell from 133 in 1904[13] to 111 in 1922,[14] the year that the two departments were merged,[15] and was 129 in 1938.[16] In 1925 the Ann Cam foundation was divided into separate funds to maintain the school buildings and assist the education of local children.[17]

Haffield National (later C. of E.) School also became a public elementary school and in 1904 it had an average attendance of 81.[18] In 1922, the year after the Henry family conveyed the building to a diocesan trust,[19] it became a mixed junior and infant school.[20] The average attendance was 54 in 1922, 12 in 1932, and 22 in 1938.[21] In that period some farmers sent their sons to a preparatory school in Kempley and some children from the Leadington went to school at Little Marcle (Herefs.).[22] Haffield School closed in 1951 when it had 12 children on its roll.[23]

Ann Cam's school obtained aided status in the mid 20th century[24] and moved to a new building on the edge of the village in 1974. Accommodation there increased as attendance grew[25] and, as Ann Cam C. of E. Primary School, there were 135 children on the roll in 2002.[26] In 2008 the number was 98.[27] The foundation's education fund was closed by 1997.[28]

SOCIAL LIFE

Public Houses

In 1596 two Dymock men kept unlicensed victualling houses and allowed illicit games in them.[29] In 1690 the magistrates closed four of Dymock's alehouses but let four old inns stay open.[30] The village had the Plough inn in 1709[31] and also the Harrow in 1754.[32] The George inn opened there after 1806[33] and, as well as the Plough, the village also had one or two cider and beerhouses including the Crown and, at Shakesfield, the Anchor in the mid 19th century.[34] The Plough, the principal inn, hosted dinners, dances, and club meetings[35] and was renamed the Beauchamp Arms in the later 1880s. The George closed in the 1880s[36] and the Anchor in the early 20th century.[37] Following the Crown's closure in 1990[38] the Beauchamp Arms was the sole public house in the village. Having been bought by the parish council in 1997,[39] it remained open in 2008.

Ryton had buildings called the Sun House and the

---

1 TNA, ED 7/34/117; OS Map 6", Glos. X.SW (1883 edn). For the school bldg., below, religious hist. (religious life).
2 *1st Rep. Com. Employment in Agric.* app. II, p. 130.
3 GA, P 125/IN 4/19.
4 *Kelly's Dir. Glos.* (1856), 281; TNA, RG 9/1761.
5 PRO, RG 10/2608; *Kelly's Dir. Glos.* (1870), 541; (1879), 639; (1885), 449; see *Slater's Dir. Glos.* (1868), 239.
6 GA, P 125/MI 17 (par. mag. Dec. 1867); TNA, RG 10/2608; *Kelly's Dir. Glos.* (1870), 540; (1879), 638.
7 TNA, ED 7/34/116; GA, P 125/SC 5.
8 GA, P 125/IN 4/19.
9 Ibid. SC 18; *Memo on Educational Arrangements in Dymock 1875*: copy in GA, ED 12.
10 *Kelly's Dir. Glos.* (1870), 540; (1879), 638.
11 GA, D 2593/2/454; P 125/SC 18; SC 35.
12 Ibid. S 125/2/2, passim.
13 *Public Elem. Schs. 1906*, 184.
14 *List 21*, 1911 (Board of Education), 161; 1922, 104.
15 GA, S 125/2/3, p. 277; 4, p. 189.
16 *List 21*, 1938 (Board of Education), 126.
17 Nat. Soc. files, Dymock.
18 *Public Elem. Schs. 1906*, 184.
19 GA, P 125/SC 4.
20 Ibid. S 125/1/1, 3; C/CE/M 2/16, p. 193.

21 *List 21*, 1922 (Board of Education), 104; 1932, 114; 1938, 126.
22 Information from Malcolm Stallard of Callow Farm and Mabel McCulloch of Hallwood Green; see below, Kempley, social hist. (education).
23 GA, S 125/1/2.
24 Nat. Soc. files, Dymock.
25 School website (accessed 30 Jan. 2003)
26 *Schools and Establishments Dir. 2002–3* (Glos. co. council), 4.
27 Ibid. *2008–9*, 6.
28 http://www.charity-commission.gov.uk/registeredcharities (accessed 10 May 2007: no 311619).
29 BL, Harl. MS 4131, f. 484.
30 GA, Q/SO 2.
31 Ibid. DC/S 34/3.
32 Ibid. D 4317/6, ct. papers (Wooding alias Shayles).
33 MCA, J 2vii, bdl. 111D, nos 26–28.
34 GA, P 125A/SD 2/1–2 (nos 586, 1514, 1543, 1549); TNA, HO 107/1960; RG 9/1761.
35 GA, P 125/IN 4/19.
36 *Kelly's Dir. Glos.* (1879 and later edns); *Licensed Houses in Glos. 1891*, 140–1; MCA, L 1i, (5) letter 21 Mar. 1887.
37 OS Map 6", Glos. X.SW (1903, 1924 edns).
38 *Village Voices*, 16 n.
39 *Citizen*, 29 Mar. 1997.

New Inn in the late 18th century.[1] In the mid 19th century beer and cider were sold at houses in many outlying places.[2] One public house in 1861 was the Royal Oak at Greenway.[3] A beerhouse at Bromesberrow Heath was called the Blue Bell in 1863[4] and later the Bell.[5] At Broom's Green a blacksmith's beerhouse[6] was known as the Horse Shoe.[7] A beerhouse at Ryton lost its licence in 1872[8] and the Bell and the Horse Shoe, the only licensed public houses outside Dymock village in the late 19th century,[9] closed in 1989[10] and in 2002 respectively.[11]

Meeting Places, Societies, Clubs, and Events

The former church house by the churchyard was long the meeting place of Dymock manor court.[12] By custom recorded in the mid 16th century the lord provided dinners for the jury at the principal courts.[13] In the mid 19th century meetings and entertainment were held in the village school and from the late 19th until the mid 20th century an outbuilding at High House, then the vicarage house, was used for church meetings.[14] In 1930 a hall by the Ledbury road east of the church, originally used by a rifle club, was converted as a village (later parish) hall.[15] It has been enlarged several times, the latest in 2000 and 2001.[16] At Broom's Green a wooden hut erected in 1920 as a memorial to the dead of the First World War provided a meeting place also for Ryton and for Donnington (Herefs.). It was replaced by a larger hall in 1998.[17]

A friendly society formed by local tradesmen in 1789 began with 45 members[18] and evidently continued with 100 members in 1803.[19] Following the rebuilding of Society Lodge in the village it met at the George inn.[20] In the early 1870s farm labourers held union meetings and demonstrations in the village and at Bromesberrow Heath. In the village a working men's club founded in 1872 had a reading room[21] and a friendly society met at the Plough from 1884.[22] The club closed in 1911 when it had 44 members.[23] At Bromesberrow Heath, where a working men's club established in 1877 closed in 1887,[24] a friendly society meeting at the Bell from 1884 was dissolved in 1893.[25] A circulating library existed in Dymock from 1882 until at least 1898.[26] In the early 1930s there were branches of the Mothers' Union and Women's Institute,[27] the former having originated as a weekly church meeting in the late 1870s.[28] In the mid 1960s the Women's Institute had branches at Dymock, Broom's Green and Donnington, and Castle Tump.[29] Those at Dymock and Castle Tump continued to meet, the latter outside the parish, in 2003.[30]

Little is known about the parishioners' early pastimes and customs. A house near the village at Shakesfield was called the Maypole in 1811[31] and a field just west of Bromesberrow heath was recorded by the name of Maypole meadow from the mid 19th century.[32] An annual race meeting was held in the parish in the mid 1870s[33] and a local horticultural society held an annual show from 1888 and into the 20th century.[34] In the late 1940s there was an annual gymkhana.[35] Dymock had a cricket club in 1867[36] and the church choir was instrumental in reviving club cricket in 1882.[37] A cricket club extended its ground east of the village in 1955[38] and enlarged its pavilion in 1987.[39] An association football club existed in 1912[40] and football clubs have been based on both

---

1 Worcs. RO, 705:99 (BA 3375), Dymock deeds 1802–13.
2 GA, P 125A/SD 2/1–2 (nos 631, 669–70, 869); *Kelly's Dir. Glos.* (1863), 262–3.
3 TNA, RG 9/1761.
4 GA, Q/RI 31, 59.
5 OS Map 1:2,500, Glos. X.11 (1884 edn).
6 *Kelly's Dir. Glos.* (1870), 541.
7 *Western Mail*, 24 Mar. 1871; *Licensed Houses in Glos. 1891*, 140–1.
8 GA, P 125/IN 4/19.
9 *Licensed Houses in Glos. 1891*, 140–1.
10 *Bromesberrow 1999–2000: Bromesberrow Parish Appraisal* (copy in VCH Glos. office), 15.
11 Local information.
12 Above, local govt. (manorial govt.).
13 Bigland, *Glos.* I, 526 n.
14 GA, P 125/MI 17 (par. mag. Dec. 1867); D 7322 (par. mag. Oct. 1880, Feb. 1959); P 125/IN 3/4.
15 Ibid. D 3168/4/7/40.
16 Ibid. D 3469/5/49; Dymock par. council, par. meeting min. book, pp. 250, 256.
17 'Broomsgreen, Donnington and Ryton Memorial Hall': leaflet in hall; *Kelly's Dir. Glos.* (1939), 158.
18 *Rules & Orders to be observed by an Amicable Society of Tradesmen & Others in Dymock* (1800: copy in Glos. Colln. R 116.1).

19 *Poor Law Abstract, 1804*, 172–3.
20 GA, Q/RZ 1; for Society Lodge, above, settlement (Dymock village).
21 GA, P 125/IN 4/19; *Glouc. J.* 26 Oct. 1872; see N. Scotland, *Agricultural Trade Unionism in Gloucestershire 1872–1950* (1991), 20, 30.
22 TNA, FS 4/13, Glos. no 1115.
23 Ibid. no 1021.
24 Ibid. FS 4/12, Glos. no 86.
25 Ibid. FS 4/13, Glos. no 1108.
26 GA, D 1785.
27 Ibid. D 3168/4/7/40.
28 Ibid. D 7322 (par. mag. Nov. 1880).
29 Gethyn-Jones, *Dymock Down the Ages*, 147.
30 Information from Mrs Thick.
31 MCA, I 6i, bdl. 93, no 21.
32 GA, P 125A/SD 2/1–2 (no 843).
33 Ibid. P 125/IN 4/19.
34 Ibid. IN 1/18, pp. 219, 257, 351; IN 1/21, ff. 52, 87.
35 Ibid. D 3168/5/8.
36 Ibid. D 3028/4.
37 Ibid. D 7322 (par. mag. Aug. 1882).
38 Gethyn-Jones, *Dymock Down the Ages*, 149.
39 C. and R. Newman, 'Watching brief and salvage work at the new cricket pavilion, Dymock', *Glevensis* 24 (1990), 22–6.
40 T. Ward, *Around Newent* (1994), 98.

Bromesberrow Heath and Broom's Green.[1] In the 1990s a golf course was laid out in the grounds of the Old Grange, the former stable block of which was adapted as a club house.

The Church was behind a society that in 1879 acquired blankets to hire in Broom's Green and Ryton.[2] In the late 19th and early 20th century the Ledbury hospital and dispensary received funds from Dymock.[3] A nurse employed by an association for Dymock, Bromesberrow, and Redmarley D'Abitot lived at Bromesberrow Heath in 1906[4] and a district nurse continued to live in Dymock until the mid 1960s.[5] From the later 1920s a doctor held a surgery in Dymock[6] and at the end of the 20th century Dymock people attended surgeries at Newent or Ledbury.[7]

In 1696 William Winter was accused with other Dymock men of clipping and counterfeiting coins.[8] A lead tablet discovered at Wilton Place in 1892 and dating possibly from the later 17th century bears an inscription invoking spirits to banish Sarah Ellis, who perhaps lived in Oxenhall.[9] In 1840 local leaders of the Latter Day Saints were shot, hanged, and burned in effigy.[10] In the 1870s, when the vicar W.C.E. Newbolt was at odds with many of the parish, the churchyard was policed on several occasions during services and in 1872 protesters demonstrating against a resident at the vicarage for defamation repeatedly paraded effigies in the village street.[11]

The local daffodils, of which large numbers were picked for London hospitals in the mid 20th century,[12] have continued to bring an influx of visitors to the area.[13] In the early 21st century refreshments were served in the parish hall during the daffodil season.

'The Dymock Poets'

In 1911 the poet Lascelles Abercrombie set up house at The Gallows in Ryton[14] and in early 1914, in collaboration with Wilfred Gibson, Rupert Brooke, and John Drinkwater, he began *New Numbers*, a quarterly magazine devoted to new writing by all four authors. Gibson had moved into The Old Nail Shop at Greenway in 1913. Among other writers to visit Dymock at that time were Robert Frost, who set up home at Little Iddens in the Leadington in 1914, Edward Thomas, and Eleanor Farjeon. *New Numbers*, published at Ryton and posted to subscribers, ran to four issues. Some poetry written during those years was inspired by the area and scenery and, although they left Dymock following the outbreak of the First World War, Abercrombie wrote later of trees behind The Gallows in 'Ryton Firs' and Gibson recalled an evening gathering at The Old Nailshop in 'The Golden Room'. Frost, who returned to America in 1915, revisited Dymock in 1928 and 1957.

RELIGIOUS HISTORY

EARLY HISTORY AND STATUS OF THE PARISH CHURCH

Dymock church, standing high above the river Leadon in a large churchyard, was built anew in the late 11th century[15] and replaced a pre-Conquest church served by a priest holding 12 a. in 1066.[16] The new building evidently took place after the church was given to Cormeilles abbey (Eure) presumably by its founder William FitzOsbern (d. 1071), lord of Dymock.[17] In the late 12th century Flaxley abbey gave the land directly north of the adjacent graveyard to its servant William 'de monasterio' and the place was known later as Minster's Croft.[18] Two of the priests with the cure of souls in Dymock in succession in the later 12th century took 2s. a year for the tithes of land cultivated by the Flaxley monks.[19] Cormeilles appropriated the church under a licence granted in 1195,[20] the appropriation having taken place by 1207 when the two abbeys reached agreement over

---

1 *Bromesberrow 1999–2000*, 8, 15.
2 GA, D 7322 (par. mag. Nov. 1880).
3 Ibid. (par. mag. Oct. 1882); P 125/CW 2/4; IN 1/18, pp. 148, 252, 284.
4 Ibid. P 125/MI 4.
5 *Kelly's Dir. Glos.* (1931), 159; GA, D 7322 (par. mag. Feb. 1965).
6 *Kelly's Dir. Glos.* (1927), 167; (1939), 159.
7 *Village Voices*, 12.
8 *Cal. SP Dom.* 1696, 384; 1698, 17.
9 Gethyn-Jones, *Dymock Down the Ages*, 104–5; B.S. Smith, '"The Dymock Curse"', *Trans. BGAS* 93 (1974), 183–4.
10 *Hereford Times*, 14 Nov. 1840: reference supplied by Mary Pochin of Burntwood (Staffs.).
11 GA, P 125/IN 4/19.
12 *The Times*, 7 Apr. 1928; Gethyn-Jones, *Dymock Down the Ages*, 65.
13 For the daffodils as a tourist attraction in the 1920s, *Heref. J.* 20 Sept. 1924; T. Ward, *Around Newent* (1994), 93.
14 This section is based on S. Street, *The Dymock Poets* (1994); L. Hart, *Once They Lived In Gloucestershire: A Dymock Poets Anthology* (1995).
15 Below (religious life).
16 *Domesday Book* (Rec. Com.), I, 164.
17 BL, Add. MS 18461, ff. 1–2v. For William, above, manors (Dymock manor).
18 *Flaxley Cart.* p. 159. For Minster's Croft, MCA, Box I 5iv, bdl. 89, no 1; GA, P 125A/SD 2/1–2 (no 1508).
19 *Flaxley Cart.* pp. 157–8.
20 *Eng. Episc. Acta VII*, pp. 136–8.

tithes,[1] and a vicarage was established in 1247.[2] There was a vicarage house in the mid 14th century.[3]

The benefice was subject to a series of reorganizations from 1938, when it was united with Kempley, and the incumbent was styled rector from 1941, when Preston was added to the united benefice.[4] At another reorganization, in 1955, Dymock and Donnington (Herefs.) were united.[5] In 1975 Kempley was added to that benefice[6] and in 2000 six more parishes merged with it.[7]

PATRONAGE AND ENDOWMENT

Cormeilles abbey and later Newent priory on its behalf exercised the patronage of the vicarage[8] but from the mid 14th century the Crown often presented by reason of the French wars.[9] The patronage passed with the rectory to Fotheringhay college (Northants.) in the early 15th century and to lay ownership in the mid 16th century.[10] In 1539 John Sylvester, a Northamptonshire clergyman, presented under a grant from Fotheringhay and in 1577 the bishop collated by reason of lapse. John Kyrle was patron for a turn in 1667 as executor of William Winter. In 1714 the two owners of the rectory made a joint presentation.[11] In 1866 the advowson was sold to the 6th Earl Beauchamp.[12] His successors' right of patronage,[13] diluted by the various unions of benefices affecting Dymock from 1938,[14] was transferred to the bishop in the late 20th century.[15]

The endowment of the vicarage in 1247 was mostly small tithes. It was intended to provide 14 marks (£9 6s. 8d.) a year[16] but the income was considerably smaller in the early 15th century when the vicarage was customarily valued at £6 13s. 4d.[17] The living was worth £9 13s. 8d. in 1535.[18] The vicar had an income of £20 in 1603[19] and of £40 in 1650,[20] the latter figure being the same as the stipend, including an increment of £10, paid to the vicar from the rectory estate in the later 1660s.[21] By the early 18th century the stipend had been increased to £60.[22] Grants from Queen Anne's Bounty in 1811 and 1812[23] were used in 1826 to buy land in Newent[24] but the vicarage had a value of only £105 in 1856[25] and part of the £60 stipend went to the rector of Preston from 1873.[26]

The vicarage house in front of the churchyard was a building of three bays in 1679[27] and was partly rebuilt during the incumbency of Joseph Symonds (1787–1800).[28] It was pulled down shortly after Earl Beauchamp gave High House to the living in 1877 in exchange for the glebe in Newent and remodelled it as the vicarage house.[29] A cottage in the village given to the living in 1893 by the earl's successor[30] was sold in 1920[31] and High House in 1955.[32] A new parsonage, known as the Rectory, was built in 1953.[33]

RELIGIOUS LIFE

The Building of the Parish Church

Dymock is the largest in a group of early Norman churches ascribed to a 'Dymock school' of sculpture.[34] The church's size, plan form, high-quality masonry and elaborate decoration indicate its importance when built. Its age has been debated but it is now widely accepted that the present building, which once had a central tower, dates from after 1070, its long nave and certain stylistic characteristics continuing Anglo-Saxon traditions.[35] The walls of the nave are decorated with pilaster buttresses and a carved string course and, inside, the remains of the sanctuary arch include cushion capitals with primitive upturned and confronted volutes. A doorway on the northern side of the former central tower, perhaps an opening into a stair

---

1 BL, Add. MS 18461, f. 86 and v.
2 Ibid. f. 14 and v.1
3 Ibid. f. 81v.
4 *London Gazette*, 25 Feb. 1938, pp. 1252–3; Gethyn-Jones, *Dymock Down the Ages*, 56.
5 GA, P 125/IN 3/12.
6 *Glouc. Dioc. Year Book* (1978), 21.
7 *Dioc. of Glouc. Dir.* (2000–1), 91; (2001–2), 24–5.
8 *Reg. Swinfield*, 535; *Reg. Orleton*, 388; *Reg. L. de Charlton*, 72.
9 *Reg. Trefnant*, 182; *Cal. Pat.* 1343–5, 143; 1354–8, 47; 1405–8, 280.
10 Above, manors (other estates); see *Reg. Lacy*, 114; *Cal. Pat.* 1547–8, 108–9.
11 Hockaday Abs. clxxxvii; TNA, PROB 11/323, ff. 328–9.
12 MCA, I 2ii, bdl. 61B, no 44.
13 *Kelly's Dir. Glos.* (1870–1939 edns).
14 *London Gazette*, 25 Feb. 1938, pp. 1252–3; GA, P 125/IN 3/12; *Glouc. Dioc. Year Book* (1955–6), 28–9; (1978), 21.
15 *Dioc. of Glouc. Dir.* (1994–5), 58.
16 BL, Add. MS 18461, f. 14 and v.
17 *Reg. Mascall*, 37, 119; *Reg. Lacy*, 17.
18 *Valor Eccl.* II, 501; the value given in *Military Surv. of Glos. 1522*, 56, was £10.
19 *Eccl. Misc.* 102.
20 C.R. Elrington, 'The Survey of Church Livings in Gloucestershire, 1650', *Trans. BGAS* 83 (1964), 98.
21 TNA, PROB 11/323, f. 328 and v.
22 Atkyns, *Glos.* 395; *Bp. Benson's Surv. of Dioc. of Glouc. 1735–50*, 5; Rudder, *Glos.* 411.
23 Hodgson, *Queen Anne's Bounty* (1826), 322.
24 GA, P 125/IN 3/4, letter 21 Aug. 1928.
25 GDR vol. 384, f. 87.
26 *London Gazette*, 18 July 1873, pp. 3385–7; GA, P 256/IN 3/2.
27 GDR, V 5/116T 2.
28 Ibid. 4; Hockaday Abs. clxxxvii.
29 MCA, J 2ii, bdl. 104, no 17; GA, P 125/IN 3/11; D 1381/54; OS Map 6", Glos. X.SW (1883 edn).
30 GA, P 125/IN 4/21.
31 Nat. Soc. files, Dymock.
32 GA, P 125/IN 3/9.
33 Verey and Brooks, *Glos.* II, 346.
34 Above, Newent and May Hill (settlement, society, and buildings). See E. Gethyn-Jones, *The Dymock School of Sculpture* (Chichester, 1979).
35 Verey and Brooks, *Glos.* II, 344–5; H.M. and J. Taylor, *Anglo-Saxon Architecture* I (Cambridge, 1965), 221–2.

39. Dymock church: the south side of the chancel

tower, has a plain monolithic tympanum. There is an original window in the nave south wall. Dymock is one of the few English churches of late 11th-century date to have had a polygonal apsidal end to the chancel. The apse was decorated with blind arcading, two bays of which remain on the south side of the chancel and contain diagonally-set masonry in the tympana.[1] Those details derive possibly from Continental churches rather than directly from Anglo-Saxon ones.[2]

In an embellishment of the church in the early 12th century, the south doorway was given a new hoodmould decorated with chevrons and a tympanum carved with a distinctive interpretation of the Tree of Life motif. Its jambs, seemingly part of the original building, were carved with capitals, which have volutes and, hanging from them, stepped triangular motifs characteristic of the so-called Dymock school.[3]

The Middle Ages

In the mid 13th century Ela Longespée, countess of Warwick, and her husband Philip Basset supported a chaplain performing a daily service in honour of the Virgin, the church's patron saint. Under their grant of the manor in 1257 Flaxley abbey was to pay him a stipend of 8s. 2d.[4] The chantry of St Mary's had its own resident chaplain in the mid 14th century[5] and its endowments later included its priest's house.[6] In

40. Dymock church: the south doorway

1 Fig. 39.
2 E. Fernie, *The Architecture of Norman England* (Oxford, 2000), 248
3 Fig. 40; Verey and Brooks, *Glos.* II, 344–5. The churches at Kempley and Pauntley contain similar decoration.
4 *Glos. Feet of Fines 1199–1299*, p. 121.
5 BL, Add. MS 18461, f. 81v.; *Cal. Pat.* 1391–6, 502.
6 *Cal. Pat.* 1549–51, 101; TNA, E 310/14/54, f. 44; C 66/1985, no 1.

the late Middle Ages a local cult of St Chad included an obit celebrated by a chaplain in the church.[1] A local spring was known as St Chad's well in 1620.[2] Early reverence for another saint may be recorded in the name the 'Back of St Clement's' used in the later 18th century for a place near the church.[3]

In the early 14th century the east end of the church was rebuilt on a rectangular plan. In other work in that century its west wall was rebuilt and new windows were inserted in the nave's north and south walls. About 1400 north and south transeptal chapels were added individually and asymmetrically to the nave, the former having a large canopied niche and the latter a piscina. In the early 15th century a west tower was added to the building. Arms displayed on its western buttresses may include those of the Ruyhale family and of John Merbury (d. 1438), lords of Dymock manor.[4] The south porch, which is of the same stone as the top of the tower, was also built then. Bells were installed in the tower and in the reign of Henry VIII the parish was in debt to the Worcester bell founder Nicholas Green (d. by 1542).[5]

The first recorded institution to the vicarage was that of John Fillot in 1304.[6] William Lestor, who became vicar in 1324, was a French man.[7] In 1397 the rector's failure to repair the chancel roof meant that the vicar was unable to celebrate Mass when it rained. The rector, presumably in the guise of Newent priory acting for Cormeilles abbey, had also for three years failed to honour the custom of providing the candle lit during Mass.[8] Robert Crawford, rector of Abbots Morton (Worcs.), became vicar by an exchange of livings in 1418[9] and resigned almost immediately with a pension of £4 and accommodation in the vicarage house.[10] Thomas Hankins, vicar 1482–1539,[11] was to be Dymock's longest serving incumbent. He came from a local family as did John Cam, who by 1517 served as a curate or chaplain for a salary of £5. Both men faced charges of sexual incontinence and in 1526, because of ill health, Hankins was absolved for not attending the consistory court.[12] Sir John Bridges (d. 1530) instructed his executors to make a marble tomb at his father Thomas's burial place by the high altar and to provide vestments and altar hangings decorated with his coat of arms. He also assigned 10s. a year for an annual obit.[13]

From the Reformation to the Restoration

In the mid 16th century the church was attended by the residents of the more distant settlements and farms in the parish.[14] The chantry of St Mary was dissolved in the late 1540s[15] and the service of St Chad ceased probably a little earlier.[16] The clergy serving in the church included Thomas Whiting, vicar from 1539, and William Greystock, a curate who did not recite the 'Ave Maria' and refused to consecrate bread and water in 1548. At that time some parishioners chattered in the churchyard during services.[17] Greystock's learning was deemed satisfactory in 1551, the year he married the mother of his daughter. Whiting, who was unable to recite the Ten Commandments,[18] was deprived of the living in 1554. Henry Wakeman, a former monk who was deprived of the neighbouring Preston living for being married, served in Dymock as curate in 1559[19] and until his death in 1569.[20]

In 1576 a chalice was still used at the church and the vicar was failing to preach quarterly sermons and to teach the catechism.[21] Walter Cowsley, who became vicar the following year, retained the living for almost 50 years.[22] By the end of the 16th century several parishioners did not attend church at Easter to receive Communion and in 1612 they included members of some of the leading families, notably the Forsters and Wynniatts. One, Catherine Cam, was said to be a recusant in 1619.[23] Richard Morgan, vicar from 1626, was replaced after his death in 1654 by Henry Kirkham, an approved public preacher.[24] Under changes introduced by the Commonwealth from 1653, the duties of register (registrar) for Dymock were undertaken by John Cam the younger of the Farm; his recording of births, civil marriages, and burials in the parish register was at first meticulous.[25] A Baptist church met in Dymock at that time.[26]

---

1 GDR dispersed wills 8; TNA, E 309/1/5 Eliz./7, no 4.
2 GA, D 2464/T 1.
3 Rudder, *Glos.* 409.
4 F. Were, 'Notes on Heraldry', *Trans. BGAS* 31 (1908), 284–5; *Trans. Woolhope Naturalists' Field Club* (1939–41), p. xxii; above, manors.
5 *Glos. Ch. Bells*, 39.
6 *Reg. Swinfield*, 535.
7 *Reg. Orleton*, 388; TNA, SC 6/1125/15, rot. 2.
8 A.T. Bannister, 'Visitation Returns of Diocese of Hereford in 1397', *EHR* 44 (1929), 453.
9 *Reg. Lacy*, 119.
10 Ibid. 114 and n.
11 *Reg. Mylling*, 192; *Reg. of Dymock*, 1.
12 *Military Surv. of Glos. 1522*, 55–6; Hockaday Abs. clxxxvii.
13 TNA, PROB 11/23, f. 166 and v.; see *Visit. Worcs. 1569* (Harl. Soc. 27), 25.
14 *Reg. of Dymock*, passim.
15 Hockaday Abs. clxxxvii; TNA, E 301/23, no 31.
16 GDR dispersed wills 8.
17 Hockaday Abs. xxx, 1544 stipendiaries, f. 7; 1545 visit. f. 2; clxxxvii.
18 J. Gairdner, 'Bishop Hooper's Visitation of Gloucester', *EHR* 19 (1904), 119; *Reg. of Dymock*, 13, 16.
19 Hockaday Abs. clxxxvii; below, Preston, religious hist. (religious life).
20 *Reg. of Dymock*, 29.
21 GDR vol. 40, f. 249.
22 Hockaday Abs. clxxxvii; see *Reg. of Dymock*, 104.
23 GA, D 2052.
24 Hockaday Abs. clxxxvii; *Reg. of Dymock*, 126.
25 *Reg. of Dymock*, pp. xix–xx, 125–33.
26 *Calamy Revised*, 214.

Under the will of Revd John Wood (d. 1640) of St James within Aldgate in London a rent charge from Dymock funded sermons in Alstone church in Overbury (Worcs.).[1]

The Established Church and Nonconformity after the Restoration

Henry Kirkham subscribed to the Act of Uniformity in 1662 but had resigned as vicar by 1664.[2] In the following decades nonconformist sentiment was probably more widespread in Dymock than in any other parish in west Gloucestershire. Sixteen parishioners were declared schismatic in 1670[3] and eighteen nonconformists were recorded in 1676.[4] In 1672 three houses were licensed for Presbyterian meetings. One belonged to John Giles, formerly a preacher in Redmarley D'Abitot and elsewhere,[5] and the others to John Hawkins and John White, who were among 16 parishioners not attending church in 1683.[6] A Baptist meeting, led c.1715 by William Drew,[7] dwindled and a Baptist was the sole nonconformist in the parish in 1735.[8]

The parish church's congregation was also depleted after the Restoration as residents of outlying places went to churches nearer their homes.[9] Between 1667 and 1761 Dymock church was served in turn by Grindal Wilson (d. 1714) and Samuel Savage, both as vicar. Savage, also rector of Poole Keynes (Wilts., later Glos.) from 1721,[10] provided full services and was the first minister to have 10s. a year for preaching at Candlemas in support of William Hooper's education charity and testing the schoolchildren on the catechism.[11]

Although three of its six bells were replaced or recast in 1707 and 1710,[12] the church's interior with the pulpit and reading desk on the south side was basically unchanged after the Restoration. The seating, all proprietary, was insufficient, partitions obstructed the view from the side chapels, the west end was empty of seats and used as a store, and the vestry room off the chancel was too small for meetings. Servants (i.e. agricultural labourers) regularly crowded into the seats and remained seated throughout services; some sat on the communion table and rails in the chancel, placing their hats and staves on the table. On at least one occasion the leaking roof forced worshippers to abandon seats in the chancel. Despite the wish of parishioners led by Richard Hill to preserve the interior, in 1727 the churchwardens obtained permission to make extensive alterations, including the construction of a vestry room and a servants' gallery at the west end. As part of the improvements in the nave the transept arches were rebuilt, a pillar was removed in what may have been a modification of the abutments of the central tower, the roof was ceiled, the south-east window was enlarged, and a new north window inserted.[13] A small early 18th-century wooden font was acquired at some point[14] and the remaining old bells were replaced in 1726 and 1731 and a sanctus was acquired later. At the end of the century the Wynniatt family had a large gallery filling the east end of the nave, the west gallery was reserved for the singers, and several seats were allotted to the recipients of a clothing charity. A new vestry room was built in the churchyard c.1801.[15] Members of leading families of the period such as the Cams, Winters, Wynniatts, and Chamberlaynes were commemorated inside the church and the churchyard monuments included many decorated chest and pedestal tombs, the largest that of William Cam (d. 1767) immediately east of the chancel.[16]

William Hayward, vicar 1761–87,[17] usually placed the parish in the care of a stipendiary curate. Jenkin Jenkins, rector of Donnington (Herefs.), served the church thus from 1766 to 1780. Evan Evans, who was briefly curate and schoolmaster in Dymock in the mid 1780s,[18] became vicar in 1800.[19] In 1816 part of the congregation accused him among other things of neglecting his duties, conducting services carelessly, providing one Sunday service instead of two as customary, and turning the churchyard into a nursery orchard.[20] Under William Beale, vicar from 1820, Church life continued to be soured by acrimony between clergy and laity after 1822 when, in response to complaints about services and the lack of a resident minister, a curate moved into the vicarage house. Beale (d. 1827) himself served

---

1 TNA, PROB 11/182, ff. 301–3; GBR, F 4/14, pp. 44–5; F 4/16, pp. 419–20.
2 Hockaday Abs. clxxxvii.
3 GA, D 2052.
4 *Compton Census*, 544.
5 *Cal. SP Dom. 1672*, 235; *Calamy Revised*, 222.
6 *Cal. SP Dom. 1672*, 379; GA, D 2052.
7 *Trans. Bapt. Hist. Soc.* 2 (1911), 99.
8 *Bp. Benson's Surv. of Dioc. of Glouc. 1735–50*, 6.
9 Below, Preston, religious hist. (religious life).
10 Hockaday Abs. clxxxvii; TNA, E 179/247/14, rot. 35d.; *Reg. of Dymock*, 184.
11 *Bp. Benson's Surv. of Dioc. of Glouc. 1735–50*, 6; GDR wills 1747/66.
12 *Notes on Dioc. of Glouc. by Chancellor Parsons*, 155; GDR, V 5/116T 4.
13 GDR, F 1/4; Hockaday Abs. clxxxvii.
14 'Visit to Dymock ch. 24 Aug. 1939', *Trans. Woolhope Naturalists' Field Club* (1939–41), p. xxii; J.E. Gethyn-Jones, *Dymock: A Royal Manor* (1950), 13. It remained in the ch. until the later 20th cent.
15 GDR, V 5/116T 4; *Glos. Ch. Bells*, 277–8.
16 Above, social hist. (social structure); Bigland, *Glos.* I, 528–31, which gives some incorrect dates; Verey and Brooks, *Glos.* II, 345–6.
17 Hockaday Abs. clxxxvii.
18 *Reg. of Dymock*, 217–29, 235, 282, 294–5, 297; GA, P 125/CH 4/1.
19 Hockaday Abs. clxxxvii.
20 GDR, B 4/1/912; GA, P 125/VE 2/2.

Newent church.[1] John Simons, the next vicar, reprimanded labourers for frequenting public houses, wakes, and dances and exhorted them to industry and frugality.[2] In the mid 1820s the church held two Sunday services or occasionally one, alternately in the morning and afternoon, and 60 people were regular communicants. Services included a new sung version of the psalms[3] and the singers' gallery was enlarged in 1830.[4] During the early 19th century there was no regular Sunday school, despite the vestry's appointment in 1819 of a salaried master,[5] and in the mid 1820s religious instruction was given during Lent and on four other Sundays.[6]

Nonconformity in the Early Nineteenth Century

Sporadic nonconformist activity took place in Dymock by the 1820s. In 1819 a preacher of the Ledbury Methodist circuit registered a house and in 1820 and 1822 a minister from Gorsley, presumably a Baptist, registered buildings in and near the village. A Ledbury man registered a house in 1825[7] and Castle Tump was on the preaching plan of the Gorsley Baptist church in 1831.[8] Between 1834 and 1844 eight nonconformist meeting places were registered, including one at Oaksbottom in 1836 and another at Hallwood green in 1838.[9] A meeting at Broom's green led in 1834 by Thomas Kington, a missionary from Castle Frome (Herefs.), belonged to a sect called the United Brethren. It built a small chapel in 1837 but Kington's followers in Dymock later met elsewhere[10] and in 1840, the year the chapel was handed to the Bible Christians,[11] a substantial number joined the Latter Day Saints.[12] Several families emigrated to America soon afterwards.[13]

From the 1840s to the First World War

In 1851 Dymock church with its 600 seats, half of them free, was attended by only a fraction of parishioners, its Easter Sunday congregations being 182 in the morning and 60 in the afternoon. Some residents of outlying places attended churches nearer their homes[14] and on the same day the Bible Christian chapel at Broom's green had a congregation of 26 in the morning and 40 in the evening[15] and a Wesleyan Methodist chapel on Bromesberrow heath, built in 1847 by a carpenter James Underwood, had a congregation of 50 in the evening.[16]

In 1862 William Charles Henry of Haffield, in Ledbury, built a school church, a single room with an apsidal east end, west of Bromesberrow heath.[17] The vicar usually delegated services there to a curate,[18] much of whose stipend Henry paid.[19] Neighbouring clergy continued to minister to inhabitants elsewhere[20] and in 1873 the north-western corner of Dymock at the Leadington and Hallwood green was transferred to Preston for ecclesiastical purposes.[21]

At the parish church the Cheltenham firm of Middleton & Goodman restored the nave and chapels in 1870 and 1871 and a north vestry and organ chamber were added to the chancel in 1874. The Gloucester firm of Waller & Son conducted later alterations but altogether the gradual changes, among them the scraping of the interior walls, the removal of galleries, the reinstatement of windows, and the introduction of new furnishings, lacked a unified plan. Prominent members of the congregation such as the Thackwells paid for many new fittings, which included a font and a pulpit, and much of the window glass was replaced by stained glass memorials to individual parishioners.[22]

During that period the 6th Earl Beauchamp (d. 1891), a strenuous High Churchman,[23] had great influence on Church life. As rector he financed alterations in the church's chancel, sharing the cost of the new organ chamber with the congregation,[24] and as patron of the living from 1866[25] he appointed a succession of vicars with High Church views. William Baird, vicar from 1867, introduced music for

---

1 Hockaday Abs. clxxxvii; GA, P 125/VE 2/2; see ibid. IN 1/10, memorandums at front of vol.
2 Hockaday Abs. clxxxvii; J. Simons, *A Friendly Address to the Labourers and Working People of the Parish of Dymock* (Worcester, 1832: copy in Glos. Colln. R 116.15).
3 GDR vol. 383, no cxi.
4 GA, P 125/CW 2/8.
5 Ibid. VE 2/2; see *Educ. of Poor Digest*, 298.
6 GDR vol. 383, no cxi.
7 Hockaday Abs. clxxxvii; see ibid. ccxciii, Newent, 1820.
8 *Gorsley Baptist Chapel 1852–1952* (copy in GA, NC 46), 8.
9 Hockaday Abs. clxxxvii.
10 Ibid.; TNA, HO 129/335/2/1/2.
11 G.E. Lawrence, *Bible Christians of the Forest of Dean*, ed. H.R. Jarrett (1985: copy in GA, NC 79), 26; see GA, P 125A/MI 1/1, p. 10.
12 Information from Mary Pochin of Burntwood (Staffs.) based on research in the archives of the Church of Jesus Christ of Latter Day Saints, Salt Lake City (Ut.).

13 *Glouc. J.* 8 Aug., 12 Sept. 1840; GA, P 125/CH 4/4.
14 TNA, HO 129/335/2/1/1.
15 Ibid. HO 129/335/2/1/2.
16 Ibid. HO 129/335/2/1/3; for Underwood, GA, reg. wills 1867, ff. 254–6.
17 TNA, ED 7/34/117.
18 MCA, L 1i, (2) letter 4 June 1866; GA, P 125/IN 4/1; IN 1/17.
19 GA, P 125/MI 17 (par. mag. July 1867); IN 1/18, p. 232.
20 Ibid. MI 17 (par. mag. Dec. 1867); MCA, L 1i, (2) letter 24 Nov. 1866.
21 Below, Preston, religious hist. (patronage and endowment; religious life).
22 GA, P 125/CW 2/3; CW 3/2; IN 1/18; VE 2/3; D 2593/2/389, 399. See Verey and Brooks, *Glos.* II, 345. A screen made of oak pews removed in 1870 stood in the vicar's house in 1911: GA, D 2299/2/10/6, p. 8.
23 *Oxford DNB*; see *VCH Worcs.* IV, 121.
24 GA, P 125/CW 2/3.
25 Above (patronage and endowment).

41. *Dymock church the interior looking east in 1948*

which the barrel organ in the west gallery was unsuited but within two years he had returned to the East End of London.¹ Under William Charles Edmund Newbolt (1870–7),² whose practices faced strong opposition, the church acquired new altar furnishings and plate, the west gallery was pulled down, an instrument was placed in the new organ chamber, and the choir began wearing surplices. Differences with the bellringers culminated in 1873 with their exclusion from the belfry and the formation of a new band;³ new rules were made in 1879 for managing the belfry and encouraging change ringing.⁴ Under Reginald Horton (1883–1911)⁵ a pipe organ was donated in 1885 by C.H. Palairet of Berkeley⁶ and screens were erected at the entrances to the chancel and south chapel.⁷

In the late 19th century one or more curates usually assisted the vicar.⁸ Services continued in Haffield school near Bromesberrow heath⁹ and Anglicans held missions elsewhere, including Broom's green,¹⁰ where they used the nonconformist chapel in the early 20th century,¹¹ and Hallwood green, where in the same period Revd A.P. Doherty from Preston conducted open-air services during the summer.¹²

Nonconformist activity was confined to small meetings. Although the chapel on Bromesberrow heath closed, probably on the death of its owner in 1867,¹³ Wesleyans established a mission to Dymock village in 1875¹⁴ and preachers of the Ledbury circuit held services at Greenway House in 1884.¹⁵ The Broom's green chapel, which was not on the Bible Christian circuit plan for 1858,¹⁶ was taken over by the Primitive Methodist mission from Gloucester in 1875. The mission, which also held services at Hallwood green and Bromesberrow heath, closed the chapel in 1894. Wesleyan Methodists used it in 1900¹⁷ and it was reopened as an Anglican mission room the following year.¹⁸ Baptists were active in Dymock in the early 1870s¹⁹ and the Gorsley church began holding services at Four Oaks in 1887.²⁰ A Congregational minister living at Hill Grove in 1901²¹ presumably served the church formed in Dymock the previous year.²²

---

1 MCA, L 1i, (2) letters 7 Dec. 1866–4 May 1867; W. Baird, *Feeding the Lambs* (London, 1870: copy in Glos. Colln. SR 3.32).
2 *Alumni Oxon.* 1715–1886, III, 1014. For Newbolt, also see *Oxford DNB*.
3 GA, P 125/ IN 4/19.
4 *Glos. Ch. Bells*, 279–80; see GA, P 125/MI 5.
5 GA, P 125/IN 1/18, pp. 1, 14; IN 1/21, f. 142.
6 Ibid. IN 4/20.
7 Ibid. P 125/CW 3/5; CW 3/15; IN 1/18, p. 222; IN 1/21, f. 95. Fig. 41.
8 GA, P 125/IN 1/31; IN 4/19; D 2593/2/399 (par. mag. Feb. 1880).
9 Ibid. P 125/CW 3/3; IN 1/21.
10 Ibid. IN 1/18, p. 112; IN 1/19.
11 Ibid. IN 1/21, ff. 28, 55; below (next para.).

12 Grace Ruck, *Preston: A Guide and History* (1953: copy in GA, PA 256), 16.
13 GA, G/NE 160/3/1, f. 93; reg. wills 1867, ff. 254–6.
14 Ibid. P 125/IN 4/19.
15 Ibid. D 2689/1/2/4.
16 Lawrence, *Bible Christians of the Forest of Dean*, 29.
17 GA, D 3689/3/1/2–3; P 125/IN 1/21, f. 28; OS Map 6", Glos. X.SW (1903 edn).
18 GA, P 125/IN 1/21, f. 28.
19 Ibid. IN 4/19.
20 *Gorsley Baptist Chapel 1852–1952*, 10.
21 TNA, RG 13/2422.
22 GA, D 2052.

After the First World War

Sidney Marston, who until his appointment as vicar in 1911 had been chaplain to the 7th Earl Beauchamp at Madresfield (Worcs.),[1] served Dymock church in person. Elements of High Church ritual that he reintroduced to worship[2] were dropped after he left Dymock in 1937.[3] Haffield school was used from 1923 for a Sunday school formerly held at Bromesberrow Heath but regular church services apart from harvest festivals ceased in it.[4] Bromesberrow Heath was transferred, together with Lintridge and part of Ryton, to Bromesberrow for ecclesiastical purposes in 1935.[5] John Eric Gethyn-Jones, who succeeded his father Daniel as rector in 1955, was Dymock's resident clergyman from 1937 until 1967, apart from the war years, and the author of several local history books, including *Dymock Down the Ages* first published in 1951.[6] In the late 20th century Dymock was served with several other parishes by a priest resident in the village and from 2000 it was part of a larger team ministry led by a woman living in Redmarley D'Abitot.[7]

About 1920 an evangelical group put up a small wooden hall at Shakesfield. The building, which later was clad in iron and had a porch added,[8] was described as a gospel hall in 1939[9] and remained in use in the early 1970s.[10] In 1973 a former railway shed on the south side of the village was adapted as a chapel (Western Way Chapel)[11] and in 2006 the hall at Shakesfield stood long abandoned. From 1924 the Baptist mission to Four Oaks held its services in a new chapel just within Oxenhall.[12]

HUNTLEY

HUNTLEY is a small rural parish lying under May hill 11 km west of Gloucester. The parish, the suffix *ley* in its name denoting a woodland clearing,[13] came to cover 1,439 a.[14] (582 ha) in a compact area with its southern boundary following the Ley brook in the west and a Roman road leading westwards from Gloucester in the east.[15] North of that road Huntley's eastern boundary was the tract of land known in the 13th century as the wood of Birdwood[16] and beyond the main road from Gloucester to Ross-on-Wye (Herefs.) it passed the place known by the late 18th century as Solomon's Tump.[17]

LANDSCAPE

From the eastern side of the parish, which is fairly flat and lies at just over 30 m, the land rises gradually before climbing steeply, under May hill, to 200 m on Huntley hill in the west and 170 m on Bright's hill in the north-west. Off the sandstone hills of the west[18] the land lies on the Keuper Marl and in places gravel terrace.[19] The south of the parish is drained by a stream flowing off May hill between Huntley and Bright's hills into a ravine known as Deep Filling and continuing south-eastwards past Woodend to join the Ley brook midway along the south boundary. Off the hills the stream was canalized in the mid 19th century and the lower of two ponds created high up between Huntley and Bright's hills at that time was adapted c.1900 as a reservoir to supply water to houses below.[20] On the north side of the parish a stream flowing eastwards from springs in the centre was known as Butterwall brook in the early 18th century.[21]

The wood that according to Domesday Book measured two leagues by one on William son of Baderon's estate was a substantial remnant of

---

1 GA, P 125/IN 1/21, ff. 142, 144.
2 Ibid. MI 27 (par. mag. Feb. 1921).
3 Ibid. D 3028/1; Gethyn-Jones, *Dymock Down the Ages*, 56.
4 GA, P 125/MI 27 (par. mags. Apr. and May 1919, Aug. 1923); D 3028/1.
5 Ibid. P 125/IN 4/11; Gethyn-Jones, *Dymock Down the Ages*, 126.
6 Gethyn-Jones, *Dymock Down the Ages* (1966 edn), pp. viii, 56; 'Obituaries', *Trans. BGAS* 114 (1996), 217–18.
7 *Dioc. of Glouc. Dir.* (2000–1), 43, 91; (2001–2), 24, 122.
8 Information from 'Glimpses of Life in Kempley' (exhibition in Kempley Baptist chapel 13–16 Oct. 2006).
9 *Kelly's Dir. Glos.* (1939), 158.
10 OS Maps 1:25,000, SO 63 (1957 edn); 1:2,500, SO 6831–6931 (1973 edn).
11 GA, D 3295/I/6.
12 Below, Oxenhall, religious hist. (religious life); see OS Map 6", Glos. XVII.NW (1901, 1924 edns).
13 *PN Glos.* III, 191. This account was written in 2006.
14 *OS Area Book* (1883).
15 I.D. Margary, *Roman Roads in Britain*, II (1957), 59–60.
16 C.E. Hart, 'The Metes and Bounds of the Forest of Dean', *Trans. BGAS* 5 (1945), 185. For the wood of Birdwood, see *VCH Glos.* X, 11.
17 GA, P 184/MI 4; OS Map 1", sheet 43 (1831 edn).
18 See C. Callaway, 'Longmyndian Inliers at Old Radnor and Huntley', *Quarterly J. Geol. Soc.* 56 (1900), 511–20.
19 Geol. Surv. Map 1:50,000, solid and drift, sheet 234 (1972 edn).
20 GDR, T 1/106; OS Map 6", Glos. XXIV.SW (1889, 1903, 1924 edns).
21 Hockaday Abs. ccxlviii, 1806; see GA, D 1297, survey of Huntley, Netherley, and Longhope 1717, Huntley no 4.

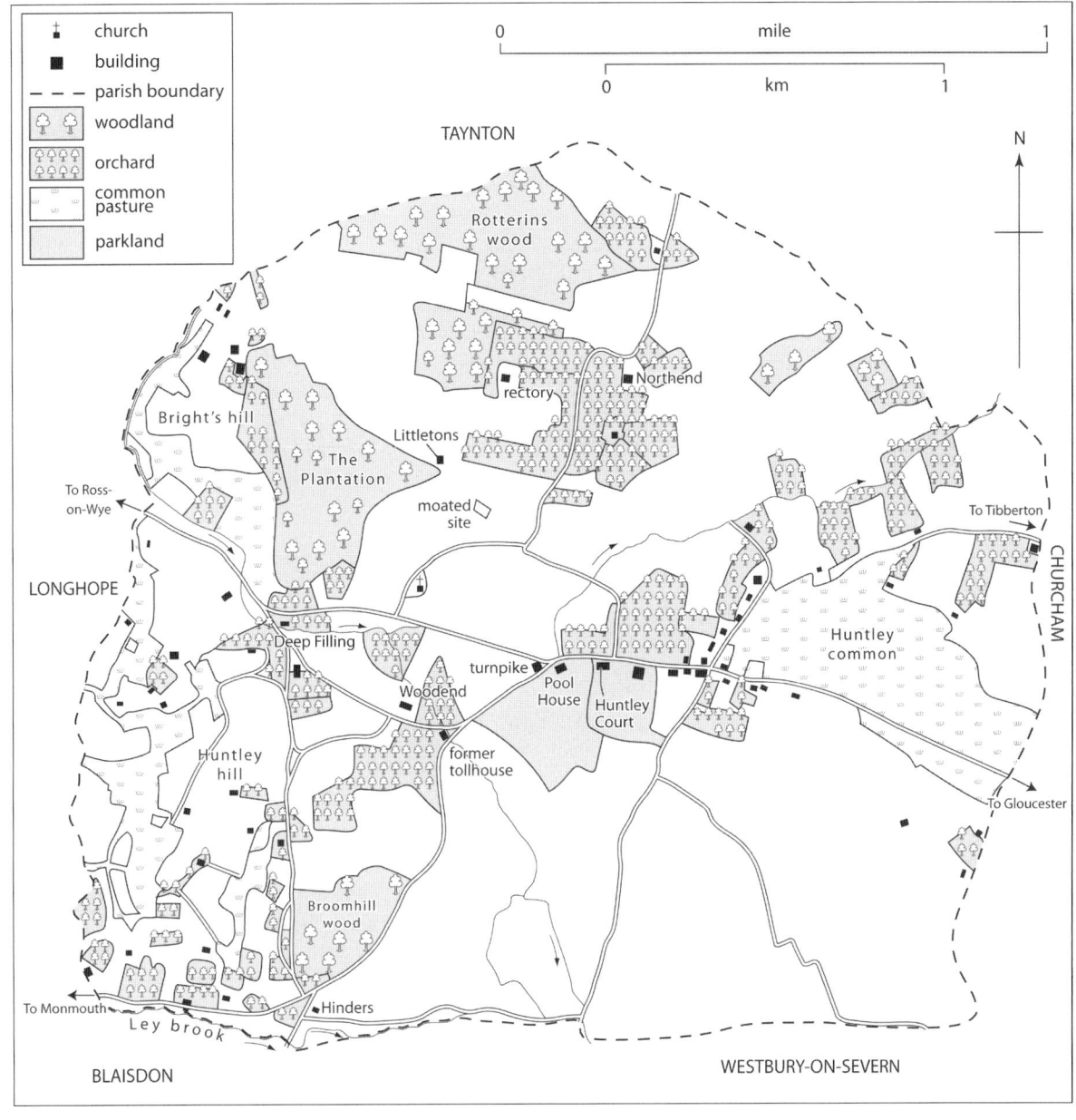

Map 9. *Huntley 1840*

ancient woodland that extended westwards into Longhope.[1] Felling of the wood in Huntley included clearances by Walter of Huntley in the mid 13th century, one alongside the main road to hinder the activities of robbers and another above his court house.[2] In early modern times a third of Huntley was partly wooded common or waste land.[3] Part of Huntley Wood common, which ran over Huntley and Bright's hills, was turned into a woodland nursery in the mid 18th century[4] and the summit of Huntley hill, called Elm Head hill on a map of 1777,[5] had a crown of one or more fir trees at the end of the century.[6] Huntley common, on the east side of the parish, was confined to 57 a. mostly on the north side of the Gloucester–Ross road when it was inclosed in the 1850s and Huntley Wood common covered 95 a. at its final inclosure in the 1870s.[7] The parish had a few small patches of waste land, including part of Gander's green behind Bright's hill, at the time of the Commons Registration Act of 1965.[8]

1 *Domesday Book* (Rec. Com.), I, 167.
2 TNA, E 32/31, m. 15.
3 Bigland, *Glos.* II, 111; see GA, D 1297, surv. 1717, Huntley nos 3, 5–6; Longhope no 16.
4 Bigland, *Glos.* II, 111; below, econ. hist. (woodland management).
5 Taylor, *Map of Glos.* (1777).
6 GA, P 184/MI 4; Bryant, *Map of Glos.* (1824).
7 GA, Q/RI 83–4.
8 Ibid. DA 30/132/11.

In 1841 there was an estimated 148 a. of woodland in the parish, most of it in the north in the Plantation (44 a.) and Rotterins (later Cherry) wood (44 a.) and smaller areas in the north-east and in Broomhill wood in the south-west.[1] In a redrawing of the boundaries of the northern woodland following exchanges of land in 1857 and 1866[2] part of Rotterins wood was felled for farmland and land around the rectory house (Huntley Manor) to its south was imparked.[3] The park was extended eastwards following a road diversion in 1902 and 1903.[4] Much of the remaining open land on Bright's and Huntley hills was covered with woodland in the late 19th and early 20th century, most of the new planting there happening after 1905 when woodland accounted for 160 a. in Huntley and included small new woods in the south-east of the parish.[5] A golf course was created in the east of the parish in 1996.[6]

ROADS

The main road to Ross-on-Wye and Hereford, a branch off the Roman road from Gloucester,[7] crosses the middle of the parish from east to west, passing along the south side of Huntley common into the village's main street. West of the village the road formerly ran south-westwards to a fork near Woodend, from where the Monmouth road branched southwards on a curving course through cuttings up to Little London, in Longhope. The Ross road continued south of Woodend and climbed north-westwards through Deep Filling between Huntley and Bright's hills towards Dursley Cross, in Longhope.[8] In the mid or late 1820s it was diverted north of Woodend to take a more direct line at the start of its ascent west of the village[9] and a tollhouse opened at the junction near Woodend c.1770[10] was replaced by a new building at the new junction with the Monmouth road.[11] The Ross road had been turnpiked through Huntley in 1726 and the Monmouth road in 1747;[12] they remained turnpikes until 1880.[13] In the later 17th century traffic from Gloucester also followed the Roman road along the south side of the parish. That route, which joined the Monmouth road east of Little London,[14] fell into disuse early in the turnpike era[15] and it survives mostly as a track or footpath.

Of the lanes leading from the crossroads at the east end of the village, that to the north ran along the side of Huntley common, from which there were early routes north-westwards towards Newent and north-eastwards towards Tibberton.[16] In 1856, on the eve of the common's inclosure, the road was remade as the entrance (North Road) to a new road towards Tibberton.[17] The lane southwards from the crossroads, the beginning of which was once part of an ancient way to Huntley mill and Blaisdon,[18] is called Grange Court Lane. It leads to Upper Ley and Lower Ley in Westbury-on-Severn and was straightened in the south-east of Huntley in the late 1880s when it was a way to Grange Court railway station.[19]

Further west, out of a network of lanes north of the main road,[20] a road to Newent, described as a highway in 1584[21] and making several sharp turns,[22] was straightened past Northend in 1902 and 1903, the diversion taking it further east away from Huntley Manor.[23] In the west of the parish Hinders Lane, running southwards from the Ross road at Deep Filling and across the Monmouth road into Blaisdon, and the road running northwards from the Ross road to Gander's green and Glasshouse hill were deemed ancient public rights of way at inclosure in 1872.[24]

POPULATION

Ten tenant households were recorded on the Huntley estate in 1086[25] and seven men and women were assessed for tax in the parish in 1327.[26] A muster

---

1 GDR, T 1/106.
2 GA, Q/RI 83; *Morris's Dir. Glos.* (1876), 505–6; *Kelly's Dir. Glos.* (1870), 584, dated the second exchange to 1865.
3 GDR, T 1/106; OS Map 6", Glos. XXIV.SW (1889 edn).
4 OS Map 6", Glos. XXIV.SW (1903, 1924 edns); GA, Q/SRh 1902C.
5 OS Map 6", Glos. XXIV.SW (1889, 1903, 1924 edns); Acreage Returns, 1905.
6 *Huntley Parish Plan July 2004* (copy in Glos. Colln. 49658), 80.
7 Margary, *Roman Roads in Britain*, II, 59–62.
8 Taylor, *Map of Glos.* (1777).
9 Bryant, *Map of Glos.* (1824); Greenwood, *Map of Glos.* (1824); OS Map 1", sheet 43 (1831 edn).
10 See GA, D 204/2/2; Taylor, *Map of Glos.* (1777).
11 GDR, T 1/106 (nos 120, 396).
12 Glouc. & Heref. Roads Acts, 12 Geo. I, c. 13; 20 Geo. II, c. 31.
13 Annual Turnpike Acts Continuance Act, 1880, 43 & 44 Vic. c. 12.
14 Ogilby, *Britannia* (1675), plate 15; GA, D 1297, surv. 1717, Huntley nos 1, 2, 8; see *VCH Glos.* X, 12.
15 See Taylor, *Map of Glos.* (1777); OS Map 1", sheet 43 (1831 edn).
16 GA, D 1297, surv. 1717, Huntley no 3; GDR, T 1/106.
17 GA, Q/RI 83; Q/SR 1857 A.
18 Ibid. D 1297, surv. 1717, Huntley nos 1, 2, 8; Hart, 'The Metes and Bounds of the Forest of Dean', 185. For the mill, below, econ. hist. (other mills).
19 GA, P 184/OV 2/1; OS Map 6", Glos. XXIV.SW (1888, 1903 edns). For the station, *VCH Glos.* X, 85.
20 GA, D 1297, surv. 1717, Huntley nos 4–6; Taylor, *Map of Glos.* (1777).
21 GDR, V 5/170T 1.
22 GA, P 184/MI 4.
23 Ibid. Q/SRh 1902C; OS Map 6", Glos. XXIV.SW (1903, 1924 edns).
24 GA, Q/RI 84.
25 *Domesday Book* (Rec. Com.), I, 167.
26 *Glos. Subsidy Roll, 1327*, 35.

of 1542 named 31 men[1] and the parish had c.120 communicants in 1551[2] and 40 households in 1563.[3] The number of communicants was put at 150 in 1603[4] and the number of families at 50 in 1650.[5] The population, estimated at 240 c.1710[6] and 269 c.1775,[7] stood at 313 in 1801 and grew to 555 in 1851. It then declined, particularly in the 1870s, before rising from 416 in 1881 to 445 in 1901. Another decline in the early 20th century was checked in the 1920s but the population did not recover fully until the later 20th century, when, as a result of new building in the village, it rose from 498 in 1961 to 1,161 in 1981. After that it dropped back slightly and in 2001 it was 1,023.[8]

SETTLEMENT

Early farmsteads in Huntley were scattered throughout the parish below the steeper slopes on its west side. The pattern of settlement was also determined by the survival until the later 19th century of extensive commons on both sides of the parish. Thus the parish church stands apart from the village, which grew up later on the fringes of Huntley common.

THE VILLAGE

The village of Huntley stands in the eastern half of the parish. It developed on a simple plan formed by the main Gloucester–Ross road and a line of encroachments to the north along the edge of Huntley common on what has become the west side of North Road.[9] Just off the main road east of North Road, opposite the junction of Grange Court Lane, is the base of a wayside cross. In the late 16th century a poorhouse stood nearby next to a horse pool and well.[10] There was also a pound on the edge of the common.[11] At the crossroads the Red Lion inn facing east to North Road was known as the George in the mid 17th century and had expanded onto the site of another inn, the Crown, by the 1730s.[12] To its north was a dwelling called the Pale or Paled House in the mid 17th century,[13] and one of the cottages standing on the edge of the common in the early 18th century survives in Ivydene House.[14] West of the crossroads Huntley Court, south of the main road, is a substantial house built, apparently in the mid 17th century, in the grounds of the White Hart inn,[15] where the manor court was held in the mid 18th century;[16] it was remodelled in the late 18th century as a landowner's residence.[17]

East of the crossroads a few houses were built south of the main road from the early 19th century and several villas were built further out in the 1860s and 1870s following the inclosure of Huntley common.[18] Forest Gate (formerly Pool House), at the west end of the village, occupies the large site of a farmhouse that was rebuilt as a residence for the Probyn family in the early 19th century[19] and became the rectory house in 1866.[20] To its west, beyond the former line of the Monmouth road, a polygonal toll house erected c.1830[21] has an extension added in 1881 when it was a private house.[22] In the 20th century, and more particularly after the Second World War, the village was enlarged considerably by private and council development. While detached houses and bungalows were built on the main road and on Grange Court Lane, most of the new building took place north of the main road where several fields were covered with housing estates in the 1960s and 1970s.[23]

OUTLYING SETTLEMENT

The parish church stands off the Ross road 1 km west of the village. The Court House, a dwelling standing to its west[24] presumably on the site of Walter of Huntley's court house recorded in 1282,[25] was sold in 1725 to (Sir) Edmund Probyn[26] and was demolished, presumably by 1752 when the manor court was held elsewhere.[27] From that time the church stood on its

---

1 *L&P Hen. VIII*, XVII, 499.
2 J. Gairdner, 'Bishop Hooper's Visitation of Gloucester', *EHR* 19 (1904), 120.
3 Bodleian, Rawl. C. 790, f. 27v.
4 *Eccl. Misc.* 101.
5 C.R. Elrington, 'The Survey of Church Livings in Gloucestershire, 1650', *Trans. BGAS* 83 (1964), 98.
6 Atkyns, *Glos.* 486.
7 Rudder, *Glos.* 505.
8 *Census*, 1801–2001.
9 GA, D 1297, surv. 1717, Huntley no 3; GDR, T 1/106.
10 GA, P 184/IN 1/1, terrier 1692 at front of vol.; MI 4; see below, social hist. (charities for the poor).
11 GA, D 1297, surv. 1717, Huntley nos 3, 13.
12 Below, social hist. (social life).
13 GA, D 365/T 4.
14 Ibid. D 1297, surv. 1717, Huntley no 3.
15 Ibid. Huntley nos 7, 11.
16 Ibid. D 23/T 10.
17 Below, manor.
18 GA, Q/RI 83; OS Map 6", Glos. XXIV.SW (1889 edn).
19 GA, D 1230/1; P 184/MI 4; GDR, T 1/106 (no 420); for the Probyns at Pool House, below, social hist.
20 Below, religious hist.
21 Above, introd. (roads).
22 TNA, RG 11/2525.
23 Below (bldgs.).
24 GA, D 23/T 14, deed 25 Dec. 1719; D 1297, surv. 1717, Huntley nos 6, 9.
25 TNA, E 32/31, m. 15.
26 GA, D 1230/1.
27 Ibid. D 23/T 10.

42. Huntley church from the south-east: the school is on the left

own until the early 1840s[1] when a school and school house were built to its west.[2] On the hillside to the north, the 17th-century house of a farmstead called Littletons at the eastern corner of the plantation established in the mid 18th century[3] became a gamekeeper's cottage.[4] Lower down to its south-east is a rectangular moated site.[5] Huntley Manor,[6] further to the north-east, occupies the site of the early rectory house and dates from a rebuilding for Daniel Capper in 1862 and 1863.[7] A farmstead established by Capper north of the house close up to Rotterins wood[8] was known in 1861 as Exhibition Farm[9] and later, after its acquisition by Edmund Probyn in 1866, as Home Farm.[10]

North of Huntley common a cottage stood among a group of closes called the Billes in the mid 17th century[11] and a farmstead (Yew Tree Farm) was established nearby following the common's inclosure in 1857.[12] South of the main road a farmhouse on the parish boundary, known as Coppice Cottage in the 1880s,[13] dated probably from the 18th century.[14] The house at Frogland, on the lane leading north-westwards from Huntley common,[15] was recorded from 1637[16] and demolished with its outbuildings in the mid 20th century, the lane having become a cul-de-sac (Frog Lane) by the mid 19th century.[17] Out on the Newent road at Northend, where there was at least one house in 1509,[18] the farmhouse occupied by William Hopton in 1673[19] has been rebuilt. The cottage at Little Northend, a little higher up to the south, dates from the 17th century[20] and was known as Pain's Knapp in 1728.[21] A few houses stand further along the road, one being built on the parish boundary in the early 19th century. A house known as Alma Villa in 1891[22] that became the property and residence of the Elton family[23] was converted as four flats by C.P. Ackers in 1946.[24]

In the west of the parish the farmstead at Woodend served the largest farm on the manor

---

1 GDR, T 1/106.
2 GA, P 184/SC 1; below, social hist. Fig. 42.
3 GA, D 4869/1/1/2; P 184/MI 4; see ibid. D 1297, surv. 1717, Huntley no 6; GDR, T 1/106 (no 68). For the plantation, above, introd. (landscape).
4 TNA, RG 9/1758; GA, SL 10.
5 OS Map 6", Glos. XXIV.SW (1889 edn).
6 See below, manor.
7 Below, religious hist. (patronage and endowment: rectory houses).
8 See GDR, T 1/106 (no 71).
9 TNA, RG 1758. In 1863 it was Rectory Farm: *Kelly's Dir. Glos.* (1863), 297.
10 GA, SL 10; see OS Map 1:2,500, Glos. XXIV.10 (1883 edn).
11 GA, D 23/T 7; see ibid. D 1297, surv. 1717, Huntley nos 3, 11.

12 Ibid. Q/RI 83; P 184/OV 2/1, min. 12 Dec. 1862; see TNA, RG 10/2605.
13 GDR, T 1/196 (no 479); OS 6", Glos. XXIV.SW (1889 edn).
14 See GA, D 1297, surv. 1717, Huntley no 2; D 4869/1/1/2.
15 OS Map 6", Glos. XXIV.SW (1889 edn).
16 GDR wills 1637/51.
17 OS Maps 6", Glos. XXIV.SW (1924 edn); 1:2,500, SO 7219–7319 (1972 edn); GDR, T 1/106.
18 Hockaday Abs. ccxlviii.
19 TNA, PROB 11/347, f. 109 and v.
20 DoE List, Huntley (1985), 3/50.   21 GA, D 23/T 15.
22 TNA, RG 12/2007.
23 GDR, T 1/106 (nos 81–2); GA, D 2428/1/65, f.5.
24 GA, DA 24/100/14, min. 28 Aug. 1946; M. Hamlen, 'History of Huntley' (1981: typescript in Glos. Colln. 45959), 244.

estate in the early 18th century.¹ Its house dates from the 17th century and among the outbuildings are substantial ranges provided in the late 1850s by Edmund Probyn.² In 2006, when the farmstead was the centre of a riding school, the house accommodated offices, a house, and rooms for eight students and the outbuildings included an indoor arena completed in 1979.³ In 1936 the Huntley Manor estate built two log cabins north of the farmstead by the Ross road, one for offices and the other for an estate cottage.⁴

On the Monmouth road the Lower House, a copyhold standing east of the stream flowing south-eastwards past Woodend,⁵ was demolished in the 18th century.⁶ Further along the road another farmhouse, low down beside the Blaisdon road, was called the Sheepscot in the early 18th century.⁷ Known later as Hinders,⁸ it was rebuilt on a larger scale in the late 19th century. In the same period two new houses were built nearby, on the north side of the Monmouth road.⁹ Further along the road towards Little London, where there was a number of cottages in the late 18th century,¹⁰ are several 20th-century houses.¹¹

Scattered settlement had begun on Huntley hill by the early 17th century, when a dwelling on its lower slopes was known as Wood House or Woods,¹² and had penetrated Smokey bottom, a dell high above Deep Filling, by the early 18th.¹³ By that time there were several dwellings on or near the old Ross road in Deep Filling¹⁴ and in the late 18th century one at the junction of the road with Hinders Lane was known as Roughcast House. Cottages were also built at and below Gander's green.¹⁵ More dwellings, mostly small squatter cottages, were erected high up on the commons and in the dells in the early and mid 19th century.¹⁶ Among the few built there after inclosure in the 1870s the Firs, above Hinders Lane, was for Albert Knight in 1903.¹⁷ Many of the dwellings have been enlarged, one (Brook Villa) being rebuilt by Edmund Probyn as early as 1857,¹⁸ and some of the earlier cottages have been abandoned. The Rest House overlooking the Ross road was erected c.1930 by Forest Products Ltd for tea rooms and had a wooden annex, higher up, with ten bedrooms.¹⁹

BUILDINGS

The only medieval fabric in Huntley appears in the church tower and as the base of a medieval cross near the junction of the main road and North Road, which serves as the centre of the village. Of the surviving timber-framed houses The Old Rectory, in the village just off North Road, was called Newhall in the mid 19th century²⁰ and appears to be the late 16th-century two-storeyed cross wing of a house of high status. It had oriel windows and close studding on its gable ends.²¹ The other, smaller houses were built in the 17th century with their frames infilled with both wattle and daub and brick. They include the former farmhouse of Littletons and the cottage at Little Northend.²² Ivydene House, one of the village's timber-framed houses, occupies an early encroachment on the edge of Huntley common.²³ The outbuildings north of the former farmhouse at Northend include an early 18th-century timber-framed barn.²⁴

The first extensive use of brick is found at Huntley Court²⁵ and at the two-storeyed Red Lion inn. The latter, built on an L plan in the late 17th or early 18th century when it was known as the George,²⁶ was extended by a range of farm buildings and later a western residential block was added.

During the 19th century cottages were enlarged, small stone and brick houses were built randomly on the commons and hills, and the appearance of the main road through the village was transformed by the building of terraced cottages and plain, three-bayed red brick villas. The villas, then the smartest small houses in the parish, include a group of three on the south side,²⁷ one being larger and L-plan, and a later, more elaborately finished house dated 1888. The Laurels, further east, is one of three villas on a series of regular plots laid out on the north side of the road following the inclosure of Huntley common in 1857.²⁸

1 GA, D 1297, surv. 1717, Huntley nos 7, 10; D 3921/I/58.
2 Below (bldgs.).
3 Information from Mrs Torill Freeman of Home Farm.
4 Hamlen, 'Huntley', 17; see GA, D 2299/8665.
5 GA, D 23/T 6; D 1297, surv. 1717, Huntley no 7.
6 See ibid. P 184/MI 4.
7 Ibid. D 23/T 6; D 1297, surv. 1717, Huntley no 8.
8 Ibid. P 184/MI 4; GDR, T 1/106 (no 26).
9 OS Map 1:2,500, Glos. XXXIV.14 (1884, 1903 edns); see GA, SL 10.
10 GA, P 184/MI 1.
11 One is dated 1912 with the inits. 'R' and 'S'.
12 GA, D 1230/2; see D 1297, surv. 1717, Huntley no 7.
13 Ibid. D 23/T 15; see Hamlen, 'Huntley', 202, 232.
14 GA, D 1230/2; see D 1297, surv. 1717, Longhope no 16.
15 GA, P 184/MI 4.
16 GDR, T 1/106; GA, Q/RI 84; see Hamlen, 'Huntley', 203.
17 Datestone with inits. on ho.; see GA, D 2299/1434.
18 GDR, T 1/106 (no 140); Hamlen, 'Huntley', 234.
19 *Kelly's Dir. Glos.* (1931), 230; (1935), 231; information from Mrs Freeman.
20 GA, D 177, Wilton, Huntley papers 1855–6; GDR, T 1/106 (nos 528–9).
21 DoE List, Huntley, 7/53.
22 Ibid. 7/48; 3/50.
23 GA, D 1297, surv. 1717, Huntley no 3.
24 DoE List, Huntley, 3/51.
25 Below, manor.
26 See below, social hist. (social life).
27 e.g. DoE List, Huntley, 7/45–6.
28 GA, Q/RI 83; OS Map 6", Glos. XXIV.SW (1889 edn).

Several major building projects were undertaken within the parish in the mid 19th century. In the late 1850s Edmund Probyn created at Woodend the largest and most systematically planned farmstead on his estates in the area. The existing farmhouse, screened on the south in the earlier 19th century by a longer brick range, was remodelled and enlarged and new buildings were placed to the north. The new outbuildings, designed by J. & J. Girdwood,[1] are of orange-red brick with slate roofs and form an E which opens to the south and has more elaborately treated outer façades. The east–west spine incorporates a hay barn, a two-storeyed granary and feed store that contained probably water-powered machinery for feed preparation, and stables that return as the west wing. The east wing has other stables and a trap house. The central range is a double cowhouse, its wide-span roof of composite timber and iron construction.

The rector Daniel Capper, who in 1862 and 1863 employed S.S. Teulon as the architect for a rebuilding of the church and the rectory house (later Huntley Manor)[2] as well as for his rebuilding of the village of Hunstanworth (Co. Dur.),[3] established Home Farm (in 1861 Exhibition Farm) north of the rectory and provided several other new buildings. Those at Home Farm, which Edmund Probyn acquired in 1866,[4] were arranged with an enclosed central courtyard for the house and an open-sided farmyard to the west.[5] Henry Miles, Capper's successor in 1866, adapted another house (later Forest Gate) as the rectory house[6] and rebuilt Capper's school,[7] which together with the new church formed a picturesque enclave in a parkland setting.[8]

After 1945 house building was concentrated in the village, where small brick houses and bungalows filled empty sites along the main road and covered the fields to the north. The first council houses, four pairs on North Road, were built in 1952[9] and, about the same time, C.P. Ackers, owner of the Huntley Manor estate, built a row of six flat-fronted bungalows with generous gardens on the Tibberton road.[10] In the 1960s and 1970s small estates of modest houses were laid out, mainly in *culs-de-sac*, east and west of North Road[11] and the remaining plots along the main road were filled by individual detached houses and bungalows. Some building also took place on Grange Court Lane. Among the buildings in North Road, which became a focus for social activity, is a plain brick village hall opened in 1970.[12] C.P. Ackers's conversion of the former Alma Villa on the Newent road as four flats in 1946 was to provide accommodation for men training in forestry at Huntley Manor.[13]

MANOR AND ESTATES

Following the Norman Conquest Huntley, like neighbouring Longhope, was among the possessions of the lords of Monmouth that passed eventually to the dukes of Lancaster. Among early landholders under Huntley manor was Peter de Somervill, whom the Crown restored to his lands in 1322.[14] Later property owners included nine freeholders resident *c.*1710.[15] The Probyns of Newland, who were investing in land in Huntley by the late 17th century, continued to buy up land there after acquiring the manor in the mid 1720s[16] and among the few properties to be independent of them in the mid 19th century[17] was an estate created at Huntley Court in the late 18th century. On the break up of the Probyns' estate in 1884 much of their land was bought with the house called Huntley Manor by the Ackers family, whose descendants sold off parts of that land in the later 20th century.

HUNTLEY MANOR

In 1066 Alwin held an estate of two hides in Huntley from Archbishop Ealdred of York. In 1086 the estate belonged to William son of Baderon,[18] lord of Monmouth, and in 1144 William's son Baderon of Monmouth confirmed Huntley church to Monmouth priory, founded by Wihanoc of Monmouth in

---

1 Verey and Brooks, *Glos.* II, 545. One outbldg. is dated 1858 with Probyn's inits.
2 Below, religious hist. (patronage and endowment; religious life).
3 N. Pevsner and E. Williamson, *County Durham* (Bldgs. of England, 1983), 333–4.
4 Above (outlying settlement).
5 GA, SL 10; OS Map 1:2,500, Glos. XXIV.10 (1883 edn).
6 Below, religious hist. (patronage and endowment; religious life).   7 Below, social hist. (education).
8 An illustration of the new church by Randall Druce (copy in the church) shows part of the original school.

9 GA, DA 24/602/1.
10 Ibid. DA 24/100/19, pp. 248, 435.
11 *Dean Forest Mercury*, 14 Mar. 1969; OS Maps 1:2,500, SO 7019–7119 (1973 edn); SO 7219–7319 (1972 edn); *Huntley Parish Plan*, 8.
12 Below, social hist. (social life).
13 GA, DA 24/100/14, min. 28 Aug. 1946; Hamlen, 'Huntley', 244.
14 *Cal Close* 1318–23, 420.
15 Atkyns, *Glos.* 486.
16 GA, D 1230/3.
17 See GDR, T 1/106.
18 *Domesday Book* (Rec. Com.), I, 167.

William I's reign.[1] Huntley descended to John of Monmouth (d. 1248)[2] and the overlordship of the manor, which owed the service of ½ knight's fee in the early 14th century,[3] passed with the lordship of Monmouth to the earls, later dukes, of Lancaster.[4]

Walter of Huntley, who acted for the Crown in 1255 as a seller of wood in the Forest of Dean,[5] had the manor in 1270 and 1282.[6] John of Huntley, son and heir of Thomas of Huntley, answered for the ½ knight's fee in 1303 and relinquished his right in the manor, in which Thomas's widow Ela had dower, to Robert de Sapy and his wife Aline by 1313.[7] Robert, under whom part of the manor was held by his father-in-law Nicholas of Bath,[8] was granted free warren on the demesne in 1317.[9] He added to his land in 1315 and 1320[10] and, having for a time been deprived of the manor by Thomas of Huntley and his wife Iseult,[11] died c.1336.[12] Aline was patron of Huntley church in 1340[13] and Thomas of Huntley's son Thomas quitclaimed the manor to Richard Talbot in 1344.[14]

Richard Talbot (d. 1356) was succeeded in the manor by his son Gilbert.[15] Following the latter's death in 1387 the manor descended with the Talbots' Longhope manor,[16] passing with it in the early 17th century to the Grey family, under which Huntley manor was being farmed in 1624 and 1628 by William Purefey and Benjamin Hale.[17] Sir Edmund Probyn of Newland bought both manors from Henry Grey, duke of Kent, in the mid 1720s[18] and added land in the adjoining part of Taynton to his estate.[19] His descendant Edmund Probyn, who became lord of Huntley in 1855,[20] took up residence in the parish and, having acquired it by exchange in 1866, moved into the new rectory house and renamed it Huntley Manor.[21] He sold most of the estate in 1884[22] but remained lord of the manor until his death in 1890,[23] after which the manorial rights apparently passed to Wilmot Inglis Jones.[24]

HUNTLEY MANOR (ACKERS ESTATE)

At the sale of Edmund Probyn's estate in 1884 Huntley Manor was bought with 1,100 a. in Huntley and Taynton, much of it woodland, by Benjamin St John Ackers.[25] Benjamin, who was MP for West Gloucestershire in 1885,[26] died in 1915. His son Charles Penrhyn Ackers,[27] who had bought 700 a. of woodland near by in Newent before the First World War,[28] enlarged the estate to about 2,000 a. by the purchase of woodland in Blaisdon in the early 1930s.[29] After his death in 1960[30] the estate passed to his daughter Torill. She married Michael Freeman and in 2006, with the sale of the estate's outlying parts and of land in Huntley, including in 1988 Huntley Manor, owned the farmland north of the Ross road with 1,200 a. of woodland in Huntley, Taynton, and Newent. Her sons had sold most of the farmland south of the Ross road.[31]

Huntley Manor was Revd Daniel Capper's rectory house built in 1862 and 1863. Designed as a small country house in a North French style by S.S. Teulon,[32] it had a broken skyline, diapered roof tiles, and iron balconies, finials, and lamps and its walls were of rendered brick.[33] The plan was rectangular, the rooms linked by a corridor around a small light well in which the main staircase rose on the east side. Very large rooms, including a library, were on the south and west and the main entrance was in a north-western projection that partly screened northern service rooms. The room closest to the front door served as a study.[34] The interior decoration included Minton tiles in the staircase hall and carved stone chimneypieces with marble jewels,

---

1 *Cal. Doc. France*, 409–10; For the lordship of Monmouth, I.J. Sanders, *English Baronies* (1960), 64–5 and nn.
2 *Book of Fees*, I, 50.
3 *Feudal Aids*, II, 250, 285.
4 *Inq. p.m. Glos.* 1302–58, 255, 361; 1359–1413, 153, 200, 245; *Cal. Close* 1360–4, 210; TNA, C 139/179, no 58; C 140/46, no 52. For the earls and dukes, *Complete Peerage*, VII, 378–418.
5 *Cal. Lib.* 1251–60, 224, 232.
6 TNA, E 32/29, rot. 8; E 32/30, rot. 23d.
7 *Cal. Close* 1307–13, 574; *Feudal Aids*, II, 250.
8 *Inq. p.m. Glos.* 1302–58, 197.
9 *Cal. Chart.* 1300–26, 363.
10 *Glos. Feet of Fines* 1300–59, pp. 43, 64.
11 *Cal. Pat.* 1324–7, 61.
12 *Inq. p.m. Glos.* 1302–58, 254–5.
13 *Reg. T. de Charlton*, 81, which names her as Alice de Sapy.
14 *Glos. Feet of Fines* 1300–59, no 753. Richard had acquired an estate of Aline's inheritance in Westbury-on-Severn: *VCH Glos.* X, 86.
15 *Inq. p.m. Glos.* 1302–58, 361.
16 Ibid. 1359–1413, 153, 200–1, 245; BL, Add. Ch. 72671; TNA, C 140/46, no 52; C 142/231, no 106. For the full descent, see below, Longhope, manor.
17 GA, D 23/T 6; Atkyns, *Glos.* 485.
18 GA, D 23/T 5, T 15, T 18.
19 Ibid. T 32.
20 Ibid. D 4869/1/1/6.
21 TNA, RG 9/1758; RG 10/2605; below, religious hist. (patronage and endowment).
22 GA, SL 10.
23 *Kelly's Dir. Glos.* (1885), 508; *Burke's Landed Gentry* (1898), II, 1218.
24 GA, P 184A/PC 1/1, pp. 7, 10, 14, 16.
25 GA, SL 10.
25 Williams, *Parl. Hist. of Glos.* 79.
27 For the Ackers fam., see *Burke's Landed Gentry* (1952), I, 2.
28 C.P. Ackers, *Practical British Forestry* (1947), p. viii; GA, G/NE 159/5/6, p. 56; 20, p. 56.
29 *VCH Glos.* X, 8.
30 *The Times*, 14 Nov. 1960.
31 Information from Mrs Freeman of Home Farm; N. Kingsley and M. Hill, *The Country Houses of Glos.* III (2001), 169.
32 *Glouc. J.* 18 Apr., 27 June 1863; Verey and Brooks, *Glos.* II, 545.
33 Below, Fig. 43.
34 GA, D 2593/2/475.

43. Huntley Manor in 1884

work comparable with that in the contemporary church. Ornamental gardens lay south and west of the house and a large kitchen garden to the north-west.[1]

In the late 19th and early 20th century the house was enlarged, a single-storeyed north hall for servants and billiard and smoking rooms being among the additions. Changes to its interior decoration included the introduction of 18th-century chimneypieces and stained glass designed in 1923 to display the Ackers family coat of arms in the staircase window. In 1964 many of the additions were removed to return the house to its original size.[2] The house's park was enlarged in the early 20th century[3] and an east lodge designed by Walter B. Wood was built on the Huntley–Newent road in 1923 and 1924[4] and was matched by a second lodge erected to its south in the late 1940s.[5] Mr Richard Gabriel, owner of the house from 1988, constructed an indoor swimming pool and a helicopter hangar in the grounds and sold the property in 2004 to Professor T. Congdon.[6]

HUNTLEY COURT

Huntley Court stands south of the main road in the grounds of the former White Hart inn,[7] which was kept by Giles White in 1657.[8] The house's compact double-pile plan[9] with central passage and its symmetrical elevations with crow-stepped gables suggest that it was built in the mid 17th century. There were four heated rooms on each of its two floors; a Mr White was taxed on 8 hearths in Huntley in 1672.[10] To the west a seven-bayed barn alongside the road has a series of cruck trusses evidently predating the house.[11] Thomas Blunt, a Mitcheldean surgeon,[12] bought the house with land in Huntley and Longhope from Edmund Probyn in 1794[13] and gave it the name Huntley Court.[14] He died in 1811 and after the death of his widow Mary in 1828[15] his lands passed to his daughter Harriet and the three sons of his late daughter Frances Nayler.[16] Harriet, who bought out her nephews' interests in Huntley Court in 1844, died in 1859 and the house and its land (25 a.), which she left to her nephew Revd Thomas Nayler, were sold in 1867 to Edmund Probyn. Charlotte Constance Blood bought them from him in 1884 and her son John Neptune Blood sold the house in 1925 to Spencer Shelley[17] (d. 1941). His son Spencer retained Huntley Court in 1975[18] but its ownership changed hands several times in the late 20th and early 21st century.[19]

After acquiring the house in 1794, Thomas Blunt altered its façade by inserting sash windows, tripartite on the ground floor, and a pedimented

---

1 OS Map 6", Glos. XXIV.SW (1889 edn).
2 Kingsley and Hill, *Country Houses of Glos.* III, 168–9.
3 Above, introd. (landscape).
4 GA, D 7942/414; see Verey and Brooks, *Glos.* II, 545.
5 M. Hamlen, 'History of Huntley' (1981: typescript in Glos. Colln. 45959), 241.
6 Information from Prof. Congdon.
7 GA, D 1297, survey of Huntley, Netherley, and Longhope 1717, Huntley nos. 7, 11.
8 TNA, E 134/1657/Mich. 47.
9 See GA, D 2593/2/488.
10 TNA, E 179/247/14, rot. 36d.
11 DoE List, Huntley (1985), 7/55; see GDR, T 1/106 (no 423).
12 GA, D 1280/5/21.
13 Ibid. D 2714, Shelley fam., Huntley Court deeds 1794–1947.
14 Ibid. P 184/MI 4; Rudge, *Hist. of Glos.* II, 55.
15 Ibid. D 2714, Shelley fam., Huntley Court deeds 1794–1947.
16 Ibid. D 6/F 3/9.
17 Ibid. D 2714, Shelley fam., Huntley Court deeds 1794–1947.
19 *The Times*, 4 Nov. 1941; 20 Mar. 1946; 18 Dec. 1975.
20 Information from Maureen and Richard Blakemore of Forest Gate.

44. Huntley Court: the south front in 1924

doorcase, created a west staircase, and added a stable court and probably the east service wing. Later hoodmoulds were added to the sashes in the main façade and bay windows to the three main reception rooms.[1] In the mid 19th century the house was occupied by tenants and for a time accommodated a school.[2] In changes designed for Charlotte Blood by James Dolman in 1885 a new porch and mullioned windows were put on the north front, a porch was constructed to link the bay windows on the south garden front, the service accommodation was enlarged, and there was minor remodelling inside both house and stables.[3]

ECONOMIC HISTORY

In Huntley's economy woodland management and crafts long played a central role alongside farming and orcharding.

AGRICULTURE

The Middle Ages

In 1086 William son of Baderon's estate in Huntley was worth 30s. compared with 40s. in 1066. In demesne it had one plough and one slave and its tenants were 4 villans and 6 bordars working a total of 3 ploughs.[4] In 1220 there were six ploughteams in Huntley.[5] In 1326 the estate that Nicholas of Bath had held from the lord of the manor included 80 a. of arable, 2 a. of meadow, 2 a. of pasture, and 3s. in rents of assize from three free tenants[6] and in 1337 the manor included 120 a. of arable, 6 a. of meadow, 40 a. of woodland pasture, and 30s. in rents of assize.[7]

The Early Modern Period

Most of the cultivated land was in old closes and paddocks. A block of closes south-east of the church was known as Church field and closes called Ginger's dole and Red dole in the south and Lady Furlong meadows and Day dole in the north, north-east of Northend, may formerly have been parts of early open fields and common meadows.[8] By the early 18th century large tracts of common woodland had been mostly cleared of trees and small

---

1 See GA, D 2593/2/488.
2 GDR, T 1/160 (no 424); *Kelly's Dir. Glos.* (1863), 297; (1870), 584; (1879), 688.
3 GA, D 2593/2/488. Fig. 44.
4 *Domesday Book* (Rec. Com.), I, 167.
5 *Book of Fees*, I, 307.
6 *Inq. p.m. Glos.* 1302–58, 197.
7 Ibid. 255.
8 GA, D 1297, survey of Huntley, Netherley, and Longhope 1717, Huntley passim.

inclosures, some growing potatoes, had encroached on them.[1] Huntley common covered 80 a. stretching eastwards from the village to the parish boundary[2] and Huntley Wood common, where trees had been felled in the early 1630s,[3] covered 346 a. on Huntley and Bright's hills in the west and was open to extensive common pastures in Longhope.[4] Piecemeal inclosure and cultivation on the western slopes was facilitated by the pragmatism of the Probyns, lords of the manor from the mid 1720s, in granting leases to cottagers[5] and a substantial part of Bright's hill was inclosed in the later 18th century to make a timber plantation.[6]

In 1717 the earl of Kent's manor had 18 tenants holding for lives by copy or lease, with heriots payable, and 2 tenants at will. The principal holding, the farm at Woodend, had 142 a.; seven tenants, including Edmund Probyn, had 39–64 a.; and the rest together with one holding in hand had 30 a. or less. Some of the tenants were among 21 persons owing rent to the manor as freeholders.[7] By 1763 the farm at Northend had absorbed a holding called Adams[8] and in 1794 the manor estate had nine farms ranging in size from 200 a. to 15 a. and six smaller holdings. The largest farms were those at Woodend and Northend and of the others two were based on the White Hart and the Red Lion and one included land in Taynton. Some Huntley land was farmed from Upper and Lower Ley, in Westbury-on-Severn.[9]

Pastoral farming was evidently important at the beginning of the period. A clothier lived in the parish in the early 17th century[10] and one farmhouse was known as the Sheepscot in the early 18th.[11] The farmhouse at Northend had a cheese vat in 1673.[12] In the late 18th century, when the commons were grazed by a few sheep and small cattle,[13] many of the principal farms had a greater proportion of arable land.[14] Four fifths of 278 a. reported as being cropped in 1801 were under corn, nearly all wheat of which more than usual had been sown, and very little barley. Scarcely any turnips were grown and potato cultivation included small patches adjoining the commons.[15] There were orchards for both apples and pears[16] and tithing customs in 1680 dealt with the collection of fruit tithes.[17] In the early 18th century Round hill, on the south side of the parish, was known as Honey Pear hill and there were several orchards next to the Court House, by the church.[18] Many if not all farms had cider mills in the 17th and 18th centuries.[19]

The Nineteenth and Twentieth Centuries

The land continued to be farmed in holdings that ranged from a few to several hundred acres well into the 20th century. In 1831 six out of ten farmers in Huntley did not employ labour and there were 57 agricultural labourers in the parish.[20] In 1851, when there was a resident farm bailiff, the principal farmers worked 245 a. (Woodend), 130 a. (Northend), 86 a. (the Red Lion), and 61 a. (Littletons).[21] Northend and Woodend farms were taken into the home farm of the Huntley Manor estate in the 1880s and 1900s respectively[22] and the number of agricultural occupiers in Huntley, most tenant farmers, fell from 35 in 1896 to 26 in 1926, when the agricultural workforce also included 31 labourers in regular employment. Apart from the home farm the farms in 1926 comprised one with between 100 and 150 a., two with between 50 and 100 a., five with between 20 and 50 a, and seventeen with less, some much less, than 20 a.[23] The estate took several more farms in hand in the following years[24] and its home farm covered more than 500 a. in 1956, when four other farms had between 50 and 100 a., two between 20 and 50 a., and nineteen less than 20 a.[25] In 1986 there were three farms of over 40 ha (*c*.100 a.) and six of under 10 ha (*c*.25 a.) among a total of ten holdings returned for the parish. The farms gave employment to 24 workers, including a manager, and the smaller farms were worked on a part-time basis.[26]

In 1838 Huntley contained 522 a. of arable and 545 a. of meadow and pasture. Much of the latter was planted with fruit trees and there were numerous small orchards on the sides of Huntley hill. Of the commons, then covering 110 a.,[27] Huntley common

---

1 GA, D 23/E 5, T 15.
2 Ibid. D 1297, surv. 1717, Huntley no 3.
3 BL, Harl. MS 4850, f. 65.
4 GA, D 1297, surv. 1717, Longhope no 16.
5 Ibid. D 23/T 15; Rudge, *Hist. of Glos.* II, 54.
6 Below (woodland management).
7 GA, D 1297, surv. 1717, Huntley nos 9–15. For Probyn's holding, see ibid. D 23/T 6.
8 Ibid. D 23/T 15.
9 Ibid. D 4869/1/1/2.
10 See below (other industry and trade).
11 GA, D 23/T 6; see above, settlement (outlying settlement).
12 TNA, PROB 11/347, f. 109.
13 Turner, *Agric. of Glos.* 50.
14 GA, P 184/IN 3/3.
15 *1801 Crop Returns Eng.* I, 173, 189.
16 GA, D 23/T 15.
17 GDR, V 5/170T 3.
18 GA, D 23/T 14; D 1297, surv. 1717, Huntley nos 2, 6.
19 TNA, PROB 11/347, f. 109; GA, D 23/E 22
20 *Census*, 1831.
21 TNA, HO 107/1959.
22 *Kelly's Dir. Glos.* (1885 and later edns); see M. Hamlen, 'History of Huntley' (1981: typescript in Glos. Colln. 45959), 5.
23 TNA, MAF 68/1609/15; MAF 68/3295/15.
24 Hamlen, 'Huntley', 37.
25 TNA, MAF 68/4533/166.
26 Ibid. MAF, 68/6005/166.
27 GDR, T 1/106.

was inclosed in 1857 at the expense of Edmund Probyn. He received 54 a., including, by exchange for an old inclosure, 3 a. that were allotted to the rector for the glebe, and two other landowners were given 1 a. each. The Poor's Land charity and 15 people, mostly cottagers, took even smaller allotments, some of only a few perches, and 15 others money payments of £1–£5 for their rights of common. Two pieces of land totalling 8 a. were assigned to the churchwardens and overseers as a recreation ground and as allotments for the labouring poor.[1] The remnants of Huntley Wood common were finally inclosed in 1872 under an award which also dealt with some old inclosures. Again Edmund Probyn was the main beneficiary, taking 85 a., including 5 a. for his manorial rights. The charity received 5 a. and 21 landholders, including the rector, minute allotments, of which 13, in all 3 a., were sold to Probyn.[2]

In 1866, when 56 a. was returned as fallow or uncultivated, the farmland again contained almost equal areas of arable and grassland, the area of permanent grass being 454 a., and wheat was the main crop in the rotation, which also included legumes, turnips, and grass leys.[3] The livestock reported that year were 110 cattle, including 38 dairy cows, 326 sheep, and 136 pigs.[4] In the later 19th century the dairy herds, a major feature of the principal farms,[5] increased and the area of arable decreased as more land was put permanently to grass. The livestock reported in 1896, when 872 a. was returned as permanent grassland, included 259 cattle, among them 97 dairy cows, 296 breeding ewes, and 32 breeding sows. Arable farming was restricted to 200–300 a. in the early 20th century and the livestock numbers reported in 1926 were similar to those of 1896.[6] C.P. Ackers started a herd of black pigs on the Huntley Manor estate's home farm and in the late 1920s he established a flock of sheep on it.[7] He also maintained a stud of percheron horses, a breed used by the Army, until the 1930s.[8]

A poultry farm recorded in 1910 was short lived.[9] Market gardening, one resident's main business by 1881,[10] was on a small scale and devoted to growing soft fruit, of which 2 a. was reported in 1896 and 6 a. in 1926. In the same period the reported area of orchards increased from 45 a. to 86 a.[11] Although more plum trees were being planted,[12] several farmers continued to make large quantities of cider and perry[13] and after the First World War a factory in Deep Filling, a business founded by Albert Knight in the late 19th century, took apples from local producers and from further afield and delivered cider in barrels and bottles to many parts of the county and to Ross-on-Wye. In the mid 20th century more land was turned to orchards and to blackcurrant and other soft fruit cultivation[14] and in 1956 272 a. of orchards and 79 a. of soft fruit were returned as opposed to 175 a. of rotated crops and 3 a. of fallow. Dairying and livestock farming remained well represented and 534 a. were returned as permanent grassland and 80 a. as rough grazing.[15]

More fields were planted with fruit trees and bushes in the 1960s and 1970s and the Huntley Manor estate employed a shepherd into the 1980s,[16] when sheep farming, fruit farming, and horticulture were each the speciality of one of the three principal farms. The totals returned for the parish in 1988 included, in addition to 100 ha (*c.*250 a.) of corn, 1,402 sheep and lambs, 95 ha (*c.*235 a.) of horticultural crops, 68 ha (*c.*168 a.) of orchards, mostly plums but also apples, pears, and cherries, and 27 ha (*c.*57 a.) of blackcurrants.[17] Fruit farming decreased in the late 20th century, many of the trees and bushes grubbed being in the east in the area laid down as a golf course in 1996.[18]

WOODLAND MANAGEMENT

Huntley contained extensive woodland in 1086.[19] Trees were felled when the woodland was in the hands of the Crown in the mid 13th century[20] and Walter of Huntley had made two clearings in his wood by 1282.[21] The manor included 40 a. of great timber and pasture in 1337.[22] The rector, whose glebe included half of a coppice acquired by exchange in the mid 17th century, was one of several coppice owners in the parish later that century[23] and he reserved all his woodland for himself when letting

---

1 GA, Q/RI 83; for the Poor's Land charity, below, social hist. (charities for the poor).
2 GA, Q/RI 84.
3 TNA, MAF 68/26/9.
4 Ibid. MAF 68/25/20.
5 GA, D 2299/2/3/17; 2/7/12.
6 TNA, MAF 68/1609/15; MAF 68/3295/15; Acreage Returns, 1905.
7 Hamlen, 'Huntley', 16, 37–8.
8 Ibid. 11; *The Times*, 26 Nov. 1928.
9 *Kelly's Dir. Glos.* (1910), 225; (1914), 231.
10 TNA, RG 11/2525.
11 Ibid. MAF 68/1609/15; MAF 68/3295/15.
12 Hamlen, 'Huntley', 16.
13 See GA, D 2299/2/3/17; 2/7/12.
14 *Kelly's Dir Glos.* (1889–1939 edns); Hamlen, 'Huntley', 212–14.
15 TNA, MAF 68/4533/166.
16 Hamlen, 'Huntley', 288.
17 TNA, MAF 68/6005/166.
18 See OS Map 1:2,500, SO 7219–7319 (1972 edn); *Huntley Parish Plan July 2004* (copy in Glos. Colln. 49658), 80.
19 *Domesday Book* (Rec. Com.), I, 167.
20 TNA, E 32/29, rot. 8.
21 Ibid. E 32/31, m. 15.
22 *Inq. p.m. Glos.* 1302–58, 255.
23 GDR, V 5/170T 2, 6–7.

the glebe in the 1720s and 1730s.[1] In 1608 four charcoal burners, described as colliers, were listed in the parish[2] and the tithe customs of 1680 and 1698 included bark sold from coppice crops.[3]

In the early 18th century, when parts of Huntley Wood common including Broom hill in the south-west remained wooded,[4] the manor's unshared woodland comprised Rotterins (later Cherry) wood in the north and some small coppices in the north-east. Edmund Probyn, the leaseholder of those woods by 1719,[5] acquired them with the manor in the mid 1720s[6] and two small nurseries cultivating timber and fruit trees were recorded from 1732.[7] John Probyn included his Huntley woods in his charcoal concession of 1761 to the agent of the owner of the Flaxley ironworks[8] and about that time a large part of Huntley Wood common was inclosed for a timber nursery.[9] In 1794 Edmund Probyn's main woods were Rotterins (40 a.), the Plantation (30 a.) on Bright's hill, and Broomhill (15 a.) in the south-west.[10] They remained mostly oak plantations until the later 19th century,[11] when part of Rotterins wood was felled for farmland in the 1860s and 1870s and new areas of woodland, including coniferous plantations, were created on the Huntley Manor estate.[12] The estate employed up to five gamekeepers at the end of the century.[13]

C.P. Ackers, who began managing the estate's woodland before the First World War, increased its area considerably and came to run 2,000 a. of commercial woodland and nurseries in and around Huntley. His book *Practical British Forestry*, published in 1938, described his system of management. He first planted 30 a. of hilly scrub with fir and larch[14] and by the 1920s had covered much of Huntley hill with trees.[15] In the 1930s, when most new planting was of spruces, he irrigated and treated with farmyard manure 20 a. for growing willows for cricket bats. Other ventures included businesses to manufacture and sell woodland products (Forest Products Ltd) and to assist landowners in the development of their woodland (Woodland Improvement Ltd). For several years from 1946 Ackers ran a forestry school at Huntley Manor.[16] Following his death in 1960 some outlying woods were sold and Broomhill wood was bought by Cyril Hart, his former secretary, and in the early 1980s, when its policy was to fell 15 a. of conifers a year, the estate employed seven men in its woods. In 2006 the estate's woodland, 1,200 a. in Huntley, Newent, and Taynton mostly of conifers with some sweet chestnut coppice, supplied the building trade through a single dealer and a nursery in Huntley was run as a separate business.[17]

WOODLAND CRAFTS AND SAW MILLS

Cask and hoop makers supported at least two families in the late 17th and early 18th century[18] and a rake maker was recorded in 1771.[19] In the mid 19th century, when several men were employed as wood fellers and cutters, a smaller number, perhaps two or three, practised crafts such as lath cleaving and hoop and hurdle making.[20] A besom maker was among the few woodland craftsmen, all among the hill population, in 1881.[21] Under C.P. Ackers's management of the Huntley Manor woods in the early 20th century the crafts of making wattle hurdles and cleaving chestnut wood for fence pales were revived and Forest Products Ltd, founded in 1927, manufactured fences, gates, and garden furniture at a mill on the Ross road west of the village.[22] Following Ackers's death that business was sold and, for a few years, the Huntley Manor estate had a saw mill on the Newent road.[23] Forest Products, which had come to use mostly sawn wood,[24] opened a shop at its mill in 1987[25] and continued to trade in 2006.

OTHER MILLS

Huntley mill, known as 'Stinderforthemilne' in the mid 13th century, stood midway along the parish's south boundary[26] where the Ley brook is joined by the stream flowing south-eastwards from May hill

---

1 GA, P 184/IN 3/3.
2 Smith, *Men and Armour*, 71.
3 GDR, V 5/170T 3, 7.
4 GA, D 1297, surv. 1717, Longhope no 16; D 23/E 7.
5 Ibid. D 1297, surv. 1717, Huntley nos 5, 11; D 23/T 6, T 14.
6 Above, manor.
7 GA, D 23/T 15.
8 Ibid. D 23/E 8; see below, Longhope, econ. hist. (woodland management).
9 Bigland, *Glos.* II, 111.
10 GA, P 184/MI 4; D 4869/1/1/2.
11 TNA, IR 18/2766.
12 GDR, T 1/106; OS Map 6", Glos. XXIV.SW (1889, 1903 edns).
13 Hamlen, 'Huntley', 50; for the head keeper, see *Kelly's Dir. Glos.* (1897 and later edns).
14 C.P. Ackers, *Practical British Forestry* (1947 edn), pp. vii–xi, being the preface to the first edition dated Dec. 1937; see H. Phelps, *The Forest of Dean* (1983), 146.
15 OS Map 6", Glos. XXIV.SW (1924); information from Mrs Torill Freeman of Home Farm.
16 *The Times*, 19, 23 July 1937; Hamlen, 'Huntley', 10–22; see GRO, DA 24/100/14, min. 28 Aug. 1946.
17 Hamlen, 'History of Huntley', 288; information from Mrs Freeman; http://www.woodland-improvement.co.uk/about.htm (accessed 17 Mar. 2006).
18 GA, P 184/IN 1/1; GDR, B 4/1/1479.
19 GA, D 23/T 15.
20 TNA, HO 107/361; HO 107/1959; GA, P 184/IN 1/3.
21 TNA, RG 11/2525.
22 Ackers, *Practical British Forestry*, pp. viii–ix; Hamlen, 'Huntley', 12–15, 41–3. See Fig. 45.
23 Information from Mrs Freeman.
24 Phelps, *Forest of Dean*, 146.
25 Information from Mrs Freeman; *Citizen*, 23 Mar. 1987.
26 C.E. Hart, 'The Metes and Bounds of the Forest of Dean', *Trans. BGAS* 66 (1945), 185.

45. Making tent pegs at Forest Products Ltd in 1939

past Woodend. Part of the manor, it was being leased with Woodend farm in 1717[1] and was demolished before the end of the 18th century.[2]

Elsewhere, the pond of a mill at Woodend had been filled and planted as a woodland nursery by 1732.[3]

OTHER INDUSTRY AND TRADE

A number of sandstone quarries have been opened on the west side of the parish. The largest workings were on the south side of Bright's hill[4] where quarrying continued in the early 20th century.[5]

A cinder deposit, identified by field names in use in the early 18th century,[6] points to ironworking in Roman and perhaps earlier times. In 1608, when some residents derived their livelihood from traffic along the main road,[7] a smith, a carpenter, a shoemaker, a tailor, and a coverlet weaver were included in a muster roll for Huntley. Joseph White, a leading parishioner at that time,[8] was a clothier[9] and weaving, the craft of a parishioner who made his will in 1547,[10] gave employment to a few men in the late 17th and early 18th century.[11] William Hopton, the farmer at Northend, was one of several tanners in the early 1670s.[12] The industry, in which Hopton's son had worked in 1666, was dependent on the bark trade and continued to employ Huntley men in the early 1680s.[13] Masons and other usual rural craftsmen were resident in the late 17th and early 18th century and there was a distiller in the mid 1680s.[14]

In 1851 Huntley's master craftsmen included 7 wheelwrights and carpenters, 2 blacksmiths, 2 masons, 3 shoemakers, a plumber and glazier, a tailor, and a hat maker.[15] Huntley had a saddler in 1863.[16] A farmer made agricultural implements in 1889 and an engineering business produced incubators and other poultry appliances in 1897. A basket maker was recorded from 1894.[17] The decline of traditional crafts outside the woodland economy included the closure of a saddlery in the early 1930s[18] and only a builder and a blacksmith were recorded in a trade directory of 1939.[19] In 2006 the main employers in Huntley were Forest Products and a plant nursery[20] and other local businesses included an equestrian centre and an agricultural engineering firm. Nearly half of the working population travelled to Gloucester for employment.[21]

Huntley's economic benefit from its position on main roads from Gloucester into Herefordshire and

---

1 GA, D 1297, surv. 1717, Huntley nos 8, 10.
2 No bldgs. were recorded on the site in Taylor, *Map of Glos.* (1777); OS Map 1", sheet 43 (1831 edn).
3 GA, D 23/T 15; see ibid. D 1297, surv. 1717, Huntley no 7.
4 OS Map 6", Glos. XXIV.SW (1889, 1903, 1924 edns).
5 Hamlen, 'Huntley', 215.
6 GA, D 1297, surv. 1717, Huntley no 6; see ibid. D 23/E 5, T 14.
7 See below, this section.
8 Smith, *Men and Armour*, 71.
9 GDR wills 1637/51
10 Hockaday Abs. ccclviii.
11 GA, P 184/IN 1/1
12 TNA, PROB 11/347, f. 109 and v.; E 134/22 Chas. II/East. 3.
13 GDR wills 1667/168; 1690/300; GA, P 184/IN 1/1.
14 GA, P 184/IN 1/1.
15 TNA, HO 107/1959.
16 *Kelly's Dir. Glos.* (1863), 297.
17 Ibid. (1889 and later edns).
18 Hamlen, 'Huntley', 132–7.
19 *Kelly's Dir. Glos.* (1939), 237.
20 See above (woodland management; woodland crafts and saw mills).
21 *Huntley Parish Plan*, 6.

south Wales was evident before the turnpike era. It had at least one inn in the late 16th century[1] and three carriers, one an innkeeper's younger namesake, were recorded in 1608.[2] A carrier from Monmouth married at Huntley in 1682[3] and the parish was a staging post for Herefordshire and Monmouthshire wagons and had several good inns for travellers in the early 18th century.[4] In the mid 18th century, when the White Hart hosted business meetings,[5] the Red Lion's keeper supplied grass for cattle and, in 1771, ran weekly carrying services to Gloucester and Ross-on-Wye.[6] In the mid 19th century, when an ostler lived at the Red Lion,[7] two Huntley men provided carrying services to Gloucester on market days.[8]

Two badgers were recorded in Huntley in the 1680s, one being licensed in 1689, and a chandler died in 1702.[9] Three shopkeepers were resident in 1851[10] and a post office was open in 1856.[11] A machine owner, a castrator, a butcher, and several cattle dealers were among residents supplying agricultural services in 1851.[12] In the 20th century traffic on the main roads continued to support local businesses. A garage opened in the mid 1920s and Forest Products Ltd erected tea rooms and a lodging house overlooking the Ross road c.1930. Huntley had two garages, a bakery, a butchery, and three other shops, one also the post office, in 1939[13] and it retained a post office, a butcher's shop, and two garages in 2004.[14]

LOCAL GOVERNMENT

MANORIAL GOVERNMENT

The lord of the manor had a court house in 1282[15] and the business of the manor court, recorded in the mid 14th century,[16] apparently included some tenurial matters in Longhope in the late Middle Ages.[17] The Huntley court had leet jurisdiction and was held by the farmers of the manor in 1624 and 1628.[18] The Court House by the church was demolished in the 18th century[19] and the court met at the White Hart in 1752.[20]

PAROCHIAL GOVERNMENT

In 1576 Huntley's two churchwardens were censured for spending church money on other business.[21] A parish charity established by that time supported the poor and was later applied solely in poor relief, thus offsetting its cost to the parish; by 1726 it had given up part of a cottage for use as a parish poorhouse.[22] The amount spent by the parish on administering the poor law, £44 in 1776, rose considerably in the late 18th century and stood at £108 in 1803, when 16 people received regular and 22 occasional help.[23]

In the early 19th century the cost of relief was usually contained. The number of people receiving regular assistance was 12 in 1815[24] and much the same in the mid 1820s when annual expenditure was often just over £130. Occasional payments were made to tramping poor. In the early 1830s the parish employed a salaried overseer and engaged a doctor on several occasions and in 1835, when it paid for accommodation in the Taynton workhouse and in a deaf and dumb institute at Edgbaston (Warws.), expenditure was at its highest (£210).[25] Huntley became part of the new Westbury-on-Severn poor-law union later in 1835.[26]

The parish vestry's business in the later 18th century included annual nominations of men to serve as petty constable. In 1803 a petition from leading inhabitants secured the replacement of the constable on the grounds of age and infirmity.[27] The vestry remained active in the mid 19th century. In 1844 it chose an assistant overseer by tender and the following year reappointed him as a salaried officer. In 1851 it ordered a complete census of dogs to ensure that all were kept muzzled. In 1852 it required animals trespassing on the commons to be impounded and in 1857, the year Huntley common was inclosed, it set the tariff for keeping animals on the east side of the parish higher than that for animals on the west side. Following that

---

1   TNA, E 134/36 Eliz./Hil. 21; GDR wills 1598/162.
2   Smith, *Men and Armour*, 71; GDR wills 1598/162.
3   GA, P 184/IN 1/1.
4   Bodleian, Top. Glouc. c. 3, f. 194.
5   Below, social hist. (social life).
6   *Glouc. J.* 20 Feb. 1753; 21 Oct. 1771.
7   TNA, HO 107/1959; RG 9/1758.
8   *Kelly's Dir. Glos.* (1856), 313.
9   GA, P 184/IN 1/1; Q/SO 2.
10 TNA, HO 107/1959.
11 *Kelly's Dir. Glos.* (1856), 313.
12 TNA, HO 107/1959.
13 *Kelly's Dir. Glos.* (1923 and later edns).
14 *Huntley Parish Plan*, 6.
15 TNA, E 32/31, m. 15.
16 *Inq. p.m. Glos.* 1302–58, 255.
17 TNA, DL 7/2, no 33.
18 GA, D 23/T 6, T 10.
19 Above, settlement (outlying settlement).
20 GA, D 23/T 10.
21 GDR vol. 40, f. 261v.
22 Below, social hist. (charities for the poor); GA, P 184/CH 2.
23 *Poor Law Abstract, 1804,* 180–1.
24 Ibid. *1818,* 152–3.
25 *Poor Law Returns* (1830–1), 69; (1835), 68; GA, P 184/OV 2/1.
26 *Poor Law Com. 2nd Rep.* p. 524.
27 GA, Q/SR 1786 D; 1799 D; 1803 A.

inclosure the vestry oversaw the creation of the recreation ground and in 1868 it entrusted its management to the surveyor of the highways. In 1880 it appointed a salaried surveyor for the former turnpike roads but his immediate successors did not take a salary until 1884. The parish's improvement of the Grange Court road in late 1880s was partly funded by a loan from rector Henry Miles.[1]

A parish council was first elected in 1894. Its main business included the management of the allotment gardens and the recreation ground with the pound and the pond at its corner.[2] Stocks recorded from 1828[3] stood north of the main road next to the pound[4] and were moved eastwards to the side of the recreation ground c.1970.[5]

A police constable lived in Huntley in 1901[6] and a cottage there served as a police station after the First World War.[7]

SOCIAL HISTORY

SOCIAL STRUCTURE

Little is known of the division of landholding in Huntley in the Middle Ages.[8] In 1327, when Robert de Sapy, the lord of the manor, was assessed there for tax at 6s. 9d., Walter of Hauville was assessed for 8s. and Robert of Hauville for just over 3s. Three other men and one woman, Margery of Hauville, were also assessed, two at just over 2s. and two at just over 1s.[9] Later lords of the manor, the Talbots,[10] were non-resident.

In 1522 Huntley's wealthier inhabitants included members of the Bird family, relatives of Richard Bird who in 1470 had owned a holding called Awbery's.[11] John Bird of Northend, who had a servant, and Thomas Hyett each had goods worth £20. Of some thirty other inhabitants excluding the rector more than half had goods worth £3 or less and for several no valuation was provided.[12] The Bird family, of which William Bird became a woollen draper in Bristol and by will proved 1590 left part of his wealth to Huntley's poor and the repair of the road to Gloucester,[13] continued to farm in Huntley in 1608. None of the 42 men then deemed fit for militia service was described as a gentleman. The farming community was represented by 2 yeomen, 5 husbandmen, and 1 bailiff and there were 13 craftsmen and tradesmen as well as 7 labourers and 1 shepherd. Of the 9 servants named, 4 were employed by farmers, 1 by an innkeeper, and 4 by Joseph White, the constable[14] and a clothier.[15] The White family later held the White Hart inn[16] and in 1672 a member was assessed on eight hearths for the site with its new house (Huntley Court). The 45 other parishioners assessed all had fewer hearths, 21 of them only one each.[17]

The number of cottagers increased in the 18th and early 19th century as squatter development on the commons increased.[18] About 1710 the population included nine freeholders[19] and in the later 18th century among the leading tenant farmers were members of the Drinkwater family at Woodend,[20] of whom Richard kept the Red Lion inn by 1771[21] and Ann became overseer of the poor in 1837.[22] Few members of the gentry were resident, notably William Ellis of Northend, who by will proved 1689 left moneys for rebuilding the parsonage and for the poor,[23] and Thomas Blunt, a Mitcheldean surgeon who made the house at Huntley Court his residence in the late 18th century.[24] Most rectors were resident, their house destroyed in the mid 17th century having been rebuilt in the early 18th, and the household of Daniel Capper, rector from 1839,[25] included half a dozen servants.[26] In 1817 the lessees of the tithes undertook collectively to provide free carriage for coal for the rector, John Morse.[27] The Probyns, lords of the manor from the 1720s, were non-resident but after they moved to Longhope in the early 19th

---

1 GA, P 184/OV 2/1.
2 Ibid. P 184A/PC 1/1.
3 Ibid. P 184/OV 2/1.
4 OS Map 1:2,500, Glos. XXIV.14 (1884 edn).
5 DoE List, Huntley (1985), 7/47.
6 TNA, RG 13/2418.
7 Kelly's Dir. Glos. (1919 and later edns); GA, D 2299/3547.
8 See above, econ. hist.
9 Glos. Subsidy Roll, 1327, 35.
10 Above, manor.
11 BL, Campbell Ch. XVIII.14*, 15.
12 Military Surv. of Glos. 1522, 199–200.
13 TNA, C 2/ELIZ/F 10/17; PROB 11/76, ff. 192–4.
14 Smith, Men and Armour, 71.
15 GDR wills 1637/51.
16 TNA, E 134/1657/Mich. 47; E 134/1659/East. 33; E 134/22 Chas. II/Trin. 6; GDR wills 1692/221.
17 TNA, E 179/247/14, rot. 36d. For Huntley Court, above, settlement (the village); manor.
18 Turner, Agric. of Glos. 50.
19 Atkyns, Glos. 486.
20 GA, D 23/F 3; D 4869/1/1/2.
21 Glouc. J. 21 Oct. 1771.
22 GA, P 184/OV 2/1.
23 GDR wills 1689/294.
24 Above, manor.
25 Below, religious hist.
26 TNA, HO 107/361; RG 9/1758.
27 GA, P 184/IN 3/3.

century[1] the heir to the estate lived with his family and servants at Pool House in Huntley.[2] Edmund Probyn continued to occupy the house after he took over the estate in 1855[3] and, following the departure of Daniel Capper in 1866, acquired and moved into the rectory house and renamed it Huntley Manor.[4] Capper had used part of his personal wealth in the early 1860s to rebuild both the house and the church.[5]

In the mid 19th century the working population was made up of farmers, many of them working only a few acres, craftsmen, and tradesmen. The principal farmers included the Drinkwater family at Woodend and the Red Lion.[6] Of the main houses, Huntley Manor retained a large resident staff, including 10 maids, under Benjamin St John Ackers in 1901.[7] Pool House was remodelled as the rectory house[8] and Henry Miles (d. 1906), who was a considerable benefactor to the parish,[9] and his successor George Baker (d. 1934) both employed resident staff.[10] Huntley Court, occasionally let as a gentleman's residence in the mid 19th century,[11] was occupied from 1884 by its new owner, Charlotte Constance Blood.[12] She was a manager of Huntley school alongside Miles and Ackers in 1890[13] and with her son J.N. Blood, a barrister, employed three live-in servants in 1901.[14]

As owner of the Huntley Manor estate from 1915 C.P. Ackers was landlord as well as employer of many parishioners.[15] The Shelleys, owners of Huntley Court from 1925 with interests in a Sri Lanka tea plantation,[16] became one of the few other resident gentry families[17] and in the 1920s and 1930s the population continued to be made up mostly of farmers, craftsmen, and tradesmen.[18] In the early 1950s Ackers built six bungalows for estate workers[19] but after his death in 1960 the estate's influence was diluted, in part by the growth of population as houses were built on land that no longer belonged to the estate.[20] In the early 21st century parts of the enlarged village were a dormitory and nearly half of the working population travelled to Gloucester for employment.[21] Three of Ackers's six bungalows were occupied by estate workers in 2006.[22]

CHARITIES FOR THE POOR

By 1577 a cottage north of the main road on the edge of Huntley common and two small pieces of land in Huntley were vested in feoffees for the use of the parish poor and other charitable purposes. In 1656 commissioners set the number of feoffees at six and ordered that £20 given to the poor by Henry Woodward of Gloucester be laid out on land and added to the trust. Woodward's gift was put towards the acquisition of a small piece of land in 1663 and the feoffees' body included the rector from 1726. The trust became known as the Poor's Land charity.[23] The cottage was let to two tenants before 1683, when it was described as the church house,[24] and the trust income from rents was distributed among the poor at Christmas in the late 17th century.[25] In the early 18th century an income of £5 5s. benefited over a score of people and some payments were earmarked for clothes and rents. A prisoner was among recipients in the mid 1720s.[26] The parish used part of the cottage as a poorhouse[27] and the charity continued to let the other part after rebuilding it in the early 1760s. In 1770 15 people received cash doles[28] and in 1828 the charity was shared between up to 60 people regardless of whether or not they were in receipt of parish relief.[29] Under a Scheme of 1898, when its annual rental was £22 15s. 3d.,[30] the charity gave cash to 45 or more people and from 1920 it had 28 or fewer recipients.[31] Its property was sold in 1928.[32]

William Ellis by will proved 1689 left £10 for the poor.[33] The charity as augmented by a gift of £2 from Lord Kennedy was distributed in bread at Christmas

---

1 Below, Longhope, manor; for the Probyn fam., see pedigree in J. Maclean, 'The History of the Manors of Dene Magna and Abenhall', *Trans. BGAS* 6 (1881–2), 194–7; *Burke's Landed Gentry* (1898), II, 1217–18.
2 GDR, T 1/106 (no 420); TNA, HO 107/361.
3 Above, manor, TNA, RG 9/1758.
4 TNA, RG 10/2605.
5 Above, settlement; below, religious history (patronage and endowment; religious life).
6 TNA, HO 107/1959.
7 Ibid. RG 13/2418.
8 Below, religious hist. (patronage and endowment).
9 See below (education; social life).
10 Below, religious hist. (religious life); TNA, RG 10/2605; RG 13/2418; M. Hamlen, 'History of Huntley' (1981: typescript in Glos. Colln. 45959), 73–6.
11 TNA, RG 10/2605.
12 Above, manor; *Kelly's Dir. Glos.* (1885), 508; (1910), 225.
13 GA, S 184/1.
14 TNA, RG 13/2418.
15 Above, manor; GA, G/WE 159/7/1–11.
16 Above, manor; GA, D 177, Shelley fam. papers.
17 *Kelly's Dir. Glos.* (1927), 240; (1939), 237.
18 See Hamlen, 'Huntley', passim.
19 GA, DA 24/100/19, pp. 248, 435.
20 Information from Mrs Torill Freeman of Home Farm.
21 *Huntley Parish Plan July 2004* (copy in Glos. Colln. 49658), 6.
22 Information from Mrs Freeman.
23 GA, P 184/IN 1/1, terrier 1692 at front of vol.; Hockaday Abs. ccxlviii, 1806; *18th Rep. Com. Char.* 323–4.
24 GDR, V 5/170T 5.
25 GA, P 184/IN 1/1, terrier 1692 at front of vol.
26 Ibid. P 184/CH 2.
27 Hockaday Abs. ccxlviii, 1806; *18th Rep. Com. Char.* 324.
28 GA, P 184/CH 2.
29 *18th Rep. Com. Char.* 324.
30 GA, D 3469/5/81.
31 Ibid. P 184/CH 6.
32 Ibid. D 2299/3867, 4429.
33 GDR wills 1689/294.

and, following the loss of £5 of the principal, it was vested in Thomas Wintle in 1729 and 7s. a year was given in bread to the recipients of the Poor's Land charity. John Wyman (d. 1721) of Gloucester gave £5 for a distribution of bread on the feast of St John the Evangelist (27 December). The charity, which had 20 recipients in 1727, was dispensed by his daughter Elizabeth Ashley, who in 1752, when wife of Thomas Hartland of Newent, gave £20, 5s. of the income to supplement the charity and the remainder to teach children to read.[1] Samuel Hawkins (d. 1805) by will gave £200, part of the income for a sermon charity, £1 1s. a year for sixpenny loaves for people attending the sermon service on New Year's Day, and any residue, in default of the kindred of John Belson of Huntley, to two poor householders.[2]

Among other charitable gifts to the poor were 5s. given by Anthony Grey, Lord Harold, and shared between 17 people at Christmas in 1722[3] and a £1 legacy from John Purrock of Highnam that was shared between a similar number early in 1725.[4] In the later 19th century surplus income from the management of the parish's recreation ground was shared among the poor.[5]

Hawkins's charity and the other bread charities were distributed together in bread and cash on St Thomas's day (21 December) by 1864, when there were 18 recipients,[6] and Hawkins's charity paid for the bread until at least 1945.[7] The charities were amalgamated with the Poor's Land charity in 1975 to form the Huntley Relief in Need charity. After making fixed payments for the New Year's Day sermon, the new charity benefited the parish poor generally and individually.[8] Its income, though usually less than £100, was £150 in 2006.[9]

EDUCATION

Thomas Unwin, the rector, taught at least one local boy for several years c.1630.[10] About 1710 Huntley had a school in which ten children were taught at the expense of the rector, Abraham Morse,[11] and in 1752 Elizabeth Hartland assigned 15s. a year out of the income of a charitable gift to the teaching of two or more children to read.[12] There was a school house at Huntley Court in 1811[13] and a day school teaching two children with the Hartland gift in 1818[14] also taught eight children at their parents' expense in 1833.[15] Under Daniel Capper, rector from 1839,[16] a day school was supported in part by pence[17] and was housed from 1841 in a new building that included separate schoolrooms for the boys and the girls. There was an adjacent house for the master and mistress. That school, which was affiliated to the National Society and was almost entirely funded by Capper, taught 15 boys and 15 girls in 1847 and, having been enlarged in 1855, had an average attendance of 84, including infants, in 1860.[18] At that time the teachers were a scripture reader and his wife.[19] In 1863, when new teachers took charge, the school had mixed and infant departments and Capper's curate occasionally taught in it.[20] Elsewhere, a schoolmaster lived in the south-east of Huntley in 1851[21] and Huntley Court accommodated a private girls' school in 1863.[22]

In 1874 Henry Miles, the rector, enlarged the National school in a substantial rebuilding[23] completed to designs by J.E. Jones of Gloucester in 1875.[24] The school was attended by children from May hill[25] and had average attendances in 1885 of 111[26] and in 1904, when it was known as Huntley C. of E. school, of 149.[27] A private school, open in Huntley in the late 1870s, closed in 1887[28] but one of its teachers ran her own school there in 1894 and until at least 1902.[29] The church school was enlarged in 1912 and 1913[30] but the average attendance fell to 96 in 1922.[31] The older children were transferred to a new school in Abenhall in 1930 and a few children were later awarded scholarships to Newent grammar school.[32] Huntley school, where the average attendance fell to 57 in 1938,[33] acquired voluntary aided status after the

---

1 GA, P 184/IN 1/1, memos at front of vol.; CH 2; GDR wills 1763/18. For Wyman, see Bigland, *Glos.* II, 113.
2 *18th Rep. Com. Char.* 324; *19th Rep. Com. Char.* 107.
3 GA, P 184/CH 2. Anthony was the eldest son of the duke of Kent, the lord of the manor: *Complete Peerage*, VII, 178 and n.
4 GA, P 184/CH 2. Purrock's will was not proved until 1729: GDR wills 1729/148.
5 GA, P 184/OV 2/1.
6 Ibid. CH 3.
7 Ibid. CH 6.
8 Ibid. D 3469/5/81.
9 http://www.charity-commission.gov.uk/registeredcharities (accessed 31 May 2007: no 254793).
10 TNA, E 134/22 Chas. II/East. 3.
11 *Glos. N&Q* I, 293.
12 GA, P 184/IN 1/1, memo at front of vol.; see above (charities for the poor).
13 GA, Q/REl 1, Duchy of Lancaster hundred.
14 *Educ. of Poor Digest*, 302.
15 *Educ. Enq. Abstract*, 318.
16 Below, religious hist.
17 GA, P 184/CH 3.
18 Nat. Soc. *Inquiry, 1846–7*, Glos. 10–11; TNA, ED 7/34/175.
19 TNA, RG 9/1758.
20 GA, S 184/1.
21 TNA, HO 107/1959.
22 *Kelly's Dir. Glos.* (1863), 297.
23 GA, S 184/1; see ibid. P 184/SC1; OS Maps 1:2,500, Glos. XXIV.10 (1883 edn); 14 (1884 edn).
24 Verey and Brooks, *Glos.* II, 545. See Fig. 42.
25 GA, S 184/1.
26 *Kelly's Dir. Glos.* (1885), 508.
27 *Public Elem. Schs. 1906*, 185.
28 GA, S 184/1.
29 *Kelly's Dir. Glos.* (1894), 214; (1902), 219.
30 GA, S 184/3.
31 *List 21*, 1922 (Board of Education), 105.
32 GA, C/CE/M 2/20. p. 290; S 184/3; see *VCH Glos.* V, 190–1.
33 *List 21*, 1932 (Board of Education), 115; 1938, 127.

Second World War[1] and as Huntley C. of E. Primary school had 85 children on its roll in 2005.[2] A library and other rooms were added to the main building in 1991[3] and a classroom in 1998.[4] In 1906 the part of the Hartland charity devoted to education was made a separate fund[5] and in 2004 it had an income of c.£10.[6]

SOCIAL LIFE

In the later 16th century morris dancers attended local May Day revels presided over by a May lord and Huntley had at least one inn or alehouse.[7] An unlicensed alehouse was recorded in 1667.[8] An inn with the sign of the White Hart in 1657 stood on the south side of the main road and was used for business.[9] The manor court and turnpike trustees met there in the mid 18th century[10] but the inn had closed by the end of the century, the house in its grounds becoming known as Huntley Court.[11] The George and the Crown, recorded in 1654 and 1709 respectively,[12] stood next to each other north of the main road but by the early 1730s the Crown had been demolished and the George had taken the site for its yard and had been renamed the Red Lion.[13] It was used by friendly societies in the 19th century[14] and remained open in 2006. In the mid 19th century there were several other inns or beer and cider houses, one called the Mason's Arms being probably by the main road on Huntley common.[15] The Yew Tree in North Road, a beer house open in 1863,[16] was for sale in 1919.[17]

In 1803 a friendly society had 33 members.[18] In 1825 the parish kept a library for the use of the poor[19] and in 1885 Revd Henry Miles built a reading room for a working men's club on the south side of the village's main street.[20] At the inclosure of Huntley common in 1857 the part next to the village was reserved for a recreation ground and a smaller part further east for allotments.[21] A memorial to the dead of the First World War erected in the recreation area next to the main road took the form of a stone Calvary.[22] In 1927 a wooden building in North Road became the meeting place of a branch of the Women's Institute[23] and in 1970 a new village hall opened on the east side of the recreation ground.[24] The W.I. hut became the headquarters of a scout troop in 1959 and was replaced by a new building in 1975.[25] The reading room was demolished in the late 1970s.[26] A cricket ground was established in Grange Court Lane c.1960[27] and its pavilion, replacing a temporary building, opened in 1969.[28]

RELIGIOUS HISTORY

EARLY HISTORY AND THE STATUS OF THE PARISH CHURCH

In the mid 12th century the church at Huntley was a chapel to Longhope church, which the lords of Monmouth had given to Monmouth priory.[29] Huntley was later a separate rectory, in the gift of John of Huntley in 1304.[30] The benefice included the May hill district of Taynton to the north from 1935[31] and was united with Longhope in 1983. From 2003 the united benefice included Churcham and Bulley.[32]

PATRONAGE AND ENDOWMENT

The patronage of the rectory passed from John of Huntley to his successors in the manor and in 1336 John de Sapy evidently repeated a presentation made the preceding year by Robert de Sapy.[33] In 1477, when the lord was a minor, William Hastings, Lord

---

1 GA, C/CE/M 2/33, p. 563.
2 *Schools and Establishments Dir. 2005–6*, 25.
3 Glos. Colln RR 170.6 (order of service 28 June 1991).
4 *Forester*, 30 Oct. 1998.
5 GA, P 184/CH 6.
6 *Huntley Parish Plan*, 68.
7 TNA, E 134/36 Eliz./Hil. 21; GDR wills 1598/162.
8 GA, Q/SIb 1, f. 146.
9 TNA, E 134/1657/Mich. 47; E 134/1659/East. 33; E 134/22 Chas. II/Trin. 6.
10 GA, D 23/T 10; D 204/2/2.
11 See above, settlement (the village); manor.
12 GA, D 2957/48/3; P 184/IN 1/1, burial 2 Jan. 1709.
13 Ibid. D 1230/1.
14 Ibid. Q/RZ 1; *Glouc. J.* 31 May 1845; 1 July 1848; TNA, FS 2/3, Glos. no 399.
15 TNA, HO 107/1959.
16 *Kelly's Dir. Glos.* (1863), 297; (1870), 584; TNA, RG 10/2605.
17 *Glouc. J.* 7 June 1919.
18 *Poor Law Abstract, 1804*, 180–1.
19 GDR vol. 383, no cxiv.
20 *Kelly's Dir. Glos.* (1885), 508; (1906), 221; OS Map 1:2,500, Glos. XXIV.14 (1923 edn).
21 GA, Q/RI 83.
22 OS Map 6", Glos. XXIV.SW (1924 edn).
23 Hamlen, 'Huntley', 263–4.
24 *Citizen*, 3 Aug. 1970.
25 Hamlen, 'Huntley', 248, 259–60, 263–4.
26 *Huntley Parish Plan*, 8. Its datestone was placed on another bldg. in the village: information from Maureen and Richard Blakemore of Forest Gate.
27 *Forester*, 21 June 2001; see OS Map 1:2,500, SO 7219–7319 (1972 edn).
28 Hamlen, 'Huntley', 254–5.
29 *Cal. Doc. France*, 409–11.
30 *Reg. Swinfield*, 535, 545; *Reg. T. de Charlton*, 75, 79; *Reg. Orleton*, 163–4.
31 GA, P 326/IN 3/4.
32 *Dioc. of Glouc. Dir.* (1994–5), 59; (2003–4), 23.
33 Above, manor; *Reg. T. de Charlton*, 75, 79, 80; *Reg. Trillek*, 381; *Reg. Spofford*, 352; *Reg. Boulers*, 22. *Reg. Mascall*, 188, ascribes the patronage in 1416 to Llanthony priory in Wales.

Hastings, acted as patron[1] and in 1584 Thomas Hooper and John Fowle were patrons for a turn.[2] The advowson remained with the manor[3] until the duke of Kent sold it in 1725 or 1726 to Jackman Morse,[4] vicar of Awre. From Jackman (d. 1765)[5] it passed through his widow Anne to his son Revd John Morse[6] (d. 1797). The latter's widow Martha (d. 1826),[7] together with his daughters Martha, wife of John Morse of Newent, and Hannah, widow of Revd Richard Foley, was patron in 1817.[8] At the next vacancy, in 1839, Robert Capper of Cheltenham presented his son Daniel,[9] who was named as patron in 1863.[10] Henry Miles succeeded Daniel as rector on his own presentation in 1866[11] and the patronage was later vested in his brother Philip Miles (d. 1909). In 1914 it belonged to Benjamin St John Ackers of Huntley Manor[12] and in the mid 1960s it passed from his son's executors to the bishop.[13]

The rectory was valued at £4 in 1291[14] and £7 5s. 10d. in 1535.[15] Its glebe, made up of the parsonage closes and several detached pieces in 1584,[16] covered c.38 a. in 1692.[17] Comprising 45 a. around the rectory house in 1841,[18] it was enlarged slightly at the inclosure of Huntley common in the late 1850s[19] and Henry Miles exchanged it with Edmund Probyn in 1866[20] for land elsewhere in Huntley and a farm in Westbury-on-Severn.[21] The farm was sold before the First World War.[22] All the tithes belonged to the rectory and in the late 17th century the only established moduses were those for gardens and milk.[23] The tithes, later lessened in value by the substitution of other fixed cash payments,[24] were commuted in 1841 for a corn rent charge of £250.[25] The living, which had been valued at £35 in 1650[26] and at £60 in 1750[27] and had been augmented by Queen Anne's Bounty on gifts from the rector, John Morse, in 1826,[28] was worth £242 in 1856.[29]

Rectory Houses, including Huntley Manor and Forest Gate

An early rectory house, part of which was a separate dwelling in 1584,[30] was destroyed by fire in the mid 17th century and was replaced in 1710 with the help of donations, the largest from the lord of the manor.[31] Standing some way north of the church,[32] it was rebuilt on a larger scale in 1862 and 1863 for Daniel Capper.[33] Following the exchange of 1866 mentioned above, Edmund Probyn made the house his residence and renamed it Huntley Manor[34] and Henry Miles remodelled and enlarged Pool House, on the main road west of the village,[35] as the rectory house. Huntley Manor, designed for Capper by S.S. Teulon, is described elsewhere in this account.[36]

Pool House, which has been renamed Forest Gate, is a plain red brick house with Bath stone dressings built for the Probyns in the early 19th century on a large site. The east front has three gables, the central one marking the entrance hall which is flanked by two receptions rooms. In its conversion as the rectory house Henry Miles employed the architect Thomas Fulljames and the main changes were on the south garden front in 1866. The south-east rooms were enlarged by a canted projection and the south-west portion of the house was replaced by a gabled block containing a staircase hall and a reception room with service accommodation to the west.[37] A timber porch was added to the east entrance later. The house, which was reduced in size by the demolition of a service wing in the late 1930s, remained the rectory house until 1952. Among its

---

1 *Reg. Myllyng*, 187 and n., which names the lord, incorrectly as John, earl of Shrewsbury; see below, Longhope, manor.
2 Hockaday Abs. ccxlviii.
3 Atkyns, *Glos.* 485.
4 GA, P 184/IN 1/1, note on patrons at front of vol.
5 Bigland, *Glos.* I, 104.
6 GDR wills 1765/20; Rudder, *Glos.* 505.
7 GA, P 184/CH 3.
8 Hockaday Abs. cclxviii, 1797, 1800, 1814, 1817; for Hannah's marriage (21 Jan. 1801), GA, P 184/IN 1/4.
9 Hockaday Abs. cclxviii; *Alumni Cantab. 1752–1900*, I, 508.
10 *Kelly's Dir. Glos.* (1863), 297.
11 GDR vol. 377, f. 14.
12 *Kelly's Dir. Glos.* (1870 and later edns); *Alumni Cantab. 1752–1900*, IV, 411; for Ackers and his successor, above manor.
13 *Glouc. Dioc. Year Book* (1965–6), 28–9; (1967–8), 28–9.
14 *Tax. Eccl.* 161.
15 *Valor Eccl.* II, 501.
16 GDR, V 5/170T 1.
17 Ibid. 6.
18 Ibid. T 1/106.
19 GA, Q/RI 83.
20 *Morris's Dir. Glos.* (1876), 505–6; *Kelly's Dir. Glos.* (1870), 584, which dated the exchange to 1865.
21 GDR, V 5/170T 10.
22 *Kelly's Dir. Glos.* (1910), 225; (1914), 230; see GA, D 2299/691.
23 GDR, V 5/170T 3, 7.
24 GA, P 184/IN 3/3, memo 22 July 1821.
25 GDR, T 1/106.
26 C.R. Elrington, 'The Survey of Church Livings in Gloucestershire, 1650', *Trans. BGAS* 83 (1964), 98.
27 *Bp. Benson's Surv. of Glouc. 1735–50*, 6–7.
28 Hodgson, *Queen Anne's Bounty* (1845), pp. cclxxxiv, ccv.
29 GDR vol. 384, f. 122.
30 Ibid. V 5/170T 1.
31 GA, P 184/IN 1/1, memo at front of vol. According to Bigland, *Glos.* II, 111, the burnt ho. was rebuilt in 1720.
32 GDR, T 1/106 (no 92).
33 *Glouc. J.* 18 Apr., 27 June 1863; Verey and Brooks, *Glos.* II, 545.
34 *Kelly's Dir. Glos.* (1870), 584; (1879), 688.
35 GA, P 184/MI 4; GDR, T 1/106 (no 420).
36 Above, manor.
37 GA, D 2593/2/189; *Kelly's Dir. Glos.* (1870), 584; 1860s photog. of ho. in the possession of Maureen and Richard Blakemore of Forest Gate.

fittings is the bell for the Sunday school once held there.[1] Part of Miles's new establishment was an extensive collection of outbuildings,[2] of which a curved brick range incorporating trap house, stabling and pigsties survives.

Since 1952 three other houses have served in succession as the parsonage.[3]

RELIGIOUS LIFE

The Middle Ages

Huntley church bore its dedication to St John the Baptist by the end of the Middle Ages.[4] Its late medieval west tower, which is all that remains of the medieval church,[5] contains a bell dating from the early 15th century.[6]

Of its rectors, William de Rostele was licensed in 1310 to be non-resident for the purpose of study[7] and was later a deputy escheator.[8] In 1323 he was in a group accused of an assault at Gloucester and of forcible entry elsewhere and in 1327 his arrest was ordered for participation in an armed force that went to plunder Berkeley castle and refused to join the Crown's expedition against the Scots.[9] A new rector was instituted in 1328.[10] In 1397 both the rector and a chaplain, the latter living in Churcham, were said to lead uncelibate lives,[11] as was the rector in 1517. Robert Hemming, who was perhaps the rector instructed in 1518 to leave Churcham and serve the cure, was cited several times between 1522 and 1526 for incontinency and remained rector until his death. In 1509 it was revealed that two women had buried an unbaptized, perhaps stillborn, infant in the churchyard and afterwards had exhumed it. In 1517 another woman was accused of sorcery.[12]

From the Reformation to the Restoration

Richard Taylor, Robert Hemming's successor in 1548,[13] was unable to recite the Ten Commandments or prove the Apostles' Creed.[14] He resigned the living in 1556. Henry a Fowle, described as parson in 1557, came from a local family[15] and had been deprived of Blaisdon rectory in 1554.[16] Instituted as rector in 1559,[17] he was censured several times for haunting alehouses and playing cards and tables. Other complaints, some repeated in 1576, were that he studied the scriptures little, failed to preach quarterly sermons and teach the catechism, and admitted to the communion, held only once a year, immoral persons and others unable to say the Lord's Prayer and the Creed. In 1576 it was also reported that the church, while it lacked a psalter and the largest Bible, had a cope and other vestments, that a former churchwarden privately kept two mass books, that May Day revellers were allowed into the church, and that the churchwardens were not spending church money appropriately.[18] The church has a bell acquired in 1580 and another dated 1616.[19]

William a Fowle, Henry's son and successor as rector in 1584,[20] was a conformist and in 1593 was deemed a sufficient scholar but no preacher.[21] Under him and Thomas Unwin, his successor in 1613,[22] several parishioners regularly failed to attend church and to take communion.[23] Unwin, described as a preaching minister in 1650,[24] remained rector until his death in 1661,[25] the rectory house being burned down towards the end of his incumbency.[26]

The Established Church and Nonconformity after the Restoration

Isaac Hague was rector from 1661 until his death in 1688.[27] At that time the church, described as an entire aisle, had a plain interior with few if any wall monuments.[28] In 1680 it had a bowl, a flagon, and four bells,[29] of which the tenor was apparently acquired in 1670.[30] In 1672 Thomas Smith, the former vicar of Longhope, served a dissenting meeting in Huntley.[31] One nonconformist was recorded in the

---

1 Information from Maureen and Richard Blakemore; M. Hamlen, 'History of Huntley' (1981: typescript in Glos. Colln. 45959), 79–80.
2 GA, D 2593/2/189; OS Map 1/2,500, Glos. XXIV.14 (1884 edn).
3 OS Map 1:2,500, SO 7019–7119 (1973 edn); SO 7219–7319 (1972 edn); *Dioc. Of Glouc. Dir.* (1994–5), 18: (2003–4), 111; information from Maureen and Richard Blakemore.
4 Hockaday Abs. ccxlviii, 1544.
5 See below (rebuilding of the par. ch.).
6 *Glos. Ch. Bells*, 386.
7 *Reg. Swinfield*, 545.
8 *Reg. Orleton*, 163–4.
9 *Cal. Pat.* 1321–4, 444–5; 1327–1330, 156–7.
10 *Reg. T. de Charlton*, 75.
11 A.T. Bannister, 'Visitation Returns of Diocese of Hereford in 1397', *EHR* 44 (1929), 450, 452.
12 Hockaday Abs. ccxlviii.
13 Ibid.
14 J. Gairdner, 'Bishop Hooper's Visitation of Gloucester', *EHR* (1904), 120.

15 GDR wills 1560/62; Hockaday Abs. ccxlviii; see *Military Surv. of Glos. 1522*, 200, 207.
16 *VCH Glos.* X, 10.
17 Hockaday Abs. ccxlviii.
18 Ibid. 1563; GDR vol. 40, f. 261v.
19 *Glos. Ch. Bells*, 385–8.
20 Hockaday Abs. ccxlviii; GDR, V 5/170T 1.
21 Hockaday Abs. xlix, state of clergy 1584, f. 42; lii, state of clergy 1593, f. 7.
22 Ibid. ccxlviii. 23 GA, D 2052.
24 Elrington, 'Surv. of Church Livings', 98.
25 TNA, E 134/22Chas2/East3.
26 GA, P 184/IN 1/1, memo at front of vol.
27 Hockaday Abs. ccxlviii; GA, P 184/IN 1/1.
28 *Notes on Dioc. of Glouc. by Chancellor Parsons*, 159; see Bigland, *Glos.* II, 112.
29 GDR, V 5/170T 4.
30 *Glos. Ch. Bells*, 386; see Ellacombe, *Glos. Ch. Bells* (1881), 52.
31 *Cal. SP Dom.* 1672, 118, 234, 574; below, Longhope, religious hist.

parish in 1676[1] and 33 parishioners, some if not all dissenters, refused to pay church rates in 1687.[2]

The rectors between 1688 and 1797 represented three generations of the Morse family.[3] Abraham Morse, rector 1688–1726, built a new rectory house and lived in it in the early 18th century.[4] Richard Clark of Painswick was buried in the churchyard in 1717 and commemorated there as 'a zealous assertor of the Protestant Religion and of his Country's Liberties'.[5] Jackman Morse, rector 1727–65, lived at Awre, where he was vicar,[6] and employed a curate at Huntley, including on occasions one or other of his sons.[7] The curate provided one Sunday service, alternately in the morning and afternoon,[8] and in 1759 the rector led a perambulation of the parish bounds.[9] John Morse, rector 1765–97, held Blaisdon rectory from 1778 and employed a curate at least in his later years.[10]

The next three rectors, including Richard Foley (1800–13), held the living for a total of twenty years. John Morse (1817–39),[11] the last of his family to be rector, was also vicar of Oxenhall from 1824.[12] At Huntley a Sunday school was taught in his house[13] and in 1825 the Sunday service, alternating between the morning and the afternoon, was said to attract a congregation of over 100, particularly in the afternoon when the church, with most of its seating free, was filled to capacity. Psalms and hymns were sung to the music of John Nunn.[14] Under a sermon charity established by Samuel Hawkins (d. 1805) the singers were paid for singing the old 100th psalm on New Year's Day.[15] In 1825 there were 25 regular communicants and the parish maintained a library.[16]

Although local nonconformists registered houses in 1798 and 1822,[17] Huntley was said in 1825 to have no dissenters.[18] Another Huntley man registered his house in 1838[19] and other houses were registered in 1847 and 1850, the latter by the Baptist minister of Longhope.[20] None of those meetings continued for long.

The Rebuilding of the Parish Church

The parish church, with a chancel, a nave with south porch, and a low west tower,[21] was described in the late 18th century as very small and having nothing of architectural or antiquarian interest.[22] Increasing the church's accommodation was the first concern of Daniel Capper, rector 1839–66,[23] and at the start of his ministry the church was enlarged to hold a north gallery facing the nave and pews were installed in the chancel and benches under an old west gallery and in the belfry at the base of the tower.[24] From 1844 Capper was assisted by a succession of curates[25] and in 1851 there were morning and afternoon services with attendances of 100 and 150 respectively.[26] In 1857 there were 56 regular communicants.[27] In 1862, after the vestry had accepted Capper's offer to pay for the building's repair and restoration,[28] the church was stripped of its wall monuments, erected in the later 18th and early 19th century to commemorate among others members of the Morse and Drinkwater families, and was demolished apart from the tower. In its place Capper built a larger church, its chancel as a memorial to his father Robert (d. 1851), and he added a broach spire to the tower. The churchyard was enlarged at the same time.[29]

The new church, completed in 1863, was designed by S.S. Teulon in the Decorated style and was lavishly furnished. Built of local sandstone with Painswick stone dressings, its chancel is flanked on the north by a chapel and a vestry and on the south by a transeptal organ chamber and it has a nave with a north aisle and south porch. The polychrome interior has biblical texts throughout and carvings by Thomas Earp, notably representations of the Evangelists in medallions on the nave arcade. The glass, by Lavers & Barraud, is richly coloured in the windows of the east end and the bottom of the tower. The other windows display biblical scenes picked out on monochrome glass. The fittings, of which the reredos, pulpit,

---

1 *Compton Census*, 544.
2 GA, D 2052.
3 Hockaday Abs. ccxlvii; Bigland, *Glos.* II, 112; GDR wills 1726/266; 1765/20.
4 GA, P 184/IN 1/1, memo at front of vol.; above (patronage and endowment).
5 GA, P 184/IN 1/1; Bigland, *Glos.* II, 113.
6 *VCH Glos.* V, 43.
7 GA, P 184/IN 1/1; IN 3/3; *Alumni Oxon. 1715–1886*, III, 988–9.
8 *Bp. Benson's Surv. of Glouc 1735–50*, 7.
9 GA, P 184/IN 1/1, memo at end of vol.
10 Hockaday Abs. cxxvi, ccxlviii.
11 Ibid. ccxlviii; for Foley, GA, P 184/IN 1/6; above (patronage and endowment).
12 *Alumni Oxon. 1715–1886*, III, 989.
13 Glos. Colln RR 170.6 (letter from the National Society 18 Aug. 1975).
14 GDR vol. 383, no cxiv; for Nunn, see *Oxford DNB*, s.v. Nunn family.
15 *18th Rep. Com. Char.* 324–5
16 GDR vol. 383, no cxiv.
17 Hockaday Abs. ccxlviii.
18 GDR vol. 383, no cxiv.
19 Hockaday Abs. ccxlviii.
20 GA, Q/RZ 1; see below, Longhope, religious hist.
21 Plan of 1839 in GDR, F 1/4.
22 Bigland, *Glos.* II, 111.
23 Hockaday Abs. ccxlviii; GDR vol. 377, f. 14; see *Alumni Cantab. 1752–1900*, I, 508.
24 GA, P 184/CW 3/1; GDR, F 1/4. For the plan of ch. in 1857, see GA, P 184/IN 4/2.
25 Hockaday Abs. ccxlviii.
26 TNA, HO129/334/2/6/12.
27 GA, P 184/IN 4/2.
28 Ibid. CW 2/1.
29 Ibid. CH 3; *Glouc. J.* 27 June 1863. Brass plates on the chancel steps record the memorial to Rob. Capper.

46. Huntley church: the interior looking east

lectern, and font are in alabaster and marble and by Earp, included a wooden sanctuary arch, an organ, and pendentive lamps, the last (of which those in the nave have been removed) by Francis Skidmore.[1] The displaced wall monuments were set up in the tower.[2] The plate comprises a chalice made in 1844 and other pieces made between 1858 and 1862.[3]

From the Later Nineteenth Century

Henry Miles, rector 1866–1906[4] was resident after he had established a new rectory house[5] and regularly employed a curate. His successor George Baker served in person[6] and died in 1934.[7] At the church the tenor bell was recast and a new bell added to the peal in 1878 and the peal was augmented to six in 1884.[8] A screen was inserted in the tower arch 1908.[9] The churchyard has two late 19th-century lamp-posts.

From the 1960s the rectory changed hands more frequently[10] but even as part of a united benefice Huntley continued to have a resident clergyman in the early 21st century.[11]

KEMPLEY

KEMPLEY is a small rural parish on the county boundary midway between Gloucester and Hereford and 9 km SSW of the town of Ledbury (Herefs.). The ancient parish was a slice of land hugging Dymock to its east and extending southwards to Kempley Green and Fishpool, the latter a hamlet in Upton Bishop (Herefs.).[12] A stretch of the long western boundary against Herefordshire followed the Upton Bishop–Much Marcle road, on which Wiggin's Ash was a landmark in the late 18th century.[13] Elsewhere the parish was defined by field boundaries and streams and after gaining a small area of Much Marcle (Herefs.) on its side of the Kempley brook below Chibler's hill in the south-

---

1 *Glouc. J.* 27 June 1863; Verey and Brooks, *Glos.* II, 544–5. See Fig. 46. An old photog. of the interior looking E., in the ch. in 2006, shows lamps in the nave different in design from those in the chancel.
2 GA, P 184/CH 3.
3 *Glos. Ch. Plate*, 124.
4 *Alumni Cantab. 1752–1900*, IV, 411.
5 *Kelly's Dir. Glos.* (1870 and later edns to 1906); Hockaday Abs. ccxlviii; see above (patronage and endowment).
6 GA, P 184/IN 1/6, 15.

7 Ibid. S 184/3, p. 192.
8 *Glos. Ch. Bells*, 385–6.
9 GA, D 2593/2/692.
10 Hamlen, 'Huntley', 79–80.
11 *Dioc. of Glouc. Dir.* (1994–5), 18, 59; (2003–4), 23, 111.
12 OS Maps 6", Glos. IX.SE (1883 edn); XVI.NE (1889 edn). This account was written in 2005 and 2006 and revised in 2007.
13 MCA, M 4i, undated maps of Chievely's and the Fish Pond and of Drew's, Adams' and Matthew's farms.

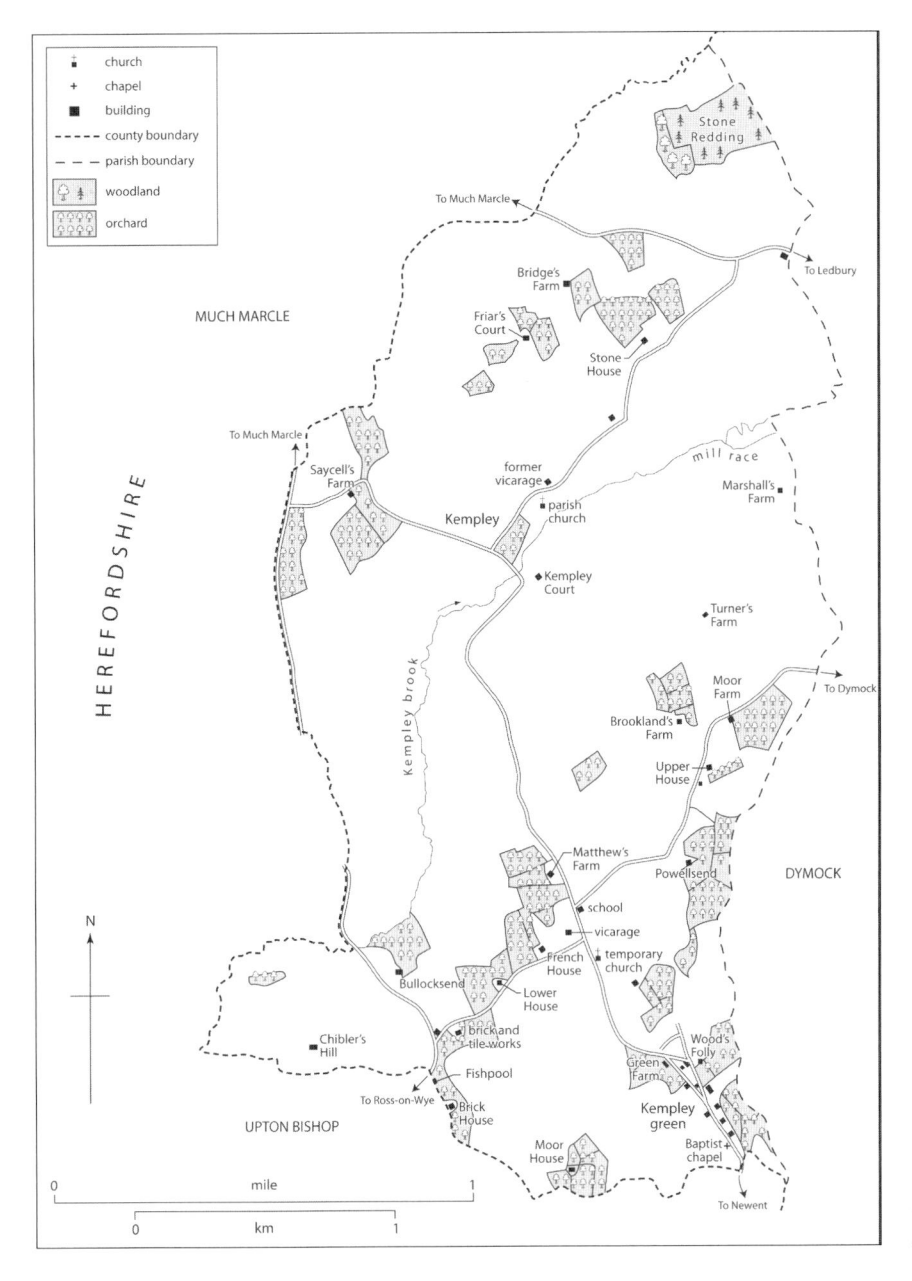

Map 10. *Kempley 1880*

western corner in the later 19th century[1] it covered 644 ha (1,593 a.).[2] In 1965 it was enlarged to 680 ha by the addition from Upton Bishop of settled farmland to the south at Kempley Green and Fishpool.[3]

LANDSCAPE

Kempley has rolling and gently undulating countryside save in the south-west where it rises more steeply on Chibler's hill. The Kempley brook flows northwards on the parish's west side before turning eastwards across its north end in a broad valley that is subject to flooding. The land, lying mostly at between 50 and 70 m, rises to 90 m at Kempley Green and to 100 m on Chibler's hill. The soil is a heavy clay mostly on the Old Red Sandstone and with gravelly deposits in the valley of the brook and a tributary joining it from the south below Chibler's hill.[4]

Although much of Kempley was under the plough at Domesday, more land was brought into cultivation through later woodland clearance. Kempley wood, in the southern end of the parish adjoining the ancient Teds wood in Upton Bishop,[5] was described as a foreign common wood in 1308.[6]

1 GDR, T 1/108; MCA, maps and plans, shelf 4, no 10.
2 *OS Area Book* (1884).
3 *Census*, 1971.
4 Geol. Surv. Map 1:50,000, solid and drift, sheet 216 (1988 edn).

5 Worcs. RO, 705:99 (BA 5540), Kempley and Wilton ct. rolls 1526–68, rott. 12d., 13, 25; see MCA, F 5v, deed 1365; I 5i, bdl. 88A, no 1, 4; I 5ii, bdl. 88, nos 17, 19.
6 *Inq. p.m. Glos.* 1302–58, 100, 185.

Piecemeal clearance continued after most of it was inclosed in the mid 16th century[1] and, with the gradual inclosure of the adjoining waste,[2] only a remnant of the common of Kempley green was left.[3] The parish retained very little woodland and only 5 a. of common land in 1839.[4]

While most of the farmland was in early closes there were several medieval open fields. Their fullest extent is unknown. Orchards, planted locally in arable land, were being established by the mid 14th century and, together with meadows and pastures, accounted for more than half the parish in the 18th century. A park containing oak saplings in 1308[5] overlooked the manor house (Kempley Court) from the hillside in the centre of the parish[6] and was laid down as 30 a. of farmland in the mid 17th century.[7] To preserve the remaining trees farming leases of Kempley Court in the early 18th century provided an allowance for the tenant to buy coal from the Forest of Dean as his fuel.[8]

Piecemeal planting begun in the later 19th century has increased the wooded area beyond the 43 a. recorded in 1905.[9] Most of the new woodland forms a block at the north end of the parish including Stone Redding,[10] once an ancient wood.[11] The number of orchards continued to grow in the 19th century but was reduced in the 20th century.

ROADS

Kempley is crossed by lanes and paths used mainly by local traffic. Even the principal lanes were muddy and impassable in winter in the mid 18th century,[12] as was a new road in 1791.[13] Only that crossing the north end of the parish from east to west, part of a route between the Gloucester–Ledbury road in Bromesberrow and the Ledbury–Ross-on-Wye road in Much Marcle, was turnpiked, from 1833[14] to 1871.[15]

The lane leading southwards past the medieval parish church and up, and along a ridge, to Kempley Green is a way to Newent. The road from Dymock to Ross-on-Wye runs from the east by way of Camomile green[16] to join the Newent road south of Matthew's Farm and continues its westerly course a short distance further south. At the north end of the parish a hollow lane, part of a highway leading southwards from a place called Broadstone's green,[17] was abandoned during the construction of Stone House c.1600.[18] Several lanes in the south, including a way to Ross-on-Wye from the Newent road north of Matthew's Farm,[19] were closed or abandoned after 1787[20] and the course of the Ross road in the far south was diverted near Lower House in 1809.[21]

POPULATION

According to the Domesday survey there were 17 tenant households on Kempley manor in 1086.[22] Fifteen persons were assessed for tax in the parish in 1327.[23] A muster in 1542 named 31 Kempley men[24] and in 1563 the parish contained 20 households.[25] The number of communicants was given as c.80 in 1551[26] and 60 in 1603.[27] There were 36 families in 1650[28] and the population was estimated at 180 c.1710.[29] About 1775 the population was given as 257[30] but that figure may have been too high, for in 1801 it was recorded as 218. In the first two decades of the 19th century it rose to 301 and, apart from a rise to 342 in 1841, the population remained just over 300 until the late 19th century when it fell to 210 in 1901. A partial revival in its size took place in the mid 20th century and in 1961 it stood at 255 with another 33 people living in those parts of Upton Bishop transferred to Kempley in 1965. The population of the enlarged parish remained the same in 2001.[31]

---

1 Worcs. RO, 705:99 (BA 5540), Kempley and Wilton ct. rolls 1526–68, rott. 33–4.
2 MCA, F 2vii, deed 829; A 2ii, no 18 (M 60–71); I 2ii, bdl. 61B, no 51; J 2vi, bdl. 107A, no 1.
3 GBR, J 4/1, no 33; MCA, M 4i, undated map of Wood and Green farms.
4 GDR, T 1/108.
5 *Inq. p.m. Glos.* 1302–58, 100.
6 Worcs. RO, 705:99 (BA 5540), Kempley and Wilton ct. rolls 1526–68, rot. 32.
7 MCA, G 1iv, bdl. 173, no 2; F 3i, deed 1044; F 4iv, deed 1108; F 5vii, deed 1585.
8 Ibid. F 5v, deed 1364; G 1ii, bdl. 172D, no 72.
9 Acreage Returns, 1905.
10 OS Map 6", Glos. IX.SE (1883–1924 edns).
11 See GA, P 188/IN 1/2, burial 29 Aug. 1678.
12 Rudder, *Glos.* 508.
13 Herefs. RO, E 69/226.
14 Ledbury Roads Act, 3 Wm. IV, c. 58 (Local and Personal); see Bryant, *Map of Glos.* (1824).
15 Annual Turnpike Acts Continuance Act, 1871, 34 & 35 Vic. c. 115.
16 HCA 6157.
17 Herefs. RO, E 12/G/20.
18 MCA, G 1iv, bdl. 173, no 1; HCA 3477/22; for Stone House, below, settlement (outlying settlement); manor.
19 See Taylor, *Map of Glos.* (1777).
20 MCA, M 4i, undated maps of Drew's, Adams' and Matthew's farms and of Wood and Green farms; OS Map 1", sheet 43 (1831 edn).
21 MCA, I 4iii, no 20.
22 *Domesday Book* (Rec. Com.), I, 167v.
23 *Glos. Subsidy Roll, 1327*, 35–6.
24 *L&P Hen. VIII*, XVII, 499.
25 Bodleian, Rawl. C. 790, f. 28.
26 J. Gairdner, 'Bishop Hooper's Visitation of Gloucester', *EHR* 19 (1904), 119.
27 *Eccl. Misc.* 101.
28 C.R. Elrington, 'The Survey of Church Livings in Gloucestershire, 1650', *Trans. BGAS* 83 (1964), 98.
29 Atkyns, *Glos.* 489.
30 Rudder, *Glos.* 509.
31 *Census*, 1801–2001.

SETTLEMENT

Early settlement in Kempley took the form of scattered farmsteads and cottages with the medieval parish church and manor house standing apart in the north end of the parish on opposite sides of the Kempley brook.[1] The peripheral situation of some dwellings was underlined by the inclusion of the suffix *end* in their names. The settlement pattern, evident in much of the parish in the mid 14th century and modified by the abandonment of some farmsteads later,[2] is more intensive in the south where the clearance of woodland continued into the early modern period and a hamlet mostly of squatter dwellings formed on Kempley green.[3] The hamlet became the southern part of a long village, the northern end of which contains a church built in the early 20th century.

THE VILLAGE

The village straggles along the ridge beside the Newent road in the south of the parish. At its northern end Matthew's Farm belonged as a copyhold on the rectory estate of St Katherine's hospital, Ledbury, to the Edwyn family in the early 14th century[4] and was occupied by the Matthews or Phipps family by the early 16th.[5] To the south a cottage called Old Saycell's, a name recorded in 1532,[6] formed a row of four poorhouses in the early 19th century[7] and was demolished before the 1880s.[8] There were a few other early dwellings immediately to the south. One or two small cottages were thrown up on waste land at the junction of the Ross road *c.*1800[9] but the development of the area as the north end of the village dates properly to the 1860s and 1870s when Earl Beauchamp built a schoolroom, a vicarage house (Kempley House), and a temporary church (the village hall) there.[10] A new church completed south of the junction of the Ross road in 1903 has become the parish church.[11] Little Adams, built east of the lane to Newent in the early 17th century,[12] served as a beerhouse in the later 19th century and has been rebuilt, first as a clubroom and later as a house (The Hollies).[13]

Building had begun higher up on Kempley green by the mid 17th century as part of the settlement of Kempley wood.[14] In the mid 18th century there were two farmsteads at the north-western end of the green or common[15] and a two-bayed farmhouse, owned by St Bartholomew's hospital in Gloucester, on its east side;[16] the last was known later as Folly Farm (Wood's Folly).[17] More cottages and small houses were built on the common in the later 18th and early 19th century[18] and the settlement had about 30 dwellings[19] when, in 1850, a nonconformist chapel was erected there.[20]

Two council house were built on the lane north of the village in 1934 and another two at Kempley Green in 1939.[21] Four more council houses were built at the green in 1949[22] and another eight, including a row of four, further north at Wantridge, towards the northern end of the village, in 1953 and 1954.[23] In the later 20th century private building of bungalows and larger houses filled vacant spaces on the green to create a linear residential settlement.[24]

OUTLYING SETTLEMENT

The farmstead at Powellsend, just off the Dymock road north-east of the village, was formerly known as Powersend,[25] after a family living in Kempley in the 14th and 15th centuries.[26] Further along the lane at Camomile green was Upper House (Parsonage Farm), part of the rectory estate,[27] where some buildings were demolished before the mid 1430s.[28] The farmhouse was pulled down after its acquisition by Earl Beauchamp in 1869. A stone cottage built near by a few

---

1 Below (outlying settlement).
2 There was a dwellings at a place known in 1601 as Sneed's End: BL, Add. Ch. 38897.
3 *1st Rep. Com. Employment in Agric.* app. II, p. 130.
4 HCA 7018/5(2), pp. 45–8, 56–7.
5 Ibid. p. 58; 7018/5(1), pp. 13–15.
6 Worcs. RO, 705:99 (BA 5540), Kempley and Wilton ct. rolls 1526–68, rott. 6, 8.
7 MCA, I 2ii, bdl. 61B, nos 56–65; GA, P 188/OV 2/2; GDR, T 1/108 (nos 206, 208, 210–11).
8 OS Map 6", Glos. XVI.NE (1889 edn).
9 MCA, H 4v, bdl. 49, no 12.
10 OS Map 6", Glos. XVI.NE (1889 edn); below, social hist. (education); religious hist. (religious life). For the earl and his bldg. projects in general, see *Oxford DNB*.
11 Below, religious hist. (religious life).
12 MCA, J 6ii, bdl. 101v, nos 166–79; GDR, T 1/108 (no 390).
13 Below, social hist.; information from Mr C. Bligh of The Hollies.
14 MCA, A 2ii, no 18 (M 60–71); F 5v, deed 1354; F 5viii, deed 1583; I 3vi, bdl. 71B, nos 5–6; J 2i, bdl. 105B, no 10; Worcs. RO, 705:99 (BA 3375), Kempley deeds 1602–66, deed 3 Feb. 1659.
15 MCA, M 4i, undated map of Wood and Green farms; G 1iv, bdl. 173, no 16.
16 GBR, J 1/2023E; J 4/1, no 33.
17 MCA, J 2vii, bdl. 111G, no 50; OS Map 6", Glos. XVI.NE (1889 edn).
18 MCA, I 2i, bdl. 61b, nos 51, 68, 70.
19 GDR, T 1/108; TNA, HO 107/1960.
20 Below, religious hist.
21 GA, DA 30/100/14, pp. 40, 384, 392.
22 Ibid. 100/17, p. 211; 100/18, pp. 33, 81.
23 Ibid. 100/21, pp. 157, 224; 100/22, p. 145; 100/23, p. 26.
24 Several houses built in the late 1990s have datestones.
25 Worcs. RO, 705:99 (BA 5540), Kempley and Wilton ct. rolls 1526–68, rot. 30; MCA, F 3iv, deed 820.
26 *Glos. Subsidy Roll, 1327*, 35; HCA 7018/5(3), p. 58.
27 OS Map 1", sheet 43 (1831 edn); HCA 6157; 7005/10, pp. 242–6.
28 HCA 7018/5(2), pp. 67–8; 1840.

years earlier[1] was known in 1866 as Camomile cottage.[2] Further along the lane a farmhouse, on the site of a cottage called the Moors in 1614,[3] was replaced after it burned down in the 1960s.[4]

North of the Dymock road Brookland's (formerly Cake's) Farm[5] belonged to the Brooke family in the mid 17th century.[6] The Perry House, a farmstead recorded in 1532, stood immediately to the west.[7] After becoming part of the Brookes' farm[8] its house was demolished but the farm retained a barn there.[9] Hillfields Farm, to the north-east, was known until the early 20th century as Print House and sometimes as Turner's Farm.[10] Presumably a medieval farmstead,[11] it was taken, together with a farmstead called Lintons, into the manor estate in 1620[12] and was sometimes called the Court House in the later 17th century.[13] Marshall's Farm, on the east side of the parish up against woodland in Dymock,[14] was on land owned in the Middle Ages by Flaxley abbey[15] and was possibly named after a family living in Kempley in the early 14th century.[16] The farmstead, occupied in the late 19th century by the gamekeeper on the Old Grange estate,[17] was abandoned in the 20th century and the ruins of its small brick house, dating perhaps from the 16th or 17th century, were demolished, apart from a chimney stack, c.1960.[18]

In the north end of the parish the 12th-century parish church, famed for its wall paintings, stands redundant and virtually solitary on the north bank of the Kempley brook. The only house near it was built for the vicarage in the late 18th century.[19] Kempley Court, across the brook some way from the church, occupies the site of the manor house used by the Grey family in the early 14th century.[20] Rebuilt as a gentleman's residence by Thomas Pyndar in the later 17th century, the Court was long a farmhouse.[21] Two bungalows have been built near by, one in the mid 1960s and the other in the mid 1980s, the latter immediately south of the Court serving as a new farmhouse.[22]

Friar's Court, some way north of the old church, was established as the main farm on the rectory estate of St Katherine's hospital by the mid 1430s.[23] Another farmstead belonging to the rectory, known as Woodward's after the family that occupied it from the later 14th century,[24] stood on the hillside north-east of the church.[25] Its house was converted as an oast house[26] soon after the lord of the manor erected a mansion called Stone House right next to it c.1600.[27] From the later 1720s the site centred on Stone House developed as the principal farmstead in the parish.[28] Further north, Bridges's Farm, part of the manor estate in the mid 17th century,[29] stands on the hillside facing north across the Much Marcle road perhaps in the place of Jack's, a farmstead sold to Henry Finch by Thomas Bridges of Sugwas (Herefs.) in 1592.[30] In the mid 1950s another house was built to the north-east.[31] North of the road an early farmstead called Tup House[32] was abandoned, and its buildings demolished, after 1720.[33]

Saycell's Farm, in the west of the parish, bears the name of a man with property in Kempley in the mid 13th century[34] and occupies the site of Saycell's Place owned in the early 15th century by the Walwyn family.[35] Further south a farmstead called Carter's Place in the mid 1430s belonged to the rectory estate.[36] It had been abandoned by the late 16th century[37] and its site, west of the Kempley brook, was cleared of buildings.[38]

In the south-west of the parish French House, on

---

1 Ibid. 7005/10, pp. 257–65; GDR, T 1/108; OS Map 6", Glos. XVI.NE (1889).
2 GA, P 188/IN 1/18.
3 MCA, J 2i, bdl. 105B, no 8; J 2iv, bdl. 105E, no 50.
4 Inf. from Mr and Mrs Cooke of Upper House.
5 OS Map 1", sheet 43 (1831 edn).
6 TNA, PROB 11/267, ff. 336v.–337; MCA, J 3i, bdl. 117, nos 14–24; GA, Q/REl 1, Botloe hundred, Kempley.
7 Worcs. RO, 705:99 (BA 5540), Kempley and Wilton ct. rolls 1526–68, rott. 5–6.
8 GDR wills 1713/78.
9 See MCA, M 4i, undated map of Cole's, Turner's, and the Perry House farms; GDR, T 1/108 (nos 153–4).
10 OS Map 6", Glos. IX.SE (1883–1924 edns); Bryant, *Map of Glos.* (1824).
11 It may be named after the Prentout family recorded in the 14th century: HCA 1899; 7018/5(2), pp. 50–1.
12 MCA, F 2vii, deed 828; F 3iv, deed 880.
13 Ibid. G 1iv, bdl. 173, no 12; HCA 3477/2.
14 OS Map 6", Glos. IX.SE (1883 edn).
15 GA, D 214/T 17, deed 3 Nov. 1630; below, manor (other estates).
16 *Glos. Subsidy Roll, 1327*, 36.
17 *Kelly's Dir. Glos.* (1889), 722–3, 825; (1894), 144, 216.
18 GA, SL 417; information from Mr Geo. Young of Hillfields Farm.
19 HCA 3496/1; see GDR, T 1/108.

20 *Inq. p.m. Glos.* 1302–58, 100, 185, 293; *Glos. Subsidy Roll, 1327*, 35.
21 Below, manor.
22 GA, DA 30/100/32, p. 217; inf. from Mrs (Rachel) Pugh of Kempley Court.
23 HCA 7018/5(2), p. 68; see below, manor (other estates: Kempley rectory). In the 18th and 19th cents. it was sometimes called Prior's Court: Rudder, *Glos.* 509; Bryant, *Map of Glos.* (1824); OS Map 6", Glos. IX.SE (1883 edn).
24 HCA 7018/5(1), pp 20–1; (2), pp. 54, 58, 67–8.
25 MCA, M 4i, terrier of hospital land 1787; maps and plans, shelf 5, map of the Stone House estate and Bridge's farm 1787.
26 HCA 3477/1, 22.
27 Herefs. RO, E 12/G/20; MCA, misc. letter 49; see below, manor.
28 Rudder, *Glos.* 508; MCA, G 1ii, bdl. 172C, no 59; bdl. 172D, nos 61, 68, 79; G 1iv, bdl. 173, no 16; maps and plans, shelf 5, map of the Stone House estate and Bridges's farm 1787.
29 MCA, F 4iii, deed 1053; G 1i, bdl. 172B, no 33.
30 Ibid. F 2i, deed 655.
31 GA, DA 30/100/23, p. 134.
32 Worcs. RO, 705:99 (BA 5540), Kempley and Wilton ct. rolls 1526–68, rot. 7.
33 MCA, G 1ii, bdl. 172C, no 53; GDR, T 1/108 (nos 8–10).
34 TNA, JUST 1/278, rot. 25d.
35 Below, manor (other estates).
36 HCA 7018/5(2), pp. 67, 56–8.
37 MCA, F 2i, deed 644.
38 HCA 3477/1, 22; 7018/4.

47. Barn at Friar's Court from the south-west

the Ross road below the village, was named presumably after John the French (*fl.* 1327).[1] The house, recorded from 1532,[2] has been replaced by a small brick farmhouse. The farmstead at Lower House, to the west, was known as Jenkins and belonged to the Baynham family in the early 16th century.[3] In the early 1820s it passed to Ephraim Blewett, a Ross-on-Wye builder who established brickworks nearby.[4] The farmhouse stands north of the lane opposite outbuildings, to the west of which a new house was built in 2002. Further west a group of cottages near the site of the brickworks includes two built in the early 19th century, one before the course of the Ross road was altered in 1809 and the other by the road from Upton Bishop to Much Marcle.[5] To the north-west Hill Brook Farm (formerly Bullocksend) stands above the Much Marcle road.[6] The site of the Bullock family's house called Hillend in 1529,[7] it was known both as Hill House and Wood's Farm in 1659 when it separated from the manor.[8]

Further south there was at least one cottage beside Teds wood in the mid 16th century,[9] probably at Fishpool where a new cottage was built within Kempley in the mid 18th century.[10] Brick House Farm, on the parish boundary to the south-east, was known as the Brick House by 1777.[11] A cottage to the south-east called the Bull Ring was demolished in the late 18th century.[12] Moor House, a small farmhouse much further south-east of Fishpool, was recorded from 1532[13] and taken into the manor estate in 1624.[14] To the west on Chibler's hill, a farmstead known as Chievely's belonged to the Baynham family in the early 16th century.[15] A barn, retained after the house was demolished, became part of the manor estate in 1692[16] and stood partly derelict next to other farm buildings in 2003.

BUILDINGS

Most early houses and outbuildings among Kempley's scattered medieval farmsteads, such as a newly rebuilt house at Upper House (Parsonage Farm) in 1581[17] and a 'great barn' near Powellsend in 1614,[18] have not survived. At Friar's Court the northern half of a six-bayed barn, formerly thatched, contains two pairs of late medieval cruck trusses flanking a stone threshing floor. The rest of the barn was added or rebuilt in the 17th century.[19]

1 *Glos. Subsidy Roll, 1327*, 36.
2 Worcs. RO, 705:99 (BA 5540), Kempley and Wilton ct. rolls 1526–68, rot. 7; MCA, F 2iv, deed 508; Taylor, *Map of Glos.* (1777).
3 Worcs. RO, 705:99 (BA 5540), Kempley and Wilton ct. rolls 1526–68, rot. 5.
4 MCA, I 4iii, bdl. 80, nos 27–34; GDR, T 1/108; for the brickworks, below, econ. hist. (industry and trade).
5 GDR, T 1/108; MCA, I 4iii, bdl. 80, nos 20, 24.
6 OS Map 6", Glos. XVI.NE (1889 edn).
7 Worcs. RO, 705:99 (BA 5540), Kempley and Wilton ct. rolls 1526–68, rot. 3.
8 Ibid. Kempley deeds 1602–66; MCA, G 1i, bdl. 172A, no 17; below, manor (other estates).
9 Worcs. RO, 705:99 (BA 5540), Kempley and Wilton ct. rolls 1526–68, rott. 12d., 25.
10 MCA, I 3vi, bdl. 71D, nos 26–45; GDR, T 1/108 (no 283).
11 GA, Q/REl 1, Botloe hundred, Kempley; Bryant, *Map of Glos.* (1824); GDR, T 1/108 (no 285).
12 MCA, I 5i, bdl. 88B, nos 23, 26; see GDR, T 1/108 (no 301).
13 Worcs. RO, 705:99 (BA 5540), Kempley and Wilton ct. rolls 1526–68, rott. 6, 26.
14 MCA, F 3ii, deed 900; GDR, T 1/108 (no 305).
15 Worcs. RO, 705:99 (BA 5540), Kempley and Wilton ct. rolls 1526–68, rot. 5; MCA, M 4i, undated map of Chievely's and the Fish Pond; OS Map 6", Glos. XVI. NE (1905 edn).
16 Worcs. RO, 705:99 (BA 3375), Kempley deeds 1671–1713; MCA, G 1ii, bdl. 172C, no 50; GDR, T 1/108.
17 HCA 3476/1.
18 MCA, F 2vii, deed 832.
19 Verey and Brooks, *Glos.* II, 554; J. Hillaby, *St Katherine's Hospital, Ledbury, c.1230–1547* (Ledbury and District Soc. Trust Ltd, 2003), 40–1. See Fig. 47.

The house at Saycell's Farm (severely damaged by fire in 2006)[1] was built in the late 16th or early 17th century with a timber frame and three rooms on each of its two storeys. Stone House, a mansion built in the early 17th century, was refurbished later in the century and soon afterwards Kempley Court, the old manor house, was rebuilt as a fashionable residence.[2] A vicarage house was built in Gothick style at the end of the 18th century.[3]

A considerable amount of renovation took place on the farms in the late 18th and early 19th century. At Saycell's Farm an outshut with kitchen and dairy was added to the house and, to the south-west, a range incorporating stables and a barn at right angles to the house was partly rebuilt reusing roofs from the earlier buildings. At Lower Farm the house was possibly rebuilt in the 19th century by Ephraim Blewett;[4] his initials are on a datestone of 1836 on a barn on the opposite side of the lane.[5]

New building and rebuilding in red brick on the estate of the 6th Earl Beauchamp in the later 19th century has given the building stock a distinctive character. It is seen at a schoolroom[6] and a new conventional vicarage house[7] as well as estate farmhouses, outbuildings, and cottages, many of which are marked with datestones bearing the initial 'B'. At Friar's Court, acquired by the earl in 1869,[8] a new house was built to a standard double-pile, two-storeyed pattern and to its west a range of farm buildings dated 1870 includes stables and cow sheds. At Hill Brook Farm the farmhouse was enlarged on its acquisition in 1871 by the addition of a taller two-storeyed block on its east.[9] At Saycell's Farm, part of the estate from 1872,[10] the house and outbuildings were cased in brick and a cider house with granary above was built to fill the space between them. A cowshed added to the outbuildings at the same time[11] has been removed.[12] At Hillfields Farm a new farmhouse was built in 1883[13] and the old farmhouse was converted as a store and cider mill.[14] A new barn was built about the same time and both store and barn were pulled down in the mid 20th century to make way for new outbuildings.[15] The house at Brick House Farm was rebuilt in 1884.[16] New labourers' cottages included a plain pair dated 1876 to the south-west of Stone House, where the early 17th-century manor house was rebuilt, with Jacobean gables, as a farmhouse in 1883.[17]

New building continued on the estate in the early 20th century, the most adventurous architecturally being a church designed for the 7th Earl Beauchamp in Arts and Crafts style.[18] A new house dated 1908 and outbuildings were provided at Matthew's Farm.[19] Although the house at Green Farm, at Kempley Green, had also been totally rebuilt, several farmhouses, including Bridge's Farm and Brookland's Farm, retained some timber framing. Among outbuildings erected during that period and removed later was a wood and corrugated iron shed used as a cider bottling plant at Saycell's Farm in 1919.[20]

New building after the break up of the estate included a number of council houses in the mid 20th century. The housing stock was increased later in the 20th century primarily by new detached houses and bungalows, most of them at Kempley Green where Green Farm became a private house (Kempley Green House). Some farm buildings were converted as dwellings, an outbuilding of the former Upper House being made into a house in the early 21st century.

MANOR AND ESTATES

The manor of Kempley was created by the union of two estates soon after the Norman Conquest and was owned by a succession of prominent families including that of Pyndar, whose name changed in the mid 18th century to Lygon. St Katherine's hospital in Ledbury (Herefs.), which was given Kempley church in the early 13th century, built up a sizeable estate in the parish and Flaxley abbey was among other landowners with possessions there in the Middle Ages. Ownership of the bulk of the land remained divided until the later 19th century when Frederick Lygon, 6th Earl Beauchamp, bought most of the farms not already in his estate. The farms were sold off individually just after the First World War.

---

1 *Citizen*, 28 Dec. 2006.
2 Below, manor.
3 Below, religious hist. (patronage and endowment: vicarage houses).
4 GDR, T 1/108; MCA, I 4iii, bdl. 80, nos 4, 6, 20, 27–34.
5 DoE List, Kempley (1987), 8/137.
6 Below, social hist. (education).
7 Below, religious hist. (patronage and endowment: vicarage houses).
8 Below, manor (other estates: Kempley rectory).
9 Below, manor (other estates); MCA, E 6ii, plans for alterations at Bullocksend.
10 Below, manor (other estates).
11 MCA, E 2ii, no 15.
12 It is shown on photogs. belonging to Mr and Mrs Thompson of Saycell's Farm.
13 Datestone on ho.
14 MCA, L 6i, no 39.
15 Information from Mr Geo. Young of Hillfields Farm.
16 Datestone on ho.
17 Below, manor.
18 Below, religious hist. (religious life: bldg. of a second ch.).
19 Datestone on ho. displays the init. 'B'.
20 GA, SL 310.

KEMPLEY MANOR

In 1086 Roger de Lacy had an estate at Kempley of three hides made up of two manors held in 1066 by Edric and Leuric.[1] Roger's estates, of which Kempley was almost certainly inherited from his father Walter (d. 1085),[2] were forfeit by his rebellion against William II in 1095 and were given to his brother Hugh (d. by 1121). They passed to Hugh's nephew Gilbert de Lacy and he was succeeded in turn by his son Hugh (d. 1186) and by Hugh's son Walter.[3] Walter's lordship over Kempley manor, assessed as ½ knight's fee,[4] was restored to him in 1215 after a period of banishment.[5] After his death in 1241 it passed with the barony or honor of Weobley to his granddaughters Margery and Maud and to their descendants,[6] but from the mid 14th century the manor was sometimes said to be held directly from the Crown.[7]

In the later 12th century the manor belonged to Emme de St Léger, wife in turn of Hugh de Longchamp (d. by 1194) and Walter de Baskerville. Walter surrendered the estate to her son Geoffrey de Longchamp in 1195[8] and Geoffrey's widow Isabel held it in the mid 1230s.[9] The manor, of which Emery de Cancellis was said in the early 1240s to hold a third from Walter de Baskerville,[10] passed with the Longchamps' main estate, at Wilton in Bridstow (Herefs.), to Maud, daughter and heiress of Henry de Longchamp, and she and her husband Reynold Grey held it in 1260.[11]

Reynold, who became Lord Grey of Wilton,[12] survived Maud and at his death in 1308 the manor passed to his son John.[13] From John (d. 1323) it descended with the title in the direct line to Henry[14] (d. 1342), Reynold[15] (d. 1370), and Henry (d. 1396). Henry settled the manor on the marriage of his younger son Reynold and on the death of Reynold's widow Joan it reverted to Reynold Grey, son of Henry's son and heir Richard (d. 1442). Reynold, who lost the manor temporarily when in 1463 an inquest found incorrectly that John Abrahall (d. 1443) had held it from the Crown,[16] died in 1494. The manor passed to his son John (d. 1499), Lord Grey,[17] and in 1502 it was settled on John's widow Elizabeth, who had married Sir Edward Stanley, created Lord Mounteagle in 1514. At Elizabeth's death in 1515 the manor reverted to Thomas, Lord Grey, son of Edmund (d. 1511), Lord Grey.[18] Thomas (d. 1517), a minor, was succeeded in turn by his brothers Richard (d. 1523) and William, also minors, and Edmund's widow Florence had custody of the manor from 1519.[19]

William, Lord Grey, was granted livery of his inheritance in 1529[20] and he conveyed the manor in 1551 to William Pigott (d. 1553). William's widow Margery (fl. 1579)[21] was succeeded in it by Anne, the daughter of her son Leonard Pigott. Anne married in turn Samuel Danvers and Henry Finch[22] and with Henry, described at the turn of the century as of Little Horwood (Bucks.),[23] occupied a new manor house (Stone House) in Kempley.[24] Following Henry's death in 1631 and Anne's soon afterwards the manor passed to their son Francis.[25] Francis, who lived in Rushock (Worcs.),[26] incurred business debts[27] and in 1659 he broke up the estate, selling the manor to Thomas Grubham (Grobham) Howe, the third son of John Howe of Little Compton (or Cassey Compton) in Withington.[28] Thomas, who took up residence in Kempley and acquired a knighthood, died without issue in 1680 and was buried in the family vault in Withington church. He left the manor to his nephew Sir Scrope Howe of Langar (Notts.),[29] who, to fund a payment to Thomas's widow, sold it in 1682 to Reginald Pyndar of Duffield (Derbs.).[30]

---

1 *Domesday Book* (Rec. Com.), I, 167v.
2 See below (other estates: Kempley rectory); religious hist. (early hist.).
3 I.J. Sanders, *English Baronies* (1960), 95.
4 *Book of Fees*, I, 439; II, 1138; *Feudal Aids*, II, 250.
5 *Rot. Litt. Claus.* (Rec. Com.), I, 241; H. Barkly, 'Testa de Nevill, Returns for the County of Gloucester', *Trans. BGAS* 12 (1887–8), 270 1.
6 Sanders, *Eng. Baronies*, 95–6; *Inq. p.m. Glos.* 1302–58, 100, 292; 1359–1413, 212; *Cal. Inq. p.m.* VI, 38; VII, 496; X, 540; TNA, C 139/19, no 26.
7 *Inq. p.m. Glos.* 1302–58, 310; *Feudal Aids*, II, 298; *Cal. Fine* 1461–71, 114, 138.
8 *Glos. Feet of Fines 1199–1299*, p. 203; W. St Clair Baddeley, 'The History of Kempley Manor and Church, Gloucestershire', *Trans. BGAS* 36 (1913), 132–3.
9 *Book of Fees*, I, 439; St Clair Baddeley, 'Kempley Manor and Church', 133; see *Cur. Reg.* XVI, 86.
10 *Book of Fees*, II, 1138.
11 *Glos. Feet of Fines 1199–1299*, p. 127; *Complete Peerage*, VI, 173 and n.
12 For the Greys and the peerage, *Complete Peerage*, VI, 171–86.
13 *Cal. Inq. p.m.* V, 18.
14 Ibid. VI, 310.
15 Ibid. VIII, 261.
16 TNA, E 159/243, Communia Trin., rot 1 and d.; see ibid. C 140/9, no 8; *Cal. Fine* 1461–71, 114, 138.
17 TNA, C 1/516/20.
18 Ibid. C 142/30, no 115; *Complete Peerage*, IX, 113–15.
19 *L&P Hen. VIII*, II (1), p. 256; III (1), p. 31; III (2), pp. 1452–3; see *Military Surv. of Glos. 1522*, 59; Worcs. RO, 705:99 (BA 5540), Kempley and Wilton ct. rolls 1526–68, rot. 1.
20 *L&P Hen. VIII*, IV (3), p. 2350.
21 TNA, C 142/111, no 74; see below, Oxenhall, manor.
22 MCA, G 1i, bdl. 172A, no 18, p. 29; see *Visit. Glos. 1623*, 61.
23 MCA, F 2viii, deed 728; Herefs. RO, E 12/G/20.
24 Below.
25 *Inq. p.m. Glos.* 1625–42, I, 158–9; *Visit. Glos. 1623*, 61; Bigland, *Glos.* II, 119.
26 Herefs. RO, E 12/G/13; MCA, G 1i, bdl. 172A, nos 9, 13–15.
27 Below, Oxenhall, manor; econ. hist. (Ellbridge furnace).
28 Worcs. RO, 705:99 (BA 3375), Kempley deeds 1602–66; for the Howes at Little Compton, *VCH Glos.* IX, 261.
29 Worcs. RO, 705:99 (BA 3375), Kempley deeds 1602–66; MCA, F 5ii, deed 1187; F 5vi, deed 1218; see GA, P 374/IN 1/8.
30 Worcs. RO, 705:99 (BA 3375), Kempley deeds 1671–1713.

Reginald Pyndar settled much of the estate in 1686 on the marriage of his son Thomas and Elizabeth Hacket.[1] Thomas, who rebuilt the old manor house (Kempley Court),[2] succeeded to the manor on Reginald's death in 1712[3] and left it to Elizabeth at his in 1722. From Elizabeth (d. 1759)[4] it passed to their grandson Reginald Pyndar, who had assumed the surname Lygon on inheriting the Madresfield estate in Worcestershire.[5] Reginald died in 1788. His only son William Lygon, elevated to the peerage as Lord Beauchamp in 1806, became Earl Beauchamp in 1815[6] and after his death in 1816 the manor descended with the earldom and the Madresfield estate.[7] William's son and heir William (d. 1823) was succeeded in turn by his brothers John (d. 1853), who had taken the surname Pindar, and Henry (d. 1863) and Henry in turn by his sons Henry (d. 1866) and Frederick. Through his purchases of farms and other property[8] Frederick (d. 1891), the 6th earl, came to own virtually the whole of Kempley. His son and heir William sold the farms and cottages in lots after the First World War[9] but retained 45 a. of woodland.[10]

Kempley Court

Following the break up of the 7th earl's estate Kempley Court and its farm (192 a.) were bought by John Houlbrooke.[11] He sold them in 1943 to W.J. Pugh, whose two grandsons were the owners in 2005.[12]

Kempley Court occupies the site of the manor house known as the Old Court in the early 16th century when let as a farmhouse and in decay, the upper part of the hall being uncovered in 1533.[13] Used as a farmhouse in the 17th century,[14] it was rebuilt by Thomas Pyndar as his residence when he took over the estate in 1686. Pyndar's house, on which his crest appears on a stone plaque dated 1689,[15] was a compact double-pile house of two storeys and attics, fashionable and superior to most local farmhouses. Although the main, north-western façade and the side walls are built of brick, the rear wall and the internal partitions are timber-framed, the former with brick infill. The roof over the front pile is hipped and covered with stone slates; that over the rear pile is in three gabled sections and tiled. The symmetrical plan contains a central entrance hall with a dog-leg staircase to its south-west. Flanking them are two parlours (the great parlour and withdrawing room reserved by Pyndar for himself in 1701[16]) on the south-western side and a parlour and kitchen on the north-eastern. The interior was probably always plainly finished, the parlours having corner fireplaces and the kitchen an external stack. The pattern is repeated upstairs but with a bedchamber over the entrance hall. The south-eastern front had two sash windows per bedchamber and, flanking the central doorcase, narrow lights for the hall. The parlour windows were altered in the early 19th century.[17] On the north-western front the flat canopy over the main door may replace a shell hood. The narrow walled forecourt has gate-piers (reduced in height) with ball finials.

To the north-east a timber-framed barn with brick nogging and an adjoining two-bayed stable may predate the house. The barn, originally of four bays, was extended by two bays in the early 18th century.

Stone House

Stone House, a mansion on Henry Finch's estate in 1604, stood on land called Stone Acre.[18] Described later as having pediments and bay windows in early 17th-century style,[19] it became the manor house[20] and with 11 hearths by far the largest dwelling in the parish in 1672.[21] The house became the Gloucestershire seat of the Pyndar family and from the late 1720s was the principal farmhouse on their estate,[22] the outbuildings making a long range to the north-east.[23] The 6th Earl Beauchamp, who made changes to the outbuildings in 1871,[24] had the house demolished and its remains incorporated in the service wing of a red brick farmhouse built in 1883.[25] The new house was designed in an estate

---

1 MCA, F 5iii, deed 1247; F 4v, deed 1249.
2 Below.
3 MCA, F 6i, deed 1361; F 5v, deed 1359.
4 Bigland, *Glos.* II, 119; GDR wills 1722/191.
5 Rudder, *Glos.* 508; *The Madresfield Muniments* (1929, Worcester), 41, 62–3.
6 For the Lygons and the earldom, *Burke's Peerage* (1963), 190.
7 GDR, T 1/108; *Kelly's Dir. Glos.* (1856 and later edns).
8 e.g. MCA, H 4v, bdl. 49, no 18; I 2iii, bdl. 64, no 5; I 3ii, bdl. 68A, no 56; I 3v, bdl. 74, no 12; I 4iii, bdl. 80, no 34; I 5i, bdl. 88C, no 53; I 5vi, bdl. 92A, no 3; J 2iv, bdl. 105E, no 50; J 2vii, bdl. 111G, no 50.
9 GA, SL 310.
10 Ibid. G/NE 159/14/1, f. 7.
11 Ibid. f. 1.
12 Information from Mr W.H. Houlbrooke of Colwall Green, Malvern (Worcs.), and from Mrs (Rachel) Pugh of Kempley Court.
13 Worcs. RO, 705:99 (BA 5540), Kempley and Wilton ct. rolls 1526–68, rott. 11, 33.
14 MCA, G 1i, bdl. 172B, nos 24, 28.
15 The crest, a crowned lion, is repeated on his monument in St Mary's ch.
16 MCA, G 1i, bdl. 172B, no 40.
17 Old photog. in possession of Mrs Pugh.
18 Herefs. RO, E 12/G/20.
19 Bigland, *Glos.* II, 118.
20 MCA, F 4iii, deed 1053.
21 TNA, E 179/247/14, rot. 36.
22 Rudder, *Glos.* 508; MCA, G 1ii, bdl. 172C, nos 46, 49, 51, 55–6, 59; bdl. 172D, nos 61, 68, 79, 79; G 1iv, bdl. 173, no 16; maps and plans, shelf 5, map of the Stone House estate and Bridge's farm 1787.
23 GDR, T 1/108.
24 MCA, E 1ii, 14; E 4ii, 9.
25 Datestone with letter 'B' on the house; *Kelly's Dir. Glos.* (1885), 510.

48. Stone House: 17th-century ceiling

style but with Jacobean shaped gables at each end of the main range.

The size and status of the early 17th-century house is indicated by a rubble wall with moulded string course from which a large chimneystack, built of finely dressed stone, projects north-east. That wall and chimney, hidden by an extension to the north-west, form the north-eastern wall of a large room (now subdivided but mainly a kitchen) with a later 17th-century plaster ceiling of six compartments filled with wreaths of fruit and flowers.[1] The ceiling was probably inserted as part of a refurbishment of the house by Sir Thomas Howe, who in the early 1670s donated timber for alterations to St Mary's church.[2] Much of the house's carved woodwork, including an overmantel dated 1610 with the initials of Henry and Anne Finch, was moved to Madresfield Court in 1883.[3]

In 1926 the farmhouse belonged with 160 a. to Charles Stackhouse.[4] A.D. Evans, who owned it in 1937, sold the house and 312 a. in 1973 to the Watkins family, which owned 620 a. in the farm in 2005. Many of the brick farm buildings erected in the later 19th century have been replaced since 1973.[5]

OTHER ESTATES

Hill Brook Farm (Bullocksend)

On the break up of the manor estate in 1659 Bullocksend and a lot of land, some of it leased from St Katherine's hospital, were included in a sale to William Bosworth of Leigh (Worcs.).[6] From William (*fl.* 1684) the new estate passed to Harry Bosworth[7] of Hereford (d. 1731) and after the death of Harry's widow Ann in 1738 to his sister Elizabeth Nash of Worcester. After her death in 1741 it was sold to John Worrall of Upton Bishop (Herefs.).[8] John (d. 1767) left Bullocksend to his grandson John Worrall Rideout[9] and in 1787 the latter, a Manchester merchant, sold it with 119 a. (178 a. by customary measure) to Daniel Hullett of Much Marcle (Herefs.).[10] Daniel died in 1808[11] and the estate passed from his widow Nancy to his nephew John Hullett the following year. In 1833 John included Bullocksend in a sale of land in Upton Bishop and Much Marcle to John Shore (d. 1834), Lord Teignmouth. The latter's son and heir Charles John Shore[12] sold Bullocksend to Earl Beauchamp in 1871.[13] In 1926, following the sale of the outlying parts

---

1 Fig. 48.
2 Below, religious hist. (religious life).
3 *Kelly's Dir. Glos.* (1885), 510; *VCH Worcs.* IV, 119.
4 GA, G/NE 159/14/1, f. 1.
5 Information from Mr R. Watkins of Stone House, where there is a photog. of the farmstead in 1973.
6 Worcs. RO, 705:99 (BA 3375), Kempley deeds 1602–66; MCA, G 1i, bdl. 172A, no 17.

7 HCA 3472/2.
8 MCA, I 3ii, bdl. 68A, nos 1–6; HCA 5229.
9 GA, P 188/IN 1/3; TNA, PROB 11/939, ff. 311v.–312v.
10 MCA, I 3ii, bdl. 68A, no 11; G 1iv, bdl. 173, no 17.
11 TNA, PROB 11/1490, ff. 48–9.
12 MCA, I 3ii, bdl. 68A, nos 47–50; *Complete Peerage*, XII (1), 656.
13 MCA, I 3ii, bdl. 68A, no 56.

of the Madresfield estate,[1] the Joneses, a farming family, owned 125 a. at Bullocksend.[2] They continued to farm at Bullocksend (Hill Brook Farm) in 2005.[3] The farmhouse was enlarged on its acquisition by Earl Beauchamp.[4]

Saycell's Farm

At his death in 1415 Thomas Walwyn of Much Marcle assigned Saycell's Farm, then called Saycell's Place, for the endowment of a chantry in Much Marcle church[5] but by 1494 the farmstead and its land had been inherited from Richard Walwyn by his son Roger.[6] In 1533 the farm belonged to Agnes Walwyn[7] and in 1579 Thomas Walwyn, whose father Sir Richard had given him land in Kempley and Dymock in 1572,[8] conveyed it to Anthony Kyrle in return for an annuity of £7 10s.[9] Anthony, later of Ross-on-Wye, died in 1590 leaving the farm to his daughter Sarah.[10] She married William Scudamore of Ballingham (Herefs.) and in 1601 Thomas Walwyn released them from the payment of the annuity.[11] William died in 1649 and Sarah in 1659. Their grandson Sir John Scudamore Bt (d. 1684) had the farm and his daughter Sarah, wife in turn of John Holmes (d. 1700) and Philip Monson,[12] sold it in 1720 to Joseph Cam, a London haberdasher.[13] From Joseph (d. 1729) the farm descended with Great Netherton in Dymock to Ann Cam (d. 1790)[14] and at a division between her heirs confirmed in 1808 became the property of John Hill of Stardens, in Newent.[15] John (d. 1825) left his Kempley land to his brother James (d. 1836) and his nephew Joseph Hill sold the farm (56 a.) to Earl Beauchamp in 1872.[16] At the sale of the Madresfield estate's Kempley farms Saycell's (87 a.) passed to the tenant R. Down[17] and in 1922 it was bought by James Price (d. 1949), whose family retained it in 2005.[18] The farmhouse dated from the late 16th or early 17th century and with its outbuildings underwent alterations in the later 19th century.[19]

Kempley Rectory

St Katherine's hospital at Ledbury appropriated the rectory after being given Kempley church by Geoffrey de Longchamp c.1230.[20] Among the church's property was a thicket or hay given to it in the early 13th century.[21] St Guthlac's priory, successor to a church founded in Hereford by Walter de Lacy (d. 1085), owned some of the tithes[22] and in 1291, when the rectory was worth £8, its portion was valued at 10s.[23] John Price acquired the priory and its estates after the Dissolution[24] and for its tithes in Kempley and Yarkhill (Herefs.) Gregory Price received a pension from the hospital in the late 16th century.[25]

St Katherine's hospital enlarged its estate by early acquisitions of land[26] and laymen held all its land on leases by the late 14th century.[27] The estate remained divided between leaseholders[28] and the principal holding, Friar's Court with its tithes, was called a manor in 1484 and later.[29] The dean and chapter of Hereford cathedral, confirmed in 1580 as the hospital's governors,[30] continued to grant leases of land[31] and from the early 18th century leases were renewed every seven years on a payment of at least 1¼ year's value.[32] Later uncertainty about the location of some of the hospital's land prompted the lord of the manor and the dean and chapter in 1810 to identify formally 95 a. held by the former and was resolved in 1819 when the owner of Bullocksend conceded ownership of 26 a.[33] The dean and chapter sold all the land (271 a.) to Earl Beauchamp in 1869.[34] Soon after the First World War Friar's Court and other land (225 a.) were acquired from the

---

1 GA, SL 310; see above (Kempley manor).
2 GA, G/NE 159/14/1, f. 6.
3 Information from Mr. R.G. Jones of Hill Brook Farm.
4 Above, settlement (bldgs.).
5 J. Duncumb, *Collections towards the History and Antiquities of the County of Hereford* (continuation by W.H. Cooke), III (1882), 63.
6 Hampshire Record Office, 44M69/C/660; TNA, C 1/234/48.
7 Worcs. RO, 705:99 (BA 5540), Kempley and Wilton ct. rolls 1526–68, rot. 11, which mentions the endowment of the chantry.
8 TNA, C 115/38, no 2324.
9 BL, Add. Ch. 1845.
10 TNA, C 115/38, no 2330.
11 Ibid. C 115/62, no 5381.
12 C.J. Robinson, *A History of the Mansions and Manors of Herefordshire* (1873), 21; BL, Add. Ch. 1963.
13 MCA, I 3v, bdl. 74, no 3.
14 Above, Dymock, manors (other estates: Great Netherton).
15 MCA, I 3v, bdl. 74, no 9.
16 Ibid. no 12.
17 GA, SL 310; see above (Kempley manor).
18 Information from Mr and Mrs Thompson of Saycell's Farm; GA, P 188/IN 1/18; see GA, G/NE 159/14/1, f. 4.

19 Above, settlement (bldgs.).
20 *Eng. Episc. Acta VII*, pp. 278–80; below, religious hist. (early hist.).
21 HCA 3707.
22 Dugdale, *Mon.* III, 620; *Eng. Episc. Acta VII*, pp. 23, 149–51, 197–9. For Walter, Sanders, *Eng. Baronies*, 95.
23 *Tax. Eccl.* 161.
24 *L&P Hen. VIII*, XIX (1), p. 285.
25 HCA 3575.
26 Ibid. 3702–4.
27 A.T. Bannister, 'Visitation Returns of Diocese of Hereford', *EHR* 45 (1930), 93.
28 HCA 1639; 1840–2; 1845; 1979; 1989–90; 3471; 3472–8; 3496; 3575; 3769; 7018/5(1), pp. 12–15, 20; (2), pp. 52–61, 67–8.
29 Ibid. 7018/5(1), pp. 12–13; (2), pp. 56–7; 7031/2, f. 16v.; 3575.
30 A.T. Bannister, 'The Hospital of St. Katherine at Ledbury', *Trans. Woolhope Naturalists Field Club* (1918–20), 66.
31 e.g. HCA 3475/2; 3476/1; MCA, F 3ii, deed 922; G 1iv, bdl. 173, nos 6, 10–11.
32 HCA 3472; 3475; 3478/1; 3623/2; MCA, misc. letter 101.
33 MCA, I 2iii, bdl. 64, nos 1–2; HCA 7018/3–4; St Catherine's Hospital Act, 59 Geo. III, c. 22 (Private).
34 HCA 7005/10, pp. 242–6, 257–65; MCA, I 2iii, bdl. 64, no 5.

Madresfield estate by the tenant W.J. Brooke, who thereby became the single largest landowner in Kempley.[1] His son Mr Kenneth Brooke owned Friar's Court in 2005.[2]

Other Medieval Monastic and Hospital Estates

Land in Kempley acquired by Flaxley abbey[3] passed with the estate centred on the abbey's grange (Old Grange) in the adjoining part of Dymock after the Dissolution.[4] The estate retained *c.*30 a. at Marshall's Farm on the east side of Kempley until 1920.[5]

Aconbury priory (Herefs.), founded in the early 13th century by Margery de Lacy,[6] received early grants of land and rent in Kempley from Geoffrey de Longchamp, Richard son of Robert le Rich of Gloucester, and William de Gamages.[7] The priory retained the estate until the Dissolution when it provided an annual income of 14*s.* 6*d.* in rents.[8] An estate belonging to Cookhill priory (Worcs.) was first recorded in 1522.[9] In 1535 it comprised rents worth 3*s.*[10] and in 1542 the Crown sold it with the priory and its lands to Nicholas Fortescue.[11] Another religious house, a commandery, with land in, or perhaps next to, Kempley in the early 1530s has not been identified.[12]

St Bartholomew's hospital in Gloucester had land in Kempley in the mid 13th century.[13] The hospital's estate comprising a farmhouse and *c.*15 a. beside Kempley green in the mid 18th century[14] was sold in 1884 to Earl Beauchamp[15] and was owned in 1926 by Joseph Patrick.[16]

ECONOMIC HISTORY

In common with those of other parishes in the area Kempley's economy was based on mixed farming and orcharding, the latter being established by the later Middle Ages. The principal industrial site was a small brickworks that operated for part of the 19th century.

AGRICULTURE

The Middle Ages

In 1086 the manor, which was worth £5 compared with £4 in 1066 for the two manors it had replaced, had 3 ploughs in demesne and 7 slaves, and the tenants, 10 villans and 7 bordars, worked a total of 12 ploughs.[17] Arable cultivation was evidently less intensive in 1220 when four ploughteams were recorded at Kempley.[18]

In the mid 14th century the parish contained several areas of open-field arable. The Rye, probably the largest and named after the principal cereal crop, was on the hillside in the centre of the parish by the Newent road and Whitley was to the west beyond the Kempley brook. Ast field was presumably on the east side of the parish[19] and Wood field, recorded in the early 16th century, in the south towards Kempley wood.[20] Woodland clearance gradually brought more land into cultivation[21] and the planting of orchards, for pears as well as for apples,[22] evidently began before the mid 14th century when some land was called Perry field.[23] One farmstead became known as the Perry House.[24]

In the early 14th century there were two large arable farms, both demesnes in hand, and numerous smaller holdings. On the manor, which included 45 diverse free tenancies in 1308, the demesne comprised 200 a. arable, 10 a. meadow, and 3 a. pasture and ten customary tenants, holding 3 yardlands, owed autumn labour services as well as cash rents.[25] St Katherine's hospital[26] had 247½ a. arable, 10 a. meadow, and 3½ a. moor in demesne and kept 2 ploughs as well as 2 horses and 12 oxen in 1316.

---

1 GA, SL 310; G/NE 159/14/1, f. 1.
2 Information from Mr Kenneth Brooke of Friar's Court.
3 TNA, SC 2/175/71, rot. 3 and d. For rents in Kempley acquired by the abbey, *Flaxley Cart.* pp. 131, 177.
4 GA, D 214/T 17, deed 3 Nov. 1630; D 4262/T 17; above, Dymock, manors (Old Grange Manor).
5 GDR, T 1/108; GA, SL 417.
6 Dugdale, *Mon.* VI (1), 489.
7 TNA, E 315/55, pp. 40–4, 53–4.
8 *Valor Eccl.* III, 18.
9 *Military Surv. of Glos. 1522*, 63; Worcs. RO, 705:99 (BA 5540), Kempley and Wilton ct. rolls 1526–68, rot. 8.
10 *Valor Eccl.* III, 263. In 1536 the Crown received 13*s.* 6*d.* in rents from the estate: TNA, SC 6/Hen. VIII/7319, rott. 32d.–33.
11 *L&P Hen. VIII,* XVII, 319.
12 Worcs. RO, 705:99 (BA 5540), Kempley and Wilton ct. rolls 1526–68, rott. 7–8, 10, 33.
13 *Glouc. Corp. Rec.,* p. 244; see *Valor Eccl.* II, 489–90.
14 GBR, J 4/1, no 33.
15 MCA, J 2vii, bdl. 111G, no 50.
16 GA, G/NE 159/14/1, f. 3.
17 *Domesday Book* (Rec. Com.), I, 167v.
18 *Book of Fees,* I, 307.
19 HCA 7018/5(2), pp. 50–3; R 1164; see MCA, F 2i, deed 644.
20 Worcs. RO, 705:99 (BA 5540), Kempley and Wilton ct. rolls 1526–68, rot. 3.
21 Above, introd. (landscape).
22 Worcs. RO, 705:99 (BA 5540), Kempley and Wilton ct. rolls 1526–68, rott. 22, 28.
23 TNA, SC 2/175/71, rott. 1–3.
24 Worcs. RO, 705:99 (BA 5540), Kempley and Wilton ct. rolls 1526–68, rot. 5. See *PN Glos.* IV, 161.
25 *Inq. p.m. Glos.* 1302–58, 100–1.
26 A fuller account of the hospital's land and tenants is given in J. Hillaby, *St Katherine's Hospital, Ledbury, c.1230–1547* (Ledbury and District Soc. Trust Ltd, 2003).

Its grange held wheat, oats, and peas and vetches[1] and in 1322 its bailiff was granted a bushel of wheat a week from Kempley for life in addition to a salary of 10s.[2] Two tenants held a half and a quarter yardland (30 and 15 a.) for cash rents and labour services. A few other tenants had smaller holdings. The half-yardlander's services included 16 days' harvest work and sending two men to mow a meadow but by 1312 tenants were withholding such services. A few acres of 'forlet' land held for cash rents in 1369 were perhaps among areas more recently cleared for cultivation. In the later 14th century parts of the hospital's demesne were let for cash rents for terms of three lives. The hospital grew crops in Kempley in 1380,[3] but by 1397 it had leased the whole of the demesne[4] and in the mid 1430s the estate was made up of nine tenanted holdings, the principal one at Friar's Court. Two of the farms, based on Edwyn's (later Matthew's Farm) and Carter's Place, were merged before 1497[5] and the hospital's leases were frequently for terms of up to 99 years by the early 16th century.[6]

On the manor the demesne was leased to Thomas Walwyn of Much Marcle before 1530, when he was in dispute with Lord Grey, the lord, over the mowing of a meadow.[7] Aconbury priory had seven tenants on its small estate in the early 14th century[8] and Cookhill priory three tenants at the Dissolution.[9]

The Early Modern Period

The manorial demesne was leased to the Bridgeman family of Mitcheldean in the mid 16th century.[10] The land owned by St Katherine's hospital remained divided between leaseholders and in 1580 contained four farms, one (Friar's Court) of 1½ yardland, another of 1 yardland, and two of ½ yardland each, and several smaller holdings.[11] Pigs continued to be kept in the parish; in 1554 the manor court ordered all tenants to ring those hogs intended for slaughter and to yoke store swine.[12]

Following the Restoration Sir Thomas Howe kept part of the manorial demesne in hand with Stone House but from 1674[13] the whole of it (437 a.) was divided between several farmers. Most of it was in Stone House and Kempley Court farms, which were held on leases for years;[14] Thomas Pyndar himself farmed at Kempley Court for several years until 1701.[15] The manorial estate, which included land held under lease from St Katherine's hospital,[16] also contained 307 a. divided between 18 tenants holding leases for lives, most of them having under 10 a. and only three (based on Bridge's Farm, Edwyn's, and Print House) more than 70 a. The manor also had five copyhold tenants with holdings ranging from 5 to 37 a. and three tenants at will with considerably smaller holdings. In addition some 19 freeholders had land in the parish.[17]

Many small farms had been absorbed into larger units by the later 18th century, when there were c.20–25 farms in the parish.[18] Stone House farm with 260 a. was the largest and in 1787 at least five other farms, including Kempley Court, Matthew's, and Friar's Court, had over 100 a. each. Two of the smallest farms comprising between 10 and 20 a. were on the manorial estate, on which Chibler's hill was farmed from Upton Bishop. Although some owned land, most farmers, especially the principal ones, were tenants. John Brooke's farm, for example, included over 100 a. belonging to the lord of the manor.[19] Land (26 a.) conceded by the owner of Bullocksend to St Katherine's hospital in 1819[20] was later added to Matthew's farm.[21]

At the beginning of the period open-field land survived among Kempley's small fields and closes. Some holdings had been consolidated[22] and the piecemeal inclosure of more substantial remnants, such as the Rye and Wood field, continued.[23] An area of ridge and furrow on the west side of the parish beyond the Kempley brook[24] had been divided into closes and small fields by the mid 17th century[25] and the park on the hillside above the Rye

---

1 HCA 1658A.

2 Ibid. 1899.

3 Ibid. 7018/5(2), pp. 45–61; R 1164. The interpretation of 'forlet' land is based on a suggestion (2009) by Prof. C. Dyer of the University of Leicester. For the size of the yardland on the hospital's estates, Hillaby, *St Katherine's Hospital*, 23.

4 A.T. Bannister, 'Visitation Returns of Diocese of Hereford in 1397', *EHR* 45 (1930), 93.

5 HCA 7018/5(2), pp. 58, 67–8.

6 Ibid. 1639; 1840–1; 1979; 3292, 7018/5(1), pp 12–22.

7 TNA, STAC 2/16, ff. 322–3; see Worcs. RO, 705:99 (BA 5540), Kempley and Wilton ct. rolls 1526–68, rot. 9.

8 TNA, E 315/55, p. 139.

9 Ibid. SC 6/Hen. VIII/7319, rott. 32d.–33.

10 Worcs. RO, 705:99 (BA 5540), Kempley and Wilton ct. rolls 1526–68, rott. 26, 32–3. For the Bridgemans, see *VCH Glos.* V, 181.

11 HCA 3575.

12 Worcs. RO, 705:99 (BA 5540), Kempley and Wilton ct. rolls 1526–68, rot. 35.

13 MCA, G 1i, bdl. 172B, no 27. Ibid. F 5vii, deed 1585, shows that Sir Thos. stored hay in a barn at Kempley Court.

14 Ibid. A 2i, 16 (Misc. Roll 30, rot. 1); F 5vii, deed 1589; G 1i, bdl. 172B, no. 33.

15 Ibid. G 1i, bdl. 172B, no 40.

16 HCA 3477/2–5; see MCA, G 1iv, bdl. 173, nos 4, 6, 8.

17 MCA, A 2i, 16 (Misc. Roll 30, rott. 2–4); see ibid. F 5vii, deed 1589; G 1i, bdl. 172B, no. 33.

18 GA, Q/REl 1, Botloe hundred, Kempley.

19 Ibid.; MCA,G 1iv, bdl. 173, no 16; M 4i, five undated maps of parts of Reginald Lygon's estate; maps and plans, shelf 5, two maps dated 1787 of parts of Reginald Lygon's estate.

20 Above, manor.

21 HCA 3475/28; 6157.

22 MCA, F 2i, deed 644.

23 Ibid. G 1i, bdl. 172a, nos 4, 6; Herefs. RO, E 12/G/20.

24 HCA 7018/3–4.

25 Ibid. 3472/1.

was laid down as farmland at that time.[1] A good proportion of the land was meadow and pasture[2] and in the 1650s and 1660s several landowners, including Sir Thomas Howe, reserved a right to water such land themselves.[3]

Orchards, particularly for cider apples, were numerous[4] and by custom, as recorded in 1705, apple and pear tithes were handed to the vicar at the foot of the trees during the harvest.[5] In the later 17th century the manorial demesne contained extensive orchards in the area of the former park[6] and both of its main farms produced great quantities of cider.[7] The cider made from Red Streak apples was highly regarded[8] and in 1674 Sir Thomas Howe included a hogshead in the rent of Stone House farm.[9] Farming leases stipulated the preservation of existing orchards and sometimes new planting of stocks and in 1721 Thomas Pyndar himself undertook to plant 50 fruit trees on Bridge's farm.[10] By the 18th century many farms had their own cider mills and presses[11] and, although cereal production, dairying, and sheep farming continued,[12] cider production became the main business of farming and the watering and draining of farmland was neglected. Together with the meadows and pastures the orchards, planted traditionally on arable land, covered more than half the parish in the 1770s. Even the churchyard was full of apple trees.[13] From the later 18th century new orchards were increasingly planted on grassland[14] and a few were created on land newly inclosed from Kempley green.[15] Hops were grown in various places in the parish[16] and in the early 17th century an old farmhouse next to Stone House was adapted as an oast house.[17] Of 275 a. recorded as under crops in 1801 all but a few grew cereals, mostly wheat, and pulses.[18]

The Nineteenth and Twentieth Centuries

In the mid 19th century, while most of the land was cultivated by tenant farmers, Stone House farm, which with over 200 a. remained the largest unit, was managed by a bailiff employing six labourers in 1851. In addition to the other farms, of which five contained over 100 a., seven men worked smallholdings of between 1 and 5 a.[19] From 1866, when he became lord of the manor, the 6th Earl Beauchamp[20] systematically purchased more land for his Madresfield estate[21] and reorganized many of the farms. In 1875 two of the estate's tenants had farms of over 200 a., six had over 100 a., and three over 50 a.[22] More land was brought into the estate in the next few years and few farms and smallholdings remained outside it.[23] Of the 20 agricultural occupiers returned for the whole parish in 1896 only one owned any part of his farm.[24] In 1901 farming remained the chief source of employment for the majority of parishioners, including several cattlemen, wagoners, and carters, and one farmer's son worked as an engine driver.[25]

In 1919, when the farms on the Madresfield estate were up for sale, three tenants each worked 200 a. or more and, of the ten others, four had over 100 a. and four under 30 a.[26] One of the smallest holdings, Moor House farm, was bought by the county council smallholdings' committee.[27] In 1926, when four of the 22 holdings returned for Kempley had over 150 a., four over 100 a., and six under 20 a., several farms, including most of the largest, were worked by their owners. Altogether the farms employed 27 full-time and 7 casual workers.[28] Of the 19 farms returned in 1956, one had over 300 a., three over 150 a., two over 100a., and five under 20 a. The agricultural workforce shrank in the later 20th century and only four labourers were hired full-time on some of the 13 farms returned for the parish in 1986. One farm had over 100 ha (*c.*250 a.) and two over 50 ha (*c.*125 a.), and of the smaller holdings, several of which were worked by part-time farmers, six had over 30 ha (*c.*75 a.) and three under 10 ha (*c.*25 a.).[29] In the late 20th century larger farming units were created, some landowners renting out land they had once worked themselves,[30] and in 2005 the largest, Stone House farm, covered 810 ha (2,000 a.).[31]

---

1 Above, introd. (landscape).
2 Atkyns, *Glos.* 489.
3 Worcs. RO, 705:99 (BA 3375), Kempley deeds 1602–66, deed 14 April 1656; MCA, F 5i, deed 1087; G 1i, bdl. 172B, no 24.
4 GDR wills 1599/14; MCA, F 3i, deed 985; G 1i, bdl. 172A, no 13; G 1iii, bdl. 172C, no 47A; Atkyns, *Glos.* 489.
5 GDR, V 5/175T 3.
6 MCA, G 1i, 172B, no 33.
7 Ibid. A 2i, 16 (Misc. Roll 30, rot. 1).
8 Bodleian, Top. Glouc. c. 3, f. 196v.
9 MCA, G 1i, bdl. 172B, no 27.
10 BL, Add. Ch. 1963; MCA, G 1iii, bdl. 172C, nos 46, 47A, 55.
11 MCA, G 1i, bdl. 172B, no 39; GDR wills 1729/439.
12 See MCA, F 5v, deed 1364; G 1i, bdl. 172b, no 39.
13 Rudder, *Glos.* 508–9; see ibid. 409; above, Dymock, econ. hist.
14 See above, Dymock, econ. hist.
15 MCA, I 2ii, bdl. 61B, no 51.
16 GDR, T 1/108 (nos 11, 131, 140, 150, 300).
17 HCA 3477/1, 22; above, settlement (outlying settlement).
18 *1801 Crop Returns Eng.* I, 174.
19 GDR, T 1/108; TNA, HO 107/1960.
20 Above, manor.
21 e.g. MCA, H 4v, bdl. 49, no 18; I 2iii, bdl. 64, no 5; I 3ii, bdl. 68A, no 56; I 3v, bdl. 74, no 12; I 4iii, bdl. 80, no 34.
22 Ibid. L 1i, no 5.
23 Ibid. I 5ii, bdl. 88C, no 53; J 2iv, bdl. 105E, no 50; J 2vii, bdl. 111G, no 50; see GA, SL 310.
24 TNA, MAF 68/1609/6.
25 Ibid. RG 13/2422.
26 GA, SL 310.
27 Ibid. C/CC/M 5/31, p. 125; M 5/36, p. 81.
28 TNA, MAF 68/3295/15; see GA, G/NE 159/14/1.
29 TNA, MAF 68/4533/167; MAF 68/6005/14/167.
30 Information from Mr Kenneth Brooke of Friar's Court.
31 Information from Mr R. Watkins of Stone House.

In 1840, when 764 a. was devoted to arable crops and 642 a. to grass including leys, the usual three-course rotation included a fallow and, although a larger number of sheep was kept, the main livestock were milch cows and young beef cattle.[1] In 1866, when 303 sheep, 210 dairy and beef cattle, and 97 pigs were returned for the parish,[2] upwards of 400 a. was permanent grassland, over 650 a. was planted with crops, mostly cereals and grass seeds, and 38 a. was fallow.[3] Dairy herds were sufficiently large to employ a resident dairyman at Kempley Court in 1841[4] and a resident dairymaid at Stone House in 1861.[5] In the later 19th century and the early 20th cereal cultivation decreased and numbers of dairy and beef cattle grew. More land was laid down as permanent pasture[6] and in the late 1880s the Madresfield estate improved the drainage of a number of fields.[7] During that period the farm at Upper House was used for breaking in horses.[8]

Orcharding remained important and in the early 1840s there were several nurseries, one of them on Moor House farm.[9] The area of orchards, given as 106 a. in 1896, remained constant.[10] Saycell's Farm, from where Henry Tandy marketed cider and perry commercially,[11] acquired its own bottling plant[12] and in the 1920s and 1930s the business of James Price & Sons made cider and perry there for sale locally.[13] In the later 20th century orcharding declined considerably and in 1986 only 10 ha (c.25 a.) was returned as being commercial orchards, mostly for apples and pears.[14]

In 1956, when 242 a. was returned as growing corn, 763 a. was described as permanent grassland and 683 a. was used as pasture. The livestock that year included 767 dairy and beef cattle, 482 ewes, and 177 pigs.[15] Thirty years later, when 360 ha (890 a.) was returned as grassland and at least 164 ha (405 a.) was under corn, three farms were primarily dairy units, another raised beef cattle, another both cattle and sheep, and two specialized in horticulture.[16] Poultry farming, introduced by 1926, was mainly for chickens and in 1986 2,845 birds were kept for egg production and larger numbers were reared for the table.[17] While cereal growing and sheep farming have continued, at Kempley Court beef cattle gave way to a dairy herd, introduced in 1994,[18] and at Stone House livestock farming was abandoned and in 2005 production centred primarily on potatoes and included sugar beet and cereals.[19] Three dairy farms remained in 2006.[20]

WOODLAND MANAGEMENT

Oaks were felled in the mid 12th century to construct Kempley's parish church[21] and one or more foresters were among local inhabitants in the early 13th century.[22] In the early 14th century Kempley wood, part of an extensive tract of ancient woodland in the south of the parish, was used as a common by people living near by.[23] Attempts at the time by St Katherine's hospital to extract pannage from its tenants point to the use of local woodland as swine pasture[24] and the manor court's order of 1554 was probably intended to limit common pasture to pigs intended for slaughter.[25] In the mid 16th century bark was cropped from felled oaks and the lessee of the manorial demesne, having cut down trees, mostly oaks, in the lord's park and elsewhere, sold timber to people in Dymock, Newent, and Much Marcle. In 1549 Kempley wood was leased to John Abrahall of Eaton Tregoes (Herefs.) and by 1553 he had inclosed 60 a. in it.[26] That land remained in the hands of a lessee in the early 17th century.[27]

In the later 16th century timber was dressed if not felled in Kempley for use by St Katherine's

---

1 TNA, IR 18/2771.
2 Ibid. MAF 68/25/4.
3 Ibid. MAF 68/26/16; MAF 68/62/5.
4 Ibid. HO 107/350/8.
5 Ibid. RG 9/1761.
6 Ibid. MAF 68/1609/6; MAF 68/3295/15; Acreage Returns, 1905.
7 MCA, maps and plans, shelf 4, no 16 (undated map of Kempley).
8 TNA, RG 13/2422; GA, P 188/IN 1/6; see *Kelly's Dir. Glos.* (1889), 824; (1906), 244.
9 GDR, T 1/108.
10 TNA, MAF 68/1609/6; MAF 68/3295/15.
11 GA, D 7799/1; *Kelly's Dir. Glos.* (1894–1923 edns); TNA, RG 13/2422.
12 GA, SL 310.
13 Poster and photogs. in possession (2005) of Mr and Mrs Thompson of Saycell's Farm.
14 TNA, MAF 68/4533/167; MAF 68/6005/14/167.
15 Ibid. MAF 68/4533/167.
16 Ibid. MAF 68/6005/14/167.
17 Ibid. MAF 68/3295/15; MAF 68/6005/14/167.
18 Information from from Mrs (Rachel) Pugh of Kempley Court.
19 Information from Mr Watkins.
20 'Glimpses of Life in Kempley' (exhibition in Kempley Baptist chapel 13–16 Oct. 2006).
21 B.M. Morley, 'The Nave Roof of the Church of St Mary, Kempley, Gloucestershire', *Antiq. J.* 65 (1985), 101–11; B.M. Morley and D.W.H. Miles, 'The Nave Roof and Other Timberwork at the Church of St Mary, Kempley, Gloucestershire: Dendochronological Dating', ibid. 80 (2000), 294–6.
22 HCA 3707; BL, Add. Ch. 1310.
23 *Inq. p.m. Glos.* 1302–58, 100; above, introd. (landscape).
24 HCA 7018/5(2), pp. 45–6.
25 Worcs. RO, 705:99 (BA 5540), Kempley and Wilton ct. rolls 1526–68, rot. 35.
26 Ibid. rott. 13, 32–4.
27 Ibid. rott. 38, 43; MCA, F 3iv, deed 800.

hospital.[1] In the late 1670s timber was felled in Stone Redding in the north end of the parish.[2] Throughout Kempley woodland was cleared gradually[3] but after the mid 19th century the process was reversed with piecemeal planting, including conifers, in and around Stone Redding.[4] The Madresfield estate retained some woodland after selling its farmland in the early 20th century.[5]

MILL AND FISHPONDS

Saycell had a mill in Kempley in the mid 13th century[6] and Kempley mill, built on the manorial demesne,[7] belonged with Saycell's farm to Roger Walwyn in 1494.[8] Thomas Walwyn retained the mill in 1579[9] and the lords of the manor were in possession by 1601.[10] The mill stood on the Kempley brook south-east of Saycell's Farm and upstream of Kempley Court[11] and a new ditch dug for the brook in the mid 17th century was presumably intended to improve its water supply.[12] Reserved as a corn mill in farming leases of Kempley Court in the early 18th century, it was let to a carpenter in 1721[13] and was standing, though possibly not in use, in 1787.[14]

Saycell's farm included two fishponds that Sir John Scudamore reserved for his own use in 1665.[15]

INDUSTRY AND TRADE

A smith was living in Kempley in 1564[16] and a gunsmith there died in 1693.[17] A smithy operating for many years at the junction of the lane to Kempley green and the Ross road[18] closed c.1870.[19] A tailor was recorded in 1589[20] and the trades and crafts of the carpenter, shoemaker, cook, and butcher were also practised in the parish in 1608.[21] A mason lived there in 1707[22] as did a wheelwright in 1758.[23] Textile manufacture has not been recorded in Kempley but in 1567 the manor court expressly forbade the washing of flax and hemp in the Kempley brook.[24] In 1851 eighteen tradesmen and craftsmen excluding brick makers were counted in the parish. Most of them, including a carrier and a shopkeeper as well as a sawyer and thatcher, lived at or near Kempley Green.[25] A few men and boys were employed at a brick yard by the Ross road in the south of the parish.[26] The works, opened in the 1820s or 1830s by the builder Ephraim Blewett,[27] produced tiles and drain pipes as well as bricks.[28] They closed in the mid 1890s.[29]

A blacksmith at Fishpool and a builder at Brookland's Farm in business at the turn of the 20th century both worked on Kempley's new church.[30] Other parishioners included a hurdle maker[31] and later a wheelwright[32] and in 1939 a carpenter. Carrying services linking Kempley with Newent and Gloucester, Ledbury, and Ross-on-Wye were run from Brick House Farm at Fishpool from the 1870s and continued at a reduced level in the 1930s after a motor haulage business had been established in the parish. Kempley always had at least one shop in the later 19th and early 20th century, residents at Kempley Green including a grocer in 1895, and there was a post office in 1927. Kempley retained three shops, one a bakery and another a tobacconist, in 1939[33] but it lacked both a shop and a post office in 2002. An insurance agent lived in the parish in 1903.[34]

---

1 F.C. Morgan, 'The Accounts of St Katherine's Hospital, Ledbury, 1584–1595', *Trans. Woolhope Naturalists' Field Club* 34 (1952–4), 101.
2 GA, P 188/IN 1/2, burial 29 Aug. 1678.
3 Above, introd. (landscape).
4 OS Map 6", Glos. IX.SE (1883–1924 edns).
5 GA, G/NE 159/14/1, f. 7; above, manor (manor).
6 TNA, JUST 1/278, rot. 25d.
7 Worcs. RO, 705:99 (BA 5540), Kempley and Wilton ct. rolls 1526–68, rot. 11.
8 Hampshire RO, 44M69/C/660.
9 BL, Add. Ch. 1845.   10 Ibid. 38897.
11 MCA, maps and plans, shelf 5, map of the Kempley Court estate 1787.
12 Worcs. RO, 705:99 (BA 3375), Kempley deeds 1602–66.
13 MCA, G ii, bdl. 172B, no 40; G iii, bdl. 172C, nos 49, 56.
14 Ibid. maps and plans, shelf 5, map of the Kempley Court estate 1787.
15 BL, Add. Ch. 1963.
16 MCA, F 2iv, deed 508.
17 GDR wills 1685/20; GA, P 188/IN 1/2.
18 MCA, H 4v, bdl. 49, nos 2, 12; GDR, T 1/108 (no 212); GDR wills 1761/29.
19 *Kelly's Dir. Glos.* (1863), 299; (1870), 585–6.
20 Herefs. RO, E 12/G/20.
21 Smith, *Men and Armour*, 65.
22 GDR wills 1711/196.
23 MCA, G iii, bdl. 172D, no 80.
24 Worcs. RO, 705:99 (BA 5540), Kempley and Wilton ct. rolls 1526–68, rot. 45.
25 TNA, HO 107/1960.
26 GDR, T 1/108; see TNA. HO 107/350/8; RG 9/1761; GA, P 188/IN 1/6.
27 Above, settlement (outlying settlement).
28 *Kelly's Dir. Glos.* (1870), 585.
29 OS Map 6", Glos, XVI.NE (1889 edn); *Kelly's Dir. Glos.* (1889), 824; (1894), 216–17.
30 Below, religious hist. (religious life: bldg. of a second ch.).
31 *Kelly's Dir. Glos.* (1889), 825; (1906), 224.
32 GA, SL 310.
33 *Kelly's Dir. Glos.* (1863–1939 edns); GA, P 188/IN 1/6.
34 GA, P 188/IN 1/6.

LOCAL GOVERNMENT

MANORIAL GOVERNMENT

In the mid 16th century the manor court, in an important part of its business, handed down punishments for trespasses on the lord's demesne and waste, particularly woodland, for illicit felling of trees, and for poaching of partridges and fish. In 1542 it fined a man for picking apples and pears in the wood and making cider and in 1554 it issued an instruction for the ringing and tethering of pigs. The court also dealt with the maintenance of highways and watercourses. In 1539 three men kept unmarried women in their homes in defiance of an earlier court order.[1] The court, which was held at Stone House in the 17th century,[2] was summoned until at least 1746. Encroachments within Kempley wood were a large part of its business in the 1660s and 1670s and the lord of the manor and William Bosworth were both presented in 1666 for not scouring the mill leat.[3] Deodands were automatically seized for the lord of the manor in the late 17th century.[4] There is no evidence that gallows were erected in Kempley although the hillside on the eastern side of the parish below the road north of the Kempley brook was known as Gallows hill in the mid 19th century.[5]

St Katherine's hospital and Aconbury priory held courts at Kempley in the later Middle Ages. The hospital's court, convened in 1307 and until at least 1515, was concerned almost exclusively with tenurial and agrarian matters. In 1325 it heard a case concerning the felling of trees and assarting of land and in 1380 it was notified that four men had fished in the hospital's fishery.[6] The priory's court, recorded from 1361, dealt invariably with the holdings of its tenants at Kempley and Ketford, although in 1509 presentments were made about excessive pasturing of livestock and the disrepair of a ditch.[7]

PAROCHIAL GOVERNMENT

Kempley's two churchwardens were first recorded in 1446.[8] The parishioners' warden came to be chosen by rotation and in 1689, when the post fell to a labourer, the parish in consultation with the lord of the manor, Reginald Pyndar, appointed a deputy in his place. In the late 17th century the churchwardens submitted separate accounts, one being responsible for repairs to the church steeple in 1700, and there was a salaried parish clerk. To prevent mistakes in the selection of its overseers of the poor and petty constable, the parish determined in 1687 that both offices should be served from house to house according to different rotas. In 1692 Reginald Pyndar and other leading inhabitants chose the overseer for Bullocksend, then the possession of an absentee. Later the duties of both offices were occasionally discharged by deputies and in 1749 the constable also served as one of the parish's two surveyors of the highways.[9] In 1815 a woman's service as overseer was postponed a year because of a 'recent affliction'.[10]

Following a public meeting convened by the vicar in 1686 the parish indemnified itself against any obligation to provide relief for a family of five living elsewhere. At that time the parish supported one or two residents on a regular basis and made occasional payments for cottage repairs, medical expenses, funerals, and the like.[11] From the mid 18th century the number of paupers receiving regular help increased and the overseers apprenticed several children to local farmers. The poor, who were put to work spinning flax, numbered eight in 1770. In 1783 they were sent to the Dymock workhouse as a temporary measure and on their return the following year a salaried overseer was employed for a short period.[12] In the late 1790s the families of two militia men were among those receiving regular help and in 1800 and 1801, when many families sought assistance, the parish bought corn and flour for distribution to the poor. John Forty acted as deputy overseer in the early 19th century and Old Saycell's, a cottage he owned, was adapted as poorhouses.[13] The parish also acquired a cottage at Kempley Green for the use of the poor.[14]

Annual expenditure on relief, which had rarely exceeded £10 in the 1730s and 1740s,[15] rose from £45 in 1776 to £83 in 1803, when 20 people received permanent help,[16] and to £234 in 1814, when 13 people received permanent and 24 occasional help. The

---

1 Worcs. RO, 705:99 (BA 5540), Kempley and Wilton ct. rolls 1526–68.
2 Herefs. RO, E 12/G/9.
3 MCA, A 2ii, no 18 (M 60–71).
4 GA, P 188/IN 1/2, burials 29 Aug. 1678, 8 Oct. 1681.
5 GDR, T 1/108.
6 HCA 7018/5 (2), pp. 45–61; R 1164.
7 TNA, SC 2/175/71; SC 2/175/72.
8 Hockaday Abs. ccl.
9 GA, P 188/CW 2/10.
11 Ibid. CW 2/10.
12 Ibid. OV 2/1.
13 Ibid. 2.
14 GDR, T 1/108.
15 GA, P 188/OV 2/1.
16 *Poor Law Abstract, 1804*, 172–3.
10 Ibid. OV 2/2.

following year, when the comparable numbers were 15 and 19, it was £135[1] and in the decade before, in 1835, Kempley joined the Newent poor-law union,[2] it hovered around that level.[3]

Works undertaken by Kempley and funded partly by ratepayers in Dymock under an agreement of 1819 presumably improved the chief road between the two parishes.[4] From 1850 the parish paid a salary for the collection of rates, first to the surveyor of the highways and from 1865 to an assistant overseer of the poor. In 1848 and 1879 ratepayers opposed proposals to use rates for the repair of roads at Kempley Green.[5] In 1895 the parish meeting was given the powers of a parish council.[6]

SOCIAL HISTORY

SOCIAL STRUCTURE

In the early 14th century the lords of the manor, the Greys of Wilton, were occasionally resident[7] and in 1327, when Henry Grey was assessed for tax in Kempley at 10s., two other men were assessed there at 3s. 6d., six others at 2s. or more, three at 1s., and three at 6d.[8] At that time the principal tenants of St Katherine's hospital disclaimed any duty to perform labour and other customary services and by 1316 one had his sons ordained and his daughters married without licence.[9] In the late Middle Ages with the Greys as absentees the manor house fell into disrepair[10] and the farmers were the principal residents. According to a valuation of goods and chattels in 1522, John Matthews (£6 13s. 4d.), whose family held the farmstead called Edwyn's (later Matthew's Farm),[11] was, with the possible exception of the vicar, the wealthiest inhabitant. He was followed by William Berkeley and Thomas Bullock (£5 each) and among other residents nine had goods valued at £2 or more, eight at £1 or more, and five at less than £1.[12]

In the early 17th century the lord of the manor was resident and the rest of the community, as represented by thirty-seven men named in 1608, was made up of yeoman farmers, husbandmen, and labourers with a few craftsmen and tradesmen.[13] Henry Finch, who as lord lived in a new manor house (Stone House),[14] employed three domestic and four farm servants. William Poole, whose family farmed at Friar's Court by 1567,[15] employed two servants. In 1676 Henry Poole, whose family remained at Friar's Court until the late 17th century,[16] was high constable of Botloe hundred.[17] Following the Restoration, after an absence of several decades, the parish again had a resident lord of the manor in Sir Thomas Howe.[18] In 1672 he was assessed for tax on 11 hearths, another parishioner on 4, three on 3, four on 2, and thirteen on 1.[19]

On acquiring the manor in 1682 Reginald Pyndar moved with his family from Derbyshire to Kempley[20] and in 1689 his son Thomas rebuilt the old manor house (Kempley Court) as his residence.[21] The Pyndars lived in Kempley until the early 1720s and Elizabeth Pyndar fulfilled the role of lady of the manor from Ludlow (Salop.) in the following decades,[22] establishing a number of charities for the parish.[23] In the early 18th century Kempley's population of c.180 included 10 freeholders[24] and a number of tenant farmers.[25] In the mid 1740s Elizabeth Pyndar had 18 tenants in Kempley owing rents ranging from £120 to 10s., and on her behalf George Palmer, the farmer at Kempley Court, regularly gave £1 1s. to the poor at Christmas, provided meat and drink for an annual dinner for the tenants, and paid 16s. a year for teaching two children.[26]

After Elizabeth Pyndar (d. 1759) the lords of the manor lived at Madresfield (Worcs.)[27] and Kempley, which was rendered inaccessible by poor roads in

---

1 Ibid. *1818*, 146–7.
2 *Poor Law Com. 2nd Rep.* p. 523.
3 *Poor Law Returns* (1830–1), 66; (1835), 64.
4 GA, P 125/VE 2/2.
5 Ibid. P 188/VE 2/1.
6 *Minutes of Gloucestershire County Council 1894–5* (copy in Glos. Colln. D 10590), order no 53.
7 *Inq. p.m. Glos.* 1302–58, 100, 185, 293.
8 *Glos. Subsidy Roll, 1327*, 35–6.
9 HCA 7018/5(2), pp. 45–50; see ibid. p. 52.
10 Worcs. RO, 705:99 (BA 5540), Kempley and Wilton ct. rolls 1526–68, rott. 9, 11.
11 HCA 7018/5(1), pp. 13–15; (2), p. 58.
12 *Military Surv. of Glos. 1522*, 59–60, 63. For Berkeley and Bullock, see Worcs. RO, 705:99 (BA 5540), Kempley and Wilton ct. rolls 1526–68, rott. 1–3.
13 Smith, *Men and Armour*, 64–5.
14 Above, manor.
15 HCA 7031/2, f. 16v.
16 GDR wills 1629/146; 1668/59; see rate assessments in GA, P 188/CW 2/10.
17 GA, Q/SO 1, f. 129v.
18 Above, manor.
19 TNA, E 179/247/14, rot. 36.
20 GA, P 188/IN 1/2.
21 Above, manor.
22 *The Madresfield Muniments* (1929, Worcester), 62–3; see deeds in MCA, G 1i, bdl. 172B; G 1iii, bdls. 172C and 172D.
23 Below (education); religious hist. (religious life).
24 Atkyns, *Glos.* 489.
25 See MCA, G 1i, bdl. 172B, no 40; G 1iii, bdl. 172C, nos 47A, 49, 52; HCA 3476/7.
26 MCA, L 1vi, no 2; F 5vii, deeds 1444, 1463.
27 Above, manor; Rudder, *Glos.* 508; Rudge, *Hist. of Glos.* II, 33.

winter, remained a society dominated by farmers.[1] Most, if not all, vicars from the late 17th century had been non-resident but following the building of a new vicarage house c.1800 there was a clergyman in the parish.[2] In 1851 eleven farmers had servants living in and eight of them each employed a domestic servant.[3] In 1861 four servants lived with Revd A.J. Street and his family at the vicarage house[4] and in 1901 five farmers and the vicar each had one domestic servant living with them.[5] The Palmers, who took a lease of Kempley Court in 1722,[6] farmed there until the 1920s.[7]

Frederick Lygon (d. 1891), who inherited the manor on becoming 6th Earl Beauchamp in 1866, was active as a landlord in Kempley. He enlarged his estate and provided many new buildings on it. He also built a school, a church, and a vicarage house close to the parish's main centres of population.[8] In 1872, to celebrate the birth of his son William, he entertained his tenant farmers at Madresfield and organized a distribution of meat, bread, tea, sugar, and cash to his lesser tenants in their parishes.[9] In 1893, when William (then 7th earl) came of age, a tree was planted at crossroads near St Mary's church to mark the event[10] and the farmers and cottage tenants attended separate celebrations at Madresfield,[11] many of them subscribing to the presentation of a loving cup to him.[12] William Lygon built Kempley a new church, completed in 1903 as a permanent replacement for his father's temporary structure,[13] and let a field to the parish for use as allotments from 1905.[14] He relinquished his estate soon after the First World War.[15]

CHARITIES FOR THE POOR

The parish built up a stock of money from gifts and let it out at interest for the use of the poor. It included £3 given in 1609 by Richard Gwynne, a clothworker, for lending to poor parishioners. The stock, to which John Lewes, the vicar, added 14s. in 1675 and John Wood, a shoemaker, added £1 by will in 1684,[16] totalled £7 10s. in 1698[17] and £8 10s. in 1726.[18] The interest was shared among the poor, four men and five widows being the recipients at Christmas in 1691, as was money collected at holy communion services and an annual gift by the Pyndar family at Christmas. Up to ten people usually benefited from the collections in the later 17th and early 18th century but there were only three beneficiaries in 1721.[19]

In 1677 Richard Mayle of Much Marcle (Herefs.) made a gift to provide seven twopenny loaves a year.[20] The charity, to be distributed on Good Friday, was not recorded after 1705.[21] Joan Wotton by will proved 1707 gave 10s. a year, charged on Old Saycell's, for the relief of the poor.[22] In 1744 the charity was shared in cash between nine people and the following year, together with 8s. 6d. interest from the parish stock, between ten people. In 1750 the charity, supplemented by the interest from the stock and a donation of £2 2s. from Elizabeth Pyndar and Reginald Lygon, provided clothing for six people.[23] In 1753 the parish stock, then £12 10s., was used by John Worrall to buy 2 a. as an endowment for a schoolmistress. The land, charged initially with paying 6s. a year to the poor,[24] was later devoted solely to helping the poor[25] and in 1810 the income from it, £1 10s., was distributed with Joan Wotton's charity in bread. In 1818 the two charities and a collection box provided £3 17s. 6d. that was distributed in cash among 23 people, the minimum payment being 2s. In 1825, when the available money included the surplus income from Elizabeth Pyndar's educational charity, £5 13s. 6d. was shared between 25 people.[26]

The three charities together provided cash payments until at least 1838 and handed out clothes, sheets, and blankets at Christmas by 1854. In the later 1870s they made some cash payments and grants to a local clothing club, but from 1879, when because of severe agricultural depression 18 people received payments totalling £4 1s. 6d., they provided only cash. Payments came to be made on the feast of St Thomas (21 December) and the total sum varied from year to year. In the late 19th century the number of beneficiaries occasionally exceeded 30 and most individual payments were 5s.[27] In the early

---

1 Rudder, *Glos.* 508.
2 Below, religious hist. (religious life).
3 TNA, HO 107/1960.
4 Ibid. RG 9/1761.
5 Ibid. RG 13/2422.
6 MCA, G 1ii, bdl. 172C, no 57; bdl. 172D, no 72.
7 TNA, HO 107/1960; RG 9/1761; RG 13/2422; *Kelly's Dir. Glos.* (1856–1927 edns).
8 Above, settlement (bldgs.); manor; econ. hist.; below (education); religious hist.
9 GA, D 5292, 26 Aug. and 6 Sept. 1872; see above, Dymock, social hist. For the earl as landlord, see also *Oxford DNB*.
10 Plaque at tree.
11 GA, D 5292, 1 and 3 Aug. 1893.
12 MCA, P 1, no 4.
13 Below, religious hist. (religious life).
14 GA, SL 310; see OS Map 6", Glos. XVI.NE (1924 edn).
15 Above, manor.
16 GA, P 188/IN 1/2, memos.
17 MCA, F 4v, deed 1306; see GDR, V 5/175T 4.
18 GA, P 188/OV 2/1.
19 Ibid. P 188/CW 2/10; for the Pyndars' Christmas gift, see also MCA, F 5vii, deed 1444.
20 GA, P 188/IN 1/2.
21 GDR, V 5/175T 4.
22 Ibid. wills 1706/34; GA, P 188/CW 2/10; MCA, J 3ii, bdl. 114b, no 5.
23 GA, P 188/OV 2/1.
24 MCA, G 1ii, bdl. 172D, no. 78; below (education).
25 *20th Rep. Com. Char.* 14.
26 GA, P 188/CW 2/10; *20th Rep. Com. Char.* 13–14.
27 GA, P 188/CH 1; VE 2/1; D 5292, 21 Dec. 1886.

years of his incumbency Edward Denny, vicar 1886–98, handed out beef, tea, and sugar on Christmas Eve.[1] Following the closure of Kempley school in 1919[2] Elizabeth Pyndar's educational charity was applied solely to helping needy residents. The tariff of individual payments from the three charities was reduced in 1938 and at one Christmas in the 1960s 26 people received 4s. each, 11 had 10s. each, and one person received £1.[3] In 1997 the charity originating as the parish stock lapsed and the funds of Joan Wotton's charity were transferred to Elizabeth Pyndar's charity, which under the name of the Kempley charity, had an income of £283 in 2006.[4]

EDUCATION

In 1605, when Henry Finch employed an unlicensed teacher for his children, the parish clerk was entirely unlearned.[5] In 1753 John Worrall, following the wishes of his mother Mary, bought 2 a. in Kempley to support a mistress teaching four boys or girls to read, knit, and sew[6] and in 1755 Elizabeth Pyndar, who had been giving 16s. a year for the education of two children,[7] donated 4 a. in Much Marcle as an endowment to teach two children to read.[8] Although the Kempley land was used for other purposes,[9] in the early 19th century the Much Marcle land provided the salary of the mistress of a day school for which the parish occasionally bought books. The teacher's salary was increased in 1808 from four to five guineas.[10] From 1818, when it had 12 pupils and was the only school in the parish,[11] the school was sometimes taught by a local man in collaboration with his wife.[12] In 1825, when its subjects were reading, sewing, and the catechism,[13] eighteen Kempley children had a day school education[14] but in 1833 only six attended the parish's school.[15] In 1847 the school taught 26 infants on weekdays and Sundays and some older children went to Ann Cam's school in Dymock.[16] In the 1850s a shoemaker and his wife living at Kempley Green taught the Kempley school.[17]

In 1866 Earl Beauchamp built a schoolroom some way north of Kempley Green near the centre of the parish.[18] The school established there in 1867 was managed by Revd A.J. Street as a National school and was funded by the earl, voluntary contributions, pence, and Elizabeth Pyndar's charity.[19] In 1871 the earl undertook to underwrite the school's cost on condition that local people raised a quarter of it by subscription.[20] Almost from the outset the managers, led by vicars with High Church views, had difficulty in engaging and retaining acceptable teachers. Attendance was often low and there were several unsuccessful attempts to establish a night school.[21] In 1904 the day school had an average attendance of 40 in a single mixed department.[22] An infants' class was later held in a separate room. The school, which changed its name from Kempley National to Kempley Church of England school in 1906,[23] closed in 1919.[24]

In the 1920s and 1930s the vicar D. Gethyn-Jones ran a boys' preparatory school in Kempley for sons of local farmers.[25]

SOCIAL LIFE

Kempley had several beershops or inns in the mid 19th century, including in 1841 the Yew Tree and the Plough at and near Kempley Green. Only that at Little Adams[26] was open, as the Cross Keys inn, in 1871.[27]

For long, as in the late 17th century, St. Mary's church was the parishioners' main meeting place.[28] The schoolroom built in 1866 was used for meetings and in 1874 the schoolmistress helped the vicar to run a club. There was a mothers' meeting in 1890. Among regular events in Kempley was a biennial flower show established by 1886 and enjoying the patronage of Earl Beauchamp. Events for the Golden Jubilee of 1887 were funded by public subscription. A cricket club was formed in 1899.[29] In 1899 the Cross Keys, which had recently closed,[30] became the premises of a new club for the men of the parish[31] and in 1903,

---

1 Ibid. D 5292.
2 Below (education).
3 GA, D 3469/5/84.
4 http://www.charity-commission.gov.uk/registeredcharities (accessed 15 June 2007: nos 205124–5, 202981).
5 GDR vol. 97, f. 244 and v.
6 MCA, G 1iii, bdl. 172D, no. 78.
7 Ibid. F 5vii, deeds 1444, 1463; L 1vi, no 2.
8 Bigland, Glos. II, 118; 20th Rep. Com. Char. 14.
9 Above (charities for the poor).
10 GA, P 188/CW 2/10.
11 Educ. of Poor Digest, 302.
12 GA, P 188/CW 2/10; CH 1.
13 20th Rep. Com. Char. 14.
14 GDR vol. 383, no cxv.
15 Educ. Enq. Abstract, 318.
16 Nat. Soc. Inquiry, 1846–7, Glos. 10–11.
17 GA, P 188/CH 1; TNA, HO 107/1960.
18 OS Map 6", Glos. XVI. NE (1889 edn); datestone on bldg.
19 TNA, ED 7/37, Kempley National School; 1st Rep. Com. Employment in Agric. app. II, p. 130.
20 GA, P 188/VE 2/1.
21 Ibid. D 5292; P 188/SC 1/1.
22 Public Elem. Schs. 1906, 185.
23 GA, P 188/SC 1/1.
24 TNA, ED 7/37, Kempley National School.
25 Kelly's Dir. Glos. (1931), 233; (1939), 239; information from Malcolm Stallard of Callow Farm, Dymock, and from Mabel McCulloch of Hallwood Green, Dymock.
26 TNA, HO 107/350/8; Kelly's Dir. Glos. (1856), 315.
27 TNA, RG 9/1761; RG 10/2609; OS Map 6", Glos. XVI.NE (1889 edn); Licensed Houses in Glos. 1891, 140–1.
28 GA, P 188/CW 2/10.
29 Ibid. D 5292.
30 cf. Licensed Houses in Glos. 1891, 140–1; 1903, 124.
31 GA, D 5292; Kelly's Dir. Glos. (1902), 222; OS Map 6", Glos. XVI.NE (1905 edn).

on the building of St Edward's church, the nearby temporary church it replaced became the church hall.[1] The clubhouse closed soon after the First World War[2] and the church hall, which came to serve as a village hall for Kempley and the neighbourhood,[3] was rebuilt in 1994.[4] Two bus shelters were erected in 1949, one on the Ross road and the other at Kempley Green, as memorials to villagers killed during the First and Second World Wars.[5]

RELIGIOUS HISTORY

EARLY HISTORY AND STATUS OF THE PARISH CHURCH

When Kempley's medieval church was completed in the mid 12th century some tithes there belonged to St Guthlac's priory, successor to the church founded in Hereford by Walter de Lacy (d. 1085).[6] Geoffrey de Longchamp, lord of the manor and patron of Kempley,[7] gave its church to St Katherine's hospital, Ledbury, c.1230. The hospital appropriated the rectory after the death of its then incumbent Robert, also styled dean,[8] who in 1234 paid the hospital an annual rent of a pound of incense specified in Geoffrey's gift,[9] and the church was served by a chaplain.[10] In 1447, because of its inefficient use by the hospital, the consistory court sequestered the income and a vicarage was created.[11]

The benefice was united with Dymock in 1938[12] and with Oxenhall in 1955.[13] In 1975 Kempley was added to the united benefice of Dymock with Donnington[14] and the parish church was declared redundant and its place taken by a church opened in 1903 in the more populous southern end of the parish.[15] From 2000 Kempley was part of a benefice embracing nine former ecclesiastical parishes.[16]

PATRONAGE AND ENDOWMENT

St Katherine's hospital was confirmed in its ownership of the advowson by Reynold and Maud Grey in 1260.[17] The first presentation to the vicarage, in 1448, was by the bishop[18] but the patronage remained with the hospital.[19] The bishop presented by reason of lapse in 1471 and 1479.[20] Although it was claimed that the lord of the manor had the right to present at every third vacancy,[21] Margery Pigott was patron for only a turn in 1575[22] and exercise of the patronage passed from the hospital's master to its governors, the dean and chapter of Hereford, in the late 16th century.[23] A move by the dean and chapter to secure the succession to the vicarage led to an intervention by the archbishop of Canterbury in 1606 on the ground of lapse of time.[24] In the 1640s Francis Finch apparently exercised the patronage[25] and in 1660, after Charles II had presented to the living by reason of lapse,[26] the dean and chapter's nomination was rejected.[27] In 1869 the dean and chapter sold the advowson with the hospital's Kempley lands to the 6th Earl Beauchamp.[28] The next earl conveyed the patronage to H.L. Roberts of Newent in 1937[29] and Revd J.E. Gethyn-Jones acquired Roberts's right c.1970.[30] Mr R.D. Marcon owned it in 2002.[31]

---

1 MCA, D 2i (7); OS Map 6", Glos. XVI.NE (1924 edn).
2 GA, SL 310; OS Map 6", Glos. XVI.NE (1924 edn).
3 http://www.charity-commission.gov.uk/registeredcharities (accessed 1 May 2002: no 1005524).
4 Photogs. in hall.
5 Of the shelters, provided by the parish council, that on the Ross road has been rebuilt following its accidental demolition: information from Mr K. Brooke of Friar's Court.
6 Dugdale, *Mon.* III, 620; *Eng. Episc. Acta VII*, pp. 23, 149–51, 197–9. For Walter, I.J. Sanders, *English Baronies* (1960), 95; W.E. Wightman, *The Lacy Family in England and Normandy* (1966), pedigree at end.
7 Above, manor; *Cur. Reg.* XIII, 193.
8 *Eng. Episc. Acta VII*, pp. 278–80. See BL, Add. MS 18461, f. 78 for the style 'dean of Kempley'.
9 A.T. Bannister, 'Descriptive Catalogue of Manuscripts Dealing with St. Katherine's, Ledbury', *Trans. Woolhope Naturalists' Field Club* (1921–3), 253.
10 A.T. Bannister, 'Visitation Returns of Diocese of Hereford in 1397', *EHR* 44 (1929), 453; Hockaday Abs. ccl, 1446.
11 Hockaday Abs. ccl.
12 *London Gazette*, 25 Feb. 1938, pp. 1252–3.
13 GA, P 125/IN 2/12.
14 *Glouc. Dioc. Year Book* (1978), 21.
15 GA, D 7322; below (religious life).
16 *Dioc. of Glouc. Dir.* (2001–2), 24–5.
17 *Glos. Feet of Fines 1199–1299*, p. 127.
18 *Reg. Spofford*, 368.
19 *Reg. Stanbury*, 175, 179; *Reg. Myllyng*, 197; *Reg. Bothe*, 340, 346.
20 *Reg. Stanbury*, 187; *Reg. Myllyng*, 189.
21 Worcs. RO, 705:99 (BA 5540), Kempley and Wilton ct. rolls 1526–68, rot. 24.
22 Hockaday Abs. ccl.
23 See above, manor (other estates: Kempley Rectory).
24 HCA 7031/3, p. 22; GDR vol. 1B, pp. 52–3.
25 MCA, G 1iv, bdl. 173, no 17.
26 GDR vol. 1B, p. 83.
27 HCA 7031/3, p. 193; MCA, F 4vii, deed 1137.
28 HCA 7005/10, pp. 242–6, 257–65.
29 GA, P 188/IN 4/5.
30 *Glouc. Dioc. Year Book* (1969), 28–9; (1970), 28–9.
31 *Dioc. of Glouc. Dir.* (2001–2), 24.

The vicarage, which had all the tithes apart from those from Friar's Court,¹ was valued at £5 4s. 7½d. in 1535,² £40 in 1650, when it was described as a rectory,³ and £60 in 1750.⁴ The vicarage tithes were commuted for a corn rent charge of £226 12s. 3d. in 1842 on an agreement which left 143 a. belonging to St Katherine's hospital tithe free and set aside 6 a. of hospital land next to the vicarage house for the use of the vicar.⁵ The living was worth £213 in 1856.⁶

Vicarage Houses

In 1680 the vicarage house had three bays, one of them newly built, a central stone stack, and three hearths. Its outbuildings included several adjacent sheds and a barn of six bays.⁷ The house, to which another heated bay had been added by 1705, was recorded in 1737 but its location is unknown.⁸

About 1800 the vicar Robert Squire built a house opposite the medieval churchyard on land belonging to St Katherine's hospital.⁹ Designed as a compact gentleman's residence with Gothick details on a stuccoed three-storeyed and three-bayed façade, it was superseded in the mid 1870s by a new house provided by the 6th Earl Beauchamp in the southern part of the parish¹⁰ and was extended in the later 20th century in the style of a coach house. The Victorian house, designed in brick in a conventional gabled Gothic manner by the Cheltenham firm of Middleton & Goodman,¹¹ was sold in the late 20th century.

RELIGIOUS LIFE

The Middle Ages

Built between c.1120 and 1150, Kempley's medieval church is one of the most complete small 12th-century churches in England, retaining not only its tunnel-vaulted chancel, chancel arch, and nave with south and west doorways but also much original timberwork and a remarkably complete scheme of painted wall decoration. One of four local churches sharing sculptural details ascribed to a 'Dymock school' of craftsmen,¹² its lavish construction has been attributed to the Lacy family but may have been by a predecessor of Emme de St Léger, lady of the manor later in the century,¹³ The south and west doorways are flanked by attached columns with capitals and have tympana, that over the south door

49. *St Mary's church: the south doorway with original ironwork on the door*

decorated with a carving of the Tree of Life.¹⁴ The nave roof is the earliest to survive in England and the west door is original.¹⁵ The east window seems to have been enlarged shortly after the church was built and the chancel decoration representing the vision of the Apocalypse and Christ in Majesty described in the Book of Revelation remained untouched until the Reformation.¹⁶ The paintings on the nave walls were altered in the Middle Ages to display at various times a Doom, imagery related to particular saints, and the Wheel of Life.¹⁷ The fabric was altered by the addition of a short west tower without an external entrance in the later 13th century and the construction of a timber-framed south porch and the enlargement of a nave window in the 14th century.

---

1   GDR, V 5/175T 1, 3; see HCA 7018/5(1), pp. 12–13.
2   *Valor Eccl.* II, 501.
3   C.R. Elrington, 'The Survey of Church Livings in Gloucestershire, 1650', *Trans. BGAS* 83 (1964), 98.
4   *Bp. Benson's Surv. of Dioc. of Glouc. 1735–50*, 7.
5   GDR, T 1/108.
6   Ibid. vol. 384, f. 125.
7   Ibid. V 5/175T 1.
8   Ibid. 3, 5.
9   HCA 3496/1.
10 GA, D 5292.
11 Ibid. D 2970/1/78.
12 See above, Newent and May Hill (settlement, society, and buildings).
13 Verey and Brooks, *Glos.* II, 552; see above, manor.
14 Fig. 49.
15 B.M. Morley, 'The Nave Roof of the Church of St Mary, Kempley, Gloucestershire', *Antiq. J.* 65 (1985), 101–11; B.M. Morley and D.W.H. Miles, 'The Nave Roof and Other Timberwork at the Church of St Mary, Kempley, Gloucestershire: Dendochronological Dating', ibid. 80 (2000), 294–6.
16 Below, Fig. 50.
17 Verey and Brooks, *Glos.* II, 552–4.

50. *St Mary's Church: the chancel*

In the early 13th century, when the daughters of a forester gave it a thicket in return for an annual mass, the church had a dedication to St Leonard.[1] The date of its dedication to St Mary is unknown but in the late 14th century St Katherine's hospital withheld its annual gift of wax to the light of St Leonard[2] and one of two early 15th-century bells in the church bore an inscription invoking the protection of the Virgin.[3] The church also retains a chest made from an oak felled in the later 15th or early 16th century.[4]

Following its appropriation in the 13th century the church was presumably served by chaplains from the hospital at Ledbury.[5] Much later it was claimed that the lords of the manor gave the hospital its land in Kempley to support two beadsmen and one other serving at the lord's request as well as a priest celebrating mass on three days a week.[6] The parishioners were without ready access to the chaplain in the late 14th century as there was no manse near the church.[7] Among the parishioners cited before the court in 1446 were seven men said to have withheld ecclesiastical rights and a woman accused of adultery with the chaplain. Most of the vicars serving the church from 1448 were in place for

---

1 HCA 3707.
2 Bannister, 'Visitation Returns in 1397', 453.
3 H.T. Ellacombe, *Glos. Ch. Bells* (1881), 53. The dedication to St Mary is first recorded in *Kelly's Dir. Glos.* (1856), 315.
4 Morley and Miles, 'Nave Roof and Other Timberwork at the Church of St Mary', 296.
5 See HCA 1658A.
6 Worcs. RO, 705:99 (BA 5540), Kempley and Wilton ct. rolls 1526–68, rot. 24.
7 Bannister, 'Visitation Returns in 1397', 453.

less than ten years.[1] George Blundell (1515–27) was succeeded by Thomas Blundell,[2] the hospital's previous master. He resigned the living after two years with a pension[3] charged in 1531 on his successor John Cam.[4]

From the Reformation to the Restoration

At or soon after the Reformation the paintings in the church were covered with whitewash and texts were later painted on the nave walls.[5] In 1551 there were c.80 communicants and John Cam and his curate were equally ignorant, both unable to recite the Ten Commandments.[6] In 1552, during a vacancy in the vicarage, Edward Baskerville, the hospital's master, had the church key removed so that services could not take place there. William Scull, the next vicar,[7] was non-resident and employed a curate.[8] Humphrey Craddock (or Taylor), vicar from 1575,[9] was not a preacher but, although not a graduate in 1584, was considered a sufficient scholar in 1593.[10] He died in 1605 but his designated successor, his son John,[11] was not instituted until 1607 and only after the resignation of Richard Atkins, to whom the archbishop had given the living because of the delay.[12]

The church was reported in 1576 incorrectly as lacking a table of the Commandments and a book of homilies.[13] Responsibility for maintaining the chancel belonged to the lessees of Friar's Court, including several generations of the Poole family.[14] Two parishioners were described as recusant in 1577[15] and several people, including the landowner Richard Kyrle, failed to attend church and take communion in the late 16th century.[16] Although it was claimed in 1603 that there were no recusants in the parish,[17] at least two parishioners absented themselves from church in 1605[18] and a larger number, at least eight in 1639, regularly failed to take communion in the 1620s and 1630s[19] In the late 1640s the landowner William Kyrle was included in a list of Roman Catholics in the county.[20] A memorial to Henry and Anne Finch, lord and lady of the manor, was erected in the chancel by their son in 1633[21] and the parish retains a paten acquired the following year.[22] John Craddock, who succeeded his father John as vicar in the 1640s,[23] was a preaching minister[24] and remained in post until his death.[25] Paul Frewen, a leading member of a Baptist church in Dymock, became vicar in 1658 and was ejected at the Restoration.[26]

The Established Church and Nonconformity after the Restoration

John Lewes, vicar 1666–93, was resident.[27] His successor Peter Senhouse, a vicar choral in Hereford cathedral, was also vicar of Linton (Herefs.) from 1703 and resigned his cathedral post in 1705.[28] Religious dissent during that period was limited, three men being described in 1669 as schismatics[29] and only three nonconformists being reported among 100 parishioners in 1676,[30] and may have died out entirely by the mid 18th century.[31]

Following the Restoration the church nave was given new windows, one on the south side lighting the pulpit next to the chancel arch, and new pews and a ceiling and west gallery were inserted in it. In the latter work, undertaken in the early 1670s largely at the cost of Sir Thomas Howe who supplied much if not all of the timber,[32] the ceiling was supported on beams, brackets, and pilasters that appear to have been designed to stand on panelling.[33] Among acquisitions for the church were a baluster font,[34] a bell cast in 1680,[35] and a silver tazza by gift from Bridget Morgan in 1705.[36] The lords of the manor worshipped in a large pew in the north side of the

---

1 Hockaday Abs. ccl.
2 *Reg. Mayew*, 283; *Reg. Bothe*, 340.
3 J. Hillaby, *St Katherine's Hospital, Ledbury, c.1230–1547* (Ledbury and District Soc. Trust Ltd, 2003), 127.
4 *Reg. Bothe*, 346 and n.; Hockaday Abs. ccl.
5 Verey and Brooks, *Glos.* II, 554.
6 J. Gairdner, 'Bishop Hooper's Visitation of Gloucester', *EHR* 19 (1904), 119.
7 Hockaday Abs. ccl; for Baskerville, *Alumni Oxon. 1500–1714*, I, 81.
8 Bodleian, Rawl. C. 790, f. 28; Hockaday Abs. xliv, 1572 visit. f. 6.
9 Hockaday Abs. ccl.
10 Ibid. xlix, state of clergy 1584, f. 43; lii, state of clergy 1593, f. 6.
11 HCA 7031/3, p. 22; for the Craddocks, MCA, G 1iv, bdl. 173, no 17.
12 GDR vol. 1B, pp. 52–3; Hockaday Abs. ccl.
13 GDR vol. 40, f. 245.
14 HCA 3475/2-27; see MCA, G1iv, bdl. 173, no 17 (letter 16 Dec. 1672).
15 R.H. Clutterbuck, 'Bishop Cheyney and the Recusants of the Diocese of Gloucester', *Trans. BGAS* 5 (1880–1), 236.
16 GA, D 2052; for Kyrle, of Much Marcle, MCA, F 3iv, deed 800; F 3vi, deed 886.
17 *Eccl. Misc.* 101.
18 GDR vol. 97, f. 244v.
19 GA, D 2052.
20 *Cal. Cttee for Compounding*, I, 87.
21 Bigland, *Glos.* II, 119.
22 *Glos. Ch. Plate*, 127.
23 MCA, G 1iv, bdl. 173, no 17; see *Alumni Oxon. 1500–1714*, I, 344.
24 Elrington, 'Surv. of Church Livings', 98.
25 MCA, G 1iv, bdl. 173, no 17; F 4vii, deed 1137.
26 Hockaday Abs. ccl; *Calamy Revised*, 214; GDR vol. 1B, p. 83.
27 Hockaday Abs. ccl; GA, P 188/IN 1/2.
28 Hockaday Abs. ccl; HCA 7003/4/3, no 17.
29 GA, D 2052.
30 *Compton Census*, 544.
31 *Bp. Benson's Surv. of Dioc. of Glouc. 1735–50*, 7.
32 GA, P 188/IN 1/2.
33 Parts of the woodwork are dated 1670 and 1671.
34 GA, P 188/CW 2/10.
35 *Glos. Ch. Bells*, 393.
36 GA, D 5292.

nave in front of the chancel arch;[1] in the 18th century a memorial to the Pyndar family was placed on the wall before the pew.[2] The Poole family continued to be responsible for the chancel's fabric.[3] The vicar received a rent charge of 5s. for church purposes[4] but the payment was discontinued in 1682 because the land from which it was owed could not be identified.[5] In 1735 Elizabeth Pyndar assigned a rent charge of £3 to support a communion service on the second Sunday of each month, £2 2s. for the vicar or curate conducting the service and the rest for bread and wine.[6]

Peter Senhouse, who retained the vicarage until his death in 1760,[7] regularly employed a curate at Kempley by 1735[8] and the church had the required number of services in 1750.[9] Curates continued to serve the church well into the 19th century. J. Jenkins, the curate from 1772 until 1800,[10] lived in Donnington. Robert Squire, vicar 1787–1821, lived in Hereford[11] and, although he built a new vicarage house near the church c.1800[12] and sometimes served in person, remained non-resident. Richard Brooke, employed as curate from 1817 by Squire and his successor,[13] was resident and in 1825 the church had two Sunday services, conducted in the morning and afternoon without singing and followed by religious instruction. Ten communicants attended the monthly communion service.[14] A new painting of royal arms was placed in the church in the later 18th century.[15] A spire, supporting in 1733 a ball and weathercock, was taken off the tower in 1824[16] and replaced by a pyramidal roof.

Nonconformists were active in Kempley in the early 19th century, among them Abraham Whatmough, a Wesleyan minister from Newent, in 1816.[17] In 1831 the Baptist church at Gorsley under its minister John Hall held cottage meetings at Kempley Green[18] and in 1836 Thomas Kington, a missionary from Castle Frome (Herefs.) active in the area, registered a house there.[19]

In 1839 a new vicar, William Servante, took up residence. He served in person until 1851,[20] when the living was placed under sequestration to recover his debts and the bishop appointed A.J. Street as resident curate in charge.[21] A Sunday school was held at that time[22] but the church, remote from the bulk of the population and occasionally cut off by floods,[23] was usually less than half full during services and many people attended nonconformist meetings. In 1851 the church's congregation was 40 in the morning and 30 in the afternoon and its morning Sunday school had 11 scholars.[24] A Baptist chapel built at Kempley Green in 1850 and served by John Hall had a congregation of 40 at an afternoon service.[25] In 1856 Hall with other members of the Gorsley church bought a piece of land at the green and built on it a chapel called Bethel.[26] A meeting for which a Ledbury man registered a house in 1852 has not been identified.[27] Parishioners also attended a Methodist chapel opened within Upton Bishop at Fishpool by 1860.[28]

The Later Nineteenth Century

From 1866, when he became lord of the manor, church life had an active champion in Frederick Lygon, 6th Earl Beauchamp,[29] and its focus shifted from the church towards the more populous southern end of the parish. Occasional evening prayers and religious meetings were held in a new schoolroom on the lane to Kempley Green.[30] In 1872 A.J. Street was followed as minister by Arthur Hislop Drummond, the first of three vicars appointed by the 6th earl,[31] a staunch High

---

1 *Ledbury Reporter*, 29 Nov. 1913 (offprint in Glos. Colln., RR 175.2).
2 Bigland, *Glos.* II, 119.
3 HCA 3475/3–4; MCA, G 1iv, bdl. 173, no 17.
4 GA, P 188/IN 1/2.
5 GDR, V 5/175T/2, 4; see MCA, misc. letter 85.
6 MCA, F 6iii, deed 1425.
7 HCA 7003/4/3, no 17.
8 Hockaday Abs. ccl; GA, P 188/IN 1/3.
9 *Bp. Benson's Surv. of Dioc. of Glouc. 1735–50*, 7.
10 GA, P 188/IN 1/3, 6; Hockaday Abs. ccl.
11 GDR vol. 382, f. 17; Hockaday Abs. ccl.
12 HCA 3496/1; above (patronage and endowment: vicarage houses).
13 GA, P 188/IN 1/3, 6; Hockaday Abs. ccl.
14 GDR vol. 383, no cxv.
15 E. Fawcett, 'Royal Arms in Gloucestershire Churches', *Trans. BGAS* 55 (1933), 118.
16 GA, P 188/CW 2/10.
17 Hockaday Abs. ccl; for Whatmough, also ibid. ccxciii, Oxenhall, 1816.
18 *Gorsley Baptist Chapel 1852–1952* (copy in GA, NC 46), 8. For Hall, see *Glouc. J.* 28 May 1881; P. Goodland, *The Greening of Wild Places: English Village Life Over Two Centuries – The Story of Gorsley Baptist Church 1800–2002* (2002).
19 Hockaday Abs. ccl; see above, Dymock, religious hist. (religious life).
20 GA, P 188/IN 1/6; GDR, T 1/108.
21 GDR, D 16/3/16; Hockaday Abs. ccl.
22 *Nat. Soc. Inquiry, 1846–7*, Glos. 10–11.
23 J.E. Gethyn-Jones, *St. Mary's Church, Kempley, and its Paintings* (1961), 33.
24 TNA, HO 129/335/2/2/4.
25 Ibid. HO 129/335/2/2/5.
26 Copy of deed dated 8 Aug. 1856 in 'Glimpses of Life in Kempley' (exhibition organized by Ms E.M. Goulding in Kempley Baptist chapel 13–16 Oct. 2006); datestone on bldg.
27 GA, D 2052.
28 Ibid. D 5292; MCA, I 5iv, bdl. 88C, no 50; OS Map 6", Glos. XVI. NE (1924 edn).
29 Above, manor.
30 TNA, ED 7/37, Kempley National School; GA, P 125/MI 17.
31 GA, P 188/IN 1/6; GDR vol. 385, p. 130; *Kelly's Dir. Glos.* (1885), 510; (1889) 826.

51. *Church of St Edward King and Confessor from the north-west*

Churchman,[1] and within two years the earl had built a vicarage house[2] and a temporary church further south on the lane. The parish church continued to be used save, within a few years, during the winter.[3]

Drummond immediately introduced changes in church services and started a choir. In the parish church the gallery was removed and the pews altered and Drummond himself scraped the church's walls to reveal its medieval paintings.[4] A chalice and paten of 1876 were bought by subscription.[5] Drummond's successors, particularly Edward Denny from 1886, made other innovations, including sung masses, the occasional use of vestments and incense, and services at Corpus Christi and other festivals. Denny faced vehement opposition, led by a churchwarden, and church life was seriously disrupted. The impasse was solved by Denny's departure in 1898,[6] his resignation apparently being forced by a noisy demonstration around the vicarage house for three days and nights.[7] On his arrival in Kempley Denny's successor received an address pleading for a simpler and more traditional Sunday morning service but he agreed only to conduct the monthly communion service, by then on the first Sunday, without music. There were several Protestant missions to Kempley Green during the 1890s and 1900s and local people continued to attend the nonconformist chapels there and at Fishpool.[8] In 1885 stock was substituted for Elizabeth Pyndar's endowment of the monthly communion service[9] and by 1890 the income from it fell short of £3.[10]

The Building of a Second Church

In 1902 work began on a new church near the temporary church. A project of William Lygon, 7th Earl Beauchamp, its foundations were laid before the earl entrusted its design to A. Randall Wells, recently clerk of works for the architect William Lethaby at Brockhampton church in Herefordshire.[11] The church, intended for High Church worship, was built of Forest of Dean sandstone and local timber with direct local labour. Wells's designs, in adopting Lethaby's 'primitive' style, adapted several elements used at Brockhampton and included a lychgate at the entrance to the churchyard. The chancel and nave are enveloped by a single steep roof, which drops

---

1 *Oxford DNB*; see *VCH Worcs.* IV, 121.
2 Above (patronage and endowment: vicarage houses).
3 GA, D 5292; OS Map 6", Glos. XVI.NE (1889 edn).
4 GA, D 5292; P 188/VE 2/1.
5 *Glos. Ch. Plate*, 128.
6 GA, D 5292; P 188/CW 2/1.
7 Theodora C. Reeves, 'History of Little Marcle and of Preston Parish' (1972: typescript in Glos. Colln. 36709), 124–5.
8 GA, D 5292.
9 MCA, J 3ii, bdl. 114C, nos 7–8.
10 GA, P 188/CH 1.
11 Ibid. D 5292. For the ch. and its fittings, see C. Nicholson and C. Spooner, *Recent English Ecclesiastical Architecture* (n.d. [1911]), 127: photocopy in GA, D 7322; *Country Life*, 19 Aug. 1916, suppl. 2, 4; Verey and Brooks, *Glos.* II, 551–2.

almost to the ground on the south side and was covered with stone slates (replaced with clay pantiles c.1970). On the north side the building incorporates from east to west a lady chapel, a vestry, and a tall porch entrance beneath a tower. The chamber west of the tower was added in 1908 to accommodate heating apparatus.[1] The dominant architectural features are the west window filled with a diamond grid of mullions and transoms and the scissor-trusses of the open roof. The east wall is windowless. Simple details include triangular window heads and a saddle-back roof over the tower and the plain masonry is punctuated by carvings by Laurence Turner. A figure of Christ over the porch was executed by Wells assisted by the builder, Richard James of Brookland's Farm.[2]

The furnishings are mostly products of the Arts and Crafts Movement made by collaborators of Lethaby and Wells such as Ernest Gimson and Ernest Barnsley.[3] George Smallman of Fishpool was responsible for the ironwork.[4] The two rood figures which together with the decoration of a roof truss mark the division between nave and chancel were carved by David Gibb of London, a maker of ship figureheads. Earl Beauchamp donated a high-altar baldachin supported on baroque columns.

The Twentieth Century

Services were held in the new church from 1903 but before dedicating it to St Edward King and Confessor the bishop ordered the removal of an altar stone from the lady chapel and several other fittings;[5] they were reinstated soon after the bishop's resignation in 1905.[6] In 1907 an incoming vicar decided to use vestments only at principal festivals and not to revive the practice of sung masses every Sunday, and the number of candlesticks on the main altar of St Edward's was reduced to two. The new vicar also agreed, at the bishop's request, to use St Mary's church for the monthly communion service and in the summer for two Sunday services a month.[7]

Following a major restoration in 1913 St Mary's was used every Sunday. The restoration, funded primarily by voluntary donations, had widespread support within the diocese and beyond on account of the church's ancient frescoes.[8] Under the architect Temple Moore the tower was strengthened, the nave ceiling was raised, and the 12th-century south and west doors, which had been kept in the tower, were reinstated in the nave's doorways. New fittings and furnishings were acquired or given, a harmonium being installed in the place of the pew north of the chancel arch, and Blaisdon parish donated its old, 16th-century, font and Earl and Countess Beauchamp returned the tazza donated in 1705,[9] having bought it at a private sale in 1908.[10] One of the medieval bells, long damaged, was recast.[11]

Daniel Gethyn-Jones, vicar 1921–60, played a key role in the restoration of the frescoes in St Mary's between 1955 and 1958.[12] St Edward's was consecrated in 1934 and licensed for marriages in 1943,[13] and in 1975 it was made the parish church and St Mary's was declared redundant.[14] Kempley had a resident Anglican clergyman until the union of benefices in 1975.[15] After that the church was served from Dymock[16] and from 2000 by a team of ministers headed by a woman living in Redmarley D'Abitot.[17] The monthly communion service established by Elizabeth Pyndar's charity was supported by the Kempley charity in 2006.[18] The Baptist chapel at Kempley Green, where regular Sunday evening services ceased by the 1980s, was used for a Sunday school and occasional services in 2006.[19]

---

1 GA, D 5292.
2 Above, Fig. 51; Verey and Brooks, *Glos.* II, 551, names Wells's assistant as Wal. James. For Ric. James as builder, see GA, D 5929; *Kelly's Dir. Glos.* (1889), 825; (1906), 224.
3 M. Greensted, *Gimson and the Barnsleys* (Stroud, 1991) 178–80.
4 For Smallman at Fishpool, see GA SL 310.
5 GA, P 188/IN 1/1; D 5292.
6 Gethyn-Jones, *St. Mary's Church* (1961), 37.
7 GA, D 5292.
8 Ibid. P 188/CW 2/2.
9 *Ledbury Reporter*, 29 Nov. 1913; MCA, D 2i, no 7. St Mary's baluster font stood in the porch of St Edward's ch. in 2002.
10 GA, D 5292.
11 *Glos. Ch. Bells*, 393.
12 Gethyn-Jones, *St. Mary's Church* (1961), passim.
13 GA, P 188/ IN 2/3.
14 Ibid. D 7322.
15 *Glouc. Dioc. Year Book* (1955–6), 10, 28–9; (1965–6), 28–9, 66; (1977), 23, 42.
16 Ibid. (1978), 21, 42.
17 *Dioc. of Glouc. Dir.* (2001–2), 24–5, 122
18 http://www.charity-commission.gov.uk/registeredcharities (accessed 15 June 2007: no 202981); for the Kempley charity, above, soc. hist. (charities for the poor).
19 Information from 'Glimpses of Life in Kempley' and from Ms E.M. Goulding of Newent.

LONGHOPE

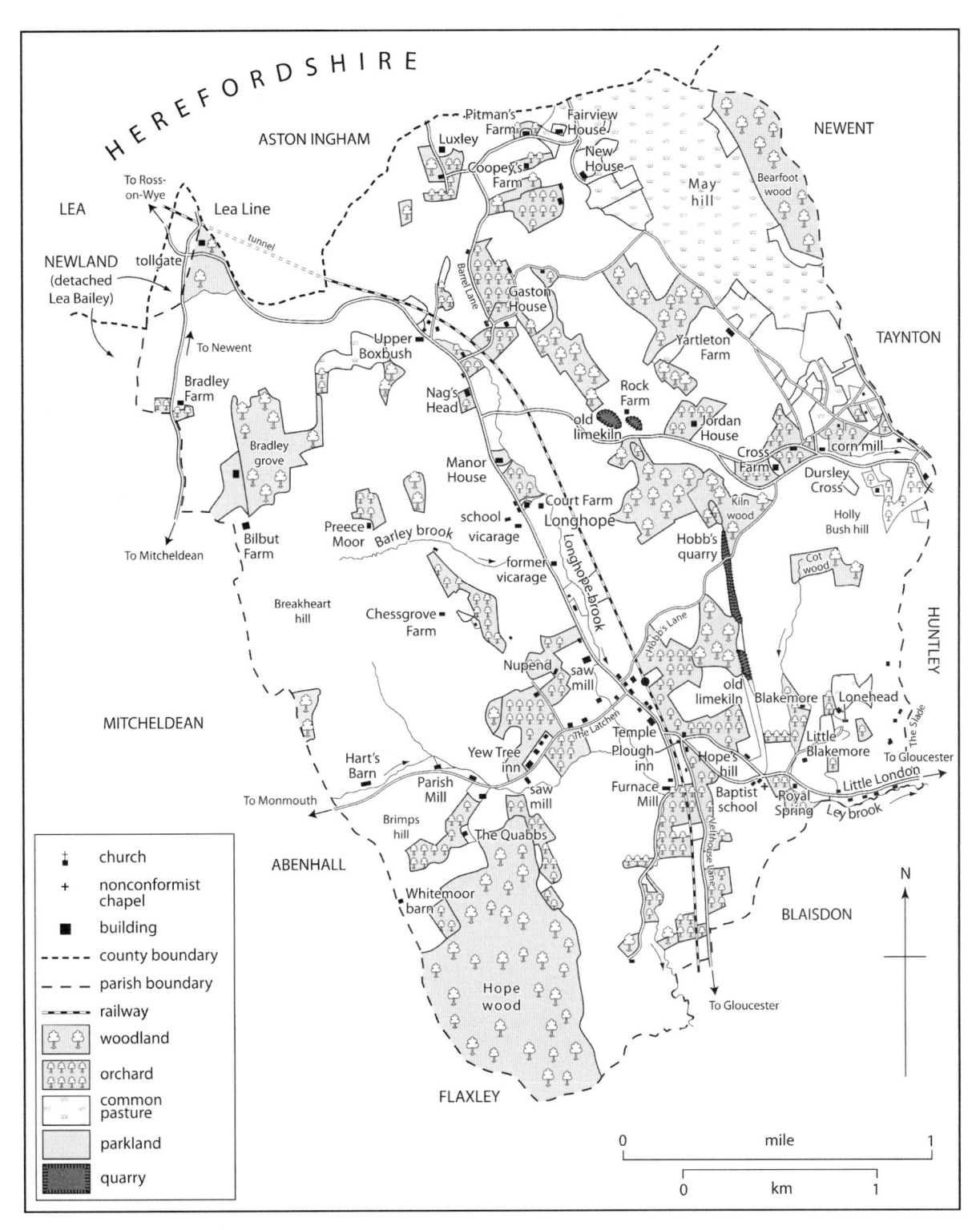

Map 11. *Longhope 1870*

LONGHOPE is a hilly and wooded parish lying 15 km west of Gloucester on Gloucestershire's ancient boundary with Herefordshire close to the Forest of Dean. Taken into the jurisdiction of the Forest in the early Middle Ages and among the places disafforested in the early 14th century,[1] Longhope was known after early lords as Hope Baderon in the mid 12th century and Hope Monmouth in the early 13th.[2] Woodland and carrying trades provided employment for many inhabitants and in the 17th century ironworks operated on several sites. In more recent times wood turning remained among the mainstays of the economy.

BOUNDARIES AND DIVISIONS

The ancient parish covered 3,153 a. (1,276 ha) in a rough circle taking in the summit of May hill in the north-east.[3] Its boundaries, marked mostly by ancient paths and streams, included on the south a tributary of the Longhope brook dividing Hope wood from the Flaxley woods and called 'Tinbridge Sith' in 1667[4] and on the south-east the uppermost stretch of the Ley brook. In the north-west the parish projected between the old route of the Gloucester–Hereford road on the east and the Mitcheldean–Newent road on the west to a point at Lea Line.[5]

The parish contained two divisions for the purposes of civil government in the early modern period.[6] Although the precise boundary between the two parts was unknown at the end of the 19th century,[7] the lower division, in the south, was the larger. The upper division covered the northern end of the parish, including Dursley Cross, and contained the parish church.[8]

In 1935 106 a. below Bradley grove in the north-west was transferred to Mitcheldean.[9] In 1965 the small projection to the north at Lea Line was added to Lea (Herefs.) to leave Longhope with 3,034 a. (1,228 ha).[10]

LANDSCAPE

As indicated in its name the parish's primary feature is the valley of the Longhope brook.[11] It falls from 110 m in the north to 45 m in the south, and on both sides steep hills, cloven by small streams, rise above 150 m, reaching 217 m on Breakheart hill to the west and 296 m on May hill to the north-east. On the west the land is formed by Old Red sandstones of the Devonian period and on the north-east by older Silurian sandstones.[12] May hill was formerly known as Yartledon (later Yartleton)[13] and its summit, the site of a beacon where the neighbourhood traditionally kept watch and ward,[14] was the place for ancient May Day rites enacted by men from surrounding parishes.[15] Springs on Breakheart hill feed a tributary stream known in the early 17th century as Barley brook.[16] Another stream running down from Mitcheldean between Breakheart hill and Brimps hill to the south was, like the Longhope brook, dammed in several places to form ponds to power mills and ironworks. The east of the parish is drained by the Ley brook, which flows eastwards from a source at Royal Spring.[17]

Most cultivation in Longhope has always been in closes and orchards were being established by the end of the Middle Ages. The ancient woodland, of which Hope wood in the south was recorded in 1227,[18] was extensive and subject to common pasture rights. The top of May hill was cleared of its woodland, apart from Bearfoot (formerly Fairfoot) wood on the east side,[19] and remained common land until 1874.[20] At the inclosure a clump of fir trees on the summit, possibly first planted in the mid 18th century,[21] was reserved in a circle of 4 a. for the recreation of the inhabitants of Longhope and its neighbourhood.[22] Since then the clump has been occasionally renewed, trees to mark the Golden Jubilee of 1887 and the Silver Jubilee of 1977 being

---

1 *VCH Glos.* V, 295–7. This account was written between 2005 and 2007.
2 *Pipe R* 1167 (PRS 11), 143; *Pleas of the Crown for Glos.* ed. Maitland, 80. See below, manor. The forms Hallilda Hope and Hope Eilildis were also recorded in the mid 12th cent.: *Cal. Doc. France*, 403–4, 409–10.
3 *OS Area Book* (1880).
4 C. Hart, *The Forest of Dean: New History 1550–1818* (1995), 180. The Flaxley woods included Timbridge wood, in which Longhope's vicar claimed tithes in 1542: *VCH Glos.* V, 138; Hockaday Abs. cclxiii.
5 Hart, *Forest of Dean: New History*, 180; Bryant, *Map of Glos.* (1824). See above, Map 11.
6 Below, local govt. (parochial govt.).
7 See GA, DA/24/100/2, p. 23. The divisions are described here from rate and tax assessments of the mid 18th cent. and the census of 1841: GA, D 3436/1; Q/REl 1, Duchy of Lancaster hundred 1776; TNA, HO 107/361.
8 GDR vol. 383, no cxvii.
9 *Census*, 1931 (pt. ii).
10 Ibid. 1971; see GA, D 2428/1/65, ff. 23, 38, 42.
11 *PN Glos.* III, 191.
12 Geol. Surv. Maps 1:50,000, solid and drift, sheet 216 (1988 edn); sheet 234 (1972 edn).
13 Above, Newent, introd. (landscape). See *PN Glos.* III, 192–3.
14 GA, D 1803/1.
15 Rudder, *Glos.* 533; Fosbrooke, *Glos.* II, 224.
16 GA, D 36/T 18; GDR, V 5/193T 5.
17 OS Map 6", Glos. XXIV.SW (1889 edn).
18 *Flaxley Cart.* pp. 108–9.
19 Birmingham City Archives, Barnard Colln. 940; GA, D 1297, survey of Huntley, Netherley, and Longhope 1717, Longhope no 16.
20 GA, Q/RI 91.
21 Ibid. D 1297, surv. 1717, Longhope no 16; Taylor, *Map of Glos.* (1777). The prominence of the crown of trees in the wider landscape is evident in an illus. of 1790: Bigland, *Glos.* I, 426.
22 GA, Q/RI 91.

among new plantings.[1] The rest of the top of the hill was acquired by the National Trust in 1935.[2]

In 1841 there was an estimated 460 a. of woodland in Longhope. The largest area was Hope wood with 177 a.[3] and among the smaller areas were those south of Dursley Cross known in 1785 as Kiln and Coleshare (later Cot) woods.[4] Bradley grove, covering 52 a. on a spur in the north-west of the parish, was reduced in area in the mid 19th century[5] and again in the later 20th.[6] Woodland accounted for 392 a. in Longhope in 1905[7] and new planting took place on the upper slopes of May hill in the 20th century. The land has been quarried in many places, particularly along the sides of May hill where continuous limestone outcrops[8] were extensively worked in the 18th and 19th centuries.[9] Earlier quarrying presumably created Crocket's Hole, a place near the hill's summit reputed in the early 18th century to have been a hiding place in time of religious persecution and civil war.[10]

ROADS AND RAILWAY

Two main roads from Gloucester wind through Longhope as continuations of a Roman road leading westwards from the city.[11] In the later 17th century, despite following narrow and in places very steep lanes, both were major routes towards Wales. That to Ross-on-Wye (Herefs.) and Hereford[12] ran over the southern end of May hill, on which a wayside cross marked a crossroads at Dursley Cross,[13] and continued on a curving course to Lea Line. There it crossed the road from Mitcheldean to Newent and descended Lea hill, once known as the devil's bowling green.[14] The Monmouth road, further south,[15] climbed from Little London before descending Hope's hill into the Longhope valley by way of Old Hill, a steep drop at a place known in the later 19th century as the Steps[16] near the bottom of which stood a wayside cross.[17] The road continued north-westwards up the valley for a short distance before turning west, away from the road leading up the valley to the parish church and a junction with the Ross road, to run along the Latchen and up the tributary valley towards Mitcheldean and the Forest of Dean.[18]

The Ross and Monmouth roads were turnpiked through Longhope in 1726 and 1747 respectively.[19] Both roads, together with the road from Mitcheldean to Lea Line which was part of the same trust from 1769,[20] remained turnpiked until 1880.[21] In the mid or late 1820s the Ross road, the route of which was likened to one of the plagues of Egypt,[22] was moved southwards at Dursley Cross and the Monmouth road was straightened through Little London and diverted southwards on its descent on Hope's hill to Longhope village.[23] Under an Act of 1833, the Ross road was diverted in the north-west corner of Longhope to take an easier route down Lea hill in a cutting south of Lea Line. The course there of the Mitcheldean–Newent road was also altered.[24] In the 1850s a section of the Ross road in the north-west was shifted again to the south to accommodate a railway.[25] A tollhouse erected near Hopesbrook in the 1840s was altered to face the new road to its south[26] but in 1871 the tollgate was further west, just outside the parish at the crossroads south of Lea Line.[27] In 1975 the road over Hope's hill was widened and a new road built south of the village to carry through traffic on the Monmouth road.[28]

Many old lanes and paths cross and climb the sides of the Longhope valley and of May hill, some later abandoned. Justy Path recorded on the western boundary in 1667[29] may have been the Monmouth

---

1 *Kelly's Dir. Glos.* (1889), 833; GA, D 3921/III/15.
2 *Properties of the National Trust* (1974), 79.
3 GDR, T 1/116.
4 GA, D 2123, pp. 145, 147.
5 GDR, T 1/116; OS Map 6", Glos. XXIII.SE (1883 edn).
6 OS Maps 1:25,000, SO 61, SO 62 (1957 edn); personal observation.
7 Acreage Returns, 1905.
8 Geol. Surv. Maps 1:50,000, solid and drift, sheet 216 (1988 edn); sheet 234 (1972 edn).
9 D. Bick, 'Lime-Kilns in North-West Gloucestershire', *Glos. Soc. Ind. Archaeol. J.* (1984), 4–9.
10 Bodleian, Top. Glouc. c. 3, f. 140v.; GA, D 4869/1/2/6; GDR, T 1/116 (no 147). See D. Bick, 'The Enigma of Crocket's Holes, Newent', *The New Regard* 5 (Forest of Dean Local History Soc., 1989), 62–4.
11 I.D. Margary, *Roman Roads in Britain*, II (1957), 59–62.
12 Ogilby, *Britannia* (1675), plate 71.
13 The cross's remains, its base, are at the place marked on OS Map, Glos. XXIV.SW (1889 edn).
14 *The Times*, 11 June 1835.
15 Ogilby, *Britannia* (1675), plate 15.
16 OS Map 6", Glos. XXIV.SW (1889 edn).
17 The position of the cross's base has been moved from that shown on ibid. (1924 edn).
18 Taylor, *Map of Glos.* (1777): Bryant, *Map of Glos.* (1824).
19 Glouc. & Heref. Roads Acts, 12 Geo. I, c. 13; 20 Geo. II, c. 31.
20 Glouc. & Heref. Roads Act, 9 Geo. III, c. 50.
21 Annual Turnpike Acts Continuance Act, 1880, 43 & 44 Vic. c. 12.
22 C. Heath, *The Excursion down the Wye* (1826), s.v. May Hill.
23 Bryant, *Map of Glos.* (1824); Greenwood, *Map of Glos.* (1824); OS Map 1", sheet 43 (1831 edn).
24 Huntley, Mitcheldean, & Elton Roads Act, 3 Wm. IV, c. 75 (Local and Personal); GA, Q/Rum 128. See D. Bick, 'Two More Tollhouses', *The New Regard* 17 (Forest of Dean Local Hist. Soc., 2002), 34.
25 GDR, T 1/116; OS Map 6", Glos. XXIII.SE (1883 edn). For the railway, below, this section.
26 Bick, 'Two More Tollhouses', 31–4. There was a resident gate keeperin 1851: TNA, HO 107/1959.
27 TNA, RG 10/2605; OS Map 6", Glos. XXIII.SE (1883 edn).
28 *The Longhope Village Appraisal 1991* (copy in VCH Glos. office), 4.
29 Hart, *Forest of Dean: New History*, 180.

road. Jane Shell Lane, recorded in 1797, ran south-westwards to join the Monmouth road near the foot of Old Hill.[1]

A route from Dursley Cross to Mitcheldean, described in 1692 as a market way, ran south-westwards down the side of the Longhope valley[2] and was later known as Hobb's Lane. Yartleton Lane, which emerges from a criss-cross of lanes just above Dursley Cross,[3] runs north-westwards along the side of May hill and its highest section, over boggy ground, was made a public highway when the hill's summit was inclosed in 1874.[4] Lower down to the west Barrel Lane is the road branching off the Ross road northwards towards Aston Ingham (Herefs.). In the late 19th century the principal minor roads out of the village were Velthouse Lane leading southwards to Blaisdon and Hobb's Lane leading north-eastwards up to Dursley Cross.[5] Hobb's Lane has been reduced to a footpath for part of its course. Mill Lane leads southwards to Furnace Mill, where a stone bridge surviving over the Longhope brook provided a way towards the southern end of the parish below Hope wood.[6]

The railway line from Gloucester to Hereford opened up the Longhope valley as far as Hopesbrook by the Ross road in 1853. On the line's completion in 1855 a station opened beside the village.[7] The line closed in 1964.[8] The bridge that carried it over Barrel Lane was in place in 2005.

POPULATION

There were at least 13 tenant households on the Longhope estate in 1086[9] and 54 men and women were assessed for tax in Longhope and its hamlet of Blaisdon in 1327.[10] In Longhope alone 45 men were named in a muster of 1542[11] and there were c.180 communicants in the parish in 1551[12] and 63 households in 1563.[13] Two hundred and ten communicants were recorded in 1603[14] and one hundred families in 1650.[15] The population was estimated at 500 c.1710[16] and 470 c.1775,[17] the latter figure possibly an underestimate for in 1801 the population was 636. There was steady growth to 1,104 in 1861 but the population then declined to 971 in 1881 and 863 in 1901. After the First World War it rose to 957 in 1931 and, with only small losses from the boundary changes of 1935 and 1965, it grew from 1,031 in 1951 to 1,491 in 1991, most of that increase accompanying new building in the village after 1971. The population in 2001 was 1,474.[18]

SETTLEMENT

Medieval settlement in Longhope was scattered. The village developed much later where the road to the parish church branched off the Monmouth road in the Longhope valley. The high ground was sparsely settled but encroachments on the commons on the eastern side of the parish in the 18th and 19th centuries led to the creation of groups of cottages on some of the hillsides there.

THE VILLAGE

The medieval parish church, 1 km from the old Monmouth road, stands low down by the line of a former road across the valley. Court Farm, to the east, occupies the site of the medieval manor[19] and was known as the Court House in the early 18th century, when the Longhope brook flowed between it and the churchyard.[20] The vicarage house, recorded from the early 15th century, stood a little to the south.[21] The house there ceased to be used by the vicars at the end of the 18th century[22] and became a farmhouse.[23]

During the later 18th and early 19th century several houses and cottages were built along the Monmouth road into the southern end of the road to the church (Church Road). Of the older dwellings strung out on the two roads most are of the 17th or early 18th century but The Cruck House in Church Road contains the remains of a 15th-century hall.[24] Further

---

1 GA, D 5412/III/91.
2 Ibid. D 36/T 23; D 2123, p. 147.
3 OS Map 1", sheet 43 (1831 edn).
4 GA, Q/RI 91; see *Glouc. J.* 12 June 1875.
5 GA, DA 24/100/2, pp. 233–4.
6 OS Maps 1", sheet 43 (1831 edn); 6", Glos. XXIV.SW (1889 edn).
7 E.T. MacDermot, *Hist. GWR*, revised C.R. Clinker (1964), I, 207, 454–5; OS Maps 6", Glos. XXIII.SE (1883 edn); XXIV.SW (1889 edn).
8 *VCH Glos.* X, 6.
9 *Domesday Book* (Rec. Com.), I, 167.
10 *Glos. Subsidy Roll*, 1327, 43.
11 *L&P Hen. VIII*, XVII, 499.
12 J. Gairdner, 'Bishop Hooper's Visitation of Gloucester', *EHR* 19 (1904), 120.
13 Bodleian, Rawl. C. 790, f. 27v.
14 *Eccl. Misc.* 100.
15 C.R. Elrington, 'The Survey of Church Livings in Gloucestershire, 1650', *Trans. BGAS* 83 (1964), 98.
16 Atkyns, *Glos.* 546.
17 Rudder, *Glos.* 534.
18 *Census*, 1801–2001.
19 GDR, V 5/193T 1.
20 GA, D 1297, surv. 1717, Longhope nos 9, 19.
21 Reg. Lacy, 115 n.; GDR, V 5/193T 1.
22 C. Dighton, *The Dightons of Clifford Chambers* (1902), 28.
23 TNA, HO 107/1959; RG 9/1758.
24 Below (bldgs.).

north, in a small cluster opposite the church, Marle Cottage, once the property of the parish,[1] dates from the 16th century and Court Leet, to its north, was built in the later 17th century.[2]

On the Monmouth road the Plough inn, that stood opposite Knapp House near the foot of Old Hill,[3] survived until road widening in 1975.[4] Of the newer houses by the Monmouth road Coglan House, opposite the entrance to the Latchen, was occupied by the landowner Robert Coghlan[5] (d. 1803 or 1804).[6] The Temple, an early 19th-century gentleman's residence, has become a hotel.

Elsewhere the Manor House, to the north beyond the church, occupies the site of the seat of the Yate family.[7] Rebuilt for the Probyns in the early 19th century,[8] it is set in grounds intersected by the Longhope brook and with an approach from the Ross road[9] and was a hotel in the mid 20th century[10] and a nursing home later. The Old Rectory, south-west of the church, was built as the vicarage house in the later 1820s with a schoolroom in an outbuilding.[11] The house became a nursing home in the late 20th century.

From the mid 19th century more houses were built at the south end of Church Road and to the south-east by the new line of the Monmouth road up Hope's hill. New building also took place on the Monmouth road in the Latchen. There a small house opposite a pound[12] was rebuilt by the Norwich Union Fire Office in 1852, the year after it had burnt down,[13] and another house, further west, was replaced in the 1860s by Tyndale Villa, built by Evan Butler, a Cheltenham carpenter.[14] A horse trough placed by parishioners opposite the entrance to the Latchen in 1904[15] was used for a floral display in 2007. A memorial to local men killed in the First World War, taking the form of a recumbent lion on a stone pedestal at the foot of Old Hill, was given by its creator, Walter Davis of Hereford, and unveiled in 1928.[16] Private and council building both contributed to the development of the village in the 20th century. Council houses were built on Church Road, the first being three pairs near the church in the early 1930s[17] and several more, including an estate of six pairs,

52. *Pound House*

following in the late 1940s and early 1950s.[18] Other new buildings after the Second World War included a police station on Church Road.[19] In the 1970s and 1980s more houses were built in the Latchen[20] and private developers built many bungalows and detached houses on the west side of the village. Some of the new houses encroached on Nupend, an ancient farmstead[21] where the house had been rebuilt in the early 19th century.[22] Private development continued on land in Church Road in the early 21st century.

OUTLYING SETTLEMENT

The East Side

Several farmhouses and cottages stood on Hope's hill in the early 18th century.[23] Zion House, below the brow of the hill, dates from the mid 19th century, being the manse of a chapel built there earlier, in

---

1 GDR, T 1/116 (no 479); GA, D 2299/1977.
2 Below (bldgs.).
3 OS Map 6", Glos. XXIV.SW (1889 edn).
4 See above, introd. (roads and railway).
5 Rudge, *Hist. of Glos.* II, 57; GA, D 5412/III/91.
6 TNA, PROB 11/1404, ff. 276–279v.; see GDR, T 1/116 (no 1003).
7 Below, manor (manor: the Manor Ho.).
8 Below (bldgs.).
9 See Bryant, *Map of Glos.* (1824); GDR, T 1/116.
10 *Kelly's Dir. Glos.* (1939). 252; OS Map 1:2,500, SO 6820–6920 (1970 edn).
11 GA, D 23/E 43; Dighton, *Dightons of Clifford Chambers*, 28–9; GDR, V 6/64B.

12 GDR, T 1/118; OS Map 6", Glos. XXIV.SW (1889 edn).
13 Inscr. on ho., shown in Fig. 52.
14 GA, D 1819; see TNA, RG 10/2604.
15 Inscr. on trough; see Richardson, *Wells and Springs of Glos.* 113.
16 *Glouc. J.* 30 June 1928; Verey and Brooks, *Glos.* II, 575.
17 GA, DA 24/600/1.
18 Ibid. DA 24/602/1.
19 Ibid. DA 24/100/15, f. 56; G. Sindrey and T. Heath, 'Forest of Dean Police Stations 1840 to 2000', *The New Regard* 15 (Forest of Dean Local Hist. Soc., 2000), 52.
20 GA, DA 24/602/3.
21 *Military Surv. of Glos.* 1522, 207.
22 GA, D 2174/7; GDR, T 1/116 (no 602).
23 GA, D 3436/1, burials 18 Mar. 1711, 30 May 1717, 5 Mar. 1723.

1846.[1] To the east Royal Spring, a farmhouse south of the Monmouth road at the place called Blackmoor (or Blackmire) green in the early 18th century, was rebuilt by William Kendale (d. 1778), a Gloucester innholder.[2] In the mid 1950s an estate of ten council houses was built on the opposite side of the road right up against Little Blakemore,[3] a farmhouse that was copyhold until 1913.[4] The house at Blakemore, to the north, was part of one of the larger farmsteads in Longhope in the mid 19th century[5] and was the centre of a farm park in 2006. Several small farmhouses used to stand at Lonehead, high up to the north-east of Little Blakemore;[6] the last remaining house there was enlarged in the late 20th century.

Towards the eastern boundary small farmhouses and cottages straggle along the Monmouth road in the place known as Little London by the early 18th century.[7] In the late 19th and early 20th century a number of dwellings there were rebuilt or refronted and new buildings included a house with a shop in matching style. Building on the common on the hillsides north of the road had begun by the early 18th century[8] and led to the creation of the scattered settlement called the Slade.

In the south-east of the parish a few houses stand at irregular intervals along Velthouse Lane. The oldest is Peach Tree Cottage, a small 17th-century dwelling, at the north end.[9] Those built in the later 20th century face west across the valley towards Hope wood. In Mill Lane the principal buildings are associated with the former Furnace Mill and the tannery that operated next to it in the 19th century.[10]

The West Side

On the west side of the parish several farmsteads and mills were built along the valley leading up to Mitcheldean. The house at Brook Farm, sandwiched between the Monmouth road and the stream, dates from the 17th century.[11] The farmstead at Hart's Barn, further up the valley, was probably named after the family of Robert the Hart (*fl.* 1380).[12] Its house, long the property of the Sergeaunt family,[13] was enlarged in the early 18th century[14] and the outbuildings, mostly dating from the 18th and 19th centuries, were converted in mid 1990s as a craft and veterinary centre.[15] Set back in a combe on the south side of the valley the Quabbs was a copyhold cottage in the early 18th century.[16]

Three early farmsteads stand high on Breakheart hill, to the north. Chessgrove Farm, to the east of which was a common with only one other dwelling on its edge in the early 18th century,[17] had a large collection of buildings in the 19th century.[18] Preece Moor, further north, is recorded from 1608[19] and Bilbut Farm, over the brow of the hill looking to the west was called Great Bilbut in 1619.[20] To the north Forest Court, on the west side of Bradley grove, was built as a country house, on land taken from the wood, shortly before 1870 and was known originally as Bradley Grove and later as Bradley Court.[21] In the 20th century it was in turn an agricultural college, a riding school,[22] a hotel, and a nursing home.[23] The farmstead at Lyndors Farm, north-east of Bradley grove, was established in the 20th century.[24] Lower down to the west two farmsteads stood on the Mitcheldean–Newent road. Known as Great and Little Bradley, both belonged to the curates (later vicars) of Flaxley from 1737[25] and Little Bradley, the southern one, was demolished before the mid 19th century.[26]

There are also small groups of houses in the west of Longhope by the Ross road in the area known in the late 19th century as the Upper End.[27] The older houses date mostly from the 18th and 19th centuries and included clusters of farmsteads at the end of Barrel Lane and further along the road at the place originally called Boxbush.[28] Upper Boxbush House, south-west of the road, is a mid 17th-century farmhouse that belonged to the curates (later vicars)

1 TNA, RG 11/2525; date on chapel. For the chapel, below, religious hist.
2 GA, D 7631, Longhope deeds 1720–1853.
3 Ibid. DA 24/602/1; OS Map 1/2,500, SO 6818–6918 (1972 edn).
4 GA, D 2667.
5 GDR, T 1/116 (no 948).
6 Ibid. (nos 909A, 925); see GA, D 2667.
7 GA, D 3436/1, burials 6 Oct. 1719, 24 Apr. 1726.
8 GA, D 1297, surv. 1717, Longhope no 16.
9 DoE List, Longhope (1985), 6/139.
10 See below, econ, hist. (corn mills and ironworks; other industry and trade).
11 DoE List, Longhope, 6/130.
12 *Cal. Pat.* 1377–81, 453.
13 Below, manor (other estates: Hart's Barn).
14 Below (bldgs.).
15 Verey and Brooks, *Glos.* II, 575; *Citizen*, 13 May, 1993; 29 May 1996; *Forester*, 9 Aug., 13 Sept. 1996.
16 GA, D 3436/1, burial 23 May 1712; D 1297, surv. 1717, Longhope no 24.
17 GA, D 1297, surv. 1717, Longhope no 8.
18 GDR, T 1/116 (no 527); OS Map 6", Glos. XXIII.SE (1883 edn).
19 TNA, PROB 11/112, ff. 225v.–226v.
20 J. Maclean, 'The History of the Manors of Dene Magna and Abenhall', *Trans. BGAS* 6 (1881–2), 207.
21 *Kelly's Dir. Glos.* (1870), 598; GA, D 543, Longhope deeds 1828–80, deed 24 Dec. 1880.
22 *Kelly's Dir. Glos.* (1906–39 edns).
23 P. Mason, *A Glance Back at Mitcheldean* (2001), 14; OS Map 1:2,500, SO 6620–6720 (1970 edn).
24 OS Maps 6", Glos. XXIII.SE (1924 edn); 1:2,500, SO 6620–6720 (1970 edn).
25 GA, D 2362, deeds 1718–1892; for the Flaxley curacy (later vicarage), see *VCH Glos.* V, 147–8.
26 GA, D 1297, surv. 1717, Longhope nos 6, 17, 25; GDR, T 1/116.
27 GA, D 10336; *Kelly's Dir. Glos.* (1894), 226.
28 GA, D 6/E 4, no 4; GDR, T 1/116.

of Maisemore between 1745 and 1925.[1] The Farmer's Boy opposite it was a small farmhouse in the mid 18th century.[2] Further along the road Dean End high up at Lea Line was built in the early 19th century to replace a dwelling on a slightly different site and was known originally as Blenheim House.[3]

The North End: May Hill

Scattered settlement has taken place on the lower slopes of May hill in the north-east of the parish. On the southern slopes dwellings probably existed at Rock Farm and Jordan House, above the Ross road, by 1327 when John and Sibyl Hunter and Roger Jordan were recorded in Longhope;[4] Rock Farm (sometimes the Rock) was called Hunter's in 1633.[5] A residential park lower down to the west on the road originated as a caravan park in the mid 1950s.[6]

There was also early settlement higher up to the east at Dursley (sometimes Durley) Cross.[7] Roger of Durley was among those recorded in the parish in 1327[8] and the name Durley was used for land some way south of the Ross road.[9] Cross Farm, a copyhold known as Lower House in 1667,[10] stands south of the old line of the Ross road and its house, probably of late medieval date, was rebuilt in the early 18th century.[11] In the early 18th century a few cottages and small farmsteads stood higher up to the north-east on the edges of the commons on May hill.[12] More cottages were built by squatter development on the commons in the later 18th and early 19th century[13] and much scattered building has taken place in the area since the inclosure of 1874.[14] To the north, higher up the hill, there was a house in Bearfoot wood in the early 18th century[15] and a few cottages on the wood's edge, including at Crocket's Hole, in the mid 19th.[16] A cottage, formerly the keeper's lodge,[17] remained at the southern edge in 2005.

May Hill House, standing north-west of Dursley Cross on the site of Yartleton Farm,[18] perhaps the copyhold Yartleton House in 1642,[19] took its name on its creation as the residence of H.A. Pringle in the 1930s. May Hill Lodge, further along Yartleton Lane, was an entirely new house built for Pringle.[20] The few dwellings further north-west were built on the edge of the common, Wingate's Farm being in 1826 a cottage known as the New House.[21] Of the farmsteads below the lane Coopey's Farm, near the foot of the hill, contains a cottage of the early 17th century. The former farmhouse of Pitman's Farm is later and in stone, and a stone outbuilding to the south-east has been converted as a dwelling. The house at Fairfield, higher up to the east, was built in the mid 19th century[22] and was known originally as Fairview House.[23]

Lower down to the west a few houses are spaced irregularly on Barrel Lane. While some cottages there were rebuilt in the 19th century, the older surviving buildings include The Old Farm and Gaston Cottage in a cluster of dwellings at the bottom of a lane off May hill, the latter being where the vicar C.M. Dighton lived in 1825.[24] The cottage at Luxley, in the north, was part of a copyhold farmstead in the 19th century.[25]

BUILDINGS

Early Buildings

Two of Longhope's oldest surviving domestic buildings were substantial houses with open halls. The stone-walled Cruck House in Church Road retains a cruck truss and the remains of a spere truss from a 15th-century hall, into which a floor and a chimney were inserted in the 16th or 17th century. Marle Cottage opposite the church has a complete 16th-century cross wing. The wing, which retains close studding indicative of a high-status house, was extended westwards by a bay in the 17th century.[26]

Court Leet, north-west of the church, has three bays with two whole storeys and attics and a lobby entrance and a rear outshut.[27] It was built perhaps for Thomas Nourse (d. 1675), who was assessed on three hearths in 1672. Nourse Yate, his successor as lay

---

1 GA, D 2299/1112; P 210/IN 3/2.
2 Ibid. D 543, Longhope deeds 1740–1862; GDR, T 1/116 (no 329).
3 GA, D 1297, Longhope ct. book 1828–91, pp. 193–5; GDR, T 1/116 (no 374A).
4 *Glos. Subsidy Roll, 1327*, 43.
5 GA, D 23/T 18.
6 Ibid. DA 24/100/21, p. 276; OS Map 1:2,500, SO 6820–6920 (1970 edn).
7 GA, D 36/T 23
8 *Glos. Subsidy Roll, 1327*, 43.
9 GA, D 1297, surv. 1717, Longhope no 12; D 36/T 23.
10 GA, D 36/T 23.
11 DoE List, Longhope, 6/121; GA, D 36/E 12, ff. 36v.–37; D 2123, p. 147.
12 GA, D 1297, surv. 1717, Longhope no 16.
13 Turner, *Agric. of Glos.* 50; *Glos. Chron.* 29 Aug. 1868 (letter).
14 Below, econ. hist.
15 GA, D 1297, surv. 1717, Longhope no 16.
16 GDR, T 1/116 (nos 142, 147, 147A, and 149); GA, D 4869/1/2/6.
17 See Bick, 'Enigma of Crocket's Holes', 63.
18 GDR, T 1/116 (no 245); OS Map 6", Glos. XXIV.SW (1889–1924 edns).
19 GA, D 36/T 23.
20 R. Green, 'May Hill' (1992: TS hist. in GA, GMS 264), 7; *The Times*, 17 June 1939 (obituary of H.A. Pringle). See GA, DA 24/100/11, p. 239.
21 OS Maps 6", Glos. XXIV.NW (1887 edn); XXIV.SW (1889 edn); GA, D 4869/1/2/4.
22 GDR, T 1/116; GA, Q/RI 91.
23 OS Map 6", Glos. XXIV.NW (1887 edn).
24 Dighton, *Dightons of Clifford Chambers*, 29.
25 GA, D 2714, Longhope deeds 1726–1919.
26 Below, Fig. 53; Verey and Brooks, *Glos.* II, 574; DoE List, Longhope, 6/117.
27 DoE List, Longhope, 6/118.

rector,[1] had a 'good seat near the church' c.1710.[2] The construction and accommodation of the mid 17th-century Upper Boxbush House is also of high quality with a lobby-entrance plan, three rooms on each of its two floors, and some decoration in the heated room over the parlour. A west bay of rougher construction appears to have been built as a single-storeyed lean-to workshop or service room with a separate entrance.[3] In the southern part of the village Knapp House, on the Monmouth road, is of two storeys with attic and four rooms in line and was also large enough to have been among the 12 houses that in 1672 had three or more hearths.[4] Two smaller 17th-century houses on the old Monmouth road, and one further west, have, like Upper Boxbush, upper rooms partly within their roofs[5] and Peach Tree Cottage in Velthouse Lane has only two rooms and an attic.[6] On the lower slopes of May hill the similar house at Coopey's Farm was originally two-bayed[7] and Rock Farm has a house that was first built on the same scale.[8] Dam Barn Cottages in Church Road occupy a long timber-framed range erected in the late 17th or early 18th century[9] possibly for industry and used in the mid 19th century as a farm building.[10]

The 17th-century houses described above were timber-framed structures with chimneys and gable walls on stone plinths. Hart's Barn appears to have

53. *Marle Cottage*

54. *Upper Boxbush House*

1 TNA, E 179/247/14, rott. 36d.–37; below, manor (manor: the Manor Ho.; other estates: Longhope rectory).
2 Atkyns, *Glos.* 545.
3 Fig. 54; DoE List, Longhope, 2/138.
4 TNA, E 179/247/14, rott. 36d.–37; see below, social hist. (social structure).
5 DoE List, Longhope, 6/128–30.
6 Ibid. 6/139.
7 Ibid. 2/140.
8 GA, D 2299/5934.
9 DoE List, Longhope, 6/106.
10 GDR, T 1/116 (no 1031).

55. *Hart's Barn from the south-east in 1996*

been rebuilt entirely in stone in the middle of the century by Edward Sergeaunt.[1] With Edward one of only two householders assessed on four hearths in 1672,[2] it was two-storeyed and had at least three bays, attics, and cellar. A surviving window in the gable end has an ovolo-moulded mullion.

Domestic and Other Buildings from the Eighteenth Century

Most probably after 1702 by William Sergeaunt, Hart's Barn was extended west to become the most fashionable house in the parish. Its front was slightly raised and, above the cellar, was given a two-storeyed brick façade, with a central pediment that rests on a coved cornice, a plain semicircular doorhood, and timber cross-casement windows. A rear projection was added to house a staircase with twisted balusters. New stone outbuildings included a cowhouse with hayloft and stables and a granary south-west of the house.[3] The farmhouse at Dursley Cross was also rebuilt in the early 18th century, when part of the Colchester family's estates;[4] the new two-storeyed front range has attics and cellars and a gabled stair projection, is almost entirely faced in Flemish-bond brick, and has timber windows. The house retains a cruck within the stone-cased rear wing.[5] In the south of the village the remains of a tall 18th-century brick house, perhaps also with a stair projection, can be discerned at Coglan House, which was built as a gentleman's residence probably by Robert Coghlan (d. 1803 or 1804).[6]

Although timber framing continued to be used into the 18th century for poorer dwellings such as the two-room Walnut Cottage at Little London,[7] most new building in Longhope was in stone or brick. Stone rubble quarried from the slopes of May hill was much used for small houses, such as the early 18th-century Gaston House, and for outbuildings. Brick was often used to form openings in rubble walls, as can be seen in the small house and outbuildings at Pitman's Farm. In the early to mid 19th century unsquared stone was used for a field barn and cattle shed at Preece Moor.[8] Court Farm was rebuilt in the same manner but on a larger scale with farm buildings round three sides of a yard and Bilbut Farm, through improvements funded by the landowner Edmund Probyn, acquired a new house, a plain three-bayed villa dated 1857, and a symmetrical layout of outbuildings.[9] At Hart's Barn by the late 1870s a large barn and associated buildings had been built north-east of the house around a new farmyard higher up the slope.[10]

In the early 19th century several large houses were built in stuccoed classical style. The four-square Manor House, north of the church, was provided most probably for John Probyn about the time he became lord of the manor in 1819[11] The house, which had a stable court to the south and a pleasure ground with a fishpond to the north,[12] is of 2½ storeys with a hipped roof with projecting eaves and its main east façade is unadorned except for a slender doorcase with open pediment and a central first-floor window with intersecting glazing bars, a pattern repeated in some windows of the stable block.[13] The Old Rectory, south-west of the church, was begun in

1 For the Sergeaunts, below, manor (other estates: Hart's Barn).
2 TNA, E 179/247/14, rott. 36d.–37.
3 Fig. 55; DoE List, Longhope, 6/131–3.
4 GA, D 36/E 12, ff. 36v.–37; D 2123, p. 147.
5 DoE List, Longhope, 6/121.
6 See above (the village).
7 DoE List , Longhope, 7/125.
8 GDR, T 1/116 (nos 463–4); DoE List, Longhope, 6/104.
9 Datestone has Probyn's inits.; see GDR, T 1/116 (no 449); OS Map 6", Glos. XXIII.SE (1883 edn).
10 OS Map 6", Glos. XXIII.SE (1883 edn).
11 See below, manor; social hist. (social structure).
12 GDR, T 1/116.
13 GA, GPS 206/5.

1825 by the vicar C.M. Dighton and completed by 1829 by his successor Edmund Probyn. Its neo-classical main façade, with recessed centre and porch with Tuscan columns *in antis*, originally had two projectings bows. An outbuilding erected at the same time for a schoolroom[1] is joined to a simple single-storeyed rock-faced range with red brick dressings built as a school in 1911 to a design by R.S. Phillips.[2] The Temple, in the south of the village on the old Monmouth road, was built as a gentleman's residence probably by the solicitor Solomon Coleman, its occupant in the late 1830s.[3] It has a slightly irregular five-bayed façade with two storeys and a Tuscan porch. Its outbuildings in 1913 included a range that had accommodated a coach house and stabling.[4]

Increasingly builders took advantage of the parish's topography to choose sites that commanded views. The classical Blenheim House (Dean End) at Lea Line had been built by 1841, when it was a boarding school,[5] and was much enlarged later in the same late Georgian style. Bradley Grove (later Bradley Court and in 2007 Forest Court) was built high up in the west in the late 1860s as a country house for Osman Barrett, a Forest of Dean mine owner. Designed by T.H. Rushforth of London in an unambitious Tudor-Gothic style, it was built of red sandstone with Bath stone dressings[6] on an L plan with a northern service court. The double-pile main block has to the west a long façade of 2½ storeys varied only by gables and shallow bay windows and to the east a two-storeyed entrance front with a Gothic doorcase and staircase window. The interior of the house, where Barrett and his family lived with seven servants in 1871,[7] was equally conventional, the main hall containing an overmantel in Jacobethan style.[8] The house had two lodges,[9] one of them in a U-plan coach and stable block with tourelle on the southern edge of the small park.

Throughout the 19th century small villas in late classical style were built on the main roads, such as Jordan House and Hopebrook on the Ross road, both three-bayed and early 19th-century.[10] The red brick Zion House on the Monmouth road on Hope's hill was the mid 19th-century manse of the Baptist chapel there. The chapel, built back from the road in 1845 and 1846,[11] is modest with a rendered north façade with gable and a door flanked by two round-headed windows. A schoolroom added in 1866 and enlarged in 1893 is at the rear.[12] In the village a number of villas built in the southern part after the railway station opened there in 1855 were occupied by private residents.[13] In the Latchen the rebuilding in 1852 of Pound House as a Gothic two-roomed 1½-storeyed cottage standing end on to the road presumably repeated in stone the form of the timber-framed cottage that burned down on the site in 1851.[14] The development of the village, and particularly its southern end, was supported in the early 20th century by the provision of a hall; built of stone and brick on a slope in the Latchen, its basement housed committee and store rooms.[15] The mission room at the Upper End in 1901 was a small wooden building with Gothic windows attached to a house off the Ross road at the bottom of Barrel Lane.[16]

The practice of building on May hill to command a wide prospect continued in the 20th century. In the 1930s the landowner H.A. Pringle added to the buildings at Yartleton Farm to create May Hill House, using ashlar to face a new austere block of reception rooms that look south-westwards over the Longhope valley. May Hill Lodge, one of several new houses built by Pringle near by, is pebble-dashed and in more conventional cottage style.[17] Since the Second World War older dwellings such as Yartleton Oak Cottage have been enlarged. One of the new houses, constructed on the prefabricated Huf system, incorporates large areas of glass.

Industrial Buildings

The once prolific industrial activity in Longhope has left little built evidence although many of its sites alongside the Longhope brook and the main tributary can be traced.[18] In the village the turnery of James Constance & Sons included a tall chimney and other buildings[19] that were pulled down in the late 20th century. South of the village stone buildings stand east of the Longhope brook at Furnace Mill, where a corn mill and a tannery operated side by side

---

1 Dighton, *Dightons of Clifford Chambers*, 28–9; GA, D 23/E 43; GDR, V 6/64B.

2 Verey and Brooks, *Glos.* II, 574; below, social hist. (education).

3 GDR, T 1/116 (no 718); for Coleman, below, econ. hist.; social hist. (social structure).

4 GA, D 2299/1177.

5 Below, social hist. (education).

6 *Kelly's Dir. Glos.* (1870), 598. For Barrett, see *VCH Glos.* V, 333.

7 TNA, RG 10/2605.

8 Mason, *Glance Back at Mitcheldean*, 14.

9 OS Map 6", Glos. XXIII.SE (1883 edn); TNA, RG 11/2525; RG 12/2007.

10 DoE List, Longhope, 2/120, 136.

11 *Glouc. J.* 2 Aug. 1845; 18 July 1846.

12 Verey and Brooks, *Glos.* II, 575; see below, social hist. (education).

13 *Kelly's Dir. Glos.* (1856 and later edns).

14 Inscription on ho.; see above, Fig. 52.

15 *Glouc. J.* 6 Oct. 1906; see below, social hist. (social life).

16 Below, religious hist. (religious life).

17 Green, 'May Hill', 7; see GA, DA 24/100/11, p. 239.

18 Below, econ. hist.

19 Below, Fig. 56.

in the mid 19th century.[1] The mill house, of the late 18th or early 19th century, has a plain three-bayed west front of three storeys and an east range spanning the mill race.[2] The tannery buildings to the north, between brook and leat, have not survived and a house, to the north-east, has been almost concealed by late 19th- and 20th-century additions. At Dursley Cross a two-storeyed house with attics on the Ross road was built in 1850 to accommodate a steam flour mill.[3]

MANOR AND ESTATES

During the Norman settlement in the later 11th century Longhope became the possession of the lords of Monmouth. Under the manor, which was acquired by the Talbot family in the mid 13th century and passed to the Grey family in the early 17th, the parish was divided between numerous landholders,[4] including the Baynhams in the early 16th century.[5] In the 16th and 17th centuries the Nourse and Sergeaunt families built up estates in Longhope[6] and William Steventon (d. 1647) of Dothill in Wellington (Salop.) owned land on the boundary with Mitcheldean.[7] In the early 18th century, when Longhope had 36 resident freeholders,[8] the Colchesters of Westbury-on-Severn were among its more prominent landowners[9] and the Probyns of Newland became the chief landowners on their acquisition of the manor.[10] Small gifts of land and cottages beginning in the late 14th century created an endowment for parish charities (the Parish Charity Lands trust) that eventually covered over 70 a. in scattered pieces in Longhope.[11]

Although much copyhold was enfranchised on the sale of the manor in the mid 1720s[12] and in the 1880s,[13] some land remained copyhold until after the First World War.[14] Most of the Probyns' land was sold to the Sharpe family in 1872[15] and among the many other landowners in the early 20th century[16] were M.W. Colchester-Wemyss, who owned a farm at Bradley that had belonged to the curates of Flaxley from 1737 to 1880,[17] and the trustees of Osman Barrett (d. 1890).[18] Barrett, a colliery owner in the Forest of Dean,[19] had acquired land at Chessgrove and Preece Moor that had been part of the Blunt family's Huntley Court estate.[20]

LONGHOPE MANOR

An estate at Longhope held in 1066 by the royal thegns Forne and Wulfheah (Ulfeg)[21] probably also covered Blaisdon.[22] It was presumably among the lands that after the Conquest came to Wihanoc, lord of Monmouth, for his nephew and successor William son of Baderon held the estate in 1086, when it was assessed for geld at five hides.[23] William's son Baderon of Monmouth confirmed Longhope church to Wihanoc's foundation Monmouth priory[24] and the Longhope part of the estate passed to Baderon's son Gilbert of Monmouth[25] (d. 1190). Gilbert's son and heir John of Monmouth (d. 1248) owed the service of a knight's fee from Longhope[26] and the widow of his son John (d. 1257) held the estate in dower.[27] In 1267 Prince Edward granted the lordship of Monmouth to his brother Edmund[28] (d. 1296) and the overlordship of Longhope manor thereby descended with the earldom (later dukedom) of Lancaster.[29]

Gilbert Talbot, who held the manor by grant from Prince Edward, died in 1274 and was succeeded in it

---

1 GDR, T 1/116 (nos 737–9).
2 OS Map 6", Glos. XXIV.SW (1889 edn); C. Hart, *The Industrial History of Dean* (1971), 373, which gives a date of 1799 for a cottage; see ibid. pl. facing p. 309.
3 Inscription on bldg.; OS Map 6", Glos. XXIV.SW (1889 edn).
4 TNA, DL 7/2, no 33.
5 Ibid. REQ 2/116/54.
6 Below (Longhope manor: the Manor Ho.; other estates: Hart's Barn).
7 TNA, CP 43/131, Carte rott. 13d.–14d.; *VCH Shropshire* XI, 215.
8 Atkyns, *Glos.* 546.
9 GA, D 1297, survey of Huntley, Netherley, and Longhope 1717, Longhope nos 8, 11, 12, 18, 26. For the Colchesters' estates, *VCH Glos.* X, 87; V, 180.
10 See GDR, T 1/116.
11 *18th Rep. Com. Char.* 326–7; GDR, T 1/116; see below, social hist. (charities for the poor); religious hist.
12 GA, D 543, Longhope deeds 1738–95, deed 27 Dec. 1738; D 892/T 43; D 2362, deeds 1718–1892; D 2714, Longhope deeds 1726–1919.
13 Ibid. D 1297, Longhope ct. book 1828–91.
14 Ibid. D 2714, Longhope deeds 1726–1919.
15 Below, this section (the Manor Ho.).
16 GA, G/WE 159/9; DA 24/500/9.
17 Ibid. D 2362, deeds 1718–1892; see *VCH Glos.* V, 148.
18 GA, D 8966.
19 *VCH Glos.* V, 333.
20 Above, Huntley, manor; GDR, T 1/116; see Rudge, *Hist. of Glos.* II, 57.
21 *Domesday Book* (Rec. Com.), I, 167.
22 Taylor, *Domesday Glos.* 203. Blaisdon was regarded as a hamlet of Longhope until at least 1327: *Feudal Aids*, II, 268; *Glos. Subsidy Roll, 1327*, 43.
23 *Domesday Book* (Rec. Com.), I, 167. For the lordship of Monmouth, I.J. Sanders, *English Baronies* (1960), 64–5 and nn.
24 *Cal. Doc. France*, 409–10.
25 *Flaxley Cart.* p. 133.
26 *Book of Fees*, I, 50, 439; *Flaxley Cart.* pp. 108–9.
27 *Rot. Hund.* I, 176.
28 For Edmund and Longhope, see TNA, JUST 1/275, rott. 17, 39.
29 *Complete Peerage*, VII, 381–418; *Cal. Pat. 1272–81*, 422, 442; *Feudal Aids*, VI, 576; *Inq. p.m. Glos.* 1302–58, 354; 1359–1413, 153, 200, 245.

by his son Richard[1] (d. 1306). Richard's son and heir Gilbert, Lord Talbot, forfeited it temporarily following his capture at the battle of Boroughbridge in 1322[2] and was granted free warren in the demesne in 1328.[3] From Gilbert (d. 1346) the manor descended evidently in direct line to successive Lords Talbot, Richard[4] (d. 1356), Gilbert[5] (d. 1387), and Richard[6] (d. 1396). Richard's widow Ankaret, who married Thomas Neville, Lord Furnivale (d. 1407),[7] retained the manor and was succeeded in it in 1413 by her son Gilbert Talbot, Lord Talbot[8] (d. 1418). His heir, his infant daughter Ankaret,[9] died in 1421 and the manor passed to her uncle John Talbot, who was created earl of Shrewsbury in 1442. The manor then descended with that earldom,[10] Catherine, widow of John Talbot (d. 1473), holding it in dower,[11] and it was inherited from the 7th earl, Gilbert Talbot (d. 1616), by his daughter Elizabeth, wife of Henry Grey (d. 1639), Lord Grey of Ruthin and from 1623 earl of Kent. After Elizabeth's death in 1651[12] it passed to Anthony Grey, earl of Kent,[13] and his mother Amabel, dowager countess of Kent, held it during his minority.[14] Anthony (d. 1702) was succeeded by his son Henry. He rose to the status of duke of Kent in 1710 and sold off his family estates in and around Longhope in the mid 1720s.[15]

Sir Edmund Probyn of Newland, who acquired the manor,[16] died in 1742 leaving it to his nephew John Hopkins. From John, who took the surname Probyn[17] and died in 1773,[18] it descended, from father to son,[19] to Edmund Probyn[20] (d. 1819), Ven. (later Very Revd) John Probyn (d. 1843),[21] and John Probyn[22] (d. 1863). His son and heir Edmund, who became lord of the manor in 1855,[23] sold most of the land in 1872 to F.W. Sharpe, a Derbyshire clergyman, but kept some of it, notably Hope and Bearfoot woods, with the manorial rights[24] and retained most of the top of May hill when common rights there were extinguished.[25] In 1891, the year after Edmund's death, the manor belonged to Wilmot Inglis Jones[26] of Derry Ormond (Cardiganshire). Jones, who changed his surname to Inglis-Jones in 1899,[27] sold the land in 1917 to H.A. Pringle.[28] Pringle sold Hope wood to the Crown in 1918[29] and Jones, the last recorded lord of the manor, died in 1949.[30]

The Manor House

Away from the site of the manor east of the parish church[31] the Manor House stands 265 m to the north towards the Ross road. Presumably in the place of the house with five hearths occupied in 1672 by Thomas Master (d. 1682), a member of a Cirencester gentry family,[32] it dates from rebuilding in the early 19th century of a house that had belonged to Yate Bromwich, a relative of Master according to heraldic evidence[33] and a descendant of the Nourse family. The Nourses were established in Longhope by the mid 16th century[34] and Richard Nourse by will dated 1590 left his house and land there to his grandson Thomas Nourse, a minor.[35] Thomas, described in 1651 as a gentleman, enlarged his estate, acquiring land from John Ayleway in 1669[36] and the rectory. At his death in 1675 he was succeeded by his grandson Nourse Yate, who gave the impropriation to the vicarage in 1701[37] and retained a substantial estate c.1710.[38] His widow Priscilla (d. 1720)[39] owned the estate in 1717 and the main house and 120 a. were copyhold[40] until 1726 when his son and heir Charles

---

1 *Inq. p.m. Glos.* 1236–1300, 91; for the Talbot fam., see *Complete Peerage*, XII (1), 608–20.
2 *Cal. Fine* 1319–27, 96–7; see *VCH Glos.* V, 61.
3 *Cal. Chart.* 1327–41, 81.
4 *Inq. p.m. Glos.* 1302–58, 354.
5 Ibid. 361, which does not mention Longhope.
6 Ibid. 1359–1413, 153.
7 Ibid. 200–1, 245–6. .
8 *Cal. Inq. p.m.* XX, 34–5.
9 TNA, C 138/41, no 68.
10 *Complete Peerage*, XI, 698–716; see TNA, C 139/154, no 29; C 139/179, no 58; C 142/231, no 106; *Military Surv. of Glos. 1522*, 206.
11 TNA, C 140/46, no 52; *Cal. Pat.* 1467–77, 397, 541.
12 GA, D 23/T 18; *Inq. p.m. Glos.* 1625–42, I, 196; for the Grey fam., see *Complete Peerage*, VII, 173–8.
13 GA, D 23/T 18.
14 *Glos. N&Q* I, 399–400.
15 GA, D 543, Longhope deeds 1738–95, deed 27 Dec. 1738; D 892/T 43; D 2362, deeds 1718–1892; D 2714, Longhope deeds 1726–1919; see above, Huntley, manor.
16 GA, D 23/T 18; for Sir Edm., see *VCH Glos.* V, 214; *Oxford DNB*.
17 GA, D 637/II/1/T 1.
18 Bigland, *Glos.* II, 262.
19 For the Probyn fam., see pedigree in J. Maclean, 'The History of the Manors of Dene Magna and Abenhall', *Trans. BGAS* 6 (1881–2), 194–7; *Burke's Landed Gentry* (1898), II, 1217–18.
20 Rudder, *Glos.* 533; Rudge, *Hist. of Glos.* II, 57.
21 GDR, T 1/116; TNA, PROB 11/1988, ff. 357v.–361.
22 GA, D 4869/1/1/3–5.
23 Ibid. D 1297, Longhope ct. book 1828–91; see ibid. D 4869/1/1/6.
24 Ibid. D 4869/1/1/17, 19.
25 Ibid. Q/RI 91; D 4869/1/2/9–27.
26 Ibid. D 1297, Longhope ct. book 1828–91.
27 *Burke's Landed Gentry* (1952), I, 1401.
28 GA, D 177, Pringle fam., Longhope deeds 1872–1917.
29 C.E. Hart, *Royal Forest: A History of Dean's Woods as Producers of Timber* (1966), 235.
30 GA, D 2714, Longhope deeds 1726–1919; *Burke's Landed Gentry* (1952), I, 1401.
31 Above, settlement (the village).
32 TNA, E 179/247/14, rott. 36d.–37; Rudder, *Glos.* 534; Bigland, *Glos.* II, 170.
33 Bigland, *Glos.* II, 170.
34 GDR wills 1568/14.
35 Ibid. 1592/156.
36 GA, D 23/E 23.
37 TNA, PROB 11/349, ff. 308v.–312v., below (other estates: Longhope rectory).
38 Atkyns, *Glos.* 545.
39 Bigland, *Glos.* II, 170.
40 GA, D 1297, surv. 1717, Longhope nos 5, 11–12, 21, 25–6.

acquired their freehold. At Charles's death in 1730 the estate passed to his surviving sisters, Mary (d. 1761), Priscilla (d. 1763) wife of Lancelot Bromwich (d. 1752), Henrietta (d. 1752), Arethusa (d. 1752), and Frances (d. 1747).[1] The sisters sold some land and on Priscilla's death the rest passed with the main house to her son Yate Bromwich, vicar of Longhope. In 1774, soon after his death, his sister Priscilla Bromwich sold the estate to John Howell[2] (d. 1778) and from him it passed to his grandson Edmund Probyn, the lord of the manor.[3]

The Yates' house, part of which had been leased in 1759 to a farmer,[4] was rebuilt as the Probyns' residence and became known as the Manor House about the time John Probyn, rector of Abenhall and archdeacon (later dean) of Llandaff, inherited the manor in 1819.[5] In 1872 Edmund Probyn sold the house with 687 a. to Revd Francis William Sharpe[6] (d. 1873). Sharpe's widow Mary (d. 1880) retained the estate and his eldest son William Granville Sharpe (d. 1890) devised it to a cousin, John Charles Sharpe of Byfleet (Surrey). In 1909 he conveyed the estate to his son Revd. Charles Henry Sharpe,[7] the founder of a religious community at More Hall in Stonehouse,[8] and in 1918, at the break up of the estate, the house was bought with some land by Henry Arthur Pringle,[9] already a landowner in the parish.[10] Pringle, who moved to a new house on May hill in the mid 1930s,[11] died in 1939 and was survived by his only child Margaret, wife of R.W.J. Pringle-Nicholson (d. 1940).[12]

OTHER ESTATES

Hart's Barn

The house called Hart's Barn, in the west of Longhope by the Monmouth road, was part of an estate or farm owned by Nicholas Rowles (d. 1608), a merchant whose son Arthur lived in Longhope in 1608.[13] The house was acquired by John Sergeaunt of Mitcheldean, who had inherited land at Whitemoor[14] and at his death in 1615 was succeeded by his son Edward, a minor.[15] Edward, who was a Longhope churchwarden immediately after the Restoration,[16] lived at Hart's Barn and left the house and its lands at his death in 1698 to his son John. John released the estate in 1702 to his son William and William settled it in 1731 on the marriage of his son John[17] (d. 1765).[18] John's son John,[19] vicar of Awre, left Hart's Barn at his death in 1780 in turn to his brother Richard and to Richard's son John.[20] Richard died in 1802 and after John's death, in Philadelphia in 1820, the estate passed in turn to his mother Margaret (d. 1837) and his sisters Margaret, Ann, Joanna, and Mary. Margaret, who married Hugh Thompson Martin, died in 1845 leaving her share to her grandson Martin Wheeler Hooper (d. 1859). In 1859 Mary conveyed her share to her nephew Richard Hall, then of Baglan House in Neath (Glam.). From Richard, who acquired the other interests in the estate (*c*.96 a.),[21] Hart's Barn passed to his daughter Mary, the wife of John Hobart Culme-Seymour (d. 1887), and she sold it[22] in 1921 to Charles C. Few[23] (d. 1965).[24]

Longhope Rectory

In 1291 Monmouth priory's portion in Longhope church as rector (£3 6s. 8d.) was worth less than that of the vicar (£4).[25] In 1324 the prior took two thirds of the church's income and received a pension from the other third.[26] Later the vicar paid the priory a pension of 5s. and in 1525 the then vicar acquired a lease of the priory's rectory estate, made up of the tithes of the parish, for the term of his incumbency for a rent of 21s. 8d.[27]

In 1549 the Crown sold the rectory to Robert Wood[28] and he sold it, together with the patronage of the vicarage, to Thomas Baker of Milton Keynes

---

1 GA, D 23/E 23; GDR wills 1747/170; for deaths, see Bigland, *Glos*. II, 170; GA, P 206/IN 1/1–3.
2 GA, D 23/E 23; T 18; GDR wills 1774/102.
3 Bigland, *Glos*. II, 260; Rudge, *Hist. of Glos*. II, 57.
4 GA, D 23/T 18.
5 Above, settlement (bldgs.); see below, social hist. (social structure). For the Probyns, see Maclean, 'Hist. of Dene Magna and Abenhall', 195–8.
6 GA, D 4869/1/1/17, 19.
7 Ibid. D 177, Pringle fam., Longhope deeds 1872–1917.
8 *The Times*, 16 Sept. 1913 (obituary of J.C. Sharpe); *VCH Glos*. X, 276.
9 GA, D 177, Pringle fam., Longhope deeds 1872–1917, sale partics. 1917; D 2299/1421, sale partics. 1930.
10 Above, this section.
11 Above, settlement (bldgs.).
12 *The Times*, 6 Apr. 1927 (marriages); 17 June, 1939 (obituary of H.A. Pringle); 29 June 1940 (obituary of R.W.J. Pringle-Nicholson).
13 TNA, PROB 11/112, ff. 225v.–226v.; Smith, *Men and Armour*, 68.

14 TNA, C 142/383, no 114; C 142/413, no 95; W.T. Sargeaunt, 'The Family of Sargeaunt, of Hart Barn, Longhope', *Trans. BGAS* 78 (1959), 117–18. For the ho. above, Fig. 55.
15 *Inq. p.m. Glos*. 1625–42, I, 186.
16 Hockaday Abs. lviii, 1661 visit. f. 3.
17 Bigland, *Glos*. I, 448; GA, D 543, Hart's Barn papers.
18 John's death is given in an undated history in Glos. Colln. RR 193.1.
19 GA, D 1202.
20 GDR wills 1780/142; Bigland, *Glos*. I, 105.
21 GA, DC/S 34/2; TNA, PROB 11/1664, ff. 497v.–498. For Margaret Martin, see GA, D 1297, Longhope ct. book 1828–91, p. 79.
22 GA, D 2299/1975; *Burke's Peerage and Baronetage* (1900), II, 1352.
23 See NRA Report, Longhope (C.C. Few); *Kelly's Dir. Glos*. (1923), 244.
24 Monument in churchyard.
25 *Tax. Eccl.* 161; see below, religious hist. (early hist.).
26 TNA, SC 6/1125/15.
27 *Valor Eccl*. III, 16; TNA, SC 6/Hen. VIII/7319, rot. 5d.
28 *Cal. Pat*. 1549–51, 95

(Bucks.).¹ Although he left land in west Gloucestershire to John Nourse of Milton Keynes, the history of the Longhope impropriation after Thomas's death in 1559² is unclear. John Baker presented to the vicarage in 1577³ and Richard Nourse's duty at that time to maintain the church's chancel passed with the farm of the rectory to Nicholas Rowles before 1600.⁴ In 1603 the rectory belonged to a Worcester man surnamed Hall (Hawle)⁵ and in 1616 John Hall of Longhope conveyed it to James Cadell, a Bristol pewterer. James was succeeded a year later by his brother John, similarly a pewterer. Following his bankruptcy the rectory, which included many cash payments from parishioners,⁶ was sold in 1630 to Nicholas Roberts, owner of an estate near by in Westbury-on-Severn.⁷ It later passed to Thomas Nourse, to whom Richard Halford and his wife Joan, Margery Morgan, and Walter Hugill or Hubarne and his wife Cecily quitclaimed it in 1674.⁸ Thomas (d. 1675) left it with his lands in Longhope to his grandson Nourse Yate⁹ and he settled the impropriation, made up mostly of the tithes of the parish, on the vicarage in 1701.¹⁰

ECONOMIC HISTORY

Although primarily a rural parish Longhope had a long industrial tradition embracing iron making, quarrying, wood turning and other woodland crafts, and tanning.

AGRICULTURE

The Middle Ages

In 1086 the Longhope estate, which may have included Blaisdon, was worth £5 compared with £8 in 1066. It had two ploughs in demesne and 3 slaves, and its tenants, 12 villans and 1 bordar, had 12 ploughs between them.¹¹ While eight ploughteams were recorded in Longhope in 1220¹² the manorial demesne comprised 60 a. of arable and 8 a. of meadow in 1274. At that time free tenants held other land and customary tenants held 16½ yardlands for cash rents and, at Christmas, a render of pepper. In addition two mondaymen, presumably holding land once subject to Monday work, owed the same smaller cash rents as five cottagers.¹³ In 1322, during the Crown's temporary seizure of the manor, wheat was sown on 36 a. of the demesne.¹⁴

While the steeper land is not suited for ploughing, medieval and later ridge and furrow covers some gentler slopes and hilltops of the parish.¹⁵ The regular pattern of the closes high on Breakheart hill near Chessgrove Farm suggests that their origin was much earlier. Orchard cultivation¹⁶ produced yields substantial enough for pear and apple tithes to merit mention alongside corn and hay tithes in the late Middle Ages.¹⁷ Sheep farming provided employment for at least one shepherd 1327.¹⁸ The extensive woodland, recorded in 1086 as part of William son of Baderon's estate in Huntley,¹⁹ was common pasture throughout the year²⁰ and in the late 13th century the lord of the manor claimed an entitlement to common rights within Flaxley abbey's woods in adjoining Flaxley.²¹ Longhope maintained rights of common on the royal demesne woodland of the Forest of Dean after it was taken out of the Forest's jurisdiction in the early 14th century.²²

The Early Modern Period

Names recorded in 1780 might indicate that the parish once had a north field and a south field²³ but in the early 18th century, when there were several strips of land on the side of May hill, most cultivated land was in closes.²⁴ Despite piecemeal encroachment much land, both woodland and pasture, remained common. On the east side of the parish a string of commons, largely cleared of woodland, extended northwards above the Monmouth road, where they were open to Huntley Wood common to the east, and over Holly Bush hill to Yartleton on May hill. In the early 18th century,

---

1 TNA, CP 40/1142, Carte rott. 2–3.
2 Ibid. PROB 11/42A, f. 256 and v. For John Nourse, ibid. PROB 11/73, ff. 248v.–50.
3 Hockaday Abs. cclxiii.
4 GDR, vol. 40, f. 247; vol. 87, f. 287; V 5/193T 1.
5 *Eccl. Misc.* 100.
6 TNA, C 3/412/111; GA, D 36/E 36.
7 GA, D 36/E 3, p. 234; see VCH *Glos.* X, 87.
8 TNA, CP 25/2/658/26 Chas. II Easter, no 6.
9 Ibid. PROB 11/349, ff. 308v.–312v.
10 GDR, V 5/193T 4.
11 *Domesday Book* (Rec. Com.), I, 167; Taylor, *Dom. Glos.* 203.
12 *Book of Fees*, I, 306.
13 *Inq. p.m. Glos.* 1236–1300, 90–1.
14 TNA, SC 6/1145/15.
15 Archaeology Data Service (http://ads.ahds.ac.uk/catalogue: accessed 3 May 2005).
16 See GA, D 36/T 17/3; T 18.
17 TNA, C 1/749/17.
18 *Glos. Subsidy Roll, 1327*, 43.
19 *Domesday Book* (Rec. Com.), I, 167.
20 Below (woodland management).
21 *Cal. Close 1272–9*, 569; *Flaxley Cart.* p. 42.
22 VCH *Glos.* V, 295–7, 361; see below.
23 GA, D 6/E 4, no 4.
24 Ibid. D 1297, survey of Huntley, Netherley, and Longhope 1717, Longhope no 2.

when there were clusters of encroachments at Dursley Cross and elsewhere, they covered some 441 a.[1] and Chessgrove common covered 21 a. in the west, on the far side of the Longhope valley.[2] From the later 1720s small-scale piecemeal inclosure and cultivation was facilitated by the pragmatism of the Probyns, the lords of the manor, in granting leases to cottagers.[3] In the mid 18th century the parish paid 3s. 4d. herbage money for common rights in the Forest of Dean.[4]

Longhope's numerous farms[5] varied considerably in size. Some were owner-occupied; 36 freeholders lived there c.1710[6] and there were 25 freeholders, some of them also tenants, under the manor in 1717. At that time, when two leaseholds were in hand, the manor had 22 tenants by lease or agreement for lives with heriots payable, 81 copyhold tenants, and 3 free benchers without heirs. At least two holdings, one of them centred on the Court House, were over 100 a. and several, including Bilbut, Hunter's, Great Bradley, and Boxbush, were over 50 a. Most of the rest were much smaller, usually less than 20 a., and many copyholders were cottagers with 1 or 2 a.[7] In 1794 the largest farm on Edmund Probyn's estate was made up of holdings of 172 a. and 77 a. The estate's smaller tenancies, all held separately, contained 81 a., 73 a., 64 a., 44 a., 23 a., and 19 a.[8]

Farming leases granted by the lord of the manor often required planting of new broadleaved trees but in the 17th and 18th centuries they increasingly requested regular planting of new stocks for apples and pears.[9] Local cider did not keep long[10] and apples from Longhope were being transported along the Severn in the mid 17th century.[11] The area of orchards increased[12] and former common land at Dursley Cross and elsewhere on the lower slopes of May hill had been planted with fruit trees by 1728.[13] Nursery cultivation was considerable in 1780, when it was reported that 1,000 young stocks had been sent to one purchaser, probably Thomas Crawley-Boevey of Flaxley.[14]

Although much farmland was used as pasture, and much of that also as orchard, more land was devoted to arable farming in the middle if not at the end of the 18th century.[15] On the Hart's Barn estate crops were grown on parts of Whitemoor, the hillside south of the Monmouth road extending westwards into Abenhall, and among the closes there were a barn, a sheepcot, and two folds.[16] A sheepcot on May hill at Dursley Cross[17] may have been standing in 1667.[18] At least 499 a. of Longhope were under arable crops in 1801, over half devoted to wheat and most of the rest to other cereals and to pulses.[19]

The Nineteenth and Twentieth Centuries

In 1831 14 farmers in Longhope employed labour and there were 82 agricultural labourers in the parish.[20] The land continued to be farmed in holdings ranging from a few to several hundred acres. Of 22 resident farmers identified in 1851 one worked 200 a., six over 100 a., and two over 50 a. One farmer's wife was a poultry dealer.[21] More farmland was under grass than arable crops and there was over 400 a. of common land, over half of it open pasture on May hill, where inclosures on the upper slopes were limited to a few small pieces adjoining Bearfoot wood.[22] The payment of herbage money for common rights in the royal Forest had continued[23] and in 1860 two parishioners exercised those rights.[24] In 1866 the livestock returned for Longhope were 249 cattle, including 66 milch cows, 996 sheep, and 205 pigs; wheat was the main arable crop and over 100 a. was devoted to turnips and other root crops; and some 96 a. was returned as fallow or uncultivated.[25] Within Longhope common rights on May hill were extinguished in 1874 on the initiative of Edmund Probyn and by a series of exchanges and purchases he became sole owner of the hill's summit apart from its circle of trees.[26] The status of the manor's main woods as commons ended at the same time.[27]

In the late 19th and early 20th century there were c.70 agricultural occupiers in Longhope. At the beginning of the period most were tenant farmers and in 1926, when just under a half were owner occupiers, forty had under 20 a. and only one more than 150 a. Similarly most of the 99 holdings returned in 1956 had under 20 a. and only one over

---

1 Ibid. Longhope nos 2, 12, 16; see D 36/T 23.
2 Ibid. D 1297, surv. 1717, Longhope no 8.
3 Ibid. D 23/T 18; Rudge, *Hist. of Glos.* II, 54.
4 GA, P 206/CW 2/1; see *5th Rep. Dean Forest Com.* 65 and n.
5 See GA, D 23/E 4; D 3436/1–3.
6 Atkyns, *Glos.* 546.
7 GA, D 1297, surv. 1717, Longhope nos 17–26.
8 Ibid. D 4869/1/1/2.
9 Ibid. D 23/T 18.
10 J. Beale, 'Aphorisms Concerning Cider', in J. Evelyn, *Sylva, or a Discourse of Forest-Trees, and the Propagation of Timber in His Majesties Dominions* (London, 1664), 22.
11 TNA, E 134/1659/Mich. 13.
12 GA, D 23/E 23, recital of deed 2 Oct. 1669.
13 Ibid. D 23/T 18.
14 Ibid. D 3436/3.
15 Rudder, *Glos.* 533; Rudge, *Hist. of Glos.* II, 56.
16 GA, D 149/T 1155; D 543, misc. deeds 1694–1876.
17 GDR wills 1777/138.
18 GA, D 36/T 23.
19 *1801 Crop Returns Eng.* I, 174.
20 *Census*, 1831.
21 TNA, HO 107/1959.
22 GDR, T 1/116.
23 *5th Rep. Dean Forest Com.* 65 and n.
24 GA, D 9096/F 3/128, letter 29 Nov. 1860.
25 TNA, MAF 68/25/20; MAF 68/26/9.
26 GA, Q/RI 91; D 4869/1/2/9, 11–27; see *Glos. Chron.* 29 Aug. 1868 (letter).
27 Below (woodland management).

150 a. The agricultural workforce in 1926 included 33 labourers in regular employment.[1]

Cereal farming declined in the late 19th century, the acreage for it being returned as 252 in 1896 compared with 509 in 1866. In the same period the area of permanent grassland increased from 813 to 1,773 a. and the number of dairy cattle grew, 121 dairy animals being among 351 cattle recorded in 1896.[2] Livestock numbers continued to grow as more dairy herds were established and in 1956 213 milch cows were returned along with large numbers of other cattle, sheep, and pigs and 25 goats.[3] One poultry farmer was recorded in 1931[4] and commercial farming was represented in 1956 by 10,136 birds, mostly fowls.[5] A market gardener lived in Longhope in 1881[6] and a small area was used as nursery gardens in 1896, when 173 a. was returned as orchards and 11 a. as given over to small fruit cultivation. The number of fruit trees increased considerably in the early 20th century, the area of orchards being returned as 368 a. in 1956.[7] In the early 1930s, when two fruit growers were recorded,[8] a Manchester fruit company owned a farm[9] and in the late 1940s one fruit farm was owned by the county council's smallholdings committee.[10] Many orchards grew the local Blaisdon Red variety of plum.[11]

Later there was a retreat from orchard cultivation and in 1986, when the area of fruit trees and small fruit together accounted for at least 60 ha (c.150 a.), the commercial orchards grew mostly plums but included apples and pears, a few for making cider and perry, and cherries. The agricultural farms declined in number in the later 20th century but many remained small. Of 48 holdings declared in 1986 twenty-seven had under 10 ha (c.25 a.) and eight over 30 ha (c.75 a.), the largest having over 200 ha (c.500 a.). Most of the smaller farms were worked by part-time farmers. The principal holdings included two dairy units, four sheep or cattle farms, and one mixed farm, the livestock returned that year including 1,114 cattle, 210 of them in milk, and 7,022 sheep and lambs. Most land was laid down to grass and 55 ha (c.136 a.) was classified as rough grazing. Two farms covering 61 ha (c.150 a.) raised horticultural crops and there were three fruit farms and one poultry farm, most of some 50,000 birds being kept for egg production.[12] There was a mushroom farm in the early 1970s[13] and a flock of Angora goats was established in the mid 1980s for the production of mohair.[14] Another farm was used for the display of rare breeds in the 1990s.[15]

WOODLAND MANAGEMENT

Although not all of Longhope's extensive woodland was in the lord's hands,[16] that belonging to the manor was given in 1274 as 200 a. in extent and, subject to common rights throughout the year,[17] provided the lord with timber for building work.[18] In 1322, while the manor was in Crown hands, a man was paid for keeping its woodland as well as for sowing corn,[19] and in 1350 one of the manor's tenants was a woodward.[20] Care of woodland was among the main tasks of the manorial bailiff in the mid 17th century[21] and the larger woods, including Hope wood and Bearfoot (Fairfoot) wood with its house on the far side of May hill, remained in hand.[22] Custody of Bradley grove was the responsibility of the farmer at adjoining Bilbut in the early 18th century.[23] Custom, as recorded in 1660, excluded commoners from the lord's plantations in Hope wood and Bearfoot wood during the first seven years of their growth.[24] Common rights in both woods were abolished in 1874.[25]

Charcoal burners, described in early records as colliers, were active in Longhope, one being buried there in 1606[26] and three being named in 1608.[27] In the mid 17th century the ironmaster Thomas Foley obtained charcoal for his iron-making operations in the area locally[28] and he and his successors managed a number of woods in their possession,[29] harvesting and charcoaling cordwood cut on a 14-year cycle.[30] Bradley grove, which Revd Thomas Mantle acquired on the break up of the manorial estate in 1726, supplied charcoal to Flaxley and Gloucester in the

---

1 TNA, MAF 68/1609/15; MAF 68/3295/16; MAF 68/4533/181.
2 Ibid. MAF 68/25/20; MAF 68/26/9; MAF 68/1609/15.
3 Ibid. MAF 68/3295/16; MAF 68/4533/181; 'Village on the Air' (transcript of a BBC radio programme on 6 Oct. 1948: Glos. Colln. RF 193.4).
4 *Kelly's Dir. Glos.* (1931), 245.
5 TNA, MAF 68/4533/181.
6 Ibid. RG 11/2525.
7 Ibid. MAF 68/1609/15; MAF 68/3295/16; MAF 68/4533/181.
8 *Kelly's Dir. Glos.* (1931), 245–6; (1935), 246.
9 GA, D 2299/L 104.
10 GA, DA 24/100/17, f. 11.
11 'Village on the Air'; *Longhope, Gloucestershire, Coronation Year 1953* (Longhope W.I. parish guide: copy in ibid. R 193.4), 2; see *VCH Glos.* X, 9.
12 TNA, MAF 68/6005/181.
13 OS Map 1:2,500, SO 6818–6918 (1972 edn).
14 *Citizen*, 23 Sept. 1987; 12 Nov. 1993.
15 *Forester*, 29 Jan. 1993.
16 *Glos. Feet of Fines 1300–59*, p. 3.
17 *Inq. p.m. Glos.* 1236–1300, 90–1.
18 *Cal. Close* 1279–88, 36; see TNA, E 32/29, rot. 8d.
19 TNA, SC 6/1145/15.
20 Shakespeare Birthplace Trust, Stratford-upon-Avon (Warws.), DR 37/2/Box 118/29.
21 GA, D 23/T 18, deed 30 Sept. 1684.
22 Ibid. D 1297, surv. 1717, Longhope nos 6, 15–16.
23 Ibid. D 23/T 18, deed 26 Mar. 1711.
24 *Glos. N&Q* I, 401–2; see Bigland, *Glos.* II, 169 and n.
25 GA, Q/RI 91.
26 GDR, V 1/149.   27 Smith, *Men and Armour*, 68–9.
28 C. Hart, *The Industrial History of Dean* (1971), 20.
29 GA, D 2528, p. 16, plan E; see ibid. D 2184; D 3666/1.
30 Herefs. RO, E 12/G/12, table of woods 1698–1711.

56. *The turnery and timber store of James Constance & Sons Ltd, Longhope, in the early 20th century*

early 1740s and was sold to the Gloucester ironmaster Rowland Pytt in 1744.[1] In 1761 the agent of Thomas Crawley-Boevey, the owner of the Flaxley ironworks, secured a near monopoly for 17 years of the cordwood felled in John Probyn's woods, which included Hope and Bearfoot woods,[2] and in 1785 the operators of the Ayleford ironworks in Newnham obtained the right to the next cordwood crop in Coleshare and Kiln woods on Maynard Colchester's estate.[3] Coleshare wood had presumably got its name from charcoal burning. In the mid 19th century Longhope's numerous coppices were generally managed on a cycle of cutting at 15 years' growth.[4] Charcoal burning was last recorded in Longhope, on May hill, in 1930.[5]

Oak bark, which figured alongside coppice wood in the tithe customs in 1705,[6] was a valuable product of the timber crop in Hope wood in 1739. At that time Longhope's woods, Bradley grove among them, were also exploited for the manufacture locally of handles, hoops, and laths[7] and later they sustained the Constance family's saw mill in the village.[8] A timber merchant lived in Longhope in 1738[9] and members of the Constance family were among resident timber dealers in the mid 19th century.[10] Woods were also used for raising game and a keeper lived on the west side of May hill in 1861 and 1881.[11] Shooting rights in Bradley grove were included in 1880 in a tenancy of the adjoining country house (Bradley Court)[12] and those in Hope wood were let in the early 20th century to Sir Thomas Crawley-Boevey of Flaxley Abbey.[13] Silver foxes were bred in Bearfoot wood in the 1930s.[14]

In 1924 Hope wood was one of the Crown woods transferred with the Forest of Dean to the Forestry Commission,[15] under which it has been managed as part of the Forest[16] and much of it has been planted with conifers.[17] Similarly, under the National Trust broadleaf plantations on May hill were replaced with conifers from the 1960s.[18] The business of James Constance & Sons Ltd continued to own woodland and supply timber in 2006.[19]

WOODLAND CRAFTS AND SAW MILLS

Longhope's woodland has supported a variety of crafts and trades other than charcoal burning.[20] In 1608 a cooper, a turner, and two sawyers lived in Longhope[21] and in the mid 18th century the parish

---

1 GA, D 543, Longhope deeds 1726–92; D 3436/2. For Pytt, see *VCH Glos.* IV, 127; V, 73, 342.
2 GA, D 23/E 7–8; *VCH Glos.* V, 146.
3 GA, D 36/E 7/3; *VCH Glos.* X, 42.
4 TNA, IR 18/2788.
5 *The Times*, 4 Sept. 1930.
6 GDR, V 5/193T 5.
7 GA, D 3436/2; see also, ibid. D 36/E 7/5.
8 Below (woodland crafts and saw mills).
9 GA, D 543, Longhope deeds 1738–95.
10 TNA, HO 107/1959; RG 9/1758.
11 Ibid. RG 9/1758; RG 11/2525.
12 GA, D 543, Longhope deeds 1828–80.
13 Ibid. D 2428/1/65, f. 23.
14 *Kelly's Dir. Glos.* (1935), 246; (1939), 252.
15 TNA, CRES 36/266; see *VCH Glos.* V, 375.
16 C.E. Hart, *Royal Forest: A History of Dean's Woods as Producers of Timber* (1966), 240.
17 *The Longhope Village Appraisal 1991*, 4.
18 J. Graves, 'Planting on May Hill, Gloucestershire', *Quarterly J. of Forestry* (Jan. 1972), 31–2.
19 Notice in Longhope village; personal observation.
20 For charcoal burning, see above (woodland management).
21 Smith, *Men and Armour*, 68–9.

57. Products of James Constance & Sons exhibited at the Royal Agricultural Show, Newport, 1927

was an important producer of handles for mops, brooms, and rakes, hoops for casks and barrels, and laths, many of the products being sent for sale to Bristol and Bewdley (Worcs.) as well as Gloucester.[1]

Theophilus Constance was a turner at the turn of the century and his son James (d. 1890),[2] who in 1835 ran the family's workshop by the Longhope brook north of the village centre (in the later Church Road),[3] had 20 employees in 1851. At that time, when perhaps as many labourers were employed in wood turning and other woodland crafts as in agricultural work, Peter Constance ran a smaller turnery.[4] Earlier, in 1821, in a short-lived venture Benjamin Constance operated a paper mill in Longhope.[5] James Constance's business mostly making handles for domestic, garden, and agricultural tools[6] grew after the opening of the railway. The mill in Church Road was enlarged and at the end of the century, under S.W. Constance, most of its products were for markets outside the county.[7] Another saw mill operated south of the Monmouth road on the site of a water mill[8] and hoop and hurdle making continued in the early 20th century next to the railway station.[9]

The firm of James Constance & Sons, which absorbed a number of smaller local businesses,[10] increased its workforce in the late 1920s[11] and, having been sold in the 1940s, employed 40 men and women in the early 1970s.[12] The mill, which mainly used birch wood, ceased to be a turnery in 1981 and its site was adapted as an industrial estate.[13] In the 1960s, when a number of other businesses, two of them new in 1953, made ladders and interwoven fencing,[14] there were saw mills by the Ross road west of Dursley Cross and at Upper End as well as that by the Monmouth road.[15] A timber merchant had been based at Upper End in the 1920s and 1930s.[16]

CORN MILLS AND IRONWORKS

Corn mills have operated at a number of sites on the Longhope brook and its main tributary flowing down from Mitcheldean. Several blast furnaces or bloomery hearths situated by the streams in the 17th century probably smelted cinders as well as ore from

---

1 GA, D 3436/2; D 36/A 6.
2 GDR wills 1848/205; GA, P 206/IN 1/11. According to *Kelly's Dir. Glos.* (1870), 592 the Constances' business started in 1788. James was baptized in 1805: GA, P 206/IN 1/3.
3 GA, D 2174/2; GDR, T 1/116 (nos 607A–208A).
4 TNA, HO 107/1959.
5 F.J.T. Harris, 'Paper and Board Mills', *Trans. BGAS* 94 (1976), 133.
6 *Kelly's Dir. Glos.* (1870), 592. See Fig. 57.
7 OS Map 6", Glos. XXIV.SW (1889 edn); *Industrial Gloucestershire 1904*, 40–1: copy in GA, IN 11. See above, Fig. 56.,
8 OS Map 6", Glos. XXIV.SW (1889 edn): see GDR, T 1/116 (nos 696–9).
9 GA, D 2428/1/65, f. 29; D 177, Pringle fam., Longhope deeds 1872–1917, sale particulars 1917.
10 Hart, *Ind. Hist. of Dean*, 333–4.
11 GA, DA 24/114/1, p. 199.
12 Hart, *Ind. Hist. of Dean*, 334.
13 H. Phelps, *The Forest of Dean* (1983), 146 n; *Longhope Village Appraisal*, 3.
14 *Longhope, Coronation Year*, 3; *Dean Forest Mercury*, 14 Mar. 1969.
15 OS Maps 1:2,500, SO 6820–6920 (1970 edn); SO 6620–6720 (1970 edn); SO 6818–6918 (1972 edn).
16 *Kelly's Dir. Glos.* (1923), 244; (1939), 252.

the Forest of Dean.[1] One heap of cinders, the refuse of earlier ironworks, was recorded by the Monmouth road in 1726.[2] Iron making in Longhope ceased in the late 17th or early 18th century and corn milling there ended in the mid 20th century.

Longhope manor had a mill in 1086.[3] Gilbert of Monmouth (d. 1190) and his wife Bertha charged Longhope mill with the payment of 5s. during Lent to Flaxley abbey for buying wine or repairing books.[4] The manor's tenants included a millward in the mid 14th century[5] and the manorial mill,[6] perhaps that held in the early 16th century by the Dobbs family,[7] was on the Longhope brook in the south of the parish. A lease of the corn mill passed to the farmer Thomas Daw (d. by 1587)[8] and a blast furnace, presumably that being built on the earl of Shrewsbury's estate in 1609,[9] operated next to it in the early 17th century.[10] The mill, which was still held by the Daw family in the early 18th century, became known as Furnace Mill.[11] Its operation, as part of the business of the Prince family, was interrupted during local bread riots in 1795.[12] John Kearsey, the miller in 1841, was also a farmer.[13] Flour milling ceased there probably in the early 1880s.[14] Cowman's Mill, downstream, was demolished before 1717.[15]

A furnace operated higher up the brook just upstream of the Court House (later Court Farm) in 1656.[16] In 1661 Thomas Nourse, who occasionally used it by agreement with his tenant Thomas Foley, undertook to keep a mill on the stream in constant operation. Paul Foley operated the furnace later, in partnership with his brother Philip from 1674,[17] and, while there was sufficient power to drive the bellows, shifts of men laboured day and night in 1682. The owner then was Nourse Yate.[18] The furnace had been demolished by 1717[19] but a large pond created by damming the brook existed there in 1777.[20] A field downstream was known as Dam Meadow,[21]

At his death in 1608 Nicholas Rowles had a mill on the tributary stream next to Hart's Barn and also a furnace.[22] The mill, grinding corn, passed as part of the Hart's Barn estate to John Sergeaunt (d. 1615)[23] and, accommodating two pairs of millstones in the mid 18th century,[24] was worked as part of the house's farm in the mid 19th century.[25]

Longhope or Parish Mill, downstream of Hart's Barn by the Monmouth road,[26] was a corn mill belonging to the parish in the mid 16th century.[27] In leasing it as part of a small farm to William Yate of Colethrop, in Standish, in 1661 the parish feoffees required him to restore its water supply, which Thomas Weale had diverted to his furnace.[28] Nathaniel Vaughan worked the mill in the late 18th century.[29] With two pairs of stones in the late 19th century, it was sold by the parish in the early 1920s[30] and it finally ceased operating soon after the Second World War. Its machinery remained in place in 1974.[31]

Elsewhere in 1717 James Sansom, the owner of a freehold called Bird's Mill, held two water corn mills, perhaps two pairs of stones in one building, by copy and William Welch owned another water corn mill, also copyhold.[32] A mill, perhaps that working in 1780,[33] possibly stood downstream of Parish Mill at the place south of the Monmouth road where a saw mill worked in the later 19th century.[34]

In 1850 a flour mill was built on the Ross road at Dursley Cross.[35] Occupying three storeys and powered by steam,[36] it closed at the turn of the century;[37] its machinery, including two pairs of stones, remained in place in 1911.[38] In the mid 1890s

---

1 See C. Hart, *The Free Miners of the Royal Forest of Dean and the Hundred of St. Briavels* (2002), 71, 93.
2 GA, D 892/T 43.
3 *Domesday Book* (Rec. Com.), I, 167.
4 *Flaxley Cart.* p. 133.
5 Shakespeare Birthplace Trust, DR 37/2/Box 118/29.
6 *Inq. p.m. Glos. 1236–1300*, 91; TNA, SC 6/1145/15.
7 *Military Surv. Of Glos. 1522*, 206; Hockaday Abs. cclxiii, 1545.
8 Hockaday Abs. cclxiii.
9 C. Hart, *The Forest of Dean: New History 1550–1818* (1995), 86.
10 TNA, E 134/3 Jas. II/Easter 22.
11 GA, D 1297, surv. 1717, Longhope no 18.
12 H.G. Nicholls, *The Forest of Dean: an Historical and Descriptive Account* (1858), 84–5. Richard Prince, a mealman in 1797, was the son of Robert Prince, a local landowner: GA, D 892/T 43; D 6/E 4, no 5.
13 TNA, HO 107/361; *Kelly's Dir. Glos.* (1856), 321.
14 *Kelly's Dir. Glos.* (1879), 697; (1885), 519; OS Map 6", Glos. XXIV. SW (1889, 1903 edns).
15 GA, D 1297, surv. 1717, Longhope no 10.
16 Hart, *Free Miners*, 71; GA, D 1297, surv. 1717, Longhope no 5.
17 Hart, *Ind. Hist. of Dean*, 20–1, 43.
18 Ibid. 74.
19 GA, D 1297, surv. 1717, Longhope nos 5, 21.
20 Taylor, *Map of Glos.* (1777).
21 GDR, T 1/116 (no 1034); see B.C. Cave, 'Mill Sites on the Longhope–Flaxley–Westbury Streams', *Glos. Soc. for Industrial Archaeol. J.* (1974), 14.
22 TNA, PROB 11/112, ff. 225v.–226v.
23 Ibid. C 142/383, no 114.
24 *Glouc. J.* 30 Dec. 1765.
25 GA, D 3436/3, account for 1780; GDR, T 1/116.
26 OS Map 6", Glos. XXIII.SE (1883 edn); GA, D 2299/1977.
27 TNA, C 93/1/34.
28 GA, D 23/T 19.
29 Ibid. D 3436/3, account for 1780.
30 *Kelly's Dir. Glos.* (1889), 833; GA, D 2299/1977.
31 Cave, 'Mill Sites', 15–16.
32 GA, D 1297, surv. 1717, Longhope nos 24, 26. The mill mentioned in Sansom's will was in Abenhall, upstream of Hart's Barn: GDR wills 1727/104; GA, D 36/T 1.
33 GA, D 3436/3.
34 GDR, T 1/116 (nos 696–9); above (woodland crafts and saw mills).
35 OS Map 6", Glos. XXIV.SW (1889 edn); inscription on bldg.
36 *Kelly's Dir. Glos.* (1870), 592.
37 Ibid. (1897), 230; OS Map 6", Glos. XXIV.SW (1903 edn).
38 GA, D 2299/889.

the Palmers, a farming family, operated a steam and water mill elsewhere in Longhope.[1]

The location of a windmill on one of the lord of the manor's estates in 1569 and 1640 is not known.[2]

QUARRYING

Longhope's soils, particularly those on May hill, were long dug for lime and marl.[3] In the 18th century limestone was quarried for building as well as agricultural use[4] and quarrying on the western slopes of May hill was in many places accompanied by lime burning. In 1735 a quarry and adjacent limekiln belonging to Hunter's (later Rock) farm were reserved by Sir Edmund Probyn, the tenant being allowed to use them for the farm, and in 1757 John Probyn kept a new quarry on the farm with the right to erect another kiln and to remove stone for road repairs and other uses.[5] In the later 18th century there were also kilns south of the Ross road, one being in the area of Hobb's quarry,[6] and in the mid 19th century, when twelve men worked at the quarry and kiln on Rock farm,[7] large quarries were open on both sides of the road, gouging long channels southwards along the limestone outcrop towards the Monmouth road or craters to the north-west, further around the hill.[8] Several farmers were in business also as stone and lime merchants in the 1870s[9] and, although many of the quarries and kilns had gone out of use by 1880, Hobb's quarry and several workings below it, all by the line of a long wooded incline running straight down to the Monmouth road, remained open.[10] Quarrying for road stone continued intermittently into the 20th century,[11] the main quarries south of the Ross road being reopened by H.A. Pringle in 1919.[12] In the late 20th century, following their abandonment, sections of those quarries were filled in and landscaped.[13] In 2005, when cliff faces up to 20 m deep were visible in places, the Gloucestershire Wildlife Trust managed Hobb's quarry as a nature reserve.

The parish also contains small abandoned sandstone quarries in the west.[14]

OTHER INDUSTRY AND TRADE

A man surnamed Smith (*Faber*) lived in Longhope in 1221.[15] Three smiths were listed in Longhope in 1608 among some 24 craftsmen and tradesmen, of whom several pursued other rural trades and woodland crafts and a tanner represented an industry associated with the bark trade.[16] Tanning took place at several sites in the 17th century.[17] That used by the Birkin family in the early 18th century[18] was evidently on the tributary of the Longhope brook by the Monmouth road[19] and there were tanhouses by the brook itself near Boxbush[20] and in the village, where a house in Church Road was known in the early 20th century as the Old Tanhouse.[21] A tannery established by the brook next to Furnace Mill by 1824[22] was owned by John Coleman and operated by Frederick Coleman in 1841.[23] The latter's business, which employed six men and a boy in 1851,[24] continued until the 1860s.[25] Weaving was another industry recorded at Longhope in the later 17th century.[26]

Of 194 families resident in Longhope in 1831 42 depended chiefly on trades or crafts and 109 on agriculture.[27] A large proportion of the former relied on wood turning and only a small minority of residents was supported by more usual rural crafts. Several masons lived in the parish in the mid 19th century, including Robert Field, whose son Robert[28] had three employees as a mason in 1871 and whose grandson Frederick Field[29] (*fl.* 1939) ran a building business.[30] A nailmaker lived at Dursley Cross in 1861 and 1889.[31]

At the end of the First World War a factory for pulping and bottling fruit was built in the village close to the railway station. It closed soon afterwards[32] and was used as a fruit depot in the early 1950s[33] and as a welding workshop in 2006. In the later 20th century a number of small businesses were

---

1 *Kelly's Dir. Glos.* (1894), 226.
2 TNA, CP 25/2/142/1799, no 7; CP 25/2/423/15 Chas. I Hil. no 18.
3 GA, D 36/T 18, deed 25 Oct. 1699; T 23, copy court roll 1 May 1667.
4 Rudge, *Agric. of Glos.* 22.
5 GA, D 23/T 18.
6 Ibid. D 6/E 4, no 4; D 2528, p. 16, plan E.
7 TNA, HO 107/1959.
8 GDR, T 1/116; D. Bick, 'Lime-Kilns in North-West Gloucestershire', *Glos. Soc. for Industrial Archaeol. J.* (1984), 4–7.
9 TNA, RG 10/2605; *Morris's Dir. Glos.* (1876), 514.
10 OS Map 6", Glos. XXIV.SW (1889 edn).
11 GA, D 2957/193/4; DA 24/100/3, p. 42; DA 30/100/12, p. 59.
12 Ibid. DA 30/100/12, p. 162; see ibid. GA, D 177, Pringle fam., Longhope deeds 1872–1917, sale partics. 1917.
13 Bick, 'Lime-Kilns', 4–7.
14 OS Map 6", Glos. XXIII.SE (1883 edn).
15 *Pleas of the Crown for Glos.* ed. Maitland, p. 80.
16 Smith, *Men and Armour*, 68–9.
17 GDR wills 1608/120; 1615/147; 1685/175.
18 GA, D 892/T 43, deed 22 May 1713.
19 Ibid. D 2671.
20 Ibid. D 6/E 4, no 4; GDR, T 1/116 (no 313).
21 GA, D 2428/1/65, ff. 16, 21.
22 Cave, 'Mill Sites on the Longhope–Flaxley–Westbury Streams', 16.
23 GDR, T 1/116 (nos 737–9); TNA, HO 107/361.
24 TNA, HO 107/1959.
25 *Kelly's Dir. Glos.* (1863), 305; (1870), 592.
26 GDR wills 1666/99; 1678/168; 1686/4.
27 *Census,* 1831.
28 TNA, HO 107/1959.   29 Ibid. RG 10/2605.
30 *Kelly's Dir. Glos.* (1889 and later edns); cat. of GA, D 4380, which includes business records of Robert Field (d. 1891).
31 TNA, RG 9/1758; *Kelly's Dir. Glos.* (1889), 833.
32 GA, DA 24/500/9, f. 43; D 2299/3020: OS Map 6", Glos. XXIV.SW (1903, 1924 edns).
33 *Longhope, Coronation Year*, 2.

established, some on the site of the former turnery in the village and in the craft centre at Hart's Barn, and in 2006 manufacturers included makers of garden ornaments, furniture, windows and doors, and trailers, handcarts, and trolleys.

The inclusion of three sailors and three carriers among the inhabitants listed in Longhope in 1608 shows that much trade was organised from the parish. Thomas Dobbs's carrying business prospered,[1] moving goods between London and Abergavenny and Monmouth, and was continued after his death in 1613 by his son Richard (d. 1614).[2] In the mid 19th century several carrying and haulage businesses operated from the Little London area. One was run by a fruiterer by 1861[3] and a farmer provided a regular carrying service to Gloucester in the late 1870s. Although Mitcheldean carriers later offered a regular service to Gloucester, hauliers continued to operate from Longhope. Richard Read, whose father Henry had established a motor transport business in the 1920s,[4] founded his own haulage firm in 1946 and broadened his business to include the sale of commercial vehicles, building warehouses on a site on the Monmouth road.[5] In 2006 another haulage firm, started by Richard's brother Harold, operated from Church Road[6] and the warehouses of a storage and transport business occupied the saw mill site at Upper End.

The railway built along the Longhope valley in the mid 1850s provided some employment, the staff of the village station including a night watchman in 1871.[7] In the early 20th century several refreshment rooms catered for increasing road and tourist traffic[8] and in 1927 a garage on the Ross road at Boxbush served motor traffic.[9] A caravan and camping site established just off the road in the mid 1950s has become a residential park.[10] For a time there were tea rooms on May hill, on Yartleton Lane.[11]

Longhope's inhabitants in the mid 19th century included several shopkeepers and a newsman.[12] There was a postmistress in 1856[13] and a second telegraph office, the first being at the railway station, opened in 1897.[14] In the later 19th century shopkeepers lived in several places, including Dursley Cross, Little London, and Gaston House in Barrel Lane.[15] A grocery business established at Little London by 1881[16] was combined with a bakery for many years and continued after the First World War.[17] In the late 1930s six shopkeepers, grocers, and bakers were recorded in the parish.[18] In 2006 the village had the only shop and a post office. In 1969 there had also been a post office on May hill.[19]

An excise officer lived in Longhope in 1861.[20] Professional services were provided by Solomon Coleman, who ran his practice as a solicitor from Longhope until his death in 1878.[21] The professions were also represented by a surgeon in 1906,[22] at which time a Mitcheldean doctor was the medical officer for the parish.[23] In 2006 livery and veterinary services were available in Longhope.

LOCAL GOVERNMENT

MANORIAL GOVERNMENT

The manor court provided profits for the lord in the mid 13th century[24] and was presumably held at the manor house, the site of Court Farm known as the Court House in the early 18th century.[25] In the late Middle Ages the lord's court for Huntley manor apparently dealt with some tenurial matters in Longhope.[26] Custom required the Longhope court to meet twice a year[27] but tenurial business necessitated additional occasional meetings in the 17th century. Of the twice-yearly general sessions as both court leet and court baron that in October, convened in a local inn in the later 1680s and early

---

1 Smith, *Men and Armour*, 68–9.
2 TNA, PROB 11/122, ff. 381–382v.; GA, D 36/T 18, deed 24 Jan. 1614; GDR wills 1614/159.
3 TNA, HO 107/1959; RG 9/1758; RG 10/2605; *Morris's Dir. Glos.* (1876), 514–15.
4 *Kelly's Dir. Glos.* (1879 and later edns).
5 *Forester*, 20 June 1997; http://www.richardreadtransport.co.uk (accessed 23 May 2005).
6 http://www.longhopevillage.co.uk (accessed 2 Jan. 2007).
7 TNA, RG 9/1758; RG 10/2604; RG 11/2525.
8 *Kelly's Dir. Glos.* (1910), 240.
9 Ibid. (1927), 256.
10 Above, settlement (outlying settlement: the north end).
11 Information from Mrs Torill Freeman of Home Farm, Huntley.
12 TNA, HO 107/1959.
13 *Kelly's Dir. Glos.* (1856), 321.
14 GA, DA 24/100/1, pp. 236, 249; P 206A/PC 1/1, p. 73.
15 *Morris's Dir. Glos.* (1876), 514.
16 TNA, RG 11/2525; RG 12/2007
17 Ibid. RG 12/2007; GA, DA 24/100/13, p. 4; *Kelly's Dir. Glos.* (1923), 244; (1927), 256.
18 *Kelly's Dir. Glos.* (1939), 252.
19 OS Map 1:2,500, SO 7020–7120 (1970 edn).
20 TNA, RG 9/1758.
21 GA, D 1791/4, min. 15 Sept. 1843; reg. wills 1878, ff. 193v.–194v.
22 *Kelly's Dir. Glos.* (1906), 235.
23 Plaque in Longhope ch. to N.F. Searancke, MOH for the district 1883–1931; see *Kelly's Dir Glos.* (1910 and later edns).
24 *Inq. p.m. Glos.* 1236–1300, 91.
25 Above, settlement (the village).
26 TNA, DL 7/2, no 33.
27 *Glos. N&Q* I, 399–402. For another transcript of the manor customs of 1660, see Birmingham City Archives, Barnard Colln. 940.

1690s, elected a petty constable.[1] Later the court, which was held until at least 1891, met in general session only in October but continued its occasional sessions. In that period the October court elected two constables until 1841 and a hayward on a few occasions. It dealt with the repair of bridges but its main business until 1874 concerned encroachments on common land, primarily on May hill. In 1842 both the lord of the manor and the vicar were fined for cutting turf on the hill. Fines were also imposed for removing dung from the hill. In the mid 19th century the steward convened the occasional courts in a number of places, often away from Longhope but including the Yew Tree in 1865.[2]

PAROCHIAL GOVERNMENT

Longhope's two churchwardens, named in 1469,[3] repaired the parish church, distributed alms, and provided military equipment using the income from parish property held in trust and known later as the Parish Charity Lands. Their role in the trust's business being defined in 1599,[4] the churchwardens were much involved in later poor relief within the parish and they continued to supply military accessories in the late 17th century. Apart from the trust's contributions, which were divided equally between them, the wardens were funded occasionally from rates and they made separate accounts.[5]

There were two overseers of the poor long before the 1700s,[6] each having responsibility for one of the parish's two divisions in which rates were collected separately. Each division also had its own surveyor of the highways.[7] The burden of poor relief was eased considerably by the Parish Charity Lands trust and from the late 17th century a charity provided funds for apprenticeships arranged by the parish officers, of whom the overseers were partly eclipsed in their work by the churchwardens. Two other charities provided clothing for the poor.[8] Frequent assistance was given to vagrants and the poor with passes tramping along the main roads. Many of those helped in the mid 1720s were sailors. From the mid 18th century poor residents were sometimes treated in the Gloucester infirmary. A local workhouse, the articles of which were signed in 1774,[9] had closed by 1803.[10] In 1811 the vestry agreed an *ex gratia* payment of £10 to a labourer, who after being chosen by ballot to serve in the militia had hired a substitute to save his family from becoming dependent on the parish. Another workhouse opened after 1816 was in use in 1835[11] when Longhope became part of the new Westbury-on-Severn poor-law union.[12]

The rise in the cost of relief in the later 18th century was marked and in 1803, when 22 parishioners received regular and 12 occasional help, Longhope supported 63 outsiders, presumably squatters living on May hill among them. The cost, £222, was double that twenty years earlier, but included £16 spent trying to recover money paid to the hundred's high constable.[13] Ten years later, when the trust funded expenditure only in the parish's upper division, the poor were even more numerous and £638 was used to help 129 people, 66 of them permanently; in 1815 £287 was spent on a similar number of people.[14] The cost of relief remained over £220 in the 1820s and 1830s and was almost £350 in the early 1830s.[15] The parish employed a salaried assistant overseer after 1835[16] and the Parish Charity Lands trust, although it ceased to pay house rents,[17] made an appreciable contribution to the business of relief well into the 20th century.[18]

Longhope, with its two main roads, was presented in 1598 for letting the Monmouth road fall into disrepair[19] and was fined in 1682 for not repairing its highways.[20] Road maintenance remained a considerable financial burden in the turnpike era, particularly for the parish's upper division which included the Ross road,[21] and on occasions was financed by fines on the whole parish.[22] After assuming responsibility for the turnpike roads in 1880 the two surveyors each received a salary but from 1886 the vestry employed a single surveyor for the two divisions, reducing his salary in 1889 after the county council took over the main roads.[23]

The vestry remained at the forefront of parish government until the election of a parish council in 1894.[24] The council, which immediately became

---

1 GA, D 36/T 23; D 23/E 1; D 1281/1.
2 Ibid. D 1297, Longhope ct. book 1828–91. For 19th-cent. ct. records, see also ibid. Longhope deeds 1796–1859; D 891, steward's papers 1800–21.
3 Hockaday Abs. cclxiii.
4 *18th Rep. Com. Char.* 326–7; GDR, V 5/193T 3; see above, social hist. (charities for the poor).
5 GA, P 206/CW 2/1; *18th Rep. Com. Char.* 327.
6 GA, P 206/CW 2/1; see ibid. Q/SO 1, f. 191.
7 Ibid. D 3436/1; VE 2/1–2.
8 Above, social hist. (charities for the poor); GA, P 206/CW 2/1; D 3436/1.
9 GA, P 206/CW 2/1.
10 *Poor Law Abstract, 1804*, 180–1.

11 GA, P 206/VE 2/1–2.
12 *Poor Law Com. 2nd Rep.* p. 524.
13 *Poor Law Abstract, 1804*, 180–1; GA, P 206/VE 2/1, min. 9 Mar. 1802.
14 *Poor Law Abstract, 1818*, 152–3.
15 *Poor Law Returns* (1830–1), 70; (1835), 68.
16 GA, P 206/VE 2/2.
17 Ibid. D 1791/4.
18 Above, social hist. (charities for the poor).
19 BL, Harl. MS 4131, f. 527v.
20 GA, Q/SO 2, f. 5v.
21 Ibid. P 206/VE 2/1.
22 Ibid. Q/SR 1767 B; 1769 C.
23 Ibid. P 206/VE 2/2.
24 Ibid.

embroiled in the affairs of the trustees of the Parish Charity Lands,[1] had regular meetings to deal with its own business, including the appointment of parish officers and the oversight of public rights of way and springs, and the assistant overseer usually acted as its clerk. In 1898 the council took over the management of the summit of May hill,[2] which had been the responsibility of the churchwardens and overseers since 1874,[3] and from 1900 it paid a groundsman to look after the land and its clump of trees. It also took over the running of some allotment gardens and in 1901 it succeeded the lord of the manor in maintaining the parish pound and appointing the hayward. In 1906 it moved its regular business meetings from the British schoolroom on Hope's hill to the Latchen Room (the village hall),[4] which it bought in 1924.[5]

Longhope had a number of police stations in succession.[6] The earliest recorded was accommodated in the former vicarage house in 1899.[7]

SOCIAL HISTORY

SOCIAL STRUCTURE

In the later 13th century customary tenants on Longhope manor owed cash rents and five cottagers and two mondaymen were among those with smaller holdings.[8] Fifty-four people were assessed for tax in Longhope and Blaisdon in 1327, two, including Sarah Talbot, for just over 6s. and five, among them the two lords of Blaisdon manor, for between 4s. and 4s. 8d. Eleven people were taxed for 2s., two for 1s. 6d., twenty-three for 1s., one for 9d., and ten for 6d.[9] Despite Sarah Talbot's inclusion in the assessment, the Talbots, lords of Longhope manor and later earls of Shrewsbury,[10] were invariably non-resident.

Few wealthy people lived in Longhope. In 1522 of fifty-five men other than the vicar one (William Dobbs) had goods valued at £20, two at £10, and two at £8. Of the rest the great majority had goods worth £3 or less and for eight parishioners no valuation was provided.[11] In 1608 three residents, Henry Acton, Arthur Rowles, and John Bower, were described as gentlemen. Among the rest, a community of small farmers, craftsmen, tradesmen, and cottagers, the carrier Thomas Dobbs employed two of the eight men described as servants.[12] In 1672, when 48 of 115 residents were excused the payment of hearth tax, the great majority of parishioners had a single hearth and 23 including the vicar two hearths. Nine householders each had 3 hearths, two 4 hearths, and one (Thomas Master) 5 hearths.[13] The farmer Thomas Bright, one of the resident manorial bailiffs in the mid 17th century, was reputed to be well over 110 years old at his death in 1708.[14] Among the leading local landowners Thomas Nourse (d. 1675) and his successor Nourse Yate[15] made substantial donations to the church and the poor.[16]

In 1769 the parishioners needed to defray much of the cost of rebuilding the church by soliciting funds from elsewhere.[17] In the later 18th and early 19th century the number of cottagers increased as squatters settled on the commons below the summit of May hill to live off the local woods[18] and the burden of poor relief rose considerably.[19] During local bread riots in 1795 Foresters intercepted wheat destined for a flour mill in Longhope and demonstrated at the mill.[20] In 1814 a small farm at Lonehead formerly owned by John Stephens, a master mariner, belonged to Duncan Thompson Stephens, his son by Mary Thompson, a free quadroon woman living in Jamaica. Duncan, who had been in England, had returned to Jamaica as a saddler and on his death there in 1821 the land passed to his father's legitimate heirs.[21]

John Probyn, rector of Abenhall and archdeacon (later dean) of Llandaff, moved to Longhope about the time he inherited the manor in 1819[22] and made

---

1 Ibid. CH 1.
2 Ibid. P 206A/PC 1/1.
3 Ibid. Q/RI 91.
4 Ibid. P 206A/PC 1/1.
5 Ibid. D 3168/4/7/144.
6 G. Sindrey and T. Heath, 'Forest of Dean Police Stations 1840 to 2000', *The New Regard* 15 (Forest of Dean Local History Soc., 2000), 49, 52, 57.
7 GA, S 206/1/2/1; see TNA, RG 13/2418.
8 *Inq. p.m. Glos. 1236–1300*, 91.
9 *Glos. Subsidy Roll, 1327*, 43. For the lords of Blaisdon, see *VCH Glos.* X, 7.
10 Above, manor.
11 *Military Surv. of Glos. 1522*, 206–7.
12 Smith, *Men and Armour*, 68–9.
13 TNA, E 179/247/14, rott. 36d.–37. For Master, above, manor (Longhope manor: the Manor Ho.).
14 TNA, E 134/3 Jas. II/Easter 22; GA, D 3436/1. On his tombstone his age was given as 124: Rudder, *Glos.* 534.
15 Above, manor (manor: the Manor Ho.).
16 Below (charities for the poor); religious hist.
17 GA, Q/SR 1769 B; see BL, Church Brief B.XI.4.
18 Turner, *Agric. of Glos.* 50; *Glos. Chron.* 29 Aug. 1868 (letter); see GA, D 36/E 7/5.
19 Above, local govt. (parochial govt.).
20 H.G. Nicholls, *The Forest of Dean: an Historical and Descriptive Account* (1858), 84–5.
21 GA, D 2667; TNA, PROB 11/1463, f. 278 and v.
22 Hockaday Abs. xcv, Abenhall; above, manor; information from the Revd Canon Dr B.M. Lodwick of Neath.

the Manor House his home.[1] On the death of his brother William in 1825 he gave the vicarage to his son-in-law Charles Mein Dighton and, after Charles's premature death, in turn to his son Edmund Probyn (d. 1837) and son-in-law Robert Napier Raikes (d. 1851).[2] John's son and heir John also lived in Longhope, patronizing local societies and groups.[3] In 1851 his household included six servants and his sisters Caroline Raikes and Elizabeth Probyn maintained smaller establishments at the vicarage and the Temple. Several other parishioners, including the landowner John Coleman, the curate, the Baptist minister, and ten farmers, also employed domestic servants. The adult male population was mostly tradesmen, craftsmen, and manual workers, with a handful of businessmen headed by the wood turner James Constance and many of the farmers being employers of labour.[4] While the solicitor Solomon Coleman (d. 1878) lived permanently in Longhope,[5] members of the professions were usually a transient presence, Jordan House being home to a barrister in 1851 and a clergyman in 1861.[6]

Although Elizabeth Probyn lived in Longhope until her death in 1897,[7] after John Probyn's death in 1863 the lord of the manor was again non-resident, Edmund Probyn living in Huntley before moving to Staffordshire.[8] In the later 19th century the Manor House was occupied by a succession of tenants and the number of private residents increased as incomers moved into houses in the village and on May hill. Widows and spinsters headed a number of households,[9] the largest of which was at Bradley Grove (later Bradley Court), built in the late 1860s for the colliery owner Osman Barrett[10] and from 1880 the home of the family of Thomas Miller (d. 1882), formerly a merchant in the Cape Verde Islands.[11] During that period the vicar F.C. Guise, a member of a leading county family, chaired much parish business until the eve of the first election, in 1894, of a parish council.[12]

H.A. Pringle, who took a lease of the Manor House in 1916 before becoming the main landowner in Longhope,[13] was among several military officers to move to Longhope at that time. W.S. Davis, who settled at Coglan House,[14] was formerly of the Indian civil service. His son Admiral Sir William Davis (d. 1987) took a leading part in youth and other organizations within the county.[15] Among local businessmen representing the parish in local government were the timber merchant William Constance, elected as vice-chairman of the rural district council in 1918,[16] and the baker and grocer William Armstrong Bradley (d. 1939), a member of the district council for over 20 years after his retirement.[17] New building in the later 20th century, particularly the development of a housing estate on the edge of the village after 1971, drew many new families into Longhope and retired people made up a quarter of the households in the village at the end of the century.[18] Several of the larger houses in the parish, including the Manor House, the Temple, and Bradley Court, were turned into hotels or nursing homes, a process under way by the mid 20th century.[19]

CHARITIES FOR THE POOR

A charitable trust used land and cottages acquired by the parish from a series of gifts beginning in the late 14th century[20] to finance repairs to the parish church, equipment for soldiers, and help for poor and orphaned parishioners, maimed soldiers, and prisoners in the county gaol. The body of feoffees, in which the property was vested, renewed itself by the grant of its two surviving members in the mid 16th century. Rules imposed in 1599, after improper handling of trust affairs, set the minimum number of feoffees at 12 and required the churchwardens and at least six other parishioners to approve leases of trust property, which comprised scattered pieces in Longhope and a share in a cottage in Mitcheldean.[21] The feoffees' body regularly renewed itself from that time and the trust became known as the Parish Charity Lands.[22] In spending the income of the trust the churchwardens were much involved in poor relief and in the late 17th and early 18th century, when the rental was usually just over £35, they made

---

1 GDR, T 1/116; TNA, PROB 11/1988, ff. 357v.–361; above, settlement (bldgs.).
2 Hockaday Abs. cclxiii; C. Dighton, *The Dightons of Clifford Chambers* (1902), 28–9. See below, religious hist.
3 *Glouc. J.* 23 May, 18 July 1846; 20 May 1848.
4 TNA, HO 107/1959.
5 Ibid. HO 107/361; RG 9/1758; GA, reg. wills 1878, ff. 193v.–194v.
6 TNA, HO 107/1959; RG 9/1758.
7 *The Times*, 13 May 1897; GA, D 2299/2/6/53.
8 *Kelly's Dir. Glos.* (1870), 584; (1889), 833; GA, SL 10.
9 *Kelly's Dir. Glos.* (1870–1902 edns); GA, D 2299/2/3/74.
10 *Kelly's Dir. Glos.* (1870), 598; TNA, RG 10/2605. For Barrett, see *VCH Glos.* V, 333.
11 GA, D 543, Longhope deeds 1828–80; TNA, RG 11/2525; RG 12/2007; RG 13/2418. For Miller's date of death, see his tombstone in Longhope churchyard.
12 GA, D 2174/1; P 206/CH 1; VE 2/2; P 206A/PC 1/1, pp. 6–7, 35.
13 GA, D 177, Pringle fam., Longhope deeds 1872–1917; above, manor.
14 *Kelly's Dir. Glos.* (1919), 231; (1923), 244.
15 Inscriptions in Longhope ch.; *Who Was Who 1981–90*, 191.
16 *Kelly's Dir. Glos.* (1919), 231; GA, DA 24/100/8, p. 111.
17 GA, DA 24/100/13, p. 4.
18 *The Longhope Village Appraisal 1991* (copy in VCH Glos. office), 5.
19 Above, settlement (the village).
20 *18th Rep. Com. Char.* 327.
21 TNA, C 93/1/34; see GDR, V 5/193T 5; T 1/116.
22 *18th Rep. Com. Char.* 326–7.

cash payments typically of 6d. to soldiers and sailors as well as to parishioners.[1]

The amount regularly available to the churchwardens for Longhope's poor was increased by legacies from Thomas Nourse, who by will proved 1675 left £5 a year for coats or other garments for 10 people at Christmas and £5 a year for apprenticeships for one or two children in London, Bristol, Gloucester, or a market town. The payments, as charges on the rectory estate,[2] were from Nourse Yate until 1701 and from the vicar thereafter[3] and the apprenticeships were arranged, usually one a year, in London and elsewhere. In 1695, while churchwarden, Nourse Yate supplemented the premium paid to a Coleford tailor.[4] To enable eight elderly people to have shirts at Christmas, farmer Thomas Hodges by will proved 1736 left a piece of land called Broom's Pool for buying linen cloth in the great market held at Ross-on-Wye after Michaelmas.[5] By the mid 1820s, when that land produced a rent of £4,[6] Thomas Nourse's clothing charity was restricted to five people, the same ones receiving it every other year, and his apprenticeship charity funded a new apprenticeship every two or three years.[7]

Apart from the repair of its buildings and the church, the Parish Charity Lands used its income of between £130 and £140 in the mid 1820s for the poor.[8] After the demolition of the Mitcheldean cottage and until 1865 the trust received 25s. a year from Mitcheldean parish.[9] Under rules agreed in 1835 the trustees (formerly feoffees) appointed a treasurer and started holding quarterly meetings. Those meetings were frequently adjourned because a quorum of three was not present and from 1843 the vicar and churchwardens were co-opted as acting trustees with responsibility for much of the administration. In 1844, with payments to the poor an almost daily event, a salaried relieving officer (later almoner) was employed[10] and the dispensing of the clothing and apprenticeship charities passed from the treasurer back to the churchwardens.[11] At that time those charities provided coats for five men and clothing material including duck and calico for over 30 men and women at Christmas. The occasional apprenticeships were served by boys locally but usually outside the parish.[12] Thomas Nourse's clothing charity provided three coats and cloth for men's frocks from 1858[13] and together with the Hodges charity supplied, in addition to the coats, cloth to 43 people in 1875 and 50 people in 1890.[14] Under a Scheme of 1913 the apprenticing charity could give cash support for Longhope children in apprenticeships in market towns more than 15 miles away.[15]

From 1866, under a Scheme which established the vicar and churchwardens among its governors, the Parish Charity Lands applied its substantial income in equal parts to the church, the church school, and the poor.[16] For the poor its almoner made individual weekly and occasional cash payments with freeholders ineligible for poor-law relief being favoured for regular help. Weekly pay was raised from 2s. to 2s. 6d. in 1906, when there were four recipients, and was according to need from 1909, following the introduction of State old-age pensions. In 1913 the trust assigned part of its subscription to the Gloucester infirmary to a local nursing association.[17] From 1896 a third of the trust's income was reserved for the maintenance of the parish church and the rest was used for the school and the poor by a separate charity with representatives of the parish council on its board.[18] Distinct from the trust property was a piece of woodland (6 a.) held for charitable purposes in the mid 19th century[19] and an acre on May hill near Dursley Cross set aside by the Inclosure Commissioners in 1874 for the benefit of the parish's labouring poor.[20] Rose Barton by will dated 1951 left £1,000 for a Christmas party for the poor and infirm.[21]

From 1957 the Parish Charity Lands trust, which had sold its land,[22] could apply a third of its income to the poor, another third to the church fabric, and the final third to the poor or church repairs as thought fit. In practice only a third went to the church and under the new Scheme 13 mostly elderly people received weekly pensions of 5s., paid monthly, in 1969. In 1976 the Nourse and Hodges clothing charities and the charity for the labouring poor were merged to form the Longhope Relief in Need charity providing individual and general help. The new charity's income was augmented by a third of that of

---

1 GA, P 206/CW 2/1; D 3436/1.
2 TNA, PROB 11/349, ff. 308v.–312v.
3 GDR, V 5/193T 4–5.
4 GA, P 206/CW 2/1; D 3436/1.
5 TNA, PROB 11/678, ff. 78v.–80.
6 *18th Rep. Com. Char.* 325–6.
7 Ibid. 325.
8 Ibid. 326–7.
9 GA, P 206/CH 2; *VCH Glos.* V, 191 and n.
10 GA, D 1791/4; D 2174/1.
11 Ibid. D 2174/1; P 206/CW 2/3.
12 Ibid. D 2174/1.
13 Ibid. P 206/CW 2/3.
14 Ibid. CW 2/3.
15 Glos. Colln. RF 193.1.
16 GA, P 206A/PC 1/1, pp. 13–15.
17 Ibid. P 206/CH 1; for the nursing association, below (social life).
18 GA, P 206/CH 1; P 206A/PC 1/1.
19 GDR, T 1/116.
20 GA, Q/RI 91.
21 Ibid. D 3469/5/96.
22 See ibid. D 2299/1977.

EDUCATION

Longhope had a public school in 1679.[3] A schoolmaster lived there in 1803[4] but in 1818, while there was a Sunday school, there was no day school for the poor.[5] Edmund Probyn, who built a schoolroom next to his new vicarage house in the late 1820s,[6] employed a teacher with 63 day pupils paying pence in 1833. At that time 185 children attended the Sunday school.[7] In 1836 Edward Goff's (or Gough's) trust appointed a master for a day school at the Baptist chapel at Little London. The master and his successor also served as the chapel's minister[8] and from 1846 the free day school and a Sunday school were taught in the meeting's new chapel on Hope's hill.[9] At that time there were also two small dame schools in the parish.[10] A school for boys from a wealthier background, opened by John Irving at Blenheim House, Lea Line, by 1841, had 33 boarding pupils in 1851.[11]

At the vicarage schoolroom, where over 100 children attended Sunday school in the mid 1840s,[12] Revd F.C. Guise ran a day school attended on average in the early 1860s by c.68 children including infants. Known as Longhope Church of England school, it was funded in part by annual sermons[13] and from 1866 it received a third of the income of the Parish Charity Lands trust.[14] It was also supported by pence and voluntary contributions and in 1874 the average attendance was 50.[15]

The Baptist chapel on Hope's hill had a schoolroom in 1855 and its Sunday school taught 119 children in 1866.[16] A new schoolroom was added to the chapel in 1866. The day school, supported by pence and receiving £50 a year from Goff's trust for the teacher's salary, taught boys, girls, and infants and had an average attendance of 40 in 1874, when it became a British school[17] with the minister as the chief manager and its first female teacher was appointed.[18] The boarding school at Lea Line closed in the 1870s.[19] Among later, smaller schools one at Upper End for girls, established by 1891,[20] remained open in 1916.[21]

The church and the British schools respectively had average attendances of 52 and 40 in 1885[22] and 60 and 69 in 1904.[23] The British school, which was enlarged in 1893 to provide separate infant accommodation,[24] became known as Longhope Council school on its transfer to the county council in 1906[25] and the average attendance in 1910 was 86 in mixed and infant departments.[26] The church school, with an average attendance of 55 in 1910,[27] was altered and given a new playground to its west in 1911[28] and had in mixed and infant departments an average attendance of 46 in 1922 and 43 in 1938.[29] There were 78 children on its roll in 2000.[30] The council school, where average attendance declined from 67 in 1922 to 49 in 1938,[31] was known as Hopes Hill Community Primary school and had 40 children, some from Blaisdon, on its roll in 2000.[32] In 2001 the two schools were amalgamated to form Hope Brook C. of E. Primary school, which moved in 2003 to a new building in the centre of the village off Church Road.[33] It had 110 children on its roll at the beginning of 2005.[34]

An agricultural college established at Bradley Court in the early 20th century was superseded by a riding school in the later 1930s.[35]

---

1 GA, D 3469/5/96.
2 http://www.charity-commission.gov.uk/registeredcharities (accessed 4 June 2007: nos 254952, 262340).
3 Hockaday Abs. cclxiii.
4 GA, D 3398/1/7/14, abstract of title 1846 (will of William Bullock).
5 *Educ. of Poor Digest*, 303.
6 GDR, V 6/64B; OS 6" Maps, Glos. XXIII.SE (1883 edn); XXIV.SW (1889 edn).
7 *Educ. Enq. Abstract*, 320.
8 J. Stanley, *In Days of Old. Memories of the Ejected Ministers of 1662* (Hereford, 1913), 42; T. Bright, *Rise of Nonconformity in the Forest of Dean* (Forest of Dean Local History Soc. 1953), 29–30.
9 *Glouc. J.* 2 Aug. 1845; 18 July 1846; TNA, HO 129/334/7/14.
10 Nat. Soc. *Inquiry, 1846–7*, Glos. 12–13.
11 TNA, HO 107/361; HO 107/1959; GDR, T 1/116 (no 374A).
12 Nat. Soc. *Inquiry, 1846–7*, Glos. 12–13.
13 TNA, ED 7/34/198.
14 GA, P 206A/PC 1/1, pp. 13–15.
15 TNA, ED 7/345/198.
16 *Glouc. J.* 25 Aug. 1855; 27 Jan. 1866.
17 TNA, ED 7/34/199.
18 GA, S 206/2/1/1.
19 TNA, RG 10/2605; RG 11/2525.
20 *Kelly's Dir. Glos.* (1879–1902 edns); TNA, RG 12/2007.
21 GA, S 206/1/1/1, p. 31.
22 *Kelly's Dir. Glos.* (1885), 519.
23 *Public Elem. Schs. 1906*, 186.
24 GA, S 206/2/1/1, pp. 270–3.
25 Ibid. C/CE/M 2/4, pp. 215–16
26 *List 21*, 1911 (Board of Education), 164.
27 Ibid. 163.
28 GA, P 206/SC 1; the date on bldg.; see GA, S 206/1/3/1.
29 *List 21*, 1922 (Board of Education), 105; 1938, 128.
30 *Schools and Establishments Dir. 2000–1* (co. educ. dept), 28.
31 *List 21*, 1922 (Board of Education), 105; 1932, 116; 1938, 128.
32 *Schools and Establishments Dir. 2000–1*, 25; see *Longhope Village Appraisal*, 6.
33 Information from school website (http://www.hopebrook.gloucs.sch.uk: accessed 1 June 2006).
34 *Schools and Establishments Dir. 2005–6*, 25.
35 *Kelly's Dir. Glos.* (1902–39 edns); E. Gaskell, *Glos. Leaders* (1906), s.v. William Hunter Gandy.

SOCIAL LIFE

Morris men have long gathered on the summit of May hill to greet the dawn of May Day.[1] The ancient custom was for men from surrounding parishes to enact in mock battle a contest, originally between the forces of winter and spring, for possession of the hill.[2] In 1875 a morris dance ended workmen's celebrations for the construction of the top part of Yartleton Lane.[3]

The Yew Tree inn, standing west of the village on the Monmouth road, had evidently opened by 1608.[4] In the 1660s Longhope had three unlicensed alehouses.[5] At least one of them was open in the mid 1680s[6] and the manor court met at a local inn in 1688 and 1692.[7] A house below Bradley grove was known as the Bear in 1717[8] and the parish also had houses called the Leather Bottle in 1736[9] and the Cock in 1743.[10] A victualler lived at Dursley Cross in 1727.[11]

In the village a public house on the Monmouth road was known as the Plough by 1856[12] and there were beerhouses next to the railway station and in the Latchen in 1861. Little London had the King's Head inn in 1861.[13] An inn at Dursley Cross recorded in 1830[14] was known as the Eight Bells in 1841[15] and beerhouses further along the Ross road were known as the Farmer's Boy and the Nag's Head in 1851 and 1871 respectively.[16] Of the five public houses licensed in Longhope in the late 19th century[17] that at Dursley Cross closed in the mid 20th century[18] and the Plough was demolished in the mid 1970s. The Yew Tree, Nag's Head, and Farmer's Boy served Longhope and passing traffic in 2005.

The Yew Tree was the meeting place of a friendly society formed in 1845.[19] Later societies met there or at the Plough, one having 39 members at its dissolution in 1881.[20] A friendly society based on the Cross inn on May hill in 1864 had 37 members when it was wound up in 1884.[21] In the mid 19th century local festivals and annual treats occasionally enlivened social life. Such events usually followed a service in the parish church or the Baptist chapel and were accompanied by sports and marked by processions which, as in 1855 during the Crimean War, afforded displays of patriotism.[22]

From the mid 19th century parish business was generally conducted in the schoolroom near the church.[23] In 1895 the new parish council chose to do its business in the schoolroom at the Baptist chapel[24] and from 1906 it met at the Latchen Room, a new hall built for the parish at the bottom of the village on the Monmouth road by William Henry Powell of Hill House.[25] A hall was built at the chapel in 1922.[26] The Latchen Room accommodated a variety of clubs and societies including a branch of the Women's Institute recorded in 1923 and a drama society formed in the early 1930s and has remained the village hall. Longhope also had a band and a branch of the British Legion in the late 1930s [27] and local groups in 2005 included a gardening club as well as the drama society and the Women's Institute. A hall erected in the parsonage grounds near the church in the mid 20th century[28] has been demolished to make way for a small housing estate.

A football club made the Latchen Room its headquarters in 1906.[29] A cricket club was founded soon afterwards[30] and a bowling club existed in the late 1930s.[31] Blacksmith's Meadow, just north of the village centre, was made a recreation ground on its purchase by public subscription in 1947 as a memorial to local men killed in the Second World War.[32] It continues to be used by football, cricket, and tennis clubs.

A medical officer appointed in 1883 provided services from Mitcheldean[33] and in 1939 one of two visiting physicians held a surgery in Longhope twice a week.[34] A nursing association was formed for Longhope and Blaisdon in 1907.[35]

---

1 N. Spencer, *The Complete English Traveller* (1771), 364.
2 Rudder, *Glos.* 533; Fosbrooke, *Glos.* II, 224.
3 *Glouc J.* 12 June 1875.
4 Smith, *Men and Armour*, 68; GA, D 1297, survey of Huntley, Netherley, and Longhope 1717, Longhope no 24.
5 GA, Q/SIb 1, ff. 44, 113, 146v., 166v., 168v.
6 GDR wills 1686/344.
7 GA, D 36/T 23; D 23/E 1.
8 Ibid. D 1297, surv. 1717, Longhope no 26; D 543, Longhope deeds 1726–92.
9 TNA, PROB 11/678, ff. 78v.–80.
10 GA, D 3436/2, agreement 10 June 1743.
11 GDR wills 1730/37.
12 TNA, HO 107/1959; *Kelly's Dir. Glos.* (1856), 321; OS Map 6", Glos. XXIV.SW (1889 edn).
13 TNA, RG 9/1758.
14 GA, Q/REl 1, Duchy of Lancaster hundred.
15 TNA, HO 107/361.
16 Ibid. HO 107/1959; RG 10/2605.
17 *Licensed Houses in Glos. 1891*, 152–3.
18 See *Kelly's Dir. Glos.* (1939), 252.
19 *Glouc. J.* 23 May 1846.
20 TNA, FS 2/3, Glos. nos 694, 738, 818; FS 4/13, Glos. no 1081.
21 Ibid. FS 2/3, Glos. no 825; FS 4/13, Glos. no 825.
22 *Glouc. J.* 20 May 1848, 7 June 1851, 25 Aug. 1855.
23 GA, P 206/VE 2/2; P 206/CH 1.
24 Ibid. P 206A/PC 1/1.
25 *Glouc. J.* 6 Oct. 1906; above, settlement (bldgs.).
26 *Dean Forest Mercury*, 14 Mar. 1969.
27 GA, D 3168/4/7/144; *Kelly's Dir. Glos.* (1923), 244.
28 OS Maps 1: 2,500, Glos. XXIV.9 (1923 edn); SO 6819–6919 (1972 edn).
29 *Glouc. J.* 6 Oct. 1906.
30 'Village on the Air' (transcript of a BBC radio programme on 6 Oct. 1948: Glos. Colln. RF 193.4).
31 GA, D 3168/4/7/144.
32 Plaque in recreation ground; GA, DA 24/100/16, f. 14.
33 Plaque in Longhope ch. to N.F. Searancke; see *Kelly's Dir. Glos.* (1885), 525; (1931), 246, 259.
34 *Kelly's Dir. Glos.* (1939), 252.
35 Glos. Colln. R 48.1–2.

RELIGIOUS HISTORY

EARLY HISTORY AND STATUS OF THE PARISH CHURCH

The church at Longhope, to which that at Huntley was a chapel in the mid 12th century, was given to Monmouth priory presumably in William I's reign by the priory's founder Wihanoc of Monmouth.[1] The priory appropriated the church[2] and a vicarage had been established by 1291.[3] The impropriate rectory, which included the tithes of the parish, was added to the vicarage's endowments in the early 18th century[4] and the style of the benefice changed from vicarage to rectory in the late 19th century.[5] The benefice was united with Huntley with May Hill in 1983 and the united benefice included Churcham and Bulley from 2003.[6]

PATRONAGE AND ENDOWMENT

Until the Dissolution the vicarage was in the gift of Monmouth priory.[7] The Crown presented to the living in 1340, when the priory, a cell of the abbey of St Florent at Saumur (Maine-et-Loire), was in the king's hands by reason of war with France,[8] and in 1391.[9] Following the Dissolution the patronage passed with the rectory,[10] with Raphael Rawlins of Gloucester being patron at the first vacancy, in 1541, under a grant from the priory[11] and the Crown being patron for a turn in 1626.[12] On giving the rectory to the vicarage in 1701 Nourse Yate reserved the patronage[13] and in 1703 Joseph Venn was patron for a turn.[14]

After Yate's death the patronage descended with his Longhope estate[15] to his granddaughter Priscilla Bromwich. In 1774 she and William Matthews presented David Jones,[16] and he acquired the patronage shortly afterwards.[17] After Edmund Probyn bought it, probably in 1783,[18] it descended with the manor until the later 1840s.[19] From Sir John Wright Guise Bt, patron in 1851,[20] it passed to his son and heir Sir William Vernon Guise, and by 1879 it was apparently vested in the widow of Vernon George Guise (d. 1861), a former vicar of Longhope.[21] After belonging to F. Burrow of Cullompton (Devon) in 1894, it was acquired by J.C. Sharpe and after his death in 1913 it passed to the National Church League.[22] The Church Society was successor to the league[23] but the bishop became sole patron of the benefice of Huntley with May Hill and Longhope created in 1983 and shared the patronage with the dean and chapter of Gloucester after Churcham and Bulley were merged with the united benefice in 2003.[24]

Longhope vicarage, valued at £4 in 1291,[25] had a house in the early 15th century.[26] It included a lease of the rectory tithes in 1535, when it was worth £9 7s. 11½d. clear,[27] and in the 1540s Thomas Baker claimed its glebe and house to be his as rector.[28] The vicarage was worth £30 a year in 1650.[29]

Thomas Nourse by will proved 1675 left £10 a year from the rectory to future resident vicars[30] but his successor Nourse Yate, on adding the tithes with the rectory to the vicarage's endowments in 1701, ensured that the annuity was paid to George Venn, the vicar of Sherborne, until he became vicar of Longhope in 1703.[31] Payments of tithes in kind[32] had largely ceased by 1719 but some of fruit remained in kind and those of wood continued in kind under the agreements for cash rents tithe payers negotiated

---

1 *Cal. Doc. France*, 409–10.
2 For the descent of the rectory appropriated by the priory, above, manor (other estates).
3 *Tax. Eccl.* 161.
4 Below (patronage and endowment).
5 *Kelly's Dir. Glos.* (1894), 225; (1897), 229; see GA, P 206/IN 4/1.
6 *Dioc. of Glouc. Dir.* (1994–5), 59; (2003–4), 23.
7 *Reg. Lacy*, 115; *Reg. Stanbury*, 178; *Reg. Bothe*, 335.
8 *Cal. Pat.* 1340–3, 29, 63; see *Cal. Doc. France*, 409–10.
9 *Cal. Pat.* 1388–92, 472; *Reg. Trefnant*, 176.
10 TNA, CP 40/1142, Carte rott. 2–3; see above, manor (other estates).
11 Hockaday Abs. cclxiii.
12 TNA, E 331/GLOUC/11.
13 GDR, V 5/193T 4.
14 Hockaday Abs. cclxiii.
15 Above, manor (manor: the Manor Ho.).
16 Hockaday Abs. cclxiii; *Bp. Benson's Surv. of Dioc. of Glouc. 1735–50*, 9; Bigland, *Glos.* II, 170 (monument to Yate Bromwich).
17 Rudder, *Glos.* 533.
18 GA, D 3436/1, letter 3 Sept. 1783.
19 Ibid. D 4869/1/1/4; above, manor.
20 Hockaday Abs. cclxiii.
21 *Kelly's Dir. Glos.* (1870), 592; (1879), 696). For the Guises, *Burke's Peerage* (1963), 1087–8. A presentation in 1861 was by trustees: Hockaday Abs.cclxiii.
22 *Kelly's Dir. Glos.* (1894 and later edns); *The Times*, 25 Feb. 1897 (eccles. intelligence); 16 Sept. 1913 (obituary of J.C. Sharpe); 9 Feb. 1925 (eccles. news). For Sharpe, above, manor (manor: the Manor Ho.).
23 *Glouc. Dioc. Year Book* (1950–1), 34–5; (1951–2), 34–5.
24 *Dioc. of Glouc. Dir.* (1994–5), 59; (2003–4), 23.
25 *Tax. Eccl.* 161.
26 *Reg. Lacy*, 115 n.
27 *Valor Eccl.* II, 501; see ibid. III, 16; TNA, SC 6/Hen. VIII/7319, rot. 5d.
28 TNA, E 321/41/322; Hockaday Abs. cclxiii.
29 C.R. Elrington, 'The Survey of Church Livings in Gloucestershire, 1650', *Trans. BGAS* 83 (1964), 98.
30 TNA, PROB 11/349, f. 309.
31 GDR, V 5/193T 4; Hockaday Abs. cclxiii.
32 GDR, V 5/193T 5.

with a new vicar in 1774 and 1775.¹ In 1825 a new vicarage house was begun near the church² and in 1829 part of the glebe, including the old house, was exchanged for land adjoining the new house and containing a new schoolroom.³ The vicar was awarded a corn rent charge of £403 3s. for the tithes in 1841⁴ and the living, which had been worth £120 in 1750,⁵ was valued at £394 in 1856.⁶ Most of the glebe, which contained 23 a. in the mid 19th century,⁷ was sold in the 1920s⁸ and another part in the late 1940s.⁹ The house was sold in the late 20th century.

RELIGIOUS LIFE

The Middle Ages

Longhope's church, which was dedicated to All Saints by the mid 12th century,¹⁰ was built perhaps in the late 11th century and comprised chancel, nave, and west tower, all with walls of thin-bedded sandstone rubble and dark red quoins, perhaps from Mitcheldean. The nave retains single-light windows (blocked) with monolithic heads and the original tower, which had pilaster buttresses, survives up to the first string course. The chancel was extended in the 13th century and its medieval fabric, re-used in major repairs in the early 1770s,¹¹ includes two lancet windows (one blocked) and a south door. North and south transeptal chapels, about equal in length and with matching double-chamfered arches towards the nave, were built and traceried windows inserted in the south side of the nave, all probably in the early 14th century. Probably about the same time an octagonal spire was placed on the tower¹² and a new tower arch created. A south porch was added later, as were some nave windows in Perpendicular style.¹³ A series of gifts of lands to the parish from the late 14th century provided funds for the maintenance of the church and other purposes in the mid 16th century and became known as the Parish Charity Lands.¹⁴

The earliest known vicar of Longhope is Nicholas of Tibberton in 1318.¹⁵ Geoffrey Marshall, who became vicar in 1340¹⁶ and possibly retained the living in 1390,¹⁷ was from a local landowning family.¹⁸ John Sabyn, a parishioner who took orders as an acolyte in 1349,¹⁹ became vicar in 1391 and was allowed to occupy the main part of the vicarage's hall on his retirement in 1419.²⁰ The next two incumbencies spanned over a century.²¹

From the Reformation to the Restoration

William Trigge, vicar from 1541,²² was fully knowledgeable on the Lord's Prayer but unable to recite the Ten Commandments and adduce scriptural authority for the Apostles' Creed in 1551.²³ He was deprived of the living early in Mary's reign. Before that, in 1548, the parish sold a chalice, a pyx, and a cross to fund equipment for soldiers in the army and repairs to the highway to Huntley.²⁴ Among the church's acquisitions was a copy of Foxe's *Book of Martyrs*.²⁵

Henry Deyce, vicar from 1561, was a poor Latinist²⁶ and was reported in 1576 for providing only one sermon in the previous year, allowing another man to deliver the communion cup, not teaching the catechism, wearing a surplice on perambulations, and churching unmarried women.²⁷ Although not considered a preacher, Thomas Rudge,²⁸ vicar 1577–1618,²⁹ preached regularly in the church and instructed children in the catechism. During his time a parish clerk was unable to read lessons and psalms publicly and a few families were negligent in attending church.³⁰ Edward Potter, vicar from 1626, was the rector of Abenhall. Deprived of both livings, he was succeeded at Longhope in 1656 by Thomas Smith.³¹

The Established Church and Nonconformity after the Restoration

After the Restoration Smith was ejected from the vicarage and was succeeded by George Ditton in 1664.³² It was possibly in that period when a large mortar was installed in the church for use as a font in

---

1 GA, D 3436/2.
2 Above, settlement (bldgs.); see OS Map 6", Glos. XXIV.SW (1889 edn).
3 GDR, V 6/64B.
4 Ibid. T 1/116.
5 Bp. Benson's Surv. of Dioc. of Glouc. 1735–50, 10.
6 GDR vol. 384, f. 136.
7 Ibid. T 1/116.
8 *Kelly's Dir. Glos.* (1923), 244; (1927), 256.
9 GA, DA 100/16, ff. 95, 264, 297.
10 *Cal. Doc. France*, 411.
11 See below.
12 See *Glos. Ch. Notes*, 65.
13 Verey and Brooks, *Glos.* II, 574.
14 TNA, C 93/1/34; see above, social hist. (charities for the poor).
15 *Reg. Orleton* (Cant. & York Soc. 1908), 82–3.
16 *Reg. T. de Charlton*, 81.
17 Hockaday Abs. cclxiii.
18 *Glos. Feet of Fines 1199–1299*, no 962; *1300–59*, nos 749–50.
19 *Reg. Trillek*, 480.
20 *Reg. Trefnant*, 176; *Reg. Lacy*, 115 and n.
21 *Reg. Lacy*, 115; *Reg. Stanbury*, 178; *Reg. Bothe*, 335.
22 Hockaday Abs. cclxiii.
23 J. Gairdner, 'Bishop Hooper's Visitation of Gloucester', *EHR* 19 (1904), 120.
24 Hockaday Abs. cclxiii.
25 See below.
26 Hockaday Abs. cclxiii; xlvii, 1576 visit. f. 120.
27 GDR vol. 40, f. 247.
28 Hockaday Abs. xlix, state of clergy 1584, f. 42; lii, state of clergy 1593, f. 7.
29 Ibid. cclxiii.
30 GDR, V 5/193T 1.
31 *Walker Revised*, 176.
32 *Calamy Revised*, 449; Hockaday Abs. cclxiii.

place of one destroyed before the Restoration.[1] Smith remained in Longhope, ministering in his own house[2] until at least 1672 when it was licensed for Congregational meetings. Longhope also had a Presbyterian meeting in 1672.[3] Although no dissenters were recorded in the parish in 1676,[4] perhaps a score of people regularly absented themselves from church at that time[5] and a house was registered for worship by Presbyterians in 1710.[6]

George Ditton, whom Thomas Nourse expressly excluded from enjoyment of the annuity he left for future vicars,[7] remained vicar until his death in 1700.[8] The annuity, intended to ensure that Longhope was served by an able and orthodox preaching minister, was denied also to Charles Hopkins, Ditton's successor, and lapsed in 1703 when George Venn succeeded Hopkins and resigned the living of Sherborne.[9] In Venn's early years at Longhope Bibles, prayer books, and religious literature were occasionally presented to a handful of children and adults.[10]

In 1695 in work commissioned, and partly paid for, by churchwarden Nourse Yate a new painting of the king's arms and new tables displaying the Lord's Prayer, the Creed and the Ten Commandments were installed in the church. At the same time the church's copy of Foxe's *Book of Martyrs* was bound.[11] The church's bells, numbering four in 1680,[12] were replaced by a ring, probably of five, cast in 1700 by Abraham Rudhall.[13]

Church and Chapel after 1715

Thomas Mantle, vicar from 1718, was also rector of Abenhall from 1723.[14] In 1742 the patrons, the Yate sisters, gave the vicarage to Yate Bromwich, the son of one of them. Bromwich, who was instituted as vicar anew in 1754, inherited the sisters' estate in Longhope in 1763 and remained vicar until his death in 1774, employing his son William as his curate from 1769.[15] From 1786, and until 1851, all the vicars were members and relatives of the Probyn family. William Probyn (1786–1825) became vicar of Pershore (Worcs.) in 1797 and from there employed a curate at Longhope.[16]

The church, in which a parishioner gained permission in 1716 to erect an additional private pew, had a damaged ceiling in 1730.[17] Despite occasional repairs the building's condition deteriorated further and part of its roof collapsed. The ceiling and some fittings were removed early in 1769 and extensive repairs were carried out in 1770 and 1771 under the supervision of local craftsmen. During that work, for which deals were brought from Bristol, the tower and steeple were repaired and parts of the church, including the chancel, were entirely rebuilt. Among the fittings introduced were new seats and a replacement table of the Articles.[18] A gallery recorded later was probably at the west end.[19] In later work the spire was partially rebuilt in 1808[20] and the tenor bell recast in 1829.[21]

Seventeen Independents recorded in the parish in 1735[22] were presumably members of the nonconformist church in Mitcheldean, which in the later 18th century counted deacon Nathaniel Vaughan among its Longhope adherents.[23] In 1799 under Stephen Philipps, its acting pastor, the Mitcheldean meeting registered a house at Little London for worship.[24] Another group had a new chapel in Longhope in 1807 and a congregation established in 1823 by G.B. Drayton, minister of the Baptist church in Gloucester, built a meeting house at Little London. That chapel, registered in 1824,[25] used a nearby stream as its baptistery and from 1836 it had a resident minister and schoolmaster.[26] There was also a meeting of Wesleyans in Longhope in 1825[27] and John Horlick, minister of the Mitcheldean Independent church, registered a farmhouse there in 1829.[28]

In 1825, when Charles Mein Dighton became vicar,

---

1 A.C. Fryer, 'Gloucestershire Fonts: Post-Reformation Period', *Trans. BGAS* 49 (1927), 146.

2 GA, D 2052.

3 *Cal. SP Dom.* 1672, 197, 299.

4 *Compton Census*, 544.

5 GA, D 2052.

6 Ibid. Q/SO 3.

7 TNA, PROB 11/349, f.309.

8 GDR wills 1700/230

9 Hockaday Abs. cclxiii; GDR, V 5/193T 4; above (patronage and endowment).

10 GA, D 3436/1.

11 Ibid. P 206/CW 2/1.

12 GDR, V 5/193T 2.

13 H.T. Ellacombe, *The Church Bells of Gloucestershire* (1881), 54; see GA, P 206/CW3/17; M. Bliss, 'The Last Years of John Rudhall, Bellfounder of Gloucester, 1828–35', *Trans. BGAS* 121 (2003), 17.

14 Hockaday Abs. cclxiii.

15 Ibid.; above, manor (manor: the Manor Ho.).

16 Hockaday Abs. cclxiii; GA, P 206/IN 1/10; see pedigrees in J. Maclean, 'The History of the Manors of Dene Magna and Abenhall', *Trans. BGAS* 6 (1881–2), 194–8; above, social hist. (social structure).

17 Hockaday Abs. cclxiii.

18 GA, Q/SR 1769 B; P 206/CW 2/1; Rudder, *Glos.* 534.

19 The gallery was first mentioned in 1856: GA, P 206/VE 2/2.

20 Ibid. VE 2/1.

21 Ellacombe, *Church Bells*, 54; Bliss, 'Last Years of John Rudhall', 17.

22 *Bp. Benson's Surv. of Dioc. of Glouc. 1735–50*, 10.

23 GA, D 2297; P 220/CH 5/1; for the Mitcheldean meeting see *VCH Glos.* V, 192.

24 Hockaday Abs. cclxiii; J. Stratford, *Good and Great Men of Gloucestershire* (1867), 409.

25 Hockaday Abs. cclxiii; *VCH Glos.* IV, 321.

26 T. Bright, *Rise of Nonconformity in the Forest of Dean* (Forest of Dean Local History Soc. 1953), 29–30; J. Stanley, *In Days of Old. Memories of the Ejected Ministers of 1662* (Hereford, 1913), 42. For the school, above, social hist. (education).

27 GDR vol. 383, no cxvii.

28 Hockaday Abs. cclxiii; see *VCH Glos.* V, 192.

the average congregation at the parish church, which then had few free sittings, was said to be 250, the number of communicants was put at 30, and between 70 and 80 children received religious instruction from the church on Sundays. Sunday services, in which psalms and anthems were sung, were reduced during the winter from two to one, conducted in the morning and afternoon alternately. Dighton started building a new vicarage house but fell ill and died not long after leaving Longhope for Madeira in 1826.[1] His successor Edmund Probyn (d. 1837) became rector of Abenhall at the same time and lived at Longhope until 1834.[2]

The Reign of Victoria (1837–1901)

Robert Napier Raikes, vicar from 1837, remained resident after acquiring the living of Old Sodbury with Chipping Sodbury soon afterwards.[3] The Baptist chapel at Little London had been abandoned by 1844 when the home of its minister Henry Clement Davies, within Blaisdon, was licensed for services.[4] In 1846 the meeting opened a new chapel called Zion built with financial help from John Probyn and other Anglicans on land on Hope's hill donated by James Constance, a farmer.[5] Although a Wesleyan minister registered John Constance's house in 1840, the later story of Methodism in Longhope is not recorded.[6] A house on the Monmouth road towards Mitcheldean was later known as the Old Chapel.[7]

In 1850 congregations at the parish church then with 350 sittings, 210 of them free, were small but were said to have increased recently under a curate, nearly doubling to 70 in the morning and 120 in the afternoon. In 1851 the Easter Sunday congregations were 198 in the morning and 100 in the afternoon.[8] At the Baptist chapel, which had 130 sittings, all free, the congregations on the same day were 71 in the morning, 84 in the afternoon, and 102 in the evening,[9] some of those present being from outside Longhope.[10] A new schoolroom was added to the chapel in 1866[11] and the meeting, which had 36 members in 1868,[12] continued to have a resident minister.[13]

Vernon George Guise, who became vicar later in 1851, and his cousin Frederick Charles Guise, who succeeded him in 1861,[14] both served in person.[15] The church, much of the outside of which had been coated in yellow stucco,[16] was extensively restored from 1858 to designs in 13th-century style by the Gloucester firm of Medland & Maberly. In replacing windows and many other post-Reformation changes those architects remade a chancel arch, took down the gallery, and unblocked the tower arch. They also added a north vestry and organ loft and included a stone pulpit and font among the new fittings.[17] In 1869, on the advice of A.W. Maberly, the spire was removed and the tower was buttressed and its upper stages rebuilt with crocketed angle pinnacles and battlements and a cusped west window. A screen was placed in the tower arch and the five bells were repaired in 1870.[18] V.G. Guise (d. 1861) was commemorated in new glass in the chancel east window.[19] Much of the restoration work was funded by the Parish Charity Lands trust. Church rates had ceased to be collected in 1861.[20]

There were further alterations to the parish church in the later 19th century and it was cleaned and redecorated in 1889, with Revd F.C. Guise paying a third of the cost of the renovation of the chancel. A repair of the tower was funded in 1891 mainly by subscriptions.[21] A new organ was installed in 1893[22] and an oak lectern was carved, depicting an angel, and given to the church by R.S. Kearsey, a churchwarden, in 1897.[23]

The Twentieth Century and Later

The church continued to be served by a resident incumbent after F.C. Guise's resignation of the living in 1896. George Barr, his immediate successor,[24] remained rector until 1916[25] and there was a mission

---

1 GDR vol. 383, no cxvii; Dighton, *Dightons of Clifford Chambers*, 28–9.
2 Hockaday Abs. cclxiii; xcv; *VCH Glos.* V, 99.
3 Hockaday Abs. cclxiii; GDR, T 1/116; see above, social hist. (social structure).
4 Hockaday Abs. cxxvi. No chapel is recorded in the Longhope tithe award: GDR, T 1/116.
5 *Glouc. J.* 2 Aug. 1845; 18 July 1846.
6 Hockaday Abs. cclxiii.
7 TNA, HO 107/1959: RG 10/2604.
8 Ibid. HO 129/334/2/7/13.
9 Ibid. HO 129/334/7/14.
10 See *Glouc. J.* 7, 28, Feb., 23 Oct. 1852; 8 Jan., 16 July 1853; 22 July 1854.
11 Above, social hist. (education).
12 GA, D 2052.
13 *Kelly's Dir. Glos.* (1863–1902 edns).
14 Hockaday Abs. cclxiii; *Burke's Peerage* (1963), 1087–8.
15 *Kelly's Dir. Glos.* (1856), 321; (1963), 305; (1870), 592; GA, P 206/IN 1/10–11.
16 *Glos. Ch. Notes*, 64.
17 Ibid.; GA, P 206/VE 2/2; Verey and Brooks, *Glos.* II, 574. The redundant 'font' was taken to Court Farm and used as a pig trough before being placed in the churchyard on the base of an old cross (from where it has been removed): Fryer, 'Glos. Fonts: Post-Reformation Period', 146–7; GA, P 206/VE 2/3, entry 11 Apr. 1912.
18 GA, P 206/VE 2/2; CW 2/3; Verey and Brooks, *Glos.* II, 574; *Glos. Ch. Bells*, 418–19.
19 *Kelly's Dir. Glos.* (1879), 696
20 GA, P 206/CW 2/3; VE 2/2; see above, social hist. (charities for the poor).
21 GA, P 206/CW 2/3; VE 2/2–3.
22 *Kelly's Dir. Glos.* (1894), 225.
23 Inscription on lectern; Verey and Brooks, *Glos.* II, 574.
24 *Kelly's Dir Glos.* (1894–1939 edns). For Guise's resignation, see GA, P 206/VE 2/2.
25 GA, P 206/IN 1/11.

room at the Upper End in 1901.[1] Bible classes and lectures were held in the Latchen Room after 1906[2] and funds collected for a church institute were used in 1910 to build a vestry and purchase surplices and cassocks for the church choir.[3] In 1912 the organ was enlarged at the expense of Constance Miller,[4] whose family had lived at Bradley Court (formerly Bradley Grove),[5] and a weekly collection to increase the organist's salary began.[6] Members of the Miller family are commemorated in glass fitted in the chancel south window in 1911.[7] Barr, who himself spent the moneys collected at early morning services and the first main Sunday service of each month on the church and the poor, purchased a silver flagon in 1915 and a paten in 1916.[8] The church plate had included a chalice and paten made in 1898.[9] In 1922 a sixth bell was added to the church's peal.[10]

Successive rectors in the mid 20th century resided and served in person[11] but after Longhope ceased to be a benefice on its own in 1983 its church was served from Huntley.[12] Church repairs continued to receive funds from the Parish Charity Lands trust[13] and in work completed in 1987 the peal of bells was increased from six to eight, a ringing chamber was inserted in the tower and a kitchen installed in its base, and the windows in the nave and the south transept were restored.[14] From 2003 the church was part of a ministry including four other churches[15] and in 2005 it had at least one service every Sunday. The Baptist chapel on Hope's hill, where the adjoining elementary school closed in 2001,[16] had a resident minister in 2005. The mission room at the Upper End stood long abandoned in 2005. Roman Catholics attended services at the Salesian Society's school established in Blaisdon in the mid 1930s.[17]

OXENHALL

OXENHALL, a small parish of scattered farmsteads, lies on the north-west boundary of Gloucestershire, its south side adjoining Newent town. The ancient parish covered 1,909 a.[18] (772 ha). Part of its west boundary and a longer part of its south boundary followed a stream which skirted the wood called Hay wood and joined Ell brook at about the mid point of the south boundary.[19] From that confluence the boundary followed the leat of Crooke's Mill, diverged southwards to take in a tract of land formerly known as the Hides, and rejoined Ell brook near Newent town at a bridge called Ell bridge. From near the bridge the east boundary followed a lane leading from Newent towards Botloe's green and then a track that joined the Newent–Dymock road near a place called Three Ashes. Leaving that road, it ran north-westwards across an area where in the early Middle Ages the lords of the manor formed a park incorporating land in both Oxenhall and Newent manors.[20] At Gospel Oak, named from a tree that stood there until 1893,[21] the boundary turned westwards to follow a lane along a ridge in the area known as Hillend and then a track running through woodland towards Kempley.

In 1883 Oxenhall parish was enlarged to include a detached part of Pauntley parish comprising 341 a. (138 ha)[22] between the Ell brook and its tributary and the Newent hamlets of Kilcot and Gorsley to the south.[23] This account includes the history of that part of Pauntley.

LANDSCAPE

Oxenhall parish (as enlarged in 1883) occupies rolling countryside rising generally to around 60–70 m but forming a more pronounced ridge, reaching almost 100 m, at Hillend in its north-east corner. The north-western part of the parish is formed of the Old Red Sandstone and the south-eastern of the newer Triassic sandstone, which is visible in the sides of some of the lanes. Between the two formations occur

---

1 TNA, RG 13/2418.
2 GA, P 206/CW 2/3. For the Latchen Room, above, social hist. (social life).
3 GA, P 206/VE 2/3.
4 *Kelly's Dir. Glos.* (1931), 245.
5 Ibid. (1885–97 edns), s.v. Mitcheldean.
6 GA, P 206/VE 2/3.
7 Ibid.; *Kelly's Dir. Glos.* (1931), 245.
8 GA, CW 2/3; VE 2/3.
9 *Glos. Ch. Plate*, 139.
10 GA, P 206/CW 3/17; *Glos. Ch. Bells*, 418–19.
11 *Kelly's Dir. Glos.* (1939), 251–2; *Glouc. Dioc. Year Book* (1950–1), 16, 34–5; (1978), 21, 43.
12 *Dioc. of Glouc. Dir.* (1994–5), 18, 59; (2003–4), 11, 23.
13 Above, social hist. (charities for the poor).

14 *Citizen*, 4 Mar. 1987; inscriptions on windows.
15 *Dioc. of Glouc. Dir.* (2003–4), 23.
16 Above, social hist. (education).
17 *The Longhope Village Appraisal 1991* (copy in VCH Glos. office), 16; *VCH Glos.* X, 8.
18 Area calculated by deducting from 2,250 a., the area given in *OS Area Book* (1883), the 341 a. added to the par. in 1883: below. This account, written in 2005 and 2006, was revised in 2008.
19 For the boundaries of the ancient parish, GDR, T 1/137.
20 Below (landscape).
21 OS Map 6", Glos. XVII. NW (1884 edn); GA, P 125/IN 1/18, p. 271.
22 Local Govt. Board Order, 20 Dec. 1882: copy in GA, P 241/VE 2/1.
23 GDR, T 1/140.

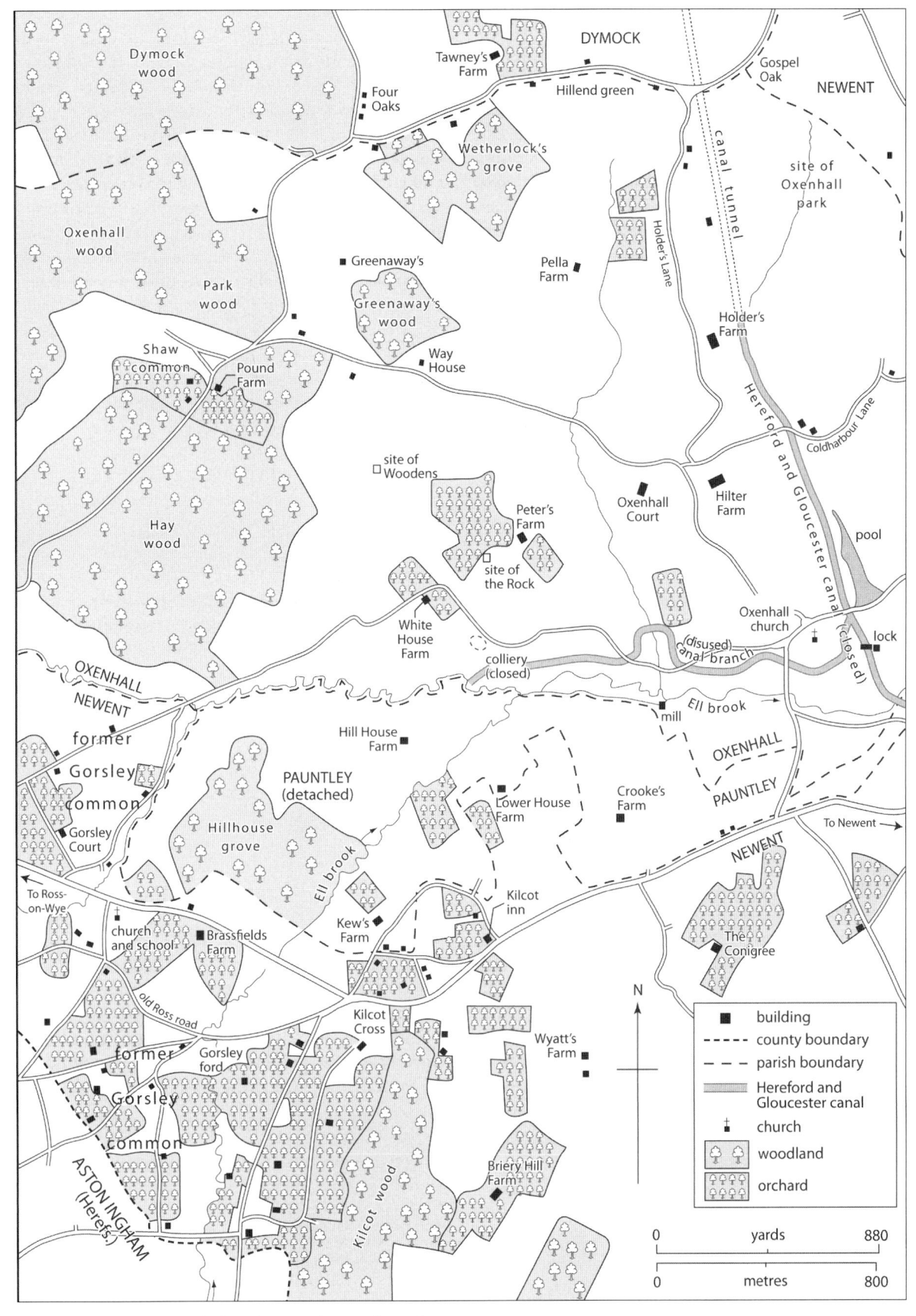

Map 12. Oxenhall, Kilcot, and part of Gorsley, 1882

thin coal seams, which were worked with no great success in the late 18th and the 19th century.[1] The soil is mainly a sandy loam of the type known as 'the ryelands' from the principal cereal crop once raised on it, but there are also areas of heavy clay.[2] The drainage system centres on the Ell brook into which fall some minor streams rising in the north of the parish. Field names suggest that the stream flowing down the centre of the parish and parting the lands of the farms called Oxenhall Court and Peter's Farm was once called Ash brook and that another further east, forming a valley that was used in the late 18th century as the course of the Hereford and Gloucester canal, was called Hub (or Up) brook.[3] On the latter stream a long pond, just above the road leading from Oxenhall church to the Newent–Dymock road, is a remnant of a system of ponds and watercourses that once powered Ellbridge (or Elmbridge) iron furnace, in the south-east corner of the parish.[4] Beside the Ell brook to the south of the parish church Gloucester corporation built a waterworks in 1896, pumping water from a borehole to a reservoir at Madam's wood in Newent parish, near Upleadon. Under the agreement for the purchase of the site from the Oxenhall manor estate the main tenant farms were provided with a free supply.[5]

Over a quarter of the ancient parish comprises woodland, which was predominantly oak before the introduction of conifer plantations by the Forestry Commission in the mid 20th century. The western side of the parish is part of an extensive tract of woodland that straddles the county boundary. Within Oxenhall the main components were Hay wood in the south, covering 194 a. in 1775, and Brandhill, Oxenhall, and Park woods further north, together covering 176 a. in 1775.[6] In 1615 the bulk of Brandhill wood and a part of Hay wood near the parish boundary were on lease from the lord of the manor to individual tenants,[7] and further leases which included permission to fell the timber and convert the land to farmland were granted in the 1650s, mainly to a branch of the Hill family. By 1659 Park wood (50 a.) was on lease to Richard Messenger,[8] from whom it took its later name of Messenger's park. After 1659 the bulk of the woodland was retained in hand by the Foleys, lords of the manor, to produce charcoal for Ellbridge furnace,[9] but parts of Brandhill remained under cultivation in the hands of tenants, creating a belt of closes extending diagonally through the centre of the woodland (on the line taken in the mid 20th century by the M50 motorway).[10] An area at the north-east end of those closes, called in 1615 Little wood[11] and later Shaw common, was the only part of the woods where tenants were permitted to exercise commoning rights in the post-medieval period. As a result it was encroached and settled by cottagers from the mid 17th century. In 1775 24 a. remained common land, but by the mid 19th century most of that had been absorbed by further encroachment.[12]

Smaller woods, outliers of the main tract, included Cumming's grove (later Betty Daw's wood), Colonel's grove, and Wetherlock's grove, which lay together near the north boundary, and Rayer's grove, Coather's wood, and Wayhouse grove (later known collectively as Greenaway's wood), further south. Most of those woods were named from tenants who had held them under the manor as parts of copyhold and leasehold farms, but Colonel's grove was probably named from Col. Maynard Colchester (d. 1715) who owned it as part of the Oxenhall rectory estate.[13] In the detached part of Pauntley Hillhouse grove, covering 53 a. in 1775,[14] belonged to the lords of Newent and was kept in hand by the Foleys after they acquired that manor in 1659.[15] In the mid 20th century it was felled except for a small clump of trees and the land turned over to agriculture.[16]

Park wood in the main tract of woodland was called the new park in 1659,[17] evidently to distinguish it from a park enclosed by the lords of Oxenhall in the north-east of the parish. That park straddled the boundary with Newent and in the mid 13th century William of Evreux, lord of Oxenhall, gave Cormeilles abbey, lord of Newent, 4 a. of land to compensate for 2½ a. of the abbey's land enclosed within it.[18] In 1335, when it was grazed by the lord's deer, it was described as small[19] and in 1435 it was extended at 40 a.,[20] but later evidence shows it was larger, incorporating a substantial tract extending as far as the Newent–

---

1 Geol. Surv. Map, solid and drift, sheet 216 (1988 edn); below, econ. hist. (coal mining).
2 Rudge, *Agric. of Glos.* 20, 138.
3 GA, D 2528, pp. 9–10, 12, 14; photocopy 5.
4 Below, econ. hist. (Ellbridge furnace).
5 *VCH Glos.* IV, 264; *Chapters in Newent's History* (Newent Local Hist. Soc. 2003), 111–17.
6 GA, D 2528, pp. 10–11.
7 Ibid. photocopy 1194/1.
8 Herefs. RO, E 12/G/9, rental 1659; G/24, leases 27 Oct.1651, 6 May 1656, 28 Aug. 1657.
9 Below, econ. hist. (woodland management and woodland crafts; Ellbridge furnace).
10 GA, photocopy 5.
11 Ibid. photocopy 1194/1.
12 Ibid. D 2528, p. 10; photocopy 5; GDR, T 1/137.
13 GDR, T 1/137; Rudder, *Glos.* 795.
14 GA, D 2528, p. 7.
15 Herefs. RO, E 12/G/15, mortgage 1660; G/12, table of woods 1698–1711.
16 OS Map 1:25,000, SO 62 (1957, 1977 edns).
17 Herefs. RO, E 12/G/9, rental 1659 (s.v. Oxenhall leaseholders).
18 BL, Add. MS 18461, f. 77.
19 *Inq. p.m. Glos.* 1302–58, 253.
20 TNA, C 139/70, no 34.

Dymock road. It was leased in two halves by 1527,[1] and in 1659 six tenants held portions totalling over 150 a.[2] By the late 18th century it comprised arable and pasture closes indistinguishable from other farmland in the parish.[3] Further south on the same side of the parish, a small farm called Marshall's was converted as a golf course at the end of the 20th century, and a field near by, adjoining the lane from Oxenhall church to the Newent–Dymock road, was used by the Newent cricket club.

COMMUNICATIONS
Roads

Of the roads crossing the parish only that on the east side, leading from Newent town through Dymock to Ledbury, was used by other than very local traffic. It was a turnpike from 1769 until 1874.[4] The southern part, running past Lambsbarn, was apparently improved substantially by the trust c.1832.[5] Ell bridge, on the Ell brook where the road enters the parish, was repaired jointly by Oxenhall and Newent parishes.[6] It and another bridge further upstream, evidently at the crossing known as Ellford (or Ollifordes) south of Oxenhall church,[7] were both recorded in 1282 as landmarks on what was then the northern boundary of the Forest of Dean.[8] Various lanes running westwards from the Newent–Dymock road were used mainly for access to the parish's scattered farmsteads, though they also continued through the wooded area into adjoining parishes. A continuation of Furnace Lane, running from the site of the Ellbridge ironworks northwards to Winter's Farm,[9] is among minor lanes to be abandoned in the late 18th or early 19th century, most becoming disused with the disappearance of the farmsteads they served. The M50 motorway, opened in 1960 between the M5 and Ross-on-Wye (Herefs.),[10] crosses the north-west part of Oxenhall, but, screened by woodland and with no direct access from the parish, has had little impact on its landscape or settlement pattern.

Canal and Railway

The Hereford and Gloucester canal, begun in 1793 and opened between Gloucester and Ledbury in 1798, traversed the parish, with a tunnel, 2 km long, taking it under the high land at Hillend. A branch was constructed running west from the main line near Oxenhall church to serve small collieries near Hill House Farm in the detached part of Pauntley, but the lack of success of those workings led to the early abandonment of the branch.[11] Some time before 1812 a horse tramroad was laid through the west part of the parish across Shaw common and towards Gorsley common, probably following the lane through Hay wood.[12] It was probably built specifically to carry materials from quarries in the Linton (Herefs.) part of Gorsley for the building of the canal and its tunnel, and no later record of it has been found. The canal was closed and replaced in 1885 by the Gloucester and Ledbury railway, which was built on the line of the canal where it entered the parish at Ellbridge but then diverged on a more westerly course up the valley of the Ash brook. Oxenhall was served by Newent station just over the parish boundary near Ellbridge, and a halt was opened in 1937 at Four Oaks where the railway left the parish on the north. Passenger services ceased in 1959 and the railway was closed in 1964.[13] Among surviving remains on the line of the canal are a lock and its keeper's brick cottage of 1838 east of Oxenhall church.[14]

POPULATION

Eight agricultural tenants were recorded on Oxenhall manor in 1086[15] and 23 people were assessed for the subsidy in Oxenhall in 1327.[16] A figure of 24 households given in 1563[17] seems a considerable underestimate given the number of small farmhouses that existed at that date. Population estimates of 50 families in 1650[18] and around 200 inhabitants c.1710[19] seem to accord more accurately with the evidence of the settlement pattern at those

---

1 Ibid. SC 6/Hen.VIII/6044.

2 Herefs. RO, E 12/G/9, rental 1659 (leaseholds of Thos. Addis and Hen. Wetherlock, copyholds of John Comin, Wm. Wood, Mary Price, and Francis Fidoe); and see, ibid. cts. 14 Oct. 23 Chas. I, 1 Dec. 1649; G/23, leases D 2, D 32.

3 GA, D 2528, pp. 9–5; photocopy 5: the farm tenanted by Phil. Valender and parts of those tenanted by Ric. Hunt and Wm. Cumming evidently comprised former parkland.

4 Glouc. and Heref. Roads Act, 9 Geo. III, c. 50; Newent Roads Act, 5 Geo. IV, c. 11 (Local and Personal); Annual Turnpike Acts Continuance Act, 1874, 37 & 38 Vic. c. 95.

5 GA, D 412/Z 3, Newent notes, 1900, where it is implied that this was a new stretch of road, but it existed and was used as the way between Newent and Dymock in 1693: GA, D 127/588.

6 GDR wills 1559/360.

7 Ibid.; Herefs. RO, E 12/G/ 23, lease D 30; G/24, lease 1 Oct. 1645.

8 C.E. Hart, 'Metes and Bounds of the Forest of Dean', *Trans. BGAS* 66 (1945), 175–6.

9 Herefs. RO, E 12/G/23, lease D 30; G/24, lease 1Oct. 1645; GA, photocopy 5.

10 *Citizen*, 29 Nov. 1960.

11 D.E. Bick, *The Hereford & Gloucester Canal* (Newent, 1979), 8–16.

12 GA, D 1882/5/2 (and for the field called Pertens mentioned in the source, GDR, T 1/137).

13 Bick, *Heref. & Glouc. Canal*, 58–62.

14 Ibid. 50; below, Fig. 58.

15 *Domesday Book* (Rec. Com), I, 167v.

16 *Glos. Subsidy Roll, 1327*, 35.

17 Bodleian, Rawl. C. 790, f. 29.

18 C.R. Elrington, 'The Survey of Church Livings in Gloucestershire, 1650', *Trans. BGAS* 83 (1964), 98.

19 Atkyns, *Glos.* 595.

58. *Lock Cottage*

later dates. About 1775 a figure of 202 people in 46 families was given, apparently by an exact local enumeration.[1] During the next 35 years there appears to have been proportionately a rapid growth, with the declining number of small farmhouses more than offset by the building of new cottages in outlying parts of the parish: 313 people were returned in 1801 and 347 in 1811. The population then began a steady fall, reaching 218 in 1891 (the boundary change of 1883 having added only 28 people on the few farms of the detached lands of Pauntley). During most of the next century it diverged little from that figure, 223 people being enumerated in the parish in 1991, but by 2001 it had fallen to 185.[2]

SETTLEMENT

Oxenhall has no village and is unlikely ever to have had one. The ancient pattern of settlement was scattered small farmsteads. In 1659 a manorial survey[3] enumerated 21 dwellings on the small copyhold farms that formed the core of the tenantry, but several of the copyholds, though having only one house, were described, following an ancient description, as comprising two or three messuages. Altogether the survey suggests that the copyholds had at one time included 31 houses, the number being reduced by a process of amalgamation of farms into larger units begun in the late Middle Ages. That process continued during the next two centuries and by 1841 the sites of only about a third of the copyhold houses recorded in 1659 were still occupied. The total of dwellings listed in 1659, including the houses of some freehold farms and various leasehold cottages, mainly on the fringes of Hay wood, was 45, and *c*.1710 the parish was said to contain 40 houses.[4] Later, although the number of farmhouses was reduced, new cottages were built on the edge of woodland and elsewhere in the parish, so that Oxenhall had 63 inhabited dwellings in 1831.[5]

ANCIENT SETTLEMENT

Oxenhall's parish church occupies an isolated site in the south of the parish on a small, well-defined hill above the valley of the Ell brook. A church house standing at the edge of the churchyard,[6] built probably in the late 1550s when a legacy was left for that purpose,[7] was pulled down in 1841[8] when a small school building was built across the lane from the church.[9] On higher ground further north, near the junction of a number of lanes including Coldharbour Lane leading from the

---

1 Rudder, *Glos.* 590.
2 *Census*, 1801–2001.
3 The account that follows is based on: a rental of 1659 (Herefs. RO, E 12/G/9); a plan and survey of 1775 (GA, photocopy 5; D 2528, pp. 9–15); and the tithe award of 1841 (GDR, T 1/137).
4 Atkyns, *Glos.* 595.
5 *Census*, 1831.
6 Fig. 59.
7 GDR wills 1559/360; GA, D 1791/8.
8 GA, P 241/VE 2/1.
9 Below, social hist. (education).

59. *Oxenhall church from the south with the church house in the background c. 1840*

Newent–Dymock road in the east and Holder's Lane leading from Hillend on the north boundary, are two ancient sites: Hilter Farm (formerly Yeldhall) was possibly the site of an early medieval manor house and Oxenhall Court was the farmhouse of the rectory estate.[1]

The main spread of ancient farmhouses lay in the west of the parish in the area traversed by lanes leading from the parish church towards Gorsley and from near Hilter Farm to Shaw common. That area once had a more complex pattern of closes, interspersed by coppices, orchards, and minor tracks to the farmhouses. Among the few surviving houses, White House Farm on the lane to Gorsley was recorded from 1443[2] and was in 1659 the centre of the largest copyhold farm on the manor. On higher ground north of that lane stands a farmhouse once called Briary House but later known as Peter's Farm from the surname of the family that occupied it in 1549 and until 1688 or later.[3] South-west of Peter's Farm, on a small hill where the underlying sandstone outcrops, stood a farmhouse called the Rock (later Hilltop),[4] and near the head of a small stream *c*.500 m north-west of White House was another called Goodwins (later Woodens);[5] both those houses survived as the centres of small farms in 1775[6] but were demolished before 1841. Another small farmstead called Carter's, occupied by a branch of the Hill family in 1549 and until the late 17th century,[7] stood south-east of White House beside the lane leading from the parish church.[8] It survived until the mid 19th century and was probably removed in the 1870s when a coal mine (Newent colliery) was established close to its site.[9]

Field names in the south-west of the parish recall and probably mark the sites of other copyhold farmhouses recorded in the mid 16th century by the names 'Smith's', 'Loveridge's', 'Yardsley's', and 'Woodnutt's (later Ashbrook)'.[10] Way (or Wain) House, on the north side of the lane to Shaw common, was recorded from 1509 as the centre of a small freehold but was acquired *c*.1607 by the manor estate,[11] on which it remained a smallholding.[12] In 2006 the cottage at the site had a small commercial vineyard attached. Two copyhold farmhouses in the area to the north of the same lane were both known as Thraper's in the 17th century. One was in decay by 1713 but the other, then known as Greenaway's[13] from an earlier tenant, remained the centre of a small farm in 1775; there was still a cottage on the site in 2006.

---

1 Below, manor (other estates).
2 Westminster Abbey Mun. 3535.
3 Herefs. RO, E 12/G/9, ct. 20 Feb. 3 Edw. VI; GDR wills 1640/98; GA, D 1791/8.
4 GDR wills 1601/86; 1648/93; Herefs. RO, E 12/G/32, agreement 22 Dec. 1669; Bryant, *Map of Glos*. (1824).
5 Herefs. RO, E 12/G/9, ct. 24 Oct. 4 Edw.VI; GDR wills 1698/73.
6 For the identification of those two in the 1775 survey, see also GA, Q/REl 1, Botloe hundred 1776.
7 Herefs. RO, E 12/G/9, ct. 20 Feb. 3 Edw. VI; G/12, deed 1 Mar. 1628; GDR wills 1680/27.
8 A field to the south was called Carter's meadow in 1775; Bryant, *Map of Glos*. (1824) marked the house as 'Court House', perhaps a corruption or mishearing of the name.
9 GDR, T 1/137; below, econ. hist. (coal mining).
10 Herefs. RO, E 12/G/9, ct. 20 Feb. 3 Edw. VI; and for Ashbrook, ibid. G/23, lease D 12; G/24, lease 7 Apr. 1682.
11 Ibid. G/11, deeds of Weyhouse grove and Gyles Croft.
12 Ibid. G/23, lease D 18; GDR wills 1685/498.
13 Herefs. RO, E 12/G/23 leases D 6, D 23; GDR wills 1765/136.

On the north boundary of the parish a dwelling called the Shaw was the centre of a copyhold that included Betty Daw's wood (formerly Cumming's grove); the Cummings (Comin) family were its tenants in 1602[1] and until the late 18th century.

On the generally higher and more open land in the north of the parish the surviving farmsteads include Holder's Farm, standing on the east side of Holder's Lane, and Pella Farm, west of Holder's Lane. Both were recorded from the 1440s (assuming Pella to be the house then called *Pilleysplace*),[2] and in 1659 each farm comprised the land of three former tenant houses but only one farmhouse remained on each. One of the sites absorbed into Holder's farm was probably at a place called Sandfords[3] (later Sandford Orchard) near Hillend green, and one of those absorbed by Pella at a field called Woodhall[4] on the parish boundary north of Pella farmhouse. The houses of three of the smaller copyholds of the 16th[5] and 17th centuries — Backs, held for many years by a branch of the Wood family,[6] Cook's Place (later Wilses), and Boar's Place[7] — stood further south in the upland fields bounded on the west by Ash brook and on the east and south-east by Holder's Lane. By 1775 all three had been absorbed into Hilter farm and only a house called Little Pella (Pellow) survived in that area; it too had been demolished by 1841. In the mid 17th century several of the tenants farming parts of the lord of the manor's park had dwellings in the north-east of the parish. One, held by Henry Wetherlock,[8] was probably the farmhouse later called Waterdynes or Waterlocks, north of Holder's Farm.[9] In 1775 there was also a small farmhouse in the former parkland east of Waterdynes, close to the parish boundary. It was demolished before 1882, by which time the owners of the manor had built a larger house called the Parks near by, within Newent.[10]

In the 17th century a few houses stood east of Hilter Farm where Coldharbour Lane crossed the stream in the valley later used as the course of the canal. On the east bank of the stream, in an area then known as Overbrooks or Upbrooks End, a branch of the Wood family had a copyhold farmhouse called More's Place;[11] it was possibly the house that in 1775 stood at the end of the pool that the stream forms south of Coldharbour Lane. Dwellings called in 1659 Hathaway's and Overbrooks are evidently represented by the two 17th-century houses (Brook Cottage and its neighbour) which stand by the crossing on the north side of the lane. They were among the few small independent freeholds in the parish and remained so until the 1820s when bought by Samuel Beale, owner of Oxenhall Court farm; his successors sold them with the farm to the lord of the manor in 1859.[12]

In the south-east part of the parish there were relatively few dwellings. Most of the land there belonged in the late Middle Ages to a large freehold called Marshall's, based on a house near Ellbridge. In the early 17th century, when the lord of the manor built an ironworks at Ellbridge, the farm was broken up, the name Marshall's passing to a farmhouse established at the north end of its land, on Coldharbour Lane. Adjoining the remains of the ironworks at Ellbridge is a substantial house once called the Furnace (later Oakdale House) occupied by members of the Onslow family, owners of the manor in the 19th century and the early 20th. Winter's Farm, on the lane leading from the Newent–Dymock road towards Oxenhall church, was another site occupied by the late Middle Ages.[13] Lambsbarn, on the east side of the Newent–Dymock road, was so called by 1693,[14] taking its name from a former owner of the adjoining group of fields. A small farmhouse was added beside the barn before 1841.

The detached part of Pauntley added to Oxenhall in 1883 has a number of ancient farmsteads.[15] Hill House Farm, on a low hill overlooking the confluence of the Ell brook with the tributary that marked the old parish boundary, is on a site apparently occupied from the 13th century. Its late medieval tenants, the Hills, probably took their name from the location and may have been the ancestors of the many branches of the family who later farmed in the Oxenhall area. Kew's Farm, on the boundary with Newent close to Kilcot, and Crooke's Farm, further east, were both recorded from the early 15th century, and Lower House, across Ell brook from Hill House Farm, had been established by the 17th century. A few other dwellings were recorded in the mid 17th century: they included two cottages in a close called Peppercorn, between

---

1 Herefs. RO, E 12/G/9, ct. 20 Apr. 44 Eliz.; G/23, lease D 32; GDR, V 5/226T 1 (where James Cumming's grove lay west of the rectory grove, the later Colonel's grove).
2 Westminster Abbey Mun. 3535; Herefs. RO, E 12/G/9, ct. 24 Oct. 4 Edw. VI; G/19, copy of ct. roll 3 Mar. 20 Eliz. I.
3 Herefs. RO, E 12/G/23, lease D 21.
4 Ibid. lease D 35.
5 Ibid. G/9, ct. 24 Oct. 4 Edw. VI.
6 GDR wills 1685/498; Bigland, *Glos.* II, 304.
7 Herefs. RO, E 12/G/23, lease D 34; G/24, lease 2 Jan. 1674; GA, Q/REl 1, Botloe hundred 1776.
8 Herefs. RO, E 12/G/24, lease 27 Dec. 1666.
9 Bryant, *Map of Glos.* (1824); TNA, RG 12/2008.
10 OS Map 6", Glos. XVII.NW (1884 edn).
11 Herefs. RO, E 12/G/9, ct. 14 Oct. 23 Chas. I; G/24, lease 13 May 1674; GA, P 241/IN 1/1, burial 1706.
12 GA, D 1882/1.
13 Below, manor (other estates: Marshall's and Winter's farms). For the Onslows at the Furnace, below, social hist. (social structure).
14 GA, D 127/588; Herefs. RO, E 12/G/9, rental 1659 (s.v. Oxenhall freeholders).
15 Below, manor (estates in detached part of Pauntley).

60. Quince Cottage near Shaw common

Hillhouse grove and the brook that formed the west boundary of the detached lands of Pauntley, and a house called Spillman's, on the east side of the grove.[1] All had been demolished by 1775.[2]

SETTLEMENT IN MODERN TIMES

The building of cottages in outlying parts of Oxenhall, mainly on the fringes of its western woodlands, was a feature of its early modern history, though in no part did it create a hamlet of any size or compactness. By 1615 seven cottages were spaced out around the southern edge of Hay wood in closes of land varying from 3 to 8 acres.[3] Held from the manor by leasehold rather than copyhold, they were presumably of fairly recent origin. The encroachment of Shaw common, north-east of Hay wood, had begun by the 1640s, when two cottages there were leased under the manor,[4] and in 1659 there were at least two more further north, adjoining Oxenhall wood. In the course of the next century almost all of the cottages along the south side of Hay wood vanished. Presumably their abandonment was not the result of policy by the landlords, the Foleys, who permitted cottage development in other parts of their estate and perhaps actively encouraged it to provide a labour force for cording and charcoaling their coppices. The Foleys granted leases of cottages on encroachments on Shaw common in the early and mid 18th century,[5] and in 1775 there were seven dwellings there and another three further east on waste beside the lane leading back towards the centre of the parish.[6] Others were added later, and by 1851 there were 10 households living around Shaw common and another 12 in the area, then distinguished as Shaw green, around the lane further east;[7] presumably some of the cottages were then in more than one occupation.

One cottage at Shaw common in 1775 was rebuilt on a larger scale as the centre of Pound farm, one of the main farms of the manor estate in the 19th century. It was named from the pound established near by for livestock found straying in the woods;[8] the original cottage at the site was possibly that occupied by the lord of the manor's woodward in the 17th century.[9] Most of the dwellings in the area were abandoned and demolished in the later 19th century and the 20th, and in 2006 the only survivors on the former common were Pound Farm and a cottage near by, once the centre of a smallholding called Little Pound farm, and four cottages further east, around the entrance of the lane leading towards the centre of the parish. One of the latter, adjoining the east side of a grove called Haine's Oak wood, was occupied by the manor estate's head gamekeeper in the 19th century.[10] It became known as Crown Lodge after the Oxenhall woods passed to Crown estate in 1914[11] and as Old Crown Lodge after the mid 20th century, when a new lodge and small forestry depot were established to the north of Pound Farm.

A few cottages were built, widely spaced out, on

---

1 Herefs. RO, E 12/G/31.
2 GA, D 2528, p. 7; photocopy 5, where field names identify the sites.
3 Ibid. photocopy 1194/1.
4 Herefs. RO, E 12/G/24, leases 22 Aug. 1645, 2 Feb. 1647.
5 Ibid. G/23, leases D 5, D 31, D 45.
6 See Fig. 60.
7 TNA, HO 107/1960; Bryant, *Map of Glos.* (1824).
8 GA, D 1882/5/2, deed 27 Jan. 1812; GDR, T 1/137.
9 GA, D 147/2; Herefs. RO, E 12/G/23, lease D 20.
10 GA, SL 79.
11 TNA, CRES 38/674; F 9/5.

the Oxenhall side of the lane that marks the north boundary of the parish. By 1775 there were two at Hillend green, where one near the junction with Holder's Lane had been leased from the manor in 1749,[1] and another three further west where the lane adjoined Wetherlock's grove. A small and more concentrated group of cottages was established on freehold land near the road junction at Three Ashes on the east boundary. One was built shortly before 1733, and Richard Peters, a wheelwright, added four others on an adjoining plot that he bought in 1815.[2] There were six households at Three Ashes in 1851.[3] In 1856 a larger house was built as a vicarage near by, on the Newent–Dymock road.[4]

The 20th century made little impact on the settlement pattern of Oxenhall. Six council houses were built adjoining Four Oaks, a hamlet on the north boundary mainly within Dymock, during 1953 and 1954.[5] Later in the century a few private houses were added in various parts of the parish, and some of the farms were given modern dwellings after old farmhouses were sold away from the land.

BUILDINGS

Most of the sites of the farmhouses in Oxenhall and the adjoining part of Pauntley can, as described above, be traced from the 17th century and several from the 15th, though the present appearance of most of the houses is the result of remodelling or rebuilding in brick in the late 18th century and the early 19th. For the majority, the farmhouses on the Oxenhall manor estate, a fairly standard pattern was used, but Crooke's Farm, the principal freehold, was transformed at that period into a small country house.

Crooke's Farm stands on a site that slopes steeply up from almost west to east and the house platform has been terraced, perhaps in the 17th century when the house was enlarged to accommodate parallel northern and southern ranges at different levels. Its northern range incorporates at its western end the cross wing of a substantial medieval house, which may have had an H plan. Built probably in the first quarter of the 15th century, the two-storeyed wing is of high quality with part of its western wall and large western chimneystack built of stone and the gable end timber-framed, partly close-studded. The northern end was probably the principal chamber, comprising four narrow bays open to a roof which has cusped windbraces; at the apex the principals are cusped and together with curved struts springing from the collar form a trefoil. The southern end has remains of slightly simpler trusses, of which one at each end and some re-used rafters are smoke-blackened, perhaps the result of an 18th-century fire.[6] There is another late medieval farmhouse at Furnace Farm, apparently the house of the substantial freehold called Marshall's.[7] Originally on an L plan,[8] it may have been built in the late 15th century, and has a two-bayed hall with arch-braced trusses and cusped windbraces.

Rebuilding in the Sixteenth and Seventeenth Centuries

In the mid 17th century, probably before 1672 when it was assessed on 8 hearths,[9] Crooke's Farm was enlarged. An east–west range was built at the north-eastern end of the cross wing, perhaps replacing or incorporating the medieval hall range, and a large stack with six diamond shafts was inserted within its eastern end. The eastern wing was probably rebuilt or remodelled then.[10] A parallel two-storeyed, two-bayed range with western chimneystack and staircase was added at a right angle to the other, south-eastern end of the cross wing, almost detached from it. The gap between the two east–west ranges and the difference in floor levels were reconciled by inserting a broad dog-leg staircase with turned balusters and ball finials between them. In the farmyard to the north-east a barn was built. At Furnace Farm at the same period the medieval hall was floored and a large stack built at the western end.

Other farmhouses were built anew with timber frames in the 17th century, including Winter's, Lower House, Kew's, White House, and Oxenhall Court (the rectory farmhouse). Winter's Farm is an L-plan, two-storeyed house with a tall, stone-built cellar under the cross wing to take advantage of the site's fall. Lower House is on a similar plan but of 1½ storeys. Two of its three rooms are divided by a stack, and the beam over one fireplace has a rough inscription of 1619. Kew's Farm,[11] of three bays and two storeys, was probably built in the mid to late 17th century and has brick infilling. Contemporary farm buildings include an attached cider house and a barn which encloses a farmyard on a south-eastern terrace. White House Farm was built on a similar plan but had one storey with additional rooms within the roof. Sandstone was used, perhaps later, for the eastern gable wall which may have curtailed

---

1 Herefs. RO, E 12/G 23, lease D 42.
2 GDR wills 1733/135; GA D 2079/III/215.
3 TNA, HO 107/1960.
4 Verey and Brooks, *Glos.* II, 628.
5 GA, DA 30/100/22, p. 83; 100/23, p. 47.
6 Below.

7 Below, manor (other estates: Marshall's and Winter's farms).
8 GA, photocopy 5.
9 TNA, E 179/247/14, rot. 36.
10 The interior of the E. wing was not seen.
11 Fig. 61.

61. *Kew's Farm, near Kilcot*

the house that in 1672 was assessed on 5 hearths.¹ Some of the hearths may have been in detached buildings, for in 1659 White House was described as a house of four bays, with an old two-bay kitchen, a two-bayed (cider)-mill house, and a four-bayed barn;² one of those outbuildings may have been the single-storeyed southern wing which was later joined to the house. Oxenhall Court seems to have been built with some stone outer walls and mullioned windows as an L-plan house, its main southern range being of three bays and two storeys and attic. Brook Cottage and the adjoining cottage, standing in Coldharbour Lane by the bridge over the disused canal, both timber-framed with large end chimneys, are surviving examples of smaller dwellings of the period.

Rebuilding after 1750

White House Farm was subjected to extensive work in the mid 18th century, at least some of it in 1752 and 1761 when much building material, including brick and tile from Gorsley, was supplied by the Foley estate.³ The timber frame was faced with brick, the high end of the house raised to two storeys, and the roof hung with clay tiles. Much of the fabric of the outbuildings may be of similar date. Marshall's Farm, on Coldharbour Lane, combines brick and stone in a shallow-roofed building that could be of the 18th or early 19th century. Elsewhere 18th-century work seems to have been confined to outbuildings, and to building by squatters of cottages with light timber frames, such as at Quince Cottage, near Shaw common,⁴ and the former Way House (in 2006 St Anne's Vineyard), or of brick alone, as at Little Pound Farm at Shaw common.

The farmhouses at Holder's and at Hilter were completely rebuilt in brick c.1800. At Holder's the work was probably in two stages close in date, for the front range, which has a plain two-storeyed, three-bayed façade with segmental-headed casement windows and end stacks, appears to have been raised slightly when a back range was added.⁵ The L plan was infilled later by a lean-to dairy. At Hilter Farm the old farmhouse was replaced by a house similar in plan and elevation to that at Holder's, but larger and with an extra storey. It was remodelled later in the 19th century when it was given a roof with overhanging eaves and a front porch. Blue brick diapering on the western gable wall was repeated in a cider house to the east. Pound Farm at Shaw common was rebuilt in the late 19th century, probably in the 1870s when it was occupied by William Onslow, a younger son of the lord of the manor,⁶ and is a late version of the same pattern as Holder's.

Crooke's Farm was made to resemble a small country house in the late 1820s or 1830s; it had for some time been leased as a farmhouse, as it was again for many years afterwards, but possibly the owner, Benjamin Hooke, intended at that time to use it as a

---

1 TNA, E 179/247/14, rot. 36.
2 Herefs. RO, E 12/G/9, rental 1659.
3 Ibid. G/29, disbursements 1752, Newent and Oxenhall receipts 1761.
4 Above, Fig. 60.
5 Below, Fig. 62.
6 GA, P 241/VE 2/1, min. 28 Mar. 1878; *Burke's Peerage* (1963), 1863.

62. *Holder's Farm from the south*

residence.[1] The northern façade was rendered and given sashes and a Doric portico, and much of the roof was reconstructed. The main rooms were fashionably decorated and given chimneypieces and doorcases with reeded architraves and lions' head paterae, as on the portico. The lowest flight of the staircase, which had apparently already been replaced after a fire in the early 18th century,[2] was remade as a plain swept flight.

Alterations to other farmhouses were minor. Winter's was reroofed (one rafter has a date 1860), a gable wall and large chimneystack were rebuilt, and a veneer of Victorian style was applied. Kew's was doubled in size by the addition to the north of two plain brick piles of rooms, and Lower House was cased in brick in the late 19th century when one bay was extended and barn and stables of Gorsley stone provided. The northern front of Oxenhall Court was refaced in brick and the angle of its two ranges filled with service rooms. At Furnace Farm, where the back range was removed before 1841 and the house became two cottages,[3] the high end of the surviving range was rebuilt in brick.

Most farms were provided with brick outbuildings in the early and mid 19th century. Some timber-framed buildings were retained or improved, for example a barn at Pound Farm, and at Holder's a 17th-century bull house (attached to a brick barn which before rebuilding was possibly the five-bayed barn mentioned there in 1659) and a long, low timber-framed range.[4] New work at Hilter Farm included a courtyard of brick buildings close to the house, and a six-bayed barn which stood until the mid 20th century.[5] At Oxenhall Court a long range was built to incorporate a pigsty, stable and hayloft, cider-mill house, five-bayed threshing barn, and cart shed: a cider mill on site is dated 1838. Part of that range of building was converted to residential use in the late 20th century. The houses most extensively altered in the late 20th century were White House and Winter's Farm after their farmland was sold.

MANOR AND ESTATES

Oxenhall formed a separate manor from before the Norman Conquest, and for most of its history the manor estate included the bulk of the ancient parish. Some independent freeholds[6] emerged by the late Middle Ages, including a block of land on the east side of the parish owned by the Porter family. Most of those lands were, however, bought in later by the Foley family of Stoke Edith (Herefs.), which acquired Oxenhall manor in 1658. During the 18th and 19th centuries the only farm of any size in the ancient

---

1 Below, manor (estates in detached part of Pauntley).
2 *The Oxenhall Anthology* (Oxenhall Parish History Group, 1999), 5.
3 GDR, T 1/137; GA, SL 79.
4 Herefs. RO, E 12/G/9, rental 1659.
5 Aerial photog. at house.
6 In 1522 a tax assessment on Llanthony priory, Gloucester, for £8-worth of lands was included under Oxenhall but it appears to be a misplaced entry for Okle Clifford manor in Newent: *Military Surv. of Glos. 1522*, 62.

parish outside the manor estate was the rectorial glebe based on the farmhouse called Oxenhall Court. The pattern of landholding changed radically with the sale of the manor estate in 1913 when most of the farms were bought by the tenants. In the detached portion of Pauntley added to Oxenhall in 1883 the most significant farm was Crooke's, which belonged to the Hooke family by 1435 and remained in its possession in the early 21st century.

OXENHALL MANOR

In 1066 Oxenhall manor was held from Earl (i.e. King) Harold by Thorkell. In 1086 it was part of the extensive Gloucestershire estates of Roger de Lacy,[1] having presumably belonged to his father Walter (d. 1085). After Roger's rebellion and banishment in 1096 his lands were forfeited and granted to his brother Hugh de Lacy.[2] Oxenhall had apparently been subinfeudated by 1202 when the tenants of Walter de Lacy's honor included the 'lady of Oxenhall',[3] and in 1236 the widow of Stephen of Evreux held it from Walter.[4] The overlordship has not been found recorded again until 1335 when the manor was held from the heirs of Geoffrey de Genevyle.[5] By 1358 Roger Mortimer, earl of March, was overlord, and his right descended with his earldom[6] to be assumed by the Crown on the accession of his descendant as Edward IV.[7]

By 1251 Oxenhall manor had passed to William of Evreux.[8] After his death at the battle of Evesham in 1265 it was granted for life to his widow Maud,[9] who in 1292 approved a grant by a younger William of Evreux of his reversionary right to William de Grandison and his wife Sibyl.[10] William de Grandison was in possession of the manor in 1316[11] and died c.1335 to be succeeded by his son Peter.[12] Peter (d. 1358)[13] settled the manor on his nephew Thomas de Grandison (d. 1375) with remainder to Elizabeth le Despenser, whose son Guy de Brian succeeded at Thomas's death.[14] After Guy's death in 1386 his widow Alice retained Oxenhall manor[15] until her death in 1435, when the heir was Elizabeth Lovell.[16] Elizabeth died in 1437, leaving as heir to Oxenhall her grandson Humphrey FitzAlan, earl of Arundel,[17] who died a minor in 1438. In 1445 Oxenhall was settled on James Butler and his wife Amice, evidently in her right. She died in 1457[18] and James, who had been created earl of Wiltshire in 1449, retained the manor until his execution and attainder after the battle of Towton in 1461. The following year it was included in an extensive grant of forfeited Lancastrian lands to Walter Devereux, created Lord Ferrers, who may have retained it until his death at Bosworth in 1485.[19] The manor passed to Henry Percy (d. 1489), earl of Northumberland, perhaps by virtue of his marriage to Devereux's niece Maud Herbert.[20] In 1492 it was in the hands of the Crown during the minority of the earl's son and heir Henry,[21] who came of age in 1499. That Earl Henry (d. 1527) was succeeded by his son Henry, who sold Oxenhall to the Crown with other Gloucestershire possessions in 1535.[22]

In 1544 the Crown mortgaged Oxenhall to a group of London merchant tailors, of whom Thomas Broke[23] owned it at his death in 1546. He left it to Richard Tonge but his will was voided and it was given to his sister Joan Arrowsmith.[24] She conveyed Oxenhall in 1547 to William Grey, Lord Grey of Wilton,[25] and he conveyed it in 1551, with his manor of Kempley, to William Pigott (d. 1553). His widow Margery[26] retained it in 1579,[27] when his son Leonard settled the reversion on the marriage of his daughter Anne to Samuel Danvers[28] of Culworth (Northants). The couple had apparently succeeded to Oxenhall by 1586[29] and Anne and her second husband Henry Finch, of Little Horwood (Bucks.) and later of Kempley, were dealing with the manor in 1600.[30] Two years later Finch bought out the reversionary right of Samuel Danvers, Anne's son by her first marriage,[31] and at his death in 1631 he was succeeded

---

1 *Domesday Book* (Rec. Com.), I, 167v.
2 W.E. Wightman, *The Lacy Family in England and Normandy* (1966), pedigree at end.
3 *Pipe R.* 1202 (PRS N.S. 15), 179.
4 *Book of Fees*, I, 439.
5 *Inq. p.m. Glos.* 1302–58, 253.
6 Ibid. 366–7; *Cal. Close* 1396–9, 457; TNA, C 139/164, no 16.
7 TNA, C 142/357, no 21.
8 *Cal. Chart.* 1226–57, 369; *Close* 1254–6, 36.
9 *Cal. Pat.* 1258–66, 462.
10 *Glos. Feet of Fines 1199–1299*, p.192.
11 *Feudal Aids*, II, 265.
12 *Inq. p.m. Glos.* 1302–58, 252–3.
13 Ibid. 366–7.
14 Ibid. 1359–1413, 102; *Cal. Close* 1374–7, 481.
15 *Inq. p.m. Glos.* 1359–1413, 146; *Cal. Close* 1385–9, 190.
16 TNA, C 139/70, no 34.
17 Ibid. C 139/87, no 46.
18 Ibid. C 139/164, no 16.
19 *Cal. Pat.* 1461–7, 153, 486; *Complete Peerage*, V, 322–4.
20 *Cal. Inq. p.m. Hen. VII*, I, p. 231; *Complete Peerage*, X, 401, 718.
21 *Cal. Pat.* 1485–94, 388.
22 *L&P Hen. VIII*, VIII, p. 147; TNA, SC 6/Hen. VIII/6044.
23 *L&P Hen. VIII*, XIX (2), pp. 78–9.
24 TNA, C 142/75, no 3; *Cal. Pat.* 1547–8, 142–3.
25 *Cal. Pat.* 1547–8, 166.
26 TNA, C 142/111, no 74.
27 Herefs. RO, E 12/G/9, copy of ct. roll 3 Mar. 20 Eliz.I; G/15, lease 18 Nov. 1579.
28 *Cal. Pat.* 1575–78, p. 417; MCA, G 1i, bdl. 172A, no 18, p. 29.
29 Herefs. RO, E 12/G/11, Weyhouse grove and Gyles Croft deeds (deed 4 July 1607).
30 J. Maclean, 'Pedes Finium or Excerpts from the Feet of Fines, in the County of Gloucester', *Trans. BGAS* 17 (1892–3), 186; above, Kempley, manor.
31 Worcs. RO, 705:99 (BA 3375), Kempley deeds 1602–66.

by his son Francis Finch,[1] later of Rushock (Worcs.), who in the late 1640s and early 1650s held manor courts for Oxenhall and granted leases jointly with John Blurton of Redditch (Worcs.), perhaps a mortgagee.[2] Francis, who set up ironworks at Ellbridge, incurred large business debts and in 1658 he sold the manor to the ironmaster Thomas Foley.[3]

Thomas Foley shortly afterwards bought the adjoining manor of Newent, with which Oxenhall descended in the Foleys and their successors, the Onslows, for the next two and a half centuries.[4] In 1775 the Oxenhall estate comprised 1,668 a.,[5] and in the mid 19th century there were eight principal farms totalling 972 a., various smallholdings, and 480 a. of woodland.[6] The estate was put up for sale by Andrew Richard Onslow in 1913 and most of the farms, including Holder's, Winter's, Peter's, Pella, White House, and Waterdynes, were bought by the sitting tenants.[7] In 1914 639 a. of woodland in Oxenhall and Dymock was sold, with Little Pound farm, to Archibald Weller of Malvern; he sold the woods in the same year to the Crown[8] and they were subsequently managed as part of the large tract known later as Dymock Woods.[9] A.R. Onslow (d. 1950) retained the manorial rights of Oxenhall.[10]

As suggested below, the original manor house of Oxenhall may have been at Hilter Farm. A capital messuage recorded on the manor in 1358[11] and worth nothing in 1435, when it was waste,[12] was more likely in Oxenhall park in the north-east corner of the parish. There it was said c.1700 that a house had once been a residence of the Grandisons.[13] A field called Moat field, north-east of Waterdynes Farm, may have been its site.[14]

OTHER ESTATES IN OXENHALL

Hilter Farm

A man called Roger of the Guildhall (*de la Ghildhalle*) witnessed Oxenhall deeds in 1316[15] and in 1327 Roger 'atte Yeldhalle' and two others similarly surnamed were assessed for tax in the parish.[16] Those men evidently occupied a building or buildings at the prominent site near the centre of the parish where in the 17th century stood the farmhouse called Yeldhall; the name later mutated to Illto or Ilthall and finally, by the early 19th century, to Hilter (or Hilters) Farm.[17] If the name Guildhall was being used in its original sense — as a building where payments or dues were rendered[18] — it seems likely that Hilter was the site of the original manor house, perhaps alienated or leased away by the lords before the early 14th century. The existence of a dovehouse among the buildings at the site in the 17th century and a coney warren in one of its fields[19] further supports the suggestion of former manorial status.

Yeldhall (later Hilter) Farm passed to John Hill, who sold it in 1596, together with his Hill House estate in Pauntley, to Sir Edward Winter, owner of Newent manor.[20] In 1657 the Winters sold Yeldhall, with 25 a. of land adjoining, to Thomas Rogers and in 1668 he sold that estate with other lands to the lord of Oxenhall manor, Thomas Foley, who as part of the transaction granted it back on a lease for lives. Rogers died in 1671 and his son William surrendered his life interest to Paul Foley in 1680.[21] The house, which was assessed for tax on six hearths in 1672,[22] was apparently then the largest in the parish. It remained the centre of one of the principal farms on the manor estate until the sale of 1913,[23] but ceased to be a farmhouse in the 1970s when the farmland was sold to a fruit farmer, who built a new house near by.[24]

Marshall's and Winter's Farms

An estate called Marshall's farm, based on a house near Ellbridge, may have derived from an early medieval subinfeudation: at the death of its owner in 1612 it was said to be held from the lord of Oxenhall manor by fealty and suit of court but a second inquisition revised that finding to tenure by knight service from the Crown as overlord of the manor.[25] Roger the marshal (*mareschal*) who was assessed for tax at a high rate at Oxenhall in 1327[26] was

---

1 *Inq. p.m. Glos.* 1625–42, I, 158–9.
2 Herefs. RO, E 12/G/9; G/24, leases 4 Oct. 1647, 1 May 1651, 14 Sept. 1652.
3 Ibid. G/13; MCA, F 4iii, deed 1050; below, econ. hist. (Ellbridge furnace).
4 Above, Newent, manors (Newent manor).
5 GA, D 2528.
6 GDR, T 1/137.
7 GA, SL 79.
8 TNA, CRES 38/674.
9 Above, Dymock, econ. hist. (woodland management).
10 *Kelly's Dir. Glos.* (1923), 276; (1939), 285; *Burke's Peerage* (1963), 1863.
11 *Inq. p.m. Glos.* 1302–58, 366–7.
12 TNA, C 139/70, no 34.
13 *Notes on Dioc. of Glouc. by Chancellor Parsons*, 182. According to Atkyns (*Glos.* 594) part of the house remained standing at the start of the 18th cent. but his account confuses entries taken from the preceding source concerning it and Hilter Farm.
14 GA, photocopy 5.
15 'Cal. of Earlier Heref. Cathedral Mun.' (TS, Nat. Lib. Wales 1955), II, pp. 761, 767, 769.
16 *Glos. Subsidy Roll, 1327*, 35.
17 Herefs. RO, E 12/G/11; GDR wills 1671/150; *Notes on Dioc. of Glouc. by Chancellor Parsons*, 182; OS Map 1", sheet 43 (1831 edn).
18 *OED*.
19 Herefs. RO, E 12/G/11, deed 19 Mar. 1656/7.
20 GA, D 421/T 34; and see ibid. E 13, f. 16; M 81 (s.v. Oxenhall).
21 Herefs. RO, E 12/G/11; and for Rogers's death, GA, P 241/IN 1/1.
22 TNA, E 179/247/14, rot. 36.
23 GA, SL 79.
24 Information from Ms E.M. Goulding of Newent.
25 TNA, C 142/348, no 121; C 142/357, no 21.
26 *Glos. Subsidy Roll, 1327*, 35.

presumably an early occupant, but the estate has not been found recorded before 1525, when with Winter's farm it belonged to Arthur Porter.[1] Possibly the two farms had been acquired by his father Roger Porter (d. 1523) of Newent, who was steward of Oxenhall manor for the earl of Northumberland.[2] Both farms descended, presumably with Arthur's extensive estate in Newent, to his grandson Sir Arthur Porter.[3] In 1604 Sir Arthur with others, presumably trustees or mortgagees, sold Marshall's farm (110 a.) to Christopher Hooke, its tenant since 1586.[4] Christopher died in 1612 and, subject to his widow Anne's third share in dower, the farm passed to his son Thomas.[5] Thomas sold it in 1634 to Edward Clarke of Newent, a haberdasher; it then included Ellbridge mill which later, under a lease by Clarke, Francis Finch converted to form part of his ironworks. In 1647 Clarke settled the farm on the marriage of his son Edward with Mary Chinn.[6]

By 1659 the farm had been dispersed among several owners, and the farmhouse, then styled Marshall's or Ellbridge, was said to belong to William Chinn.[7] In 1672, however, the younger Edward Clarke confirmed to Paul Foley a grant he had formerly made of the house and Ellbridge mill to Paul's father Thomas.[8] The house was evidently the remodelled 15th-century farmhouse[9] that was known later as Furnace Farm from the nearby ironworks, though it stands some way north of that site on the west side of Furnace Lane. Furnace Farm remained part of the manor estate after the mid 17th century. It was attached to Winter's farm in 1775[10] and later, reduced in size, it was occupied as farm cottages.[11] In 1913 the house with a farm of 105 a. was bought by the widow of the former tenant James Lodge,[12] and in 2006 it was owned and farmed by Mr R.G. Heath. Another former part of Marshall's farm passed to a branch of the Hill family, which sold it to the Foleys in 1758,[13] and another former part, adjoining Coldharbour Lane west of the Dymock road, acquired its own small farmhouse, which assumed the name Marshall's Farm. The latter was owned by members of the Clarke family in the mid 19th century[14] but was added to the Oxenhall manor estate in 1890.[15]

Winter's farm, based on a farmhouse on the lane running between Oxenhall church and the Newent–Dymock road and originally including a second farmhouse called Gillhouse, was sold by Sir Arthur Porter in 1604 to Roger Hill. It passed to Roger's son Arthur Hill of Highnam, who settled the 70-a. farm in 1635 on the marriage of his daughter Martha and Henry Stranke of Highnam.[16] In 1659 Winter's was held by a lawyer William Sheppard[17] and in 1677 and 1688 by Joseph Morwent of Ledbury.[18] Nevertheless, it descended to the Strankes' grandson, John Rawlinson of Dartmouth (Devon), who sold the farm in 1718 to Thomas Foley, the lord of the manor.[19] From that time until the sale of 1913 it remained one of the principal farms of the manor estate.[20]

Oxenhall Rectory and Oxenhall Court

In the mid 12th century the tithes of Oxenhall belonged, probably by gift of one of the Lacy family, to St Guthlac's priory, Hereford, which had confirmation of its right from the bishop of Hereford.[21] By 1291, however, Oxenhall church, apparently with all its tithes and profits, belonged to the Knights Hospitaller,[22] who attached it to their preceptory of Dinmore (Herefs.). In 1338 the church, including four 'bovates' of glebe land, was let at farm under the preceptory for £10 a year.[23] Following the Dissolution the rectory estate was held by the Crown before being granted in 1548 to Robert Curzon, one of the Barons of the Exchequer.[24] He conveyed it the same year to John Bridges (d. 1561), with whose Boyce Court estate, in Dymock, it passed to his nephew Humphrey Forster and then to Humphrey's son Giles.[25] Giles incurred debts in his post of royal receiver for several Midland counties, leading to the Crown taking possession of the rectory estate[26] and conveying it in 1610 to feoffees to use the profits for repayment. Nevertheless the same year Giles made a conveyance of the estate to William Burrows, who in 1612, together with Sir Clement Throckmorton, assignee of the Crown's feoffees, sold it to Sir Robert Baugh (also known, apparently, by the surname Banister), John Worsley, and Launcelot Salfield. Those parties sold it in 1625 to Nicholas Roberts,[27]

---

1 Herefs. RO, E 12/G/11, bdl. marked 'Winter's'.
2 *Military Surv. of Glos. 1522*, 62.
3 Above, Newent, manors (Boulsdon manor).
4 Herefs. RO, E 12/G/32.
5 TNA, C 142/348, no 121; REQ 2/297, no 8.
6 Herefs. RO, E 12/G/13.
7 Ibid. G/9, rental 1659.
8 Ibid. G/13.
9 Above, settlement (bldgs.).
10 GA, D 2528, p. 9; photocopy 5.
11 GDR, T 1/137.
12 GA, SL 79.
13 Herefs. RO, E 12/G/12, bdl. marked 'writings of lands purchased of William Hill'.
14 GDR, T 1/137; GA, D 1882/5/2.
15 GA, SL 79 (notes of title).
16 Herefs. RO, E 12/G/11; GDR wills 1640/155.
17 Herefs. RO, E 12/G/9, rental 1659.
18 Ibid. G/24, lease 20 Feb. 1677; GA, D 1791/8.
19 Herefs. RO, E 12/G/11.
20 GA, SL 79.
21 *Eng. Episcopal Acta* VII, pp. 23, 149–51.
22 *Tax. Eccl.* 161; *Reg. T. de Charlton*, 53.
23 *The Knights Hospitallers in England*, ed. L.B. Larking (Camd. Soc. 1st ser. 65, 1857), p. 30.
24 *Cal. Pat.* 1547–8, 383–4.
25 TNA, C 142/129, no 99; Hockaday Abs. xlvii, 1576 visit. f. 118; see above, Dymock, manors (other estates: Boyce Ct.).
26 GA, D 36/E 56.
27 Ibid. E 1, ff. 122–3; and for Banister, GDR, V 5/226T 1.

from whom it descended until 1801 with an estate in Westbury-on-Severn in the Roberts and Colchester families.[1]

The rectory included all the tithes of the parish with a glebe farm, described in 1613 as comprising a parsonage house (that later called Oxenhall Court), a tithe barn, three orchards, seven inclosed fields, and a meadow; there were also some outlying parcels of land and woodland leased separately,[2] as was the case later. The whole rectory was valued at £30 in 1600,[3] and in 1629 Nicholas Roberts granted a lease to John Beale at the rent of £70. In 1708 the rectory was leased to John Dobbins, who then also tenanted the adjoining Hilter farm on Oxenhall manor.[4] In 1738, when Oxenhall Court farm comprised 74½ a., it was leased to Arthur Clarke, whose family remained lessees until the mid or later 19th century.[5]

In 1801 the trustees of John Colchester sold the rectory estate to Samuel Beale, an attorney of Upton upon Severn (Worcs.).[6] Beale died in 1840, having entailed it on his daughter Mary Symonds and her descendants,[7] and in 1841 she was awarded a corn rent charge of £440 a year in place of the tithes.[8] In 1857 Mary with other family members and Samuel's trustees sold Oxenhall Court and the rectory lands to R.F. Onslow, heir to the Oxenhall manor estate.[9] At the sale of that estate in 1913 Oxenhall Court farm was bought by George Gurney,[10] who still owned and farmed it in 1931. By 1939 the farmer was John Cummins,[11] and the Cummins family sold it in 1982 to Dr and Mrs P.H. Wright, the owners in 2006.[12] The tithe rent charge was retained by Mary Symonds (d. 1859) and passed to her daughter Mary Tennant (d. 1903) and grandson Edmund William Tennant (d. 1923), whose trustees held it until tithe redemption in the 1930s.[13]

ESTATES IN THE DETACHED PART OF PAUNTLEY

In 1086 Ansfrid of Cormeilles, lord of Pauntley, held a manor called Kilcot, extended at 1 hide.[14] Later evidence suggests that it included the whole of what became the detached part of Pauntley parish, lying south of Oxenhall, together with adjoining lands in Gorsley that belonged to Newent parish, though the evidence is rendered difficult to interpret by the overlapping, and probably changing, application of the place names Kilcot and Gorsley. In the late 12th century William de Solers, probably then lord of Pauntley manor,[15] made a grant of ½ yardland and 10 a. in Kilcot, which a later owner gave to Cormeilles abbey, lord of Newent.[16] In the mid 13th century Roger de Solers granted to Cormeilles all the rents and services owed by four tenants 'in Kilcot in the parish of Pauntley' as well as remitting to the abbey the rent from the estate alienated by William. Later, Richard, son of Walter de Solers of Pauntley, remitted all right in the lands Cormeilles held from him, except for royal service and a rent of 8s.[17] Those lands presumably comprised the ⅓ knight's fee 'in Gorsley' that in 1398 the prior of Newent, administrator of Cormeilles' Newent manor, was said to have held from the earl of March, the overlord of the de Solers family in Pauntley.[18] By that time the 8s. rent reserved to the lords of Pauntley under Richard's grant was paid from land on Newent manor known as the 'court of Gorsley', which adjoined and was sometimes itself regarded as lying within the detached part of Pauntley.[19] It is clear, however, that the rights that the abbey had acquired from the de Solers family extended also over the whole western part of the detached lands of Pauntley, for in 1419 farms there called Hill's Place (later Hill House) and Kew's, together with land called 'freres', were held from Newent manor as free tenancies by a family surnamed Hill.[20] Their estate presumably included holdings once of John 'de Monte' and Roger 'le Frere', two of the four tenants mentioned in Roger de Solers's grant. The eastern part of the detached lands of Pauntley, forming Crooke's farm, was probably not included in the de Solers' grants to Cormeilles, for the farm's owners held it directly from the lords of Pauntley.

Crooke's Farm

Crooke's farm, which was held from the lords of Pauntley by fealty and a small chief rent,[21] was recorded from the early 15th century. A tradition, recorded in the early 18th century, stated that the farm was given, together with a sword and the right

---

1 *Inq. p.m. Glos.* 1625–42, II, 44, 161; GA, D 36/E 56; *VCH Glos.* X, 87.
2 GA, D 36/E 12, ff. 40v.–41; GDR, V 5/226T 1; T 1/137.
3 GA, D 36/E 1, f. 122v.
4 Ibid. E 3, p. 55.
5 Ibid. E 11, ff. 29v.–30; Herefs. RO, E 12/G/9, rental 1683/4.
6 GA, D 36/E 12, ff. 40v.–41; E 7/10; GDR, T 1/137; *Glouc. J.* 23 Feb. 1801.
7 GA, D 1882/1; GDR, V 5/226T 6.
8 GDR, T 1/137.
9 GA, D 1882/1.
10 Ibid. SL 79.
11 *Kelly's Dir. Glos.* (1931), 279; (1939), 285.
12 Information from Dr and Mrs Wright.
13 *Kelly's Dir. Glos.* (1885 and later edns); *Burke's Landed Gentry* (1937), II, 2200, 2219–20.
14 *Domesday Book* (Rec. Com.), I, 170.
15 Below, Pauntley, manor.
16 BL, Add. MS 18461, ff. 118v.–119.
17 Ibid. f. 122 and v.
18 *Inq. p.m. Glos.* 1359–1413, 212.
19 Above, Newent, manors (Kilcot: Gorsley and Brassfields).
20 Herefs. RO, E 12/G/2, ct. 12 Feb. 6 Hen. V.
21 *Inq. p.m. Glos.* 1625–42, III, 84–5; J.N. Langston, 'The Pastons of Horton', *Trans. BGAS* 77 (1958), 124.

to a coat of arms, to a member of the Hooke family who served in Henry VIII's French campaign and helped rescue the king after he was surrounded by the enemy.[1] A version of the tradition current by the mid 20th century maintained, however, that those events featured a Hooke who served with and aided Henry V at Agincourt.[2] An ancient sword which remains in possession of the family is thought to date from the early 16th century[3] but, as the Hookes held Crooke's by 1435, the second version seems more likely to contain an element of truth.

In 1435 Thomas Hooke and his trustees settled Crooke's farm, together with the site of a house called Callowhill (in Compton, Newent), on his son Thomas and his wife Margaret. The deed was witnessed by his overlord, Guy Whittington of Pauntley,[4] said to be the father of Margaret in family pedigrees, which trace a descent in direct line to Guy Hooke (*fl.* 1470) and Richard Hooke.[5] Richard Hooke was a large taxpayer in Pauntley parish in 1522,[6] and Christopher Hooke of Crooke's died *c.*1579, leaving his lands to his son Thomas.[7] The son was apparently the Thomas who had three servants in Pauntley at the muster of 1608[8] and died in 1628, holding Crooke's and 60 a. in Pauntley parish and another 193 a. in adjoining parishes, including Callowhill and land at Mantley and Picklenash in Newent. He was succeeded by his son Edward[9] (d. 1651) and Edward by his son John[10] (d. 1705), who devised Crooke's to his grandson Philip Fincher and his heirs on condition they adopted the surname Hooke.[11] John's widow Anne may have retained the farm until her death in 1722,[12] and Philip was in possession in 1734.[13] It apparently passed later to Edward Hooke (d. 1762), who was succeeded by his brother Benjamin Hooke of Worcester, and from that period Crooke's farm was leased while its owners lived in Worcester or on their estate at Norton, near that city. From Benjamin (d. 1771) Crooke's passed in succession to his sons John (d. 1795) and Benjamin (d. 1796).

John, son of the last Benjamin, succeeded but in 1826 he sold the farm to his younger brother Benjamin,[14] who also acquired lands near by in Newent, including Briery Hill farm,[15] a gift from his mother Elizabeth Hooke (d. 1823).[16] Benjamin (d. 1848) left his Gloucestershire estates to his second son John Brewer Hooke, but they passed later to his eldest son Thomas T.B. Hooke (d. 1898). Crooke's then passed in direct line to Thomas C.B. Hooke (d. 1942), Douglas T.H. Hooke (d. *c.*1971), Michael R.D.H. Hooke (d. 2004), and Mr Richard Hooke. The family returned to live at Crooke's Farm in the 1970s, but in 2006 the farmland, comprising *c.*100 a., remained on lease.[17]

Hill House Farm

Hill House farm, in the west of the Pauntley lands, was owned by Walter Hill (d. *c.*1419). Kew's farm, lying further south, was then in the same ownership,[18] but in later centuries usually followed a different descent. James Hill owned Hill House in 1539[19] and, although John Hill sold it in 1596 to Edward Winter, lord of Newent manor,[20] members of the Hill family occupied it as lessees until 1640 or later.[21] The Winters sold Hill House, probably in the late 1650s, to John Brock, a carpenter. Brock died in 1668 leaving it to his wife Margery and then to his two daughters,[22] of whom Margery, wife of John Hill (d. 1687), later succeeded. Margery and her son Thomas Hill both died in 1712, leaving apparently as heir to the farm Margery's grandson John Warr. John came of age *c.*1717 and he settled Hill House, with the farm adjoining called Lower House, in 1731 on his marriage with his wife Anne.[23] He died in 1734 and she in 1765, when the property was evidently divided among the families of John's sisters, Mary Mayo, Margery Wood, and Margaret Phillips.[24] In 1780 Mary Mayo and her son Thomas sold a third share to Thomas Wood,[25] presumably Margery's heir, and in 1795 parts were owned by Thomas Wood and John Phillips, Margaret's heir.[26] Later Hill

---

1 GA, D 412/Z 3, Nourse MS, p. 12.
2 *Burke's Landed Gentry* (1952), 1277.
3 Letters from D.T.H. Hooke and J.N. Taylor to Dr K.M. Tomlinson of Newent, 1957 (in 2005 in possession of Dr Tomlinson).
4 GA, D 2245 (acc. 7541), envelope no 8 (copy of deed 7 July 1435).
5 The descent given here is based on *Burke's Landed Gentry* (1952), 1277–8, and on GA, D 2245 (acc. 7541), envelope containing copies of Hooke fam. wills.
6 *Military Surv. of Glos, 1522*, 61.
7 GDR wills 1579/16.
8 Smith, *Men and Armour*, 66.
9 *Inq. p.m. Glos.* 1625–42, III, 84–5; GDR wills 1628/155.
10 TNA, PROB 11/217, ff. 112v.–113v.; GA, D 2245/E 5.
11 GDR wills 1706/49.
12 Langston, 'Pastons of Horton', 124.

13 Herefs. RO, E 12/G/23, lease D 30.
14 GA, D 2245 (acc. 7541), envelope no 4.
15 GDR, T 1/126,140.
16 GA, D 2245 (acc. 7541), envelope no 10A.
17 Information from Mr Richard Hooke.
18 Herefs. RO, E 12/G/2, ct. 12 Feb. 6 Hen. V.
19 Ibid. G/5, rental 1539.
20 GA, D 421/T 34, where Thos. Baynham and Geo. Huntley acted as trustees for Winter.
21 Herefs. RO, E 12/G/31, lease 1609; GA, D 421/M 81 (s.v. Pauntley tenants).
22 GDR wills 1668/72.
23 GA, D 1882/1, marr. settlement 1731; P 241/IN 1/1, burials 1687, 1712; GDR wills 1688/237; 1711/60–1; 1712/327.
24 Bigland, *Glos.* II, 304; GDR wills 1734/206.
25 GA, D 1882/1.
26 TNA, RAIL 836/3, pp. 155–6, 264, 286.

House farm in its entirety was acquired, together with Kew's farm, by Samuel Beale (d. 1840), owner of the Oxenhall rectory estate, and in 1857 Beale's family sold Hill House and 82 a. (including some fields of Kew's farm) to R.F. Onslow, heir to the Oxenhall manor estate.[1] At the sale of that estate in 1913 Hill House farm was bought by S. Goulding,[2] whose family remained owners in 2006.

ECONOMIC HISTORY

While it remained overwhelmingly an agricultural parish with a significant woodland economy, Oxenhall for a period contained ironworks. Later, canal construction was associated with the mining of coal locally.[3]

AGRICULTURE

To the Late Seventeenth Century

In 1086 the manor of Oxenhall had two ploughs and two slaves on its demesne, and the tenants were five villans and three bordars with five ploughs between them. Three burgesses in Gloucester were attached to the manor.[4] In 1335 the demesne comprised one ploughland and 3 a. of meadow. By 1386 the demesne ploughland had reduced in value, from 20s. to 16s., but the meadow, extended then at 6½ a., had increased in value, from 14d. to c.20d. per acre.[5] In 1435 the demesne arable comprised two ploughlands and was valued at the same total sum as in 1386,[6] presumably reflecting the falling in of tenant land to the lord and the decline in corn prices. According to the 14th-century extents the third part of the demesne arable that was left fallow each year, and the whole of it after the harvest, lay in common, suggesting that the demesne formed part of a fairly extensive tract of open fields. By the mid 17th century, however, the manor owned only a group of inclosed fields, lying in the southern part of the parish, bordered on the north by the lands of the rectory farm (Oxenhall Court) and the freehold called Hilter and on the east by the lands of the freehold called Winter's. That area contained fragments of open fields in the early modern period and may have been the location of larger open fields, perhaps inclosed in the late Middle Ages by a collaboration of the lords of the manor and the owners of those three other estates. In 1659 the manor closes in that area — the Woolastons lying between Oxenhall Court farm and the road from the parish church to Gorsley, Dropping Orchard south of that road, fields known later as Church fields adjoining the church, Hornifords meadow and Broad meadow on the north side of Ell brook, and lands called the Hides south of the brook — were on lease among manor tenants and other landowners.[7] In the 14th-century extents the demesne meadowland also was said to lie in common after the hay harvest, so part at least of the meadows bordering Ell brook was presumably once farmed in common.

In 1335 there were free tenants on the manor owing rents of 60s. a year and customary tenants owing rents of 13s. 4d.[8] By 1358 the figures were 100s. and 42s. 6d.,[9] the latter increase presumably the result of the commutation of unwanted labour services. A process of amalgamation of customary tenancies under way in the late Middle Ages is reflected in the copyholds that formed the main class of manor tenancies in the 16th and early 17th century: the descriptions given to them indicate that most then incorporated the lands once attached to two or three separate holdings. In 1659 the manor contained a total of 24 copyhold farms. The largest, based on White House Farm, comprised 66 a., four others, including those based on Holder's and Pella Farms, had between 50 and 56 a., another based on Briary House (later Peter's Farm) had 32 a., and the remainder were under 30 a. There were also leaseholds, most of them small and based on cottages adjoining Hay wood but including some larger ones comprising parkland, woodland, and former demesne lands.[10] Under the Foleys in the later 17th century copyhold tenure was phased out, but in most cases it was replaced by leasehold for 99 years or three named lives with heriots payable, so the change for the tenants was probably not that significant.[11]

Only fragments of open-field land survived into the early modern period. In 1635 Winter's farm included five 'doles' of arable in Pool field, which probably adjoined the east side of Oxenhall pool,[12]

---

1 GA, D 1882/1.
2 Ibid. SL 79.
3 Above, introd. (communications).
4 *Domesday Book* (Rec. Com), I, 167v.
5 *Inq. p.m. Glos.* 1302–58, 252–3; 1359–1413, 146.
6 TNA, C 139/70, no 34.
7 For those demesne closes, Herefs. RO, E 12/G/9, ct. 20 Feb. 3 Edw. VI; rental 1659 (s.v. Oxenhall leaseholders); G/15, lease 18 Nov. 1579; G/24 leases 1 Oct. 1645, 28 Jan. 1651, 31 July 1663; and for their location, GA, photocopy 5; GDR, T 1/137.
8 *Inq. p.m. Glos.* 1302–58, 252–3.
9 Ibid. 366–7.
10 Herefs. RO, E 12/G/9, cts. 20 Feb. 3 Edw. VI, 14 Oct. 23 Chas. I; rental 1659.
11 Ibid. G/23–4; G/9, rental 1683–4.
12 Ibid. G/11, deed 18 June 1635; GA, photocopy 5.

and at the same period a small open field called Six Acres lay in the valley of Ash brook south-west of the lands of Oxenhall Court farm.[1] It is that area of the parish, extending from Six Acres on the west to the land of Winter's farm on the east, that seems the most likely site of the larger system of fields that apparently existed in the 14th century. Six Acres remained uninclosed in 1775 when five tenants owned land there. By then known simply as 'the common field',[2] it was presumably the last uninclosed arable to survive in Oxenhall. The meadowland along the Ell brook was all inclosed by the mid 17th century, the manorial demesne having a large part and most of the copyholders small closes.[3] The woodland in the west of the parish was subject to common rights of the tenants in the 14th century,[4] but by the 17th century all but the area that later formed Shaw common was several to the lord of the manor.[5]

The sandy soil of much of Oxenhall favoured the growing of rye, rather than wheat, as the winter corn crop.[6] In parishioners' wills of the 16th and 17th centuries rye featured regularly in the form of gifts to family members and charitable bequests,[7] and rye, barley or other spring crops, and a fallow were the usual courses of the three-year rotation that continued as the practice in the early modern period.[8] Some wheat was grown, however, where the soil was suitable:[9] Woodens farm in the south-west part of the parish and Holder's farm in the north-east both had closes named Wheat field in the 1670s.[10] All or most Oxenhall farmers kept sheep in the 16th and 17th centuries,[11] though the lack of common pasture or large open fields must have restricted the flocks to modest proportions. A sheephouse was among new buildings put up at Oxenhall Court in 1630s by its tenant John Beale,[12] and in 1659 the outbuildings on four of the copyhold farms included sheephouses.[13] Cider was another staple product, with cider mills (must mills), presses, and casks (hogsheads and pipes) among items passed down in the farming families.[14] Most leases of farms in the late 17th and early 18th century provided for the planting of apple and pear stocks in each year of the term.[15] A writer at the start of the 18th century identified rye, wool, and cider as the main products of the parish.[16]

From c.1700

Under the Foley family the amalgamation of the tenant farms of the manor continued, though the groupings of lands sometimes changed over the years and the new farms were not all ring-fenced, suggesting that the process resulted more from the ambition of particular tenants rather than a policy of reorganization on the part of the landlords.[17] Two new farms were formed on the estate after the purchase of the freehold of Hilter and Winter's farms. In 1775 Hilter, comprising the former freehold with some manorial demesne lands and the land of several of the smaller copyholds, had 156 a. and Winter's, with most of the land in the south-east corner of the parish, had 155 a. Another five farms — White House, Peter's, Pella, Holder's, and Waterdynes — then had between 80 and 102 a., another six had between 39 and 51 a., and there were a few smaller holdings.[18] Oxenhall Court farm with c.75 a., tenanted under the lay rectors, was the only substantial farm in the parish remaining outside the manor estate. In the adjoining detached part of Pauntley most of the land had long been divided between three farms, Crooke's, which was tenanted under its owners by the late 18th century, Hill House, and Kew's.[19] Further modifications in the pattern of farms on the manor occurred later, probably during the prosperous period for farming during the Napoleonic Wars when several of the Oxenhall farmhouses were rebuilt. William Deykes, the Foleys' land agent, who lived in the parish during those years,[20] presumably directed those changes. The long leases were probably phased out and replaced by annual tenancies at that period. By 1841 Hilter farm had been enlarged to 215 a. by the inclusion of Pella farm, Holder's to 152 a., and White House to 130 a., and Pound farm, based on a house at Shaw common and formed from a number of smaller holdings adjoining the woodlands in the western part of the parish, had 117 a. Winter's then had 96 a., the rest of its land being farmed from a small house near the remains of Ellbridge furnace, and the other main farms

---

1 Herefs. RO, E 12/G/23, leases D 17, D 27; GDR, V5/226T 1.
2 GA, D 2528, p. 10; photocopy 5.
3 Herefs. RO, E 12/G/9, rental 1659 (s.v. Oxenhall leaseholders); G/19, list of occupiers of lands adjoining watercourse, 8 Mar. 1670/1.
4 *Inq. p.m. Glos.* 1302–58, 252–3; 1359–1413, 146.
5 GA, photocopy 1194/1; above introd. (landscape).
6 Rudge, *Agric. of Glos.* 20, 138.
7 e.g. GDR wills 1556/108; 1563/29; 1584/116; 1620/12; 1626/79; 1648/93; 1682/53.
8 Ibid. 1573/246; 1609/158; Herefs. RO, E 12/G/24, lease 13 May 1674, articles of agreement 2 Feb. 1667.
9 GDR wills 1556/108; 1601/156.
10 Herefs. RO, E 12/G/24, leases 21 Apr. 1673, 28 Feb.1679.
11 e.g. GDR wills 1560/173; 1562/90; 1573/246; 1609/158; 1626/79; 1661/125; 1674/60.
12 TNA, E 134/16 Chas. I/Mich. 9.
13 Herefs. RO, E 12/G/9, rental 1659.
14 e.g. GDR wills 1587/271; 1601/156; 1626/79; 1640/98; 1662/105; 1673/98; 1698/73.
15 Herefs. RO, E 12/G/23–4.
16 *Notes on Dioc. of Glouc. by Chancellor Parsons*, 182.
17 Herefs. RO, E 12/G/23–4.
18 GA, D 2528, pp. 9–15; photocopy 5.
19 Above, manor.
20 Above, settlement (bldgs.); for Deykes, below, social hist. (social structure).

on the estate were Peter's (103 a.) and Waterdynes (71 a.).[1] The Onslows, the Foleys' successors, continued the policy of buying in freehold land when it became available, adding to the estate Oxenhall Court and Hill House farms in 1857, Lambsbarn farm before 1864, and Marshall's farm in 1890.[2]

As with much of western Gloucestershire, adoption of the new agricultural techniques of the 18th century was slow. The main change in practice was the replacement of the rye crop by wheat, made possible by the use of lime and other forms of manuring;[3] only 3 a. of land was returned as under rye in 1801. The crops returned then — 289 a. of wheat, 195 a. of barley, and 65 a. of other crops (including less than 5 a. of turnips and no clover or grass seeds)[4] — suggest that the traditional rotation of two crops and a fallow still obtained. By 1866 a more sophisticated rotation had been introduced, with the land mainly under wheat, barley, root crops, peas, and beans, and with vetches, clover, and grass-seeds also playing a part. The total land under crops returned in 1866 was 816 a. compared with 249 a. of permanent grass. The later years of the 19th century saw the usual decline in arable, mainly accounted for by a fall in the amount of wheat grown: by 1896 in the parish (as enlarged by the detached land of Pauntley in 1883) 620 a. was returned as under crops and 580 a. as permanent grassland. The number of cattle kept rose during that period, from 47 in 1866 to 116 in 1896, and sheep, with total flocks of 575 returned in 1896, remained a significant part of the local farming enterprise.[5]

In the parish (as enlarged) the pattern of c.15 principal farms of between 50 and 150 a. established by the mid 19th century continued during the 20th. At the sale of the manor estate in 1913 a number of the farms were bought by their tenants,[6] and in 1926 of the larger farms (over 50 a.) eight were owner-occupied and seven were tenanted; there were then nine smaller units. The farmers of the parish then employed a total of 39 workers full-time and another 24 on a casual basis.[7] There was little change in the pattern later in the century, apart from a rise in the amount of owner-occupied land and a trend for some of the smaller holdings to be worked on a part-time basis: in 1986 there were 13 farms of over 20 ha (c.50 a.) and eight smaller units and 46 people (including the farmers and their families) were employed on the land full-time and another 10 on a seasonal or casual basis.[8]

There was the usual recovery in the amount of arable in the mid and later years of the 20th century with 875 a. returned as under crops compared to 930 a. of permanent grassland in 1956, by which time sugar beet (83 a.) had become a significant cash crop. Livestock farming, particularly dairying, was, however, the dominant enterprise. In 1956 907 cattle were returned, including 215 cows described as in milk or calf for the dairy herds and 68 in milk or calf for the beef herds. In 1986, when 1,132 cattle were returned, the equivalent figures were 495 and 175; of the 15 main farms four then specialized in dairying, three were mainly engaged in dairying, and one reared beef cattle. Sheep raising was an expanding enterprise, with 238 breeding ewes returned in 1926, 473 in 1956, and 506 in 1986. Fruit growing also continued: 20 a. of orchard was returned in 1926 when the parish had at least one specialist fruit grower, and in 1986 26.6 ha (66 a.) of orchard produced cider and dessert apples and pears. Oxenhall shared with adjoining parts of Herefordshire and Gloucestershire in the expansion of the horticultural sector of farming during the 20th century. Soft fruit was grown commercially by the 1920s, and in 1986 29.1 ha (72 a.) was returned as under small fruit, vegetables, and nursery stock: two occupiers then specialized in fruit, one in vegetables, and one in general horticulture.[9] In the last years of the 20th century and the first of the 21st the dairy herds of the parish were given up. In 2006 most of the farms raised beef cattle and sheep and one farm supported a large flock of goats.[10] The parish then had several fruit farms, a nursery for young trees, and a small vineyard which had begun production in 1984.[11]

WOODLAND MANAGEMENT AND WOODLAND CRAFTS

All of Oxenhall's woodland was apparently open to rights of common by the tenants in the 14th century[12] but by the 17th all but a small part, the later Shaw common, was reserved in severalty to the lord of the manor. As mentioned above, parts were leased to tenants in the early 17th century, leading to the felling and clearing of some areas.[13] After the establishment of the furnace at Ellbridge, however, the bulk was used for coppicing for charcoal production,[14] a practice probably already followed in some parts of the woodland by 1608 when two 'colliers' lived in the parish.[15] Francis Finch, who by

---

1   GDR, T 1/137.
2   Above, manor; GA, D 1882/5/2.
3   Rudge, *Agric. of Glos.* 138.
4   *1801 Crop Returns Eng.* I, 176.
5   TNA, MAF 68/26/12; MAF 68/1609/15.
6   GA, SL 79.
7   TNA, MAF 68/3295/15.
8   Ibid. MAF 68/6005/14/169.
9   Ibid. MAF 68/3925/15; MAF 68/4533/169; MAF 68/6005/14/169.
10 Information from the farmers.
11 *Glos. and Avon Life*, July 1985, 30–1.
12 *Inq. p.m Glos.* 1302–58, 253; 1359–1413, 90.
13 Above, introd. (landscape).
14 Below (Ellbridge furnace).
15 Smith, *Men and Armour*, 67.

1634 employed a woodward to preserve the woods on his manor from depredation by local cottagers and their animals,[1] cut and charcoaled large quantities of cordwood in Hay wood in the late 1630s.[2] In 1659 in the manor coppices, then extended at 240 a., the practice was to fell 20 a. at 12 years' growth each year,[3] and intensive use of the woods for charcoal continued under the Foleys during the late 17th and early 18th century. At the turn of the century the Oxenhall woods, with those belonging to the estate in Newent and Longhope, were managed on a perpetual cycle of cutting at 14 years' growth.[4] Some of the smaller groves attached to tenant farms were also used for the same purpose, and leases granted by the manor usually reserved all timber on the farms except for that traditionally allowed as 'bote' for the upkeep of buildings and hedgerows.[5] In 1670 Thomas Foley while on a visit to the manor encouraged his tenants to plant acorns on their lands.[6]

The large quantities of oak bark produced by Francis Finch's cording operations in the 1630s were sold to Gloucester city tanners,[7] and in the early 18th century the estate produced bark for tanneries in Newent and elsewhere, as well as wood for making hoops (for barrels), laths, and broomsticks.[8] A cooper occupied one of the cottages adjoining the woods in 1773,[9] and most of the cottagers living around Shaw common were probably supported in part by woodland crafts. Among them during the 19th century were woodcutters, lath makers, wood turners, hoop makers, a chair maker, and a hurdle maker.[10] The canal, which had a timber yard on its bank near Oxenhall pool in 1841,[11] aided the distribution of woodland products. In the late 19th century annual sales of timber and coppice wood were held by a local firm of auctioneers, and in 1913 most of the woodland was still managed as coppice, cut at 16 years' growth.[12] The sporting rights in the woods were exploited in the late 19th century under the Onslows, who employed several gamekeepers.[13] Those rights were valued at £100 a year in 1902,[14] and at the sale of the estate the woods were offered in a single lot as a sporting and agricultural estate;[15] but in the event the purchaser in 1914 sold them a few months later to the Crown, and in 1924 with the adjoining woodland (the whole known collectively as Dymock Woods) they were transferred to the Forestry Commission for commercial management.[16]

COAL MINING

The coal seams that underlie Oxenhall and the former detached land of Pauntley in a thin band running between Hillend, on the Dymock boundary on the north-east, and Kilcot, on the south-west, were worked sporadically during the 18th and 19th centuries. A field adjoining Peter's Farm, where old shafts were visible in the 1880s,[17] was known as Mine Pit field by 1729.[18] The main attempts to develop the coal deposits were associated with the building of the Hereford and Gloucester canal in the 1790s. During 1794 and 1795 the canal company sank shafts on the lands of Lower and Hill House farms in Pauntley,[19] and in 1796 it built a branch of the canal through Oxenhall to serve those mines. The company transferred its lease of the mining rights on the two farms to Richard Perkins, who formed a partnership with John Moggridge of Boyce Court, in Dymock. Perkins set up a steam engine and sank further shafts in 1796 and two years later purchased four of the canal company's barges, but the company became increasingly impatient with his slowness in supplying the coal they needed to burn bricks and lime for the work then continuing on the main line of the canal and Oxenhall tunnel. In 1799 it also complained that some of the coal he raised was being taken out by wagon and not by the canal. Perkins's mining operations came to an end soon after 1800.[20] The canal branch leading to the works was disused and leased in sections to adjoining farmers before 1841,[21] but the pits on Lower and Hill House farms were being worked again that year when the census recorded two miners occupying a cabin in the area and a coal merchant living in a cottage.[22]

A more substantial project was begun in the neighbouring part of Oxenhall in 1875, when the lord of the manor R.F. Onslow granted a lease of mining rights to William Aston. The following year Aston and investors from the industrial Midlands formed the Newent Colliery Co. and secured a wider lease covering a large part of Onslow's estate. The

---

1 GA, D 147/2.
2 TNA, E 134/16 Chas.I/Mich. 9.
3 Herefs. RO, E 12/G/9, rental 1659.
4 Ibid. G/12, table of woods 1698–1711.
5 Ibid. G/23–4.
6 Ibid. G/6, note on back of rental 1659–70.
7 TNA, E 134/16 Chas. I/Mich. 9.
8 Herefs. RO, E 12/G/25.
9 Ibid. G/23, lease D 56.
10 GA, P 241/IN 1/6, baptisms 1824, 1826; VE 2/1, min. 16 Mar. 1948; TNA, HO 107/1960; RG 9/1759; RG 12/2008.
11 GDR, T 1/137.
12 GA, SL 79.
13 *Kelly's Dir. Glos.* (1894), 257; (1910), 273.
14 GA, D 1882/5/3.
15 Ibid. SL 79.
16 TNA, CRES 36/266; CRES 38/674. See above, Dymock, econ. hist. (woodland management).
17 OS Map 6", Glos. XVII.SW (1884 edn).
18 Herefs. RO, E 12/G/23, lease D 17.
19 TNA, RAIL 836/3, pp. 101, 141, 168–9, 212, 237.
20 Ibid. pp. 264, 286, 319–20, 340, 350–1, 359, 422, 434–5; RAIL 836/4, pp. 33–4, 46; D. Bick, *The Mines of Newent and Ross* (Newent, 1987), 27.
21 GDR, T 1/137.
22 TNA, HO 107/350.

company opened a mine (Newent colliery) beside the lane south-east of White House Farm; in 1879 it was employing 60 workmen but the venture was unsuccessful and the company was wound up in 1880.[1] No serious attempts to exploit the coal in Oxenhall are recorded later, although a firm of investment brokers issued an optimistic prospectus soon after the sale of the Onslow estate in 1913.[2] In 2006 the overgrown shafts and waste tip of the 1870s colliery provided the main reminders of mining operations in Oxenhall.

MILLS

A corn mill belonging to Hill House farm stood on the brook below and just to the north of the farmhouse.[3] It was sold with the farm in 1596 to Sir Edward Winter[4] and was leased in 1609 to Thomas Hill. In 1639 Sir John Winter leased the watercourse running to the mill to Francis Finch,[5] evidently to facilitate water supply to the latter's Ellbridge furnace. The next owner of Hill House, John Brock, conveyed the mill in 1660 to John Spicer,[6] the manager of the furnace under Thomas Foley, and the following year he and Spicer renewed the lease of the watercourse to Foley.[7] Probably from that date the mill ceased working; it had been demolished by 1731.[8]

Further east, a mill on the Ell brook belonged to Crooke's farm. In 1645 the farm's owner, Edward Hooke, leased its leat to Francis Finch, with an undertaking that water from the brook would only be directed down it to the mill at times when Ellbridge furnace was not in blast.[9] Edward's son John renewed the lease to the Foleys on the same terms later in the century.[10] Crooke's Mill was recorded as a working corn mill in 1882[11] and is thought to have ceased operation when Gloucester corporation built its waterworks a short way downstream in the 1890s.[12]

A mill called Ellbridge Mill, standing just upstream of the bridge of that name, was recorded from 1444.[13] In the early 17th century it formed part of Marshall's farm and in 1638 Edward Clarke leased it to Francis Finch, who converted it as part of his ironworks. In 1659, under Thomas Foley, the mill was used as a steelworks in connexion with the furnace.[14] It remained in use for that purpose in 1670, when there was a suggestion that it should be turned back to corn milling to make up a shortage of capacity in the area,[15] to which the abandonment (or partial abandonment) of the Hill House and Crooke's mills had evidently contributed.

ELLBRIDGE FURNACE

The iron-smelting furnace at Ellbridge (often called Elmbridge furnace) was established by the lord of the manor Francis Finch before 1638. It was built on waste land between the Ell brook and the lane that became known as Furnace Lane, and, as mentioned above, the works incorporated the nearby Ellbridge mill.[16] In the late 1630s Finch bought cinders (the residue of ancient iron workings) from local landowners[17] and took leases to secure his supplies of water to power the bellows.[18] By 1655, partly by the purchase of coppice wood, he had incurred debts of £4,000 and in an attempt to recover his position he made an agreement with the Midland ironmaster Thomas Foley under which, in return for Foley standing security for his debts, he mortgaged the furnace and its sources of supply of cinders and charcoal to Thomas Lowbridge of Wilden (Worcs.), Foley's agent or partner. Finch was to continue to work the furnace but supply Lowbridge with pig-iron to the value of the debts, the iron to be delivered to Ashleworth on the river Severn for shipping upstream to ironworks of Foley and his partners at Wilden and the adjoining Stour valley. Most of Finch's debts remained outstanding in October 1658 when the same three parties made a further agreement on similar lines,[19] but a few months later Finch sold Oxenhall manor with his residual rights in the furnace to Foley.[20]

Under Foley and his descendants the furnace was worked on an extensive scale, and the operation of powering and charging it employed resources from an area extending well beyond their manors of Oxenhall and Newent. The use of water from the Ell brook and its tributaries was secured by a series of leases and agreements with other landowners and

---

1 Bick, *Mines of Newent and Ross*, 44–52.
2 GA, D 3398/1/12/18.
3 Ibid. D 1882/1, marr. settlement 1731; and for Pale field, which its site adjoined, GDR, T 1/ 40.
4 GA, D 421/T 34.
5 Herefs. RO, E 12/G/31.
6 Note of foot of fine in possession of VCH Glos. (the bdl. containing the original, TNA, CP 25/2/656/12 Chas. II Trin., had been misplaced in 2006).
7 Herefs. RO, E 12/G/24, lease 21 Mar. 1661.
8 GA, D 1882/1, marr settlement 1731.
9 Herefs. RO, E 12/G/24, lease 1 Oct. 1645.
10 GA, D 2245/E 5.
11 *Kelly's Dir. Glos.* (1879), 720; OS Map 6", Glos. XVII.SW (1884 edn).

12 G.M. Davies, 'Mills of the River Leadon and Tributaries', *Glos. Soc. Ind. Archaeol. Newsletter* 7 (Apr. 1966), p. 40.
13 Westminster Abbey Mun. 3535.
14 Herefs. RO, E 12/G/13.
15 Ibid. G/13, notes 30 Aug. 1670.
16 Ibid. G/11, deed 28 Jan. 1653; G/13, lease 1 Apr. 1638.
17 Ibid. G/15, deed 20 Apr. 1639.
18 Herefs. RO, E 12/G/24, leases 1 Oct. 1645, 10 May 1659; G/31, lease 3 Aug. 1639.
19 Herefs. RO, E 12/G/13. For the Foleys and their ironworks, B.L.C. Johnson, 'New Light on the Iron Industry of the Forest of Dean', *Trans. BGAS* 72 (1953), 129–143; ' The Stour Valley Iron Industry in the late 17th Century', *Trans. Worcs. Archaeol. Soc.* N.S. 27 (1950), 35–46.
20 Above, manor.

63. Building at the former Ellbridge ironworks

Foley tenants holding lands bordering the streams.¹ Part of the supply came from a 5-a. pool in the valley east of the parish church. It was apparently constructed or enlarged by Francis Finch,² and he, or possibly Foley, built a long leat to bring water to the pool from Ell brook near Hill House Farm; the leat followed a course north of the brook similar to that taken later by the colliery branch of the Hereford and Gloucester canal. In addition the Foleys built three storage ponds on feeder streams of the Ell brook about 4 km distant from the furnace, on Gorsley common at the boundary of Newent and adjoining parishes.³

As well as the extensive tracts of woodland belonging to the Foleys' own manors of Oxenhall and Newent, much woodland belonging to nearby estates was coppiced and charcoaled. In the 1660s a total of 1,475 a. in Newent, Dymock, Pauntley, Linton (Herefs.), Bromesberrow, and Upleadon was managed by agreement with other landowners,⁴ and at the same period Thomas Foley and his manager John Spicer felled and charcoaled timber on Woolridge common in Hartpury.⁵ In the quest for every available source even a little 5-a. grove on the copyhold farm called Hilltop in Oxenhall was earmarked for charcoaling in 1669.⁶ Cinders were acquired from many adjoining landowners, including in Newent, Tibberton, Taynton, and Upton Bishop (Herefs.),⁷ and both cinders and iron ore were brought from the Forest of Dean. Some of the pig-iron produced by the furnace was processed in a forge at Upleadon, but the bulk continued to be carried to Ashleworth to be shipped upstream.⁸ About 1710 the Oxenhall furnace was said to produce 20 tons of pig-iron each week it was in blast.⁹ It remained in use until at least 1751, continuing to supply the works of the Foleys and their partners in the Stour valley.¹⁰ A ruined building that survives on the south side of Furnace Lane was possibly the bellows-house adjoining the furnace, and a substantial barn-like building near by is thought to have been a charcoal store.¹¹ Oakdale House (formerly the Furnace), standing on the lane to the east of those buildings may have originated as the works manager's house but was extensively remodelled in the 19th century when used as a residence by the Onslows.¹²

---

1 Herefs. RO, E 12/G/24.
2 Ibid. G/19, bond Oct. 1660; G/23, leases D 25–6.
3 Ibid. G/19, list of occupiers of lands adjoining watercourse, 8 Mar. 1670/1; *Chapters in Newent's History* (Newent Local Hist. Soc. 2003), 156–8.
4 Herefs. RO, E 12/G/19, survey of woods around Newent c.1668.
5 TNA, E 134/20 Chas.II/East. 37.
6 Herefs. RO, E 12/G/32.
7 Ibid. G/12.
8 Johnson, 'Iron Ind. of Forest of Dean', 135–6.
9 Atkyns, *Glos.* 594.
10 Johnson, 'Iron Ind. of Forest of Dean', 142–3.
11 D.E. Bick, 'Remnants of Newent Furnace', *Glos. Soc. Ind. Archaeol. J.* (1980), pp. 29–37: Fig. 63.
12 Below, social hist. (social structure).

OTHER INDUSTRY AND TRADE

In 1608 only six non-agricultural tradesmen were listed for the muster,[1] and in 1831 only seven families were supported by trade compared with 50 by agriculture.[2] Apart from the woodland crafts mentioned above,[3] a few parishioners followed the usual rural trades, such as tailoring, joinery and carpentry, and smithing;[4] the more sophisticated trades and retail services were supplied by the adjoining town of Newent. A tradesman of a wealthier class than the norm was the carpenter John Brock (d. 1668), who, though illiterate, amassed sufficient capital to buy Hill House farm.[5] In the 1630s, when he lived at Taynton, he provided a set of new farm buildings at Oxenhall Court and built a new vicarage house,[6] and presumably he enjoyed a wide building practice in those days of predominantly timber-framed dwellings. In 1659 and until the 1720s the Addis family of blacksmiths worked a smithy near Hillend in the north-east of Oxenhall.[7] The canal company established a smithy at Hillend green during the building of the canal tunnel in the 1790s,[8] and one continued in use there until the 1920s.[9] In the mid and later 19th century a few tradesmen, including smiths and wheelwrights, occupied the group of cottages on the Newent–Dymock road at Three Ashes.[10]

LOCAL GOVERNMENT

MANORIAL GOVERNMENT

Leet jurisdiction over Oxenhall manor was exercised by the Botloe hundred court, at which the parish was represented by a constable and a tithingman in the 1640s.[11] The court baron for the manor, which met two or three times a year in the 1440s, dealt almost exclusively with tenurial matters.[12] In the 16th century and the early 17th it was held together with the court for Okle Grandison manor in Newent.[13] It still met occasionally in the early 19th century,[14] though, with the phasing out of copyhold tenure, it probably had little business to transact.

PAROCHIAL GOVERNMENT

As a small and sparsely populated parish, Oxenhall may have found it difficult to find the full complement of parish officers. From the mid 17th century or earlier it had only a single churchwarden,[15] and in the early 18th century, when his accounts included payments to vagrants, the same man was apparently performing the duties of overseer of the poor. From 1719, however, a separate overseer was appointed.[16] In the early 1780s a total of *c.*20 paupers were receiving relief each year,[17] and in 1803 12 were on permanent relief and 13 on occasional relief at an annual cost of £65.[18] By the close of the Napoleonic Wars the total numbers relieved had risen to over 30 and annual expenditure to over £200,[19] and expenditure varied between £170 and £260 in the late 1820s and early 1830s.[20] The parish was included in the Newent poor-law union in 1835.[21]

SOCIAL HISTORY

SOCIAL STRUCTURE

For most of its history Oxenhall was essentially a community of small tenant farmers under a single estate. After the 14th century probably no lord resided on the manor until the 19th century, though the Foleys, owners from 1658, were based not far away at Stoke Edith (Herefs.) and managed

---

1 Smith, *Men and Armour*, 67.
2 *Census*, 1831.
3 Above (woodland management and woodland crafts).
4 e.g. Smith, *Men and Armour*, 67; GDR wills 1722/64; 1732/23; 1768/107; GA, P 241/IN 1/6.
5 GDR wills 1668/72; above, manor (estates in detached part of Pauntley).
6 TNA, E 134/16 Chas.I/Mich. 9.
7 Herefs. RO, E 12/G/9, rental 1659 (s.v. Oxenhall leaseholders); G/23, lease D 23; G/24, lease 7 Aug. 1668; GDR wills 1729/181.
8 TNA, RAIL 836/4, pp. 38, 51.
9 OS Map 6", Glos. XVII.NW (1884 edn); GA, P 241/VE 2/1, min. 16 Mar. 1848; *Kelly's Dir. Glos.* (1879 and later edns).
10 TNA, HO 107/1960; *Kelly's Dir. Glos.* (1856 and later edns).
11 Herefs. RO, E 12/G/9.
12 Westminster Abbey Mun. 3535; it is not known why the abbey's muniments contain Oxenhall court rolls (for 1443–7).
13 Herefs. RO, E 12/G/9.
14 Fosbrooke, *Glos.* II, 230.
15 Hockaday Abs. lxviii, 1661 visit. f. 2; GDR, V 5/226T 3; GA, P 241/IN 1/1.
16 GA, P 241/CW 2/1.
17 Ibid. OV 2/1–2.
18 *Poor Law Abstract, 1804*, 172–3.
19 Ibid. *1818*, 146–7.
20 *Poor Law Returns* (1830–1), 66; (1835), 65.
21 *Poor Law Com. 2nd Rep.* p. 523.

ironworks and woodlands in Oxenhall and Newent. During the later 18th century and the early 19th their agents, namely Edward James (d. 1768)[1] and William Deykes (d. 1827),[2] lived at Ellbridge in the house called the Furnace (in 2006 Oakdale House) and were presumably a controlling influence in local affairs. After Deykes's death the Furnace became the residence of Richard Foley Onslow, who succeeded to the manor estate in 1861.[3] In the mid 1860s he leased the Furnace to a tenant and moved to Stardens, near by in Newent,[4] but his son A.G. Onslow returned to live at the Furnace before 1889 and was followed there by his son A.R. Onslow.[5] The incumbents of Oxenhall, who were poorly beneficed and usually lived in adjoining parishes, were of little note in its affairs before the mid 19th century.

In 1522 the most prosperous inhabitants of Oxenhall were Richard Hill, probably lessee of the main freehold farms called Marshall's and Winter's, with land worth 40s. and goods worth £16, and William Hill with goods worth £10. Most of the other inhabitants assessed then had goods worth between £1 and £4 and were mainly copyholders under the manor. They included three more members of the Hill family and five members of the Wood family,[6] and the Hills and Woods continued the most numerous farming families until the 18th century. Others long represented among Oxenhall's farmers were the Peter, Wetherlock, and Cumming families.[7] At the muster for the county in 1608 the copyholders were represented by 21 men styled husbandmen who comprised over half of all those listed. Only one man, Christopher Hooke, owner of the Marshall's farm freehold, merited the style gentleman, and one other, Roger Hill, owner of Winter's farm, that of yeoman. The dominance of the manor estate in Oxenhall was augmented later by the Foleys' purchase of those two farms[8] and other freehold land. In the adjoining detached part of Pauntley parish, which was essentially a group of three or four farms, one gentry family, the Hookes of Crooke's Farm, was resident between the early 15th century and the early 18th.[9] The owners and tenants of the farms there evidently looked to Oxenhall for some purposes long before their land was added to that parish in 1883.

During the early modern period, the farms in Oxenhall were gradually enlarged, resulting in fewer and larger units and the employment of more labourers. The labouring class remained, however, fairly independent in character, as their cottages were mostly held on leases for lives under the lord of the manor and the cottagers had other opportunities of employment, particularly in trades connected with the adjoining woodlands.[10] The influence of various industrial developments — the Ellbridge ironworks and, later and less successfully, coal mining and the building of the canal — brought relatively little change to the essentially rural and agricultural nature of the parish or its pattern of settlement; those developments depended for the most part on labour imported temporarily from elsewhere. In 1851 among the heads of the households enumerated in the parish 9 were farmers, 27 were agricultural labourers, 9 were craftsmen, and the remaining 11 included a gamekeeper, a gardener, a lock keeper, and R.F. Onslow of Furnace House.[11] The farmers, who were enabled to buy their farms at the break-up of the Onslows' estate in 1913, remained the core of the community throughout the 20th century. Among them were several branches of the Goulding family,[12] deriving their descent from Daniel Goulding, who became tenant of Kew's farm in the 1880s.[13]

SOCIAL LIFE

No public house or shop has been found recorded in Oxenhall or in the detached land of Pauntley, and for most social activities, as for their marketing, the inhabitants looked to the nearby Newent town. Oxenhall church was the main meeting place, together with a church house, built probably in the 1530s. The church house was removed in 1841,[14] from which time a schoolroom built close by was the venue for meetings, including those of the parish vestry.[15] In 1955 the school building was sold to the vicar and churchwardens for use as a church hall,[16] which purpose it had presumably served since its closure as a school in 1935. In 1998 it was settled on trustees for general use as a parish hall.[17] A Baptist chapel at Four Oaks provided a community focus for some cottagers of outlying parts of the parish in the mid 20th century.[18]

---

1 Bigland, *Glos.* II, 303; Herefs. RO, E 12/G/29, receipts 1756, 1761.

2 TNA, RAIL 836/3, p. 139; GDR, V 5/226T 6; inscription in Newent churchyard.

3 GDR, T 1/137; TNA, HO 107/1960; above, manor.

4 TNA, RG 10/2607; above, Newent, manors (other manors and estates).

5 *Kelly's Dir. Glos.* (1889 and later edns); *Burke's Peerage* (1963), 1863.

6 *Military Surv. of Glos. 1522*, 62.

7 Ibid.; Herefs. RO, E 12/G/9, ct. 20 Feb. 3 Edw. VI, rental 1659; G/23; GA, P 241/IN 1/1; D 2528, pp. 9–15.

8 Smith, *Men and Armour*, 67; above, manor (other estates).

9 Above, manor (estates in detached part of Pauntley).

10 Above, econ. hist.

11 TNA, HO 107/1960.

12 GA, SL 79; *Kelly's Dir. Glos.* (1906 and later edns).

13 Information from Ms E.M. Goulding of Newent (formerly of Holder's Farm, Oxenhall); TNA, RG 12/2008.

14 Above, settlement (ancient settlement); also Fig. 59.

15 GA, P 241/VE 2/1.

16 Ibid. SC 2.

17 http://www.charity-commission.gov.uk/registeredcharities (accessed 20 Mar. 2008: no 1072614).

18 Below, religious hist. (religious life); *The Oxenhall Anthology* (Oxenhall Parish History Group, 1999), 32, 35, 37.

EDUCATION

Before 1712 Maynard Colchester of Westbury-on-Severn, a founder of the Society for Promoting Christian Knowledge[1] and owner of the Oxenhall rectory estate, started a charity school for 20 children at Oxenhall; the lessee of his estate was allowed £4 out of the rent to support it. It apparently lapsed a few years after Colchester's death in 1715.[2] There was no school in the parish in 1818, but the vicar Thomas Davies was then teaching eight children from each of his three cures, Oxenhall, Pauntley, and Upleadon, probably at the house he then occupied in Newent town. His successor at Oxenhall, John Morse,[3] started a Sunday school in 1826, teaching it with the help of two poor women of the parish.[4]

In 1842 a day school, in association with the National Society, was opened in a building put up on a site given by the lady of the manor Elizabeth Foley close to the church, at the entrance to Winter's Lane.[5] In 1847 the school, popularly known later as the Vicar's school, had an income from subscriptions and school pence and taught 21 boys.[6] It had closed, presumably through lack of funds, by 1868, but the Oxenhall children were not left entirely without instruction: some then attended Newent's National school, others, perhaps girls and infants, were taught in the schoolroom twice a week by the daughters of the lord of the manor R.F. Onslow, and c.6 boys attended a night school taught by the vicar T.P. Little. In addition there was a small dame school attended by c.15 children.[7] In 1873 to meet government requirements under the Education Act the parishioners raised funds by a voluntary rate to send children to the Newent school. After the formation of a school board for Newent in 1882, however, Oxenhall failed to agree terms for the continuing accommodation of its children, and in 1883 the Oxenhall National school was reopened under the management of the vicar and a temporary committee of parishioners. It then had an average attendance of 38 boys and girls in a single class.[8] The school was taken over by the county education authority in 1903, and in 1905 the building was enlarged to provide a separate infants' classroom.[9] Styled Oxenhall C. of E. school from 1907, it had an average attendance of 44 in 1910. Attendance had fallen to 15 by 1935 when the school was closed.[10]

RELIGIOUS HISTORY

ORIGIN AND STATUS OF THE PARISH CHURCH

Oxenhall church was probably of early Norman or pre-Conquest origin, for, unlike several neighbouring churches, there is no evidence that it originated as a chapel to Newent. The earliest surviving part of its fabric and fittings is a 12th-century lead font. When first found recorded, in 1291, the church was in the possession of the Knights Hospitaller.[11] No details of the arrangements by which the cure was served in the Middle Ages have been found, and in the post-Reformation period the status of the living was unclear. It was usually assumed by the diocesan officials to be a vicarage[12] and the right to present to one was included in the Crown's grant of the rectory to a lay impropriator in 1548,[13] but there is apparently no record of a vicarage being ordained or of any endowment or fixed stipend being given by the Hospitallers for serving the cure.

After the Dissolution all the tithes passed, together with a glebe farm, to lay impropriators,[14] who found a curate to serve the church. Giles Forster, the impropriator in the late 16th century, is said to have 'compounded' on two occasions with claimants to the vicarage for the abandonment of their claims. One of those cases apparently occurred in 1597 when a cleric was refused institution by the bishop unless evidence for a vicarage could be produced.[15] Another claimant secured institution in 1636 and his attempts to establish his right to a portion of the profits resulted in a decree which secured a salary to the incumbent.[16] The official status of the living, however, remained in doubt: some who later served it were called vicars and others curates (or, following

---

1 *VCH Glos.* X, 87.
2 *Glos. N&Q* I, 294; GA, D 36/E 11, ff. 29v.–30.
3 *Educ. of Poor Digest*, 305, 315; Hockaday Abs. cccviii, 1817, 1824.
4 *Educ. Enquiry Abstract*, 323.
5 GA, P 241/SC 1; TNA, ED 7/35/248.
6 Nat. Soc. *Inquiry, 1846–7*, Glos. 14–15.
7 *1st Rep. Com. Employment in Agric.* app. II, p. 133.
8 GA, P 241/VE 2/1; TNA, ED 7/35/248.
9 GA, P 241/SC 2; *Kelly's Dir. Glos.* (1910), 273.
10 GA, P 241/SC 3; *List 21*, 1911 (Board of Education), 165; 1932, 117.
11 *Tax. Eccl.* 161; *Reg. T. de Charlton*, 53.
12 Hockaday Abs. cccviii.
13 TNA, C 66/811, mm. 25–6; the statement in *Notes on Dioc. of Glouc. by Chancellor Parsons*, 181, that the Crown reserved the advowson in this grant is mistaken.
14 Above, manor (other estates: Oxenhall rectory).
15 Hockaday Abs. cccviii, 1597; GA, D 36/E 54.
16 Below (endowment and patronage).

augmentations in the late 18th century and the early 19th, perpetual curates),[1] and in 1750 the living was described as a former vicarage held since 1636 by sequestrators and licensees of the bishop.[2] In 1918 Oxenhall was made a united benefice with the perpetual curacy of Pauntley[3] but that union was dissolved in 1955 when Oxenhall was united with Kempley.[4] Following later amalgamations, Oxenhall formed in 2006 part of a large benefice of nine parishes.[5]

ENDOWMENT AND PATRONAGE

In 1522 the curate serving Oxenhall was receiving a salary of £5 13s. 4d.[6] In 1603 his salary was said to be £12[7] but in 1629 only £8 a year was assigned to him by the impropriator when granting a new lease of the rectory.[8] In 1636 Robert Kerfoot secured institution as vicar on the presentation of the Crown and succeeded in getting some parishioners to pay him tithes.[9] Following a suit in the Exchequer court between Kerfoot and the impropriator Caesar Roberts and his lessee John Beale, the matter was referred to the judgement of the diocesan ordinary. The bishop's decision, incorporated in a decree of 1638, was that the impropriator should pay Kerfoot and his successors an annual stipend of £13 6s. 8d. and build him a house on 1 a. of land, assigned out of the rectory estate; the incumbent was to be entitled also to the fees for marriages and churchings.[10] The house was built in that or the following year by the lessee of the rectory[11] on a plot of land on the lane leading north from the church alongside the land of the rectory farm, Oxenhall Court. About 1644, however, it burnt down, and it was never rebuilt.[12] In 1793 the curate Thomas Davies attempted unsuccessfully to compel the impropriator to build him a new house. Davies also failed in an attempt to enlarge his income by claiming Easter offerings, tithes of gardens, and 'hearth money' from the parishioners, and, it was said, he intended to lay claim to all the small tithes. In the rebuttal of Davies's demands the decree of 1638, which had declared the stipend then assigned to be in full satisfaction of any further claim on the profits of the church, proved decisive.[13]

The stipend and fees assigned by the decree remained the incumbent's only income until 1767, when Queen Anne's Bounty made a capital grant of £200 to the living. Further grants of similar sums were made in 1785, 1810, and 1825,[14] most of those funds being used to buy land, including a house and 7 a. in Byton (Herefs.) in 1783, a barn and c.8 a. near Haines Oak wood in Oxenhall in 1787, and a house and 2 a. in Dymock in 1818.[15] In 1844 the Ecclesiastical Commissioners augmented the living with a grant of £26 a year, which raised the curate's income to £80.[16] In 1850 funds were granted to provide a vicarage house, the Commissioners giving £200 to match a benefaction from the bishop, Revd S.W. Warneford giving £391, and the General Parsonage House fund £100.[17] The house was built in 1856 on the east side of the Newent–Dymock road at Three Ashes,[18] and in 1863, using part of £200 given by a private benefactor and a matching sum from the Ecclesiastical Commissioners, a field adjoining was bought.[19] A further benefaction of £100 was made to the living in 1885,[20] and in 1903 the vicar's annual income, derived from the glebe land and some stock, was £119.[21]

The question of the right to appoint to the living was not addressed in the litigation of the 1630s and the subsequent decree. The impropriators continued to regard the choice of a curate as their right, delegating that responsibility in a new lease of the rectory estate in 1697, and they or their lessees appear to have nominated all the curates until the first augmentation of the living in 1767.[22] At the vacancy following, in 1782, Thomas Davies was licensed as perpetual curate on the collation of the bishop, and in 1795, evidently as part of his attempts to enhance his position, Davies secured institution as 'vicar' on a presentation from the Crown, described then as patron for that turn by lapse. The bishop collated again in 1824[23] and by the mid 19th century seems to have been regarded as patron in his own right.[24]

RELIGIOUS LIFE

Robert the chaplain of Oxenhall, who in 1360 was among those accused of trespass and acts of violence on the property of the prior of Newent,[25] may have been serving the church by appointment of the

---

1 Hockaday Abs. cccviii.
2 *Bp. Benson's Surv. of Diocese of Glouc. 1735–50*, 14.
3 *Kelly's Dir. Glos.* (1931), 279; *Glouc. Dioc. Kalendar* (1920), 50.
4 *Glouc. Dioc. Year Book* (1970), 28.
5 *Dioc. of Glouc. Dir.* (2003–4), 24.
6 *Military Surv. of Glos. 1522*, 62.
7 *Eccl. Misc.* 100.
8 GA, D 36/E 3, p. 55.
9 Ibid. p. 56; TNA, E 134/16 Chas. I/Mich. 9.
10 GA, D 36/E 54.
11 Ibid. E 3, p. 150; TNA, E 134/16 Chas. I/Mich. 9.
12 GDR, V 5/226T 5; GA, D 412/Z 3, Nourse MS, p. 6.
13 GA, D 36/E 56; Hockaday Abs. cccviii, 1809.
14 Hodgson, *Queen Anne's Bounty* (1826), 324; (1845), p. cclxxxv.
15 GA, P 241/IN 3/4.
16 *London Gazette*, 3 May 1844, p. 1511.
17 Hodgson, *Queen Anne's Bounty* (1845, suppl. 1864), pp. xxii, lxvi. For Warneford, *Oxford DNB*.
18 Verey and Brooks, *Glos.* II, 628.
19 *London Gazette*, 20 Nov. 1863, pp. 5563–70; GA, P 241/IN 3/3, letter 21 Feb. 1884.
20 *London Gazette*, 15 May 1885, p. 2221.
21 GA, P 241/IN 3/4.
22 Ibid. D 36/E 56.
23 Hockaday Abs. cccviii.
24 GDR vol. 384, f. 155; *Kelly's Dir. Glos.* (1856), 339.
25 E.G. Kimball, 'Gloucestershire Peace Rolls', *Trans. BGAS* 62 (1940), 65.

Knights Hospitaller. The lord of the manor Peter de Grandison had licence to found a chantry in the church in 1347[1] and a Carmelite friar of Gloucester, who was described in 1446 as celebrant of divine service in the chapel of Oxenhall, presumably served the chantry.[2] It appears to have lapsed before the Reformation.

William Adys who was serving Oxenhall church in 1522[3] remained curate in 1551 when he was found to be thoroughly ignorant.[4] The curate in 1576 had not preached a sermon for the last 12 months and employed an illiterate parish clerk,[5] and John Taylor, curate in 1593, was classed as a sufficient scholar but no preacher.[6] Robert Kerfoot, who secured the Exchequer decree establishing the incumbent's salary in 1638, remained in post until his death in 1670;[7] he was described as a preaching minister in 1651.[8] Abraham Morse, who was curate in the 1680s, served the church together with the curacy of Pauntley,[9] as did many of his successors. Later the curacy was usually combined with Upleadon also[10] and the three parishes were held together until 1823. Thomas Davies, whose efforts to enhance his status as incumbent are mentioned above, was perpetual curate from 1782 until his death in 1823. Also a school teacher, he lived in or near Gloucester and later at Newent.[11] Under his successor John Morse, who lived on his benefice at Huntley, one service was held at Oxenhall each Sunday in the morning or evening alternately.[12] Thomas Sherwood, perpetual curate 1839–48, employed a stipendiary curate to serve Oxenhall and allowed him the whole income of the living.[13] Thomas Palling Little, perpetual curate (or vicar) 1848–83,[14] was probably the first incumbent to reside in the parish for many years. He lodged in a farmhouse until the new vicarage house at Three Ashes was completed in 1856.[15] In the 1860s he oversaw the restoration and partial rebuilding of the church.[16] After 1955 the incumbent of the united benefice resided at Kempley,[17] and in 2006 the large benefice of which Oxenhall formed a part was served from Redmarley D'Abitot.[18]

No early evidence of dissent from the established church has been found in the parish and in 1703 it was said to contain no dissenters.[19] In 1726 a mission from the Gloucester Independent church met at Crooke's Farm, in the detached part of Pauntley, then tenanted by William Warr; the house was again licensed for use by followers of the same church in 1740.[20] George Whitefield preached in Oxenhall churchyard in 1739 at the invitation of the curate John Pauncefoot.[21] A Newent Wesleyan minister, Abraham Whatmough, registered a house in Oxenhall for worship in 1816,[22] Thomas Kington registered a house at Shaw common in 1836, and a house at Three Ashes was registered in 1845.[23] Baptists attached to the church at Gorsley, in Linton (Herefs.), held services at Four Oaks from 1887[24] and in 1924 built a small chapel there, just within the Oxenhall boundary.[25] It had closed by 1993 and was later converted to a dwelling.[26]

THE CHURCH BUILDING

Oxenhall church, dedicated to St Anne, surmounts a small, pronounced hill above the Ell brook in the south of the parish. The medieval church had chancel, tall nave with south porch, and a west tower with a small, recessed spire.[27] The nave was probably built in the 11th century or the 12th, as it had a Norman south doorway with a tympanum.[28] The 12th-century lead font is one of six which were cast from the same mould, probably in the Bristol area.[29] The tower was added in the early 14th century and contains two bells of around that period.[30] Other medieval features, including a pointed chancel arch without imposts, a square-headed Perpendicular window, and a timber and brick south porch, were identified in a description of 1857 but some, possibly extensive, changes had already been made. The walls of nave and chancel probably had

---

1 *Cal. Pat.* 1345–8, 434.
2 Hockaday Abs. cccviii.
3 *Military Surv. of Glos. 1522*, 62.
4 J. Gairdner, 'Bishop Hooper's Visitation of Gloucester', *EHR*, 19 (1904), 121; Hockaday Abs. xxx, 1544 stipendiaries, f. 8.
5 GDR vol. 40, f. 246.
6 Hockaday Abs. lii, state of clergy 1593, f. 7.
7 Ibid. cccviii, 1662; GA, P241/IN 1/1.
8 C.R. Elrington, 'The Survey of Church Livings in Gloucestershire, 1650', *Trans. BGAS* 83 (1964), 98.
9 GA, P 241/IN 1/1.
10 *Bp. Benson's Surv. of Dioc. of Glouc. 1735–50*, 15, 19.
11 Hockaday Abs. cccviii, cccx, ccclxxxiv.
12 GDR vol. 382, f. 20; vol. 383, no. cxxvii.
13 Hockaday Abs. cccviii.
14 Ibid.; *Crockford's Clerical Dir.* (1894), 822.
15 TNA, HO 107/1960.
16 Below (ch. bldg.).
17 *Glouc. Dioc. Year Book* (1970), 28.
18 *Dioc. of Glouc. Dir.* (2003–4), 24.
19 Hockaday Abs. cccviii.
20 Ibid. cccx; those signing the certificates were Gloucester church members: GA, D 6026/6/6.
21 *George Whitefield's Journals*, ed. W. Wale (1905), 246.
22 Hockaday Abs. ccxciii.
23 Ibid. cccviii; for Kington, above, Dymock, religious hist.
24 Above, Dymock, religious hist.
25 Date on bldg.
26 *Citizen*, 4 Mar. 1993.
27 Copy of a painting of the ch. from the S., c.1840, reproduced above, Fig. 59.
28 *Glos. Ch. Notes*, 107.
29 G. Zarnecki, *Eng. Romanesque Lead Sculpture* (1957), 10–14; Fig. 64.
30 *Glos. Ch. Bells*, 479–80.

been rendered or partly rebuilt, and some windows had been renewed or inserted, including a mullioned window to light a west gallery[1] erected in 1743.[2]

Chancel, nave, and south porch were rebuilt during 1866 and 1867 to designs by John Middleton of Cheltenham.[3] The two-bayed chancel and three-bayed nave are in Decorated style, built in contrasting red sandstone with grey dressings; the porch is mainly of timber. The interior is lavishly decorated with foliage and figurative ornament by R.L. Boulton and polychromatic details, including a reredos carved by John Roddis.[4] The lychgate is in the same manner. The tower, described in 1864 as in such a state that the bells could not be rung with safety, was restored at the same time.[5] It was again restored in 1912[6] when the tenor of its three bells was recast by Llewellins & James of Bristol.[7] In the early 1970s the spire was found to be in need of expensive repairs, and the top part was removed in 1972 and the remainder a few years later.[8] The pulpit, one of the few fittings to survive the 19th-century rebuilding, is dated 1632 and is made up of 17th-century sections of panelling. A few wall monuments, mainly to the Clarke family, tenants of the rectory farm, were removed from the chancel at the rebuilding and fixed under the tower.[9]

64. *Font at Oxenhall church*

PAUNTLEY

PAUNTLEY is a small rural parish 14 km north-west of Gloucester. In the later Middle Ages it contained the principal seat of the Whittington family,[10] of whom Richard (d. 1423) is celebrated as mayor of London.[11] The ancient parish had two parts.[12] The larger one, north-east of Newent, covered 1,630 a. (660 ha)[13] bounded on the north by the twisting course of the river Leadon, which there formerly divided Gloucestershire from Worcestershire. Irregular in shape and with long north and south boundaries, that main part of Pauntley rose above the river in two areas joined together by a narrow band of land west of its church. The southern, upland boundary, running from near Baldwin's Oak in the west to Collin Park wood in the east, crossed common land at Botloe's green, Pool hill, and Brand green and its line was disputed with Newent in the early 17th century.[14]

The other part of Pauntley, referred to as Little Pauntley in the later 18th century,[15] was sandwiched between Oxenhall and Newent by the Ell brook west of Newent town. Very irregularly shaped and containing 341 a. (138 ha) after a minor adjustment of its boundary with Newent, it was transferred in 1883

---

1 *Glos. Ch. Notes*, 107–8; GA, P 225A/MI 1/13.
2 Bigland, *Glos.* II, 303.
3 GA, P 241/VE 2/1, mins. 21 Apr. 1865, 5 Feb. 1866; P 125/MI 17 (Dymock par. mag. July 1867).
4 Verey and Brooks, *Glos.* II, 628.
5 GA, D 2592, letter 12 Dec.1864; P 241/VE 2/1, min. 21 Apr. 1865.
6 *Kelly's Dir. Glos.* (1914), 279.
7 *Glos. Ch. Bells*, 479–80.
8 Oxenhall notes by B.S. Smith: notes and papers on spire repairs.
9 Bigland, *Glos.* II, 303.
10 Below, manor (manor); social hist. (social structure). This account was written between 2004 and 2007 and revised in 2009.
11 *Oxford DNB*; S. Lysons, *The Model Merchant of the Middle Ages* (1860).
12 GDR, T 1/140.
13 *OS Area Book* (1884). See below, Map 13.
14 Herefs. RO, E 12/G/7; GA, D 1803/1; above, Newent, introd. (boundaries and divisions).
15 GA, Q/REl 1, Botloe hundred, land tax returns for Pauntley.

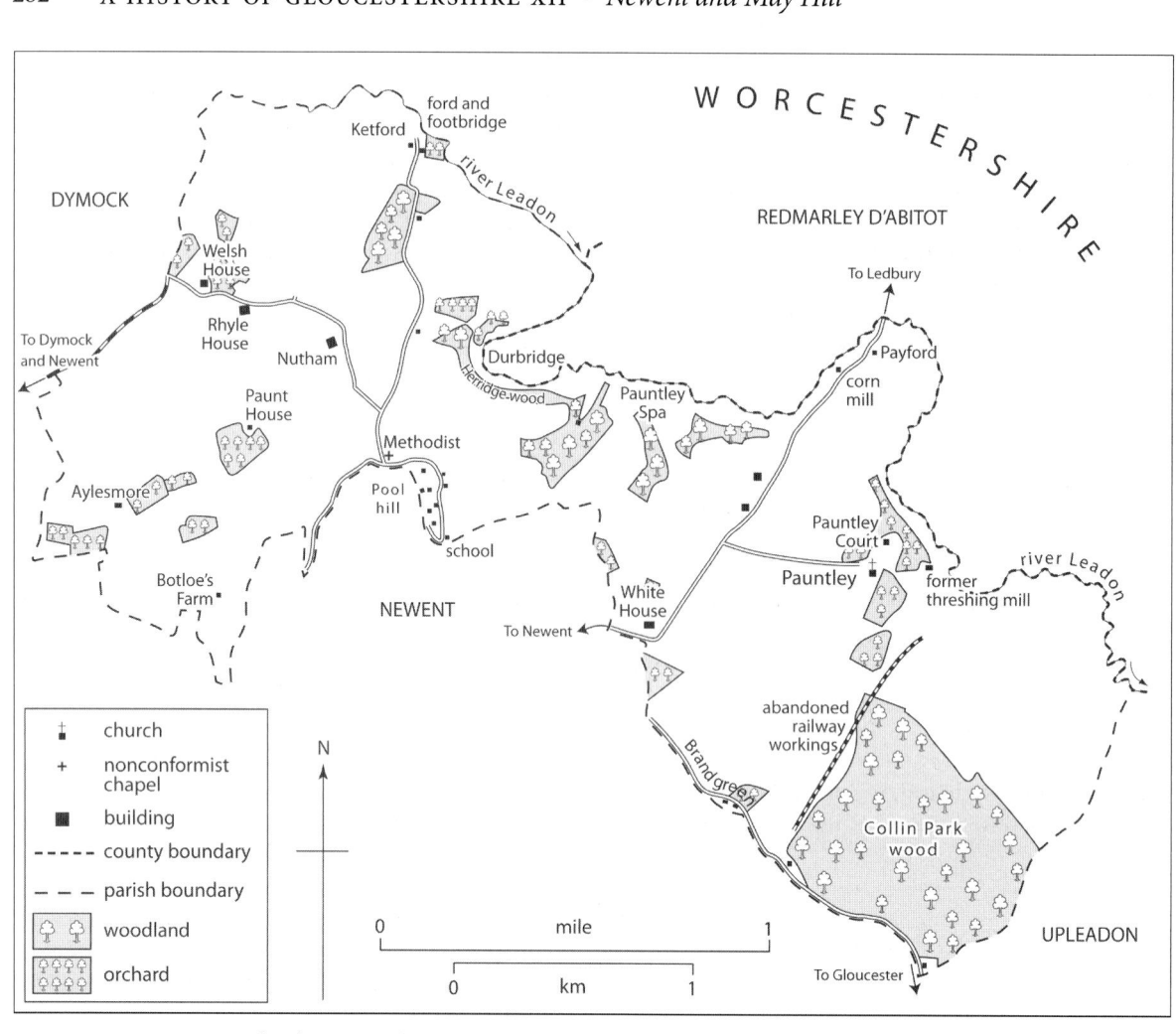

Map 13. *Pauntley (main part) 1880*

to Oxenhall[1] and its history is given with that parish.[2] The following history deals with Pauntley's larger part within its ancient boundaries. Hamlets at Pool hill and Brand green were brought entirely within Pauntley in 1992, when an area of settled farmland on its south side, including Compton green, was added from Newent and part of Collin Park wood in the south-east was transferred to Upleadon.[3]

LANDSCAPE

Pauntley rises steeply above the Leadon in hills and dells at between 20 and 75 m. The soil is formed of sandstone save at the east end where it is on the Keuper Marl,[4] and the higher land with its lighter soils formed part of the area known as 'the ryelands'.[5] Downstream of Ketford, in the west, the river flows between Pauntley and Redmarley D'Abitot (Worcs., later Glos.) under precipitous banks past Durbridge and Payford and the sites of several mills. To mitigate the effects of flooding weirs damaged by flood waters in 1947 were not restored.[6] A tributary stream rising in the south-west emerges from a narrow valley on the north side of Pool hill in a series of fish ponds. The oldest was created from the remains of a mill pond[7] and the remainder, lower down, were formed in the late 20th century.[8]

Although land close to the Leadon was settled before the later 11th century some of the steeper river banks and hillsides remained wooded.[9] Among early named woods Solers Grove stood by a way to Ketford

---

1 GDR, T 1/140; Local Govt. Board Order, 20 Dec. 1882: copy in GA, P 241/VE 2/1.
2 Above.
3 The Forest of Dean (Parishes) Order 1991 (unpublished Statutory Instrument 1992 no 2283); information (Sept. 2003) from Mr Gareth Ellison (environment directorate, Glos. co. council). See E. Warde, *They Didn't Walk Far: a History of Pool Hill* (priv. printed, 2000), 127.
4 Geol. Surv. Map 1:50,000, solid and drift, sheet 216 (1988 edn).
5 Rudder, *Glos.* 597; Rudge, *Agric. of Glos.* 20.
6 R. and P. Palmer, *Secret River: an exploration of the Leadon Valley* (2004), 44.
7 OS Map 6", Glos. XVII.NE (1889, 1903 edns); GDR, T 1/140 (no 81).
8 See OS Map 1:1,250, SO 7229–7329 (1972 edn).
9 Below, settlement.

in 1382[1] and Great (Muckle) Herridge pressed close to the river downstream of Durbridge in 1410.[2] The wooded park belonging to the lords of the manor in the early 14th century[3] was presumably the same as the great park that the Whittingtons maintained in woodland at the east end of the parish, apart from their manor house, in the late Middle Ages.[4] In the early 17th century a warrener lived in Pauntley.[5] Collin Park wood, which incorporates part of the area of the great park, covered 158 a. in 1840[6] and was slightly enlarged in late 19th century by planting up to the line of abandoned railway workings to the west.[7] In 1905 Pauntley had 222 a. of woods and plantations.[8] Collin Park wood was designated a Site of Special Scientific Interest in 1966 and part of it was managed as a nature reserve in 2004.[9]

Several saline springs rise by the river in and below Herridge wood.[10] The source known in 1382 as 'Thornbacheswell' was evidently among them. One spring, possibly the source of the stream called 'salbrook' in 1410,[11] issued water with strong purgative properties[12] and became the focus of a May Day custom.[13] Known as Pauntley Spa in the 1880s, it had been abandoned by the end of the 19th century.[14] In 1911 Gloucester city corporation began pumping water from a new well at Ketford to supplement its supply from reservoirs in Madam's wood in Newent. It completed a second well at Ketford in 1915[15] and built a small reservoir next to Collin Park wood a few years later.[16]

ROADS, BRIDGES, AND RAILWAY

Pauntley is crossed by narrow, and in places deep, lanes and footpaths. Among the lanes are roads from Newent running down to the Leadon at Ketford and Payford, that by way of Payford possibly being a continuation of a Saxon salt way coming southwards through Redmarley.[17] At Ketford, where a bridge was in place in the later 12th century,[18] the ford continued in use alongside a footbridge[19] until 1928 when a wider bridge was built partly at the cost of Gloucester corporation.[20] At Payford the maintenance of a bridge was supported by a bequest from Guy Whittington (d. 1440), lord of Pauntley.[21] In the early 19th century flood and frost damage caused the landowner John Stokes to rebuild a new bridge there[22] and in 1901, after the bridge had been washed away, Gloucestershire and Worcestershire county councils contributed towards the cost of rebuilding it.[23] Ketford and Payford bridges were both replaced in 2003, the latter being raised slightly to alleviate flooding.[24] The river crossing at Durbridge has long been on a track used by farm traffic.[25]

Construction of a railway to link Worcester and Monmouth, authorized in 1863,[26] began across the Leadon valley in Pauntley but was abandoned there to leave an embankment and, higher up, a cutting.[27]

POPULATION

Early population figures included residents in both parts of the parish. Ten tenants were recorded on the estates at Pauntley, Ketford, Kilcot, and Hayes in 1086[28] and 27 people were assessed for tax in the parish in 1327.[29] A muster in 1542 named 35 men in Pauntley[30] and in 1563 the parish was said to contain 16 households.[31] The number of communicants in the parish was given as *c.*60 in 1551[32] and 80 in 1603[33] and there were 40 families in 1650.[34] The parish's population, estimated at 115 *c.*1710,[35] was reckoned to have fallen to 87 *c.*1775[36] but that figure presumably

---

1 BL, Add. Ch. 24767.
2 Ibid. 74874.
3 *Inq. p.m. Glos.* 1302–58, 116.
4 TNA, C 142/46, no 22; see GDR, T 1/140.
5 Smith, *Men and Armour*, 66.
6 GDR, T 1/140.
7 OS Map 6", Glos. XVII.NE (1889, 1903 edns).
8 Acreage Returns, 1905.
9 *Wildlife News* (Glos. Wildlife Trust, May–August 2004), 10–11.
10 C. Duncan and L. Richardson, 'Mineral Springs of Newent and Pauntley', *Proc. CNFC* 21.2 (1922), 151–9; see Bryant, *Map of Glos.* (1824).
11 BL, Add. Ch. 24767, 74874.
12 Rudder, *Glos.* 597.
13 Below, social hist. (social life).
14 OS Map 6", Glos. XVII. NE (1889, 1903 edns).
15 Richardson, *Wells and Springs of Glos.* 133; VCH Glos. IV, 264.
16 OS Map 1:1,250, SO 7427–7527 (1972 edn); see GA, G/NE 159/7/1–3.
17 *PN Glos.* III, 189.
18 BL, Add. Ch. 24752; see ibid. Add. MS 18461, f. 87.
19 OS Map 6", Glos. XVII.NW (1903 edn); see R. and P. Palmer, *Secret River*, 40.
20 GA, DA 30/100/13, pp. 91, 155–6, 158, 204, 207.
21 Hockaday Abs. cccx.
22 GA, P 246/OV 2/1–2.
23 Ibid. DA 30/100/7, pp. 71, 82–3, 97–8, 121–2, 176.
24 Personal observation; information from Johnnie Vizor of Payford Mill.
25 GDR, T 1/140.
26 Worcester, Dean Forest, and Monmouth Railway Act, 26 & 27 Vic. c. 185 (Local and Personal).
27 GA, Q/RUm 305; OS Map 6", Glos. XVII.NE (1889 edn).
28 *Domesday Book* (Rec. Com.), I, 170.
29 *Glos. Subsidy Roll, 1327*, 36.
30 *L&P Hen. VIII*, XVII, 499.
31 Bodleian, Rawl. C. 790, f. 28.
32 J. Gairdner, 'Bishop Hooper's Visitation of Gloucester', *EHR* 19 (1904), 120.
33 *Eccl. Misc.* 101.
34 C.R. Elrington, 'The Survey of Church Livings in Gloucestershire, 1650', *Trans. BGAS* 83 (1964), 98.
35 Atkyns, *Glos.* 601.
36 Rudder, *Glos.* 599.

accounted for only part of the parish as in 1801 the total population was 215. Pauntley's population grew to 280 in 1831 and it was 249 in 1841.[1] The population of the main part of the parish fell from 217 in 1841[2] to 155 in 1891[3] and remained roughly the same throughout much of the 20th century, standing in 1991 at 158. In 2001, following the boundary changes of 1992, it was 305.[4]

SETTLEMENT

The names Pauntley and Ketford, both recorded from the later 11th century, indicate early settlement along the Leadon valley with the parish name representing a woodland clearing or perhaps meaning, in a Celtic form, a dell or valley.[5] In the 14th century a pattern of scattered, isolated farmsteads existed across Pauntley and the presence then of men surnamed of Clevegrove suggests settlement among the woods clothing the steep banks above the river.[6] A number of inhabited sites had been abandoned by the early 18th century.[7] Two new farmsteads were established in the 20th century.

The early 12th-century parish church occupies an elevated site overlooking the Leadon valley in the eastern end of Pauntley.[8] Although Pauntley Court, its only near neighbour, stands lower down to the north the church's main entrance was originally from the south. Pauntley Court, which is also on a platform, is a fragment of a large manor house that was the home of the Whittington family in the later Middle Ages. In the mid 20th century it was briefly a home for wayfarers.[9] Upstream at Payford a former mill stands beside the Leadon at the foot of a wooded cliff. In the early 19th century a lodge of Pauntley Court stood east of the lane near Payford bridge[10] and in 1838 a school was built next to it.[11] The hamlet included a wooden bungalow in the 1920s[12] and comprised the former mill and school and a modern house in the early 21st century.[13] Higher up a cottage standing near the lane was a gamekeeper's house in 1841.[14]

There were several early farmsteads high up in the eastern end of Pauntley, at least one being next to the boundary at Brand green in an area known in the later 14th century as Hollins[15] (later the Hollend).[16] Pauntley Place, to the north-west on the boundary next to Compton green, is a large 17th-century house known originally as the White House.[17] Leadon Vale Farm, to the north-east on the lane to Payford, was established in the 20th century; its house was built in 1977. Redlea is one of several bungalows built further along the lane in the same period.[18] A prefabricated building standing at the entrance to the way to the church and Pauntley Court was erected as a pair of farm cottages c.1929.[19] A house to its east, overlooking the Leadon valley, dates from the later 20th century.

In the western end of the parish there was one cottage on the lane leading down towards the river at Ketford in the early 19th century.[20] A man lived at or near the bridge at Ketford in the later 12th century[21] and there was evidently more than one dwelling on the Pauntley side of the river in the early 14th.[22] Little Ketford Farm, the oldest surviving building, stands east of the lane and in the early 19th century its land included the site of an abandoned farmstead at Ketford.[23] The few other dwellings at Ketford include a pair of cottages built in the early 20th century following the establishment of Gloucester corporation's waterworks near by[24] and a house provided for a new farmstead (Barn Farm) in 1982.[25]

On the higher land in the west of Pauntley there was early settlement in an area known anciently as Ryley. Men surnamed of Ryley were recorded from the late 12th century and a house there was called Malyn Place in 1399.[26] Welsh House, near the western

---

1 *Census*, 1801–41.
2 TNA, HO 107/350/12.
3 Ibid. HO 107/1960; RG 9/1760; RG 10/2607; *Census*, 1851–91.
4 TNA, RG 13/2421; *Census*, 1901–2001.
5 *PN Glos.* III, 182–3; see A. Breeze, 'Chaceley, Meon, Prinknash and Celtic Philology', *Trans. BGAS* 120 (2002), 103–4.
6 *Glos. Subsidy Roll, 1327*, 36; BL, Add. Ch. 24765; Sloane Ch. XXXIII.43, 52.
7 GA, Q/RNc 1, pp. 132–5.
8 The land below the ch. is shown in Fig. 1, above.
9 *Glos. Countryside* Jan. 1937, 197–8; see below, econ. hist. (agric.: the 19th and 20th cents.).
10 GA, photocopy 192; GDR, T 1/140 (nos 46–7).
11 TNA, ED 7/35/254; see GA, D 2299/3041.
12 See GA, D 2299/3086.
13 Ibid. DA 30/100/21, p. 189.
14 Ibid. photocopy 192; TNA, HO 107/350/12, s.v. Pauntley, Hill House.
15 BL, Add. Ch. 74873, 24778.
16 TNA, PROB 11/320, f. 191v.; Atkyns, *Glos.* 601.
17 GA, P 246/IN 1/1, list of taxpaying properties at beginning of vol. See below (bldgs.).
18 Information from Brenda Bainbridge, chairman of Pauntley par. council; OS Maps 1:1,250, SO 7228–7328, SO 7429–7529 (1972 edns).
19 GA, DA 30/100/13, p. 263.
20 GDR, T 1/140.
21 BL, Add. Ch. 24752.
22 *Glos. Subsidy Roll, 1327*, 36; see *Glos. Feet of Fines 1300–59*, p. 51.
23 GA, D 1618, Pauntley deeds 1803–18; D 2080/126.
24 Above, introd. (landscape).
25 Datestone reported by Brenda Bainbridge.
26 BL, Add. Ch. 24752; Sloane Ch. XXXIII.23, 52; see GA, D 6322/1; *Glos. Subsidy Roll, 1327*, 36.

boundary, is presumably named after the family of William le Waleys, who lived in Pauntley in 1248.[1] Rhyle House, a little to the east on Welsh House Lane, formerly was known as Ryleys or Rylas[2] and belonged to a copyhold estate.[3] Further east on the lane at Nutham, which was inhabited in the later 12th century,[4] a small farmhouse known as Mason's in 1570 was part of a farm acquired in 1862 by Guy Hill of Dymock.[5] The house was demolished and a cottage was built near by in the mid 20th century.[6] Further east a bungalow was erected by the road from Pool Hill to Ketford for Herridge's farm c.1920.[7] In the mid 17th century there were three farmsteads in the south-west of the parish, namely Paunt House, Aylesmore, and Botloe's Farm,[8] the last nestling in a fold of the hills below Botloe's green.[9] Only Aylesmore has remained the centre of a working farm.

The hamlets of Brand Green and Pool Hill on the southern boundary with Newent formed in the 18th and 19th centuries with the building of cottages on waste land, where in the early 17th century two cottages erected by Pauntley parish stood as poorhouses, one of them at the Hollend.[10] Most of the houses in Brand Green belonged to Newent,[11] but Hollin's Court Farm built as a private house c.1930[12] and a village hall erected in 1950[13] were within Pauntley. More houses and bungalows were added to the hamlet in the later 20th century, several of them next to Collin Park wood,[14] at the south tip of which a dwelling was recorded at a tower from 1820.[15] The hillside hamlet of Pool Hill was created by the building of cottages higgledy-piggledy on the common there, all, save a few on the west side, within Pauntley.[16] In the mid 19th century the settlement had more than a score of cottages and an early 19th-century nonconformist chapel stood lower down to the north-west.[17] At the hamlet's top, southern end is a school chapel built for Pauntley and the adjoining part of Newent in 1869.[18]

BUILDINGS

Several former farmhouses retain fabric dating from their rebuilding in the 17th century. At Pauntley Place (formerly the White House), a substantial two-storeyed house with attics that was first the home of the Pauncefoot family,[19] the L was infilled in the 18th century. In the 19th century, when the house was let as a private residence,[20] a brick wing was added to recreate an L plan and painted to imitate timber framing. Of the 17th-century farm buildings a granary survives. Of the smaller 17th-century houses the most complete is Botloe's Farm.[21] At Little Ketford Farm the cross wing of the farmhouse has survived the rebuilding of the rest.

Rhyle House had a new farmhouse in 1814 shortly after ownership of the farm reverted to the lord of the manor.[22] An outbuilding to its east that has been converted as a house (Old Winery) dates from the mid 19th century. In the late 19th century the Attwood family provided new buildings on its property in Pauntley, namely a brick farmhouse at Welsh House[23] and a new house with a set of brick outbuildings at Paunt House.[24] One of the latter's outbuildings was converted as a cottage in the mid 20th century.[25] At Aylesmore the farmhouse had been enlarged by the mid 19th century,[26] and the farmstead included large modern outbuildings in the early 21st century.

At Payford the fabric of the former mill house appears to be mostly 17th-century.[27] With its west wall and large stone chimneystack standing partly on an outcrop right against a cliff, the house originally had two rooms on each of its two floors and a floored attic. In the early 19th century the east wall was rebuilt, and the other walls were encased, in brick. The adjoining mill building of one bay, which together with the house was bought in the early 1930s by the artist Robert Herdman-Smith for his home and studio,[28] has been floored and ceiled. To the east

---

1 TNA, JUST 1/274, rot. 10; see *Glos. Subsidy Roll, 1327*, 36.

2 GA, Q/RNc 1, p. 133; TNA, PROB 11/555, f. 192v.; GDR, T 1/140.

3 Below, manor (other estates); GA, D 1618, Pauntley deeds 1811–14, deed 24 Oct. 1814.

4 BL, Add. Ch. 24752

5 GA, D 3672/3; DC/S 35; GDR, T 1/140.

6 cf. OS Map 1:1,250, SO 7229–7329 (1972 edn); GA, DA 30/100/18, p. 107.

7 GA, D 2299/5292.

8 Ibid. P 246/IN 1/1, list at beginning of vol.

9 For ownership of Botloe's Farm, see below, manor (other estates).

10 GA, D 1803/1.

11 Above, Newent, introd. (outlying settlements: Compton).

12 *Kelly's Dir. Glos.* (1931), 282; OS Map 1:1,250, SO 7428–7528 (1972 edn).

13 Below, social hist. (social life).

14 GA, DA 30/100/26, p. 201.

15 Ibid. P 246/IN 1/6; photocopy 192.

16 Ibid. SL 79; see above, Newent, introd. (outlying settlements: Compton).

17 GDR, T 1/140.

18 Below, social hist. (education).

19 See TNA, PROB 11/339, ff. 288–291v.

20 See GDR, T 1/140; TNA, HO 107/1960.

21 DoE List, Pauntley (1985), 3/208.

22 GA, D 1618, Pauntley deeds 1811–14, deed 24 Oct. 1814; below, manor (other estates).

23 GA, D 2299/452; G/NE 160/8/1.

24 Ibid. D 2299/452; G/NE 160/8/1. A barn has a datestone of 1888 with the inits. 'TA'.

25 Information from Elizabeth Shepherd of Paunt House.

26 GDR, T 1/140.

27 Below, Fig. 67.

28 *Kelly's Dir. Glos.* (1935), 283; G.M. Davies, 'Mills of the River Leadon and Tributaries', *Glos. Soc. Ind. Archaeol. Newsletter* 7 (Apr. 1966), 30.

65. Little Place, Pool Hill

a single-storeyed range of timber-framed buildings contains the former stables and a complete cider mill and press. Downstream, a mill building erected east of Pauntley Court in the early 19th century has a crow-stepped gable towards the house.[1]

Among the cottages making up the scattered settlement of Pool Hill are later 17th- and 18th-century dwellings often with spindly timber framing. A two-roomed single-storeyed hovel, unheated, perhaps represents the parish poorhouse that stood there in the early 17th century.[2] In the 19th and early 20th century several cottages were enlarged and improved. Little Place, a two-bayed thatched house of 1½ storeys, was doubled in size in the mid 19th century by the insertion of a brick two-storeyed bay with end stacks between the house and its outbuilding, possibly a cider house and granary, to the east.[3] The whole made a single house and a short north-west wing was rebuilt in the 1930s on a larger scale using old timber and brick.[4] Beggar's Roost, built as a row of three thatched timber-framed cottages in the early 1840s,[5] was converted as a single picturesque house after 1910.[6] Of the new brick cottages one (Walden Villa) is dated 1855.[7] In the later 20th century some cottages were demolished but most were enlarged or rebuilt, a large timber-framed wing being added to the 18th-century Cherry Tree Cottage, and the nonconformist chapel below the hill was converted as a house.[8] At the beginning of the 21st century the hamlet had few entirely new houses.

MANOR AND ESTATES

Pauntley manor was created out of several pre-Conquest estates and in the early 14th century it included 16 freehold properties,[9] including substantial estates in the detached part of the parish. Copyhold estates were located mostly if not entirely in the main part,[10] where the manor house, in the east at Pauntley Court, was the residence of the Whittington family in the later Middle Ages.[11]

Members of the d'Abitot family of Redmarley D'Abitot (Worcs., later Glos.) had land there in the later 15th century and the mid 17th.[12]

The manorial estate centred on Pauntley Court was broken up in the early 20th century. In the west large holdings were formed by piecemeal purchases several times in the 19th and 20th centuries. Four farms acquired by Jonas Symonds passed separately

---

1 Verey and Brooks, *Glos.* II, 634. Shown in frontispiece.
2 GA, D 1803/1.
3 Fig. 65. See GDR, T 1/140 (nos 279–80); OS Map 6", Glos. XVII.NW (1884 edn).
4 Warde, *They Didn't Walk Far*, 48.
5 GDR, T 1/140; Warde, *They Didn't Walk Far*, 5–10.
6 Photog. c.1910 in possession of Mr and Mrs Holland of Beggar's Roost (2005).

7 Datestone (not visible) reported by Lesley Harding of Walden Villa.
8 Warde, *They Didn't Walk Far*, 119–20; information from Eric Warde (formerly of Little Place).
9 *Inq. p.m. Glos.* 1302–58, 116.
10 GA, D 1803/1; Q/RNc 1, pp. 131–4.
11 See below, social hist. (social structure).
12 BL, Add. Ch. 24776, 24781; TNA, PROB 11/280, f. 267

after his death in 1830,[1] one eventually to the industrialist M.L. Attwood (d. 1915) of Stourbridge (Worcs.).[2] Other principal landowners were J.T.W.S. Holder in the mid 20th century and Mr David L. Dennis in the early 21st.[3]

PAUNTLEY MANOR

The medieval manor included the whole of Pauntley and small parts of Newent and Redmarley D'Abitot.[4] Its origins were four manors that Wulfhelm, Alfward, and Wiga held at Pauntley, Kilcot, Ketford, and Hayes (*Hege*) on the eve of the Norman Conquest and that Ansfrid of Cormeilles received on his marriage to a niece of Walter de Lacy. Ansfrid retained them in 1086, when they were assessed at a total of 4½ hides.[5] The medieval manor was held from the honor of Clifford for a knight's fee,[6] described sometimes as in Pauntley and Kilcot,[7] and in the late 14th and early 15th century the Mortimers, earls of March, were its overlords.[8] In the late 16th century part of the manor was said to be held of the manor of Dymock.[9]

Pauntley manor appears to have passed in the later 12th century from William de Solers to his son Richard. Richard's son Walter claimed the advowson of Pauntley church in 1208[10] and Walter's son Richard remitted to Cormeilles abbey (Eure) services it owed for land held of him at Kilcot.[11] Walter de Solers held the manor in 1248[12] and John de Breuse was its custodian in 1258 and 1265.[13] It passed to Thomas de Solers[14] and his son John de Solers (d. 1311) was succeeded in it by William of Whittington.[15] From William (*fl.* 1330) the manor passed to his son William[16] on whose death in 1358 it was retained by his widow Joan. Their eldest son William,[17] lord of Pauntley in 1377, died without issue. His brother Robert, lord in 1379,[18] was succeeded in 1423 or 1424 by his son Guy (d. 1440)[19] and the manor passed to Guy's grandson William Whittington (d. 1470) and to William's son John[20] (d. 1525). John's son and heir Thomas,[21] who settled it for a term on the marriage of his daughter Elizabeth (d. 1543) to (Sir) Giles Poole,[22] died in 1546 and the manor was inherited by Elizabeth's son (Sir) Henry Poole and her sisters Anne, wife of Brian Berkeley, Joan, wife of Roger Bodenham, Margaret, wife of Thomas Throckmorton, Alice, and Blanche, wife of John St Aubyn.[23] Henry, who succeeded his father at Sapperton in 1589,[24] acquired his aunts' interests[25] and at his death in 1616 the manor passed to his son Henry.[26] He sold it in 1620 to Edward Somerset, earl of Worcester.[27]

Edward Somerset died in 1628 and his son and heir Henry[28] settled the manor on his second son Sir John Somerset in 1632.[29] John, who fought on the royalist side in the Civil War,[30] evidently regained the sequestered estate in 1655[31] and was alive in 1671.[32] In 1694 his son and heir Henry gave the manor to his son Edward.[33] Edward died in 1709[34] and his widow Anne, who married John Paston of Horton in 1713,[35] retained the manor[36] until her death in 1731.[37] It then passed to the daughters of the third marriage of Charles Somerset (d. 1712), brother of Henry Somerset, namely Jane, widow of James Hooper, Frances, wife of Henry Scudamore, Carolina, later wife of Richard Brickenden, Clare,

---

1 GA, D 2356; TNA, PROB 11/1776, ff. 170v.–172v.
2 GA, G/NE 160/8/1; D 2299/4561; *The Times*, 13 Mar. 1916.
3 Information from Elizabeth Shepherd of Paunt House; see GA, DA 30/516/10/3, p. 180.
4 GA, D 1803/1.
5 *Domesday Book* (Rec. Com.), I, 170; see *Domesday Book; Glos.* ed. and trans. Moore.
6 *Close 1227–31*, 217; *Inq. p.m. Glos. 1302–58*, 115; *Cal. Fine R. 1307–19*, 91.
7 *Feudal Aids*, II, 250, 285.
8 *Cal. Inq. p.m.* XVII, 450; XXII, 473.
9 TNA, C 142/189, no 90; C 142/203, no 40.
10 *Cur. Reg.* IV, 233–4.
11 BL, Add. MS 18461, f. 122v.; above, Oxenhall, manor (estates in detached part of Pauntley).
12 *Glos. Feet of Fines 1199–1299*, p. 95.
13 *Cal. Pat. 1247–58*, 634; *Close 1261–4*, 315; *Cal. Inq. Misc.* I, 209.
14 *Feudal Aids*, II, 250.
15 *Cal. Inq. p.m.* V, 139. Atkyns, *Glos.* 600, states that William had married John's daughter and heiress Maud; see Fosbrooke, *Glos.* II, 231.
16 See *Glos. Feet of Fines 1300–59*, p. 108.
17 *Cal. Inq. p.m.* X, 370.
18 BL, Sloane Ch. XXXIII.43, 45–6; pedigree in S. Lysons, *The Model Merchant of the Middle Ages* (1860).
19 Hockaday Abs. cccx.
20 TNA, C 142/46, no 22; E. Conder, 'Pauntley Manor and the Pauntley Custom', *Trans. BGAS* 40 (1917), 116–17. Feoffees held the manor in 1472: BL, Add. Ch. 24778.
21 TNA, C 142/44, no 156.
22 Ibid. C 142/74, no 79; Bigland, *Glos.* II, 315.
23 TNA, C 142/74, no 79. GA, P 246/IN 1/1, gives 1545 as the year of Thos. Whittington's burial.
24 *VCH Glos.* XI, 91.
25 TNA, CP 40/1372, Carte rott. 26–7; E 315/411, ff. 10v., 13–14; see ibid. C 142/189, no 90; C 142/203, no 40.
26 Ibid. C 142/365, no 153.
27 Badminton Muniments OA/8.
28 TNA, C 142/442, no 26. For the Somerset fam., see pedigree in Badminton Muniments FmL 4/5/5.
29 Badminton Muniments OA/8.
30 *Bibliotheca Glos.* I, p. xxxvi; *Complete Peerage* XII (2), 860 and n.; see H. Dunant, *The Somerset Sequence* (1951), 60, 65–7, 79.
31 *Cal. Cttee. for Compounding*, I, 85; P.N. Gladwish, 'The Sales of Confiscated Properties after the English Civil War in Five Counties' (Cambridge Univ. Ph.D. thesis, 2002), 185.
32 GA, D 2700/QA 4/6.
33 Ibid. D 1618, Dymock, Pauntley, and Redmarley deeds 1663–1812.
34 Ibid. P 32/IN 1/1. According to Badminton Muniments FmL 4/5/5 Edward died in 1711 but his will was proved in 1710: TNA, PROB 11/517, ff. 66–67v.
35 GA, P 246/IN 1/1.
36 Ibid. Q/RNc 1, pp. 131–5.
37 Ibid. P 182/IN 1/1.

66. *Pauntley Court from the north-east in 1996*

later wife of John Southcote, Ann, and Henrietta Maria, later wife of John Frederick[1] (*fl.* 1771). In 1748 Clare's share was acquired by her five surviving sisters. Henrietta Maria died later that year and Ann and Carolina, the last surviving sisters, in 1764 and 1770 respectively. In 1773 Henry Blachford Scudamore, grandson of Frances (d. 1760) and heir of Carolina, bought Ann's share of the manor from Henry Somerset, duke of Beaufort,[2] and at his death in 1795 he left his share to his wife Tamar.[3] She bought out the other owners[4] and broke up the estate by sales, Pauntley Court and most of the land being acquired under an agreement of 1807 by John Lindsay of Edgware (Middx).[5]

Lindsay, to whom no deed of conveyance was made, sold his estate, including the manor, to John Stokes of Sheriff's Lench (Worcs.) in a series of transactions in 1810 and 1811.[6] In 1819 Stokes sold it with a deed of indemnity to David Ricardo, the political economist,[7] who owned 110 a. at Ketford that Tamar Scudamore had sold to Richard Loveridge in 1803.[8] After Ricardo's death in 1823 Pauntley Court descended with his Bromesberrow estate to Frank Ricardo,[9] who beginning in 1920 sold off the Pauntley Court estate. J.C. Davies of Ledbury bought the Court and its farm and his son H.J.P. Davies[10] sold the house in 1933, to the council of the Gloucestershire Home for Wayfarers,[11] and the rest of his land in 1937, part with the house's outbuildings to John Goulding and part to the Land Settlement Association.[12] J.R. Clapham bought the association's land in 1955[13] and his son D.J. Clapham sold it to Simon Skelding in 2000.[14] Pauntley Court, which John Goulding bought after the Second World War,[15] was owned from 1970 by David Ayshford Sanford. He sold it in 1990 to the Skelding family which, following piecemeal purchases of adjoining land, owned 182 ha (450 a.) in 2007.[16]

Pauntley Court

The manor house was largely rebuilt in the late 16th and 17th century but it incorporates fragments of its late medieval predecessor. Foundations discovered under the garden north-east of the house indicate that the medieval complex was once more extensive. The present house[17] comprises ranges on three sides of a courtyard open to the south. Most of it is timber-framed and, except for the eastern range, of

1 GA, D 2356; D 1618, Dymock, Pauntley, and Redmarley deeds 1663–1812; for Charles Somerset's burial, ibid. P 246/IN 1/1.

2 Ibid. D 2356; D 2700/NQ 2/2–3; TNA, PROB 11/963, ff. 50–52; for the burials of Henrietta Maria, Frances, and Ann, GA, P 246/IN 1/1.

3 GDR wills 1795/116; Bigland, *Glos.* II, 316.

4 Rudge, *Hist. of Glos.* II, 42.

5 GA, D 1618, Pauntley deeds 1803–18; 1811–14.

6 Ibid. Dymock, Pauntley, and Redmarley deeds 1663–1812; Pauntley deeds 1811–14; D 2356.

7 Ibid. D 2245/E 6; for Ricardo, *Oxford DNB*.

8 GA, D 1618, Pauntley deeds 1803–18; D 2080/126.

9 Above, Bromesberrow, manor (manor); *Burke's Landed Gentry* (1937), II, 1912; GDR, T 1/140; *Kelly's Dir. Glos.* (1863 and later edns), where the manorial rights in Pauntley are said to belong to the Crown. The Crown owned the woodland in the detached part of the parish: GA, P 246/MI 1/5.

10 GA, D 2299/2331, 2723.

11 Ibid. D 5426/17.

12 Ibid. D 2299/6532, 8054.

13 GA, D 2299/8054.

14 Information from J.S. Luard (land agent), of The Hill, Staunton.

15 GA, D 5426/16–17; DA 30/100/23, p. 92.

16 Information from Christine Skelding of Pauntley Court and from Mr Luard; see sale particulars of 1990 in National Monuments Record, Swindon, file BF83620.

17 Fig. 66.

two storeys. The five-bayed western range, which has been truncated to the south, is reported to have an arch-braced roof with two tiers of windbraces and at the southern end smoke-blackened timbers.[1] The northern range, which is aligned differently to the other two and connected to them by later work, was built in at least three phases. It contains a narrow range with an external stack on the southern side and a parallel northern row of rooms under a separate, pitched roof; the upper floor of the southern part and the northern pile appear to have been added to earlier fabric in the 16th century. The upper floor on the north side may have been rebuilt in the 17th or 18th century. The house, where the Somerset family abandoned new building in stone after the Restoration,[2] was reduced in size as a farmhouse in the 18th century.[3] In the late 18th and 19th centuries much of the building was refaced in brick and render and new roofs were provided and in the 19th the western end of the northern range was rebuilt or enlarged as a four-bayed brick-built block. The eastern range was used as a farm building and has an external stone staircase.

In the early 19th century the house had a lodge at Payford, to the north, and another drive reached the house from Brand green, higher up to the south.[4] Immediately south of the house a large gabled dovecot in stone may have been among the buildings erected by the Somersets after the Restoration. A two-storeyed five-bayed range of stables, timber-framed with a brick infill, dates from the 17th century.[5]

OTHER ESTATES

Rhyle House and Botloe's Farm

William Wall of Ledbury, who may have been the descendant of Pauntley inhabitant Thomas Wall (*fl.* 1522),[6] died in 1717 leaving Rhyle House and Botloe's Farm, copyholds under the manor, to his daughter Dorothy, the widow of Thomas Jauncey[7] of Whitwick in Stretton Grandison (Herefs.). After Dorothy's death in 1743[8] the combined estate belonged to her daughter Dorothy, wife of Revd Samuel Bethell (d. 1766) of Dinedor (Herefs.).[9] From Dorothy (d. 1776) it passed to her daughters Dorothy and Mary Bethell of Hereford[10] and *c*.1807 it reverted to the lord of the manor.[11] In 1812 John Stokes sold Botloe's Farm to Jonas Symonds (d. 1830), from whom the farm (40 a.) passed in turn to his daughter Mary Cummins (d. 1846) and her son Joseph Cummins (d. 1889). It was retained by Joseph's widow Emma in 1894[12] and was owned by J.L. Stelfox in 1910.[13] Rhyle House (84 a.),[14] which John Stokes retained,[15] passed with the Pauntley Court estate[16] and was among parts of the estate offered for sale in 1921.[17] J.T.W.S. Holder owned the farm in the early 1970s.[18]

Pauntley Rectory

Pauntley church, to which a yardland as well as the Pauntley tithes belonged in the early 13th century,[19] was appropriated by Cormeilles abbey.[20] In the late Middle Ages Fotheringhay college (Northants.) administered the tithes as part of its Newent estate[21] and following the college's surrender of its possessions in 1547[22] the tithes descended with Newent manor[23] until 1664 when Sir John Winter conveyed them to Thomas Awbrey.[24] At the turn of the century the impropriation belonged to Anthony Meeke[25] before passing by 1704 to Edward Somerset, the lord of the manor.[26] Edward by will proved 1710 left the impropriation to William Higford and others in trust to sell[27] and William's daughter Frances, widow of Henry Wakeman,[28] devised it by 1784 to her daughters Margaret, wife of Charles Welch of Evesham (Worcs.), and Winifred. It passed to

---

1 M.A. Johnson and B. Fallon, 'The History of Pauntley Court, Gloucestershire' (1992: copy at Pauntley Court in 2005).
2 GA, D 412/Z 3, Nourse MS, p. 14; *Notes on Dioc. of Glouc. by Chancellor Parsons*, 183;
3 Rudder, *Glos.* 598.
4 Greenwood, *Map of Glos.* (1824); GDR, T 1/140.
5 See DoE List, Pauntley (1985), 3/205–6.
6 *Military Surv. of Glos. 1522*, 61.
7 TNA, PROB 11/557, ff. 192–3; *Reg. of Dymock*, 252.
8 For Dorothy Jauncey and her descendants, see http://www.geocities.com/sjkelsey2001/whitwick (accessed 26 Oct. 2004).
9 GA, D 2700/NQ 2/2; *Alumni Oxon. 1500–1714*, I, 118.
10 See TNA, PROB 11/924, f. 103 and v.
11 GDR wills 1795/116; GA, D 1618, Dymock, Pauntley, and Redmarley deeds 1663–1812.
12 GA, D 2356; GDR, T 1/140; TNA, PROB 11/1776, ff. 170v.–172v.
13 GA, D 2428/1/17, f. 62.
14 Ibid. D 2356.
15 Ibid. D 1618, Pauntley deeds 1811–14.
16 Above (Pauntley manor); see GDR, T 1/140; GA, D 2428/1/17, f. 62.
17 GA, D 2299/2723.
18 Ibid. DA 30/516/10/3, p. 180.
19 BL, Add. MS 15668, f. 72.
20 Below, religious hist. (early hist.): see *VCH Glos.* II, 105.
21 Herefs. RO, E 12/G/2, 5; *Valor Eccl.* IV, 287.
22 *L&P Hen. VIII*, XXI (2), p. 381.
23 Above, Newent, manors; see *Cal. Pat.* 1547–9, 108–9; 1555–7, 94; 1566–9, p. 42; GA, D 421/T 1–2, T 23; TNA, C 142/118, no 54; C 142/227, no 204; C 142/378, no 147. Sirs Nicholas Arnold and Henry Poole, named as owners of the Pauntley impropriation in 1551 and 1603 respectively, were its lessees: J. Gairdner, 'Bishop Hooper's Visitation of Gloucester', *EHR* 19 (1904), 120; TNA, C 3/195/2; *Eccl. Misc.* 101; TNA, E 315/411, f. 33.
24 GA, D 3526; TNA, CP 25/2/656/16 Chas. II Mich. no 9.
25 TNA, CP 25/2/831/3 Wm and Mary Trin. no 24; *Notes on Dioc. of Glouc. by Chancellor Parsons*, 183.
26 GDR, V 5/250T 5; Atkyns, *Glos.* 601.
27 TNA, PROB 11/517, ff. 66–67v.
28 See GDR wills 1737/131.

Margaret's son Charles Welch, later of Hawford in Ombersley (Worcs.),[1] and in 1838 his widow Anne and Charles Willoughby Osborne were its owners. The tithes were commuted in 1841 for a corn rent charge of £450[2] and Anne (d. c.1844) left her share to C.W. Osborne.[3] He was sole owner in 1865[4] as was Emma Willoughby-Osborne in 1936 when tithe rent charges were redeemed.[5]

ECONOMIC HISTORY

Pauntley's economy depended almost entirely on agriculture with some variation provided by woodland crafts and rural trades.

AGRICULTURE

The Middle Ages

Lands in Pauntley, Kilcot, Ketford, and Hayes (*Hege*) worth £3 10s. in 1066 were valued at £4 and contained nine ploughteams in 1086. Two of the teams belonged to Ansfrid of Cormeilles's demesne, which employed 2 slaves, and the other seven to his tenants, namely 7 villans and 3 bordars.[6] Six ploughteams were recorded in Pauntley in 1220.[7] In the late 12th century one yardland belonged to a house at Nutham.[8]

In 1311 Pauntley manor had 100 a. of arable in demesne, as well as 6 a. of meadow, a several pasture, and a wooded park. Of the customary tenants, ten each held a half-yardland for a cash rent of 5s. and owed two days' work during mowing and four bedrips during the harvest. Another eleven tenants, four cottagers among them, owed smaller cash rents and three bedrips each. Sixteen various freehold estates or farms owed rents of assize totalling 22s. 2d.[9] Holdings with a half-yardland of arable changed hands in the later 14th century.[10]

Although Pauntley contained areas of open-field land in the later medieval period,[11] their precise location is undetermined and the dispersed nature of medieval settlement together with the remains of ancient woodland suggests that a substantial part of Pauntley was cleared for cultivation in closes. Of the parish's meadows one known in 1379 as Buckley was in divided ownership.[12] Meadowland lay all along the bank of the river Leadon. That below Great Herridge was not part of the manor estate in 1410, when it was known as Salbrook's mead,[13] and was possibly the land later called Sawbridge meadow.[14] Apple cultivation was under way by the later 15th century when John d'Abitot, in granting access to his woods in Pauntley, reserved the apple trees growing in them for his own use.[15] In 1522 John Whittington's household at Pauntley included his steward[16] but it is not known if any of his manorial demesne was in hand.

The Early Modern Period

Giles Poole, who farmed the manor at the beginning of the period,[17] from Sapperton confirmed his bailiff and rent collector at Pauntley in his post for life in 1561.[18] In the early 17th century, when six husbandmen were described as servants of Sir Henry Poole and a warrener was present, the manorial demesne was worked by several farmers and at least twelve others cultivated freehold or tenanted land.[19] Eight landholders had freehold farms, some if not most of them in the detached portion of the parish and several created by the amalgamation of smaller holdings. On the manor four tenants held land other than the demesne, and including mills at Payford, by lease. Copyhold estates granted for up to three lives conferred no right of free bench and the integrity of holdings was possibly long maintained, for the jury at a court of survey in 1619 disclaimed knowledge of any customary holdings having been divided into smaller parcels.[20]

More farms throughout the parish had been amalgamated by 1717, when four freeholders owed rent to the manor and five tenants held land on leases for years on lives. One leasehold, based on Paunt House, contained the sites of four other homesteads and two others were each made up of two holdings. A majority of nine copyholds also included the sites of more than one homestead. One of five cottage tenants occupied a cottage on the demesne and the principal leasehold farm, based on

---

1 Fosbrooke, *Glos.* II, 233; Rudge, *Hist. of Glos.* 43; Birmingham City Archives, Barnard Colln. 362469.
2 TNA, IR 18/2830; GDR, T 1/140.
3 TNA, PROB 11/2026, ff. 79v.–81v.
4 GA, P 246/MI 1/3; see ibid. D 1815/Box 15/1.
5 Ibid. P 246/CW 2/3.
6 *Domesday Book* (Rec. Com.), I, 170.
7 *Book of Fees*, I, 307.
8 BL, Add. Ch. 24752.
9 *Inq. p.m. Glos.* 1302–58, 115–16.
10 BL, Sloane Ch. XXXIII.45, 51.
11 Ibid. 45, 51, 56.
12 Ibid. 45.
13 Ibid. Add. Ch. 74874.
14 Herefs. RO, E 12/G/5.
15 BL, Add. Ch. 24776, 24781.
16 *Military Surv. of Glos.* 1522, 59–60, 61.
17 *Acts of PC* 1547–50, 247; see above, manor.
18 BL, Sloane Ch. XXXIII.85.
19 Smith, *Men and Armour*, 66.
20 GA, D 1803/1.

part of Pauntley Court, included a second cottage on the demesne.[1] In the 1770s Pauntley Court farm covered 536 a., four other farms had between 100 and 200 a., and about a dozen holdings were of less than 50 a. each. Of the larger farms those based on the White House, Aylesmore, and Paunt House were part of the Pauntley Court estate. The fourth took in Rylas (Rhyle House) and Botloe's Farm on the Bethells' estate.[2]

Dairying as well as corn and sheep husbandry were among the staples of Pauntley's larger farms throughout the period. Flocks of geese were also kept in the early 17th century[3] and new orchards were being planted before the mid 1680s.[4] In the early 17th century a meadow under Great Herridge was part of John d'Abitot's estate.[5] There was little meadowland in Pauntley away from the banks of the river Leadon and in the early 18th century the Pastons, owners of the manor, had five parcels in one of Hasfield's common meadows by the river Severn.[6] The manorial tenants had common rights on the pastures at Botloe's green, Pool hill, and Brand green where ancient intercommoning arrangements had been superseded by the early 17th century by counter accusations of encroachments during perambulations of the Pauntley and Newent parish boundaries.[7]

In 1771 Pauntley Court farm contained almost equal areas of arable and pasture and most of the available meadowland. The four other large farms were mostly arable.[8] At that time most of the land was used for growing wheat and other grain and was grazed regularly by flocks of sheep, a few turnips being included in the crop rotation as feed for both sheep and horned cattle. Little rye was grown despite the traditional association of that crop with the lighter, sandy soils of the area. The sheep kept were of a small species noted for its fine wool and sweet meat. Farmers devoted themselves principally to the cultivation of orchards, the production of cider being their main concern, and they eschewed the draining of wet lands as well as the watering of meadows.[9] The 445 a. recorded as under crops in 1801 grew mostly wheat and barley and included 35 a. of turnips.[10]

The Nineteenth and Twentieth Centuries

In 1839 the largest farms, both on Osman Ricardo's estate, were at Pauntley Court (458 a.) and Ketford (255 a.).[11] In 1851, when several hundred acres on the estate were farmed from Compton House in Newent,[12] John Butler, the farmer at Pauntley Court (460 a.), employed 18 men and boys on his land and farmers in the west at Aylesmore (145 a.), Rylas (88 a.), Paunt House (47 a.), and Nutham (20 a.) between them hired 15 farm labourers.[13] A bailiff managed Paunt House in the 1860s and 1870s and Henry Butler, the farmer at Pauntley Court, himself employed a bailiff in the 1900s.[14] In 1896 nine agricultural occupiers, all tenants, were returned for Pauntley[15] and in 1926 14 holdings, seven of them with under 20 a. each, and 21 full-time and 16 part-time agricultural workers were recorded.[16] Similar numbers of farms were returned in 1956 and 1986. In 1986, when one had over 50 ha (*c.*125 a.), three over 30 ha (*c.*75 a.), and two between 10 and 20 ha (*c.*25 and 50 a.), several of the smaller holdings were worked by part-time farmers and the larger farms hired in all six full-time workers.[17]

In 1813 John Stokes was in dispute with two flax dressers of Bengeworth (Worcs.) over part of the Pauntley Court estate set aside for their use.[18] In 1839 the parish contained 1,239 a. of arable and 326 a. of pasture and meadow.[19] Arable farming followed a four-course rotation, including grass leys, and lime was used commonly for manure. Although prone to flooding, the meadows by the Leadon were a source of hay. A list of animals that year included 1,500 sheep, 100 store bullocks, 30 stock cows, 50 oxen, and 70 horses.[20] Orchard cultivation remained important and at that time there were several hop gardens in Pauntley.[21] Turnips were grown on at least 272 a. in 1866, when wheat and barley covered over 700 a. and oats and rye 33 a. Some 405 a. in the parish was permanent pasture[22] and among the livestock returned in 1866 were 145 cattle, including 33 milch cows, 974 sheep, and 99 pigs.[23] The farm bailiff's wife at Paunt House in 1861 was a dairymaid.[24]

The area of arable in the main part of Pauntley shrank markedly in the later 19th century and that of

---

1 Ibid. Q/RNc 1, pp. 131–4.
2 Ibid. D 2700/NQ 2/2; P 246/CW 2/1.
3 GDR, B 4/3/977.
4 GA, D 2957/230/1.
5 Ibid. D 1803/1.
6 Ibid. Q/RNc 1, pp. 134–5; see *VCH Glos.* VIII, 286.
7 GA, D 1803/1; Herefs. RO, E 12/G/7.
8 Ibid. D 2700/NQ 2/2.
9 Rudder, *Glos.* 597.
10 *1801 Crop Returns Eng.* I, 176.
11 GDR, T 1/140.
12 Above, Newent, econ. hist. (agric.).
13 TNA, HO 107/1960.
14 Ibid. RG 9/1760; RG 10/2607; *Kelly's Dir. Glos.* (1863–1914 edns).
15 TNA, MAF 68/1609/16.
16 Ibid. MAF 68/3295/15.
17 Ibid. MAF 68/4533/120; MAF 68/6005/14/170.
18 Birmingham City Archives, Barnard Colln. 364299.
19 GDR, T 1/140.
20 TNA, IR 18/2830.
21 GDR, T 1/140; *Kelly's Dir. Glos.* (1863), 326.
22 TNA, MAF 68/26/17.
23 Ibid. MAF 68/25/4.
24 Ibid. RG 9/1760.

permanent grass continued to increase in the early 20th. In 1926, when permanent pasture accounted for 622 a. and rough grazing for 29 a., 211 cattle, including 67 milch cows, 522 sheep, and 84 pigs were returned, the livestock numbers being higher than those recorded in 1896. Sugar beet filled a quarter of the area, less than 300 a., returned as under arable crops in 1926. Orchards covering 41 a. were reported in 1896[1] and there was a cider mill at Payford mill in 1921.[2] Small areas of soft fruit and hops were also grown during the period and commercial poultry farming was introduced.[3] At the turn of the century Pool Hill's residents included a fruit dealer.[4] There was a specialist poultry unit at Redlea in 1939.[5] In 1933, in a venture involving an Anglican religious order and counting poet laureate John Masefield among its chief patrons, 40 a. was acquired with Pauntley Court to provide work and shelter for young male vagrants. The scheme, for which the Land Settlement Association purchased Pauntley Court farm in 1937, provided training in general agricultural work, market gardening, and orcharding and continued until the Second World War.[6]

In 1956 Pauntley remained predominantly pastoral in character, with 310 dairy and beef cattle and 618 sheep and lambs returned, and pig and poultry farming continued. Orchards covering 64 a. were also returned along with areas of soft fruit, mostly blackcurrants, and a market garden with a nursery.[7] In the following decades the areas devoted to fruit farming and horticulture grew. Large orchards were cultivated in several places, including Welsh House Lane where an outbuilding of Rhyle House was for a time the centre of a fruit farm[8] on which in 1972 the Three Choirs Vineyard was started.[9] A market garden was established at Ketford by the mid 1960s.[10] In 1986, when 209 ha (516 a.) of grassland, 9 ha (22 a.) of rough grazing, 503 cattle, and 665 sheep and lambs were returned, two of the principal farms specialized as dairy units and two were concerned mainly with fruit growing; 25 ha (62 a.) of orchards and soft fruit, including grapes, was returned and market gardens covered at least 27 ha (67 a.).[11] In the late 20th century, while some orchards were grubbed up, the area given over to viticulture at Welsh House Lane increased.

WOODLAND MANAGEMENT

Little is known of the management of Pauntley's woodland during the Middle Ages. In 1382 John Hard of Cheltenham granted two men the right to fell and take wood in Solers Grove and Kyndene for two years.[12] In granting similar access to a number of woods for slightly longer terms in 1466 and 1489 John d'Abitot reserved the apple trees as well as the principal timbers and their replacements.[13]

In the early 17th century the manorial demesne included 240 a. woodland[14] and the lord had a woodward on his staff. Some of the woodland was held by a tenant[15] but later the woodland on the Pauntley Court estate was usually all in hand.[16] In 1631 at least two charcoal burners, described as colliers, were working in Herridge wood.[17] Collin Park wood, the largest single area of woodland, supplied cordwood for the ironmaster Thomas Foley in the later 17th century[18] and the right there to harvest bass, bark from lime trees used in mat and basket making, provided a regular income in the early 18th.[19] Cordwood commanded a higher price in Pauntley than in Monmouth in 1771. A timber park created by 1765[20] accounted for 34 of the 313 acres of woodland on the estate in 1803.[21] Much of the woodland was oak coppice felled every 20 years.[22] In the late 19th and early 20th century there were annual sales of timber and coppice wood from Collin Park and of alders, oaks, and ashes from elsewhere in Pauntley.[23] A Pool Hill resident dealing in wood in 1839 remained in business in 1861.[24] The estate's woods were patrolled by a gamekeeper in the later 18th century[25] and there was a resident keeper in the early 20th century,[26] when sporting rights over the estate were in the hands of a lessee.[27] Collin Park,

---

1 TNA, MAF 68/1609/16; MAF 68/3295/15; see also, Acreage Returns, 1905.
2 GA, D 2299/2723.
3 TNA, MAF 68/1609/16; MAF 68/3295/15.
4 GA, P 246/IN 1/6.
5 *Kelly's Dir. Glos.* (1939), 289.
6 *Glos. Countryside* Jan. 1937, 197–8; GA, D 2299/6532, 6886, 8054. For photogs. and other records of the training scheme at Pauntley Court, see GA, D 5426.
7 TNA, MAF 68/4533/170.
8 OS Maps 1:1,250, SO 7229–7329 (1972 edn); SO 7230–7330 (1970 edn).
9 *Citizen*, 21 Oct. 1975; *Glos. Life*, Aug. 1989, 468. See above, Newent, econ. hist. (agric.); also Fig. 20.
10 GA, P 246/IN 1/6.
11 TNA, MAF 68/6005/14/170.
12 BL, Add. Ch. 24767.
13 Ibid. 24776, 24781.
14 TNA, E 315/411, f. 12.
15 GA, D 1803/1.
16 Ibid. Q/RNc 1, p. 134; GDR, T 1/140.
17 GA, P 246/IN 1/1.
18 Herefs. RO, E 12/G/19.
19 GA, Q/RNc 1, p. 134; *OED*.
20 GA, D 2700/NQ 2/2.
21 Ibid. D 2957/212/161.
22 TNA, IR 18/2830.
23 GA, D 2299/2/8/36; D 2299/2/11/84.
24 Ibid. P 246/IN 1/6; TNA, HO 107/35012; HO 107/1960; RG 9/1760.
25 GA, D 1618, fam. papers, deposition of Ric. Lloyd 3 May 1817.
26 *Kelly's Dir. Glos.* (1906), 272; (1910), 277; (1927), 294.
27 GA, D 2299/2331, 2723.

67. Payford Mill

where charcoal burning was temporarily re-established in 1997, continued to be maintained as deciduous plantation, mainly lime and oak, under traditional coppice management and in 2004 the Gloucestershire Wildlife Trust managed part of it as a reserve.[1]

MILLS

Ansfrid of Cormeilles had a mill on his estate in 1086[2] and the manor included a water mill in the early 14th century.[3] In 1358 the lord of Redmarley D'Abitot owned a corn mill called Pauntley mill[4] and in 1410 a water mill stood below Great Herridge wood at a place called Thurbache, perhaps on the Redmarley side of the Leadon at Durbridge.[5] A mill operating within Pauntley on a tributary stream below the wood in the later 18th century[6] belonged to a farm on the Pauntley Court estate.[7] It had been abandoned by the late 1880s[8] and little remained of the building in the mid 20th century.[9] In 1605 George and Martha Wood quitclaimed a mill in Pauntley to Sir Edward Winter.[10]

In the early 17th century, when he was served by a miller,[11] the lord's corn mill on the Leadon at Payford had several pairs of stones and was used traditionally by most of the manor's tenants even though they were not bound by custom to do so.[12] In the early 19th century the miller, William Holland, acquired the mill and in the early 1830s he left it to Richard Birt.[13] Later the mill was back in the Pauntley Court estate and, with two pairs of stones,[14] was used regularly until the early 1920s.[15] The mill equipment, which was damaged by floods in 1947, was restored in the 1980s.[16] The wheel pit and undershot wheel, apparently of the 19th century, also survive and the sluice gate has been reconstructed.[17]

In the early 19th century a mill was built by the river east of Pauntley Court to house a threshing machine[18] powered by water from a pond fed by a stream rising in Collin Park wood.[19] Part of Pauntley Court farm,[20] the mill was not used by the late 19th century[21] but remained standing in the early 21st.

---

1 *Wildlife News* (Glos. Wildlife Trust, May–August 2004), 10–11.
2 *Domesday Book* (Rec. Com.), I, 170.
3 *Inq. p.m. Glos. 1302–58*, 116.
4 *Cat. Ancient Deeds*, V, 138.
5 BL, Add. Ch. 74874; see *VCH Worcs*. III, 485.
6 Taylor, *Map of Glos.* (1777); Greenwood, *Map of Glos.* (1824).
7 GDR, T 1/140 (no 83).
8 OS Map 6", Glos. XVII.NE (1889 edn).
9 G.M. Davies, 'Mills of the River Leadon and Tributaries', *Glos. Soc. Ind. Archaeol. Newsletter* 7 (Apr. 1966), 30.
10 TNA, CP 25/2/297/3 Jas. I Trin. no 12.
11 Smith, *Men and Armour*, 66.
12 GA, D 1803/1; see GDR wills 1610/44.
13 GA, D 2957/212/161; TNA, PROB 11/1793, f. 45 and v.; see GDR, T 1/140 (no 52).
14 GA, D 2299/2723, 3086.
15 See *Kelly's Dir. Glos.* (1923), 280; (1927), 294.
16 R. and P. Palmer, *Secret River*, 44.
17 See Fig. 67.
18 Verey and Brooks, *Glos.* II, 634.
19 Greenwood, *Map of Glos.* (1824); Davies, 'Mills of River Leadon and Tributaries', 31.
20 GDR, T 1/140 (no 359).
21 OS Map 6", Glos. XVII.NE (1889, 1903 edns).

INDUSTRY AND TRADE

Digging in the coal deposits near the ground surface in the west of Pauntley[1] had begun by 1797, when a miner died in the parish.[2] Ten years later prospecting had not led to mining on any significant scale.[3]

In 1608 Pauntley's men included a smith and a turner.[4] A smith lived at Brand green in the mid 17th century and the first recorded shoemaker in the parish died in 1778.[5] A smithy operated next to a new house below Pool hill in 1815[6] and the hamlet's residents in 1851 included a sawyer, a shoemaker, a glovemaker, and a stone mason.[7] Traditional crafts such as thatching, basket making, and hurdle making were practised in Pauntley in the later 19th century[8] and residents in the early 20th century included a farm machinery operator, two road workmen, and a railway fireman.[9] A man at Pool hill kept a shop in 1819[10] and a grocer living there in 1861 was among a number of shopkeepers recorded in Pauntley in the later 19th century.[11] Residents in 1863 included a postman[12] and in the mid 1870s a local man ran a weekly carrying service between Pauntley and Gloucester.[13] The farmer at Rhyle House traded as a threshing machine proprietor and a guano and sack merchant in the 1880s.[14]

The smithy below Pool hill closed during the First World War and a local carrying business ceased at the same time. After the war, as agriculture and traditional crafts together provided ever fewer jobs, some residents found employment in engineering, transport, and public services. A hurdle maker lived at Pool Hill in the 1930s. There was a post office and shop at Pool Hill in 1906. In the 1920s the hamlet gained a second shop[15] but from the mid 1970s it was without both and from the mid 1980s a post office.[16] In 2000 most of the hamlet's residents worked away in a variety of professional, managerial, and skilled jobs, including law, education, nursing, personnel services, engineering, and computing.[17] Businesses in Pauntley included a riding school and, at Payford mill, the studio of a garden equipment designer.[18]

LOCAL GOVERNMENT

MANORIAL GOVERNMENT

There was a manor court in 1311.[19] The only evidence of its jurisdiction is a copy of the articles of enquiry for, and the presentments at, a court of survey held in 1619 for Henry Poole. The manor court, which custom designated the sole forum for recording transactions in copyhold land,[20] presumably convened until at least the early 18th century.[21]

PAROCHIAL GOVERNMENT

In the early 17th century two churchwardens, two overseers of the poor, and two surveyors of the highways were chosen from among landowners in the two parts of the parish. Deputies occasionally served.[22] Later one churchwarden, one overseer, and one surveyor were appointed, all three offices, together with that of constable, being filled by rota between 16 farmhouses, including Pauntley Court. The rota system was abandoned by the mid 1780s.[23]

By 1619 two poorhouses had been built on waste land on Pool hill and at the Hollend.[24] The parish's expenditure on poor relief in 1776 was higher than that of many of its neighbours but was much less in the mid 1780s,[25] when about five adults received weekly pay. Much larger numbers received occasional help from the late 18th century, corn being given to the poor in 1795 and 1796, and about 15 people were usually on relief in the 1820s and early 1830s. Occasional measures taken by the parish in the late 18th century included apprenticing children to local farmers, employing women to spin flax or

---

1 Geol. Surv. Map, 1:50,000, solid and drift, sheet 216 (1988 edn).
2 GA, P 246/OV 2/1.
3 Rudge, *Agric. of Glos.* 21.
4 Smith, *Men and Armour*, 66.
5 GA, P 246/IN 1/1, burials 8 Mar. 1666/7, 14 July 1778.
6 Ibid. IN 1/6; GDR, T 1/140 (no 257).
7 TNA, HO 107/1960.
8 GA, P 246/IN 1/6.
9 TNA, RG 13/2421.
10 GA, P 246/IN 1/6.
11 TNA, RG 9/1760; RG 10/2607; *Kelly's Dir. Glos.* (1863–1902 edns).
12 GA, P 246/IN 1/6.
13 *Morris's Dir. Glos.* (1876), 560.
14 *Kelly's Dir. Glos.* (1885), 547; (1889), 864.
15 Ibid. (1902–39 edns); GA, P 246/IN 1/6.
16 E. Warde, *They Didn't Walk Far: a History of Pool Hill* (priv. printed, 2000), 2, 67.
17 Ibid. 145.
18 Personal observation; information from Johnnie Vizor of Payford Mill.
19 *Inq. p.m. Glos.* 1302–58, 116.
20 GA, D 1803/1. For a transcription of the document, see E. Conder, 'Pauntley Manor and the Pauntley Custom', *Trans. BGAS* 40 (1917), 118–31.
21 GA, Q/RNc 1, pp. 132–5, confirms that copyhold tenure persisted in 1717 under John and Anne Paston.
22 GA, P 246/IN 1/1.
23 Ibid. CW 2/1.
24 Ibid. D 1803/1.
25 *Poor Law Abstract*, 1804, 172–3.

hemp, and paying for a family's lodging at Rudford. In 1785 the parish decided to assist a man with the cost of a new house on Pool hill including that of a lease of land for its site. In 1812 and 1813 the parish made several payments to the Ledbury overseers and in 1820, the year the poorhouse on Pool hill was rebuilt, it settled a substantial doctor's bill and reimbursed a man for a payment to the Gloucester infirmary. An annual allowance of two guineas to the overseer, started in 1794, was withdrawn in 1798, following objections from magistrates, but had been reinstated by 1803 and was gradually increased.[1] In the early 19th century the annual cost of relief more than doubled[2] but by the mid 1820s it had fallen back slightly.[3] At that time the rent of a garden at Pool Hill supplemented the income available for relief. Among moves to limit expenditure was a stipulation in 1830 that only the churchwarden or overseer could authorize the services of a doctor attending the parish.[4] In 1835 administration of relief passed to the guardians of the new Newent poor-law union.[5]

In 1676 a former surveyor of the highways sought reimbursement of his expenses on works at Ketford and Payford bridges.[6] Pauntley shared responsibility for Payford bridge with Redmarley D'Abitot (Worcs., later Glos.) and in 1815, after John Stokes had built a new bridge there, it decided to pay him £20 for bridle rights across it and to share with him the maintenance cost for the part within Pauntley.[7] Responsibility for Ketford bridge was shared with Dymock.[8]

In the late 18th century the churchwarden's, surveyor's, and constable's expenses and also the parish clerk's salary were funded at least in part from the poor rate and for over ten years until 1798 the churchwarden's expenditure was included in the overseer's account. The constable alone continued to be paid from the poor rate after 1798.[9] From 1843 the vestry appointed a salaried surveyor of highways and there were again two churchwardens, one chosen by the vicar and the other by the parish.[10]

SOCIAL HISTORY

SOCIAL STRUCTURE

In 1327 William of Whittington, lord of the manor and a knight, was assessed for tax in Pauntley at just over 6s. Of the other men and women there, including landholders in the main part of the parish, one was assessed at just over 5s. 5d., one at 4s., three at 3s., and four between 2s. and 2s. 6d. The lower assessments were eleven at 1s. or more and six between 6d. and 8d.[11] At that time there were some 16 free and 21 customary tenants on the manor. Some if not most of the free tenants lived in the detached part of the parish. All of the customary tenants owed labour services as well as cash rents.[12]

The Whittingtons maintained the manor house as their principal residence and by the time of Robert Whittington (d. 1423 or 1424), the owner of estates elsewhere,[13] lived in considerable opulence.[14] Robert's younger brother Richard (d. 1423), the third son of William Whittington (d. 1358), went to London where he achieved fame as merchant and mayor,[15] and Robert's son and heir Guy (d. 1440) added to the family's estates by marriage.[16] In 1522 John Whittington, with goods and chattels worth £100, was the wealthiest lay person in the region let alone the parish. Including two chaplains, most of the other inhabitants assessed in Pauntley for the military subsidy that year had goods worth between £1 and £4. For six men no assessment was made. Of two men with goods valued at £20,[17] James Hill probably owned Hill House in the detached part of the parish[18] and Thomas Wall may have been a copyholder at Rhyle House or Botloe's Farm.[19]

In the later 16th century the lords of the manor were at least occasionally resident. Sir Henry Poole raised his family there in the 1570s and 1580s and his eldest daughter Elinor (d. c.1647), wife of Sir Richard Fettiplace and author of a treatise on household management, lived there in 1602.[20] Among other gentry families in Pauntley at that time the

---

1 GA, P 246/OV 2/1–2.
2 *Poor Law Abstract, 1804*, 172–3; *1818*, 146–7.
3 *Poor Law Returns* (1830–1), 66.
4 GA, P 246/OV 2/2.
5 *Poor Law Com. 2nd Rep.* p. 523.
6 GA, Q/SO 1, f. 106.
7 Ibid. P 246/OV 2/1–2.
8 Ibid. P 125/SU 2/2.
9 Ibid. P 246/OV 2/1; CW 2/1.
10 Ibid. VE 2/1.
11 *Glos. Subsidy Roll, 1327*, 36.

12 *Inq. p.m. Glos.* 1302–58, 115–16; above, econ. hist. (agric.).
13 See *VCH Glos.* XI, 92, 111; *VCH Worcs.* IV, 199–200
14 Hockaday Abs. cccx, 1424, 1440, 1452.
15 *Oxford DNB*; S. Lysons, *The Model Merchant of the Middle Ages* (1860).
16 See *VCH Glos.* VI, 80; VIII, 62; IX, 148; XI, 222.
17 *Military Surv. of Glos. 1522*, 59–60, 61–2.
18 Above, Oxenhall, manor (estates in detached part of Pauntley).
19 Above, manor (other estates).
20 GA, P 246/IN 1/1; for Elizabeth Fettiplace, see *Oxford DNB*.

Pauncefoots, headed by William (d. 1617), lived in the main part of the parish.[1] Of 41 people listed in Pauntley in 1608 at least 18 being described as husbandmen were farmers, of whom six together with a gardener and a miller were described as Sir Henry's servants. Of seven other servants, three worked for Thomas Hooke, a landowner in the detached part of the parish, and one for William Pauncefoot.[2]

In 1672, when 18 persons in the whole parish were assessed for hearth tax, the only houses in the main part with more than 3 hearths were those occupied by the Attwoods (12 hearths), the Cruyses (8 hearths), and the Pauncefoots (6 hearths). The majority of the other houses had only 1 hearth.[3] While the Cruyses lived at the Hollend[4] and the Pauncefoots at the White House,[5] the Attwoods occupied Pauntley Court in the absence of Sir John Somerset. He was living in Belgium in 1671[6] and his son Henry, described as of Pauntley Court in 1694,[7] also lived out his days abroad.[8] Edward Somerset was resident and William Attwood resided at the White House in the early 18th century.[9] Edward's widow Anne remained at the Court when married to John Paston[10] but the Somerset heiresses, although several of them were, like their parents, buried at Pauntley, were non-resident[11] and from the Court farmer Daniel Dew (*fl.* 1771) acted as local agent, collecting rents and maintaining the estate's woods.[12] Ann Somerset (d. 1764) is commemorated in the church by a monument by Thomas Symonds of Hereford.[13] Other memorials of the period, those to members of the Attwood and Pauncefoot families included, were more modest with carved headstones marking some farmers' graves in the churchyard.[14] During the whole period there was no resident clergyman.

John Stokes (d. 1828), owner of the Pauntley Court estate, farmed much of the land from Pauntley Court himself even after he sold the estate in 1819.[15] The Ricardos, owners of the estate from 1819, were non-resident[16] but Osman Ricardo established and sustained a day school at Payford in the mid 19th century.[17] Away from Pauntley Court, the principal farmers occupied the main farmsteads in the west of Pauntley. Alexander Symonds, whose father Jonas (d. 1830) bought four of the farms there,[18] lived at Aylesmore[19] and from 1827 to 1843 was the churchwarden. Mary Perkins, whose family farmed at Rylas (Rhyle House) by the late 1770s,[20] served as the overseer several times, the first in 1827.[21] A later farmer at Rylas, John Cowmeadow (d. 1863),[22] is commemorated at the church in the glass of the chancel east window.

In the mid 19th century the households of most of the five main farmers, headed by John Butler at Pauntley Court, included domestic servants and some also included farm servants. Elsewhere in 1851, out of a population of 210, there were 27 agricultural labourers, 16 of them on Pool hill where a small community of labourers, craftsmen, and tradesmen, most of them tenants, occupied some 24 small cottages.[23] In the whole parish the number of households receiving regular support through the poor law, about five in the mid 1780s, had doubled by the end of the century and was about 15 in the 1820s and early 1830s.[24] In 1845 ten of the poorest men were exempted from all parish rates on account of poverty.[25]

In the later 19th century a few members of the gentry and the professional and officer classes as well as new farming families moved into Pauntley.[26] The White House, which had been occupied by the parish priest in the later 1830s,[27] was let as a private residence,[28] occupants briefly including Charles Griffin[29] (d. 1879), a former deputy chief constable

---

1 GA, P 246/IN 1/1.
2 Smith, *Men and Armour*, 66. For Hooke, above, Oxenhall, manor (estates in detached part of Pauntley: Crooke's Farm).
3 TNA, E 179/247/14, rot. 36.
4 Ibid. PROB 11/320, f. 191v.; Atkyns, *Glos.* 601.
5 See TNA, PROB 11/339, ff. 288–291v.
6 GA, D 2700/QA 4/6.
7 Ibid. D 1618, Dymock, Pauntley, and Redmarley deeds 1663–1812.
8 TNA, PROB 11/506, ff. 312v.–313v.; Badminton Muniments FmN 3/3/19.
9 *Notes on Dioc. of Glouc. by Chancellor Parsons*, 183; Atkyns, *Glos.* 601; TNA, PROB 11/595, f. 4.
10 *Remarks and Collections of Thomas Hearne* IX, ed. H.E. Salter (Oxford Hist Soc. 65, 1914), p. 236; J. Fendley, 'The Pastons of Horton and the Horton Court Library', *Recusant Hist.* 22 (1995), 508.
11 GA, P 246/IN 1/1, 3; see the Somerset fam. pedigree in Badminton Muniments FmL 4/5/5.
12 GA, D 2700/NQ 2/2.
13 Verey and Brooks, *Glos.* II, 633.

14 Bigland, *Glos.* II, 315–16. Several headstones have been preserved laid in a row on the S. side of the churchyard.
15 Above, manor (manor); GA, D 4647/8/3; Q/REl 1, Botloe hundred, Pauntley 1817, 1821.
16 Above, manor (manor); *Burke's Landed Gentry* (1937), II, 1912.
17 Below (education).
18 TNA, PROB 11/1776, ff. 170v.–172v.; GA, D 2356.
19 TNA, HO 107/350/12.
20 GA, P 246/CW 2/1; GDR, T 1/140.
21 GA, P 246/OV 2/2.
22 Ibid. IN 1/7; TNA, HO 107/350/12; RG 9/1760
23 TNA, HO 107/1960; for ownership of the Pool Hill cottages, see GDR, T 1/140.
24 GA, P 246/OV 2/1–2.
25 Ibid. VE 2/1.
26 TNA, HO 107/1960; RG 9/1760; RG 10/2607; GA, G/NE 160/8/1.
27 GDR, T 1/140.
28 TNA, HO 107/1960; RG 9/1760; RG 10/2607.
29 GA, G/NE 160/8/1.

for the county.[1] In the later 1880s it became the residence of W.P. Thackwell (d. 1922), the younger son of a landowner in Dymock,[2] and with Pauntley Court, the farmhouse of Henry Butler in 1901, remained among the chief houses in Pauntley in the early 20th century.[3] Pauntley Court, which from 1933 was a transient home for young men being trained on the land for regular work,[4] was a hostel for refugees during the Second World War[5] and reverted to domestic use afterwards.

CHARITIES FOR THE POOR

Charles Griffin by will proved 1879 left £300 to fund weekly payments of 1s. to six elderly people from Pauntley, Pool Hill, and Brand Green for six months over the winter and 10s. to each of them for a Christmas dinner.[6] From 1886, when the individual Christmas bonus was reduced from 5s. to 3s., the charity distributed £8 2s. a year in cash[7] and in 1942 and following years the six recipients shared £6 18s. given as a single Christmas gift.[8] The charity helped fewer people in the early 1970s[9] and was restricted to Pauntley parish by a Scheme of 1975. It lapsed in 2006.[10]

Pauntley's celebrations to mark the Golden Jubilee of 1887 included the gift to cottagers of 41 blankets paid for by collections.[11] From 1903, if not earlier, a fund raised by church collections met altar expenses and assisted the sick and needy. Managed by the vicar, it mostly helped widows and it continued in 1918.[12] A similar fund provided Christmas payments, mostly of 3s. 6d., to 11 people in 1935 and, having increased individual payments to 5s., had 8 beneficiaries in 1945 and 6 in 1952.[13]

EDUCATION

In 1798 William Holland, the miller at Payford, ran a school.[14] In 1817 the parish provided clothing and books for 8 poor children from Pauntley attending a school taught by Thomas Davies, the perpetual curate, probably at the house he occupied in Newent.[15] A church Sunday school was established in Pauntley in 1824 and Wesleyan Methodists also ran a Sunday school there in 1833.[16] In 1838 Osman Ricardo opened a day school at Payford. It taught boys and girls separately and its teaching staff included the master's wife and an assistant in 1851.[17] In 1868, when with Ricardo's continued support it taught 60–70 boys from a wide area, girls attended schools in Newent and Upleadon.[18] Two women teachers lived on Pool hill in 1861[19]

In 1869 a room was built at the top of Pool hill for a National school to serve both Pauntley and the adjoining part of Newent.[20] The school, on land donated by J.H. Frowde of Walden Court,[21] opened in 1870 under the management of T.P. Little, the vicar of Pauntley, and was supported mainly by voluntary contributions and pence.[22] It had an average attendance of 55 in 1885[23] and of 53 in 1904.[24] The building was altered, possibly in 1895, to accommodate a room for the infants.[25] The school was later known as Pauntley C. of E. school and after the First World War the average attendance fell to 40 or less.[26] The older children went to school in Newent from 1950[27] and Pauntley school, where attendance fell to 16 in the mid 1970s,[28] had 53 children on its roll in 2005.[29]

During the Second World War there was a school at Payford mill for French and Belgian refugee children living at Pauntley Court.[30]

SOCIAL LIFE

In the early 19th century farm labourers in Pauntley maintained the custom of assembling in a wheat field on the eve of Twelfth Night to light twelve fires in a row at the ends of twelve lands and to toast the harvest and their masters in cider around the largest fire. On returning home they feasted on caraway cakes, soaked in cider, claimed as their reward for sowing the corn.[31] In the mid 19th century people from Newent, Ledbury, and elsewhere congregated at a spring (Pauntley Spa) by the river Leadon

---

1 Ibid. reg. of wills 1879, ff. 167–168v.
2 *Kelly's Dir. Glos.* (1885), 547; (1889), 864; *Burke's Landed Gentry* (1898), II, 1452; *The Times*, 12 Oct. 1922.
3 TNA, RG 13/2421.
4 *Glos. Countryside* Jan. 1937, 197–8; see above, econ. hist. (agric.: the 19th and 20th cents.).
5 GA, DA 30/100/15, p. 278.
6 GA, reg. of wills 1879, ff. 167–168v.
7 Ibid. P 246/VE 2/1.
8 Ibid. CW 2/2.
9 Ibid. D 3469/5/120.
10 http://www.charity-commission.gov.uk/registeredcharities (accessed 31 May 2007: no 201478).
11 Ibid. P 246/VE 2/1.
12 Ibid. CW 2/5; see ibid. VE 2/1; CW 2/2.
13 Ibid. CW 2/4.
14 *Glouc. J.* 14 May 1798; for Holland at Payford, see GA, D 2957/212/161.
15 GA, P 246/CW 2/1; *Educ. of Poor Digest*, 306, 315. For Davies, above, Oxenhall, religious hist.
16 *Educ. Enquiry Abstract*, 324.
17 TNA, ED 7/35/254; HO 107/350/12; HO 107/1960.
18 *1st Rep. Com. Employment in Agric.* app. II, p.133.
19 TNA, RG 9/1760.
20 GA, P 246/SC 1; *Kelly's Dir. Glos.* (1870), 617.
21 GDR, A 17/10/121. For Frowde, see *Glouc. J.* 2 Sept. 1899.
22 TNA, ED 7/35/254.
23 *Kelly's Dir. Glos.* (1885), 547.
24 *Public Elem. Schs. 1906*, 188.   25 GA, P 246/SC 1.
26 *List 21*, 1922 (Board of Education), 106; 1932, 117; 1938, 129.
27 GA, P 246/SC 2.
28 Ibid. S 246/1.
29 *Schools and Establishments Dir. 2005–6* (co. educ. dept), 36.
30 R. and P. Palmer, *Secret River: an exploration of the Leadon Valley* (2004), 44–5.
31 Rudge, *Hist. of Glos.* II, 42–3.

upstream of Payford to warm and drink its waters at first light on May Day and run about a field in a figure of eight to obtain the desired, laxative result. The custom was waning by 1893 after a farmer's objections to his hedges being stripped for firewood.[1] In 1933 fishing rights in a stretch of the Leadon belonged under lease to a Gloucester angling club.[2]

Pauntley appears never to have had a licensed public house. There was a church house in 1610.[3] The parish vestry met in the later 18th century in the church and sometimes in the mid 19th century at the incumbent's house. The schoolroom built in 1869 became the usual place for meetings.[4] In 1950 a village hall for Pauntley was opened at Brand Green. Erected as a memorial to the dead of the Second World War, the wooden hut was the gift of R. Smith of Pauntley Place and was intended as a temporary structure.[5] Among the groups using it was a local branch of the Women's Institute formed in 1950.[6] The hall, which has been modified, remained in use in 2007.

RELIGIOUS HISTORY

EARLY HISTORY AND STATUS OF THE PARISH CHURCH

Pauntley church was a chapel confirmed among the possessions of Cormeilles abbey (Eure) in 1181[7] and appropriated by the abbey together with the church at Newent under an episcopal licence of 1195.[8] It was served in the late Middle Ages by a resident, stipendiary chaplain[9] and in 1522 two chaplains had salaries of £5 6s. 8d. each.[10] Although Pauntley continued as a chapelry of Newent in the mid 16th century,[11] it then was sometimes described as a separate vicarage[12] and later was served by its own curate with a stipend paid by the owner of the Pauntley tithes.[13] The stipend was £7 in 1603[14] and was set at £13 6s. 8d. by 1650.[15]

After endowment in the mid 18th century[16] the living became a perpetual curacy[17] and from 1868 was officially styled a vicarage.[18] It was united with Oxenhall in 1918[19] and with Upleadon in 1955.[20] Pauntley and Upleadon were united with Oxenhall and Redmarley D'Abitot in 1977[21] and other parishes were added to the united benefice later.[22]

PATRONAGE AND ENDOWMENT

In the early 13th century the abbot of Cormeilles defended his house's rights in Pauntley church against Walter de Solers, who, having asserted that it had belonged to his grandfather William de Solers,[23] quitclaimed any right in the church, its property, and advowson to the abbey.[24] The patronage passed with the church to Fotheringhay college[25] and from the mid 16th century with the Pauntley tithes in lay hands.[26] With Edward Somerset and his successors in the 18th century being Roman Catholics, the bishop appointed clergy to serve the church[27] and the living remained in his gift after he collated to the perpetual curacy in 1782.[28]

Apart from fees, the curate's income in the 17th century and in much of the 18th was the stipend paid by the impropriator.[29] Occasional grants from Queen Anne's Bounty to augment the curate's income began in 1767[30] and were used to buy land in Newent and Dymock.[31] In 1844 the Ecclesiastical Commissioners granted the living £14 a

---

1 A.R. Winnington-Ingram, 'On the Origins of Names of Places', *Proc. CNFC* 11.1 (1893), 35; C. Duncan and L. Richardson, 'Mineral Springs of Newent and Pauntley', ibid. 21.2 (1922), 157.
2 GA, D 2299/5292.
3 GDR wills 1610/44.
4 GA, P 246/OV 2/1–2; VE 2/1.
5 Ibid. D 3168/4/7/61; DA 30/100/17, p. 97.
6 Ibid. D 2933/20.
7 BL, Add. MS 18461, ff. 1–2v.; see *VCH Glos.* II, 105.
8 *Eng. Episc. Acta VII*, pp. 136–8.
9 Herefs. RO, E 12/G/5.
10 *Military Surv. of Glos. 1522*, 62.
11 *Tax. Eccl.* 161; *Nonarum Inquisitiones*, 415; *Reg. Foxe*, 367, 371; Bodleian, Rawl. C. 790, f. 28.
12 *L&P Hen. VIII*, XXI (2), p. 381; *Cal. Pat.* 1547–9, 108–9; 1555–7, 94; 1566–9, p. 42.
13 For ownership of the tithes, above, manor (other estates: Pauntley rectory).
14 *Eccl. Misc.* 101.
15 C.R. Elrington, 'The Survey of Church Livings in Gloucestershire, 1650', *Trans. BGAS* 83 (1964), 98; GDR, V 5/230T 1; GA, D 1815/Box 15/1.
16 Below (patronage and endowment).
17 Hockaday Abs. cccx, 1763; *London Gazette*, 3 May 1844, pp. 1511.
18 District Church Tithes Act Amendment Act, 31 & 32 Vic. c. 117; see GA, P 246/IN 1/6.
19 *London Gazette*, 19 Nov. 1918, pp. 13,598–9.
20 B. & G. Par. Rec. 218; *Glouc. Dioc. Year Book* (1955–6), 30–1.
21 GDR, V 15/1/110; see *Glouc. Dioc. Year Book* (1978), 22.
22 *Dioc. of Glouc. Dir.* (1989), 52; (2001–2), 24–5.
23 *Cur. Reg.* IV, 233–4.
24 BL, Add. MS 15668, ff. 3v., 72.
25 *L&P Hen. VIII*, XXI(2), p. 381.
26 *Cal. Pat.* 1547–8, 108–9; 1555–7, 94; 1566–9, 42; see E. Conder, 'Pauntley Manor and the Pauntley Custom', *Trans. BGAS* 40 (1917), 130; Bodleian, Top. Glouc. c. 3, f. 196v.
27 Bp. Benson's Surv. of Dioc. of Glouc. 1735–50, 15 and n.; Rudder, *Glos.* 598; see TNA, IR 18/2830. For the Wakeman family's Catholicism: *VCH Glos.* VIII, 261.
28 Hockaday Abs. cccx; *Kelly's Dir. Glos.* (1863 and later edns); GDR vol. 384, f. 156; D 17/7/6.
29 GDR, V 5/230T 1, 4–5.
30 Hodgson, *Queen Anne's Bounty* (1826), 324.
31 GDR, V 5/230T 6–7; GA, P 246/IN 3/1.

68. *Pauntley church: the south doorway in 1996*

year[1] but its value in 1856 was only £64, raised by 1864 to £80.[2] No house or building belonged to the perpetual curacy.[3]

RELIGIOUS LIFE

The Middle Ages

The ornate decoration of the church's chancel arch and south doorway, which have capitals and a range of ornament characteristic of the 'Dymock school',[4] indicates the high quality of Pauntley's early 12th-century chapel.[5] Enlargement resulted in a three-bayed nave with a 13th-century north doorway, which is sheltered by a timber-framed porch of the 14th century and retains medieval ironwork on the door. The nave windows were enlarged and given Decorated tracery in the 14th century. A late medieval west tower, of two stages, contains two 14th-century bells in a frame capable of supporting four bells.[6]

In the later Middle Ages the Whittingtons were regular benefactors of the church, which was dedicated to St John the Evangelist by 1423.[7] A chapel of St George, described in 1440 as new, was built on the south side of the chancel to house a chantry founded by Guy Whittington and to serve as his family's mortuary chapel.[8] It has a west doorway and contains a pillar piscina. The chancel, which may have been enlarged in the 13th century, was remodelled in the same style as the chapel and given a wagon roof and an aumbry with a piscina. Windows in the chancel and the tower contain fragments of glass displaying the Whittingtons' arms.[9] Thomas Whittington (d. 1491) of Over Lypiatt endowed a service of Our Lady in the church and in the later 1520s Thomas Whittington maintained a right to appoint its priest on the authority of its feoffees.[10]

Of the chaplains that served the church Thomas, who possibly became the bishop's constable at Bishop's Castle (Salop.), was assaulted midway between Pauntley and Hereford in 1346.[11] In 1397, when several parishioners absented themselves from church, the chaplain was non-resident, the church's manse having fallen down through the rector's neglect, the baptistery or font was left unlocked, and the rector was failing to honour an obligation to supply two processional candles.[12] The farmer of the rectory paid for repairs to the chaplain's house in 1409[13] and received parishioners' offerings for the purchase of wax in the late 15th century.[14]

From the Reformation to the Restoration

In 1544 Pauntley had as curate Thomas Twinning, formerly a monk at Tewkesbury,[15] who was unlearned, being unable in 1551 to recite the Ten Commandments.[16] There were 90 communicants in 1548 when, at its dissolution, the chantry of St George was served by Hugh Dowsing, vicar of Tirley.[17]

In 1576 the curate was unlicensed,[18] there had been no sermons for a long time, and the young were not taught the catechism.[19] William Whitcott, curate in 1593, was classified as a sufficient scholar but no preacher[20] and was said in 1609 to be

---

1 *London Gazette*, 3 May 1844, p. 1511.
2 GDR vols. 384, f. 156; 385, p. 163.
3 *Bp. Benson's Surv. of Dioc. of Glouc. 1735–50*, 15; GDR, V 5/230T 6.
4 See above, Newent and May Hill (settlement, society, and buildings).
5 Fig. 68.
6 *Glos. Ch. Bells*, 495–8.
7 Hockaday Abs. cccx, 1424, 1440, 1452, 1525.
8 Ibid. 1440; TNA, C 1/917/31.
9 F. Were, 'A Few Notes on the Heraldry Seen June 2nd 1908', *Trans. BGAS* 31 (1908), 286–7.
10 TNA, C 1/582/41; *VCH Glos*. XI, 111.
11 *Reg. Trillek*, 17, 91–2.
12 A.T. Bannister, 'Visitation Returns of Diocese of Hereford in 1397', *EHR* 44 (1929), 452–3.
13 Herefs. RO, E 12/G/5.
14 Ibid. 2.
15 Hockaday Abs. xxx, 1544 stipendiaries, f. 7; G. Baskerville, 'The Dispossessed Religious of Gloucestershire', *Trans. BGAS* 49 (1927), 85.
16 J. Gairdner, 'Bishop Hooper's Visitation of Gloucester', *EHR* 19 (1904), 120.
17 Hockaday Abs. cccx; Baskerville, 'Dispossessed Religious', 121; *VCH Glos*. VIII, 103.
18 GDR vol. 39, p. 117.
19 Ibid. vol. 40, f. 255v.
20 Hockaday Abs. lii, state of clergy 1593, f. 7, where he is called John Whitcott.

unlearned in scripture and Latin and to have conducted marriages irregularly.[1] He resigned in 1613 on account of age. Local gentry from both parts of parish attended the church,[2] members of the Pauncefoot family taking their place in the south chapel.[3] In 1603, when the number of communicants was put at 80, one man was recusant[4] and in 1625, when the parish clerk read prayers in the church although suspended from his duties, six people failed to take communion at Easter and another man did not come to church.[5] In 1610 the miller at Payford had a copy of *The Imitation of Christ* as well as a Bible.[6] In the mid 1640s John Skinner, who later conducted a nonconformist ministry elsewhere, was curate[7] and in 1650 his successor was an accepted preaching minister.[8]

The Parish Church and Roman Catholicism after the Restoration

Following the Restoration the church was almost invariably served by a non-resident curate and often with Oxenhall.[9] It acquired a new pulpit and a third bell in 1676[10] and its wooden chest is dated 1679. Among its plate at that time was a silver chalice,[11] perhaps that dated 1651 that was later returned to the church from a nearby farmhouse.[12]

Although only conformists were recorded in Pauntley in 1676[13] Roman Catholics gathered occasionally in an upper room of Pauntley Court,[14] the manor having been in Catholic ownership since Henry Somerset's accession in 1628.[15] According to a later writer popular sentiment during the Popish Plot of 1678 led to the abandonment of plans to enlarge the house.[16] Although some members of the Somerset family lived on the Continent,[17] there was a Catholic presence in Pauntley in the early 18th century[18] and a building at Pauntley Court was known as the chapel house.[19] In the mid 1720s a priest was a member of the Pastons' household at Pauntley Court[20] and their steward Richard Redfearn (d. 1727), a co-religionist, was buried in the chancel of the church.[21]

The Established Church and Nonconformity from the Mid Eighteenth Century

In the mid 18th century the parish church had one Sunday service, held alternately in the morning and afternoon. From that time the curacy was usually combined with Upleadon as well as Oxenhall[22] and the three parishes were held together until 1823. Pauntley continued to be served with Upleadon until 1841.[23] In the mid 1780s a west gallery and a ceiling were inserted in the church and the Ten Commandments were drawn for display in it.[24] A new painting of the royal arms was acquired in 1817, the first of two years in which the parish employed a singing teacher for the church choir. The choristers were instructed in psalmody in 1830 and the choir received more instruction in the mid 1830s.[25] In 1825, when the perpetual curate was resident, the church still had a weekly service and a communion service every other month attracted between 10 and 14 communicants. A church Sunday school started in 1824 taught up to 60 children, some of them from Upleadon.[26]

In 1814 a nonconformist minister from Newent registered a field on the hillside north-west of Pool Hill as a place of worship[27] and the next year a new Wesleyan Methodist chapel opened below it.[28] At that time John Stokes, whose Pauntley Court estate included the field, was refusing to contribute towards the repair of the parish church.[29] Although a preacher on the Ledbury circuit had registered several houses in the Pauntley area by 1820,[30] the chapel below Pool Hill was the only nonconformist meeting place in the parish in 1825.[31] A Sunday school run by the Wesleyans taught 38 children in 1833.[32]

---

1 GDR, B 4/1/2039.
2 GA, P 246/IN 1/1.
3 *Notes on Dioc. of Glouc. by Chancellor Parsons*, 183.
4 *Eccl. Misc.* 101.
5 GDR vol. 158, ff. 15–16, f. 28.
6 GDR wills 1610/44.
7 *Calamy Revised*, 444; see *VCH Glos.* V, 228.
8 Elrington, 'Surv. of Church Livings', 98.
9 See above, Oxenhall, religious hist. (religious life).
10 Bigland, *Glos.* II, 314; *Glos. Ch. Bells*, 495.
11 GDR, V 5/230T 2.
12 J. Douglas, *Historical Notes on Newent with Oxenhall and Pauntley* (1912), 19; see also inventory 1906, in GA, P 246/CW 2/2.
13 *Compton Census*, 544.
14 M.B. Rowlands (ed.), *English Catholics of Parish and Town 1558–1778* (Catholic Rec. Soc. 1999), 96.
15 *Complete Peerage* XII (2), 857; fam. pedigree in Badminton Muniments FmL 4/5/5; *Bp. Benson's Surv. of Dioc. of Glouc. 1735–50*, 15 n.
16 GA, D 412/Z 3, Nourse MS, p. 14.
17 Above, social hist. (social structure).
18 GA, Q/SO 4.
19 Ibid. Q/RNc 1, p. 132.
20 *Remarks and Collections of Thomas Hearne* IX, ed. H.E. Salter (Oxford Hist Soc. 65, 1914), p. 236.
21 Bigland, *Glos.* II, 315–16; GA, Q/SO 4, list of papists s.v. Horton.
22 *Bp. Benson's Surv. of Dioc. of Glouc. 1735–50*, 15, 19.
23 Hockaday Abs. cccviii, cccx, ccclxxxiv.
24 GA, P 246/OV 2/1. According to Bigland, *Glos.* II, 314, the gallery was built in 1783.
25 GA, P 246/CW 2/1. In 2004 the royal arms were displayed high in the base of the ch. tower.
26 GDR vol. 383, nos cxxviii, cxxxvi; *Educ. Enquiry Abstract*, 324.
27 Hockaday Abs. cccx; GDR, T 1/140 (nos 252, 254).
28 *Glouc. J.* 17 Apr. 1815; TNA, HO 129/335/1/14/16.
29 GDR, B 4/3/978; for Stokes, above, manor (manor).
30 Hockaday Abs. cccx, 1819; ccxciii, 1820.
31 GDR vol. 383, nos cxxviii.
32 *Educ. Enquiry Abstract*, 324.

From 1841 the parish church was served again with Oxenhall. T.M. Sherwood, the incumbent,[1] had the gallery removed in 1845 but his offer to fund two thirds of the cost of restoring the church was narrowly rejected by the vestry. In 1847 and 1848 the south wall and east gable were rebuilt, the south doorway being reset, and the nave was reroofed in a less costly plan from a London architect, possibly Richard Armstrong.[2] R. Hodges donated a new font[3] and in 1850 the Incorporated Church Building Society made a grant for reseating the whole church.[4] Restoration of the south chapel was inhibited by uncertainty over its ownership.[5] On Easter Sunday 1851 the church with 134 sittings, two thirds of them free, had a congregation of 65 at an afternoon service. The Methodist chapel below Pool hill, with seats for 204, held three services on that day and usually had smaller congregations.[6] In 1856 residents of Redmarley D'Abitot (Worcs., later Glos.) gave the church a chalice and paten in return for the accommodation afforded them while their church was being rebuilt.[7] Charles Griffin by will proved 1879 made a bequest for heating the parish church[8] and in 1907 an organ was acquired to replace the harmonium there.[9]

In the early 1870s the vicar of Pauntley held occasional evening services in the new schoolroom at Pool Hill[10] and in the mid 1880s, after the initiation of a Sunday church service near by at Walden Court in Newent,[11] regular Sunday evening services were held at the school.[12] In the late 19th century the Methodist chapel below Pool hill[13] had occasional weekday as well as Sunday services and in 1911 its Sunday congregation numbered eight.[14]

After the First World War

The parish church continued to be served from Oxenhall[15] and in the 1930s and 1940s, when donations paid the organist's salary, occasional services were held in the Pool Hill schoolroom.[16] Restoration of the church was renewed in the 1950s and the corporation of the City of London made several gifts in memory of Richard Whittington, including an alms dish in 1959, when the lord mayor of London and representatives of the Mercers' Company attended celebrations marking the supposed 600th anniversary of Whittington's birth.[17] Both the corporation and the company contributed in 1968 to funds for restoration of the fabric and windows, and new fittings in 1989 included a stall and carpets given by the corporation to mark the 800th anniversary of the office of mayor of London.[18] Services, provided from Upleadon from 1955,[19] were arranged from Redmarley D'Abitot from 1977[20] and a small congregation attended a regular Sunday service in 2004.

The Methodist chapel below Pool hill fell into disuse and although it was re-opened in 1950 it closed finally four or five years later. The last burial took place there in 1965 and the chapel, having become derelict, was sold in 1977 and converted as a house.[21]

PRESTON

PRESTON, situated 22 km north-west of Gloucester and 5 km south-west of the Herefordshire town of Ledbury, covered 897 a.[22] and was one of Gloucestershire's smallest rural parishes. It lay at the end of a wide salient of the county jutting north-westwards into Herefordshire. Its ownership by Gloucester abbey, from which it took its name, meaning the priests' settlement, by the late Anglo-Saxon period,[23] accounted for its inclusion in the hundred of Longbridge (later part of Dudstone and

---

1 Hockaday Abs. cccx, cccviii; GA, D 1815/Box 15/1.
2 GA, P 246/VE 2/1; CW 2/1; Verey and Brooks, *Glos.* II, 633.
3 GA, P 246/VE 2/1. The Hodges fam. owned Upleadon Court: GA, D 2094/31/4.
4 Incorporated Church Bldg. Society: http://www.churchplansonline.org (accessed 25 Sept. 2003).
5 GA, P 246/VE 2/1.
6 TNA, HO 129/335/1/14/15–16.
7 *Glos. Ch. Plate*, 165. See GA, P 246/IN 1/6, entries in 1855 and 1856.
8 GA, reg. of wills 1879, ff. 167–168v. The Griffin bequest was spent by 1999: http://www.charity-commission.gov.uk/registeredcharities (accessed 31 May 2007: no 247766).
9 GA, P 246/CW 2/2.
10 TNA, ED 7/35/254.
11 *Kelly's Dir. Glos.* (1879), 722; (1885), 547. See E. Warde, *They Didn't Walk Far: a History of Pool Hill* (priv. printed, 2000), 130–1.
12 GA, P 246/CW 2/2.
13 Marked incorrectly on OS Map 6", Glos. XVII.NW (1884 edn) as a Baptist chapel.
14 Warde, *They Didn't Walk Far*, 117.
15 *Kelly's Dir. Glos.* (1885), 547; (1897), 265; (1906), 271; (1939), 289.
16 GA, P 246/CW 2/2.
17 *Pauntley Church Guide* (n.d. [1970s]): copy in GDR, V 15/1/100.
18 Information from notices in ch.
19 *Glouc. Dioc. Year Book* (1955–6), 9, 30–1: (1976), 36–7, 82.
20 Ibid. (1978), 22, 42; *Dioc. of Glouc. Dir.* (1989), 4, 52; (2001–2), 24–5, 122.
21 Warde, *They Didn't Walk Far*, 117–20.
22 *OS Area Book* (1884). This account was written in 2002 and 2003.
23 *Domesday Book* (Rec. Com.), I, 165v.; *PN Glos.* III, 184.

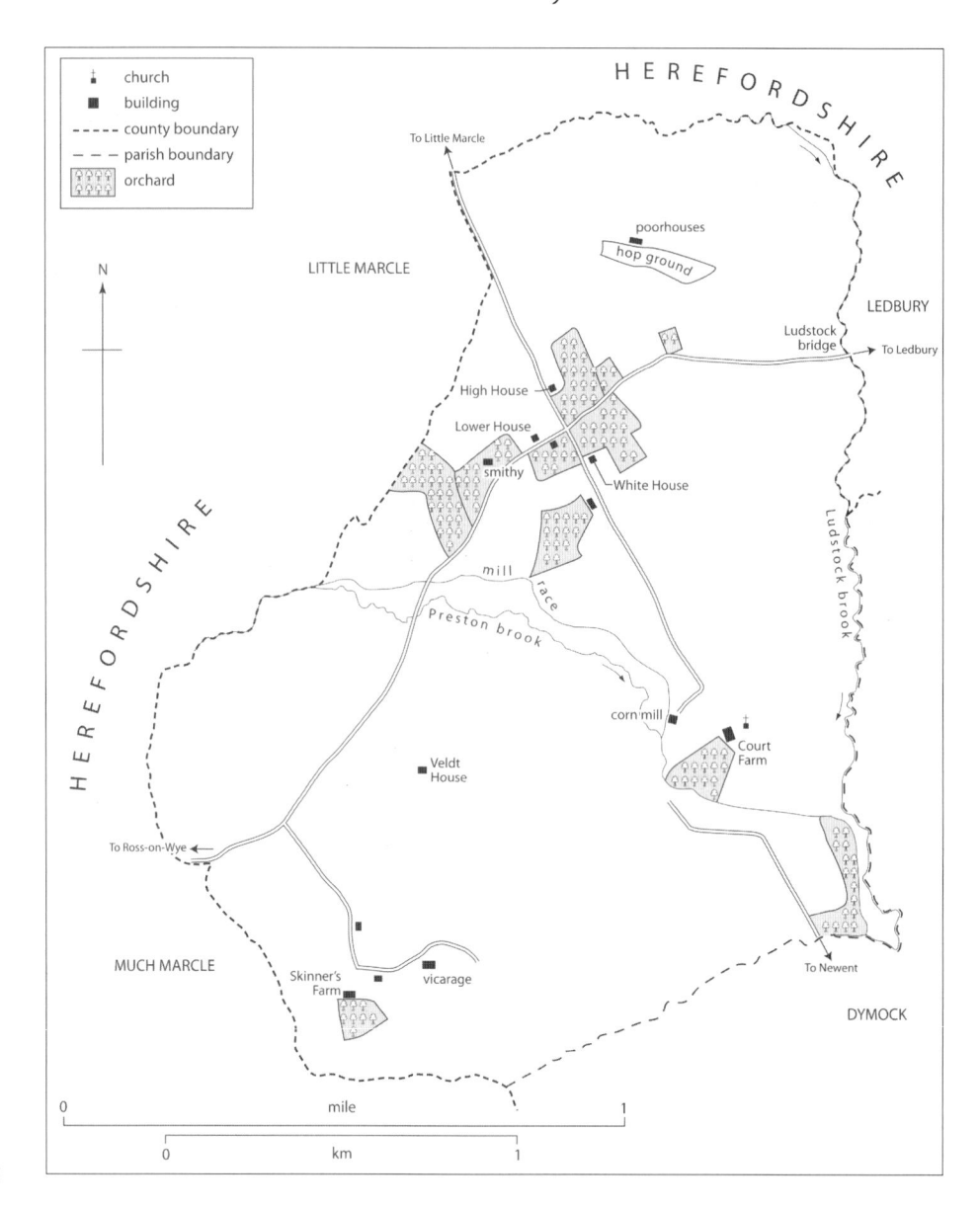

Map 14. Preston 1834

King's Barton).¹ As a civil parish Preston was absorbed in 1935 by Dymock, its much larger neighbour to the south-east.²

LANDSCAPE

Save on the west Preston is bounded by streams,³ that on the east being the Ludstock brook.⁴ In the north the very end of the western boundary is a straight road leading into Herefordshire on the line of a Roman route by way of Dymock.⁵ The land is generally flat lying at between 40 and 50 m and rising gently in the north and the south-west to over 60 m. The highest point, at 68 m, is in the south-west where the fields on much of the hill were known as the Castle Grounds in the late 18th century.⁶ Most of the parish drains towards the Preston brook flowing across the centre of the parish from north-west to south-east. In the east the Ludstock brook, its principal tributary, was diverted a few hundred metres short of their confluence long before 1790.⁷

---

1 *Domesday Book*, I, 165v.; Taylor, *Domesday Glos.* 31.
2 *Census*, 1931 (pt. ii).
3 OS Maps 6", Glos. IX.NE and SE; X.NW and SW (1883 edn).
4 Worcs. RO, 705:99 (BA 5540), Dymock ct. book 1784–1822, cts. 9 and 10 June 1790.
5 SMR Glos. no 7677; I.D. Margary, *Roman Roads in Britain*, II (1957), 60; see E. Gethyn-Jones, 'Roman Dymock. A Personal Record', *Trans. BGAS* 109 (1991), 97–8.
6 GDR, G 2/3/15932; G 3/42.
7 See perambulation of Dymock manor in Worcs. RO, 705:99 (BA 5540), Dymock ct. book 1784–1822, cts. 9 and 10 June 1790.

The land is on the Old Red Sandstone with alluvial deposits on the banks of the Preston brook and its tributaries.[1] The soil is mostly a deep heavy loam suited to arable farming and the land bordering the banks of the Preston brook and its tributaries is made up of meadows and pastures.[2] The parish contains no woodland[3] but the manor court dealt with the unauthorized felling of oak and other trees in the late 13th century[4] and pannage was among payments owed by medieval tenants.[5] The extent and number of Preston's medieval open fields are not known. Their inclosure was a long process partly determined by the local practice, adopted by the 16th century, of planting orchards in arable land.[6] Most of Preston's orchards in the mid 17th century were next to farmhouses. Inclosure was completed essentially in the later 18th century and scattered orcharding, although reduced in area in the later 20th century, has remained a feature of the landscape.[7] In the late 20th century a private air strip was created in a field west of the main road to Dymock in the south of Preston.[8]

ROADS AND BRIDGES

The main road between Ledbury and Ross-on-Wye (Herefs.) enters the north of Preston from the east at Ludstock bridge and runs westwards to crossroads at Preston Cross and from there continues south-westwards to cross the Preston brook. The road, which probably follows the course of a highway mentioned in the early 16th century,[9] was a turnpike road from 1722 to 1871.[10] Ludstock bridge, first mentioned in 1500,[11] was in considerable disrepair in 1824.[12] Regarded as a county bridge, it was widened in 1839[13] and it was rebuilt, in brick, in 1897.[14] The junction at Preston Cross was made a roundabout in 1996 and just beyond it the Ross road was diverted slightly to the south.[15]

In the early 19th century the turnpike road was the only good road in the parish, the other routes being almost impassable in the winter.[16] From Preston Cross a road or lane ran southwards to the parish church and Preston Court and another ran northwards into Little Marcle (Herefs.),[17] both roads observing the line of the Roman route mentioned above. The church and Court stood together at the centre of a network of minor lanes or tracks,[18] some of which were presumably carried over ditches by bridges mentioned in the early 16th century.[19] About 1835 the lane leading northwards to Preston Cross and Little Marcle was incorporated in a new road constructed as part of a route from Newent to Leominster (Herefs.) by way of Dymock.[20] The new road, entering Preston from the south,[21] was a turnpike until 1871.[22]

POPULATION

In 1086 there were at least twelve tenant households in Preston[23] and in 1327 eight persons were assessed for tax there.[24] In 1539 a muster named 11 men in Preston[25] and in 1563 the parish contained 13 households.[26] The number of communicants was given as c.60 in 1551[27] and 48 in 1603.[28] Preston's population was estimated at 60 c.1710[29] and at 40 c.1775.[30] The latter figure may have been an underestimate, for in 1801 the recorded population was 87. In the 19th and 20th centuries the population was usually smaller and in 1881 it was as low as 61. In 1931, at the last national census to treat Preston separately, it was 77.[31] Preston's population fell even lower in the mid 20th century for in 1953 it was said to be 54[32] and in 1972 it was 53.[33]

---

1 Geol. Surv. Map 1:50,000, solid and drift, sheet 216 (1988 edn).
2 GDR, G 3/24, ff. 1–2.
3 See ibid. G 3/19, pp. 8–14; TNA, IR 29/13/159; Acreage Returns, 1905.
4 GA, D 936A/M 1, rot. 5.
5 Below, econ. hist.
6 Rudder, *Glos.* 408–9, 607; Rudge, *Hist. of Glos.* II, 188.
7 Below, econ. hist.
8 OS Map 1:25,000, SO 63/73 (1982 edn); Dymock par. council, par. meeting min. book, pp. 202, 222.
9 GDR vol. 1A, pp. 46, 47.
10 Ledbury Roads Act, 7 Geo. I, c. 23; Annual Turnpike Acts. Continuance Act, 1871, 34 & 35 Vic. c. 115.
11 GDR vol. 1A, p. 4.
12 GA, Q/SO 15, f. 244.
13 Ibid. 17, ff. 148v., 152v.
14 Datestone on bridge.
15 Dymock par. council, par. meeting min. book, p. 222.
16 GDR, G 3/24, f. 1.
17 Ibid. G 3/42.
18 Bryant, *Map of Glos.* (1824); OS Map 1", sheet 43 (1831 edn).
19 GDR vol. 1A, pp. 46, 57.
20 Ledbury Roads Act, 3 Wm. IV, c. 58 (Local and Personal); GA, Q/RUm 129.
21 GDR, G 3/43; see Bryant, *Map of Glos.* (1824); OS Map 1", sheet 43 (1831 edn).
22 Annual Turnpike Acts Continuance Act, 1871, 34 & 35 Vic. c. 115.
23 *Domesday Book* (Rec. Com.), I, 165v.
24 *Glos. Subsidy Roll, 1327*, 33.
25 TNA, E 101/59/9.
26 Bodleian, Rawl. C. 790, f. 28.
27 J. Gairdner, 'Bishop Hooper's Visitation of Gloucester', *EHR* 19 (1904), 119.
28 *Eccl. Misc.* 101.
29 Atkyns, *Glos.* 608.
30 Rudder, *Glos.* 608.
31 *Census*, 1801–1931.
32 Grace Ruck, *Preston: A Guide and History* (1953: copy in GA, PA 256), 5.
33 Theodora C. Reeves, 'History of Little Marcle and of Preston Parish' (1972: typescript in Glos. Colln. 36709), 2.

SETTLEMENT

Preston has few houses. Several form a small hamlet around the crossroads at Preston Cross and the rest are scattered through the parish. Personal surnames in the late 13th and early 14th century, including 'on the hill', indicate the antiquity of some of the inhabited sites.[1] In the mid 17th century there were apparently just over 20 houses in the parish[2] but by the early 19th century several farmsteads had been long abandoned[3] and in 1801 the parish contained 16 houses.[4] Despite further demolitions, new building in the later 19th century increased the number of houses to 18 in 1901.[5] There were 14 houses in 1953[6] and 23 dwellings in 2000.[7]

Preston's medieval church stands on the east side of the parish behind Preston Court, an imposing timber-framed house built on the site of the manor in the late 16th or early 17th century.[8] The cluster of buildings at Preston Cross was made up of farmsteads. White House Farm and High House, east of the Dymock and Leominster roads respectively, were named in 1779.[9] Outbuildings north of the Ross road mark the site of Lower House,[10] where the farmhouse was demolished in the mid 19th century.[11] In the early 19th century there were two other farmhouses at Preston Cross. One, once part of an estate called Hooper's, was by the lane to Preston Court and was occupied as two cottages. The other, formerly part of an estate called Roper's, was on the Ross road and was used as a blacksmith's house and workshop.[12] Across the fields north-east of Preston Cross were two relatively new cottages built by the parish.[13]

On the west side of the parish the Veldt House (formerly Felt or Velt House)[14] stands south of the Ross road on a site where parishioners surnamed 'at' or 'in the field' in the late 13th and early 14th century may have lived.[15] Once there were also several houses and cottages further south some distance off the Ross road. In the early 19th century they included a farmhouse and two small cottages and a barn near by, in Upper Castle Ground, marked the site of an abandoned farmstead.[16] The farmhouse, known in 1780 as Green House,[17] was later called Skinner's,[18] after the family having the farm in the 18th century.[19] One cottage, north of the farmhouse, had the name Old Wytch in the mid 19th century.[20] The farmhouse, its outbuildings, and the cottages were all demolished in the late 19th century, apart from a barn[21] that remained standing until the late 20th century.[22] The Parsonage, to the east, began as a small house or cottage that was enlarged in the 1830s when it served as the vicarage house.[23] In the late 20th century it was restored and a private drive running northwards to the Ross road was created.[24]

Preston Priory, on the Leominster road north-west of Preston Court, was built as the vicarage house in 1864.[25] At that time the parish was short of cottage accommodation, two of its eight cottages having been built by squatters.[26] At the end of the century four new pairs of estate cottages were built, one at Preston Cross on the Ledbury road, another in the west on the Ross road, and two in the south on the Dymock road, and the two cottages just south of Preston Cross were rebuilt, all in the same style.[27] A new house was built at Preston Cross in 1960 and the old smithy on the Ross road was pulled down a few years later to be replaced by an engineering workshop.[28] Apart from a pair of cottages lower down to the west few other entirely new houses have been built in Preston.

---

1 GA, D 936A/M 1, rot. 5; M 2, rot. 4; *Glos. Subsidy Roll, 1327*, 33; below, this section.
2 GDR, G 3/19, pp. 8–14.
3 Ibid. G 3/24, ff. 2, 6.
4 *Census*, 1801.
5 TNA, RG 13/2422.
6 Ruck, *Preston*, 5.
7 GA, Q/REr.
8 Below, manor.
9 GA, Q/REl 1, Dudstone & King's Barton hundred.
10 GDR, G 3/42; OS Map 6", Glos. IX.NE (1883 edn).
11 cf. TNA, HO 107/355; HO 107/1960.
12 GDR, G 3/24, f. 8; G 3/42.
13 Ibid. G 3/24, f. 19; below, local govt.
14 GDR, G 3/24, f. 7; OS Maps 6", Glos. IX.NE (1883, 1904 edns); 1:25,000, SO 63/73 (1982 edn).
15 GA, D 936A/M 1, rot. 5; M 2, rot. 4; *Glos. Subsidy Roll, 1327*, 33.
16 GDR, G 3/24, ff. 6, 12, 14; G 3/42.

17 GA, Q/REl 1, Dudstone & King's Barton hundred. On OS Map 1", sheet 43 (1831 edn) it was called Neverwood.
18 OS Map 6", Glos. IX.SE (1883 edn).
19 GA, Q/REl 1, Dudstone & King's Barton hundred 1779; GDR, G 2/3/16702.
20 TNA, HO 107/355; HO 107/1960.
21 OS Maps 6", Glos. IX.NE and SE (1883, 1904 edns).
22 Reeves, 'Little Marcle and Preston', 51, 63; OS Map 1:25,000, SO 63/73 (1982 edn).
23 GDR, G 3/42; below, religious hist.
24 Information from Mr David Teague, finance director of Velcourt, the Veldt House.
25 Datestone on porch; see GDR, F4/1; GA, D 2593/2/175, 410.
26 *1st Rep. Com. Employment in Agric.* app. II, p. 130.
27 OS Map 6", Glos. IX.NE (1883, 1904 edns); see GA, DA 30/100/6, p. 220.
28 Information from Mrs Gillian Thomas of White House Farm; GA, DA 30/100/29, p. 20; 100/32, p. 166.

BUILDINGS

Apart from Preston Court[1] three early farmhouses survive. In the early 19th century farm buildings on the estate were generally deemed to be in a poor or indifferent condition[2] and later all three farmhouses were improved and supplemented with extensive red brick outbuildings. Some of the new building presumably formed part of the programme providing new estate cottages at the end of the century.[3] High House, the oldest and most elaborate of the three farmhouses, incorporates a late 16th-century two-storeyed cross wing from an L or H plan. The frame has close studding and in the main rooms intersecting beams. The hall was replaced, probably soon after 1803,[4] by a tall three-storeyed block, one room deep with a shallow external stack and a lean-to dairy. White House Farm, a later 17th-century house on an L plan, has been subjected to a remodelling similar to that of Preston Court. One gable end was rebuilt in brick with segment-headed sashes and the main front was rendered in work, illustrated on a painting of 1843 in the house, that may have been finished by 1779 when the term White House was used.[5] The Veldt House was a smaller 17th-century dwelling of 2½ storeys with square-panel framing and a two-room plan with central stack and through passage. The house, occupied by a farm labourer in 1803,[6] was extended by two bays later in the 19th century and was much remodelled, using some old timbers, in the late 20th century when it was turned into offices.[7] The hipped roof at one end has been extended to link to what may have been the mill and granary mentioned in 1803.[8] The houses at Lower House and Skinner's, both demolished in the 19th century,[9] were recorded in 1803 as small dwellings, at least partly timber-framed and thatched and with three rooms on a floor.[10]

At White House Farm a substantial timber-framed barn contemporary with the house survives. Of three bays and three panels high, it has some woven wattle infill.[11] At High House timbers from a five-bayed barn[12] were re-used in a 19th-century barn, which is probably contemporary with five large animal shelters there. At the Veldt House a five-bayed barn[13] was replaced by a new courtyard of buildings, which were converted as six dwellings at the end of the 20th century.[14] A small timber-framed barn is among buildings surviving at the site of Lower House.

MANOR AND ESTATES

Although Preston's only manor remained an ecclesiastical possession until the mid 20th century, it was in lay hands from the later 16th to the mid 19th century by virtue of leases to a lord farmer. Copyhold estates made up a good part of the manor[15] but by the mid 18th century some had been combined and the lord farmer had taken others in hand.[16] Most of the rest came in hand later on the expiry of their terms[17] and the last surviving copyhold, White House farm owned by the Elton family of Much Marcle (Herefs.),[18] lapsed soon after 1803.[19] The manor estate was broken up by sales in the mid 20th century and there were two main landowners in Preston at the turn of the century.

PRESTON MANOR

Gloucester abbey evidently acquired the manor before the Norman Conquest. It formed an estate of two hides in 1086[20] and remained the abbey's property until the Dissolution.[21] In 1541 it was included in the endowment of the new bishopric of Gloucester.[22]

In 1583 the bishop granted the Crown a lease of the manor subject to an interest in it of the Powell family.[23] Thomas Powell had lived in Preston in the

---

1 Below, manor.
2 GDR, G 3/24, passim.
3 Above (settlement).
4 See GDR, G 3/24, f. 17.
5 GA, Q/REl 1, Dudstone & King's Barton hundred.
6 GDR, G 3/24, f. 7.
7 Information from Mr Teague.
8 GDR, G 3/24, f. 7.
9 Above (settlement).
10 GDR, G 3/24, ff. 12, 15.
11 DoE List, Dymock (1987), 1/98.
12 GDR, G 3/24, ff. 17.
13 Ibid. f. 7.
14 Information from Mr Teague.
15 GDR, G 3/19, pp. 8–14.
16 GA, P 256/OV 2/2.
17 GDR, G 2/3/15932.
18 GA, Q/REl 1, Dudstone & King's Barton hundred 1779–1804; for the Eltons of Much Marcle, J. Duncumb, *Collections towards the History and Antiquities of the County of Hereford* (continuation by W.H. Cooke), III (1882), 43; cf. GDR wills 1728/85.
19 Rudge, *Hist. of Glos.* II, 188; GDR, G 3/24, ff. 2, 10–11; cf. ibid. G 2/3/16694.
20 *Domesday Book* (Rec. Com.), I, 165v.
21 *Valor Eccl.* II, 417.
22 *L&P Hen. VIII*, XVI, p. 572.
23 GDR, G 3/19, p. 8.

mid 1570s[1] and his son John had acquired a turn in the patronage of Preston church in 1576.[2] In 1585 the queen granted her interest to Fulke Greville and the following year he relinquished it to John Powell, who became his agent as secretary to the council of the Welsh marches.[3] John, described in 1587 as of Cheltenham,[4] resided at Preston by 1604[5] and remained lord farmer of the manor until his death in 1632.[6] Anne Robins, the widow of Thomas Rich (d. 1607) and of Henry Robins (d. 1613), both of Gloucester,[7] acquired a lease of the manor probably by 1639[8] and she retained the estate despite being listed in 1648 as a royalist sympathizer.[9] At her death in 1659 she left the manor to her grandson Henry Clements[10] and for a few years following the Restoration John Clements paid the rent owed by the lessee.[11] Henry Clements, who lived in Epsom (Surrey), died in 1696 leaving the manor to Anne Pauncefoot,[12] the widow of William Pauncefoot (d. 1691) of Carswalls, in Newent.[13] After Anne's death in 1715[14] it passed to Sarah, the daughter of her son William Pauncefoot (d. 1711), and she married William Bromley of Worcester, later of Abberley (Worcs.). By that time the manor was held under the bishop for a term of three lives, the lease being renewed periodically with a variation in the named lives, and for the same rent as earlier.[15] The bishop's income came from the renewal fine, calculated at 1¾ year's valuation.[16]

William Bromley died in 1769 and his son and heir Robert (d. 1803) was succeeded in the manor by Sir George Bromley Bt, the owner of Carswalls in Newent. Sir George, who became known as Sir George Pauncefote after that inheritance,[17] died in 1808[18] and left the manor for life to his companion Elizabeth Lester, known as Mrs Edwards.[19] She married Thomas Rickards[20] (d. 1832)[21] and at her death, by 1834, the manor reverted to Sir George's cousin Robert Pauncefote (formerly Smith) of Swansea.[22] Robert (d. 1843) was succeeded by his son Robert Pauncefote (d. 1847), and he by his brother Bernard. In 1855 Bernard, who lived in India, conveyed his estate to his brother Julian in order to relinquish it to the bishop, but the death of the bishop delayed the transaction until 1857, by which time the Ecclesiastical Commissioners had taken over the bishop's estate.[23]

The Ecclesiastical Commissioners included Preston in the estates given back to the bishopric on its re-endowment in 1867[24] but they regained the Preston estate later in the century.[25] In the early 1950s their successors, the Church Commissioners, broke up the estate, selling its four farms to their tenants, and in the early 1970s the principal landowners in Preston were John Rhys Thomas of Preston Court and Michael Thomas of White House Farm.[26] While Rhys Thomas's land was sold after his death in 1982, Michael Thomas's land was retained by his family in 2004.[27]

Preston Court

Preston Court stands next to the parish church on the site of the manor, an earth platform[28] on which a house known as 'the parlour' (*le parlure*) was rebuilt *c*.1501.[29] The Court is a large three-storeyed timber-framed house which, although its north end is separately framed in the manner of a cross wing, appears to have been built in a single phase by John Powell in the late 16th or early 17th century. In its U plan with the wings to the rear and its display of close studding and decorative gables it follows local patterns.[30] The façade design with a jettied second floor and row of six gables is related to urban buildings in the region as well as to some Herefordshire country houses. The central two bays accommodate a hall and screens passage entered by a two-storeyed porch. The wings extend eastwards and a newel stair fills a north-eastern projection axial

---

1 Hockaday Abs. cccxvi, Preston (unidentified): in the mid 1570s John was in the household of Richard Pate, recorder of Gloucester (*VCH Glos.* IV, 85).
2 GA, D 936/E 12/1, ff. 40v.–41.
3 GDR, G 3/19, p. 8; HMC 23, *12th Rep. I, Cowper*, I, pp. iv–v. For Greville, *Oxford DNB*.
4 Hockaday Abs. cccxvi, Preston (Forest).
5 HMC, *Cowper*, I, pp. 47, 59, 63, 66.
6 GDR, G 3/19, pp. 8–9; Bigland, *Glos.* III, no 205.
7 Bigland, *Glos.* III, no 205; *VCH Glos.* IV, 377, 468.
8 GDR vol. 205, depositions 4 Nov. 1639; see ibid. G 3/19, pp. 8–9.
9 *Cal. Cttee for Compounding*, I, 86; GDR, G 3/19, pp. 8–14.
10 TNA, PROB 11/295, ff. 124–7.
11 GDR, G 3/12.
12 TNA, PROB 11/432, ff. 33v.–34.
13 *Visit. Glos. 1682–3*, 131.
14 Bigland, *Glos.* III, no 205.
15 Ibid. II, 316; GDR, G 2/3/15925–36.
16 Ibid. G 3/24.
17 *Complete Baronetage*, V, 108 and n.; GDR, G 2/3/15932. See above, Newent, manors (Carswalls manor).
18 GA, P 256/IN 1/4.
19 GDR, G 2/3/16692–3.
20 Ibid. 16698.
21 GA, P 256/IN 1/8.
22 GDR, G 3/42; G 2/3/15935, 16693.
23 Ibid. G 2/3/16712–14; see *London Gazette*, 9 Dec. 1856, pp. 4159–60.
24 *London Gazette*, 23 Aug. 1867, pp. 4680, 4687–90.
25 *Kelly's Dir. Glos.* (1879), 725; (1885), 551.
26 Theodora C. Reeves, 'History of Little Marcle and of Preston Parish' (1972: typescript in Glos. Colln. 36709), 103–4; Grace Ruck, *Preston: A Guide and History* (1953: copy in GA, PA 256), 14.
27 Information from Mrs E.M. Delahay of Ledbury, and from Mrs Gillian Thomas of White House Farm.
28 In the early 19th cent. the field immediately to the S. was called Moat Croft: GDR, G 3/24, f. 4; TNA, IR 29/13/159; IN 30/13/159.
29 Glouc. Cath. Libr., Reg. Abb. Braunche, ff. 8v.–9.
30 Fig. 69.

69. Preston Court: the west front in 1945

with the screens passage. The south wing, built over a cellar, has two parlours, the main one panelled and with an original overmantel. The north wing has two service rooms. On the west front the service wing and the four bays of the hall and high end are distinguished by different styles of framing: the former has large square panels, the latter close studding and downward braces. The north front of the north wing has close studding below square panels. The three brick stacks have diamond-set chimneys, two clusters of three at the high end and a cluster of six on the north wing, which together correspond to the 12 hearths recorded in 1672.[1]

In the early 18th century the south front of the south wing was faced in brick and given moulded stringcourses, segment-headed window surrounds, and a classical doorcase. The south windows have been altered and in the 1930s rendering added to the main front and a sash window inserted in the west end of the south wing, perhaps also in the 18th century, were removed.[2] The centre of the north front was made to look Georgian after 1982.[3]

Extensive outbuildings stand north-east of the house. They include timber-framed stables, a partly rebuilt cider house, and further east a courtyard of 19th-century red brick farm buildings wrapped around an older stone barn.

ECONOMIC HISTORY

The economy of the small parish was devoted to meeting the immediate farming needs of its inhabitants. More specialist services were obtained elsewhere.

AGRICULTURE

The Middle Ages

In 1086 there were ten ploughteams in Preston, two belonging to Gloucester abbey's demesne, which employed 4 slaves, and the others to the abbey's tenants, who were 8 villans and 4 bordars.[4] In the mid 13th century the abbey's tenants owed 66s. 2½d. in rent and 36s. 10½d. in aid and their services were valued at 8s.[5] The abbey granted one customary tenant, a carter, 23 a. arable and ½ a. meadow for a cash rent of 8s., the service of a man performing three bedrips, i.e. reaping services, and customary payments including pannage.[6] In the early 1290s there was a collective duty to mow the abbey's meadow in Gloucester and a woman was presented in the manor court for not repairing the abbey's nets. At that time several tenants were in arrears with their services and several as well as the carter kept cattle.[7] Tenant holdings included yardlands, one of which was held for a rent of 14s. 2½d.,[8] half-yardlands, and quarter-yardlands. A yardland contained 48 a. In 1351 a dozen holdings, among them several mondaylands, were in hand

---

1 TNA, E 179/247/14, rot. 34d.
2 Verey and Brooks, *Glos.* II, 641.
3 Information from Mrs Rosemary Ford, owner of the ho. since 1982.
4 *Domesday Book* (Rec. Com.), I, 165v.
5 *Hist. & Cart. Mon. Glouc.* III, 105.
6 Ibid. II, 87.
7 GA, D 936A/M 1, rott. 2, 5.
8 *Hist. & Cart. Mon. Glouc.* II, 274–5.

and a few tenants held some of their land by grant from the abbey. Earlier in 1351 the abbey had granted Richard of Ledbury, archdeacon of Gloucester, a yardland for nine years at a cash rent and the custody of another holding during the minority of the tenant.[1]

Most land in Preston was used for arable farming in the Middle Ages.[2] What little meadow land and pasture there was adjoined the Preston brook and its tributaries. In the later 13th century Gloucester abbey's demesne included land in open arable fields and in meadows called South Mead and Pond Mead.[3] At that time parts of Preston were cultivated in closes and the abbey, which included oats among its crops, had meadow land and pasture in severalty.[4] There were several open fields. In 1351 a holding of 4 a. was divided between the south field and another place[5] and in 1512 the tenants were ordered to close the fields sown with corn before All Saints and the other fields before Candlemas.[6] There was common pasture in the parish[7] and in 1515 a tenant was presented for overburdening it. In 1518 Thomas Hankins and fellow tenants agreed that he might hold a pasture called Hales Meadow in severalty every third year.[8]

The demesne, which covered c.250 a. according to later measurements,[9] was leased with other land in severalty to John Sibles and his sons in 1501 for a rent of 27 quarters of wheat to the abbey cellarer and of 20 each of geese, ducks, capons, and pullets and 44 measures of green pulse to the abbey kitchener. Among the land leased with the demesne were four meadows and pastures, of which Broad Bridge[10] was next to the site of the manor by the Ludstock and Preston brooks.[11] The maintenance of ditches to ensure effective drainage of the land was a major concern of the manor court during the period.[12] In 1535 Richard Sibles's rent, still in kind, was worth £8 3s. 11d. and those of the abbey's other tenants, free and customary, were valued at £13 3s. 7½d.[13]

In the late Middle Ages there were fewer tenants than earlier and in the early 16th century a dozen paid pannage. Some copyholds had been amalgamated and one tenant held demesne land in the open fields called Brink field and Clan field as part of her farm. The holdings varied in size and one of the smallest comprised a cottage and a few acres.[14] The decline in the number of small copyholders continued after the Middle Ages and was in all likelihood related to piecemeal inclosure of the open fields, which became small and scattered.[15]

The Early Modern Period

In the early 17th century John Powell employed four farmers on the demesne and another three men had sizeable farms in the parish.[16] The demesne remained in hand in the mid 17th century, when it was surveyed as 145 a. and most of the other land was copyhold granted by the lord farmer. Of eleven copyholds recorded in 1647, nine ranged in size from 9 to 68 a. and the others comprised a cottage and a little land. The largest holdings or farms, including four with c.52 a. each and one with 68 a., had probably been created by the amalgamation of smaller units for they each had more than one messuage, one as many as four. The tenants retained the customary rights of ploughbote, hedgebote, and firebote.[17]

The parish remained predominantly arable with the demesne made up of 120 a. arable, 10 a. meadow, and 15 a. pasture in 1647. Most of the demesne arable was in four places, principally Church field and Great field, and the tenants' arable included pieces of various sizes in the remnants of the medieval open fields, including Brink field in the west, Clan field in the north-east, and Link field in the north. Piecemeal consolidation and inclosure of holdings in open-field land was far from complete; several of the pieces were surveyed as ½ a. Among the many small fields and closes in Preston in the mid 17th century was one called Pease Croft.[18] The local practice of planting orchards in the fields[19] presumably began in Preston before the later 16th century; in 1578 a Preston widow left cider as part of her property.[20] In the mid 17th century one tenant had three orchards next to his house and a cider house among his outbuildings.[21]

Further reorganizations of tenant holdings took place and in the mid 18th century some copyhold land was farmed with the demesne from Preston Court.[22] In the later 18th century, when he allowed

---

1 GA, D 936A/M 2, rott. 3d.–4.
2 Above, this section.
3 *Hist. & Cart. Mon. Glouc.* II, 87–8.
4 GA, D 936A/M 1, rott. 2, 5.
5 Ibid. M 2, rot. 4.
6 GDR vol. 1A, p. 85.
7 GA, D 936A/M 2, rot. 3d.
8 GDR vol. 1A, pp. 102, 125.
9 Ibid. G 3/24, ff. 4–5; TNA, IR 29/13/159.
10 Glouc. Cath. Libr., Reg. Abb. Braunche, ff. 8v.–9.
11 See TNA, IR 29/13/159; IR 30/13/159.
12 GDR vol. 1A, passim.
13 *Valor Eccl.* II, 417. For Richard Sibles, see Glouc. Cath. Libr., Reg. Abb. Newton, ff. 66–7; Reg. Abb. Malvern, II, ff. 126v.–127.
14 GDR vol. 1A, passim.
15 Below, this section.
16 Smith, *Men and Armour*, 11.
17 GDR, G 3/19, pp. 8–14.
18 Ibid.; see TNA, IR 29/13/159; IR 30/13/159.
19 Rudder, *Glos.* 408–9, 607; Rudge, *Hist. of Glos.* II, 188.
20 GDR wills 1578/28.
21 Ibid. G 3/19, pp. 12–13.
22 GA, P 256/OV 2/2.

copyhold tenure to lapse and replaced it with leasehold tenure, the lord farmer added more land to Preston Court farm.[1] The last remaining copyhold lapsed in the early 19th century.[2] The tenant farms continued to be reorganized and their number was gradually reduced.[3] In 1803 Preston Court farm had increased in area to 495 a. and the other four farms comprised 116 a. (High House), 87 a. (White House), 77 a. (Lower House), and 50 a. (Skinner's). A bailiff managed White House farm for Samuel Cooper of Ledbury.[4]

The inclosure of the open fields continued as land was exchanged between the various farms and was virtually complete by the end of the 18th century; in 1803 only one farm was made up of scattered pieces. The land was best suited to growing wheat and beans[5] and over half of the 220 a. recorded as being under crops in 1801 was devoted to wheat and the rest comprised small areas of barley and oats, 53 a. of peas and beans, and 11 a. of turnips.[6] With meadow land of middling quality and poor pasturage, in 1803 pastures called Cow Leaze and Lower Cowleaze on White House farm had not long been converted to arable. The livestock at that time presumably included several dairy herds. The outbuildings of Preston Court farm included a cheese chamber and cattle sheds as well as pig sties and several other farms also had cow sheds.[7]

Although there were many orchards, each farm usually containing one or more next to the farmhouse, by the beginning of the 19th century some had been grubbed up and others were old and in decline. There were few new orchards at that time. Some of the best were at Preston Cross. Although some pear trees had been planted, most farms made cider for local consumption.[8] Hops were also grown in Preston and in the early 19th century there were two hop gardens, one of them old, in the north and another old one near Preston Court.[9]

The Nineteenth and Twentieth Centuries

Farm reorganization continued in the early 19th century. By 1824 the entire northern end of the parish beyond the Ledbury–Ross road was farmed from High House[10] and in 1834 Preston Court farm contained 322 a. and the rest of the farmland (apart from the glebe) was divided between farms centred on High House (208 a.), the Veldt House (109 a.), Skinner's (94 a.) and White House Farm (76 a.).[11] Veldt House and Skinner's farms, making up the western side of the parish, were amalgamated before 1842[12] and Preston's four farmers worked 322 a., 200 a., 190 a., and 110 a. and employed a total of 22 labourers in 1851.[13] The four farms remained much the same size in the later 19th century.[14]

In 1842 the parish contained 368 a. of arable and 482 a. of meadow and pasture.[15] In 1866, when the crop rotation included some clover or grass, cereals, particularly wheat, remained the main crop but there was as much permanent pasture as there was arable.[16] Each farm had a resident dairy maid in 1861[17] and among the livestock returned in 1866 were 117 cattle, including 56 milch cows, 164 sheep, and 49 pigs.[18] In the late 19th century cereal production declined and in 1896, when at least 34 a. was fallow, livestock in the parish included 196 cattle, among them 37 milch cows, and 158 ewes and 67 pigs.[19] Cattle farming continued to grow in importance in the early 20th century, and in 1926, when permanent grassland accounted for 506 a. and cereal production for 212 a., 243 cattle, including 64 milch cows, were returned. The numbers of ewes and pigs had fallen to 61 and 15 respectively.[20] During that period the area of orchards (27 a.) was little changed but blackcurrant bushes were planted in a few of their acres. The agricultural workforce in 1926 included 12 labourers employed full time.[21]

For a period beginning in the mid 1920s the number of farms was reduced to three[22] but after the Second World War Preston's farmland was again cultivated in four units. Farming was mixed and in 1951 two farms specialized in dairying and the others raised beef cattle. Sheep and pigs were also reared on two farms. Some land was used as grass leys and the arable crops included potatoes as well as cereals. Mushrooms were cultivated in some places.[23] By 1972

---

1 Ibid. Q/REl 1, Dudstone & King's Barton hundred; GDR, G 2/3/15932.
2 Rudge, *Hist. of Glos.* II, 188; GDR, G 2/3/16694.
3 See GDR, G 2/3/16694, 16695, 16702, 16703.
4 Ibid. G 3/24, ff. 3–18.
5 Ibid. ff. 1–2.
6 *1801 Crop Returns Eng.* I, 176.
7 GDR, G 3/24, ff. 2–19.
8 Ibid.
9 Ibid. f. 5; TNA, IR 29/13/159; IR 30/13/159.
10 GDR, G 2/3/16707.
11 Ibid. G 3/42.
12 TNA, IR 29/13/159; IR 30/13/159.
13 Ibid. HO 107/1960.
14 Ibid. RG 9/1761; RG 10/2609; *London Gazette*, 28 Aug. 1867, p. 4680.
15 TNA, IR 29/13/159.
16 Ibid. MAF 68/26/17; MAF 68/62/5.
17 Ibid. RG 9/1761.
18 Ibid. MAF 68/25/4.
19 Ibid. MAF 68/1609/6.
20 Ibid. MAF 68/3295/15.
21 Ibid. MAF 68/1609/6; MAF 68/3295/15.
22 Ibid. MAF 68/3295/15; *Kelly's Dir. Glos.* (1923–39 edns).
23 Grace Ruck, *Preston: A Guide and History* (1953: copy in GA, PA 256), 8, 14–15.

Preston was divided into two large farms.[1] The parish retained many of its orchards in the mid 20th century[2] but most had been grubbed up by the beginning of the 21st century. A new orchard was planted by the Ross road, in front of the Veldt House, in the later 20th century.

MILLS

There was a water mill in Preston by the mid 13th century.[3] Roger the millward lived in the parish in 1327[4] and Gloucester abbey granted a water mill to a man from Redmarley D'Abitot for a term of 60 years in 1351.[5] In 1511 and 1512 a miller was presented in the manor court for taking excess toll.[6]

Two places in Preston have been associated with water mills. One, on the Preston brook west of Preston Court, was possibly the site of a little mill held with the house in 1647.[7] The mill there stood at the end of a long leat[8] and was leased as part of Preston Court farm in the late 18th century. It usually operated as a corn mill,[9] although in 1832 it was described as a grist or clover mill,[10] and in 1803 it was housed in a small timber and boarded building and was powered by an overshot wheel.[11] Replaced by a brick and weather-boarded building, it was abandoned in the early 20th century and the empty mill pond was used as a chicken run in 1951. The building was demolished after 1966[12] and the site was entirely overgrown in 2002.

The other mill stood on the Preston brook in the south-eastern corner of the parish where the Ludstock brook was diverted to increase the flow of the Preston stream.[13] It was held by the Cam family and the fields on either side of the Preston brook became known as Cam's Mill Orchard and Cam's Mill Meadow.[14] In 1515, following William Cam's failure to repair it, the mill was declared ruinous.[15] It was presumably never rebuilt and in 1647 John Cam held land adjoining an old mill.[16]

TRADES AND SERVICES

Among residents of Preston in the early 14th century was a female dressmaker (shipster).[17]

Although trades allied to farming have provided employment in Preston evidence for them is almost entirely lacking. An abandoned kiln at High House in 1803[18] had possibly been used solely for the purposes of the farm. In the early 19th century, when a blacksmith and a wheelwright lived and worked in Preston,[19] four of the parish's fourteen families were supported by trade or crafts.[20] A carpenter named in 1815[21] remained in business in the mid 19th century and Preston's residents in 1851 also included a drainer and a dressmaker.[22] One parishioner worked as a sawyer in 1833 and 1841.[23] The smithy, on the north side of the Ross road at Preston Cross, continued to operate into the 20th century[24] and its site was occupied by a small engineering firm servicing and selling agricultural machinery in 2002.

Velcourt, a land management company originally founded by John Rhys Thomas at Preston Court, moved to the Veldt House in 1982 and employed ten people there, seven of them full time, in 2004.[25] An antiques business established at Preston Court in 1983 continued in 2004.[26]

Preston has never had a post office and no evidence of a shop has been found.[27]

---

1 Theodora C. Reeves, 'History of Little Marcle and of Preston Parish' (1972: typescript in Glos. Colln. 36709), 103–4.
2 OS Maps 6", Glos. IX.NE and SE (1883 edn); 1:25,000, SO 63 (1957 edn).
3 *Hist. & Cart. Mon. Glouc.* II, 88; III, 105.
4 *Glos. Subsidy Roll, 1327*, 33.
5 GA, D 936A/M 2, rot. 4.
6 GDR vol. 1A, pp. 72, 85.
7 Ibid. G 3/19, p. 9.
8 Taylor, *Map of Glos.* (1777).
9 GDR, G 2/3/16689.
10 Ibid. 16708.
11 Ibid. G 3/24, f. 5.
12 G.M. Davies, 'Mill of the River Leadon and Tributaries', *Glos. Soc. Industrial Archaeol. Newsletter* 7 (Apr. 1966), 29; OS Map 6", Glos. IX.NE (1883–1924 edns).
13 See Worcs. RO, 705:99 (BA 5540), Dymock ct. book 1784–1822, cts. 9 and 10 June 1790, perambulation of Dymock manor.
14 GDR, G 3/42.
15 Ibid. vol. 1A, pp. 20, 101.
16 Ibid. G 3/19, f. 10.
17 GA, D 936A/M 2, rot. 4.
18 GDR, G 3/24, f. 17.
19 Ibid. f. 8.
20 *Census*, 1811.
21 GA, P 256/IN 1/5.
22 TNA, HO 107/1960; RG 9/1761.
23 GA, P 256/IN 1/5; TNA, HO 107/355.
24 GDR, G 3/42; GDR, OS Map 6", Glos. IX.NE (1883–1924 edns).
25 Information from Mrs. E.M. Delahay of Ledbury and from Mr David Teague, finance director of Velcourt, the Veldt House.
26 Information from Mrs Rosemary Ford of Preston Court.
27 Ruck, *Preston*, 6.

LOCAL GOVERNMENT

MANORIAL GOVERNMENT

Gloucester abbey held a manor court for Preston.[1] In addition to tenurial and agrarian business, in the early 16th century it enforced the assize of ale, supervised the maintenance of roads, streams, and ditches and dealt with stray animals. It also regularly heard pleas of assault and affray and on a few occasions it elected a constable. In 1505 the abbey's tenants were ordered to seek justice only in the manor court and through the abbot, a member of his council, or the manorial bailiff.[2] Members of the Sibles family, as lessees of the site of the manor and demesne, were required to provide hospitality for the abbey cellarer and steward when they came to Preston to hold the court.[3]

In the early modern period the court belonged to the lord farmer of the manor[4] and, as indicated in a lease of 1793, the main parlour of Preston Court was its traditional meeting place.[5] No records of the court survive from the period; its work as a court baron would have largely ceased with the final extinction of copyhold tenure in the early 19th century.[6]

PAROCHIAL GOVERNMENT

Parish government was in the hands of Preston's few farmers, who between them filled the offices of churchwarden, overseer of the poor, and constable.[7] There were two churchwardens in 1540[8] and in 1626, but by the later 17th century only one churchwarden was appointed and he often remained in office for several years. In the later 18th century John Wood, the farmer at Preston Court, was churchwarden for many years.[9] From the mid 19th century there were again two churchwardens and farmers continued to hold the office for a number of years.[10] William Hartland resigned as rector's churchwarden in 1898 after 43 years of almost continuous service.[11]

Poor relief was administered in Preston by a single overseer. He was traditionally chosen by rotation among the farmers but in the later 18th century John Wood, whose farm took in many former copyholds, usually held the post, occasionally serving on behalf of another farmer. In the early 19th century the overseer remained in office for several years. In the mid 18th century relief was dispensed regularly to two people and a few apprenticeships to local farmers were arranged. Occasional medical expenses included a doctor's bill in 1759–60 for treating a case of smallpox. The overseer also made several payments for building or repairing cottages.[12] Two cottages erected at parish expense for the use of the poor stood next to each other in the fields in the north of the parish and each was let with a garden near by in 1803.[13] For several years from 1810 the churchwarden's and the constable's expenses were met out of the poor rate.[14]

The small size of the parish and its population meant that the cost of relief was among the lowest in the area,[15] even though by the 1780s it included the expense of keeping a parishioner in an asylum.[16] Between 1776 and 1784 the amount spent by Preston on the poor fell from £28 to £14, and in 1803, when three people received regular and six occasional assistance, the cost of relief was £52.[17] About half of that figure went to the asylum keeper, to whom payments continued until 1806.[18] In the following years expenditure on the poor increased as more families turned to the parish for support and in 1811 £108 was spent and weekly help was given to ten people. In 1813, when nine people received regular payments, the total cost of relief was £81.[19] It was at the same level in the late 1820s and fell well below £50 a year in the early 1830s.[20] Preston joined the Newent poor-law union in 1835.[21]

While an annual parish meeting or vestry appointed the churchwardens and dealt with matters concerning the church and churchyard in the mid 19th century, a separate meeting was convened regularly from 1877, if not earlier, to appoint two overseers and a waywarden for Preston. In 1873 and 1881 the parish also elected a poor-law guardian. Preston's few farmers of necessity often held several

---

1 GA, D 936A/M 1, rott. 2, 5; M 2, rott. 3d.–4.
2 GDR vol. 1A, pp. 4, 6, 9, 16, 20, 28–30, 36–7, 44–6, 56–7, 59–60, 65–6, 72–3, 84–5, 91–4, 101–2, 108–9, 112–13, 125–6.
3 Glouc. Cath. Libr., Reg. Abb. Braunche, ff. 8v.–9; Reg. Abb. Newton, ff. 66–7.
4 GDR, G 3/19, p. 9; G 2/3/15925.
5 Ibid. G 2/3/16689.
6 Above, econ. hist.
7 Below, this section; see Theodora C. Reeves, 'History of Little Marcle and of Preston Parish' (1972: typescript in Glos. Colln. 36709), 106–8, 119–20.
8 Hockaday Abs. xxix, 1540 subsidy, f. 8.
9 GDR, V 1/186.
10 GA, P 256/CW 2/5.
11 Ibid. VE 2/1.
12 Ibid. OV 2/2.
13 GDR, G 3/24, f. 19; see ibid. G 3/42.
14 GA, P 256/OV 2/2.
15 Poor Law Abstract, 1804, 170–3; 1818, 146–9.
16 GA, P 256/OV 2/2.
17 Poor Law Abstract, 1804, 170–1.
18 GA, P 256/OV 2/2.
19 Poor Law Abstract, 1818, 148–9.
20 Poor Law Returns (1830–1), 68; (1835), 66.
21 Poor Law Com. 2nd Rep. p. 523.

offices simultaneously and on several occasions the rector was waywarden. From 1894, when the ratepayers unanimously favoured the parish's transfer to Herefordshire and the Ledbury poor-law union,[1] the appointment of officers other than the churchwardens belonged to a civil parish meeting. That meeting was held annually and conducted little business. It convened less regularly after 1927[2] and the civil parish ceased to exist when Preston became part of Dymock in 1935.[3]

SOCIAL HISTORY

SOCIAL STRUCTURE

For most of its history Preston was the possession of an absentee ecclesiastical landowner.[4] The eight people assessed for tax there in 1327 were all presumably tenants of Gloucester abbey. One, John in the field, was assessed for 4s. 2¼d., another for 1s. 8½d., and the rest for amounts ranging from 1s. 3½d. to 10½d.[5] In the early 16th century the site of the manor was leased to John Sibles and his sons, of whom Richard was tenant in 1537.[6] Richard's widow Elizabeth was named in a muster for Preston in 1539.[7]

By the late 16th century the principal resident was the lessee, and *de facto* lord, of the manor. While the residence of John Powell, one of the first lords farmer,[8] Preston Court was visited many times in the early 17th century by his son-in-law (Sir) John Coke, who became a secretary of state in 1625.[9] In the late 1640s Anne Robins lived there with her son-in-law John Hanbury, a royalist and a former MP for Gloucester.[10] After the Restoration the lords farmer, apart from Anne Pauncefoot (d. 1715),[11] were non-resident and Preston Court became a farmhouse.[12] Visits by the lord farmer were rare enough for Sir George Pauncefote's presence at a church service in 1804 to be noted in the parish register. That visit sealed the family's association with Preston and Sir George and his successors, including Robert Pauncefote (d. 1843) who lived in Paris, were buried there.[13] In 1899, long after the family had relinquished the estate,[14] Sir Julian Pauncefote took the title Baron Pauncefote of Preston on his elevation to the peerage.[15]

In the early modern period much of Preston's small population belonged to farming families, such as the Drews and Gundeys, and there were apparently few landless labourers. Of fifteen men listed in 1608 one, John Cam, was a yeoman, six were husbandmen, and one was a labourer. Cam and three of the husbandmen were in the service of John Powell and one other man was also a servant.[16] A majority of the 12 people assessed for hearth tax in Preston in 1672 had 1 or 2 hearths, a few had 3 or 4 hearths, and William Vobes at Preston Court had 12 hearths.[17] From the late 17th century there was no resident clergyman[18] and in the mid 18th century the parish was run by a handful of farmers headed by the Wood family of Preston Court.[19] John Wood organized improvements in the parish church in 1773[20] and agreed in 1796 to pay part of the cost of hiring the man whom Preston and Dymock were to provide for service in the navy.[21] In the early 19th century John and his son Charles farmed more than half of the parish from Preston Court[22] and one of the four other farmers was non-resident.[23]

The Wood family departed Preston in 1810 or 1811,[24] and from the mid 1830s, following a few years' occupation by Elizabeth Rickards,[25] Preston Court was the home of William Hartland, Preston's chief farmer.[26] In 1851 the population of 80 included 4 farmers, 18 agricultural labourers, 12 of whom lived with one or other of the farmers, and a few women in domestic service at Preston Court and White House Farm.[27] The vicar was resident from 1855[28] and a new parsonage (later Preston Priory) built in

---

1 GA, P 256/CW 2/5.
2 Ibid. PC 1/1.
3 *Census*, 1931 (pt. ii).
4 Above, manor.
5 *Glos. Subsidy Roll, 1327*, 33.
6 Glouc. Cath. Libr., Reg. Abb. Braunche, ff. 8v.–9; Reg. Abb. Malvern, II, ff. 126v.–7.
7 TNA, E 101/59/9. See Glouc. Cath. Libr., Reg. Abb. Newton, ff. 66–7.
8 Above, manor.
9 HMC 23, *12th Rep. I, Cowper*, I, pp. iii–v, 57, 59, 62–4; *Oxford DNB*.
10 *Cal. Cttee for Compounding*, I, 85–6; III, 2207; Williams, *Parl. Hist. of Glos.* 193.
11 TNA, PROB 11/546, f. 148v.
12 GA, P 256/OV 2/2; GDR, G 2/3/16689; G 3/24, f. 3.
13 GA, P 256/IN 1/4, 8.
14 Above, manor.
15 *Complete Peerage*, X, 317–18.
16 Smith, *Men and Armour*, 11.
17 TNA, E 179/247/14, rot. 34d.; for Vobes, MCA, F 4iv, nos 1089–91.
18 Below, religious hist.
19 Below, local govt.; see Theodora C. Reeves, 'History of Little Marcle and of Preston Parish' (1972: typescript in Glos. Colln. 36709), 106–9.
20 GA, P 256/IN 1/4.
21 Ibid. P 125/VE 2/2.
22 GDR, G 3/24, ff. 3–8; GDR wills 1813/153; Rudge, *Hist. of Glos.* II, 188.
23 GDR, G 3/24, ff. 10–18.
24 Ibid. G 2/3/16696, 16700.
25 Ibid. 15933, 16707–8; for Elizabeth Rickards, above, manor.
26 GDR, G 3/42.
27 TNA, HO 107/1960.
28 Below, religious hist.

1864[1] provided jobs in domestic service. In the late 19th century most Preston men were agricultural labourers and in 1901 ten of the 16 households were headed by farm workers and one by the blacksmith.[2] The population continued to be made up mostly of farmers and labourers until after the Second World War.[3] In the later 20th century the number of farmers fell to two[4] and agriculture ceased to be the chief source of employment.

SOCIAL LIFE

Ale was brewed and sold in Preston in the early 16th century.[5] There is no record that Preston ever had a licensed public house but in the early 19th century two of the farmsteads at Preston Cross had drink houses for the consumption, and perhaps sale, of cider.[6] Preston received no charitable endowments for the relief of poverty but the parish itself built two cottages for the use of the poor[7] and paid for wheat distributed to parishioners in 1800.[8] J.M. Niblett, the parson, ran a clothing club in 1892.[9]

There have been few schools in Preston and the parish clerk in 1605 was unable to read and write.[10] The parish was without a school in 1818[11] but a Sunday school was started by 1825.[12] H.H. Hardy, the vicar, opened a day school in 1859.[13] A schoolmistress lodged with the blacksmith at Preston Cross[14] but the school was short lived as there were too few children for it to succeed[15] and in 1868 children went to schools in Little and Much Marcle (both Herefs.).[16] The new parsonage built in 1864 became a focus of church and parish life especially after 1879 when Revd Alfred Newton added a room to the stable block for use as a church hall.[17] Parish meetings were held in the room after 1894[18] and A.P. Doherty, rector 1895–1912, taught labourers reading and writing in it.[19] A men's club used the room between the First and Second World Wars.[20] Scout and guide groups started by C.W. Dixon, rector 1913–16, lapsed under his successor.[21] Preston's children attended schools in neighbouring parishes, including Dymock and Little Marcle, during that period[22] and the older children later went to school in Newent.[23]

Immediately after the Second World War the church remained at the centre of social life and there was no public house. The nearest public telephone boxes were in Dymock and Little Marcle. Among the community groups in the area was a Women's Institute.[24] In the 1950s there were organized cricket matches in Preston and, to remedy the lack of a meeting place following the sale of the Victorian parsonage, Revd Daniel Gethyn-Jones obtained the use of an upper floor of an outbuilding at Preston Court as a church room.[25] The room remained a meeting place in 2004, being used by the Women's Institute for its monthly meetings.[26] A preparatory school opened at Preston Priory, the former Victorian parsonage, in 1959 closed a few years later.[27]

RELIGIOUS HISTORY

EARLY HISTORY AND STATUS OF THE PARISH CHURCH

Preston church originated as a chapel built by Gloucester abbey. It had its own graveyard in the 1130s[28] and the abbey had established a vicarage to serve it by 1291.[29] Following the abbey's dissolution the impropriate rectory, to which the manorial demesne tithes belonged,[30] passed like the manor to the bishopric of Gloucester[31] and by 1603 was

---

1 Above, introd.
2 TNA, RG 10/2609; RG 13/2422.
3 Grace Ruck, *Preston: A Guide and History* (1953: copy in GA, PA 256), 14–15.
4 Reeves, 'Little Marcle and Preston', 103–4.
5 GDR vol. 1A, pp. 20, 60.
6 Ibid. G 3/24, ff. 8, 15.
7 Below, local govt.
8 GA, P 256/OV 2/2.
9 Ibid. IN 3/2.
10 GDR vol. 97, f. 239v.
11 *Educ. of Poor Digest*, 306, s.v. Preston (Crowthorne and Minety hundred).
12 Below, religious hist.
13 GA, P 256/CW 2/2.
14 TNA, RG 9/1761.
15 GA, P 125/SC 5, report 19 Nov. 1870.
16 *1st Rep. Com. Employment in Agric.* app. II, p. 130.
17 GA, D 2593/2/175; P 256/CW 2/5.
18 Ibid. P 256/PC 1/1.
19 Reeves, 'Little Marcle and Preston', 54, 86; *Kelly's Dir. Glos.* (1910), 281.
20 Information from Mabel McCulloch of Hallwood Green, Dymock.
21 Reeves, 'Little Marcle and Preston', 54, 96.
22 *Kelly's Dir Glos.* (1885 and later edns.); *Kelly's Dir. Herefs.* (1879), 1021; (1891), 130; (1926), 160.
23 Ruck, *Preston*, 6.
24 Ibid.
25 Reeves, 'Little Marcle and Preston', 100.
26 Information from Mrs Rosemary Ford of Preston Court and Mrs Jennifer Thick of Dymock, sec. to Dymock par. council.
27 Information from Mrs Elizabeth Drew of Preston Priory.
28 *Eng. Episc. Acta VII*, p. 47.
29 *Tax. Eccl.* 161.
30 Glouc. Cath. Libr., Reg. Abb. Newton, ff. 66–7; Reg. Abb. Malvern, II, ff. 126v.–127.
31 *L&P Hen. VIII*, XVI, p. 572; J. Gairdner, 'Bishop Hooper's Visitation of Gloucester', *EHR* 19 (1904), 119.

annexed to the vicarage.[1] Although called a rectory in 1538,[2] the living continued to be styled a vicarage until it was designated a rectory officially in 1867.[3]

Preston was added to the united benefice of Dymock with Kempley in 1941[4] but was reconstituted a separate benefice in 1955.[5] In 2000 it merged with eight other benefices in Gloucestershire and Herefordshire.[6]

PATRONAGE AND ENDOWMENT

Gloucester abbey retained the advowson of the vicarage until the Dissolution.[7] In 1378, during a vacancy in the abbey, the Crown made two presentations to the living on one day[8] and later that year it ratified the estate of a new vicar instituted on the abbey's gift.[9] In 1538 the abbey granted three Gloucester men the patronage at the next vacancy, which occurred in 1546.[10]

Ownership of the advowson passed with the manor to the bishopric of Gloucester in 1541.[11] In 1575 Anthony Higgins was patron for a turn[12] and the following year the bishop granted the next turn to John Powell.[13] John, who became lord farmer of the manor,[14] was patron in the early 17th century[15] and Anne Robins had both manor and advowson at her death in 1659.[16] The bishopric had the advowson after the Restoration[17] and the Crown presented to the vicarage during a vacancy in the see in 1690.[18] Leases of the manor granted between 1717 and 1730 included the patronage but the living did not fall vacant until after the bishop had reserved the advowson in 1734.[19] The bishop, who from 1941 had the right to present at the second of every three turns in the united benefice,[20] was confirmed as Preston's patron in 1955.[21]

In 1291 the church was worth £3 6s. 8d.[22] The vicarage, which included all the tithes save those of the manorial demesne, was worth £6 3s. 5d. in 1535.[23] Later, after the impropriate rectory was attached to his living,[24] the vicar received 30s. a year for the demesne tithes and in 1750 the living's worth was £40, including £11 rent for the glebe and vicarage house.[25] The tithes were commuted in 1844 for a corn rent charge of £127 3s.[26] and the living was valued in 1856 at £146.[27] Following an enlargement of the ecclesiastical parish in 1873 the incumbent received £10 8s. 7d. a year out of a stipend of the vicar of Dymock.[28]

The glebe comprised 31 a. in the mid 19th century, much of it in closes next to the vicarage house in the south-west of the parish some way from the church.[29] The house described as 'very mean' in 1750[30] had two ground-floor rooms, one a kitchen, and two rooms above. In 1836 it was remodelled as the entrance and kitchen of a new house (The Parsonage) designed by Robert Jones of Ledbury for Charles Bryan; the additions comprised a west block, which projected beyond the line of the south front, and rooms on the north side.[31] The enlarged house was occupied for a time by a curate[32] but by 1851 it was used as a labourer's cottage[33] and in 1864 Alfred Newton built a new house (Preston Priory), to a Gothic design by Thomas Fulljames, on the Leominster road north-west of Preston Court.[34] The glebe and the old house were sold in 1886[35] and the new house was sold in 1945.[36]

RELIGIOUS LIFE

Preston church was a simple rectangular structure of squared rubble until it was elaborated in the mid 19th century. Original fabric of the late 11th or very early 12th century survives on the north side and indicates that the eastern end was extended or rebuilt in the 13th century. The Norman material incorporates one high window (blocked), corbel heads, and a square-headed doorway. The decoration on the doorway's

---

1 *Eccl. Misc.* 101.
2 Glouc. Cath. Libr., Reg. Abb. Malvern, II, f. 151v.
3 *Bp. Benson's Surv. of Dioc.of Glouc. 1735–50*, 16; GDR vol. 382, f. 20; *London Gazette*, 12 July 1867, p. 3917; for use of the style rector before 1867 see also TNA, IR 18/2836.
4 *London Gazette*, 25 Feb. 1938, pp. 1252–3; J.E. Gethyn-Jones, *Dymock Down the Ages* (1966 edn), 56.
5 GA, P 125/IN 3/12.
6 *Dioc. of Glouc. Dir.* (2001–2), 24–5.
7 *Reg. Swinfield*, 532; *Reg. Mayew*, 206, 283; Glouc. Cath. Libr., Reg. Abb. Braunche, f. 66.
8 *Cal. Pat.* 1377–81, 86, 104.
9 Ibid. 263.
10 Glouc. Cath. Libr., Reg. Abb. Malvern, II, 151v.; Hockaday Abs. cccxvi, Preston (Forest).
11 *L&P Hen. VIII*, XVI, p. 572; see GA, D 936/E 12/1, ff. 40v.–41.
12 Hockaday Abs. cccxvi, Preston on Stour.
13 GA, D 936/E 12/1, ff. 40v.–41
14 Above, manor.
15 *Eccl. Misc.* 101.
16 TNA, PROB 11/295, ff. 124–7.
17 Atkyns, *Glos.* 608.
18 Hockaday Abs. cccxvi, Preston (Forest).
19 GDR, G 2/3/15925–8; Hockaday Abs. cccxvi, Preston (Forest).
20 *London Gazette*, 25 Feb. 1938, pp. 1252–3.
21 GA, P 125/IN 3/12.
22 *Tax. Eccl.* 161.
23 *Valor Eccl.* II, 501; Glouc. Cath. Libr., Reg. Abb. Newton, ff. 66–7; Reg. Abb. Malvern, II, ff. 126v.–7.
24 Above (early hist.).
25 *Bp. Benson's Surv. of Dioc.of Glouc. 1735–50*, 16; TNA, IR 18/2836.
26 TNA, IR 29/13/159.
27 GDR vol. 384, f. 159.
28 *London Gazette*, 18 July 1873, pp. 3385–7; GA, P 256/IN 3/2.
29 TNA, IR 29/13/159; IR 30/13/159.
30 *Bp. Benson's Surv. of Dioc. of Glouc. 1735–50*, 16.
31 GDR, F 4/1.
32 Hockaday Abs. cccxvi, Preston (Forest).
33 PRO, HO 107/1960; RG 9/1761.
34 GDR, F 4/1; GA, D 2593/2/175, 410.
35 GA, P 256/IN 3/1.
36 Information from Mrs Elizabeth Drew of Preston Priory; see Grace Ruck, *Preston: A Guide and History* (1953: copy in GA, PA 256), 11.

70. Preston church: the north doorway tympanum

tympanum is carved in the style of the 'Dymock school'[1] with dummy voussoirs and an Agnus Dei; the lamb carries a Maltese cross rather than the more usual flag.[2] The 13th-century walling has pierced lancets. In the 14th century a timber-framed porch was added to shelter the north door and painted glass depicting the Crucifixion with St Mary and St John was set in the only window on the south side of the Norman nave.[3] The church's dedication to St John the Baptist is not recorded until the mid 19th century. The lessee of the manorial demesne maintained the chancel in the early 16th century[4] when there was no partiton between it and the nave.[5] The church, which retains an old, probably medieval, bell,[6] had a low wooden west tower in the early 18th century.[7]

Of the early vicars John Harper (? Barbour) was deprived of the living in 1437.[8] James Jones, regularly cited in the manor court in the early 16th century for offences including affray and bloodshed,[9] retained the living until his death. John Smith, his successor in 1507,[10] resigned in 1515 having permission to negotiate a pension to be paid by William Davies, his successor.[11] Davies was accused of keeping a woman in 1526.[12]

Henry Wakeman or Worcester, who succeeded Davies in 1546,[13] was formerly a monk of Tewkesbury.[14] Unable to recite the Ten Commandments, in 1551, when the church had c.60 communicants,[15] he did penance for 'naughty living'[16] and in 1554 he was removed for being married.[17] His successor Richard Wheeler had been a chantry priest and a schoolmaster in Ledbury.[18] In 1576, when the vicar Edward Carwardine was non-resident, a curate wore a surplice on perambulation and issued an unheeded summons to children to learn the catechism. Carwardine, who was ordered to repair the vicarage house, not to let the living, and to preach quarterly sermons,[19] was neither a graduate nor a preacher.[20] His successor Nicholas Drew[21] was described in 1593 as a sufficient scholar but no preacher.[22] Although no recusants were recorded in Preston in 1603,[23] several parishioners, including a preacher, failed to take communion at Easter in 1605.[24] George Dixon, employed as Drew's curate for 20 years,[25] succeeded him as vicar in 1629[26] and was among those resisting the 1635 writ of ship money.[27]

By the later 17th century Preston church was attended by the residents of the outlying parts of neighbouring parishes, notably Dymock.[28] The chancel was maintained by the lords farmer of the manor[29] and ornate monuments were erected in it to Anne Robins (d. 1659) and her son Richard (d. 1650) and plainer monuments to her grandson Sir Thomas Hanbury (d. 1708) of Little Marcle (Herefs.) and to Anne Pauncefoot (d. 1715).[30]

Edward Rogers, who subscribed to the Act of Uniformity as vicar in 1662, retained the living in 1666 but had resigned by 1671[31] and became a nonconformist preacher in London; he was active in the Preston area in 1683, at the time of the Rye House

1 See above, Newent and May Hill (settlement, society, and buildings).
2 Fig. 70; Verey and Brooks, *Glos.* II, 641.
3 Rudge, *Hist. of Glos.* II, 189; the glass is now in a window in the S. aisle.
4 Glouc. Cath. Libr., Reg. Abb. Newton, ff. 66–7.
5 Hockaday Abs. cccxvi, Preston (Forest), 1563.
6 *Glos. Ch. Bells*, 507.
7 Atkyns, *Glos.* 608.
8 *Reg. Spofford*, 361; see ibid. 354 and n.
9 GDR vol. 1A, pp. 4, 16, 29, 37, 44.
10 Glouc. Cath. Libr., Reg. Abb. Braunche, f. 66.
11 *Reg. Mayew*, 206, 283.
12 Hockaday Abs. cccxvi, Preston (Forest).
13 Ibid.
14 G. Baskerville, 'The Dispossessed Religious of Gloucestershire', *Trans. BGAS* 49 (1927), 86.
15 Gairdner, 'Hooper's Visitation of Gloucester', 119.
16 F.D. Price, 'Gloucester Diocese under Bishop Hooper, 1551–3', *Trans. BGAS* 60 (1938), 92, 117.
17 Baskerville, 'Dispossessed Religious', 86.
18 Hockaday Abs. cccxvi, Preston (Forest); J.G. Hillaby, *The Book of Ledbury* (1982), 90.
19 GDR vol. 40, f. 240.
20 Hockaday Abs. xlix, state of clergy 1584, f. 43, where his forename is given as Ric.
21 Ibid. cccxvi, Preston (Forest).
22 Ibid. lii, state of clergy 1593, f. 6.
23 *Eccl. Misc.* 101.
24 GDR vol. 97, f. 239v.
25 HMC 23, *12th Rep. I, Cowper*, I, p. 381.
26 Hockaday Abs. cccxvi, Preston (Forest).
27 *Cal. SP Dom.* 1635–6, 396.
28 GA, P 256/IN 1/4.
29 Bp. Benson's *Surv. of Dioc. of Glouc. 1735–50*, 16.
30 Bigland, *Glos.* III, no 205.
31 Hockaday Abs. cccxvi, Preston (Forest); Hereford Cathedral Archives 7031/3, p. 249.

Plot.¹ From the 1690s Preston's vicars were non-resident and pluralists² and in 1750, when the vicar, Robert Symonds, was a schoolmaster in Colwall (Herefs.), the church had one Sunday service, alternately in the morning and afternoon.³ In 1730 one parishioner refused to pay church rates and attend services.⁴ Among projects undertaken by John Wood as churchwarden were the acquisition in 1764 of a new bell cast by Thomas Rudhall⁵ and a refurbishment of the church in 1773, when a Bible, prayer book, and surplice were purchased as well as a pulpit, reading desk, and other new furniture. Wood also donated railings for the churchyard.⁶ In the later 18th and early 19th century curates usually served the church,⁷ although Jenkin Jenkins, vicar 1780–1817, at first came in person from Donnington (Herefs.).⁸ In the early 19th century the Pauncefotes, non-resident lords farmer of the manor, supported a subscription for a chalice⁹ and several of them were buried at Preston. A memorial to Robert Pauncefote (d. 1843)¹⁰ carved by Edward Gaffin of London was placed in the chancel.

Under John Kempthorne (1817–20), the evangelical protégé of Bishop Henry Ryder,¹¹ and Charles Bryan (1820–55) the church was served until 1834 from Donnington by P.G. Blencowe.¹² In 1825, when Kempthorne's version of the psalms was sung, the Sunday service was still held alternately in the morning and afternoon and the average congregation, swelled by the presence of people from outside Preston, was 30–50, including children. The number of communicants at the four communion services a year was 20. All the 14 children in the parish attended a Sunday school in the church where religious instruction was given once a fortnight.¹³ In 1833 a Sunday school provided free education to 9 boys and 9 girls.¹⁴

Clergy had a more permanent presence in the parish from the mid 19th century. Curates occupied the vicarage house following its enlargement in 1836 but W.J. Morrish was required from 1846 to be resident for only three months a year and to live in the neighbourhood of Ledbury at all other times.¹⁵ Morrish was probably the master paid in 1847 to teach 12 boys and 13 girls in the Sunday school in the church.¹⁶ In 1851 the church's average congregation numbered 54.¹⁷ H.H. Hardy, vicar 1855–63,¹⁸ lodged at White House Farm¹⁹ and energetically promoted religion and education.²⁰ In particular he secured money, mostly voluntary contributions, for the restoration and enlargement of the church in 1859 and 1860 to designs by the London partnership of Hugall & Male.²¹ In that work a separate chancel was created by inserting a wall pierced by a wide arch fitted with a low timber screen, the nave south wall was dismantled to make way for a lean-to three-bayed aisle in plain 13th-century style, and the west wall was buttressed to support a stone bellcot. The many new fittings and furnishings included an octagonal stone font and an old-fashioned pulpit and reading desk.²² Among gifts from the Hardy family was carved furniture and William Drew, a farmer, donated the window containing the 14th-century glass previously in the nave.²³ The church's dedication to St John the Baptist is recorded from 1863; in 1856 it was said to be to St Matthew.²⁴ The church had a pipe organ in 1878.²⁵

Alfred Newton, Hardy's successor,²⁶ built a new vicarage house much nearer the church than the old one²⁷ and provided a meeting place for the parish at

71. *Preston church from the north*

---

1 *Cal. SP Dom.* July–Sept. 1683, 133–4.
2 Hockaday Abs. cccxvi, Preston (Forest).
3 *Bp. Benson's Surv. of Dioc. of Glouc. 1735–50*, 16.
4 Hockaday Abs. cccxvi, Preston (Forest).
5 *Glos. Ch. Bells*, 507.
6 GA, P 256/IN 1/4.
7 GDR, V 1/186; GA, P 256/IN 1/5, 8.
8 GDR vol. 382, f. 20.
9 GA, P 256/CW 3/3; see *Glos. Ch. Plate*, 167.
10 GA, P 256/IN 1/4, 8.
11 See *VCH Glos.* IV, 158.
12 Hockaday Abs. cccxvi, Preston (Forest); GA, P 256/IN 1/5, 8.
13 GDR vol. 383, no cxxix.
14 *Educ. Enquiry Abstract*, 324.
15 Hockaday Abs. cccxvi, Preston (Forest); above (patronage and endowment).
16 Nat. Soc. *Inquiry, 1846–7*, Glos. 14–15; see GA, P 256/CW 3/3.
17 TNA, HO 129/335/2/3/6.
18 *Alumni Oxon. 1715–1886*, II, 606.
19 *Kelly's Dir. Glos.* (1856), 344; (1863), 328; TNA, RG 6/1761.
20 See above, social hist (social life).
21 GA, P 256/CW 2/2; D 2593/2/476.
22 Verey and Brooks, *Glos.* II, 640–1. See Fig. 71.
23 GA, P 256/CW 2/2. For Drew, *Kelly's Dir. Glos.* (1856), 344; (1863), 328 .
24 *Kelly's Dir. Glos.* (1856), 344; (1863), 328.
25 GA, P 256/CW 2/5.
26 Hockaday Abs. cccxvi, Preston (Cirencester).
27 Above (patronage and endowment); see OS Map 6", Glos. IX.NE (1883 edn).

the new house.[1] In 1873 his parish was enlarged by the addition of the Hallwood green and Leadington area of Dymock and the Ludstock area of Ledbury.[2] From 1870, when church income came to depend on voluntary subscriptions, Newton and William Hartland provided most of the money but following the parish's enlargement more people contributed to the funds and from the later 1880s the Ecclesiastical Commissioners, the principal landowners, were regular contributors. There were also occasional collections at services and extraordinary items of expenditure, such as the erection of rails around the churchyard in 1898, were financed by subscription. Weekly church collections were introduced in 1914.[3] In the church in 1885 the chancel was almost entirely rebuilt and fenestration in both chancel and nave was altered to match the trefoil-headed lights in the aisle, all to designs by the firm of Waller, Son, & Wood. The new, enlarged east window was filled with memorial glass to Alfred Newton (d. 1884).[4] In 1896 a south-east vestry designed by F.W. Waller was added and, to compensate for its blocking the chancel south-east window, a north-east window was made.[5]

A.H.A. Camm, rector from 1931, was Preston's last resident incumbent and after his resignation in 1941 continued for a time to live in the Victorian parsonage and take church services. Under Daniel Gethyn-Jones, incumbent of Dymock with Kempley and Preston from 1941, the churchyard was enlarged in 1945. In 1955, when Preston became a separate benefice again, Gethyn-Jones remained rector and H.A. Edwards, formerly rector of Donnington, moved into the former Victorian parsonage to act as curate until his death in 1958.[6] From 1959 the church was served from Little Marcle[7] and from 1992 by a priest-in-charge living in Dymock.[8] On the union of benefices in 2000 it came under team ministry led from Redmarley D'Abitot.[9]

In 1994 a plaque displaying a bust of the poet John Masefield (d. 1967), who was baptized in the church in 1878, was placed on the nave north wall.[10] The church has been given an old chair in memory of Geoffrey Houlbrooke (d. 1991).

TAYNTON

THE Gloucestershire parish of Taynton lies 10 km WNW of Gloucester in rolling countryside below May hill. Although parts contained ancient tree cover and supported woodland crafts, it was predominantly agricultural in character and in the 17th and 18th centuries was known particularly for the growing of pears. Its medieval church was destroyed in military action during the Civil Wars and its replacement, dating from the 1650s, is a rare example of a parish church aligned north–south.[11]

BOUNDARIES AND DIVISIONS

The ancient parish covered 2,521 a. (1,020 ha) extending south-westwards from the hamlet of Kent's Green to a tongue of land climbing Glasshouse hill on the lower slopes of May hill.[12] Irregular boundaries included the Glasshouse brook on the north-west and the Tibberton brook on the south-east. On the north, where a relatively straight road marked the boundary west of Kent's Green, the long boundary with Newent was adjusted in two places in 1992 to bring the whole of Kent's Green and Clifford Manor below Glasshouse hill within Taynton.[13]

Taynton was anciently divided between the manors of Great and Little Taynton.[14] Little Taynton, assessed for tax separately in 1327,[15] was much the smaller. Comprising the north-east corner of the parish, it extended westwards to Norman's Farm and south-westwards to Taynton Court[16] and was bounded on the south by a lower stretch of the Glasshouse brook.[17] Although not administered apart from the rest of the parish in the early modern period, Little Taynton asserted its

---

1 Above, social hist.
2 *London Gazette*, 18 July 1873, pp. 3385–7; GA, P 256/IN 3/2.
3 GA, P 256/CW 2/5; VE 2/1; CW 2/3.
4 Ibid. CW 3/1; *Kelly's Dir. Glos.* (1889), 867.
5 GA, P 256/CW 3/1; CW 2/5; D 2593/2/476
6 Theodora C. Reeves, 'History of Little Marcle and of Preston Parish' (1972: typescript in Glos. Colln. 36709), 96–100.
7 *Glouc. Dioc. Year Book* (1959–60), 12, 30–1.
8 *Dioc. of Glouc. Dir.* (2000–1), 43, 91.
9 Ibid. (2001–2), 24–5, 122.
10 Plaque in ch.; see GA, P 256/IN 1/5.

11 Below, settlement; religious hist. This account was written in 2005 and 2006.
12 *OS Area Book* (1883). See below, Map 15.
13 The Forest of Dean (Parishes) Order 1991 (unpublished Statutory Instrument 1992 no 2283); information (Sept. 2003) from Mr Gareth Ellison (environment directorate, Glos. co. council).
14 *Notes on Dioc. of Glouc. by Chancellor Parsons*, 188.
15 *Glos. Subsidy Roll, 1327*, 35.
16 See Taynton land-tax assessments 1776–1832 in GA, Q/REl 1, Botloe hundred.
17 GDR, V 5/299T 1.

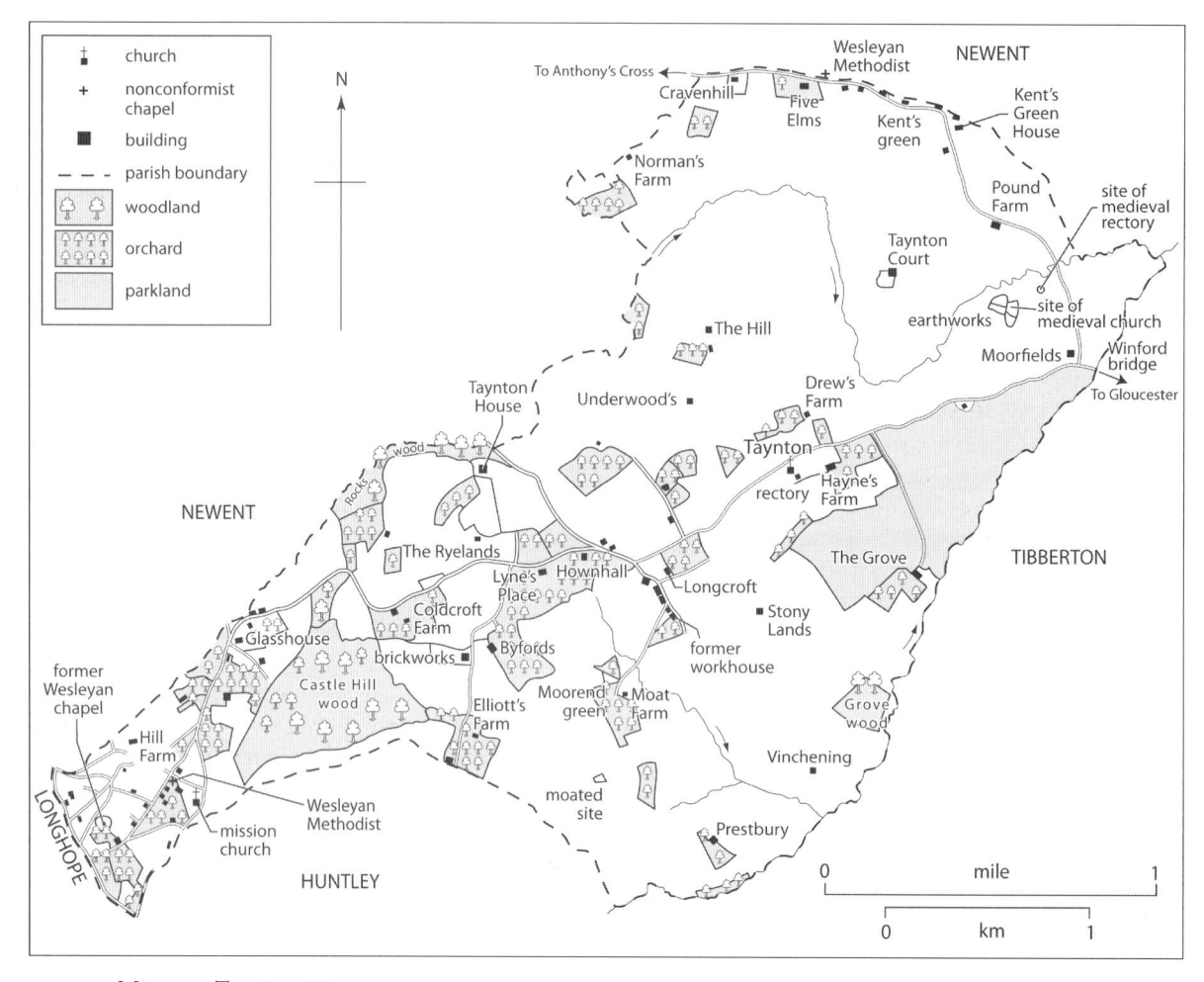

Map 15. *Taynton 1880*

separate identity in some aspects of parish government in the mid 19th century.[1]

LANDSCAPE

The east end of Taynton is open country rising gently to 40 m on the ridge followed by the boundary west of Kent's Green and to 50 m in the centre of the parish. Further west the topography becomes hilly, the land rising in places to over 86 m before it ascends steeply to reach 213 m on Glasshouse hill. Streams flowing off May hill from west to east drain the parish into tributaries of the river Leadon and are prone to flood across low land.[2] The Glasshouse brook runs south of Norman's Farm across the eastern end of the parish. Another stream, fed by a spring at the foot of Glasshouse hill called Monk's well in the early 18th century, emerges from its valley and turns south-eastwards in the centre of the parish near Hownhall to flow past Moorend green and join the Tibberton brook.[3] Except for areas in the east with alluvial soil the land is formed by marls and shales with sandstone formations and limestone outcrops making the higher ground of the west.[4]

The scattered nature of settlement indicates that much of it followed the clearance of ancient woodland. King John (1199–1216) extended forest law to the covert of Taynton[5] and the parish remained within the official bounds of the Forest of Dean until the early 14th century.[6] By that time Taynton's woods were presumably confined to its south-western end, where commonable woodland and waste called Taynton wood once covered Glasshouse hill. The hill was denuded of trees probably by the early 18th century when the main wood was below it on Castle hill.[7] Inclosed by the late 16th century[8] and extended at 89 a. in 1840,[9] Castle Hill wood was

---

1 Below, local govt.
2 Rudder, *Glos.* 725.
3 *Notes on Dioc. of Glouc. by Chancellor Parsons*, 188.
4 Geol. Surv. Map 1:50,000, solid and drift, sheet 216 (1988 edn).
5 *Eng. Episc. Acta VII*, pp. 256–7.
6 *VCH Glos.* V, 295–7.
7 GA, D 23/T 32; D 1230/4–5.
8 BL, Harl. MS 4131, f. 481v.
9 GDR, T 1/177 (no 223).

enlarged to the south in the early 20th century[1] and has remained by far the largest piece of woodland. Lewis grove (40 a.) recorded in the late 16th century[2] was cleared and inclosed in the mid 17th.[3] Among woodland remaining in the mid 19th century were Tuns wood (8 a.) on the north side of Castle Hill wood, Rocks wood (14 a.) along the north-western boundary of the parish, and Hayne's wood (4 a.) and Grove wood (10 a.) in the east;[4] Hayne's wood was grubbed up a few years later. A covert of 8 a. planted at the end of the century on the Newent Court estate at Cravenhill in the north[5] was grubbed up in the mid 20th century.[6] Field names in the early 19th century suggest that land in the east next to earthworks marking perhaps the original site of Great Taynton manor may have been parkland.[7] By the time of the Commons Registration Act of 1965 the former commons of the parish had been reduced to a few small patches of roadside waste, including remnants of Glasshouse green below Glasshouse hill and of Kent's green on the Newent boundary.[8]

ROADS

Taynton's roads are narrow lanes used by local traffic. That from Tibberton to May hill running from east to west through the centre of the parish past its 17th-century church was a highway from Gloucester in 1648.[9] It enters Taynton at the stream crossing known as Winford bridge $c.$1703,[10] where a lane branches northwards towards Kent's Green. A way further south, perhaps another route from Gloucester, ran westwards past the Grove.[11] Further west, where it was known in the later 17th century as Puck Lane,[12] it joined Moat Lane, which runs from Moorend green to the south[13] to a junction with the road to May hill just before Hownhall. In the west the road to May hill, curving through the hills before its ascent of Glasshouse hill, was the way to Mitcheldean in the mid 17th century[14] and a section became known as Gatling Lane (the Gatling).[15]

The principal ancient route from south to north through the parish was probably that in the west followed in places by the road from Huntley, and earlier Newnham, to Newent.[16] South of Taynton House, where in 1694 John Holder filled up the lane leading to the house with earth,[17] the road turns eastwards to follow the east–west route back to Hownhall. From there it continues north-westwards past Taynton House and its grounds down to a bridge built on the parish boundary in 1813.[18]

POPULATION

Sixteen tenant households were recorded on the Great Taynton and six on the Little Taynton estates in 1086.[19] In 1327 20 men were assessed for tax in Great Taynton and 8 in Little Taynton,[20] and a muster of 1542 named 22 men for Great Taynton and 11 for Little Taynton.[21] The parish had $c.$140 communicants in 1551[22] and 41 households in 1563,[23] and the number of communicants was put at 60 in 1603[24] and the number of families at 86 in 1650.[25] The total population, estimated at 200 $c.$1710[26] and 250 $c.$1775,[27] rose from 378 in 1801 to 634 in 1841. From 689 in 1861 it declined to 463 in 1901 and, after a small increase, to 394 in 1961. Despite the boundary changes of 1992 it remained 405 in 2001.[28]

SETTLEMENT

Much of Taynton is settled in scattered farmsteads, many with medieval origins. The farmsteads were once more numerous and the locations of some of those that have been abandoned, for example Welsh Place and Over House recorded in the later 17th century, the latter at a place called Allow End,[29] have not been identified. In later centuries few houses were erected on entirely new sites.

---

1 OS Map 6", Glos. XXIV.SW (1903, 1924 edns).
2 BL, Harl MS 4131, f. 514v.
3 GA, D 2957/299/109.
4 GDR, T 1/177 (nos 31, 49, 489, 497).
5 OS Map 1:2,500, Glos. XXIV.3 (1883, 1903 edns); Glos. Colln. RX 212.2.
6 See OS Map 1:2,500, SO 7223–7333 (1972 edn).
7 BL, Add. MS 15648E; below, settlement.
8 GA, DA 30/132/11.
9 *LJ* 9, 665.
10 *Notes on Dioc. of Glouc. by Chancellor Parsons*, 188.
11 See OS Maps 6", Glos. XXIV.NE (1888 edn); NW (1887 edn).
12 GA, D 892/T 81; see GDR, T 1/177 (nos 39, 96).
13 Greenwood, *Map of Glos.* (1824).
14 GA, D 2957/299/128.
15 Ibid. D 413/T 3.
16 See Ogilby, *Britannia* (1675), plate 71.
17 GA, D 1371.
18 Below, local govt.; see above, Newent, introd. (communications: roads).
19 *Domesday Book* (Rec. Com.), I, 167 and v.
20 *Glos. Subsidy Roll, 1327*, 35.
21 *L&P Hen. VIII*, XVII, 499.
22 J. Gairdner, 'Bishop Hooper's Visitation of Gloucester', *EHR* 19 (1904), 120.
23 Bodleian, Rawl. C. 790, f. 27.
24 *Eccl. Misc.* 101.
25 C.R. Elrington, 'The Survey of Church Livings in Gloucestershire, 1650', *Trans. BGAS* 83 (1964), 98.
26 Atkyns, *Glos.* 710.
27 Rudder, *Glos.* 727.
28 *Census*, 1801–2001.
29 GA, D 892/T 81; GDR wills 1674/155.

The church recorded from the mid 12th century[1] stood on the east side of the parish within substantial earthworks between an ancient lane and, to the north, the stream that marked the southern boundary of Little Taynton.[2] The earthworks probably originated in the late 11th or early 12th century as a ringwork that was remodelled as a motte and bailey fortification, probably with a moat.[3] The likely builders were the lords of Great Taynton, William Goizenboded and his successors of whom Maud de Wateville relinquished her rights in the church by 1148.[4] In the early 18th century the bulk of the earthworks belonged to the Little Taynton estate, part of which was in Great Taynton.[5] The church was destroyed along with the nearby rectory house, which stood inside a circular moat to the north-east within Great Taynton,[6] by royalists soon after the raising of siege of Gloucester in 1643.[7] A thatched building on the south side of the churchyard, described in 1704 as the parish house,[8] accommodated several dwellings when in private ownership[9] and was removed in the mid 20th century.[10]

In the early 19th century a farmhouse (Moorfields) was built to the south by the road leading westwards from Winford bridge on land temporarily out of the ownership of a Dumbleton charity.[11] Two pairs of council houses were built on the south side of the road in 1936[12] and a third pair a few years later. More houses and bungalows were built there in 1963.[13] Further west on the road farm buildings on the Cinders estate were remodelled after their absorption by the Grove estate in 1849[14] as a farmstead with a single-storeyed dwelling (the Stalls).[15]

The Grove, across the fields to the south-west, stands south of the line of an old east–west route and probably on the site of a medieval dwelling; two men surnamed 'at the grove' were assessed for tax in Great Taynton in 1327.[16] The house, which probably served the demesne farm of Great Taynton in the late 16th century, became the residence of Thomas Pury (d. 1693)[17] and later was the principal farmhouse on a substantial estate.[18] In the mid 19th century fields to the north were planted as a park with a drive southwards from the road leading westwards from Winford bridge[19] and in the mid 1920s M.P. Price built a pair of cottages at the entrance to the drive[20] and enlarged the house.[21] To the south-west at Vinchening, formerly known as Vinchend or Vinchingend, was a farmhouse called Awberry's in 1716.[22] A barn remained standing after the house became derelict in the early 20th century.[23] In the same general area a farmstead called Drinkwater's probably after a family resident in Taynton in the early 18th century was abandoned before the mid 19th century[24] and other cottages in the fields to the north were also abandoned long ago, the site of a homestead in the place called Stony Lands being covered by a copse.[25]

Two farmsteads set back on opposite sides of the road leading westwards from Winford bridge are named after the families of Giles Haynes and John Drew, who in the mid 1640s were among petitioners for a church in the centre of the parish.[26] The new church, standing near by on the south side of the road, was in use in 1659.[27] A rectory house was built next to it in 1849 and 1850[28] and a schoolroom, later the parish room (church hall), on the north side of the road in 1883.[29] Further west along the road Marchfield (formerly March Croft) dates from 1912[30] and one of its outbuildings was enlarged in the late 20th century to make a house.

Further west a few cottages stand east of a small green at Hownhall where the road to Newent turns north-westwards. On the south side of the green Hownhall Farm, the chief dwelling on the Ayleway family's estate in the 16th century,[31] presumably marks the spot occupied in 1327 by Walter of Hownhall (Heuwenhulle).[32] In 1953 an oak tree was planted on the green to replace an old one that had been destroyed by fire.[33]

---

1 Below, religious hist.
2 GDR, T 1/177 (nos 668 and 666); V 5/299T 1, 4.
3 S. Williams, 'Taynton Parva', *Glevensis* 30 (1997), 27–32.
4 Below, manors; religious hist.
5 GDR, V 5/299T 4; ibid. wills 1745/57.
6 Ibid. V 5/299T 1; T 1/177 (no 675).
7 *LJ* 9, 665.
8 GDR, V 5/299T 4: Bigland, *Glos.* III, no 266.
9 In the mid 18th cent. four gardens there were in the same ownership as the bldg.: GDR, T 1/177 (nos 669, 671–3).
10 OS Maps 6", Glos. XXVI.NE (1888, 1924 edns); 1:2,500, SO 7422–7522 (1972 edn).
11 *12th Rep. Com. Char.* 67–8.
12 GA, D 2176/2/6/10; DA 30/100/14, pp. 64, 98, 214.
13 Ibid. DA 30/100/17, p 245; 100/30, p. 111; 100/31, pp. 7, 168; OS Maps 1:2,500, SO 7422–7522 and 7423–7523 (1972 edns).
14 GA, D 608/13/14; D 1589/1.
15 Ibid. D 2176/2/4/3, f.30.
16 *Glos. Subsidy Roll, 1327*, 35.
17 Below, manors (other estates: the Grove).
18 See GDR, T 1/177.
19 cf. ibid.; OS Map 6", Glos. XXIV.NE (1888 edn).
20 GA, D 2176/2/6/4.
21 Ibid. DA 30/711/6.
22 Ibid. D 892/T 81.
23 Ibid. D 2176/2/3/6, ff. 5–6; 2/6/8.
24 Ibid. D 892/T 81; D 1859/1.
25 See GDR, T 1/177 (nos 66–7, 78); N. Currer-Briggs, 'Taynton and the Holder Family 1538–1950' (1956 typescript in GA, PA 326/1), 18; information from Mr Donald Sherratt of Green Croft Farm.
26 Parliamentary Archives, HL/PO/JO/10/1/243.
27 Below, religious hist.
28 Verey and Brooks, *Glos.* II, 707.
29 Below, social hist.
30 D.R. Sherratt, *Taynton's Industrial Past: The Brickworks, Potteries and Brass Mill* (1998), 11–12; OS Map 6", Glos. XXIV.NE (1924 edn).
31 *Notes on Dioc. of Glouc. by Chancellor Parsons*, 189; below, manors (other estates).
32 *Glos. Subsidy Roll, 1327*, 35.
33 GA, P 326A/PC 1/1, pp. 161–4.

Longcroft, the largest house at the top of Moat Lane, south-east of Hownhall, in the mid 19th century, stands north of the line of Puck Lane[1] in the place of a cottage recorded from 1655.[2] Musgrove Cottage, one of two timber-framed cottages to the south, belonged to a parish charity[3] and Hill View House, next to it, was built in 1818 as a parish workhouse.[4] Later houses on Moat Lane include a pair of council houses built opposite the former workhouse by 1945.[5]

Further south stands a couple of houses at Moorend green, south of a stream at the bottom of a lane that in 1323 was a way called 'Crowelone' street. The area, known in the later Middle Ages as the mere end, included in 1452 the home of William Horn's widow Agnes.[6] Moat Farm, the principal house, is timber-framed. The rectangular moat next to it, enclosing an orchard in the mid 19th century,[7] was destroyed in the late 1960s to make way for turkey sheds.[8] Further south, in the fields some way north-west of the farmstead at Prestbury, a rectangular earthwork within a moat was covered in trees in the mid 19th century.[9]

In the north-east of the parish, in Little Taynton, the farmhouse at Taynton Court stands within the remains of a rectangular moat and was the principal dwelling of Kilpeck's tithing,[10] the lords of Kilpeck being the owners of Little Taynton in the early Middle Ages.[11] In 2006 a new house stood to the north-east. Further north-east a cottage was built at the entrance to the drive from the road from Winford bridge to Kent's Green c.1900.[12] Pound Farm, further east on the road, has a house dating from the 17th century.

Kent's Green The hamlet of Kent's Green formed with the building of small farmhouses and cottages by and on a green at the boundary between Taynton and Newent. Settlement there began by the early 17th century[13] and a homestead adjoining the Taynton side of the green was called Ittons in 1684.[14] In 1828 a roadside cottage being built on the waste was demolished.[15] At the east end Kent's Green House, the principal house, dates mainly from the mid 19th century.[16] Five Elms Farm, to the west by the road to Anthony's Cross, belonged to the Nelme family until Joseph Clarke (d. 1738) added the farm to his estate.[17] The house at Cravenhill (Craven Hill), further along the road, occupies a site that was the centre of an estate recorded in the later 13th century[18] and was occupied by John of Cravenhill in 1327.[19] The present house dates from a rebuilding, probably as a gamekeeper's lodge, in the late 19th century.[20] Norman's Farm, across the fields to the south-west on the boundary with Newent, was part of a farm acquired by Joseph Clarke (d. 1705).[21]

To the south, back in Great Taynton, the small timber-framed cottage by Haskins stands between the sites of two farmsteads that Thomas Underwood left to William Haskins in the late 18th century. The southern farmstead, where Underwood had lived,[22] was provided with new outbuildings in the later 19th century and the old house at the northern farmstead was adapted as a farm building and its name, the Hill, transferred to its southern neighbour after a fire in the 20th century.[23] Further south the house at Green Croft Farm, known in the early 19th century as Palmer's,[24] has brick additions of the 1920s.[25] Taynton Villa, near by, is a brick house of c.1850.[26]

In the west of the parish Elliott's Farm, near the southern boundary by the Huntley–Newent road, was long owned by the Elliott family, whose property in the late 18th century included Adams,[27] a farm that Peter Charles had owned at the beginning of that century.[28] At Elliott's Farm, also known as New House Farm after it was taken into Edmund Probyn's Huntley estate in 1861,[29] the oldest building

---

1 GDR, T 1/177; above (roads). See K. and W. Thomas, *Our Story of Taynton* (Taynton Society, 1981), 10.
2 GA, D 1272, Taynton deeds.
3 Below, social hist. (charities for the poor); GDR, T 1/177 (no 90).
4 Date on bldg.: K. and W. Thomas, *Our Story of Taynton*, 16; below, local govt.
5 GA, P 184/IN 1/15.
6 Ibid. D 23/T 31.
7 GDR, T 1/177 (nos 133–4).
8 Information from Mr Sherratt.
9 GDR, T 1/177 (no 154).
10 Ibid. (no 777).
11 Below, manors (Little Taynton manor; other estates: medieval monastic estates).
12 Glos. Colln. RX 212.2; OS Map 6", Glos. XXIV.NE (1888, 1903 edns).
13 See GA, D 2528, p. 4, plan C; above, Newent, settlement (outlying settlements: Malswick).
14 GA, D 2176/1/2/2.
15 Ibid. P 326/CW 2/1, survey 14 June 1828.
16 In 1861 it was called New House: TNA, RG 9/1760. See below (bldgs.).
17 Below, manors (other estates: Norman's Farm); see GDR wills 1659/2; 1738/17.
18 Below, manors (other estates).
19 *Glos. Subsidy Roll, 1327*, 35.
20 See OS Map 1:2,500, Glos. XXIV.3 (1883, 1903 edns); Glos. Colln. RX 212.2.
21 Below, manors (other estates).
22 TNA, PROB 11/1302, ff. 359v.–360v.; GDR, T 1/117 (nos 620, 616, 582).
23 GA, D 2299/2/6/48; Glos. Colln. RX 212.2; information from Mr Sherratt.
24 OS Map 1", sheet 43 (1831 edn); see GA, Q/REl 1, Botloe hundred 1832; GDR, T 1/177 (no 586).
25 Information from Mr Sherratt.
26 Sherratt, *Taynton's Industrial Past*, 9.
27 GDR, T 1/177 (no 205); see GA, Q REl 1, Botloe hundred 1776, 1832.
28 GDR wills 1707/262.
29 GA, SL 10; TNA, RG 9/1760; RG 10/2607; *Kelly's Dir. Glos.* (1885), 591.

is an 18th-century barn.[1] In the later 20th century a house was built between the farmstead and the road. Further north there was presumably a dwelling at Byfords before the early 14th century, when John of Byford was among Great Taynton's wealthiest residents.[2] The farmhouse, one of the Whittington family's possessions in the early 16th century,[3] stands on a rock outcrop overlooking a crossing of a stream[4] and its yard occupies a terrace immediately below.[5] The farmstead at Lyne's Place, to the north-east by the road leading westwards down from Hownhall, belonged to the Hartland family in the early 18th century[6] and was part of the Cadle family's estate in the early 19th.[7]

Taynton House, standing near the northern boundary west of Newent road, was a farmhouse known as Jack's House owned by the Holder family from the later 17th century.[8] In the early 19th century it was extensively remodelled as a country house and to the south another gentleman's residence (the Ryelands) was built on the edge of its grounds on the site of a cottage[9] taken into the Holders' estate in 1822.[10]

A number of buildings in the area were pulled down by John Holder after he inherited Jack's House in 1684.[11] South of the road to May hill at Kingetts (or Kingketts),[12] where a dwelling probably existed by the early 14th century,[13] he dismanted a barn and a cider house in 1696 and the farmhouse, having been sold in 1699, was removed to Little Taynton.[14] The farmstead a little further west at Coldcroft Farm was known until the mid 19th century as Tuns, a name that has been transferred to a cottage on the road near by.[15] Among other dwellings scattered on the hills of the west a cottage called Thornton (or Thornington) in the late 16th century stood at Crockett's orchard on the north boundary with Newent.[16]

Glasshouse The hamlet of Glasshouse at the foot of May hill is named after glassworks that opened within Newent in the late 16th century.[17] Of the dwellings there in the 17th century at least one was a copyhold of Great Taynton manor.[18] Cottages were built next to the site of the works on waste land (Glasshouse green) and those within Newent, the majority,[19] were removed by the mid 19th century.[20] Cottages north of the lane to Hownhall were demolished in the late 19th century during the creation of the grounds of the new Clifford Manor, in Newent.[21] To the south Monk's Spout Cottage, next to Castle Hill wood, stands near the spring called Monk's well and the spot where, according to tradition, a chapel, presumably the woodland hermitage acquired by Gloucester abbey in the 12th century, once stood.[22] Within the wood a circular earthwork above the north side of a small valley was probably formed with a watchtower in the late 11th or early 12th century.[23]

Although scattered building had taken place on the common on Glasshouse hill by the early 18th century,[24] the oldest surviving houses there date from the late 18th century. That at Hill Farm was built with outbuildings near an older barn.[25] Higher up a farmhouse known as the Folly in 1799[26] was home to a curate in the 1890s and 1900s.[27] Building, which also took place at Gander's green on the boundary with Huntley in the valley to the south, continued in higgledy-piggledy fashion in the early 19th century[28] and among new buildings in the 1860s and 1870s were a chapel on what was to become the main road over the hill and a mission church.[29] In the 20th century more houses and bungalows were built among the lanes on the hill and the scattered settlement, extending into Longhope, became recognised as the village of May Hill.

BUILDINGS

Among physical evidence of medieval building in Taynton are the earthworks raised on the east side of the parish after the Norman Conquest, part of which was the site of the parish church, and the moat around the rectory house near by. The medieval farmsteads have been redeveloped. Taynton Court, where the house stood within a moat, presumably

---

1 DoE List, Taynton (1985), 7/249.
2 *Glos. Subsidy Roll, 1327*, 35; see *Inq. p.m. Glos. 1236–1300*, 232.
3 Below, manors (other estates).
4 For a footbridge down-stream of the road bridge, see OS Map 6", Glos. XXIV.SW (1889 edn).
5 See below (bldgs.).
6 GA, D 214/B 9/14.
7 GDR, F 1/4; T 1/177; see TNA, PROB 11/2148, f. 293 and v.
8 Below, manors (other estates).
9 Below (bldgs.); see Bryant, *Map of Glos.* (1824).
10 GA, D 2957/299/98, 102.
11 Ibid. D 1371; see below, manors (other estates: Taynton Ho.).
12 Currer-Briggs, 'Taynton and the Holder Family', 4.
13 Surnames derived from the place name are recorded in TNA, E 142/31, rot. 4d.; *Glos. Subsidy Roll, 1327*, 35.
14 GA, D 1371; see ibid. D 2957/299/128.
15 GDR, T 1/177 (nos 537–8); OS Map 6", Glos. XXIV.NW (1887 edn); see Sherratt, *Taynton's Industrial Past*, 3–5; 12–13.
16 GA, D 413/T 1; see GDR, T 1/177 (no 495).
17 See above, Newent, econ. hist. (other industry and crafts).
18 GA, D 413/T 2–4.
19 Ibid. D 2528, pp. 1–2, plan A.
20 Above, Newent, settlement (outlying settlements: Cugley).
21 OS Map 6", Glos. XXIV.NW (1887, 1903 edns).
22 *Notes on Dioc. of Glouc. by Chancellor Parsons*, 188; see below, religious hist. (religious life).
23 A.F. Dodd, 'Taynton: Castle Hill Earthwork', *Glevensis* 14 (1980), 32.
24 GA, D 1230/4.
25 Ibid. D 413/T 4.
26 Ibid. T 7.
27 *Kelly's Dir. Glos.* (1897), 316; (1906), 319.
28 GA, D 413/T 3, T 10; D 4869/1/4/1.
29 Below, religious hist.

72. Byfords from the south

marks the site of Little Taynton manor.¹ Its house, for which Henry Westerdale was assessed on five hearths for tax in 1672,² was altered using material brought in 1699 by John Viney from the dismantled house at Kingetts³ and it has four bays and is of stone with one mullioned window. The church and the rectory house were destroyed in 1643. A new church, erected on a different site in the 1650s, was transformed from a single-cell preaching box into a conventional medieval-style church during the 19th century.⁴

Of the principal houses of Great Taynton Hownhall Farm contains a fragment of the house occupied by the Ayleways in the 16th century. The Grove and Taynton House (formerly Jack's House) seem to have been rebuilt in the late 16th or early 17th century with timber frames and brick infill. Both were **H**-plan houses⁵ and at Taynton House at least the outlines of Jack's House have survived, together with a record that in 1672 the owner Robert Holder had four hearths.⁶ The Grove faced north-west and the square panels of a substantial two-storeyed house are evident on its north-west and south-east fronts. The high end of the house was to the north-east, where a large chimney stack was shared by a central hall and parlour and chambers in a north-east wing.

South-east of the stack a dog-leg staircase in a gabled projection served the hall. The house's south-western end, possibly jettied and slightly different in date, had a projecting stack.⁷

Among the smaller farmhouses Byfords and Pound Farm are 17th-century timber-framed dwellings. Byfords, built for a farm on a larger estate,⁸ looks taller and more striking because of its position on an outcrop on the side of a steep slope.⁹ On the south and west fronts the house is two-storeyed and on the north and east it has three storeys and an attic and a high cellar. The square panelled frame is varied on the south and north by bands of close studding and is infilled with large local bricks. Some of the original stone roof tiles survive. The **L** plan accommodates two large but plain main rooms with intersecting beams on each floor. In the longer west range the hall is heated by a west chimney stack. Behind the hall and chamber above are a small unheated room and an oak winder staircase. The kitchen, at a slightly lower level to the east, has at its north end a massive external chimney stack. In the semicircular farmyard below the house the oldest buildings, a cider house and stable with raised cruck roof, were probably built in the early 18th century, part of the improvements made by John Holder, who

---

1   See above (settlement).
2   TNA, E 179/247/14, rot. 36d.; for Westerdale, below, manors (Little Taynton manor).
3   GA, D 1371; see K. and W. Thomas, *Our Story of Taynton*, 10.
4   Below, religious hist. (religious life: bldg. of new par. ch., transformations of par. ch.).
5   See N. Kingsley, *The Country Houses of Gloucestershire*, I (2001), 240–1, 251.
6   TNA, E 179/247/14, rot. 36d.
7   GA, DA 30/711/6.
8   Below, manors (other estates).
9   Fig. 72.

73. Brick outbuildings at Taynton House, namely the oxhouse (1699) and (left) the barn (1695)

installed a new cider press in 1705 and erected a cart house and dairy in 1707.[1] One barn is dated 1864.[2]

The smaller house at Pound Farm stands on a fairly level site. It has a simple plan of three rooms and attics in line. The hall was heated by an external brick chimney stack on the north wall and the east room was probably unheated until a north stack was added in the 19th century to warm a bread oven. In the late 17th century the west room was rebuilt as a chamber block of two full storeys with end chimney stack and framed newel staircase. A long range south-east of the house incorporates a cider house and, together with a three-bayed barn further south-east, dates probably from the 17th century.

In the later 17th century the principal farmhouses had up to four or five heated rooms. One or two may have been considerably larger but most houses in the parish were very small.[3] Surviving examples include Tudor Cottage at Glasshouse, Monk's Spout Cottage, and the, perhaps slightly later, cottage by Haskins. All three have two-bayed, 1½-storeyed cores.[4]

The use of brick for external walls rather than for the infilling of timber frames is seen in Taynton from the late 17th century, notably in buildings erected on John Holder's estate. At Taynton House he created a walled farmyard immediately north of the house with a symmetrical arrangement of a six-bayed barn of 1695 on the north and an oxhouse (later stables) and a cider house with cellar of 1699 on the east and west respectively. The buildings, of brick with stone roof tiles and finials,[5] are of a standard above most of the area's domestic buildings at that time and are matched in quality and ambition only at the farmhouse at Hownhall, which Holder bought in 1698.[6] There one room of the old house, which had been repaired in the mid 17th century after 1643,[7] was retained as the north service wing of a new red brick house.[8] With a single pile of rooms raised on a brick vaulted basement well ventilated for storing produce, the house from the east has a fashionable symmetrical five-bayed façade of two storeys and attics, timber sashes, and a small forecourt with a low wall swept up to higher piers. The south façade, comparable in style, has three bays of blind windows in front of a chimney stack, the blank panels filled with the local orange brick that is used for all the dressings. Only the south-eastern corner of the roof is hipped. The west elevation is distinctly the back, its three wide gabled bays accommodating an extra storey and its windows having (replaced) cross-casements. A projecting east bay contains a dog-leg service staircase. The main staircase, plain but handsomely made, fills a central entrance hall flanked by two

1 GA, D 1371.
2 The datestone bears the inits. of C.B. Atherton, owner of the Taynton Ho. estate: below, manors (other estates).
3 See TNA, E 179/247/14, rot. 36d.
4 DoE List, Taynton, 7/245, 244, 234.

5 GA, D 1371; see DoE List, Taynton, 7/240–2. See Fig. 73.
6 Below, manors (other estates).
7 TNA, E 134/1657/Mich. 47.
8 DoE List, Taynton, 7/235. The ho. was described as newly built in 1779: GA, D 2957/299/66.

parlours.¹ Near by a brick building with details matching those of the house and a datestone inscribed 1723 was built by Holder as stables and cattle sheds. A timber-framed barn to the south has full cruck trusses taken in 1720 by Holder from a barn he dismantled at a place called Collards.²

Among houses rebuilt as compact brick dwellings in the late 17th or early 18th century, that at Five Elms Farm has two storeys and a projecting porch linked by band courses. Few other new houses were built in the 18th century. The Grove was partly refaced in brick and a timber-framed dairy and scullery were added on the north-east possibly as late as the 1730s or 1740s. In those changes the high and low ends of the house were reversed, the hall was divided into hall and sitting room, service rooms were added to the south-eastern front of the hall, and a brick cider house and granary were built close to the south-eastern angle of the house.³

In the early 19th century both Taynton Court and Taynton House were refaced, the former modestly with sash windows. At Taynton House, in work probably undertaken for William Holder,⁴ the east front of the house was turned into that of a *cottage ornée* with rendered walls, an extra gable over the hall, sash windows, and a trellis porch (since replaced by a timber verandah) and a ha-ha was dug in front of it. The interior was stripped and gutted and a new staircase built at the back. The refitting included doorcases with lions' heads⁵ and in 1825 the house was advertised for letting, under the name of the Ryelands, with entrance hall, dining and drawing rooms, and six bedrooms.⁶ The house now called the Ryelands, standing on the edge of the grounds of Taynton House, was built slightly later by the Holders as a smaller gentleman's residence and was sometimes known also as Irelands.⁷ In the mid 20th century pineapple finials were added to the east front⁸ and a lodge was built half way along the drive from the Newent road.⁹

Kent's Green House was embellished with scalloped bargeboards when it was built or enlarged on an L plan in the mid 19th century.¹⁰ With the exception of the rectory house completed in 1850 most other houses in Taynton dating from

74. The hall at Hownhall

the 19th century were small plain dwellings of red brick.¹¹ Hill View House, built as a workhouse in 1818, has three storeys with few windows towards Moat Lane.¹²

Few new houses were built in the 20th century. Marchfield (formerly March Croft), the largest, was constructed in 1912 using locally made bricks.¹³ Of the principal houses only the Grove was much altered, it being enlarged to designs made in 1924 by Harold Trew for M.P. Price, who the previous year had built a pair of cottages at the entrance of the drive to the house. The drawing room was to become the study and the entrance hall a dining room and a new south-west wing was to contain a drawing room, a sitting room, a west loggia, and a hall entered from the south and interconnecting with a new staircase in the place of an earlier study.¹⁴

---

1 Fig. 74.
2 GA, D 1371; K. and W. Thomas, *Our Story of Taynton*, 8; DoE List, Taynton, 7/236–7.
3 GA, DA 30/711/6.
4 The name Taynton House is written in the record of his burial: ibid. P 326/IN 1/9.
5 Currer-Briggs, 'Taynton and the Holder Family 1538–1950', 19; Verey and Brooks, *Glos.* II, 707; see DoE List, Taynton, 7/239.
6 *The Times*, 7 Apr. 1825.
7 GA, D 2957/299/98, 102; *The Times*, 6 Feb. 1841; 24 June, 28 Aug. 1848. See Bryant, *Map of Glos.* (1824).
8 DoE List, Taynton, 7/238.
9 cf. OS Maps 6", Glos. XXIV.NW (1924 edn); 1:2,500, SO 7221–7321 (1972 edn).
10 GA, SL 13.
11 Above (settlement).
12 Date on bldg.; below, local govt.; also Fig. 75.
13 Sherratt, *Taynton's Industrial Past*, 11–12.
14 GA, DA 30/711/6; D 2176/2/6/4; see Verey and Brooks, *Glos.* II, 707.

MANORS AND ESTATES

Of the two estates in Taynton described in Domesday Book the larger became the manor of Great Taynton, which covered most of the parish. The manor of Little Taynton derived from the other estate, which the lords of Kilpeck held in the 12th and 13th centuries, and included Cravenhill, the subject of a grant from the Crown c.1270. The manor of Taynton that passed from Richard Lister (d. 1558) to his son Michael remains to be identified.[1]

Gloucester abbey owned land in the parish from the mid 12th century and the changing pattern of landownership under the manors produced a number of estates,[2] some based in the 16th and 17th centuries on the Grove and other houses in the parish. Much of the land, some of which was copyhold,[3] belonged to farming families, notably the Holders from the mid 17th century. Non-resident owners included the Gloucester lawyer and politician Thomas Pury (d. 1666).[4] His contemporary William Sivedale, landowner in Taynton and Malswick, in Newent, was fined for his support of the Royalist cause during the Civil Wars.[5] In the shifting pattern of landownership the Probyn family added Castle Hill wood to its possessions in the early 1740s[6] and remained among the principal landowners in the parish[7] until 1884, when on the sale of the Huntley estate its land passed to the Ackers family.[8] In the mid 19th century, when the Probyns had 148 a., four landowners, including two members of the Holder family and the politician Benjamin Disraeli, each had over 300 a. in the parish.[9] In the later 19th century P.R. Cocks, Lord Somers, made piecemeal purchases of land in the west of Taynton in creating an estate that centred on the house he built at Clifford Manor, in Newent.[10] Land elsewhere was taken into the Newent Court estate built up by Andrew Knowles and split up after his death in 1909. The Grove became part of the Price family's Tibberton Court estate in the early 20th century and was sold off towards the end of it.

GREAT TAYNTON MANOR

An estate of 6 hides that Alwin held immediately before the Conquest was one of the possessions of William Goizenboded in 1086.[11] William and his immediate successors, of whom Maud de Wateville was lady of Taynton in the mid 12th century,[12] probably raised the substantial earthworks on the east side of Taynton that included the medieval parish church.[13] William's main estates descended to Arnald du Boys, a tenant of the honor of Leicester[14] and a landholder in Taynton in 1236.[15] Later Great Taynton manor, claimed in 1287 to be part of the honor,[16] was held for a knight's fee of William du Boys[17] but by 1303 it was held together with an estate in Kilcot, in Newent, from the king in chief as ½ knight's fee.[18]

Ralph Avenel, who required Ralph the clerk of Taynton to pay an annuity to St Bartholomew's hospital in Gloucester until it received land in Longford from him,[19] died by 1217[20] and his widow Margaret had dower in his Taynton estate. The estate passed to Douce, the daughter of his son William, by 1236 when she was made the ward of Robert de Mucegros. Under the name Cecily, she married Robert's son John (d. c.1275)[21] and was succeeded in Great Taynton manor at her death c.1301 by her granddaughter Hawise, daughter of Robert de Mucegros and wife of John de Ferrers[22] (d. 1312) of Chartley (Staffs.).[23] Hawise's next husband John de Bures survived her and at his death in 1350 the manor passed to her grandson John de Ferrers,[24] a minor.[25] John died in 1367 and at the death in 1375 of his widow Elizabeth, who had married Reynold of

---

1 TNA, C 142/123, no 83.
2 For early unidentified estates, *Glos. Feet of Fines 1199–1299*, p. 181; *1300–59*, pp. 3, 30, 128, 148, 168–9.
3 See GA, D 324; D 413/T 2; D 2957/299/10, 76–7, 98, 108–9.
4 TNA, PROB 11/326, ff. 176v.–177; for Pury, see *Oxford DNB*.
5 *Cal. Cttee for Compounding*, I, 85–6; III, 2016.
6 GA, D 23/T 32.
7 Rudge, *Hist. of Glos.* II, 47; GDR, T 1/177.
8 GA, SL 10.
9 GDR, T 1/177.
10 GA, D 413/T 2–5, 7–12; above, Newent, manors (Boulsdon manor: Clifford Manor).
11 *Domesday Book* (Rec. Com.), I, 167.
12 *Eng. Episc. Acta VII*, pp. 19, 59. The Wateville family also acquired an interest in William's estate in Guiting Power: Rudder, *Glos.* 462–3; Dugdale, *Mon.* VI (2), 836.
13 See above, settlement.

14 J.S. Moore, 'The Gloucestershire section of Domesday Book: geographical problems of the text, part 2', *Trans. BGAS* 106 (1988), 99.
15 *Close 1234–7*, 297; see *Cal. Inq. p.m.* I, 82.
16 *Plac. de Quo Warr.* 246.
17 *Cal. Inq. p.m.* IV, 9.
18 *Feudal Aids*, II, 250, 284, 298; for the Kilcot estate, above, Newent, manors.
19 *Glouc. Corp. Rec.* pp. 92–3.
20 *Pat. 1216–25*, 127.
21 *Close 1234–7*, 297; *Cal. Close 1272–9*, 172; J. Maclean, 'Notice of Earthworks in the Parish of English Bicknor', *Trans. BGAS* 4 (1879–80), 311–17, which includes a discussion of the identity of Margaret's husband.
22 *Cal. Inq. p.m.* IV, 8–9.
23 For the Ferrers fam., *Complete Peerage*, V, 307–21.
24 *Cal. Inq. p.m.* IX, 402; see *Glos. Feet of Fines 1300–59*, p. 66.
25 *Cal. Fine 1347–56*, 292.

Cobham, the manor passed to his son Robert, a minor.[1] Robert (d. 1413) was succeeded by his son Edmund[2] and Edmund (d. 1435) by his son William[3] After William's death in 1450 without male issue the manor was awarded to his brother Edmund Ferrers[4] (d. 1453), from whom it passed in turn to his brothers Martin[5] (d. 1484), Henry[6] (d. 1486), and Richard.[7] Richard died in 1494 and from his widow Elizabeth[8] the manor reverted to the direct descendants of William de Ferrers, a line represented in 1503 by the infant Walter Devereux, Lord Ferrers.[9]

Lord Ferrers, who thus became the principal landowner in Taynton,[10] was created Viscount Hereford in 1550. He died in 1558 and his grandson and heir Walter Devereux, created Lord Bourchier in 1571 and earl of Essex in 1572, died in 1576. Although Walter's son Robert, the next earl, granted a lease of the demesne,[11] the manor was retained by Walter's widow Lettice, who married in turn Robert Dudley (d. 1588), earl of Leicester, and Sir Christopher Blount (ex. 1601). The Crown seized the manor on Blount's attainder[12] and granted it in 1603 to Sir Simon Weston and John Wakeman.[13] Weston was the lord in 1608[14] and by reason of its grant the Crown in 1617 rescinded a gift of the manor to George Villiers, then earl of Buckingham.[15]

In 1627 Great Taynton belonged to Robert Parkhurst,[16] a London alderman who was knighted and died in 1636. He was succeeded by his son Robert,[17] who was also knighted, and the latter's son Robert[18] quitclaimed the manor to Jerome Smith in 1656.[19] Jerome conveyed it to Abraham Shapton, a London cheesemonger, and his wife Judith in 1673[20] and they broke up the estate by sales in 1687. Part, including the manorial rights, was bought by Thomas Pury,[21] a former MP for Gloucester who had inherited land in Taynton from his father Thomas (d. 1666) and had sponsored the building of a new parish church in the 1650s.[22] Thomas died in 1693[23] and the manor was settled in 1695 on his daughters Elizabeth Whittington and Sarah Pury and their infant niece Sarah Huggins.[24] Sarah Pury died in 1709[25] and Elizabeth Whittington in 1733. In the late 18th century the manor was ascribed to Morgan Price, owner of the Grove in Taynton,[26] but in the early 19th century there was no agreed lord, the estate having been much divided.[27]

LITTLE TAYNTON MANOR

The manor of Little Taynton originated in an estate that was held by Wulfgar in 1066 and by William son of Norman in 1086. A yardland in the Forest of Dean attached to that estate[28] became the hay of Hereford, which was in the keeping of the lord of Little Taynton in the mid 13th century.[29] William's estate passed to his son Hugh (*fl.* 1130) and descended with the lordship of Kilpeck (Herefs.)[30] to Hugh of Kilpeck (d. *c.*1244).[31] In 1258 in a division of Hugh's property between his daughters Joan and Isabel, respectively the wives of Philip Marmion and William Walrond, Little Taynton was assigned with Kilpeck to Isabel[32] and the following year, as part of an exchange, she and William gave it to Robert Walrond.[33] Bevis de Knovill, who married William Walrond's granddaughter Joan, held the manor in 1273 and was granted free warren in the demesne in 1285.[34] The manor was held for ¼ knight's fee in the early 14th century[35] and Henry of Pembridge had a mesne lordship in it as of the inheritance of Robert Walrond in 1338.[36] In 1364 the overlordship belonged to the earl of Ormonde, as lord of Kilpeck.[37]

Bevis de Knovill (d. 1307) was succeeded by his son Bevis.[38] He forfeited his lands for taking part in a

---

1 *Cal. Inq. p.m.* XII, 116–17; XIV, 102.
2 Ibid. XX, 10–11.
3 TNA, C 139/75, no 33.
4 Ibid. C 44/29/26; *Cal. Pat.* 1446–52, 413–14.
5 TNA, C 139/151, no 50.
6 Ibid. C 141/2, no 20.
7 *Cal. Inq. p.m. Hen. VII*, I, 19–20.
8 Ibid. 539–40.
9 Ibid. III, 412; see *Complete Peerage*, V, 327 and n.
10 *Military Surv. of Glos. 1522*, 57–8.
11 See below (other estates: the Grove).
12 *Complete Peerage*, V, 140–2; TNA, E 178/952.
13 *Cal. SP Dom.* 1603–10, 27.
14 Smith, *Men and Armour*, 65.
15 *Cal. SP Dom.* 1611–18, 444; see TNA, C 66/2090, no 7; C 66/2115, no 1.
16 A document at Forthampton Court, Gloucestershire, refers to a manor ct. held for Robert in that year.
17 TNA, PROB 11/173, ff. 103v.–105; C 142/543, no 21.
18 GA, D 2957/299/10.
19 TNA, CP 25/2/554/1656/57 Hil. no 32.
20 Ibid. CP 25/2/658/25 Chas. II Trin. no 16.
21 GA, D 2957/299/109; Atkyns, *Glos.* 709.
22 *Oxford DNB*, s.v. Thomas Pury (d. 1666); TNA, PROB 11/326, ff. 176v.–177; below, religious hist.
23 Bigland, *Glos.* III, no 266.
24 Shakespeare Birthplace Trust, Stratford-upon-Avon (Warws.), DR 18/1/1720.
25 GA, P 326/IN 1/2.
26 Bigland, *Glos.* III, no 266. For the Grove, below (other estates).
27 Rudge, *Hist. of Glos.* II, 47.
28 *Domesday Book* (Rec. Com.), I, 167v.
29 *Book of Fees*, II, 1407–8; see *Cal. Inq. p.m.* V, 74–5, 78.
30 See F.B. Welch, 'Gloucestershire in the Pipe Rolls', *Trans. BGAS* 57 (1935), 90; I.J. Sanders, *English Baronies* (1960), 73.
31 *Close 1242–7*, 155; *Book of Fees*, II, 1407–8.
32 *Glos. Feet of Fines 1199–1299*, p. 123.
33 *Cal. Inq. p.m.* V, 74–5.
34 Ibid. II, 8; *Complete Peerage*, VII, 347.
35 *Feudal Aids*, II, 250, 285.
36 *Cal. Inq. p.m.* VIII, 108.
37 Ibid. XI, 396.
38 Ibid. IV, 335–6.

rebellion against Edward II but was restored to them[1] and at his death in 1338 he held Little Taynton jointly with his wife Joan. His son and heir John de Knovill[2] was in possession in 1343.[3] John's widow Margery married Thomas Moyne and on her death in 1361 the manor was divided between the descendants of John's paternal aunts Margaret and Elizabeth, the wives of Thomas Verdun and Thomas Maudit.[4] Margaret's son John Verdun granted the reversion of a moiety of the manor to Richard of Pembridge in 1363.[5] The other moiety was settled in 1385 on the marriage of Henry and Maud Green[6] and was acquired in 1397 by John Cassey of Wightfield in Deerhurst parish.[7] In 1393 he had acquired a reversionary right to a quarter of the manor previously owned by Richard Burley and retained by Richard's widow Beatrice, wife of Hugh Waterton.[8] The remaining quarter of the manor passed to John Barre (d. 1483) and on the death of his widow Joan was inherited by his daughter Isabel, wife in turn of Humphrey Stafford, earl of Devon, and Thomas Bourchier[9] (d. 1491). Isabel died in 1489[10] and after Thomas's death her share of the manor was divided between Richard Delabere, Edward Hanmer, and Thomas Cornwall.[11] It has not been traced later.

John Cassey died in 1400 and his descendant John Cassey[12] had a substantial estate at Little Taynton in 1451.[13] Little Taynton manor, which Ursula, the widow of John Cassey (d. 1508), retained in 1530,[14] passed to her husband's grandson Robert Cassey (d. 1547) and to Robert's son Henry[15] (d. 1595). Henry's son Thomas sold the manor in 1604 to Robert Atkinson[16] of Stowell. Robert (d. 1607) was succeeded in turn by his sons Henry (fl. 1630) and John[17] and the latter, who held his first manor court in 1631,[18] sold the manor in 1656 to Charles Pitfield of Hoxton (Middx).[19] The next sale, in 1669, was to Robert Holder (d. 1684) and he left the manor to his grandson John Holder,[20] who sold it in 1698 to John Viney of Gloucester.[21]

The site of the manor, presumably at Taynton Court, followed a different descent from 1577 when Henry Cassey sold it with its land to Christopher Westerdale[22] (d. 1581). Christopher's eldest son Christopher (d. 1655)[23] left the estate to his grandson Henry Westerdale[24] (d. 1681)[25] and it was presumably thorough the marriage of Henry's daughter Mary to John Viney that the site was re-united with the manor.[26]

John Viney (d. 1719) was succeeded in the manor by his son William[27] (d. 1744) and on the death of William's widow Mary in 1760 the estate, including land in Great Taynton,[28] passed to their son Revd James Viney[29] (d. 1767). James's son and heir James, a Royal Artillery officer who was made a knight, died in 1841,[30] his estate of 330 a. at Taynton Court and Pound Farm[31] having passed to his niece Mary Anne Evans, wife in turn of Wyndham Lewis (d. 1838) and the politician Benjamin Disraeli.[32] The Disraelis sold the estate in 1862 to William Laslett[33] (d. 1884).[34] In 1889 Robert Bridges Bellers sold it with Kent's Green House, part of the estate from 1874, to Andrew Knowles[35] and when his Newent Court estate was split up after his death in 1909 Taynton Court farm was sold, with Kent's Green House, to its tenant F. Smith and Pound farm to its tenant A. Wintle.[36] Smith died in 1944 and Taynton Court passed from Joseph Harrison (d. 1975) to his son-in-law Brian Griffiths, whose son, Mr James Griffiths, farmed there in 2006.[37]

---

1 *Cal. Fine* 1319–27, 96–7, 175; *Complete Peerage*, VII, 348–9.
2 *Cal. Inq. p.m.* VIII, 108.
3 *Glos. Feet of Fines 1300–59*, p. 139.
4 *Complete Peerage*, VII, 349 and n.
5 *Cal. Close* 1360–4, 532; see TNA, CP 25/1/78/72, no 415.
6 TNA, CP 25/1/289/54, no 120.
7 Ibid. CP 25/1/79/83, no 141; *Cat. Anct. D.* I, p. 444.
8 TNA, CP 25/1/78/82, no 112; *Cal. Inq. Misc.* V, 139–40.
9 TNA, C 140/84, no 39; *Cal. Inq. p.m. Hen. VII*, I, 3–4, 47.
10 *Cal. Inq. p.m. Hen. VII*, I, 200, 214; *Complete Peerage*, IV, 328.
11 *Cal. Fine* 1485–1509, 175–6.
12 For John (d. 1400) and his successors, *VCH Glos.* VIII, 40.
13 TNA, CP 25/1/79/91, no 118.
14 Ibid. C 142/50, no 89.
15 Ibid. C 142/84, no 77.
16 Ibid. CP 25/2/297/2 Jas. I Mich. no 42.
17 Ibid. C 142/306, no 150; *Inq. p.m. Glos. 1625–42*, III, 85; *VCH Glos.* IX, 211.
18 GA, D 324.
19 TNA, CP 25/2/554/1656/57 Hil. no 35; for Charles Pitfield, GA, D 247/31.
20 GA, D 1371; GDR wills 1684/222.
21 GA, D 1371; R.W. Stewart, 'Notes on the Viney Family of Gloucester' (n.d.): ibid. GE 138.
22 TNA, CP 25/2/143/1829/19 Eliz. I Trin. no 1; GA, D 324, f. 1v.
23 Bigland, *Glos.* III, no 266.
24 TNA, PROB 11/245, f. 111 and v.
25 Bigland, *Glos.* III, no 266.
26 D. Allen, 'Pedigree of Westerdale' (2001): GA, GE 406.
27 GDR wills 1719/144.
28 Ibid. 1745/57; Fosbrooke, *Glouc.* 133.
29 TNA, PROB 11/1270, f. 378.
30 Stewart, 'Notes on Viney Family'.
31 BL, Add. MS 15648E.
32 *Oxford DNB*, s.v. Disraeli, Mary Anne; *Glos. N&Q* II, 104–5; GDR, T 1/177.
33 GA, D 8502/1.
34 W.R. Williams, *The Parliamentary History of the County of Worcester* (Hereford, priv. printed 1897), 112.
35 NRA Report, Taynton (J.T. Harrison).
36 Above, Newent, manors (Newent manor: Newent Court); Glos. Colln. RX 212.2.
37 Information from Mr Donald Sherratt of Green Croft Farm; memorials to Smith and Harrison in Taynton churchyard.

OTHER ESTATES

Byfords

The house at Byfords was the centre of an estate that John Whittington (d. 1525), lord of Pauntley, settled on the marriage of his son Thomas (d. 1546).[1] In 1583, in a Chancery suit to which George Burrell and John Ayleway were a party, (Sir) Thomas Throckmorton of Tortworth and Thomas Bodenham of Rotherwas (Herefs.), descendants of two of Thomas Whittington's coheirs, were confirmed in their titles to parts of the estate.[2] Throckmorton's share, which included Castle Hill wood,[3] passed at his death in 1608 to his son William,[4] who was made a baronet in 1611.[5] Ayleway was the owner of Hownhall with which Byfords was sold as a farmhouse in 1698 to John Holder.[6] The Athertons owned the farmhouse with Taynton House in the early 20th century,[7] after which it had a succession of owners. Mr Eric Freeman, the owner from 1982, kept it with 20 ha (50 a.) in 2006.[8]

Cravenhill

About 1270 Henry III granted Bevis de Knovill an estate called Gravenhull.[9] The estate, which was held from the king in chief for 1/20 knight's fee, descended with Little Taynton manor to John de Knovill (*fl.* 1349)[10] and was based on the house in Little Taynton at Cravenhill (Craven Hill), by the road leading westwards from Kent's Green.[11] The house with its land passed to Richard Hooper (d. 1577)[12] and to Thomas Nelme (*fl.* 1630).[13] John Pritchard sold it to Thomas Burgis of Gloucester, who by will proved 1715 left it to his son Thomas (d. 1718).[14] Cravenhill belonged with 31 a. to James Clarke in 1840[15] and was sold as part of Norman's farm in 1910.[16]

The Grove

The Grove, a farmhouse on the east side of Taynton, stands probably on the site of the demesne farm of Great Taynton manor leased from Robert, earl of Essex, to John Addis in the late 16th century.[17] The residence of Thomas Pury (d. 1693),[18] the Grove passed with the manor to his daughters Elizabeth and Sarah[19] and in 1742 it belonged with its land to John Grove.[20] From John, a parishioner in 1737,[21] the Grove passed to Samuel Grove by 1769.[22] Samuel (d. 1787)[23] was succeeded by his daughter Catherine[24] (d. 1820). Her husband, Revd Morgan Price of Knebworth (Herts.), died in 1830 and the estate passed to their son Samuel Grove Price who bought the adjacent Hayne's farm in 1826.[25] Samuel, MP for Sandwich (Kent), lived at Sunninghill (Berks.)[26] and died in 1839 leaving the estate, which covered 333 a. of Taynton, to his widow Marianne.[27] After her death in 1868 their son Stanhope Grove Price acquired the estate.[28] He changed his name to Stanhope Grove Grove in 1870[29] and at his death in 1909 was succeeded by his son Stanhope Pury Grove.[30] In 1911 the Grove and its land were bought by Morgan Philips Price, owner of the adjoining Tibberton Court estate, and in 1926, soon after he had moved into the farmhouse,[31] he owned 437 a. in Taynton.[32] Price, who became a Labour MP and represented the Forest of Dean (later West Gloucestershire) from 1935 to 1959, died in 1973.[33] His son (William Philips) Peter sold the farmland in the early 1980s and, on the death of M.P. Price's widow Elisa in 1985, their daughter Margaret Tatiana Rose sold the house at the Grove.[34] In 2006 house and farm were owned by Col. R.H. Ker.

---

1 TNA, C 1/813, no 41. For John Whittington and his successors, above, Pauntley, manor.

2 TNA, C 78/77, no 5.

3 BL, Harl. MS 4131, f. 481v.

4 TNA, C 142/304, no 96.

5 *Complete Baronetage*, I, 65; see GA, D 2957/299/128.

6 Below (Hownhall); GA, D 1371, f. 5.

7 Ibid. D 2428/1/24, ff. 75–6.

8 Information from Mr Freeman; see sale particulars of 1949 in National Monuments Record, Swindon, file SA01004.

9 *Rot. Hund.* I, 176.

10 *Inq. p.m. Glos.* 1302–58, 97–8, 270–1; *Complete* Peerage, VII, 349.

11 OS Map 1:2,500, Glos. XXIV.3 (1883, 1903 edns); Glos. Colln. RX 212.2.

12 GA, P 326/IN 1/1.

13 GDR wills 1577/119; GA, D 324, f. 10v.; TNA, C 3/214/33.

14 GDR wills 1715/83; 1718/266; Fosbrooke, *Glouc.* 173.

15 GDR, T 1/177.

16 Glos. Colln. RX 212.2.

17 TNA, E 178/952.

18 *Notes on Dioc. of Glouc. by Chancellor Parsons*, 188–9. Pury's arms are displayed in the ho.: DoE List, Taynton (1985), 7/233.

19 Above (Great Taynton manor); *Notes on Dioc. of Glouc. by Chancellor Parsons*, 188.

20 TNA, C 108/3.

21 GDR wills 1739/200.

22 GA, D 3398/1/3/1, 16.

23 *The Times*, 17 Sept. 1787.

24 TNA, PROB 11/1158, f. 7 and v.

25 GA, D 1589/1.

26 Ibid. D 3398/1/3/16.

27 TNA, PROB 11/1916, ff. 283v.–284; GDR, T 1/177.

28 GA, D 1589/1.

29 Ibid. D 3398/1/3/16.

30 Ibid. D 1589/1; D 1865.

31 M.P. Price, *My Three Revolutions* (1969), 246; *Kelly's Dir. Glos.* (1914), 331.

32 GA, G/NE 159/11, f. 15.

33 *The Times*, 25 Sept. 1973.

34 Information from Mr Gordon Fluck of Tibberton, executor of Peter Price (d. 1987).

Hownhall

An estate based on Hownhall, in the centre of the parish, was built up by the Ayleway family. In 1268 Henry Ayleway and his wife Joan granted a yardland in Taynton to Geoffrey Ayleway, who may have acquired 5 a. there in 1254.[1] Walter Ayleway was a juror on an inquisition *post mortem* conducted at Taynton in 1301[2] and the reversion of his estate, which included a yardland, was settled in 1306 on Reynold Ayleway.[3] John Ayleway owned land in Great Taynton in the early 16th century[4] and Roger Ayleway was Taynton's wealthiest resident landowner in 1522.[5] John Ayleway[6] (d. 1599), who was similarly wealthy, lived at Hownhall and was succeeded by his son Christopher (d. 1605). Hownhall and its estate passed from the latter's son Richard (d. 1654)[7] to his son Thomas[8] and he mortgaged them in 1666 to his brother-in-law Richard Cocks (d. 1670). Richard's son Richard, who owned Hownhall in 1682, inherited a baronetcy with Dumbleton manor in 1684 and sold Hownhall in 1698 to John Holder,[9] the owner of Jack's House.[10] John (d. 1734) left Hownhall to his youngest son Robert (d. 1769), who left it to his son John. John (d. 1801), who lived in Ross-on-Wye (Herefs.), was succeeded in his Gloucestershire estates by his nephew John Holder.[11] He owned 331 a. in Taynton in 1840[12] and was succeeded in 1850 by his son John.[13] Hownhall became part of Edmund Probyn's Huntley Manor estate in 1872 and following the sale of the estate in 1884[14] was possibly acquired by William Viner Ellis (d. 1888) of Minsterworth.[15] Mrs A. Viner Bradford, the owner c.1910,[16] sold the farm in 1920 to Albert House[17] (d. 1929).[18] In 1994 the farm was broken up and sold, part being bought by Col. Ker, owner of the Grove.[19] John House remained at the farmhouse in 2006.

Norman's Farm

Norman's Farm, standing on Taynton's northern boundary with Newent, was the centre of an estate owned in 1677 by John Crockett[20] and in 1691 by Joseph Clarke[21] (d. 1705). Joseph's son Joseph (d. 1738) enlarged the estate, purchasing Five Elms farm from Thomas Nelme, and left Norman's farm to his wife Elizabeth (d. 1754) and Five Elms to his son Thomas (d. 1789).[22] Norman's farm descended to Joseph Clarke of Newent and after his death in 1833[23] it was sold to John Cocks Bower (d. 1860). He left it to Sophia Maile and Harriet Elizabeth Radclyffe and the latter sold her share to Caleb Maile, Sophia's husband. In 1863 the Mailes sold the farm (161 a.) to a trust for the family of Sir John Owen Bt (d. 1861) and in 1895 the trust sold it to Andrew Knowles.[24] In 1910, on the break up of his Newent Court estate which also included Five Elms farm, Norman's farm was bought by Selwyn Smith.[25]

Taynton House

Taynton House, so called in 1819,[26] is a country house created by the remodelling of a farmhouse known as Jack's House for the Holder family.[27] Robert Holder, who bought the reversion of the farmhouse from Robert Parkhurst in 1655, laid the foundations of the Holders' estate, his purchases including a group of fields in the east of Taynton called the Cinders from Thomas Pury in 1668. At his death in 1684 his lands passed with Little Taynton manor to his grandson John Holder.[28] From John (d. 1734) the house and its estate passed in turn to his sons John (d. 1752), William (d. 1758) and Robert (d. 1769) and then to Robert's son William.[29] William (d. 1819) left Taynton House and its land to his nephew William Charles Holder.[30] In 1826 he, prior to taking Holy Orders,[31] transferred the estate to his uncle Edward Howell (d. 1834)[32] who devised it, subject to

---

1 *Glos. Feet of Fines 1199–1299*, pp. 103, 146.
2 *Inq. p.m. Glos.* 1236–1300, 232.
3 *Glos. Feet of Fines 1300–59*, p. 13. For members of the fam. in 1415 and 1452, see GA, D 23/T 31.
4 TNA, C 1/276, no 17.
5 *Military Surv. of Glos. 1522*, 57–8.
6 For John and his descendants, *Visit. Glos. 1623*, 229–30.
7 *Notes on Dioc. of Glouc. by Chancellor Parsons*, 189; GDR wills 1599/58; 1605/27.
8 GA, D 2957/299/19–20.
9 Ibid. 26–38; *Complete Baronetage*, III, 242. See Ayleway pedigree in A.W. Crawley-Boevey, *The 'Perverse Widow'* (1898), 263.
10 Below (Taynton Ho.).
11 GA, D 1371; D 2957/299/48, 116.
12 GDR, T 1/177.
13 GA, D 2957/299/101; see below (Taynton Ho.).
14 GA, D 4869/1/1/20; SL 10.
15 William Viner Ellis owned land in Taynton in 1885: *Kelly's Dir. Glos.* (1885), 591. See *Glouc. J.* 5 May 1888.
16 GA, D 2428/1/24, f. 70.
17 Ibid. D 2299/2019; G/NE 159/11, f. 12.
18 Monument in Taynton churchyard.
19 D.R. Sherratt, *Taynton's Industrial Past: The Brickworks, Potteries and Brass Mill* (1998), 15.
20 GA, D 2957/299/79.
21 Ibid. D 247/34.
22 Bigland, *Glos*. III, no 266; GDR wills 1738/17.
23 GDR wills 1833/234.
24 GA, D 5241/1.
25 Glos. Colln. RX 212.2.
26 GA, P 326/IN 1/9.
27 Above, settlement (bldgs.).
28 Ibid. GA, D 1371; GDR wills 1684/222. Above (Little Taynton manor). For the Cinders, GDR, T 1/177 (nos 6, 11–12).
29 GA, D 1371; D 2957/299/109–11.
30 Ibid. P 326/IN 1/9; D 2957/299/71.
31 *Alumni Cantab. 1752–1900*, III, 410.
32 GA, D 2957/299/98.

a life interest of his widow Hester, back to his nephew. W.C. Holder died in 1837 leaving the estate (314 a.) to his brother John[1] (d. 1850), who left it to his daughter Louisa Henrietta Holder.[2] She died in 1888 and at the death of her husband Charles Bernard Atherton in 1904 Taynton House passed to her son Henry Holder Atherton (d. 1913) and later her daughters Catherine (d. 1939) and Henrietta (d. 1950).[3] Henrietta left the estate of 210 a. to a nephew, Hamilton Alexander Gardner, and following his death in 1951 it was broken up by sales.[4] Taynton House was owned by Mr Richard Ashcroft in 2006.

Medieval Monastic Estates

Through its gift of Taynton church in the mid 12th century Gloucester abbey acquired a man and his family as well as a chapel and a yardland there.[5] By its acquisition of Kilpeck church in the 1130s it also obtained tithes from Taynton given to Kilpeck probably by Hugh of Kilpeck.[6] About 1158 Samson, the abbey sacrist, was instituted in Taynton church[7] and later sacrists received a pension of 2 marks (26s. 8d.) from it. The Kilpeck tithes were worth 16s. in 1291.[8] Following the Dissolution the sacrist's pension was granted, in 1541, to the bishop of Gloucester[9] and the Kilpeck tithes passed to the dean and chapter of Gloucester. Those tithes, used during the Interregnum to support St Mary de Lode church in Gloucester,[10] became known as Kilpeck's tithing and, taken from Taynton Court and 142 a. in Little Taynton, were commuted in 1843 for a corn rent charge of £27.[11] Gloucester abbey's land in Taynton was included, as part of the manor of Tibberton, Taynton, and Bulley, in the endowment of the dean and chapter in 1541.[12] That manor, an account of which will be given under Bulley in another volume, passed to the Ecclesiastical Commissioners who in 1860 enfranchised 52 a. at the Ryelands.[13]

In 1244 Studley priory (Warws.) held ½ yardland in Little Taynton.[14]

ECONOMIC HISTORY

AGRICULTURE

Although much of Taynton was under the plough in the Middle Ages pastoral farming and orcharding were long significant in Taynton.

The Middle Ages

In 1086 eleven ploughs were recorded in Taynton. The Great Taynton estate, worth £3 compared with £6 in 1066, had one in demesne and its tenants, 9 villans and 7 bordars, had nine between them. The other plough belonged to 6 bordars on the Little Taynton estate, which was worth 20s.[15] Five ploughteams were recorded in Great Taynton and one in Little Taynton in 1220.[16]

In 1301 the manor of Great Taynton had 100 a. arable, 8 a. meadow, and 5 a. pasture in demesne. Its tenants, apart from 12 freeholders with 9½ yardlands and 4 a. between them, owed labour services. Fourteen holding in all 7 yardlands for cash rents and customary payments were expected to perform services during winter and spring ploughing and haymaking and harvest bedrips. Similar services were required of eight tenants holding 2 yardlands between them. Five bondmen with ½ yardland and 6 a. owed a day's work a week and a day's work carrying hay. During August and September their weekly duty increased to two days, four cottars owed a day's work a week, and another cottar was expected to perform six harvest bedrips.[17] In 1307 the manor of Little Taynton, extended at two ploughlands, had 120 a. arable, 6 a. meadow, 2 a. several pasture, and 3 a. woodland in demesne. Seven customary tenants holding 1½ yardland owed cash rents and labour services that increased during August and September and three cottars owed autumn services as well as cash rents. One tenant on the manor was a freeholder and seven tenants on the lord's estate at Gravenhull also owed only cash rents.[18] A three-course rotation was evidently followed on the lord's demesne estate at Little Taynton and Kilcot in 1338; of 60 a. arable on the demesne, a third was cultivated,

---

1 Ibid. 101; TNA, PROB 11/1837, ff. 174–175v.; PROB 11/1892, ff. 180v.–183; GDR, T 1/177.
2 TNA, PROB 11/2122, f. 822 and v.
3 Monuments in Taynton churchyard; *Kelly's Dir Glos.* (1863–1939 edns); GA, reg. wills 1905, f. 55 and v.
4 H.P.R. Finberg, 'Three Studies in Family History', *Glos. Studies* (1957), 183; *The Times*, 2 Jan. 1952.
5 *Hist. & Cart. Mon. Glouc.* I, 116, 224, 228; II, 136–7; see below, religious hist. (early hist.; religious life).
6 *Hist. & Cart. Mon. Glouc.* I, 91; *Eng. Episc. Acta VII*, p. 58.
7 *Eng. Episc. Acta VII*, p. 59
8 *Tax. Eccl.* 161.
9 *L&P Hen. VIII*, XVI, 572.
10 Hockaday Abs ccxviii, 1657.
11 GA, D 936/Y 20; GDR, T 1/177.
12 *L &P Hen. VIII*, XVI, 572; see *Valor Eccl.* II, 412, 417.
13 GA, D 2957/299/102.
14 *Book of Fees*, II, 1157.
15 *Domesday Book* (Rec. Com.), I, 167 and v.
16 *Book of Fees*, I, 307.
17 *Inq. p.m. Glos.* 1236–1300, 232–4.
18 Ibid. 1302–58, 97–8.

another third was fallow during Lent, and the last third was to lie fallow until the following year.[1]

A north field by a highway in the early 16th century was possibly an open field[2] and open fields and common meadows in the eastern half of the parish are attested by later evidence.[3] In the Moorend green area part of a field or close called Clark's field was an orchard in 1530.[4] Apples were grown in Taynton for cider and eating and in the later Middle Ages the rector or the farmer of the rectory collected tithes of cider and of 'hoarding fruit' from parishioners' houses. Hemp was among other crops mentioned in statements made about tithe customs in 1552.[5]

The Early Modern Period

Taynton had numerous farms of varying sizes. In Great Taynton manor by the late 17th century many customary tenements had been enfranchised and a pattern of farms based on whole, and fractions of, yardlands had been obscured by amalgamation and division of holdings. A yardland had covered 64 a.[6] The Hownhall estate was made up of three farms, including Byfords,[7] and in the mid 18th century the Grove estate contained two principal farms.[8] In the late 18th century the Probyn family's estate had two farms with land in Taynton,[9] and in Little Taynton one farm represented the manorial demesne and two other holdings belonged to the lord's estate.[10]

Much of the farmland was in closes but the retention of a dole of land and the division of fields called Stony field and the Wire in the early 17th century represent the remnants of open fields in the south of the parish.[11] In 1655 a half yardland in Great Taynton comprised two pieces of land, the smaller of which was in a common meadow.[12] At that time Great Taynton had two common meadows, both beside the stream on the parish's eastern boundary north-east of the Grove: Chare (or Chard) meadow included a piece called Orley dole; Middle Ditch was to its south-west.[13] Both probably ceased to be common meadows by the mid 18th century through consolidation of holdings.[14] In Little Taynton the disposition of the lands of Kilpeck's tithing in 1562 indicates several areas of ridge and furrow and common meadow, one called Berry field being by the road to Kent's green.[15]

In the 17th century farming was a mixture of arable and pastoral husbandry with sheep and dairy cattle, and perhaps also pigs, reared in numbers. Some flax was grown.[16] There was a sheepcot at the Ryelands, then a close on the Gloucester dean and chapter estate.[17] John Holder, after coming of age in 1691, enlarged and consolidated his farm at Jack's House (later Taynton House) in a series of purchases, sales, and exchanges of land, and managed the land directly, pulling down redundant farmhouses, planting and replanting hedges and brakes, ploughing up several fields before returning them to grass in the 1710s, and digging channels to water the meadows below his house. He added to his land in Chare meadow and dug drainage trenches, and in 1713 inclosed 2 a., there. He undertook new planting and building around his house and garden, where notably he built a large barn in 1695 and an oxhouse and a cider house in 1699, and he provided new outbuildings on two farms that he acquired in 1698, namely a cart house and a dairy at Byfords in 1707 and stables and cattle sheds at Hownhall in 1723.[18]

Fruit growing was widespread and, although walnuts, cherries, and plums were mentioned along with hops in the tithe customs in 1704,[19] the orchards were mostly of apples and pears for the table and for drink. In the mid 17th century pears were the main fruit crop with a variety of squash pear making what was regarded as the best perry locally.[20] Farmsteads usually had their own cider mills[21] and when cider and perry were made the rector was entitled to the twelfth part, bringing his own vessels for it.[22] John Holder, who planted new orchards on his farm and in 1700 installed a mill and press in a new outbuilding, reckoned that 200 of his fruit trees were blown down by the great storm of 1703. He planted and grafted new apple and pear trees, including a nursery of stocks begun in 1720, and in 1705 he installed new cider presses at the farmsteads at Hownhall and Byfords.[23] In the later 18th century the parish continued to be esteemed for the excellence of its cider and perry,

---

1 *Inq. p.m. Glos.* 1302–58, 271.
2 TNA, C 78/77, no 5.
3 Below, this section.
4 GA, D 23/T 31.
5 GDR vol. 8, pp. 227–9; see Hockaday Abs. ccclxv, 1552.
6 GA, D 247/31, 34–5; D 413/T 2; D 2957/299/22, 109.
7 Ibid. D 1371, f. 5.
8 Ibid. D 23/E41.
9 Ibid. E 4.
10 Ibid. D 127/656.
11 Ibid. D 2957/299/15; for the Wire, GDR, T 1/177 (nos 149, 156).
12 GA, D 247/31.
13 Ibid. D 2957/299/128; D 247/31–2; D 892/T 81; see ibid. D 608/13/14.
14 Ibid. D 2957/299/13.
15 Ibid. D 936/Y 56; for Berry field, BL, Add. MS 15648E.
16 GDR, V 5/299T 4.
17 GA, D 1740/E 1, f. 117 and v.
18 Ibid. D 1371, passim; H.P.R. Finberg, 'Three Studies in Family History', *Glos. Studies* (1957), 176–9.
19 GDR, V 5/299T 4.
20 D. Colwall, 'An Account of Perry and Cider out of Gloucestershire', in J. Evelyn, *Sylva, or a Discourse of Forest-Trees, and the Propagation of Timber in His Majesties Dominions* (London, 1679), 401.
21 Finberg, 'Three Studies in Family History', 174.
22 GDR, V 5/299T 4.
23 GA, D 1371, passim.

that made from the Taynton Squash pear having a market in London.[1]

In the later 18th century the farmland was divided almost equally between arable and pasture. According to Samuel Rudder in the mid 1770s the farmers, assured of sufficient crops from the naturally fertile soil, were deficient in their management of the land and as a result the grass on the wet lands was poor in quality and yield. Farmers were also encouraged to poll young oak trees by their entitlement to the loppings.[2] Nearly three quarters of 516 a. reported as being cropped in 1801 were under corn, mostly wheat of which a third more than usual had been sown. Peas, beans, and turnips were all grown but potato cultivation was limited to gardens and the holdings of the poor.[3]

The Nineteenth and Twentieth Centuries

In the early 19th century the remnants of the common on Glasshouse hill were inclosed[4] and in 1840 barely any waste was left in the parish, the farmland being reckoned as 1,200 a. of pasture and 900 a. of arable.[5] In 1866, when at least 1,030 a. was permanent grassland, 301 cattle, including 119 milch cows, 488 sheep, and 178 pigs were returned for the parish. Wheat was the main arable crop and some 71 a. lay fallow or uncultivated.[6] In the later 19th and early 20th century dairying increased and there was a corresponding decline in cereal farming. The parish contained 453 a. of arable and 1,640 a. of permanent grassland in 1905[7] and reported livestock numbers in 1926 were 581 cattle, including 226 dairy cows, 292 ewes, and 280 pigs.[8]

The farmers, of whom 10 of 26 identified in 1831 did not employ labour, had holdings that varied considerably in size. The agricultural workforce at that time included 72 labourers.[9] The larger farms were in the east and centre of the parish, where in 1851 the Grove estate was divided between the Grove farm (350 a.) and Hayne's farm (170 a.) and the Disraelis' estate between Taynton Court farm (300 a.) and Pound farm (120 a.). The other large farms were Hownhall (281 a.), Lyne's Place (140 a.), Norman's (120 a.), and Drew's (120 a.). Several other farms, also employing labour, had more than 70 a. and there were smaller units, some of a few acres only, throughout the parish.[10] In 1889 Taynton Court farm, then newly part of the Newent Court estate, was run by a bailiff[11] and in the early 20th century the estate had six farms of between 62 a. and 159 a. in the north-east of Taynton.[12] In 1924 M.P. Price took the farm at the Grove in hand.[13] In 1926 23 farms of over 20 a. were returned, three of them having more than 150 a. and one more than 300 a., and 58 agricultural labourers were reported, 42 of them in regular employment.[14] By the later 20th and early 21st century the creation of larger units had led to a reduction in the number of farms and the sale or abandonment of unwanted farmhouses. A total of 23 holdings returned for the parish in 1986 included 15 farms of over 10 ha (c.25 a.), three of them having over 50 ha (c.125 a.) and one over 100 ha (c.250 a.). The farms, of which the smaller ones were part-time businesses, were worked by a total of 49 people.[15] On the break up of Hownhall farm in 1994 much of its land passed to Grove farm.[16]

Apple and pear cultivation remained important[17] and the reported area of orchards increased from 98 a. in 1896 to 190 a. in 1956. Small fruit was also grown, 4 a. being returned in 1926. In the mid 20th century greater numbers of pigs and poultry were reared, 401 pigs being returned in 1956.[18] Dairying remained the main business of farming in the 1980s, with six specialist dairy units among the holdings returned in 1986. Several other farms raised cattle and sheep and some wheat and barley were grown, the return recording 1,304 cattle, including 621 dairy cows, 1,320 sheep and lambs, 25 pigs, and 129 ha (c.319 a.) of cereals. Two farms were primarily poultry units, nearly 50,000 birds being reared for egg production or for the table.[19] Rare livestock breeds were raised at Hill farm (formerly the Hill).[20] Many fruit trees had been grubbed up by the 1980s and less than 5 ha (c.12 a.) of apple orchards, of which only part was being cultivated commercially, was returned in 1988.[21] The remaining orchards were mainly in the Kent's Green area, where a vineyard had been planted in 1979.[22] In 1994 a sapling of the Taynton Squash pear, then a rarity, was planted on Hownhall green.[23] By 2006 the

---

1 Rudder, *Glos.* 725; Turner, *Agric. of Glos.* 53; W. Marshall, *The Rural Economy of Gloucestershire* (1796), II, 222, 229.
2 Rudder, *Glos.* 724–5; Rudge, *Hist. of Glos.* II, 46.
3 *1801 Crop Returns Eng.* I, 178.
4 GA, D 413/T 3, T 10: D 4869/1/4/1.
5 GDR, T 1/177.
6 TNA, MAF 68/25/5; MAF 68/26/7.
7 Acreage Returns, 1905.
8 TNA, MAF 68/1609/16; MAF 68/3295/15.
9 *Census*, 1831.
10 TNA, HO 107/1960; see GDR, T 1/177; *Kelly's Dir. Glos.* (1856), 368.
11 *Kelly's Dir. Glos.* (1889), 909; above, manors (Little Taynton manor).
12 GA, D 2428/1/24, ff. 72–4.
13 M.P. Price, *My Three Revolutions* (1969), 246.
14 TNA, MAF 68/3295/15.
15 Ibid. MAF 68/6005/172.
16 Above, manors (other estates).
17 *Kelly's Dir. Glos.* (1870), 650.
18 TNA, MAF 68/1609/16; MAF 68/3295/15; MAF 68/4533/172.
19 Ibid. MAF 68/6005/172.
20 K. and W. Thomas, *Our Story of Taynton* (Taynton Society 1981), 21; *Citizen*, 3 Nov. 1988.
21 TNA, MAF 68/6005/172.
22 J. Hudson, 'Last of the Summer Wine', *Glos. & Avon Life* (Jan. 1987), 40–2.
23 http://www.taynton.btinternet.co.uk/roots.htm (accessed 29 July 2005).

number of dairy farms had fallen to three, the largest herd being at Taynton Court. Among recent farming ventures was the conversion of an intensive poultry-laying unit to free-range egg production.[1]

WOODLAND MANAGEMENT

Castle Hill wood, the largest wood in Taynton, belonged to the Whittingtons of Pauntley in the early 16th century when it included an area known as Cut wood.[2] The woodland, which contained crab stocks in 1595 when it belonged to Sir Thomas Throckmorton,[3] passed to the three surviving daughters of William Acton of Sneedham, in Upton St Leonards, on his death in 1674[4] and William Sergeaunt of Hart's Barn, in Longhope, had acquired a two-thirds interest in it by 1727. Sir Edmund Probyn added the wood to his estates in the early 1740s[5] and John Probyn included it in his concession of 1761 allowing the agent of the owner of the Flaxley ironworks to make charcoal in his woods.[6] Fifty-five acres of oak coppice grown for 16 years were sold in 1797.[7] In the early 18th century John Holder had the wood above his house coppiced for the sale of cordwood;[8] earlier charcoal production accounts for the presence of a collier in Great Taynton in 1608.[9]

A timber dealer from Newent lived in Taynton in 1819[10] and one or two parishioners were wood dealers in the mid 19th century.[11] In Castle Hill wood, part of the Ackers family's Huntley estate from 1884,[12] 42 a. of ash and oak coppice were for sale in 1899.[13] Farmland between the wood and Cherry wood, to the south in Huntley, was filled with trees in the early 20th century[14] and the estate's woods were managed mostly as coniferous plantations in 2006.[15]

In the early 20th century a gamekeeper on the Newent Court estate lived at Cravenhill next to a newly planted covert.[16] A charcoal burner was among parishioners in 1925.[17]

WOODLAND CRAFTS

Two coopers were listed in Great Taynton in 1608.[18] Illicit felling in Castle Hill wood and elsewhere in the late 16th century[19] and the clearance of Taynton wood on Glasshouse hill probably by the early 18th century[20] were possibly the piecemeal endeavours of local people engaged in woodland crafts. Hoop makers were recorded in 1738 and 1790[21] and a large part of the population of Glasshouse hill, notably members of the Hook family, was involved in making hoops, hurdles, mop handles, and brooms in the early 19th century.[22] The number of people on the hill employed in those crafts and in wood cutting, about a score in 1851,[23] fell in the later 19th century and one hoop maker and a handful of woodcutters were recorded in 1901.[24] A besom maker worked in Castle Hill wood in the 1920s.[25] A turnery established on Glasshouse hill by H.V. Barnes in 1932 employed 45 people in 1950 and closed in 1961.[26] In the late 20th and early 21st century tent pegs were made by hand at Hill Farm.[27]

MILLS

A mill was recorded on Walter Ayleway's estate in 1306[28] and two mills on an estate in Great Taynton and Byfords that Henry Wyville and his wife Catherine quitclaimed to Walter of Cirencester in 1339.[29] A miller was assessed for tax in Great Taynton in 1327.[30]

A mill called the Brass Mills stood south-east of Moorend green by a stream rising at the foot of Glasshouse hill.[31] Manufacturing brass wire, it was established by 1638, when a wire drawer was resident[32] and its customers included John Tilsley

---

1 Information from Mr Donald Sherratt of Green Croft Farm and Mr Eric Freeman of Byfords.
2 TNA, C 78/77, no 5.
3 BL, Harl. MS 4131, f. 481v.
4 GDR wills 1674/155; GA, P 347/IN 1/2.
5 GA, D 23/T 32; D 1230/4–5.
6 Ibid. D 23/E 8; see above, Longhope, econ. hist. (woodland management).
7 GA, D 23/E 7.
8 Ibid. D 1371, ff. 19, 33, 46.
9 Smith, *Men and Armour*, 65.
10 GA, P 326/IN 1/5.
11 TNA, HO 107/350; HO 107/1960.
12 GA, SL 10.
13 Ibid. D 2299/2/8/19.
14 OS Map 6", Glos. XXIV.SW (1903, 1924 edns).
15 Information from Mrs Torill Freeman of Home Farm, Huntley; see above, Huntley, econ. hist. (woodland management).
16 Glos. Colln. RX 212.2; OS Map 1:2,500, Glos. XXIV.3 (1883, 1903 edns).
17 GA, S 326/3.
18 Smith, *Men and Armour*, 65–6.
19 BL, Harl. MS 4131, ff. 481v., 514v.
20 GA, D 23/T 32; D 1230/4–5.
21 Ibid. D 1272, Taynton deeds; D 1819.
22 Ibid. P 326/IN 1/5; TNA, HO 107/350.
23 TNA, HO 107/1760.
24 Ibid. RG 13/2421.
25 M. Hamlen, 'History of Huntley' (1981: typescript in Glos. Colln. 45959), 41.
26 C. Hart, *The Industrial History of Dean* (1971), 334; *Kelly's Dir. Glos.* (1939), 337.
27 http://www.taynton.btinternet.co/uk/tourpic/images/pegs.jpg (accessed 13 Oct. 2006); H. Phelps, 'Historical Sojourn from Huntley to May Hill', *Gloucestershire: the County Magazine* (Sept. 1988), 31.
28 *Glos. Feet of Fines 1300–59*, p. 13.
29 Ibid. p. 128.
30 *Glos. Subsidy Roll, 1327*, 35.
31 *Notes on Dioc. of Glouc. by Chancellor Parsons*, 188; see GDR, T 1/177 (nos 158–9, 167); G.M. Davies, 'Mills of the River Leadon and Tributaries', *Glos. Soc. Ind. Archaeol. Newsletter* 7 (Apr. 1966), 32–6.
32 Hockaday Abs. ccclxv.

and his brother, pinmakers in Gloucester and Bristol.[1] A pinmaker lived in Taynton in 1658.[2] Part of the Hownhall estate, the mill was evidently used as a corn mill by 1661.[3] John Holder sold the mill house in 1702 and pulled down the mill in 1706.[4] The site, which became overgrown with trees and bushes, was cleared and levelled in the 1960s.[5]

OTHER INDUSTRY AND TRADE

Stone has been quarried in several places[6] and that used for building at the parish church in the mid 1820s came from W.C. Holder's land.[7] May hill also yielded substantial deposits of iron ore, which were reputed to contain traces of silver and gold.[8] Discoveries that Abraham Shapton claimed to have made while prospecting for coal on his acquisition of Great Taynton manor in 1673 led the Society of Mines Royal and Mineral and Battery Works to grant a lease of mines in the manor to John Claypole.[9] The mining rights passed through several hands from 1677 but the refining of the ore, mined perhaps in Rocks wood, was given up on proving unprofitable.[10]

Large quantities of cinders observed in Taynton *c*.1700 contained the discarded slag from ironworking in Roman and perhaps earlier times.[11] Some deposits in the eastern half of the parish were listed *c*.1670 for possible use at the Foleys' Ellbridge furnace[12] and field names on the parish's eastern boundary beyond the Grove[13] record an area of slag that also spread across part of Tibberton.[14]

Personal names suggest that craftsmen in Taynton included a thatcher or weaver in 1287, a tailor in 1306,[15] and possibly a lead beater in 1327.[16] A woman was making thatch in 1522[17] and a weaver lived in Taynton in 1543.[18] Other weavers were recorded until the early 18th century.[19] A smith, a baker, and a butcher were among men listed in Great Taynton in 1608.[20] Later smiths, some of whom were described as gunsmiths,[21] included a blacksmith at Kent's Green in 1737,[22] and a smithy operated by the green at Hownhall in the later 18th century.[23] A mason was one of several builders working in the parish in the mid 17th century.[24] Glass making was under way at the foot of May hill in the late 16th century. The glasshouse, from which the hamlet there took its name, was in Newent[25] but the site of an old quarry and glasshouse was recorded within Taynton in the mid 19th century.[26]

As well as blacksmiths, carpenters, masons, and practitioners of other common crafts, Taynton's inhabitants in the early 19th century included a drainer in 1835 and a brazier in 1841.[27] A brick maker lived at Glasshouse in 1827[28] and there was a brick yard by the Huntley–Newent road in the early 1830s.[29] The yard, part of a farm on which John Smith employed 8 men in 1851,[30] was acquired in 1862 by Edwin Phillips (d. 1908). Under him it also produced tiles, pipes and a range of pottery, some of it ornamental. It closed finally during the First World War. In the late 19th century there was also a brick yard in Moat Lane.[31] The population of Glasshouse hill included several craftsmen in the early 20th century,[32] a carpenter and a baker remaining there in 1923 and a boot repairer in 1939.[33]

A sailor present in Taynton in 1608 was possibly engaged in local trade.[34] Mention in 1632 of a market was probably a reference to trading that took, or used to take, place by the medieval churchyard.[35]

A haulier lived in the parish in 1832[36] and a shopkeeper at Hownhall carried goods to and from Gloucester on three days a week in 1856. At the turn of the 20th century there was also a carrying service

---

1 W.B. Willcox, *Gloucestershire: A Study in Local Government 1590–1640* (New Haven, Yale University Press, 1940), 255–6 and n.
2 GA, D 5554/10.
3 Ibid. D 2957/299/34, 42.
4 GA, D 1371.
5 Davies, 'Mills of River Leadon and Tributaries', 32; D.R. Sherratt, *Taynton's Industrial Past: The Brickworks, Potteries and Brass Mill* (1998), 16.
6 GA, P 326/CW 2/1, survey 4 May 1809.
7 Ibid. ch. improvement acct. 1825–6.
8 Bodleian, Top. Glouc. c. 3, f. 194; Rudder, *Glos.* 504.
9 *Cal. SP Dom.* 1682, 223–4; above, manors.
10 D. Bick, *The Mines of Newent and Ross* (1987), 71–2; see *Cal. Treasury Books* 1681–5, 492; 1685–9, 354, 442, 467. Later writers dated the mining episode to *c*.1700: Rudder, *Glos.* 725.
11 *Notes on Dioc. of Glouc. by Chancellor Parsons*, 188.
12 Herefs. RO, E 12/G/12. For the furnace, above, Oxenhall, econ. hist.
13 GDR, T 1/177 (nos 6, 11–12); see GA, D 247/32.
14 Diane Charlesworth, 'Mapping the landscape: the Iron Age and Roman periods in part of north-west Gloucestershire' (2006 typescript, in VCH Glos. office), 9–10, 13–14.
15 TNA, JUST 1/278, rot. 58; JUST 1/286, rot. 8d.
16 *Glos. Subsidy Roll, 1327*, 35.
17 Hockaday Abs. ccclxv.
18 GA, P 326/IN 1/1.
19 GDR wills 1592/90; Smith, *Men and Armour*, 65; Hockaday Abs. ccclxv, 1662, 1679; GA, P 326/IN 1/2, burial 5 Feb. 1725.
20 Smith, *Men and Armour*, 65–6.
21 Memorial in churchyard to Gilbert Beale (d. 1704) and his son John (d. 1723).
22 GA, D 3113/1; GDR wills 1764/32.
23 GA, D 2957/299/66.
24 TNA, E 134/1657/Mich. 47.
25 Above, Newent, econ. hist. (other industry and crafts).
26 GDR, T 1/177 (no 435).
27 GA, P 326/IN 1/5.
28 Ibid. D 413/T 5; TNA, HO 107/350
29 OS Map 1", sheet 43 (1831 edn).
30 TNA, HO 107/1960.
31 GDR, T 1/177 (no 218); Sherratt, *Taynton's Industrial Past*, 3–13.
32 GA, P 326/IN 1/6.
33 *Kelly's Dir. Glos.* (1923), 326–7: (1939), 337–8.
34 Smith, *Men and Armour*, 66.
35 GA, D 324, f.11.
36 Ibid. P 326/IN 1/5.

between Glasshouse hill and the city. In the later 1930s Taynton was served by a carrier from outside the parish and by buses running between Ledbury and Gloucester.[1] In 1799 and 1826 a farmer on Glasshouse hill acted as a news carrier.[2] Taynton had several shops in the mid 19th century,[3] shopkeepers being recorded on Glasshouse hill from 1841 and at Kent's Green in 1861.[4] The parish also had a post office in 1856. In 1906 there was a post office in Moat Lane and in 1939 a shop on Glasshouse hill served as a post office.[5] A shop on Hownhall farm was accommodated from 1988 in a former cider house[6] and remained open in 2006.

There was an insurance agent in Taynton in 1888.[7] Farming brothers on Glasshouse hill offered veterinary services in 1889[8] and the farmer at Tuns and a resident at Glasshouse both undertook horse breaking in 1891.[9] A fruiterer lived at Kent's Green in 1891.[10] In the early 21st century there were an equestrian school, stables, and livery yard at Coldcroft Farm.

LOCAL GOVERNMENT

MANORIAL GOVERNMENT

In 1287 Cecily de Mucegros claimed view of frankpledge and waifs in Great Taynton manor and excused her lack of gallows and a tumbrel by her ownership of those at English Bicknor. Bevis de Knovill, who claimed the assize of bread and ale and pleas concerning hue and cry and bloodshed in Little Taynton manor, was also without the necessary instruments of punishment.[11]

The Little Taynton manor court held views of frankpledge, in 1607 conducting a joint session as leet and court baron in April and in the next three decades convening in similar session in October. A book covering those courts until 1638 is probably a complete record of meetings in that period, during which the court several times abandoned leet, and in 1629 all, business for lack of attendance. The court elected a constable, the choice presumably determined by a rota of farmers, and frequently ordered the repair of a pound and stocks. It was unable to ensure that the archery butts were maintained, no men in its jurisdiction having bows and arrows as required by law. The court dealt with the obstruction and repair of lanes and paths and of streams, in addition to the usual business of a manor court. In 1634 it required the landowner Christopher Westerdale to remove an inclosure from a meadow, to restore the adjoining stream to its original course, and to remove a family he had placed in a cottage without licence. Presentments occasionally included the felling of trees.[12] The court continued to hold a leet session in the early 18th century.[13] The court of Great Taynton manor and its view of frankpledge were summoned in April 1713 to their usual meeting place.[14]

The court for the manor of Tibberton, Taynton, and Bulley recorded grants of land in Taynton until at least 1822.[15]

PAROCHIAL GOVERNMENT

The earliest surviving records of parish government are the churchwardens' accounts for the years 1794–1841.[16] The accounts included the expenditure of rents from property in the parish that had been assigned by the later 17th century to poor relief and became known as Dame Cecilia Musgrove's charity.[17]

Supported by the income from the rents, the cost to the parish of relief rose little in the late 18th century.[18] A cottage in Moat Lane, part of the property, was used as a poorhouse[19] and in 1803 the parish, in spending £105 on relief, paid a subscription to the Gloucester infirmary and gave regular help to 24 people.[20] In 1813 expenditure on relief was £201, although only 11 people received regular help, and in the next two years it reduced.[21] A workhouse built next to the Moat Lane cottage in 1818[22] was shared in its first two years with Tibberton parish, which paid the governor a weekly salary.[23] In 1822, when Taynton maintained the governor and his family in

---

1 *Kelly's Dir. Glos.* (1856 and later edns).
2 GA, D 413/T 7, T 4.
3 *Kelly's Dir. Glos.* (1856), 368.
4 TNA, HO 107/350; HO 107/1960; RG 9/1760.
5 *Kelly's Dir. Glos.* (1856 and later edns); information from Mr Sherratt.
6 *Citizen*, 13 Dec. 1988.
7 GA, P 326/IN 1/6.
8 *Kelly's Dir. Glos.* (1889), 909.
9 TNA, RG 12/2008.
10 GA, P 326/IN 1/6.
11 *Plac. de Quo Warr.* 243–4, 246.
12 GA, D 324; D 2957/299/79.
13 Atkyns, *Glos.* 710.
14 GA, D 2957/299/47.
15 Ibid. 98.
16 Ibid. P 326/CW 2/1.
17 GDR, V 5/299T 3; below, social hist. (charities for the poor).
18 *Poor Law Abstract, 1804,* 172–3.
19 GA, P 326/CW 2/1; *18th Rep. Com. Char.* 288–9; see GDR, T 1/177 (no 90).
20 *Poor Law Abstract, 1804,* 172–3.
21 Ibid. *1818,* 146–7.
22 Date on bldg.; K. and W. Thomas, *Our Story of Taynton* (Taynton Society, 1981), 16; GDR, T 1/177 (no 89). Fig. 75.
23 GA, P 332/OV 2/1.

75. Hill View House (formerly Taynton workhouse)

return for a weekly payment, the acting overseer of the poor was awarded an annual allowance or salary and in 1826 he was left to agree terms with Paul Barnard, a local hurdle maker, as the new governor and the vestry appointed a workhouse visitor. From 1831 Barnard was also employed as assistant overseer with a salary replacing that of the overseer. In the early 1830s the vestry decided to restrict relief in aid of house rents, a surgeon contracted to attend parishioners, and Tibberton and Huntley parishes were allowed to use the workhouse. Work in the parish quarry was among forms of relief. Although repayment of a debt of £200 was charged on the poor rate in 1823,[1] the vestry's striving to contain parish expenditure on relief meant that during the late 1820s and the early 1830s, when charity income was used to provide the poor with cheap coal,[2] the highest annual figure recorded was £269.[3]

Taynton became part of the Newent poor-law union in 1835[4] and the parish, which had a cottage on Glasshouse hill among its property in the mid 19th century,[5] employed a salaried assistant overseer and rate collector from 1845, Paul Barnard being the first holder of the posts. In 1888 the vestry decided not to publish the list of persons receiving outdoor relief on the church door.[6] The parish retained ownership of the former workhouse (Hill View House) until 1960, latterly with the parish council letting its rooms to tenants.[7]

In the late 18th and early 19th century parish government also included the regulation of encroachments on common land and the highways. Landowners made several surveys of the encroachments[8] but, despite an agreement in 1829 by 22 landholders for concerted action, an ultimatum of 1838 from the vestry for the removal of encroachments on Glasshouse hill[9] was not implemented.[10]

Historically Taynton shared the cost of repairing Winford bridge with Tibberton.[11] In 1813 it contributed towards the cost of building a bridge on the Newent road[12] and in the 1820s and 1830s the highest rate burden it imposed was for road repairs on Glasshouse hill and elsewhere. The landowner Edward Howell, who oversaw the repairs from 1827, was allowed to employ a deputy surveyor and, although the vestry placed a cap on his total annual expenditure, when he stood down as surveyor in 1832 the parish owed him moneys. His successor received a salary. In the mid 1840s the parish elected two surveyors, one for Little Taynton, and from 1847 it again employed a salaried surveyor. Little Taynton residents re-elected their own surveyor in 1856. After the formation of Newent highway district in 1863 Taynton elected one waywarden to its board.[13]

SOCIAL HISTORY

SOCIAL STRUCTURE

In 1327, a time when most of Taynton's population were customary tenants owing labour services on its manorial demesnes,[14] John de Bures and Bevis de Knovill, the lords of Great and Little Taynton, were assessed for a subsidy at 8s. and 4s. 3d. respectively.

Of the other men taxed one (John of Byford) was assessed at 6s. 6d. and the remainder at 3s. or less.[15] In the absence of later lords of the manors Taynton had few wealthy inhabitants. In 1522, when the goods of landowner Roger Ayleway and the rector were valued at £20 and £12 respectively and those of ten others were worth between £3 and £10, seventeen

---

1 GA, P 326/VE 2/1; for Paul Barnard, TNA, HO 107/350; HO 107/1960.
2 GA, P 326/CW 2/1.
3 *Poor Law Returns* (1830–1), 66; (1835), 65.
4 *Poor Law Com. 2nd Rep.* p. 523.
5 GDR, T 1/177 (no 293); GA, P 326/VE 2/1, min. 9 Mar. 1868.
6 GA, P 326/VE 2/1.
7 Ibid. P 326A/PC 1/1, pp. 1, 4, 135–6, 199.
8 Ibid. P 326/CW 2/1.
9 Ibid. VE 2/1.
10 See above, econ. hist. (agric.: the 19th and 20th cents.).
11 *Notes on Dioc. of Glouc. by Chancellor Parsons*, 188; Bigland, *Glos.* III, no 266.
12 GA, P 225/VE 2/1.
13 Ibid. P 326/VE 2/1.
14 *Inq. p.m. Glos.* 1236–1300, 232–4; 1302–58, 97–8.
15 *Glos. Subsidy Roll, 1327*, 35.

men had goods valued at less than £3 and for eight others no valuation was given.[1]

In the later 16th and early 17th century the Ayleways and the Westerdales were among Taynton's few established gentry families. The Ayleway household employed Alice Ciprian (d. 1590) as a servant,[2] and a servant of Christopher Westerdale was among the men named for Taynton in the muster roll of 1608. In the roll Westerdale and two others were described as gentlemen, 9 as yeomen, 6 as husbandmen, 8 as labourers, 8 as craftsmen and tradesmen, and 3 more as servants, the last being in the employ of a yeoman, a husbandman, and a butcher.[3] Between 1634 and 1643 several 'Dutchmen' were recorded in Taynton.[4] For the hearth tax of 1672 a simple majority of 31 parishioners had a single hearth and six had 2 hearths. Three others each had 3 hearths, three more each 4 hearths, Henry Westerdale 5 hearths, a Mr Burge 8 hearths, and Peter Charles, a farmer who owned a house and farm called Adams, 10 hearths.[5] Thomas Pury was resident in 1687 when he became lord of Great Taynton[6] and the Grove became the main house on his estate.[7]

Details of the family life of the farmer John Holder of Jack's House (later Taynton House) from 1691 are reported in a volume of annals, in which he also recorded his land dealings and farming activities and wrote verses composed by himself and Latin quotations.[8] Following his death in 1734 a memorial to himself and his late wife was by his instruction carved by Thomas Ricketts of Gloucester with a Latin inscription and erected in the parish church.[9] Other resident landowners included Joseph Clarke (d. 1705), a property owner in Newcastle upon Tyne and elsewhere in Northumberland.[10] Among non-resident landowners were Dorothy Cocks (d. 1714) and John Cocks (d. 1728), members of an established county family; she used Taynton land to endow charity schools in Dumbleton and Gloucester and he did similarly for an apprenticing charity in Dumbleton.[11]

The parish community was predominantly one of farmers and labourers but the settlement of Glasshouse hill, under way by the early 18th century,[12] produced in the far west a society largely of cottagers and squatters living off local woods and seasonal employment and accounting for more than half of the population in the mid 19th century.[13] Social and geographical divisions were reflected in the church's seating plan in the early 19th century; the seats closest to the pulpit were reserved for the owners or occupants of Taynton House, the Grove, and other farmsteads in the east and centre of the parish and those at the opposite end of the building were free.[14] Taynton House was used as a country house by the Holders and their relative Edward Howell (d. 1834), formerly a builder in Chelsea (Middx). Revd W.C. Holder (d. 1837), who inherited the family estate in 1819,[15] left Paul Barnard, governor of the parish workhouse, and his wife Hannah £10 each.[16] Barnard, a craftsman and native of the parish, lived on Glasshouse hill.[17] In 1868 6 a. provided by a landowner was let as allotments of ¼ a. each.[18]

Taynton had a resident clergyman from 1829, when W.C. Holder became curate, and the rector was resident from 1864.[19] In the mid 19th century, when several farming households included one or two domestic servants, there were larger private households at Taynton House and its daughter house, the Ryelands.[20] Taynton House was let to tenants,[21] including the impecunious baronet John Owen (d. 1861), MP for Pembroke Boroughs,[22] before the Athertons settled finally in it.[23] The Ryelands,[24] occupied by a curate in 1841,[25] was in 1879 the home of Philip Reginald Cocks.[26] He played a part in church life in Taynton after he moved to his new house at Clifford Manor, in Newent, and joined the peerage, as Lord Somers.[27] Other houses used as

---

1 *Military Surv. of Glos. 1522*, 57–8.
2 GA, P 326/IN 1/1.
3 Smith, *Men and Armour*, 65–6.
4 GA, P 326/IN 1/1.
5 TNA, E 179/247/14, rot. 36d. For Peter Charles, GDR wills 1707/262.
6 Above, manors (Great Taynton manor); GA, D 2957/299/109.
7 *Notes on Dioc. of Glouc. by Chancellor Parsons*, 188.
8 Copy in GA, D 1371; see H.P.R. Finberg, 'Three Studies in Family History', *Glos. Studies*, 174–83.
9 GA, D 2957/299/48.
10 TNA, PROB 11/485, f. 122v.; see above, manors (other estates: Norman's Farm).
11 GDR wills 1717/193; 1728/561; Bigland, *Glos.* I, 502; see *12th Rep. Com. Char.* 65–70; *16th Rep. Com. Char.* 26.
12 Above, settlement.
13 *1st Rep. Com. Employment in Agric.* app. II, p. 126; *Glos. Chron.* 29 Aug. 1868 (letter). See MS notes on the parish by Revd C.Y. Crawley (c.1868) in GA, P 326/MI 1.
14 GDR, F 1/4.
15 Above, manors (other estates: Taynton Ho.); for Howell, TNA, PROB 11/1364, f. 109; PROB 11/1837, ff. 174–175v.
16 TNA, PROB 11/1892, f. 182.
17 Ibid. HO 107/350; HO 107/1960; see above, local govt.
18 *1st Rep. Com. Employment in Agric.* app. II, p. 126.
19 Below, religious hist.
20 TNA, HO 107/1960; RG 9/1760; RG 10/2607.
21 GA, D 2957/299/98.
22 TNA, HO 107/1960; *The Times*, 11 Feb. 1861; *Hist. Parl. Commons 1790–1820*, IV, 702–3.
23 *Kelly's Dir. Glos.* (1856 and later edns).
24 See *The Times*, 7 Apr. 1825; 6 Feb. 1841; 28 Aug. 1848.
25 TNA, HO 107/350.
26 *Kelly's Dir. Glos.* (1879), 759; TNA, RG 11/2527.
27 GA, P 326/VE 2/1; *Complete Peerage*, XII (1), 34–5; above, Newent, manors (Boulsdon manor: Clifford Manor).

private dwellings included Longcroft and Kent's Green House, the latter in 1851 the home of the solicitor Henry Evans.[1] The Grove continued to serve as a farmhouse before being occupied permanently by its owners, the Prices (later Groves), towards the end of the century.[2]

Although the number of domestic servants in farming households declined in the later 19th century, Taynton's farmers remained among its principal inhabitants. Taynton House, the main private residence,[3] passed to the Misses Atherton, the last of whom died in 1950.[4] Another spinster active in parish business was Mary Cockburn, for whom March Croft (later Marchfield) was built.[5] The daughter of a Birkenhead (Ches.) man, she died in 1937[6] having been a patron of the school and a member of the parish council.[7] In the 1920s several Taynton men were in service, in posts such as butler and chauffeur, in houses in the area.[8] M.P. Price, who moved into the Grove to take up farming in the mid 1920s, balanced the life of a radical politician with that of a landowner, including the pursuit of traditional country sports, and lived there until his death in 1973.[9] Taynton ceased to have a resident clergyman in 1963[10] and the number of farming and labouring families declined in the late 20th century as professional and retired people moved into former farmhouses and other buildings in the parish.[11]

CHARITIES FOR THE POOR

In the late 17th century an income of 40s. from a cottage and three small closes, by tradition the gift of Cecily Musgrove for the tenants of Great Taynton manor, was used for the parish poor. Its application was determined at public meetings of the tenants and before 1683 it funded apprenticeships.[12] The cottage was in Moat Lane and the land included the pieces called Keptepot and the Poor's Meadow (later the Poor's Patch), some way to the east and south respectively.[13] In the late 18th century the cottage, having been rebuilt after a fire, was used as a poorhouse and the churchwardens distributed the same income, sometimes allowed to accumulate for two or three years, in cash. Thirteen people received up to 3s. each in 1798. In the early 19th century the income was increased and the churchwardens occasionally applied it in other ways, as in 1801 for midwifery and a distribution of potatoes and in 1809 for inoculating children. In 1820, to distinguish the industrious from the idle poor, it was spent on white hats for eight men who had supported their families during the previous year without parish relief. From the mid 1820s, when it was known as Dame Cecilia Musgrove's charity, it was used at Christmas to provide coal at a reduced price as well as cash doles. The income then included a rent for the use of the cottage garden by the inmates of the neighbouring parish workhouse. The charity had 32 recipients in 1830 and 44 in 1840.[14]

William Gilding (d. 1793) of Linton (Herefs.) by will left £100 to fund an apprenticeship every other year for boys from Taynton.[15] The charity was augmented by a legacy of £160 from Revd W.C. Holder, by will proved 1838,[16] but was in abeyance in 1848.[17] A bequest of £50 for the poor from Edward Howell's widow Hester, by will proved 1847,[18] was assigned by a Scheme approved in 1857 to support a day school.[19] The Scheme also regulated the Musgrove and the Gilding and Holder charities.[20] The latter funded a couple of apprentices and in 1896 the vestry selected masters in Gloucester and Newent for two of three apprentices.[21] The charity was the subject of a new Scheme in 1906 and provided financial help for school leavers in the late 1960s.[22] It continued as an education charity after the Scheme was amended in 1976 and its income, £119 in 2004,[23] paid for books in 2006.[24] The Musgrove charity, which accommodated two dwellings in its cottage in 1825,[25] was the subject in 1907 of a Scheme that eschewed cash payments. It distributed coal to a dozen or more elderly or widowed people in the

---

1 TNA, HO 107/1960; *Kelly's Dir. Glos.* (1856), 368.
2 *Kelly's Dir. Glos.* (1856 and later edns); TNA, RG 9/1760; RG 12/2008.
3 TNA, RG 13/2421.
4 Above, manors (other estates); *The Times*, 4 Dec. 1950.
5 D.R. Sherratt, *Taynton's Industrial Past: The Brickworks, Potteries and Brass Mill* (1998), 12.
6 Headstone in Taynton churchyard.
7 GA, S 326/1, pp. 179–80, 245; 2, pp. 11, 32; P 326A/PC 1/1, pp. 29, 52.
8 GA, S 236/3.
9 M.P. Price, *My Three Revolutions* (1969), passim; *The Times*, 25 Sept. 1973.
10 Below, religious hist.
11 Information from Mr Donald Sherratt of Green Croft Farm.
12 GDR, V 5/299T 3. The alleged donor was Cecily de Mucegros, lady of Great Taynton in the late 13th cent.: above, manors; see *18th Rep. Com. Char.* 288.
13 GDR, V 5/299T 4; see ibid. T 1/177 (nos 81, 86, 90); information from Mr Sherratt.
14 GA, P 326/CW 2/1; *18th Rep. Com. Char.* 288–9.
15 Bigland, *Glos.* III, no 266; GDR, B 4/1/2423.
16 TNA, PROB 11/1892, f. 182.
17 GA, P 326/VE 2/1.
18 TNA, PROB 11/2052, ff. 270v.–272.
19 GA, P 326/CH 6; VE 2/1.
20 Ibid. D 3469/5/151.
21 Ibid. P 326/VE 2/1.
22 Ibid. D 3469/5/151.
23 http://www.charity-commission.gov.uk/registeredcharities (accessed 29 Nov. 2005: no 311476).
24 Information from charity correspondent, Mrs Amanda Rawson of Pound Farm.
25 GA, P 326/CW 2/1; GDR, T 1/177 (no 90).

EDUCATION

In 1712 fourteen children were taught to read in Taynton, ten of them at the expense of the rector, Benjamin Newton.[4] By will proved 1739 Robert Aldridge, a tailor, provided 52s. a year to instruct four poor children to read the Bible.[5] The charity was administered by the owners of property in Elton, in Westbury-on-Severn, on which the payment was charged and the teacher was usually a poor woman living in Taynton.[6] In 1818 two other schools taught between them 56 children, attendance varying according to the season of the year,[7] and in 1833 three day schools had 50 pupils, of whom 4 were paid for by the charity and 20 by subscriptions.[8] A Sunday school started in 1823 was supported by donations and from 1831 was held in the new vestry at the parish church. It had 70 pupils in 1833.[9]

One of two infants' school in the parish in 1856[10] was presumably the school managed by the curate, William Hughes, that was supported under a Scheme of 1857 by the charity of Hester Howell.[11] A school established in the church vestry under the management of the rector in 1866 had rules modelled on those of a school at Newent and was supported by pence and subscriptions as well as the Hester Howell charity. On its opening it taught 42 boys and girls in a single department.[12] The other infants' school in 1856 was kept on Glasshouse hill by Hannah Barnard for many years[13] and was supported for some time by voluntary contributions and pence. By the late 1860s attendance had fallen from 30 to five or six and some children from the hill went to Huntley school.[14] In 1861 there was a small boarding school at Kent's Green House.[15]

From 1883 the Taynton school was held in a new building erected near the church on glebe land donated by A.D. Bagshawe.[16] It had an average

late 1960s[1] and with an income (£304 in 2004)[2] that included the rent of Keptepot paid fuel bills in 2006. The cottage was sold in 1959.[3]

76. Taynton: the former school built in 1883

attendance of 45 in 1885,[17] 63 in 1904,[18] and 30 in 1922,[19] and it was among the beneficiaries of the Lady Wedderburn Prize Fund established in 1910 to reward practical work by children in the Newent area.[20] In 1931 the older children were transferred to schools in Newent[21] and the following year the 19 children remaining on the roll were sent to schools in Tibberton and Newent.[22]

SOCIAL LIFE

A church house stood next to the medieval churchyard. It was the parish house in 1704[23] but was occupied as cottages by the mid 19th century.[24] The schoolroom erected near the 17th-century parish church in 1883 was used as a church hall after the day school's closure in 1932[25] and following its sale in 1979 was run by the parochial church council as a parish room.[26] In 1933 a village hall for Taynton and Tibberton was built near Winford bridge on land given by M.P. Price. A committee room, the first of several extensions, was added to the hall in 1938 and a playing field opened next to it in 1953.[27]

In 1923 the landowner C.P. Ackers[28] built a hall on Glasshouse hill as a reading room and meeting place

---

1 GA, D 3469/5/151.
2 http://www.charity-commission.gov.uk/registeredcharities (accessed 29 Nov. 2005: no 237689).
3 Information from charity correspondent, Mrs Rawson, and from Mr Sherratt.
4 *Glos. N&Q* I, 294; Bodleian, Top. Glouc. c. 3, f. 196v. For Newton, below, religious hist.
5 GDR wills 1739/200.
6 *18th Rep. Com. Char.* 289.
7 *Educ. of Poor Digest*, 313.
8 *Educ. Enq. Abstract*, 328.
9 Ibid.; GA, P 326/VE 2/1, min. 6 July 1865; see below, religious hist.
10 *Kelly's Dir. Glos.* (1856), 368.
11 GA, P 326/VE 2/1; CH 6; see above (charities for the poor).
12 TNA, ED 7/35/315.
13 *Kelly's Dir. Glos.* (1856), 368; see TNA, HO 107/1960.
14 *1st Rep. Com. Employment in Agric.* app. II, p. 126–7.
15 TNA, RG 9/1760.
16 GA, P 326/SC 1. Fig. 76.
17 *Kelly's Dir. Glos.* (1885), 591.
18 *Public Elem. Schs. 1906*, 189.
19 *List 21*, 1922 (Board of Education), 107.
20 GA, P 326/SC 2, pp. 36–7; S 326/1, pp. 141, 149–51, 166–7; P 165/SC 4/3.
21 Ibid. S 326/3.
22 Ibid. S 326/2, p. 79.
23 GDR, V 5/299T 4: Bigland, *Glos.* III, no 266.
24 Above, settlement.
25 Above (education); GA, P 326/CH 6; *Tibberton, Gloucestershire: A History of Our Village*, ed. L.W. Davis (2001), 78, 80.
26 K. Thomas and D. Sherratt, *Taynton and Education: The Era of the Schools* (1998), 22.
27 *Tibberton: History of Our Village*, 40–1, 75–85.
28 For Ackers, above, Huntley, manor.

for the May hill district.¹ A cross in memory of the men of the district killed during the First World War was erected on the hill by 1921² and a parish memorial was erected in St Lawrence's churchyard in 1922.³

With the possible exception of an inn near Kent's green in the early 18th century⁴ the first indications of there being a public house in Taynton are from the mid 19th century⁵ when Glasshouse had the New inn.⁶ In 1872 agricultural labourers formed a union at the Glasshouse inn.⁷ Then a beerhouse run by a shoemaker,⁸ it remained open in 2006.

Although sports were part of Taynton's celebrations to mark the Golden Jubilee of 1887 and the coronation of 1902⁹ there are no earlier references to sports clubs. In the early 20th century a boy's club met in an outbuilding at the rectory.¹⁰ Taynton had a football club and a young men's club in 1933 and the building that year of a village hall led to clubs and societies for Taynton and Tibberton together, including a branch of the Women's Institute. Football, cricket, and tennis clubs used the hall and the playing field opened in 1953¹¹ and a horticultural society held its annual show in the hall in the later 20th century.¹² In 2006 a snooker club meeting at Green Croft Farm had recently celebrated its 40th anniversary.¹³ In 1981 the Taynton Society, formed to foster the parish's identity, published a local history.¹⁴

In 1933 a pageant based on accounts of the sacking of the parish church in 1643 was held in the grounds of Taynton House.¹⁵ In the early 1960s opera, ballet, and theatre were staged in the great barn there.¹⁶

Part of Taynton was included in a nursing association for the Tibberton district formed in 1903.¹⁷ An endowment by M.P. Price in 1922 continued to finance care for the sick after the association lapsed¹⁸ and under a Scheme of 1978 paid for goods and services for ill and disabled people of the district.¹⁹

RELIGIOUS HISTORY

EARLY HISTORY AND STATUS OF THE PARISH CHURCH

The medieval parish church stood near Taynton's eastern boundary within earthworks probably raised first soon after the Norman Conquest for the lord of Great Taynton.²⁰ Its early history was evidently as a chapel of Newent church, for together with Newent it was claimed as a possession of Cormeilles abbey (Eure) in 1181²¹ and Newent priory had a portion in it worth 2s. in 1291. The portion passed to Fotheringhay college (Northants.).²²

Maud de Wateville, lady of Taynton, endowed Taynton church and gave it to Gloucester abbey in 1134 × 1148.²³ The abbey also acquired tithes in Little Taynton that were granted by its lord to Kilpeck church and became known as Kilpeck's tithing. Although Maud persuaded its priest to resign in favour of the abbey sacrist c.1158 and later sacrists had a portion in it,²⁴ Taynton church remained a rectory.²⁵

The medieval church was burnt down in 1643 and a new parish church was built on a more central site after a few years. The benefice, from which the May hill district in the west of the parish was removed in 1935,²⁶ was united with Tibberton in 1975²⁷ and the united benefice was merged with Highnam with Lassington and Rudford in 1984.²⁸

---

1 GA, G/NE 159/11, f. 18; *Kelly's Dir. Glos.* (1927), 344, which erroneously dates the hall to 1922. The foundation stone is dated 1923 with the inits. of Ackers's wife: see *Burke's Landed Gentry* (1937), I, 2.
2 OS Map 6", Glos. XXIV.SW (1924 edn).
3 *Kelly's Dir. Glos.* (1927), 344.
4 GA, D 2176/1/2/2, will of Wm. Nelme.
5 See *Kelly's Dir. Glos.* (1856), 368.
6 GA, P 326/IN 1/5, baptism 25 Oct. 1857.
7 *Glouc. J.* 20 Apr. 1872; see N. Scotland, *Agricultural Trade Unionism in Gloucestershire 1872–1950* (1991), 18–20.
8 *Kelly's Dir. Glos.* (1870), 650; TNA, PROB 10/2607; *Licensed Houses in Glos. 1891*, 140–1.
9 GA, P 326/VE 2/1.
10 K. and W. Thomas, *Our Story of Taynton* (Taynton Society, 1981), 24.
11 *Tibberton: History of Our Village*, 79, 81, 88.
12 Programme for 1961 show (copy in Glos. Colln. R 505.1); 'All About the Community' (Tibberton and Taynton W.I., n.d. [c.1988]: copy in ibid. R 305.4).
13 Information from Mr Sherratt.
14 K. and W. Thomas, *Our Story of Taynton*.
15 D.J. Parker, *Taynton, Gloucestershire. A Story of Two Churches* (1998), 6–7.
16 *Lady*, 18 May 1961; *Glos. Countryside*, Apr.–May 1963, p. 20; *The Times*, 25 July 1964.
17 GA, D 4277/12/1.
18 Ibid. D 2176/2/6/5.
19 http://www.charity-commission.gov.uk/registeredcharities (accessed 29 Nov. 2005: no 238450).
20 GDR, T 1/177 (nos 668 and 666); above, settlement.
21 BL, Add. MS 18461, ff. 1–2v.
22 *Tax. Eccl.* 161; *Valor Eccl.* II, 500.
23 *Eng. Episc. Acta* VII, p. 19; see *Hist. & Cart. Mon. Glouc.* I, 116; II, 136–7; III, 5.
24 Above, manors (other estates: medieval monastic estates); *Eng. Episc. Acta* VII, p. 59.
25 *Reg. Orleton* (Cant. & York Soc., 1908), 188–9; *Reg. T. de Charlton*, 83.
26 Below (religious life).
27 GA, P 326/IN 3/9.
28 *Glouc. Dioc. Year Book* (1976), 34–7; *Dioc. of Glouc. Dir.* (1989), 50–1.

PATRONAGE AND ENDOWMENT

Gloucester abbey's patronage of the rectory[1] was exercised by the king in 1306 during a vacancy in the abbacy[2] and was granted to the dean and chapter of Gloucester in 1541.[3] At the next vacancy, in 1545, Thomas Payne, a Gloucester draper, was patron by grant from the abbey. John Veale of Longford was patron under the dean and chapter for a term of years in 1560 and members of his family presented in 1585 and 1597; the Crown presented in 1595 following the rector's deposition for simony. Revd Edward Savacre exercised the patronage in 1602 and 1613[4] and Giles Fowler was patron for a turn in 1633.[5] The dean and chapter presented from 1677, apart from 1864 when the Crown was patron,[6] and were with Peter Price joint patrons of the benefice of Tibberton with Taynton created in 1975. They retained an interest in the larger benefice of which Taynton was part from 1984.[7]

The rectorial tithes excluded Kilpeck's tithing and were commuted in 1843 for a corn rent charge of £444 19s. 4d.[8] The glebe was measured at 26 a. in 1612[9] and 29 a. in 1840.[10] Most of it, including the old churchyard, was sold in the early 1920s.[11] The rectory was worth £5 15s. 4d. in 1291,[12] £8 5s. 9d. in 1535,[13] £45 in 1650,[14] £100 in 1750,[15] and £349 in 1856.[16]

The rectory house, recorded from 1525,[17] stood north-east of the medieval church[18] and was burnt down with it in 1643.[19] The living remained without a house[20] until the rector Francis Jeune built one next to the 17th-century church.[21] The new house, to designs in Tudor Gothic style by John Hayward of Exeter, was completed in 1850 and enlarged in 1881.[22] It was divided into two flats c.1957[23] and was restored as a single dwelling after it was sold in the late 20th century.

RELIGIOUS LIFE

The Middle Ages

A woodland chapel or hermitage in Taynton was an adjunct of Taynton's church on its acquisition by Gloucester abbey in the 12th century.[24] The church was dedicated to St Lawrence by 1148.[25] The priest who resigned it in favour of the Gloucester abbey sacrist c.1158 was evidently to remain the celebrant with a pension of 10 marks (£6 13s. 4d.).[26]

In 1346 Elizabeth Coly of Taynton was licensed to have mass celebrated in an oratory in her house.[27] Richard Phipps or Phillips, accused of incontinence in 1468, resigned as rector in 1481. David Phipps, rector from 1484,[28] was presumably the same as Richard Phillips, priest in Taynton at his death in 1506.[29] Richard Ede, rector in 1508, faced several accusations of incontinence and, having confessed in 1522, was given a penance of six beatings, three each at Taynton and Hereford. Roger Brayne, his successor in 1524, was also vicar of Lydney and rector of Staunton-on-Wye (Herefs.).[30]

From the Reformation to the Civil Wars

George Blundell, rector from 1527 until his death in 1545, employed a curate at Taynton in his last years.[31] At that time services included two annual obits, both perhaps recent foundations; one was for Margaret Falconer and the other for a member of the Horn family.[32] Blundell's immediate successors were both former monks of Gloucester abbey; Walter Stanley (d. 1551), who married, was resident and Thomas Kingswood (d. 1559), a prebendary of Gloucester cathedral,[33] had in 1551 a curate who was generally satisfactory but was unable to prove the Apostles' Creed from Scripture.[34]

John Yannes (James), rector 1560–85,[35] was in

---

1 See *Reg. Swinfield*, 525, 528; *Reg. Lacy*, 118.
2 *Cal. Pat.* 1301–7, 431.
3 *L&P Hen. VIII*, XVI, 572–3.
4 Hockaday Abs. ccclxv.
5 TNA, E 331/GLOUC/13.
6 Hockaday Abs. ccclxv.
7 GA, P 326/IN 3/9; *Glouc. Dioc. Year Book* (1976), 36–7; *Dioc. of Glouc. Dir.* (2003–4), 22.
8 GDR, T 1/177.
9 Ibid. V 5/299T 1.
10 Ibid. T 1/177.
11 GA, D 2299/2312; G/NE 159/11, ff. 16–16.
12 *Tax. Eccl.* 161.
13 *Valor Eccl.* II, 500.
14 C.R. Elrington, 'The Survey of Church Livings in Gloucestershire, 1650', *Trans. BGAS* 83 (1964), 98.
15 *Bp. Benson's Surv. of Dioc. of Glouc. 1735–50*, 18.
16 GDR vol. 384, f. 197.
17 Hockaday Abs. ccclxv.
18 GDR, V 5/299T 1; T 1/177 (nos 675 and 668).
19 *LJ* 9, 668.
20 GDR, V 5/299T 4; *Bp. Benson's Surv. of Dioc. of Glouc. 1735–50*, 18.
21 See GDR, T 1/177; OS Map 6", Glos. XXIV. NE (1888 edn).
22 Verey and Brooks, *Glos.* II, 707; GDR, F 4/1; GA, D 2593/2/419.
23 GA, DA 30/100/26, p. 101.
24 *Hist. & Cart. Mon. Glouc.* I, 116, 224, 228, 352; II, 127–8, 136–7; III, 5.
25 *Eng. Episc. Acta VII*, p. 19.
26 Ibid. p. 59.
27 *Reg. Trillek*, 59.
28 Hockaday Abs. ccclxv.
29 TNA, PROB 11/15, ff. 43v.–44.
30 Hockaday Abs. ccclxv.
31 Ibid. ccclxv; xxx, 1544 stipendiaries, f. 8; 1545 visit. f. 5.
32 Ibid. ccclxv; TNA, C 54/3768, no 26.
33 Hockaday Abs. ccclxv; G. Baskerville, 'The Dispossessed Religious of Gloucestershire', *Trans. BGAS* 49 (1927), 74, 83.
34 J. Gairdner, 'Bishop Hooper's Visitation of Gloucester', *EHR* 19 (1904), 120.
35 Hockaday Abs. ccclxv.

dispute with his curate and parishioners in 1575.[1] In 1576, when an unlicensed minister held services and read the Gospels on perambulations, the churchwardens were lax in enforcing church attendance, there was one communion service a year, and the catechism was not regularly taught.[2] Richard Wood, who became rector in 1585 by the gift of Thomas Veale of Gloucester, was deprived for simony. William Masters, his successor in 1595, resigned in 1597[3] after many parishioners boycotted services[4] and a mob including Veale's wife entered the rectory house.[5]

The Building of a New Parish Church

In 1643, a few days after the raising of the siege of Gloucester, Royalists burnt down the parish church and neighbouring rectory house.[6] Although parts of the church remained standing[7] parishioners headed by Ferdinando Stratford, rector 1634–77,[8] obtained a parliamentary ordinance in 1648 for building a new church and house on glebe in a more central position, the old church having been inaccessible to most inhabitants especially in winter.[9] The building of the new church, under way in 1657 when Gloucester corporation made a gift of the seats remaining in Holy Trinity church in the city,[10] was sponsored by Thomas Pury the younger, MP for the city and a former parliamentary soldier.[11] The first baptism in it was that of his daughter Deborah in 1659, the first burial there that of his son Theophilus in 1665.[12]

The new church, built of local rubble, was a narrow rectangular box oriented, contrary to Laudian principles, north–south. It had a tiebeam roof and its east and west fronts were of four bays with regularly spaced windows marked by roughly finished quoins and lintels and, on both fronts, a doorway in the north bay. There may also have been a north doorway as one was reinstated in the 1820s.[13] The original interior plan is unknown but surviving elements of the woodwork, among them late medieval panels from the Holy Trinity seats, suggest that the furnishings were of high quality and that some were in a fashionable style. A new bell, recorded in 1681,[14] was housed in a wooden north bellcot. The church kept the dedication to St Lawrence[15] and among its goods were a chalice and paten cover from the old church.[16]

From the Restoration to 1800

Two families attended a small Quaker meeting in Taynton in 1669[17] and two nonconformists were recorded in the parish in 1676.[18] Abraham and Judith Shapton, who bought Great Taynton manor in 1673, were Quakers[19] but his children by a new marriage in 1689[20] were baptized at Taynton.[21] Quaker farmer Augustine King lived in Taynton at his death in 1720 or 1721.[22]

From the late 17th century the parish was often served by a stipendiary curate,[23] the rectors being usually prebendaries of Gloucester cathedral and invariably non-resident. Benjamin Newton, who succeeded his father John as rector in 1710, was master of the cathedral school from 1712 to 1718 and cathedral librarian from 1731. He resigned the living in 1733.[24] Of his curates the first, in 1713, was Samuel Whittington,[25] the son of Elizabeth Whittington, lady of Great Taynton manor.[26] Benjamin Newton's son John, rector 1737–54,[27] was also cathedral librarian but officiated at Taynton church and provided full services except in winter.[28] Thomas Parker, rector from 1755, was also rector of Welsh Bicknor (Mon., later Herefs.) at his death in 1800.[29]

Church and Chapel in the Nineteenth Century: missions to Glasshouse Hill and Kent's Green

John Luxmoore, dean of Gloucester, had the rectory from 1800 to 1806 and George William Hall (d. 1843) and Francis Jeune, masters of Pembroke College,

---

1 *The Commission for Ecclesiastical Causes in the Dioceses of Bristol and Gloucester, 1574*, ed. F.D. Price (BGAS Records Section 10, 1972), 84–5, 100.
2 GDR vol. 40, f. 256v.
3 Hockaday Abs. ccclxv.
4 GA, D 2052.
5 BL, Harl. MS 4131, ff. 514v.–515.
6 *LJ* 9, 665.
7 See TNA, PROB 11/245, f. 111.
8 Hockaday Abs. ccclxv; GA, P 326/IN 1/2.
9 Parliamentary Archives, HL/PO/JO/10/1/243; *LJ* 9, 665.
10 GBR, B 3/3, p. 41. For Holy Trinity ch., *VCH Glos.* IV, 294–5.
11 *Notes on Dioc. of Glouc. by Chancellor Parsons*, 189; *Oxford DNB*, s.v. Thomas Pury (d. 1666).
12 GA, P 326/IN 1/1.
13 Below (transformations of par. ch.).
14 GDR, V 5/299T 2; *Glos. Ch. Bells*, 603.
15 Atkyns, *Glos.* 709, which suggests incorrectly an E–W alignment.
16 GDR, V 5/299T 2; *Glos. Ch. Plate*, 205.
17 Ibid. D 2052.
18 *Compton Census*, 544.
19 GA, D 2052.
20 Information from Arthur Hopkins of Federal Way, Washington State, USA.
21 GA, P 326/IN 1/2.
22 GDR wills 1721/251; see ibid. B 4/1/2606.
23 Ibid. V 1/240.
24 *Oxford DNB*, s.v. Benjamin Newton; J. Newton, 'A Short Account of the Author's Life', in *Sermons on Several Occasions by the Revd Benjamin Newton* I (1736), pp. v–xxii: copy in Glos. Colln. 17014.
25 GDR, V 1/240; Hockaday Abs. ccclxv.
26 Churchyard monument to Samuel (d. 1724) in Bigland, *Glos.* III, no 266; see above, manors.
27 *Oxford DNB*, s.v. Benjamin Newton.
28 *Bp. Benson's Surv. of Dioc. of Glouc. 1735–50*, 18.
29 Hockaday Abs. ccclxv; GDR, V 1/240; *Alumni Oxon. 1715–1886*, III, 1068.

Oxford, had it in turn between 1810 and 1864.[1] During that period the parish remained in the care of a stipendiary curate[2] and in 1825 the church had one Sunday service, alternately in the morning and afternoon, and the average congregation was said to be 150 and the number of regular communicants was put at between 40 and 50. Religious instruction was given every other Sunday;[3] a Sunday school had been started in 1823.[4] Nonconformists registered houses in the parish in 1797 and 1802[5] and Wesleyan Methodists built a chapel on Glasshouse hill in 1820.[6] In 1836 Kent's Green was among many places around Newent visited by the evangelist Thomas Kington.[7]

William Charles Holder of Taynton House,[8] who instigated alterations to the church in the mid 1820s while churchwarden,[9] became Taynton's minister as curate in 1829[10] and with his uncle Edward Howell donated several pieces of church plate.[11] In 1834 a meeting of 47 men, mostly farmers, craftsmen, and labourers, declared their attachment to the Established Church and its role in the State.[12] Holder's successors as curate from 1835 were also resident, William Hughes (1850–64) being the first occupant of Francis Jeune's new glebe house.[13] In 1851 the church had morning and afternoon services with congregations averaging between 70 and 80.[14] The Wesleyan chapel on Glasshouse hill, served from Ledbury, had an average attendances of 65 and 60 at morning and afternoon services and another Methodist meeting on the hill, using a building erected in 1810, had similar attendances.[15] In the late 1840s the Newent Congregational church conducted cottage meetings at Kent's Green.[16]

In 1864 Wesleyans built a new chapel lower down Glasshouse hill[17] and a year or two later moved a wooden chapel from Highleadon to Kent's Green. The latter building, placed north of the road to Anthony's Cross, was also part of the Ledbury circuit but was occasionally off its plan for lack of support.[18] The Anglicans, for whom Charles Yonge Crawley, rector 1864–76,[19] was the first in a succession of resident incumbents,[20] held a monthly service on Glasshouse hill.[21] A mission room built there in 1879[22] was served by Alfred Drake Bagshawe, rector 1877–91,[23] and had an adjacent burial ground.[24] Under Norman Shelton, rector 1891–1903, a curate lived on the hill[25] and the mission took in Kent's Green.[26]

Transformations of the Parish Church

In the early 19th century the church had proprietary seats at its south end, where the pulpit rose behind the communion table on the west side, and free seats at the north end, where the area under a small singers' gallery stored lumber.[27] The gallery was in place in the later 18th century[28] and the decoration of the church included royal arms paid for in 1796.[29] In 1825 the pulpit, which together with the clerk's desk and reading desk formed a three-tiered arrangement, was moved to the south wall and the communion table to the east wall for liturgical reasons, an east window was painted, and the font was embellished. At the north end the east and west doorways were blocked, the gallery was enlarged and free seats placed below it, and a porch was built to shelter a reinstated north doorway. The alterations, made without a faculty, were sponsored primarily by churchwarden W.C. Holder. The remaining cost was met by a grant and donations and by a rate which several parishioners refused to pay.[30]

In 1830 and 1831 the pulpit was moved forward and the south window was adapted to create a doorway into a vestry. The new room was also used for a Sunday school, part of its cost having been met by a

---

1 Hockaday Abs. ccclxv; *Oxford DNB*, s.vv. Francis Jeune and John Luxmoore; *Alumni Oxon. 1715–1886*, II, 587.
2 GDR, V 1/240; GA, P 326/IN 1/5–6, 9.
3 GDR vol. 383, no cxxxiii.
4 *Educ. Enq. Abstract*, 328.
5 Hockaday Abs. ccclxv. According to K. and W. Thomas, *Our Story of Taynton* (Taynton Society, 1981), 10, the house registered in 1802 was Longcroft, the home of a Quaker.
6 Date on bldg.; GDR, T 1/177 (no 330).
7 Hockaday Abs. ccxciii. For Kington, above Dymock, religious hist. (religious life).
8 See above, manors (other estates).
9 See below (transformations of par. ch.).
10 Hockaday Abs. ccclxv.
11 *Glos. Ch. Plate*, 205; for Howell, above, manors (other estates: Taynton Ho.).
12 GA, P 326/VE 2/1.
13 Hockaday Abs. ccclxv; *Alumni Cantab. 1752–1900*, III, 438; TNA, HO 107/350/14; HO 107/1760; RG 9/1760; above (patronage and endowment).
14 TNA, HO 129/335/1/9/9.
15 Ibid. HO 129/335/1/9/10; HO 129/335/1/8/8.
16 GA, D 6026/9/1.
17 Inscr. on chapel; see OS Map 6", Glos. XXIV.SW (1889 edn).
18 W. Balmforth, 'The Story of Kents Green Chapel' (1992: copy in GA, P 332/2), 2–5, 12; G.R. Hine, *Methodist Church Gloucester Circuit Records* (1971), 31; see OS Map 6", Glos. XXIV.NE (1903 edn).
19 *Alumni Oxon. 1715–1886*, I, 314.
20 *Kelly's Dir. Glos.* (1870 and later edns).
21 GA, P 326/MI 1.
22 *Kelly's Dir. Glos.* (1885), 591; OS Map 6", Glos. XXIV.SW (1889 edn). See below, Fig. 78.
23 GA, P 326/MI 2; IN 1/6, 9.
24 Ibid. SL 10.
25 *Kelly's Dir. Glos.* (1897), 316; (1906), 319.
26 *Rural Deanery of the North Forest Church Monthly and Parochial Visitor* (Jan. 1896: copy in Glos. Colln. (H)E 13.13).
27 GDR, F 1/4; B 4/1/2423.
28 The position of a monument to James Parker (d. 1789) high on the N. wall provides a *terminus ante quem* for the erection of the gallery.
29 GA, P 326/CW 2/1.
30 GDR, F 1/4; B 4/1/2423; GA, P 326/VE 2/1; CW 2/1. See Fig. 77.

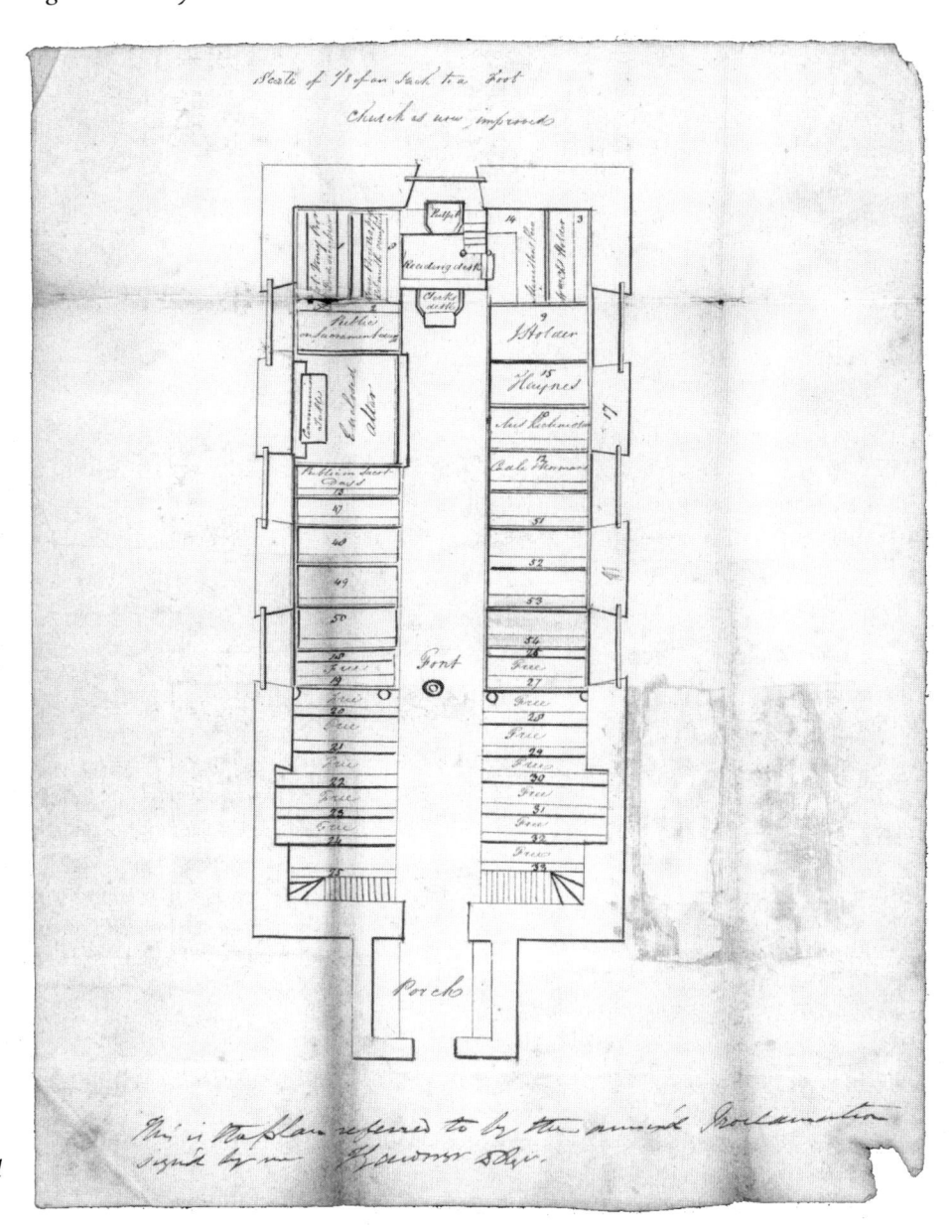

77. Taynton church: ground-floor plan (south to the top) as laid out in 1825

grant from the National Society.¹ In extensive alterations in 1865 the church ceiling was removed and battens and a plaster lining were added to the roof, the wooden windows were replaced by stone mullions with Pependicular style tracery, a window was inserted above the porch to light the gallery, and the height of the pews was reduced.² The bellcot was replaced in stone in 1875 after it was struck by lightning.³ In the later 19th century the church had a succession of organs,⁴ one being donated in 1880 by P.R. Cocks (later Lord Somers).⁵

In 1893 and 1894, against local opposition,⁶ a chancel was created in place of the vestry. In its design, by the Gloucester firm of Medland & Son, the south wall was refaced, the roof was raised to a higher pitch, a Gothic chancel arch and south window were inserted, and a west organ chamber was added. At the same time the gallery was removed, the entire church was reseated, and the old oak pews were re-used as a reredos behind the communion table, which was moved into the chancel, and as a dado around the nave. An oak lectern was made and presented by Revd W.B. Atherton as a memorial to his mother and other members of the Holder family. The north doorcase is probably made from the frame of a reredos, a

1 GA, P 326/VE 2/1; GDR, F 1/4. See plan in GA, D 2593/2/490.
2 GA, P 326/VE 2/1; *Church Builder* N.S. 14 (1893), 70.
3 GA, P 326/VE 2/1; Bigland, *Glos.* III, no 266.
4 See *VCH Glos.* IX, 90.
5 GA, P 326/VE 2/1; *Complete Peerage*, XIII (1), 34–5.
6 See GA, P 326/VE 2/1; *Glouc. J.* 16 May 1908.

78. All Saints' church, May Hill

'curious erection' installed in 1825 and dismantled in 1893.[1] The single-decker pulpit is fashioned out of late medieval panels from the seats from Holy Trinity, Gloucester, and 17th-century pieces, and a combination of linen-fold panelling and classical carving is repeated in the reredos panelling and on two chairs in the chancel. The font, one of the church's mid 17th-century fittings, has a bowl carved with cherubs' heads and acanthus and resting on a fluted pedestal.

The Twentieth Century and Later

At the beginning of the 20th century a chancel was added to the mission church on Glasshouse hill, the work being financed by Revd Norman Shelton, in part from donations.[2] With a dedication to All Saints in 1919,[3] the church was served until 1930 by a curate-in-charge, the last of whom, J.R. Rimes,[4] donated a pulpit.[5] A medieval bell is said to have come from Westbury-on-Severn.[6] The church, which with its district was part of Huntley for ecclesiastical purposes from 1935,[7] had a weekly Sunday morning service in 2006. The parish church, where a new organ was installed in 1909,[8] was served with Tibberton church from 1946 and had a resident rector until 1969.[9] Taynton church was later in the care of priests-in-charge living in Tibberton and from 1984 in Highnam.[10]

The chapel at Kent's Green, which from 1912 to 1921 housed a mission run by the rector, B.K. Foster, closed in 1969.[11] It stood abandoned and overgrown in 2006. The Methodist chapel on Glasshouse hill, to which a new schoolroom was added in 1922,[12] had a weekly Sunday morning service in 2006.

---

1 *Church Builder* N.S. 14 (1893), 70; *Glos. Chron.* 14 Apr. 1894; *Glouc. J.* 16 May 1908.
2 Glos. Colln. RR 76.1; *Kelly's Dir. Glos.* (1906), 319.
3 GA, P 326/VE 2/1. See Fig. 78.
4 *Kelly's Dir. Glos.* (1906 and later edns); *Crockford's Clerical Dir.* (1939), 1132.
5 GA, D 3028/1.
6 *Glos. Ch. Bells*, 427–8; information from Miss Mary Bliss, of Beech Pike, Winstone.
7 GA, P 326/IN 3/4.
8 D.J. Parker, *Taynton, Gloucestershire. A Story of Two Churches* (1998), 32.
9 *Glouc. Dioc. Year Book* (1947–8), 15, 34–5; (1969), 30–1, 71.
10 Ibid. (1970), 30–1, 73; *Dioc. of Glouc. Dir.* (1989), 11, 50–1; (2003–4), 22, 103.
11 Balmforth, 'Kents Green Chapel', 6–7.
12 Inscr. on chapel extension. The addition of a schoolroom was considered in 1875: GA, D 2689/1/2/4.

INDEX

NOTES: Page numbers in **bold** indicate the main entry for a place.
Page numbers in *italic* denote an illustration.

The following abbreviations and contractions have been used: Alex., Alexander; And., Andrew; Ant., Anthony; Benj., Benjamin; Bucks., Buckinghamshire; Cath., Catherine; cent., century; Chas., Charles; Chris. Christopher; d., died; Dan., Daniel; dau., daughter; Derbs., Derbyshire; Edm., Edmund; Edw., Edward; Eliz., Elizabeth; *fl.*, *floruit*; Fred., Frederick; Geo., George; Geof., Geoffrey; Glam., Glamorgan; grds., grandson; Hants, Hampshire; Hen., Henry; Herefs., Herefordshire; Herts., Hertfordshire; Humph., Humphrey; Jas., James; Jos., Joseph; m., married; Matt., Matthew; Middx, Middlesex; Mic., Michael; Mon., Monmouthshire; n, note; Nat., Nathaniel; Nic., Nicholas; Northants., Northamptonshire; Notts., Nottinghamshire; Oxon., Oxfordshire; Phil., Philip; Reg., Reginald; Ric., Richard; Rob., Robert; Rog., Roger; s., son; Salop., Shropshire; Sam., Samuel; Staffs., Staffordshire; Steph., Stephen; Thos., Thomas; Tim., Timothy; w., wife; Wal., Walter; Warws., Warwickshire; Wilts., Wiltshire; Wm., William; Worcs., Worcestershire.

Abberley (Worcs.), named as an address, 45, 306
Abbot, John, 118
Abenhall, 191, 235, 237, 241 n, 245, 251, 253
Abercrombie, Lascelles, 167
Abergavenny (Mon.), carrier to, 243
Abitot, *see* d'Abitot
Abrahall, John, 203, 210
Ackers:
    Benj. St John, 181, 190, 193
    Chas. Penrhyn, 5, 62, 178, 180–1, 185–6, 190, 340
    Torill, m. Mic. Freeman, 181
    family, 3, 40, 180, 182, 193, 326, 334
Aconbury priory (Herefs.), 148, 154, 207, 208, 212
Acton:
    Hen., 245
    Wm., 334
    family, 334
Addis (Adys):
    John, 329
    Wm., curate of Oxenhall, 280
    family, 276
Agincourt, battle of, 269
Ainsworth, Oliver, 69
air strip, 303
Albright:
    Dinah, 103–4, 115, 117–18, 122
    Geo. Stacey, 104, 106, 115, 117, 122
Albright & Wilson, manufacturer of phosphorus, 115
Alderley, named as an address, 138
Aldridge, Rob., 340
Alfward (*fl.* 1066), 287
Alley:
    Eliz., *see* Boulsdon
    John, 42
Almeley (Herefs.), named as an address, 40
Almondsbury, named as an address, 52
America, 167
    emigration to, 172
Amyrable, Ric., 133
Anketil, John (one or more late 13th cent.), 17, 68
architects, *see* Armstrong, Ric.; Basevi, Geo.; Dancey, H.A.; Dolman, Jas.; Elrington, Jean; Fulljames, Thos.; Girdwood, J. & J.; Hamilton, Craig; Harris, E. Swinfen; Hayward, John; Hugall & Male; Jones, J.E.; Jones, Ric.; Jones, Rob.; Lethaby, Wm.; Maberly, A.W.; Medland, Jas.; Medland & Maberly; Medland & Son; Middleton, John;

Middleton & Goodman; Millard, Jas.; Moore, Temple; Phillips, R.S.; Preedy, Fred.; Price, J.G.; Rees, Wm.; Rollinson, S., & Son; Rushforth, T.H.; Scott, Gilbert; Stratford, Ferdinando; Teulon, S.S.; Trew, Harold; Waller, F.W.; Waller & Son; Waller, Son, & Wood; Wells, A. Randall; Wood, Wal. B.; Wren, Sir Chris.
Arlingham, named as an address, 103–4
Armstrong, Ric., 301
Arnold, Sir Nic., 39, 49, 54
Arrowsmith, Joan, *see* Broke
Arts and Crafts Movement, 94
Arundel, earl of, *see* FitzAlan, Humph.
Ashcroft, Ric., 331
Ashleworth, 274–5
    named as an address, 47
Ashley, Eliz., *see* Wyman
Astman:
    John, 33
    family, 33, 77
Aston, Wm., 273
Aston Ingham (Herefs.), 6, 8–10, 36–7, 57, 61, 79, 90, 226
Atherlard family, 50
Atherton:
    Cath., 331
    Chas. Bernard, 331
    Hen. Holder, 331
    Henrietta, 331
    Louisa Henrietta, *see* Holder
    Revd W.B., 345
    family, 329, 338–9, 345
Atkins, Ric., vicar of Kempley, 219
Atkinson:
    Hen., 328
    John, 46, 328
    Rob., 328
attorneys, 69; *see also* solicitors
Attwood:
    M.L., 287
    Wm., 296
    family, 296
Aubrey (Awbrey):
    Thos., 289
    Wal., 114
    family, 99
Australia, emigrant to, 51
Avenant, Thos., vicar of Newent, 81, 83
Avenel:
    Douce (later Cecily), m. John de Mucegros, 5, 326, 336, 339 n
    Margaret, 326

    Ralph, 326
    Wm., 326
Awbrey, *see* Aubrey
Awre, 193, 195, 235
Aycrigg, Benj., 19
Ayleford, *see* Newnham
Ayleway:
    Chris., 330
    Geof., 330
    Hen., 330
    Joan, 330
    John (*fl.* early 16th cent.), 330
    John (d. 1599), 329–30
    John (*fl.* 1669), 234
    Reynold (*fl.* 1306), 330
    Reynold (*fl.* c.1315, ? same as last), 52
    Ric. (*fl.* 1639), 64
    Ric. (d. 1654, ? another), 330
    Rog., 330, 337
    Thos., 330
    Wal., 330, 334
    family, 320, 323, 330, 338

Baderon of Monmouth, 180, 233
Bagshawe, Alfred Drake, rector of Taynton, 340, 344
Baird, Wm., vicar of Dymock, 172
Baker:
    Geo., rector of Huntley, 190, 196
    John, 236
    Rob., 99
    Thos., 235–6, 250
Ballingham (Herefs.), named as an address, 206
Bampton (Oxon.), named as an address, 139
Banister, *see* Baugh
banks, 69
Baptists, 84, 88, 90, 170–4, 195, 219–20, 222, 232, 246, 248, 252–4, 280
Barbados, 139
Barber:
    Marianne, *see* Leigh
    Rob., 53
Barbour, *see* Harper
Barnard:
    Hannah, w. of Paul, 338, 340
    Paul, 337–8
Barnes, H.V., 334
Barnsley, Ernest, 222
Barnsley, 142
Barr, Geo., vicar of Longhope, 253
Barre:
    Isabel, m. 1 Humph. Stafford, earl of Devon, 2 Thos. Bourchier, 328
    Joan, w. of John, 328
    John, 328

Barrett:
    Osman, 232–3, 246
    family, 232
Barrington, Great, named as an address, 54
Barton:
    Edith, w. of Wilfred, 50
    Rose, 247–8
    Wilfred, 50
Basevi, Geo., 105
Baskerville:
    Edw., 219
    Emme de, see St Léger
    Wal. de, 203
Basset, Phil., 138. 169
Bath:
    Aline of, m. Rob. de Sapy, 181.
    Nic. of, 181, 183
Battersea (Surrey), named as an address, 139
Baugh (or Banister), Sir Rob., 267
Baynham family, 201, 233
Beach, John, 63
Beale:
    Isabella, see Morse
    John (fl. 1467–75), 106, 108, 114
    John (fl. 1487, son of last), 106
    John (fl. 1506, ? another), 106
    John (fl. 1629–36), 268, 271, 279
    John (d. 1775), 40
    Mary, m. Wm. Symonds, 145–6, 268
    Miles (d. 1698), 66
    Miles (d. 1713), 40, 66
    Miles (d. 1748), 40
    Sam, 139, 145, 260, 268, 270
    Theophilus, 51
    Wm., vicar of Dymock, 51, 84, 88, 171
    family, 31, 270
Bearcroft:
    Edw., 48
    Eliz., see Rogers
    Eliz., m. Jas. de Visme, 48, 54
    Phil. Rogers, 48
Beauchamp:
    Guy de (d. 1315), earl of Warwick, 103
    Ric. de (d. 1422), earl of Worcester, 103
    Ric. de (fl. 1423), earl of Warwick, 103
    Ric. (fl. late 15th cent.), Lord
        Beauchamp, 100
    Rog. (d. 1380), 138
    Rog. (s. or grds. of last), 138
    Thos. (d. 1401), earl of Warwick, 103
Beauchamp, Earls, see Lygon
Beaufort, duke of, see Somerset, Hen.
Beckford (Worcs., formerly Glos.), named
    as an address, 39
Belgium, 296
    refugees from, 297
Bellamy, Geo., 132
Bellers, Rob. Bridges, 328
bellfounders, see Green, Nic.; Llewellins &
    James; Pennington, John; Rigby,
    Alex.; Rudhall, Abraham and
    Thos.
Belson, John, 191
Bengeworth (Worcs.), 291
Bennion:
    S.W. (? same as next), 146
    Sam., 162
    family, 162
Benson, Rachael, m. Decimus Weale, 144
Berkeley:
    Anne, see Whittington
    Brian, 287
    Wm., 213

Berkeley, 194
    named as an address, 173
Berkshire, see Sunninghill
Berrow (Worcs.), 97, 100, 104, 147
    school, 116
    Whiteleaved Oak, 100
Bethell:
    Dorothy, w. of Revd Sam., see Jauncey
    Dorothy, dau. of Revd Sam., 289
    Mary, 289
    Revd Sam., 289
Bewdley (Worcs.), 240
Bicknor, English, 336
Bicknor, Welsh (Herefs., formerly Mon.),
    343
Billinghurst (Sussex), named as an address, 51
Bird:
    John, 189
    Wm., 189
    family, 189
Birkenhead (Ches.), 339
Birmingham, named as an address, 115
Birt, Ric., 293
Birtsmorton (Worcs.), 106, 147
    named as an address, 81
Blaisdon, 91–2, 176, 181, 194–5, 222, 226, 236,
        245, 253–4
Blaisdon Red, plum called, 238
Blakeney, Wal. of, 119
Blencowe, P.G., 316
Blewett, Ephraim, 201–2, 211
Blindman's Gate, see Linton
Blisworth (Northants.), named as an
    address, 138
Blood:
    Charlotte Constance, 182–3, 190
    John Neptune, 182, 190
Blount:
    Sir Chris., 139, 327
    Sir Edm., 138
    Lettice, see Devereux
Blundell:
    Geo., vicar of Kempley and later rector
        of Taynton, 219, 342
    Thos., vicar of Kempley, 219
Blunt:
    Frances, m. —— Nayler, 182
    Harriet, dau. of Thos., 182
    Mary, w. of Thos., 182
    Thos., 182, 189
Blurton, John, 266
Bodenham:
    Joan, see Whittington
    Rog., 287
    Thos., 329
Bodenham (Herefs.), 141
Bohun, Hen. de, earl of Hereford, 138
Bolonies, see Bulnoys
Boroughbridge, battle of, 234
Bosworth:
    Ann, w. of Harry, 205
    Eliz., m. —— Nash, 205
    Harry, 205
    Wm., 205, 212
Botloe hundred, 2, 5
    court, 71, 276
    meeting place, 5–6
Botloe's Green, in Newent and Pauntley,
    8–9, 29–30, 69, 91
Botte, Revd Wm., 103
Boughton, Rutland, 78
Boulsdon:
    Eliz., m. John Alley, 42

Thos. of (fl. 1258), 42
Thos. (d. 1473), 42
Wm. of, 42
Boulsdon, see Newent
Boulton, R.L., 281
Bourchier:
    Ant., 85
    Barbara, see Richardson
    Isabel, see Barre
    Thos., 328
    Wal., 142
    Wm., 142
Bourchier, Lord, see Devereux, Wal.
Bourne:
    Dorothy, m. Wal. Nourse (d. 1743), 47
    John, 47
Boverel family, 34
Boverton (Glam.), named as an address, 139
Bower:
    Edw., 66
    John, 245
    John Cocks, 330
    family, 25, 66
Boyce, see Boys
Boyd, Fr. Wm., 91
Boys (Boyce):
    Arnald du, 46, 326
    Edm. du, 141
    Ric. du (fl. 1200), 141
    Ric. du (fl. 1286, 1299), 103, 118–19, 141
    Wal. du, 141
    Wal. (fl. 1385), 141
    Wm. du, 326
Bradford:
    Edm. 105
    John (d. 1561), 104
    John (fl. 1640), 49
    Phil., 49
    Rob., 111
    Rog., 104
    Wm., 104–5
    family, 37, 160
    see also Viner Bradford
Bradford-on-Avon (Wilts.), named as an
    address, 139
Bradley, Chris., 50
Brand Green, in Newent and Pauntley, 8,
    27, 29–30, 39, 62, 69, 90–1, 284–5,
    289
    village hall, 298
brass wire manufacture, 334
Bray:
    Sir Edm. (d. 1684), 41, 54, 87
    Edm. (d. 1725), 54
    Edm. (d. 1728), 54
    Reg., 54
    Reg. Morgan, 54
    family, 64
Brayne, Rog., rector of Taynton, 342
bread and ale, assize of, 71, 336
Breteuil, Rog. of, earl of Hereford, 38, 137
Breuse, John de, 287
Brian;
    Alice, w. of Guy de, 49, 265
    Guy de, 265
Brickenden:
    Carolina, see Somerset
    Ric., 287
brick making, 63–4, 201, 211, 335
Bridges:
    Edm., 141
    Ellen, w. of Edm., 141
    Sir John (d. 1530), 163, 170

John (d. 1561), 141, 267
Maud, *see* Henbarrow
Thos. (*fl.* 1457), 141
Thos. (d. by 1530, ? same as last), 170
Thos. (*fl.* 1592), 200
Wm. (d. 1523), 141, 160
Wm. (*fl.* 1530), 141
family, 141
Bridstow (Herefs), Wilton, named as an address, 3, 203, 213, 265
Bright, Thos., 245
Brindle:
Thos., 146
Wm., 146
Bristol, 157, 189, 240, 247, 335
named as an address, 236, 281
British Legion Housing Association, 21
Brock:
John, 269, 274, 276
Margery, w. of John, 269
Margery, m. John Hill, 269
see also Broke; Brooke
Brockhampton (Herefs.), 221
Broke:
Joan, m. —— Arrowsmith, 265
Thos., 265
see also Brock; Brooke
Bromesberrow, 1–2, 4–5, *95–122*, 143, 152, 167, 198
advowson, 118
agriculture, 108–10
boundaries, 95–7
Bromesberrow Court, 99, 101–2, 104, 114
Bromesberrow Place, *see* Bromesberrow, Hook House
Brookend, 97
Lower Brookend, 99, 101
Upper Brookend, 99, 101, 106, 114–15
Brown's End, 99–100, 106
charities, 100, 113, 115–16, 120–1
Chase End, 100, 102
church, 97, 99, 113, 115, 118–22, 174
church house, 117
commons, 97–8, 108–10,
courts, 113–14
domestic architecture, 101–2, 104–5, 106–7
farms, 108–10
fields, 97, 108–9
fishponds, 97, 111
friendly society, 117
Hook House (Bromesberrow Place), 97, 99–100, 102, 104–*105*, 115–16
inclosure, 97, 110
manors, 102–4
manor houses, 115; *see also* Bromesberrow, Bromesberrow Court *and* Hook House (Bromesberrow Place)
mills, 97, 99, 111
named as an address, 150, 164
nonconformity, 120–1
parish officers, 113–14
park, 97
poor relief, 113–14
poorhouse, *see* Bromesberrow, workhouse
population, 98
pound, 100
reading room and library, 117
rectors, 119–22; *see also* Eaton, Ric.; Hayward, Wm.; Hill, Reg. Pyndar; Rigby, F.F.; Yate, Hen. Gorges Dobyns

rectory, 118
rectory houses, 100, 102, 118
roads, 97–8
road repairs, 114
schools, 100, 102, 115–17
settlement, 98–100
social structure, 114–16
societies and clubs, 117
tithes, 118
Toney's Farm, 96–7, 102, *107*
trades, 112
village hall, 117
Woodend, 97, 100, 116
woodland, 96–7, 275
woodland management, 110–11
workhouse (formerly poorhouse), 100, 113–14
Bromesberrow Heath, in Bromesberrow and Dymock, 2, 4, 96, 98, 118, 122–3, 126, 131–2, 155–7, 160, 162–3, 166–7, 174
public house, 117, 166
school, 116–17; *see also* Dymock, schools, Haffield
Bromley:
(formerly Smith), Sir Geo., Bt, *see* Pauncefote
Rob., 45, 306
Sarah, *see* Pauncefoot
Sir Rob. Howe, 45
Wm., 45, 306
Bromwich:
(or Dyer), Rob., 114–15
Ann (or Agnes), *see* Payne
Constance, w. of John (d. 1388), m. 2 Hugh Waterton, 3 Rog. Leech, 103
Edm., 103
Edw., 103, 115
Isaac, 103
Jas., 115
John (d. 1388), 103, 114
John (*fl.* 1447), 103
John (d. 1485, ? another), 103
John (d. 1512), 103
John (d. 1567), 103, 110–11, 118
John (d. 1592), 99, 103, 114–15, 119
Lancelot, 235
Maud, w. of John (d. 1485), 103
Priscilla, *see* Yate
Rob., 103, 113, 115–16
Thos. (*fl.* 1420), 103
Thos. (*fl.* 1467), 103
Wm., 252
Yate, vicar of Longhope, 234–5, 252
family, 115
Brooke:
Revd Jas., 134
John (*fl.* 1617), 101
John (*fl.* 1787), 208
Kenneth, 207
Ric., 109–10, 117
Ric., curate of Kempley, 220
Rupert, 167
W.J., 207
Wm., 99
family, 200
see also Brock; Broke
Broom's Green, *see* Dymock
Broughton, John, 64
Bruton:
Hen. (d. 1894), 67
Hen. (*fl.* 1908), 59
family, 67

Bruton & Knowles, auctioneers, 62
Bryan, Chas., vicar of Preston, 314, 316
Buckingham, earl of, *see* Villiers, Geo.
Buckinghamshire, *see* Horwood, Little; Milton Keynes
Bulley, 192, 250
manor of Tibberton, Taynton, and Bulley, 331, 336
Bullock (Bulloc):
Thos., 213
Wm., 28
family, 201
Bulnoys (or Bolonies), John, 65
Bures:
Hawise de, *see* Mucegros
John de, 326, 337
Burge, ——, 338
Burgh, Hubert de, 127, 156, 158
Burgis:
Thos. (d. *c*.1715), 329
Thos. (d. 1718), 329
Burland:
John B.H., 41
Morris, vicar of Gorsley with Clifford's Mesne, 89
Burley:
Beatrice, w. of Ric., m. 2 Hugh Waterton, 328
Ric., 328
Burrell:
C.J.K., rector of Newent, 85
Geo., 329
Burrow, F., 250
Burrows, Wm., 267
Bushley (Worcs.), named as an address, 106
Butler:
Amice, w. of Jas., 265
Evan, 227
Hen., 291, 297
Jas., earl of Wiltshire, 265
John, 291, 296
Byfleet (Surrey), named as an address, 235
Byford, John of, 322, 337
Byron, J.M., 89
Byton (Herefs.), 279

Cadbury Ltd, chocolate maker, 59
Cadle (Cadell):
Harriet, 51
Jas., 236
John (*fl.* 1617), 236
John (d. 1859), 51–2
Jos., 51
Jos. Draper, 51
Thos. (*fl.* 1849), 20, 69
Thos. (d. 1859), 51, 53
family, 322
Caerleon, Morgan of, 138, 158
Callow, Wm., 143
Callowhill, Rob. of, 27
Cam:
Ann, 139, 142, 145, 147, 161, 164, 206
Ann, m. Abraham Whittaker, 146
Cath., 170
John (*fl.* 1517), vicar of Dymock, 170
John (*fl.* 1551), vicar of Kempley, 219
John (*fl.* 1608), 312
John (d. 1662), 147, 310
John (d. 1680), 147, 161, 170
John (d. 1707), 147
John (d. 1739), 147
John (d. 1753), 146
John (d. 1767), 147

John (d. 1769), 146
John (d. 1809), 146
Jos., 145, 161, 206
Mary, w. of Jos., 145
Mary, m. Wm. Cam (d. 1767), 145
Mary, m. Nicholas Sykes, 146
Wm. (fl. 1515), 310
Wm. (d. 1623), 146
Wm. (d. 1767), 145, 147, 161, 171
family, 3, 130, 132, 137, 160–1, 310
see also Camm
Cambie, S.R., vicar of Gorsley with Clifford's Mesne, 89
Cambridge, 87
St Catherine's college, 85
Camm, A.H.A., rector of Preston, 317
canal, see Hereford and Gloucester canal
Cancellis, Emery de, 203
Cannock, John, 47
Canterbury, archbishop of, 216, 219
Cape Verde islands, 246
Capper:
Dan., rector of Huntley, 4, 178, 180–1, 189–1, 193, 195
Rob., 193, 195
Cardiganshire, see Derry Ormond
Carmarthenshire, see Llangandeirne
Carswalls:
Ingram of, see Solers, Ingram de
John of (? John Ingram), 45
Ric., 45
Carswalls, see Newent
Carter family, 45
Carwardine, Edw., vicar of Preston, 315
Cassey:
Hen., 46, 328
John (d. 1400), 328
John (fl. 1451), 328
John (d. 1508), 328
Rob., 328
Thos., 46, 328
Ursula, 328
family, 46, 328
Castle, Bishop's (Salop.), constable of, 299
castle, see Dymock
Castlemorton (Worcs.), named as an address, 107
Casynton, Steph. de, 103
Cauvey, Wm., 141
Chamberlayne:
Edw. Pye, 139
Edw. Pye (d. 1729, s. of last), 139
Edw. Pye (s. of last), 139, 142
Eliz., w. of Edw. Pye (d. 1729), 139
family, 150, 161, 171
Chance, Geo. 104
charcoal production, 62–3, 65, 111, 153–4, 186, 238–9, 256, 272, 275, 292–3, 334
Charles II, 87, 216
Charles, Peter, 321, 338
Chartley (Staffs.), named as an address, 326
Chelsea (Middx), named as an address, 338
Cheltenham, 69, 81
named as an address, 53, 72, 92–3, 172, 193, 217, 227, 281, 292, 306
Cheshire, see Birkenhead
Chew:
A.H., 143–4, 159, 162
R.S., 143
Cheyne, John, 39, 51, 55
Chichester, Wm., 137
Chinn:
Edw. (d. by 1768), 51

Edw. (d. 1791), 51
Edw. (fl. 1802), 51
Eliz., see Woodward
Mary, m. Edw. Clarke, 267
Wm., 267
Christchurch (Dorset, formerly Hants), Bure Homage, 104
Christian Brethren, 90–1
Church Commissioners, see Ecclesiastical Commissioners
church houses, see Bromesberrow; Dymock; Huntley; Oxenhall; Pauntley; Taynton
Churcham, 192, 194, 250
cider and perry, 4, 51, 58–9, 85, 110, 151, 153, 157, 184, 209–10, 237, 271–2, 291–2, 308–9, 332–3; see also orchards
cider tax, repeal, 58, 79
Cinderford, 90
Ciprian, Alice, 338
Cirencester, Wal. of, 334
Cirencester, 234
named as an address, 104
Civil War
cavalry standards, 120
incidents, 3; see also Gloucester; Newent; Taynton
Claines (Worcs.), named as an address, 144
Clapham:
D.J., 288
J.R., 288
Clark (Clarke):
Arthur, 268
Chas., 47
Edw. (fl. 1634), 267, 274
Edw. (fl. 1647, s. of last), 267
Eliz., 330
Jas. (fl. 1840), 329
Jas. (fl. 1913), 67
Jos. (d. 1705), 321, 330, 338
Jos. (d. 1738), 321, 330
Jos. (d. 1833), 330
Mary, see Chinn
R.F., 106
Ric., 195
Thos., 330
Woodchurch, 155
family, 267, 281
Claypole, John, 335
Clements:
Hen., 306
John, 306
Clifford:
A.W., 50
Jas., 42
Wal. de, 138
family, 42, 48
Clifford, honor of, 287
Clifford's Mesne, see Newent
Clinton:
Agnes, see Peneys
Ives of, 155
John, 111
family, 155
Clive, Francis Windsor, 107
cloth making, 65–6, 112, 156, 187, 242, 335
Coates, see Tarlton
Cobham:
Eliz. of, see Ferrers
Reynold of, 326–7
Cockburn, Mary, 339

Cocks:
Dorothy, 338
John, 338
John Somers, Earl Somers, 115
Phil. Reg., Lord Somers, 34, 43, 326, 338, 345
Ric. (d. 1670), 330
Sir Ric. (fl. 1684), Bt, 330
Rob., 113
see also Coxe
Coghlan, Rob., 227, 231
Coke, Sir John, 312
Colchester:
John, 268
Maynard (d. 1715), 265, 278
Maynard (fl. 1785), 239
family, 231, 233, 268
Colchester-Wemyss, M.W., 233
Coleford, 247
named as an address, 85
Coleman:
Fred., 242
John, 242, 246
Solomon, 232, 243, 246
Colethrop, see Standish
Collins, Mary, see Evans
Colwall, Arnold, 49
Colwall (Herefs.):
Hope End, 144
named as an address, 148
schoolmaster, 316
Coly, Eliz., 342
commandery (religious house), 207
Commonwealth period:
'Barebones' Parliament, Gloucestershire members, 161
civil register (registrar), 161, 170
Compton, Rob. of, 28
Compton, see Newent
Compton, Little (or Cassey), see Withington
Compton Green, in Newent and Pauntley, 8–9
Compton House, 27, 39, 291
Conches abbey (Eure), 103, 118
Conder:
Bertha, w. of Edw. (d. 1934), 47
Edw. (d. 1910), 47, 72
Edw. (d. 1934), 47
family, 20
Congdon, Professor T., 182
Congregationalists, 26, 88, 90, 173, 344
Constance:
Benj., 240
Jas. (fl. 1846), 253
Jas. (d. 1890), 240, 246
John, 253
Peter, 240
S.W., 240
Theophilus, 240
Wm., 246
family, 5, 239
Constance, Jas., & Sons, turners, 232, 239, 240
Cooke:
Chas. Jas., 40
family, 28
Cookhill priory (Worcs.), 207–8
Cooper, John, 155
Coppe family, 28
Corfe (Dorset), constable of castle, 119
Cormeilles, Ansfrid of, 46, 49, 268, 287, 289, 293

Cormeilles abbey (Eure), 2, 65, 68, 85, 170, 256
   abbots, 56
   as lord of Newent, 7, 10, 18, 66, 70–1, 76
   churches, 84, 167–8, 289, 298, 341
   estates, 13, 34, 37–8, 46, 54–5, 86, 147, 149, 268, 287, 289
Cornwall, Thos., 328
Corsham (Wilts.), named as an address, 146
Cowcher, Geo., 35
Cowmeadow:
   as a surname, 30
   John, 296
Cowsley, Wal., vicar of Dymock, 170
Coxe:
   John, 107
   Ric., 107
   Wm. (d. 1666), 107
   Wm. (*fl.* 1667), 107
   see also Cocks
Coxmore, John of, 30
Cracknell:
   Alfred, 90
   family, 91
Craddock:
   (or Taylor), Humph., vicar of Kempley, 219
   John (*fl.* 1607), vicar of Kempley, 219
   John (s. of last), vicar of Kempley, 219
Craister, John, vicar of Newent, 81, 85, 87–8
Cravenhill, John of, 321
Cravenhill, *see* Taynton
Crawford, Rob., vicar of Dymock, 170
Crawley, Chas. Yonge, rector of Taynton, 344
Crawley-Boevey:
   Thos. (d. 1769), 239
   (Sir) Thos. (d. 1818), 23.
   Sir Thos. (d. 1912), 239
Criketot:
   Geo. de, 119
   Rog. de (?), 119
Cripps family, 156
Crocket (Crockett):
   John (*fl.* 1556), 86
   John (*fl.* 1677), 330
Crocket's Hole, *see* May hill
Cross, F.N., 145
Crow Hill, *see* Upton Bishop
cruck framing, 23, 35, *101*, 106–*107*, 128, 134–5, 182, 201, 229, 231, 323, 325
Cruys family, 296
Cugley, Jordan, *see* Jordan, Rob.
Cugley, *see* Newent
Cullompton (Devon), named as an address, 250
Culme-Seymour:
   John Hobart, 235
   Mary, *see* Hall
Culworth (Northants.), named as an address, 265
Cummings (Cumming; Comin) family, 260, 277
Cummins:
   Emma, w. of Jos., 289
   Jas., 45
   John, 268
   Jos., 289
   Mary, *see* Symonds
   Wm., 145
   family, 28, 268
Curtis:
   John, 19

Thos., 35
Curzon, Rog., 267
Cutler, John, vicar of Newent, 87

d'Abitot:
   John (*fl.* 1466–89), 290, 292
   John (another), 291
   family, 286
daffodils, 4, 80, 153, 157, 167
Dalton, Geo., 53, 64
Damerham (Hants, formerly Wilts.), 43
Dance, Thos., 156
Dancey, H.A., 24
Dancocks:
   Hercules Hailes (d. 1818), 145
   Hercules Hailes (*fl.* 1849), 145
   Sarah, w. of Hercules Hailes (d. 1818), 145
Danvers:
   Anne, *see* Pigott
   Sam. (*fl.* 1586), 203, 265
   Sam. (s. of last), 265
Dartmouth (Devon), named as an address, 267
Davenport, Revd Jas., 106
Davies:
   H.J.P., 288
   Hen. Clements, 253
   J.C., 288
   Jos., 137
   Thos., perpetual curate of Oxenhall and Pauntley, 278–80, 297
   Wm., vicar of Preston, 315
Davis:
   Francis, 65
   Sir Wm., 246
   W.S., 246
   Wal., 227
   family, 65
Daw:
   Thos., 241
   family, 241
Dean, Forest of, 48, 62–3, 74, 87, 181, 198, 224–5, 232–3, 241, 275, 327
   bounds, 9, 61–2, 257, 318
   common rights, 236–7
   MP for, 329
Dean, Forest of, district, 6, 74–5
Deane:
   Caroline Drummond, *see* Wynniatt
   Geo. Onslow, 142
   Georgiana Matilda, *see* Drummond
   Horace Drummond, *see* Deane-Drummond
Deane-Drummond:
   (formerly Deane), Horace Drummond, 140, 142
   John Drummond, 142
   family, *see* Drummond
Deerhurst, John 17
Deerhurst, Wightfield, named as an address, 46, 328
Delabere, Ric., 328
Dene, Wm., 110
Dennis, David L., 287
Denny, Edw., vicar of Kempley, 215, 221
Derby, earl of, *see* Lancaster, Hen. of
Derbyshire, 3, 213, 234; *see also* Duffield
Derry Ormond (Cardiganshire), named as an address, 234
Despenser:
   Eliz. le, 265
   Isabel le, 103

Devall:
   Hester, *see* Winter
   John, 148
Devereux:
   Anne (d. 1469), w. of Wal. (d. 1485), Lord Ferrers, 138
   Eliz., *see* Merbury
   Jane (or Joan), w. of Wal. (d. 1485), Lord Ferrers, m. 2 Thos. Vaughan, 3 Sir Edm. Blount, 4 Thos. Poyntz, 138
   John, 39–40
   Lettice, w. of Wal. (d. 1576), m. 2 Rob. Dudley, earl of Leicester, 3 Sir Chris. Blount, 139, 327
   Rob., earl of Essex, 327, 329
   Sir Wal. (d. 1459), 138
   Wal. (d. 1485), Lord Ferrers, 138, 265
   Wal. (d. 1558), Lord Ferrers, later Viscount Hereford, 139, 327
   Wal. (d. 1576), Lord Ferrers, later Lord Bourchier and earl of Essex, 139, 327
   family, 39
Devon, earl of, *see* Stafford, Humph.
Devon, *see* Cullompton; Dartmouth
Dew, Dan., 296
Dewchurch, Much (Herefs), named as an address, 139
Dewell:
   Chas. Goddard, 146
   Thos., 146
Deyce, Hen., vicar of Longhope, 251
Deykes:
   Wm. (d. 1827), 30, 72, 76, 271, 277
   Wm., nephew of last, 30
Dighton, Chas. Mein, vicar of Longhope, 229, 232, 246, 252–3
Dinedor (Herefs.), named as an address, 289
Dinmore preceptory (Herefs), 267
Disraeli:
   Benj., 326, 328
   Mary Anne, *see* Evans
   family, 333
Ditton, Geo., vicar of Longhope, 251–2
Dixon:
   C.W., rector of Preston, 313
   Geo., vicar of Preston, 315
Dobbins, *see* Dobyns
Dobbs:
   Ric., 243
   Thos., 243, 245
   Wm., 245
   family, 241
Dobyns (Dobbins):
   Alex., 85
   Bridget, w. of Guy (d. 1682), 50
   Eliz., w. of Sam. (d. by 1743), m. 2 Edw. Sergeaunt, 50
   Guy (d. 1544), 54
   Guy (*fl.* 1607), 50
   Guy (d. 1682), 50
   Hester, w. of Sam. (d. 1709), 50
   John (*fl.* 1544), 54
   John (*fl.* 1708), 268
   Phil., 54
   Randall, 54, 72, 81
   Rob. (*fl. c.*1240), 27
   Rob. (d. 1766), *see* Yate
   Sam. (d. 1679), 50
   Sam. (d. 1709), 50
   Sam. (d. by 1743), 50

Wm., 49, 54
  family, 27, 77
Dodd, Nat., vicar of Newent, 87
Doherty, A.P., rector of Preston, 173, 313
Dolman, Jas., 183
Donne, Hen., vicar of Newent, 87
Donnington (Herefs), 118, 125, 166, 168, 171, 216, 220, 316–17
Dormington (Herefs.), 54
Dorset, see Corfe; Studland; see also Christchurch
Down, R., 206
Dowsing, Hugh, vicar of Tirley, 299
Drayton:
  G.B., 252
  see Grimké-Drayton
Drew:
  John, 320
  Nic., vicar of Preston, 315
  Wm. (*fl. c.*1715), 171
  Wm. (*fl.* 1859), 316
  family, 312
Drinkwater:
  Ann, 189
  John, 167
  Ric., 189
  family, 189–90, 195, 320
Drummond:
  Georgiana Matilda, m. George Onslow Deane, 142
  John (d. 1835), 142
  John (d. 1875), 142, 148
  John Hislop, vicar of Kempley, 220–1
  (later Deane-Drummond) family 3, 162
Dublin, Trinity college, 85
Duchy of Lancaster hundred, 5
Dudley:
  Lettice, see Devereux
  Rob., earl of Leicester, 139, 327
Dudstone and King's Barton hundred, 5, 301–2
Duffield (Derbs.), named as an address, 203
Dulle:
  Maud, m. John Roberts, 48
  Wm., 48
Dumbleton, 320, 330, 338
Durbridge, in Pauntley and Redmarley D'Abitot. *see under* Redmarley D'Abitot
Dursley, 66
  named as an address, 50
Dutchmen, men described as, 338
Dyer, Rob., see Bromwich
Dyke:
  Alice, 99
  Rob., 99
Dymock, 1–2, 6, **122–74**, 200, 206, 210, 213, 222, 279, 297, 298, 302, 317
  advowson, 168
  agriculture, 148–53
  boundaries, 122–3
  Boyce Court, 124, 126, 128–9, 139, 142–*143*, 150, 161–3, 267
  Broom's Green, 132, 153, 156–7, 160, 166–7
    nonconformist chapel, 91, 172–3
  burgages, 127, 149, 158, 160
  Callow Farm, 130, 143
  canal, 126–7, 142, 148, 157
  castle, 129
  Castle Tump, 123–4, 129–30, 155, 172
  chantries, 169–70
  charities, 148, 163–4, 171
  church, 84, 87, 127, 147, 161, 167–74 (*169, 173*), 216, 314

church house (later workhouse), 113, 127, 159–60, 164, 166, 212
clubs and societies, 166–7
commons, 124, 126, 149–50, 152–3
courts, 125, 158–9, 166
Cut Mill, 122, 131
divisions, 124, 159–60
domestic architecture, *128*, 134–7, 140–7, 154–5
Edulus Place, *see* Dymock, Pitt House Farm
fair, 127, 156–7
Farm, the, *see* Dymock, Wilton Place
farms, 149–53
fields, 124, 149–50, 152
Flaxley tithing, 124, 158
friendly societies, 117, 166
Gamage Hall, *128*, 141, 144, 150–3, 156, 159; *see also* Dymock, Little Dymock manor tithing, *see* Dymock, Woodend
golf course, 124, 167
Gospel Oak, 123–4, 254
Great Dymock (Dymock) manor, 130–1, 133, 137–9, 141–2, 149–50, 154, 158
Greenway, 125, 132, 156–7, 165–7
Greenway House, 132, 134–6 (*135*), 161–3, 165
halls and meeting places, 166
Hallwood Green, 133–4, 156–7, 160, 316
Hillash, 125, 130, 136–7, 158, 162
inclosure, 150, 152
inns and public houses, 165–6
Leadington:
  division, 124, 159–60
  settlement, 132–4
  tithing, 124, 158
library, 166
Lintridge, 50, 118, 122, 150, 152, 155, 174
  Great Lintridge, 144, 151, 161
  Little Lintridge, 144
Little Dymock (Gamage Hall) manor, 128, 137, 139, 141, 150, 154, 158
Long bridge, 125
manors, 102, 124, 137–41, 287; *see also* Dymock: Great Dymock, Little Dymock, *and* Old Grange
manor houses, *see* Dymock: Gamage Hall *and* Old Grange, *also* Boyce Court
market, 66, 127, 156–7
mills, 130–1, 148, 154–5
Netherton, 125
  Great Netherton, 133, 145, 206
  Little Netherton, 133, 135
nonconformity, 170–4, 219
Ockington, 130, 135, 137, 157, 163
  tithing, 124, 158
Old Grange, 124, 126, 129, *140*, 150, 158, 162–3, 167
  estate, 129, 151–2, 154–5, 161, 200, 207
  manor, 137, 139–41
Old Rock, 129, 145, 151, 162
parish officers, 159–60
parks, 124, 142, 161
Pitt House Farm (Edulus Place), 129, 136, 145–6, 161, 164
poor relief, 159–60
poorhouses, 159
population, 126
Pound Farm, 132, *146*
pounds, 125, 127, 158
railway and tramroad, 126, 128, 157
reading room, 166

rector, 170, 172
rectory estate, 147–50, 158, 161, 168; *see also* Dymock, White House
roads, 11, 124–6, 198, 254, 302–3
  road repairs, 160, 213
Ryeland:
  division, 124, 159–60
  settlement, 130–2
  tithing, *see* Dymock, Ryton
Ryton, 118, 130–1, 149–52, 154–5, 157, 165–7, 174
  mill, 154
  (Ryeland) tithing, 124, 158
schools, 161, 163–5, 171
  Ann Cam's, 127, 134, *164*–165, 215
  Haffield, 117, 132, 155, 164–5, 172–4
settlement, 126–34
social structure, 160–3
Tiller's Green, 132, 156–7
tithes, 147–9, 151, 167–8
tithings, 124, 158
trades, 156–8
Upham House, 133, 137, 162–3, 165
vicarage, 168
vicarage (later rectory) houses, 127, 134–5, 162, 166–8, 170
vicars (later rectors), 148, 164, 170–4; *see also* Beale, Wm.; Evans, David *and* Evan; Gethyn-Jones, Dan. *and* John Eric; Hayward, Wm.; Newbolt, Wm. Chas. Edm.; Symonds, Jos.
stipend, 148, 168, 314
White House, 127, 134, 148, 161
Wilton Place (the Farm), 130, 147, 151, 154, 161–2, 164
Wintour's green, 127, 162
Woodend:
  division, 124, 159–60, 163
  settlement, 128–30
  (Gamage Hall) tithing, 124, 158
woodland, 124, 154, 200, 275
woodland management, 153–4
workhouse, *see* Dymock, church house
working men's clubs, 166
see also Bromesberrow Heath; Four Oaks; Hillend green; Ketford; Preston
Dymock 'school' of sculpture, 4, 168, 217, 299, 315
Dymock 'Poets', 167
Dymock Woods, 154, 266, 273
Dyne, John, 33

Ealdred, archbishop of York, 180
Earp, Thos., 195–6
East family, 165
East Dean and United Parishes (later East Dean) rural district, 6
  housing, 227–8
Eastnor (Herefs), 96, 102, 111–12, 116
  Eastnor Castle, 155
  Bronsil castle, 102
  estate, 99, 103, 108–9, 111
  named as an address, 155
  roads, 97
Eaton Tregoes (Herefs.), named as an address, 210
Eaton:
  Ric. (d. 1709), rector of Bromesberrow, 116, 120
  Ric. (d. 1745), rector of Bromesberrow, 120

Ecclesiastical (later Church) Commissioners, 89, 279, 298, 306, 317, 331
Eckley, Thos., 116
Ede, Ric., rector of Taynton, 342
Edgbaston (Warws.), 188
Edgware (Middx), named as an address, 288
Edmonds, Edm., 20, 47, 50, 69, 77, 145
Edmund Crouchback (d. 1296), earl of Lancaster, 233
Edric (*fl.* 1066), 203
Edward the Confessor, 38, 137
Edward I, 39, 138
    as Prince Edward, 233
Edward II, 66
Edward IV, 265
Edward, duke of York, 39
Edwards:
    H.A., curate of Preston, 317
    Mrs, *see* Lester, Eliz.
Elizabeth I, 306
Ell bridge, in Newent and Oxenhall, 6, 11–12, 61, 254, 257
Elliott family, 321
Ellis:
    Sarah, 167
    Wm., 189–90
    Wm. Viner, 330 and n
Elrington, Jean, 21, 135
Elton family, 178, 305
Elton, *see* Westbury-on-Severn
Ely, Adam, 33
Emlett (a surname), 33
Epsom (Surrey), 306
Essex, earls of, *see* Devereux, Rob. *and* Wal.
Estcourt:
    Ric., 43
    Thos., 43
Evans:
    A.D., 205
    David, vicar of Dymock, 148
    Evan, vicar of Dymock, 148, 171
    Hen., 339
    Mary, m. —— Collins, 148
    Mary Anne, m. 1 Wyndham Lewis, 2 Benj. Disraeli, 328
Evesbatch (Herefs.), 120
    named as an address, 104
Evesham (Worcs.), named as an address, 289
Evesham, battle of, 265
Evesham, Vale of, 68
Evreux:
    Maud, w. of Wm. of (d. 1265), 265
    Steph. of, w. of, 265
    Wm. of (d. 1265), 256, 265
    Wm. of (*fl.* 1292), 265
Exchequer Baron, 267
Exeter, bishop of, *see* Grandison, John de
Exeter, named as an address, 342

Falconer, Margaret, 342
fairs, *see* Dymock; Newent
Farjeon, Eleanor, 167
Farley, tenants surnamed of, 33
Fauconberge, Thos., 138
Fawcett:
    Sir Chas., 106
    Marion Edith, *see* Fry
Fawke:
    Jos., 137 n
    family, 133
Ferrers:
    Edm. (d. 1435), 327
    Edm. (d. 1453), 327
    Eliz., w. of John (d. 1367), m. 2 Reynold of Cobham, 326
    Eliz., w, of Ric., 327
    Hawise de, *see* Mucegros
    Hen., 327
    John de (d. 1312), 326
    John de (d. 1367), 326
    Martin, 327
    Ric., 327
    Rob., 327
    Wm. (d. 1450), 327
    family, 46
Ferrers, Lord, *see* Devereux, Wal.
Fettiplace:
    Elinor, *see* Poole
    Sir Ric., 295
Few, Chas. C., 235
Field:
    Fred., 242
    Rob., 242
    Rob. (*fl.* 1871, s. of last), 242
Fillol, Geof., 17
Fillot, John, vicar of Dymock, 170
Finch:
    Anne, *see* Pigott
    Francis, 49, 65, 203, 216, 266–7, 272, 274–5
    Hen., 200, 203, 213, 215, 219, 265
Fincher, *see* Hooke
Fisher:
    Chas. Hawkins, 45
    Jane, *see* Wenman
    Paul Hawkins, 45
    Thos., 139
Fishpool, *see* Upton Bishop
FitzAlan, Humph., earl of Arundel, 265
FitzOsbern:
    Rog., *see* Breteuil, Rog. of
    Wm., earl of Hereford, 38, 137, 167
flax, crops of, 108, 151
    flax dressers, 291
Flaxley, 2, 228, 233, 238
    abbey, 102, 137–8, 147, 153, 158, 160, 167, 169, 236, 241
        estates and grange, 124, 129, 139–40, 149–50, 153, 155, 200, 202, 207
    Flaxley Abbey, named as an address, 239
    ironworks, 111, 154, 186, 239, 334
    named as an address, 237
    woods, 224, 236
Flaxman, John, 93
Foley:
    And., 40, 58, 88, 154
    Eliz., dau. of And., 40, 83, 278
    Hannah, *see* Morse
    Harriett, m. Richard Onslow, 40
    John, vicar of Newent, 76, 82, 88
    Paul, 39, 54, 85, 87, 241, 266–7
    Phil., 241
    Ric., rector of Huntley, 195
    Rob., vicar of Newent, 88
    Thos. (d. 1677), 10, 34, 37, 39, 49, 53, 62, 111, 153, 238, 241, 266–7, 273–5
    Thos. (d. 1737), 39, 67, 85, 267, 292
    Thos. (d. 1749), 39
    Thos. (d. 1822), 40
    Thos., Lord Foley (d. 1777), 39–40, 88
    Wm. And., 40
    family, 3, 5, 34, 37–8, 40, 46, 57, 62–3, 72, 76, 256, 261, 264, 266–7, 270–7, 335
Foote, Anne, *see* Yate
Ford, And., 59

Forest of Dean, *see* Dean, Forest of
Forest Products Ltd, 179, 186–8
Forestry Commission, 154, 256, 273
Forne (*fl.* 1066), 233
Forster:
    Giles, 139, 141, 150, 161, 267, 278
    Humph., 141, 267
    Martha, w. of Humph., 141
    family, 170
Fortescue, Nic., 207
Forty:
    John, 212
    Thos., 156
Foster, K.B., rector of Taynton, 346
Fotheringhay college (Northants.), 54, 148–9, 168, 289, 298, 341
    as lord of Newent, 10, 22, 39, 55, 62, 76
Four Oaks, in Dymock and Oxenhall, 125–6, 130, 173, 257
    nonconformist chapel, 174, 277, 280
Fowke, Hen., 51, 53
Fowle:
    Hen. a, rector of Huntley, 194
    John, 193
    Wm. a, rector of Huntley, 194
Fowler, Giles, 342
Foxcote, Margery of, 42
Frampton on Severn, 42, 115
    named as an address, 103
France:
    natives of, 76, 170
    refugees from, 297
    wars with, 39, 76, 147, 168, 250
franchises, *see* bread and ale, assize of; gallows; infangthief; pillory; tumbrel
Frederick:
    Henrietta Maria, *see* Somerset
    John, 288
Freeman:
    Eric, 329
    Mic., 181
    Nigel, 50
    Torill, *see* Ackers
    family, 60, 181
Fretherne, 120
    named as an address, 42
Frewen, Paul, vicar of Kempley, 219
Frome, Castle (Herefs.), 172, 220
Frost, Rob., 167
Frowde:
    Jas. Chas. Wm., 50
    Jas. Hen., 50, 54, 88, 297
    Susan, *see* Harrison
Fry, Marion Edith, m. Sir Chas. Fawcett, 106
Fulljames, Thos., 193, 314
Furnivale, Lord, *see* Neville, Thos.

Gabriel, Ric., 182
Gael, Amice de, m. Rob., earl of Leicester, 38
Gaffin, Edw., 316
gallows, 71, 212, 336
Gamages:
    Eliz. de, m. Hen. of Pembridge, 141
    Euphemia de, m. Wm. of Pembridge, 141
    Godfrey de, 141
    Wm. de, 137–9, 141, 154, 207
Gambier Parry, *see* Parry
Gamond family, 133, 160
Gander's green, in Huntley and Taynton, 176, 179, 332
Gardino, Wm. de, 34
Gardner, Hamilton Alex., 331
Garnett, Wm., 48

Gatcombe Park, see Minchinhampton
Gate, Revd Tim., 48
General Parsonage House fund, 279
Genevyle, Geof. de, 265
Gethyn-Jones:
    Dan., vicar of Dymock and of Kempley and rector of Preston, 174, 215, 222, 313, 317
    John Eric, rector of Dymock, 174, 216
Gibb, David, 222
Gibson, Wilfred, 167
Gilbert of Monmouth, 233, 241
    w. Bertha, 241
Gilding, Wm., 339
Giles, John, 171
Gimson, Ernest, 222
Girdwood, J. & J., 180
Gladwin, John Hartland, 155
Glamorgan, see Boverton; Llandaff; Neath; Swansea
glass making, 34, 65, 322, 335
Glasshouse, see Taynton
Glasson, John Ric., 43
Glendower, revolt of Owen, 39
Gloucester:
    Durand of, 42, 55
    Miles of, earl of Hereford, 137
    Rog. of, earl of Hereford, 137–9
Gloucester, bishops of, 3, 222, 278–9, 298, 305–6, 313, 331
    as patron, 85, 118, 168, 193, 298, 314
    see also, Ryder, Hen.
Gloucester, 4, 5, 13, 59, 63, 66–9, 75, 77, 80, 115, 187, 190, 194, 238, 240, 247, 273, 280, 307, 335, 339, 342
    abbey, 54, 322, 326, 331, 341–2
        as lord of Preston, 301, 305, 307, 310–11, 313–14
        cellarer and steward, 311
        sacrists, 331, 341–2
    archdeacon, 308
    burgesses in, 270
    cathedral:
        dean, see Luxmoore, John
        dean and chapter, 250, 331–2, 342
        librarian, 343
        school, 343
        prebendaries, 342–3
    Civil War siege, 320, 343
    corporation, 5, 63, 74, 256, 274, 283–4, 343
    Holy Trinity church, 343, 346
    infirmary, 159, 244, 247, 295, 336
    Llanthony priory, 42, 48, 86
    MPs, 139, 312, 327, 343
    municipal charity trustees, 48–9
    named as an address, 24, 35, 52, 62–3, 67, 73, 93–4, 103, 105, 118, 120, 134, 143, 148, 172, 190–1, 207, 227, 239, 250, 253, 306, 328–9, 338, 343, 345
    nonconformity, 89–90, 173, 252, 280
    roads to, 2, 11–12, 98, 122, 124, 174–6, 198, 224–5, 319
    schools, 41, 83, 338
    St Bartholomew's hospital, 86, 199, 207, 326
    St Kyneburgh's hospital, 48
Gloucestershire:
    county council, 128–9, 144, 152, 209, 244, 238, 283
    county gaol, 246
    deputy chief constable, 296–7
    MPs, 114, 161, 181

    sheriffs, 42, 45, 48, 104, 144
    see also inshire
Gloucestershire Banking Co., 69
Gloucestershire Home for Wayfarers, 288
Gloucestershire Wildlife Trust, 242, 293
Goff (Gough), Edw., nonconformist trust, 248; for school see Gorsley, school
Goizenboded, Wm., 320, 326
Gooding:
    Eliz. w. of John and formerly of ―― Haverd, 45
    John, 45
Gordon, Wm., 132
Gore:
    Chas., 148
    Ellen, see Humphreys
    Mary, see Humphreys
    Thos., 148
Gorsley, nomenclature, 8, 268
Gorsley, in Newent and Linton (Herefs.), 2, 4, 7–9, 11, 39, 46, 62, 69, 254, 257, 263, 268
    Anglican chapel, 88–9
    church, 89, 94
    Gorsley Court, 10, 46
    nonconformity, 84, 88, 90, 172–3, 220, 280
    school, 83–4, 89
    vicarage house, 89
Gorsley common, in Newent, Linton, and Aston Ingham (Herefs.), see Newent
Gorsley with Clifford's Mesne ecclesiastical district, 84–5, 89
    vicarage, 89
Gorsley and Kilcot civil parish, 9, 74
Goulding:
    Arthur, 90
    Dan., 277
    G.H., 142
    John, 288
    S., 270
    Sylvia, dau. of G.H., 142
    family, 91, 146, 270, 277
Goupillières, Simon of, prior of Newent, 76
Grafton (Worcs.), 102
Grafton, Francis Fred., 43
Grandison:
    John de, bishop of Exeter, 138
    Peter de, 138, 265, 280
    Sibyl, w. of Wm. de, 138, 147, 265
    Thos. de, 138, 149, 265
    Wm. de, 138, 147, 265
    family, 49, 92, 266
Great Western railway, 13
Green:
    Dorothy, see Pauncefoot
    Eleanor, 81–2, 87
    Hen., 328
    Maud, w. of Hen., 328
    Nic., 170
    Ric. (d. by 1596), 45
    Ric. (s. of last), 45
    Thos., 64
    Wal., 99
Greenall, Dr the Hon. Gilbert, 104
Greene, Ric., 115
Greville, Fulke, 306
Grey:
    Amabel, dowager countess of Kent, 234
    Ant. (d. 1702), earl of Kent, 234
    Ant. (fl. 1722), Lord Harold, 191
    Edm., Lord Grey, 203

    Eliz., w. of John (d. 1499), m. 2 Sir Edw. Stanley, Lord Mounteagle, 203
    Eliz., see Talbot
    Florence, w. of Edm., Lord Grey, 203
    Hen. (d. 1342), Lord Grey, 203, 213
    Hen. (d. 1396), Lord Grey, 203
    Hen. (d. 1639), Lord Grey and earl of Kent, 234
    Hen., earl (and from 1710 duke) of Kent, 181, 234
    Joan, w. of Reynold (d. 1370), 203
    John (d. 1323), Lord Grey, 203
    John (d. 1499), Lord Grey, 203
    Maud, see Longchamp
    Reynold (d. 1308), Lord Grey, 203, 216
    Reynold (d. 1370), Lord Grey, 203
    Reynold (d. 1494), Lord Grey, 203
    Ric. (d. 1442), Lord Grey, 203
    Ric. (d. 1523), Lord Grey, 203
    Thos., Lord Grey, 203
    Wm., Lord Grey, 203, 208, 265
    family, 3, 181, 213, 233
Greystock, Wm., curate of Dymock, 170
Griffin, Chas., 296–7, 301
Griffith, Jas., vicar of Newent, 88
Griffiths:
    Brian, 328
    Jas., 328
Grimké-Drayton, Theodore, 43
Grove:
    Cath., m. Revd Morgan Price, 329
    John, 329
    Ric. (fl. 1487), 99
    Ric. (fl. 1522, ? same as last), 114
    Rob., 99
    Sam., 329
    (formerly Price), Stanhope Grove, 329
    Stanhope Pury, 329
    Wm., 106
    see also Price
Guildhall, Roger of the, 266
Guise:
    Fred. Chas., vicar of Longhope, 243, 246, 248
    Sir John Wright, Bt, 250
    Sir Wm. Vernon, Bt, 250
    Vernon Geo., vicar of Longhope, 253
    widow of last, 250
Guiting Power, 326 n
Gundey family, 312
Gurney, Geo., 268
Guy, Ric., 158
Gwillim Edw., 44, 65
Gwynne, Ric., 214

Habgood, Alice, 160
Hacket, Eliz., m. Thos. Pyndar (d. 1722), 204, 213–15, 220
Hacqueville, Wm. of, prior of Newent, 76
Haffield, see Ledbury; also Dymock, schools
Hague, Isaac, rector of Huntley, 194
Hale, Benj., 181
Halford:
    Joan, w. of Ric., 236
    Ric., 236
Hall:
    Geo. Wm., master of Pembroke College, Oxford, and rector of Taynton, 343–4
    John (fl. 1616), 236
    John, Baptist minister, 90, 220
    Mary, m. John Hobart Culme-Seymour, 235

Ric. (d. 1780), 144, 151
Ric. (*fl.* 1861), 144, 235
Hamilton, Craig, 106
Hampshire, *see* Christchurch; *see also* Damerham
Hanbury:
  John, 85, 312
  Sir Thos. (d. 1708), 315
Hankins:
  Edw., 146
  Jos., 50, 54, 73
  Mary, w. of Jos., 54
  Thos. (*fl.* 1500)., vicar of Dymock, 170
  Thos. (*fl.* 1776), 136
  Thos. (d. 1864), 50, 54
  Wm., 161
  family, 54, 77, 132, 160
Hanley Castle (Worcs.), 95, 103, 121
  constable, 113
  named as an address, 144
Hanmer, Edw., 328
Hard, John, 292
Harden, Rob., rector of Bromesberrow, 120
Hardy:
  H.H., vicar of Preston, 313, 316
  family, 316
Harold, Earl (King), 2, 103, 265
Harper (? Barbour), John, vicar of Preston, 315
Harris:
  E. Swinfen, 94
  Jos., 144
  Mary, *see* Terrett
Harrison:
  Jos., 328
  Mary, 50
  Susan, m. Jas. Hen. Frowde, 50
Hart, Cyril, 186
Hartland:
  Edw., 44, 63
  Eliz., *see* Wyman
  Hen., 34
  John, 53, 155
  Thos., 34
  Thos. (*fl.* 1752, ? same as last), 191
  Thos. (d. 1844), 53
  Wm. (*fl.* 1840), 312
  Wm. (*fl.* 1870–98), 311, 317
  family, 58, 77, 322
  see also Gladwin
Hartpury:
  named as an address, 31
  Woolridge common, 275
Harwell, Thos., rector of Bromesberrow, 119–20
Hasfield, 291
  named as an address, 92
Haskins, Wm., 321
Hastings, Wm., Lord Hastings, 192–3
Hauville:
  Margery of, 189
  Rob. of, 189
  Wal. of, 189
Haverd:
  Anne, w. of Phil., 45
  Isabel, *see* Heylond
  John, 45
  Phil., 45
Hawkins:
  John, 171
  Sam., 191, 195
  family, 145
Haynes, Giles, 320

Hayward:
  John, 342
  Wm., rector of Bromesberrow and vicar of Dymock, 120, 171
Heath, R.G., 267
Hege, see Newent, Hayes estate
Hemming, Rob., rector of Huntley, 194
Hempsted, the Newark, 42
Henbarrow:
  Maud, m. Thomas Bridges, 141
  Thos., 141
Henry II, 38, 65, 138–9
Henry III, 11, 66, 86, 153, 156, 329
Henry IV, 39
Henry V, 269
Henry VIII, 67, 170, 269
Henry:
  Wm. Chas., 132, 162, 164, 172
  family, 165
Herbert, Maud, m. Hen. Percy, earl of Northumberland, 265
Herdman-Smith, Rob., 285
Hereford, Wal. of, 138
Hereford, bishops of, 84, 267
  as patron, 118, 216
Hereford, earls of, 42; *see also* Bohun, Hen. de; Breteuil, Rog. of; FitzOsbern, Wm.; Gloucester, Miles of *and* Rog. of
Hereford, diocese of, chancellor, 163
Hereford, 13, 59, 146, 220, 299, 342
  cathedral:
    dean and chapter, 206, 216
    precentor, 86
    vicar choral, 219
  coaches, 78
  hay of, 327
  named as an address, 154, 205, 227, 289, 296
  roads to, 2, 11–12, 176, 224–5
  St Guthlac's priory, 206, 216, 267
  St Peter's church, 54
Hereford, Viscount, *see* Devereux, Wal.
Hereford and Gloucester canal, 7, 13, 41, 63, 81, 126, 142, 148, 157, 256–7, 273, 275
Herefordshire, *see* Aconbury priory; Almeley; Aston Ingham; Ballingham; Bodenham; Bridstow; Brockhampton; Byton; Colwall; Dewchurch, Much; Dinedor; Dinmore preceptory; Donnington; Dormington; Eastnor; Eaton Tregoes; Evesbatch; Frome, Castle; Gorsley; Holme Lacy; Kilpeck; Kingstone; Lea; Ledbury; Leominster; Linton; Llanwarne; Madley; Marcle, Little *and* Much; Mordiford; Norton; Ross-on-Wye; Rotherwas; 'ryelands', 'the'; Staunton-on-Wye; Stoke Edith; Stretton Grandison; Sugwas; Tarrington; Upton Bishop; Weston under Penyard; Wigmore; Woolhope; Wormsley priory; Yarkhill: *see also* Bicknor, Welsh
Hertfordshire, *see* Knebworth
Heye:
  Peter de, 50
  Thos. de, 50
Heylond:
  Isabel, m. John Haverd, 45

Joan, m. John Westerdale, 45
John, 45
Higford:
  Frances, m. Hen. Wakeman, 289
  Wm., 289
Higgins, Ant., 314
Higgs, Thos., rector of Bromesberrow, 120
Highleadon, *see* Rudford and Highleadon
Highnam, 341, 346
  named as an address, 28, 39, 86, 191, 267
Hill:
  Arthur, 267
  Chas., rector of Bromesberrow, 121
  Guy, 144–5, 151, 285
  Hen., 144–5, 162
  Jas. (*fl.* 1522), 295
  Jas. (*fl.* 1539), 269
  Jas. (*fl.* 1670s), 92
  Jas. (*fl.* 1805), 154
  Jas. (d. 1836), 206
  John (*fl.* 1596), 266, 269
  John (d. 1687), 269
  John (*fl.* 1800), 159
  John (d. 1825), 206
  Jos. (d. 1800), 144
  Jos. (d. 1833), 144
  Jos. (*fl.* 1858), 144
  Jos. (*fl.* 1872), 206
  Margery, *see* Brock
  Martha, m. Hen. Stranke, 267
  Mary, w. of Ric. (d. 1772), 145
  Reg. Pyndar, rector of Bromesberrow, 117, 121
  Revd Thos., 115
  Ric. (*fl.* 1522), 277
  Ric. (*fl.* 1727), 171
  Ric. (d. 1772), 145, 161, 164
  Ric. (d. 1794), 145, 161
  Rog. (*fl.* 1604–8), 267, 277
  Rog. (*fl.* 1608), 65
  Thos. (*fl.* 1522), 150
  Thos. (*fl.* 1539), 145
  Thos. (*fl.* 1607), 42
  Thos. (*fl.* 1609), 274
  Thos. (*fl.* 1624), 46
  Thos. (d. 1712), 269
  Thos. (*fl.* 1715), 145
  Thos. (*fl.* 1746–69), 144
  Thos. (d. 1756), 155
  Thos. (d. 1815 or 1816), 145
  Thos. (d. 1843), 145
  Wal. (d. *c.*1419), 269
  Wal. (*fl.* mid 15th cent.), 46
  Wm. (*fl.* 1522), 277
  Wm. (d. 1631), 145
  family, 3, 128, 130, 145, 160, 162, 256, 260, 267–9, 277
Hillend green, in Dymock and Oxenhall, 130, 260, 262, 276
Hinds:
  Hen., 54
  family, 54
Hodges:
  R., 301
  Sarah, 116
  Thos., 247
  family, 132, 301 n
Hog, Rob., 31
Holbrook, Thos., 136, 162
Holbrooke (Houlbrooke):
  Geof., 317
  John, 204

Holder:
    J.T.W.S., 287, 289
    John (d. 1734), 319, 322–5, 328–30, 332, 334–5, 338
    John (d. 1752), 330
    John (d. 1801), 330
    John (d. 1850), 330, 331
    John (s. of last), 330
    Louisa Henrietta, m. Chas. Bernard Atherton, 331
    Rob. (d. 1684), 323, 328, 330
    Rob. (d. 1769), 330
    Wm. (d. 1758), 330
    Wm. (d. 1819), 325, 330
    Revd Wm. Chas. (d. 1837), 330–1, 335, 338–9, 344
    family, 3, 322, 325–6, 330, 338, 345
Holes, Rob., 133
Holland, Wm., 293, 297
Holloway, T.B., 45
Holme Lacy (Herefs.), 4
Holmes:
    John (d. by 1685), 145
    John (d. 1700), 145, 206
    Rob., 145, 161
    Sarah, *see* Scudamore
    Wm., 145
    family, 130
Home Office, 75
Hook (Hooke):
    Ann, w. of Chris. (d. 1612), 267
    Anne, w. of John (d. 1705), 269
    Benj. (d. 1771), 269
    Benj. (d. 1796), 269
    Benj. (d. 1848), 263, 269
    Chris. (d. *c*.1579), 106, 269
    Chris. (d. 1612), 277, 267
    Douglas T.H., 269
    Edw. (d. 1651), 269, 274
    Edw. (d. 1762), 269
    Eliz., w. of Benj. (d. 1796), 35, 269
    Guy (*fl*. 1470), 269
    Guy (*fl*. 1487), 104
    John (*fl*. 1826), 269
    John (d. 1705), 269, 274
    John (d. 1795), 269
    John (? another), 86
    John, vicar of Newent, 86
    John Brewer, 269
    Margaret, *see* Whittington,
    Mic. R.D.H., 269
    (formerly Fincher), Phil., 269
    Reynold, 104
    Ric. (*fl*. 1522), 269
    Ric. (*fl*. 2006), 269
    Rob., vicar of Newent, 86
    Thos. (*fl*. 1435), 269
    Thos. (s. of last), 269
    Thos. (*fl*. 1463), 104
    Thos. (d. 1628), 72, 269, 296
    Thos. (*fl*. 1634), 267
    Thos. C.B., 269
    Thos. T.B., 269
    Wm. (*fl*. 1424), 104
    Wm., rector of Bromesberrow and Redmarley D'Abitot, 119
    family, 20, 27, 34–5, 86, 269, 277, 334
Hooper:
    Hen., rector of Bromesberrow, 120
    Jane, *see* Somerset
    Jas., 287
    Martin, Wheeler, 235
    Ric., 329

Thos., 193
Wm., 163
family, 133
Hope End, *see* Colwall
Hopkins:
    Chas., vicar of Longhope, 252
    John, *see* Probyn
hops, 110, 151–3, 209, 291–2, 309, 332
Hopton, Wm., 178, 187
Horlick, John, 252
Horn (Horne):
    Agnes, w. of Wm., 321
    Wm., 321
    Edw., 86
    family, 342
horse racing, 166
Horsman, John, 30
Horton, Reg., vicar of Dymock, 173
Horton, named as an address, 287
Horwood, Little (Bucks.), named as an address, 203, 265
Houlbrooke, *see* Holbrooke
House:
    Albert, 330
    John, 330
House of Commons, Speaker, 39
Howe:
    John, 203
    Sir Scrope, 203
    Sir Thos. Grubham (Grobham), 203, 205, 208–9, 213, 219
Howell:
    Edw., 330, 337, 338–9, 344
    Hester, w. of Edw., 331, 339–40
    John, 235
    Ric., 158
Hownhall, Wal. of, 320
Hoxton (Middx), named as an address, 328
Hubarne, *see* Hugill
Hugall & Male, 316
Huggins, Sarah, 327
Hugh son of Wm. son of Norman, 327
Hughes:
    Rob., 72
    Wm., curate of Taynton, 340, 344
Hugill (or Hubarne):
    Cecily, w. of Wal., 236
    Wal., 236
Hullett:
    Dan., 205
    John, 205
    Nancy, w. of Dan., 205
Humphreys:
    Ellen, m. Chas. Gore, 148
    Mary, m. 1 Wm. Ball Waring, 2 Thos. Gore, 148
    Rob., 148
    Sir Orlando, Bt, 148
    Sir Wm., Bt, 148
Humpidge, Jas., 49
Hunstanworth (Co. Durham), 180
Hunter:
    John, 229
    Sibyl, 229
Huntley:
    Ela, w. of Thos. of, 181
    Sir Geo., 139, 141
    Iseult, w. of Thos. of (*fl*. 1344), 181
    John of, 181, 192
    Thos. of, 181
    Thos. of (*fl*. 1344, s. of last), 181
    Wal. of, 175, 181, 185
    Wm., 139

Huntley, 1–2, 4–5, 11, **174–96**, 251, 280, 337
    advowson, 192–3
    agriculture, 183–5
    allotments, 185, 189, 192
    boundaries, 174
    charities, 185, 188–91
    church, 177–181 (*178*), 190, 192–196
    church house, *see* Huntley, poorhouse
    commons, 175–7, 179, 183–5
    court, 177, 188, 243
    court (manor) house, 175
        the Court House, 177, 188
    cricket ground, 192
    cross, 177
    domestic architecture, 179–83
    farms, 178, 184–5
    fields, 183
    Forest Gate (formerly Pool House), 177, 180, 190, 193–4
    friendly societies, 192
    golf course, 176, 185
    Huntley Court, 3, 177, 179–80, 182–*183*, 189–92, 233
    Huntley Manor, 176, 178, 180–*182*, 185–6, 190, 193
        estate, 9–10, 40, 62, 180, 326, 330, 334
    inclosure, 175, 177–9, 184–6, 188, 192–3
    inns, 177, 179, 182, 188–9, 192
    library, 192
    manor, 180–1
    manor house, *see* Huntley, court house
    mills, 176, 186–7
    nonconformity, 194–5
    parish officers, 188–9
    park, 176, 182
    Pool House, *see* Huntley, Forest Gate
    poor relief, 188–9
    poorhouse (also called church house), 177, 188, 190
    population, 176–7
    pound, 177, 189
    reading room, 192
    recreation ground, 185, 189, 192
    rectors, 189, 194–6; *see also* Baker, Geo.; Capper, Dan.; Miles, Hen.; Morse, Abraham, Jackman, *and* John; Unwin, Thos.
    rectory, 192, 196
    rectory houses, 176, 178, 180–1, 189–90, 193; *see also* Huntley, Forest Gate *and* Huntley Manor
    roads, 11, 14, 174–6
        road improvement, 189
        road traffic and trades, 187–8
    schools, *178*, 183, 191–2, 195, 340
        forestry, 180, 186
        riding, 179
    settlement, 177–9
    social structure, 189–90
    tithes, 189, 193
    trades, 187–8
    village hall and meeting places, 192, 180
    war memorial, 192
    Woodend, 174, 176, 178–80
    woodland, 62, 174–6, 181, 183–4, 334
    woodland crafts, 186, *187*
    woodland management, 185–6
    working men's club, 192
    see also Gander's green
Huntley with May Hill, benefice, 192, 250, 346
Husey:
    Ernest Wynniatt, 140, 145, 162

Harriett, *see* Wynniatt
Hen. Mildmay, 140
Hussemane:
  Wal. de, 44
  Wm. de, 44–5
Hutchinson:
  Amy, 40
  Clara, 40
  Gertrude, 40
Hyett:
  John, 103
  Rob., 48
  Thos., 189

Incorporated Church Building Society, 301
India, 31, 306
  see Madras civil service
Indies, West, 161; *see also* Barbados; Jamaica
  West India merchant, 41
industry, *see* brass wire manufacture; brick making; charcoal production; glass making; ironworks; mining; nail making; quarrying; tanning
infangthief, 71
Inglis-Jones, *see* Jones
Ingram, John, *see* Carswalls, John of
inshire, 5
Ireland, 107, 115
  justiciar of, 114
ironworks, *see* Flaxley; Longhope; Lydney; Newnham, Ayleford; Oxenhall, Ellbridge furnace; Powick; Wilden
Irving, John, 248
Isett (Ysett):
  Hen., 18
  Wal., 28
  family, 16–17

Jackman, Thos., vicar of Newent, 87
Jamaica, 245
James I, 67
James:
  Edw., 277
  John, *see* Yannes
  Ric., 222
Jauncey:
  Dorothy (d. 1743), *see* Wall
  Dorothy (d. 1776), m. Revd Sam. Bethell, 289
  Jas., 111
  Thos., 289
Jenkins, Jenkin, rector of Donnington and vicar of Preston, 171, 220, 316
Jennings:
  John, rector of Bromesberrow, 119
  Rob., 119
Jeune, Francis, master of Pembroke College, Oxford, and rector of Taynton, 343–4
John, King, 138, 318
John 'de Monte', 268
John in the field, 312
John of Monmouth (d. 1248), 181, 233
John of Monmouth (d. 1257), 233
John the French, 201
John the fuller, 64
Johnstone, W.M.L., 80
Jones:
  Anne, w. of John, 111
  Chas. (*fl.* 1710), 82
  Chas. (d. 1716), 49
  Chas. (d. 1740), 49
  Chas. (*fl.* 1763), 48
  David, 250
  Francis, 92
  Jas., vicar of Preston, 315
  J.E., 191
  John, 111
  Laetitia, *see* Rogers
  Ric., 93, 134
  Rob., 314
  (later Inglis-Jones), Wilmot Inglis, 181, 234
  family, 206
  see also Gethyn-Jones
Jordan:
  Rob. (Jordan of Cugley), 10, 34
  Rog. 229

Kearsey
  John, 241
  R.S., 253
Keene:
  Harold, 52
  M.H., 52
Kempe, John, 121–2
Kempley, 1–5, 118, 125, 154–5, 160, 162, **196–222**, 280
  advowson, 216
  agriculture, 207–10
  architecture:
    domestic, 201–2
    Madresfield estate, 202
  boundaries, 196–7
  Bullocksend, *see* Kempley, Hill Brook End
  charities, 213–15, 222
  churches, 168, 216–222, 279, 314
    St Edward King and Confessor, 202, 221–222
    St Mary (medieval), 199–200, 210, 217–22
      wall paintings, 217–*218*, 221, 222
    temporary, 199, 216
  clubroom, 199, 215–16
  clubs and societies, 215
  commons, 197–8, 210
  courts, 212
  farms, 207–10
  fields, 198, 207–8
  Friar's Court, 200, *201*, 202, 206–7, 208, 213, 219
  Hill Brook Farm (formerly Bullocksend), 202, 205–6
  inclosure, 197–9, 207–8,
  inns and beerhouses, 199, 215
  Kempley Court, 198, 200, 202, 204, 208, 210–11, 213–14
  Kempley Green, 197, 199, 202, 211, 215–16
    nonconformist chapel, 220, 222
  manor, 202–4, 265
  manor houses, 199; *see also* Kempley, Kempley Court *and* Stone House
  mills and fishponds, 211
  nonconformity, 219–22
  parish officers, 212–13
  park, 198, 208–10
  poor relief, 212–13
  poorhouses, 199, 212
  population, 198
  rectory estate, 199, 200, 206–7, 216; *see also* Kempley, Friar's Court
  roads, 198
    road repairs, 213
  Saycell's Farm, 202, 206, 210–11
  schools, 165, 199, 202, 213–15
  settlement, 199–201
  social structure, 213–14
  Stone House, 198, 200, 202, 204–*205*, 208–10, 213
  tithes, 206, 216–17
  trades, 211
  vicarage, 216–17
  vicarage houses, 199–200, 202, 214, 217
  vicars, 215, 218–21, 222; *see also* Denny, Edw.; Lewes, John; Squire, Rob.
  woodland, 197–8
  woodland management, 210–11
Kempthorne, John, vicar of Preston, 316
Kendale, Wm., 228
Kennedy, Lord, 190
Kent, duke of, 193; *see also* Grey, Hen.
Kent, earl of, 184; *see also* Grey, Ant. *and* Hen.
Kent, *see* Sandwich
Kent's Green, in Newent and Taynton, 8, 11, 32, 90, 317, 321, 333, 336
  nonconformist chapel, 344, 346
Ker, R.H., 329–30
Kerfoot, Rob., vicar of Oxenhall, 279–80
Ketford:
  Rob., 131, 149
  Wal. of, 131
Ketford, in Dymock and Pauntley, 11, 29, 122, 124–5, 130–1, 149–50, 160, 212, 282–4, 288, 295
  Domesday estate, 2, 287, 290
  Great Ketford, 131
  Little Ketford, 131
  Little Ketford Farm, 285
  mills, 148, 154, 155
  waterworks, 283
Keys:
  Barbara, w. of John, 48, 64
  John, 48
  Wm., 48, 64
  family, 100
Kidder:
  Matt., 144
  Rachael, *see* Weale
Kidderminster (Worcs.), 88
Kilcot, *see* Pauntley *and* Newent
Kilpeck:
  Hugh of, 327, 331
  Isabel of, m. Wm. Walrond, 327
  Joan of, m. Phil. Marmion, 327
Kilpeck (Herefs.), lords of, 3, 321, 326–7
  church, 331, 341
Kilpeck's tithing, *see* Taynton
King, Augustine, 343
Kingham (Oxon.), 88
Kingston upon Hull (Yorkshire, East Riding), named as an address, 146
Kingston:
  Sir Ant., 139
  Sir Wm., 139
Kingstone (Herefs.), 84
Kingswood, Thos., rector of Taynton, 342
Kington, Thos., 91, 172, 220, 280, 344
Kirkham, Hen., vicar of Dymock, 170–1
Knebworth (Herts.), named as an address, 329
Knight, Albert, 179, 185
Knights Hospitaller, 267, 278, 280
Knovill:
  Bevis de (d. 1307), 5, 46, 327, 329, 336
  Bevis de (d. 1338), 327–8, 337
  Eliz. de, m. Thos. Maudit, 328
  Joan, w. of Bevis de (d. 1338), 328

Joan de, *see* Walrond
John de, 328–9
Margaret de, m. Thos. Verdun, 328
Margery, w. of John de, m. 2 Thos. Moyne, 328
Knowles:
  And., 20, 38, 40–1, 52, 53, 77, 80, 88, 93, 326, 328, 330
  Ann, 82
Kyrle:
  Ant., 206
  John (*fl.* 1665–7, ? same as next), 153, 168
  John (d. 1724), 'Man of Ross', 127
  Ric., 219
  Sarah, m. Wm. Scudamore, 206
  Wm., 219

Lacy:
  Gilbert de, 203
  Hugh de (d. by 1121), 203, 265
  Hugh de (d. 1186), 203
  Margery de (*fl.* early 13th cent.), 207
  Margery de (*fl.* 1241, ? another), 203
  Maud de, 203
  Rog. de, 44, 203, 265
  Wal. de (d. 1085), 203, 206, 216, 265
  Wal. de (d. 1241), 44, 203, 265
  family, 3, 217, 267, 287
Lambert:
  Hen., 148
  Jane, *see* Pritchard
  Susan (known as Susan Pritchard), m. Sir Henry Tempest Bt, 144, 148
Lancashire, *see* Manchester
Lancaster:
  Hen. of, earl of Derby, 39
  Herbert, 63
Lancaster, earldom (later dukedom), 233
  earl of, *see* Edmund Crouchback
  see also Duchy of Lancaster hundred
Land Settlement Association, 7, 29, 50, 60, 80, 288, 292
landscape designer, *see* Moggridge, Hal
Langar (Notts.), named as an address, 203
Lark, A.E., 85
Laslett:
  Sophia, 144
  Wm., 144, 152, 328
Lassington, 341
Latter Day Saints, 121, 172
Latton:
  Edw., 43
  John (*fl.* 1615), 42–3
  John (*fl.* 1626), 43
Lavers & Barraud, glass makers, 195
Layne family, 30
Lea (Herefs., formerly Glos. and Herefs.), 224
Lea Line, *see* Longhope
Leadington family, 116
Leadon, river, 1, 9, 11, 13, 122, 124–6, 130–3, 149–50, 154, 167, 281, 283–4, 291, 293, 298, 318
  valley, *frontispiece*, 160, 284
Ledbury, Richard of, archdeacon of Gloucester, 308
Ledbury (Herefs.), 13, 21 n, 59, 66, 68, 91, 112, 115, 117, 155–7, 164, 159, 167, 211, 295, 297, 315–17, 336
  Haffield, 103, 132
    named as an address, 162, 172
  named as an address, 92, 121, 134, 144, 146, 163, 267, 288–9, 309, 314
  nonconformity, 89–90, 172–3, 300, 344

roads to, 11–12, 98, 122, 125, 131, 198, 257, 303
St Katherine's hospital, 3, 199–200, 202, 205–8, 210–12, 216–18
workhouse, 159
see also Ludstock bridge
Ledbury poor-law-union, 312
Lee, Sir Ric., 39, 54
Leech, Rog., 103
Leicester, earl of, 84; *see also* Dudley, Rob.; Robert (d. 1168); Robert ès Blanchemains
Leicester, named as an address, 105
Leigh:
  Marianne, w. of Wm. (d. by 1658), m. 2 Rob. Barber, 53
  Peter, 53
  Wm. (*fl.* 1653), 53
  Wm. (d. by 1658), 53
Leigh (Worcs.), named as an address, 205
Lench, Sheriff's (Worcs.), named as an address, 288
Leominster (Herefs.), road to, 125, 303
Lester, Eliz., (known as Mrs Edwards), m. Thos. Rickards, 306, 312
Lestor, Wm., vicar of Dymock, 170
Lethaby, Wm., 221–2
Leuric (*fl.* 1066), 203
Lewes, John, vicar of Kempley, 214, 219
Lewis:
  John (*fl.* 1782), 47
  Mary, w. of John and mother of last, 47
  Mary Anne, *see* Evans
  Wyndham, 328
Lightfoot, Revd John, 78
Lindsay, John, 288
Linton (Herefs.), 6, 8–10, 12, 37, 57, 63, 85, 89, 219, 275
  Blindman's Gate, 90
  named as an address, 64, 339
  see also Gorsley; Gorsley with Clifford's Mesne
Liscourt, Abraham, 65
Lister:
  Mic., 326
  Ric., 326
Little, Thos. Palling, perpetual curate of Oxenhall and Pauntley, 280, 297
Llandaff, archdeacon and dean of, 235, 245
Llangadeirne (Carmarthenshire), named as an address, 105
Llanthony priory, *see* Gloucester
Llantilio Crossenny (Mon.), named as an address, 47
Llanwarne (Herefs.), named as an address, 146
Llewellins & James, bellfounders, 281
Lodge, Jas., 267
London, 115, 121, 156, 161, 163, 167, 173, 247, 295, 315, 327, 333
  carrier to, 243
  corporation of City of, 301
  Fleet Street, St Bride's church, 87
  haberdashers of, 161, 163, 206
  mayor (later lord mayor), 281, 295, 301
  Mercers' Company, 301
  merchant of, 161
  merchant tailors of, 265
  named as an address, 75, 106, 145. 147, 171, 222, 282, 301, 316, 327
Longbridge hundred, 2, 5, 301
Longchamp:
  Emme de, *see* St Léger

Geof. de, 203, 206–7, 216
Hen. de, 203
Hugh de, 203
Isabel, w. of Geof. de, 203
Maud de, m. Reynold Grey, 203, 216
family, 203
Longespée, Ela, countess of Warwick, m. Phil. Basset, 138, 153, 169
Longford, 326
  named as an address, 342
Longhope, 1–3, 5, 175, 182, 184, 188–9, 192, **223–54**
  advowson, 235, 250
  agriculture, 236–8
  architecture:
    domestic, 227, 229–32 (*230, 231*)
    industrial, 230, 232–4, 239
  allotment gardens, 245
  boundaries, 224
  Bradley Grove (later Bradley Court), *see* Longhope, Forest Court
  charities, 233, 244–8, 251, 253–4
  church, 192, 226, 233, 245, 250–4
  clubs and societies, 249
  commons, 224, 226, 228–9, 236–8, 244–5
  court, 243–4, 249
  Court Farm (the Court House), 226, 231, 237, 243
  Crocket's Hole, *see* May hill
  Dursley Cross, 176, 224–6, 229, 231, 233, 237, 241–3, 247, 249
  farms, 237–8
  fields, 236
  Forest Court (formerly Bradley Grove and Bradley Court), 228, 232, 246, 254
  Furnace Mill, 228, 232–3, 241
  friendly societies, 249
  Hart's Barn, 144, 228, 230–231, 235, 237, 334
    named as an address, 334
  inclosure, 224, 226, 237
  industry and trades, 236, 239–40, 242–3; *see also* Longhope, ironworks, mills, *and* turneries
  inns (and alehouses), 249
  ironworks, 240–1
  Lea Line, 12, 224–5, 229, 232, 248
  Little London, 176, 179, 225, 228, 231, 243, 248, 253
  Lower Longhope, 224
  manor, 181, 233–4
  manor house, *see* Longhope, Court Farm *and* Manor House, the
  Manor House, the, 227, 231, 234–5, 246
  May hill, *see* May hill
  mills, 228, 232–3, 239–41, 245
  mission room, 232, 253–4
  nonconformity, 195, 227, 232, 246, 248–9, 252–4
  parish officers, 244–5
  poor relief, 244, 246–7
  population, 226
  pound, 227, 245
  railway, 225–6, 232, 240, 242–3, 249
  rectory estate, 235–6, 250
  roads, 225–6
  schools, 227–8, 232, 245, 248, 253
  settlement, 226–9
  social structure, 245–6
  tithes, 235–6, 250–1
  turneries, 232, 239–240
  Upper Longhope, 224

vicarage (later rectory), 235–6, 250
vicarage (later rectory) houses, 226, 227, 230–1, 246, 248, 251
vicars (later rectors), 194, 251–4; *see also* Bromwich, Yate; Dighton, Chas. Mein; Guise, Fred. Chas.; Mantle, Thos.; Probyn, Edm. *and* Wm.; Raikes, Rob. Napier; Smith, Thos.
village hall (the Latchen Room), 232, 245, 249
war memorials, 227, 249
wayside crosses, 225
woodland, 224–5, 273
woodland crafts, 239–40
woodland management, 238–9
workhouses, 244
Lovell, Eliz., 265
Loveridge:
 Ric., 288
 family, 128
Lowbridge, Thos., 274
Ludlow (Salop.), 213
Ludstock bridge, in Preston and Ledbury, 303
Luxmoore, John, dean of Gloucester, rector of Taynton, 343
Lydney, 342
 ironworks, 111, 154
 named as an address, 3, 39–40, 76
Lygon:
 Fred., 6th Earl Beauchamp, 127, 134, 144, 148, 152, 162, 167, 172, 199, 202, 204–7, 209, 214–16, 220–1
 Hen. (d. 1863), 4th Earl Beauchamp, 152, 204
 Hen. (d. 1866), 5th Earl Beauchamp, 204
 John, *see* Pindar
 (formerly Pyndar), Reg., 204, 214
 Wm. (d. 1816), Lord Beauchamp of Powick, later Earl Beauchamp, 139, 143, 154, 204
 Wm. (d. 1823), 2nd Earl Beauchamp, 204
 Wm., 7th Earl Beauchamp, 162, 167, 174, 202, 204, 214, 216–17, 221–2
 Wm., 8th Earl Beauchamp, 139
 family, 4, 122, 137; *see also* Lygon
Lynde ('Linde'), de la, family, 28, 128
Lypiatt, Over, *see* Stroud
Lythe, family, 100

Maberly, A.W., 253
Maddocks (Maddox):
 Gerald, 50
 John, 31
 Wal., 50
Madeira, 253
Madley (Herefs), Carwardine, named as an address, 145
Madras civil service, 162
Madresfield (Worcs.), 3, 121, 174, 213–14
 Madresfield Court, 205
 estate, 4, 130–1, 139, 143–4, 151–2, 154–5, 202, 204, 206–7, 209, 211
 named as an address, 122, 137, 162
Maile:
 Caleb, 330
 Sophia, w. of Caleb, 330
Maisemore, 229
Malet, Rob., 155
Malvern (Worcs.):
 Great Malvern priory, 118
 named as an address, 266
 stone, 107

Malvern Chase, 95, 97, 103, 111
Malvern Hills Area of Outstanding Natural Beauty, 96
Malvern urban district council, waterworks, 97, 99
Manchester, 238
 merchant of, 205
Mantle, Thos., vicar of Longhope, 238, 252
March, earls of, 268, 287; *see also* Mortimer
Marches of Wales:
 council, 306
 court, 111
Marcle;
 John, 86
 Wal., 86
Marcle, Little (Herefs.), 303, 313, 317
 named as an address, 315
 school, 165, 313
Marcle, Much (Herefs.), 7, 124, 133, 196, 198, 205, 210, 215
 chantry, 206
 named as an address, 205–6, 208, 214, 219 n, 305
 roads to, 98, 125, 196
 school, 313
Marcon, R.D., 216
markets, *see* Dymock; Newent
market gardening, 60–61, 153, 185, 238, 292
Marmion:
 Joan, *see* Kilpeck
 Phil., 327
Marsh, Wal., 119
Marshall family, 200
Marston, Sidney, vicar of Dymock, 174
Martin:
 Hugh Thompson, 235
 Mary, *see* Sergeaunt
Martley, Hugh of, vicar of Newent, 86
Masefield, John, 292, 317
Master:
 Thos. (*fl.* 1660), 24
 Thos. (d. 1682), 234, 245
Masters, Wm., rector of Taynton, 343
Matthews:
 John (*fl.* 1522), 213
 John (*fl.* 1816–41), 50
 John (*fl.* 1849), 50
 Wm., 250
 family, 20
 (or Phipps) family, 199
Maudit:
 Eliz., *see* Knovill
 Thos., 328
May Day revels, 192, 194, 224, 249
May hill (formerly Yartledon and Yartleton), 1, 9–10, 36, 38, 42, 57, 65, 74, 186, 191, 224–6, 229–30, 232, 235–9, 242–5, 247, 249, 317–19, 322, 335
 Crocket's Hole, 86, 225, 229
Mayle:
 John, 50–1
 Ric., 214
Mayo:
 Mary, *see* Warr
 Thos., 269
McClellan, Ant., 106
McKechnie, Alan, 106
Medland, Jas., 26
Medland & Maberly, 253
Medland & Son, 44, 345
Meek (Meeke):
 Ant. 289

Rob. ('Joe'), 78
Mendip coalfield, 63
Merbury:
 Eliz., m. Wal. Devereux, 138
 John, 138, 170
Mercia, sculpture from, 92
Messenger, Ric., 256
Methodists:
 Bible Christian, 172–3
 Primitive, 173
 Wesleyan, 84, 88–90, 172–3, 220, 280, 297, 300–1, 344
Middlesex, *see* Chelsea; Edgware; Hoxton
Middleton, John, 53, 281
Middleton & Goodman, 117, 172, 217
Midland Electricity Board, 75
Mile, Reynold, 31
Miles:
 Francis, 104–5
 Hen., rector of Huntley, 180, 189–94, 196
 Phil., 193
Millard, Jas., 118
Miller:
 Constance, 254
 Thos., 246
 family, 246, 254
mills, *see* Bromesberrow; Dymock; Huntley; Kempley; Ketford; Longhope; Newent; Oxenhall; Pauntley; Preston; Taynton; *see also* windmills.
Millward family, 111
Milton Keynes (Bucks.), named as an address, 235–6
Min, Col. Nic., 76
Minchinhampton, Gatcombe Park named as an address, 104
mining, 9, 13, 63, 85, 155–6, 256–7, 259, 273–4, 277, 294, 335
 see also Society of Mines Royal and Mineral and Battery Works
Minsterworth, 151, 224–5, 233
 named as an address, 330
Minton, Hollins, & Co., tilemakers, 121
Mitcheldean, 69, 182, 189, 224, 240, 243, 246–7, 249, 252
 Forest Court (formerly Bradley Grove and Bradley Court), *see* Longhope
 market, 68
 named as an address, 50, 62, 208, 235
 nonconformity, 252
 roads to, 12, 125, 224–6, 319
moated sites, 30, 32, 45, 48–9, 52, 99, 126, 129, 130, 178, 306 n, 320–2
Moggridge:
 Hal, 97
 John, 139, 273
 John Hodder, 139, 142
Monmouth, 2, 188, 292
 carrier to, 243
 lords of, 3, 180–1, 233; *see also* Baderon of Monmouth; Gilbert of Monmouth; John of Monmouth; Wihanoc; William son of Baderon
 named as an address, 63
 priory, 180, 233, 235, 250
 road to, 176, 225–6
Monmouthshire, *see* Abergavenny; Bicknor, Welsh; Llantilio Crossenny
Monson:
 Phil. 206

Sarah, *see* Scudamore
Montagu:
    Ric. de, 138
    Wm. de, earl of Salisbury, 138
Moore:
    Hen., 115, 117
    Temple, 222
Mordiford (Herefs.), 54
Morgan:
    Bridget, 219
    Cath., *see* Grove
    John, 48
    Margery, 236
    Ric., vicar of Dymock, 170
Morris, Mr and Mrs R., 40
morris men, 192, 249
Morrish, Revd W.J., 316
Morse:
    Abraham, curate of Oxenhall and Pauntley, later rector of Huntley, 191, 195, 280
    Anne, w. of Jackman, 193
    Edw., 69
    Hannah, m. Revd Ric. Foley, 193
    Isabella, m. —— Beale, 47
    Jackman, vicar of Awre and rector of Huntley, 193, 195
    Jas., 23, 64
    John (d. 1797), rector of Huntley, 193, 195
    John (*fl.* 1839), perpetual curate (vicar) of Oxenhall and rector of Huntley, 189, 193, 195, 278, 280
    John (d. 1842), 43, 51
    John Nourse, 37–38, 43–4, 47, 51, 58, 63, 69, 72
    Martha, m. John Morse, 193
    Martha, w. of John (d. 1797), 193
    Wm., 44
    family, 23, 77, 88, 195
Mortimer:
    Rog., earl of March, 265
    family, earls of March, 287
Morton:
    Ant., 141
    Eliz., *see* Pembridge
    Humph., 105
    Ric., 141
    Sir Roland, 141
Morton, Abbots (Worcs.), 170
Morwent, Jos., 267
motorway (M50), 2, 12, 96, 98, 123, 126, 257
Mounteagle, Lord, *see* Stanley, Sir Edw.
Moyaux:
    John of, prior of Newent, 76
    Simon of, prior of Newent, 76
Moyne:
    Margery, *see* Knovill
    Thos., 328
Mucegros:
    Cecily de, *see* Avenel, Douce
    Hawise de, m. 1 John de Ferrers, 2 John de Bures, 326
    John de, 46, 326
    Rob. de, 46, 326
Murrell (Murzell), Thos., 129
    charity of, 163
Musgrove, Cecily, charity of, 336, 339

nail making, 65, 156
Nanfan:
    Giles (*fl.* 1580), 81
    Revd Giles (*fl.* 1742), 106
    John (*fl.* 1635), 81

    John (d. by 1749), 106
    John (d. by 1775), 106
    Margaret, m. 1 Thos. Webb, 2 Revd. Jas. Davenport, 106
    Margaret, *see* Walford
    Mary (d. 1767), *see* Stone, Mary
    Mary, w. of John (d. by 1749), 106
Nash, Eliz., *see* Bosworth
National Society, 345
National Trust, 225
Nayler:
    Frances, *see* Blunt
    Revd Thos., 182
    family, 182
Neale, Noah Hill, 145
Neate, Sam., 145
Neath (Glam.), Baglan House, named as an address, 235
Nelme:
    Thos. (*fl.* 1630), 329
    Thos. (*fl.* early 18th cent.), 330
    Wm., 58, 69
    family, 321
Neville:
    Ankaret, *see* Talbot
    Thos., Lord Furnivale, 234
New Numbers, 167
Newbolt, Wm. Chas. Edm., vicar of Dymock, 167, 173
Newcastle upon Tyne, 338
Newent, 1–6, **7–94**, 123, 167–8, 210–11, 254, 269, 276–8, 281–2, 285, 287, 289, 297–8, 317, 334, 339, 344
    advowson, 85
    agriculture, 55–61
    Almshouse Green, mission room, 88
    almshouses, 25–26, 81
    Anglo-Saxon cross shaft, 84, *91–92*
    Anthony's Cross, 12, 32
    Atherland's Place, *see* Newent, Scarr, the
    Baldwin's Oak, 28, 281
    boothall, 18, 21–3 (*22*), 67; *see also* Newent, market house
    borough, 8, 70–1; *see also* Newent, Newent tithing
    Boulsdon, 8, 11, 35, 38, 42, 45, 57, 63, 66, 72, 85–6
        settlement, 34–6
        see also Newent, manors
    Briery Hill Farm, 35
    boundaries, 7–9
    burgages, 17, 70
    Caerwent's Farm, 11
    canal, 7, 13, 32, 63, 69
    Carswalls, 2, 8, 36
        named as an address, 306
        see also Newent, manors
    Carswalls Manor, 45–46
    cemetery, 20
    chantries, 50, 86
    charities, 81–2
    churches:
        parish church, 17, 77, 80, 84–9, 91–4 (*93*), 172, 341
        see also Gorsley; Newent, Clifford's Mesne *and* Kilcot
    Civil War incident, 76
    Clifford Manor, 34, 38, 43–44, 317, 322, 326, 338
    Clifford's Mesne, 2, 4, 7–10, 12, 26, 36, 42–3, 62–3, 69, 90
        Anglican chapel, 88–9
        church, 89, *94*

        school, 83, 89
        see also Gorsley with Clifford's Mesne ecclesiastical district
    clubs and societies, 79–80
    cricket club, 257
    coalfield, 69, 155; *see also* mining
    commons, 7, 8, 10–11, 26, 29–30, 36, 42, 55, 57–9
    Compton, 8, 10, 12, 20, 27–8, 38, 44–5, 54, 56–7, 62, 65, 72
        settlement, 26–30
    Compton House, *see* Compton Green
    Conigree Court (the Conigree), 8–10, 20, 36–7, 46–8 (*47*), 57
    Court House, the (Old Court), 19, 39–*41*, 88
        named as an address, 31
    court officers, 71–2
    courts, 18, 70–2
    crafts, *see* Newent, industry and crafts
    Cugley, 8, 10–11, 36–8, 51, 56, 58, 62, 65, 66, 72
        settlement, 32–4
        named as an address, 42
    distributive and service trades, 68–9
    domestic architecture:
        town, 23–6, 40–2,
        outlying, 26–38, (*29*), 44–54
    fairs, 66–8
    farms, 39–3, 45, 55–61
    fields, 55, 57
    forge, 65
    gallows, 71
    Glasshouse Green, 8, 34, 322
    glassworks, 34, 65 , 322, 335
    Gorsley common, 7–11, 26, 36, 46–7, 57, 63, 65, 72, 77, 257
        settlement, 37–8
    Great Boulsdon Farm, 34, *44*
    Hayes (*Hege*) estate, 2, 49, 287, 290
    Hayes Farm, 27, 49–50
    high cross, 18
    inclosure, 58
    industry and crafts, 62–6
    inns and public houses, 78–9
        Black Dog, 24, 78
        George, 78–80
        King's head, 78
        Red Lion, 23, 78, 79
    Kilcot, 7–11, 36–7, 47, 57, 62–3, 69, 78, 90–1, 254, 326, 331
        chapel-of-ease, 88
        inn, 59, 79
        medieval chapel, 86
        nonconformist chapel, 90
        school, 83
        settlement, 36–7
        wood, 10, 46–7
        see also Newent, manors
    Madam's wood, 8, 10, 74, 256, 283
    Malswick, 8, 10–11, 38, 48–9, 56, 61, 66, 326
        settlement, 30–2
        named as an address, 49
    manor houses, *see* Newent, Carswalls Manor; Conigree Court; Court House, the; Great Boulsdon Farm; Moat, the; *and* priory, precinct
    manors, 38
        Boulsdon, 8–10, 34, 36, 38, 42–3, 47, 51, 55, 57, 62–3
        Carswalls, 8, 28, 38, 44–5, 55, 57

Index

Kilcot, 9–10, 36–7, 46–7, 56–7, 62, 71, 268
Newent, 8, 10, 38–40, 42, 48–50, 52, 55–7, 62, 64, 71, 76, 85, 266
Okle Clifford, 10, 41, 48–9, 56–7, 64
Okle Grandison, 49, 56–7
   court, 276
Southorles (Lower Southerns), 8, 32, 42, 51–2; *see* Newent, Moat, the
market house, 18, 22–23, 67, 74, 79, 91; *see also*, Newent, boothall
market place, 16–19, 44, 67, 70, 77, 79–80
markets, 7, 15, 66–8, 108, 156
meeting places, 79–80
mills, 32, 40, 49, 64–5
Moat, the, 8, 9, 32, 41, 51–3 (52), 65, 85
   named as an address, 52
named as an address, 191, 193, 267, 330
Nelfields Farm, 11, 13
   named as an address, 53
Newent Court (New Court), 16, 20–1, 40–2, 77
   estate, 319, 326, 328, 330, 333–4
Newent tithing (borough or liberty of Newent), 8, 18, 37, 56–7, 72, 77
Newent (Yartleton) woods, 8–10, 12, 33–4, 36, 38, 40, 52, 61–2, 85
nonconformity, protestant, 88–91, 220, 280, 300, 344
Okle, 8, 30, 38, 55
   manors, *see* Newent, manors
Okle Pitchard, (Pitcher), 30, 49
Old Court, *see* Newent, Court House, the
parish council (Newent town council), 74, 76
parish officers, 72–4
parks, 55, 80
Parks, the, 260
poor relief, 72–3
pound, 18
priory, 12, 19, 30, 38, 40, 49, 52, 55, 62, 64, 76, 85–6, 147, 158, 168, 170, 341
   farm buildings, 30, 49
   precinct, 15–19, 40, 55, 67, 85; *see also* Newent, Court House, the
   priors, 11, 46, 64, 163, 268, 279; *see also* Moyaux, John of *and* Simon of; Goupillières, Simon of; Hacqueville, Wm. of
population, 13
Porter's Place, 18–19, 42–4
prison (of the manor), 71
public services, 74–6
railway, 13, 257
recreation ground, 74, 80
rectors, 70, 76
rectory estate, 54
roads, 11–12
   road repairs, 73–4
roads to, 124–5, 176, 198, 224–5, 256–7, 303, 319
Roman Catholicism, 91, 94
Scarr, the (formerly Atherlard's Place), 28, 50, 60, 91
school board, 83
schools, 74, 77, 80, 82–4, 164, 191, 278, 297, 313, 340; *see also* Gorsley; Newent, Clifford's Mesne
settlement:
   town, 13–21 (15)
   outlying, 26–38
streets, 13–17 (16), 25, 79
social structure, 76–7

Southends (Southerns), 50–1
spa, 69, 81
stagecoach services, 78
Stalling (Stallions) estate, 8, 32, 38, 52–3, 55
Stardens, 28, 38–40, 53–54, 77, 277
   named as an address, 40, 206
Tan House, the, 19, 24–25
tithes, 54, 84–5
tithings, 8, *see also* Newent, Newent tithing
town bailiff and other officers, 70–2
vicarage (later rectory), 54, 84–5
vicarage house, 19, 85, 87
vicars (later rectors), 76, 86–8; *see also* Avenant, Thos.; Craister, John; Foley, John; Onslow, Ric. Francis
Walden Court, 27, 41, 49–50, 54, 88, 297, 301
waterworks, 74
woodland, 9–10, 42, 57, 181; *see also* Newent, Madam's wood *and* Newent woods
woodland management and crafts, 61–3, 186, 273, 275
workhouse (parish, later union), 25, 73–4, 83
see also Botloe's Green; Brand Green; Compton Green; Ell bridge; Gorsley; Gorsley and Kilcot civil parish; Gorsley with Clifford's Mesne ecclesiastical district; Kent's Green; Pool Hill
Newent county court district, 74
Newent Gas Light & Coke Co., 75
Newent highway district (and board), 114, 160, 337
Newent petty sessional division, 74
Newent poor-law union, 6, 74, 114, 160, 213, 276, 295, 311, 337
Newent rural district, 6, 74, 77
   council, 26, 74–6, 85, 97
   housing, 20–1, 30, 36, 99–100, 102, 127–8, 130–1, 133–5, 199, 202, 262, 320
Newland, 3, 180
   named as an address, 48, 180–1, 233–4
Newnham:
   Ayleford ironworks, 239
   market, 66
   named as an address, 51
   road to, 319
Newton:
   Alfred, vicar (and rector) of Preston, 313–14, 316–17
   Benj., rector of Taynton 1710–33, 340, 343
   John (father of last), rector of Taynton, 343
   John (grds. of last), rector of Taynton 1737–54, 343
Niblett, J.M., parson of Preston, 313
Noel, Wm. Fred., 53
nonconformity, protestant, *see* Baptists; Christian Brethren; Congregationalists; Latter Day Saints; Methodists; Presbyterians; Quakers; United Brethren
Norman, Wm. son of, *see* William
Northamptonshire, 168; *see also* Blisworth; Culworth; Fotheringhay college
Northumberland, earls of, *see* Percy
Northumberland, 338; *see also* Newcastle upon Tyne

North-West Gloucestershire Water Board, 74–5
Northwood:
   John, 138
   Rog., 138
Norton (Herefs.), 103
Norton (Worcs.), 269
Nottinghamshire, *see* Langar; Stoke, East
Nourse:
   Dorothy, *see* Bourne
   Eliz., 43, 47
   John (fl. 1559), 236
   Revd John (d. 1754), 43, 47
   John (fl. 1789), 43, 51
   Lucy, w. of Tim., m. 2 —— Stokes, 51, 82
   Mary, w. of Wal. (d. 1663), 43, 87
   Ric. (fl. 1570s), 236
   Ric. (fl. 1590, ? same as last), 234
   Thos., 229, 234, 236, 241, 245, 247, 250, 252
   Revd Tim., 51, 78, 82, 87
   Wal. (fl. 1597), 19
   Wal. (d. 1652), 43, 51, 63, 81
   Wal. (d. 1663), 43
   Wal. (d. 1743), 43–4, 47, 51, 78, 87
   Wm., 43, 63
   family, 44, 77, 81, 233–4
Nunn, John, 195
nursing associations, 167, 249, 341

Odo (fl. 1086), 44
Okle:
   as a surname, 48–9
   Joan 'ate', 48
   John of, 48
   Reynold of, 48
Old Sodbury with Chipping Sodbury, 253
Oldcastle:
   Eliz., *see* Ruyhale
   Ric., 138
Ollney, John Harvey, 82
Ombersley (Worcs.), Hawford, named as an address, 290
Onslow:
   And. Geo., 40, 277
   And. Ric., 40, 266, 277
   Arthur And., vicar of Newent, 88
   Harriett, *see* Foley
   Ric. Foley, 40, 53, 67, 76–7, 83, 268, 270, 273, 277
   Ric. Francis, vicar of Newent, 40, 76, 79, 83, 88
   Wm., 263
   family, 3, 38, 40, 46, 62–3, 77, 85, 89, 260, 266, 272–3, 275, 277
   see also Deane
orchards, 4, 59, 97, 109–10, 124, 150–3, 184–5, 198, 207, 209–10, 224, 236–8, 272, 291–2, 303, 308–10, 321–2; *see also* cider and perry
Ormonde, earl of, 327
Osborne, Chas. Willoughby, 290; *see also* Willoughby-Osborne
Owen:
   Sir John, Bt, 330, 338
   family, 330
Oxenhall, 1–3, 5–6, 9, 11, 40, 57, 74, 76, 80, 118, 123, 130, 153, 130, **254–81**, 300–1
   advowson, 278–9
   agriculture, 270–2
   boundaries, 254
   canal, 257–258, 273, 276–7
   canal tunnel, 126
   chantry, 280

church, 216, 258–259, 278–81 (281), 298, 300–1
church house, 258–259, 277
commons, 270–1
    Shaw common, 256–7, 259, 261, 263, 271–3, 280
court, 276
Crooke's Farm, *see* Pauntley
Crooke's Mill, *see* Pauntley
curacy (later vicarage), 130, 278–9
curates (perpetual curates and vicars), 195, 277, 279–80; *see* Davies, Thos.; Little, Thos. Palling; Morse, Abraham *and* John; Sherwood, Thos.
domestic architecture, *261*, 262–264
Ellbridge furnace, 7, 9, 38–9, 62, 65, 76, 111, 256–7, 260, 271–2, 274–275, 277, 335
    water supply to, 9, 256, 275
farms, 270–2, 277
fields, 270–1
Furnace, the, *see* Oxenhall, Oakdale House
golf course, 257
Gospel Oak, *see* Dymock
Hill House Farm, *see* Pauntley,
Hilter Farm (formerly Yeldhall), 259, 266
inclosure, 256, 261
ironworks, *see* Oxenhall, Ellbidge furnace
Kew's Farm, *see* Pauntley
manor, 39, 49, 57, 260, 262, 264–6, 267, 271–2, 280
manor house, *see* Oxenhall, Hilter Farm
Marshall's Farm, 260, 263, 266–7
mills, 274
mining, 63, 273–4, 277
named as an address, 42
nonconformity, 277, 280
Oakdale House (formerly the Furnace), 40, 260, 275, 277
Oxenhall Court, 256, 259–60, 262–4, 268, 271, 276
parish officers, 276
park, 28, 254, 256–7
poor relief, 276
population, 257–8
pound, 261
railway and tramroad, 257
rectory estate, 256, 265, 267–8, 270, 278; *see also* Oxenhall, Oxenhall Court
roads, 11, 257
schools, 258, 277–8
settlement, 258–62
social structure, 276–7l
tithes, 266–9
trades, 276
vicarage, *see* Oxenhall, curacy
vicarage houses, 262, 276, 279–80
waterworks, 256
Winter's Farm, 260, 266–7
woodland, 10, 62, 154, 256–7, 261, 271
woodland crafts, 272
woodland management, 272–3
Yeldhall, *see* Oxenhall, Hilter Farm
see also Ell bridge; Four Oaks; Hillend green
Oxford, 51
    Hertford college, 120
    named as an address, 51
    Pembroke College, masters of, 343
    Sheldonian Theatre, 87
Oxfordshire, *see* Bampton; Kingham; Witney

Painswick:
    named as an address, 195
    stone, 195
Palairet, C.H., 173
Palmer:
    Geo., 213
    family, 214–2
Paris, 312
Parker, Thos., rector of Taynton, 343
Parkhurst:
    Sir Rob. (d. 1636), 327
    Sir Rob. (s. of last), 327
    Rob. (*fl.* 1655–6, s. of last), 327, 330
parks, *see* Bromesberrow; Dymock; Huntley; Kempley; Newent; Oxenhall; Pauntley; Taynton
Parry:
    E. Gambier, 155
    Thos. Gambier, 133
Parsons, Ailway, 66
Paston:
    Anne, *see* Somerset
    John, 287, 296
    family, 291, 300
Patrick, Jos., 207
Paul, Matt., 69
Pauncefoot:
    Anne, w. of Wm. (d. 1691), 306, 312, 315
    Dorothy, m. Ric. Green, 45
    Grimbald, 45
    Hen., 48
    John, curate of Oxenhall, 280
    N. (*fl. ante* 1501), 48
    Poole, 45, 87
    Sarah, m. Wm. Bromley, 45, 306
    Wm. (d. 1617), 53, 296
    Wm. (d. 1691), 45, 306
    Wm. (d. 1711), 45, 306
    family, 27, 81, 285, 296, 300
Pauncefote
    Bernard, 306
    (formerly Smith and Bromley), Sir Geo., Bt, 45, 49, 70, 306, 312
    Sir Julian, later Baron Pauncefote of Preston, 306, 312
    (formerly Smith), Rob. (d. 1843), 306, 312, 316
    Rob. (d. 1847), 306
    family, 312, 316
Pauntley, 1–3, 5–9, 13, 20, 27, 29, 38, 46, 54, 57–8, 61, 86, 118, 145, 160, 254, 256, 265, *281–301*, 329
    advowson, 287, 298
    agriculture, 271–2, 290–2
    Botloe's Farm, 285, 289, 291, 295
    boundaries, 254, 281–2
    canal, 257, 273
    chantries, 299
    charities, 297
    church (chapel), 54, 84, 279, 281, 284, 287, 298–301 (*299*)
    church house, 298
    Collin Park wood, 10, 281–3, 292–3
    commons, 281, 291
    court, 294
    Crooke's Farm, 260, 262–4, 268–9
    Crooke's Mill, 254, 274
    curacy (later vicarage), 280, 298
    curates (perpetual curates and vicars), 299–301; *see* Davies, Thos.; Little, Thos. Palling; Morse, Abraham; Sherwood, Thos.
    customs, 297–8
    domestic architecture, 262–4 (*263*), 285–6
    Durbridge, *see* Redmarley D'Abitot
    farms, 268, 271–2, 277, 290–1
    fields, 290
    fish ponds, 282
    Hayes estate, *see* Newent
    Hill House Farm, 257, 260, 269–70
    Kew's Farm. 260, 262–4 (*263*)
    Kilcot, 2, 8, 283, 287, 290
    Little Pauntley, 281
    manor, 8, 49, 286–8, 288 n, 289
    manor house, 283, 295; *see* Pauntley, Pauntley Court
    mills, 274, 282, 285–6, 290, 293
    mining, 63, 257, 273, 294
    named as an address, 50, 103, 268–9, 334
    nonconformity, protestant, 90, 280, 285, 297, 300–1
    parish officers, 294–5
    park, 283, 290
    Pauntley Court, 284, 286, 288–9 (*288*), 291–3, 296–7, 300
        estate, 27, 58, 63
    Pauntley Place (formerly the White House), 285, 296–8
    Pauntley Spa, 283, 297
    Payford, 282, 284, 289
        bridge, 283, 295
        mill, 284, 285–6, 290, 292–293
    poor relief, 294–6
    poorhouses, 285–6, 294
    population, 258, 283–4
    railway, 283
    rectory estate, 289–90
    Rhyle House, 285, 289, 291–2, 294–5
    roads, 283
    Roman Catholicism, 300
    schools, 116, 278, 285, 296–7, 300
    settlement, 260–1, 282, 284–5
    social structure, 277, 295–7
    tithes, 289–90, 298
    trades, 294
    vicarage, *see* Pauntley, curacy
    White House, the, *see* Pauntley, Pauntley Place
    woodland, 256, 275, 282–3, 288 n; *see also* Pauntley, Collin Park wood
    woodland management, 292–3
    see also Brand Green; Botloe's Green; Ketford; Pool Hill
Payford, *see* Pauntley
Payne:
    Ann (or Agnes), m. 1 John Bromwich, 2 Wm. Whittington, 103, 114, 118
    Thos., 342
Peacock family, 9
Pembridge:
    Eliz. of, m. Sir Roland Morton, 141
    Eliz. of, *see* Gamages
    Euphemia of, *see* Gamages
    Hen. of (*fl.* mid 13th cent.), 141
    Hen. of (*fl.* 1338, ? same as next), 327
    Hen. of (d. 1362), 141
    John of (d. 1376), 141
    John of (*fl.* 1388), 141
    John of (d. 1505), 141
    Margaret, w. of Hen. of (d. 1362), 141
    Ric. of, 328
    Thos. of, 141

Wal. of, 141
Wm. of (*fl.* 1285), 141
Wm. of (*fl.* 1317–42), 141, 160
family, 149
Pembroke Boroughs, MP for, 338
Pendock, Joan, 106
Pendock (Worcs.), 119
Peneys:
    Agnes de, m. Ives of Clinton, 155
    John de, 155
    Rose, w. of John de, 155
Pennington, John, bellfounder, 93
Percy:
    Hen. (d. 1489), earl of Northumberland, 265
    Hen. (d. 1527), earl of Northumberland, 265
    Hen. (*fl.* 1535, s. of last), 265
    Maud, *see* Herbert
Perkins:
    Mary, 296
    Ric., 273
    family, 296
Pershore (Worcs.), 252
Peter family, 259, 277
Peters, Ric., 262
Peyer, Everard Chas. de, 41
Phelps:
    N., 50
    Wm. John, 50
Philadelphia, 235
Phillips (Philipps):
    Edwin, 335
    John, 269
    Margaret, *see* Warr
    R.S., 232
    Steph., 252
Phipps:
    David (or Ric.), rector of Taynton, 342
    (or Phillips), Ric., rector of Taynton, 342
    Ric., *see* Phipps, David
    family, *see* Matthews
Pigott:
    Anne, m. 1 Sam. Danvers, 2 Hen. Finch, 203, 205, 219, 265
    Leonard, 203, 265
    Margery, w. of Wm., 203, 216, 265
    Wm., 203, 265
pillory, 72
Pindar (formerly Lygon), John, 3rd Earl Beauchamp, 204
Pirton (Worcs.), named as an address, 134
Pitfield, Chas., 328
Pitt (Pytt):
    John (*fl.* 1607), 42, 63
    John (*fl.* 1640), 35
    Jos., 104
    Rowland, 239
    Sarah, 165
Pludie, John de la, 18
Plumtree, Ric., 17
police stations, 26, 127, 135, 189, 227, 245
Pool Hill, in Newent and Pauntley, 8–9, 11, 29, 88, 285–286, 292, 294, 296
    school, 285, 301
Poole:
    Elinor, m. Sir Ric. Fettiplace, 295
    Eliz., *see* Whittington
    Sir Giles, 287, 290
    Sir Hen. (d. 1616), 287, 290, 295–6
    Hen. (*fl.* 1620), 287, 294
    Hen. (*fl.* 1676), 213
    Wm., 213

family, 213, 219–20
Poole Keynes (formerly Wilts.), 171
Pope, Wm., 146
Porter:
    Arthur (d. 1558), 42, 267
    Sir Arthur (*fl.* 1610), 42–4, 51, 267
    Rog., 18, 34, 42, 44, 54, 77, 86, 92, 267
    Sir Thos., 42
    Wm., vicar of Newent, 86
    family, 38, 57, 264
Portes:
    Matt. de, 103
    Ric. de, 103, 118,
    Rog. de, 103
Potter, Edw., vicar of Longhope, 251
Powell:
    John, 306, 308, 312, 314
    Rob. ap, and w., 50
    Thos., 305
    Wm. Hen., 249
    family, 305
Power family, 199
Powick (Worcs.):
    ironworks, 111, 154
    Lord Beauchamp of, *see* Lygon
    named as an address, 148
Poyntz, Thos., 138
Prank family, 17
Preedy, Fred., 121
Presbyterians, 88, 121, 171
Preston, 1–2, 5, 112, 118, 123, 125, 170, 172–3, **301–17**
    advowson, 314
    agriculture, 307–10
    Baron Pauncefote of, *see* Pauncefote, Sir Julian
    boundaries, 302
    church, 155, 168, 170, 303–4, 313–17 (*315, 316*)
    court, 311
    domestic architecture, 304–7
    farms, 308–9
    fields, 303, 308
    inclosure, 303, 308–9
    manor, 305–6
    manor house, *see* Preston, Preston Court
    mills, 310
    nonconformity, 315
    parish officers, 311–12
    poor relief, 311
    poorhouses, 311, 313
    population, 303
    Preston Court, 303–7 (*307*), 310, 312
        named as an address, 28
    roads, 302, 303
    schools, 313, 316
    settlement, 304
    social life, 313
    social structure, 312–13
    tithes, 313–14
    trades and services, 310
    vicarage (later rectory), 313–14
    vicarage (later rectory) houses, 304, 312–14
    vicars (later rectors), 168, 315–17; *see* Bryan, Chas.; Dixon, C.W.; Doherty, A.P.; Gethyn-Jones, Dan.; Hardy, H.H.; Jenkins, Jenkin; Newton, Alfred; Niblett, J.M.
    woodland, 303
    see also Ludstock bridge

Price:
    Elisa, w. of Morgan Philips, 329
    Gregory, 206
    J.G., 102, 106
    Jas., 206
    Jas., rector of Bromesberrow, 119
    Margaret Tatiana, m. —— Rose, 329
    Marianne, w. of Sam. Grove, 329
    Morgan, 327
    Revd Morgan, 329
    Morgan Philips, 320, 325, 329, 333, 339–41
    Octavius, 44
    Peter (Wm. Philips Peter), 329, 342
    Sam. Grove, 329
    Stanhope Grove, *see* Grove
    family, 206, 326
    (later Grove) family, 339
Price, Jas., & Son, cider and perry makers, 210
Priday:
    Chas., 52
    family, 52
Prince:
    Ric., 241 n
    Rob., 214 n
    family, 241
Pringle:
    Hen. Arthur, 229, 232, 234–5, 242, 246
    Mary, w. of R.W.J. Pringle-Nicholson, 235
Pringle-Nicholson:
    Mary, *see* Pringle
    R.W.J., 235
prisoners-of-war, 91
    camp site, 20
Pritchard:
    Geo., 144, 148
    Jane, m. Henry Lambert, 148
    Jane, *see* Skipp
    John, 329
    Susan, *see* Lambert
Probyn:
    Caroline, m. Rob. Napier Raikes, 246
    Sir Edm. (d. 1742), 177, 181, 184, 186, 234, 242, 334
    Edm. (d. 1819), 182, 186, 234–6, 250
    Edm. (d. 1837), vicar of Longhope, 232, 246, 248, 253
    Edm. (d. 1890), 178–82, 185, 190, 193, 231, 234–5, 237, 246, 321, 330
    Eliz., 246
    (formerly Hopkins), John (d. 1773), 186, 234, 239, 242, 334
    John (d. 1843), dean of Llandaff, 231, 234–5, 245–6
    John (d. 1863), 246, 253
    Wm., vicar of Longhope, 246
    family, 3–5, 180, 184, 189–90, 193, 233, 326, 332
professions, *see* architects; attorneys; solicitors; surgeons
Puckmore, Edw., 130
Puff (Pouf) family, 17
Pugh:
    W.J., 204
    family, 204.
Pullen, John, 152
Purefey, Wm., 181
Purrock, John, 191
Pury:
    Deborah, 343
    Eliz., m. —— Whittington, 327, 329, 343
    Sarah, 327, 329

Theophilus, 343
Thos. (d. 1666), 326–7
Thos. (d. 1693), 320, 327, 329–30, 338, 343
Pye:
    Edw. (d. 1692), 139, 142, 158, 161
    see also Chamberlayne
Pyndar:
    Eliz., see Hacket
    Reg. (d. 1712), 203–4, 212–13,
    Reg. (d. 1788), see Lygon
    Thos., 200, 204, 208–9, 213
    (later Lygon) family, 3, 202, 204, 213–14, 220
Pytt, see Pitt

Quakers, 88, 343
quarrying:
    cinders, 65, 187, 240–1, 274–5, 335
    stone, 63, 96, 112, 114, 155, 187, 225, 242, 257, 335
Quedgeley, 120
Queen Anne's Bounty, 168, 193, 279, 298

races, see horse racing
Radclyffe, Eliz., 330
Raikes:
    Caroline, see Probyn
    Rob. Napier, vicar of Longhope, 246, 253
    Stanley Napier, 162
railways, 126, 226, 257, 283, 283; see also Great Western
Ralph the clerk of Taynton, 326
Rawlins, Raphael, 250
Rawlinson, John, 267
Read:
    Harold, 243
    Hen., 5, 243
    Ric., 243
    see also Reed
Redditch (Worcs.), named as an address, 266
Redfearn, Ric., 300
Redmarley D'Abitot (formerly Worcs.), 6, 96, 100, 104, 110, 112, 118–19, 122–3, 131, 167, 171, 174, 222, 280, 282–3, 287, 293, 298, 295, 301, 310, 317
    Durbridge, 282–3, 293
    named as an address, 143, 286
Reed, Geo., 41; see also Read
Rees, Wm., 94
religious houses, see Aconbury priory; commandery; Conches abbey; Cookhill priory; Cormeilles abbey; Dinmore preceptory; Flaxley, abbey; Gloucester, abbey and Llanthony priory; Hereford, St Guthlac's priory; Malvern, Great Malvern priory; Monmouth, priory; Newent, priory; St Florent abbey; Studley priory; Wormsley priory
Ricardo:
    David, 104, 288
    Frank (d. 1897), 104, 122
    Frank (fl. 1929), 104, 288
    Harriet, w. of Osman, 115–17
    Mortimer, 104
    Osman, 102, 104–5, 110, 115–17, 121, 291, 296–7
    family, 3, 100, 128, 296
Rice (Reece), Wm., 19
Rich:
    Anne, see Robins

Thos., 306
Ric, son of Robert le, 207
Richard I, 138, 141
Richardson:
    Barbara, m. —— Bourchier, 93
    Chas., 52
    Jas., 93
    Sam., 40
    Thos., 81
    family, 40
Rickards:
    Eliz., see Lester
    Thos., 306
Ricketts, Thos., 338
Rideout:
    John Worrall, 205
    see also Worrall
Rigby:
    Alex., 120
    F.F., rector of Bromesberrow, 116
Rimes, Revd J.R., 346
riots, bread, 245
roads, see salt way; motorway; turnpike roads
Robert (d. 1168), earl of Leicester, 38
Robert ès Blanchemains, earl of Leicester, 38
Robert the Hart, 228
Robert, chaplain of Oxenhall, 279
Robert, dean of Kempley, 216
Roberts:
    Caesar, 279
    H.L., 216
    John, 48
    Maud, see Dulle
    Nic., 236, 267–8
    family, 268
Robins:
    Anne, w. of Hen. and also of Thos. Rich, 306, 312, 314–15
    Hen., 306
    Ric., 315
Robinson, W.P., 122
Roddis, John, 281
Rodmarton, see Tarlton
Roger 'de la Hulle', 27
Roger 'le Frere', 268
Roger of Durley, 229
Roger the marshal, 266
Roger the millward, 310
Rogers:
    Edw. (d. 1763), 48
    Edw., vicar of Preston, 315
    Eliz., ? w. of Wm. (d. 1662), 87 and n
    Eliz., m. Edward Bearcroft, 48
    Eliz., w. of Edw. (d. 1763), 48
    John (d. 1721), 48
    John (d. 1735), 48, 54
    Laetitia, m. Charles Jones, 48
    Ric., 8, 87
    Thos., 266
    Wm. (d. 1662), 48, 87 n
    Wm. (d. 1690, s. of last), 48, 81–2, 87
    Wm. (fl. 1680, s. of Thos.), 266
    family, 64, 77, 81
Rollinson, S., & Son, 94
Roman Catholicism, 91, 219, 254, 298, 300
    Salesian Fathers, 92, 254
Roman remains, 65, 122, 125–6, 133, 156, 174, 176, 187, 225, 302–3
Rome, 86
Rose, Margaret Tatiana, see Price
Ross-on-Wye (Herefs.), 2, 8, 11, 91, 157, 185, 188, 211, 330

'Man of Ross', see Kyrle, John
market, 66–8, 247
named as an address, 51, 145, 201, 206
roads to, 11–12, 37, 125, 174–6, 198, 225, 257, 303
Rostele, Wm. de, rector of Huntley, 193
Rotherwas (Herefs.), named as an address, 329
Rowden:
    A.R., 104, 106
    Beatrice, see Waudby-Griffin
Rowles:
    Arthur, 235, 245
    Nic., 235–6, 241
Rudder, Sam., 12, 333
Rudford and Highleadon, 9
    Highleadon, 9, 11, 31, 55, 344
    Rudford, 11, 295, 341
Rudge:
    Edm. (d. 1843), 44
    Edm. (d. 1886), 44
    Frances, w. of Edm. (d. 1886), 44
    Thos., vicar of Longhope, 251
Rudhall:
    Abraham, 93, 252
    Thos., 120, 316
Rushforth, T.H., 232
Rushock (Worcs.), 203
    named as an address, 266
Ruyhale:
    Edm., 138
    Eliz., w, of Ric. (d. 1408), m. 2 Ric. Oldcastle, 138
    Ric. (d. 1408), 138
    Ric. (d. 1415), 138
    family, 170
Ryder, Hen., bishop of Gloucester, 316
Rye House Plot, 316–16
'ryelands', 'the', in Glos. and Herefs., 4, 108, 124, 256, 282
Ryeland breed of sheep, 58, 149
Ryley, as a surname, 284
Ryton, see Dymock

Sabyn, John, vicar of Longhope, 251
Sadler family, 156
Salesian Fathers, see Roman Catholicism
Salfield, Launcelot, 267
Salisbury, earl of, see Montagu, Wm. de
salt way, 2
Samson, sacrist of Gloucester abbey, 331
Samuel:
    J.F., 146
    L., 146
Sandhurst, 103
Sandwich (Kent), MP for, 329
Sanford, David Ayshford, 288
Sansom, Jas., 241
Sapperton, 287, 290
Sapy:
    Aline de, see Bath
    John de, 191
    Rob. de, 181, 189, 191
Sargeant:
    Peter, 104, 144
    Wm., 104
    see also Sergeaunt
Savacre, Revd Edw., 342
Savage, Sam., vicar of Dymock, 171
Saycell (fl. mid 13th cent.), 200–11
Scots, expedition against, 194
Scott:
    Gilbert, 93

Scudamore:
Revd H.D.Y., 122
Scudamore:
  Frances, *see* Somerset
  Hen., 287
  Hen. Blachford, 288
  Sir John, Bt, 206, 211
  John, Viscount Scudamore, 4
  Sarah, m. 1 John Holmes, 2 Phil. Monson, 206
  Sarah, *see* Kyrle
  Tamar, w. of Hen. Blachford, 288
  Wm., 206
Scull, Wm., vicar of Kempley, 219
secretary of state, 312
Senhouse, Peter, vicar of Kempley, 219–20
Sergeaunt:
  Ann, 235
  Edw. (d. 1698), 230, 235
  Edw. (d. 1800), 50
  Eliz., *see* Dobyns
  Joanna, 235
  John (d. 1615), 235, 241
  John (*fl.* 1702), 235
  John (d. 1765), 235
  Revd John (d. 1780), 144, 235
  John (d. 1820), 235
  Margaret, w. of Ric., 235
  Margaret, m. Hugh Thompson Martin, 235
  Mary, 235
  Ric., 235
  Wm., 231, 235, 334
  family, 228, 233
  see also Sargeant
Servante, Wm., vicar of Kempley, 220
Severn, river, 291
  trade, 237, 274–5
Severne, Hester, 81
Severn-Trent Water authority, 75
Seys, Evan, 139, 142, 161
Shapton:
  Abraham, 327, 335, 343
  Judith, w. of Abraham, 327, 343
Sharpe:
  Revd Chas. Hen., 235
  Revd Francis Wm., 234–5
  John Chas., 235, 250
  Mary, w. of Revd Francis Wm., 235
  Wm. Granville, 235
  family, 233
Shaw, as a surname, 18
Shayle:
  Edw., 128
  Eliz., w. of Thos. (d. 1540), 143
  John, 143
  Thos. (d. 1540), 143
  Thos. (s. of last), 143
  Thos. (*fl.* 1687), 143
  family, 128, 142
Shelley:
  Spencer (d. 1941), 182
  Spencer (*fl.* 1975), 182
  family, 190
Shelton, Norman, rector of Taynton, 344, 346
Sheppard, Wm., 267
Sherborne, 250, 252
Sherbourne (Warws.), named as an address, 106
Sherwood, Thos., perpetual curate of Oxenhall and Pauntley, 280, 301
ship money, 315
Shore:
  Chas. John, Lord Teignmouth, 205

John, Lord Teignmouth, 205
Shrewsbury, earldom of, 234, 241; for earls, *see* Talbot, Gilbert *and* John
Shropshire, *see* Castle, Bishop's; Ludlow; Wellington
Shropshire, Worcestershire, & Staffordshire Electric Power Co., 75, 159
Sibles:
  Eliz., w, of Ric., 312
  John, 308. 312
  Ric., 308, 312
  family, 308, 311–12
Simon 'Atennasse', 27
Simons, John, vicar of Dymock, 172
Sivedale, Wm., 326
Skally, John, curate of Newent, 88
Skelding:
  Simon, 288
  family, 288
Skelton, Margaret, 248
Skenfrith, Wal., chaplain of Bromesberrow, 119
Skidmore, Francis, 196
Skinner:
  John, curate of Pauntley, 300
  Steph. (d. 1674), 37, 64, 66
  Steph. (*fl.* 1705, s. of last), 24, 87
  Wm. (d. 1647), 163
  Wm., 119
  family, 19, 24, 37, 64–5, 304
Skipp:
  Jane, m. George Pritchard, 144
  John, 144
Slowe, as a surname, 30
Smallman, Geo., 222
Smith:
  as a surname, 242
  David, 121
  Eleanor, w. of Ric. and formerly of Roland Wrenford, 107
  F., 328
  G.H., 67
  Sir Geo., Bt, *see* Pauncefote
  J.M., 47
  Jerome, 327
  John (*fl.* 1390), prior of Newent, 39
  John (*fl.* 1507–15), vicar of Preston, 315
  John (*fl.* 1851), 335
  M.J., 47
  R., 298
  Ric., 107
  Rob., *see* Pauncefote
  Selwyn, 330
  Thos., vicar of Longhope, 194, 251–2
Sneedham, *see* Upton St Leonards
Society for Promoting Christian Knowledge, 278
Society of Mines Royal and Mineral and Battery Works, 335
Solers
  Ingram de (Ingram of Carswalls), 44–5
  John de, 287
  Parnel, w. of Randal de, 44
  Randal de, 44
  Ric. de (*fl.* late 12th cent.), 287
  Ric. de (grds. of last), 268, 287
  Rog. de, 45, 268
  Thos. de, 287
  Wal. de (*fl.* 1208), 287, 298
  Wal. de (*fl.* 1248, ? another), 287
  Wm. de, 268, 287, 298
solicitors, 20, 50, 69, 243, 246, *see also* attorneys

Somers, Earl, *see* Cocks, John Somers
Somers, Lord, *see* Cocks, Phil. Reg.
Somerset:
  Ann (d. 1764), 288, 296
  Anne, w. of Edw.(d. 1709), m. 2 John Paston, 287, 296
  Carolina, m. Ric. Brickenden, 287–8
  Chas., 287
  Clare, m. John Southcote, 287–8
  Edw. (d. 1628), earl of Worcester, 287
  Edw. (d. 1709), 287, 289, 296, 298
  Frances, m. Hen. Scudamore, 287–8
  Hen. (*fl.* 1632, s. of Edw. d. 1628), 287, 300
  Hen. (*fl.* 1694, s. of Sir John), 287, 296
  Hen. (*fl.* 1773), duke of Beaufort, 288
  Henrietta Maria, m. John Frederick, 288
  Jane, m. Jas.Hooper, 287
  Sir John, 3, 287, 296
  family, 3, 296, 289, 298, 300
Somerset, *see* Mendip coalfield
Somervill, Peter de, 180
sorcery, 194
Southcote:
  Clare, *see* Somerset
  John, 288
Southern, Wm., see Southorle, Wm.
Southorle:
  John of, 51
  Rog. of, 51
  Wm. (? same as Wm. Southern), 51
South-West Gas Board, 75
Spicer, John, 76, 274–5
Squire, Rob., vicar of Kempley, 217, 220
Sri Lanka, 190
St Aubyn:
  Blanche, *see* Whittington
  John, 287
St Florent abbey (Maine-et-Loire), 250
St Léger, Emme de, m. 1 Hugh de Longchamp, 2 Wal. de Baskerville, 203, 217
Stackhouse, Chas., 205
Stafford:
  Humph., earl of Devon, 328
  Isabel, *see* Barre
Staffordshire, 246; *see also* Chartley
stagecoach services, *see* Newent
Stallard:
  John, 143
  Malcolm, 143
Stallard Bros., poultry and egg producers, 60
Stalling:
  John of, 52
  Rob. of (one or more), 52, 85
Standish, Colethrop, named as an address, 241
Stanley:
  Eliz., *see* Grey
  Sir Edw., Lord Mounteagle, 203
  Wal., rector of Taynton, 342
Stanton, 140
Stardens, Nic. of, 53
Staunton (formerly Worcs.), 6, 115, 145
Staunton-on-Wye (Herefs.), 342
Stelfox, John Leather, 50, 54, 289
Stephens:
  Duncan Thompson, 245
  John, 245
  W.H., 161
Steventon, Wm., 233
Stock:
  Chris., rector of Bromesberrow, 120
  Eliz., w. of Chris., 120

John (fl. 1601), rector of Bromesberrow, 120
John (fl. 1733), 121
Jos., 121
family, 111
stocks, 113, 158, 189, 336
Stoke, East (Notts.), named as an address, 45
Stoke Edith (Herefs.), 39, 276
   named as an address, 40, 76, 264
Stokes, John, 283, 288–9, 291, 295–6, 300
Stone:
   Eliz., 106
   Guy (d. 1743), 106
   Revd Guy (d. 1779), 106
   Guy (d. 1862), 106
   Joan, 119
   John (d. 1578), 106
   John (d. 1632), 106
   John (d. 1633), 106
   John (d. 1695), 106
   John (d. 1742), 106
   Mary (d. 1767), m. Revd Giles Nanfan, 106
   Ric., 118
   Rog., 106
   Sam. (d. 1758), 106
   Sam. (d. 1825), 106
   Sam. (d. 1921), 106
   Thos. (d. 1546), 106
   Thos. (d. c.1658), 106
   Thos. (d. 1693), 106
   Wm. (fl. 1475), 106
   Wm. (d. 1683), 106
   Wm. (d. by 1702), rector of Eastnor, 116
   family, 115
Stonehouse, 235
Story:
   Edm., 162
   Miss, 165
Stour valley (Worcs.), 274–5
Stourbridge (Worcs.), 104
   named as an address, 287
Stowell, named as an address, 46, 328
Stranke:
   Hen., 267
   Martha, see Hill
Stratford:
   Ferdinando, architect, 105
   Ferdinando, rector of Taynton, 343
   John, 139
Stratford-upon-Avon (Warws.), named as an address, 106
Street, A.J., curate at Kempley, 214–15, 220
Stretton Grandison (Herefs.), 125–6
   Whitwick, named as an address, 289
Stroud, 66
   named as an address, 45, 53
   Over Lypiatt, named as an address, 299
Stuart:
   Rob. Fielding, 145
   Wm. Hen., 145
Studland (Dorset), 119
Studley priory (Warws.), 331
Suckley:
   Anne, w. of Edw., 48
   Edw., 48–9
   Jeffrey, 48–9
   Peter, 49
   Roland, 49
Sugwas (Herefs.), named as an address, 200
Sunninghill (Berks.), named as an address, 329

surgeons, 69, 182, 189
Surrey, see Byfleet; Epsom
Sussex, 138; see Billinghurst
Swansea, named as an address, 306
Swift, Hezekiah, 63
Sykes:
   Mary, see Cam
   Nic., 146
Sylvester, John, 168
Symonds:
   Alex., 296
   Eliz., see Weale
   Jas. Fred., 146
   Jonas, 286–7, 289, 296
   Jos., vicar of Dymock, 168
   Mary (d. 1846), m. —— Cummins, 289
   Mary (d. 1859), see Beale
   Mary (d. 1903), m. —— Tennant, 268
   Rob. (fl. 1746), 144
   Rob. (fl. 1750), vicar of Preston, 316
   Thos., 296
   Wm., 145–6
   family, 268

Talbot:
   Ankaret (d. 1421), 234
   Ankaret, w. of Ric. (d. 1396), m. 2 Thos. Neville, Lord Furnivale, 234
   Cath., w. of John (d. 1473), 234
   Eliz., m. Hen. Grey, Lord Grey and earl of Kent, 234
   Gilbert (d. 1274), 233
   Gilbert (d. 1346), Lord Talbot, 234
   Gilbert (d. 1387), Lord Talbot, 181, 234
   Gilbert (d. 1418), Lord Talbot, 234
   Gilbert (d. 1616), earl of Shrewsbury, 234
   John (fl. 1442), earl of Shrewsbury, 234
   John (d. 1473), earl of Shrewsbury, 234
   Ric. (d. 1306), 234
   Ric. (d. 1356), Lord Talbot, 181, 234
   Ric. (d. 1396), Lord Talbot, 234
   Sarah, 245
   family, 3, 102, 189, 233, 245
Tandy, Hen., 210
tanning, 62, 66, 154, 187
   tanneries, 228, 232–3, 242, 273
Tarlton, in Rodmarton and Coates, 107
Tarrington (Herefs.), 119
   named as an address, 103
Tawney family, 128
Taylor:
   Edw., 87, 92
   John, curate of Oxenhall, 280
   Ric., rector of Huntley, 194
   Wm., 64
   see also Craddock
Taynton, 1–3, 5, 8, 11, 34, 41, 46, 55, 181, 192, 276, *317–46*
   advowson, 342
   agriculture, 331–4
   boundaries, 317
   Byfords, 322–5 (*323*), 329, 332
   Castle Hill wood, 318–19, 322, 326, 329, 334
   chantries, 342
   chapels:
      hermitage, 322, 331, 342
      nonconformist, see Taynton, Glasshouse hill
   charities, 321, 336, 339–40
   churches, 84, 331, 341–6
      medieval, 317, 320, 322–3,

      mid 17th-cent., 317, 320, 323, 334, 342–5 (*345*)
      see also Taynton, Glasshouse hill
   church house (later parish house), 320, 340
   Civil War incident, 317, 320, 343
   clubs and associations, 341
   commons, 319
   courts, 336
   Cravenhill (Gravenhull), 319, 321, 326, 329, 331, 334
   divisions, 317–18
   domestic architecture, 322–5
   earthworks, 319–20, 322, 326
   farms, 332–4
   fields, 332
   Glasshouse, 8, 322, 324
   Glasshouse hill, 317–19, 322, 334–5, 337–8, 340, 344
      mission church, 322, 344, *346*
      nonconformist chapels, 322, 344
   Gravenhull, see Taynton, Cravenhill
   Great Taynton, 320, 323, 328, 332, 334, 337–8
      manor, 46, 317, 319, 322, 326–7, 329, 331–2
   Grove, the, 319–20, 323, 325–7, 329–30, 332–3, 338–9
   Hownhall, 319, 322, 329, 332, 335
   Hownhall Farm, 320, 323–325, 330, 332–3
   inclosure, 333
   inns, 341
   Kilpeck's tithing, 321, 331, 332, 341–2
   Little Taynton, 317–18, 320, 322, 331, 337
      manor, 46, 317, 323, 326–9, 331–2
   manors, 326–8; see also Taynton, Great Taynton *and* Little Taynton; manor of Tibberton, Taynton, and Bulley *under* Bulley
   manor house, see Taynton, Taynton Court
   meeting places, 340–1
   mills, 334–5
   named as an address, 43
   nonconformity, 343–4, 346; see also Taynton, Glasshouse hill
   Norman's Farm, 317, 321, 330, 333
   parish house, see Taynton, church house
   parish officers, 336–7
   park, 319
   poor relief, 336–7
   poorhouse, 336
   population, 319
   pound, 336
   rectors, 342–4, 346; see Bagshawe, Alfred Drake; Blundell, Geo.; Foster, K.B.; Hall, Geo. Wm.; Jeune, Francis; Luxmoore, John; Newton, Benj.; Stratford, Ferdinando; Shelton, Norman
   rectory, 341
   rectory houses, 320, 342–4
   reading room, 340
   roads, 319
   schools, 339–*340*, 344
   settlement, 319–22
   social structure, 337–8
   societies, 341
   Taynton Court, 317, 321–3, 325, 328, 331, 333
   Taynton House, 319, 322–5 (*324*), 329–32, 338–9, 344

tithes, 331, 332, 342; *see also* Taynton, Kilpeck's tithing
trades and industry, 334–6
war memorials, 341
woodland, 62, 181, 186, 318–19; *see also* Taynton, Castle Hill wood
woodland management, 334
workhouse, 188, 321, 325, 336–9 (*337*)
see also Gander's green; Kent's Green; Winford bridge
Teds wood (*Tedeswode*), 10, 38, 124, 201
Teignmouth, Lord, *see* Shore, Chas. John *and* John
Tempest:
> Sir Hen., Bt, 144, 148
> Susan, *see* Lambert

Tennant:
> Edm. Wm., 268
> Mary, *see* Symonds

Terrett:
> John, 50, 144
> Mary, w. of John, m. 2 Jos. Harris, 50, 144

Terry, Geo., 154
Teulon, S.S., 4, 180–1, 193, 195
Tewkesbury:
> bellfounder, 120
> monks of, 299, 315
> named as an address, 44, 51, 148
> roads to, 12, 125

Thackwell:
> E.J., 152
> John (d. 1808), 147
> John (d. 1829), 147, 160, 162–4
> John (d. 1914), 147
> John Cam., 147
> John Hen. Cam, 147
> Jos., 129, 147
> W.P., 297
> family, 3, 137, 162, 172, 297

The Imitation of Christ, 300
Thomas, chaplain at Pauntley, 299
Thomas:
> Edw., 167
> John Rhys, 306, 310
> Mic., 306
> family, 306

Thompson:
> Abraham, 148
> Hen. (one or more of name), 50–1, 53
> Mary, 245

Thompson, Hen., & Co., cider and perry makers, 59
Thorkell (*fl.* 1066), 265
Three Choirs Vineyard, *see* vineyards
Throckmorton:
> Sir Clement, 267
> Margaret, *see* Whittington
> Thos. (*fl.* 1546), 287
> Sir Thos. (d. 1608), 329, 334
> Sir Wm., Bt, 329

Thurston:
> Cornelius, 80
> Jas., 156
> family, 162

Tibberton, Nic. of, vicar of Longhope, 251
Tibberton, 11, 55, 176, 275, 319, 335–7, 340–2, 346
> manor of Tibberton, Taynton, and Bulley, *see* Bulley
> Tibberton Court estate, 326, 329
> *see also* Winford bridge

Tilley, W.J., London firm of, 75

Tilsley:
> John, 334
> family, 334–5

Tirley, 299
> Rye manor, 137

Todenham:
> Cath., w. of Rob., 138
> John, 138

Tomlinson, K.M., 84
Toney:
> Hen., 107
> John, 107
> Ric., 107
> Rob. (*fl.* 1424), 107
> Rob. (*fl.* 1487), 107
> family, 107
> *see also* Tony

Tonge, Ric., 265
Tony:
> Alice, dau. of Ralph de, 103
> (Tosny), Ralph de, 103, 118
> Ralph de (d. *c.*1126, s. of last), 103
> Rob. de, 103
> Rog. de, 118
> family, 102
> *see also* Toney

Tortworth, named as an address, 329
Towton, battle of, 265
Tracy:
> Frances, *see* Wrenford
> Sir Ric., 118
> Thos., 107

trade unionism, agricultural, 166, 341
tramroads, 126, 257
Trew, Harold, 325
Trigge, Wm., vicar of Longhope, 251
Trouncell, Thos., 64
tumbrel, 336
Turberville, Geo., rector of Bromesberrow, 121
Turner, Laurence, 222
turnpike roads, 11–12, 98, 125, 131, 160, 176, 198, 225, 257, 303
Twinning, Thos., curate of Pauntley, 299
Twyning, named as an address, 48

Ulfeg, *see* Wulfheah
Underwood:
> Jas. 172
> Thos., 321

Unett:
> Jane, *see* Wenman
> Ric., 140

United Brethren, 172
Unwin, Thos., rector of Huntley, 191, 194
Upleadon, 8–10, 12, 31–2, 55, 64, 118, 256, 275, 278, 280, 282, 298, 301
> curacy, 280, 300
> forge, 275
> named as an address, 50
> school, 297
> Upleadon Court, 301 n

Upton Bishop (Herefs.), 10, 197–8, 205, 208, 275
> Crow Hill, 12
> Fishpool, 196, 201, 211, 222
> nonconformity, 220–1
> named as an address, 205
> Teds wood, 197

Upton St Leonards, Sneedham, named as an address, 334
Upton upon Severn (Worcs.), named as an address, 145, 268

Vaughan:
> Nat., 241, 252
> Thos., 138

Veale:
> John, 342
> Thos., 343
> family, 342–3

Venn:
> Geo., vicar of Sherborne, later of Longhope, 250, 252
> Jos., 250

Verdun:
> John, 328
> Margaret, *see* Knovill
> Thos., 328

Villiers, Geo., earl of Buckingham, 327
Viner Bradford, Mrs A., 330.
Viney:
> Revd Jas. (d. 1767), 328
> Sir Jas. (d. 1841), 328
> John, 323, 328
> Mary (d. 1760), w. of Wm., 328
> Mary, *see* Westerdale
> Wm., 328

vineyards, 108, 110, 259, 272, 333
> Three Choirs, *61*, *81*, 292

Visme:
> Eliz. de, *see* Bearcroft
> Jas. de, 40–2, 48, 54
> Revd Jas. Edw. de, 41, 48
> family, 64

Vobes, Wm., 312

Wake:
> Alice, w. of Thos., 138
> Thos., 138

Wakeman:
> Frances, *see* Higford
> Hen., 289
> (or Worcester), Hen., vicar of Preston and curate of Dymock, 170, 315
> John, 327
> Margaret, m. Chas. Welch, 289
> Winifred, 289

Wales:
> cattle drovers from, 11, 79
> chief justice, 138
> coalfields, 98
> roads to, 2, 12, 187–8, 225
> *see also* Marches of Wales

Walford:
> Hugh of, 119, 120
> Margaret, m. John Nanfan, 106

Walker:
> S.J.S., 145
> Wm., 111

Wall:
> Cath., m. Rice Yate, 155
> Dorothy, m. Thos. Jauncey, 289
> Thos. (*fl.* 1522), 289, 295
> Thos. (d. 1665), 144, 155, 161
> Wm. (*fl.* 1542), 50
> Wm. (*fl.* 1640), 50. 144
> Wm. (d. 1717), 50, 144, 161, 163, 289
> Wm. (*fl.* 1727), 144

Waller, F.W., 317
Waller & Son, 93, 122, 147, 172
Waller, Son, & Wood, 134, 317
Wallys family, 27
Walrond:
> Isabel, *see* Kilpeck
> Joan, granddaughter of Wm., m. Bevis

de Knovill, 327
    Rob., 327
    Wm., 327
Walter, chaplain of Bromesberrow, 119
Walwyn:
    Agnes, 206
    Ric. (d. by 1494), 206
    Sir Ric. (*fl.* 1572), 206
    Rog., 206, 211
    Thos. (d. 1415), 206
    Thos. (*fl. ante* 1530) 208
    Thos. (*fl.* 1579–1601), 206, 211
    family, 200
Ward:
    Ric. le, 42
    Ric., vicar of Newent, 87
Waring:
    Mary, *see* Humphreys
    Wm. Ball, 148
Warjohn, Ric., 80
Warne:
    Thos. (*fl.* 1737), 93
    Thos. (*fl.* 1805), 89
Warneford, Revd S.W., 279
Warr:
    Ann, w. of John, 268
    John, 269
    Margaret, m. — Phillips, 269
    Margery, m. — Wood, 269
    Mary, m. — Mayo, 269
    Wm., 280
warrener, 283, 290
Warwick, countess of, *see* Longespée, Ela
Warwick, earls of, *see* Beauchamp, Guy de, Ric. de, *and* Thos. de
Warwickshire, *see* Birmingham; Edgbaston; Sherbourne; Stratford-upon-Avon; Studley priory
Waterton:
    Beatrice, *see* Burley
    Hugh (*fl.* 1393), 328
    Hugh (d. 1409, ? another), 103
Wateville:
    Maud de, 320, 326, 341
    family, 326 n
Watkins family, 205
Waudby-Griffin, Beatrice, m. A.R. Rowden, 104, 106, 122
Weale:
    Decimus (*fl.* 1721), 144
    Decimus (s. of last), 144
    Eliz., m. Robert Symonds, 144
    John (*fl.* 1721), 144
    John (*fl.* 1727), 154
    Jos., 116
    Rachael, m. Matthew Kidder, 144
    Rachael, *see* Benson, 144
    Thos., 241
    Wm., 163
    family, 130, 144, 160
Webb:
    Elias, 106
    John, 106
    John Elias Nanfan, 106, 115
    Thos. (*fl.* 1709), 118
    Thos. (*fl.* later 18th cent.), 106
    Thos. Townsend, 106
Wedderburn, Lady, Prize Fund, 340
Welch:
    Anne, w. of Chas. (d. by 1838), 290
    Chas. (*fl.* 1784), 289
    Chas. (d. by 1838, s. of last), 290
    Margaret, *see* Wakeman

Wm., 241
Weller, Archibald, 266
Wellin, ? Wm., 90
Wellington (Salop.), Dothill, named as an address, 233
Wells, Randall A., 4, 221–2
Wenman:
    Jane, m. John Wynniatt, 140
    Jane (or Joan), w. of Thos., m. 2 Thos. Fisher, 3 Ric. Unett, 139–41
    Ric., 140
    Sir Thos. (*fl.* 1544), 139
    Thos. (d. 1582), 139, 141
Weobley, barony or honor of, 203
West Indies, *see* Indies, West
Westbury-on-Severn, 176, 236, 346
    Elton, 340
    estates and farms, 2, 13, 38, 193, 268
    Grange Court railway station, road to, 176
    named as an address, 51, 278
    Upper and Lower Ley, 176, 184
Westbury-on-Severn poor-law union, 6, 188, 244
Westbury hundred, 2
Westerdale:
    Chris. (d. 1581), 328
    Chris. (d. 1655), 328, 336, 338
    Hen., 323, 328, 338
    Joan, *see* Heylond
    John, 45
    Mary, m. John Viney, 328
    family, 338
Weston under Penyard (Herefs.), 90
    named as an address, 43
Weston, Sir Simon, 327
Wetherlock:
    Hen., 260
    family, 277
Whatmough, Abraham, 220 and n, 280
Wheeler, Ric., vicar of Preston, 315
Whitaker, Gertrude, 41
Whitcott, Wm., curate of Pauntley, 299
White:
    Giles, 182
    John, 171
    Jos., 187, 189
    Revd Jos., 84, 165
    Wm., 82
    family, 108, 182
Whitefield:
    Constance, w. of Wm. de, m. 2 Steph. de Casynton, 103
    Geo., 280
    Wm. de, 103, 114
Whiteleaved Oak, *see* Berrow
Whiting, Thos., vicar of Dymock, 170
Whittaker:
    Abraham, 146
    Ann, *see* Cam
Whittington:
    Alice, 287
    Ann, *see* Payne
    Anne, m. Brian Berkeley, 287
    Blanche, m. John St Aubyn, 287
    Eliz., m. Sir Giles Poole, 287
    Eliz. (d. 1753), *see* Pury
    Guy, 269, 283, 287, 295, 299
    Guy, rector of Bromesberrow, 119
    Joan (*fl.* 1358), 287
    Joan, m. Rog. Bodenham, 287
    John, 103, 287, 290, 295, 329
    Margaret, m. Thos. Hooke, 269

Margaret, m. Thos. Throckmorton, 287
    Ric., 281, 295, 301
    Rob., 287, 295
    Revd Sam., 343
    Thos. (d. 1491), 299
    Thos. (d. 1546), 287, 299, 329
    Wm. of (*fl.* 1327–30), 287, 295
    Wm. (d. 1358), 287, 295
    Wm. (*fl.* 1377), 287
    Wm. (d. 1470), 287
    Wm. (*fl.* 1522), 103, 108, 114, 118–19
    family, 3, 283–4, 286, 295, 299, 322, 334
Wiga (*fl.* 1066), 287
Wightfield, *see* Deerhurst
Wigmore (Herefs.), 21 n
Wihanoc, lord of Monmouth, 180, 233, 255
Wilden (Worcs.):
    ironworks, 274
    named as an address, 274
Wildsmith & Son, builders, 21
Wilkins, John, 51
William I, 38, 181, 250
William II, 203
William 'de monasterio', 167
William le Waleys, 285
William son of Baderon, 174, 180, 183, 233, 236
William son of Norman, 327
William the smith, 160
Willoughby-Osborne, Emma, 290; *see also* Osborne
Wills:
    John (*fl.* mid 16th cent.), 133
    John (*fl.* mid 17th cent.), 145
    family, 129, 145, 160; *see also* Wilse
Wilmot:
    Alex., 39
    Christian, 39
    Edw. (d. 1558), 39
    Edw. (*fl.* 1567), 39
Wilse John, vicar of Newent, 87
Wilson, Grindal, vicar of Dymock, 171
Wilton:
    John of, 147
    John (d. 1560), 147
    Thos. (*fl.* 1522), 147
    Thos. (*fl.* 1560), 147
    family, 130, 147, 160
Wilton, *see* Bridstow
Wiltshire, earl of, *see* Butler, Jas.
Wiltshire, *see* Bradford-on-Avon; Corsham; Poole Keynes; *see also* Damerham
windmills, 155, 242
Winford bridge, in Taynton and Tibberton, 319–20, 337, 340
Winter:
    Sir Edw., 20, 39, 266, 269, 274, 293
    Giles, 148
    Hester, m. John Devall, 148
    Sir John, 3, 39, 57, 62, 76, 139, 274, 289
    Margaret, 148
    Rob., 148, 161, 163
    Sir Wm. (d. 1589), 39, 148
    Wm. (d. 1626), 85, 148
    Wm. (d. 1667), 148
    Wm. (*fl.* 1696, s. of last), 148, 167
    Wm. (*fl.* 1659, s. of Sir John), 39
    family, 3, 40–1, 52, 57, 64, 76, 127, 161, 171, 266
Winterbotham, Lindsey, 53
Wintle:
    A., 328

Thos. (1729), 191
witchcraft, *see* sorcery
Withington, Little (or Cassey) Compton, 203
Witley, Great (Worcs.), named as an address, 39
Witney (Oxon), named as an address, 39
Wodley:
  John, 107
  Wm., 107
Wood:
  Chas., 312
  Geo., 293
  Revd John (d. 1640), 171
  John (d. by 1684), 214
  John (*fl.* 1800), 28, 311–12, 316
  Margery, *see* Warr
  Martha, 293
  Peter, rector of Newent, 88
  Ric., rector of Taynton, 343
  Rob., 235
  Thos., 269
  Wal. B., 182
  family, 260, 277
woodland crafts, *see* Huntley; Longhope; Newent; Oxenhall
Woodland Improvement Ltd, 186
Woodward:
  Acton (*fl.* 1686–1714), 69
  Acton (d. 1718, s. of last), 69
  Chris. (d. 1656 or 1657), 51–2
  Chris. (d. 1699), 51–2, 87
  Chris. (d. 1710), 51n
  Chris. (d. 1731), 51
  Eliz., m. Edward Chinn, 51
  Hen., 190
  Thos. (d. 1623), 42, 51
  Thos. (s. of last), 51
  Thos. (*fl.* 1717), 51
  family, 32–3, 62, 77, 200
Woolhope (Herefs.), named as an address, 140
Worcester, Hen., *see* Wakeman
Worcester, earls of, *see* Beauchamp, Ric. de; Somerset, Edw.
Worcester, 51, 66, 170, 236, 269
  archdeacon, 88
  dean, 88
  MP for, 144
  named as an address, 51, 144, 161, 205, 306, 315
  road to, 98
Worcestershire, 1–2, 6, 74, 86, 95, 281

county council, 283
see Abberley; Bengeworth; Berrow; Bewdley; Birtsmorton; Bushley; Castlemorton; Claines; Cookhill priory; Evesham; Grafton; Hanley Castle; Kidderminster; Leigh; Lench, Sheriff's; Madresfield; Malvern; Morton, Abbots; Norton; Ombersley; Pendock; Pershore; Pirton; Powick; Redditch; Rushock; Stour valley; Stourbridge; Upton upon Severn; Wilden; Witley, Great; *see also* Beckford; Redmarley D'Abitot; Staunton
workhouses, *see* Bromesberrow; Dymock; Ledbury; Longhope; Newent; Taynton
Wormsley priory (Herefs.), 148
Worrall:
  John, 205, 214–15
  Mary, mother of John, 215
  see also Rideout
Worsley, John, 267
Wotton, Joan, charity, 214, 215
Wren, Sir Chris., 87, 92
Wrenford:
  Frances, m. Thos. Tracy, 107
  Ric., 107
  Roland, 107
  Thos., 107
Wright, Dr and Mrs P.H., 268
Wulfgar (*fl.* 1066), 327
Wulfheah (Ulfeg) (*fl.* 1066), 233
Wulfhelm (*fl.* 1066), 44, 287
Wyman:
  Eliz., m. 1 — Ashley, 2 Thos. Hartland, 191
  John, 191
Wynniatt:
  Caroline, w. of Reg. (d. 1881), m. 2 Horace Drummond Deane, 140
  Harriett, m. Henry Mildmay Husey, 140
  Jane, *see* Wenman
  Jas. John, 133, 140, 145
  John (*fl.* 1522–31), 140, 150, 155, 160
  John (*fl.* 1522, another), 133
  John (d. 1670), 140–1, 151, 155, 161
  John Wenman, 145
  Penelope, w. of Wenman (d. 1731), 140
  Reg. (d. 1762), 140
  Revd Reg. (d. 1819), 140–1
  Reg. (d. 1881), 140, 145

Thos. (two of the name *fl.*1539), 133
Thos. (*fl.* 1649), 155
Thos. (d. 1830), 140
Wenman (d. 1676), 140
Wenman (d. 1731), 140
family, 3, 137, 150, 161–2, 170–1
Wynn-Lloyd, W., rector of Bromesberrow, 122
Wyville:
  Cath., w. of Hen., 334
  Hen., 334

Yannes (James), John, rector of Taynton, 342
Yarkhill (Herefs.), 206
Yartleton (Yartledon), *see* May hill
Yartleton woods, *see* Newent, Newent woods
Yate:
  Anne, m. —— Foote, 116
  Arethusa, 235
  Cath. (d. 1711), 104, 116
  Cath., *see* Wall
  Chas. (d. 1730), 234–5
  Chas., of Arlingham, 103–4
  Frances, 235
  Hen. Gorges Dobyns, rector of Bromesberrow, 115–16, 118, 120, 164
  Henrietta, 235
  John (d. 1749), 103, 115
  John (d. 1758), 102–5
  Mary, 235
  Nourse, 229, 234, 241, 245, 247, 250, 252
  Priscilla (d. 1720), 234
  Priscilla, m. Lancelot Bromwich, 235, 250
  Ric., 103
  Rice, 99–100, 105, 107, 113, 115, 120, 143, 155
  (formerly Dobyns, Rob.), Rob. Dobyns, 104
  Rob. Gorges Dobyns, 104, 113, 115, 120
  Wal., 103, 105, 115–16, 118, 120, 143
  Wal. Honywood, 104, 111, 115, 118, 143
  Wm. (*fl.* 1661), 241
  Wm., vicar of Longhope, 252
  family, 3, 103, 115, 131, 150–1, 227, 252
Ysett, *see* Isett
York, archbishop of, *see* Ealdred
York, duke of, *see* Edward
Yorkshire, East Riding, *see* Kingston upon Hull
Young, Freeman, 48
Younghusband, F.C.R.R., 43